PRENTICE HALL COURSE 2

MATHEMATICS

Randall I. Charles
Judith C. Branch-Boyd
Mark Illingworth
Darwin Mills
Andy Reeves

PEARSON
Prentice Hall

Needham, Massachusetts
Upper Saddle River, New Jersey

Authors

Series Author

Randall I. Charles, Ph.D., is Professor Emeritus in the Department of Mathematics and Computer Science at San Jose State University, San Jose, California. He began his career as a high school mathematics teacher, and he was a mathematics supervisor for five years. Dr. Charles has been a member of several NCTM committees and is the former Vice President of the National Council of Supervisors of Mathematics. Much of his writing and research has been in the area of problem solving. He has authored more than 75 mathematics textbooks for kindergarten through college.
Scott Foresman-Prentice Hall Mathematics Series Author Kindergarten through Algebra 2

Program Authors

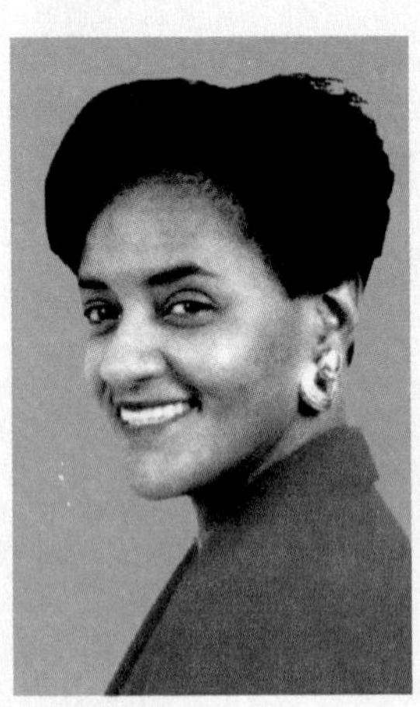

Judith C. Branch-Boyd, Ph.D., is the Area 24 Mathematics Coordinator for the Chicago Public School District. She works with high school teachers to provide quality instruction to students who are mandated to take Algebra, Geometry, and Advanced Algebra-Trigonometry. She also works with middle school and high school teachers to help students transition to Algebra 1. Dr. Branch-Boyd is active in several professional mathematics organizations at the state and national levels, including the National Council of Teachers of Mathematics. She believes,"All children can learn to love mathematics if it is taught with energy!"

ISBN 0-13-068554-2

6 7 8 9 10 07 06 05 04

Mark Illingworth has taught fifth-graders and enrichment programs for fifteen years. During this time, he received the Christa McAullife sabbatical to develop problem-solving materials and projects for middle-grades math students, and he was granted the Presidential Award for Excellence in Mathematics Teaching. In addition to serving as the district math task force coordinator for the last six years, he has written two of his own books and has contributed to both math and science textbooks at Prentice Hall. Mr. Illingworth has recently shifted from teaching fifth-graders to teaching math to high school students.

Darwin Mills is a mathematics lead teacher for the public schools in Newport News, Virginia, and a mathematics adjunct professor at Thomas Nelson Community College in Hampton, Virginia. He has received various teaching awards, including teacher of the year for the 1999–2000 school year and an Excellence in Teaching Award from the College of Wooster, Ohio, in 2002. He is a frequent presenter for staff development, especially in the area of graphing calculator usage in the classroom. He believes that all students can learn mathematics if given the proper instruction.

Andy Reeves, Ph.D., teaches at the University of South Florida in St. Petersburg. His career in education spans 30 years and includes seven years as a middle grades teacher. He subsequently served as Florida's K-12 mathematics supervisor and more recently he supervised the publication of the *Mathematics Teacher*, *Mathematics Teaching in the Middle School*, and *Teaching Children Mathematics* for NCTM. Prior to entering education, he worked as an engineer for Douglas Aircraft.

Contributing Author

Denisse R. Thompson, Ph.D., is Associate Professor of Mathematics Education at the University of South Florida. She has particular interests in the connections between literature and mathematics and in the teaching and learning of mathematics in the middle grades. Dr. Thompson contributed to the Reading Math lessons and features.

Reviewers

Course 1 Reviewers

Donna Anderson
Math Supervisor 7–12
West Hartford Public Schools
West Hartford, Connecticut

Nancy L. Borchers
West Clermont Local Schools
Cincinnati, Ohio

Kathleen Chandler
Walnut Creek Middle School
Erie, Pennsylvania

Jane E. Damaske
Lakeshore Public Schools
Stevensville, Michigan

Frank Greco
Parkway South Middle School
Manchester, Missouri

Rebecca L. Jones
Odyssey Middle School
Orlando, Florida

Marylee R. Liebowitz
H. C. Crittenden Middle School
Armonk, New York

Kathy Litz
K. O. Knudson Middle School
Las Vegas, Nevada

Don McGurrin
Wake County Public School System
Raleigh, North Carolina

Ron Mezzadri
K–12 Mathematics Supervisor
Fair Lawn School District
Fair Lawn, New Jersey

Sylvia O. Reeder-Tucker
Prince George's County Math Department
Upper Marlboro, Maryland

Julie A. White
Allison Traditional Magnet Middle School
Wichita, Kansas

Charles Yochim
Bronxville Middle School
Bronxville, New York

Course 2 Reviewers

Cami Craig
Prince William County Public Schools
Marsteller Middle School
Bristow, Virginia

Donald O. Cram
Lincoln Middle School
Rio Rancho, New Mexico

Pat A. Davidson
Jacksonville Junior High School
Jacksonville, Arkansas

Yvette Drew
DeKalb County School System
Open Campus High School
Atlanta, Georgia

Robert S. Fair
K–12 District Mathematics Coordinator
Cherry Creek School District
Greenwood Village, Colorado

Michael A. Landry
Glastonbury Public Schools
Glastonbury, Connecticut

Nancy Ochoa
Weeden Middle School
Florence, Alabama

Charlotte J. Phillips
Wichita USD 259
Wichita, Kansas

Mary Lynn Raith
Mathematics Curriculum Specialist
Pittsburgh Public Schools
Pittsburgh, Pennsylvania

Tammy Rush
Consultant, Middle School Mathematics
Hillsborough County Schools
Tampa, Florida

Judith R. Russ
Prince George's County Public Schools
Capitol Heights, Maryland

Tim Tate
Math/Science Supervisor
Lafayette Parish School System
Lafayette, Louisiana

Dondi J. Thompson
Alcott Middle School
Norman, Oklahoma

Candace Yamagata
Hyde Park Middle School
Las Vegas, Nevada

Course 3 Reviewers

Linda E. Addington
Andrew Lewis Middle School
Salem, Virginia

Jeanne Arnold
Mead Junior High School
Schaumburg, Illinois

Sheila S. Brookshire
A. C. Reynolds Middle School
Asheville, North Carolina

Jennifer Clark
Mayfield Middle School
Putnam City Public Schools
Oklahoma City, Oklahoma

Nicole Dial
Chase Middle School
Topeka, Kansas

Christine Ferrell
Lorin Andrews Middle School
Massillon, Ohio

Virginia G. Harrell
Education Consultant
Hillsborough County, Florida

Jonita P. Howard
Mathematics Curriculum Specialist
Lauderdale Lakes Middle School
Lauderdale Lakes, Florida

Patricia Lemons
Rio Rancho Middle School
Rio Rancho, New Mexico

Susan Noce
Robert Frost Junior High School
Schaumburg, Illinois

Carla A. Siler
South Bend Community School Corp.
South Bend, Indiana

Kathryn E. Smith-Lance
West Genesee Middle School
Camillus, New York

Kathleen D. Tuffy
South Middle School
Braintree, Massachusetts

Patricia R. Wilson
Central Middle School
Murfreesboro, Tennessee

Patricia Young
Northwood Middle School
Pulaski County Special School District
North Little Rock, Arkansas

Content Consultants

Courtney Lewis
Mathematics
Prentice Hall Senior National Consultant
Baltimore, Maryland

Deana Cerroni
Mathematics
Prentice Hall National Consultant
Las Vegas, Nevada

Kimberly Margel
Mathematics
Prentice Hall National Consultant
Scottsdale, Arizona

Sandra Mosteller
Mathematics
Prentice Hall National Consultant
Anderson, South Carolina

Rita Corbett
Mathematics
Prentice Hall Consultant
Elgin, Illinois

Cathy Davies
Mathematics
Prentice Hall Consultant
Laguna Niguel, California

Sally Marsh
Mathematics
Prentice Hall Consultant
Baltimore, Maryland

Addie Martin
Mathematics
Prentice Hall Consultant
Upper Marlboro, Maryland

Rose Primiani
Mathematics
Prentice Hall Consultant
Brick, New Jersey

Loretta Rector
Mathematics
Prentice Hall Consultant
Foresthill, California

Charlotte Samuels
Mathematics
Prentice Hall Consultant
Lafayette Hill, Pennsylvania

Margaret Thomas
Mathematics
Prentice Hall Consultant
Indianapolis, Indiana

Contents in Brief

Letter From the Authors xix

Connect Your Learning xx

Using Your Book for Success xxiv

Chapter 1 Decimals and Integers 2

Chapter 2 Algebra: Equations and Inequalities 68

Chapter 3 Exponents, Factors, and Fractions 128

Chapter 4 Operations With Fractions 184

Chapter 5 Ratios, Rates, and Proportions 238

Chapter 6 Percents 288

Chapter 7 Geometry 344

Chapter 8 Geometry and Measurement 400

Chapter 9 Algebra: Patterns and Rules 466

Chapter 10 Algebra: Graphing in the Coordinate Plane 518

Chapter 11 Displaying and Analyzing Data 570

Chapter 12 Using Probability 626

Chapter Projects 678

Extra Practice 684

Skills Handbook

Comparing and Ordering Whole Numbers 696
Rounding Whole Numbers 697
Multiplying Whole Numbers 698
Dividing Whole Numbers 699
Place Value and Decimals 700
Reading and Writing Decimals 701
Rounding Decimals 702
Multiplying Decimals 703
Zeros in the Product 704
Dividing a Decimal by a Whole Number 705
Powers of 10 706
Zeros in Decimal Division 707
Adding and Subtracting Fractions With Like Denominators 708
Metric Units of Length 709
Metric Units of Capacity 710
Metric Units of Mass 711

Tables

Measures 712
Reading Math Symbols 713
Squares and Square Roots 714

Formulas and Properties 715

English/Spanish Illustrated Glossary 717

Answers to Instant Check System 755

Selected Answers 772

Index 793

Acknowledgments 807

Chapter 1

Decimals and Integers

Student Support

Instant Check System

Diagnosing Readiness, 4

Check Skills You'll Need, 5, 11, 17, 23, 30, 34, 39, 45, 50, 56

Check Understanding, 5, 6, 7, 11, 12, 13, 17, 18, 19, 23, 24, 25, 31, 34, 35, 40, 41, 46, 47, 51, 52, 56, 57, 58

Checkpoint Quiz, 28, 49

Comprehensive Test Prep

Daily Test Prep, 9, 15, 22, 27, 33, 38, 44, 49, 54, 60

Test-Taking Strategies, 61

Cumulative Test Prep, 65

Reading Math

Reading Math, 6, 23, 24, 46, 51, 57

Reading Your Textbook, 10

Understanding Vocabulary, 62

Reading Comprehension, 60, 65

Writing in Math

Daily Writing Practice, 8, 14, 21, 26, 37, 43, 48, 54, 59, 64

Writing to Explain, 29

Real-World Problem Solving

Strategy: Using a Problem-Solving Plan, 30–33
Eagle Rays, 5
Skating, 14
Math at Work, 28
Cars, 47
. . . and more!

	Diagnosing Readiness	**4**
1-1	**Using Estimation Strategies** • Reading Math: Reading Your Textbook, 10	**5**
1-2	**Adding and Subtracting Decimals** • Extension: Mental Math: Compensation, 16	**11**
1-3	**Multiplying and Dividing Decimals**	**17**
1-4	**Measuring in Metric Units** • Writing in Math: Writing to Explain, 29	**23**
	Checkpoint Quiz 1	**28**
1-5	**Using a Problem-Solving Plan** Problem Solving	**30**
1-6	**Comparing and Ordering Integers** Algebra	**34**
1-7	**Adding and Subtracting Integers** Algebra	**39**
1-8	**Multiplying and Dividing Integers** Algebra	**45**
	Checkpoint Quiz 2	**49**
1-9	**Order of Operations and the Distributive Property** • Technology: Using a Scientific Calculator, 55	**50**
1-10	**Mean, Median, and Mode**	**56**
	Assessment • Test-Taking Strategies: Writing Gridded Responses, 61 • Chapter Review, 62 • Chapter Test, 64 • Test Prep: Reading Comprehension, 65	
DK	**Real-World Snapshots:** Applying Integers	**66**

Chapter 2

Algebra

Equations and Inequalities

Student Support

Instant Check System

Diagnosing Readiness, 70

Check Skills You'll Need, 71, 77, 83, 88, 93, 98, 102, 107, 112, 116

Check Understanding, 72, 73, 78, 79, 84, 85, 89, 90, 93, 94, 95, 98, 99, 103, 107, 108, 109, 112, 113, 117, 118

Checkpoint Quiz, 92, 111

Comprehensive Test Prep

Daily Test Prep, 75, 81, 87, 92, 97, 101, 105, 111, 115, 120

Test-Taking Strategies, 121

Cumulative Test Prep, 125

Reading Math

Reading Math, 84, 90, 107, 110

Understanding Word Problems, 106

Understanding Vocabulary, 122

Reading Comprehension, 75

Writing in Math

Daily Writing Practice, 74, 76, 80, 86, 91, 96, 100, 104, 110, 115, 119, 124

Writing Short Responses, 121

Real-World Problem Solving

Strategy: Write an Equation, 102–105
Public Service, 73
Practice Game, 75
Nutrition, 109
Fishing, 113
. . . and more!

Diagnosing Readiness **70**

2-1 Evaluating and Writing Algebraic Expressions Algebra **71**
- Technology: Using Spreadsheets, 76

2-2 Using Number Sense to Solve Equations Algebra **77**

2-3 Solving Equations by Adding or Subtracting Algebra . **83**
- Investigation: Modeling Equations, 82

2-4 Solving Equations by Multiplying or Dividing Algebra **88**

Checkpoint Quiz 1 . . . . **92**

2-5 Exploring Two-Step Problems Algebra **93**

2-6 Solving Two-Step Equations Algebra **98**

2-7 Write an Equation Problem Solving **102**
- Reading Math: Understanding Word Problems, 106

2-8 Graphing and Writing Inequalities Algebra **107**

Checkpoint Quiz 2 . . . . **111**

2-9 Solving Inequalities by Adding or Subtracting Algebra **112**

2-10 Solving Inequalities by Multiplying or Dividing Algebra **116**

Assessment
- Test-Taking Strategies: Writing Short Responses, 121
- Chapter Review, 122
- Chapter Test, 124
- Test Prep: Cumulative Review, 125

Real-World Snapshots: Applying Inequalities **126**

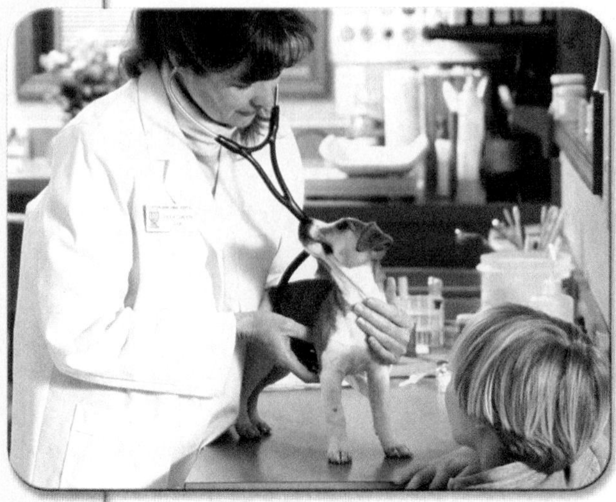

Chapter 3

Exponents, Factors, and Fractions

Student Support

Instant Check System
Diagnosing Readiness, 130

Check Skills You'll Need, 131, 136, 141, 145, 151, 156, 160, 164, 168, 173

Check Understanding, 132, 133, 137, 141, 142, 145, 146, 147, 151, 152, 156, 157, 161, 165, 169, 170, 173, 174

Checkpoint Quiz, 155, 176

Comprehensive Test Prep
Daily Test Prep, 135, 139, 144, 149, 155, 159, 163, 167, 172, 176

Test-Taking Strategies, 177

Cumulative Test Prep, 181

Reading Math
Reading Math, 131, 156, 169, 170, 174

Reading a Math Lesson, 150

Understanding Vocabulary, 178

Reading Comprehension, 155, 181

Writing in Math
Daily Writing Practice, 134, 139, 143, 148, 153, 158, 162, 167, 172, 175, 180

Writing Extended Responses, 177

Real-World Problem Solving
Strategies: Solve a Simpler Problem and Look for a Pattern, 160–163

Math in the Media, 138

Birds, 157

Practice Game, 163

Fitness, 166

. . . and more!

Diagnosing Readiness 130

3-1 **Exponents and Order of Operations** 131

3-2 **Scientific Notation** 136
- Extension: Negative Exponents, 140

3-3 **Divisibility Tests** 141

3-4 **Prime Factorization** 145
- Reading Math: Reading a Math Lesson, 150

3-5 **Simplifying Fractions** 151

Checkpoint Quiz 1 155

3-6 **Comparing and Ordering Fractions** 156

3-7 **Solve a Simpler Problem and Look for a Pattern** Problem Solving 160

3-8 **Mixed Numbers and Improper Fractions** 164

3-9 **Fractions and Decimals** 168

3-10 **Rational Numbers** 173

Checkpoint Quiz 2 176

Assessment
- Test-Taking Strategies: Writing Extended Responses, 177
- Chapter Review, 178
- Chapter Test, 180
- Test Prep: Reading Comprehension, 181

DK **Real-World Snapshots:** Applying Fractions 182

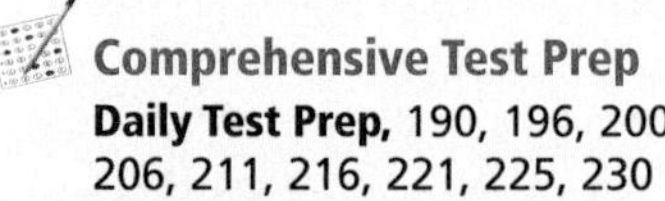

Operations With Fractions

Student Support

Instant Check System

Diagnosing Readiness, 186

Check Skills You'll Need, 187, 192, 197, 202, 207, 213, 218, 222, 227

Check Understanding, 187, 188, 192, 193, 197, 198, 203, 204, 207, 208, 213, 214, 219, 222, 223, 228, 229

Checkpoint Quiz, 201, 225

Comprehensive Test Prep

Daily Test Prep, 190, 196, 200, 206, 211, 216, 221, 225, 230

Test-Taking Strategies, 231

Cumulative Test Prep, 235

Reading Math

Reading Math, 192, 204, 207, 215, 222, 228

Understanding Word Problems, 217

Understanding Vocabulary, 232

Reading Comprehension, 206, 225, 231

Writing in Math

Daily Writing Practice, 189, 195, 199, 205, 210, 215, 221, 224, 230, 234

Real-World Problem Solving

Strategies: Try, Check, and Revise and Work Backward, 218–221
Carpentry, 193
Math at Work, 196
Science, 205
Cycling, 223
. . . and more!

Diagnosing Readiness 186

4-1 **Estimating With Fractions and Mixed Numbers** 187

4-2 **Adding and Subtracting Fractions** 192
- Investigation: Using Fraction Models, 191

4-3 **Adding and Subtracting Mixed Numbers** 197

Checkpoint Quiz 1 201

4-4 **Multiplying Fractions and Mixed Numbers** 202

4-5 **Dividing Fractions and Mixed Numbers** 207
- Technology: Using a Fraction Calculator, 212

4-6 **Solving Equations With Fractions** Algebra 213
- Reading Math: Understanding Word Problems, 217

4-7 **Try, Check, and Revise and Work Backward** Problem Solving 218

4-8 **Measurement: Changing Units in the Customary System** 222

Checkpoint Quiz 2 225

4-9 **Precision** 227
- Extension: Estimating in Different Systems, 226

Assessment
- Test-Taking Strategies: Reading-Comprehension Questions, 231
- Chapter Review, 232
- Chapter Test, 234
- Test Prep: Cumulative Review, 235

DK **Real-World Snapshots:** Applying Fractions 236

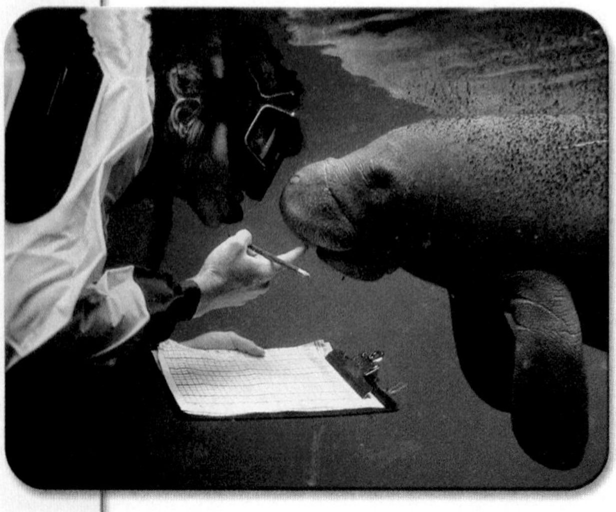

Chapter 5

Ratios, Rates, and Proportions

Student Support

Instant Check System
Diagnosing Readiness, 240
Check Skills You'll Need, 241, 246, 252, 256, 260, 267, 275
Check Understanding, 242, 243, 246, 247, 248, 253, 256, 257, 258, 260, 261, 268, 269, 275, 276
Checkpoint Quiz, 255, 272

Comprehensive Test Prep
Daily Test Prep, 245, 250, 255, 259, 264, 271, 279
Test-Taking Strategies, 281
Cumulative Test Prep, 285

Reading Math
Reading Math, 260, 275
Learning Vocabulary, 274
Understanding Vocabulary, 282
Reading Comprehension, 279, 285

Writing in Math
Daily Writing Practice, 244, 249, 254, 259, 263, 270, 273, 277, 284
Writing to Compare, 266

Real-World Problem Solving
Strategies: Draw a Diagram and Solve a Simpler Problem, 252–255
Music, 242
Sports, 247
Math at Work, 265
Geography, 276
. . . and more!

Diagnosing Readiness **240**

5-1 **Ratios** **241**

5-2 **Unit Rates and Proportional Reasoning** **246**
- Extension: Dimensional Analysis, 251

5-3 **Draw a Diagram and Solve a Simpler Problem** Problem Solving **252**

Checkpoint Quiz 1 . . . . **255**

5-4 **Proportions** Algebra **256**

5-5 **Solving Proportions** Algebra **260**
- Writing in Math: Writing to Compare, 266

5-6 **Using Similar Figures** **267**
- Technology: Creating Similar Figures, 273
- Reading Math: Learning Vocabulary, 274

Checkpoint Quiz 2 . . . . **272**

5-7 **Maps and Scale Drawings** **275**
- Investigation: Plan a Trip, 280

Assessment
- Test-Taking Strategies: Using a Variable, 281
- Chapter Review, 282
- Chapter Test, 284
- Test Prep: Reading Comprehension, 285

DK **Real-World Snapshots:** Applying Ratios **286**

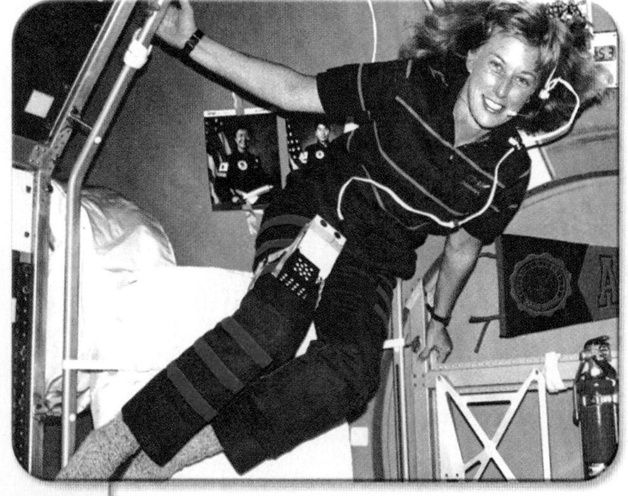

Chapter 6

Percents

Diagnosing Readiness 290
6-1 Understanding Percents 291
6-2 Percents, Fractions, and Decimals 295
6-3 Percents Greater Than 100 or Less Than 1 301
6-4 Finding a Percent of a Number 305
Checkpoint Quiz 1 310
6-5 Solving Percent Problems Using Proportions (Algebra) 311
• Reading Math: Understanding Word Problems, 317
6-6 Solving Percent Problems Using Equations (Algebra) 318
6-7 Applications of Percent (Algebra) 322
Checkpoint Quiz 2 326
6-8 Finding Percent of Change (Algebra) 327
6-9 Write an Equation (Problem Solving) 333

Assessment
• Test-Taking Strategies: Work Backward, 337
• Chapter Review, 338
• Chapter Test, 340
• Test Prep: Cumulative Review, 341

DK Real-World Snapshots: Applying Percents 342

Student Support

Instant Check System

Diagnosing Readiness, 290

Check Skills You'll Need, 291, 295, 301, 305, 311, 318, 322, 327, 333

Check Understanding, 291, 292, 296, 297, 301, 302, 306, 307, 311, 312, 313, 318, 319, 322, 323, 324, 328, 329, 334

Checkpoint Quiz, 310, 326

Comprehensive Test Prep

Daily Test Prep, 294, 300, 304, 310, 316, 321, 326, 332, 336

Test-Taking Strategies, 337

Cumulative Test Prep, 341

Reading Math

Reading Math, 291, 315, 333

Understanding Word Problems, 317

Understanding Vocabulary, 338

Reading Comprehension, 326

Writing in Math

Daily Writing Practice, 293, 300, 303, 309, 315, 320, 325, 331, 335, 339, 340

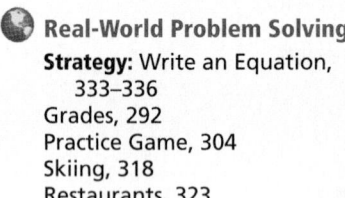

Real-World Problem Solving

Strategy: Write an Equation, 333–336
Grades, 292
Practice Game, 304
Skiing, 318
Restaurants, 323
. . . and more!

Chapter 7

Geometry

Student Support

Instant Check System

Diagnosing Readiness, 346

Check Skills You'll Need, 347, 351, 357, 363, 369, 374, 378, 383, 388

Check Understanding, 347, 348, 351, 352, 353, 358, 359, 363, 364, 365, 370, 371, 375, 379, 380, 384, 388, 389

Checkpoint Quiz, 367, 382

Comprehensive Test Prep

Daily Test Prep, 350, 356, 361, 367, 373, 377, 382, 386, 392

Test-Taking Strategies, 393

Cumulative Test Prep, 397

Reading Math

Reading Math, 352, 384

Learning Vocabulary, 387

Understanding Vocabulary, 394

Reading Comprehension, 356, 397

Writing in Math

Daily Writing Practice, 349, 355, 360, 366, 372, 376, 381, 385, 391, 396

Writing to Justify, 368

Real-World Problem Solving

Strategies: Draw a Diagram and Look for a Pattern, 374–377

Math at Work, 350

Physical Therapy, 355

Architecture, 363

Amusement Parks, 384

. . . and more!

Diagnosing Readiness **346**

7-1 Lines and Planes **347**

7-2 Measuring and Classifying Angles **351**

7-3 Constructing Bisectors **357**
- Extension: Angles and Parallel Lines, 362

7-4 Triangles **363**
- Writing in Math: Writing to Justify, 368

Checkpoint Quiz 1 . . . . **367**

7-5 Quadrilaterals and Other Polygons **369**

7-6 Draw a Diagram and Look for a Pattern Problem Solving **374**

7-7 Congruent Figures **378**

Checkpoint Quiz 2 . . . . **382**

7-8 Circles **383**
- Reading Math: Learning Vocabulary, 387

7-9 Circle Graphs **388**

Assessment
- Test-Taking Strategies: Drawing a Diagram, 393
- Chapter Review, 394
- Chapter Test, 396
- Test Prep: Reading Comprehension, 397

Real-World Snapshots: Applying Geometry **398**

Chapter 8

Geometry and Measurement

Diagnosing Readiness 402

8-1 Estimating Length and Area 403

8-2 Areas of Parallelograms and Triangles 407

8-3 Areas of Other Figures 413

8-4 Circumferences and Areas of Circles 419
- Reading Math: Making a Concept Map, 425

Checkpoint Quiz 1 424

8-5 Square Roots and Irrational Numbers 426

8-6 The Pythagorean Theorem 432
- Investigation: Exploring the Pythagorean Theorem, 431

8-7 Three-Dimensional Figures 437
- Extension: Three Views of an Object, 441

8-8 Surface Areas of Prisms and Cylinders 442
- Extension: Patterns in 3-Dimensional Figures, 448

8-9 Volumes of Rectangular Prisms and Cylinders 449

Checkpoint Quiz 2 454

8-10 Try, Check, and Revise and Write an Equation (Problem Solving) 455

Assessment
- Test-Taking Strategies: Finding Multiple Correct Answers, 459
- Chapter Review, 460
- Chapter Test, 462
- Test Prep: Cumulative Review, 463

Real-World Snapshots: Applying Volume 464

Student Support

Instant Check System
Diagnosing Readiness, 402

Check Skills You'll Need, 403, 407, 413, 419, 426, 432, 437, 442, 449, 455

Check Understanding, 403, 404, 407, 408, 409, 410, 414, 415, 420, 421, 426, 427, 428, 433, 437, 438, 442, 443, 444, 449, 450, 451, 456

Checkpoint Quiz, 424, 454

Comprehensive Test Prep
Daily Test Prep, 406, 412, 418, 424, 430, 436, 440, 447, 453, 458

Test-Taking Strategies, 459

Cumulative Test Prep, 463

Reading Math
Reading Math, 414, 421, 426

Making a Concept Map, 425

Understanding Vocabulary, 460

Reading Comprehension, 406

Writing in Math
Daily Writing Practice, 405, 411, 417, 420, 423, 429, 435, 439, 445, 452, 458, 462

Real-World Problem Solving
Strategies: Try, Check, and Revise and Write an Equation, 455–458

Quilting, 410

Practice Game, 430

Recreation, 433

Boat Building, 455

. . . and more!

Chapter 9

Patterns and Rules

Student Support

Instant Check System

Diagnosing Readiness, 468

Check Skills You'll Need, 469, 474, 480, 484, 489, 494, 499, 503, 507

Check Understanding, 469, 470, 471, 475, 476, 480, 481, 484, 485, 489, 490, 494, 495, 499, 500, 503, 504, 507, 508

Checkpoint Quiz, 488, 502

Comprehensive Test Prep

Daily Test Prep, 473, 478, 483, 488, 492, 498, 502, 506, 510

Test-Taking Strategies, 511

Cumulative Test Prep, 515

Reading Math

Reading Math, 475, 477, 484, 507

Understanding Word Problems, 479

Understanding Vocabulary, 512

Reading Comprehension, 498, 515

Writing in Math

Daily Writing Practice, 472, 477, 482, 486, 491, 497, 502, 505, 509, 514

Real-World Problem Solving

Strategy: Write an Equation, 503–506
Gas Mileage, 480
Plants, 490
Consumer Decisions, 504
Math at Work, 506
. . . and more!

	Diagnosing Readiness	**468**
9-1	**Patterns and Graphs**	**469**
9-2	**Number Sequences** • Reading Math: Understanding Word Problems, 479	**474**
9-3	**Patterns and Tables** (Algebra)	**480**
9-4	**Function Rules** (Algebra)	**484**
	Checkpoint Quiz 1	**488**
9-5	**Using Tables, Rules, and Graphs** (Algebra) • Technology: Three Views of a Function, 493	**489**
9-6	**Interpreting Graphs** (Algebra)	**494**
9-7	**Simple and Compound Interest**	**499**
	Checkpoint Quiz 2	**502**
9-8	**Write an Equation** (Problem Solving)	**503**
9-9	**Transforming Formulas** (Algebra)	**507**

Assessment
- Test-Taking Strategies: Using Estimation, 511
- Chapter Review, 512
- Chapter Test, 514
- Test Prep: Reading Comprehension, 515

Real-World Snapshots: Applying Graphs **516**

Chapter 10

Algebra

Graphing in the Coordinate Plane

Student Support

Instant Check System

Diagnosing Readiness, 520

Check Skills You'll Need, 521, 527, 533, 540, 544, 549, 554, 559

Check Understanding, 522, 523, 527, 528, 534, 535, 540, 541, 545, 549, 550, 551, 555, 559, 560

Checkpoint Quiz, 538, 558

Comprehensive Test Prep

Daily Test Prep, 525, 531, 537, 543, 547, 553, 558, 562

Test-Taking Strategies, 563

Cumulative Test Prep, 567

Reading Math

Reading Math, 521, 523, 533, 534, 549, 550, 559

Learning Vocabulary, 532

Understanding Vocabulary, 564

Reading Comprehension, 531

Writing in Math

Daily Writing Practice, 524, 530, 536, 543, 546, 552, 556, 561, 566

Real-World Problem Solving

Strategies: Make a Table and Make a Graph, 544–547

Beekeeping, 529

Avalanches, 534

Practice Game, 547

Computer Animation, 551

. . . and more!

Diagnosing Readiness **520**

10-1 Graphing Points in Four Quadrants (Algebra) **521**
- Extension: Geometry in the Coordinate Plane, 526

10-2 Graphing Linear Equations (Algebra) **527**
- Reading Math: Learning Vocabulary, 532

10-3 Finding the Slope of a Line (Algebra) **533**
- Technology: Exploring Slope, 539

Checkpoint Quiz 1 . . . . **538**

10-4 Exploring Nonlinear Relationships (Algebra) **540**

10-5 Make a Table and Make a Graph (Problem Solving) **544**

10-6 Translations **549**
- Investigation: Exploring Slides, Flips, and Turns, 548

10-7 Symmetry and Reflections **554**

Checkpoint Quiz 2 . . . . **558**

10-8 Rotations **559**

Assessment
- Test-Taking Strategies: Answering True/False Questions, 563
- Chapter Review, 564
- Chapter Test, 566
- Test Prep: Cumulative Review, 567

Real-World Snapshots: Applying Coordinates. **568**

Chapter 11

Displaying and Analyzing Data

Student Support

Instant Check System
Diagnosing Readiness, 572
Check Skills You'll Need, 573, 579, 585, 592, 596, 602, 606, 613
Check Understanding, 573, 574, 575, 579, 580, 581, 585, 586, 587, 593, 597, 603, 606, 607, 608
Checkpoint Quiz, 590, 618

Comprehensive Test Prep
Daily Test Prep, 578, 584, 589, 595, 599, 605, 611, 617
Test-Taking Strategies, 619
Cumulative Test Prep, 623

Reading Math
Reading Math, 574, 597
Understanding Word Problems, 601
Understanding Vocabulary, 620
Reading Comprehension, 589, 623

Writing in Math
Daily Writing Practice, 578, 582, 583, 588, 594, 598, 599, 604, 610, 616, 622
Writing to Persuade, 612

Real-World Problem Solving
Strategies: Make a Table and Use Logical Reasoning, 592–595
Social Studies, 573
Math at Work, 600
Sharks, 604
Trees, 614
. . . and more!

Diagnosing Readiness 572

11-1 **Reporting Frequency** 573

11-2 **Spreadsheets and Data Displays** 579

11-3 **Other Displays** 585
- Extension: Venn Diagrams, 591

Checkpoint Quiz 1 590

11-4 **Make a Table and Use Logical Reasoning** Problem Solving 592

11-5 **Random Samples and Surveys** 596
- Reading Math: Understanding Word Problems, 601

11-6 **Estimating Population Size** Algebra 602

11-7 **Using Data to Persuade** 606
- Writing in Math: Writing to Persuade, 612

11-8 **Exploring Scatter Plots** 613

Checkpoint Quiz 2 618

Assessment
- Test-Taking Strategies: Answering the Question Asked, 619
- Chapter Review, 620
- Chapter Test, 622
- Test Prep: Reading Comprehension, 623

Real-World Snapshots: Applying Data Analysis 624

Chapter 12

Using Probability

Diagnosing Readiness 628

12-1 Probability 629

12-2 Experimental Probability 636
- Investigation: Exploring Experimental Probability, 635
- Technology: Random Numbers, 642

12-3 Make an Organized List and Simulate a Problem (Problem Solving) 643

12-4 Sample Spaces 647

Checkpoint Quiz 1 652

12-5 Compound Events 653
- Reading Math: Understanding Word Problems, 659

12-6 Permutations 660

12-7 Combinations 664

Checkpoint Quiz 2 668

Assessment
- Test-Taking Strategies: Eliminating Answers, 669
- Chapter Review, 670
- Chapter Test, 672
- Test Prep: Cumulative Review, 673

Real-World Snapshots: Applying Probability. 676

Student Support

Instant Check System

Diagnosing Readiness, 628

Check Skills You'll Need, 629, 636, 643, 647, 653, 660, 664

Check Understanding, 629, 630, 631, 637, 638, 644, 647, 648, 649, 654, 655, 660, 661, 664, 665

Checkpoint Quiz, 652, 668

Comprehensive Test Prep

Daily Test Prep, 633, 641, 646, 651, 658, 663, 667

Test-Taking Strategies, 669

Cumulative Test Prep, 673

Reading Math

Reading Math, 629, 631, 657, 660

Understanding Word Problems, 659

Understanding Vocabulary, 670

Reading Comprehension, 641

Writing in Math

Daily Writing Practice, 633, 639, 645, 650, 657, 663, 667, 672

Real-World Problem Solving

Strategies: Make an Organized List and Simulate a Problem, 643–646

Coins, 631

River Travel, 648

Practice Game, 634

Hobbies, 661

. . . and more!

End-of-Book Features

For a complete list, see Contents in Brief on page vi.

From the Authors

Dear Student,

We have designed this unique mathematics program with you in mind. We hope that Prentice Hall Mathematics will help you make sense of the mathematics you learn. We want to enable you to tap into the power of mathematics.

Examples in each lesson are broken into steps to help you understand how and why math works. Work the examples so that you understand the concepts and the methods presented. Then do your homework. Ask yourself how new concepts relate to old ones. Make connections! As you practice the concepts presented in this text, they will become part of your mathematical power.

The many real-world applications will let you see how you can use math in your daily life and give you the foundation for the math you will need in the future. The applications you will find in every lesson will help you see why it is important to learn mathematics. In addition, the Dorling Kindersley Real-World Snapshots will bring the world to your classroom.

This text will help you be successful on the tests you take in class and on high-stakes tests required by your state. The practice in each lesson will prepare you for the format as well as for the content of these tests.

Ask your teacher questions! Someone else in your class has the same question in mind and will be grateful that you decided to ask it.

We wish you the best as you use this text. The mathematics you learn this year will prepare you for your future as a student and your future in our technological society.

Sincerely,

Randy Charles.
Andy Reeves
Darwin E. Mills
Mark Illingworth
Judith C. Branch-Boyd

Connect Your Learning

Through Problem Solving, Activities, and the Web

Applications: Real-World Applications

Animals
Alligators, 604
Animals, 13, 14, 103, 175, 546
Bees, 529
Birds, 74, 157
Deer Population, 602
Dinosaurs, 278
Dogs, 86
Fish, 604
Sharks, 604
Wildlife, 544, 610
Zoo, 505

Careers
Careers, 385, 665
Employment, 476, 491
Engineering, 417
Jobs, 100, 219, 254, 331, 340, 376, 594
Journalism, 154
Masonry, 124, 234
Work, 314, 473, 506

Cars
Cars, 47, 48, 162, 244, 245, 315, 536, 567, 645
Driving, 152, 545
Gasoline, 90, 281, 284, 480, 482

Consumer Issues
Consumers, 9, 114, 119, 323, 331, 504
Discounts, 234
Shopping, 6, 20, 22, 58, 63, 80, 101, 124, 220, 233, 248, 251, 260, 283, 322, 324, 325, 326, 328, 339, 340, 494
Tickets, 81, 102, 106

Entertainment
Aquariums, 453
Band Concerts, 123
Broadcasting, 657
Circus, 421
Entertainment, 20, 91, 100, 104, 149, 219, 302, 330, 577, 583
Games, 42, 143, 495, 654, 655, 670
Movies, 104, 114, 616
Rides, 119
Theater, 321

Food
Baking, 119, 166
Calories, 491
Cooking, 26, 228, 244, 336, 650
Dining, 361
Farming, 32
Food, 20, 26, 59, 95, 320, 583, 612, 649
Groceries, 64, 124, 179, 330
Meal Planning, 208
Nutrition, 26, 109, 115, 243, 297, 299, 300, 301, 497, 585, 609, 671
Party Planning, 165, 200, 218, 281
Recipe, 567
Restaurants, 323, 339, 340

Money Matters
Banking, 21, 48, 154, 500
Budgeting, 313, 392
Business, 53, 74, 145, 162, 215, 221, 262, 330, 331, 505, 545, 583
Coins, 104, 631
Earnings, 32, 234, 324
Fund-Raising, 73, 220, 331, 513, 546, 588, 593
Investment, 48
Loans, 501
Money, 16, 21, 27, 32, 36, 42, 54, 64, 87, 91, 96, 104, 124, 175, 214, 220, 254, 376, 457, 487, 530, 558, 590, 645, 675
Prices, 247
Profit, 122, 607
Salary, 220, 309, 510, 646
Sales, 21, 303, 308, 309, 314, 325, 326, 505, 509
Savings, 14, 123, 505, 508, 546
Small Business, 262
Stocks, 85
Tax, 314
Utilities, 284
Wages, 622

Recreation
Amusement Park, 115, 384
Ballooning, 139, 284
Boating, 195, 455
Camping, 435, 446
Cycling, 223
Chess, 553
Fishing, 113
Hiking, 199, 224, 226
Jogging, 513
Mountain Climbing, 230, 594
Photography, 554
Recreation, 319, 340, 433
Running, 476
Skating, 14
Skiing, 318
Sky Diving, 542
Swimming, 188, 665
Television, 579, 580
Tourism, 662

Sports
Baseball, 79, 509, 639
Basketball, 86, 95, 151, 637, 641
Bowling, 80, 94, 609
Cross-Country, 198
Golf, 37, 589
Gymnastics, 13, 283
Olympics, 101
Soccer, 662
Softball, 105
Sporting Goods, 84
Sports, 36, 42, 58, 64, 114, 124, 161, 220, 244, 247, 249, 253, 282, 306, 315, 320, 330, 497, 514, 565, 593, 661
Tennis, 435
Track and Field, 609

. . . And Over 100 More Topics! See Real-World Applications in the Index, Page 801

Applications: Careers

Amusement Park Designer, 265
Archaeologist, 515
Architect, 350
Artist, 506
Atmospheric Scientist, 244
Aviation Survival Technician, 411
Bricklayer, 509
Computer Aided Spacesuit Designer, 279
Costume Designer, 583
Detective, 28
Financial Planner, 530
Landscape Architect, 21
Librarian, 89
Marine Biologist, 210
Park Ranger, 599
Physical Therapist, 355
Pollster, 600
Research Scientist, 331
Sculptor, 427
Songwriter, 196
Spacesuit Designer, 279
Surveyor, 270
Tailor, 650
Tour Boat Driver, 662
Veterinarian, 78
Waiter or Waitress, 323

Applications: Interdisciplinary Connections

Anatomy, 153, 250, 257
Archaeology, 423, 515
Architecture, 53, 277, 348, 352, 363, 371, 438
Art, 271, 427, 551
Astronomy, 137, 138, 139, 181
Biology, 86, 139, 171, 203, 210, 220, 243, 297, 477, 602, 603, 617, 621
Botany, 171, 490
Chemistry, 169, 244, 514
Engineering, 331, 417
Geography, 26, 36, 132, 171, 206, 217, 224, 225, 249, 276, 284, 293, 404, 414, 417, 591, 594
Geology, 594
Government, 293, 302, 314, 631, 633
History, 263, 293, 423, 573, 596
Journalism, 154
Languages, 32, 157, 309, 594
Music, 7, 11, 48, 97, 189, 242, 312, 320, 329, 331, 388, 417, 446, 482, 597, 617, 667
Physical Science, 32, 259
Physics, 47, 48, 86, 87, 181, 542
Science, 13, 43, 59, 205, 389, 483, 632, 638, 640
Social Studies, 77, 242, 254, 422, 573
Zoology, 175

Problem-Solving Strategies

The Problem-Solving Lessons in each chapter of Prentice Hall Mathematics progress in depth and sophistication within a course and from course to course.

Course 1 Students learn to apply a single problem-solving strategy in each lesson.

Course 2 Students learn to use more than one strategy to solve a problem. They also compare strategies to determine which one is most appropriate in a given situation.

Course 3 Students continue to combine and compare strategies to solve problems. Throughout the text, a greater focus on the strategy "write an equation" helps prepare students for success in algebra.

Using a Problem-Solving Plan 30–33, 81
Write an Equation 72, 73, 78, 82, 83, 84, 85, 88, 89, 94, 95, 102–103, 109, 112, 113, 117, 203, 213, 214, 318, 319, 324, 333–334, 490, 503–504, 602, 621, 660–661, 665
Solve a Simpler Problem 160–162, 252–255
Look for a Pattern 160–163, 374–377, 393
Try, Check, and Revise 31, 218–221, 455–458
Work Backward 218–221, 233, 337, 508
Draw a Diagram 31, 252–255, 374–377, 393
Make a Table 31, 544–547, 592–595, 621
Make a Graph 544–547
Use Logical Reasoning 31, 592–595, 621
Make an Organized List 643–646, 671
Simulate a Problem 643–646, 671

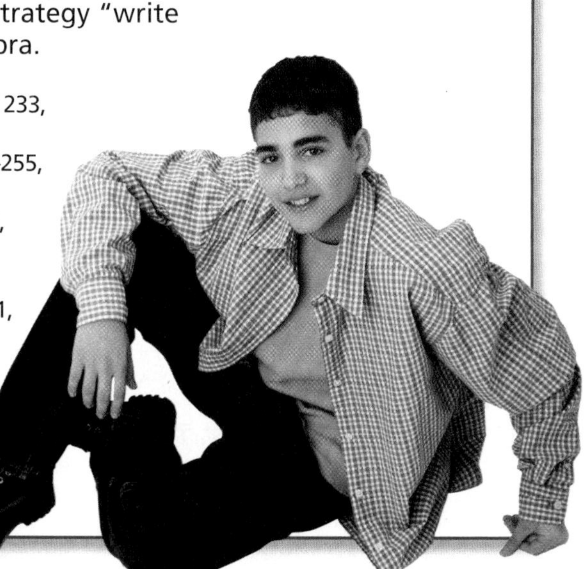

Prentice Hall Mathematics contains ample opportunities for you to actively explore mathematics, either working as a whole class, in groups, or individually.

Activities: Investigations

10–20-minute activities that either introduce or provide practice with lesson concepts

Estimates and Exact Answers, 5
Modeling Decimal Multiplication, 17
Combining Operations, 50
Algebraic Expressions, 71
Exploring Estimation, 77
Modeling Equations, 82
Exploring Inequalities, 116
Exploring Exponents, 131
Powers of Ten, 136
Ordering Fractions, 168
Using Fraction Models, 191
Modeling Multiplication of Fractions, 202
Modeling Equations with Fractions, 213
Precision in Measurements, 227
Birthday Data, 241
Exploring Similar Figures, 267
Planning a Trip, 280
A Matter of Scale, 286
Relating Fractions, Decimals, and Percents, 295
Using Percent Data from Graphs, 305
Exploring Percent of Change, 327
Folding Bisectors, 357
Angles of a Triangle, 364
Exploring Congruent Figures, 378
Area of a Parallelogram, 407
Area of a Trapezoid, 413
Relating the Area of a Circle to the Radius, 420
Squares and Square Roots, 426
Examining the Pythagorean Theorem, 431
Finding a Pattern, 474
Graphing a Function, 489
Exploring Patterns in the Coordinate Plane, 523
Exploring Slope, 533
Slides, Flips, and Turns, 548
Exploring Tesselations, 551
Making Graphs, 581
Writing Unbiased Questions, 597
Exploring Experimental Probability, 635
Experimenting with Probability, 636
Exploring Multiple Events, 653
Exploring Arrangements, 660

Activities: Real-World Snapshots

20–40-minute activities that apply the math from a chapter to real-world settings

Energy Field, 66
It's a Dog's Life, 126
Photographic Memory, 182
Into the Earth with Integers, 236
A Matter of Scale, 286
Fractal Facts, 342
Mini Golf Math, 398
Musical Shapes, 464
Through the Ages, 516
On Your Mark, 568
Bicycle Math, 624
Against the Odds?, 676

Activities: Chapter Projects

Fun projects that allow you to show off the math you've learned

Boardwalk, 678
Read All About It!, 678
Making the Measure, 679
Toss and Turn, 679
Weighty Matters, 680
Chills and Thrills, 680
Raisin' the Roof, 681
Shape Up and Ship Out, 681
Happy Landings, 682
People's Choice, 682
Too Many To Count, 683
Everybody Wins, 683

Activities: Technology

20–40-minute activities that use calculators or software to introduce math concepts

Using a Scientific Calculator, 55
Using Spreadsheets, 76
Using a Fraction Calculator, 212
Creating Similar Figures, 273
Three Views of a Function, 493
Exploring Slopes, 539
Random Numbers, 642

Plus timely calculator and graphing calculator hints

Take It to the Net

Throughout this book you will find links to the Prentice Hall Web site. Use the Web Code provided with each link to gain direct access to online material.

Here's how to **Take It to the NET**:
- Go to **www.PHSchool.com**.
- Enter the Web Code.
- Click Go!

For a complete list of online features, use Web Code abk-0099

Lesson Quiz Web Codes

There is an online quiz for each lesson. Access these quizzes with Web Codes aba-0101 through aba-1207 for Lesson 1-1 through Lesson 12-7. *See page 9.*

106 Lesson Quizzes
Web Code format: aba-0204 02 = Chapter 2 04 = Lesson 4

Chapter Resource Web Codes

Chapter	Vocabulary Quizzes *See page 62.*	Chapter Tests *See page 64.*	Dorling Kindersley Real-World Snapshots *See pages 66-67.*	Chapter Projects
1	abj-0151	aba-0152	abe-0153	abd-0161
2	abj-0251	aba-0252	abe-0253	abd-0261
3	abj-0351	aba-0352	abe-0353	abd-0361
4	abj-0451	aba-0452	abe-0453	abd-0461
5	abj-0551	aba-0552	abe-0553	abd-0561
6	abj-0651	aba-0652	abe-0653	abd-0661
7	abj-0751	aba-0752	abe-0753	abd-0761
8	abj-0851	aba-0852	abe-0853	abd-0861
9	abj-0951	aba-0952	abe-0953	abd-0961
10	abj-1051	aba-1052	abe-1053	abd-1061
11	abj-1151	aba-1152	abe-1153	abd-1161
12	abj-1251	aba-1252	abe-1253	abd-1261
End-of-Course		aba-1254		

Additional Resource Web Codes

Data Updates Use Web Code abg-2041 to get up-to-date government data for use in examples and exercises. *See page 37.*

Math at Work For information about each Math at Work feature, use Web Code abb-2031. *See page 28.*

iTEXT Complete student textbook available online. Includes interactivities and videos.

Using Your Book for Success

Welcome to *Prentice Hall Mathematics, Course 2*. There are many features built into the daily lessons of this text that will help you learn the important skills and concepts you will need to be successful in this course. Look through the following pages for some study tips that you will find useful as you complete each lesson.

Instant Check System™
An *Instant Check System*, built into the text and marked with a ✓, allows you to check your understanding of skills before moving on to the next topic.

✓ Diagnosing Readiness
Complete the *Diagnosing Readiness* exercises to see what topics you may need to review before you begin the chapter.

✓ Check Skills You'll Need
Complete the *Check Skills You'll Need* exercises to make sure you have the skills needed to successfully learn the concepts in the lesson.

✓ Check Understanding
Every lesson includes several *Examples*, each followed by a *Check Understanding* question that you can do on your own to see if you understand the skill being introduced. Check your progress with the answers at the back of the book.

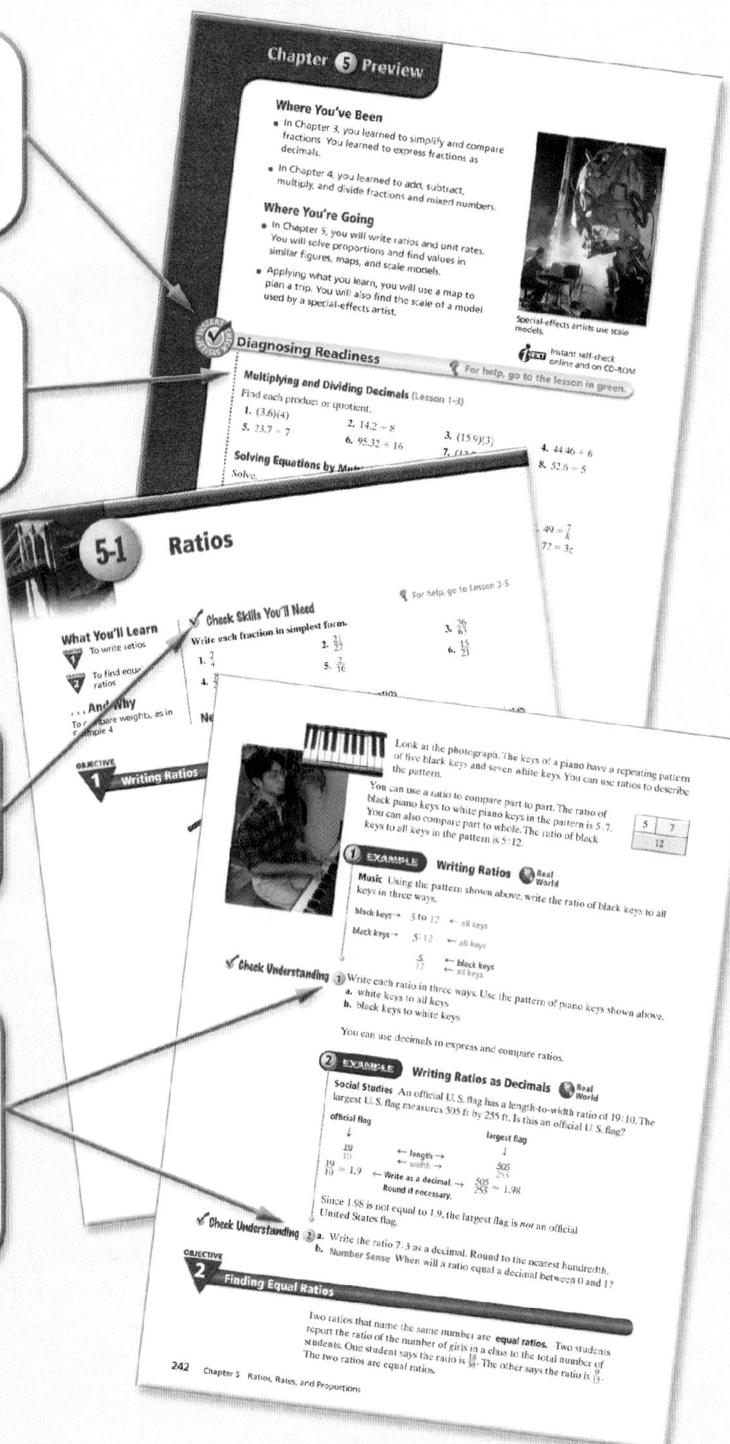

Chapter 5 Preview

Where You've Been

- In Chapter 3, you learned to simplify and compare fractions. You learned to express fractions as decimals.
- In Chapter 4, you learned to add, subtract, multiply, and divide fractions and mixed numbers.

Where You're Going

- In Chapter 5, you will write ratios and unit rates. You will solve proportions and find values in similar figures, maps, and scale models.
- Applying what you learn, you will use a map to plan a trip. You will also find the scale of a model used by a special-effects artist.

Special-effects artists use scale models.

Instant self-check online and on CD-ROM

Diagnosing Readiness

For help, go to the lesson in green.

Multiplying and Dividing Decimals (Lesson 1-3)

Find each product or quotient.

1. (3.6)(4) 2. 14.2 ÷ 8 3. (15.9)(3) 4. 44.46 ÷ 6
5. 23.7 ÷ 7 6. 95.32 ÷ 16 7. … 8. 52.6 ÷ 5

Solving Equations by …

5-1 Ratios

What You'll Learn

1. To write ratios
2. To find equal ratios

… And Why

To compare weights, as in Example 4

✓ Check Skills You'll Need

For help, go to Lesson 3-5.

Write each fraction in simplest form.

OBJECTIVE 1 Writing Ratios

Look at the photograph. The keys of a piano have a repeating pattern of five black keys and seven white keys. You can use ratios to describe the pattern.

You can use a ratio to compare part to part. The ratio of black piano keys to white piano keys in the pattern is 5:7. You can also compare part to whole. The ratio of black keys to all keys in the pattern is 5:12.

1 EXAMPLE Writing Ratios

Music Using the pattern shown above, write the ratio of black keys to all keys in three ways.

black keys → 5 to 12 ← all keys
black keys → 5 : 12 ← all keys
$\frac{5}{12}$ ← black keys ← all keys

✓ Check Understanding 1 Write each ratio in three ways. Use the pattern of piano keys shown above.
a. white keys to all keys
b. black keys to white keys

You can use decimals to express and compare ratios.

2 EXAMPLE Writing Ratios as Decimals

Social Studies An official U.S. flag has a length-to-width ratio of 19:10. The largest U.S. flag measures 505 ft by 255 ft. Is this an official U.S. flag?

official flag: $\frac{19}{10}$ ← length → ← width → ; $\frac{19}{10} = 1.9$ ← Write as a decimal. Round if necessary. → largest flag: $\frac{505}{255} \approx 1.98$

Since 1.98 is not equal to 1.9, the largest flag is *not* an official United States flag.

✓ Check Understanding 2 a. Write the ratio 7:3 as a decimal. Round to the nearest hundredth.
b. Number Sense When will a ratio equal a decimal between 0 and 1?

OBJECTIVE 2 Finding Equal Ratios

Two ratios that name the same number are **equal ratios**. Two students report the ratio of the number of girls in a class to the total number of students. One student says the ratio is $\frac{18}{30}$. The other says the ratio is $\frac{9}{15}$. The two ratios are equal ratios.

242 Chapter 5 Ratios, Rates, and Proportions

Need Help?

Need Help? notes provide a quick review of a concept you need to understand the topic being presented. Look for the green labels throughout the book that tell you where to "Go" for help.

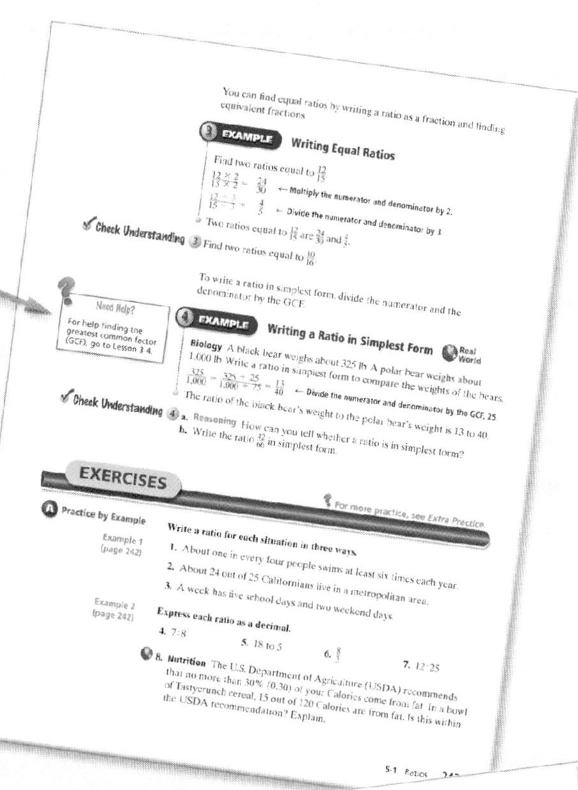

More Than One Way

The *More Than One Way* features show you two different methods to solve a problem. By analyzing each student's method, you can think critically about the solution and then choose the method you would use to solve a similar problem.

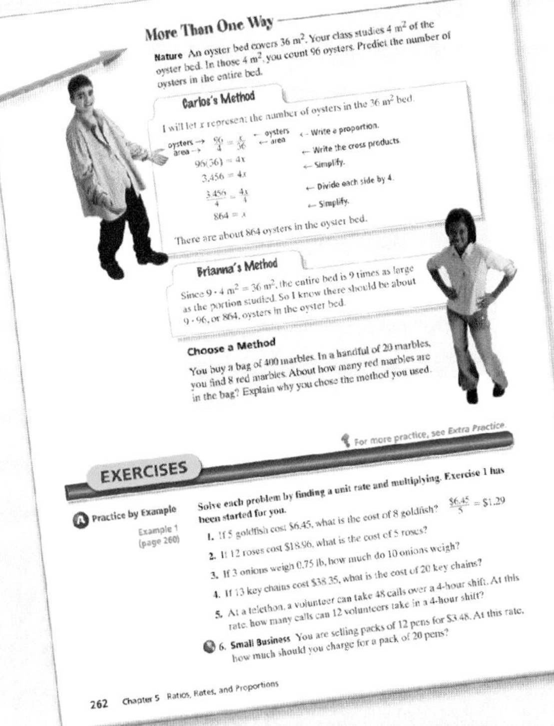

Exercise Sets

Exercises
There are numerous *Exercises* in each lesson that give you the practice you need to master the concepts in the lesson. Each practice set includes the following sections.

A: Practice by Example
The *A: Practice by Example* exercises refer you to the Examples in the lesson, in case you need help completing these exercises.

B: Apply Your Skills
The *B: Apply Your Skills* exercises combine skills from earlier lessons to offer you richer skill exercises and multi-step application problems.

C: Challenge
The *C: Challenge* exercises give you an opportunity to solve problems that extend and stretch your thinking.

Test Prep
The *Test Prep* exercises give you daily practice with the types of test question formats that you will encounter on state and national tests.

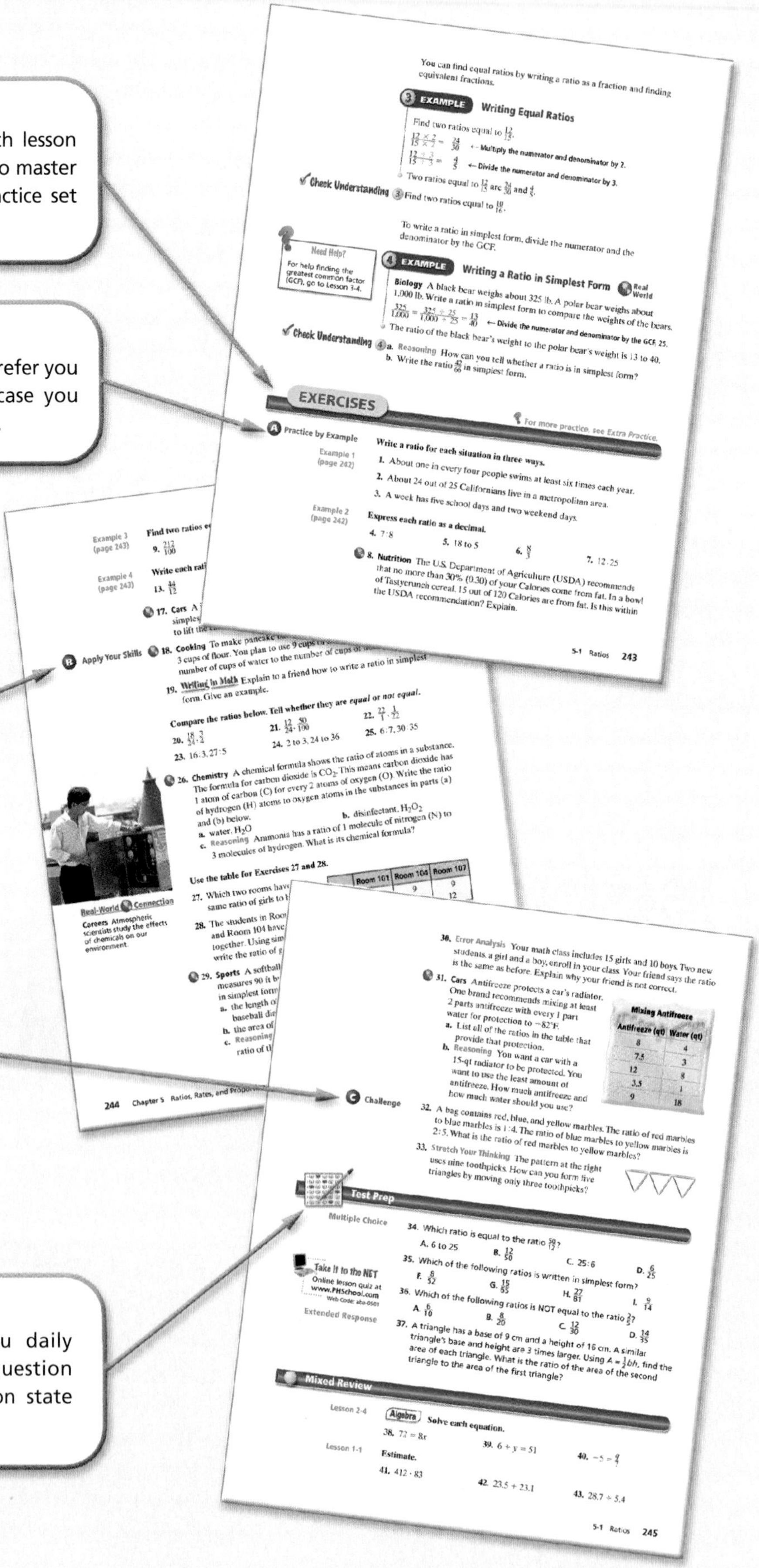

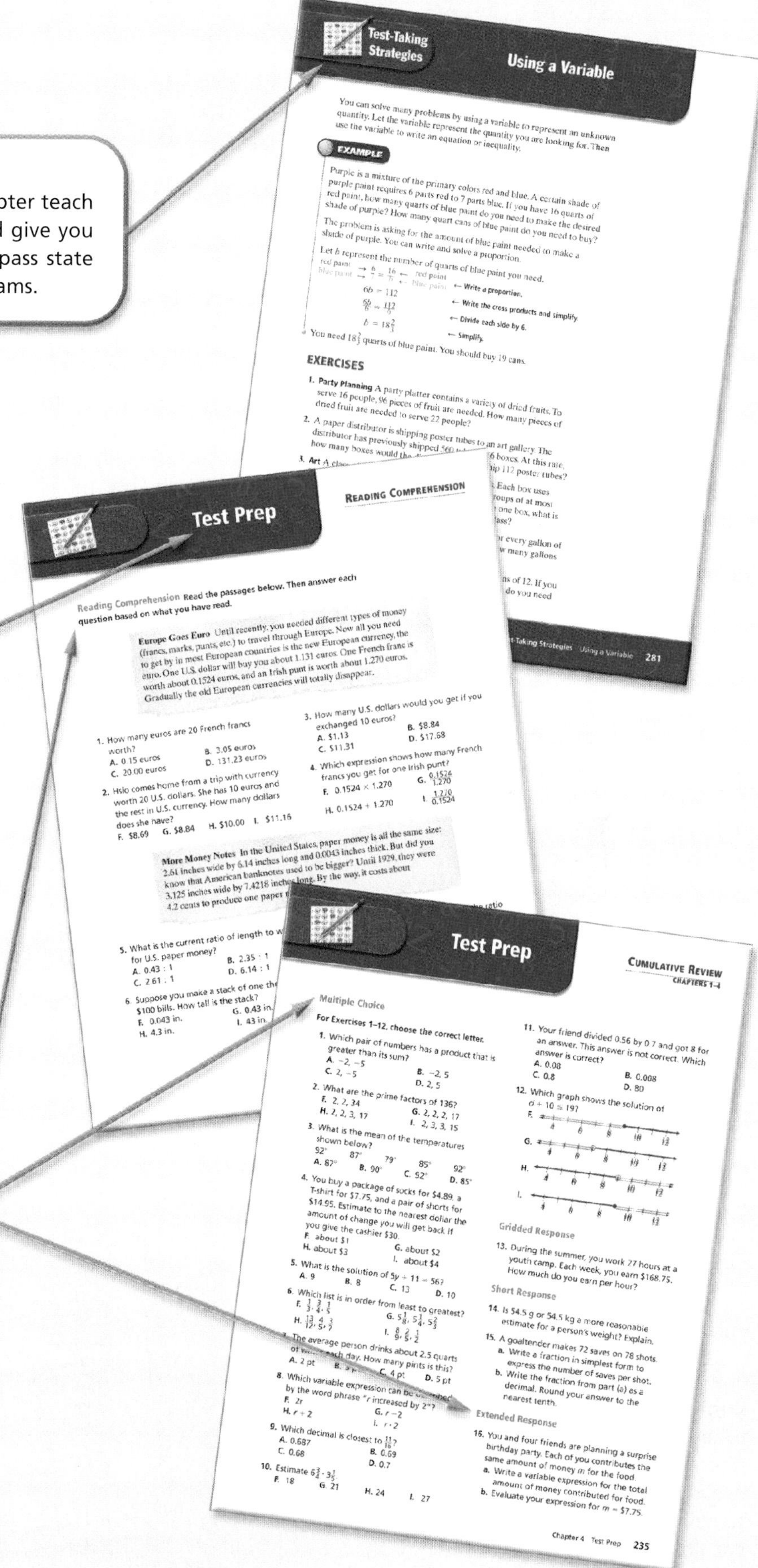

Test-Taking Strategies
Test-Taking Strategies in every chapter teach you strategies to be successful and give you practice in the skills you need to pass state tests and standardized national exams.

Test Prep
In addition to the exercises in every lesson, the *Test Prep* pages in every chapter give you more opportunities to prepare for the tests you will have to take.

Test Item Formats
The *Test Prep* exercises in your book give you the practice you need to answer all types of test questions.

- *Multiple Choice*
- *Gridded Response* (answers are written in a grid)
- *Short Response* (answers are scored with a rubric)
- *Extended Response* (answers are scored with a rubric)
- *Reading Comprehension*

Reading and Writing to Learn

Your *Course 2* text provides even more ways for you to develop your ability to read and write mathematically so that you are successful in this course and on state tests.

New Vocabulary
New Vocabulary is listed for each lesson so you can pre-read the text. As each term is introduced, it is highlighted in yellow.

Reading Math hints
These *hints* help you to use the mathematical notation correctly, understand vocabulary, and translate symbols into everyday English so you can talk about what you've learned.

Reading Math lessons
Reading Math lessons focus on a variety of topics to help you read more effectively, so that you can write, speak, and think mathematically.

Writing in Math lessons
Writing in Math lessons help you write more effectively about the mathematics you are learning.

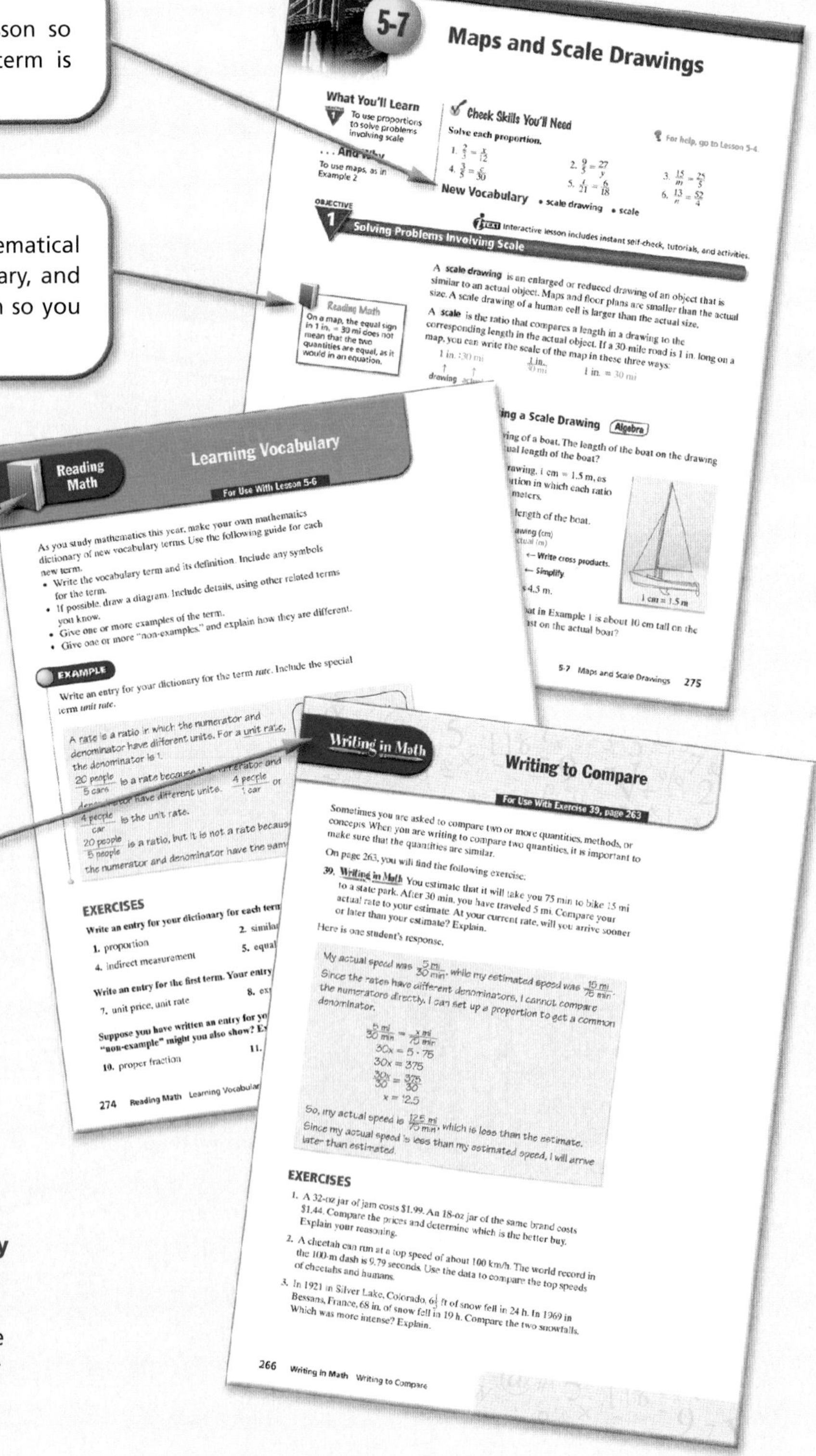

For more help:

- **Reading Math exercises**
  Reading Math exercises in the Chapter Review help you to understand and correctly use the vocabulary presented in the chapter.
- **English/Spanish Illustrated Glossary**
  While you are learning, use this handy reference that contains a written explanation and an illustrated example to help you understand and remember each term.

Dorling Kindersley (DK) is an international publishing company that specializes in the creation of high-quality, illustrated information books for children and adults. DK is part of the Pearson family of companies.

Real-World Snapshots
The *Real-World Snapshots* feature applies the exciting and unique graphic presentation style found in Dorling Kindersley books to show you how mathematics is used in real life.

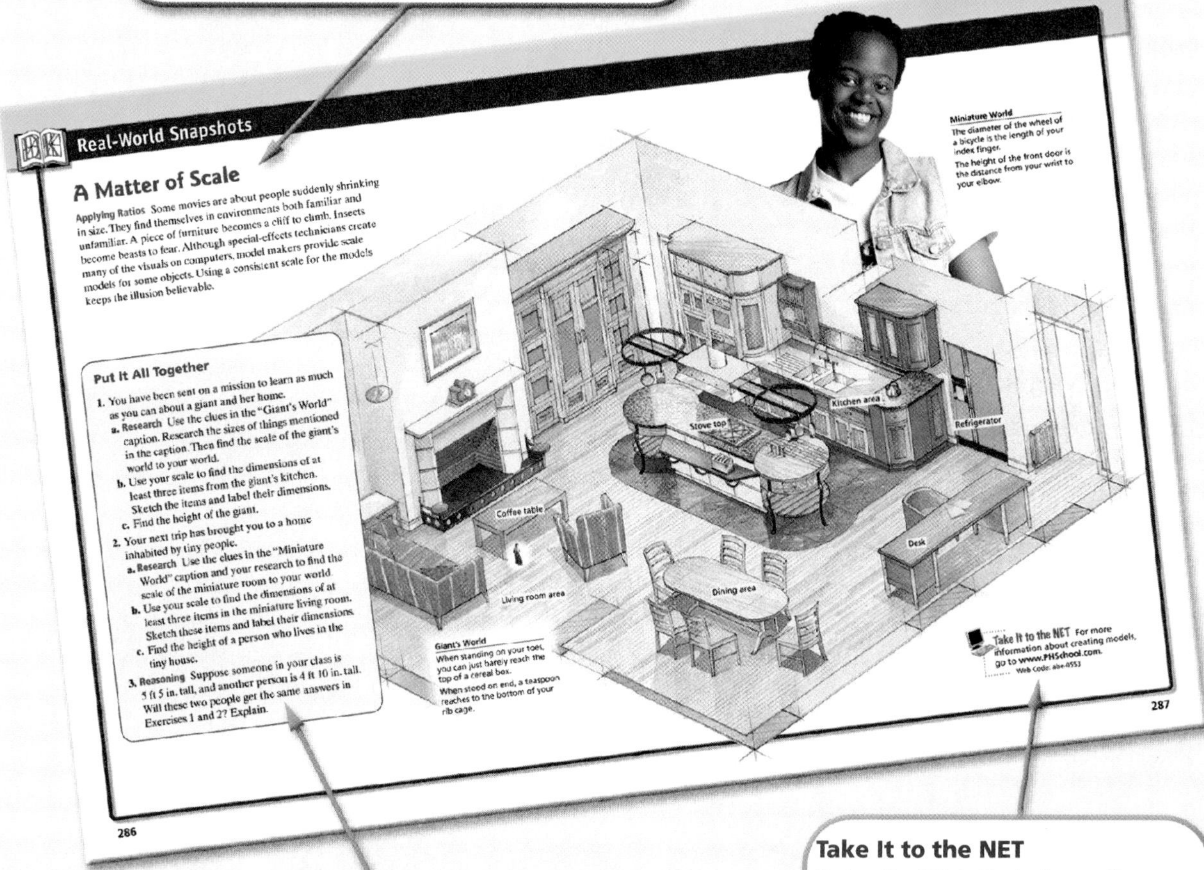

Real-World Snapshots

A Matter of Scale

Applying Ratios Some movies are about people suddenly shrinking in size. They find themselves in environments both familiar and unfamiliar. A piece of furniture becomes a cliff to climb. Insects become beasts to fear. Although special-effects technicians create many of the visuals on computers, model makers provide scale models for some objects. Using a consistent scale for the models keeps the illusion believable.

Put It All Together

1. You have been sent on a mission to learn as much as you can about a giant and her home.
   a. **Research** Use the clues in the "Giant's World" caption. Research the sizes of things mentioned in the caption. Then find the scale of the giant's world to your world.
   b. Use your scale to find the dimensions of at least three items from the giant's kitchen. Sketch the items and label their dimensions.
   c. Find the height of the giant.
2. Your next trip has brought you to a home inhabited by tiny people.
   a. **Research** Use the clues in the "Miniature World" caption and your research to find the scale of the miniature room to your world.
   b. Use your scale to find the dimensions of at least three items in the miniature living room. Sketch these items and label their dimensions.
   c. Find the height of a person who lives in the tiny house.
3. **Reasoning** Suppose someone in your class is 5 ft 5 in. tall, and another person is 4 ft 10 in. tall. Will these two people get the same answers in Exercises 1 and 2? Explain.

Giant's World
When standing on your toes, you can just barely reach the top of a cereal box.
When stood on end, a teaspoon reaches to the bottom of your rib cage.

Miniature World
The diameter of the wheel of a bicycle is the length of your index finger.
The height of the front door is the distance from your wrist to your elbow.

Take It to the NET For more information about creating models, go to www.PHSchool.com.
Web Code: abe-0553

286

287

Take It to the NET
Enter the Web Code for online information you can use to learn more about the topic of the feature.

Put It All Together
Using data that you gather as well as data from these pages and the Data File, complete the hands-on activities to apply the mathematics you are learning in real-world situations.

CHAPTER 1

Decimals and Integers

Lessons

1-1 Using Estimation Strategies

1-2 Adding and Subtracting Decimals

1-3 Multiplying and Dividing Decimals

1-4 Measuring in Metric Units

1-5 Problem Solving: Using a Problem-Solving Plan

1-6 Comparing and Ordering Integers

1-7 Adding and Subtracting Integers

1-8 Multiplying and Dividing Integers

1-9 Order of Operations and the Distributive Property

1-10 Mean, Median, and Mode

Key Vocabulary

- absolute value (p. 34)
- additive inverse (p. 39)
- compatible numbers (p. 6)
- integers (p. 34)
- mean (p. 56)
- median (p. 57)
- mode (p. 58)
- opposites (p. 34)
- order of operations (p. 50)
- outlier (p. 57)
- range (p. 41)

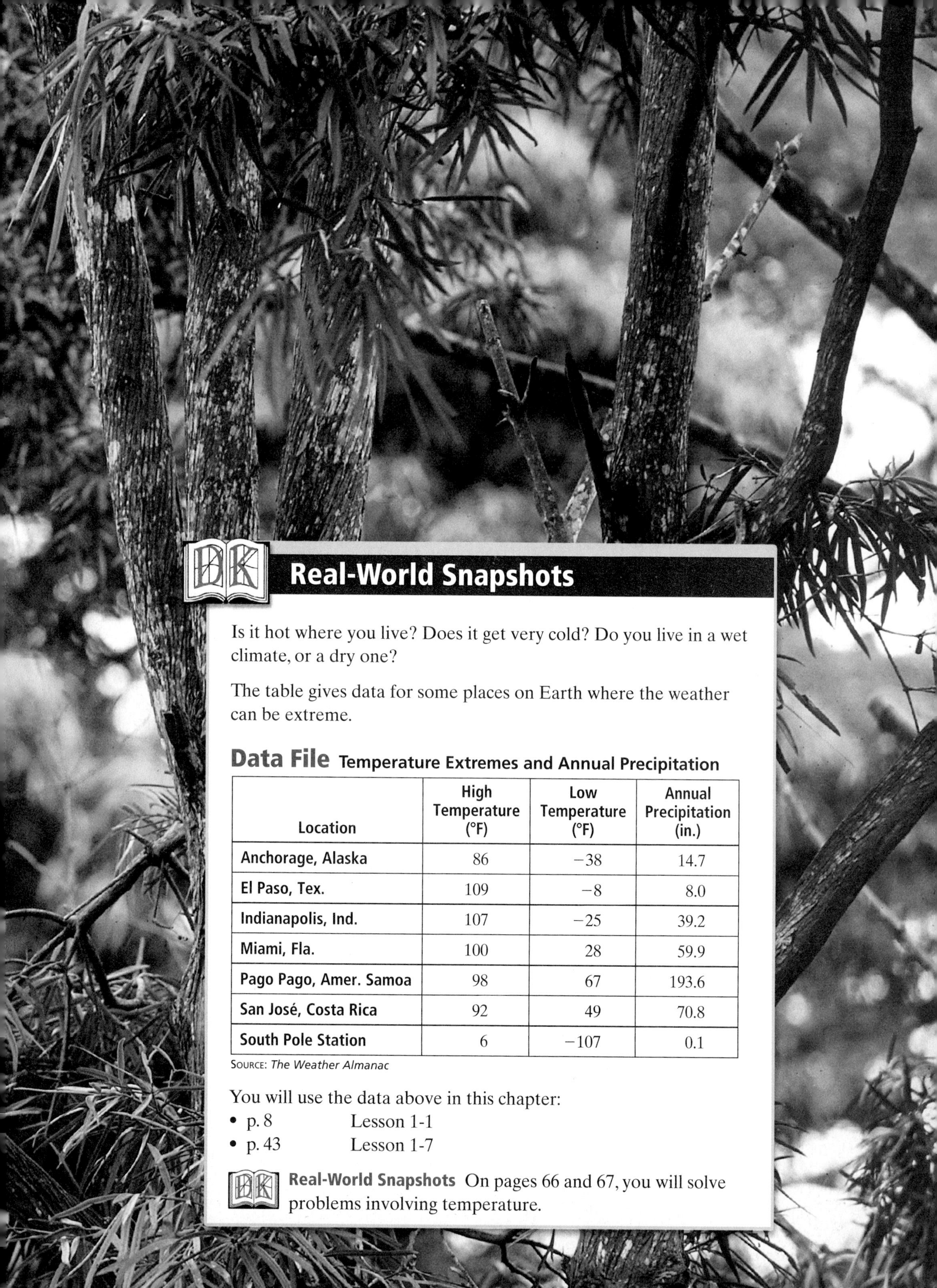

Real-World Snapshots

Is it hot where you live? Does it get very cold? Do you live in a wet climate, or a dry one?

The table gives data for some places on Earth where the weather can be extreme.

Data File Temperature Extremes and Annual Precipitation

Location	High Temperature (°F)	Low Temperature (°F)	Annual Precipitation (in.)
Anchorage, Alaska	86	−38	14.7
El Paso, Tex.	109	−8	8.0
Indianapolis, Ind.	107	−25	39.2
Miami, Fla.	100	28	59.9
Pago Pago, Amer. Samoa	98	67	193.6
San José, Costa Rica	92	49	70.8
South Pole Station	6	−107	0.1

SOURCE: *The Weather Almanac*

You will use the data above in this chapter:

- p. 8 Lesson 1-1
- p. 43 Lesson 1-7

Real-World Snapshots On pages 66 and 67, you will solve problems involving temperature.

Chapter 1 Preview

Where You've Been

- In your previous course, you learned to add, subtract, multiply, and divide decimals and integers.

Where You're Going

- In Chapter 1, you will use the properties of addition and multiplication as well as the order of operations to add, subtract, multiply, and divide decimals and integers.
- Applying what you learn, you will compare the temperatures of various places.

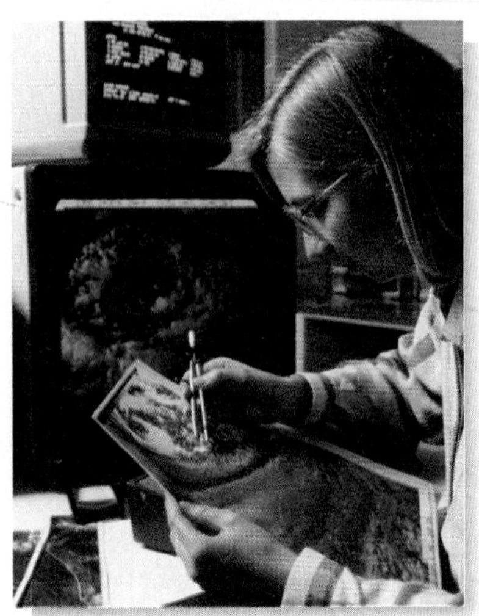

Meteorologists study weather, which includes temperatures.

Instant self-check online and on CD-ROM

Diagnosing Readiness

For help, go to the Skills Handbook.

Comparing and Ordering Whole Numbers (Skills Handbook page 696)

Use > or < to compare the numbers.

1. 72 ■ 720 **2.** 3,972 ■ 3,927 **3.** 30,000 ■ 200,000

4. 14,056 ■ 1,456 **5.** 5,010 ■ 5,001 **6.** 245,999 ■ 254,000

Dividing Whole Numbers (Skills Handbook page 699)

Find each quotient.

7. $8\overline{)296}$ **8.** $93\overline{)6{,}882}$ **9.** $71\overline{)39{,}902}$ **10.** $82\overline{)22{,}960}$

Place Value and Decimals (Skills Handbook page 700)

What is the value of the underlined digit?

11. $24.\underline{3}5$ **12.** $4.08\underline{6}$ **13.** $17\underline{9}.8$ **14.** $59.0\underline{3}$ **15.** $1.046\underline{7}$

Reading and Writing Decimals (Skills Handbook page 701)

Write each number in words.

16. 421.5 **17.** 5,006.25 **18.** 15.004 **19.** 0.329 **20.** 710.413

Rounding Decimals (Skills Handbook page 702)

Round to the nearest hundredth.

21. 34.124 **22.** 278.786 **23.** 3.602 **24.** 81.796 **25.** 16.999

1-1 Using Estimation Strategies

What You'll Learn

To estimate by rounding

To use front-end estimation and compatible numbers

. . . And Why

To estimate the cost of a gift, as in Example 3

Check Skills You'll Need

For help, go to Skills Handbook, p. 697.

Round to the place of the underlined digit.

1. 3,528 **2.** 24,106 **3.** 54
4. 131,295 **5.** 449 **6.** 4,951
7. 229,999 **8.** 82,729 **9.** 998

10. Round 3,507 to the nearest ten, nearest hundred, and nearest thousand.

New Vocabulary

- compatible numbers

Interactive lesson includes instant self-check, tutorials, and activities.

OBJECTIVE 1 Estimating by Rounding

Investigation: Estimates and Exact Answers

1. Suppose you are writing a news article. Your notes contain some data that may be estimates. For each situation, decide whether you have an estimate or an exact value. Explain your decision.
   a. The population of Florida is 16,000,000.
   b. Florida has 25 representatives in the U.S. House of Representatives.
2. Describe a situation for which an estimate is acceptable.
3. Describe a situation for which an exact answer is necessary.

Real-World Connection

Eagle rays have large fins that look like wings.

You can estimate an answer before you calculate it. Sometimes an estimate is all you need. Use the symbol ≈, which means "is approximately equal to."

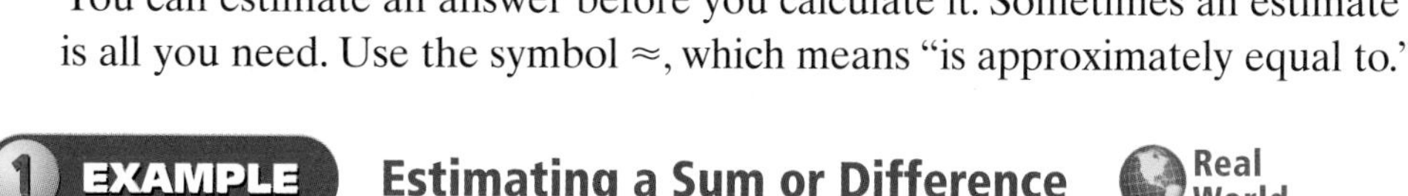

1 EXAMPLE Estimating a Sum or Difference (Real World)

Eagle Rays The span of an eagle ray's fins is 3.27 m. The span of her baby's fins is 0.88 m. Estimate the difference between the spans. Round each span to the nearest whole number before you find the difference.

$3.27 - 0.88 \approx 3 - 1$ ← **Round to the nearest whole number.**

≈ 2 ← **Subtract.**

The difference is about 2 m.

Check Understanding **1** Estimate the difference between stingrays with spans of 1.75 m and 0.92 m.

You can use rounding to estimate products.

2 EXAMPLE Estimating a Product

A living room is 10.5 ft by 9.25 ft. Use rounding to estimate the room's area in square feet.

$10.5 \approx 11$ ← **Round each factor to the nearest whole number.**

$9.25 \approx 9$

$11 \times 9 = 99$ ← **Multiply.**

The area of the living room is about 99 ft^2.

Check Understanding 2 Estimate. Round to the nearest whole number before you multiply.

a. 7.65×3.12 **b.** 11.09×4.85

OBJECTIVE

2 Using Front-End Estimation and Compatible Numbers

Front-end estimation is particularly useful for finding sums. First, add the front numbers. Then estimate the sum of the lesser numbers and adjust the estimate.

3 EXAMPLE Estimating by Front-End Estimation

Shopping Suppose you want to purchase and wrap a birthday gift. You select a kaleidoscope for \$5.39, gift wrap for \$1.49, and a greeting card for \$2.95. Estimate the total cost of your selections.

Step 1 Add the front-end digits.

\$5.39
\$1.49
+\$2.95
\$8

Step 2 Estimate the total amount of cents to the nearest dollar.

\$5.39, \$1.49	← about \$1
\$2.95	← about \$1
	\$2

\$8 + \$2 = \$10

The total cost is about \$10.

Check Since 5.39 + 2.95 + 1.49 = 9.83 ≈ 10, the answer checks.

Real-World Connection

A kaleidoscope is a tube that uses mirrors to show patterns like the one above.

Check Understanding 3 Estimate the total cost of a dog collar for \$5.79, a dog toy for \$2.48, and a dog dish for \$5.99.

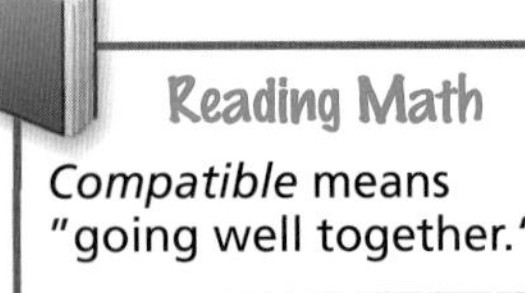

Reading Math

Compatible means "going well together."

Compatible numbers are numbers that are easy to compute mentally. You can use compatible numbers to estimate. Simply change the numbers of the problem to make the calculation easier. Compatible numbers are particularly useful for finding quotients.

4 EXAMPLE Using Compatible Numbers

Music Suppose you have \$50.25. About how many CDs can you buy from category D?

$\frac{50.25}{7.95}$ ← **Set up the quotient.**

$\frac{48}{8}$ ← **Choose compatible numbers such as 48 and 8.**

6 ← **Simplify.**

You can buy about six CDs from category D.

CD Price List

Category	Price
A	\$23.95*
B	\$15.95
C	\$12.95
D	\$7.95

*Double CD

Check Understanding 4 **a.** **Number Sense** Why are 48 and 8 compatible numbers?

b. About how many CDs can you buy from category B? Explain.

c. **Reasoning** Is an estimate of the price good enough to decide if you have enough money to buy the CDs you want? Explain.

EXERCISES

For more practice, see *Extra Practice*.

A Practice by Example

Example 1 (page 5)

Estimate. Round to the nearest whole number before you add or subtract.

1. 10.13 + 1.46 **2.** 9.82 − 1.76 **3.** 11.53 + 7.23

4. 14.17 − 10.92 **5.** 21.18 − 17.92 **6.** 9.35 − 0.81

Example 2 (page 6)

Estimate. Round to the nearest whole number before you multiply.

7. 4.9 × 12.2 **8.** 25.123 × 4.79 **9.** 98.68 × 9.13

10. 6.07 × 3.29 **11.** 13.93 × 11.68 **12.** 7.65 × 5.33

13. **Transportation** One of the world's fastest trains is France's TGV (*train à grande vitesse*, or "train of great speed"). It travels about 132 miles each hour. About how far can it travel in 4.75 hours?

Example 3 (page 6)

Use front-end estimation to estimate each sum.

14. 5.43 + 2.67 **15.** 8.09 + 11.24 **16.** 7.18 + 5.89

17. 4.39 + 9.57 **18.** 24.21 + 16.03 **19.** 3.62 + 2.31

Example 4 (page 7)

Use compatible numbers to estimate each quotient.

20. 76.5 ÷ 8.8 **21.** 19.45 ÷ 4.92 **22.** 27.36 ÷ 3.14

23. 103.6 ÷ 9.72 **24.** 32.2 ÷ 7.56 **25.** 3.963 ÷ 1.79

26. **Cooking** It took 75.75 lb of shredded cheese to make the world's largest burrito. Use compatible numbers to estimate how many 10-lb boxes of shredded cheese the cooks needed.

Apply Your Skills

Use any estimation strategy to estimate. Tell which strategy you used and why.

27. $71.43 - 28.098$ **28.** 24.32×179.12 **29.** $345.124 \div 8.98$

30. $726.27 + 699.05$ **31.** 4.27×1.6 **32.** $7.59 \div 2.143$

Real-World Connection

Chicago is called the "Windy City" because of political speeches, not because of the weather.

33. Weather In Chicago, Illinois, the average wind speed is 10.4 mi/h. In Great Falls, Montana, the average wind speed is 13.1 mi/h. About how much greater is the average wind speed in Great Falls than in Chicago?

34. Error Analysis Suppose you use a calculator to find the sum 362.9 + 42.8 + 35.46. Your display reads 826.36. Explain how an estimate would help you realize that you have made an error.

35. a. Freight Suppose you have 12 boxes that weigh 287.2 lb each and 15 boxes that weigh 198.7 lb each. Estimate the total weight of the boxes.

b. An elevator has a weight limit of 4,000 lb. What is the maximum number of boxes from part (a) that you can load on the elevator?

36. Travel On vacation, you wish to send eight postcards to friends at home. You find cards costing \$.59 each. Eight postcard stamps cost about \$2 total. About how much will it cost to buy and mail the cards?

Estimate the cost of each group of items below.

37. **38.** **39.**

The sample below shows the estimation technique called *clustering*. Since each addend clusters close to 2.5, the sum is approximately equal to 5 × 2.5. Use clustering to estimate each sum in Exercises 40–42.

Sample $2.8 + 2.6 + 2.2 + 2.4 + 2.5 \approx$
$2.5 + 2.5 + 2.5 + 2.5 + 2.5$
$5 \times 2.5 = 12.5$ ← **Multiply.**

40. $6.3 + 5.9 + 6.09 + 6.33 + 5.68 + 6.1$

41. \$14.25 + \$13.75 + \$14.53 + \$13.69

42. $33.15 + 37.95 + 34.63 + 36.29 + 34.08$

43. Data File, p. 3 Estimate the total precipitation each city gets in 3 years.

44. Writing in Math Explain how you use compatible numbers to estimate.

C Challenge

Estimate.

45. 36.92 − 12.03 + 7.5

46. 2.034 × 9.76 × 10.22

47. 497.625 ÷ 4.9138

48. 2.371 + 23.71 + 237.1 + 2,371

Estimate to decide which product is the better buy. Explain your reasoning.

49. one bucket of 3 doz practice baseballs for $89.99 plus $10.42 shipping or 8 doz practice baseballs for $221.60 plus $19.75 shipping

50. 12 pairs of socks for $34.68, or 3 pairs of socks for $9.57

51. **Consumers** Your family is driving 359.2 mi from your home. The family car gets 29.6 miles per gallon of gasoline. If the price of a gallon of gas is $1.459, about how much will the gasoline for the trip cost?

52. **Stretch Your Thinking** I am a three-digit number. The sum of my digits is 26. My last two digits are the same. What number am I?

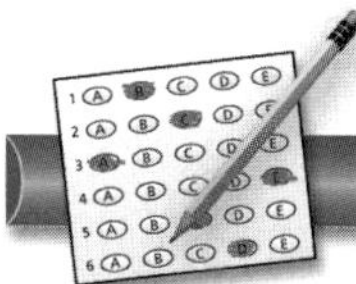

Test Prep

Multiple Choice

53. A reasonable estimate of a sum is 900. Which numbers could have been used to get this estimate?

A. 682.14 + 65.21 + 142.65
B. 734.3 + 201.79 + 55.22
C. 421.5 + 337.948 + 275.801
D. 225.06 + 275.8 + 269.7

54. Which of the following situations may use an estimate instead of an exact number?

F. time allowed for each class
G. number of classrooms at school
H. time needed to do homework
I. number of seats in a bus

Take It to the NET
Online lesson quiz at
www.PHSchool.com
Web Code aba-0101

55. You earn $612 in a year at a part-time job. Which is the best estimate for your weekly earnings?

A. $18
B. $16
C. $14
D. $12

Short Response

56. Estimate the sum of $23.58 + $13.07 + $16.85 to the nearest dollar. Justify your choice of method.

Mixed Review

Skills Handbook (page 696)

Write the numbers from least to greatest.

57. 4 4,004 40 403

58. 7,618 7,681 7,680 7,068

Skills Handbook (page 701)

Write each number in words.

59. 248.9

60. 431.85

61. 4.28

62. 130.396

Reading Your Textbook

Your textbook has many features designed to help you as you read it. In addition to these features, keep the following hints in mind.

- ***Read carefully.*** You will sometimes need to read a section several times to understand all of the information in it. Pay attention to math symbols. Make sure you understand their meaning. Also, read graphs carefully.
- ***Pay attention to mathematical terms.*** Sometimes a word that you already know is used in a new way. It may be used in more than one way because of its use with different mathematical topics.
- ***Read with pencil and paper.*** You should work through the examples as you read to make sure you understand the steps shown.

The following exercises will introduce you to the different features of your textbook. They will help you practice strategies you will use all year.

EXERCISES

Every lesson starts with "What You'll Learn. . . And Why," "Check Skills You'll Need," and "New Vocabulary." Find these in Lesson 1-2.

1. What two skills will you learn in this lesson?

2. What new vocabulary terms are introduced in the lesson?

Each lesson contains a section of worked-out examples. This section may also contain Key Concepts boxes. Go to this section in Lesson 1-3.

3. There are four worked-out examples. What are their titles?

4. How can example titles help you as you work on exercises?

5. What is the purpose of the bold text next to arrows in each example?

Find the Exercises section in Lesson 1-4.

6. To the left of Exercises 7–10, you see **"Example 2 (page 24)."** How is this information helpful as you work on exercises?

7. Find the Chapter Review. How will this help you review the chapter?

8. Locate *median* in the Glossary at the back of the book. What information is given for the word?

1-2 Adding and Subtracting Decimals

What You'll Learn

 To add and subtract decimals

 To use the properties of addition

. . . And Why

To select music for a CD, as in Example 2

Check Skills You'll Need

For help, go to the Skills Handbook p. 696.

Use < or > to compare the numbers.

1. 203 ■ 230 **2.** 1,047 ■ 147 **3.** 989 ■ 998

4. 245,641 ■ 255,614 **5.** 504,214 ■ 502,414 **6.** 1,260 ■ 126

New Vocabulary

- Identity Property of Addition
- Commutative Property of Addition
- Associative Property of Addition

OBJECTIVE

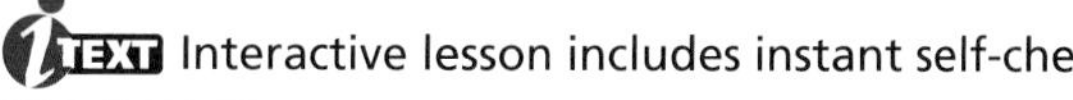

1 Adding and Subtracting Decimals

When you add and subtract decimals, be sure to align the decimal points.

1 EXAMPLE Aligning Decimal Points

Find 2.31 + 19.1 + 1.882.

Estimate 2.31 + 19.1 + 1.882 ≈ 2 + 19 + 2, or 23

Align the decimal points.

$$\begin{array}{r} 2.310 \\ 19.100 \\ +\ 1.882 \\ \hline 23.292 \end{array}$$

← **Insert zeros so each addend has the same number of decimal places.**

Check for Reasonableness 23.292 is reasonable since it is close to 23. ✔

Check Understanding 1 **a.** Number Sense How do you align the decimal points in 7.42 and 10?
b. Find 9.75 + 14.851 + 2.

2 EXAMPLE Subtracting Decimals

Real World

Music You have 8.34 min left on a CD. How much time will you have left after you burn "Born in the USA"?

Title	Min
"76 Trombones"	3.12
"Stars and Stripes Forever"	3.52
"Born in the USA"	4.65
"America the Beautiful"	3.63
"Yankee Doodle Dandy"	2.5
"Star-Spangled Banner"	4.5

$$\begin{array}{r} \scriptstyle 7\ \ \overset{12}{2}\ 14 \\ 8.34 \\ -\ 4.65 \\ \hline 3.69 \end{array}$$

← **Regroup.**

You will have 3.69 min left on the CD.

Check Understanding 2 Find 36.901 − 27.824.

Real-World Connection

A digital tape measure can store and add measurements in meters or in feet.

You can subtract a decimal from a whole number. Place a decimal point after the whole number and align the decimal points. Insert, or "annex," as many zeros as needed to have the same number of decimal places.

3 EXAMPLE Annexing Zeros to Subtract

Measurement You guess that the length of a room is 5 m. You use a digital tape measure to find that the actual length is 3.9 m. Find the difference between your guess and the actual measurement.

Insert a decimal point and one zero.	Regroup.	Subtract.
$\begin{array}{r} 5.0 \\ -\ 3.9 \\ \hline \end{array}$	$\begin{array}{r} \scriptstyle 4\,10 \\ \not{5}.\not{0} \\ -\ 3.9 \\ \hline \end{array}$	$\begin{array}{r} \scriptstyle 4\,10 \\ \not{5}.\not{0} \\ -\ 3.9 \\ \hline 1.1 \end{array}$

Your guess is 1.1 m greater than the actual measurement.

Check Understanding 3 **Health** Normal body temperature is 98.6°F. You are ill and your temperature is 102°F.

a. Estimate the difference between your temperature and normal body temperature.

b. Find the actual difference between your temperature and normal body temperature.

OBJECTIVE

2 Using the Properties of Addition

You can use the properties of addition to add mentally.

Key Concepts Properties of Addition

Identity Property of Addition

The sum of zero and a is a.

Arithmetic $5.6 + 0 = 5.6$
$0 + 5.6 = 5.6$

Algebra $a + 0 = a$
$0 + a = a$

Commutative Property of Addition

Changing the order of the addends does not change the sum.

Arithmetic $1.2 + 3.4 = 3.4 + 1.2$

Algebra $a + b = b + a$

Associative Property of Addition

Changing the grouping of the addends does not change the sum.

Arithmetic $(2.5 + 6) + 4 = 2.5 + (6 + 4)$

Algebra $(a + b) + c = a + (b + c)$

4 EXAMPLE Using Properties of Addition

Mental Math Find 0.7 + 12.5 + 1.3.

What you think

I should look for compatible numbers that add up to a whole number. The sum of 0.7 and 1.3 is 2. Then, I can add 2 and 12.5 for a total of 14.5.

Why it works

$$
\begin{aligned}
0.7 + 12.5 + 1.3 &= 0.7 + 1.3 + 12.5 && \leftarrow \text{Commutative Property} \\
&= (0.7 + 1.3) + 12.5 && \leftarrow \text{Associative Property} \\
&= 2 + 12.5 \\
&= 14.5
\end{aligned}
$$

4 Use mental math to find each sum.

a. 4.4 + 5.3 + 0.6 **b.** 5.2 + 0 + 3.8 **c.** 6.1 + 8.4 + 1.6

EXERCISES

For more practice, see *Extra Practice*.

Examples 1, 2 (page 11)

Find each sum or difference.

1. 4.56 + 2.9 **2.** 5.3 − 0.12 **3.** 102.8 + 3

4. 3.061 + 1.8 **5.** 0.56 + 0.8 + 3.1 **6.** 12.46 − 7.2

7. 3.102 − 0.89 **8.** 0.75 + 3.8 + 4 **9.** 25.1 − 15.06

10. The original price for a jacket is $79.95. The sale price for the same jacket is $62.79. What are your savings if you buy the jacket on sale?

11. Animals The record length of a king cobra is 5.58 m. The average length is 3.7 m. How much longer than average is the record holder?

Example 3 (page 12)

Find each difference.

12. 7 − 2.4 **13.** 9 − 1.8 **14.** 45 − 14.7

15. 28 − 13.29 **16.** 50 − 19.47 **17.** 100 − 31.93

18. Gymnastics For compulsory routines in gymnastics, a gymnast starts with a score of 10. If a gymnast scores 8.1 for a routine, how much was deducted?

Example 4 (page 13)

Use mental math to find each sum.

19. 16.2 + 23.5 + 3.8 **20.** 24.4 + (5.6 + 11) **21.** 27.4 + 0 + 12.1

22. 9.2 + 1.8 + 0 **23.** (4.7 + 10.6) + 0.3 **24.** 8.5 + 6.3 + 1.5

B Apply Your Skills

Find each sum or difference.

25. 0.1305 − 0.066 **26.** 0.582 + 7 **27.** 0 + 4.13

28. 0.08 − 0.002 **29.** 3.29 + 2 + 6.71 **30.** 1.913 + 0.08 + 3

Real-World Connection

Inline skating requires special safety gear.

31. Skating Lisa, Ana, and Lisa's brother Jacob go to the skating rink. Admission is $3.50 for those 12 and older and $1.75 for those under 12. They all rent skates for $2.75 a pair. Lisa and Ana are 13 years old and Jacob is 10.

a. How much more does Lisa pay than Jacob?

b. What is the total cost of admission?

c. What is the total cost of renting skates?

32. Animals The fastest fish, the sailfish, can swim as fast as 67.92 mi/h. The fastest mammal, the cheetah, can run as fast as 67.912 mi/h. Which animal is faster? How much faster?

33. Weather During a three-day storm in Florida, the rainfall was measured in several cities. Tallahassee recorded 8.91 in. and St. Augustine recorded 4.24 in. How much more rain was there in Tallahassee than in St. Augustine?

Identify each property shown.

34. (46.8 + 32.7) + 7.3 = 46.8 + (32.7 + 7.3)

35. 1.97 + 31.2 − 1.97 = 31.2 + 1.97 − 1.97

36. 70.5 + 0 = 0 + 70.5 **37.** 60.2 + 0 = 60.2

38. Use the photos at the right. Find the difference in the heights of the Empire State Building and the Eiffel Tower.

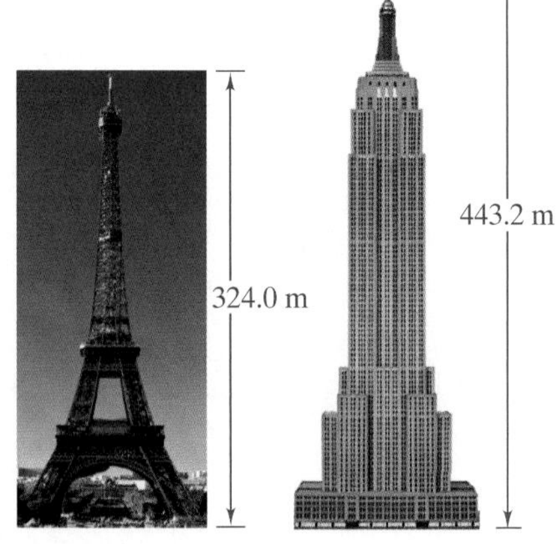

39. Savings You decide to save some money. In week 1 you save $4.20, in week 2 you save $3.85, in week 3 you save $2.50, and in week 4 you save $3.30. How much have you saved by the end of week 4?

40. Writing in Math How can you use the Identity Property of Addition to find 5.238 − 5.238 + 17.9?

41. Open-Ended Find two numbers with a sum of 0.005.

Use <, >, or = to complete each statement.

42. 3.45 + 2.9 ■ 8.9 − 2.75 **43.** 12.8 − 1.35 ■ 5.12 + 5.79

44. 15 − 6.82 ■ 32.18 − 24 **45.** 7.8 + 4.02 ■ 6.95 + 5.05

46. 42.6 − 7.52 ■ 14.92 + 18.65 **47.** 81.35 + 26.71 ■ 58.02 + 50.04

Geometry **Find the perimeter of each figure.**

48.

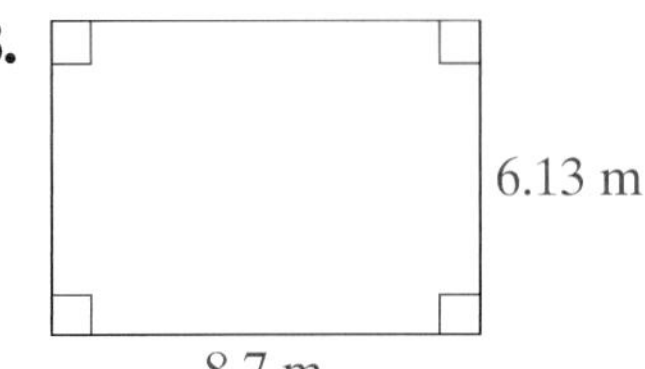

49.

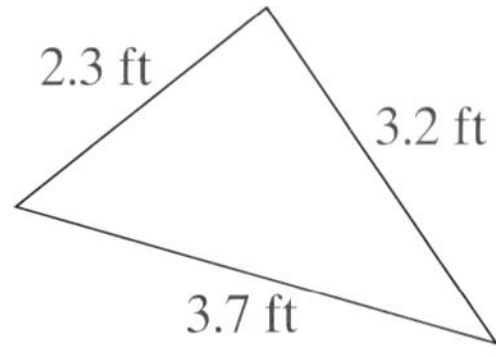

C Challenge

50. **Number Sense** Place decimal points in these numbers so that their sum is 519.654.   329   913   477   624

51. **Number Sense** Place decimal points in 190563 and 865 so that their difference is 181.913.

52. The decimal system is a place-value system. In a non-place-value system, such as the system using Roman numerals, the number of places does not determine the value.

Roman Numeral	I	V	X	L	C
Decimal	1	5	10	50	100

a. Find the sum of XXIV and CLX (Recall: IV = 4, VI = 6).

b. Find the equivalent sum using the decimal system.

c. **Reasoning** Explain the advantages of a place-value system over a non-place-value system.

53. **Stretch Your Thinking** All the markers in a desk drawer are black, red, or purple. All but two are black, all but two are red, and all but two are purple. How many markers are in the drawer?

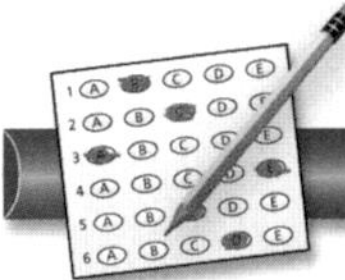

Test Prep

Gridded Response

54. Find the sum of 34.07 and 12.95.

55. Find the difference between 40.09 and 18.6.

56. The average rainfall for Charleston, West Virginia, is 2.91 in. for January, 3.04 in. for February, and 3.63 in. for March. Find the total average rainfall in inches for the first three months of the year.

57. Your grandmother gives you $50 for your birthday. You buy a book for $14.95 and a cap for $24.95. How many dollars do you have left?

Take It to the NET
Online lesson quiz at
www.PHSchool.com
Web Code aba-0102

Mixed Review

Lesson 1-1

Estimate. Round to the nearest whole number before you add or subtract.

58. 3.78 − 1.87   **59.** 14.23 − 9.82   **60.** 12.06 + 13.95

Skills Handbook (page 700)

Write the value of the underlined digit.

61. $3.0\underline{9}1$ **62.** $10.\underline{5}6$ **63.** $25.37\underline{8}$

Mental Math: Compensation

For Use With Lesson 1-2

You can use compensation to find sums and differences. Compensation allows you to adjust the numbers and make the expressions easier to calculate mentally.

The sum of two numbers remains the same if you add a number to one addend and subtract the same number from another addend.

Subtract 3: 2 ← 5   Add 3: 7 → 10

$7 + 5$
↓ ↓
$10 + 2 = 12$

The difference between two numbers remains the same if you add (or subtract) the same number from both numbers.

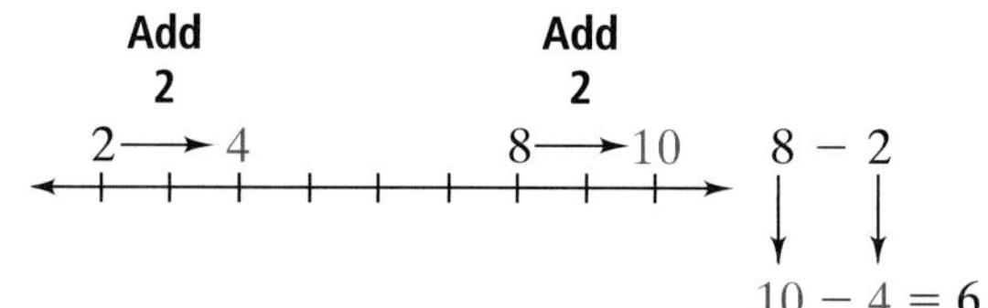

$8 - 2$
↓ ↓
$10 - 4 = 6$

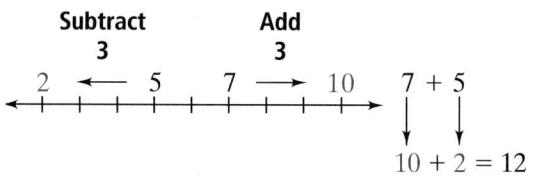

EXAMPLE Using Compensation

Find each sum or difference using compensation.

a. \$4.96 + \$3.79

\$4.96 + \$3.79
↓ ↓
+ 0.04 − 0.04 ← **Add 0.04 to one addend and subtract 0.04 from the other addend.**
↓ ↓
\$5.00 + \$3.75 = \$8.75

b. $6.1 - 1.3$

$6.1 - 1.3$
↓ ↓
$+ 0.7 + 0.7$ ← **Add 0.7 to both numbers so that you subtract a whole number.**
↓ ↓
$6.8 - 2 = 4.8$

EXERCISES

Use compensation to find each sum or difference.

1. $0.95 + 1.45$

2. $2.54 + 8.16$

3. $3.89 + 1.73$

4. $72.2 + 14.9$

5. $38.0 - 11.1$

6. $9.3 - 6.8$

7. $102 - 77$

8. $41.6 - 0.7$

9. $0.4 + 7.8$

10. $117 + 96$

11. $74.6 - 35.8$

12. $12.4 - 8.3$

13. $11.7 - 6.9$

14. $2.9 + 10.5$

15. $984 - 852$

16. $72.3 + 8.1$

17. Money You have five items to purchase at the grocery store. The prices are \$.98, \$3.95, \$2.08, \$4.99, and \$1. Use compensation to determine the amount you owe at the check-out.

18. Open-Ended Find three numbers, not ending in zero, with a sum of 1,000.

1-3 Multiplying and Dividing Decimals

What You'll Learn

 To multiply decimals

 To divide decimals

. . . And Why

To find the number of servings, as in Example 4

Check Skills You'll Need

For help, go to Lesson 1-1.

Estimate each quotient using compatible numbers.

1. 24.8 ÷ 4.9 **2.** 103.8 ÷ 13.2 **3.** 128.62 ÷ 9.86 **4.** 41.77 ÷ 6.07

New Vocabulary

- **Identity Property of Multiplication**
- **Zero Property**
- **Commutative Property of Multiplication**
- **Associative Property of Multiplication**

OBJECTIVE 1

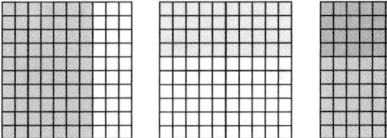

 Interactive lesson includes instant self-check, tutorials, and activities.

Multiplying Decimals

Investigation: Modeling Decimal Multiplication

The grid models show 0.7 and 0.4 and their product.

0.7 × 0.4 = 0.28

1. Draw models for each product.
   a. 0.2 × 0.9 b. 0.3 × 0.5
2. a. Is each product greater than or less than each factor?
   b. Describe the product of decimals less than 1.

To multiply decimals, first multiply as if the factors are whole numbers. Then add the number of the decimal places in both factors to find the number of decimal places in the product.

1 EXAMPLE Multiplying Decimals

Find the product of 2.43 and 2.5.

Step 1 Multiply as with whole numbers.

$$\begin{array}{r} 243 \\ \times\ 25 \\ \hline 1215 \\ 486 \\ \hline 6075 \end{array}$$

Step 2 Locate the decimal point.

$$\begin{array}{rl} 2.43 & \leftarrow \text{two decimal places} \\ \times\ 2.5 & \leftarrow \text{one decimal place} \\ \hline 1215 & \\ 486 & \\ \hline 6.075 & \leftarrow \text{three decimal places} \end{array}$$

The product of 2.43 and 2.5 is 6.075.

 **1** **a.** Find 3.7 × 9 **b.** Find 14.3 × 0.81

There are several ways to use symbols to indicate multiplication. Four ways to write "3 times 5" are shown below.

3×5 $\quad$ $3 \cdot 5$ $\quad$ $3(5)$ $\quad$ $(3)(5)$

Key Concepts **Properties of Multiplication**

Identity Property of Multiplication

The product of 1 and a is a.

Arithmetic $5 \cdot 1 = 5$
$1 \cdot 5 = 5$

Algebra $a \cdot 1 = a$
$1 \cdot a = a$

Zero Property

The product of 0 and any number is 0.

Arithmetic $5 \cdot 0 = 0$
$0 \cdot 5 = 0$

Algebra $a \cdot 0 = 0$
$0 \cdot a = 0$

Commutative Property of Multiplication

Changing the order of factors does not change the product.

Arithmetic $5 \cdot 2 = 2 \cdot 5$ **Algebra** $a \cdot b = b \cdot a$

Associative Property of Multiplication

Changing the grouping of factors does not change the product.

Arithmetic $(3 \cdot 2) \cdot 5 = 3 \cdot (2 \cdot 5)$ **Algebra** $(a \cdot b) \cdot c = a \cdot (b \cdot c)$

You can use the properties of multiplication to multiply mentally.

2 EXAMPLE Using Multiplication Properties

Mental Math Use mental math to find $0.25 \cdot 3.58 \cdot 4$.

What you think

I should choose compatible numbers with a product of 1. The product of 0.25 and 4 is 1. Then, the product of 1 and 3.58 is 3.58.

Why it works

$0.25 \cdot 3.58 \cdot 4 = 0.25 \cdot 4 \cdot 3.58$ ← **Commutative Property of Multiplication**

$= (0.25 \cdot 4) \cdot 3.58$ ← **Associative Property of Multiplication**

$= 1 \cdot 3.58$ ← **Simplify.**

$= 3.58$ ← **Identity Property of Multiplication**

Check Understanding 2 Use mental math to find each product.

a. $2.5 \cdot 6.3 \cdot 4$ **b.** $3.625 \cdot 58.42 \cdot 0$ **c.** $5 \cdot 9.1 \cdot 0.4$

d. **Reasoning** What property would you use first when finding $4.3 \cdot 2.5 \cdot 2$? Explain.

OBJECTIVE

2 Dividing Decimals

Need Help?
Recall the names of the parts of a division problem.

$$\begin{array}{r} 3 \\ 6\overline{)18} \end{array} \leftarrow \text{quotient}$$

divisor ↑ ↑ dividend

Three ways to write "12 divided by 3" are shown below.

$$12 \div 3 \qquad 3\overline{)12} \qquad \frac{12}{3}$$

Suppose you want to divide 1.2 by 0.3. You can first multiply each number by 10. This moves each decimal point one place to the right. Then you can divide 12 by 3, which is an equivalent and easier way of dividing 1.2 by 0.3.

$$\frac{1.2}{0.3} = \frac{1.2}{0.3} \times \frac{10}{10} = \frac{1.2 \times 10}{0.3 \times 10} = \frac{12}{3} = 4$$

To divide decimals, rewrite the divisor as a whole number by multiplying both the divisor and the dividend by a power of 10.

3 EXAMPLE Dividing a Decimal by a Decimal

Find 26.04 ÷ 3.1.

Estimate 26.04 ÷ 3.1 ≈ 27 ÷ 3, or 9

$$3.1\overline{)26.04} \rightarrow \begin{array}{r} 8.4 \\ 31\overline{)260.4} \\ \underline{248} \\ 12\,4 \\ \underline{12\,4} \\ 0 \end{array}$$

← **Multiply the divisor and the dividend by 10. Place the decimal point in the quotient above the decimal point in the dividend.**

Check for Reasonableness The quotient 8.4 is close to the estimate of 9. The answer is reasonable.

Check Understanding 3 Find each quotient.

a. 12.42 ÷ 5.4 **b.** 67.84 ÷ 6.4 **c.** 144.06 ÷ 9.8

When you divide by a decimal, sometimes you need to annex extra zeros in the dividend.

4 EXAMPLE Annexing Zeros to Divide

Nutrition According to the American Academy of Pediatrics, a 2-year-old child drinks about 6.8 oz of juice per day. If you set aside a daily amount for each child, how many children can you serve from one 48-oz bottle of juice?

$$\begin{array}{r} 7 \\ 6.8\overline{)48.0} \\ \underline{47\,6} \\ 4 \end{array}$$

← **Multiply divisor and dividend by 10. Annex zeros when needed.**

← **The remainder does not represent a full serving.**

You can serve seven children with a 48-oz bottle of juice.

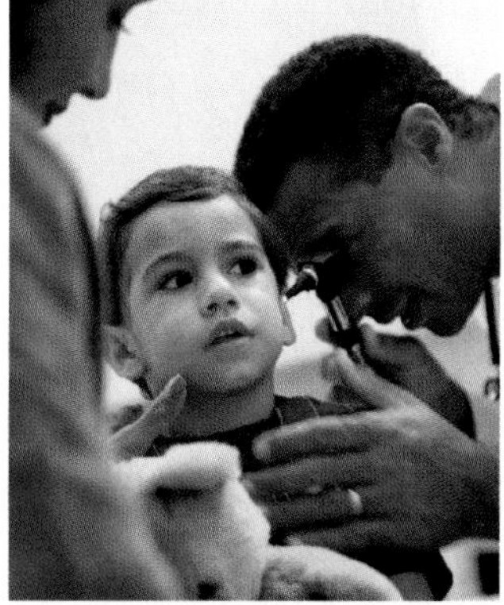

Real-World Connection

Careers Pediatricians provide health care for children.

Check Understanding 4 Find each quotient.

a. 0.27 ÷ 12 **b.** $0.04\overline{)1}$ **c.** $\frac{0.119}{0.34}$

Can you divide by zero? Consider these related problems.

$$6 \div 3 = 2 \qquad 3 \cdot 2 = 6$$

$$6 \div 0 = \blacksquare \qquad 0 \cdot \blacksquare \stackrel{?}{=} 6$$

There is no value for ■ that makes sense! So, division by zero is undefined.

EXERCISES

For more practice, see *Extra Practice.*

A Practice by Example

Example 1 (page 17)

Find each product.

1. 0.2×0.7 **2.** 0.4×0.6 **3.** 0.3×0.5 **4.** 1.02×3.6

5. 8.7×0.45 **6.** 1.45×2.6 **7.** 41×7.5 **8.** 1.3×0.05

9. Fitness If you walk 3.5 miles per hour, how far will you walk in 1.2 hours?

Example 2 (page 18)

Mental Math **Find each product.**

10. $0.2 \cdot 3.41 \cdot 5$ **11.** $1.09 \cdot 23.6 \cdot 0$ **12.** $(2.3 \cdot 0.5) \cdot 4$

13. $5 \cdot (4.3 \cdot 1)$ **14.** $0 \cdot 2.78 \cdot 1$ **15.** $0.4 \cdot 3.29 \cdot 25$

Example 3 (page 19)

Find each quotient.

16. $17.172 \div 3.24$ **17.** $1.89\overline{)5.103}$ **18.** $\frac{53.58}{4.7}$

19. $\frac{186.9}{8.9}$ **20.** $62.37 \div 2.7$ **21.** $5.47\overline{)41.572}$

22. Hobbies You spend $13.92 for fabric. Each yard costs $4.35. How many yards of fabric do you buy?

23. Entertainment You buy five movie tickets for $23.75. How much does each ticket cost?

Example 4 (page 19)

Find each quotient.

24. $0.04\overline{)10}$ **25.** $0.054 \div 0.72$ **26.** $\frac{0.078}{1.2}$ **27.** $592 \div 0.8$

28. $0.0282 \div 0.6$ **29.** $\frac{0.003}{0.5}$ **30.** $224.5 \div 0.05$ **31.** $1.25\overline{)0.1}$

32. Shopping If peanuts cost $1.75 per jar, how many jars can you buy with $14?

B Apply Your Skills

Mental Math **Find each quotient.**

33. $0.9 \div 100$ **34.** $236.7 \div 0.1$ **35.** $5.02 \div 0.01$ **36.** $0.7 \div 10$

37. a. Food Rice costs $1.33 per kilogram. How much will 1.3 kg of rice cost?
b. Milk costs $.71 per liter. How many liters can you buy with $3?
c. Reasoning How are part (a) and part (b) different?

38. **Money** A penny weighs about 0.1 oz. How much is a pound of pennies worth? (*Hint:* 1 lb = 16 oz)

Find the missing numbers. Name the property of multiplication shown.

39. 3.6 · ■ = 0

40. ■ · 1 = 25.5

41. ■ · 4 = 4 · 3

42. (2.5 · ■) · 2.3 = 2.5 · (1.4 · 2.3)

43. a. **Patterns** Look at the division problems at the right. What pattern do you see in the divisors?
    b. Copy the table. Fill in the missing divisors. Find each quotient.
    c. **Reasoning** As the divisor gets closer and closer to zero, what happens to the quotient? Why?

Dividend		Divisor		Quotient
50	÷	100	=	0.5
50	÷	10	=	■
50	÷	1	=	■
50	÷	0.1	=	■
50	÷	0.01	=	■
50	÷	0.001	=	■
50	÷	■	=	■
50	÷	■	=	■
50	÷	■	=	■

44. **Sales** A dozen pens cost a store \$11.28. Each pen sells for \$1.99.
    a. What is the profit per pen?
    b. How many pens does the store need to sell to get back its cost?

45. Find the missing numbers.
    a. 1.2 × ■ = 588
    b. ■ × 2.7 = 3.51
    c. 0.37 × ■ = 23.68
    d. **Number Sense** Explain how you found the missing numbers. How did you know that your method would work?

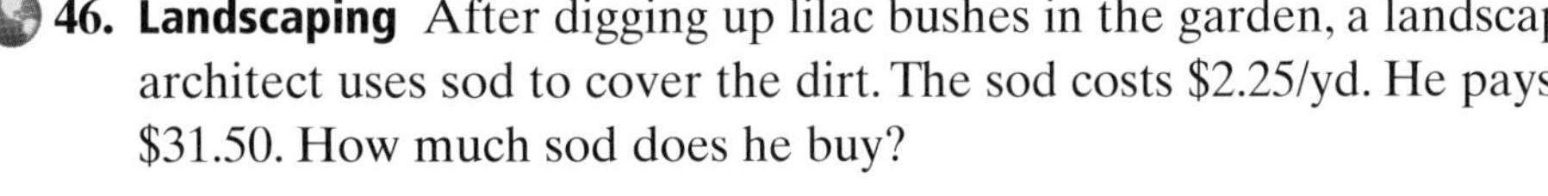

46. **Landscaping** After digging up lilac bushes in the garden, a landscape architect uses sod to cover the dirt. The sod costs \$2.25/yd. He pays \$31.50. How much sod does he buy?

Real-World Connection

Landscape architects use their knowledge of design and construction to develop a landscape project.

Find each product or quotient.

47. 641.7 ÷ 9
48. 2.07 · 15
49. 14.8 × 9.1
50. 8.4(6.2)
51. 0.0882 ÷ 6
52. 325.28 ÷ 30.4
53. 82.3 · 2.9
54. 15.6 × 7.4
55. 20.08 ÷ 25.1

56. **Writing in Math** How are the identity properties of multiplication and addition similar? How are they different?

57. a. Find $75\overline{)300}$.
    b. Find $7.5\overline{)300}$.
    c. Find $0.75\overline{)300}$.
    d. **Patterns** Describe what happens to a quotient when the dividend remains the same and the divisor decreases.

58. **Banking** You decide to take the coins that you have been saving to the bank. You count 17 pennies, 31 nickels, 22 dimes, and 14 quarters. How much money will you deposit into your account?

Real-World Connection

Tennis was originally called lawn tennis and grass courts are still in use.

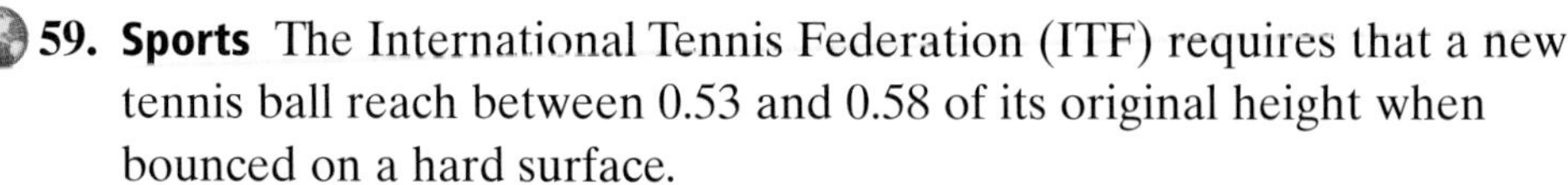

59. **Sports** The International Tennis Federation (ITF) requires that a new tennis ball reach between 0.53 and 0.58 of its original height when bounced on a hard surface.
   a. A new tennis ball is dropped from a height of 200 cm. Find the range of acceptable heights after the first bounce.
   b. A tennis ball dropped from a height of 150 cm reaches 79 cm after one bounce. Does the ball meet ITF standards?

60. **Shopping** You buy four packages of sneaker laces. You pay with a $10 bill and receive $3.24 in change. What is the price of each package?

Divide. Round each quotient to the nearest hundredth.

61. 10,000 ÷ 3.14 **62.** 6,104 ÷ 1.47 **63.** 700 ÷ 0.32

Challenge

64. **Reasoning** Do you think there is a commutative property of division? Why or why not? Give examples.

65. **Stretch Your Thinking** Marika calls two members of her softball team to schedule a practice. Each of those team members calls three other team members. Then, each of those members calls two more team members. How many team members are called? Do not count Marika.

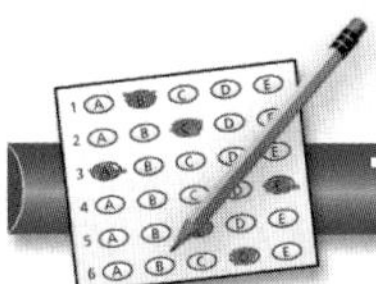

Test Prep

Multiple Choice

66. You ride a bicycle for 2.4 h at an average speed of 10.8 mi/h. How many miles do you ride?
   A. 4.5 **B.** 8.4 **C.** 13.2 **D.** 25.92

67. You receive $10 for your birthday. You wish to buy goldfish that cost $1.40 each. How many goldfish can you buy?
   F. 14 **G.** 8 **H.** 7.2 **I.** 7

Take It to the NET
Online lesson quiz at **www.PHSchool.com**
Web Code aba-0103

68. Which example shows the Commutative Property of Multiplication?
   A. $0.5 \cdot 7.2 \cdot 1 = 0.5 \cdot 7.2$ **B.** $(8.7 \cdot 5.4) \cdot 3.9 = 8.7 \cdot (5.4 \cdot 3.9)$
   C. $4.8 \cdot 0 \cdot 7.9 = 0$ **D.** $5.6 \cdot 1.4 \cdot 8.9 = 5.6 \cdot 8.9 \cdot 1.4$

Short Response

69. A bookstore receives a carton that contains 12 copies of a dictionary. Each dictionary weighs 2.3 kg, and the carton weighs 1.3 kg. Find the total weight of the filled carton. Show your work.

Mixed Review

Lesson 1-2

Find each sum or difference.

70. 8.56 + 3.11 **71.** 9.843 − 8.2 **72.** 9.4 − 7.024 **73.** 17.1 + 3.09

Skills Handbook (page 700)

Write the value of the digit 7 in each number.

74. 71,095 **75.** 274.8 **76.** 3.127 **77.** 98.716

1-4 Measuring in Metric Units

What You'll Learn

OBJECTIVE 1 To use metric units of measure

OBJECTIVE 2 To change metric units

. . . And Why

To choose appropriate measures, as in Example 1

Check Skills You'll Need

For help, go to Skills Handbook, p. 706.

Simplify.

1. 0.25 · 10
2. 4.567 · 1,000
3. 0.03 · 100
4. 45.8 ÷ 10
5. 290.97 ÷ 100
6. 18.09 ÷ 1,000
7. 4.67 ÷ 100
8. 0.07 · 1,000

Interactive lesson includes instant self-check, tutorials, and activities.

OBJECTIVE 1 Using Metric Units

The metric system is a decimal system of measurement. The chart below is a guide for choosing an appropriate unit of metric measurement.

Reading Math
Meter comes from the Latin word for measure.

Type	Unit	Reference Example
Length	millimeter (mm) centimeter (cm) meter (m) kilometer (km)	about the thickness of a dime about the width of your little finger about the distance from a doorknob to the floor about the length of 11 football fields
Capacity	milliliter (mL) liter (L)	a small spoon holds about 5 mL a little more than 1 quart
Mass	milligram (mg) gram (g) kilogram (kg)	about the mass of a mosquito about the mass of a paper clip about the mass of a bunch of bananas

1 EXAMPLE Choosing a Metric Unit

Real World

Choose an appropriate metric unit of measurement. Explain your choice.

a. mass of a bicycle

Kilogram; the mass of a bicycle is many times the mass of a bunch of bananas.

b. the capacity of a kitchen sink

Liter; it takes several quarts to fill a kitchen sink.

Check Understanding 1 Choose an appropriate unit of metric measurement. Explain your choice.

a. mass of a pencil
b. thickness of a wire
c. capacity of an eyedropper
d. length of fencing for a field

You can use appropriate units to choose reasonable estimates.

2 EXAMPLE Choosing a Reasonable Estimate

Choose a reasonable estimate. Explain your choice.

a. height of a classroom 3 cm 3 m 3 km

3 m; a classroom is about 3 times as high as the distance from a doorknob to the floor.

b. mass of a bag of flour 2.3 mg 2.3 g 2.3 kg

2.3 kg; a bag of flour is much heavier than a few paper clips.

c. capacity of a soup bowl 180 mL 180 L 180 kL

180 mL; a soup bowl holds less than a quart.

Check Understanding 2 Choose a reasonable estimate.

a. length of a shoe 28 mm 28 cm 28 m

b. mass of a butterfly 500 mg 500 g 500 kg

OBJECTIVE 2 Changing Metric Units

Reading Math

Metric measures can be written with spaces instead of commas.

Use a space for 5 or more digits:

46 117 kg

No space for 4 digits:

8732 m

The basic unit for length in the metric system is the meter. All other units are based on the meter. The prefixes deci-, centi-, and milli- describe measures that are less than one meter. The prefixes deca-, hecto-, and kilo- describe measures that are greater than one meter.

The table shows that each unit is 10 times the value of the unit to its right.

Unit	kilo-meter	hecto-meter	deca-meter	meter	deci-meter	centi-meter	milli-meter
Symbol	km	hm	dam	m	dm	cm	mm
Value	1,000 m	100 m	10 m	1 m	0.1 m	0.01m	0.001 m

The basic unit of mass is the gram. The basic unit of capacity is the liter.

You can change a measure from one unit to another by finding the relationship between the two units and multiplying.

3 EXAMPLE Multiplying to Change Units

Change 245 milliliters to liters.

245 mL = ■ L

245 · 0.001 = 0.245 ← **Since 1 mL = 0.001 L, multiply 245 by 0.001.**

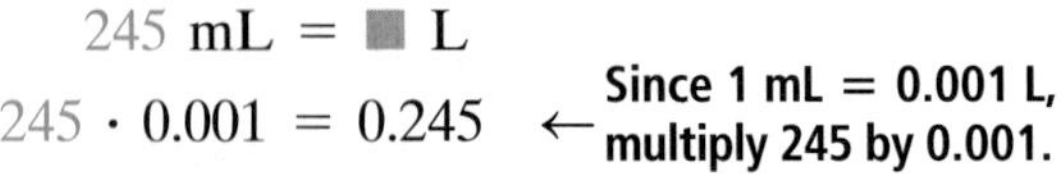

245 milliliters equals 0.245 liters.

Check Understanding 3 Write the number that makes each statement true.

a. 789 mL = ■ L **b.** 459 cm = ■ m **c.** 324 g = ■ kg

You can write metric measurements that have two units as a single unit.

4 EXAMPLE Combining Metric Units

a. Change 5 kg 32 g to kilograms. **b.** Change 5 kg 32 g to grams.

a.		b.
5 kg 32 g		5 kg 32 g
1 g = 0.001 kg	← **Find a relationship between the units.** →	1 kg = 1,000 g
$5 + 32 \cdot 0.001$	← **Multiply.** →	$5 \cdot 1{,}000 + 32$
5.032	← **Simplify.** →	5,032

5 kg 32 g equals 5.032 kg or 5,032 g.

Check Understanding 4 **a.** Change 3 m 15 mm to meters. **b.** Change 2 L 198 mL to milliliters.
c. **Reasoning** Suppose you want to change 125 kg 84 g to a single unit. Would you choose kilograms or grams? Explain your choice.

More Than One Way

A fruit punch recipe calls for 1 L of orange juice, 400 mL of pineapple juice, 60 mL of lemon juice, 2 L of apple juice, and 840 mL of water. Can you make this punch in a 5-L punch bowl?

Anna's Method

I can start by subtracting 1 L of orange juice and 2 L of apple juice from the 5 L available. That leaves 2 L of capacity in the punch bowl.

400 mL + 60 mL + 840 mL = 1,300 mL ← **Add the ingredients in mL.**

$2 \text{ L} \cdot 1{,}000 = 2{,}000$ mL ← **Change remaining capacity of punch bowl to mL.**

Since 1,300 mL < 2,000 mL, I can make the punch in the punch bowl.

Ryan's Method

I can convert all the measures to liters.

$400 \text{ mL} = 400 \cdot 0.001 = 0.4 \text{ L}$

$60 \text{ mL} = 60 \cdot 0.001 = 0.06 \text{ L}$ ← **Change milliliters to liters.**

$840 \text{ mL} = 840 \cdot 0.001 = 0.84 \text{ L}$

1 L + 0.4 L + .06 L + 2 L + 0.84 L = 4.3 L ← **Add the ingredients.**

The capacity of the punch bowl is 5 L. I can make the punch in the punch bowl.

Choose a Method

For a craft project, you need ribbon in lengths of 3 m, 25 cm, 4 m, 58 cm, 1.5 m, and 70 cm. You have 10 m of ribbon. Is that enough? Explain why you chose the method you used.

EXERCISES

For more practice, see *Extra Practice*.

A Practice by Example

Example 1 (page 23)

Choose an appropriate metric unit of measurement. Explain your choice.

1. the length of this book

2. the mass of a CD

3. the mass of a pumpkin seed

4. the capacity of a watering can

5. the capacity of a test tube

6. the thickness of a birthday card

Example 2 (page 24)

Choose a reasonable estimate.

7. capacity of a small bottle	250 mL	250 L	250 kL
8. height of an oak tree	22 cm	22 m	22 km
9. mass of an adult bullfrog	0.5 mg	0.5 g	0.5 kg
10. width of a freckle	4 mm	4 cm	4 m

Example 3 (page 24)

Write the number that makes each statement true.

11. 0.9 km = ■ g

12. ■ L = 90 mL

13. 58 m = ■ mm

14. 7,800 g = ■ kg

15. 7 m = ■ km

16. ■ L = 240 kL

Example 4 (page 25)

Change each measurement to the given unit.

17. 23 km 51 m to km

18. 48 g 19 mg to g

19. 6 L 477 mL to mL

20. 9 L 8 mL to L

21. 3 kg 329 g to kg

22. 47 m 2 cm to cm

B Apply Your Skills

23. Cooking A cookie recipe calls for 0.24 L of milk. Your measuring cup is marked in milliliters. How many milliliters of milk do you need?

24. Geography The continent of Antarctica averages 2,400 m in elevation. What is the average elevation of Antarctica in kilometers?

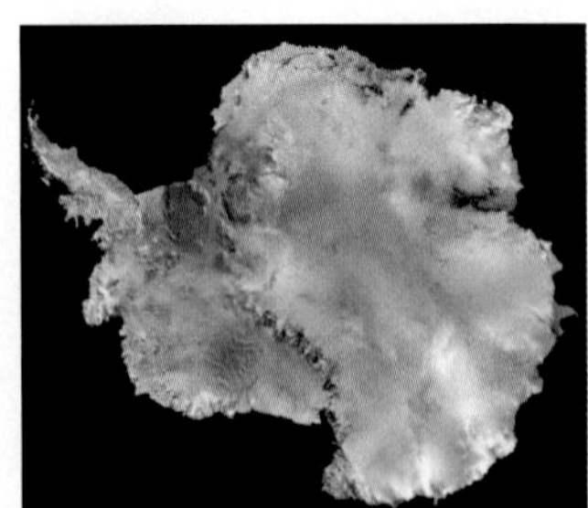

Satellite photo of Antarctica

Write the metric unit that makes each statement true.

25. 2,034 mg = 2.034 ■

26. 3.456 cm = 34.56 ■

27. 9,023 dL = 90.23 ■

28. Design You are making a drawing of a family crest from a book. You have a piece of paper that is 21.5 cm wide and want to leave a 35 mm margin on either side. How wide can you draw the crest?

29. Food The capacity of a coffee mug is 350 mL. How many coffee mugs can you fill from a 2 L container?

30. Nutrition You need 1.3 g of calcium per day. You get 290 mg of calcium per glass of milk. If you drink 4 glasses of milk, how much more calcium do you need from other sources?

31. Writing in Math Explain how to change units in the metric system.

Writing in Math

For help with writing to explain, as in Exercise 31, see p. 29.

Real-World Connection
About 55 million Americans provide feed for birds.

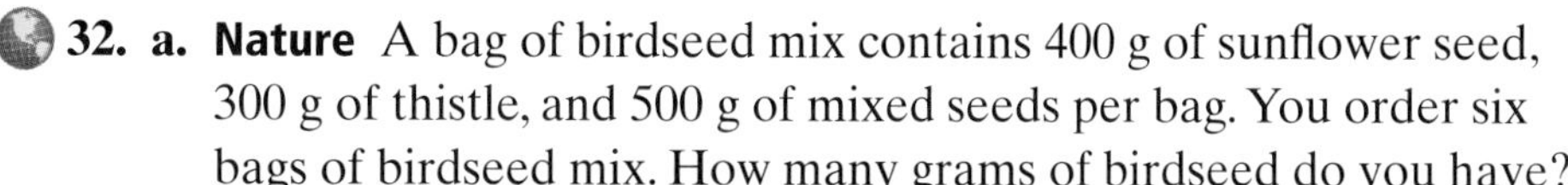

32. a. **Nature** A bag of birdseed mix contains 400 g of sunflower seed, 300 g of thistle, and 500 g of mixed seeds per bag. You order six bags of birdseed mix. How many grams of birdseed do you have?
    b. Change the units of your answer from part (a) to kilograms.
    c. **Reasoning** Which metric unit of measurement is the more appropriate for birdseed? Explain.

Match each measurement in the first column with one in the second column.

33. 25 mL	**A.** 0.025 kg
34. 2,500 g	**B.** 25 cm
35. 2.5 km	**C.** 2.5 kg
36. 0.25 L	**D.** 0.025 L
37. 250 mm	**E.** 25 cL
38. 25,000 mg	**F.** 2,500 m

39. **Money** A roll of 50 pennies has a mass of 125 g. Find the mass of $5 in pennies.

C Challenge

Order the measurements from the least to the greatest.

40. 3,752 mm   142 cm   2 m   **41.** 0.42 kg   478 g   48,103 mg

42. **Crafts** A recipe for modeling clay requires 470 mL of baking soda, 240 mL of cornstarch, and 300 mL of water. Can you make a double batch in a 1.9-L pan? Explain

43. **Stretch Your Thinking** Ulysses began with a number, multiplied his number by 2, divided the product by 5, and then added 9. The result was 19. With what number did Ulysses begin?

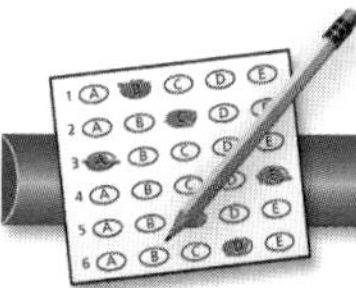

Test Prep

Multiple Choice

44. A carpenter cuts a 3-meter board into four equal pieces. What is the length in centimeters of each piece?
    A. 0.75 cm   **B.** 12 cm   **C.** 75 cm   **D.** 133 cm

45. Your school is 350 m from your house. You walk to school and home again each school day. For a 5-day school week, how far do you walk?
    F. 1750 km   **G.** 70 km   **H.** 3.5 km   **I.** 1.75 km

46. You want to change 675 cm into meters. Which fact could you use for the conversion?
    A. 100 cm = 1 m   **B.** 1 km = 1,000 m
    C. 1 m = 1,000 mm   **D.** 10 mm = 1 cm

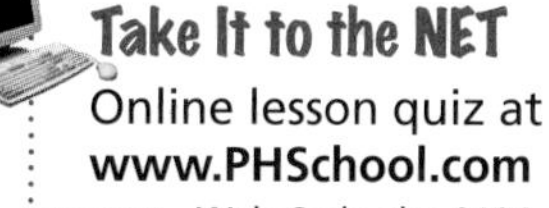

Take It to the NET
Online lesson quiz at **www.PHSchool.com**
Web Code aba-0104

Short Response

47. Which is a more reasonable estimate for the capacity of a birdbath, 11.4 mL or 11.4 L? Explain.

Mixed Review

Lesson 1-3 Mental Math **Find each product or quotient.**

48. $0.5 \cdot 6.7 \cdot 2$ **49.** $5.3 \cdot 4.9 \cdot 0$

50. $8.2 \cdot 2.5 \cdot 4$ **51.** $21.09 \div 0.1$

52. $10.92 \div 0.01$ **53.** $3{,}197.3 \div 100$

Lesson 1-2 **Find each sum or difference.**

54. $3.41 + 2.06 + 4.84$ **55.** $9.641 - 3.14$ **56.** $5.08 - 2.725$

Checkpoint Quiz 1 — Lessons 1-1 through 1-4

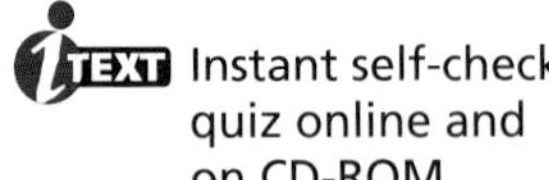

Instant self-check quiz online and on CD-ROM

Use each strategy to estimate \$3.07 + \$3.48 + \$4.24.

1. rounding to the nearest dollar **2.** front-end estimation

Simplify.

3. $2.99 + 3.08 + 18.5642$ **4.** $9.7418 + 4.603$

5. $1.36 \cdot 8.94$ **6.** $2.4 \cdot 0.04$ **7.** $15 \div 1.2$

Change each measurement to the given unit.

8. 7 kg 68 g to kilograms **9.** 14 m 8 cm to centimeters

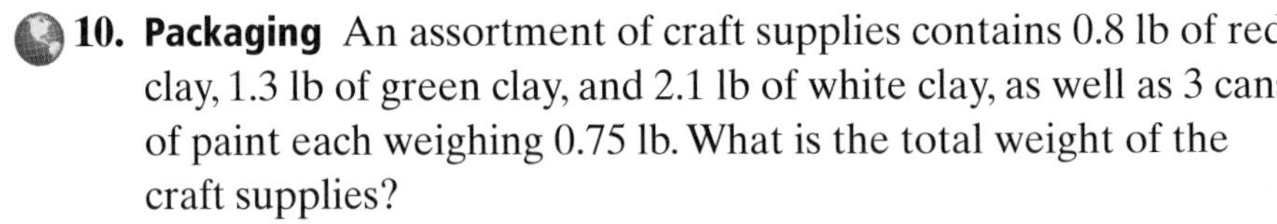

10. **Packaging** An assortment of craft supplies contains 0.8 lb of red clay, 1.3 lb of green clay, and 2.1 lb of white clay, as well as 3 cans of paint each weighing 0.75 lb. What is the total weight of the craft supplies?

Math at Work

Detective

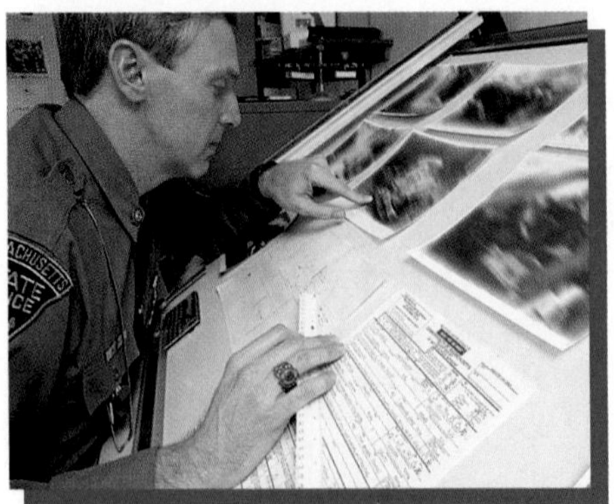

Most people think of a detective as a person in a trench coat, looking for clues. In reality, detectives can work for lawyers, government agencies, and businesses. Detectives may gather information, trace debtors, or do background investigations.

Detectives use mathematics to locate stolen funds, develop financial profiles, or monitor expense accounts.

Take It to the NET For more information about detectives, go to **www.PHSchool.com.**

Web Code abb-2031

Writing to Explain

For Use With Page 26, Exercise 31

Sometimes you are asked to explain how to use a certain math skill. When you write to explain, you should first give a general description. Then give one or more specific examples to illustrate your description. If possible, provide a way to check your work.

EXAMPLE

On page 26, you will find the following exercise:

31. Writing in Math Explain how to change units in the metric system.

First give a general description.

- Write an equation that shows the relationship between the units. Write one of the original units as a multiple of the new unit.
- Use the information from the equation to multiply to change units.
- Look back at your result. If you are changing to a larger unit, your answer will be a smaller number of units than the original. If you are changing to a smaller unit, your answer will be a larger number of units than the original.

Next give an example to illustrate your explanation.

Here is how to change 4.56 kg to grams.

1 kg = 1,000 g	Write one of the original units as a multiple of the new unit.
$4.56 \cdot 1{,}000 = 4{,}560$	Multiply by 1,000 to change from kilograms to grams.
4.56 kg = 4,560 g	Write the new equation. Look back. You changed to a smaller unit. The answer makes sense because it is a larger number of units than the original.

EXERCISES

Explain how to use each math skill. Give a general explanation and at least one specific example.

1. finding the product of two decimals

2. finding the quotient of two decimals

3. estimating a sum by rounding

4. estimating a sum by front-end estimation

5. estimating a quotient using compatible numbers

Problem Solving

1-5 Using a Problem-Solving Plan

What You'll Learn

To use a problem-solving plan to solve problems

. . . And Why

To provide an organized way to solve problems, as in Example 1

Check Skills You'll Need

For help, go to Skills Handbook p. 698.

Find each product.

1. 21 · 9
2. 31 · 4
3. 98 · 8
4. 2 · 61
5. 72 · 3
6. 104 · 5
7. Simplify (10 · 8) − (10 · 3).

Interactive lesson includes instant self-check, tutorials, and activities.

OBJECTIVE 1

Using a Problem-Solving Plan

You solve problems every day. Some problems require good problem-solving skills. To solve any problem, use the plan shown below. It will help you choose and apply an effective problem-solving strategy.

Key Concepts — **A Problem-Solving Plan**

1. Read and understand the problem.
2. Plan how to solve the problem, and then solve it.
3. Look back and check to see if your answer makes sense.

1 EXAMPLE Real-World Problem Solving

Antique Cycles The town of Lewiston celebrates Founder's Day with a parade of antique vehicles, including cycles. Some antique cycles have two wheels, and others have three wheels.

During the parade, 24 different antique cycles are counted. There are a total of 54 wheels on these 24 cycles. How many cycles in the parade have three wheels?

Read and Understand Determine what you know and what you need to find out.

Read the problem again. Ask yourself: "What information is given? What information is missing? What am I being asked to find or to do?"

Each cycle has two or three wheels. On 24 cycles, 54 total wheels are counted. You want to find out how many of the 24 cycles have three wheels.

Plan and Solve Choose a strategy.

> As you use problem-solving strategies throughout this book, you will decide which one is best for the problem you are trying to solve.

The total number of cycles has to equal 24. Since the number of possibilities isn't very large, you can ***try, check, and revise*** to find how many cycles have three wheels. Make a table to organize your work.

Choose a possible answer to test. You could, for example, start with 12 two-wheel cycles and 12 three-wheel cycles.

Cycles With 2 Wheels	Cycles With 3 Wheels	Total Number of Wheels	Result of Test
12	12	$(12 \cdot 2) + (12 \cdot 3) = 60$	high

Real-World Connection

Antique bicycles like this one are called "high-wheelers."

Since the result of the first test is too high, you need to reduce the total number of wheels. So decrease the number of three-wheel cycles and increase the number of two-wheel cycles. Keep testing and revising until you get 54 wheels.

Cycles With 2 Wheels	Cycles With 3 Wheels	Total Number of Wheels	Result of Test
12	12	$(12 \cdot 2) + (12 \cdot 3) = 60$	high
17	7	$(17 \cdot 2) + (7 \cdot 3) = 55$	high
20	4	$(20 \cdot 2) + (4 \cdot 3) = 52$	low
18	6	$(18 \cdot 2) + (6 \cdot 3) = 54$	✔

Six antique cycles in the parade have three wheels.

Look Back and Check Think about how you solved the problem.

> Look back at your work and compare it against the information and question(s) in the problem. Ask yourself: "Is my answer reasonable? Did I check my work?"

To check whether the answer is reasonable, look at the problem in another way. ***Use logical reasoning.*** All 24 cycles in the parade have at least two wheels. That accounts for 48 of the 54 wheels. Since $54 - 48 = 6$, 6 cycles must have three wheels. The answer is reasonable and checks.

Check Understanding 1

a. Solve Example 1 by drawing a diagram.

b. There are 16 tables of two sizes in the cafeteria. One size seats 5 people and the other size seats 8 people. At lunch 89 students sit down, leaving no empty seats. How many tables of each size are in the cafeteria?

EXERCISES

For more practice, see *Extra Practice*.

A Practice by Example

Example 1 (page 30)

Need Help?
- Reread the problem.
- Identify the key facts and details.
- Tell the problem in your own words.
- Try a different strategy.
- Check your work.

Use the problem-solving plan to solve each problem.

1. Find two whole numbers whose product is 147 and whose quotient is 3.

2. **Money** Tickets for a school play sell for $8 for floor seats and $6 for balcony seats. For one performance 72 tickets are sold, bringing in $516. How many of each ticket are sold?

3. **Farming** A farmer raises pigs and chickens. The farmer has 220 animals with a total of 700 legs. How many pigs does the farmer have?

4. Last month you made long-distance calls to two of your friends. One call lasted 8 min longer than the other. According to the phone bill, the two calls lasted a total of 42 min. How long was each call?

B Apply Your Skills

Strategies

Draw a Diagram
Look for a Pattern
Make a Graph
Make an Organized List
Make a Table
Simulate a Problem
Solve a Simpler Problem
Try, Check, and Revise
Use Logical Reasoning
Work Backward
Write an Equation

Use the problem-solving plan to solve each problem. Show your work.

5. Your cousin is 26 yr older than your sister. The product of their ages is 560. How old is your sister?

6. **Carpentry** A woodworker cuts a board in half. Then the worker cuts each piece in half again. Then each of the pieces is cut in half for a last time. How many cuts are made? How many pieces of wood are there?

7. **Physical Science** Earth's atmosphere is divided into five layers. The stratosphere is higher in altitude than the troposphere, but not as high as the thermosphere. The mesosphere is just below the thermosphere and the exosphere is the uppermost layer. Arrange the layers in order from lowest altitude to highest altitude.

8. **Geometry** How many triangles are in the diagram at the right?

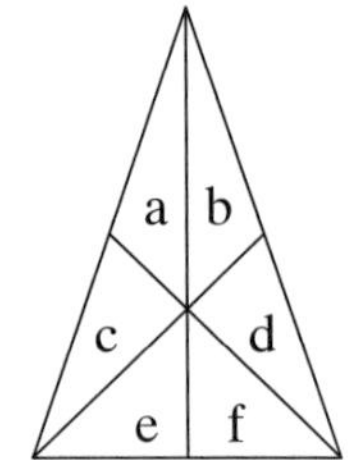

9. **Languages** In one school 65 students speak Spanish and 49 students speak Japanese. If 80 students speak either Spanish or Japanese, how many students speak both Spanish and Japanese?

10. A commuter train leaves for the city every 40 min. The first train leaves at 5:20 A.M. What is the departure time closest to 1:00 P.M.?

11. **Earnings** You and your sister work on the weekends at your parents' store. You receive $4 per hour and your sister gets $5 per hour. On Saturday both of you worked a total of 7 h and together made $32. How much money did each of you earn on Saturday?

12. **Geometry** The diagrams show the diagonals in several figures. How many diagonals are in a figure with 9 sides?

4 sides	5 sides	6 sides	7 sides
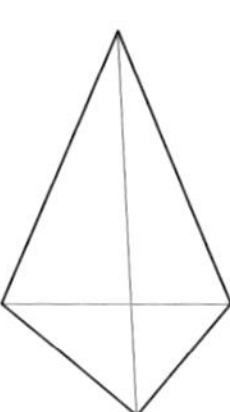	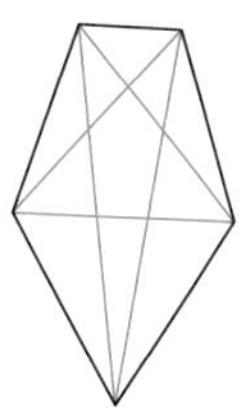	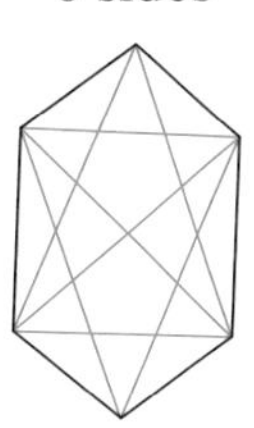	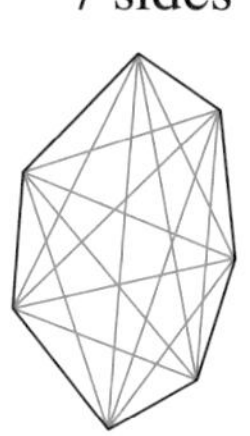
2 diagonals	5 diagonals	9 diagonals	14 diagonals

13. **Stretch Your Thinking** Each girl in the Lynberg family has the same number of brothers as she has sisters. Each boy in the Lynberg family has twice as many sisters as he has brothers. How many girls and boys are there in the Lynberg family?

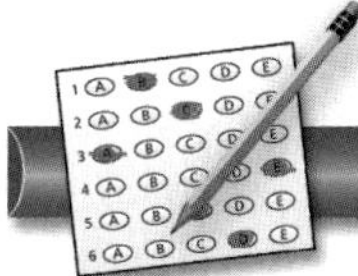

Test Prep

Multiple Choice

14. A restaurant bill is $53.67. In order to determine the tip, this amount is rounded to the nearest dollar. What is the rounded amount?
    A. $50 **B.** $53 **C.** $54 **D.** $55

15. Suppose you have a 3.79-L bottle of water to share among 8 people. About how much water will each person receive?
    F. 0.05 L **G.** 0.4 L **H.** 0.5 L **I.** 2.1 L

16. Rounding was used to estimate the sum of two prices. The estimate was $5. What were the prices?
    A. $4.51 and $0.95 **B.** $3.48 and $3.25
    C. $2.35 and $2.73 **D.** $2.10 and $2.48

Short Response

17. In a bag of nickels and dimes, there are three times as many nickels as dimes. The total value of the coins is $1.50. Find the number of dimes in the bag. Show your work.

Mixed Review

Lesson 1-4

Write a number that makes each statement true.

18. 42.3 cm = ■ m **19.** 31.7 kL = ■ L **20.** 30 kg = ■ g

Lesson 1-1

Estimate. Round to the nearest whole number before you add or subtract.

21. 9.1 + 0.578 **22.** 9.37 − 8.4 **23.** 1.562 − 0.91

24. 10.53 + 14.49 **25.** 37.14 − 7.16 **26.** 1.27 + 6.78

Algebra

1-6 Comparing and Ordering Integers

What You'll Learn

To find opposite and absolute values

To graph and order integers

. . . And Why

To compare temperatures, as in Example 4

Check Skills You'll Need

For help, go to Skills Handbook, p. 696.

Write the numbers from least to greatest.

1. 51 41 54 29

2. 203 230 302 233

3. 121 111 212 222

4. 975 982 985 970

New Vocabulary • opposites • integers • absolute value

OBJECTIVE

Interactive lesson includes instant self-check, tutorials, and activities.

1 Finding Opposite and Absolute Values

The "smoke" in many movies is really dry ice. Composed of pressurized carbon dioxide, its freezing point is −190°F. Homemade bread is ready to come out of the oven when the center of the bread reaches 190°F.

Two numbers that are the same distance from 0 on a number line, but in opposite directions, are **opposites.**

Need Help?
The whole numbers are 0, 1, 2, . . .

Integers are the set of positive whole numbers, their opposites, and zero. The table shows some real-world examples of integers.

Real World	Integer
a 5-yd loss in football	–5
a profit of $150	150
72 ft below sea level	–72

1 EXAMPLE Finding an Opposite

Find the opposite of −4.

The opposite of −4 is +4, or 4, because −4 and +4 are each four units from 0, but in opposite directions.

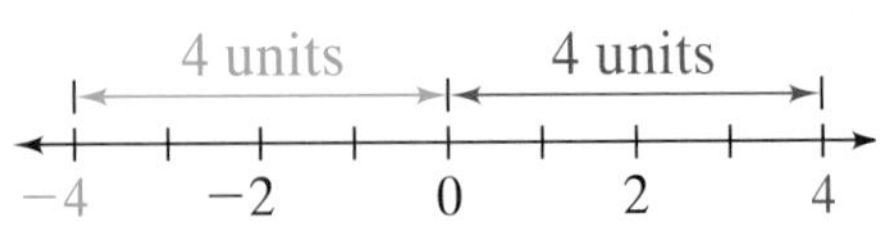

Check Understanding 1 Find the opposite of each number.

a. −8 **b.** 13 **c.** −22

The **absolute value** of a number is its distance from 0 on a number line. You write "the absolute value of −3" as $|-3|$.

2 EXAMPLE Finding Absolute Value

Find $|-3|$ and $|3|$.

3 units from 0   3 units from 0

−4 (−3) −2 −1 0 1 2 (3) 4 ← Use a number line.

$|-3| = 3$ and $|3| = 3$.

Check Understanding 2 **a.** Find $|8|$ and $|-8|$.

b. Number Sense Which two numbers have an absolute value of 1?

OBJECTIVE 2

Graphing and Ordering Integers

You can compare and order integers by graphing. Numbers increase in value from left to right.

3 EXAMPLE Comparing Integers

Compare −7 and 1 using <, >, or =.

−7 is 7 units to the left of 0.   **1 is 1 unit to the right of 0.**

−10 −8 −6 −4 −2 0 2 4 6 ← **Numbers increase in value from left to right.**

negative   zero   positive

Since −7 is to the left of 1 on the number line, $-7 < 1$.

Check Understanding 3 Compare using <, >, or =.

a. −8 ■ 2   **b.** 2 ■ −2   **c.** −3 ■ 3

4 EXAMPLE Ordering Integers

Climate Order the cities by temperature, from coldest to warmest.

Graph the temperatures on a number line.

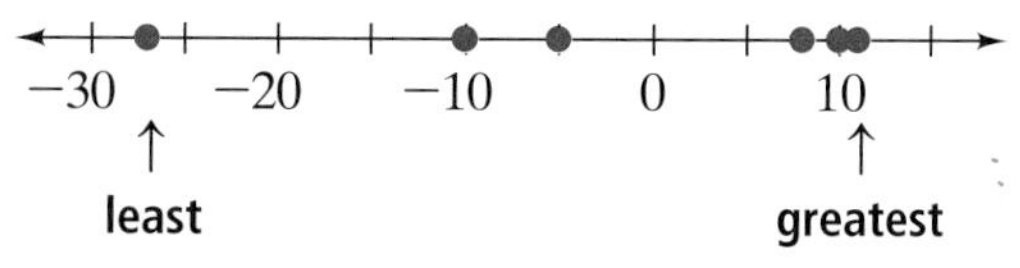

Lowest October Temperatures

ALASKA
Nome (−10°F)
Fairbanks (−27°F)
Anchorage (−5°F)
Valdez (8°F)
Juneau (11°F)
Kodiak (10°F)

SOURCE: National Weather Service

From coldest to warmest temperature, the cities are Fairbanks, Nome, Anchorage, Valdez, Kodiak, and Juneau.

Check Understanding 4 Order the numbers 3, −1, −4, and 2 from least to greatest.

EXERCISES

For more practice, see *Extra Practice.*

A Practice by Example

Find the opposite of each number.

Example 1 (page 34)

1. -1 **2.** -8 **3.** 15 **4.** 11 **5.** 90

6. -72 **7.** 21 **8.** -14 **9.** -47 **10.** 51

Find each absolute value.

Example 2 (page 35)

11. $|10|$ **12.** $|-11|$ **13.** $|-16|$ **14.** $|-1|$ **15.** $|4|$

16. $|7|$ **17.** $|-3|$ **18.** $|-5|$ **19.** $|6|$ **20.** $|-10|$

Compare using <, >, or =.

Example 3 (page 35)

21. 0 ■ -2 **22.** -6 ■ -3 **23.** -14 ■ 14 **24.** -23 ■ 0

25. -4 ■ -5 **26.** 17 ■ -18 **27.** 7 ■ -12 **28.** 5 ■ -1

Order each set of numbers from least to greatest.

Example 4 (page 35)

29. $-4, 8, -2, -6, 3$ **30.** $-2, 0, 7, -1, -5$ **31.** $2, -3, -7, 1, 10$

32. $-7, -8, 1, 9, 2$ **33.** $0, -4, 2, -9, 5$ **34.** $0, 4, -2, 9, -5$

35. Sports Scores in a golf tournament are reported by the number of strokes each player is above or below par. The scores for six players are -12, $+2$, -7, $+4$, -4, and -3. Order the scores from the lowest number under par to the greatest number over par.

B Apply Your Skills

Name the integer represented by each point on the number line.

36. *A* **37.** *B*

38. *C* **39.** *D*

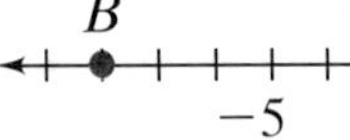
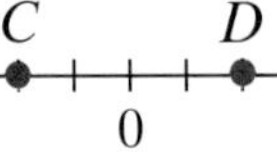
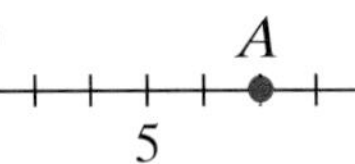

40. Number Sense On the number line above, which letters represent opposites?

Graph each integer and its opposite on a number line.

41. 2 **42.** -9 **43.** 12 **44.** -5

Write an integer to represent each situation.

45. Geography The city of New Orleans, Louisiana, is 8 ft below sea level.

46. Temperature In Miami, Florida, the average July temperature is 83°F.

47. Geography The shores of the Dead Sea are 1,345 ft below sea level.

48. Money You owe the library a fine of $3.

Use the table for Exercises 49–51.

49. **a.** Using a number line, graph the normal high temperatures for January.

b. Write the city names above the number line for coldest to warmest temperatures.

50. **a.** Using another number line, graph the normal low temperatures for January.

b. Write the city names above the number line for coldest to warmest temperatures.

Normal Temperatures for January (°F)

City	High	Low
Barrow, Alaska	–7	–19
Bismarck, N. Dak.	20	–2
Caribou, Maine	19	–2
Duluth, Minn.	16	–2
Omaha, Nebr.	31	11

SOURCE: National Climatic Data Center.
Go to **www.PHSchool.com** for a data update.
Web Code abg-2041

51. Which city has the least difference in high and low normal temperatures in January? The greatest difference?

Compare. Use <, >, or =.

52. $|-4| \blacksquare |-5|$ **53.** $|17| \blacksquare |-18|$ **54.** $|7| \blacksquare |-12|$ **55.** $|5| \blacksquare |-1|$

Real-World Connection

Tiger Woods is the first golfer to hold all four professional major golf championship titles at the same time.

56. **Sports** In golf, the person with the lowest score is the winner. By ordering their scores, rank the players at the right from first place to fourth place.

Masters Tournament 2002

Player	Score
R. Goosen	−9
J. Olazabal	−7
P. Mickelson	−8
T. Woods	−12

SOURCE: *Sports Illustrated*

57. **Writing in Math** Suppose a friend does not know how to order integers. Explain how to order the numbers 12, −4, and −5 from least to greatest.

Open-Ended **Write an integer to make each statement true.**

58. $-7 < \blacksquare$ **59.** $|12| < \blacksquare$ **60.** $-15 > \blacksquare$

61. $0 > \blacksquare$ **62.** $|-4| < \blacksquare$ **63.** $|-253| < \blacksquare$

64. **a.** **Sports** On successive plays, the home football team gained 6 yd, lost 2 yd, gained 12 yd, lost 5 yd, and then ran 27 yd for a touchdown. Represent each play as an integer.

b. Write the integers in order from least to greatest.

Find the value of each expression.

65. $|-4| + 3$ **66.** $|-1| + 3$ **67.** $|-5| - 3$ **68.** $|-2| + 2$

69. True or false?

a. The absolute value of a positive number is always positive.

b. The absolute value of a negative number is its opposite.

Challenge

70. a. Which integer is greater, −43 or 22?
b. Which has the greater absolute value, −43 or 22? Explain.

List all the integers between each pair of numbers.

71. −5.25 and 1.75 **72.** −8.99 and 0.3 **73.** −13.99 and −2.81

74. a. Reasoning Write three numbers that are between −3 and −4.
b. Are the numbers you wrote integers? Explain.

75. Stretch Your Thinking Janelle puts one piece of paper on top of another and cuts them both in half. She now has 4 pieces of paper. She stacks the pieces and cuts the stack in half to get 8 pieces of paper. Repeating this process, how many cuts will Janelle need to make in all to get 128 pieces of paper?

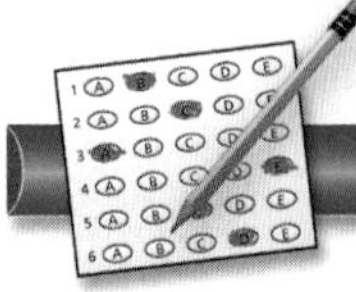

Test Prep

Multiple Choice

76. The low temperatures for Fairbanks, Alaska, for the months of November through March are −4°F, −15°F, −18°F, −14°F, and −2°F. Which shows the temperatures ordered from least to greatest?

A. −4°F −15°F −18°F −14°F −2°F
B. −2°F −4°F −14°F −15°F −18°F
C. −18°F −15°F −14°F −4°F −2°F
D. −2°F −4°F −15°F −14°F −18°F

77. When multiplied by 0.1, which number has a product that is an integer?

F. 25 **G.** 310 **H.** 2,002 **I.** 70,001

78. Which is the graph of the integers that have an absolute value of 2?

A. −4 −2 0 2 4
B. −4 −2 0 2 4
C. −4 −2 0 2 4
D. −4 −2 0 2 4

Take It to the NET
Online lesson quiz at
www.PHSchool.com
Web Code aba-0106

79. Which statement is true?

F. $-13 < -12$ **G.** $-11 > 5$ **H.** $-4 < -5$ **I.** $-2 > 0$

Mixed Review

Lesson 1-4

Write a number that makes each statement true.

80. 45.3 cm = ■ mm **81.** 26.78 mL = ■ L **82.** 256 mg = ■ g

Identify each property shown.

Lesson 1-2

83. $10.2 + 13.4 - 7.22 = 13.4 + 10.2 - 7.22$ **84.** $2.25 + 0 = 2.25$

85. $4.31 + (1.11 + 3.53) = (4.31 + 1.11) + 3.53$

Algebra

1-7 Adding and Subtracting Integers

What You'll Learn

To add integers

To subtract integers and to find range

. . . And Why

To find the range of temperatures, as in Example 5

✓ Check Skills You'll Need

For help, go to Lesson 1-6.

Find the value of each expression.

1. $|5|$ **2.** $|-2|$ **3.** $|-5|$

4. $|7|$ **5.** $|6| + 2$ **6.** $|-3| + 4$

7. $|6| - 1$ **8.** $|-8| - 3$ **9.** $|5| - 5$

New Vocabulary

- additive inverses
- range

OBJECTIVE 1

Interactive lesson includes instant self-check, tutorials, and activities.

Adding Integers

Suppose you have no money on Monday. You borrow $8 from your mother on Tuesday and pay her back from the $10 you earn babysitting on Wednesday. You can keep track of your finances on a number line.

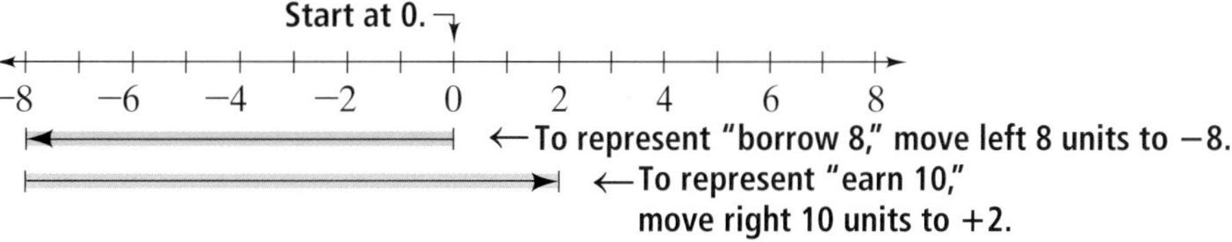

Start at 0.
−8 −6 −4 −2 0 2 4 6 8
←To represent "borrow 8," move left 8 units to −8.
←To represent "earn 10," move right 10 units to +2.

The number line shows that $-8 + 10 = 2$. You have $2.

Need Help?
Recall that addition and subtraction are inverse operations.

If you earn $8 and then spend $8, you are back where you started at zero. You can write this as the number sentence $8 + (-8) = 0$. Two numbers with a sum of 0 are **additive inverses.**

1 EXAMPLE Adding Integers With Different Signs

Use a number line to find each sum.

a. $(-4) + 5$

−4 −2 0 2 4

← Start at 0. Move 4 units left. Then move 5 units right.

The sum is 1.

b. $5 + (-4)$

−4 −2 0 2 4

← Start at 0. Move 5 units right. Then move 4 units left.

The sum is 1.

Check Understanding **1** Use a number line to find each sum.

a. $5 + (-3)$ **b.** $2 + (-5)$ **c.** $-8 + 1$

d. **Reasoning** Which property of addition is demonstrated in Example 1?

2 EXAMPLE Adding Integers With the Same Sign

Use a number line to find the sum.

$-5 + (-2)$

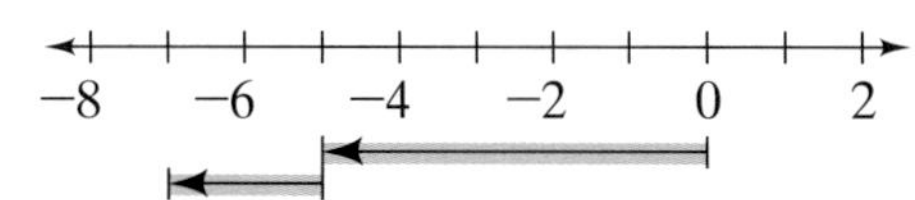

← Start at 0. Move 5 units left. Then move another 2 units left.

The sum is -7.

Check Understanding **2** Use a number line to find each sum.

a. $-4 + (-5)$ **b.** $-2 + (-3)$ **c.** $-1 + (-7)$

The following rules explain how to add two integers without using a number line.

Key Concepts Adding Integers

Same Sign The sum of two positive numbers is positive. The sum of two negative numbers is negative.

Examples $3 + 5 = 8$ $\quad -3 + (-5) = -8$

Different Signs Find the absolute value of each. Subtract the lesser absolute value from the greater. The sum has the sign of the integer with the greater absolute value.

Examples $-3 + 5 = 2$ $\quad 3 + (-5) = -2$

3 EXAMPLE Adding Integers

Test-Prep Tip
The sum of two negative integers is always negative.

Find each sum.

a. $-18 + (-16) = -34$ ← Since both integers are negative, the sum is negative.

b. $-23 + 8$

$|-23| - |8| = 15$ ← Find the difference of the absolute values.

$-23 + 8 = -15$ ← Since -23 has a greater absolute value, the sum is negative.

Check Understanding **3** Find each sum.

a. $-97 + (-65)$ **b.** $21 + (-39)$ **c.** $-49 + 54 + (-14)$

d. **Reasoning** Explain how to apply the rules to add $9 + (-6) + 8$.

OBJECTIVE

2 Subtracting Integers and Finding Range

You know that $9 - 5 = 4$, but $9 + (-5)$ also $= 4$.

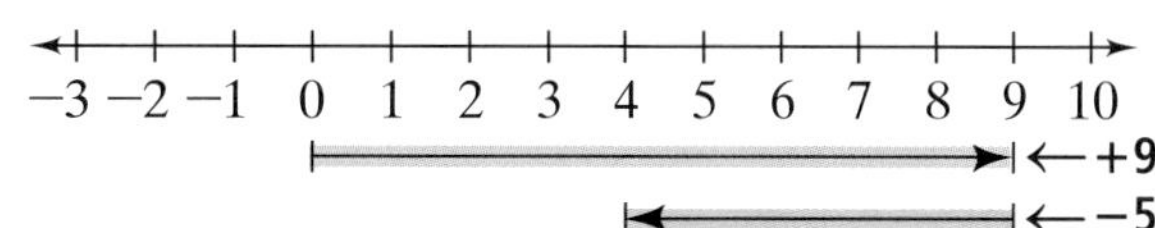

Subtract 5. Add the opposite of 5.

$9 - 5 = 4$ $9 + (-5) = 4$

The answer is 4.

Subtracting 5 is the same as adding −5. This result suggests a pattern for subtracting integers.

Key Concepts **Subtracting Integers**

To subtract an integer, add its opposite.

Examples $3 - 5 = 3 + (-5) = -2$ $-3 - 5 = -3 + (-5) = -8$

4 EXAMPLE Subtracting Integers

Find each difference.

a. $4 - 6 = 4 + (-6)$ ← **Add the opposite of 6, which is −6.**

$= -2$ ← **Simplify.**

b. $-2 - (-5) = -2 + (5)$ ← **Add the opposite of −5, which is 5.**

$= 3$ ← **Simplify.**

Check Understanding 4 Find each difference.

a. $-7 - (-3)$ **b.** $8 - 4$ **c.** $2 - 5$ **d.** $-6 - 1$

The **range** of a data set is the difference between the greatest and the least values.

5 EXAMPLE Finding Range

Climate Temperatures at Verkhoyansk, Russia, have ranged from a low of −90°F to a high of 98°F. Find the temperature range in Verkhoyansk.

$98 - (-90) = 98 + 90$ ← **Add the opposite of −90, which is 90.**

$= 188$ ← **Simplify.**

The temperature range in Verkhoyansk is 188°F.

Check Understanding 5 Find each range.

a. from 53 to −47 **b.** from −42 to −8

c. Number Sense Use a number line to show the range of temperatures of Example 5.

EXERCISES

For more practice, see *Extra Practice*.

A Practice by Example

Examples 1, 2 (pages 39, 40)

Use a number line to find each sum.

1. $-5 + (-4)$ **2.** $2 + (-8)$ **3.** $-6 + 7$ **4.** $12 + (-7)$

5. $7 + 3$ **6.** $-2 + (-3)$ **7.** $-9 + 6$ **8.** $-5 + 5$

9. $-8 + (-1)$ **10.** $5 + (-6)$ **11.** $-13 + 7$ **12.** $-14 + 16$

Example 3 (page 40)

Find each sum.

13. $-99 + 137$ **14.** $15 + (-3)$ **15.** $-10 + 4$

16. $-5 + (-13)$ **17.** $27 + (-24)$ **18.** $42 + (-42)$

19. $-15 + 20$ **20.** $28 + (-32)$ **21.** $126 + (-92)$

22. $68 + (-72) + 12$ **23.** $12 + 23 + (-5)$ **24.** $-50 + 48 + (-28)$

25. Weather At midnight, the temperature was -12°F. By 6 A.M., the temperature had risen 19 degrees. What was the temperature at 6 A.M.?

Example 4 (page 41)

Find each difference.

26. $-15 - 2$ **27.** $-3 - (-3)$ **28.** $-5 - (-9)$ **29.** $17 - (-8)$

30. $12 - (-4)$ **31.** $-14 - 14$ **32.** $-8 - (-12)$ **33.** $29 - 16$

34. $47 - 151$ **35.** $-54 - 82$ **36.** $-72 - (-22)$ **37.** $85 - (-85)$

38. Games For the game of billiards called 14.1, a penalty deducts points from a player's score. Find the difference in the scores of the winner with 50 points and the opponent with -17 points.

Example 5 (page 41)

Find each range.

39. between 24 and (-2) **40.** between 7 and (-3)

41. between 6 and (-6) **42.** between (-16) and (-6)

43. Sports Scores for a local golf tournament vary from 6 under par (-6) to 51. Find the range of the scores.

B Apply Your Skills

Find the value of each expression.

44. $3 + (-3) - 6$ **45.** $-5 - 3 + (-2)$ **46.** $3 + (-12) - 4$

47. $1 + 7 - (-7)$ **48.** $2 - 9 - 10$ **49.** $-8 - (-1) + 7$

50. $-4 - 5 + 9$ **51.** $6.5 - (-8.4)$ **52.** $-12.2 + (-9.9)$

53. Money Rosa borrowed \$10 from her sister. The next day she paid back \$5. Two days later, she borrowed \$4 more. How much does Rosa owe?

Write an expression for each model. Then find the sum.

54. −4 −2 0 2

55. 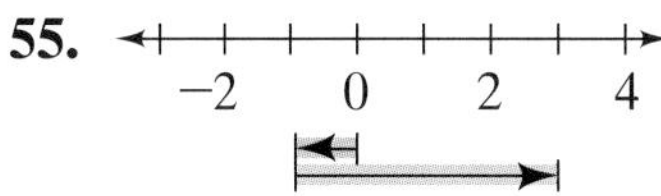

56. −2 0 2 4 6 8 10 12

57. −4 −2 0 2

Real-World Connection

Summer temperatures in Death Valley often are in excess of 120°F.

58. Temperature The highest temperature ever recorded in the United States was 134°F, measured at Death Valley, California. The coldest temperature, −80°F, was recorded at Prospect Creek, Alaska. What is the difference between these temperatures?

59. Date File, p. 3 Find the range of temperatures for each city in the table.

60. Science Use the data at the right. Which two substances have boiling points that are closest in value? Explain.

Boiling Point

Substance	Temperature (°C)
Carbon	3825
Chlorine	−34.04
Gold	2856
Helium	−268.93
Water	100

SOURCE: *CRC Handbook of Chemistry and Physics*

Number Sense Without calculating, determine whether each difference is positive or negative.

61. $-18 - 25$

62. $9 - (-2)$

63. $-7 - (-13)$

Match each equation with a property.

64. $-7 + 0 = -7$

65. $-1 + 5 = 5 + (-1)$

66. $2 = 0 + 2$

67. $-7 + (-3 + 13) = [-7 + (-3)] + 13$

A. Commutative Property of Addition

B. Identity Property of Addition

C. Associative Property of Addition

The continental United States has four time zones. Consider time changes as positive when going east and negative when going west. The time in your zone is given. Find the time in the indicated time zone.

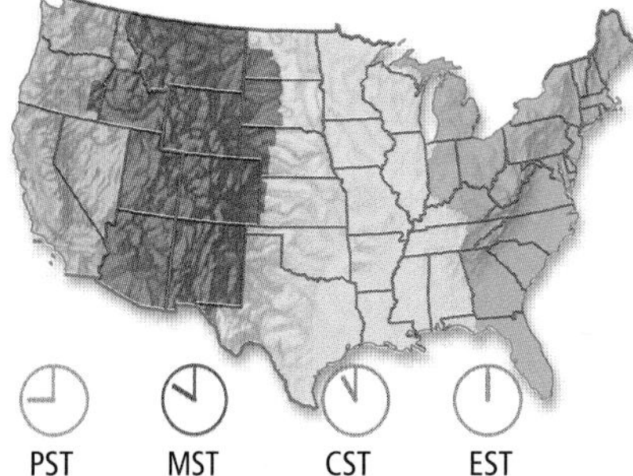

68. 6:00 A.M.; 2 time zones east

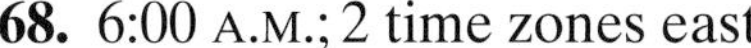

69. 9:00 P.M.; 3 time zones west

70. midnight; 2 time zones west

71. midnight; 1 time zone east

72. Writing in Math A friend has trouble simplifying $20 - (-38)$. Write an explanation to help your friend.

C Challenge

Reasoning Tell whether each subtraction sentence is *always, sometimes,* or *never* true. Support your answer with examples.

73. (positive) − (positive) = (positive)

74. (negative) − (positive) = (negative)

75. (positive) − (negative) = (negative)

76. (negative) − (negative) = (negative)

77. a. Number Sense Is $|7 - 9|$ equal to $|7| - |9|$?
b. Is $|9 - 7|$ equal to $|9| - |7|$?
c. Did you answer part (a) and part (b) the same way? Explain.

78. Stretch Your Thinking There are fewer sixth-grade students than seventh-grade students in a school district. The ninth grade has more students than either the eighth grade or the seventh grade. The number of students in the fifth grade is less than the number of students in the sixth grade. Which grade has the most students?

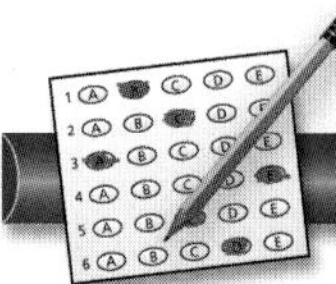

Test Prep

Multiple Choice

79. An early morning temperature is recorded at −3°F. Two hours later, the temperature has risen 20°. What is the temperature at this time?
A. −23°F **B.** −17°F **C.** 17°F **D.** 23°F

80. Which expression is NOT equal to −5?
F. −2 − 3 **G.** 2 − (−3) **H.** 3 − 8 **I.** $|-5| - 10$

81. At 8 P.M. the wind-chill temperature was −9°F. One hour later, the wind-chill temperature had fallen to −29°F. Which number sentence shows this change?
A. 29 + (−9) = 20 **B.** −9 − (−29) = 20
C. −29 − (−9) = −20 **D.** −29 − 9 = −38

Take It to the NET
Online lesson quiz at
www.PHSchool.com
Web Code aba-0107

Extended Response

82. Explain the rules for adding integers. Use examples.

Mixed Review

Lesson 1-6 **Compare. Use <, >, or =.**

83. −4 ■ −10 **84.** 0 ■ −7 **85.** 24 ■ 204

86. $|-3|$ ■ $|3|$ **87.** $|16|$ ■ $|-23|$ **88.** $|-4|$ ■ $|-2|$

Lesson 1-1 **Use front-end estimation to estimate each sum or difference.**

89. 12.78 + 4.27 **90.** 18.81 − 9.74 **91.** 13.54 + 29.48

1-8 Multiplying and Dividing Integers

What You'll Learn

To multiply integers

To divide integers

. . . And Why

To find the rate of a car's acceleration, as in Example 3

✔ Check Skills You'll Need

For help, go to Lesson 1-7.

Find each sum.

1. $5 + 5 + 5 + 5 + 5 + 5$

2. $(-3) + (-3) + (-3) + (-3)$

3. $(-12) + (-12) + (-12)$

4. $8 + 8 + 8 + 8 + 8 + 8 + 8$

5. $(-27) + (-27)$

6. $(-1) + (-1) + (-1) + (-1)$

OBJECTIVE

Interactive lesson includes instant self-check, tutorials, and activities.

1 Multiplying Integers

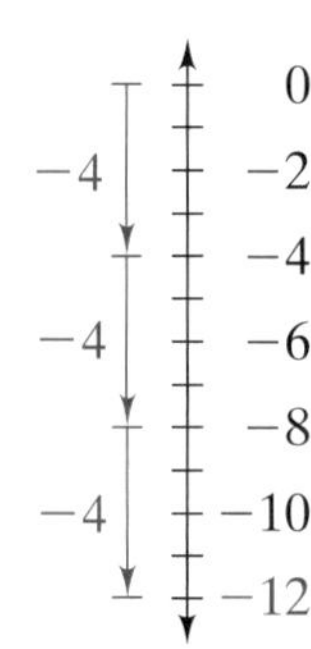

To multiply a positive and negative integer, think of multiplication as repeated addition.

A cave explorer descends 4 ft/min for 3 min.

$3(-4) = (-4) + (-4) + (-4) = -12$ ← **The explorer descends 12 ft.**

You can use number lines to multiply integers.

3(2) means three groups of 2.

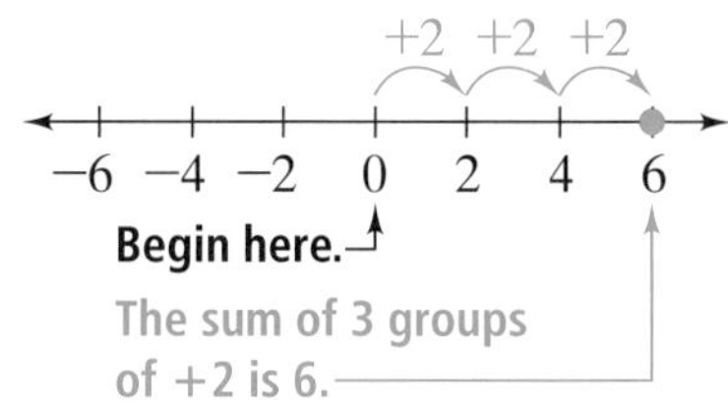

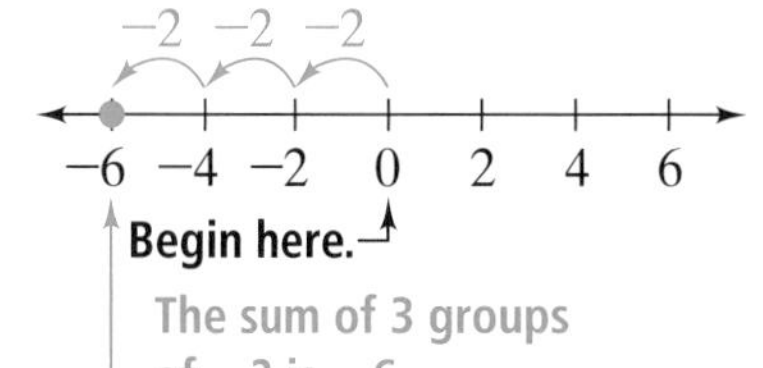

−3(2) is the opposite of three groups of 2.

−3(−2) is the opposite of three groups of −2.

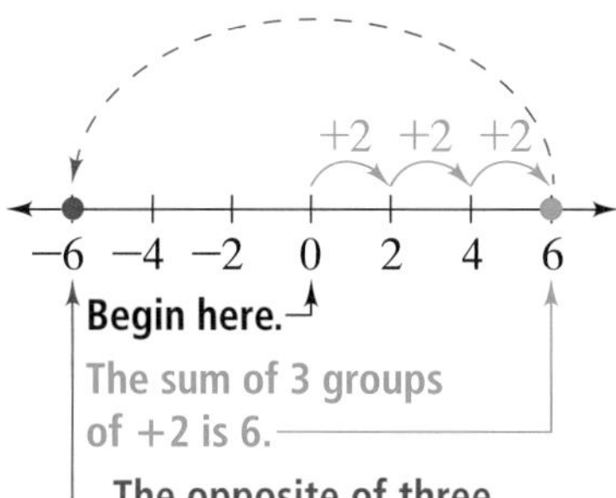

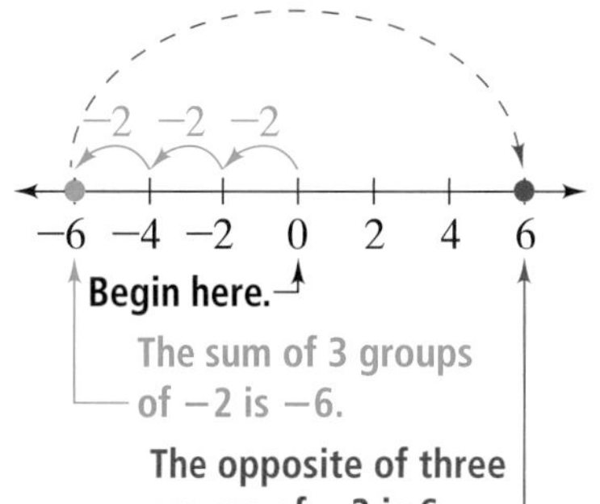

The examples on page 45 suggest rules for multiplying integers.

Key Concepts **Multiplying Integers**

The product of two integers with the same sign is positive.

Examples $3(2) = 6$ $-3(-2) = 6$

The product of two integers with different signs is negative.

Examples $-3(2) = -6$ $3(-2) = -6$

1 EXAMPLE Multiplying Integers

Find each product.

a. $5(3) = 15$ ← Factors have the same sign, positive product.

b. $5(-3) = -15$ ← Factors have different signs, negative product.

c. $-5(3) = -15$ ← Factors have different signs, negative product.

d. $-5(-3) = 15$ ← Factors have the same sign, positive product.

Check Understanding 1 Find each product.

a. $-6 \cdot (2)$ **b.** $15 \cdot (-8)$ **c.** $-12 \cdot (-6)$ **d.** $-7 \cdot (-1)$

OBJECTIVE

2 Dividing Integers

Reading Math

Inverse comes from the word *invert*, which means "to turn inside out."

Multiplication and division are inverse operations because they undo each other. Study the patterns below.

Since...	**You know that...**
$5 \cdot 2 = 10$	$10 \div 2 = 5$
$5 \cdot (-2) = -10$	$-10 \div (-2) = 5$
$-5 \cdot 2 = -10$	$-10 \div 2 = -5$
$-5 \cdot (-2) = 10$	$10 \div (-2) = -5$

Note that when two integers have the same signs, their quotient is positive. When two integers have different signs, their quotient is negative. The rules for dividing two integers are similar to the rules for multiplying.

Key Concepts **Dividing Integers**

The quotient of two integers with the same sign is positive.

Examples $10 \div 2 = 5$ $-10 \div (-2) = 5$

The quotient of two integers with different signs is negative.

Examples $-10 \div 2 = -5$ $10 \div (-2) = -5$

2 EXAMPLE Dividing Integers

Find each quotient.

a. $\frac{-24}{-8}$

$\frac{-24}{-8} = 3$ ← **The signs of the factors determine the sign of the quotient.** →

b. $\frac{18}{-3}$

$\frac{18}{-3} = -6$

Check Understanding 2 Find each quotient.

a. $\frac{14}{-2}$ **b.** $\frac{-32}{-8}$ **c.** $-56 \div (-7)$ **d.** $-121 \div 11$

Stanley Basin, Sawtooth Mountains, Idaho

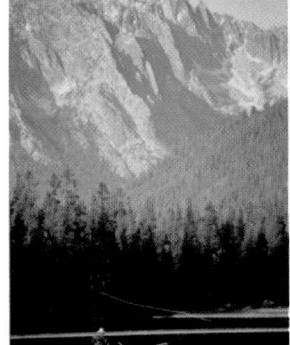

3 EXAMPLE Real-World Problem Solving

Mountain Climbing A mountain climber in the Sawtooth Mountains is at an elevation of 10,117 feet. Five hours later, he is at 7,357 feet. Find the climber's vertical speed using this formula:

$$\text{vertical speed} = \frac{\text{final elevation} - \text{initial elevation}}{\text{time}}$$

$$= \frac{7{,}357 - 10{,}117}{5}$$ ← **Substitute 7,357 for final elevation, 10,117 for initial elevation, and 5 for time.**

$$= \frac{-2{,}760}{5} = -552$$ ← **Simplify. The negative sign means the climber is descending.**

The climber's vertical speed is -552 feet per hour.

Check Understanding 3 Find the vertical speed of a climber who goes from an elevation of 8,120 feet to an elevation of 6,548 feet in three hours.

EXERCISES

For more practice, see *Extra Practice*.

A Practice by Example

Example 1 (page 46)

Find each product.

1. $-2 \cdot (-13)$ **2.** $-6 \cdot (12)$ **3.** $-5 \cdot (-6)$ **4.** $4 \cdot (-9)$

5. $-15 \cdot (-3)$ **6.** $6 \cdot (-6)$ **7.** $27 \cdot (31)$ **8.** $12 \cdot (-4)$

9. $-36 \cdot (2)$ **10.** $-12 \cdot (-14)$ **11.** $-35 \cdot (24)$ **12.** $102 \cdot (-6)$

Example 2 (page 47)

Find each quotient.

13. $\frac{36}{-12}$ **14.** $\frac{-72}{8}$ **15.** $\frac{-50}{-5}$ **16.** $\frac{-27}{9}$

17. $15 \div (-3)$ **18.** $-20 \div 10$ **19.** $-9 \div 9$ **20.** $-72 \div (-8)$

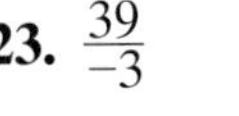

21. $\frac{-24}{4}$ **22.** $\frac{-96}{12}$ **23.** $\frac{39}{-3}$ **24.** $\frac{-66}{-11}$

Example 3 (page 47)

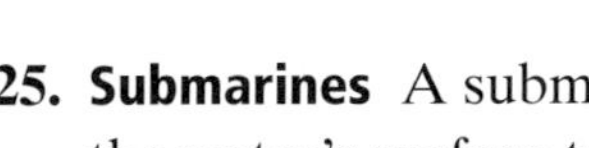

25. Submarines A submersible submarine takes 6 min to dive from the water's surface to a depth 228 m below the surface. Find the submersible's vertical speed.

26. Hiking In four hours, a hiker in a canyon goes from 892 ft above the canyon floor to 256 ft above the floor. Find the hiker's vertical speed.

B Apply Your Skills

Name the point on the number line that shows each product or quotient.

27. $-16 \div (-2)$ **28.** $(-1) \cdot (-1)$ **29.** $-4 \cdot (1)$

30. $32 \div (-4)$ **31.** $-7 \div 7$ **32.** $-5 \cdot 0$

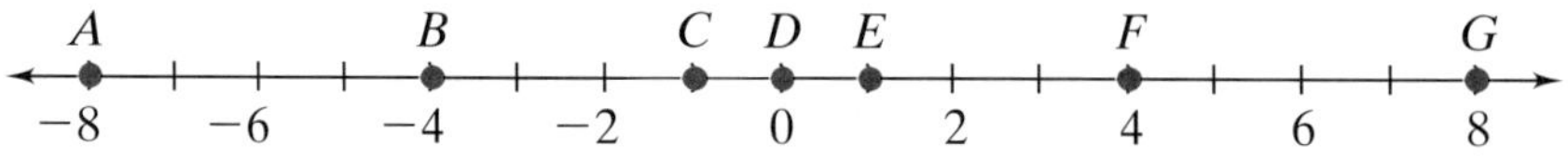

33. Investments The price of a stock falls \$2 each day for 8 days.
a. What is the total change in the price of the stock?
b. Before the price of the stock started falling, its value was \$38. What is the price of the stock after the drop?

34. Hobbies A scuba diver is 180 ft below sea level and rises to the surface at a rate of 30 ft/min. How long will the diver take to reach the surface?

Real-World Connection
The word *scuba* means **s**elf-**c**ontained **u**nderwater **b**reathing **a**pparatus.

Estimate each product or quotient.

35. $-24 \cdot 35$ **36.** $-265 \div (-129)$ **37.** $12 \cdot (-15)$

38. $-58 \div (-9)$ **39.** $19 \cdot (-5)$ **40.** $-72 \div 68$

41. Reasoning Write two related division statements for $7(-3) = -21$.

42. Banking You have \$172 in a bank account. You withdraw \$6 per week for the next 3 wk. What is your balance at the end of the 3 weeks?

43. Writing in Math Explain how you would decide whether the product of three numbers is positive or negative.

Complete each sentence.

44. (positive) · (negative) = ■ **45.** (negative) · (positive) = ■

46. (negative) · (negative) = ■ **47.** (positive) ÷ (negative) = ■

48. (negative) ÷ (positive) = ■ **49.** (negative) ÷ (negative) = ■

Use the Associative Property of Multiplication to simplify.

50. $(-2) \cdot (-5) \cdot 7$ **51.** $(-1) \cdot (-1) \cdot (-3)$ **52.** $4 \cdot 0 \cdot (-3)$

C Challenge

Find each product.

53. $1.5 \cdot (-2.25)$ **54.** $-12.3 \cdot 7.2$ **55.** $-8.75 \cdot (4.8)$

56. Stretch Your Thinking Of 100 students asked if they like rock-and-roll or country music, 7 said that they like neither, 90 said that they like rock-and-roll music, and 57 said that they like country music. How many students like both?

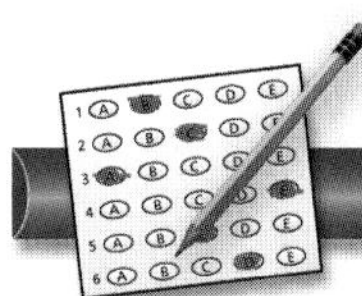

Test Prep

Multiple Choice

57. Suppose you walk down six flights of stairs each containing 12 steps. Which number sentence best describes your descent?

A. $6 \cdot 12 = 72$ **B.** $6 \cdot -12 = 72$
C. $-6 \cdot -12 = -72$ **D.** $-6 \cdot 12 = -72$

58. Find the next number in the sequence: 2, −4, 8, −16

F. 32 **G.** 16 **H.** 12 **I.** −12

59. When you divide two negative numbers, the quotient is

A. equal to one. **B.** equal to one of the numbers.
C. greater than either number. **D.** less than either number.

Extended Response

60. You swim for 25 min. Then for lunch you eat 1 c of tomato soup, 3 oz of cheese, and 8 crackers.

a. Find the number of Calories you use swimming.

b. Find the number of Calories you eat during lunch.

c. How much longer would you need to swim to use more Calories than you ate? Explain.

Food	Calories
Cheese (1 oz)	115
Crackers (4)	50
Tomato soup (1 c)	90
Activity	**Calories** used per minute
Swimming	6

Take It to the NET
Online lesson quiz at
www.PHSchool.com
Web Code aba-0108

Mixed Review

Lesson 1-7 **Find each sum or difference.**

61. $3 - (-6)$ **62.** $-23 + 9$ **63.** $-4 - (-9)$ **64.** $-1 + 8$

Lesson 1-4 **Choose a reasonable estimate.**

65. length of a banana 14 m 14 cm 14 mm

66. mass of a quarter 6.25 kg 6.25 g 6.25 mg

Checkpoint Quiz 2 — Lessons 1-5 through 1-8

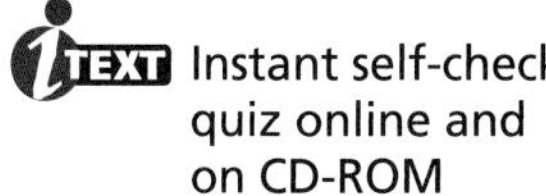

Instant self-check quiz online and on CD-ROM

Compare using <, >, or =.

1. $-4 \;■\; -5$ **2.** $-2 \;■\; 0$ **3.** $|-7| \;■\; |7|$

Find the value of each expression.

4. $-5 + 9$ **5.** $-6 + (-3)$ **6.** $-7 - (-4)$

7. $-17 - 12$ **8.** $-3 \cdot (-31)$ **9.** $84 \div (-12)$

10. **Choose a Strategy** The pages of a book are numbered from 1 to 128. How many page numbers contain the digit 6?

1-9 Order of Operations and the Distributive Property

What You'll Learn

To use the order of operations

To use the Distributive Property

. . . And Why

To find area, as in Example 2

Check Skills You'll Need

For help, go to Lesson 1-2.

Use mental math to simplify.

1. $2.5 + 7.1 + 2.5$

2. $6.2 + 6.2 + 5.6$

3. $8.1 + 3.8 + 8.1$

4. $7.3 + 4.5 + 4.5$

5. Explain how you would simplify the expression $6.8 - 2.3 + 6.8 - 2.3$.

New Vocabulary • order of operations • Distributive Property

OBJECTIVE 1

Using the Order of Operations

Investigation: Combining Operations

1. Use graph paper to draw rectangles that have the following dimensions.

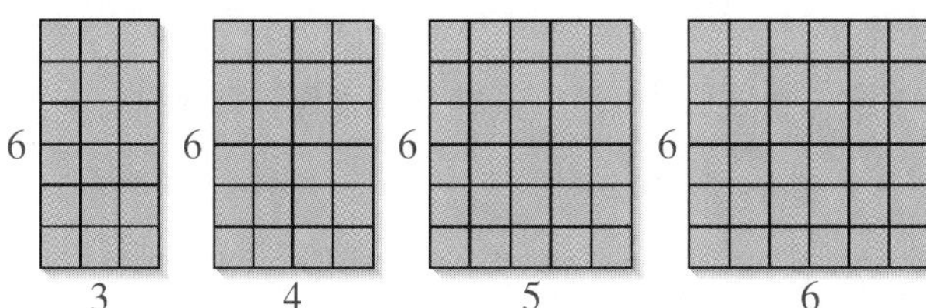

2. Cut out the rectangles. Find the area of each rectangle.
3. Combine any two rectangles to form a new rectangle. How does the area of the combined rectangle compare with the sum of the areas of the two original rectangles?

Suppose you want to simplify $5 + 2 \cdot 7$. This expression contains two operations—addition and multiplication. If you add first, your answer is 49. If you multiply first, your answer is 19. To avoid confusion, mathematicians have agreed on an order of operations.

Key Concepts **Order of Operations**

1. Work inside grouping symbols.
2. Multiply and divide in order from left to right.
3. Add and subtract in order from left to right.

Applying the Order of Operations

Reading Math

Grouping symbols include parentheses, ( ), brackets, [ ], and fraction bars, $\frac{3 + 5}{2}$.

Find the value of each expression.

a. $30 \div 3 + 2 \cdot 6$

$10 + 12$ ← **Divide and multiply.**

22 ← **Add.**

b. $30 \div (3 + 2) \cdot 6$

$30 \div 5 \cdot 6$ ← **Work inside grouping symbols.**

$6 \cdot 6$ ← **Divide.**

36 ← **Multiply.**

Check Understanding 1 Find the value of each expression.

a. $7(-4 + 2) - 1$ **b.** $\frac{-40}{4} + 2 \cdot 5$ **c.** $\frac{8 + 4}{6} - 11$

You can use the order of operations to find the area of an irregular figure.

2 EXAMPLE **Real-World Problem Solving**

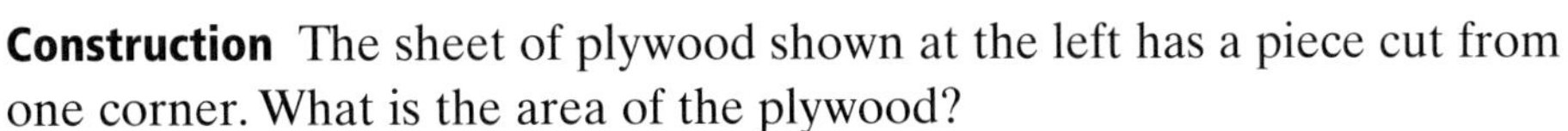

5 ft
4 ft
2 ft
8 ft

Construction The sheet of plywood shown at the left has a piece cut from one corner. What is the area of the plywood?

The length of the missing piece is 8 ft − 5 ft, or 3 ft. Its width is 4 ft − 2 ft, or 2 ft.

Words	Area of original plywood	−	Area of missing piece
Expression	$8 \cdot 4$	−	$3 \cdot 2$

$8 \cdot 4 - 3 \cdot 2 = 32 - 6$ ← **Multiply.**

$= 26$ ← **Subtract.**

The area of the plywood is 26 ft^2.

Check Understanding 2 Find the area of an 8.5 in. × 11 in. piece of paper with a 4-in. × 4-in. square removed from one corner.

OBJECTIVE

2 Using the Distributive Property

Suppose you want to simplify $3(5 + 2)$. By the order of operations, $3(5 + 2) = 3(7)$, or 21. Note also that $3(5) + 3(2) = 15 + 6$, or 21. This is an example of the Distributive Property, which combines multiplication with addition or subtraction.

Key Concepts **Distributive Property**

Arithmetic	Algebra
$9(4 + 5) = 9(4) + 9(5)$	$a(b + c) = a(b) + a(c)$
$5(8 - 2) = 5(8) - 5(2)$	$a(b - c) = a(b) - a(c)$

You can use the Distributive Property to multiply numbers mentally.

3 EXAMPLE The Distributive Property in Mental Math

Mental Math Use the Distributive Property to find 6(53).

What you think

53 is 50 + 3. Finding 6(53) is the same as finding 6(50) + 6(3). This I can do mentally, so 6(50) + 6(3) = 300 + 18, or 318.

Why it works

$6(53) = 6(50 + 3)$

$= 6(50) + 6(3)$ ← **Use the Distributive Property.**

$= 300 + 18$ ← **Multiply.**

$= 318$ ← **Add.**

Check Understanding 3 Use the Distributive Property to multiply mentally.

a. 8(21) **b.** 14(9) **c.** 48(6) **d.** 7(92)

e. **Reasoning** Does 6(50 + 3) = (50 + 3)6? Explain.

4 EXAMPLE Using the Distributive Property With Decimals

Mental Math Use the Distributive Property to find 7(5.9).

What you think

I think of 5.9 as 6.0 − 0.1. Then, 7(5.9) is the same as 7(6.0 − 0.1). I know that 7(6) − 7(0.1) = 42 − 0.7 = 41.3.

Why it works

$7(5.9) = 7(6.0 - 0.1)$

$= 7(6.0) - 7(0.1)$ ← **Use the Distributive Property.**

$= 42 - 0.7$ ← **Multiply.**

$= 41.3$ ← **Subtract.**

Check Understanding 4 Find each product mentally using the Distributive Property.

a. 4(12.1) **b.** 5(3.9) **c.** 11(9.2)

EXERCISES

For more practice, see *Extra Practice*.

A Practice by Example

Example 1 (page 51)

Find the value of each expression.

1. $6 + 1 \cdot 5$ **2.** $-4 \div 2 + 9$ **3.** $5 - 8 \div 4$

4. $3 - 0 \cdot 11$ **5.** $18 \div 3 \cdot 2$ **6.** $100 - 7 \cdot 9$

7. $-36 \div 2 + 8$ **8.** $-12 \div 6 - (1 + 4)$ **9.** $48 \div (-4 \cdot 3) + 2$

Example 2 (page 51)

10. **Supplies** A new poster board measures 30 in. × 40 in. A 12-in. square is cut from one corner. What is the area of the remaining poster board?

11. **Home Construction** You have a house lot that is 100 ft × 150 ft. You plan to build a house that is 30 ft × 50 ft. How much of the land remains for the yard?

Find each product mentally using the Distributive Property.

Example 3 (page 52)

12. 5(29) 13. 7(78) 14. 5(42)

15. 8(87) 16. 9(33) 17. 6(96)

Example 4 (page 52)

18. 6(3.9) 19. 4(10.2) 20. 7(2.6)

21. 11.6(9) 22. 9(2.2) 23. 3.4(5)

B Apply Your Skills

Find the missing numbers. Then simplify.

24. $4(-7 + 8) = 4(■) + 4(■)$

25. $-3(2 - 9) = (■)2 - (■)9$

26. $■(4.8) = 6(5) - 6(■)$

27. $■(-1 - 6) = 7(-1) - 7(6)$

28. **Architecture** Use the floor plan. Find the area of the floor.

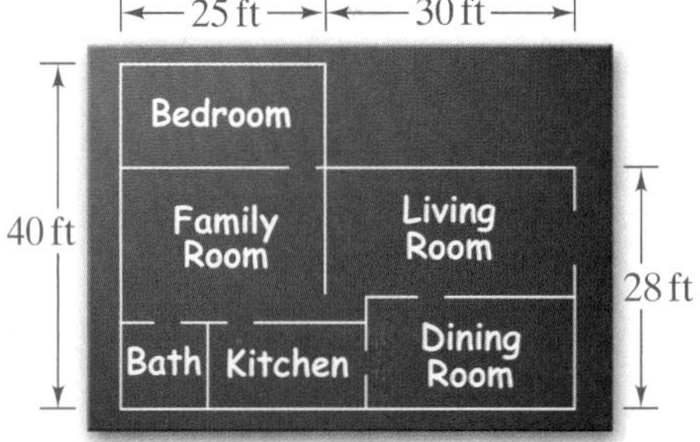

29. **Advertising** You make a poster for a school car wash. The poster measures 20 in. × 28.5 in.
    a. Use the Distributive Property to write an expression to find the area of the poster using mental math.
    b. Find the area of your poster.

30. **Open-Ended** Write an expression with three different operations. Then find the value of your expression.

31. **Business** A florist is buying flowers to use in centerpieces. Each centerpiece has 3 lilies. There are a total of 10 tables. Each lily costs $.98. Use mental math to find the cost of the lilies.

Real-World Connection

Careers Florists use many types of flowers to make centerpieces for tables.

Insert +, −, ·, or ÷ to make each equation true.

32. $-5 ■ 3 + 2 = -13$

33. $1.1 ■ 6 \cdot 0.3 = 2.9$

34. $30 - 6 ■ 6 = 29$

35. $23.1 \div 7 ■ 3.3 = 6.6$

Geometry Write two expressions to find the total area of each figure. Then find the area.

36.

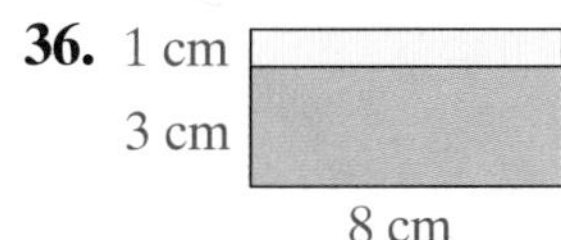

37.

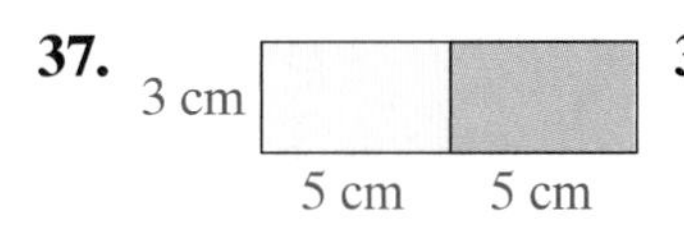

38.

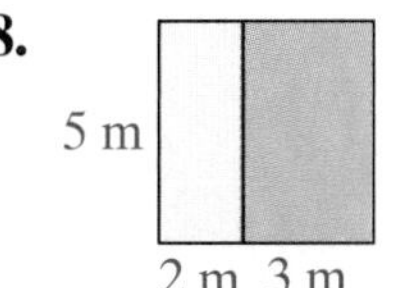

Real-World Connection Artwork is often brought to a museum for a limited time as a special exhibit.

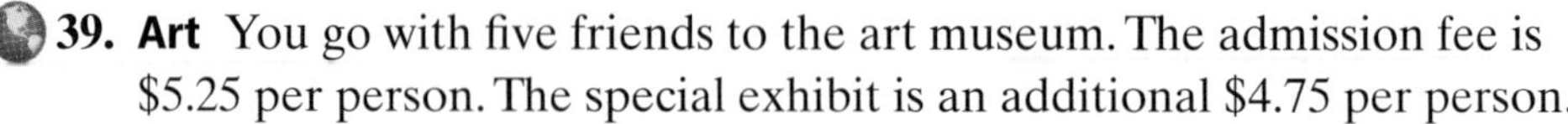

39. **Art** You go with five friends to the art museum. The admission fee is \$5.25 per person. The special exhibit is an additional \$4.75 per person.
   a. Find the admission fee for you and your friends.
   b. Find the special exhibit cost for you and your friends.
   c. Use mental math to find the total cost.

40. **Money** Use mental math to find the cost of 4 notebooks at \$.89 each.

41. **Writing in Math** Explain how you could use the Distributive Property to calculate 4(110.5) in two different ways.

Copy and place parentheses to make each statement true.

42. $4 + 4 \div 4 - 4 = -2$ 43. $4 \cdot 4 \div 4 + 4 = 2$ 44. $4 + 4 + 4 \div 4 = 3$

C Challenge

Find the value of each expression.

45. $\dfrac{3 + (-15)}{2 \cdot 3}$ 46. $\dfrac{-6(-4)}{-2 - 6}$ 47. $\dfrac{-2 \cdot 4 + 3}{7 - 2 \cdot 6}$

48. **Stretch Your Thinking** You want to place chairs along the walls in a rectangular room so that there are the same number of chairs along each wall. Describe the number of chairs you may have.

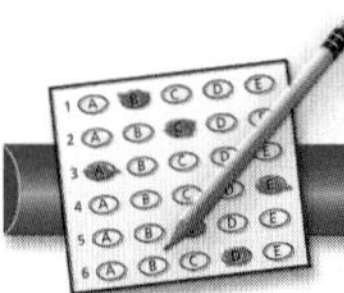

Test Prep

Multiple Choice

49. Which expression equals 7?
   A. $6 + 8 \div 2$ B. $9 + 6 \div (-3)$ C. $12 \div (2 + 1)$ D. $1 + 2 \cdot 4$

50. Which expression has the greatest value?
   F. $(5 - 2) \cdot 7$ G. $9 - 4 \cdot 2 + 1$ H. $-6 \div 2 + 4$ I. $9 + 3 \cdot 2$

Take It to the NET Online lesson quiz at www.PHSchool.com Web Code aba-0109

51. Which number sentence shows the Distributive Property?
   A. $4 \cdot 7 = 7 \cdot 4$ B. $(6 \cdot 3) \cdot 5 = 6 \cdot (3 \cdot 5)$
   C. $5(2 - 8) = 5(2) - 5(8)$ D. $-6 \cdot 1 = -6$

Short Response

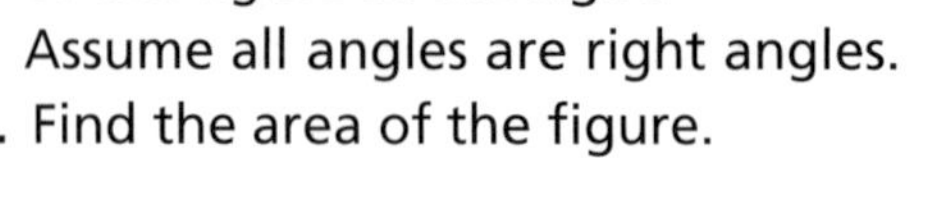

52. a. Explain how you can find the area of the figure at the right. Assume all angles are right angles.
   b. Find the area of the figure.

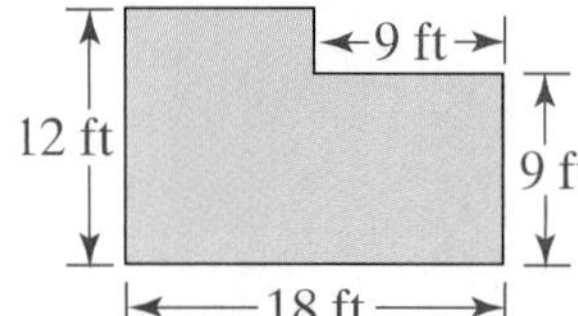

Mixed Review

Lesson 1-8 **Find each product.**

53. $-6(8)$ 54. $12(-5)$ 55. $-7(-9)$ 56. $11(13)$

Lesson 1-3 **Find each quotient.**

57. $2.21 \div 1.7$ 58. $0.75 \div 0.5$ 59. $62 \div 2.5$ 60. $7.1 \div 0.8$

Using a Scientific Calculator

For Use With Lesson 1-9

Many calculators use the order of operations. To test your calculator, try to compute $3 + 5 \cdot 2$. If the answer is 13, your calculator uses the order of operations.

You can use a scientific calculator to simplify expressions that contain more than one operation.

1 EXAMPLE Using a Calculator to Simplify Expressions

Find $6 + 18 \div 2$.

6 [+] 18 [÷] 2 [=] 15

The expression $6 + 18 \div 2$ simplifies to 15.

You can use a scientific calculator to simplify expressions that have grouping symbols.

2 EXAMPLE Using a Calculator for Grouping Symbols

Find $(5.5 - 9) \div 2$.

[(] 5.5 [−] 9 [)] [÷] 2 [=] −1.75

The expression simplifies to -1.75.

You can also simplify fractions by inserting grouping symbols.

3 EXAMPLE Inserting Parentheses

Find $\frac{-7-5}{-6+3}$.

[(] [(-)] 7 [−] 5 [)] [÷] [(] [(-)] 6 [+] 3 [)] [=] 4 ←Use the [(-)] key for negative numbers.

The quotient is 4.

EXERCISES

Use a calculator to find the value of each expression.

1. $9 + 4 \cdot 2$

2. $5.6 - 9 \div 2.5$

3. $5 \div 3.5 \cdot 8.4$

4. $(5 - 14) \div 3$

5. $7.2 \div (4.3 - 3.7)$

6. $10.9 - (6.8 + 7.1)$

7. $\frac{8 - 16}{4}$

8. $\frac{-9 - 6}{2 + 3}$

9. $\frac{10 + 8}{2 \times 3}$

Algebra

1-10 Mean, Median, and Mode

What You'll Learn

To find the mean

To find the median and the mode

. . . And Why

To describe data in a survey, as in Example 4

Check Skills You'll Need

For help, go to Lesson 1-9.

Find the value of each expression.

1. $(7 + 19) \div 2$
2. $\frac{-14 + 6}{2}$
3. $\frac{18 + 24}{2} + 5$
4. $12 - 14 \div 2$
5. $3 \cdot 6 - 4 \cdot 2$
6. $(5 + 9) \cdot 10$

New Vocabulary • mean • outlier • median • mode

Interactive lesson includes instant self-check, tutorials, and activities.

OBJECTIVE 1

Finding the Mean

Suppose your school offers piano lessons after school. About how many students do you expect will want to take lessons this year?

An average can help you make an estimate, and the most commonly used average is the mean. The **mean** of a set of data is the sum of the data divided by the number of data items.

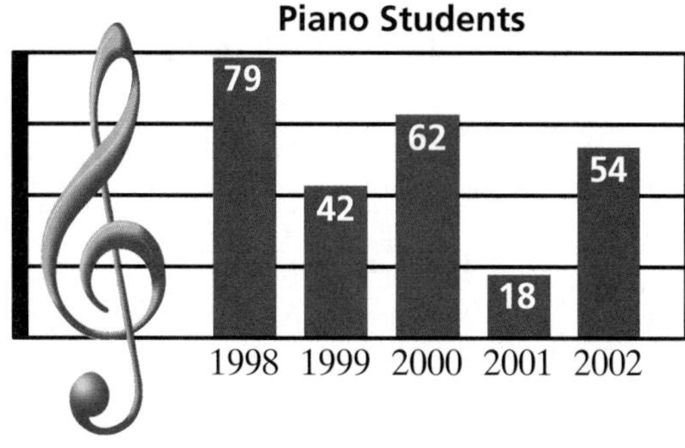

1 EXAMPLE Finding the Mean

Find the mean number of piano students from 1998 through 2002.

$\frac{79 + 42 + 62 + 18 + 54}{5}$ ← Divide the sum by the number of items.

$\frac{255}{5} = 51$ ← Simplify.

Check Understanding 1 Find the mean of 216, 230, 198, and 252.

2 EXAMPLE Applying the Mean

Real World

Health According to a study, the mean number of hours per night a typical teen sleeps is 8.8 h. How many hours per week does a typical teen sleep?

$8.8 \cdot 7 = 61.6$ ← Multiply the mean by the number of nights in a week.

A typical teen sleeps 61.6 h per week.

✓ Check Understanding 2 The average power use of a VCR is 27 watts/h when playing, but only 10 watts/h when turned off. Suppose a VCR is plugged in and ready to use. About how many additional watts will it take to watch a 2.4-hour movie?

An **outlier** is a data item that is much higher or much lower than the other items in a set of data. An outlier can greatly affect the mean of a set of data.

3 EXAMPLE Outliers

Find the outlier of the data below. How does the outlier affect the mean?

5 10 12 13 8 9 26 11 5 6

The outlier is 26, which is much higher than the other data items.

The outlier raises the mean of the data.

✓ Check Understanding 3 Find the outlier of each set of data. Describe how the outlier affects the mean.

a. −5 −1 3 −18 −2 2 **b.** 5.1 5.9 4.7 9.7 5.4

OBJECTIVE

2 Finding the Median and the Mode

Reading Math

The median of the data is like the median strip of a divided highway.

When a set of data has outliers, the mean may not be the best measure of describing the data. The **median** of a data set is the middle value when the data are arranged in numerical order. The median of a set of data always separates the data into two groups of equal size. The median for an even number of data items is the mean of the two middle values.

4 EXAMPLE Finding the Median

Data Analysis Find the median of the data in the table.

20 Responses to "How many times a day do you drink from the water fountain?"				
0	1	1	5	2
10	2	3	5	1
5	2	2	3	4
3	5	5	2	2

First write the data in order from least to greatest.

0 1 1 1 2 2 2 2 2 2 2 3 3 3 4 5 5 5 5 5 10

← The two middle values are 2 and 3.

$\frac{2 + 3}{2} = 2.5$ ← Find the mean of the two middle values.

The median is 2.5.

✓ Check Understanding 4 **a.** Find the mean of the set of data in Example 4. Identify any outlier.

b. **Reasoning** Does the mean or the median better represent the data? Explain.

c. Find the median and the mean of the data.

71 23 54 65 22 23 42 71 59 34 37

The **mode** of a data set is the item that occurs with the greatest frequency. A set of data may have more than one mode. There is no mode when all the data items occur the same number of times. The mode is a useful measure for data with values that are repetitive or non-numerical.

5 EXAMPLE Finding the Mode

Find the mode(s) of the data at the right.

Favorite Flowers of Ten People Surveyed	
rose	rose
pansy	peony
pansy	daisy
daisy	rose
daisy	orchid

Make a table to organize the data.

Rose	Pansy	Peony	Daisy	Orchid
///	//	/	///	/

There are two modes, rose and daisy.

Check Understanding 5 Find the mode(s).

a. 17 16 18 17 16 17

b. 3.2 3.7 3.5 3.7 3.5 3.2

c. pen, pencil, marker, marker, pen, pen, pen, pencil, marker, marker, pen

EXERCISES

For more practice, see *Extra Practice*.

A Practice by Example

Example 1 (page 56)

Find the mean of each set of data.

1. 8 12 6 9 5

2. 3.4 0.53 1.3 2.9 1.47 0.24

3. −6 3 −2 6 7 −3 −5 8

4. −17 32 −9 0 52 12 −14

5. Shopping You select four items in a store. Their prices are \$5.29, \$3.89, \$4.25, and \$4.97. What is the mean price?

Example 2 (page 56)

6. Sports There are 21 players on a football team. Their mean weight is 130 lb. What is the total weight for the team?

7. Transportation The average fuel mileage of your family car is 25.6 mi/gal. How many miles can you expect to travel on 12 gal of gasoline?

8. Climate Records on the cloud cover have been kept in Raleigh, North Carolina, for 47 years. The mean for cloudless days in October is 13. How many cloudless days occurred in October during those 47 years?

Example 3 (page 57)

Find the outlier of each set of data. Describe how the outlier affects the mean.

9. 75 72 74 46 77 70 80 68

10. −15 −12 −19 0 −20 −14

11. 5.3 5.1 5.2 14.7 5.8 5.9 5.4

12. 4 −1 −16 2 0 −3 6 −2

Example 4 (page 57)

Find the median of each set of data.

13. 23 18 67 32 54 41 70 11 56 33 41 58

14. −5 10 18 −3 6 −2 9 −1 −8 15 −10

15. −4 −1 −8 −5 −6 −2 7 2 0 −1 −7 2

16. 2.1 −41.2 0.13 −7.1 −1.68 8.32 2.45 7.89 3.19

Example 5 (page 58)

Find the mode(s).

17. 51 58 54 58 51 57 55 58 51 54

18. red, blue, white, white, red, red, red, blue, white, blue

B Apply Your Skills

Find the mean, median, and mode for each situation.

19. hours of practice before a concert
2 1 0 1 5 3 4 2 0 3 1 2

20. daily low temperatures (°F) for a week
55 58 62 62 65 67 72

Average Life Expectancy

Animal	Years
Bison	15
Cow	15
Deer	8
Donkey	12
Elk	15
Goat	8
Horse	20
Moose	12
Pig	10
Sheep	12

SOURCE: *The World Almanac*

21. a. **Science** Find the mean life expectancy for the animals in the table.
b. Find the median of the data.
c. Find the mode.
d. Reasoning Which measure best describes the data? Explain.

22. **Food** According to the U.S. Department of Agriculture, the mean annual egg consumption is 258.2 eggs per person. Find the number of cartons of eggs needed in a year for a family of four. Each carton holds one dozen eggs.

Open-Ended **Create a data set for each condition.**

23. median $<$ mean

24. mode $>$ median

25. mean $=$ mode

26. median $=$ mean

27. When you join a music club, you get six tapes for 1¢ each. You buy eight more tapes at \$7.99 each. What is the mean price you pay for a tape?

28. Reasoning In a data set of six items, can four of the items be greater than the median? Explain.

Find the mean. Identify an outlier, then find the mean without the outlier.

29. 2.4 3.4 6.1 4.7 2.9 2.6 3.3 3.6 2.7 3.2

30. −1.83 −7.71 −1.54 −2.61 −1.52 −2.01

31. **Writing in Math** Explain how it is possible for two sets of data to consist of different numbers, and yet have the same mean, the same median, and the same mode. Give an example.

Challenge **Find the missing data item.**

32. 12, 6, 14, 16, 8, ■; median of 11 **33.** 34, 41, 25, 43, ■; mean of 38

34. −2, −1, −2, 1, 0, −1, ■; mode of −2

35. a. Animals There are eight dogs in a kennel. The two small dogs need 1 c of dry food each day. The three medium-sized dogs need 2 c each day. The remaining three dogs are larger and need 4 c each day. What is the total amount of dog food required daily?

b. What is the mean amount of food required per dog each day?

36. Stretch Your Thinking Students from four classes of about the same size are going on a tour of a historical center. The largest class has 29 students. If the students divide into groups of 9 for the tour, then 2 students are left over. If the students divide into groups of 15, then 5 students are left over. How many students are going on the tour?

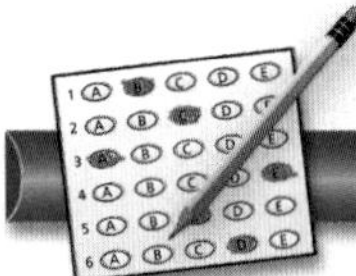

Test Prep

Reading Comprehension **Read the passage and answer the questions below.**

Birthday Bash

The Rose Hill Retirement Home celebrated seven birthdays last Sunday. Mrs. Ullsca turned 102, while the "baby" of the group, Mrs. Hansen, turned a mere 78. Family members and friends gathered for the party. Other birthdays celebrated were Mr. Harlem, 79; Mr. Joyla, 84; Mr. Ajayi, 85; Miss Rugas, 81; and Mrs. Greene, 79.

37. Find the mean, median, and mode of the data found in the article. Round the mean to the nearest whole number.

Take It to the NET
Online lesson quiz at
www.PHSchool.com
Web Code aba-0110

38. Is there an outlier? If there is, identify it.

39. Does the mean, the median, or the mode best reflect the age of those celebrating a birthday? Explain.

Short Response

40. Give an example of a set of data that has a mean of 24 and includes −4.

Mixed Review

Lesson 1-9 **Find the value of each expression.**

41. $72 \div 8 \cdot 3$ **42.** $-4 - 16 \div 2$ **43.** $32 \div (-2 \cdot 8) + 4$

Lesson 1-6 **Write the numbers from least to greatest.**

44. 32 35 −21 −42 29 **45.** 213 231 312 123 213 321

Test-Taking Strategies

Writing Gridded Responses

Some tests include gridded-response questions. You find a numerical answer. Then you write the answer at the top of the grid and fill in the corresponding bubbles below. You must use the grid correctly.

1 EXAMPLE

The mean of 0.2, 0.4, 0.6, and 0.8 is 0.5 or $\frac{1}{2}$. Record this answer.

You can write the answer as $\frac{1}{2}$, 0.5, or .5. Here are the three ways to enter these answers.

		1	/	2

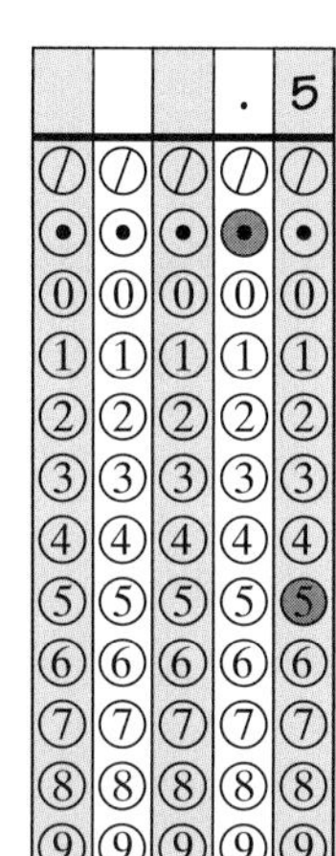

			.	5

Your answer must begin in the left column or end in the right column.

2 EXAMPLE

Find 19.25 − 18.5.

$$\begin{array}{r} 19.25 \\ -\ 18.50 \\ \hline 0.75 \end{array}$$

The answer is 0.75. You grid this as 0.75, .75, or 3/4.

EXERCISES

Write what you would grid for each answer. If you have a grid, complete it.

1. Simplify 9(7.9).
2. Find 3.37 + 2.83.
3. Find 5.8 − (−2.6).
4. Find 81.6 ÷ 2.4.
5. A bottle of apple juice holds 3.79 L. A bottle of orange juice holds 1.89 L. How many more liters does the bottle of apple juice hold?

Chapter 1 Chapter Review

Vocabulary

absolute value (p. 34)
additive inverse (p. 39)
Associative Property of Addition (p. 12)
Associative Property of Multiplication (p. 18)
Commutative Property of Addition (p. 12)
Commutative Property of Multiplication (p. 18)
compatible numbers (p. 6)
Distributive Property (p. 51)
Identity Property of Addition (p. 12)
Identity Property of Multiplication (p. 18)
integers (p. 34)
mean (p. 56)
median (p. 58)
mode (p. 57)
opposites (p. 34)
order of operations (p.50)
outlier (p. 57)
range (p. 41)
Zero Property (p. 18)

Reading Math: Understanding Vocabulary

Choose the correct term to complete each sentence.

1. The _?_ combines multiplication with sums and differences.
2. The statement $3 + (5 + 7) = (3 + 5) + 7$ demonstrates the _?_.
3. The _?_ of a number is its distance from 0 on a number line.
4. To find the _?_, take the data item that occurs most often.
5. By the _?_, you know that $4 + 7 \cdot 3$ equals 25 and not 33.

Take It to the NET
Online vocabulary quiz at **www.PHSchool.com**
Web Code abj-0151

Skills and Concepts

1-1 Objectives

- To estimate by rounding
- To use front-end estimation and compatible numbers

You can estimate decimals using rounding, front-end estimation, or **compatible numbers.**

Use any estimation strategy to calculate. Name the strategy you used.

6. $50.3 \div 6.9$
7. $98.52 - 46.91$
8. 6.9×8.92
9. $1.46 + 4.38$
10. **Writing in Math** When would you use compatible numbers to estimate the value of an expression? Explain.

1-2 and 1-3 Objectives

- To add and subtract decimals
- To use the properties of addition
- To multiply decimals
- To divide decimals

To add or subtract decimals, align the decimal points. To multiply decimals, use the sum of the number of decimal places in the factors. To divide decimals, rewrite the problem so the divisor is a whole number.

Use the **Commutative Property** to change the order in an expression. Use the **Associative Property** to change the grouping.

Simplify.

11. $23.68 \div 6.4$
12. $0.54 + 0.027$
13. $4.6 - 3.87$
14. 2.7×6.25

15. Shopping At a grocery store, you buy hamburger weighing 1.42 lb, sausage weighing 2.16 lb, and chicken weighing 3.73 lb. How many pounds of meat do you buy?

1-4 and 1-5 Objectives

- ▼ To use metric units of measure
- ▼ To change metric units
- ▼ To use a problem-solving plan to solve problems

To change a measure from one unit to another, find a relationship between the two units and then multiply.

Write the number that makes each statement true.

16. 4.56 mm = ■ cm **17.** 14.2 L = ■ mL **18.** 0.34 kg = ■ g

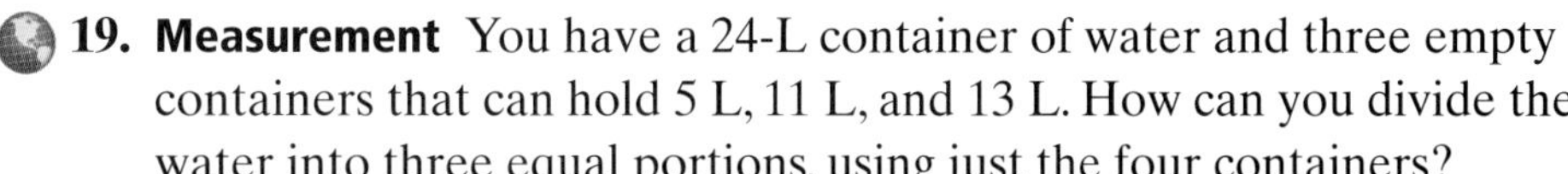

19. Measurement You have a 24-L container of water and three empty containers that can hold 5 L, 11 L, and 13 L. How can you divide the water into three equal portions, using just the four containers?

1-6, 1-7, and 1-8 Objectives

- ▼ To find opposite and absolute values
- ▼ To graph and order integers
- ▼ To add integers
- ▼ To subtract integers and to find range
- ▼ To multiply integers
- ▼ To divide integers

Opposites are two numbers that are the same distance from 0 on a number line, but in opposite directions. **Integers** are the set of positive whole numbers, their opposites, and zero. The **absolute value** of an integer is its distance from 0 on a number line.

The sum of the two positive integers is positive. The sum of two negative numbers is negative. To find the sum of two integers with different signs, subtract the lesser absolute value from the greater. The sum has the sign of the integer with the greater absolute value. To subtract an integer, add its opposite.

The product or quotient of two integers with the same sign is positive. The product or quotient of two integers with different signs is negative.

Compare. Use <, >, or =.

20. -7 ■ 7 **21.** $|-3|$ ■ $|3|$ **22.** $|-9|$ ■ -4 **23.** 8 ■ -15

Simplify.

24. $-14 + (-8)$ **25.** $17 - (-12)$ **26.** $-5 \cdot 6$ **27.** $125 \div (-5)$

1-9 and 1-10 Objectives

- ▼ To use the order of operations
- ▼ To use the Distributive Property
- ▼ To find the mean
- ▼ To find the median and the mode

Use the **order of operations** to simplify an expression. The **Distributive Property** combines multiplication with addition or subtraction. The **mean**, **median**, and **mode** of a set of data, along with any **outliers**, reflect the characteristics of the data.

Find the value of each expression.

28. $(7.3 + 4) \div 4 + 0.3 \cdot 2$ **29.** $8 - 6.2 \div 5 + 7(0.91)$

30. Pets Here are the weights, in ounces, of one-month-old hamsters. Find the mean, median, and mode. 4, 1, 3, 2, 2, 2, 1, 1, 2, 1, 2, 3.

Chapter 1

Chapter Test

Take It to the NET
Online chapter test at
www.PHSchool.com
Web Code aba-0152

Estimate using any estimation strategy.

1. 289.76 − 52 **2.** 7.532 + 2.19

3. 97.6 · 3.4 **4.** 68.5 ÷ 7.02

5. Use front-end estimation to estimate the sum of the following grocery items to the nearest dollar: \$7.99, \$2.79, \$4.15, \$2.09.

Simplify.

6. 9.53 + 3.29 **7.** 8 − 6.17

8. 10.5 − 9.67 **9.** 0.57 + 1.825

10. Money You had a balance of \$213.15 in a savings account. You make withdrawals of \$68.94 and \$128.36. Find your new balance.

11. Decorations For a class party, the student council purchases 42 balloons at \$1.85 each. Estimate the total cost of the balloons.

Identify each property shown.

12. 9.5 + 6.1 + 2.3 = 9.5 + 2.3 + 6.1

13. 7.2 × (1.6 × 3.9) = (7.2 × 1.6) × 3.9

14. 5.1(7.4 − 3.1) = 5.1(7.4) − 5.1(3.1)

Find each quotient. Round to the nearest tenth.

15. 1.2 ÷ 0.3 **16.** 1.58 ÷ 1.1

Find the value of each expression.

17. 9.5 − 7.1 + 2.4 · 0.5 − 1.3

18. $\frac{8.25}{4} \cdot (0.6 - 0.54) + 8.3$

Change each measurement to the given unit.

19. 4.2 cm = ■ m **20.** 5.17 kL = ■ L

21. 6 kg 14 g = ■ g **22.** 2 km 7 m = ■ km

Mental Math **Find each product mentally using the Distributive Property.**

23. 6(10.5) **24.** 3(98)

Write an expression for each model. Then find the sum.

25.

−4 −2 0 2 4

26.

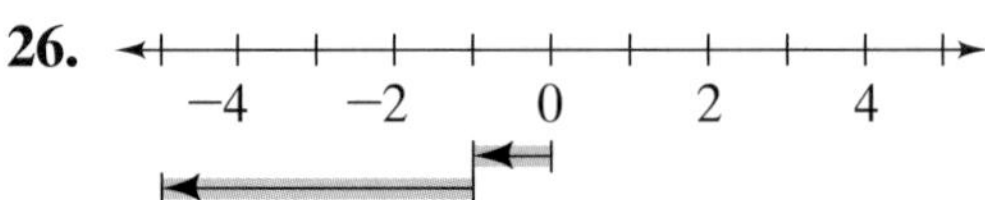
−4
−2
0
2
4

27. Write the integers in order from least to greatest. 2 5 0 −7 −3

Simplify.

28. −3 + 5 **29.** −2 + (−2)

30. −4 − 9 **31.** −8 · (−9)

32. 48 ÷ (−3) **33.** −6(11)

34. Produce The weights of four bags of apples are 3.5 lb, 3.8 lb, 4.2 lb, and 3.5 lb. What is the median weight?

35. Fitness Suppose you ride your bicycle a distance of 257.5 mi in a benefit ride. How many miles must you average each day to finish the ride in 4.5 days?

36. Writing in Math When finding an average, the sign of the quotient always depends on the sign of the dividend. Explain why.

37. Sports On successive plays, the home football team gains 12 yd, loses 3 yd, loses 5 yd, gains 15 yd, and runs 16 yd to a touchdown. What is the average gain or loss in yards per play?

38. Find the mean, the median, and the mode for the following junior league bowling scores: 45, 56, 134, 55, 78, 121, 38, 66, 56, 41.

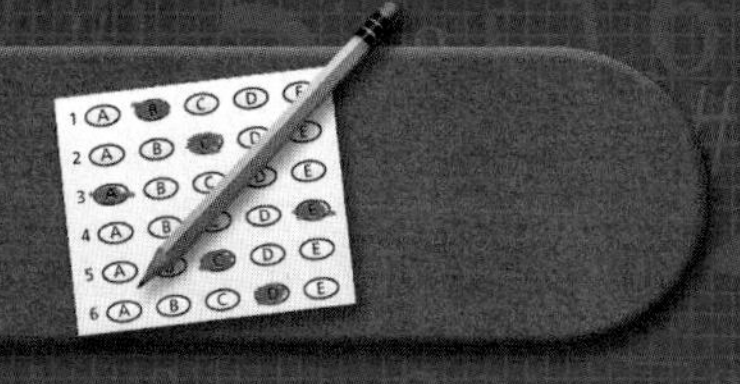

Test Prep

Reading Comprehension **Read each passage below and answer the questions that follow.**

Big Shows Successful films earn a lot of money for the studios that create them. Five movies that have earned a lot of money in the United States, and their approximate total receipts, are: *Titanic* (1997), $600 million; *Star Wars* (1977), $460 million; *Star Wars: The Phantom Menace* (1999), $430 million; *E.T.* (1982), $400 million; and *Jurassic Park* (1993), $360 million.

1. What are the mean total box office receipts of the five films?
   A. $400 million **B.** $430 million
   C. $450 million **D.** $460 million

2. *Star Wars: The Phantom Menace* sold about $64,811,000 worth of tickets on its opening weekend. Which is the best estimate of the portion of its total sales that took place the first weekend?
   F. 0.1 **G.** 0.15 **H.** 0.35 **I.** 0.5

3. What is the median earnings of the films?
   A. $400 million **B.** $430 million
   C. $450 million **D.** $460 million

4. Between which pair of films is the range in their total receipts the greatest?
   F. *Star Wars* and *Jurassic Park*
   G. *Titanic* and *Star Wars*
   H. *Star Wars* and *E. T.*
   I. *E. T.* and *Jurassic Park*

Parity We say that two integers have the same *parity* if they are both even or both odd. So 2 and 12 have the same parity, and 51 and 139 have the same parity. If one number is even and the other number is odd, then we say they have different or opposite parities. 2 and 51 have opposite parities.

5. Two intergers have the same parity. Describe the parity of their sum.
   A. same as the two numbers
   B. opposite of the two numbers
   C. same if the numbers are odd
   D. opposite if the numbers are odd

6. Two integers have the same parity. Describe the parity of their difference.
   F. same as the two numbers
   G. opposite of the two numbers
   H. same only if the numbers are even
   I. same only if the numbers are odd

7. Two integers have the same parity. Describe the parity of their product.
   A. same as the two numbers
   B. opposite of the two numbers
   C. same only if the numbers are odd
   D. opposite only if the numbers are odd

8. Two integers have different parity. Describe their product.
   F. always even
   G. always odd
   H. sometimes even
   I. odd if the smaller number is odd

Real-World Snapshots

Energy Field

Applying Integers Too hot? Open a window. Too cold? Put on a sweater. Sound familiar? Heating and air-conditioning systems can let you live more comfortably in a wide range of weather conditions, but they cost money. The cost of heating or cooling a home depends on many things, including the outdoor air temperature, the indoor air temperature, and the cost of fuel.

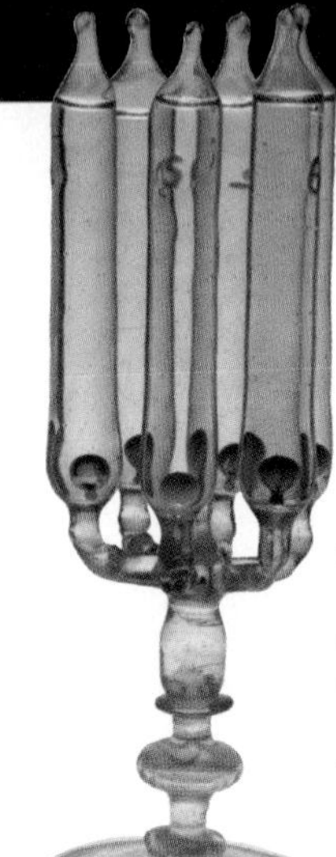

Ancient Thermometer

In this thermometer, changing temperatures cause the colored glass balls to rise and fall in the water inside the glass tubes.

Put It All Together

Data File Use the data on these two pages and on page 3 to answer these questions.

1. Use the heating cost formula to estimate the cost of heating a house to 68°F for one day when the average outside temperature is 20°F.
2. a. **Open-Ended** Choose three places from the table on page 3. Use the heating cost formula to estimate the cost of heating a house to 68°F in each place on the coldest day.
   b. Use a number line to display your answers to part (a). Include the location and the outdoor temperature.
3. You can use the equation below to calculate the cost of changing the indoor temperature from 68°F to 66°F.

   change in cost = new cost − old cost = cost at 66°F − cost at 68°F

   a. Use the low temperature for Indianapolis, Indiana. Calculate the cost of changing the temperature to 68°F.
   b. **Reasoning** Explain why your answer to part (a) is a negative number.
4. **Writing in Math** Where do you think changing the indoor temperature from 68°F to 70°F will cost the most? Why? Check your prediction by calculating the increased cost in several locations. Explain your results.

Heating Cost Formula (°F)

daily heating cost ($) = 0.15 x (indoor temperature − outdoor temperature)

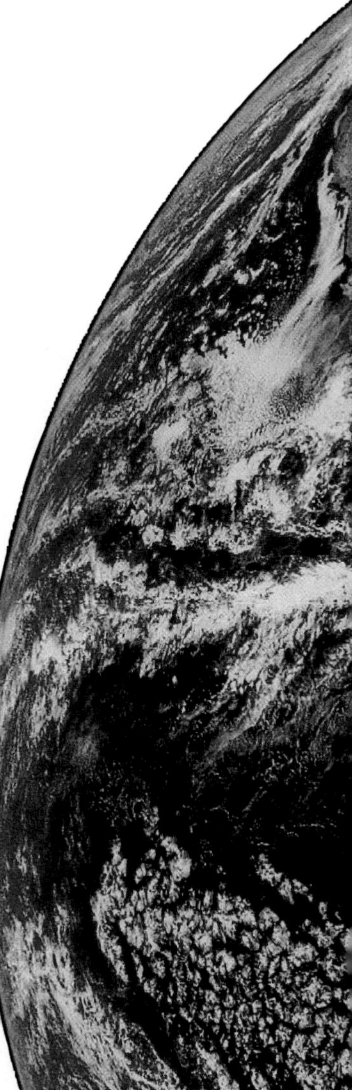

Weather Around the World

Photographs from space show giant swirls of clouds around the Earth. These swirls show the constant movement of gases that gives us our weather.

Forms of Precipitation

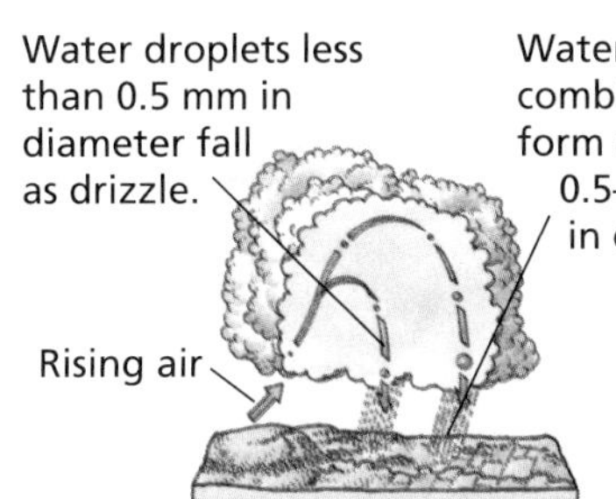

Water droplets less than 0.5 mm in diameter fall as drizzle.
Water droplets combine to form raindrops 0.5–5.0 mm in diameter.
Rising air

Rain From Clouds Not Reaching Freezing Level

Water droplets fall as rain.
Snowflakes melt to fall as rain.
Snowflakes from ice crystals fall as snow.
Rising air

Rain and Snow From Clouds Reaching Freezing Level

Vertical air currents toss frozen water droplets up and down.
Alternate freezing and melting builds up layers of ice.
Ice falls as hailstones.
Rising air

Hail

Take It to the NET For more information about weather, go to **www.PHSchool.com**.
Web Code: abe-0153

Halifax, Nova Scotia, 49°F
Reno, Nevada, 49°F
Miami, Florida, 78°F
Hurricanes spiral across the Atlantic and into the Caribbean.
Mexico City, Mexico, 60°F
San Jose, Costa Rica, 69°F
Caracas, Venezuela, 70°F
Bands of clouds form along the equator, caused by the strong rising air currents stirred up by the hot sun.

Algebra

CHAPTER 2

Equations and Inequalities

Lessons

2-1 Evaluating and Writing Algebraic Expressions

2-2 Using Number Sense to Solve Equations

2-3 Solving Equations by Adding or Subtracting

2-4 Solving Equations by Multiplying or Dividing

2-5 Exploring Two-Step Problems

2-6 Solving Two-Step Equations

2-7 Problem Solving: Write an Equation

2-8 Graphing and Writing Inequalities

2-9 Solving Inequalities by Adding or Subtracting

2-10 Solving Inequalities by Multiplying or Dividing

Key Vocabulary

- algebraic expression (p. 71)
- equation (p. 77)
- inequality (p. 107)
- inverse operations (p. 83)
- open sentence (p. 77)
- solution of an equation (p. 77)
- solution of an inequality (p. 107)
- variable (p. 71)

Real-World Snapshots

For thousands of years, dogs have lived with humans as hunting companions, protectors, and friends.

Data File Non-Sporting Dogs

Breed	Height	Weight	Life Expectancy
Boston terrier	15–17 in.	10–25 lb	13 yr
Bulldog	12–14 in.	40–50 lb	7–9 yr
Chow chow	18–20 in.	45–70 lb	11–12 yr
Dalmatian	20–24 in.	50–55 lb	12 yr
Keeshond	17–18 in.	55–65 lb	12–14 yr
Lhasa apso	9–11 in.	13–15 lb	12–14 yr
Poodle:			All:
Toy	Up to 10 in.	14–17 lb	12–15 yr
Miniature	10–15 in.	26–30 lb	
Standard	Over 15 in.	33–42 lb	
Shar-Pei	18–20 in.	40–55 lb	11–12 yr

SOURCE: *The New Encyclopedia of the Dog*

You will use the data above in this chapter:

• p. 86 Lesson 2-3
• p. 110 Lesson 2-8

Real-World Snapshots On pages 126 and 127, you will solve problems involving dogs.

Chapter 2 Preview

Where You've Been

- In Chapter 1, you learned about integers and the order of operations. You also compared integers.

Where You're Going

- In Chapter 2, you will solve equations and inequalities with variables.
- Applying what you learn, you will write equations and inequalities to solve problems involving the depth of a cave.

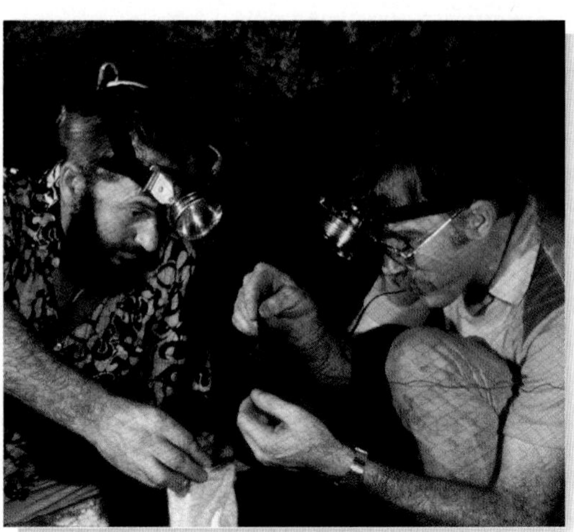

Scientists use math for measuring.

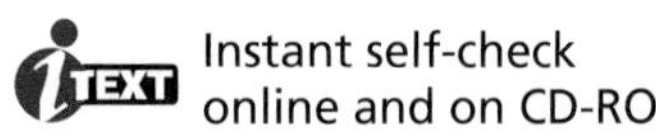

Diagnosing Readiness

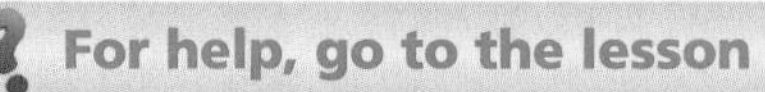

For help, go to the lesson in green.

Adding and Subtracting Decimals (Lesson 1-2)

Find each sum or difference.

1. $5.304 - 0.89$ **2.** $2.35 + 1.8 + 4.45$ **3.** $2.15 - 1.36$

4. $3.14 + 2.67 + 9.4$ **5.** $22.38 - 19.68$ **6.** $12.2 + 3.65 + 7.11$

Comparing Integers (Lesson 1-6)

Compare. Use $<$, $>$, or $=$.

7. $|-2| \blacksquare |-5|$ **8.** $|11| \blacksquare |-13|$ **9.** $10 \blacksquare |-10|$ **10.** $-8 \blacksquare |-8|$

Adding and Subtracting Integers (Lesson 1-7)

Find each sum or difference.

11. $7 - 15$ **12.** $-15 + 15$ **13.** $-20 - 20$ **14.** $27 + (-19)$

Multiplying and Dividing Integers (Lesson 1-8)

Find each product or quotient.

15. $-12 \cdot 3$ **16.** $-16 \div (-4)$ **17.** $-6 \cdot (-7)$ **18.** $-54 \div 9$

Order of Operations (Lesson 1-9)

Find the value of each expression.

19. $14 + 2(15 \div 5)$ **20.** $20 \div 2 - 3 \cdot 3$ **21.** $(5 + 4) \cdot 4 \div 36$

22. $(9 - 4) \div 5 \cdot 6$ **23.** $9 \div (18 - 15) + 4$ **24.** $6 + 8 \cdot 7 - 24$

Algebra

2-1 Evaluating and Writing Algebraic Expressions

What You'll Learn

To evaluate algebraic expressions

To write algebraic expressions

. . . And Why

To find the cost of posters, as in Example 4

Check Skills You'll Need

For help, go to Lesson 1-9.

Use the order of operations to simplify.

1. $3 + 4 \cdot 2$
2. $12 - 6 \div 3$
3. $6 \cdot (5 - 7) + 2$
4. $(4 + 3) \cdot 2 - 11$
5. $8 \div 4 + 10 \cdot 2$
6. $2 - 4(3 \cdot 2) + 10$
7. $10 - (-2) - 4 \cdot 2$
8. $4 - (18 \div 6 + 3)$

New Vocabulary • variable • algebraic expression

OBJECTIVE 1

Evaluating Algebraic Expressions

TEXT Interactive lesson includes instant self-check, tutorials, and activities.

Investigation: Algebraic Expressions

During part of its flight, an airplane rises 12 feet in altitude each second.

1. Look at the table. Explain how to find the distance the plane rises for each amount of time.
2. Copy and complete the table.
3. At t seconds, how many feet has the plane risen?

Time (s)	Distance (ft)
1	12
5	■
10	■
20	■
25	■
50	■
100	■
200	■
300	■

A **variable** is a symbol that represents one or more numbers. Variables are usually letters. An **algebraic expression** is a mathematical phrase with at least one variable.

variables →	g	z	x
algebraic expressions →	$13 - g$	$\frac{z}{2}$	$3x + 8$

The value of an algebraic expression varies, or changes, depending on the value of the variable. The expression $60m$ means $60 \times m$ or $60 \cdot m$. To evaluate an algebraic expression, substitute a number for the variable. To find the seconds in 3 minutes, substitute 3 for m in the expression $60m$.

$60m = 60 \cdot 3 = 180$ ← **Substitute 3 for *m*. There are 180 seconds in 3 minutes.**

1 EXAMPLE Evaluating Algebraic Expressions

Evaluate each expression. Use $p = 2, n = 3$, and $s = 5$.

a. $2p + 7$

$2p + 7 = 2(2) + 7$ ← **Substitute.**
$= 4 + 7$ ← **Multiply.**
$= 11$ ← **Add.**

b. $p + (n \cdot s)$

$p + (n \cdot s) = 2 + (3 \cdot 5)$ **Substitute.** →
$= 2 + 15$ **Multiply.** →
$= 17$ **Add.** →

1 Evaluate each expression. Use $n = 3, t = 5$, and $y = 7$.

a. $n + 2t$ **b.** $n + (t \cdot y)$ **c.** $3n + t - 2y$

OBJECTIVE 2

Writing Algebraic Expressions

You can use algebraic expressions to describe data. Suppose your heart beats 72 times in one minute. You can write an expression for the number of times it beats in any number of minutes.

Let *m* represent the number of minutes.
↓
$72m$ ← **The algebraic expression represents the number of heartbeats in *m* minutes.**

2 EXAMPLE Writing Algebraic Expressions

Write an algebraic expression for each word phrase.

a. a temperature of t degrees increased by 5 degrees → $t + 5$

b. five cats fewer than c cats → $c - 5$

c. the product of 5 and n nickels → $5n$

d. a dinner bill of d dollars divided among five friends → $\frac{d}{5}$

Check Understanding **2** Write an algebraic expression for each word phrase.

a. p pens decreased by 16 pens **b.** six hams more than h hams

You can translate algebraic expressions into word phrases.

3 EXAMPLE Writing Word Phrases

Write three different word phrases for $x + 2$.

A number plus two

A number increased by two

Two more than a number

Check Understanding **3** Write a word phrase for each algebraic expression.

a. $5 + n$ **b.** $\frac{p}{3}$ **c.** $c - 50$

Some school clubs work to better their community.

 Real-World Problem Solving

Public Service The Environmental Club is making posters. The materials for each poster cost \$4. Write an algebraic expression for the cost in dollars of p posters.

Words	\$4 per poster	times	the number of posters
	Let p = the number of posters.		
Equation	4	$\cdot$	p

An algebraic expression for the cost in dollars of the posters is $4p$.

 4 Each of the nine students in the club is going to hang t posters. Write an algebraic expression for the total number of posters the students will hang.

EXERCISES

For more practice, see *Extra Practice*.

A Practice by Example

Example 1 (page 72)

Evaluate each expression. Use the values $p = 4$, $n = 6$, and $s = 2$. Exercise 1 has been started for you.

1. $7n = 7(6) = \blacksquare$ **2.** $-6p$ **3.** $5 - s$ **4.** $2p + 1$

5. $\frac{n}{2}$ **6.** $8s - 16$ **7.** $3(p + n)$ **8.** $5p + 3$ **9.** $\frac{n}{(p + s)}$

Example 2 (page 72)

Write an algebraic expression for each word phrase.

10. four shirts more than s shirts **11.** the quotient of p and 5

12. the sum of t TVs and 11 TVs **13.** five times your quiz score q

14. nine cards fewer than c cards **15.** divide the total points p by 3

Example 3 (page 72)

Write a word phrase for each algebraic expression.

16. $d + 2$ **17.** $\frac{4}{n}$ **18.** $c - 9.1$ **19.** $6.5 - h$

20. $13 \cdot p$ **21.** $10 + q$ **22.** $\frac{w}{10}$ **23.** $3.5v$

Example 4 (page 73)

24. Fund-Raising The marching band is selling cases of fruit for \$11 a case. Write an algebraic expression for the total sales in dollars of c cases.

25. Your job pays \$7 per hour. Write an algebraic expression for your pay in dollars for working h hours.

B Apply Your Skills

Evaluate.

26. $7p$ for $p = 2$ **27.** $m - 8$ for $m = 20$ **28.** $\frac{b}{4}$ for $b = 8.44$

29. $3t + 7$ for $t = 0.5$ **30.** $9 \cdot 3h$ for $h = 2$ **31.** $\frac{5w}{2}$ for $w = 1.4$

Real-World Connection

The blue-throated hummingbird has the most rapid heartbeat among birds.

32. Birds The blue-throated hummingbird has a heart rate of about 1,260 beats per minute.

a. Write an algebraic expression for the number of times the blue-throated hummingbird's heart beats in m minutes.

b. How many times does the hummingbird's heart beat in 5 minutes?

c. Reasoning Explain how you would calculate the number of times the blue-throated hummingbird's heart beats in a 24-hour day. Then find the number of beats in the 24-hour day.

33. Reasoning A student baby-sitting for \$5 per hour writes the expression $5n$ to represent the money he makes for n hours. Another student writes $3n + 15$ to represent the amount in dollars she makes. How much does the second student charge for her baby-sitting services?

34. Writing in Math You can write "twelve more than a number" as $12 + n$ or $n + 12$. You can write "twelve less than a number" as $n - 12$, but not as $12 - n$. Explain why.

Evaluate each expression. Use the values $t = 1.7$ and $r = 2.4$.

35. $t + 2$	**36.** $2t - 1$	**37.** $2(t - 1)$	**38.** $2(2t)$
39. $r + 2$	**40.** $2r - 1$	**41.** $2(r - 1)$	**42.** $2(2r)$

43. Estimation This section of a page from a telephone directory shows columns with 11 names in 1 in. Each page has four 10-in. columns. Write an algebraic expression for the approximate number of names in p pages of the directory.

6-4462 **Daalling V** 8 Everett All.........
2-3302 **Daavis K** 444 Greeley R.........
4-1775 **Dabady V** 94 Burnside All.........
2-0014 **Dabagh L** 13 Lancaster R.......
6-3356 **Dabagh W** Dr 521 Weston All..
4-7322 **Dabar G** 98 River All...............
6-1530 **Dabarera F** 34 Roseland All....
2-2279 **Dabas M** 17 Riverside R.........
4-9978 **D'Abate D** 86 Moss Hill Rd All..
2-6745 **D'Abate G** 111 South Central R
4-5456 **Dabbous H** 670 Warren Dr All..
6-3064 **Dabbraccio F** 151 Century All..
6-2257 **Dabby D** 542 Walnut All..........
2-9987 **Dabcovich M G** 219 Green R..
6-5643 **Dabcovich M** 72 Main All.........

C Challenge

Evaluate each expression using the values $p = 3.5$, $n = 2$, and $s = 1.4$.

44. $\frac{s}{pn} - \frac{ps}{n}$ **45.** $\frac{pn}{s} + \frac{s}{n}$ **46.** $\frac{pn}{5s} - 1$

47. Business The boy in the photo mows one lawn each weekday after school and two lawns on Saturday.

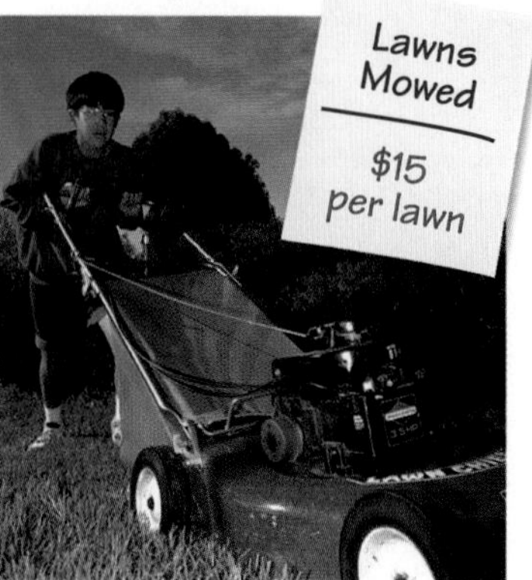

a. How many lawns does he mow in one week?

b. Write an algebraic expression for the number of lawns he mows in w weeks.

c. How much money does he make in one week?

d. Write an algebraic expression for the amount of money he makes in w weeks.

48. Stretch Your Thinking Tia's softball uniform number has 2 digits and is a multiple of 2, 4, 8, and 9. What is Tia's number?

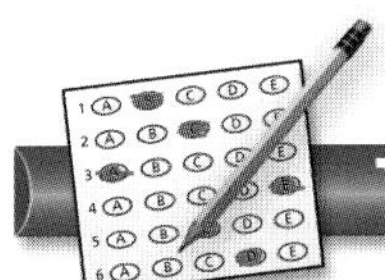

Test Prep

Reading Comprehension **Read the passage and answer the questions below.**

Cool Mints

The U.S. Mint makes coins at production facilities in Denver and Philadelphia. The Denver and Philadelphia mints together produced the following number of coins in 2001: 10,334,590,000 pennies; 1,303,384,000 nickels; 2,782,390,000 dimes; 4,806,984,000 quarters.

49. The algebraic expression for the value in dollars of n nickels is $0.05n$. Evaluate the expression using the number of nickels minted in 2001.

50. Write an algebraic expression for the value in dollars of q quarters. Evaluate the expression for the number of quarters minted in 2001.

51. Which would you rather have, the dollar value of the pennies minted in 2001, or the dollar value of the nickels? Explain.

Online lesson quiz at **www.PHSchool.com**
Web Code: aba-0201

Mixed Review

Lesson 1-9 **Find the value of each expression.**

52. $3(4 + 5) + 2(4 + 5)$ **53.** $7(1.2) + 7(0.5)$ **54.** $5(0.25 \cdot 40)$

Lesson 1-1 **Estimate. Round to the nearest whole number before you add or subtract.**

55. $239.6 - 118.43$ **56.** $26.92 + 13.267$ **57.** $765.7 - 66.7$

Practice Game

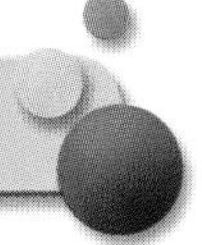

Evaluating Expressions

What You'll Need

- 24 index cards. Cut them in half so you have 48 smaller cards. On each of the smaller cards, write a different algebraic expression.
- Two number cubes

How to Play

- Deal all the cards to players. All players choose one card from their hand and place it face down on the table.
- A player rolls the number cubes. The sum of the numbers is the value of the variable for the first round.
- Each player turns over the card and announces its value. Record the value for each player.
- Play continues until all players have rolled the number cubes.
- Find each player's total. The player with the lowest total wins.

Using Spreadsheets

For Use With Lesson 2-1

You can use a computer spreadsheet to keep track of the balance in a checking account. You add deposits and subtract checks. Using the formulas you supply, the spreadsheet computes values in cells.

EXAMPLE Using Spreadsheets

Use the spreadsheet. Find the balance after each entry.

	A	B	C	D
1	Date	Deposits	Checks	Balance
2				$350
3	4/29	$100		■
4	4/30		$400	■

← Use the formula "=D2 + B3". The computer finds 350 + 100 = 450.

← Use the formula "=D3 − C4". The computer finds 450 − 400 = 50.

The first balance is $450. The second balance is $50.

EXERCISES

Use the spreadsheet at the right.

	A	B	C	D
1	Date	Deposits	Checks	Balance
2				$250
3	11/3		$25.98	■
4	11/9		$239.40	■
5	11/10	$122.00		■
6	11/13		$54.65	■
7	11/20	$350.00		■
8	11/29		$163.80	■

1. Find the account balance after each entry. Write the formulas you used.

2. Which formula can you use to find the balance in cell D9, whether or not a check has been written or a deposit has been made?
A. = D8 − B9 + C9
B. = D8 − B9 − C9
C. = D8 + B9 + C9
D. = D8 + B9 − C9

3. **Reasoning** Suppose the balance in cell D9 is $130.34. Was the amount of a deposit entered into cell B9, or was the amount of a check entered into cell C9? Support your answer.

4. **Writing in Math** Consider your answer to Exercise 2. Explain why the formula you chose works. Give examples.

5. **a.** **Reasoning** Suppose the balance in cell D8 is $250. How would you calculate the original balance in cell D2?
b. Find the original balance if cell D8 is $250.

Algebra

2-2 Using Number Sense to Solve Equations

What You'll Learn

To solve one-step equations using number sense

. . . And Why

To solve problems involving weight, as in Example 3

✓ Check Skills You'll Need

 For help, go to Lesson 2-1.

Write an algebraic expression for each word phrase.

1. four more than y **2.** six less than v **3.** eight times p

4. t decreased by 6 **5.** the product of 2 and x **6.** k divided by 9

New Vocabulary

- equation
- open sentence
- solution of an equation

 Interactive lesson includes instant self-check, tutorials, and activities.

OBJECTIVE 1

Using Number Sense

Investigation: Exploring Estimation

Use number sense to estimate the solution of each equation.

Equation	Hint
1. $\frac{y}{5} = 7.04$	What number divided by 5 is about 7?
2. $p + 34.57 = 79.78$	What number added to 35 is about 80?
3. $25.2x = 327.6$	What number times 25 is about 325?

4. What are some other number-sense techniques you can use to solve an equation?

Suppose you are asked to complete this sentence on your history test:

_?_ was the first president of the United States of America.

This sentence is neither true nor false until you substitute a name for the blank.

If you choose George Washington, the sentence is true. If you choose George W. Bush, the sentence is false.

An **equation** is a mathematical sentence with an equal sign. An equation with one or more variables is an **open sentence.** For example, $p + 12 = 34$ is an open sentence. It is neither *true* nor *false* until p is replaced with some number. A **solution of an equation** is a value for a variable that makes an equation true.

One way to find a solution of an equation is to substitute a number for the variable in the equation and determine whether the equation is then true.

1 EXAMPLE Solving Equations Using Substitution

Find the solution of $34m = 714$: 8, 11, or 21.

You can test each number by substituting for m in the equation.

$34(8) \stackrel{?}{=} 714$	$34(11) \stackrel{?}{=} 714$	$34(21) \stackrel{?}{=} 714$
$272 = 714$ **False**	$374 = 714$ **False**	$714 = 714$ ✔ **True**

Since the equation is true when you substitute 21 for m, the solution is 21.

✔ Check Understanding 1 Find the solution of $124n = 992$: 4, 8, or 18.

Sometimes you can solve an equation by using mental math.

2 EXAMPLE Solving Equations Using Mental Math

Use mental math to solve each equation.

a. $4y = 20$

What you think
What number times 4 equals 20?

Since $4 \cdot 5 = 20, y = 5$.

b. $m + 7 = 15$

What you think
What number plus 7 equals 15?

Since $7 + 8 = 15, m = 8$.

Check Understanding 2 Use mental math to solve each equation.

a. $7x = -63$ **b.** $n + 6 = -10$ **c.** $\frac{h}{4} = 8$ **d.** $t - 3 = 7$

You can solve problems by using equations and estimation.

3 EXAMPLE Estimating Solutions  Real World

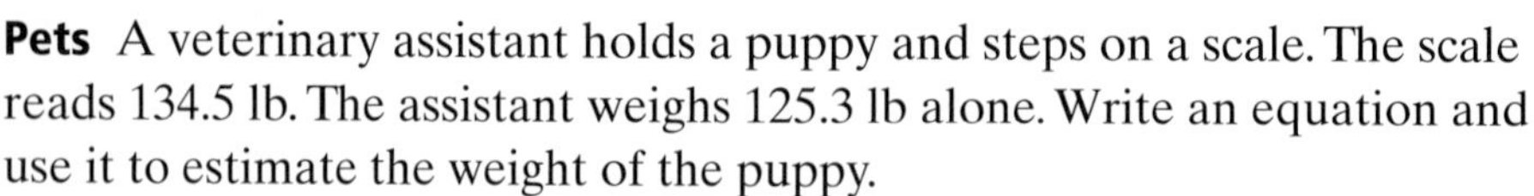

Pets A veterinary assistant holds a puppy and steps on a scale. The scale reads 134.5 lb. The assistant weighs 125.3 lb alone. Write an equation and use it to estimate the weight of the puppy.

Words assistant's weight plus puppy's weight equals total weight

Let w = the weight of the puppy.

Equation $125.3 \quad + \quad w \quad = \quad 134.5$

$125.3 + w = 134.5$

$125.3 \approx 125 \quad 134.5 \approx 135$ ← **Choose compatible numbers.**

$125 + w = 135$ ← **What number added to 125 is 135?**

$w = 10$ ← **Use mental math.**

The puppy weighs about 10 lb.

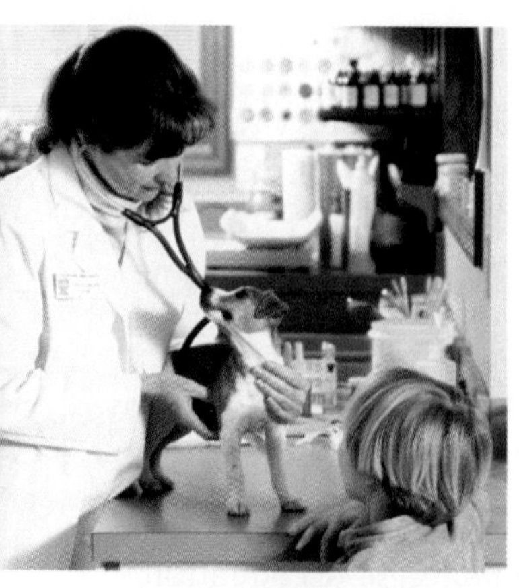

Real-World Connection

Careers A veterinarian is a health-care provider for animals.

✓ Check Understanding **3** **a.** Estimate the solution of $n - 11.67 = 35.81$ to the nearest whole number.

b. A box of machine parts weighs 14.7 lb. A forklift has a maximum weight limit of 390 lb. About how many boxes of parts can the forklift carry at one time?

EXERCISES

For more practice, see *Extra Practice*.

A Practice by Example

Example 1 (page 78)

Find the solution of each equation from the given numbers. Exercise 1 has been started for you.

1. $28h = 448$: 8, 12, 16, or 20

$28(8) \stackrel{?}{=} 448$

$224 = 448$ False

2. $\frac{y}{9} = 32$: 261, 270, 279, or 288

3. $\frac{m}{8} = 13$: 94, 104, 124, or 144

4. $143k = 1{,}573$: 11, 12, 13, or 14

5. $\ell + 17 = 56$: 19, 29, 39, or 49

6. $p + 24.1 = 72$: 47.9, 57.9, or 67.9

7. $n - 27 = 38$: 11, 51, or 65

Example 2 (page 78)

Use mental math to solve each equation.

8. $3t = 27$

9. $6d = -36$

10. $10m = 50$

11. $n + 4 = 7$

12. $k + 2 = -12$

13. $w + 7 = 11$

14. $\frac{p}{5} = 3$

15. $\frac{y}{-8} = -6$

16. $\frac{x}{4} = 5$

17. $w - 6 = 4$

18. $m - 3 = -9$

19. $n - 9 = 11$

Example 3 (page 78)

Estimate the solution of each equation to the nearest whole number.

20. $3.1g = 20.9$

21. $h - 4.9 = 13.8$

22. $7.8 + n = 38.2$

23. $\frac{t}{3.05} = 11.8$

24. $x + 12.9 = 32.6$

25. $\ell - 4.2 = 25.9$

26. Public Service Your class has collected 84.5 lb of canned food. The class record is 103.25 lb. Write an equation and use it to estimate the amount of canned food the class still needs to collect to match the record.

B Apply Your Skills

27. Baseball The total distance around a baseball diamond is 360 ft. What is the distance from first base to second base?

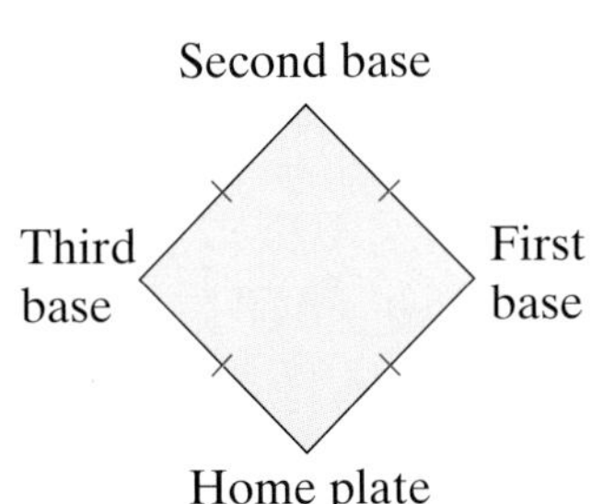

28. Moving An elevator has a maximum lift of 2,000 lb. You are moving 55-lb boxes of books. Write an equation and estimate how many boxes you can safely place on the elevator.

Solve using mental math or estimation. If you estimate, round to the nearest whole number before you add or subtract.

29. $p - 7.35 = 46.71$ **30.** $a - 20 = 14$ **31.** $122.39 + x = 343.8$

32. $n - 11 = 33$ **33.** $k - 99.89 = 463.04$ **34.** $h + 9 = 55$

35. $27 - m = 16$ **36.** $28.71 + t = 49.43$ **37.** $17 + p = -3$

Climate **Use the table for Exercises 38 and 39.**

38. The average annual precipitation for Houston, Texas, is about 1.5 times the average annual precipitation for Detroit, Michigan. Find Detroit's value.

39. The average annual precipitation for Raleigh, North Carolina, is about 4.3 times the average annual precipitation for San Diego, California. Find San Diego's value.

Average Annual Precipitation

City	Precipitation (in.)
Detroit, MI	■
Houston, TX	47.84
Raleigh, NC	43.05
San Diego, CA	■

SOURCE: National Climatic Data Center.
Go to **www.PHSchool.com** for a data update.
Web Code: abg-2041

Identify a solution for each equation from the given set of numbers.

40. $2y - 6 = 48$: 7, 17, 27, 37 **41.** $\frac{m}{6} + 11 = 12$: −8, −6, 6, 8

42. $3(t + 14) = 27$: −10, −5, 5, 9 **43.** $\frac{h + 28}{2} = 29$: 1, 30, 78, 100

44. **Writing in Math** Equations can be true or false. Can an expression be true or false? Explain.

45. **Bowling** A bowling ball has a mass of 5.54 kg. A bowling pin has a mass of 1.58 kg. About how many pins are equal in mass to one ball?

46. **Shopping** Suppose you are buying four CDs like the ones at the right. The clerk tells you that the total, before sales tax, is $67.80. Write an equation and use it to estimate the amount you are being charged for each CD. Is the clerk correct? Explain.

C Challenge

Solve each equation using mental math.

47. $-4 + h = -11$ **48.** $\frac{t}{7} = -3$ **49.** $k - 2 = -6$

50. $24 = -6w$ **51.** $\frac{c}{-3} = 8$ **52.** $z + 8 = 0$

53. **Packaging** Your family purchases a crate of oranges. Each orange weighs 0.2 kg. There are 5 kg of oranges in the crate. How many oranges are in the crate?

54. Stretch Your Thinking What is the greatest amount of change you can have and still not be able to find any combination of coins that is equal to \$1.00?

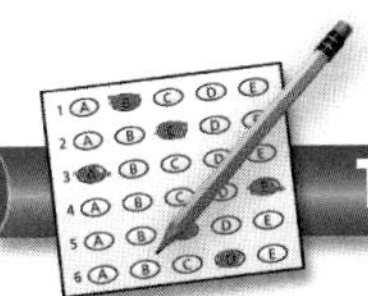

Test Prep

Multiple Choice

55. Which is the solution of $4x = 120$?
A. 3 **B.** 10 **C.** 20 **D.** 30

56. Which is the solution of $\frac{y}{6} = 8$?
F. 47 **G.** 48 **H.** 49 **I.** 50

57. Which equation has the solution 7?
A. $k + 3 = 9$ **B.** $5 - k = 12$ **C.** $k - 3 = 9$ **D.** $5 + k = 12$

Take It to the NET
Online lesson quiz at
www.PHSchool.com
Web Code aba-0202

58. Which equation has the solution –6?
F. $-8 - h = 2$ **G.** $-8h = 48$ **H.** $-8 + h = 14$ **I.** $8h = 48$

Short Response

59. Each year, the federal government spends about \$27.1 million to run Yellowstone National Park. This is \$13.5 million more than it spends to run Everglades National Park. About how much does the federal government spend to run Everglades National Park?
a. Write an equation to represent this problem.
b. Solve your equation.

Mixed Review

Lesson 2-1

Algebra **Evaluate each expression for $n = 3$, $t = 4$, and $x = 6$.**

60. $-5x$ **61.** $3tx$ **62.** $2nt - 3x$

63. $3n + 2t - x$ **64.** $t(x - n)$ **65.** $\frac{nx}{3}$

Lesson 1-7

Find the value of each expression.

66. $-5 - 4 + 9$ **67.** $3 - 6 + 8$

68. $-7 + 3 - 4$ **69.** $-9 + 10 + (-5)$

70. $-3 - (-4) + 1$ **71.** $6 - (-2) - 8$

Lesson 1-5

Use the problem-solving plan to solve each problem.

72. A restaurant has 16 tables. Some tables seat exactly 2 people, and the rest seat exactly 5 people. The restaurant is full with 44 customers. How many tables of each size does the restaurant have?

73. Tickets Tickets to an amusement park cost \$15 for adults and \$8 for children. Yesterday the park sold 170 tickets and earned \$1,675. How many tickets of each type were sold?

Investigation

Modeling Equations

For Use With Lesson 2-3

You can model and solve equations using algebra tiles.

1 EXAMPLE Solving Addition Equations

Use algebra tiles to solve $x + 4 = 12$.

$x + 4 = 12$

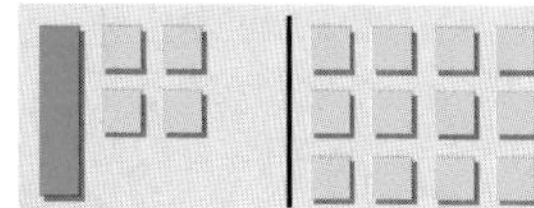

← **Model the equation. Use yellow tiles for positive integers.**

$x + 4 - 4 = 12 - 4$

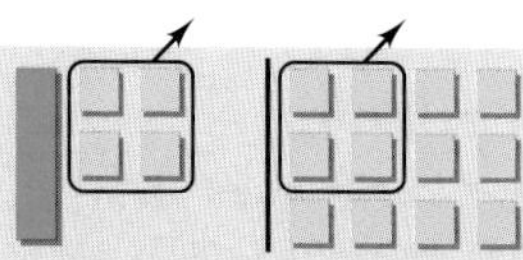

← **Remove 4 tiles from each side.**

$x = 8$

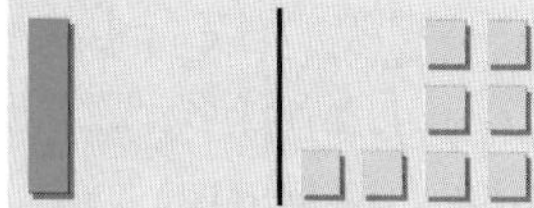

← **Simplify.**

2 EXAMPLE Solving Multiplication Equations

Use algebra tiles to solve $3x = -21$.

$3x = -21$

← **Model the equation. Use red tiles for negative integers.**

$\frac{3x}{3} = \frac{-21}{3}$

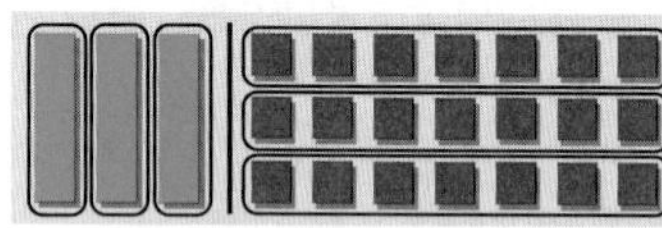

← **Divide each side into three equal groups.**

$x = -7$

← **Simplify.**

EXERCISES

Use algebra tiles to solve each equation.

1. $x + 12 = 18$ **2.** $x + 3 = 16$ **3.** $x + 8 = 17$ **4.** $x + (-7) = -13$

5. $x + (-2) = -7$ **6.** $x + (-7) = -11$ **7.** $3x = 18$ **8.** $5x = -25$

9. $7x = 21$ **10.** $2x = -18$ **11.** $4x = 28$ **12.** $2x = 24$

Solving Equations by Adding or Subtracting

What You'll Learn

To solve equations by adding

To solve equations by subtracting

. . . And Why

To find the price of stock, as in Example 4

Check Skills You'll Need

For help, go to Lesson 2-2.

Estimate the solution of each equation.

1. $y + 3.14 = 11.89$
2. $v - 4.83 = 13.12$
3. $p + 7.92 = 14.81$
4. $t - 10.21 = 21.91$
5. $x + 14.2 = 38.849$
6. $k - 9.14 = 20.03$

New Vocabulary

- Addition Property of Equality
- inverse operations
- Subtraction Property of Equality

Interactive lesson includes instant self-check, tutorials, and activities.

OBJECTIVE

1 Solving Equations by Adding

You can think of an equation as a balance scale. When you do something to one side of an equation, you must do the same thing to the other side of the equation to keep it "balanced."

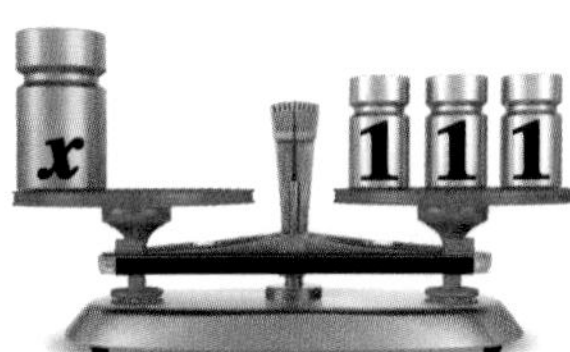

In the two scales above, two weights are added to each side of the balance scale on the left. The result is the balance scale on the right. This illustrates the following property of equality.

Key Concepts — **Addition Property of Equality**

If you add the same value to each side of an equation, the two sides remain equal.

Arithmetic	Algebra
$\frac{20}{2} = 10$, so $\frac{20}{2} + 3 = 10 + 3$.	If $a = b$, then $a + c = b + c$.

To solve an equation, you want to get the variable alone on one side of the equation. To do this, you use inverse operations. **Inverse operations** are operations that undo each other.

Addition and subtraction are inverse operations. You can add to undo subtraction.

1 EXAMPLE Solving Equations by Adding

Solve $x - 34 = -46$.

$x - 34 = -46$

$x - 34 + 34 = -46 + 34$ ← Addition Property of Equality: add 34 to each side.

$x + 0 = -12$ ← Additive Inverse Property

$x = -12$ ← Additive Identity Property

Check $x - 34 = -46$ ← Check using the original equation.

$-12 - 34 \stackrel{?}{=} -46$ ← Replace x with -12.

$-46 = -46$ ✔ ← The solution checks.

✔ Check Understanding 1 Solve each equation. Check your answer.

a. $x - 104 = 64$ **b.** $y - 129 = -72$ **c.** $-148 + h = 179$

2 EXAMPLE Real-World Problem Solving

Reading Math

The order of math symbols may differ from the order of words:

- ten fewer than $n \rightarrow n - 10$
- eight less than $r \rightarrow r - 8$
- n times $5 \rightarrow 5n$

Sporting Goods Your friend's skateboard cost \$245 less than his mountain bike. His skateboard cost \$45. How much did the mountain bike cost?

Words cost of skateboard is \$245 less than cost of bike

Let b = the cost of the mountain bike.

Equation 45 = b − \$245

$45 = b - 245$

$45 + 245 = b - 245 + 245$ ← Add 245 to each side.

$290 = b$ ← Simplify.

The mountain bike cost \$290.

✔ Check Understanding 2 A paperback book costs \$19 less than its hardcover edition. The paperback book costs \$7.95. How much does the hardcover edition cost?

OBJECTIVE 2 Solving Equations by Subtracting

Just as you use addition to undo subtraction, you can use subtraction to undo addition.

Key Concepts Subtraction Property of Equality

If you subtract the same value from each side of an equation, the two sides remain equal.

Arithmetic

$\frac{12}{2} = 6$, so $\frac{12}{2} - 4 = 6 - 4$.

Algebra

If $a = b$, then $a - c = b - c$.

3 EXAMPLE Solving Equations by Subtracting

Solve $114 + m = 249$.

$$114 + m = 249$$
$$114 - 114 + m = 249 - 114 \quad \leftarrow \text{Subtract 114 from each side.}$$
$$m = 135 \quad \leftarrow \text{Simplify.}$$

Check Understanding 3 Solve each equation. Check your answer.

a. $n + 84 = 157$ **b.** $p + 115 = -17$ **c.** $18 + h = 137$

d. Reasoning To solve the equation $249 = x + 114$, could you use exactly the same steps used in Example 3? Explain.

4 EXAMPLE Real-World Problem Solving

Stocks The final price of a stock after a day of trading is \$22.75 per share. The stock ticker indicates that the price increased by \$3.40 that day. Find the price of the stock at the beginning of the day.

Words	final price	is	3.40	more than	beginning price
	Let p = beginning price.				
Equation	22.75	=	3.4	+	p

$$22.75 = 3.4 + p$$
$$22.75 - 3.4 = 3.4 - 3.4 + p \quad \leftarrow \text{Subtract 3.4 from each side.}$$
$$19.35 = p \quad \leftarrow \text{Simplify.}$$

The price of the stock at the beginning of the day was \$19.35.

Real-World Connection

Stock traders make split-second decisions to buy or sell stocks as prices change.

Check Understanding 4 Another stock's final price is \$26.75 per share. The price decreased by \$2.40 that day. Write and solve an equation to find the stock's original price.

EXERCISES

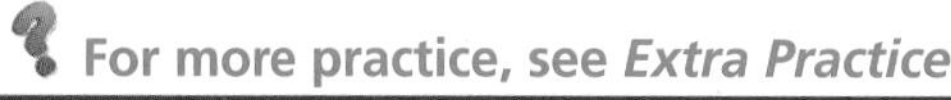
For more practice, see *Extra Practice*.

A Practice by Example

Examples 1, 2 (page 84)

Solve. Check your answer. Exercise 1 has been started for you.

1. $x - 6 = -55$
$x - 6 + 6 = -55 + 6$

2. $\ell - 12 = 23$

3. $y - 8 = 35$

4. $t - 32 = -27$

5. $h - 37 = -42$

6. $q - 16 = 40$

7. $n - 255 = -455$

8. $-83 + m = 122$

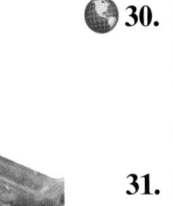

9. **Physics** At 20°C the speed of sound in air is 344 m/s. This is 1,117 m/s slower than the speed of sound in water. Write and solve an equation to find the speed of sound in water.

Example 3 (page 85)

Solve each equation. Check your answer.

10. $k + 17 = 29$
11. $b + 12 = 39$
12. $j + 33 = 48$
13. $253 + c = 725$
14. $89 + y = 100$
15. $62 + t = -77$
16. $34 + w = -24$
17. $d + 261 = -48$
18. $x + 34 = 212$

Example 4 (page 85)

19. **Basketball** A basketball player scores 15 points in the first game and p points in the second game of a tournament. She finishes the two-game tournament with a total of 33 points. Write and solve an equation to find the number of points she scores in the second game.

20. **Health** A runner's heart rate is 133 beats per minute. This is 62 beats per minute more than his resting heart rate. Write and solve an equation to find the runner's resting heart rate.

B Apply Your Skills

Use a calculator, paper and pencil, or mental math. Solve each equation.

21. $n - 35 = 84$
22. $166 = m + 97$
23. $x + 25 = 16$
24. $-17.32 = x + 6.5$
25. $16.7 = c - 5.9$
26. $3.102 = 2.023 + r$
27. $y + 76 = 67$
28. $81 + b = 102$
29. $27 = p + (-2)$

Real-World Connection

A ladybug can eat more than 5,000 aphids in a lifetime.

30. **Biology** A student collects 12 ladybugs for a science project. This is 9 fewer than the number of ladybugs the student collected yesterday. Write and solve an equation to find the number of ladybugs the student collected yesterday.

31. **Data File, p. 69** A bulldog's lower-end life expectancy is six years less than a golden retriever's life expectancy. Write and solve an equation to find the life expectancy of a golden retriever.

Match each equation with the graph of its solution.

32. $t + 14 = 18$

A. 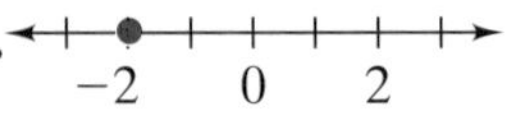

33. $x - 5 = -3$

B. 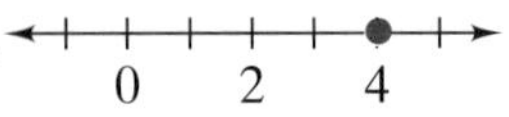

34. $w + 4 = 2$

C. 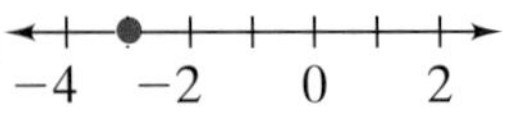

35. $y - 7 = -10$

D. 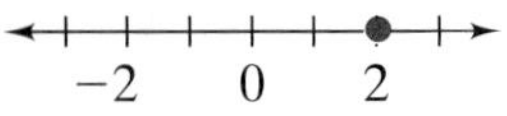

36. **Writing in Math** A student is saving money for field hockey camp. Her savings are modeled by the equation $135 + d = 250$. Explain what each part of the equation represents.

37. **Open-Ended** Write a real-world problem that $t - 3 = 10$ can model.

38. **Money** Use the advertisement. Write and solve an equation to find the original price of the sweater.

39. **Reasoning** How can you transform $5 + x = 4$ into the equation $3 + x = 2$? Support your answer with one of the properties of equality.

Challenge

Solve each equation.

40. $y + (-2) = -4$
41. $12 = q - (-7)$
42. $-11 = a + (-6)$
43. $p - (-17) = -8$
44. $-5 + m = -15$
45. $17 = h + (-9)$

46. During the first five games of a baseball season, your team scores 3, 4, 2, 6, and 8 runs. How many more runs must your team score to have a total of 30 runs? Define a variable. Then write and solve an equation.

47. **Stretch Your Thinking** A gardener plants half of the plants in her garden in rows of 18 and the other half of the plants in rows of 24. If she plants a total of 14 rows, how many plants are in her garden?

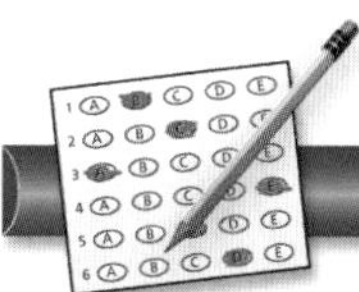

Test Prep

Multiple Choice

48. What is the solution of $n - 12 = 24$?
A. -2 B. 2 C. 12 D. 36

49. Which value of the variable makes the equation $p + 5 = 25$ true?
F. -20 G. 5 H. 20 I. 30

Take It to the NET
Online lesson quiz at
www.PHSchool.com
Web Code aba-0203

50. Which equation has the solution -10?
A. $y + 12 = -2$ B. $y - 12 = -2$
C. $y - 5 = -15$ D. $y + 5 = -15$

Extended Response

51. The boiling point of water is 212°F. This is 180°F more than its freezing point. Define a variable. Then write and solve an equation to find the freezing point of water. Show your work.

Mixed Review

Lesson 2-2

Algebra **Solve each equation using mental math.**

52. $m + 8 = 12$
53. $h - 6 = 15$
54. $5n = 45$
55. $\frac{k}{4} = 6$
56. $11 + p = 21$
57. $6w = 42$

Lesson 1-8

Simplify each expression.

58. $72 \div (-9)$
59. $-24 \div 3$
60. $4(5)(-3)$
61. $(15 \div 3)(6)$

Algebra

2-4 Solving Equations by Multiplying or Dividing

What You'll Learn

To solve equations by dividing

To solve equations by multiplying

. . . And Why

To find the number of days a library book is overdue, as in Example 2

✓ Check Skills You'll Need

For help, go to Lesson 1-8.

Find each product or quotient.

1. $-3 \cdot (-4)$ **2.** $-56 \div 8$ **3.** $7 \cdot 12$

4. $39 \div (-3)$ **5.** $13 \cdot (-2)$ **6.** $-16 \div (-8)$

7. $2 \cdot (-8) \div (-4)$ **8.** $15 \div 3 \cdot (-5)$ **9.** $-3 \cdot (-3) \cdot (-3)$

New Vocabulary

- **Division Property of Equality**
- **Multiplication Property of Equality**

Interactive lesson includes instant self-check, tutorials, and activities.

OBJECTIVE 1 Solving Equations by Dividing

After a football game you and three friends go out for pizza. An extra-large pizza and four bottles of water cost \$22.68 (including tax and a \$2 coupon). How much does each person owe if you split the bill equally?

CHECK # 325	TABLE # 12
ITEMS ORDERED	AMOUNT
X-LG PIZZA	18.60
\$2 COUPON	-2.00
BOT WTR	1.25
BOT WTR	1.25
BOT WTR	1.25
BOT WTR	1.25
TAX	1.08
TOTAL	22.68

You can represent the problem with the model below. Let p represent the amount of money each person owes.

total bill				→	22.68
p	p	p	p	→	$4p$

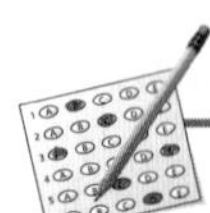

Test-Prep Tip

The words *each* and *per* are frequently used in problems that involve solving an equation by multiplying or dividing.

The model shows that you can use the equation $4p = 22.68$. To solve this equation, you can use the Division Property of Equality.

Key Concepts **Division Property of Equality**

If you divide each side of an equation by the same nonzero number, the two sides remain equal.

Arithmetic	Algebra
Since $3(2) = 6$, $\frac{3(2)}{2} = \frac{6}{2}$.	If $a = b$ and $c \neq 0$, then $\frac{a}{c} = \frac{b}{c}$.

Division is the inverse operation of multiplication. When a variable is multiplied by a number, you can use division to undo the multiplication.

Division Undoes Multiplication

$(4 \cdot 9) \div 4 = 9$ $\qquad$ $5x \div 5 = x$

1 EXAMPLE Solving Equations by Dividing

Solve $4p = 22.68$.

$4p = 22.68$ ← **Notice p is being *multiplied* by 4.**

$\frac{4p}{4} = \frac{22.68}{4}$ ← **Divide each side by 4 to get p alone.**

$p = 5.67$ ← **Simplify.**

Check $4p = 22.68$ ← **Check your solution in the original equation.**

$4(5.67) \stackrel{?}{=} 22.68$ ← **Replace p with 5.67.**

$22.68 = 22.68$ ✔ ← **The solution checks.**

Check Understanding 1 Solve each equation. Check your answer.

a. $3x = -21.6$ **b.** $-12y = -108$ **c.** $104x = 312$

You can use the Division Property of Equality and inverse operations to solve real-world applications.

2 EXAMPLE Real-World Problem Solving

Library Fines A library charges 6¢ per day for an overdue book. Your fine is 96¢. How many days late is your book?

Words 6¢ times number of days late equals fine

Let d = the number of days late.

Equation $6 \cdot d = 96$

$6d = 96$

$\frac{6d}{6} = \frac{96}{6}$ ← **Divide each side by 6.**

$d = 16$ ← **Simplify.**

The book is 16 days overdue.

Look Back and Check The fine for each day is 6¢. If the book is 16 days overdue, then the total fine is $16 \cdot \$.06$, or \$.96. The answer checks.

Real-World Connection

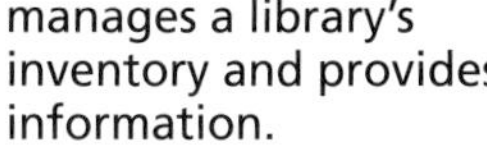

Careers A librarian manages a library's inventory and provides information.

Check Understanding 2

a. **Reasoning** The equation $0.06d = 0.96$ also represents the problem in Example 2. Explain.

b. Suppose you and four friends go to a baseball game. The total cost for five tickets is \$110. Write and solve an equation to find the cost of one ticket.

OBJECTIVE

2 Solving Equations by Multiplying

Another property you can use to solve equations is the Multiplication Property of Equality.

Key Concepts **Multiplication Property of Equality**

If you multiply each side of an equation by the same number, the two sides remain equal.

Arithmetic	**Algebra**
$\frac{12}{2} = 6$, so $\frac{12}{2} \cdot 2 = 6 \cdot 2$.	If $a = b$, then $a \cdot c = b \cdot c$.

Multiplication is the inverse operation of division. When a variable is divided by a number, you can use multiplication to undo the division.

Multiplication Undoes Division

$\frac{3}{5} \cdot 5 = 3$ $\qquad$ $\frac{n}{3} \cdot 3 = n$

3 EXAMPLE Solving Equations by Multiplying

Reading Math

Read $\frac{t}{-45} = -5$ as "t divided by negative 45 equals negative 5."

Solve $\frac{t}{-45} = -5$.

$\frac{t}{-45} = -5$ ← **Notice that t is divided by −45.**

$(-45) \cdot \frac{t}{-45} = (-45) \cdot -5$ ← **Multiply each side by −45.**

$t = 225$ ← **Simplify.**

Check Understanding 3 Solve each equation. Check your answer.

a. $\frac{x}{8} = 93$ **b.** $\frac{w}{26} = -15$ **c.** $\frac{y}{-5.5} = -23$

EXERCISES

For more practice, see *Extra Practice*.

A Practice by Example

Solve. Check your answer. Exercise 1 has been started for you.

Example 1 (page 89)

1. $5b = -235$

$\frac{5b}{5} = \frac{-235}{5}$

2. $-7h = 35$

3. $8p = -544$

4. $12t = 144$

5. $13e = -52$

6. $35q = -175$

7. $-7n = -294$

8. $0.2x = 4$

9. $-0.5r = -8$

Example 2 (page 89)

10. Gas Mileage Julie's car travels 27 miles per gallon of gasoline used. She recently traveled 324 miles. How many gallons of gasoline did her car use?

11. **Entertainment** A local park rents paddle boats for \$5.50 per hour. You have \$22 to spend. For how many hours can you rent a boat?

12. **Money** A video store charges \$2.75 per day for overdue videos. You owe a late fee of \$13.75. How many days overdue is the video?

Example 3 (page 90)

Solve each equation. Check your answer.

13. $\frac{d}{4} = 7$ 14. $\frac{m}{-5} = 3$ 15. $\frac{r}{10} = -6$

16. $\frac{z}{8} = -3$ 17. $\frac{n}{3} = 9$ 18. $\frac{t}{8} = 12$

19. $\frac{q}{2} = -14$ 20. $\frac{k}{-6} = -5$ 21. $\frac{d}{0.5} = 11$

B Apply Your Skills

Write and solve an equation for each situation.

22. **Entertainment** The world record for playgoing is held by Dr. H. Howard Hughes of Fort Worth, Texas. He saw 6,136 plays in 31 years. How many plays did Dr. Hughes see in an average year?

23. George Adrian of Indianapolis, Indiana, picked 15,830 lb of apples in 8 h. How many pounds of apples per hour is that?

24. **Trees** A growing tree absorbs about 26 lb of carbon dioxide each year. How many years will the tree take to absorb 390 lb of carbon dioxide?

Solve each equation.

25. $27 = -9w$ 26. $-3k = -18$ 27. $\frac{c}{6} = -1$

28. $\frac{y}{-12} = -12$ 29. $\frac{n}{-5} = 11$ 30. $\frac{t}{6} = -10$

31. $\frac{q}{-5} = 30$ 32. $8n = 112$ 33. $-4 = -2r$

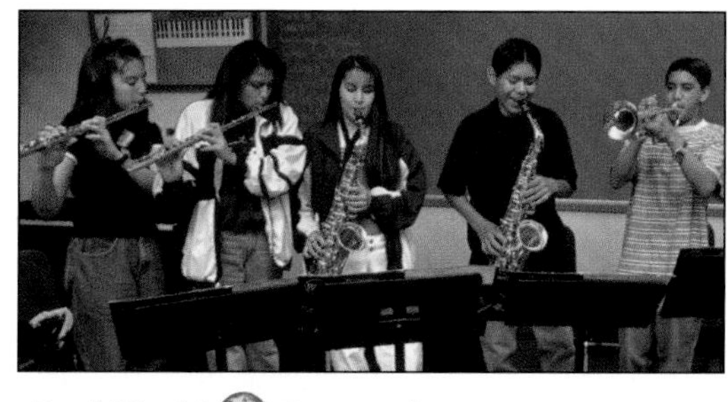

Real-World Connection

A quintet is a band with five members.

34. **Writing in Math** Explain why you can use the equation $\frac{m}{5} = 50$ to describe how much money the quintet in the photo has to earn for each member to receive \$50. What does each part of the equation represent?

35. **Estimation** What equation would you use to estimate the solution of $12x = -38$? Explain. Estimate the solution.

Use a calculator, paper and pencil, or mental math. Solve each equation.

36. $2.5m = 25$ 37. $\frac{w}{-4.2} = 10.3$ 38. $-3.25t = 19.5$

39. $\frac{k}{21.45} = 6$ 40. $7.023x = 31.6035$ 41. $\frac{y}{-5.22} = -3.11$

42. $-4y = 24$ 43. $-7 = 0.07n$ 44. $\frac{n}{3} = -4$

45. **Error Analysis** One student's solution for the equation $\frac{n}{-6} = 12$ is $n = -2$. Explain how the student may have found this solution. Then correct the student's mistake.

46. **Open-Ended** Write a problem that can be solved using $3x = 30$.

Challenge

Solve each equation for x.

47. $\frac{24}{x} = -4$ **48.** $\frac{x}{a} = b$ **49.** $ax = b$

50. Reasoning For what values of x is $5|x| = 10$ true?

51. Stretch Your Thinking I am a three-digit number. I am exactly divisible by 24 and by 36. When I am divided by 24, the quotient is 6 more than the quotient when I am divided by 36. What number am I?

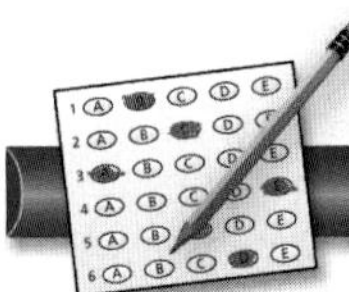

Test Prep

Gridded Response

52. You are putting glasses on shelves. You have 120 glasses. Each shelf holds 30 glasses. How many shelves will you need?

53. The restaurant bill for four people is $37. How much money, in dollars, should each person contribute to share the cost evenly?

54. The quotient of Julian's age and 3 is 4. What is Julian's age in years?

55. You write 133 invitations in 7 days. Each day you write an equal number of invitations. How many invitations do you write each day?

56. You have a part-time job after school. You earn $110.50 for 17 hours of work. How many dollars per hour do you earn?

Take It to the NET
Online lesson quiz at www.PHSchool.com
Web Code aba-0204

Mixed Review

Lesson 2-3 Algebra **Solve each equation.**

57. $m + 17 = 33$ **58.** $p - 20 = 31$ **59.** $h - 15 = 48$

Lesson 1-3 **Identify the property shown.**

60. $0(17.56) = 0$ **61.** $21 \cdot 1 = 21$ **62.** $3(48) = 48(3)$

Checkpoint Quiz 1 — Lessons 2-1 through 2-4

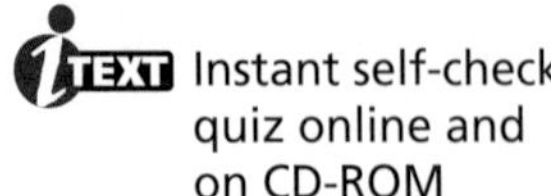

Instant self-check quiz online and on CD-ROM

Write an algebraic expression for each word phrase.

1. four less than a number
2. three times a number
3. the quotient of 4 and a number
4. nine more than a number

Solve each equation.

5. $g - 5 = -9$ **6.** $y + 10 = 12$ **7.** $-5x = 45$

8. $\frac{h}{6} = 8$ **9.** $\frac{n}{-4} = -5$ **10.** $7d = 252$

Algebra

2-5 Exploring Two-Step Problems

What You'll Learn

OBJECTIVE 1 To write and evaluate expressions with two operations

OBJECTIVE 2 To solve two-step equations using number sense

. . . And Why

To find costs for bowling, as in Example 2

Check Skills You'll Need

For help, go to Lesson 2-1.

Evaluate each expression for $n = 4$, $t = 2$, and $y = 3$.

1. $n + 3y$ **2.** nty **3.** $3y - t$

Write an algebraic expression for each word phrase.

4. 5 minutes fewer than m minutes

5. 2 times the number of points p

6. \$5 more than d dollars

OBJECTIVE

Interactive lesson includes instant self-check, tutorials, and activities.

1 Writing and Evaluating Expressions With Two Operations

In Lesson 2-1, you wrote expressions with variables using addition, subtraction, multiplication, or division. In this lesson you will write algebraic expressions that combine the operations.

1 EXAMPLE Writing Expressions With Two Operations

Define a variable and write an algebraic expression for each phrase.

a. five years more than three times your age

Let a = your age in years. ← **Define the variable.**

$5 + 3 \cdot a$ ← **Write an algebraic expression.**

$5 + 3a$ ← **Rewrite $3 \cdot a$ as $3a$.**

b. seven centimeters less than twice the span of your hand

Let s = the span of your hand in centimeters. ← **Define the variable.**

$2 \cdot s - 7$ ← **Write an algebraic expression. Note that the order is different from the order in the word phrase.**

$2s - 7$ ← **Simplify.**

c. 10 people fewer than half the population of your town

Let p = the population of your town. ← **Define the variable.**

$\frac{1}{2} \cdot p - 10$ ← **Write an algebraic expression.**

$\frac{1}{2}p - 10$ ← **Simplify.**

Check Understanding **1** Define a variable and write an algebraic expression for "two slices fewer than $\frac{1}{3}$ of a pizza."

2 EXAMPLE Evaluating Two-Step Expressions

Real-World Connection

The most common form of bowling is tenpins. Other forms include duckpins, candlepins, and skittles.

Bowling On weekday afternoons, a local bowling alley offers a special. Each bowling game costs \$2.50, and shoe rental is \$1.25. Write an expression for the total cost of the games you play, including shoe rental. Then evaluate your expression for five games.

Words	cost per game	times	number of games	plus	shoe rental
↓	Let n = the number of games played.				
Expression	2.5	$\cdot$	n	+	1.25

$2.5n + 1.25$

$2.5 \cdot 5 + 1.25$ ← **Evaluate the expression for 5 games.**

$= 12.5 + 1.25$ ← **Multiply.**

$= 13.75$ ← **Add.**

For five games and shoe rental, the total cost is \$13.75.

Check Understanding 2 **a.** Art supplies cost \$.79 for each color marker and \$1.25 for one poster board. Write an expression for the total cost of supplies, including the markers you buy and one poster board. Then evaluate your expression for seven markers.

b. **Reasoning** What expression would you use if you needed only one marker and p poster boards? Evaluate this expression for seven poster boards.

OBJECTIVE

2 Using Number Sense to Solve Two-Step Equations

Suppose your grandmother sends you five games for your birthday. The games all have the same weight. The box she mails them in weighs 8 ounces. The total weight is 48 ounces.

You can model this situation with the diagram below. Let g represent the weight of a game.

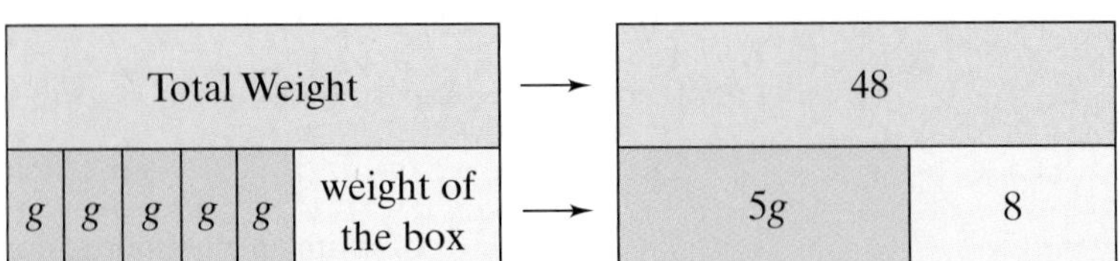

You can solve this problem using the equation $5g + 8 = 48$. Since there is more than one operation in the equation, there will be more than one step.

3 EXAMPLE Using Number Sense

Solve $5g + 8 = 48$ by using number sense.

$5g + 8 = 48$

$▢ + 8 = 48$ ← Cover $5g$. ***Think***: What number added to 8 is 48? Answer: 40

$5g = 40$ ← So ▢, or $5g$, must equal 40.

$5 \cdot ▢ = 40$ ← ***Think***: What number times 5 is 40? Answer: 8

$g = 8$ ← So ▢, or g, must equal 8.

Check $5g + 8 = 48$ ← Check your solution in the original equation.

$5(8) + 8 \overset{?}{=} 48$ ← Substitute 8 for g.

$40 + 8 \overset{?}{=} 48$ ← Multiply.

$48 = 48$ ✔ ← The solution checks.

Check Understanding **3** Solve each equation using number sense.

a. $3m + 9 = 21$ **b.** $8d + 5 = 45$ **c.** $4y - 11 = 33$

You can use two-step equations to solve real-world problems.

4 EXAMPLE Real-World Problem Solving

Need Help?
You can represent the relationships in Example 4 with this model.

share of total	
lemonade cost	share of pizza cost

↓

\$5.50	
\$1.50	$\frac{z}{3}$

Food Suppose you buy a jumbo lemonade for \$1.50 and divide the cost of a pizza with two friends. Your share of the total bill is \$5.50. Write and solve an equation to find the cost of the pizza.

Words	cost of lemonade	plus	(cost of pizza ÷ 3)	is	\$5.50
↓	Let z = the cost of the pizza.				
Equation	1.50	+	$(z \div 3)$	=	\$5.50

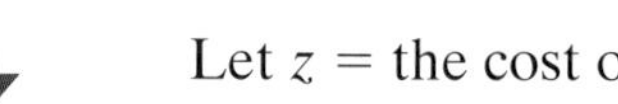

$1.50 + \frac{z}{3} = 5.50$

$1.50 + ▢ = 5.50$ ← Cover $\frac{z}{3}$. ***Think***: What number added to 1.50 is 5.50? Answer: 4

$\frac{z}{3} = 4$ ← So ▢, or $\frac{z}{3}$, must equal 4.

$\frac{▢}{3} = 4$ ← ***Think***: What number divided by 3 is 4? Answer: 12

$z = 12$ ← So ▢, or z, must equal 12.

The cost of the pizza is \$12.

Check Understanding **4** **a. Reasoning** What will the equation in Example 4 be if your share is \$6? What will be the cost of the pizza?

b. Basketball During the first half of a game you scored 8 points. In the second half you made only 3-point baskets. You finished the game with 23 points. Write and solve an equation to find how many 3-point baskets you made.

EXERCISES

For more practice, see *Extra Practice*.

A Practice by Example

Define a variable and write an algebraic expression for each phrase. Exercise 1 has been started for you.

Example 1 (page 93)

1. two points fewer than 3 times the number of points scored yesterday
Let p represent the number of points scored yesterday: 3■ − ■.

2. one meter more than 6 times your height in meters

3. seven pages fewer than half the number of pages read last week

4. 8 pounds less than five times the weight of a chicken in pounds

5. twice the distance in miles flown last year, plus 100 miles

Example 2 (page 94)

6. Money A fitness club advertises a special for new members. Each month of membership costs \$19, with an initial enrollment fee of \$75. Write an expression for the total cost. Then evaluate your expression for 8 months of membership.

7. Telephone A cellular telephone company charges \$40 per month plus a \$35 activation fee. Write an expression for the total cost. Then evaluate your expression for 10 months of service.

Example 3 (page 95)

Solve each equation using number sense.

8. $2t + 9 = 39$ **9.** $4m + 12 = 52$ **10.** $10h + 14 = 84$

11. $7w + 16 = 37$ **12.** $3y + 13 = 40$ **13.** $5v + 19 = 24$

Example 4 (page 95)

14. Six families split the cost of a family reunion. Each family also spends \$65 for a hotel room. Each family's share of the cost of the party plus the cost of the hotel room totals \$160. Write and solve an equation to find the cost of the reunion.

15. Money You want to buy a CD player that costs \$99. You already have \$15. If you save \$12 per week, when will you have enough money to buy the CD player?

B Apply Your Skills

Solve each equation using number sense.

16. $5h + 3 = 18$ **17.** $3m - 7 = 26$ **18.** $8y + 17 = 65$

19. $\frac{x}{3} - 3 = 12$ **20.** $2p - 5 = 15$ **21.** $\frac{r}{4} + 1 = 6$

22. $4n - 14 = 38$ **23.** $9d + 6 = 42$ **24.** $2y - 6 = 22$

25. Writing in Math An electrician charges a fee to come to your house, in addition to her hourly rate. This can be modeled by $40h + 35 = 115$. Explain what each part of the equation represents. Then solve the equation to find the number of hours the electrician works.

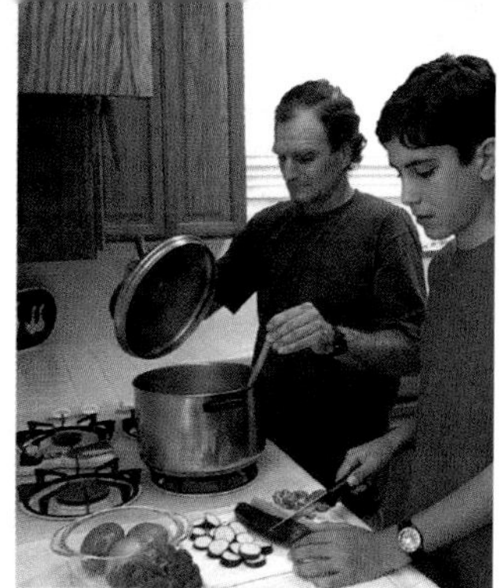

Real-World Connection
Zucchini is a good source of vitamin A and potassium.

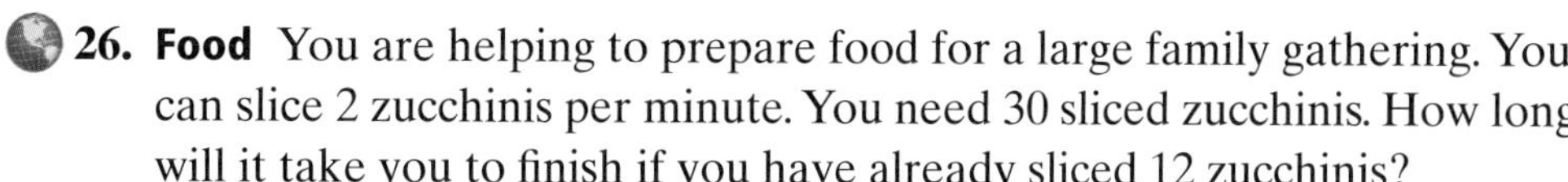

26. **Food** You are helping to prepare food for a large family gathering. You can slice 2 zucchinis per minute. You need 30 sliced zucchinis. How long will it take you to finish if you have already sliced 12 zucchinis?

27. You order 3 CDs advertised on the Internet. Each CD costs the same amount. The shipping charge is \$5. The total cost, including the shipping charge, is \$41. Find the cost of one CD.

28. **Fitness** You spend 5 minutes jogging as a warm-up for your run. Then you run 4 miles. The total time you exercise is 49 minutes. What is your average time for running a mile?

C Challenge

Solve each equation.

29. $-3x + 8 = -22$
30. $-2t - 6 = 18$
31. $15 - 3p = 9$

32. **Stretch Your Thinking** On an airline flight there is one empty seat for every three passengers. The plane has 132 passenger seats. How many passengers are on the flight?

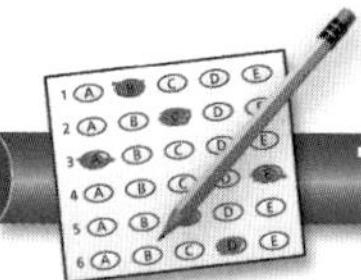

Test Prep

Multiple Choice

33. Which algebraic expression represents *five inches fewer than twice last year's rainfall in inches*?
A. $5 - 2f$ B. $2f - 5$ C. $2 - 5f$ D. $5f - 2$

34. Which algebraic expression represents *\$12 more than 3 times the number of dollars in the budget*?
F. $12b + 3$ G. $12b - 3$ H. $3b - 12$ I. $3b + 12$

35. Which word phrase is modeled by the algebraic expression $\frac{p}{3} + 5$?
A. 3 times the total price in dollars added to \$5
B. the total price in dollars divided by 5, plus \$3
C. \$5 more than 3 times the total price in dollars
D. \$5 more than the total price in dollars divided by 3

Take It to the NET
Online lesson quiz at **www.PHSchool.com**
Web Code aba-0205

Short Response

36. a. Write an equation for *six more than three times a number equals twenty-one*.
b. Solve your equation.

Mixed Review

Algebra **Solve each equation. Check your answer.**

Lesson 2-4

37. $\frac{t}{9} = 8$
38. $4m = 32.8$
39. $\frac{k}{-4} = -15$

Algebra **Solve each equation.**

Lesson 2-3

40. $200 + w = 725$
41. $r - 79 = 100$
42. $22 + t = -77$

Algebra

2-6 Solving Two-Step Equations

What You'll Learn

To solve two-step equations

. . . And Why

To solve problems involving the Olympics, as in Exercise 38

✔ Check Skills You'll Need

For help, go to Lesson 2-4.

Solve each equation.

1. $4b = 24$ **2.** $-4d = 20$ **3.** $-3c = -27$

4. $\frac{k}{4} = -16$ **5.** $8p = 48$ **6.** $\frac{h}{6} = -3$

7. $\frac{t}{-3} = 8$ **8.** $\frac{x}{-5} = -7$ **9.** $\frac{y}{-6} = -10$

OBJECTIVE

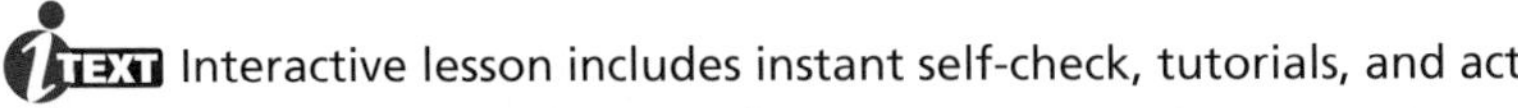

Interactive lesson includes instant self-check, tutorials, and activities.

1 Solving Two-Step Equations

In Lesson 2-5 you solved two-step equations by using number sense. Many equations are too complicated to solve by that method.

You can solve two-step equations by using inverse operations and the properties of equality to get the variable alone on one side of the equation.

Key Concepts — Solving a Two-Step Equation

Step 1 Undo addition or subtraction.

Step 2 Undo multiplication or division.

1 EXAMPLE Undoing Subtraction and Multiplication

Solve $5n - 18 = -33$.

$5n - 18 = -33$

$5n - 18 + 18 = -33 + 18$ ← To undo subtraction, add 18 to each side.

$5n = -15$ ← Simplify.

$\frac{5n}{5} = \frac{-15}{5}$ ← To undo multiplication, divide each side by 5.

$n = -3$ ← Simplify.

Check $5n - 18 = -33$ ← Check your solution with the original equation.

$5(-3) - 18 \stackrel{?}{=} -33$ ← Substitute −3 for *n*.

$-15 - 18 \stackrel{?}{=} -33$ ← Multiply.

$-33 = -33$ ✔ ← The solution checks.

✔ Check Understanding **1** Solve each equation. Check your answer.

a. $3n - 17 = 67$ **b.** $-8y - 28 = -36$ **c.** $7n - (-16) = 100$

2 EXAMPLE Undoing Addition and Division

Solve $\frac{x}{3} + 11 = 16$.

$$\frac{x}{3} + 11 = 16$$
$$\frac{x}{3} + 11 - 11 = 16 - 11 \quad \leftarrow \text{First undo addition.}$$
$$\frac{x}{3} = 5 \quad \leftarrow \text{Simplify.}$$
$$3\left(\frac{x}{3}\right) = 3(5) \quad \leftarrow \text{Then undo division.}$$
$$x = 15$$

Check Understanding 2 Solve each equation. Check your answer.

a. $\frac{x}{5} + 35 = 75$ **b.** $\frac{y}{4.25} + 15 = -17$ **c.** $\frac{d}{2} - 23 = -10$

d. Reasoning Consider the order of operations and the steps in Example 2 for solving a two-step equation. What do you notice?

More Than One Way

A family expects 85 people to attend its family reunion. There will be 13 children. Picnic tables seat 8 adults per table. The children will eat on a large blanket. How many picnic tables does the family need?

Sarah's Method

I can use number sense because the numbers are simple. First, I know that tables are needed only for adults. There are 85 − 13, or 72, adults. Each table holds 8 adults. Since 72 ÷ 8 = 9, the family needs 9 tables.

Chris's Method

I can write and solve an equation. Let t equal the number of tables. Then $8t$ is the number of adults.

adults + children = 85 people

$$8t + 13 = 85 \quad \leftarrow \text{Write the equation.}$$
$$8t + 13 - 13 = 85 - 13 \quad \leftarrow \text{Subtract 13 from each side.}$$
$$8t = 72 \quad \leftarrow \text{Simplify.}$$
$$t = 9 \quad \leftarrow 8 \cdot 9 = 72, \text{ so } t = 9.$$

The family needs 9 tables.

Choose a Method

You had $25 in your savings account seven weeks ago. You deposited the same amount of money each week for six weeks. Your balance is now $145. How much money did you deposit each week? Describe your method and explain why you chose it.

EXERCISES

For more practice, see *Extra Practice*.

A Practice by Example

Solve each equation. Check your answer. Exercise 1 has been started for you.

Example 1 (page 98)

1. $8r - 8 = -32$
$8r - 8 + 8 = -32 + 8$

2. $3w - 6 = -15$

3. $4g - 4 = 28$

4. $7t - 6 = -104$

5. $12x - 14 = -2$

6. $10m + 4 = 84$

7. $5y - 11 = 49$

8. $-2d + 17 = -39$

9. $-8a + 1 = -23$

Example 2 (page 99)

10. $\frac{w}{5} + 3 = 6$

11. $\frac{n}{4} + 2 = 4$

12. $\frac{x}{8} + 4 = 13$

13. $\frac{a}{7} + 10 = 17$

14. $\frac{m}{-11} + 1 = -10$

15. $\frac{p}{9} + 14 = 16$

16. $\frac{c}{-7} + 3 = -2$

17. $\frac{v}{-3} + 4 = -1$

18. $\frac{b}{-8} + 10 = 4$

B Apply Your Skills

Solve each equation.

19. $\frac{x}{3} - 9 = 9$

20. $3x + 6 = 12$

21. $2y + 10 = -2$

22. $10t + 10 = 90$

23. $\frac{g}{4} - 7 = -6$

24. $\frac{p}{2} - 10 = -6$

Write and solve an equation for each situation.

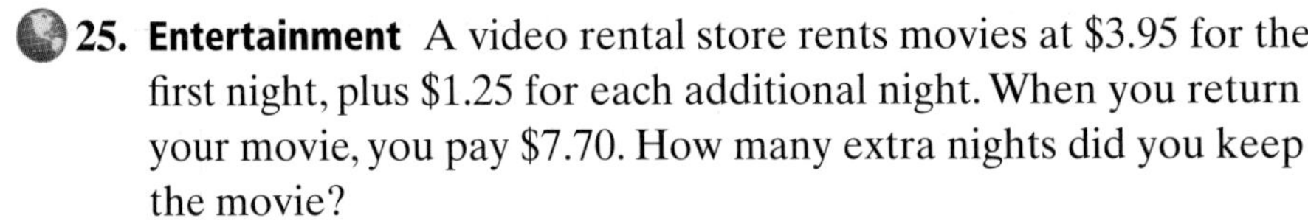

25. Entertainment A video rental store rents movies at \$3.95 for the first night, plus \$1.25 for each additional night. When you return your movie, you pay \$7.70. How many extra nights did you keep the movie?

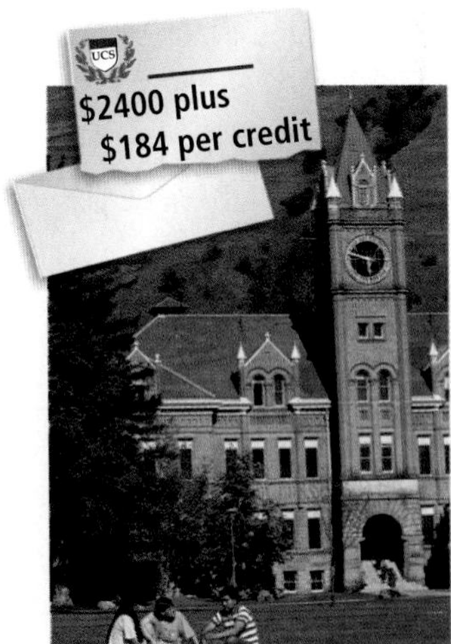

Exercise 26

26. Education To earn a college degree, you need a certain number of credits for courses taken. Tuition at a local college is \$2,400. You have \$5,160. Use the information at the left. How many credits can you take?

27. Jobs You earn \$20 per hour landscaping a yard. You pay \$1.50 in bus fare each way. How many hours must you work to end up with \$117?

Solve each equation.

28. $10h - 9 = 32$

29. $\frac{m}{-10} - 5 = 9$

30. $5t + 12 = 67$

31. $\frac{y}{-6.5} + 2 = -4$

32. $5q - 3.75 = 26.25$

33. $7.3k + 5.7 = 49.5$

34. $1.2m - 3.9 = 2.1$

35. $\frac{w}{1.02} - 3 = -5$

36. $0.5n + 3.7 = 6.12$

37. Writing in Math Your class budgets a certain amount of money from the class treasury for a dance. Expenses will include a fixed amount for decorations, plus an hourly wage for the DJ. This situation can be modeled by the equation $30x + 65 = 170$. Explain how each number and letter in the equation relates to the problem.

Write and solve an equation for each situation.

38. Olympics The first modern Olympic games were held in Greece in 1896. The 2000 Olympic games in Australia had 199 participating countries. The number of countries in the 2000 Olympic games was 4 more than 15 times the number of countries in the 1896 games. How many countries participated in the 1896 Olympic games?

39. Travel An auto rental agency offers a rate of \$38 per day plus \$.30/mile. After a one-day rental, the bill was \$74. How many miles were driven?

C Challenge

Solve each equation.

40. $\frac{x + 4}{5} = 3$ **41.** $\frac{t - 7}{-2} = 11$ **42.** $\frac{4y}{3} = 8$

43. Geometry The sum of the measures of the angles in a triangle is 180 degrees. One angle measures 45 degrees. The measures of the other two angles are equal. What are the measures of the other two angles?

44. Shopping You buy 1.25 pounds of apples and 2.45 pounds of bananas. After you use a 75¢-off coupon, the total cost is \$2.58. Apples and bananas sell for the same price per pound. Find their price per pound.

45. Stretch Your Thinking Find the value of the expression.
$1 + 1 \cdot 1 \div 1 - 1 + 1 \cdot (1 - 1) + 1$

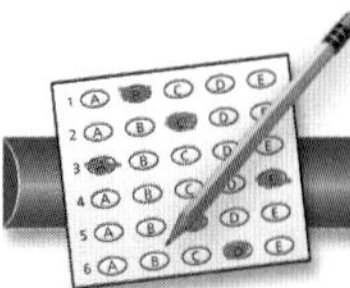

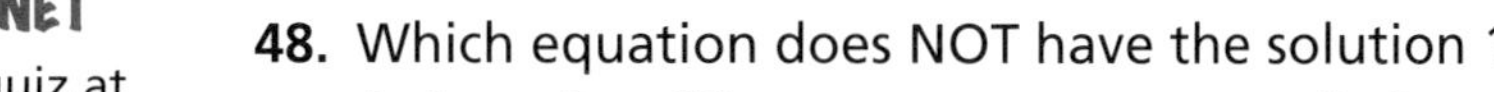

Test Prep

Multiple Choice

46. What is the solution of $4x + 8 = 24$?
A. 16 **B.** 8 **C.** 6 **D.** 4

47. What value of p makes $\frac{p}{5} - 10 = -5$ true?
F. −25 **G.** −5 **H.** 5 **I.** 25

Take It to the NET
Online lesson quiz at
www.PHSchool.com
Web Code aba-0206

48. Which equation does NOT have the solution 10?
A. $3y + 9 = 39$ **B.** $2y - 1 = 17$
C. $6y + 4 = 64$ **D.** $4y - 7 = 33$

Extended Response

49. Parts to fix your car cost \$55.35. The mechanic charges \$35 per hour for labor. The final bill is \$177.85. How long did the mechanic work on your car? Write and solve an equation. Show your work.

Mixed Review

Lesson 2-4 **Algebra** **Solve each equation.**

50. $-2x = 10$ **51.** $5y = -45$ **52.** $\frac{d}{7} = -3$ **53.** $\frac{n}{0.5} = 6$

Lesson 2-1 **Algebra** **Write a word phrase for each algebraic expression.**

54. $r + 11$ **55.** $h - 9$ **56.** $6q$ **57.** $2m + 3$

2-7 Write an Equation

What You'll Learn

To solve problems by writing equations

. . . And Why

To solve problems involving money, as in Example 1

Check Skills You'll Need

For help, go to Lesson 2-3.

Write and solve an equation for each sentence.

1. Seven fewer than a number is 12.
2. The sum of 9 and a number is equal to 36.
3. Twenty-seven is 10 less than a number.
4. Seventeen more than a number is 5.

OBJECTIVE 1

Interactive lesson includes instant self-check, tutorials, and activities.

Solving Problems by Writing Equations

When to Use This Strategy Throughout this course, you will solve real-world problems by writing and solving equations.

1 EXAMPLE Real-World Problem Solving

Tickets Suppose you have \$22.85 to spend at an amusement park. Admission costs \$12.50. How many ride tickets like the one at the right can you buy?

Read and Understand It costs \$12.50 to enter the park, plus \$.75 for every ride ticket. You have \$22.85 and need to find the number of tickets you can buy.

Plan and Solve The amount you spend cannot be more than the amount of money you have. Write an equation to solve the problem.

Words	cost of admission	plus	cost of tickets	times	number of tickets	equals	total
	Let n = the number of ride tickets you can buy.						
Equation	12.50	+	0.75	$\cdot$	n	=	22.85

$12.50 + 0.75n = 22.85$ ← Solve the equation.

$12.50 - 12.50 + 0.75n = 22.85 - 12.50$ ← Subtract 12.50 from each side.

$0.75n = 10.35$ ← Simplify.

$\frac{0.75n}{0.75} = \frac{10.35}{0.75}$ ← Divide each side by 0.75.

$n = 13.8$ ← Simplify.

Since you cannot buy 0.8 tickets, round down to a whole number. You can buy 13 ride tickets.

Look Back and Check Each ticket costs \$.75 and admission is \$12.50. The total is \$12.50 + \$.75 · 13, or \$22.25. This is \$.60 less than the amount you can spend. Since \$.60 cannot buy another ride ticket, the answer checks.

Check Understanding 1 Tulip bulbs cost \$.85 each plus \$3.25 for shipping the entire order. You have \$17 to spend on bulbs. How many bulbs can you order?

2 EXAMPLE Real-World Problem Solving

Animals An enclosure at a zoo contains both ostriches and elephants. The number of ostriches in the enclosure is 17 more than twice the number of elephants. There are 29 ostriches in the enclosure. How many elephants are there?

Real-World Connection

Ostriches live compatibly with many animals, including elephants, zebras, and giraffes.

Read and Understand Think about the information and what you are being asked to find. There are 29 ostriches. The number of ostriches is 17 more than twice the number of elephants. You need to find the number of elephants.

Plan and Solve Since you are given the relationship between the numbers, an equation can help you solve the problem.

Words	two times		number of elephants	plus seventeen	equals	number of ostriches
	Let e = the number of elephants.					
Equation	2	·	e	+ 17	=	29

$$2e + 17 = 29$$
$$2e + 17 - 17 = 29 - 17 \quad \leftarrow \text{Subtract 17 from each side.}$$
$$2e = 12 \quad \leftarrow \text{Simplify.}$$
$$\frac{2e}{2} = \frac{12}{2} \quad \leftarrow \text{Divide each side by 2.}$$
$$e = 6 \quad \leftarrow \text{Simplify.}$$

There are 6 elephants in the enclosure.

Look Back and Check To check the solution, use 6 for the number of elephants. Since $2 \cdot 6 + 17 = 12 + 17 = 29$, the answer is correct.

Check Understanding 2 A new exhibit opens that includes both harbor seals and sea otters. The number of harbor seals is 7 more than twice the number of sea otters.

a. There are 13 harbor seals in the exhibit. How many sea otters are there?

b. How does your equation change if there are 19 instead of 13 harbor seals in the exhibit?

EXERCISES

For more practice, see *Extra Practice.*

A Practice by Example

Examples 1, 2 (pages 102, 103)

Need Help?
- Reread the problem.
- Identify the key facts and details.
- Tell the problem in your own words.
- Try a different strategy.
- Check your work.

Solve each problem by writing an equation. Check your answer in the original problem.

1. **Entertainment** Lisa and Judy read mystery novels. Judy has read three fewer than five times as many as Lisa. Judy has read seventeen mysteries. How many has Lisa read?

2. A pair of boots costs $10 more than twice the cost of a pair of shoes. The boots cost $76.50. How much do the shoes cost?

3. **Money** You want to go to Africa for a photo safari. You need $2,800. You can get $1,000 from your savings and family and you can save $30 per week. How many weeks will it take you to save up for the trip?

4. **Movies** A movie ticket for an adult costs $8, and a child's ticket costs $5.50. One adult is taking a group of children to the movies. She has $35. How many children can she take with her to the movies?

5. The computer club sells 50 more than three times the number of pins the chess club sells. The computer club sells 134 pins. How many pins does the chess club sell?

B Apply Your Skills

Strategies

Draw a Diagram
Look for a Pattern
Make a Graph
Make an Organized List
Make a Table
Simulate a Problem
Solve a Simpler Problem
Try, Check, and Revise
Use Logical Reasoning
Work Backward
Write an Equation

Choose a strategy to solve each problem.

6. The band booster and the athletic booster clubs sell tickets for a fund-raiser. The band booster club sells eight more than twice the number of tickets the athletic booster club sells. The band booster club sells 280 tickets. Find the number of tickets the athletic booster club sells.

7. Ticket sales at a zoo decrease from June to December. The number of tickets sold in June is 160 more than eight times the number of tickets sold in December. The number of tickets sold in June is 80,584. Find the number of tickets sold in December.

8. **Coins** Refer to the art at the right. A quarter weighs 5.67 grams and a dime weighs 2.268 grams. There are 100 dimes. Find the number of quarters.

9. **Writing in Math** A gum tree reached a height of 150 ft in 15 years. Cathy and Darla write different equations to find the yearly average growth g of the tree. Cathy writes $15g = 150$. Darla writes $\frac{150}{15} = g$. Do these equations have the same solution? Explain.

10. **Weather** As you get ready for school, the morning weather reporter says that the temperature is expected to rise by 27°F. The high temperature is expected to be 55°F. What is the temperature now?

Kazumura Cave, Hawaii

11. Caves The deepest cave in the world is Voronja Cave in the country of Georgia. It is 5,610 ft deep. This is 1,618 ft less than twice the depth of Kazumura Cave. Find the depth of Kazumura Cave.

12. Softball This season a player scores 6 runs more than three times the number of runs she bats in. She scores 108 runs this season. How many runs does the player bat in?

13. The school choir has a fund-raiser that sells roses for \$2 each. For each rose that is sold, the choir will donate 95¢ to a children's hospital. If the choir earns \$978, how much money is donated to the hospital?

C Challenge

14. Three sisters are each less than 45 years old. The mode of their ages is 35. The range is 14. What is the mean of their ages? The median?

15. Stretch Your Thinking A survey of 40 shoppers finds that 12 like a wheat bran cereal and 23 like a crunchy cereal. Twice as many dislike both brands as like both brands. How many shoppers like both brands?

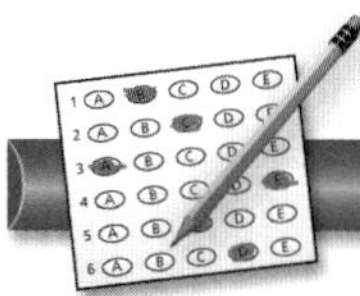

Test Prep

Multiple Choice

16. Which is an algebraic expression for 12 more than n?
A. $n - 12$ **B.** $12n$ **C.** $n + 12$ **D.** $\frac{12}{n}$

17. A container of juice contains 64 ounces. Which equation shows the remaining amount of juice left j after you have drunk d ounces?
F. $64 - d = j$ **G.** $64 + d = j$ **H.** $64d = j$ **I.** $\frac{64}{d} = j$

Take It to the NET
Online lesson quiz at
www.PHSchool.com
Web Code aba-0207

18. Evaluate $2w + 2\ell$, for $w = 3$ and $\ell = 4$.
A. 7 **B.** 10 **C.** 11 **D.** 14

Extended Response

19. A librarian has 280 returned books. Fifty of the books are reserved and kept at her desk. The remaining books are to be placed on shelves. Each shelf can hold 14 books. Define a variable. Write and solve an equation to find the number of shelves the librarian needs.

Mixed Review

Lesson 2-4

Algebra **Write an equation for each sentence. Then solve.**

20. Twice a number is 34.

21. The quotient of a number and 5 is equal to -7.

Lesson 2-1

Algebra **Evaluate each expression for $t = 4$ and $p = -2$.**

22. $3t$ **23.** $-4p$ **24.** $\frac{t}{p}$ **25.** $4p - 5$

Understanding Word Problems

For Use With Lesson 2-7

Some problems contain too much information. You need to decide which information is necessary for solving the problem. You can use the Problem-Solving Plan you learned in Lesson 1-5. Start by asking yourself "What do I know?" and "What do I need to find out?"

EXAMPLE

Identify any information not needed to solve the problem.

You have $30 to spend at a music store. You want to buy some posters to decorate your room and one new CD. New CDs cost $12.95, and used CDs cost $8.95. Posters cost $3.95 each. How many posters can you buy?

Read and Understand Read for understanding. Summarize the problem.

What do I know?

I want to buy posters and a new CD.
I have $30 to spend.
A new CD costs $12.95.
A used CD costs $8.95.
A poster costs $3.95.

What do I need to find out?

the number of posters I can buy

What information is *not* needed?

I don't want to buy a used CD, so the cost of a used CD is not needed.

Read and Understand is the first thing to do in problem solving. Once you identify the necessary information, you can *Plan and Solve* using a problem-solving strategy. For Example 1 you could ***make a table*** or ***write an equation***.

EXERCISES

For each problem, identify what you know and what you need to find out. Then identify any information *not* needed to solve the problem.

1. **Gardens** Your flower garden has 10 fewer than three times the number of plants your neighbor's flower garden has. Your flower garden has 43 plants, and your vegetable garden has 25 plants. How many plants does your neighbor's flower garden have?

2. **Tickets** The foreign language club sells 100 more than twice the number of raffle tickets the debate club sells. The chorus sells 250 tickets, and the foreign language club sells 220 tickets. How many tickets does the debate club sell?

Algebra

2-8 Graphing and Writing Inequalities

What You'll Learn

To graph inequalities

To write inequalities

. . . And Why

To write inequalities for problems involving nutrition, as in Example 4

✓ Check Skills You'll Need

For help, go to Lesson 1-6.

Compare. Use <, >, or =.

1. $0 \ \blacksquare \ -2$ **2.** $|-6| \ \blacksquare \ -3$ **3.** $14 \ \blacksquare \ -14$

4. $23 \ \blacksquare \ 0$ **5.** $-4 \ \blacksquare \ 5$ **6.** $-17 \ \blacksquare \ -18$

7. $7 \ \blacksquare \ -12$ **8.** $10 \ \blacksquare \ |-10|$ **9.** $5 \ \blacksquare \ -1$

New Vocabulary • inequality • solution of an inequality

Interactive lesson includes instant self-check, tutorials, and activities.

OBJECTIVE

1 Graphing Inequalities

Reading Math

Read > as "is greater than."

Read < as "is less than."

Read ≥ as "is greater than or equal to."

Read ≤ as "is less than or equal to."

A movie theater can hold up to 150 people, but no more than 150. You can use the inequality $p \leq 150$ to represent the capacity of the theater.

A mathematical sentence that contains $<$, $>$, $\leq$, $\geq$, or $\neq$ is an **inequality.** Sometimes an inequality contains a variable, as in $x \geq 2$.

A **solution of an inequality** is any value that makes the inequality true. The solution of an inequality can include many numbers. For example, 6, 8, and 15 are solutions of $x \geq 6$ because $6 \geq 6$, $8 \geq 6$, and $15 \geq 6$.

1 EXAMPLE Identifying Solutions of an Inequality

Find whether each number is a solution of $x \leq 2$: $-3, 0, 2, 4.5$.

$-3 \leq 2$	$0 \leq 2$	$2 \leq 2$	$4.5 \leq 2$	← **Replace *x* with each number.**
↑	↑	↑	↑	
true	**true**	**true**	**false**	

The numbers $-3, 0, 2$ are solutions of $x \leq 2$. The number 4.5 is not a solution of $x \leq 2$.

✓ Check Understanding **1** Which numbers are solutions of each inequality?

a. $m \geq -3$: $-8, -2, 1$

b. $w < -4$: $-6, -4, -1, 2$

c. **Reasoning** Is $-4 \geq -4$? Explain.

A graph can show all the numbers in a solution.

2 EXAMPLE Graphing Inequalities

Graph the solution of each inequality.

a. $n \geq -3$

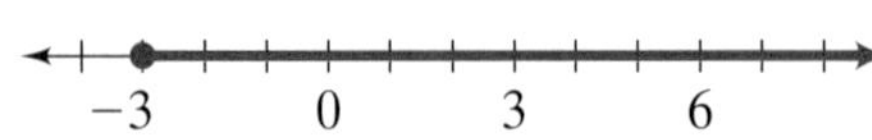

Use a closed circle at −3 to show that n can equal −3.

b. $x \leq -1$

Use a closed circle at −1 to show that x can equal −1.

c. $p > -2$

−4 −2 0 2 4 6 8

Use an open circle at −2 to show that p cannot equal −2.

d. $h < 7$

Use an open circle at 7 to show that h cannot equal 7.

Check Understanding 2 Graph the solution of each inequality.

a. $x \leq 5$ **b.** $w < -3$ **c.** $y > -4$ **d.** $g \geq 1$

OBJECTIVE

2 Writing Inequalities

You can write an inequality by analyzing its graph.

3 EXAMPLE Writing Inequalities

Write an inequality for each graph.

a. −4 −2 0 2 4 6 ←Since the circle at 2 is open, use < or >.

$x > 2$ ←Since the graph shows values greater than 2, use >.

b. −4 −2 0 2 4 6 ←Since the circle at 2 is closed, use ≤ or ≥.

$x \leq 2$ ←Since the graph shows values equal to or less than 2, use ≤.

Check Understanding 3 Write an inequality for each graph.

a.

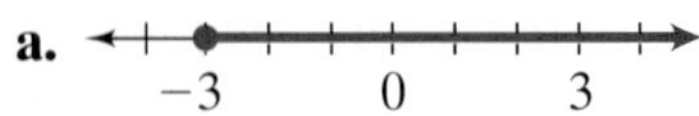

b.

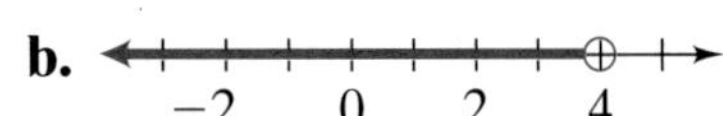

You can write inequalities to describe real-world situations. Two expressions that get confused in real-world situations are *at most* and *at least*.

At most means "less than or equal to."
A number is at most twenty translates to the inequality $x \leq 20$.

At least means "greater than or equal to."
Your salary is at least \$8.50/hour translates to the inequality $x \geq 8.50$.

Real-World Connection

The nutrition label on a food product tells you its sugar content.

4 EXAMPLE Real-World Problem Solving

Nutrition To be labeled sugar-free, a food product must contain less than 0.5 g of sugar per serving. Write an inequality to describe this requirement.

Words	amount of sugar	is less than	0.5 g of sugar
↓	Let s = the number of grams of sugar in a serving of food.		
Inequality	s	$<$	0.5

The inequality is $s < 0.5$.

✓ Check Understanding 4 Write an inequality for "To qualify for the race, your time can be at most 32 seconds."

EXERCISES

For more practice, see *Extra Practice*.

A Practice by Example

Example 1 (page 107)

Which numbers are solutions of each inequality? Exercise 1 has been started for you.

1. $x < 1$: $-2, 1, 2$
$-2 < 1$ true

2. $x > -5$: $-7, -5, -1$

3. $x \leq -9$: $-12, -4, 2$

4. $x < -8$: $-10, -5, 0$

5. $x \geq -4$: $-6, -1, 0$

6. $x \leq -1$: $-1, 1, 3$

Example 2 (page 108)

Graph the solution of each inequality.

7. $x \geq 4$ **8.** $x \leq -2$ **9.** $x < 2$ **10.** $x > -4$

11. $x \leq 0$ **12.** $h > -5$ **13.** $t \geq -5$ **14.** $p < -6$

Example 3 (page 108)

Write an inequality for each graph.

15. 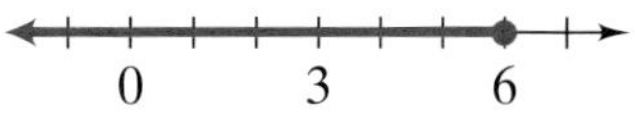

16. 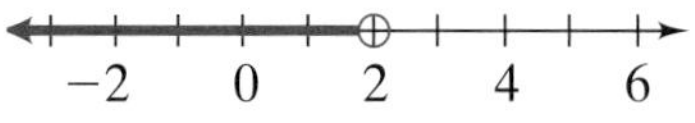

17. 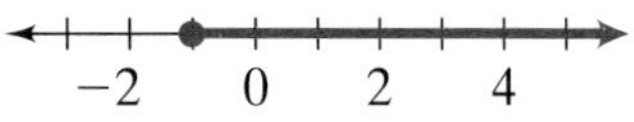

18. 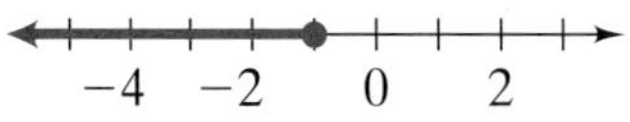

Example 4 (page 109)

Write an inequality for each statement.

19. The car ride to the park will take at least 30 minutes.

20. The space shuttle can carry more than 38,000 pounds.

Write an inequality for each statement.

21. The speed limit on the highway is at most 65 mi/h.

22. Today your break will be shorter than 15 minutes.

B Apply Your Skills

Which numbers are solutions of each inequality?

23. $3x > -5$: $-2, -1, 1, 2$

24. $x + 2 \leq -9$: $-12, -10, -8, -6$

25. $x - 4 \geq -2$: $-3, -1, 1, 3$

26. $\frac{x}{4} < 5$: $-8, -4, 4, 8$

Use a variable to write an inequality for each situation.

27.

28.

29.

30. **Data File, p. 69** Write an inequality describing the height of a toy poodle.

Write an inequality for each statement. Graph the solution.

31. A song's duration is less than 5 minutes long.

32. The temperature is over 100°F.

33. To enter the movie, you must be at least 17 years old.

34. The shelf can hold at most 250 pounds.

35. A number p is not positive.

36. A number n is not negative.

Reading Math

Not positive means a number is less than or equal to zero.

37. **Writing in Math** Explain how you know whether to draw an open or closed circle when you graph an inequality.

38. **Reasoning** Explain why $-17 > -22$.

C Challenge

Identify an integer that is a solution for the *compound inequality*.

39. $-3 \leq x < 0$

40. $-2 < y \leq 1$

41. $-6 \leq p \leq -4$

Complete each statement using <, >, ≤, or ≥.

42. If $a < b$, then b ■ a.

43. If $a \geq 9$ and $9 \geq b$, then a ■ b.

44. **Stretch Your Thinking** During basketball season, each basketball team in a 10-team conference plays every team at home. How many conference basketball games are played in a season?

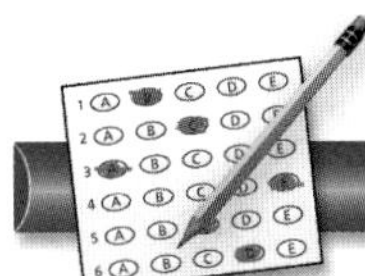

Test Prep

Multiple Choice

45. Which inequality represents *p is at least* -3?

A. $-3 < p$ **B.** $-3 \geq p$ **C.** $p < -3$ **D.** $p \geq -3$

46. Which inequality does NOT have 8 as a solution?

F. $-3 < y$ **G.** $13 \geq y$ **H.** $y < 8$ **I.** $y \geq 8$

Take It to the NET
Online lesson quiz at **www.PHSchool.com**
Web Code aba-0208

47. Which inequality is graphed below?

$-2 \quad 0 \quad 2 \quad 4 \quad 6$

A. $5 < x$ **B.** $5 \geq x$ **C.** $x < 5$ **D.** $x \geq 5$

Short Response

48. A farmer needs no less than 20 lb of seeds to plant a crop. Write an inequality for this situation. Then graph the inequality.

Mixed Review

Lesson 2-4

Algebra **Solve each equation.**

49. $\frac{p}{-5} = -8$ **50.** $\frac{n}{16} = -10$ **51.** $\frac{c}{-5} = 3.5$ **52.** $\frac{k}{3} = -41.5$

53. $208 = -8m$ **54.** $2d = 2.36$ **55.** $91 = -7a$ **56.** $4u = 112$

Lesson 1-6

Order the numbers from least to greatest.

57. $-2, 4, -4, 2, 7, -1$ **58.** $3, -8, -9, 12, -6$ **59.** $10, 0, -5, -2, 7$

Checkpoint Quiz 2 — Lessons 2-5 through 2-8

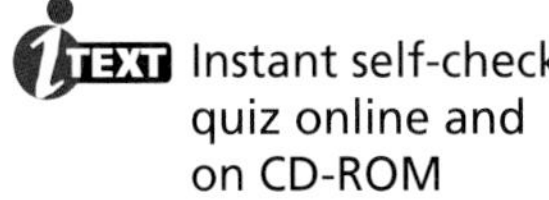

Instant self-check quiz online and on CD-ROM

Solve each equation.

1. $3x + 4 = 19$ **2.** $\frac{t}{5} - 2 = 6$

3. $-2y - 5 = -9$ **4.** $\frac{d}{-3} + 7 = 10$

Write an equation. Then solve.

5. Six less than twice a number is 10.

6. A sweater costs $12 more than twice the cost of a skirt. The sweater costs $38. Find the cost of the skirt.

Graph each inequality.

7. $x > 3$ **8.** $y \leq -2$ **9.** $d \geq -1$ **10.** $h < 6$

Algebra

2-9 Solving Inequalities by Adding or Subtracting

What You'll Learn

 To solve inequalities by adding

 To solve inequalities by subtracting

. . . And Why

To solve fishing problems, as in Example 3

✓ Check Skills You'll Need

For help, go to Lesson 2-3.

Solve each equation.

1. $c + 4 = -2$ **2.** $x + 9 = 10$ **3.** $b + (-2) = 7$

4. $g - 5 = 10$ **5.** $w - 4 = 12$ **6.** $m - (-3) = 10$

New Vocabulary

- **Addition Property of Inequality**
- **Subtraction Property of Inequality**

OBJECTIVE

Interactive lesson includes instant self-check, tutorials, and activities.

1 Solving Inequalities by Adding

You can solve inequalities using properties similar to those you used when solving equations.

If you add 3 to each side of the inequality $-3 < 2$, the resulting inequality $0 < 5$ is also true.

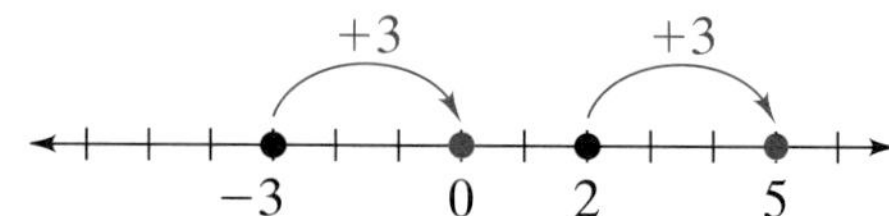

Key Concepts **Addition Property of Inequality**

You can add the same value to each side of an inequality.

Arithmetic	Algebra
Since $7 > 3, 7 + 4 > 3 + 4$.	If $a > b$, then $a + c > b + c$.
Since $1 < 3, 1 + 4 < 3 + 4$.	If $a < b$, then $a + c < b + c$.

1 EXAMPLE Solving Inequalities by Adding

Need Help?
For help with graphing inequalities, see p. 108.

Solve $n - 10 > 14$. Graph the solution.

$n - 10 > 14$

$n - 10 + 10 > 14 + 10$ ← **Add 10 to each side.**

$n > 24$ ← **Simplify.**

−8 0 8 16 24 32

Check Understanding 1 Solve each inequality. Graph the solution.

a. $x - 9 > 5$ **b.** $y - 3 < 4$ **c.** $w - 4 \leq -5$

OBJECTIVE

2 Solving Inequalities by Subtracting

To solve an inequality involving addition, use subtraction.

Key Concepts **Subtraction Property of Inequality**

You can subtract the same value from each side of an inequality.

Arithmetic	Algebra
Since $9 > 6, 9 - 3 > 6 - 3$.	If $a > b$, then $a - c > b - c$.
Since $15 < 20, 15 - 4 < 20 - 4$.	If $a < b$, then $a - c < b - c$.

Note: The Properties of Inequality also apply to $\leq$ and $\geq$.

2 EXAMPLE Solving Inequalities by Subtracting

Solve $y + 7 \geq 12$. Graph the solution.

$$y + 7 \geq 12$$

$$y + 7 - 7 \geq 12 - 7 \quad \leftarrow \text{Subtract 7 from each side.}$$

$$y \geq 5 \quad \leftarrow \text{Simplify.}$$

−2 0 2 4 6 8 10

Check Understanding 2 Solve each inequality. Graph the solution.

a. $x + 9 > 5$ **b.** $y + 3 < 4$ **c.** $w + 4 \leq -5$

d. **Reasoning** What value is a solution of $y + 7 \geq 12$ but is not a solution of $y + 7 > 12$?

Real-World Connection

In some states, children under 12 years old must be accompanied by a licensed adult in order to fish.

3 EXAMPLE Real-World Problem Solving

Fishing To win a two-day fishing tournament, you need to catch at least 25 fish. You catch 8 on the first day. How many more do you need to catch?

Words	number caught on first day	plus	number caught on second day	is at least	25
	Let c = the number you need to catch on the second day.				
Inequality	8	$+$	c	$\geq$	25

$$8 + c \geq 25$$

$$8 - 8 + c \geq 25 - 8 \quad \leftarrow \text{Subtract 8 from each side.}$$

$$c \geq 17 \quad \leftarrow \text{Simplify.}$$

You need to catch at least 17 more fish.

Check Understanding 3 To get an A, you need more than 200 points on a two-part test. You score 109 points on the first part. How many more points do you need?

EXERCISES

For more practice, see *Extra Practice*.

Practice by Example

Example 1 (page 112)

Solve each inequality. Graph the solution. Exercise 1 has been started for you.

1. $h - 19 < 15$
$h - 19 + 19 < 15 + 19$

2. $w - 14 \geq -3$

3. $a - 7 < 2$

4. $g - 2 \leq -8$

5. $m - 3 > -24$

6. $y - 5 \geq 11$

7. $x - 7 > -11$

8. $n - 10 \leq 17$

9. $p - 9 < -9$

Example 2 (page 113)

10. $j + 6 > 12$

11. $k + 4 < 3$

12. $x + 5 \geq 8$

13. $h + 8 < -13$

14. $n + 3 \geq 4$

15. $r + 9 > 4$

16. $p + 10 \leq 6$

17. $b + 22 > -1$

18. $f + 5 \geq 0$

Example 3 (page 113)

Write an inequality for each problem. Solve the inequality.

19. Movies A theater can hold at most 225 people. The theater has already admitted 132 people. How many more people can the theater admit?

20. Tests A test's total score is the sum of the scores for the multiple-choice section and the essay section. To qualify for a scholarship, you need a total score of at least 2,000. Your multiple-choice score is 1,090. What essay score do you need to qualify for the scholarship?

21. Weight The weight of a loaded dump truck must be less than 75,000 lb. An empty truck weighs 32,000 lb. What can the truck's load weigh?

Apply Your Skills

Solve each inequality.

22. $d + 0.25 \leq 2.75$

23. $c + 0.2 < -4.4$

24. $x - 0.6 > 4.8$

25. $t - 0.775 \geq 6.225$

26. $8.5 + m \leq 4$

27. $n - 3.35 \geq -5$

28. $10 > y + 11$

29. $-5 \leq w - 7$

30. $12.5 < b - 8.25$

Real-World Connection

The long jump record for junior women is 7.14 m, or 23 ft 5.25 in.

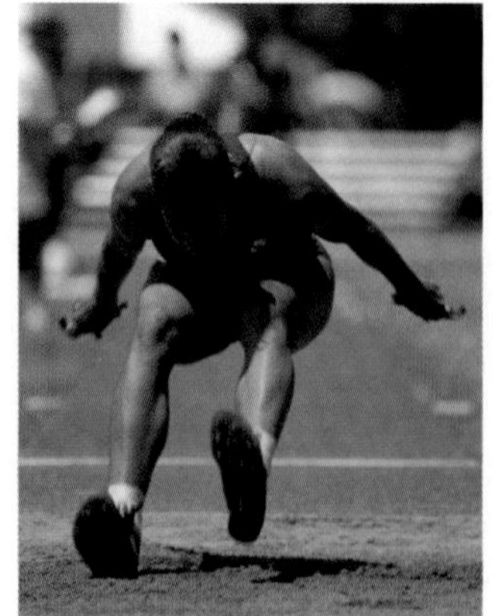

Write an inequality for each problem. Solve the inequality.

31. Sports To win the long jump, you need to jump a distance greater than 2.25 m. Your personal best jump is 2.1 m. How much farther do you need to jump to win?

32. Consumer Issues Your parents give you \$35 for a scooter that costs at least \$100. How much money do you have to save to buy the scooter?

Write an inequality for each sentence. Then solve the inequality.

33. Fifteen plus a number is greater than 10.

34. The sum of a number and 2 is at most 7.

35. The difference of a number and 6 is at most -7.

36. Reasoning Are the solutions of the inequalities $x + 5 \leq -2$ and $-2 \leq x + 5$ the same? Explain.

37. **Amusement Park** A ride at an amusement park requires a height of at least 48 in. Your little brother is 37 in. tall. How many inches must he grow in order to go on the ride?

38. Writing in Math The basketball team needs to score at least 420 points this season in order to set a new school record. It has already scored 82 points. Four players argue about which inequality represents the number of points yet to be scored: $p \geq 338$, $338 \geq p$, $p > 338$, or $338 > p$. Which inequality is correct? Explain.

C Challenge

39. **Nutrition** You want to eat no more than 3,000 Calories in a day. You consume 710 Calories for breakfast and 1,050 Calories at lunch. How many Calories can you consume at dinner?

40. An inequality can have more than one inequality symbol. Solve the inequality $-3 \leq x + 4 < 9$.

41. Stretch Your Thinking The first ten counting numbers are arranged in a triangular array like the one at the right. In what row will the number 50 appear?

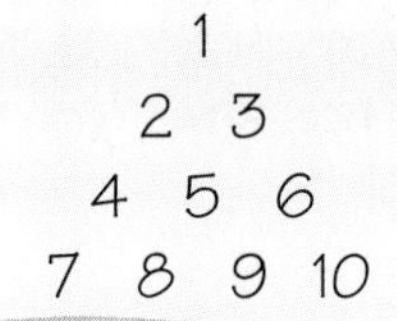

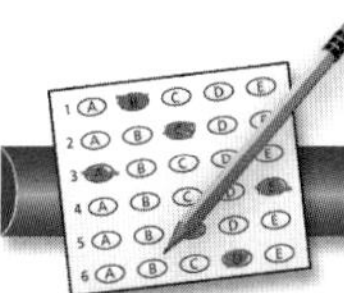

Test Prep

Multiple Choice

42. Which inequality has the solution $h > 12$?
A. $h + 13 > 1$
B. $h - 19 \leq -7$
C. $h - 24 < -12$
D. $h + 17 > 29$

43. Choose the inequality that best represents this sentence: The price is no less than $60.
F. $p \geq 60$
G. $p \leq 60$
H. $p < 60$
I. $p > 60$

Take It to the NET
Online lesson quiz at www.PHSchool.com
Web Code aba-0209

44. Solve the inequality $14 < 15 + m$.
A. $m > 29$
B. $m > -1$
C. $m < 29$
D. $m < -1$

Short Response

45. Write and solve a problem that can be represented by $x + 3 \geq 18$.

Mixed Review

Lesson 2-8

Algebra **Write an inequality for each statement.**

46. The auditorium can hold at most 250 students.

47. The number of runners in the marathon is less than 125.

Lesson 2-3

48. Algebra A pair of shoes costs $15 less than a pair of boots. The shoes cost $57.95. Write and solve an equation to find the cost of the boots.

Algebra

2-10 Solving Inequalities by Multiplying or Dividing

What You'll Learn

To solve inequalities by dividing

To solve inequalities by multiplying

. . . And Why

To calculate a maximum weight, as in Example 1

Check Skills You'll Need

For help, go to Lesson 2-4.

Solve each equation.

1. $3x = 15$ **2.** $-2p = 20$ **3.** $6w = -24$

4. $\frac{d}{5} = 8$ **5.** $\frac{r}{-2} = -8$ **6.** $\frac{n}{4} = -7$

New Vocabulary

- **Division Property of Inequality**
- **Multiplication Property of Inequality**

OBJECTIVE

Interactive lesson includes instant self-check, tutorials, and activities.

1 Solving Inequalities by Dividing

Investigation: Exploring Inequalities

Explore what happens to an inequality when you divide each side by the same number. Consider the inequality $-8 < 4$.

1. Copy and complete each statement at the right by replacing each ■ with $<$ or $>$.
2. What happens to the direction of the inequality symbol when you divide by a positive number?
3. What happens to the direction of the inequality symbol when you divide by a negative number?
4. Write a rule for dividing each side of an inequality by a negative.

$-8 \;■\; 4$

$\frac{-8}{4} \;■\; \frac{4}{4}$

$\frac{-8}{2} \;■\; \frac{4}{2}$

$\frac{-8}{-2} \;■\; \frac{4}{-2}$

$\frac{-8}{-4} \;■\; \frac{4}{-4}$

Look at the pattern you get when you divide each side of an inequality by an integer.

When the integer is positive, the direction of the inequality symbol stays the same.

$18 > 12$

$\frac{18}{6} > \frac{12}{6}$

$\frac{18}{3} > \frac{12}{3}$

$\frac{18}{-2} < \frac{12}{-2}$

$\frac{18}{-6} < \frac{12}{-6}$

When the integer is negative, the direction of the inequality symbol is reversed.

Key Concepts — Division Property of Inequality

If you divide each side of an inequality by the same positive number, the direction of the inequality symbol remains unchanged.

Arithmetic	Algebra
$9 > 6$, so $\frac{9}{3} > \frac{6}{3}$.	If $a > b$, and c is positive, then $\frac{a}{c} > \frac{b}{c}$.
$15 < 20$, so $\frac{15}{5} < \frac{20}{5}$.	If $a < b$, and c is positive, then $\frac{a}{c} < \frac{b}{c}$.

If you divide each side of an inequality by the same negative number, the direction of the inequality symbol is reversed.

Arithmetic	Algebra
$16 > 12$, so $\frac{16}{-4} < \frac{12}{-4}$.	If $a > b$, and c is negative, then $\frac{a}{c} < \frac{b}{c}$.
$10 < 18$, so $\frac{10}{-2} > \frac{18}{-2}$.	If $a < b$, and c is negative, then $\frac{a}{c} > \frac{b}{c}$.

You can solve an inequality that involves multiplication by dividing each side of the inequality by the same number.

1 EXAMPLE — Real-World  Problem Solving

Machinery A forklift can safely carry a load of up to 6,000 lb. A case of paint weighs 70 lb. At most how many cases of paint can the forklift safely carry at one time?

Words	number of cases	times	weight of one case	is at most	total weight
	Let p = the number of cases of paint.				
Inequality	p	$\cdot$	70	$\le$	6,000

$$70p \le 6{,}000$$
$$\frac{70p}{70} \le \frac{6{,}000}{70} \quad \leftarrow \text{Divide each side by 70.}$$
$$p \le 85.71428571 \quad \leftarrow \text{Simplify.}$$
$$p \le 85 \quad \leftarrow \text{Round the answer down to find a whole number.}$$

At most, the forklift can safely carry 85 cases of paint.

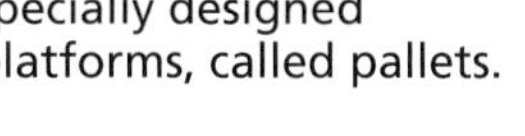

Real-World Connection Forklifts pick up loads on specially designed platforms, called pallets.

Check Understanding 1

a. Check the answer to Example 1. Is it reasonable?

b. **Reasoning** Change the words of Example 1 so the corresponding inequality uses $<$ instead of $\le$.

c. A long-distance telephone company is offering a special rate of 6¢ per minute. Your budget for long-distance telephone calls is $25 for the month. At most how many minutes of long distance can you use for the month?

2 EXAMPLE Solving Inequalities by Dividing

Solve $-3y \leq -27$. Graph the solution.

$-3y \leq -27$

$\frac{-3y}{-3} \geq \frac{-27}{-3}$ ← Divide each side by −3. Reverse the direction of the symbol.

$y \geq 9$ ← Simplify.

−12 −6 0 6 12 18

Check Understanding 2 Solve each inequality. Graph the solution.

a. $-4p < 36$ **b.** $-8m \geq -24$ **c.** $7n > -21$

OBJECTIVE

2 Solving Inequalities by Multiplying

You can solve an inequality that involves division by multiplying each side of the inequality by the same number.

Key Concepts Multiplication Property of Inequality

If you multiply each side of an inequality by the same positive number, the direction of the inequality symbol remains unchanged.

Arithmetic	Algebra
$12 > 8$, so $12 \cdot 2 > 8 \cdot 2$.	If $a > b$, and c is positive, then $a \cdot c > b \cdot c$.
$3 < 6$, so $3 \cdot 4 < 6 \cdot 4$.	If $a < b$, and c is positive, then $a \cdot c < b \cdot c$.

If you multiply each side of an inequality by the same negative number, the direction of the inequality symbol is reversed.

Arithmetic	Algebra
$6 > 2$, so $6(-3) < 2(-3)$.	If $a > b$, and c is negative, then $a \cdot c < b \cdot c$.
$3 < 5$, so $3(-2) > 5(-2)$.	If $a < b$, and c is negative, then $a \cdot c > b \cdot c$.

3 EXAMPLE Solving Inequalities by Multiplying

Solve $\frac{y}{-8} \geq 2$.

$\frac{y}{-8} \geq 2$

$-8 \cdot \frac{y}{-8} \leq -8 \cdot 2$ ← Multiply each side by −8. Reverse the direction of the symbol.

$y \leq -16$ ← Simplify.

Check Understanding 3 Solve each inequality.

a. $\frac{k}{-5} < -4$ **b.** $\frac{p}{-7} \geq 6$ **c.** $\frac{m}{9} \leq -6$

EXERCISES

For more practice, see *Extra Practice*.

A Practice by Example

Write an inequality to solve each problem. Then solve the inequality.

Example 1 (page 117)

1. A photo album page can hold six photographs. You have 296 photographs for the album. How many pages do you need?

2. A 1-ton (T) truck has the ability to haul 1 T, or 2,000 lb. At most how many refrigerators can the truck carry, if each one weighs 320 lb?

3. **Baking** A recipe for an apple pie calls for 6 apples per pie. You have 27 apples. At most how many apple pies can you make?

Example 2 (page 118)

Solve each inequality. Graph the solution.

4. $4h < 16$
5. $3p > 36$
6. $9n \leq -27$
7. $6x < -48$
8. $-8b \geq -24$
9. $-5w \leq 30$
10. $-2t > 10$
11. $-10d \geq -70$

Example 3 (page 118)

12. $\frac{p}{5} < -3$
13. $\frac{k}{4} \geq 6$
14. $\frac{w}{7} \leq -3$
15. $\frac{y}{7} > -8$
16. $\frac{n}{-2} > -5$
17. $\frac{m}{-6} \leq 5$
18. $\frac{x}{10} < -4$
19. $\frac{c}{-5} \geq -2$

B Apply Your Skills

Solve each inequality.

20. $9 < -9x$
21. $-25 > \frac{t}{-2}$
22. $-56 \leq -8p$
23. $-10 > \frac{h}{3}$

24. **Rides** A roller coaster can carry 36 people per run. At least how many times does the roller coaster have to run to allow 10,000 people to ride?

Solve each inequality.

25. $-4.9 < -7g$
26. $-3.15 > \frac{t}{-3}$
27. $-0.8n \leq -5.6$
28. $\frac{t}{3.45} > -100$

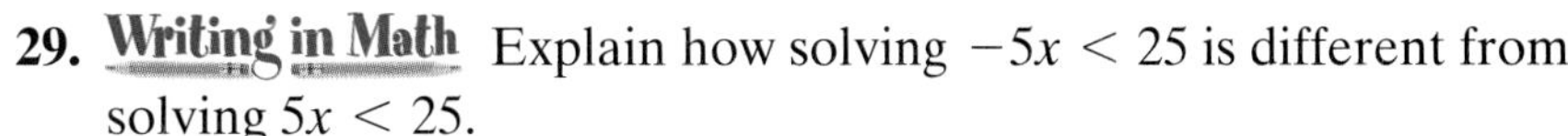

29. **Writing in Math** Explain how solving $-5x < 25$ is different from solving $5x < 25$.

30. **Error Analysis** A student solves the inequality $5n > -25$. He says the solution is $n < -5$. Explain the student's error.

Consumer Issues Use the art at the left for Exercises 31–33. You have $15.

31. At most how many hot dogs can you buy?

32. At most how many bags of peanuts can you buy?

33. You buy two hot dogs. How many bags of peanuts can you buy? How much change will you get?

34. **Reasoning** Solve and graph $-18 \geq -2y$ and $-2y < -18$. Are the solutions the same? Explain.

Write an inequality for each sentence. Solve the inequality.

35. The product of -3 and a number is greater than 12.

36. A number multiplied by 4 is at most -44.

37. A number divided by -9 is less than 10.

38. The quotient of a number and 5 is at least -8.

C Challenge

Solve each inequality.

39. $-2x + 3 < 7$ **40.** $4 - 3y > 13$ **41.** $\frac{t}{-4} + 3 \leq 5$

42. Ten more than -3 times a number is greater than 19. Solve the inequality. Graph the solution.

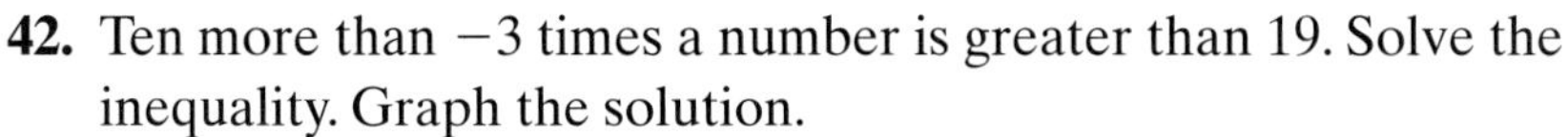

43. **Stretch Your Thinking** Amy, Ben, and Charley live in three neighboring houses on the same street. Their houses are brown, white, and green. Amy does not live in the brown house. Charley's house is white and is next to Amy's house. Ben's house is next to the green house. What color is Amy's house? Where does Amy live in relationship to Ben and Charley?

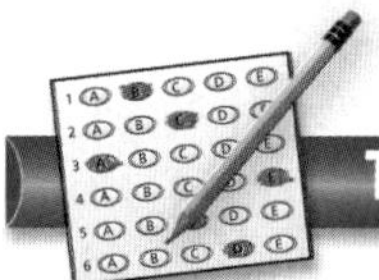

Test Prep

Multiple Choice

44. Shares of stock for a computer company cost \$12.75 per share. At most how many shares of stock can you buy if you have \$1,950?
A. 15 **B.** 16 **C.** 152 **D.** 153

45. If $x > y$, which statement is NOT always true?
F. $y < x$ **G.** $x - z > y - z$ **H.** $x + z > y + z$ **I.** $xz > yz$

Take It to the NET
Online lesson quiz at
www.PHSchool.com
Web Code aba-0210

46. Which inequality has the same solutions as $\frac{b}{8} > -20$?
A. $4n < -80$ **B.** $\frac{k}{-4} > 40$ **C.** $\frac{w}{2} < -80$ **D.** $\frac{y}{-16} < 10$

Short Response

47. No more than 50 students participated in a race. Let s represent the number of students. **(a)** Determine which of these numbers are possible values for s: 42, 46.5, 50, and 55. **(b)** Explain why some of the numbers work, while others do not.

Mixed Review

Lesson 2-9

Algebra **Solve each inequality.**

48. $k - 13 < 12$ **49.** $m + 4 \geq -5$ **50.** $y - 7 < 1$ **51.** $h + 19 > 11$

Lesson 2-4

Algebra **Solve each equation.**

52. $-6h = -18$ **53.** $\frac{p}{7} = -8$ **54.** $12w = -24$ **55.** $\frac{g}{-9} = -6$

Test-Taking Strategies: Writing Short Responses

Short-response questions are usually worth a maximum of 2 points. To get full credit you need to give the correct answer, including appropriate units. You may also need to show your work or justify your reasoning.

EXAMPLE

The cost for using a phone card is 45¢ per call plus 5¢ per minute. A recent call cost \$2.05. **(a)** Write an equation to find the length of the call. **(b)** Solve your equation.

To get full credit you must use a variable to set up an equation, solve the equation, and find the length of the call. Below is a scoring guide that shows the number of points awarded for different answers.

Scoring

[2] The equation and the solution are correct. The call took 32 minutes.

[1] There is no equation, but there is a method to show that the call took 32 minutes.

or There is an equation and a solution, both of which may contain minor errors.

[0] There is no response, or the response is completely incorrect.

Three responses are shown below with the points each one received.

2 points

Let m represent the number of minutes.

$205 = 45 + 5m$
$160 = 5m$
$32 = m$

The call took 32 minutes.

1 point

$\frac{2.05 - 0.45}{0.05}$

32 minutes

0 points

30 minutes

EXERCISES

Use the scoring guide above to answer each question.

1. Explain why each response above received the indicated points.
2. Write a 2-point response that includes the equation $0.05n + 0.45 = 2.05$.

Chapter 2

Chapter Review

Vocabulary

algebraic expression (p. 71)
equation (p. 77)
inequality (p. 107)
inverse operations (p. 83)
open sentence (p. 77)
solution of an equation (p. 77)
solution of an inequality (p. 107)
variable (p. 71)

Reading Math: Understanding Vocabulary

Match each phrase to its corresponding term.

1. a letter that represents numbers
2. a value that makes an equation true
3. a mathematical sentence with an equal sign
4. an equation with one or more variables
5. a value that makes an inequality true

A. inverse operations
B. solution of an equation
C. equation
D. inequality
E. variable
F. open sentence
G. solution of an inequality
H. algebraic expression

Take It to the NET
Online vocabulary quiz at www.PHSchool.com
Web Code: abj-0251

Skills and Concepts

2-1 Objectives

- To evaluate algebraic expressions
- To write algebraic expressions

A **variable** is a letter that stands for a number. An **algebraic expression** is a mathematical phrase that uses variables, numbers, and operation symbols. To evaluate an expression, substitute a given value for each variable and simplify.

Evaluate each expression for $n = 3, p = 5$, and $w = 2$.

6. $3n - 2w$ **7.** $\frac{4n}{w}$ **8.** $p + 4w$ **9.** $7w - 2p$

10. Profit A store makes a \$5.50 profit on each CD. Write an algebraic expression for the profit the store makes for the number of CDs it sells.

2-2 Objective

- To solve one-step equations using number sense

An **equation** is a mathematical sentence with an equal sign. An equation with one or more variables is an **open sentence**. A **solution** is a value for a variable that makes an equation true.

Use number sense to solve each equation.

11. $p + 5 = -2$ **12.** $m - 12 = 8$ **13.** $7t = 28$ **14.** $\frac{w}{8} = 9$

15. $h - 8 = 15$ **16.** $10x = 50$ **17.** $\frac{t}{7} = 5$ **18.** $n - 10 = 11$

2-3 and 2-4 Objectives

- To solve equations by adding
- To solve equations by subtracting
- To solve equations by dividing
- To solve equations by multiplying

Whatever you do to one side of an equation, you must also do to the other side of the equation. To solve a one-step equation, use **inverse operations**.

Use inverse operations to solve each equation.

19. $y + 14 = 38$ **20.** $p - 12 = 72$ **21.** $\frac{m}{11} = 9$ **22.** $-7b = 84$

23. $x - 8 = 44$ **24.** $12h = 60$ **25.** $k - 14 = 29$ **26.** $\frac{n}{6} = -9$

2-5 and 2-6 Objectives

- To write and evaluate expressions with two operations
- To solve two-step equations using number sense
- To solve two-step equations

You can also use inverse operations to solve two-step equations. Begin by undoing addition or subtraction, and then undo multiplication or division.

Solve each equation.

27. $4d + 7 = 11$ **28.** $2m - 21 = 3$ **29.** $-5y + 8 = 23$

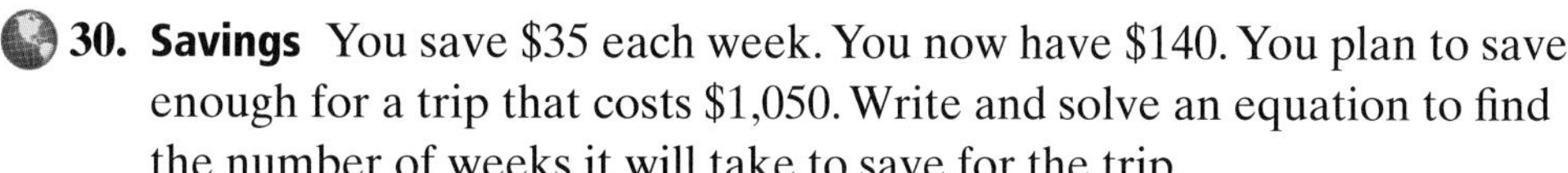

30. Savings You save $35 each week. You now have $140. You plan to save enough for a trip that costs $1,050. Write and solve an equation to find the number of weeks it will take to save for the trip.

2-7 Objective

- To solve problems by writing equations

Often you can write an equation to solve a problem.

31. Band A band made a profit of $352 from a concert. The band sold 116 tickets and spent $25 on advertising. How much did each ticket cost?

2-8 Objectives

- To graph inequalities
- To write inequalities

A mathematical sentence that contains $<, >, \leq, \geq$, or $\neq$ is called an **inequality**. A **solution of an inequality** is any number that makes an inequality true. When graphing, use an open circle for $>$ and $<$, and use a closed circle for $\geq$ and $\leq$.

Write an inequality for each statement. Then graph the inequality.

32. The ticket is at most $10. **33.** The race is less than 5 miles.

2-9 and 2-10 Objectives

- To solve inequalities by adding
- To solve inequalities by subtracting
- To solve inequalities by dividing
- To solve inequalities by multiplying

You solve inequalities just as you solve equations, but with one exception. When you multiply or divide by a negative number, you must reverse the direction of the inequality symbol.

Solve each inequality. Then graph your solution.

34. $h + 7 < -15$ **35.** $n + 11 \leq 12$ **36.** $g - 14 > 3$ **37.** $t - 9 \geq -19$

38. $-4m \leq 28$ **39.** $3p < -12$ **40.** $\frac{p}{5} \geq -3$ **41.** $\frac{x}{-7} > -2$

Chapter Test

Online chapter test at **www.PHSchool.com**
Web Code: aba-0252

Evaluate each expression for $n = 3, t = -2$, and $y = 4$.

1. $3n + 2t$ **2.** $5y - 4n$ **3.** $2(n + 3y)$

4. $ny - 6$ **5.** $\frac{2ny}{t}$ **6.** $-2t + 6n$

Solve each equation.

7. $x + 7 = 12$ **8.** $m - 3 = 6$

9. $13 + d = 44$ **10.** $p - 18 = 62$

11. $5n = 45$ **12.** $\frac{h}{7} = 8$

13. $-8t = 24$ **14.** $\frac{k}{-4} = -12$

15. $14 + 3n = 8$ **16.** $9h - 21 = 24$

17. $\frac{w}{5} - 10 = -4$ **18.** $14 + \frac{y}{8} = 10$

Define a variable. Then write and solve an equation for each problem.

19. Masonry A mason is laying a brick foundation 72 in. wide. Each brick is 6 in. wide. How many bricks will the mason need along the width of the foundation?

20. Groceries You buy 12 apples. You also buy a box of cereal that costs \$3.35. The bill is \$8.75. How much does each apple cost?

21. The music boosters sell 322 musical buttons and raise \$483 for the music department. How much does each button cost?

22. Your family drives from Austin, Texas, to Tampa, Florida. The trip is 1,145 mi and lasts four days. How many miles should your family drive each day?

23. Sports A youth soccer league recently held registration. The number of players was divided by 12 to form 13 teams. How many players registered?

24. Open-Ended Write a problem you can represent with $2k - 10 = 6$. Solve the equation. Show your work.

Define a variable and write an inequality for each statement.

25. The game's duration is at most 3 hours.

26. To rent a car you must be at least 25 years old.

27. The truck can haul more than 20,000 lb.

28. There are fewer than 10 tickets available for the concert tonight.

Solve each inequality. Graph your solution.

29. $n + 12 \geq 15$ **30.** $y - 14 > 10$

31. $m - 8 \leq -17$ **32.** $w + 22 < 14$

33. $12x < -48$ **34.** $10h \geq 90$

35. $\frac{v}{-8} > 6$ **36.** $\frac{p}{11} \leq -6$

37. $-7k \leq -84$ **38.** $\frac{x}{-15} < -4$

Define a variable. Then write and solve an inequality for each problem.

39. Transportation A ferry can safely transport at most 220 people. There are already 143 people aboard. How many more people can the ferry take aboard?

40. Money A sports drink costs \$1.49 per bottle. At most, how many bottles can you buy if you have \$12?

41. Shopping Alex and his mother spent at least \$130 while shopping for new clothes. Alex spent \$52. How much did his mother spend?

42. Writing in Math Describe the similarities and differences between solving inequalities and equations. Include examples.

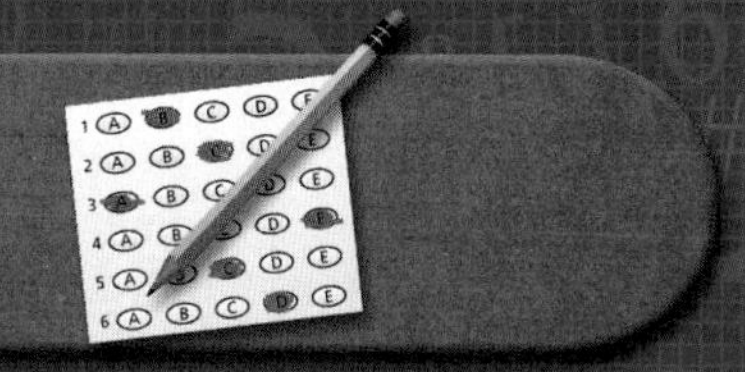

Multiple Choice

For Exercises 1–10, choose the correct letter.

1. Estimate to determine which sum is between 21 and 22.
   A. $13.71 + 1.5 + 8.2$
   B. $6.75 + 9.02 + 5.838$
   C. $5.99 + 2.69 + 15.49$
   D. $3.772 + 12.04 + 4.009$

2. Evaluate $4x - 3ny$ for $n = 2$, $x = 5$, and $y = -3$.
   F. -10 G. 2 H. 38 I. 53

3. Solve the equation $4m - 10 = 74$.
   A. -16 B. 7 C. 16 D. 21

4. If $3 + 5x = -12$, then $x =$ ■.
   F. -3 G. -1.8 H. 1.8 I. 3

5. Which numbers are all solutions of the inequality $x - 3 < -1$?
   A. $-3, 3, 6$
   B. $-1, 0, 1$
   C. 0, 1, 2
   D. 1, 2, 3

6. Which graph shows the solutions of $-5y < 30$?

   F. 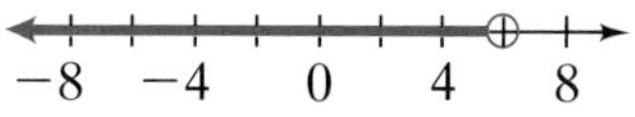

   G. 

   H. 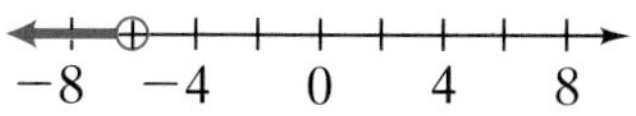

   I. 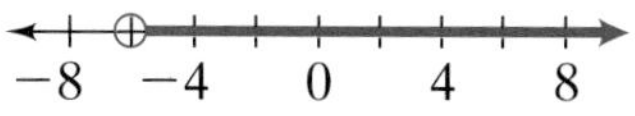

7. Which inequality's solution is represented by the graph below?

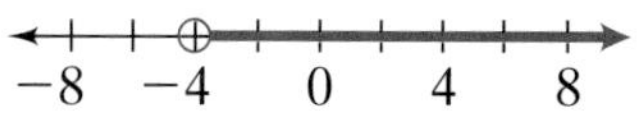

   A. $2p < -8$
   B. $20 > -5m$
   C. $3w \geq -12$
   D. $-4d > -16$

8. Which could $8m$ NOT represent?
   F. the total cost in dollars of m movie tickets if each ticket costs $8
   G. the cost in cents of m photocopies if each photocopy costs 8 cents
   H. the distance Alana rides her bike if she bikes 8 mi/h for m hours
   I. Billy's age, if Billy is m years older than his 8-year-old brother

9. The variables x, y, and z represent numbers other than zero. You know that $x > y$, $x > 0$, $y > 0$, and $z < 0$. Which must be true?
   A. $x + z < y + z$
   B. $\frac{x}{z} < \frac{y}{z}$
   C. $xz > yz$
   D. $\frac{x}{z} > \frac{y}{z}$

10. Let s equal the number of cups of sugar in a recipe. The amount of flour is 4 cups more than twice the amount of sugar. Which expression represents the amount of flour?
    F. $4 + s$
    G. $4 + 4s$
    H. $2(s + 4)$
    I. $4 + 2s$

Gridded Response

11. You want to buy a birthday card and some helium balloons. A store charges $2.25 for the card, and $3.35 per balloon. You have $20.00. How many balloons can you buy?

Short Response

12. Define a variable and write an inequality to model the word sentence "Today's temperature will be at least 55°F."

Extended Response

13. Eli buys 2 vinyl records each month. He started with 18 vinyl records.
    a. Write an expression to model the number of records Eli has after x months.
    b. How many records will Eli have after 22 months? Justify your answer.

It's a Dog's Life

Applying Inequalities Dogs come in all shapes and sizes. Different breeds have different personalities and sometimes special skills as well. Some make good guard dogs, some hunt or race, and some can pull heavy sleds. Some dogs are very friendly and make great pets. Dogs generally require a lot of attention — exercise, grooming, and, especially, feeding.

Different breeds

More than 200 different breeds of dogs exist. Most scientists believe that dogs are descendants of the wolf.

A German Shepherd's nose is usually black.

Dalmatians are born white, then develop faint smudges that become their distinctive markings.

A Healthy Pet

A healthy diet for a dog includes protein, carbohydrates, fats, fiber, water, vitamins, and minerals. In general, a puppy needs about 100 Cal/lb (Calories per pound) of body weight daily, an adult dog needs about 60 Cal/lb, and a senior dog needs about 25 Cal/lb.

Put It All Together

Data File Use the information on these two pages and on page 69 to answer these questions.

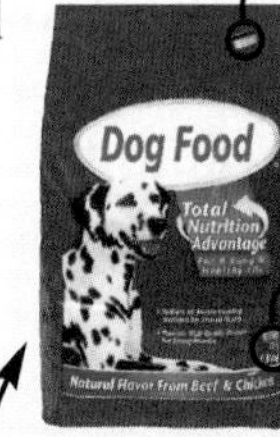

1. **Research** Use your own dog, or find information about a specific dog.
   a. How much does the dog weigh?
   b. Use the dog food label. Find the amount of food the dog will eat in a day.
   c. One cup of dog food weighs about 8 oz. About how many meals will one bag contain?
   d. About how much will it cost to feed the dog for a year?
   e. **Reasoning** Which would cost more to feed for a year: two dogs this size or one dog that is twice as large?
2. A friend decides to start a dog-care business for people who travel.
   a. Use the same dog as for Question 1. How much would it cost to feed the dog for two weeks?
   b. **Writing in Math** Suppose the dog's owners are going on vacation for two weeks. Your friend decides to charge $50/wk, which includes food, grooming, and walking the dog twice a day. Are the dog's owners likely to hire your friend? Why or why not?

Adult Dog Size	Daily Feeding
(pounds)	*Dry (cups)*
3–12 lb	1/2 to 1 1/4
13–20 lb	1 1/4 to 1 3/4
21–35 lb	1 3/4 to 2 2/3
36–50 lb	2 2/3 to 3 1/2
51–75 lb	3 1/2 to 4 3/4
76–100 lb	4 3/4 to 5 3/4
Over 100 lb	5 3/4 + 2/3 c for each 10 lb body weight over 100 lb

Take It to the NET For more information about dogs, go to **www.PHSchool.com.**
Web Code: abe-0253

CHAPTER 3

Exponents, Factors, and Fractions

Lessons

3-1 Exponents and Order of Operations

3-2 Scientific Notation

3-3 Divisibility Tests

3-4 Prime Factorization

3-5 Simplifying Fractions

3-6 Comparing and Ordering Fractions

3-7 Solve a Simpler Problem and Look for a Pattern

3-8 Mixed Numbers and Improper Fractions

3-9 Fractions and Decimals

3-10 Rational Numbers

Key Vocabulary

- composite number (p. 146)
- divisible (p. 141)
- equivalent fractions (p. 151)
- exponent (p. 131)
- greatest common factor (GCF) (p. 147)
- improper fraction (p. 164)
- least common denominator (LCD) (p. 156)
- least common multiple (LCM) (p. 145)
- mixed number (p. 164)
- prime number (p. 146)
- rational number (p. 173)
- repeating decimal (p. 169)
- scientific notation (p. 137)
- terminating decimal (p. 168)

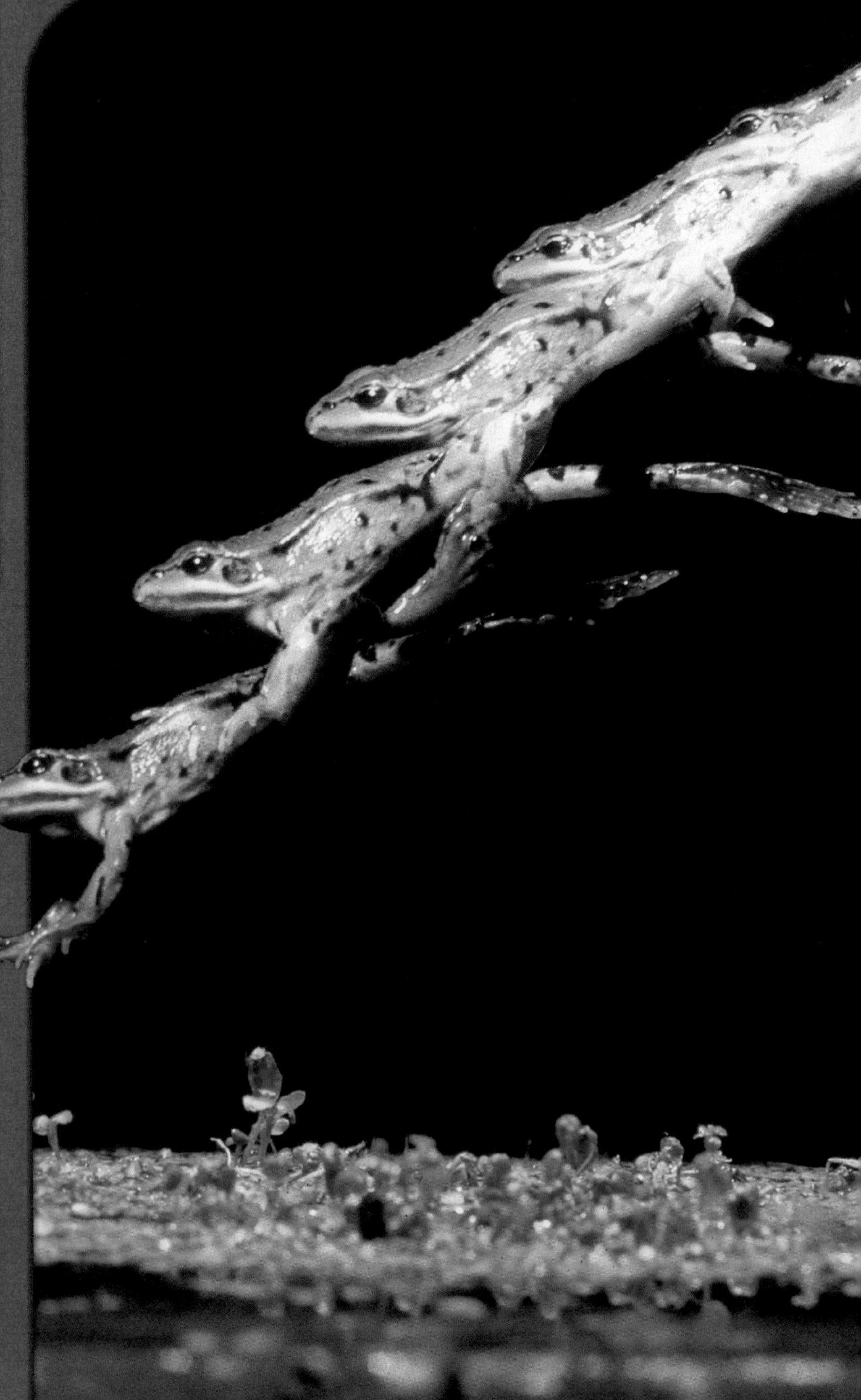

Real-World Snapshots

A camera can capture motion that our eyes see only as a blur. The shutter controls the amount of time that light is allowed to enter the camera. The rate at which a shutter opens and closes is called shutter speed.

A fast shutter speed means that the shutter opens and closes quickly. The shutter is open for a short amount of time and less light is allowed in. Fast-moving images require fast shutter speeds to prevent blurring.

Data File Shutter Opening Times (seconds)

$\frac{1}{4}$ $\frac{1}{30}$ $\frac{1}{60}$ $\frac{1}{125}$ $\frac{1}{250}$ $\frac{1}{500}$ $\frac{1}{1000}$

Slower speed—lets in more light

Faster speed—lets in less light

You will use the data above in this chapter:

- p. 153 Lesson 3-5
- p. 158 Lesson 3-6
- p. 172 Lesson 3-9

Real-World Snapshots On pages 182 and 183, you will solve problems involving photography.

Chapter 3 Preview

Where You've Been

- In Chapter 1, you performed operations with decimals and integers. You also learned how to use the Order of Operations.
- In Chapter 2, you learned to solve equations and inequalities.

Scientists use exponents to express large measurements.

Where You're Going

- In Chapter 3, you will use the Order of Operations to simplify expressions with exponents. You will simplify, compare, and order fractions and decimals.
- Applying what you learn, you will use exponents to find the magnification of an image in a microscope.

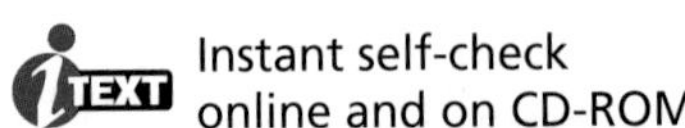

Instant self-check online and on CD-ROM

Diagnosing Readiness

For help, go to the lesson in green.

Adding and Subtracting Decimals (Lesson 1-2)

Find each sum or difference.

1. $2.1 + 3.4$ **2.** $6.02 - 4.597$ **3.** $7.0 - 3.11$ **4.** $671.02 + 6.427$

Multiplying and Dividing Integers (Lesson 1-8)

Find each product or quotient.

5. $-12 \cdot 3$ **6.** $-3 \cdot (-3)$ **7.** $27 \div (-3)$ **8.** $-16 \div (-4)$

Order of Operations and the Distributive Property (Lesson 1-9)

Find the value of each expression.

9. $10 + 4(15 \div 5)$ **10.** $30 \div 3 - 4 \cdot 2$ **11.** $(8 + 4) \div 4 - 2$

Solving Two-Step Equations (Lesson 2-6)

Algebra Solve each equation.

12. $\frac{n}{8} + 5 = 4$ **13.** $-5p - 3 = 22$ **14.** $3x + 15 = 45$

15. $-\frac{g}{7} - 6 = -4$ **16.** $3a + 1 = -17$ **17.** $-2 + \frac{b}{6} = -14$

Solving Inequalities by Multiplying or Dividing (Lesson 2-10)

Algebra Solve each inequality.

18. $4h \leq -36$ **19.** $-3t < 18$ **20.** $-\frac{m}{3} > 7$ **21.** $\frac{k}{2} \geq -5$

3-1 Exponents and Order of Operations

What You'll Learn

 To write numbers with exponents

 To simplify expressions with exponents using Order of Operations

. . . And Why

To find area in square miles, as in Example 2

Check Skills You'll Need

For help, go to Lesson 1-9.

Find the value of each expression.

1. $5 - 1 \cdot 3$ **2.** $(5 - 1) \cdot 3$ **3.** $4 \cdot (3 + 2)$

4. $10 \div 2 - 3 \cdot 2$ **5.** $10 + (2 + 4) \div 4$ **6.** $(10 + 2) \div 4 + 5$

7. Number Sense Consider any whole number greater than 2. Which produces a greater result, doubling it or multiplying it by itself?

New Vocabulary • exponent • power

Interactive lesson includes instant self-check, tutorials, and activities.

OBJECTIVE 1

Writing Numbers With Exponents

Investigation: Exploring Exponents

Suppose you're interviewing for an after-school job. The boss offers to pay you 2¢ the first day, with the amount to double each day. You investigate the offer using this table.

1. **a.** Complete the table to find how many cents you will be paid for each of the first five days.
   b. How much will you be paid for the seventh day?
   c. How much will you be paid for the tenth day?

Day	Cents
One	$2 = ■$
Two	$2 \times 2 = ■$
Three	$2 \times 2 \times 2 = ■$
Four	$2 \times 2 \times 2 \times 2 = ■$
Five	$2 \times 2 \times 2 \times 2 \times 2 = ■$

2. **Reasoning** Suppose you are offered a different job that will pay you a \$10 flat fee for 10 days of work. Which job offer would you accept? Explain.

Reading Math

You read 5^2 as "5 to the second power," or "5 squared." You read 5^3 as "5 to the third power," or "5 cubed."

You can use an exponent to show a product of equal factors. An **exponent** tells you how many times a number, or base, is used as a factor.

$$5^3 = \underbrace{5 \cdot 5 \cdot 5}_{\text{The base is used as a factor three times.}} = 125$$

exponent → 3; base → 5; value of the expression → 125

A number that can be expressed using an exponent is called a **power.** The number 125 is a power of 5 because it can be written as 5^3.

1 EXAMPLE Writing Expressions Using Exponents

Write using an exponent.

a. $3 \cdot 3 \cdot 3 \cdot 3 \cdot 3$

$= 3^5$ ← 3 is the base. 5 is the exponent.

b. $11 \cdot 11 \cdot 11$

$= 11^3$ ← 11 is the base. 3 is the exponent.

Check Understanding 1 **a.** Write $5 \cdot 5 \cdot 5 \cdot 5 \cdot 5$ using an exponent.

b. Reasoning Suppose a is a nonzero number. How would you write $a \cdot a \cdot a$ using an exponent?

You can find the value of an expression with exponents by writing it as the product of repeated factors. You can also use a scientific calculator.

2 EXAMPLE Real-World Problem Solving

Calculator Hint

You can use the ^ or y^x key to find a power. To find 4^3, use

4 ^ 3 = 64 or

4 y^x 3 = 64.

If your calculator does not have an exponent key, use

4 × 4 × 4 = 64.

Geography Gibraltar is at the western end of the Mediterranean Sea. Its area is about the same as the area of a square 1.5 mi on a side. Find Gibraltar's area.

Since $A = s^2$, find 1.5^2.

Method 1

$1.5^2 = (1.5)(1.5)$ ← Write as a product of repeated factors.

$= 2.25$ ← Multiply.

Method 2

1.5 x^2 = 2.25 ← Use the x^2 key to square numbers.

The area of Gibraltar is about 2.25 mi^2.

Check Understanding 2 Simplify. Use a calculator, paper and pencil, or mental math.

a. 3^5 **b.** 10^9 **c.** 3.1^2 **d.** 1.2^3

OBJECTIVE 2 Simplifying Expressions With Exponents

To simplify expressions with exponents, you must consider exponents in the Order of Operations.

Key Concepts **Order of Operations**

1. Do all operations within groupings first.
2. Evaluate any term(s) with exponents.
3. Multiply and divide in order from left to right.
4. Add and subtract in order from left to right.

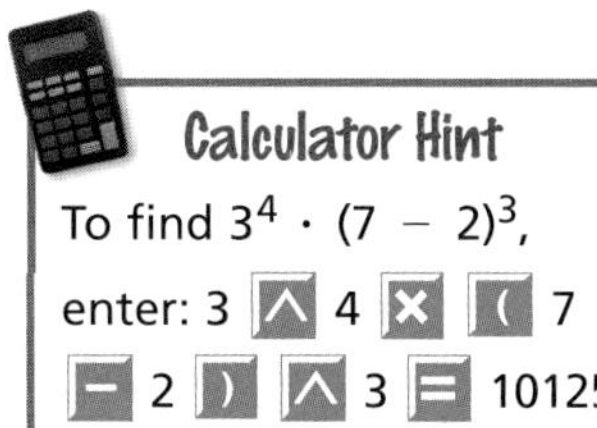
Calculator Hint
To find $3^4 \cdot (7 - 2)^3$,
enter: 3 ^ 4 × (7 − 2) ^ 3 = 10125.

3 EXAMPLE Simplifying Using Order of Operations

Simplify $3^4 \cdot (7 - 2)^3$.

$3^4 \cdot (7 - 2)^3 = 3^4 \cdot 5^3$ ← **Do operations in parentheses.**

$= 81 \cdot 125$ ← **Find the values of the powers.**

$= 10{,}125$ ← **Multiply.**

Check Understanding 3 Simplify.

a. $(3^2 + 5) - 2$ **b.** $3^2 + 5 - 2$ **c.** $(3 + 5)^2 - 2$

d. List the key strokes you use on your calculator to find $5 \cdot (9 - 2)^3$.

The expressions -5^4 and $(-5)^4$ are not equivalent. The expression -5^4 means the opposite, or the negative, of 5^4. So the base of -5^4 is 5, not -5.

4 EXAMPLE Simplifying Powers With Negatives

Simplify the expressions.

a. $-5^4 = -1 \cdot 5^4$ ← **Perform operations with exponents first.**

$= -(5 \cdot 5 \cdot 5 \cdot 5)$ ← **The base is 5, not −5.**

$= -625$ ← **Simplify.**

b. $(-5)^4 = (-5)(-5)(-5)(-5)$ ← **The base is the quantity in the parentheses, −5.**

$= 625$ ← **Multiply.**

Check Understanding 4 Simplify each expression.

a. $(-2)^3$ **b.** -2^3 **c.** -3^4 **d.** $(-3)^4$

e. **Reasoning** Does squaring a negative number always produce a positive result? Explain.

EXERCISES

For more practice, see *Extra Practice*.

A Practice by Example

Example 1 (page 132)

Write using an exponent.

1. $6 \cdot 6 \cdot 6$ **2.** $2 \cdot 2 \cdot 2 \cdot 2 \cdot 2 \cdot 2 \cdot 2$ **3.** $7 \cdot 7 \cdot 7 \cdot 7 \cdot 7$

4. $8 \cdot 8 \cdot 8 \cdot 8$ **5.** $20 \cdot 20 \cdot 20 \cdot 20 \cdot 20$ **6.** $12 \cdot 12 \cdot 12$

Example 2 (page 132)

Simplify. Use a calculator, paper and pencil, or mental math.

7. 9^2 **8.** 10^8 **9.** 0.2^6 **10.** 1.7^3

11. Each side of a sugar cube is approximately 0.6 in. long.

a. **Calculator** Find the volume of the sugar cube.

b. Which key strokes did you use?

Example 3 (page 133)

Simplify.

12. $2^3 \cdot (6 - 3)^2$ **13.** $(2^3 \cdot 6) - 3^2$ **14.** $2^3 \cdot 6 - 3^2$

15. $(2 + 6)^2 - 3^3$ **16.** $2^3 - 6 \cdot 3^2$ **17.** $(2^3 - 6) \cdot 3^2$

18. $3^2 + 2^3 \cdot 6$ **19.** $(3^2 + 2^3) \cdot 6$ **20.** $3^2 \cdot (2^2 + 6)^2$

Example 4 (page 133)

Simplify each expression.

21. $(-6)^3$ **22.** -2^4 **23.** $(-3)^7$ **24.** $(-4)^2$ **25.** -4^3

B Apply Your Skills

Use paper and pencil, mental math, or a calculator to simplify.

26. $2^5 \cdot 4^2$ **27.** $12 + 5^3$ **28.** -7^4 **29.** $8 + 3^4$

30. $(-5)^5$ **31.** $10^2 + 6^2$ **32.** $3(0.5 + 2.5)^2$ **33.** $(10 + 6)^2$

34. $3(4^2 - 10)$ **35.** $(5 - 2^2) - 1$ **36.** $4^3 + 14 \div 7$ **37.** $(20 \div 10)^2$

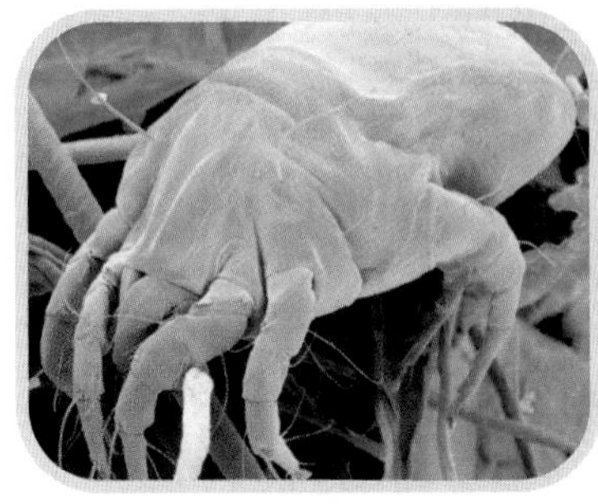

Real-World Connection

This dust mite has been magnified 1.5×10^5 times.

38. Technology A Scanning Electron Microscope (SEM) can magnify an image up to 10^5 times its size. How many times is this?

Science Match the fact with the power.

39. wheels on a unicycle **A.** 2^5

40. planets in the solar system **B.** 3^2

41. freezing point of water in degrees Fahrenheit **C.** 1^{17}

For Exercises 42–44, refer to the table.

42. Copy the table. Fill in the missing values.

43. Patterns What patterns do you notice?

44. Reasoning Predict the number of zeros in 10^{12}.

Power of 10	Value	Number of Zeros
10^1	■	1
10^2	■	■
10^3	■	■
10^4	■	■
10^5	■	■

Algebra **Evaluate each expression for $m = 3, n = 2$, and $r = 4$.**

45. $m^2 + n^2$ **46.** $(m + n)^2$ **47.** $(-r)^3$

48. $-m^3$ **49.** $n^2(m + r)$ **50.** $(n^2r^2 - m)^2$

51. a. What exponent completes the table below?

b. Calculator Find $2^0, 3^0, 4^0, 5^0$, and 10^0.

Value	16	8	4	2	1
Power of 2	2^4	2^3	2^2	2^1	$2^{■}$

52. Writing in Math Write a general rule to find the value of a nonzero expression with an exponent of 0.

53. a. Geometry How many small squares line up on one edge of the larger square?

b. How many small squares make up the whole square?

c. Reasoning Why do you think 5^2 is referred to as "5 squared"?

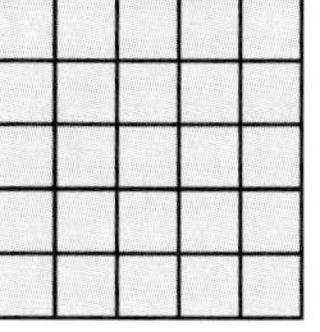

54. Estimation Write two powers that are between the values of 8^2 and 8^3.

C Challenge

Algebra **Evaluate each expression for $f = -2, g = -3$, and $h = -4$.**

55. $(f+g)^2$ **56.** $(-h)^3$ **57.** $-f^3$ **58.** $g^2(f+h)$

59. Stretch Your Thinking Paulette has six marbles that are the same size. Five of her marbles weigh the same. The sixth marble is heavier than the rest. Hahn is trying to find which marble is heavier than the rest by using a balance scale and only two weighings. How can he do this?

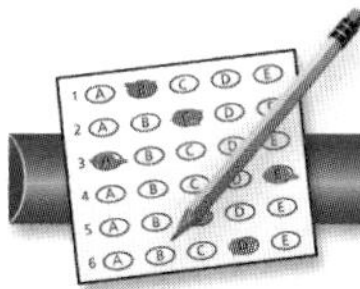

Test Prep

Multiple Choice

60. Evaluate the expression $3^3 - 24 \div 6$.
A. 0.5 **B.** 5 **C.** 21 **D.** 23

61. On a test, the class average is 3^4. Your score is 6 points above the class average. What is your score on the test?
F. 75 **G.** 81 **H.** 87 **I.** 92

62. Order from least to greatest: $4^3, 9^2, 2^7, (-5)^2$.
A. $2^7, 4^3, (-5)^2, 9^2$
B. $(-5)^2, 4^3, 9^2, 2^7$
C. $9^2, (-5)^2, 2^7, 4^3$
D. $9^2, (-5)^2, 4^3, 2^7$

Extended Response

63. Your friend sends you the following message written in a secret code.

$\underline{-8}\ \underline{-1}\ \underline{-1}\ \underline{25}$ $\underline{-8}\ \underline{-1}$ $\underline{8}\ \underline{1}\ \underline{25}\ \underline{-1}\ \underline{-27}$

Each number in the code represents a letter, as follows:

Letter	A	E	L	M	N	R	S	T
Power	1^3	$(-1)^3$	2^3	$(-2)^3$	3^3	$(-3)^3$	4^2	5^2

What does your friend's message say?

Take It to the NET
Online lesson quiz at
www.PHSchool.com
Web Code: aba-0301

Mixed Review

Lesson 2-10

Algebra **Solve each inequality.**

64. $\frac{a}{2} > 10$ **65.** $-3n < -9$ **66.** $\frac{p}{-6} \le 5$ **67.** $\frac{z}{12} \ge -1$

Lesson 1-8

Find the value of each expression.

68. $12(-2)$ **69.** $-4(-10)$ **70.** $-8 \div (-4)$ **71.** $49 \div (-7)$

Scientific Notation

What You'll Learn

To write numbers in scientific notation

To write numbers in standard form

. . . And Why

To express the moon's distance from Earth, as in Example 1

For help, go to Lesson 3-1.

Simplify.

1. 3^3 **2.** 4^2 **3.** 10^5

4. 1^{15} **5.** 10^1 **6.** 2^8

7. **Number Sense** Is 10^7 closer to a million or a billion? Answer without calculating.

OBJECTIVE

Interactive lesson includes instant self-check, tutorials, and activities.

1 Writing Numbers in Scientific Notation

Investigation: Powers of 10

1. Copy and complete the table below.

Factors	10 · 1	10 · 10	10 · 10 · 10	10 · 10 · 10 · 10
Product	10	100	■	■
Number of Zeros in Product	1	■	■	■

2. Study the pattern in your table. How is the number of zeros in the product related to the number of times 10 is used as a factor?

3. How many times should 10 be used as a factor to obtain 100,000,000,000?

4. **Calculator** Copy the table below. Use the pattern from the table above to complete the missing information in the table below.

Factors	3.5 × 1,000	7.2 × 10,000	■	36.8 × 1,000,000,000
Product	3,500	■	4,800,000	■

5. Different calculators have different ways of showing scientific notation. How does your calculator display the result in the last row of the last column of this table?

Need Help?
For practice with powers of 10, see Skills Handbook page 706.

Scientific notation is a shorthand way to write numbers using powers of 10.

Key Concepts — Scientific Notation

A number in **scientific notation** is written as the product of two factors, one greater than or equal to 1 and less than 10, and the other a power of 10.

$7{,}500{,}000{,}000{,}000 = 7.5 \times 10^{12}$

↑ **First factor is greater than or equal to 1, but less than 10.**

↑ **Second factor is a power of 10.**

1 EXAMPLE Writing in Scientific Notation

On calculators that do not display scientific notation, powers of 10 that are too large for the screen are shown with the letter "E." 2 E12 means 2×10^{12}.

Science The moon orbits Earth at a distance of 384,000 km from Earth. Write this number in scientific notation.

3.84000. ← **Move the decimal point to get a factor greater than 1 but less than 10.**

$384{,}000 = 3.84 \times 100{,}000$ ← **Write as a product of 2 factors.**

$= 3.84 \times 10^5$ ← **Write 100,000 as a power of 10.**

The moon orbits Earth at a distance of 3.84×10^5 km.

Check Understanding 1 **a.** Write 396,000,000 in scientific notation.

b. **Reasoning** Is 107×10^4 written in scientific notation? Explain.

OBJECTIVE

2 Writing Numbers in Standard Form

You can change expressions from scientific notation to standard form by simplifying the product of the two factors.

2 EXAMPLE Writing in Standard Form

Earth from space

Science The mean distance from Earth to Mars is approximately 2.3×10^8 km. Write this number in standard form.

Method 1

$2.3 \times 10^8 = 2.3 \times 100{,}000{,}000$ ← **Write as a product of 2 factors.**

$= 230{,}000{,}000$ ← **Multiply the factors.**

Method 2

$2.3 \times 10^8 = 2.30000000$ ← **The exponent is 8. Move the decimal 8 places to the right.**

$= 230{,}000{,}000$

The mean distance is approximately 230,000,000 km.

2 Write in standard form.

a. 1.2×10^2 **b.** 3.32×10^5 **c.** 6.443×10^9

EXERCISES

For more practice, see *Extra Practice.*

A Practice by Example

Example 1 (page 137)

Write in scientific notation. Exercise 1 has been started for you.

1. 7,500 $= 7.5 \times 10^{\blacksquare}$ **2.** 75,000,000 **3.** 1,250 **4.** 44,000

5. 149,000,000 **6.** 34,025 **7.** 11,020 **8.** 120,000

Example 2 (page 137)

Write in standard form.

9. 3.4×10^3 **10.** 5.9×10^2 **11.** 8.21×10^3 **12.** 6.678×10^2

13. 7.45×10^4 **14.** 9.9673×10^2 **15.** 5×10^{11} **16.** 7.02×10^1

17. 6.15×10^8 **18.** 2.439×10^7 **19.** 4.77×10^9 **20.** 2.25×10^3

B Apply Your Skills

Explain why each number is *not* in scientific notation.

21. 35.4×10^6 **22.** 8.63×2^{10} **23.** 0.387×10^7 **24.** 75.5×10^7

25. Science The table shows the planets in the solar system and their masses. List their masses in order from least to greatest.

Planet	Mass (kg)
Mercury	3.303×10^{23}
Venus	4.869×10^{24}
Earth	5.976×10^{24}
Mars	6.421×10^{23}
Jupiter	1.900×10^{27}
Saturn	5.688×10^{26}
Uranus	8.686×10^{25}
Neptune	1.024×10^{26}
Pluto	1.290×10^{22}

For Exercises 26–31, write each number in scientific notation.

26. Plants There are about 350,000 different kinds of plants on Earth.

27. Geography The Folsom Dam in California holds back 326 billion gallons of water.

28. 34.5×10^3 **29.** $1{,}228 \times 10^2$

30. 122.85×10^2 **31.** 312×10^6

Math in the Media Use the cartoon below for Exercises 32–33.

FOX TROT by Bill Amend

32. How many minutes was the warning? Write in standard form.

33. Convert the time to hours. Write in scientific notation.

Real-World Connection

This balloon's basket is made of wicker, which is sturdy but lightweight.

For Exercises 34–39, write each number in standard form.

34. 0.345×10^3 **35.** 1.203×10^{15} **36.** $0.000000312 \times 10^{10}$

37. Ballooning The first balloon to carry passengers weighed 1.6×10^3 lb.

38. Light One light-year is 5.88×10^{12} mi.

39. Science There are about 2×10^{13} red blood cells in a 125-lb person.

40. Writing in Math Explain how you would find the power of 10 to write 725,000,000 in scientific notation.

41. Biology In a laboratory experiment, two colonies of bacteria are being observed. The first is growing at a rate of 2.2×10^6 bacteria per hour. The other is growing at a rate of 6.3×10^5 bacteria per hour. Which is growing faster? How do you know?

C Challenge

42. Science An astronomical unit (AU) is approximately 9.3×10^7 mi. The average distance of Pluto from the sun is about 39 AU. Write this distance in miles in both scientific notation and standard form.

43. Stretch Your Thinking For every two goldfish you buy at the regular price, you get a third goldfish for a penny. You spend $.45 for nine goldfish. Find, in cents, the regular price of one goldfish.

Test Prep

Multiple Choice

44. How is 30,240,000,000 written in scientific notation?
A. 30.24×10^9 **B.** 30.24×10^6 **C.** 3.024×10^{11} **D.** 3.024×10^{10}

Take It to the NET
Online lesson quiz at
www.PHSchool.com
Web Code: aba-0302

45. How is 6.023×10^4 written in standard notation?
F. 60.23 **G.** 602.3 **H.** 6,023 **I.** 60,230

46. Which of the following is NOT written in scientific notation?
A. 4.127×10^1 **B.** 2.0×10^2 **C.** 3.24×10^3 **D.** 22.4×10^5

Short Response

47. A penny with a diameter of 0.75 in. is magnified to 100,000 times its size in an electron microscope.
a. Write the size that the image would be in scientific notation.
b. Write the size that the image would be in standard form.

Mixed Review

Lesson 3-1 **Simplify.**

48. $4^2 + 2^3 \cdot 3$ **49.** $(4^2 + 2^3) \cdot 3$ **50.** $4^2 \cdot (2^3 + 3)^2$

Lesson 2-9 **Algebra** **Solve each inequality.**

51. $-5 > c - 7$ **52.** $-56 \leq -7 + y$ **53.** $14 + w \geq -4$

Extension Negative Exponents

For Use With Lesson 3-2

Remember that a number in scientific notation is written as a product of two factors, one greater than or equal to 1 and less than 10, and the other a power of 10. To write a number between 0 and 1 in scientific notation, you can use a negative exponent.

1 EXAMPLE Writing in Scientific Notation

Write 0.0084 in scientific notation.

0.008.4 ← **Move the decimal point to obtain a factor greater than 1 but less than 10.**

$0.0084 = 8.4 \times 0.001$ ← **Write as a product of 2 factors.**

$= 8.4 \times 10^{-3}$ ← **The decimal point was moved 3 places to the right. Use -3 as the exponent.**

In scientific notation, 0.0084 is written as 8.4×10^{-3}.

2 EXAMPLE Writing in Standard Form

Write 3.52×10^{-5} in standard form.

Method 1

$3.52 \times 10^{-5} = 3.52 \times 0.00001$ ← **Write as a product of 2 factors.**

$= 0.0000352$ ← **Multiply the factors.**

Method 2

$3.52 \times 10^{-5} = 0.00003.52$ ← **The exponent of 10 is -5. Move the decimal 5 places to the left.**

$= 0.0000352$

The value of 3.52×10^{-5} is 0.0000352.

EXERCISES

Write each number in scientific notation.

1. 0.0008 **2.** 0.037 **3.** 0.0000422 **4.** 0.00000691

5. 0.005006 **6.** 0.00147 **7.** 0.5 **8.** 0.049562

Write each number in standard form.

9. 2.8×10^{-3} **10.** 8.55×10^{-1} **11.** 8.33×10^{-6}

12. 1.381×10^{-4} **13.** 2.005×10^{-2} **14.** 6.079×10^{-5}

15. The width of a hair is about 3×10^{-7} in.

16. A flea weighs 4.9×10^{-3} g.

3-3 Divisibility Tests

What You'll Learn

OBJECTIVE 1 To use divisibility tests

. . . And Why

To solve problems involving codes, as in Example 3

✓ Check Skills You'll Need

For help, go to Lesson 1-8.

Simplify.

1. $24 \div 6$ **2.** $-27 \div (-9)$ **3.** $55 \div 11$

4. $-150 \div 10$ **5.** $248 \div 2$ **6.** $396 \div 3$

New Vocabulary

- divisible

Interactive lesson includes instant self-check, tutorials, and activities.

OBJECTIVE 1 Using Divisibility Tests

One whole number is **divisible** by a second whole number if the remainder is 0 when you divide the first number by the second number. Since $16 \div 2 = 8$, 16 is divisible by 2.

Key Concepts — Divisibility Tests for 2, 4, 5, 8, and 10

A whole number is divisible by
- 2 if it ends in 0, 2, 4, 6, or 8.
- 4 if the number formed by the last two digits is divisible by 4.
- 5 if it ends in 0 or 5.
- 8 if the number formed by the last three digits is divisible by 8.
- 10 if it ends in 0.

1 EXAMPLE Divisibility by 2, 4, 5, 8, and 10

Is the first number divisible by the second? Explain.

a. 567 by 2 No, 567 does not end in 0, 2, 4, 6, or 8.

b. 1,015 by 5 Yes, 1,015 ends in 5.

c. 111,120 by 10 Yes, 111,120 ends in 0.

d. 934 by 4 No, 34 is not divisible by 4.

e. 29,640 by 8 Yes, 640 is divisible by 8.

✓ Check Understanding 1 Is the first number divisible by the second? Explain.

a. 160 by 5 **b.** 76 by 10 **c.** 33,560 by 4 **d.** 1,856 by 8

e. **Reasoning** Is any number that is divisible by both 2 and 5 also divisible by 10? Explain.

The table below shows a pattern for divisibility by 3 and 9.

Number	Sum of Digits	Is the *sum* divisible by 3?	Is the *sum* divisible by 9?	Is the *number* divisible by 3?	Is the *number* divisible by 9?
215	$2 + 1 + 5 = 8$	No	No	No	No
282	$2 + 8 + 2 = 12$	Yes	No	Yes	No
468	$4 + 6 + 8 = 18$	Yes	Yes	Yes	Yes

Key Concepts **Divisibility Tests for 3 and 9**

A whole number is divisible by
- 3 if the sum of its digits is divisible by 3.
- 9 if the sum of its digits is divisible by 9.

2 EXAMPLE Divisibility by 3 and 9

Is the first number divisible by the second? Explain.

a. 465 by 3 Yes, $4 + 6 + 5 = 15$, which is divisible by 3.

b. 3,016 by 9 No, $3 + 0 + 1 + 6 = 10$, which is not divisible by 9.

Check Understanding 2 Is the first number divisible by the second? Explain.
a. 262 by 3 **b.** 13,449 by 3 **c.** 586 by 9 **d.** 30,756 by 9

Use a combination of tests to find the factors by which a number is divisible.

3 EXAMPLE Real-World Problem Solving

Codes A friend sends you a message signed with the code number 5,385. Dave's number is divisible by 3, 5, and 8. Janice's number is divisible by 2 and 3, but not 4. Joshua's number is divisible by 4 and 5, but not 3. Karen's number is divisible by 3 and 5, but not 8. Who sent the message?

Use logical reasoning to see which friend's divisibility rules match the divisibility rules for 5,385.

Is 5,385 divisible by 2? No, it does not end in 0, 2, 4, 6, or 8.
Is 5,385 divisible by 3? Yes, $5 + 3 + 8 + 5 = 21$, which is divisible by 3.
Is 5,385 divisible by 4? No, 85 is not divisible by 4.
Is 5,385 divisible by 5? Yes, it ends in 5.
Is 5,385 divisible by 8? No, 385 is not divisible by 8.

5,385 is divisible by 3 and 5, but not 8, so the message is from Karen.

Real-World Connection
Ancient Egyptians used codes to represent measurements and other numerical values.

Check Understanding 3 A message is signed with the number 32,680. Who wrote it?

EXERCISES

For more practice, see *Extra Practice*.

A Practice by Example

Is the first number divisible by the second? Explain.

Example 1 (page 141)

1. 571 by 2
2. 5,605 by 10
3. 3,650 by 5
4. 3,179,144 by 4
5. 82,240 by 8
6. 6,722,540 by 10
7. 6,790 by 2
8. 3,491,660 by 4
9. 110,344 by 8

Example 2 (page 142)

10. 558 by 3
11. 675 by 9
12. 8,394 by 3
13. 2,472 by 9
14. 7,623,540 by 3
15. 7,623,540 by 9

Example 3 (page 142)

16. **Fashion** You direct marketing for a fashion magazine. To distinguish your magazine from others, you identify it with a four-digit code. The number formed by the last three digits of the code is divisible by the first digit. Determine whether each number can be used.
    a. 4,956 **b.** 5,625 **c.** 9,585 **d.** 3,173

17. **Games** In an adventure game you must correctly place three colored keys into a door to gain access to a treasure room. Each key has a number etched into it. Use the clues to find the correct keys to use.

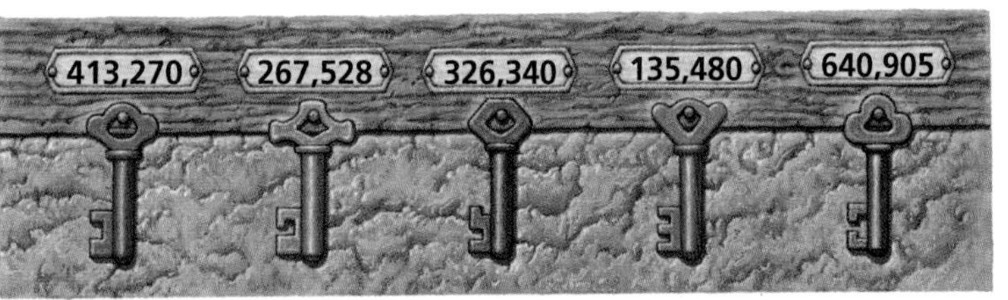

- The top lock uses a key that is divisible by 3 and 4, but not 5.
- The middle lock uses a key that is divisible by 2 and 5, but not 3.
- The bottom lock uses a key that is divisible by 3 and 5, but not 4.

B Apply Your Skills

Tell whether each number is divisible by 2, 3, 4, 5, 8, 9, or 10. Some numbers may be divisible by more than one number.

18. 324
19. 150
20. 840
21. 2,724
22. 1,430
23. 6,720
24. 81,816
25. 625
26. 7,848
27. 4,725

28. **Shipping** A company wants to ship 63,720 model airplanes. The size of a shipping carton is measured by the number of models it holds. Each carton must hold more than 3 but less than 10 models. Which sizes can the company use? How many cartons are needed for each size?

29. Refer to these numbers: 10 66 898 975 4,710
    a. Which are divisible by both 2 and 3?
    b. Which are divisible by 6?
    c. Using your results, write a divisibility test for 6.

30. **Writing in Math** Write divisibility tests for 12 and 15.

Number Sense **If you scramble the digits of a number that is divisible by 3, it is still divisible by 3. Does this work for the numbers below? Explain.**

31. numbers divisible by 2 **32.** numbers divisible by 4

33. numbers divisible by 8 **34.** numbers divisible by 9

Write the missing digit to make each number divisible by 9.

35. 22■,043 **36.** 3■, 187 **37.** 2,03■,371 **38.** 1■,012

39. Here is the divisibility rule for 11. Calculate the sum of every other digit. Then find the sum of the remaining digits of the number. Find the difference between the sums. If the result is a multiple of 11, then the number is a multiple of 11. Tell whether each is a multiple of 11.
a. 3,577 **b.** 4,818 **c.** 32,417 **d.** 361,526

40. A number is greater than 500 and less than 550. The number is a multiple of 9 and the units digit is 1. What is the number?

41. **Stretch Your Thinking** You work at a dog kennel. You use 5 lb of dog food to feed 3 dogs for 4 days. At the same feeding rate, how many pounds of dog food will you need to feed 12 dogs for 1 week?

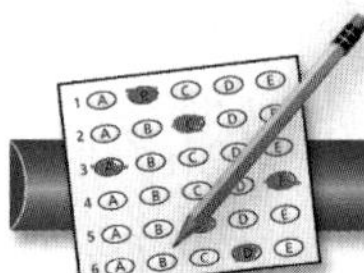

Test Prep

Multiple Choice

42. Which number is divisible by 3?
A. 18,073 **B.** 20,412 **C.** 28,412 **D.** 31,415

43. Which number is NOT divisible by 9?
F. 1,269 **G.** 2,195 **H.** 3,150 **I.** 4,761

Take It to the NET
Online lesson quiz at
www.PHSchool.com
Web Code: aba-0303

44. Which number is divisible by 4?
A. 12,542 **B.** 12,524 **C.** 12,254 **D.** 12,245

45. Eight photo albums contain an equal number of photos. Which could be the total number of photos?
F. 1,821 **G.** 1,218 **H.** 1,182 **I.** 1,128

Mixed Review

Lesson 3-2 **Write each number in scientific notation.**

46. 5,200,000 **47.** 348,000 **48.** 7,100

49. 6,125 **50.** 8,901,067,000 **51.** 123,456,789

Lesson 2-6 **Algebra** **Solve each equation.**

52. $-3y - 10 = 17$ **53.** $\frac{x}{4} + 1 = 13$ **54.** $\frac{t}{-7} + 5 = 6$

3-4 Prime Factorization

What You'll Learn

 To find multiples and factors

 To use prime factorization

. . . And Why

To determine computer delivery schedules, as in Example 1

For help, go to Lesson 3-3.

Tell whether the first number is divisible by the second number. Explain.

1. 48; 2 **2.** 48; 3 **3.** 48; 4

4. 48; 5 **5.** 48; 6 **6.** 48; 8

New Vocabulary • multiple • least common multiple (LCM) • factor • composite number • prime number • prime factorization • greatest common factor (GCF)

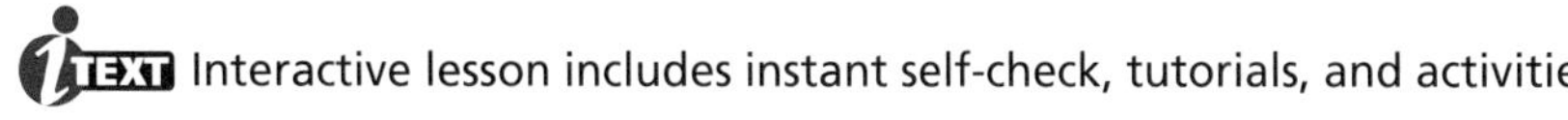

Interactive lesson includes instant self-check, tutorials, and activities.

1 Finding Multiples and Factors

Real-World Connection

Animal shelter workers rescued this baby possum from a car crash.

Suppose you and a friend volunteer at an animal shelter. Today you are both there. You volunteer every third day and your friend volunteers every fourth day. You will see each other again 12 days from today.

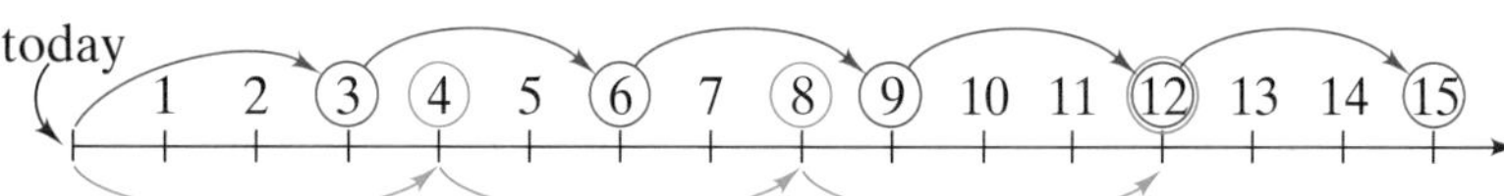

The diagram above shows multiples of 3 and 4. A **multiple** of a number is the product of that number and any nonzero whole number. The **least common multiple (LCM)** of two or more numbers is the least multiple that is common to all of the numbers. For example, the LCM of 3 and 4 is 12.

1 EXAMPLE Finding the Least Common Multiple

Business Computers are delivered to a store every 6 days. Printers are delivered every 9 days. If both printers and computers are delivered today, when will both be delivered again?

Find the least common multiple of 6 and 9.

Multiples of 6: 6, 12, 18, 24, 30, 36, . . .
Multiples of 9: 9, 18, 27, 36, . . .
← **List the first several multiples of 6 and 9.**

The LCM of 6 and 9 is 18. So, both will be delivered in 18 days.

1 Find the LCM of each pair of numbers.

a. 4, 10 **b.** 5, 7 **c.** 12, 15

d. **Reasoning** Zero is not considered a multiple of any number other than itself. Why does this make sense?

A **factor** is a whole number that divides another whole number with a remainder of 0. Any number is always divisible by all of its factors.

2 EXAMPLE Finding Factors

Find the factors of 30.

$1 \cdot 30 \quad 2 \cdot 15 \quad 3 \cdot 10 \quad 5 \cdot 6$ ←**Find pairs of numbers with a product of 30.**

The factors of 30 are 1, 2, 3, 5, 6, 10, 15, and 30.

Check Understanding 2 **a.** Find the factors of 42.
b. **Number Sense** What numbers are always factors of even numbers?

OBJECTIVE 2

Using Prime Factorization

A **composite number** is a whole number greater than 1 that has more than two factors. A **prime number** is a whole number with exactly two factors, 1 and the number itself. The number 1 is neither prime nor composite.

3 EXAMPLE Prime Numbers and Composite Numbers

Tell whether each number is prime or composite.

a. 12	Factors: 1, 2, 3, 4, 6, 12	12 is a composite number.
b. 13	Factors: 1, 13	13 is a prime number.

Check Understanding 3 Tell whether each number is prime or composite.
a. 14 **b.** 15 **c.** 11 **d.** 2
e. **Reasoning** What is the only even prime number?

Writing a composite number as the product of its prime factors shows its **prime factorization.** You can use a *factor tree* to find the prime factors.

4 EXAMPLE Writing Prime Factorization

Use a factor tree to write the prime factorization of 60.

60

Prime → (2) · 30 ←**Write 60 as the product of any two of its factors.**

Prime → (2) · 15 ←**Write 30 as the product of two factors.**

Prime → (3) · (5) ←**Write 15 as the product of two factors.**

$60 = 2 \cdot 2 \cdot 3 \cdot 5$. Or, using exponents, you can write $60 = 2^2 \cdot 3 \cdot 5$.

Need Help?
For help with writing expressions involving exponents, go to Lesson 3-1.

Check Understanding 4 Write the prime factorization of 72. Use exponents where possible.

The **greatest common factor (GCF)** of two or more numbers is the greatest number that is a factor of all the numbers.

5 EXAMPLE Finding the Greatest Common Factor

Find the GCF of 24 and 36.

$24 = 2 \cdot 2 \cdot 2 \cdot 3$ $\quad 36 = 2 \cdot 2 \cdot 3 \cdot 3$ ← **Write the prime factorizations.**

$\text{GCF} = 2 \cdot 2 \cdot 3 = 12$ ← **Find the product of the common factors.**

The GCF of 24 and 36 is 12.

Check Understanding 5 Find the GCF of 16 and 24.

More Than One Way

Two gymnastics teams are marching at an event. There are 32 members on one team and 40 on the other. They are marching in rows of equal size that are as wide as possible. How many people are in each row?

Carlos's Method

First, I'll write the prime factorizations of 40 and 32. Then I'll find the GCF.

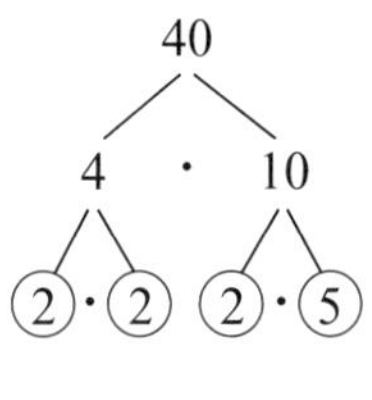

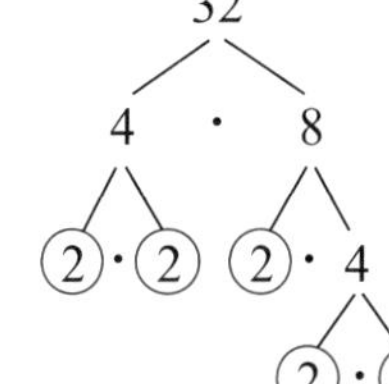

← **Write as products of two factors.**

← **Write as products of two factors.**

← **Write as a product of two factors.**

$40 = 2 \cdot 2 \cdot 2 \cdot 5$ $\quad 32 = 2 \cdot 2 \cdot 2 \cdot 2 \cdot 2$ ← **Write the prime factorizations.**

$\text{GCF} = 2 \cdot 2 \cdot 2 = 8$ ← **Find the product of the common factors.**

The teams should march in rows of 8 people.

Anna's Method

First I'll list the possible sizes of rows.
Then I'll choose the largest number in both teams.

The factors of 32 are: 1, 2, 4, 8, 16, 32
The factors of 40 are: 1, 2, 4, 5, 8, 10, 20, 40

Since 8 is the greatest factor that the two lists have in common, 8 is the GCF. The teams should march in rows of 8 people.

Choose a Method

Teams of 36 and 60 are to march in rows of equal width. How wide is the widest row possible? Describe your method and explain why you chose it.

EXERCISES

For more practice, see *Extra Practice.*

A Practice by Example

Example 1 (page 145)

Find the LCM of each pair of numbers.

1. 4, 6 **2.** 9, 12 **3.** 8, 5 **4.** 2, 5 **5.** 3, 8

6. 6, 7 **7.** 5, 10 **8.** 10, 6 **9.** 15, 9 **10.** 24, 8

11. Fitness Suppose you take aerobics classes every 3 days and martial arts classes every 7 days. If you have both classes today, when will you take both classes again on the same day?

Example 2 (page 146)

Find the factors of each number.

12. 20 **13.** 23 **14.** 32 **15.** 62 **16.** 70

17. 36 **18.** 40 **19.** 50 **20.** 44 **21.** 63

Example 3 (page 146)

Tell whether each number is prime or composite.

22. 7 **23.** 16 **24.** 21 **25.** 1 **26.** 6

Example 4 (page 146)

Write the prime factorization. Use exponents where possible.

27. 45 **28.** 64 **29.** 84 **30.** 111 **31.** 65

32. 52 **33.** 75 **34.** 48 **35.** 60 **36.** 132

Example 5 (page 147)

Find the GCF of each pair of numbers.

37. 18, 32 **38.** 12, 15 **39.** 16, 80 **40.** 10, 85

41. 38, 76 **42.** 75, 90 **43.** 54, 80 **44.** 52, 26

B Apply Your Skills

Tell whether each number is prime or composite.

45. 47 **46.** 69 **47.** 77 **48.** 165 **49.** 104

50. Error Analysis Two students made factor trees of the prime factors of 24. Are both correct? Explain.

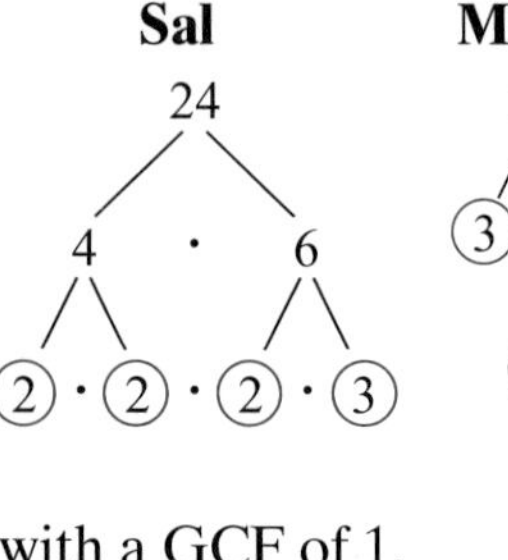

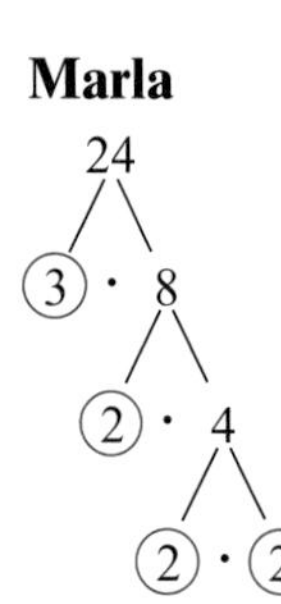

51. Writing in Math Describe the relationships between 15, 5, and 3 using the words *factor* and *multiple*.

52. Reasoning Find two composite numbers with a GCF of 1.

Write the prime factorization. Use exponents where possible.

53. 86 **54.** 144 **55.** 210 **56.** 675

57. 720 **58.** 1,000 **59.** 340 **60.** 1,234

Real-World Connection

Theater seats are staggered so people in each row do not block the views of people behind them.

61. **Entertainment** A movie theater just added two rooms. One room is large enough for 125 people, and the other can seat up to 350 people. In each room, the seating is arranged in horizontal rows with the same number of seats in each row. What is the greatest number of seats that can make up each row?

Mental Math **Find the GCF of each pair of numbers.**

62. 3, 10 **63.** 7, 12 **64.** 4, 20 **65.** 50, 1000

66. Reasoning You can express the number 100 as 10^2 using exponents. Is this the same as the prime factorization of 100? Explain.

67. The diagram shows the prime factors of 18 and 24.

18 24

3 (2 3) 2 2

a. Find the product of the factors that are in the intersection of the circles. Is the product the GCF or the LCM? Explain.

b. Find the product of all the factors in both circles. Is the product the GCF or the LCM? Explain.

Challenge

68. Number Sense Let n be any prime number. Tell whether each statement is *sometimes*, *always*, or *never* true.

a. $2n$ is composite. **b.** $2n + 1$ is prime.

c. $2n + 1$ is even. **d.** $2n + 2$ is composite.

69. Stretch Your Thinking A number is divided by 6. The quotient is doubled and then 8 is added. The answer is 24. What is the number?

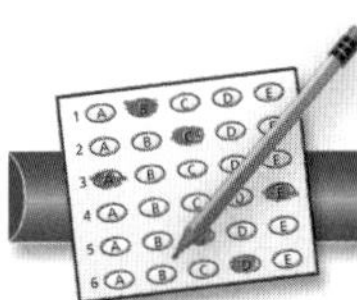

Test Prep

Gridded Response

70. Find the GCF of 21 and 15.

71. Find the GCF of 32 and 24.

72. Find the LCM of 12 and 8.

73. Find the LCM of 9 and 1.

74. What number is the greatest prime factor of 308?

Take It to the NET
Online lesson quiz at www.PHSchool.com
Web Code: aba-0304

Mixed Review

Lesson 1-7 **Find the value of each expression.**

75. $-31 - (-18)$ **76.** $21 + (-17)$ **77.** $-45 - 10$

Lesson 1-6 **Order from least to greatest.**

78. $3, -4, -5, 6$ **79.** $-7, -10, -13$ **80.** $20, -21, 21, 0$

Reading a Math Lesson

For Use With Lesson 3-4

When you read a math lesson, keep the purpose in mind. Here are some strategies you can use to help you read for the main purpose in the lesson.

Focus Before you read a lesson:

- Look at the title.
- Find the objectives.
- For each objective, write a question.

Objectives show you what is important. The questions you write can help you remember the information you are trying to find and learn.

Lesson 3-4 Prime Factorization

Objective	Questions for the Objective
1. Finding Multiples and Factors	a. What is a multiple? b. What is a factor? c. How are they similar? d. How are they different?
2. Using Prime Factorization	e. What is prime factorization? f. Why is prime factorization useful?

Read As you read:

- Try to answer your questions.
- If necessary, read the lesson or sections of the lesson again.

Reflect Suppose you are explaining the lesson to a friend who was absent from class. Make up your own example for each objective.

Ask yourself how the skills in the lesson connect to skills from earlier lessons in the chapter or book. For Lesson 3-4 you might ask, "How is finding factors like using divisibility tests?"

EXERCISES

1. Answer the questions in the table above for Lesson 3-4.
2. Make up an example for each objective in Lesson 3-4. Explain, in words, how to find the solution to each example.

Look ahead to Lesson 3-5.

3. What is the title and what are the main objectives of the lesson?
4. For each objective of Lesson 3-5, write a question that you should be able to answer after you read the lesson.

3-5 Simplifying Fractions

What You'll Learn

 To write equivalent fractions

 To simplify fractions

. . . And Why

To find a fraction of road signs, as in Example 4

Check Skills You'll Need

For help, go to Lesson 3-4.

Find the GCF of each pair of numbers.

1. 6, 10
2. 3, 7
3. 12, 24
4. 15, 25
5. 45, 50
6. 1, 2
7. Reasoning Why does $3 \div 3$ have the same result as $7 \div 7$?

New Vocabulary

- equivalent fractions
- simplest form

Interactive lesson includes instant self-check, tutorials, and activities.

Writing Equivalent Fractions

Real-World Connection

Careers Coaches encourage their team and share in the joy of winning.

A girls' basketball team won 3 out of 4 games. A boys' soccer team won 6 out of 8 games. Both teams won the same fraction of games. Fractions that name the same amount are **equivalent fractions.**

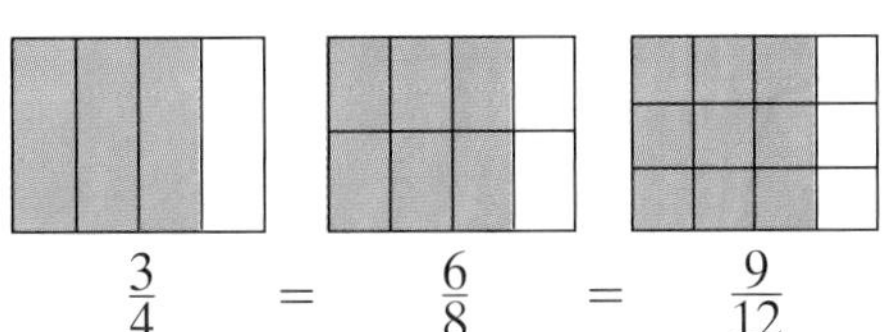

$$\frac{3}{4} = \frac{6}{8} = \frac{9}{12}$$

So $\frac{3}{4}$, $\frac{6}{8}$, and $\frac{9}{12}$ are equivalent. You can write equivalent fractions by multiplying or dividing the numerator and the denominator by the same nonzero number.

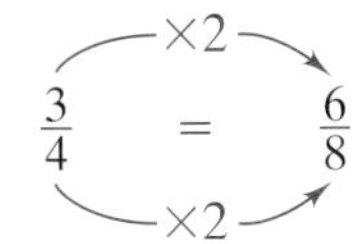

1 EXAMPLE Using Multiples to Write Equivalent Fractions

Use a table of multiples to write three fractions equivalent to $\frac{7}{8}$.

	×2	×3	×4
7	14	21	28
8	16	24	32

← **Multiples in the same column form fractions equivalent to $\frac{7}{8}$.**

Three fractions equivalent to $\frac{7}{8}$ are $\frac{14}{16}$, $\frac{21}{24}$, and $\frac{28}{32}$.

Check Understanding 1

a. Use multiples to write two fractions equivalent to $\frac{4}{5}$.

b. You can write 2 as $\frac{2}{1}$. Write three fractions equivalent to 2.

The fractions you get by dividing the numerator and denominator by a common factor are also equivalent to the original fraction.

2 EXAMPLE Using Factors to Write Equivalent Fractions

Write three fractions equivalent to $\frac{24}{30}$.

Factors of 24: 1, 2, 3, 4, 6, 8, 12, 24
Factors of 30: 1, 2, 3, 5, 6, 10, 15, 30 } ← **List the factors of each number. Look for common factors.**

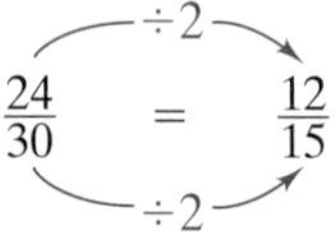

$\frac{24}{30} = \frac{12}{15}$ (÷2)

$\frac{24}{30} = \frac{8}{10}$ (÷3)

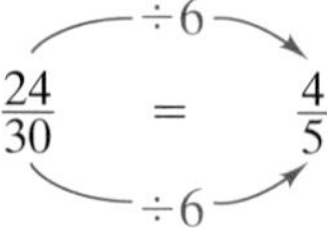

$\frac{24}{30} = \frac{4}{5}$ (÷6)

Three fractions equivalent to $\frac{24}{30}$ are $\frac{12}{15}$, $\frac{8}{10}$, and $\frac{4}{5}$.

✓ Check Understanding 2
a. Use common factors to write two fractions equivalent to $\frac{18}{30}$.
b. **Reasoning** Are $\frac{2}{4}$ and $\frac{8}{8}$ equivalent? Explain.

OBJECTIVE

2 Simplifying Fractions

A fraction is written in **simplest form** when the numerator and the denominator have no common factors other than 1. For example, $\frac{1}{3}$ and $\frac{3}{9}$ are equivalent, but only $\frac{1}{3}$ is written in simplest form.

3 EXAMPLE Simplifying by Dividing

Simplify $\frac{12}{24}$.

$\frac{12 \div 2}{24 \div 2} = \frac{6}{12}$ ← **Divide the numerator and denominator by a common factor.**

$\frac{6 \div 6}{12 \div 6} = \frac{1}{2}$ ← **If necessary, divide again by another common factor.**

In simplest form, $\frac{12}{24}$ is $\frac{1}{2}$.

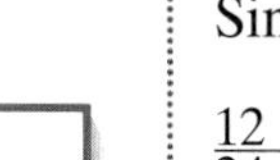

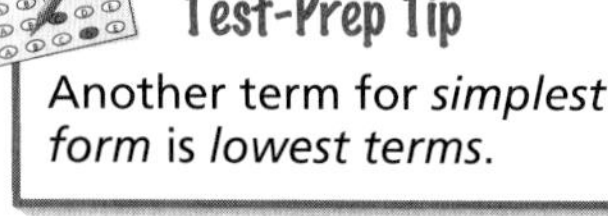

Test-Prep Tip

Another term for *simplest form* is *lowest terms*.

✓ Check Understanding 3 Write $\frac{8}{12}$ in simplest form.

You can also use the GCF to write fractions in simplest form.

4 EXAMPLE Using the GCF to Simplify a Fraction

Real World

Driving In the United States, there are 48 types of road signs. Of these, 16 are instructional, such as speed limit or stop signs. What fraction of road signs are instructional? Write your answer in simplest form.

$\frac{16}{48} = \frac{16 \div 16}{48 \div 16} = \frac{1}{3}$ ← **Divide both numerator and denominator by the GCF, 16.**

The fraction of road signs that are instructional is $\frac{1}{3}$.

✓ Check Understanding 4
a. Write $\frac{18}{45}$ in simplest form.
b. **Reasoning** Explain why it does not make sense to use the LCM of the numerator and denominator to simplify fractions.

EXERCISES

For more practice, see *Extra Practice*.

A Practice by Example

Example 1 (page 151)

Use multiples to write two fractions equivalent to each fraction.

1. $\frac{5}{6}$ **2.** $\frac{3}{8}$ **3.** $\frac{2}{9}$ **4.** $\frac{7}{10}$

5. $\frac{4}{7}$ **6.** $\frac{3}{5}$ **7.** $\frac{6}{11}$ **8.** $\frac{1}{5}$

Example 2 (page 152)

Use common factors to write two fractions equivalent to each fraction.

9. $\frac{8}{24}$ **10.** $\frac{18}{36}$ **11.** $\frac{27}{81}$ **12.** $\frac{60}{140}$

13. $\frac{30}{42}$ **14.** $\frac{45}{90}$ **15.** $\frac{24}{84}$ **16.** $\frac{36}{80}$

Examples 3 and 4 (page 152)

Write each fraction in simplest form.

17. $\frac{24}{32}$ **18.** $\frac{18}{27}$ **19.** $\frac{33}{39}$ **20.** $\frac{8}{18}$

21. $\frac{16}{28}$ **22.** $\frac{21}{28}$ **23.** $\frac{18}{30}$ **24.** $\frac{25}{35}$

25. Biology An adult's body has 206 bones. Of these, 106 are in the feet, ankles, wrists, and hands. What fraction of an adult's bones is in the feet, ankles, wrists, and hands? Write your answer in simplest form.

B Apply Your Skills

Use the table. Find the number that makes each statement true.

26. $\frac{5}{6} = \frac{20}{■}$ **27.** $\frac{25}{30} = \frac{■}{48}$

28. $\frac{30}{36} = \frac{15}{■}$ **29.** $\frac{■}{24} = \frac{35}{42}$

×	3	4	5	6	7	8
5	15	20	25	30	35	40
6	18	24	30	36	42	48

30. a. Data File, p. 129 Write the shutter opening times as equivalent fractions that all have the same denominator.

b. How could you use the fractions you wrote to compare the times?

31. a. Find the thickness of the door at the left to the nearest $\frac{1}{2}$ in.

b. Find the thickness of the door to the nearest $\frac{1}{4}$ in.

c. Reasoning A sliding door has the thickness shown at the left. If you are designing a track for the door to slide in, should you use your answer to part (a) or part (b)? Explain.

Write two equivalent fractions for each model.

32. 

33. 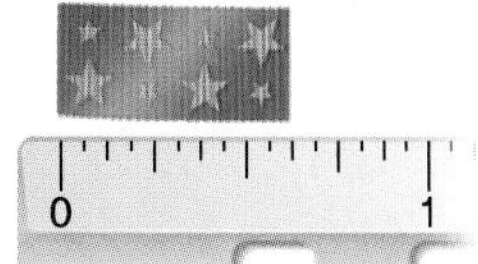

34. 

35. Writing in Math Explain how you can use divisibility rules to tell whether the fractions $\frac{9}{16}$, $\frac{10}{24}$, and $\frac{15}{35}$ are in simplest form.

36. Number Sense Which number is a factor of all positive numbers?

37. Which square does *not* have the same fraction shaded as the others?

A. 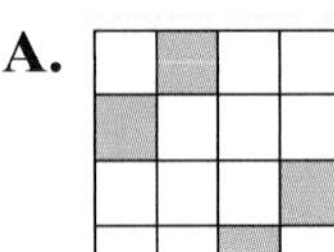 B. 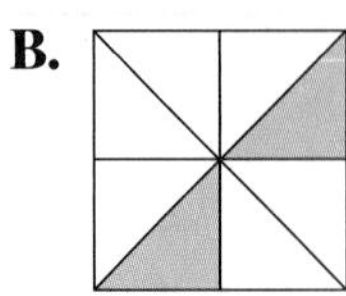 C. 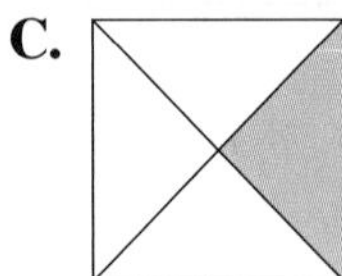 D. 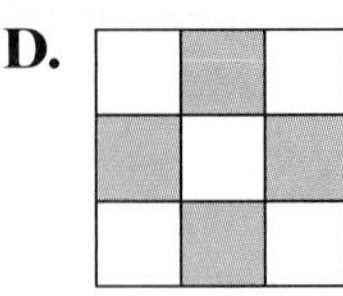

38. **Error Analysis** A math teacher asks his students to find a fraction equivalent to $\frac{5}{6}$. Shauna's answer is below. Is she correct? Explain.

$$\frac{5}{6} = \frac{5+4}{6+4} = \frac{9}{10}$$

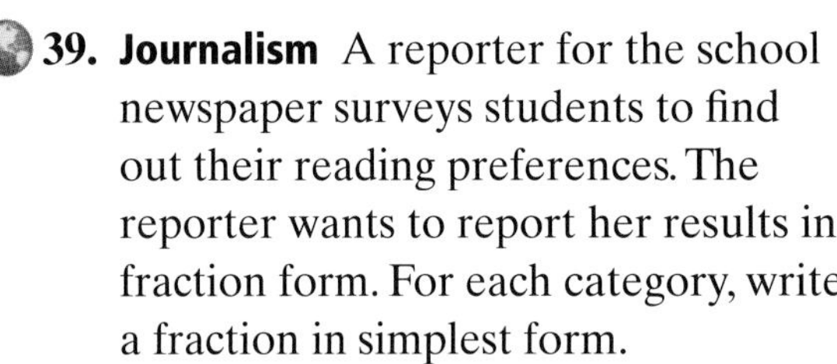

39. **Journalism** A reporter for the school newspaper surveys students to find out their reading preferences. The reporter wants to report her results in fraction form. For each category, write a fraction in simplest form.

Student Reading Preferences

Category	Number
Novels	18
Biographies	8
Science fiction	4

Real-World Connection

Careers Journalists gather information, analyze data, and write reports.

40. Find an integer that fits the following conditions: It is between 44 and 53. The sum of its digits is a prime number. It has more than 3 factors.

Find each missing number.

41. $\frac{18}{\square} = \frac{6}{7}$ 42. $\frac{5}{8} = \frac{\square}{32}$ 43. $\frac{\square}{6} = \frac{4}{1}$ 44. $\frac{35}{\square} = \frac{7}{1}$

45. The chart shows a student's daily activities. Write a fraction in simplest form for the amount of time spent on each activity.

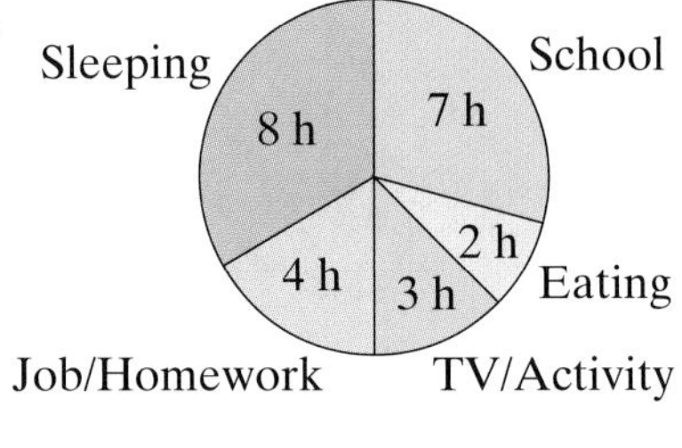

46. **Weather** The city of Houston, Texas, typically has 75 clear days out of the 365 days in a year. Houston's clear days represent what fraction of a year? Write your answer in simplest form.

Challenge

Algebra **Evaluate each expression. Let $p = 7$, $n = -3$, and $m = 2$. Write in simplest form.**

47. $\frac{p \cdot p}{p \cdot p \cdot p \cdot p}$ 48. $\frac{n^2}{n}$ 49. $\frac{n^2m^3}{n^3m}$

50. **Banking** A customer enters a four-digit number to access an ATM. The number formed by the first two digits is divisible by 4 and 7. Three of the factors of the number formed by the last two digits are 4, 5, and 12.
 a. Write three possibilities for the first two digits.
 b. Write one possibility for the last two digits.
 c. The four-digit number is divisible by 3. What is the number?

51. **Stretch Your Thinking** In the equations below, ▱ represents a two-digit number and △ represents a three-digit number. What are the numbers?

248 − ▱ = △ 64 + ▱ = △

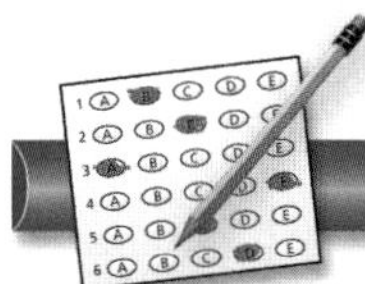

Test Prep

Reading Comprehension

Read the passage and answer the questions below.

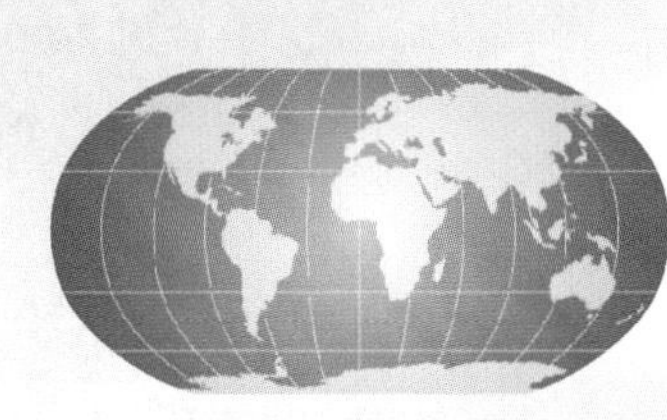

The Global Village

Think of Earth as a global village of only a thousand people. A total of 607 of them are from Asia, 132 are from Africa, 120 are from Europe, 57 are from South America, 5 are from Australia, and 79 are from North America.

Write each fraction in simplest form.

Take It to the NET
Online lesson quiz at
www.PHSchool.com
Web Code: aba-0305

52. the fraction of people from Africa

53. the fraction of people from Australia or Asia

54. the fraction of people from Europe

55. the fraction of people from South America or North America

Mixed Review

Lesson 2-6

Algebra **Solve each equation.**

56. $-5t + 7 = 62$ **57.** $\frac{s}{2} - 4 = 11$ **58.** $\frac{n}{3} + 2 = -4$

Lesson 1-2

Find each sum or difference.

59. $14.02 + 3.6$ **60.** $0.83 - 0.75$ **61.** $45.79 - 2.3$

62. $7.077 + 25.3$ **63.** $25.98 - 8.89$ **64.** $10.132 - 6.7$

Checkpoint Quiz 1 — Lessons 3-1 through 3-5

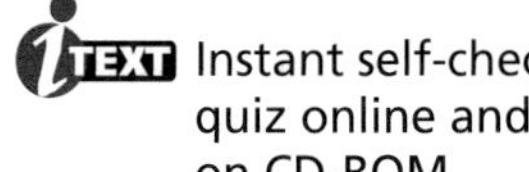

Instant self-check quiz online and on CD-ROM

Simplify each expression.

1. $8^2 + 11$ **2.** $(-2)^4$ **3.** $5 + (3^2 - 2)^2$

Write each number in scientific notation or standard form.

4. 30,500,000 **5.** 2.01×10^4 **6.** 46,110,000

7. The GCF of two numbers is 6. The prime factorization of the first one is $2^2 \cdot 3 \cdot 11$. The second is divisible by 7. What are the numbers?

Simplify each fraction.

8. $\frac{18}{36}$ **9.** $\frac{42}{60}$ **10.** $\frac{35}{56}$

3-6 Comparing and Ordering Fractions

What You'll Learn

OBJECTIVE 1 To compare and order fractions

. . . And Why

To compare the sizes of birds around the world, as in Example 2

Check Skills You'll Need

For help, go to Lesson 3-4.

Find the LCM of each pair of numbers.

1. 3, 4 **2.** 6, 5 **3.** 4, 10

4. 2, 8 **5.** 14, 7 **6.** 9, 15

New Vocabulary • least common denominator (LCD)

Interactive lesson includes instant self-check, tutorials, and activities.

OBJECTIVE

1 Comparing and Ordering Fractions

You can use a number line to compare fractions.

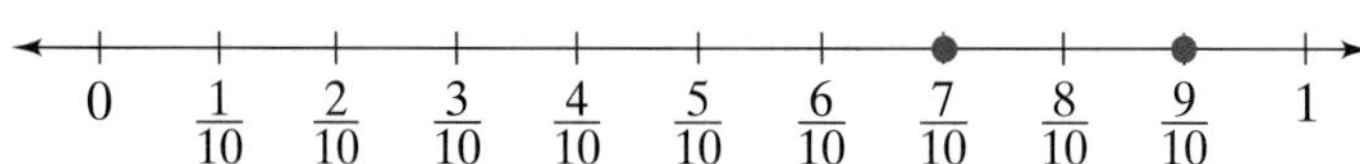

> **Reading Math**
>
> The inequality $\frac{7}{10} < \frac{9}{10}$ has the same meaning as $\frac{9}{10} > \frac{7}{10}$.

If the *denominators* are the same, the numerators tell which is greater. Use the "is greater than" (>) or the "is less than" (<) symbols.

$$\frac{7}{10} < \frac{9}{10}$$

If the *numerators* of two fractions are the same, the fraction with the lesser denominator has the greater value. For example, $\frac{3}{4} > \frac{3}{5}$.

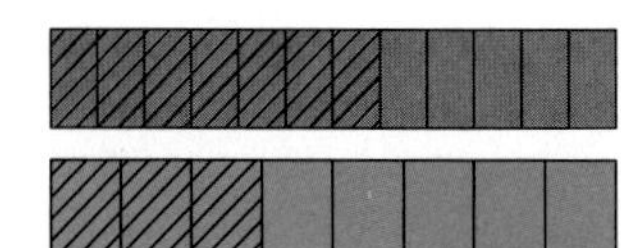

The fraction models show that $\frac{7}{12} > \frac{3}{8}$. To compare fractions with different denominators, rewrite each with a common denominator. The **least common denominator (LCD)** of two or more fractions is the least common multiple (LCM) of their denominators.

1 EXAMPLE Comparing Fractions

Compare $\frac{3}{4}$ and $\frac{9}{10}$.

The denominators are 4 and 10. Their LCM is 20. So, 20 is their LCD.

$$\left.\begin{aligned}\frac{3}{4} &= \frac{3 \times 5}{4 \times 5} = \frac{15}{20} \\ \frac{9}{10} &= \frac{9 \times 2}{10 \times 2} = \frac{18}{20}\end{aligned}\right\}$$ ← **Write equivalent fractions with a denominator of 20.**

$\frac{15}{20} < \frac{18}{20}$. So, $\frac{3}{4} < \frac{9}{10}$. ← **Compare the numerators.**

Check Understanding 1 Compare each pair of fractions. Use <, >, or =.

a. $\frac{3}{4}$ ■ $\frac{5}{6}$ **b.** $\frac{1}{6}$ ■ $\frac{2}{9}$ **c.** $\frac{4}{10}$ ■ $\frac{3}{8}$

Real-World Connection

The American phalarope is a water bird. It migrates to the Arctic in the spring.

You can use the LCD to order more than two fractions.

2 EXAMPLE **Real-World Problem Solving**

Birds There are many small birds all over the world. The American phalarope is $\frac{2}{3}$ ft long, the African cuckoo is $\frac{3}{4}$ ft long, and the Eurasian skylark is $\frac{7}{12}$ ft long. Which of these birds is the smallest? Which is the largest? Order the birds from least to greatest in length.

Order $\frac{2}{3}, \frac{3}{4}$, and $\frac{7}{12}$.

The LCM of 3, 4, and 12 is 12. So 12 is the LCD of the three fractions.

Phalarope → $\frac{2}{3} = \frac{2 \times 4}{3 \times 4} = \frac{8}{12}$

Cuckoo → $\frac{3}{4} = \frac{3 \times 3}{4 \times 3} = \frac{9}{12}$

Skylark → $\frac{7}{12}$

← **Use the LCD to write equivalent fractions.**

$\frac{7}{12} < \frac{8}{12} < \frac{9}{12}$. So, $\frac{7}{12} < \frac{2}{3} < \frac{3}{4}$. ← **Compare the numerators.**

The skylark is the smallest of these three birds. The cuckoo is the largest.

Check Understanding 2 Order from least to greatest.

a. $\frac{3}{8}, \frac{1}{2}, \frac{2}{5}$ **b.** $\frac{6}{9}, \frac{1}{3}, \frac{7}{12}$ **c.** $\frac{1}{5}, \frac{2}{6}, \frac{1}{15}$

d. **Reasoning** To order $\frac{4}{10}, \frac{3}{5}$, and $\frac{5}{25}$, it is helpful to write each fraction in simplest form first, before considering the LCD. Explain why.

EXERCISES

For more practice, see *Extra Practice*.

A Practice by Example

Example 1 (page 156)

Compare each pair of fractions. Use <, >, or =.

1. $\frac{5}{12}$ ■ $\frac{7}{12}$ **2.** $\frac{5}{6}$ ■ $\frac{3}{6}$ **3.** $\frac{1}{3}$ ■ $\frac{3}{4}$ **4.** $\frac{5}{6}$ ■ $\frac{3}{5}$

5. $\frac{3}{8}$ ■ $\frac{2}{3}$ **6.** $\frac{6}{7}$ ■ $\frac{4}{5}$ **7.** $\frac{2}{3}$ ■ $\frac{5}{8}$ **8.** $\frac{5}{6}$ ■ $\frac{7}{10}$

9. $\frac{3}{8}$ ■ $\frac{3}{5}$ **10.** $\frac{3}{9}$ ■ $\frac{1}{3}$ **11.** $\frac{3}{4}$ ■ $\frac{3}{10}$ **12.** $\frac{1}{8}$ ■ $\frac{3}{16}$

Example 2 (page 157)

Order from least to greatest.

13. $\frac{2}{3}, \frac{3}{4}, \frac{5}{6}$ **14.** $\frac{3}{8}, \frac{1}{4}, \frac{2}{3}$ **15.** $\frac{4}{9}, \frac{2}{3}, \frac{1}{2}$

16. $\frac{1}{3}, \frac{5}{6}, \frac{3}{8}$ **17.** $\frac{1}{8}, \frac{1}{6}, \frac{1}{9}$ **18.** $\frac{3}{15}, \frac{3}{10}, \frac{3}{5}$

19. $\frac{5}{8}, \frac{7}{9}, \frac{2}{1}$ **20.** $\frac{6}{10}, \frac{7}{12}, \frac{5}{8}$ **21.** $\frac{2}{5}, \frac{3}{20}, \frac{4}{5}$

22. Languages In Europe, $\frac{1}{3}$ of the languages spoken are Romance languages, $\frac{2}{15}$ are Germanic, and $\frac{8}{25}$ are Balto-Slavic. Order the language categories from least to greatest.

B Apply Your Skills

Compare each pair of fractions. Use <, >, or =.

23. $\frac{7}{12}$ ■ $\frac{5}{9}$ **24.** $\frac{10}{15}$ ■ $\frac{16}{24}$ **25.** $\frac{8}{16}$ ■ $\frac{15}{32}$ **26.** $\frac{22}{26}$ ■ $\frac{10}{13}$

Use the table at the right.

Memory Facts

People remember. . .	of. . .
three fourths	what they say.
one tenth	what they hear.
nine tenths	what they do.

27. Do people remember more of what they say or more of what they do?

28. Do people remember more of what they hear or more of what they say?

29. Order what people remember from greatest to least.

Write two fractions for the models and compare them. Use <, >, or =.

30.

31. 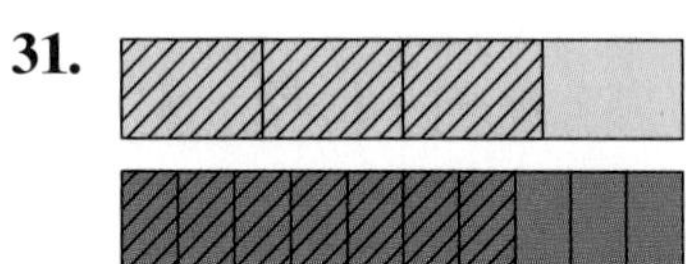

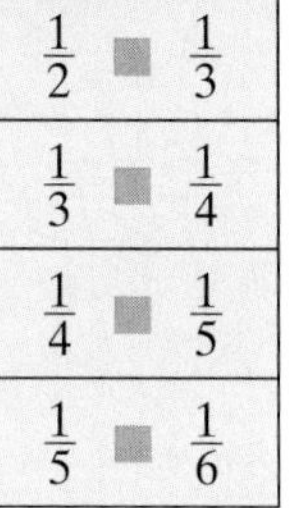

$\frac{1}{2}$ ■ $\frac{1}{3}$
$\frac{1}{3}$ ■ $\frac{1}{4}$
$\frac{1}{4}$ ■ $\frac{1}{5}$
$\frac{1}{5}$ ■ $\frac{1}{6}$

32. **Patterns** Copy the table. Compare the fractions and fill in your answers. Use <, >, or =.

33. **Writing in Math** Describe an easy way to compare fractions that have the same numerator, such as $\frac{4}{5}$ and $\frac{4}{7}$. Explain why your method works.

34. **Data File, p. 129** A fast shutter speed allows less light in because the shutter is open for less time.

a. Which shutter opening time represents the fastest shutter speed?

b. A camera is adjusted to a shutter opening time of $\frac{1}{8}$ s. Order the shutter opening times, including $\frac{1}{8}$ s, from least to greatest.

Match each fraction with a point on the number line below.

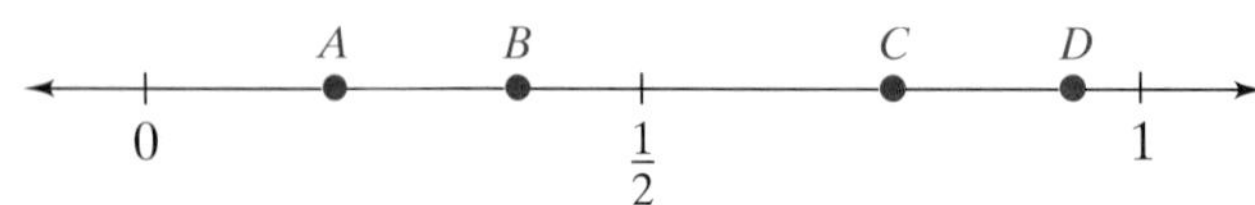

35. $\frac{3}{8}$ **36.** $\frac{11}{12}$ **37.** $\frac{3}{4}$ **38.** $\frac{3}{16}$

Order from least to greatest.

39. $1, \frac{4}{6}, \frac{1}{3}$ **40.** $\frac{10}{15}, \frac{6}{10}, \frac{1}{3}$ **41.** $2, \frac{5}{2}, \frac{4}{3}$ **42.** $\frac{1}{8}, \frac{3}{12}, \frac{4}{10}$

Which fractional part would you prefer? Explain and show your work.

43. $\frac{5}{6}$ or $\frac{3}{4}$ hours of dental work

44. $\frac{1}{6}$ or $\frac{1}{12}$ of a year on vacation

45. $\frac{2}{9}$ or $\frac{4}{15}$ of your paycheck

46. **Carpentry** You want to nail a board that is $\frac{1}{2}$ in. thick onto a wall. You can choose from nails that are $\frac{3}{8}$ in. long and $\frac{3}{4}$ in. long. Which size nail is the better choice? Explain.

47. **Reasoning** Your class orders the same number of cheese, vegetable, and meatball pizzas. There are $\frac{5}{8}$ of cheese, $\frac{2}{3}$ of vegetable, and $\frac{3}{4}$ of meatball pizza left over. Which is most popular? Explain.

Challenge

Algebra **Compare. Use <, >, or =. The variable n is a positive integer.**

48. $\frac{1}{n}, \frac{1}{n+1}$

49. $\frac{n}{2}, \frac{n+1}{2}$

50. $\frac{1}{n}, \frac{1}{2n}$

51. **Stretch Your Thinking** Draw exactly four triangles to make the figure at the right.

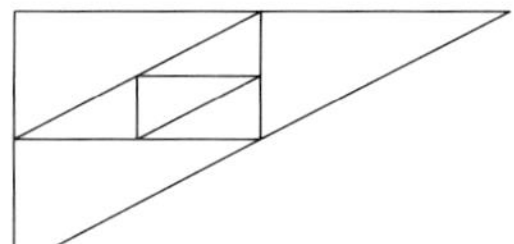

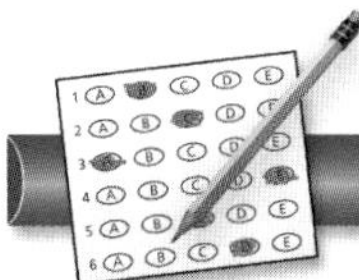

Test Prep

Multiple Choice

52. To make a noodle casserole, Jack uses $\frac{1}{3}$ cup of cream cheese, Myra uses $\frac{2}{5}$ cup, Donna uses $\frac{3}{4}$ cup, and Ferron uses $\frac{1}{2}$ cup. Who uses the most?

A. Jack B. Myra C. Donna D. Ferron

Take It to the NET
Online lesson quiz at
www.PHSchool.com
Web Code: aba-0306

53. On a group project, Richard does $\frac{1}{4}$ of the work, Bonita does $\frac{3}{16}$, Gary does $\frac{1}{8}$, and Sierra does $\frac{7}{16}$. Who does the least work?

F. Richard G. Bonita H. Gary I. Sierra

54. Which of the following is NOT written in order from least to greatest?

A. $\frac{2}{9}, \frac{3}{12}, \frac{5}{6}$ B. $\frac{1}{2}, \frac{5}{6}, \frac{3}{3}$ C. $\frac{3}{12}, \frac{5}{6}, \frac{2}{9}$ D. $\frac{2}{9}, \frac{5}{6}, \frac{3}{3}$

Short Response

55. A bank offers three types of interest-bearing savings accounts. One account increases by $\frac{1}{2}$ percent annually, another increases by $\frac{3}{5}$ percent, and a third increases by $\frac{7}{12}$ percent.

a. Order the fractions from least to greatest.

b. In which account would you prefer to invest your money?

Mixed Review

Lesson 1-7

Algebra **Find each sum.**

56. $-3 + 7$

57. $5 + (-2)$

58. $-6 + (-8)$

Lesson 1-3

Find each product or quotient.

59. $(9.4)(0.3)$

60. $1.02 \div 0.3$

61. $(8.07)(14.2)$

62. $85.92 \div 4.8$

63. $(3.01)(4.20)$

64. $15.678 \div 2.01$

3-7 Solve a Simpler Problem and Look for a Pattern

What You'll Learn

1. To solve a problem by combining strategies

. . . And Why

To solve a multi-step problem, as in Example 1

Check Skills You'll Need

For help, go to Lesson 3-1.

Simplify each expression.

1. 4^2
2. 5^4
3. 7^3
4. 3^5
5. 4^1
6. 8^2

OBJECTIVE 1

Solving a Problem by Combining Strategies

When to Use These Strategies If a problem seems to have a large number of steps, you may be able to solve a simpler problem first. Then look for a pattern that will give you a clue to the solution of the original problem.

1 EXAMPLE Combining Strategies

When you simplify 3^{50}, what number is the ones place?

Read and Understand You know that 3^{50} is a large number to calculate. You need to find out what number is in the ones place.

Plan and Solve It is not easy to simplify 3^{50} with paper and pencil. You could simplify easier expressions, like 3^2, 3^3, and 3^4, to see what number is in the ones place.

Step 1: *Solve a Simpler Problem*

Find the values of the first 10 powers of 3. Refer to the table at the right. Notice that the ones digits in the value column repeat in the pattern 3, 9, 7, 1

Power	Value
3^1	3
3^2	9
3^3	27
3^4	81
3^5	243
3^6	729
3^7	2,187
3^8	6,561
3^9	19,683
3^{10}	59,049

Step 2: *Look for a Pattern*

Organize the information to see whether there is a connection between the ones digits and the exponents. Refer to the table below.

Ones Place	Exponent of 3
3	1, 5, 9
9	2, 6, 10
7	3, 7
1	4, 8

If the exponent is divisible by 4, then the ones digit is 1. Since 48 is divisible by 4, you can start there:

Exponent:	48	49	50
Ones digit:	1	3	9

The number in the ones place of 3^{50} is 9.

Look Back and Check Look for a pattern in another row of the exponent table that might also work.

When the exponent of 3 is 2, 6, or 10, the ones digit is 9. The numbers 2, 6, and 10 are divisible by 2, but not by 4. Since 50 is divisible by 2 but not by 4, the ones digit of 3^{50} is 9.

Check Understanding 1 **a.** Describe the pattern for the ones digit of any power of 8.
b. When you simplify 8^{63}, what number is in the ones place?

EXERCISES

For more practice, see *Extra Practice*.

A Practice by Example

Solve each problem by solving a simpler problem and looking for a pattern.

Example 1 (page 160)

1. **a.** What is the pattern for the ones digit of any power of 7?
   b. When you simplify 7^{21}, what number is in the ones place?

2. The table shows the values of powers of 2 with even exponents from 10 to 20.
   a. Make a table that lists the exponents of 2 and their corresponding ones digit.
   b. What is the ones digit of 2^{80}?

Power	Value
2^{10}	1,024
2^{12}	4,096
2^{14}	16,384
2^{16}	65,536
2^{18}	262,144
2^{20}	1,048,576

3. What is the value of $(-1)^{427}$? Explain your reasoning.

4. When you simplify 10^{347}, what number is in the ones place?

B Apply Your Skills

Use any strategy or combination of strategies to solve each problem.

Need Help?
- Reread the problem.
- Identify the key facts and details.
- Tell the problem in your own words.
- Try a different strategy.
- Check your work.

5. **Sports** There are 64 teams in a state soccer tournament. A team is eliminated if it loses a game. How many games must be played to determine the state soccer champion?

6. **Cars** A new car comes in five different exterior colors and three different interior colors. How many different color combinations are available?

7. Nita, a six-year-old girl, can stretch her legs to take two stairs at one time. How many different ways can she climb six stairs using any combination of one or two stairs?

Strategies

- Draw a Diagram
- Look for a Pattern
- Make a Graph
- Make an Organized List
- Make a Table
- Simulate a Problem
- Solve a Simpler Problem
- Try, Check, and Revise
- Use Logical Reasoning
- Work Backward
- Write an Equation

8. **Writing in Math** To the amazement of his teacher and classmates, ten-year-old Carl Friedrich Gauss found the sum of the first 100 positive integers. His method is shown below for the first 8 positive integers. How would you find the sum of the first 50 positive integers using his method?

$1 + 8 = 9$

$3 + 6 = 9$

number of pairs

$$1 + 2 + 3 + 4 + 5 + 6 + 7 + 8 = 9 + 9 + 9 + 9 = 9 \cdot 4 = 36$$

$4 + 5 = 9$

$2 + 7 = 9$

9. **Business** A worker is hired for \$80 a day on the condition that if business is slow, the worker will only receive half pay. At the end of 20 days, the worker receives \$1,320. On how many days was business slow?

10. Lewis has between 3 and 100 toy cars in his collection. If he counts them three, four, or five cars at a time, he always has 2 left over. How many toy cars does Lewis have?

11. **Health** A 125-lb person burns 110 Calories walking at 2 mi/h for an hour. That same person burns 180 Calories walking at 3 mi/h, and 260 Calories walking at 4 mi/h. How many Calories do you think a 125-lb person burns in 1 hour by walking 5 mi/h?

12. a. **Patterns** How many boxes will be in the next arrangement?
    b. Draw the next arrangement.

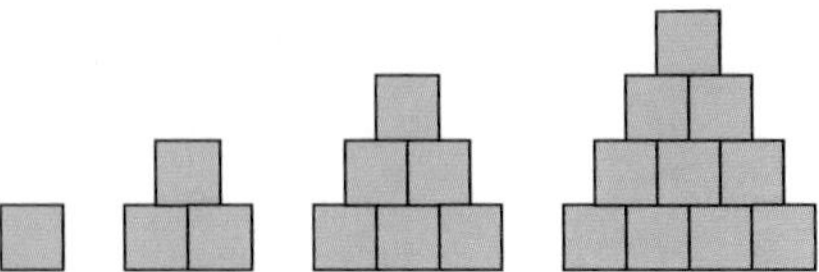

C Challenge

13. **Number Sense** Find the sum of the first 20 powers of 10, that is, the sum of $10^1 + 10^2 + 10^3 + \ldots + 10^{20}$.

14. **Stretch Your Thinking** You are sitting on chair 33 of a ski lift, which is a loop. Chairs are numbered consecutively, starting with 1. Chair 97 passes you halfway up the ski slope. How many chairs are on the lift?

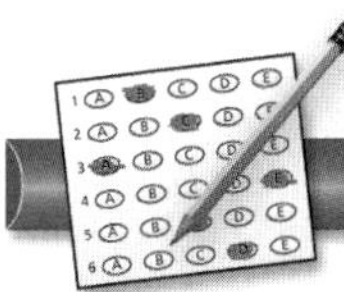

Test Prep

Multiple Choice

15. Which expression is equivalent to $9m + 9n$?
A. $18(m + n)$ **B.** $9(m + n)$ **C.** $9m + n$ **D.** $m + n$

16. Which equation is equivalent to $8p + 4.5 = 32$?
F. $8p + 4.5 = 32 + 4.5$ **G.** $8p = 36.5$
H. $8p = 27.5$ **I.** $6p = 32 - 2$

Take It to the NET
Online lesson quiz at
www.PHSchool.com
Web Code: aba-0307

17. If $4t + 13.7 = 29.9$, what is the value of t?
A. 64.8 **B.** 10.5 **C.** 4.05 **D.** 3.55

Short Response

18. Medium beverages cost \$1.39 and small beverages cost \$.89. Write an equation to find the total cost in dollars (d) of any number of medium beverages (m) and small beverages (s).

Mixed Review

Lesson 3-4

Find the LCM of each pair of numbers.

19. 7, 8 **20.** 6, 20 **21.** 11, 3 **22.** 9, 15

Lesson 3-3

Tell whether the first number is divisible by the second. Explain.

23. 216, 3 **24.** 346, 4 **25.** 315, 6 **26.** 51, 51

Lesson 2-6

Algebra **Solve each equation.**

27. $2m + 3 = 25$ **28.** $\frac{w}{4} - 3 = 3$ **29.** $6m - 7 = 29$

30. $\frac{1}{3}t + 7 = 27$ **31.** $5h - 2 = 73$ **32.** $\frac{1}{4}x - 3 = 17$

Practice Game

Factor Cards

What You'll Need

- 40 index cards numbered from 1 through 40.

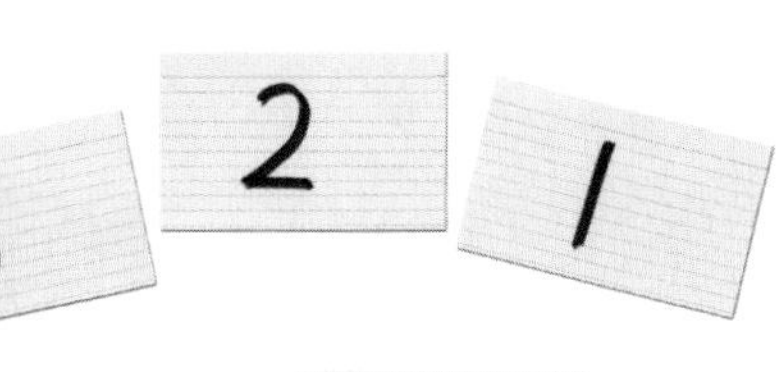

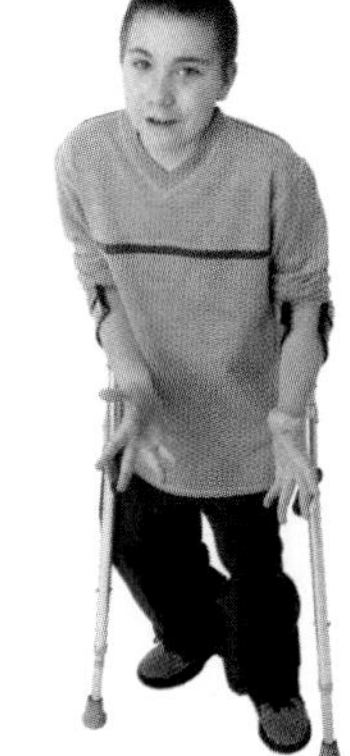

How to Play

- Divide the class into two teams.
- Team A chooses a card.
- Team B picks up any of the remaining cards that are factors of Team A's card. For example, if Team A chooses 10, Team B picks up cards 1, 2, and 5.
- Teams switch places until all of the cards are picked up. The team with the highest sum of factors on its cards wins.

3-8 Mixed Numbers and Improper Fractions

What You'll Learn

To write a mixed number as an improper fraction

To write an improper fraction as a mixed number

. . . And Why

To plan a pizza party, as in Example 3

Check Skills You'll Need

For help, go to Lesson 3-5.

Write each fraction in simplest form.

1. $\frac{12}{20}$
2. $\frac{15}{18}$
3. $\frac{24}{36}$
4. $\frac{45}{60}$
5. $\frac{20}{48}$
6. $\frac{45}{72}$

New Vocabulary • improper fraction • mixed number

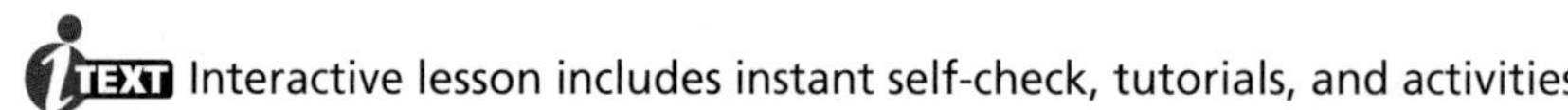

TEXT Interactive lesson includes instant self-check, tutorials, and activities.

OBJECTIVE 1

Writing Mixed Numbers as Improper Fractions

The fractions $\frac{5}{2}$, $\frac{12}{12}$, and $\frac{8}{3}$ are improper fractions. An **improper fraction** has a numerator that is greater than or equal to its denominator.

The numbers $2\frac{1}{2}$, $1\frac{2}{3}$, and $3\frac{2}{5}$ are mixed numbers. A **mixed number** is the sum of a whole number and a fraction.

The models below show that $1\frac{2}{3} = \frac{5}{3}$.

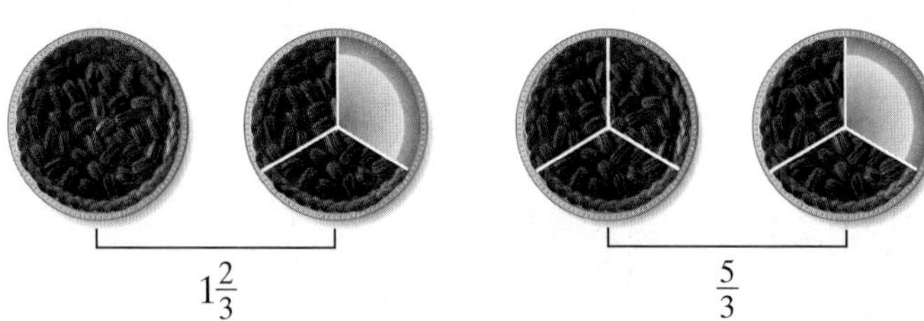

A number line can also help you understand improper fractions and mixed numbers.

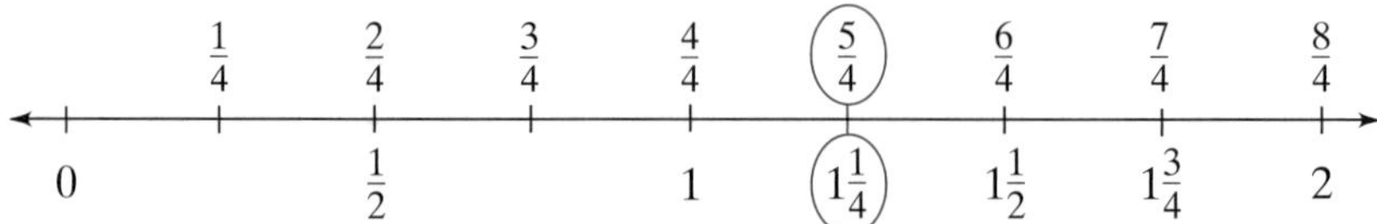

The number line shows that $1\frac{1}{4} = \frac{5}{4}$.

One way to write a mixed number as an improper fraction is to write the mixed number as a sum. Write a fraction that is equivalent to the whole number, and then find the sum of the fractions.

1 EXAMPLE Writing an Improper Fraction

Write $2\frac{3}{4}$ as an improper fraction.

$2\frac{3}{4} = 2 + \frac{3}{4}$ ← **Write the mixed number as a sum.**

$= \frac{8}{4} + \frac{3}{4}$ ← **Write 2 as a fraction with the same denominator as $\frac{3}{4}$.**

$= \frac{8 + 3}{4} = \frac{11}{4}$ ← **Add the numerators.**

Check Understanding 1 Write $3\frac{3}{4}$ as an improper fraction.

Here is another method you can use to write improper fractions.

2 EXAMPLE Using Multiplication

Write $4\frac{2}{3}$ as an improper fraction.

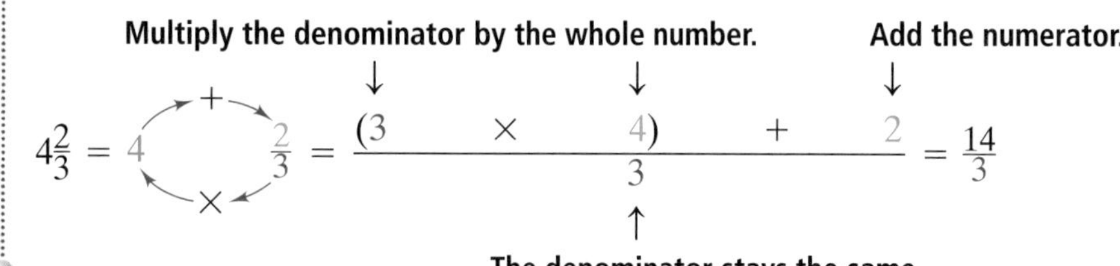

Multiply the denominator by the whole number.
Add the numerator.
$4\frac{2}{3} = 4 \; \frac{2}{3} = \frac{(3 \times 4) + 2}{3} = \frac{14}{3}$
+
×
The denominator stays the same.

Check Understanding 2 Write $2\frac{5}{8}$ as an improper fraction.

OBJECTIVE 2

Writing Improper Fractions as Mixed Numbers

To write an improper fraction as a mixed number, divide and write the remainder as a fraction of the denominator. Then simplify the fraction.

3 EXAMPLE Writing a Mixed Number (Real World)

Party Planning You are planning a pizza party. Each pizza has 8 slices. You estimate you will need 30 slices. How many pizzas should you order?

To find the number of pizzas, write $\frac{30}{8}$ as a mixed number.

$$\begin{array}{r} 3 \\ 8\overline{)30} \\ -24 \\ \hline 6 \end{array}$$

3 ← **whole number**

denominator → 8

6 ← **remainder**

$3\frac{6}{8} = 3\frac{3}{4}$ ← **Write the remainder as a fraction, $\frac{\text{remainder}}{\text{denominator}}$. Simplify.**

Since you cannot order $3\frac{3}{4}$ pizzas, you should order 4 pizzas.

Check Understanding 3 **a.** Reasoning How can you use the GCF before you divide? Explain.

b. Write $\frac{15}{12}$ as a mixed number in simplest form.

EXERCISES

For more practice, see *Extra Practice.*

A Practice by Example

Examples 1 and 2 (page 165)

Write each mixed number as an improper fraction.

1. $2\frac{3}{8}$ **2.** $5\frac{3}{4}$ **3.** $1\frac{1}{12}$ **4.** $4\frac{3}{5}$ **5.** $1\frac{3}{7}$

6. $4\frac{5}{8}$ **7.** $3\frac{2}{5}$ **8.** $2\frac{11}{12}$ **9.** $5\frac{2}{3}$ **10.** $9\frac{1}{4}$

11. $4\frac{5}{6}$ **12.** $2\frac{4}{9}$ **13.** $4\frac{7}{10}$ **14.** $7\frac{3}{5}$ **15.** $6\frac{4}{7}$

Example 3 (page 165)

Write each improper fraction as a mixed number in simplest form.

16. $\frac{16}{3}$ **17.** $\frac{25}{3}$ **18.** $\frac{42}{4}$ **19.** $\frac{31}{12}$ **20.** $\frac{28}{6}$

21. $\frac{49}{6}$ **22.** $\frac{40}{6}$ **23.** $\frac{45}{10}$ **24.** $\frac{48}{11}$ **25.** $\frac{15}{8}$

26. Baking Challah is a bread made by braiding 6 strands of dough together. What is the greatest number of loaves of challah that can be made with 40 strands of dough?

B Apply Your Skills

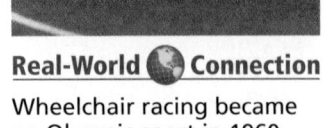

Real-World Connection

Wheelchair racing became an Olympic sport in 1960.

Fitness The distance around a track is $\frac{1}{8}$ mi. Write each distance in miles.

27. A wheelchair racer completes 36 laps around the track.

28. A jogger completes 40 laps around the track.

Write each improper fraction as a whole or mixed number in simplest form.

29. $\frac{9}{2}$ **30.** $\frac{42}{7}$ **31.** $\frac{22}{5}$ **32.** $\frac{17}{6}$ **33.** $\frac{27}{4}$

34. $\frac{19}{12}$ **35.** $\frac{18}{4}$ **36.** $\frac{21}{9}$ **37.** $\frac{32}{8}$ **38.** $\frac{29}{4}$

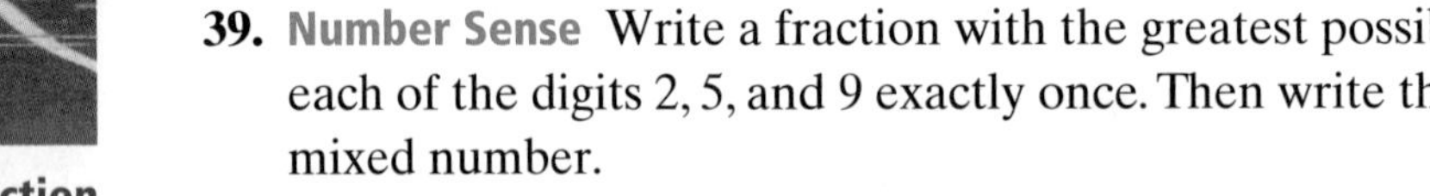

39. Number Sense Write a fraction with the greatest possible value using each of the digits 2, 5, and 9 exactly once. Then write the fraction as a mixed number.

40. Clothing A tailor designs a skirt that is $25\frac{1}{4}$ in. long. What is the length in eighths of an inch? Write your answer as an improper fraction.

Write each length as a mixed number and as an improper fraction.

41.

42.

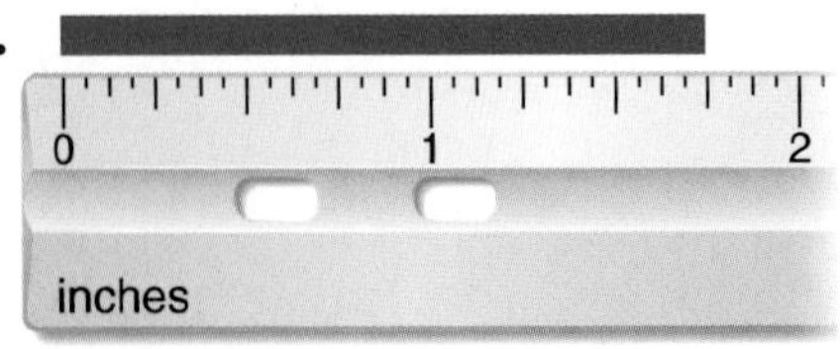

Write each mixed number as an improper fraction.

43. $8\frac{2}{3}$ **44.** $5\frac{8}{9}$ **45.** $6\frac{1}{7}$ **46.** $7\frac{3}{5}$ **47.** $12\frac{4}{7}$

48. **Writing in Math** Which is longer, $\frac{9}{4}$ miles or $1\frac{1}{2}$ miles? Explain.

49. **Modeling** Write a mixed number and an improper fraction for the model below.

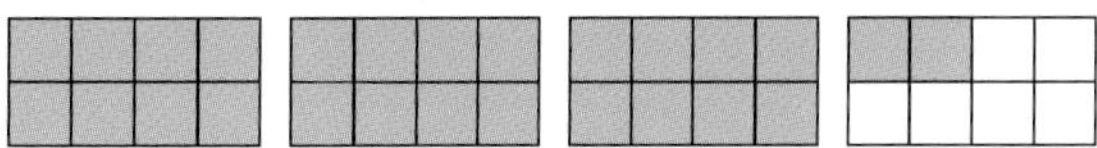

Challenge

Algebra **For Exercises 50–52, evaluate each expression for $a = 6, b = 3, c = 2$, and $d = 5$. Write your answers in simplest form.**

50. $\frac{b}{a^2}$ 51. $\frac{a^2 + b}{c}$ 52. $\frac{a + c}{b + d}$

53. **Stretch Your Thinking** Five friends are seated in a row at a concert. Shayla is sitting next to Suki. Sam is in the middle of the row and sitting next to Suki and Sari. Shar is sitting on the right end of the row. Who is sitting on the left end of the row?

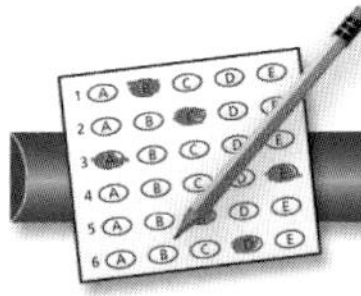

Test Prep

Multiple Choice

54. A piece of fabric measures between 3 and $3\frac{1}{4}$ ft. Which length could it be?
A. $\frac{72}{25}$ ft B. $\frac{25}{8}$ ft C. $\frac{18}{5}$ ft D. $\frac{26}{7}$ ft

Online lesson quiz at **www.PHSchool.com**
Web Code: aba-0308

55. You want to buy sports drinks for the players on your basketball team. If each drink costs $1.69, how many drinks can you buy with $22?
F. 12 G. 13 H. 14 I. 15

56. Choose the mixed number that is equivalent to $\frac{14}{6}$.
A. $2\frac{1}{3}$ B. $\frac{7}{3}$ C. $1\frac{2}{3}$ D. $\frac{6}{14}$

Extended Response

57. A carpenter spends a total of 345 minutes on a project. The carpenter is being paid $29.50 per hour.
a. Use mixed numbers to write the time in hours. Show your work.
b. Estimate the amount the carpenter is paid. Explain how you found your estimate.

Mixed Review

Lesson 2-1

Algebra **Evaluate each expression for $a = 10, b = -2$, and $c = 3$.**

58. $3a - b$ 59. $2b - 3c$

60. $abc - 1$ 61. $b + 3c - b$

Lesson 1-7

Find each difference.

62. $2 - 5$ 63. $-3 - 9$ 64. $-10 - (-18)$

65. $-8 - (-12)$ 66. $-4 - 15$ 67. $21 - (-7)$

3-9 Fractions and Decimals

What You'll Learn

To relate fractions and decimals

. . . And Why

To compare enrichment class preferences, as in Example 4

✔ Check Skills You'll Need

For help, go to Lesson 3-5.

Write each fraction in simplest form.

1. $\frac{8}{10}$
2. $\frac{10}{50}$
3. $\frac{12}{48}$
4. $\frac{70}{100}$
5. $\frac{24}{36}$
6. $\frac{125}{1{,}000}$

New Vocabulary • terminating decimal • repeating decimal

OBJECTIVE 1

Interactive lesson includes instant self-check, tutorials, and activities.

1 Relating Fractions and Decimals

Investigation: Ordering Fractions

The ball speeds toward you. Pow! You snap the bat for a hit. It doesn't happen every time. In fact, most players get a hit less than $\frac{1}{3}$ of the time.

Player	Hits	Times at Bat	Fraction of Hits	Batting Average
Shannon	57	185	$\frac{57}{185}$	.308
Jennifer	73	199	$\frac{73}{199}$	■
Sabrina	39	155	$\frac{39}{155}$	■
Tania	56	191	$\frac{56}{191}$	■

1. **Calculator** Copy the table. For each player's fraction of hits, divide the numerator by the denominator. Round to the nearest thousandth. Fill in your answers in the Batting Average column for each player.
2. Which player had the highest batting average? List the players in order, from highest to lowest batting averages.
3. **Reasoning** Which is easier to compare, the fraction of hits for each player or the decimal batting average for each player? Explain.

You can write a fraction as a decimal by dividing the numerator by the denominator. A decimal that stops, or terminates, is a **terminating decimal.**

1 EXAMPLE Writing a Terminating Decimal

Chemistry The concentration of nitrogen in a chemical sample is $\frac{5}{8}$. Write the fraction of nitrogen as a decimal.

Method 1 Paper and Pencil

$$\frac{5}{8} \text{ or } 5 \div 8 = 8\overline{)5.000} = 0.625 \leftarrow \text{quotient}$$

$$\begin{array}{r} 0.625 \\ 8\overline{)5.000} \\ -48 \\ \hline 20 \\ -16 \\ \hline 40 \\ -40 \\ \hline 0 \end{array}$$

← The remainder is 0.

Method 2 Calculator

5 ÷ 8 = 0.625

So, $\frac{5}{8} = 0.625$. The nitrogen concentration is 0.625.

Check Understanding 1 **a.** Write $\frac{4}{5}$ as a decimal.
b. Reasoning Is a remainder of 0 the same as no remainder? Explain.

Reading Math
The symbol for a repeating decimal is a bar over the repeated digit(s), such as $0.\overline{17}$.

If the same block of digits in a decimal repeats without end, the decimal is a **repeating decimal.** The repeating block can be one or more digits.

$5.355555555555\ldots = 5.3\overline{5}$ ← The digit "5" repeats.

$0.171717171717\ldots = 0.\overline{17}$ ← The digits "17" repeat.

2 EXAMPLE Writing a Repeating Decimal

Write $\frac{3}{11}$ as a decimal.

Method 1 Paper and Pencil

$\frac{3}{11}$ or $3 \div 11 = $

$$\begin{array}{r} 0.27272 \\ 11\overline{)3.00000} \\ -22 \\ \hline 80 \\ -77 \\ \hline 30 \\ -22 \\ \hline 80 \\ -77 \\ \hline 30 \end{array}$$

← The digits "27" repeat.

← There will always be a remainder.

Method 2 Calculator

3 ÷ 11 =
0.27272727273

So, $\frac{3}{11} = 0.\overline{27}$.

Calculator Hint
Most calculators display as many digits as possible of a repeating decimal and round off the final digit. For example, $0.\overline{27}$ might be shown as 0.272727273.

Check Understanding 2 Write each fraction as a decimal.

a. $\frac{2}{11}$ **b.** $\frac{1}{3}$ **c.** $\frac{5}{15}$ **d.** $\frac{5}{9}$

e. Reasoning Is 3.03003000300003... a repeating decimal? Explain.

You can write a terminating decimal as a fraction or mixed number by writing the portion of digits to the right of the decimal point as a fraction.

3 EXAMPLE Writing a Decimal as a Fraction

Reading Math

You read the decimal 1.325 as "one and three hundred twenty-five thousandths."

Write 1.325 as a mixed number with a fraction in simplest form.

Since $0.325 = \frac{325}{1{,}000}$, $1.325 = 1\frac{325}{1{,}000}$.

$1\frac{325}{1{,}000} = 1\frac{325 \div 25}{1{,}000 \div 25}$ ← **Use the GCF to write the fraction in simplest form.**

$= 1\frac{13}{40}$

Check Understanding 3 Write each decimal as a mixed number or fraction in simplest form.

a. 1.364 **b.** 2.48 **c.** 0.6 **d.** 0.275

To compare fractions and decimals, write the decimals as fractions or the fractions as decimals. You can decide which is easier for different numbers.

4 EXAMPLE Ordering Fractions and Decimals

Real World

Surveys When students are asked which enrichment class they prefer, 0.25 choose sign language, $\frac{10}{48}$ choose starting a business, $\frac{5}{12}$ choose robotics, and 0.125 choose study time. List their choices in order of preference.

business → $\frac{10}{48} = \frac{5}{24} = 0.208\overline{3}$

robotics → $\frac{5}{12} = 0.41\overline{6}$

← **Use a calculator to change the fractions to decimals.**

Since $0.41\overline{6} > 0.25 > 0.208\overline{3} > 0.125$, students' preferences are robotics, sign language, business, and study time.

Check Understanding 4 Order from greatest to least: $\frac{7}{8}$, 0.35, $\frac{8}{15}$, 0.862.

EXERCISES

For more practice, see *Extra Practice*.

A Practice by Example

Write each fraction as a decimal.

Example 1 (page 169)

1. $\frac{2}{5}$ **2.** $\frac{4}{5}$ **3.** $\frac{3}{8}$ **4.** $\frac{3}{2}$

5. $\frac{3}{4}$ **6.** $\frac{1}{8}$ **7.** $\frac{1}{5}$ **8.** $\frac{3}{16}$

Example 2 (page 169)

9. $\frac{5}{6}$ **10.** $\frac{1}{6}$ **11.** $\frac{4}{15}$ **12.** $\frac{5}{12}$

13. $\frac{1}{9}$ **14.** $\frac{6}{15}$ **15.** $\frac{7}{9}$ **16.** $\frac{9}{11}$

Example 3 (page 170)

Write each decimal as a mixed number or fraction in simplest form.

17. 0.125 **18.** 0.66 **19.** 2.5 **20.** 3.75

21. 0.32 **22.** 0.19 **23.** 0.8 **24.** 0.965

Example 4 (page 170)

Order from greatest to least.

25. $\frac{9}{22}, 0.83, \frac{7}{8}, 0.4$

26. $3.84, 3.789, 3.01, 3\frac{41}{50}$

27. $\frac{2}{3}, 0.67, \frac{5}{9}, 0.58, \frac{7}{12}$

28. $0.1\overline{2}, 0.1225, \frac{3}{25}, \frac{7}{125}$

29. Biology DNA content is measured in picograms (pg). A sea star has $\frac{17}{20}$ pg of DNA, a scallop has $\frac{19}{25}$ pg, a red water mite has 0.19 pg, and a mosquito has 0.024 pg. Order their DNA contents from greatest to least.

B Apply Your Skills

Order from least to greatest.

30. $3.\overline{6}, \frac{16}{5}, 3\frac{5}{6}$ **31.** $1.\overline{01}, 1\frac{1}{100}, 1.0101$ **32.** $\frac{3}{2}, 1\frac{2}{5}, 1.\overline{3}$

33. Science An experiment with plant seeds resulted in the data below.

Seed Type	A	B	C	D	E	F	G	H	I
Number Sprouted	15	5	22	17	18	21	14	18	8
Number Planted	48	20	44	35	52	63	55	35	15

a. For each seed type, write the fraction of $\frac{\text{number sprouted}}{\text{number planted}}$.

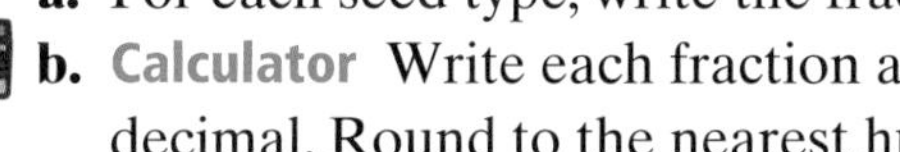

b. **Calculator** Write each fraction as a decimal. Round to the nearest hundredth.

c. Place the seed types into 3 groups: those that sprout about $\frac{1}{2}$ of the time, about $\frac{1}{3}$ of the time, and about $\frac{1}{4}$ of the time.

d. Which type(s) of seeds would you prefer to plant? Explain.

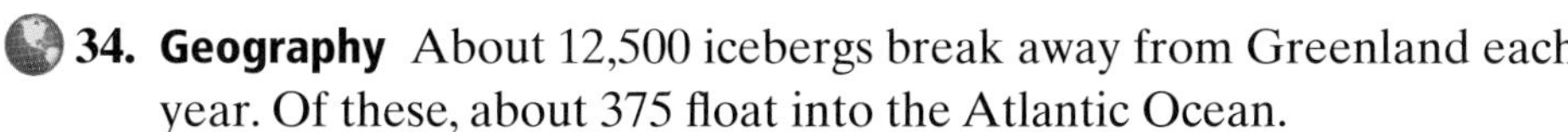

34. Geography About 12,500 icebergs break away from Greenland each year. Of these, about 375 float into the Atlantic Ocean.

a. What fraction of the icebergs float into the Atlantic Ocean?

b. Write your answer for part (a) as a decimal.

c. What fraction of the icebergs does *not* float into the Atlantic Ocean?

Real-World Connection

Greenland is the world's largest island. Its area is more than 800,000 square miles.

For Exercises 35–37, use the table at the right.

35. For each state, write a fraction that shows the $\frac{\text{number of people under age 18}}{\text{total population}}$.

36. Estimation For most of the states, would $\frac{1}{2}, \frac{1}{3}$, or $\frac{1}{4}$ best describe the fraction of the population that is under age 18?

37. Calculator Order the states from least to greatest fraction under age 18.

Population (thousands)

State	Total	Under Age 18
N.Y.	18,976	4,690
Texas	20,852	5,887
Calif.	33,872	9,250
Fla.	15,982	3,646
Ohio	11,353	2,888

SOURCE: U.S. Census Bureau. Go to **www.PHSchool.com** for a data update. Web Code: abg-2041

38. **a.** **Data File, p. 129** Write each shutter opening time as a decimal. Round to the nearest thousandth.
b. Is it easier to compare the times as decimals or fractions? Explain.

39. **Writing in Math** Describe some everyday situations in which you need to change fractions to decimals.

C Challenge

Algebra **Compare. Use <, >, or =. The variable n is a value greater than 1.**

40. $\frac{1}{n}$ ■ $\frac{n}{n}$ **41.** 1 ■ $\frac{n}{1}$ **42.** n ■ $\frac{1}{n}$ **43.** $\frac{n}{n^2}$ ■ $\frac{1}{n}$

44. **Reasoning** Divide 50 by these numbers: 100, 10, 1, 0.1, 0.01, 0.001. As the divisor gets closer to 0, what happens to the quotient? Explain.

45. **Stretch Your Thinking** I am an integer 28 units from my opposite value on the number line. What two integers could I be?

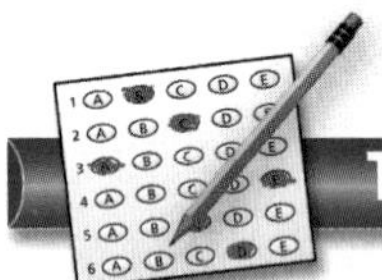

Test Prep

Multiple Choice

46. The top batting averages on a girls' softball team are Jessi $\frac{47}{164}$, Chrissy $\frac{35}{137}$, Carmen $\frac{23}{85}$, and Heather $\frac{32}{93}$. Who has the highest average?

A. Jessi **B.** Chrissy **C.** Carmen **D.** Heather

47. Order from least to greatest: $\frac{5}{9}$, $\frac{1}{5}$, 0.569, 0.21.

F. $\frac{1}{5}$, 0.569, $\frac{5}{9}$, 0.21 **G.** 0.21, $\frac{5}{9}$, $\frac{1}{5}$, 0.569
H. $\frac{5}{9}$, 0.21, $\frac{1}{5}$, 0.569 **I.** $\frac{1}{5}$, 0.21, $\frac{5}{9}$, 0.569

Short Response

48. Player C scores a free throw 51 times out of 99.
a. Write player C's free throw rate as a fraction in simplest form.
b. Write player C's free throw rate as a decimal.

Basketball Players' Statistics

Player	Free Throws	Attempts
A	52	96
B	75	120
C	51	99

Take It to the NET
Online lesson quiz at **www.PHSchool.com**
Web Code: aba-0309

Mixed Review

Lesson 3-8 **Write each mixed number as an improper fraction.**

49. $1\frac{2}{3}$ **50.** $2\frac{4}{5}$ **51.** $6\frac{4}{9}$
52. $3\frac{1}{12}$ **53.** $4\frac{2}{7}$ **54.** $1\frac{9}{9}$

Lesson 1-3 **Find each quotient.**

55. $0.45 \div 9$ **56.** $0.64 \div 0.8$ **57.** $1.75 \div 0.05$
58. $3.06 \div 0.3$ **59.** $1.8 \div 0.9$ **60.** $9.013 \div 1.0$

3-10 Rational Numbers

What You'll Learn

To compare and order rational numbers

. . . And Why

To order rational numbers from least to greatest, as in Example 3

✓ Check Skills You'll Need

For help, go to Lesson 3-9.

Compare. Use <, >, or =.

1. $\frac{8}{10}$ ■ $\frac{3}{4}$ **2.** $\frac{10}{50}$ ■ $\frac{1}{5}$ **3.** 1.3 ■ $1\frac{1}{3}$

4. $\frac{12}{48}$ ■ 0.25 **5.** 0.45 ■ $\frac{2}{5}$ **6.** 0.375 ■ $\frac{49}{50}$

New Vocabulary

- rational number

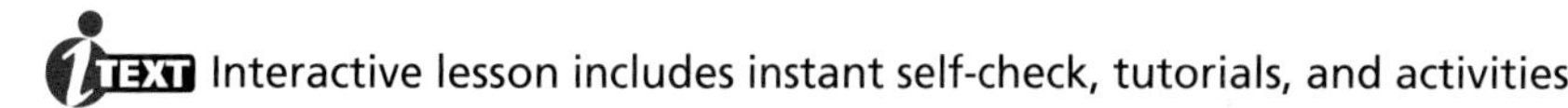

Interactive lesson includes instant self-check, tutorials, and activities.

OBJECTIVE 1 Comparing and Ordering Rational Numbers

A **rational number** is a number that can be written as a quotient of two integers, where the divisor is not 0. Examples are $\frac{2}{5}$, $0.4\overline{6}$, -6, and $3\frac{1}{2}$.

Need Help?
Integers are the set of whole numbers, their opposites, and zero.

Because you can write any integer as a quotient with a denominator of 1, all integers are rational numbers. For example, you can write 5 as $\frac{5}{1}$.

You can write a negative rational number in three ways: $-\frac{7}{9} = \frac{-7}{9} = \frac{7}{-9}$

1 EXAMPLE Comparing Negative Rational Numbers

Compare $-\frac{1}{2}$ and $-\frac{3}{4}$.

Method 1

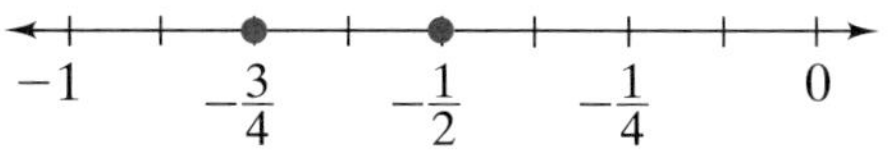

Number line: -1, $-\frac{3}{4}$, $-\frac{1}{2}$, $-\frac{1}{4}$, 0 ← Since $-\frac{3}{4}$ is farther to the left on the number line, it is the lesser number.

So, $-\frac{3}{4} < -\frac{1}{2}$.

Method 2

$-\frac{1}{2} = \frac{-1}{2}$ ← Rewrite $-\frac{1}{2}$ with a -1 in the numerator.

$= \frac{-1 \times 2}{2 \times 2}$ ← The LCD is 4. Write an equivalent fraction.

$= \frac{-2}{4} = -\frac{2}{4}$ ← The fraction $-\frac{2}{4}$ is equivalent to $\frac{-2}{4}$.

Since $-\frac{3}{4} < -\frac{2}{4}$, then $-\frac{3}{4} < -\frac{1}{2}$.

✓ Check Understanding **1** Compare. Use <, >, or =.

a. $-\frac{2}{3}$ ■ $-\frac{1}{6}$ **b.** $-\frac{1}{4}$ ■ $-\frac{1}{8}$ **c.** $-\frac{1}{5}$ ■ $-\frac{3}{10}$

Terminating and repeating decimals are rational numbers.

Reading Math
Values are greater as you move to the right on a number line.

You can use a number line to compare decimals.

−1 −0.8 −0.5 −0.2 0 0.2 0.5 1

$-0.8 < -0.5 < -0.2 < 0.2 < 0.5$

You can also compare decimals using the signs of the numbers and the digits in which they differ.

2 EXAMPLE Comparing Decimals

a. Compare 4.4 and 4.7.

$4.4 < 4.7$ ← **Both numbers are positive. Compare the digits.**

b. Compare −4.4 and 4.7.

$-4.4 < 4.7$ ← **Any negative number is less than a positive number.**

c. Compare −4.4 and −4.7.

−5 −4.7 −4.4 −4 ← **Place the decimals on a number line and compare their locations.**

$-4.4 > -4.7$

Check Understanding 2 Compare. Use <, >, or =.

a. −3.5 ■ 3.8 **b.** −4.2 ■ −4.9 **c.** −8.6 ■ −8.42

d. **Number Sense** In Example 2 (c), what do you notice about the tenths place of the greater number, −4.4, when you compare it to the tenths place of the lesser number, −4.7? Explain.

When you compare and order decimals and fractions, it is often helpful to write the fractions as decimals.

3 EXAMPLE Ordering Rational Numbers

Order these numbers from least to greatest: $\frac{1}{4}, -0.2, -\frac{2}{9}, 1.1$

$\frac{1}{4} = 1 \div 4 = 0.25$ ← **Write as a decimal.**

$-\frac{2}{9} = -2 \div 9 = -0.22222\ldots = -0.\overline{2}$ ← **Write as a repeating decimal.**

$-0.\overline{2} < -0.2 < 0.25 < 1.1$ ← **Compare the decimals.**

From least to greatest, the numbers are $-\frac{2}{9}, -0.2, \frac{1}{4}$, and 1.1.

Check Understanding 3 Order from least to greatest.

a. $\frac{2}{3}, -0.1, -\frac{5}{8}, 2.2$ **b.** $0.625, \frac{1}{8}, \frac{1}{32}, 0.025$

c. **Reasoning** Explain why rounding $-\frac{2}{9}$ to the nearest tenth would not help you compare and order the decimals in Example 3.

EXERCISES

For more practice, see *Extra Practice.*

A Practice by Example

Example 1 (page 173)

Compare. Use <, >, or =.

1. $-\frac{1}{7}$ ■ $-\frac{6}{7}$
2. $-\frac{3}{4}$ ■ $-\frac{3}{8}$
3. $-\frac{1}{2}$ ■ $-\frac{2}{10}$
4. $-\frac{3}{4}$ ■ -1
5. $-\frac{1}{2}$ ■ $-\frac{5}{6}$
6. $-\frac{4}{5}$ ■ $-\frac{1}{3}$

Example 2 (page 174)

Compare. Use <, >, or =.

7. 5.2 ■ −8.3
8. −6.5 ■ 6.2
9. −4.9 ■ −4.3
10. 1.09 ■ −1.90
11. −1.22 ■ −6.5
12. −10.2 ■ −10.23

Example 3 (page 174)

Order from least to greatest.

13. $\frac{3}{2}, 0.25, -\frac{3}{4}, -1.0$
14. $\frac{7}{3}, 2.4, -\frac{6}{25}, -1.34$
15. $\frac{6}{11}, -1.5, 0.545, \frac{1}{2}$
16. $-0.8\overline{3}, -\frac{14}{15}, \frac{1}{12}, -0.953$

B Apply Your Skills

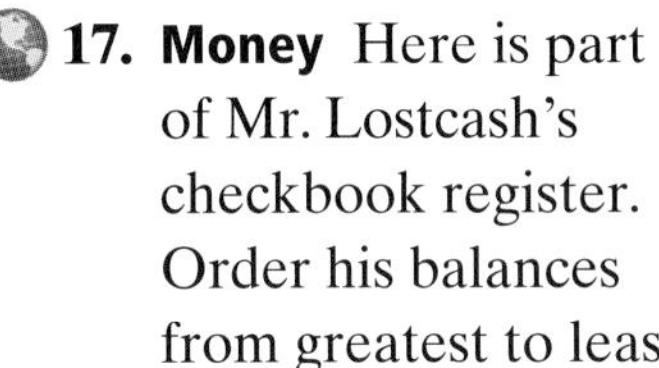

17. **Money** Here is part of Mr. Lostcash's checkbook register. Order his balances from greatest to least.

Description	Debits (−)	Credits (+)	Balance
Paycheck		122.18	122.18
Sneakers	95.00		27.18
Two outfits	68.09		−40.91
Paycheck		122.18	81.27
Insufficient funds fee	25.00		56.27
Three CDs	59.97		−3.70

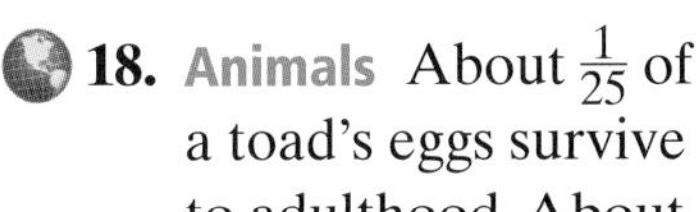

18. Animals About $\frac{1}{25}$ of a toad's eggs survive to adulthood. About 0.25 of a frog's eggs and $\frac{1}{5}$ of a green turtle's eggs survive to adulthood. Which animal's eggs have the highest survival rate?

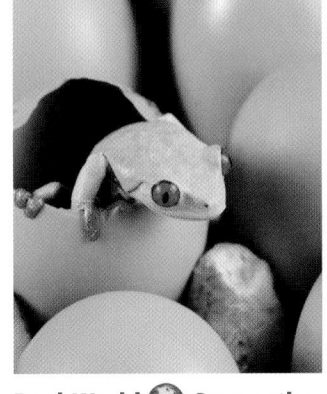

Real-World Connection
Most frogs lay their eggs in fresh water because the eggs can develop only in moist conditions.

19. **Writing in Math** Would you compare $-\frac{5}{8}$ and $-\frac{3}{4}$ by finding common denominators or by writing decimal equivalents? Explain your choice.

Compare. Use <, >, or =.

20. −5.8 ■ $-5\frac{9}{10}$
21. $-6\frac{11}{50}$ ■ −6.21
22. −10.42 ■ $-10.4\overline{2}$

Number Sense **Match each number with a point on the number line.**

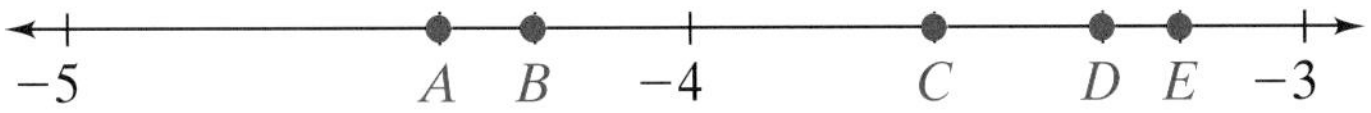

(Number line from −5 to −3 with points A, B, C, D, E; labels: −5, A, B, −4, C, D, E, −3)

23. −3.6
24. −4.25
25. $-3\frac{1}{3}$
26. −3.2
27. $-4\frac{2}{5}$

C Challenge

28. **Algebra** Evaluate $\frac{m - n}{-12}$, for $m = -3$ and $n = 6$.

29. Stretch Your Thinking A tour bus travels 400 mi on the first day of a trip. Each day after that the bus travels half the distance it went the day before. The total trip is 775 mi. How many days does the trip take?

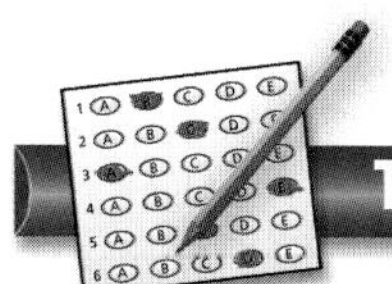

Test Prep

Multiple Choice

30. The table shows the melting points of chemical solids. Which has the highest?

A. Krypton **B.** Argon
C. Xenon **D.** Helium

Melting Points

Chemical Solid	Melting Point (°C)
Krypton	−157.36
Argon	−189.35
Xenon	−111.79
Helium	−272.2

SOURCE: *Encyclopædia Britannica*

31. Which is both an integer and a rational number?

F. $-\frac{3}{4}$ **G.** 0
H. 0.1 **I.** $3\frac{3}{5}$

Take It to the NET
Online lesson quiz at
www.PHSchool.com
Web Code: aba-0310

32. Which fraction is NOT equivalent to $-\frac{3}{8}$?

A. $\frac{-3}{8}$ **B.** $-\frac{9}{24}$ **C.** $\frac{-3}{-8}$ **D.** $\frac{-6}{16}$

33. Order from least to greatest: $\frac{1}{20}$, 0.056, −0.2, $-\frac{5}{9}$

F. $\frac{1}{20}$, 0.056, $-\frac{5}{9}$, −0.2 **G.** −0.2, $-\frac{5}{9}$, $\frac{1}{20}$, 0.056
H. $-\frac{5}{9}$, −0.2, $\frac{1}{20}$, 0.056 **I.** $-\frac{5}{9}$, −0.2, 0.056, $\frac{1}{20}$

Mixed Review

Lesson 3-9 **Order from least to greatest.**

34. 0.21, $\frac{1}{5}$, 0.212, $\frac{11}{50}$ **35.** $\frac{21}{25}$, $0.9\overline{3}$, $\frac{2}{5}$, 1.99

Lesson 3-5 **Write each fraction in simplest form.**

36. $\frac{36}{38}$ **37.** $\frac{14}{28}$ **38.** $\frac{12}{56}$ **39.** $\frac{18}{48}$

Checkpoint Quiz 2 — Lessons 3-6 through 3-10

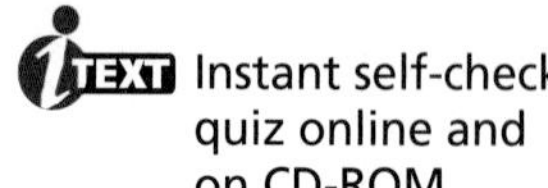

Instant self-check quiz online and on CD-ROM

Compare. Use <, >, or =.

1. $\frac{1}{8}$ ■ $\frac{2}{100}$ **2.** $\frac{5}{12}$ ■ $\frac{7}{9}$ **3.** $\frac{12}{20}$ ■ $\frac{3}{5}$ **4.** $2\frac{1}{7}$ ■ 0.146

Write each improper fraction as a mixed number and each mixed number as an improper fraction.

5. $\frac{29}{6}$ **6.** $4\frac{1}{9}$ **7.** $\frac{82}{5}$ **8.** $2\frac{5}{6}$

9. Twins occur once in every 89 births. Identical twins occur 4 times in every 1,000 births. Triplets occur once in every 7,900 births. Write each birth frequency as a decimal. Round to the nearest ten-thousandth.

10. Order from least to greatest: $\frac{7}{8}$, $-\frac{4}{9}$, −0.45, $\frac{9}{5}$, 1.89

Writing Extended Responses

An extended response question is usually worth a maximum of 4 points and has multiple parts. To get full credit, you need to answer each part and show all your work or justify your reasoning.

EXAMPLE

Without performing the division, test whether 15,534 is divisible by 3, 4, 9, and 12. Justify each response.

Below are four responses and the amount of credit each received.

4 points

Divisible by 3?
$1 + 5 + 5 + 3 + 4 = 18$
Yes, since 18 is divisible by 3.

Divisible by 4? $34 \div 4 = 8.5$
No, since 34 is not divisible by 4.

Divisible by 9? $18 \div 9 = 2$
Yes, since 18 is divisible by 9.

Divisible by 12?
No, since 15,534 is not divisible by 4.

The 4-point response shows the correct answers and justifies each one.

3 points

Divisible by 3?
$1 + 5 + 5 + 3 + 4 = 17$
No, since 17 is not divisible by 3.

Divisible by 4? $34 \div 4 = 8.5$
No, since 34 is not divisible by 4.

Divisible by 9? $17 \div 9 = 1.8$
No, since 17 is not divisible by 9.

Divisible by 12?
No, since 15,534 is not divisible by 4.

The 3-point response has a computational error, but the student completed both parts.

2 points

Divisible by 3?
$1 + 5 + 5 + 3 + 4 = 18$
Yes, since 18 is divisible by 3.

Divisible by 4? $34 \div 4 = 8$
Yes, since 34 is divisible by 4.

Divisible by 9? $18 \div 2 = 9$

Divisible by 12?
Yes, since 15,534 is divisible by 3 and 4.

The 2-point response has a computational error and is missing an answer.

1 point

Yes, 15,534 is divisible by 3.

No, 15,534 is not divisible by 4.

Yes, 15,534 is divisible by 9.

No, 15,534 is not divisible by 12.

The 1-point response shows correct answers but with no work or justification.

A 0-point response has incorrect answers and no work shown.

Chapter 3

Chapter Review

Vocabulary

composite number (p. 146)
divisible (p. 141)
equivalent fractions (p. 151)
exponent (p. 131)
factor (p. 146)
greatest common factor (GCF) (p. 147)
improper fraction (p. 164)
least common denominator (LCD) (p. 156)
least common multiple (LCM) (p. 145)
mixed number (p. 164)
multiple (p. 145)
power (p. 132)
prime factorization (p. 146)
prime number (p. 146)
rational number (p. 173)
repeating decimal (p. 169)
scientific notation (p. 137)
simplest form (p. 152)
terminating decimal (p. 168)

Reading Math: Understanding Vocabulary

Choose the correct term to complete each sentence.

1. In the expression 6^3, the number 3 represents the (power, exponent).

2. A (composite, prime) number has exactly two factors, 1 and itself.

3. (Multiples, Factors) of 28 include 1, 2, 4, 7, 14, and 28.

4. At a class party, you and two friends eat $\frac{6}{8}$ of a pizza. This can also be written as the (improper fraction, equivalent fraction) $\frac{3}{4}$.

5. The (GCF, LCM) of 24 and 36 is 12.

Take It to the NET Online vocabulary quiz at **www.PHSchool.com** Web Code: abj-0351

Skills and Concepts

3-1 and 3-2 Objectives

- To write numbers with exponents
- To simplify expressions with exponents using the Order of Operations
- To write numbers in scientific notation
- To write numbers in standard form

An **exponent** tells you how many times a number, or base, is used as a factor. A number expressed with an exponent is a **power.** A number in **scientific notation** is written as a product of a factor greater than or equal to 1 but less than 10, and another factor that is a power of 10.

Simplify.

6. -2^4 **7.** $(-4)^3$ **8.** $5^2 + 10^2$ **9.** $4(5^2 - 10)$

Write in scientific notation or in standard form.

10. 7,123,000 **11.** 9.06×10^5 **12.** 81,900 **13.** 6.015×10^8

3-3 Objective

- To use divisibility tests

One whole number is **divisible** by a second whole number if the remainder is 0 when you divide the first number by the second.

Test each number for divisibility by 2, 3, 4, 5, 8, 9, and 10.

14. 24 **15.** 56 **16.** 90 **17.** 282 **18.** 1,360

19. Test 840 for divisibility by 2, 3, 5, 9, and 10.

3-4 Objectives

- ▼ To find multiples and factors
- ▼ To use prime factorization

A **multiple** is the product of a number and any nonzero whole number. A **factor** is a whole number that divides another whole number with a remainder of 0. A whole number greater than 1 is **composite** if it has more than two factors and **prime** if it has exactly two factors, 1 and itself.

Write the prime factorization. Use exponents where possible.

20. 84 **21.** 78 **22.** 90 **23.** 92 **24.** 125

25. Groceries A grocer gets food from three suppliers. They deliver every 5 days, 6 days, and 7 days, respectively. All three came today. When will they all deliver on the same day again?

3-5 and 3-6 Objectives

- ▼ To write equivalent fractions
- ▼ To simplify fractions
- ▼ To compare and order fractions

A fraction is in **simplest form** when the numerator and denominator have no common factors other than 1. To compare and order fractions, you can use the **least common denominator (LCD),** which is the least common multiple of their denominators.

Order from least to greatest.

26. $\frac{1}{4}, \frac{1}{3}, \frac{1}{6}$ **27.** $\frac{1}{4}, \frac{2}{5}, \frac{3}{8}$ **28.** $\frac{3}{8}, \frac{5}{6}, \frac{1}{2}$ **29.** $\frac{5}{9}, \frac{2}{3}, \frac{7}{12}$

3-7 and 3-8 Objectives

- ▼ To solve a problem by combining strategies
- ▼ To write a mixed number as an improper fraction
- ▼ To write an improper fraction as a mixed number

When a problem has a large number of steps, you may be able to look for a pattern and solve a simpler problem. An **improper fraction** has a numerator that is greater than or equal to its denominator. A **mixed number** is the sum of a whole number and a fraction.

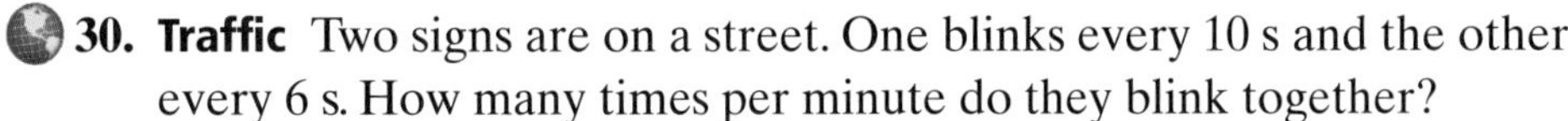

30. Traffic Two signs are on a street. One blinks every 10 s and the other every 6 s. How many times per minute do they blink together?

Write each improper fraction as a whole or mixed number in simplest form.

31. $\frac{42}{7}$ **32.** $\frac{27}{12}$ **33.** $\frac{20}{3}$ **34.** $\frac{125}{5}$ **35.** $\frac{84}{12}$

3-9 and 3-10 Objectives

- ▼ To relate fractions and decimals
- ▼ To compare and order rational numbers

To write a fraction as a decimal, you can divide the numerator by the denominator. When the division ends with a remainder of 0, the quotient is a **terminating decimal.** When the same block of digits in a decimal repeats without end, the quotient is a **repeating decimal.** A **rational number** can be written as a quotient of two integers where the denominator is not zero.

Write each fraction as a decimal.

36. $\frac{1}{3}$ **37.** $\frac{5}{9}$ **38.** $\frac{5}{2}$ **39.** $\frac{16}{20}$ **40.** $\frac{4}{50}$

Order from least to greatest.

41. $\frac{3}{4}, 0.\overline{3}, -\frac{7}{8}$ **42.** $2.7, -0.3, -\frac{4}{11}$ **43.** $-\frac{5}{6}, 2.2, -0.5$

Chapter 3

Chapter Test

Take It to the NET
Online chapter test at
www.PHSchool.com
Web Code: aba-0352

Find the value of each expression.

1. $(3^2 - 4) \div 5$
2. $5^2 - 7^2$
3. $(6 - 9)^3$
4. $54 \div 3^2$

Write using scientific notation.

5. 12,300,000
6. 75,462

Tell whether the first number is divisible by the second number.

7. 523; 3
8. 556; 5
9. 392; 4

List 3 factors and 3 multiples of each number.

10. 27
11. 36
12. 100
13. 25

Find the GCF of each pair of numbers.

14. 32, 40
15. 55, 15
16. 36, 57
17. 24, 68

18. **Reasoning** Tell whether each is true or false.
    a. Two is a composite number.
    b. Any factor of a whole number is greater than any multiple of a whole number.
    c. A number is divisible by 3 if its last digit is divisible by 3.
    d. One is neither composite nor prime.

19. Use a factor tree to write the prime factorization of 42.

Write two fractions equivalent to each fraction.

20. $\frac{1}{3}$
21. $-\frac{15}{24}$
22. $-\frac{4}{5}$
23. $\frac{16}{28}$

Write each fraction in simplest form.

24. $\frac{12}{18}$
25. $\frac{27}{54}$
26. $\frac{36}{96}$
27. $\frac{7}{42}$

28. **Writing in Math** Explain how you can use prime factorization to write a fraction in simplest form.

29. **Modeling** Draw models to represent $\frac{3}{4}$ and $2\frac{3}{5}$.

30. What fraction does the shaded part of the model represent?

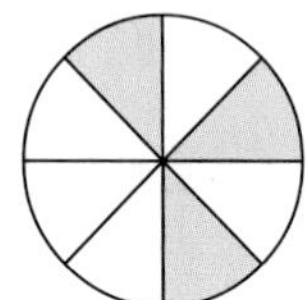

Compare. Use <, >, or =.

31. $\frac{2}{9}$ ■ $\frac{8}{9}$
32. $\frac{5}{16}$ ■ $\frac{3}{8}$
33. $\frac{7}{18}$ ■ $\frac{2}{5}$

34. **Ships** A crew finds a treasure chest with 168 gold coins and 200 silver coins. Each crew member gets an equal share of each type of coin, with none left over.
    a. What is the greatest possible number of crew members?
    b. How many of each type of coin does each crew member get?

Write as an improper fraction.

35. $5\frac{2}{3}$
36. $4\frac{5}{6}$
37. $8\frac{7}{10}$
38. $3\frac{2}{5}$

Write as a whole number or a mixed number.

39. $\frac{12}{5}$
40. $\frac{30}{9}$
41. $\frac{48}{12}$
42. $\frac{42}{30}$

Write each fraction as a decimal.

43. $\frac{2}{16}$
44. $\frac{6}{15}$
45. $\frac{5}{4}$
46. $\frac{8}{25}$

Write each decimal as a mixed number or fraction in simplest form.

47. 0.2
48. 1.3
49. 0.35
50. 3.62

51. **Mail** In one week, $\frac{5}{8}$ of your mail is advertisements and $\frac{1}{5}$ is letters from friends. What is the least number of pieces of mail you receive?

52. Order from least to greatest:

    $2.56, -2.\overline{5}, -2\frac{1}{5}, \frac{24}{10}, -2.4$

Test Prep

Reading Comprehension **Read each passage and answer the questions that follow.**

Prime Construction Jackie says, "If I multiply the first two prime numbers together and add 1, I get a new prime number." Amit says, "If I multiply the first three prime numbers and add 1, I also get a prime number. Carl says, "I bet the same will happen if I multiply the first four prime numbers and add 1." "It seems to me," says Maria, "that if I multiply any two or more prime numbers, the product is never prime."

1. What prime number does Jackie get?
A. 3 **B.** 6
C. 7 **D.** 11

2. What prime number does Amit get?
F. 16 **G.** 31
H. 41 **I.** 43

3. What number would Carl get?
A. 107 **B.** 181
C. 210 **D.** 211

4. Which numbers could NOT be used to test Maria's statement?
F. 3, 13 **G.** 2, 5, 11
H. 31, 33 **I.** 17, 29

Light Reading Light travels very quickly—at about 1.86×10^5 mi/s. This is fast enough that we do not notice any delay when we flip a light switch. However, light from distant objects in space does not arrive instantaneously. The sun is about 9.3×10^7 mi from Earth. The next nearest star system, Alpha Centauri, is about 2.5×10^{13} mi away.

5. About how far away would a lamp have to be for its light to take 2 s to reach our eyes?
A. 37,000 mi
B. 370,000 mi
C. 3,700,000 mi
D. 37,000,000 mi

6. About how long does it take light from the sun to reach Earth?
F. 5 s **G.** 5×10 s
H. 5×10^2 s **I.** 500 min

7. Which does NOT express the time in seconds it takes light from Alpha Centauri to reach Earth?
A. $\frac{2.5 \times 10^{13}}{186 \times 10^3}$ **B.** $\frac{2.5 \times 10^{13}}{186{,}000}$
C. $\frac{1.86}{2.5 \times 10^8}$ **D.** $\frac{2.5}{1.86} \cdot \frac{10^{13}}{10^5}$

8. About how many times farther is Alpha Centauri from Earth than the sun is from Earth?
F. 4 **G.** 23
H. 2.6×10^3 **I.** 270,000

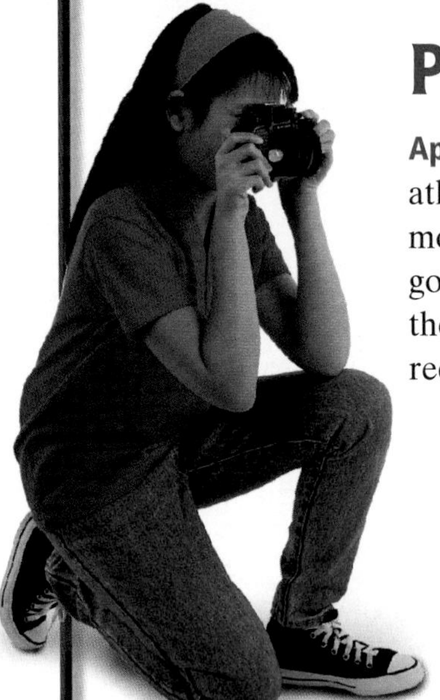

Photographic Memory

Applying Fractions You've probably seen pictures of athletes, animals, or cars that "freeze" the subject's motion but show all the excitement of the moment. A good photographer chooses the best shutter speed for the action. If the shutter stays open too long, the camera records too much movement, and the picture is blurry.

Cameras Then and Now

In the 1850s, leather bellows folded a camera into a protective case, making it easier to carry. Zoom lenses on digital cameras fold into the camera for protection.

Capturing Movement

For this photograph, the photographer used a very slow shutter speed and a strobe light. The shutter stayed open while the dancer moved.

Light Trail

For this photograph, the photographer used a very slow shutter speed and no flash. The shutter stayed open while traffic moved along the upper and lower levels of Interstate 5 in Seattle, Washington.

Put It All Together

Data File **Use the data on these two pages and on page 129 to answer these questions.**

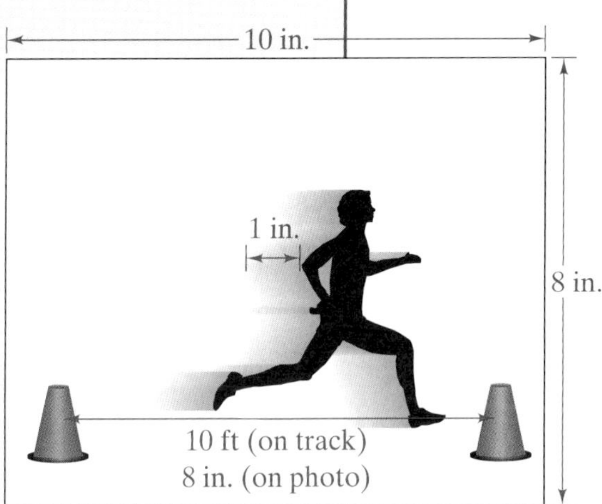

1. The image of the runner is blurry because the runner moved a visible amount during the $\frac{1}{15}$ of a second that the shutter was open.
   a. The blur for $\frac{1}{15}$ s is 1 in. long. How long would the blur be for 1 s?
   b. How long would the blur be for each shutter time on page 129?
   c. **Reasoning** At what shutter time do you think the length of the blur would be small enough that it would not show in the photo?
2. a. How many times would the blur length fit into the space between the two cones in the photo? What fraction of the distance between the cones is the blur?
   b. Use your answer to part (a) to find the distance the runner moved while the shutter was open.
   c. Maintaining the same speed, how far would the runner go in 1 s? In 1 min?

Take It to the NET For more information about photography, go to **www.PHSchool.com**.
Web Code: abe-0353

A strobe light "popped" several times per second to capture images as she danced.

CHAPTER

4

Operations With Fractions

Lessons

- **4-1** Estimating With Fractions and Mixed Numbers
- **4-2** Adding and Subtracting Fractions
- **4-3** Adding and Subtracting Mixed Numbers
- **4-4** Multiplying Fractions and Mixed Numbers
- **4-5** Dividing Fractions and Mixed Numbers
- **4-6** Solving Equations With Fractions
- **4-7** Problem Solving: Try, Check, and Revise and Work Backward
- **4-8** Changing Units in the Customary System
- **4-9** Precision

Key Vocabulary

- benchmark (p. 187)
- precision (p. 227)
- reciprocal (p. 207)

Real-World Snapshots

A canyon is a deep valley with steep sides. Carved by erosion, the exposed rocks of a canyon's walls can reveal millions of years of Earth's geology.

Data File Canyons

Location	Canyon	Maximum Depth (mi)	Length (mi)
Arizona	Grand Canyon	$1\frac{1}{8}$	277
California	Kings Canyon	$1\frac{1}{2}$	24
Colorado	Black Canyon	$\frac{1}{2}$	10
Utah	Zion Canyon	$\frac{1}{2}$	15

You will use the data above in this chapter:

- p. 200 Lesson 4-3
- p. 224 Lesson 4-8

Real-World Snapshots On pages 236 and 237, you will solve problems involving canyons.

Chapter 4 Preview

Where You've Been

- In Chapter 2, you solved equations using decimals.
- In Chapter 3, you simplified and compared fractions and mixed numbers.

Where You're Going

- In Chapter 4, you will perform operations and solve equations using fractions and mixed numbers.
- Applying what you learn, you will convert units of measure to adjust cooking recipes.

Cooks use fractions to measure ingredients.

Instant self-check online and on CD-ROM

Diagnosing Readiness

For help, go to the lesson in green.

Adding and Subtracting Integers (Lesson 1-7)

Find each sum or difference.

1. $-55 + 15$ **2.** $-3 + (-21)$ **3.** $58 - (-42)$ **4.** $-7 - (-25)$

Multiplying and Dividing Integers (Lesson 1-8)

Find each product or quotient.

5. $-3 \cdot 15$ **6.** $-12 \cdot (-5)$ **7.** $39 \div (-13)$ **8.** $-60 \div (-3)$

Solving Equations (Lessons 2-3 and 2-4)

Solve each equation.

9. $8 + x = 13$ **10.** $c - 5 = 21$ **11.** $25 = b + 3$ **12.** $p - 15 = -12$

13. $24 = 3x$ **14.** $y \div 5 = 9$ **15.** $8n = 40$ **16.** $\frac{x}{9} = 12$

Solving Two-Step Equations (Lesson 2-6)

Solve each equation using number sense.

17. $5y - 3 = 12$ **18.** $8b + 4 = 36$ **19.** $15g - 9 = 51$ **20.** $7t + 5 = 68$

Finding the Greatest Common Factor (Lesson 3-4)

Use prime factorizations to find the GCF of each pair of numbers.

21. 18, 27 **22.** 21, 42 **23.** 24, 36 **24.** 45, 36

4-1 Estimating With Fractions and Mixed Numbers

What You'll Learn

To estimate sums and differences

To estimate products and quotients

. . . And Why

To compare swimming workouts, as in Example 2

For help, go to Lesson 3-6.

Compare using <, >, or =.

1. $\frac{6}{7}$ ■ $\frac{5}{7}$
2. $\frac{2}{4}$ ■ $\frac{10}{20}$
3. $\frac{5}{12}$ ■ $\frac{3}{5}$
4. $\frac{2}{8}$ ■ $\frac{3}{15}$
5. $\frac{2}{6}$ ■ $\frac{4}{12}$
6. $\frac{2}{7}$ ■ $\frac{2}{9}$

New Vocabulary

- benchmark

Interactive lesson includes instant self-check, tutorials, and activities.

Estimating Sums and Differences

A **benchmark** is a convenient number used to replace fractions that are less than 1. You can use the benchmarks 0, $\frac{1}{2}$, and 1 to estimate fractions. Thinking of a number line can help you estimate fractions.

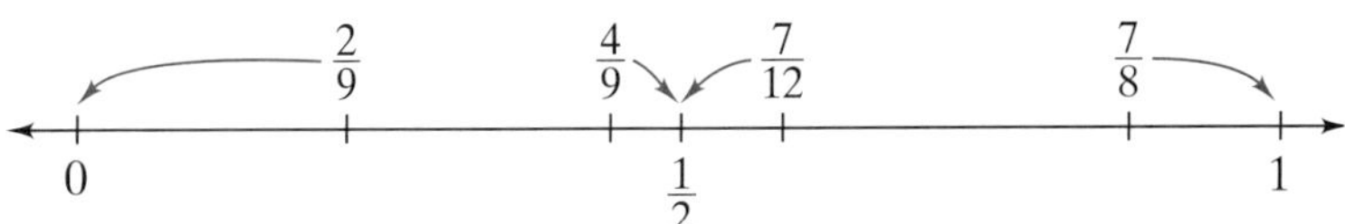

Estimate as 0 when the numerator is very small compared to the denominator.

Estimate as $\frac{1}{2}$ when the numerator is about half the denominator.

Estimate as 1 when the numerator and denominator are nearly equal.

1 EXAMPLE Using Benchmarks With Fractions

Estimate $\frac{7}{8} + \frac{4}{9}$.

$\frac{7}{8} + \frac{4}{9}$

$\downarrow \quad \downarrow$

$1 + \frac{1}{2} = 1\frac{1}{2}$ ← **Use benchmarks to estimate each fraction. Then add.**

1 Use benchmarks to estimate each sum or difference.

a. $\frac{5}{12} + \frac{1}{15}$

b. $\frac{3}{5} - \frac{1}{8}$

c. $\frac{7}{8} - \frac{5}{9}$

d. Reasoning How can you tell whether a fraction is equal to, greater than, or less than $\frac{1}{2}$? Explain.

When a sum or difference involves mixed numbers, you can make a reasonable estimate by rounding to the nearest whole number.

2 EXAMPLE **Estimating With Mixed Numbers** 

Swimming In one week, Paulo practices by swimming $8\frac{1}{5}$ mi. Allen swims $4\frac{3}{4}$ mi. About how many more miles does Paulo swim?

$8\frac{1}{5} - 4\frac{3}{4}$ ← **Estimate $8\frac{1}{5} - 4\frac{3}{4}$.**

$\downarrow \quad \downarrow$

$8 - 5 = 3$ ← **Round each mixed number. Then subtract.**

Paulo swims about 3 mi farther.

 **2** **Pets** You buy a puppy that weighs $8\frac{1}{4}$ lb. A month later, the puppy weighs $11\frac{7}{8}$ lb. About how much weight did the puppy gain?

OBJECTIVE

2 Estimating Products and Quotients

To estimate a product of mixed numbers, round each mixed number to the nearest whole number. Then multiply.

3 EXAMPLE **Estimating Products**

Estimate $2\frac{2}{5} \cdot 6\frac{1}{10}$.

$2\frac{2}{5} \cdot 6\frac{1}{10}$

$\downarrow \quad \downarrow$

$2 \cdot 6 = 12$ ← **Round each mixed number. Then multiply.**

 **3** **a.** Estimate $3\frac{5}{6} \cdot 5\frac{1}{8}$. **b.** Estimate $8\frac{1}{8} \cdot 5\frac{11}{12}$.

To estimate a quotient of mixed numbers, you can use compatible numbers. Choose numbers that are easy to divide.

Need Help?
Compatible numbers are numbers that are easy to compute mentally.

4 EXAMPLE **Estimating With Compatible Numbers**

Estimate $43\frac{1}{4} \div 5\frac{7}{8}$.

$43\frac{1}{4} \div 5\frac{7}{8}$

$\downarrow \quad \downarrow$

$42 \div 6 = 7$ ← **Use compatible numbers. Use 42 for $43\frac{1}{4}$ and use 6 for $5\frac{7}{8}$.**

Check Understanding **4** **a.** Estimate $35\frac{3}{4} \div 5\frac{11}{12}$. **b.** Estimate $22\frac{7}{8} \div 3\frac{5}{6}$.

c. **Number Sense** $30\frac{1}{7} \div 1\frac{4}{5}$ is about $30 \div 2 = 15$. Is the estimate of 15 for the quotient high or low? Explain.

EXERCISES

For more practice, see *Extra Practice*.

Ⓐ Practice by Example

Example 1 (page 187)

Use benchmarks to estimate each sum or difference. Exercise 1 has been started for you.

1. $\frac{1}{7} + \frac{3}{8} \approx 0 + \frac{1}{2}$ **2.** $\frac{3}{5} - \frac{1}{2}$ **3.** $\frac{5}{11} - \frac{1}{5}$

4. $\frac{8}{9} - \frac{5}{6}$ **5.** $\frac{1}{6} + \frac{5}{8}$ **6.** $\frac{3}{4} + \frac{5}{6}$ **7.** $\frac{3}{4} - \frac{1}{5}$

Example 2 (page 188)

Estimate each sum or difference.

8. $9\frac{1}{11} - 3\frac{7}{9}$ **9.** $5\frac{3}{5} + 3\frac{2}{3}$ **10.** $4\frac{1}{2} - 1\frac{24}{25}$ **11.** $7\frac{2}{3} - 2\frac{11}{12}$

12. $9\frac{8}{10} + 8\frac{2}{10}$ **13.** $1\frac{1}{16} - 1\frac{1}{5}$ **14.** $4\frac{5}{9} + 5\frac{9}{10}$ **15.** $1\frac{2}{7} + 6\frac{7}{9}$

16. Projects You spent $9\frac{5}{6}$ h on a take-home project. Your partner spent $4\frac{1}{5}$ h on it. About how many more hours did you spend on the project?

Example 3 (page 188)

Estimate each product.

17. $2\frac{1}{8} \cdot 3\frac{6}{7}$ **18.** $5\frac{2}{9} \cdot 4\frac{9}{10}$ **19.** $3\frac{3}{8} \cdot 5\frac{1}{6}$ **20.** $1\frac{7}{10} \cdot 8\frac{1}{12}$

21. $3\frac{2}{5} \cdot 7\frac{9}{20}$ **22.** $5\frac{3}{4} \cdot 2\frac{2}{3}$ **23.** $9\frac{5}{9} \cdot 2\frac{2}{9}$ **24.** $5\frac{4}{5} \cdot 9\frac{1}{2}$

Example 4 (page 188)

Estimate each quotient.

25. $10\frac{7}{8} \div 3\frac{1}{9}$ **26.** $36\frac{1}{3} \div 4\frac{2}{5}$ **27.** $7\frac{3}{5} \div 1\frac{1}{2}$ **28.** $8\frac{2}{12} \div 8\frac{2}{7}$

29. $22\frac{2}{12} \div 6\frac{5}{6}$ **30.** $13\frac{9}{11} \div 1\frac{4}{5}$ **31.** $16\frac{8}{11} \div 2\frac{1}{4}$ **32.** $12\frac{2}{6} \div 4\frac{1}{3}$

Ⓑ Apply Your Skills

Music The table below shows the weight of the bells of Boston's Old North Church. Use the table for Exercises 33–35.

Tone	F	E	D	C	B Flat	A	G	Low F
Weight in Tons	$\frac{3}{10}$	$\frac{3}{10}$	$\frac{7}{20}$	$\frac{2}{5}$	$\frac{11}{25}$	$\frac{19}{40}$	$\frac{3}{5}$	$\frac{3}{4}$

33. Estimate the total weight of the two heaviest bells.

34. Estimate the total weight of all eight bells.

35. Estimate the difference in the weights of the heaviest and lightest bells.

Estimate each answer.

36. $15\frac{1}{8} - 12\frac{6}{7}$ **37.** $31\frac{5}{8} - 23\frac{1}{3}$ **38.** $\frac{15}{16} + \frac{7}{19}$ **39.** $16\frac{1}{7} \div 3\frac{3}{5}$

40. $4\frac{2}{3} \cdot 15\frac{1}{3}$ **41.** $46\frac{2}{9} - 5\frac{9}{10}$ **42.** $29\frac{5}{6} \cdot 1\frac{21}{25}$ **43.** $\frac{49}{50} - \frac{1}{2}$

44. Writing in Math You need $9\frac{9}{16}$ lb of chicken. The store sells chicken in half-pound quantities. How much chicken should you order? Explain.

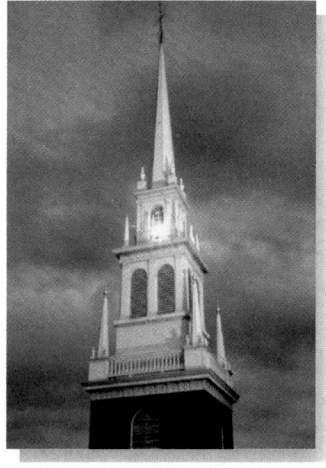

Real-World Connection

Lanterns in Old North Church signaled Paul Revere to start his ride in April, 1775.

45. **a.** Estimate $\frac{1}{8} + \frac{2}{5}$ by estimating each fraction to the nearest whole number.

b. Estimate $\frac{1}{8} + \frac{2}{5}$ by using the benchmarks 0, $\frac{1}{2}$, or 1.

c. **Reasoning** Which estimation method, part (a) or part (b), is more appropriate? Explain.

C Challenge

Algebra **Estimate the value of x.**

46. $13\frac{8}{9} - x = 9\frac{5}{8}$ **47.** $x + 5\frac{10}{12} = 15\frac{1}{7}$ **48.** $17\frac{3}{11} - x = 9\frac{4}{5}$

49. **Number Sense** Estimate the median of $9\frac{3}{5}, 5\frac{1}{4}, 7\frac{5}{10}, 1\frac{7}{8}, 6\frac{3}{4}, 3\frac{2}{8}$.

50. **Stretch Your Thinking** How many whole numbers that are made up of the digits 1, 2, 3, 4, and 5, each used exactly once, are multiples of 8? Name them.

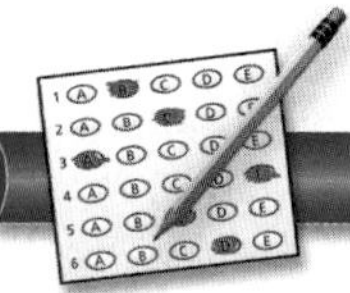

Test Prep

Multiple Choice

51. Which answer is between 6 and 7?

A. $\frac{1}{2} \cdot 14\frac{1}{2}$ B. $2 \cdot 3\frac{15}{16}$

C. $5\frac{11}{12} + \frac{24}{25}$ D. $7\frac{8}{9} - \frac{1}{2}$

52. You need $14\frac{3}{4}$ in. of fabric to make a placemat. You have $89\frac{3}{4}$ in. of fabric. Estimate the greatest number of placemats you can make.

F. 4 G. 6 H. 8 I. 10

Take It to the NET
Online lesson quiz at
www.PHSchool.com
Web Code aba-0401

53. Which answer is between 4 and 5?

A. $4\frac{1}{4} \cdot 1\frac{3}{4}$ B. $11\frac{3}{4} \div 3\frac{1}{2}$

C. $1\frac{5}{6} \cdot 2\frac{1}{4}$ D. $15\frac{1}{3} \div 5\frac{5}{6}$

Short Response

54. You want to make three kinds of pasta salad. One recipe requires $\frac{2}{3}$ c of pasta. Another requires $\frac{3}{4}$ c. The third requires $1\frac{2}{3}$ c. You have 4 c of pasta. Do you have enough? Explain.

Mixed Review

Lesson 3-4 **Write the prime factorization. Use exponents where possible.**

55. 27 **56.** 72 **57.** 56 **58.** 58

59. 162 **60.** 104 **61.** 110 **62.** 76

Lesson 3-1 **Use paper and pencil, mental math, or a calculator to simplify.**

63. -2^5 **64.** $(-5)^3$ **65.** $4^3 + 11$ **66.** $3^2 \cdot 5^2$

67. $(18 \div 6)^3$ **68.** $2^3 - 2^2$ **69.** $(4 + 3)^2 + 1$ **70.** $(2 + 1)^3 - 2^3$

Investigation Using Fraction Models

For Use With Lesson 4-2

You can use models to add and subtract fractions.

1 EXAMPLE Using Models to Add Fractions

Find $\frac{3}{10} + \frac{1}{10}$.

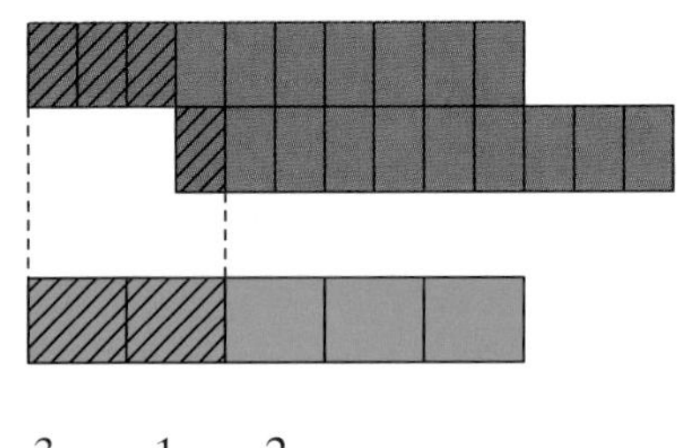

← To add, align the right side of the shaded part of the first model with the left side of the second one.

← Find a model that represents the sum of the shaded parts. If you have more than one model to choose from, use the one with the largest sections.

$\frac{3}{10} + \frac{1}{10} = \frac{2}{5}$

2 EXAMPLE Using Models to Subtract Fractions

Find $\frac{3}{4} - \frac{1}{3}$.

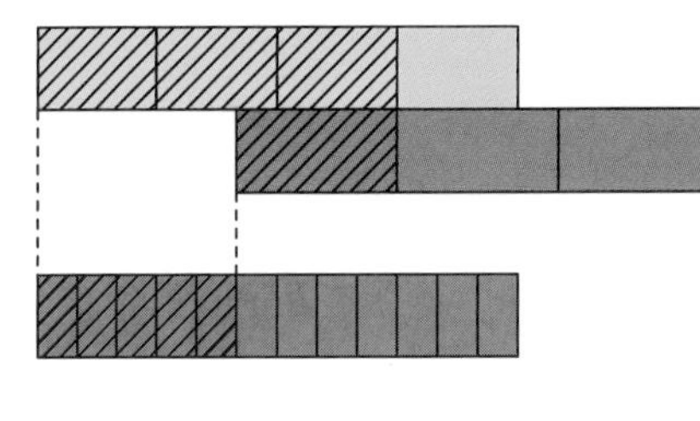

← To subtract, align the right ends of the shaded part of each model.

← Find the model that represents the difference.

$\frac{3}{4} - \frac{1}{3} = \frac{5}{12}$

EXERCISES

Write a number sentence for each model.

1. 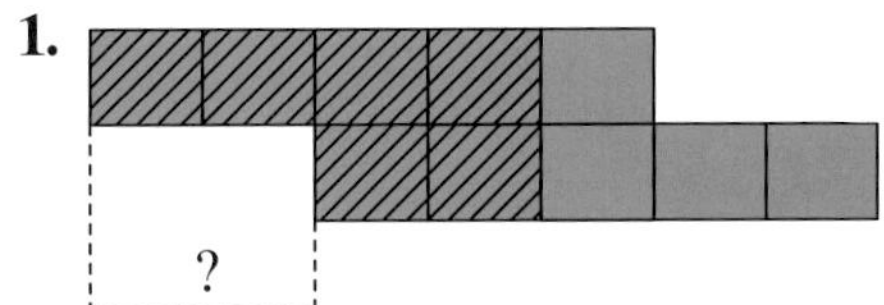

2. 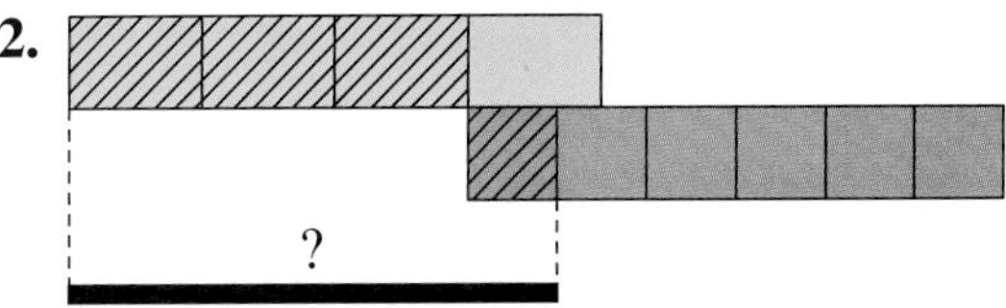

Use models to find each sum or difference.

3. $\frac{3}{8} + \frac{3}{8}$
4. $\frac{5}{6} - \frac{1}{6}$
5. $\frac{9}{10} - \frac{7}{10}$
6. $\frac{1}{6} + \frac{5}{6}$
7. $\frac{2}{5} + \frac{1}{2}$
8. $\frac{3}{4} + \frac{1}{8}$
9. $\frac{4}{5} - \frac{1}{2}$
10. $\frac{7}{10} - \frac{1}{5}$

4-2 Adding and Subtracting Fractions

What You'll Learn

To add fractions

To subtract fractions

. . . And Why

To find the difference between measurements, as in Example 3

Check Skills You'll Need

For help, go to Lesson 3-5.

Find each missing number.

1. $\frac{8}{16} = \frac{\blacksquare}{8}$

2. $\frac{\blacksquare}{10} = \frac{4}{5}$

3. $\frac{1}{6} = \frac{4}{\blacksquare}$

4. $\frac{3}{9} = \frac{\blacksquare}{3}$

5. $\frac{7}{8} = \frac{\blacksquare}{32}$

6. $\frac{1}{\blacksquare} = \frac{5}{25}$

7. Write three fractions that are equivalent to $\frac{4}{16}$.

OBJECTIVE 1

iTEXT Interactive lesson includes instant self-check, tutorials, and activities.

1 Adding Fractions

Each weekday morning, you walk $\frac{1}{10}$ mi to your friend's house. You and your friend then walk $\frac{3}{10}$ mi to school. The total distance you walk is $\frac{4}{10}$ mi.

The fractions $\frac{1}{10}$ and $\frac{3}{10}$ have the same denominator. To find their sum, add the numerators and keep the denominator the same.

Reading Math

Common denominators are sometimes called "like denominators."

1 EXAMPLE Common Denominators

Find $\frac{2}{9} + \frac{4}{9}$.

Estimate $\frac{2}{9} + \frac{4}{9} \approx 0 + \frac{1}{2}$, or $\frac{1}{2}$

$\frac{2}{9} + \frac{4}{9} = \frac{2 + 4}{9}$ ← **Keep the denominator the same.**

$= \frac{6}{9}$ ← **Add the numerators.**

$= \frac{2}{3}$ ← **Simplify. The answer is close to the estimate.**

Check Understanding 1 **a.** Find $\frac{3}{5} + \frac{1}{5}$. **b.** Find $\frac{7}{8} + \frac{3}{8}$.

You can use models to add fractions with different denominators. The model below shows the sum $\frac{1}{4} + \frac{1}{3} = \frac{7}{12}$.

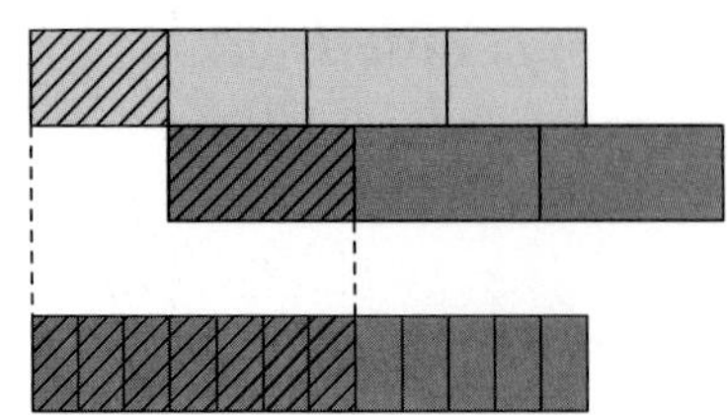

To add fractions with different denominators, you can first find their Least Common Denominator, or LCD.

Need Help?
The LCD of two fractions is the least common multiple of their denominators.

2 EXAMPLE Different Denominators

Find $\frac{4}{5} + \frac{2}{3}$.

Estimate $\frac{4}{5} + \frac{2}{3} \approx 1 + \frac{1}{2}$, or $1\frac{1}{2}$

$\frac{4}{5} = \frac{4 \cdot 3}{5 \cdot 3} = \frac{12}{15}$ ← The LCD is 15.

$+\frac{2}{3} = \frac{2 \cdot 5}{3 \cdot 5} = +\frac{10}{15}$ ← The LCD is 15.

$\frac{22}{15}$ ← Add the numerators.

$1\frac{7}{15}$ ← Write as a mixed number. The answer is close to the estimate.

Check Understanding 2 **a.** Find $\frac{1}{3} + \frac{1}{8}$. **b.** Find $\frac{3}{4} + \frac{1}{6}$. **c.** Find $\frac{4}{5} + \frac{1}{3}$.

OBJECTIVE

2 Subtracting Fractions

You can also use models to subtract fractions with different denominators. The model below shows $\frac{1}{2} - \frac{1}{3} = \frac{1}{6}$.

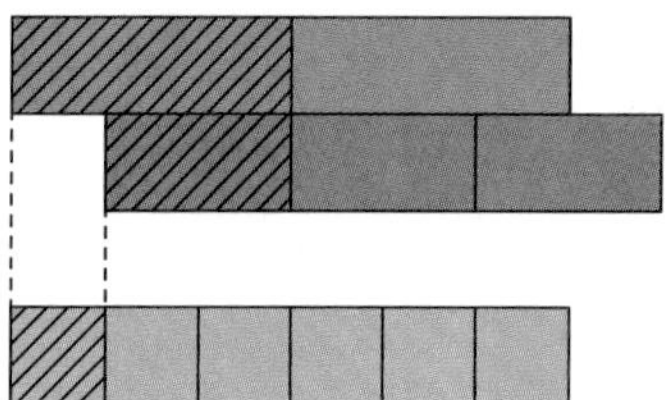

3 EXAMPLE Real-World Problem Solving

Carpentry A cabinetmaker needs a board that is $\frac{9}{16}$ in. thick. By how much must he decrease the thickness of a board that is $\frac{7}{8}$ in. thick?

Estimate $\frac{7}{8} - \frac{9}{16} \approx 1 - \frac{1}{2}$, or $\frac{1}{2}$

$\frac{7}{8} = \frac{7 \cdot 2}{8 \cdot 2} = \frac{14}{16}$ ← The LCD is 16.

$-\frac{9}{16} = -\frac{9}{16} = -\frac{9}{16}$ ← The LCD is 16.

$\frac{5}{16}$ ← Subtract the numerators.

The cabinetmaker should decrease the thickness of the board by $\frac{5}{16}$ in.

Check for Reasonableness The answer, $\frac{5}{16}$, is close to the estimate, $\frac{1}{2}$. The answer is reasonable.

Real-World Connection
Carpenters use fractions to make measurements.

Check Understanding 3 **a.** Find $\frac{3}{4} - \frac{1}{8}$. **b.** Find $\frac{5}{6} - \frac{1}{3}$.

EXERCISES

For more practice, see *Extra Practice*.

A Practice by Example

Example 1 (page 192)

Example 2 (page 193)

Example 3 (page 193)

Find each sum. Exercise 1 has been started for you.

1. $\frac{1}{7} + \frac{4}{7} = \frac{1+4}{7}$
2. $\frac{3}{4} + \frac{3}{4}$
3. $\frac{6}{8} + \frac{3}{8}$
4. $\frac{6}{7} + \frac{1}{7}$
5. $\frac{1}{4} + \frac{1}{4}$
6. $\frac{5}{6} + \frac{5}{6}$
7. $\frac{4}{3} + \frac{2}{3}$
8. $\frac{7}{12} + \frac{1}{6}$
9. $\frac{3}{3} + \frac{5}{8}$
10. $\frac{4}{5} + \frac{7}{8}$
11. $\frac{1}{2} + \frac{4}{5}$
12. $\frac{3}{2} + \frac{1}{4}$
13. $\frac{5}{6} + \frac{7}{8}$
14. $\frac{7}{10} + \frac{1}{6}$
15. $\frac{11}{12} + \frac{3}{4}$

Find each difference.

16. $\frac{4}{5} - \frac{1}{5}$
17. $\frac{7}{10} - \frac{1}{10}$
18. $\frac{7}{10} - \frac{1}{5}$
19. $\frac{9}{10} - \frac{2}{5}$
20. $\frac{5}{6} - \frac{1}{3}$
21. $\frac{3}{5} - \frac{1}{4}$
22. $\frac{5}{6} - \frac{1}{2}$
23. $\frac{2}{3} - \frac{1}{4}$

24. **Travel** The gas tank in your family's car was $\frac{9}{10}$ full when you left your house. When you arrived at your destination, the tank was $\frac{7}{15}$ full. What fraction of a tank of gas did you use during the trip?

B Apply Your Skills

Find each sum or difference.

25. $\frac{7}{12} - \frac{1}{12}$
26. $\frac{5}{24} - \frac{1}{8}$
27. $\frac{1}{2} + \frac{5}{16}$
28. $\frac{7}{6} - \frac{3}{24}$
29. $\frac{3}{5} + \frac{1}{6}$
30. $\frac{1}{3} - \frac{1}{15}$
31. $\frac{1}{5} + \frac{3}{8}$
32. $\frac{3}{4} - \frac{3}{10}$
33. $\frac{3}{6} - \frac{4}{9}$

34. **Carpentry** Suppose you are using nails $\frac{5}{6}$ in. long to nail plywood $\frac{1}{4}$ in. thick to a beam. How much of the nail extends into the beam?

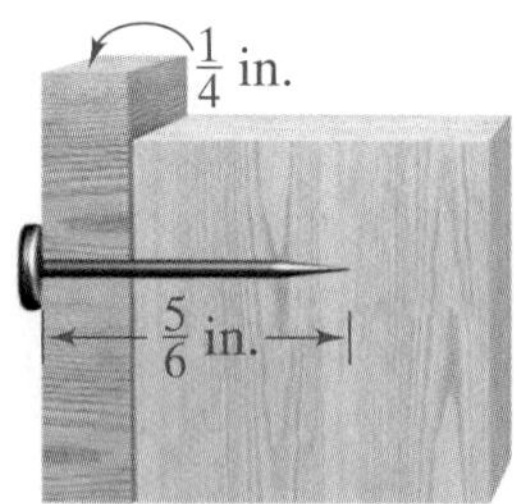

35. **Error Analysis** A student added $\frac{2}{8} + \frac{3}{8}$ and got $\frac{5}{16}$. What was the student's mistake? What is the correct answer?

Use models to find each answer.

36. $\frac{1}{8} + \frac{1}{4}$
37. $\frac{5}{6} - \frac{1}{4}$
38. $\frac{2}{3} - \frac{1}{4}$
39. $\frac{1}{2} + \frac{1}{3}$
40. $\frac{3}{4} + \frac{1}{2}$
41. $\frac{3}{4} - \frac{5}{8}$

Write a number sentence for each model.

42.

43.

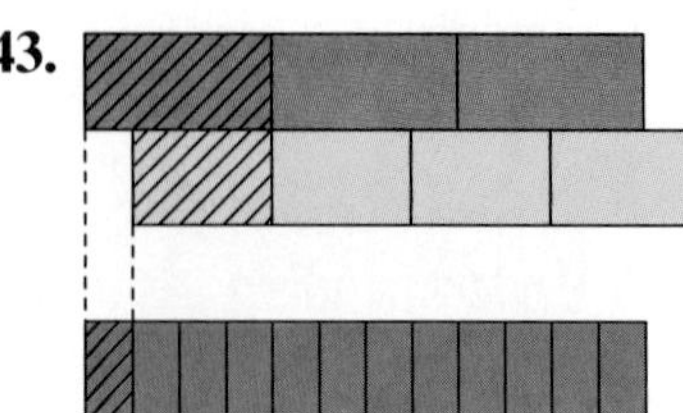

44. **Boating** You rowed $\frac{2}{3}$ mi. Your friend rowed $\frac{8}{10}$ mi. Who rowed farther? How much farther?

45. a. **Grades** One third of the students in your class got an A. One fourth of them got a B. What fraction of the students got an A or a B?
 b. Did a majority of the students get either A's or B's? Explain.

Algebra **Solve each equation.**

46. $\frac{2}{5} + x = \frac{7}{5}$ 47. $\frac{1}{7} + y = \frac{3}{7}$ 48. $p + \frac{4}{9} = \frac{9}{9}$

49. $\frac{1}{3} + k = \frac{5}{6}$ 50. $w + \frac{2}{5} = \frac{7}{10}$ 51. $r - \frac{4}{5} = \frac{1}{10}$

Use the circle graph for Exercises 52–55.

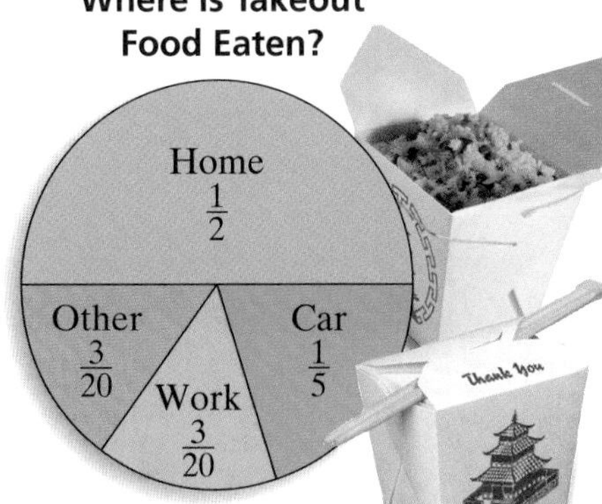

52. Data Analysis What fraction of takeout food is eaten at home or in a car?

53. How much greater is the fraction of takeout food eaten at home than the fraction eaten at work?

54. What fraction of the food is eaten at home, in a car, or at work?

55. Writing in Math Describe two ways to find the answer to Exercise 54.

56. Calculator You can use this key sequence to find $\frac{3}{5} + \frac{1}{4}$.

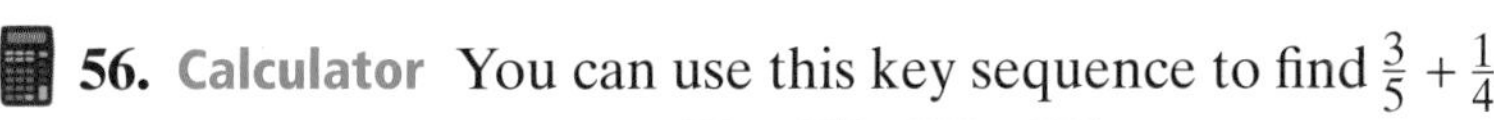

The answer the calculator displays, 0.85, can be rewritten as the fraction $\frac{85}{100}$, which can be simplified as $\frac{17}{20}$.
 a. Write the key sequence you could use to find $\frac{7}{8} - \frac{3}{5}$.
 b. Use your key sequence to find $\frac{7}{8} - \frac{3}{5}$.

C Challenge

Mental Math **Will each sum be *positive*, *negative*, or *zero*? Explain.**

57. $-\frac{2}{3} + \frac{5}{6}$ 58. $-\frac{4}{5} + \frac{8}{10}$ 59. $-\frac{7}{8} + \frac{3}{4}$ 60. $-\frac{3}{4} + \frac{3}{5}$

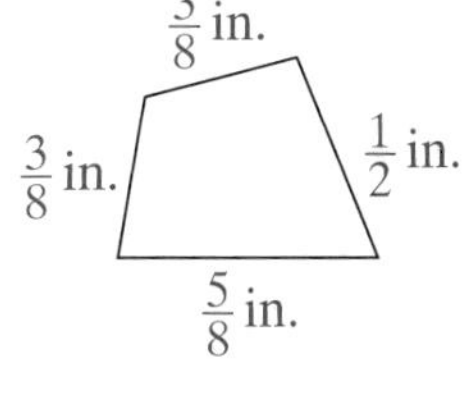

61. Geometry Find the perimeter of the figure at the left.

62. **History** The ancient Egyptians wrote fractions, but only fractions with a numerator of 1. They expressed other fractions as sums. Use sums and the Egyptian fractions at the right to express the fractions $\frac{3}{4}$ and $\frac{3}{5}$.

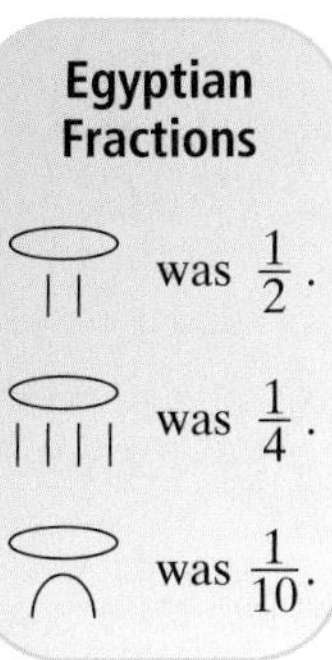

63. Stretch Your Thinking I am a fraction in simplest form. I am greater than $\frac{1}{3}$ and less than $\frac{1}{2}$. The sum of all my digits is 8. The difference between my numerator and denominator is 7. What fraction am I?

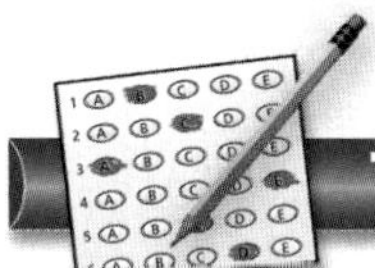

Test Prep

Gridded Response

You cannot grid a mixed number. Instead, grid an improper fraction or a decimal. To grid $1\frac{4}{5}$, grid $\frac{9}{5}$ or 1.8, as shown at the right.

9	/	5		

		1	.	8

64. After you cut off a piece $\frac{1}{5}$ m long, a bookshelf is $\frac{9}{10}$ m long. How many meters long was the bookshelf to start?

65. The bus stop is $\frac{7}{10}$ mi from your home, and the subway station is $\frac{1}{4}$ mi from your home. How many more miles is it to the bus stop than to the subway station?

66. You have a math test. You plan to study $\frac{5}{6}$ h tonight and $\frac{3}{4}$ h tomorrow. For how many hours in all are you planning to study?

Take It to the NET
Online lesson quiz at
www.PHSchool.com
Web Code aba-0402

Mixed Review

Lesson 3-9

Order from least to greatest.

67. $\frac{4}{3}, 0.52, -\frac{3}{4}, 1.0$

68. $1.34, \frac{25}{6}, -2.4, \frac{7}{3}$

69. $1.6, -0.5, \frac{8}{7}, -\frac{9}{16}$

70. $\frac{6}{5}, \frac{1}{3}, 0.32, \frac{15}{12}$

Lesson 1-10

71. Find the mean, median, and mode for the closing price of a stock in the last seven days.

$35 $37 $33 $36 $29 $39 $37

Math at Work

Songwriter

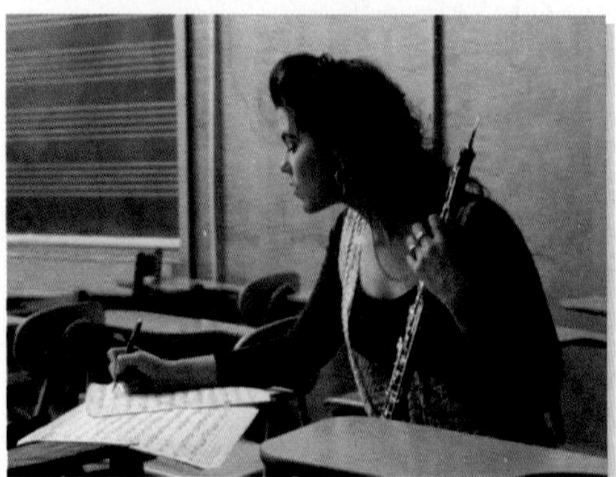

Songwriters need to know what types of music are "in" to compose a song that will sell. Then a songwriter must find a publisher willing to find an artist to record the song. Producers and record companies decide whether they will promote a song as a potential hit.

Songwriters use mathematics to design complex rhythms.

Take It to the NET For more information about songwriting and performing, go to **www.PHSchool.com.**
Web Code abb-2031

4-3 Adding and Subtracting Mixed Numbers

What You'll Learn

To add mixed numbers

To subtract mixed numbers

. . . And Why

To find running distances, as in Example 2

Check Skills You'll Need

For help, go to Lesson 3-6.

Compare each pair of fractions. Use <, >, or =.

1. $\frac{3}{12}$ ■ $\frac{5}{12}$ **2.** $\frac{1}{6}$ ■ $\frac{1}{4}$ **3.** $\frac{3}{8}$ ■ $\frac{3}{4}$

4. $\frac{5}{12}$ ■ $\frac{3}{8}$ **5.** $\frac{4}{7}$ ■ $\frac{2}{3}$ **6.** $\frac{2}{3}$ ■ $\frac{1}{5}$

7. Number Sense Two fractions have the same numerator. How can you use the denominators to compare the fractions?

OBJECTIVE 1

iTEXT Interactive lesson includes instant self-check, tutorials, and activities.

Adding Mixed Numbers

Suppose you are working on a volunteer project. On Monday you worked for $2\frac{3}{4}$ hours. On Tuesday you worked for $4\frac{3}{4}$ hours. How many total hours did you work?

The fraction parts of $2\frac{3}{4}$ and $4\frac{3}{4}$ have the same denominator. To find their sum, first add the fractions, and then add the whole numbers.

1 EXAMPLE Same Denominators

Find $2\frac{3}{4} + 4\frac{3}{4}$.

Estimate $2\frac{3}{4} + 4\frac{3}{4} \approx 3 + 5$, or 8

$2\frac{3}{4} + 4\frac{3}{4} = 6\frac{6}{4}$ ← **Add the fractions. Add the whole numbers.**

$= 6 + \frac{6}{4}$ ← **Write the mixed number as a sum.**

$= 6 + 1\frac{2}{4}$ ← **Write $\frac{6}{4}$ as $1\frac{2}{4}$.**

$= 6 + 1\frac{1}{2}$ ← **Simplify.**

$= 7\frac{1}{2}$ ← **Add the whole numbers.**

Check for Reasonableness The answer, $7\frac{1}{2}$, is close to the estimate, 8. The answer is reasonable.

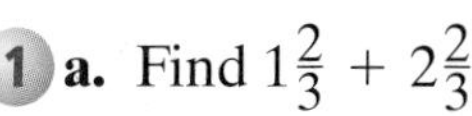

Check Understanding 1 **a.** Find $1\frac{2}{3} + 2\frac{2}{3}$. **b.** Find $2\frac{2}{5} + 3\frac{2}{5}$.

c. Mental Math Explain how to find the answer to part (b) using mental math.

Fractions in mixed numbers may have different denominators. You can use the LCD to rewrite them as fractions with common denominators.

2 EXAMPLE Different Denominators

Cross Country You are training for a cross country race. On Monday, you run $4\frac{1}{4}$ mi, and on Tuesday you run $3\frac{2}{3}$ mi. What is your total mileage?

Find $4\frac{1}{4} + 3\frac{2}{3}$.

Estimate $4\frac{1}{4} + 3\frac{2}{3} \approx 4 + 4$, or 8

$4\frac{1}{4} = 4\frac{3}{12}$ ← **Write an equivalent fraction using the LCD, 12.**

$+3\frac{2}{3} = +3\frac{8}{12}$ ← **Write an equivalent fraction using the LCD, 12.**

$7\frac{11}{12}$ ← **Add the fractions. Add the whole numbers.**

Your total mileage is $7\frac{11}{12}$ mi.

Check for Reasonableness The answer, $7\frac{11}{12}$, is close to the estimate, 8. The answer is reasonable.

Check Understanding 2 **a.** Find $2\frac{1}{4} + 1\frac{2}{3}$. **b.** Find $3\frac{1}{6} + 8\frac{7}{8}$.

c. **Reasoning** When adding mixed numbers, why do you sometimes need to rename the sum of the mixed numbers?

OBJECTIVE

2 Subtracting Mixed Numbers

When you subtract mixed numbers, you may need to rename one of the numbers before subtracting.

3 EXAMPLE Subtracting With Renaming

Find $6\frac{1}{8} - 2\frac{3}{4}$.

Estimate $6\frac{1}{8} - 2\frac{3}{4} \approx 6 - 3$, or 3

$6\frac{1}{8} = 6\frac{1}{8}$ ← **The LCD is 8.**

$-2\frac{3}{4} = -2\frac{6}{8}$ ← **Write an equivalent fraction.**

$5\frac{9}{8}$ ← **Rename: $6\frac{1}{8} = 5 + 1\frac{1}{8} = 5 + \frac{9}{8} = 5\frac{9}{8}$.**

$-2\frac{6}{8}$

$3\frac{3}{8}$ ← **Subtract.**

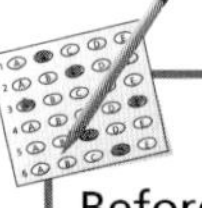

Test-Prep Tip

Before subtracting mixed numbers, decide whether you need to rename one of them.

Check for Reasonableness The answer, $3\frac{3}{8}$, is close to the estimate, 3. The answer is reasonable.

Check Understanding 3 **a.** Find $5\frac{1}{2} - 3\frac{3}{4}$. **b.** Find $4\frac{1}{3} - 2\frac{5}{6}$.

c. **Reasoning** When subtracting mixed numbers, when might you need to convert a whole number into a mixed number?

EXERCISES

For more practice, see *Extra Practice*.

A Practice by Example

Example 1 (page 197)

Find each sum. Exercise 1 has been started for you.

1. $6\frac{2}{5} + 1\frac{4}{5} = 7\frac{6}{5}$ **2.** $9\frac{3}{7} + 1\frac{2}{7}$ **3.** $3\frac{3}{8} + 4\frac{5}{8}$

4. $11\frac{10}{11} + 3\frac{5}{11}$ **5.** $7\frac{1}{3} + 2\frac{2}{3}$ **6.** $5\frac{1}{13} + 8\frac{8}{13}$ **7.** $6\frac{9}{15} + 2\frac{12}{15}$

Example 2 (page 198)

8. $6\frac{2}{5} + 1\frac{4}{10}$ **9.** $9\frac{1}{2} + 9\frac{1}{3}$ **10.** $7\frac{1}{6} + 8\frac{1}{8}$ **11.** $6\frac{1}{2} + 4\frac{5}{6}$

12. $8\frac{3}{4} + 8\frac{1}{8}$ **13.** $5\frac{5}{9} + 9\frac{1}{3}$ **14.** $17\frac{3}{4} + 3\frac{3}{8}$ **15.** $17\frac{2}{5} + 11\frac{3}{4}$

16. Construction A bolt must go through a sign and a support that together are $2\frac{1}{8}$ in. thick. An additional $\frac{5}{16}$ in. is needed for the washer and the nut. How long should the bolt be?

Example 3 (page 198)

Find each difference.

17. $7\frac{2}{3} - 1\frac{1}{6}$ **18.** $15 - 3\frac{3}{4}$ **19.** $15\frac{3}{4} - 8\frac{3}{8}$ **20.** $6\frac{9}{10} - 3\frac{2}{5}$

21. $9\frac{1}{2} - \frac{2}{3}$ **22.** $14 - 5\frac{1}{5}$ **23.** $15\frac{1}{3} - 9\frac{1}{2}$ **24.** $6\frac{3}{8} - 2\frac{3}{4}$

B Apply Your Skills

25. Calculator You can use this key sequence to find $5\frac{1}{2} + 4\frac{3}{4}$.

(5 + 1 ÷ 2) + (4 + 3 ÷ 4) = 10.25

The calculator display 10.25 can be written as $10\frac{1}{4}$.

a. Write a key sequence you can use to find $4\frac{1}{8} - 1\frac{3}{4}$.

b. Use your key sequence to find $4\frac{1}{8} - 1\frac{3}{4}$.

Real-World Connection

The distance a hiker can walk is influenced by the difficulty of the terrain and the amount of weight the hiker carries.

26. Hiking On Saturday you hiked $4\frac{3}{8}$ mi. On Sunday, you hiked $3\frac{1}{2}$ mi. How far did you hike during the weekend?

Find each sum or difference.

27. $8\frac{3}{15} - 5\frac{2}{15}$ **28.** $10 - 5\frac{18}{19}$ **29.** $11\frac{3}{4} + 15\frac{3}{4}$ **30.** $30\frac{2}{3} + 12\frac{3}{4}$

31. $13\frac{5}{8} + 25\frac{1}{2}$ **32.** $18\frac{1}{8} - 9\frac{3}{4}$ **33.** $6\frac{11}{20} - 4\frac{9}{10}$ **34.** $16\frac{7}{8} - 14\frac{3}{4}$

35. $24 - 19\frac{3}{5}$ **36.** $2\frac{11}{29} + 10$ **37.** $19\frac{11}{12} - 16\frac{3}{4}$ **38.** $22\frac{4}{5} + 44\frac{4}{7}$

39. Error Analysis A student subtracted $10\frac{1}{7} - 3\frac{5}{7}$ and got $6\frac{6}{7}$. Find the correct answer. What mistake do you think the student made?

40. Writing in Math Can you add mixed numbers by first changing them to decimals? Explain.

41. Advertising A newspaper has the following advertising space available: $2\frac{7}{8}$ c.i. (column inches), $3\frac{1}{2}$ c.i., and $4\frac{1}{4}$ c.i.

a. What is the total number of column inches available?

b. At \$20 per column inch, what is the cost of the $4\frac{1}{4}$ c.i. space?

42. **Party Planning** Your punch bowl holds 6 qt. Is it large enough to hold all the ingredients called for in the recipe at the right? Explain.

Lemon Raspberry Fizz
$2\frac{1}{4}$ qt ginger ale • $1\frac{2}{3}$ qt lemon sherbet
$1\frac{1}{2}$ qt lemonade • $\frac{1}{2}$ qt raspberry juice

43. **Data File, p.185** Use the data for maximum depth. Find the difference between the depths of the Grand Canyon and Black Canyon.

Challenge

Evaluate each expression for $a = 2\frac{1}{28}$, $b = 7\frac{1}{2}$, and $c = 5\frac{3}{7}$.

44. $a + b + c$

45. $b - c - a$

46. $(b + c) - (a + a)$

47. **Number Sense** $9\frac{x}{17} - 3\frac{y}{17}$ = a whole number. List three possible pairs of values for x and y for which $x \neq y$.

48. **Geometry** Figures A and B have a total area of $5\frac{3}{4}$ in.^{2}. Figure A's area is $1\frac{1}{4}$ in.^{2} greater than Figure B's area. Find the areas of both figures.

49. **Stretch Your Thinking** Copy the figure. Write the numbers 2, 3, 4, 5, 6, 7, 8, 9, and 10 in the squares, using each number only once, so that the numbers in the squares on each of the four circles have a sum of 27.

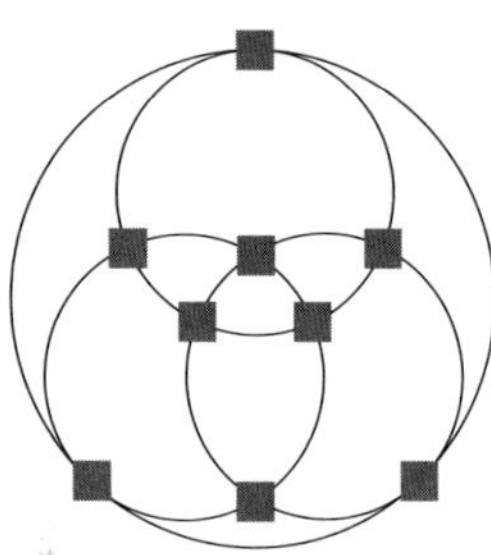

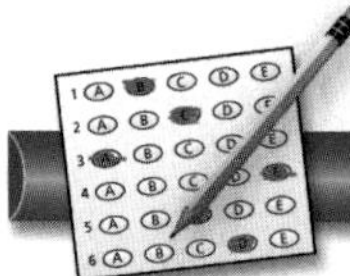

Test Prep

Multiple Choice

50. How many hours are there from 10:00 A.M. to 2:55 P.M.?
A. $4\frac{11}{20}$ h B. $4\frac{55}{100}$ h C. $4\frac{11}{12}$ h D. $5\frac{1}{12}$ h

51. To get to the library, you must travel $1\frac{1}{10}$ mi down one street, $\frac{1}{2}$ mi down another street, and $\frac{2}{5}$ mi down a third street. How many miles must you travel in all to get to the library?
F. $1\frac{4}{5}$ mi G. 2 mi H. $2\frac{1}{10}$ mi I. $2\frac{1}{2}$ mi

52. You want to be in school at 8:00 A.M. It takes you $\frac{1}{2}$ h to get dressed, 20 min to eat your breakfast, and $\frac{1}{6}$ h to bike to school. What time should you wake up?
A. 7:10 A.M. B. 7:00 A.M. C. 6:50 A.M. D. 6:40 A.M.

Take It to the NET
Online lesson quiz at
www.PHSchool.com
Web Code aba-0403

53. How much heavier is $28\frac{1}{2}$ lb than $15\frac{11}{16}$ lb?
F. $12\frac{3}{4}$ lb G. $12\frac{13}{16}$ lb H. $12\frac{7}{8}$ lb I. $13\frac{13}{16}$ lb

Short Response

54. At an animal adoption center, $\frac{1}{2}$ of the animals are dogs, and $\frac{5}{16}$ are cats. **(a)** Explain how you can find the fraction of the animals that are neither dogs nor cats. **(b)** Find the fraction.

Mixed Review

Lesson 2-8

Algebra **Write an inequality for each graph.**

55. 

56. 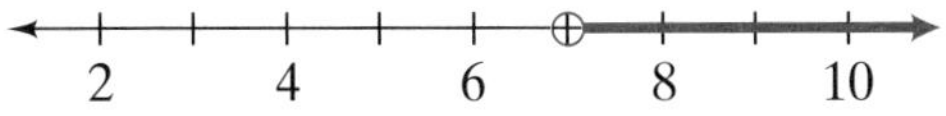

57. 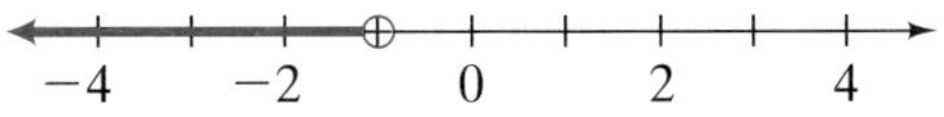

58. 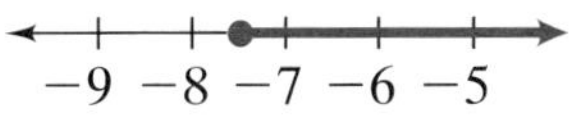

Lesson 1-9

Mental Math **Find each product using the Distributive Property.**

59. 5(23)	**60.** 7(18)	**61.** 4(62)
62. 10.2(8)	**63.** 6.5(9)	**64.** 3(−44)

65. You go shopping for a new poster for your room. You find a poster that measures 20 in. × 26.5 in.

a. Use the Distributive Property to write an expression to find the area of your poster.

b. Find the area of your poster.

Checkpoint Quiz 1 — Lessons 4-1 through 4-3

iText Instant self-check quiz online and on CD-ROM

Weather **The table shows the average rainfall in Orlando, Florida, for July through December. Use benchmarks and the table to answer Exercises 1–3.**

Month	July	August	September	October	November	December
Inches	$7\frac{7}{10}$	$6\frac{4}{5}$	$6\frac{3}{5}$	$3\frac{2}{5}$	$1\frac{9}{10}$	$2\frac{1}{10}$

1. Estimate the difference in rainfall between July and December.

2. Estimate the sum of rainfall in August and September.

3. Estimate the average rainfall for the six months.

Simplify.

4. $\frac{12}{18} - \frac{9}{18}$	**5.** $\frac{4}{3} + \frac{2}{3}$	**6.** $10\frac{7}{10} - 4\frac{4}{5}$
7. $6\frac{3}{4} + 2\frac{1}{5}$	**8.** $\frac{5}{9} - \frac{1}{3}$	**9.** $17 - 5\frac{3}{8}$

10. Measurement Five years ago, Tyler measured his height as $43\frac{7}{8}$ in. Now his height is $65\frac{1}{2}$ in. How many inches did Tyler grow in five years?

4-4 Multiplying Fractions and Mixed Numbers

What You'll Learn

To multiply fractions

To multiply mixed numbers

. . . And Why

To find a hummingbird's weight, as in Example 2

✓ Check Skills You'll Need

For help, go to Lesson 3-8.

Write each mixed number as an improper fraction.

1. $2\frac{3}{5}$ **2.** $6\frac{1}{2}$

3. $4\frac{3}{4}$ **4.** $8\frac{3}{4}$

5. $12\frac{2}{3}$ **6.** $9\frac{1}{9}$

7. Write $\frac{56}{6}$ as a mixed number in simplest form.

Interactive lesson includes instant self-check, tutorials, and activities.

OBJECTIVE 1

Multiplying Fractions

Investigation: Modeling Multiplication of Fractions

Use paper folding to find $\frac{1}{3}$ of $\frac{1}{4}$, or $\frac{1}{3} \cdot \frac{1}{4}$.

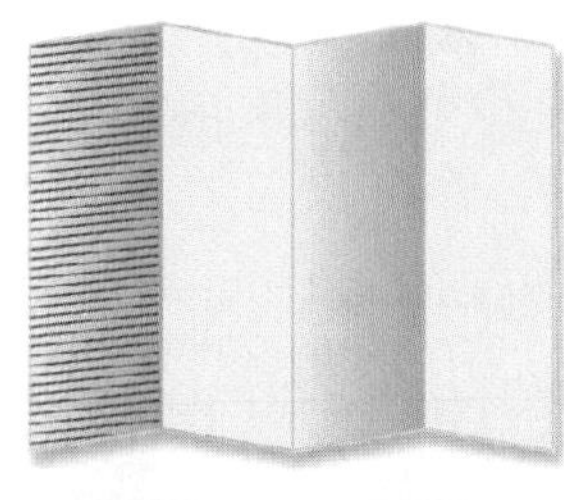

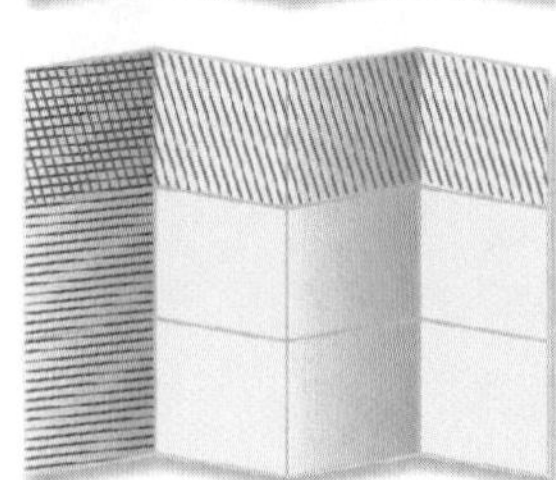

1. Fold a sheet of paper into fourths as shown in the top picture. Shade $\frac{1}{4}$ of it.
2. Fold the same paper lengthwise into thirds as shown in the bottom picture. Shade $\frac{1}{3}$ of it.
3. **a.** Count the total number of rectangles made by the folds.
   b. How many rectangles did you shade twice?
   c. What fraction of all the rectangles did you shade twice?
4. Use the model to complete: $\frac{1}{3} \cdot \frac{1}{4} = ■$. Explain how you found the product.
5. Choose two fractions from $\frac{1}{3}$, $\frac{2}{3}$, or $\frac{3}{4}$. Use modeling to find the product of the two fractions.
6. Suggest a rule for multiplying fractions.

When multiplying fractions, you do not need a common denominator as you do when adding and subtracting fractions. To multiply fractions, you multiply their numerators and multiply their denominators.

Key Concepts — Multiplying Fractions

Arithmetic	Algebra
$\frac{3}{4} \cdot \frac{1}{2} = \frac{3 \cdot 1}{4 \cdot 2} = \frac{3}{8}$	$\frac{a}{b} \cdot \frac{c}{d} = \frac{ac}{bd}$, $b \neq 0$ and $d \neq 0$

1 EXAMPLE Multiplying Fractions

Find $\frac{5}{8} \cdot \frac{2}{3}$.

Estimate $\frac{5}{8} \cdot \frac{2}{3} \approx \frac{1}{2} \cdot 1$, or $\frac{1}{2}$

$\frac{5}{8} \cdot \frac{2}{3} = \frac{5 \cdot 2}{8 \cdot 3}$ ← **Multiply the numerators. Multiply the denominators.**

$= \frac{10}{24}$ ← **Find the two products.**

$= \frac{5}{12}$ ← **Simplify.**

Check for Reasonableness The answer, $\frac{5}{12}$, is close to the estimate, $\frac{1}{2}$. The answer is reasonable.

Check Understanding 1 **a.** Find $\frac{3}{5} \cdot \frac{1}{4}$. **b.** Find $\frac{5}{6} \cdot \frac{4}{5}$. **c.** Find $\frac{2}{3} \cdot \frac{4}{5}$.

When a numerator and a denominator have a common factor, you can simplify before multiplying.

2 EXAMPLE Real-World Problem Solving

Biology The largest hummingbird is the giant hummingbird of South America. It weighs $\frac{2}{3}$ oz. The smallest hummingbird is the bee hummingbird of Cuba. Its weight is one tenth of the weight of a giant hummingbird. What is the weight of a bee hummingbird?

Words	weight of bee hummingbird	is	one tenth	of	weight of giant hummingbird

Let w represent the weight of the bee hummingbird.

Equation	w	$=$	$\frac{1}{10}$	$\cdot$	$\frac{2}{3}$

$w = \frac{1}{10} \cdot \frac{2}{3}$

$w = \frac{1}{{}_5\not{10}} \cdot \frac{\not{2}^1}{3}$ ← **Divide a numerator and a denominator by their GCF, 2.**

$w = \frac{1 \cdot 1}{5 \cdot 3}$ ← **Multiply the numerators. Multiply the denominators.**

$w = \frac{1}{15}$ ← **Simplify.**

A bee hummingbird weighs $\frac{1}{15}$ oz.

Need Help?
For help identifying the greatest common factor (GCF), go to Lesson 3-4.

Check Understanding 2 Simplify before finding the product $\frac{3 \cdot 4}{8 \cdot 5}$.

To multiply a fraction by a whole number, write the whole number as a fraction with a denominator of 1.

3 EXAMPLE Multiplying a Fraction by a Whole Number

Reading Math

When you read the expression $\frac{3}{7}$ *of 28*, think of $\frac{3}{7}$ "times" 28.

What is $\frac{3}{7}$ of 28?

$\frac{3}{7} \cdot 28 = \frac{3}{7} \cdot \frac{28}{1}$ ← **Write 28 as $\frac{28}{1}$.**

$= \frac{3}{{}_{1}7} \cdot \frac{28^{4}}{1}$ ← **Simplify before multiplying.**

$= \frac{12}{1}$ ← **Multiply the numerators. Multiply the denominators.**

$= 12$ ← **Simplify.**

Check Understanding 3 **a.** Find $\frac{5}{6}$ of 18. **b.** Find $\frac{4}{5}$ of 15.

c. Number Sense Is $\frac{5}{7}$ of 28 more or less than 28? Explain how you know without actually multiplying.

OBJECTIVE

2 Multiplying Mixed Numbers

To multiply mixed numbers, first write them as improper fractions, and then multiply as you do with fractions. Beforehand, you can round each fraction to the nearest whole number and estimate the product. Use your estimate to check whether your answer is reasonable.

4 EXAMPLE Multiplying Mixed Numbers

Find $2\frac{3}{5} \cdot 4\frac{1}{2}$.

Estimate $2\frac{3}{5} \cdot 4\frac{1}{2} \approx 3 \cdot 5$, or 15

$2\frac{3}{5} \cdot 4\frac{1}{2} = \frac{13}{5} \cdot \frac{9}{2}$ ← **Write the mixed numbers as improper fractions.**

$= \frac{13 \cdot 9}{5 \cdot 2}$ ← **Multiply the numerators. Multiply the denominators.**

$= \frac{117}{10}$ ← **Simplify.**

$= 11\frac{7}{10}$ ← **Write as a mixed number.**

Check for Reasonableness The answer, $11\frac{7}{10}$, is close to the estimate, 15. The answer is reasonable.

Check Understanding 4 **a.** Find $2\frac{1}{3} \cdot 4\frac{5}{8}$. **b.** Find $3\frac{3}{5} \cdot 1\frac{3}{10}$.

You can use this key sequence to find $6\frac{4}{5} \cdot 2\frac{1}{4}$.

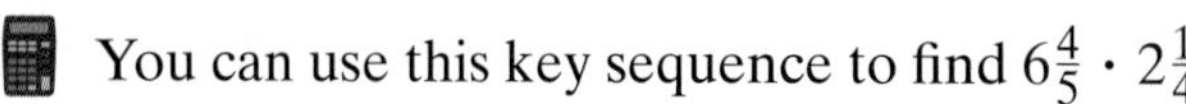

You can rewrite the answer, 15.3, as the mixed number $15\frac{3}{10}$.

EXERCISES

For more practice, see *Extra Practice*.

A Practice by Example

Example 1 (page 203)

Find each product. Exercise 1 has been started for you.

1. $\frac{1}{2} \cdot \frac{2}{3} = \frac{1 \cdot 2}{2 \cdot 3}$ **2.** $\frac{1}{4} \cdot \frac{3}{5}$ **3.** $\frac{1}{3} \cdot \frac{5}{6}$

4. $\frac{1}{4} \cdot \frac{8}{9}$ **5.** $\frac{1}{8} \cdot \frac{4}{5}$ **6.** $\frac{2}{3} \cdot \frac{2}{5}$ **7.** $\frac{2}{3} \cdot \frac{4}{9}$

Example 2 (page 203)

Simplify before finding each product.

8. $\frac{2}{3} \cdot \frac{3}{4}$ **9.** $\frac{1}{6} \cdot \frac{3}{5}$ **10.** $\frac{2}{3} \cdot \frac{1}{2}$ **11.** $\frac{2}{5} \cdot \frac{10}{11}$

12. $\frac{1}{12} \cdot \frac{8}{9}$ **13.** $\frac{7}{8} \cdot \frac{4}{5}$ **14.** $\frac{2}{5} \cdot \frac{15}{16}$ **15.** $\frac{5}{8} \cdot \frac{8}{9}$

16. The cover of your textbook is $\frac{3}{4}$ ft by $\frac{5}{6}$ ft. What is its area?

Example 3 (page 204)

Find each product.

17. $\frac{1}{4}$ of 12 **18.** $9 \cdot \frac{1}{3}$ **19.** $\frac{2}{3}$ of 18

20. $\frac{2}{5} \cdot 10$ **21.** $\frac{3}{4} \cdot 16$ **22.** $\frac{3}{5}$ of 15

Example 4 (page 204)

23. $1\frac{3}{10} \cdot 6\frac{2}{3}$ **24.** $1\frac{3}{8} \cdot 2\frac{2}{3}$ **25.** $3\frac{1}{3} \cdot 1\frac{1}{4}$

26. $2\frac{1}{2} \cdot 1\frac{3}{5}$ **27.** $4\frac{2}{3} \cdot \frac{3}{4}$ **28.** $5\frac{1}{4} \cdot 2\frac{2}{7}$

B Apply Your Skills

29. Error Analysis A student multiplies two mixed numbers, $2\frac{3}{5}$ and $1\frac{1}{3}$, and finds the product to be $2\frac{3}{15}$. Explain the student's mistake. What is the correct answer?

30. Science As a roller coaster car reaches the bottom of a slope and begins to go up the next slope, its acceleration, combined with the downward pull of gravity, can make a person feel $3\frac{1}{2}$ times as heavy. This sensation is called "supergravity."

a. How heavy would a 120-lb person experiencing supergravity feel in the roller coaster described above?

b. How heavy would a 150-lb person feel?

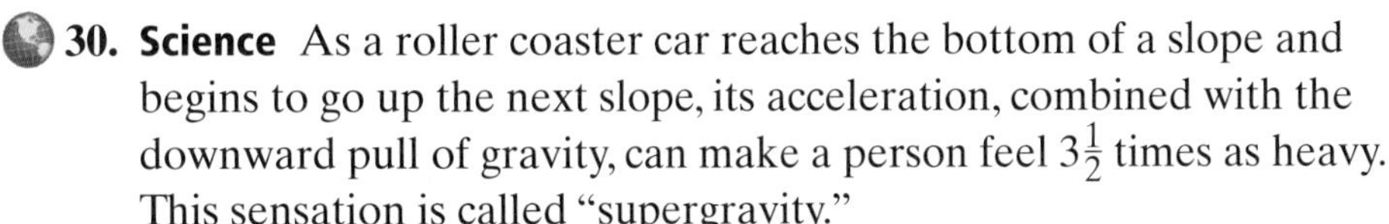

Algebra **Evaluate each expression for $a = \frac{3}{8}$ and $b = 2\frac{2}{5}$.**

31. $\frac{1}{3}a$ **32.** $2\frac{2}{5}b$ **33.** $1\frac{1}{6}a$

34. $\frac{5}{6}a$ **35.** $a \cdot b$ **36.** $a \cdot 16$

37. $5b$ **38.** $b \cdot \frac{5}{12}$ **39.** $b \cdot 50$

40. $b \cdot a$ **41.** $\frac{8}{3}a$ **42.** $b \cdot b$

Real-World Connection

Roller coasters can reach speeds as great as 100 mi/h.

43. Writing in Math How does multiplying two fractions differ from adding two fractions?

44. Fitness The length of a track around a football field is $\frac{1}{4}$ mi. You jog $3\frac{3}{4}$ times around the track. How far do you jog?

Challenge **Copy and complete the table.**

Nonfat Yogurt

	Servings	$\frac{1}{4}$	$\frac{1}{2}$	$\frac{3}{4}$	1	$1\frac{1}{2}$	2
45.	Ounces	a. ■	b. ■	c. ■	8	d. ■	e. ■
46.	Calories	a. ■	b. ■	c. ■	160	d. ■	e. ■

47. **Stretch Your Thinking** I am a two-digit number. My square is a number with its first two digits identical and its last two digits identical. What number am I?

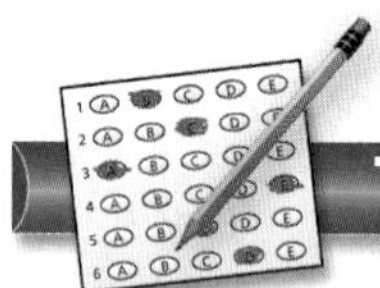

Test Prep

Reading Comprehension **Read the passage and answer the questions below.**

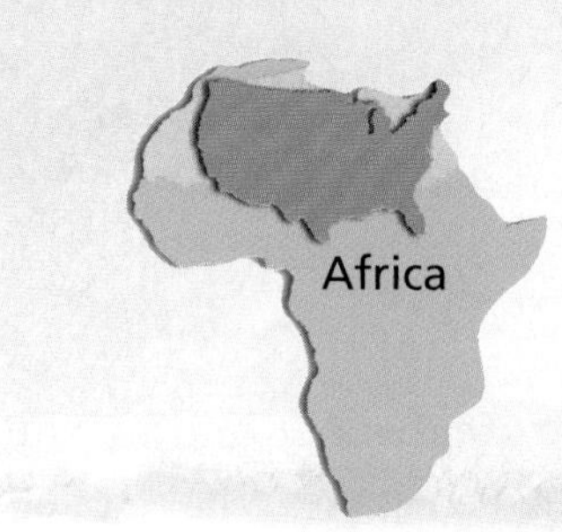

What's on Earth?

Earth has almost 200 million square miles of surface area. About seven tenths of Earth's surface is water. The remaining three tenths is land. Nearly one fifth of the land is desert. The largest desert, the Sahara in Africa, is three and a half million square miles, which is about the same area as the United States.

48. About how many square miles of Earth's surface is water?

Take It to the NET
Online lesson quiz at
www.PHSchool.com
Web Code aba-0404

49. About how many square miles is land?

50. About how many square miles is desert?

51. About what fraction of the desert surface is the Sahara Desert?

52. Africa makes up about $\frac{3}{50}$ of Earth's surface area. About how many square miles is Africa?

Mixed Review

Lesson 2-4 **Algebra** **Solve each equation. Check your answer.**

53. $5j = 30$ **54.** $\frac{r}{2} = 84$ **55.** $\frac{g}{10} = 20$

56. $3p = 150$ **57.** $\frac{m}{-4} = 21$ **58.** $0.9k = 54$

Lesson 1-1 **Estimate. Round to the nearest whole number before you calculate.**

59. $19.5 + 56.13$ **60.** $34.3 - 18.9$ **61.** $26.7 \cdot 9.9$

62. $229.5 \div 23$ **63.** $31.8 + 16.03$ **64.** $14.27 \cdot 1.81$

4-5 Dividing Fractions and Mixed Numbers

What You'll Learn

OBJECTIVE 1 To divide fractions

OBJECTIVE 2 To divide mixed numbers

... And Why

To find the number of servings, as in Example 3

✔ Check Skills You'll Need

For help, go to Lesson 4-4.

Find each product.

1. $\frac{3}{7} \cdot \frac{2}{3}$ **2.** $\frac{5}{9} \cdot \frac{1}{2}$ **3.** $\frac{13}{20} \cdot \frac{1}{3}$

4. $50 \cdot \frac{7}{10}$ **5.** $2\frac{2}{5} \cdot \frac{3}{7}$ **6.** $2\frac{2}{9} \cdot 1\frac{8}{10}$

New Vocabulary

- reciprocal

OBJECTIVE

iTEXT Interactive lesson includes instant self-check, tutorials, and activities.

1 Dividing Fractions

Asking "What is $3 \div \frac{3}{4}$?" is the same as asking "How many $\frac{3}{4}$'s are in 3 wholes?" The ruler shows there are four $\frac{3}{4}$'s in 3 wholes. So $3 \div \frac{3}{4} = 4$.

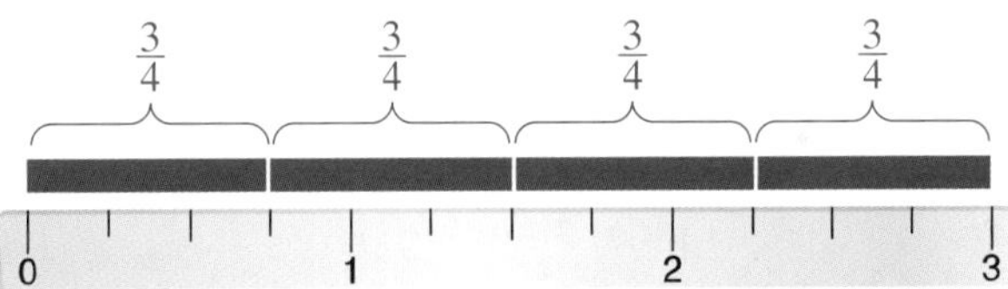

Reading Math

Reciprocal comes from a Greek word meaning "backward and forward."

The numbers $\frac{3}{4}$ and $\frac{4}{3}$ are reciprocals. Two numbers are **reciprocals** if their product is 1. To find the reciprocal of a fraction, interchange the numerator and denominator. To divide by a fraction, multiply by its reciprocal.

Key Concepts — Dividing Fractions

Arithmetic	Algebra
$\frac{5}{8} \div \frac{1}{8} = \frac{5}{8} \cdot \frac{8}{1}$	$\frac{a}{b} \div \frac{c}{d} = \frac{a}{b} \cdot \frac{d}{c}$ for $b, c,$ and $d \neq 0$

1 EXAMPLE — Dividing by a Fraction

Find $\frac{2}{3} \div \frac{5}{6}$.

$\frac{2}{3} \div \frac{5}{6} = \frac{2}{3} \cdot \frac{6}{5}$ ← Multiply by the reciprocal of $\frac{5}{6}$, which is $\frac{6}{5}$.

$= \frac{2 \cdot \cancel{6}^{2}}{{}_{1}\cancel{3} \cdot 5}$ ← Divide 6 and 3 by their GCF, which is 3.

$= \frac{4}{5}$ ← Simplify.

Check Understanding 1 **a.** Find $\frac{7}{8} \div \frac{1}{16}$. **b.** Find $\frac{5}{8} \div \frac{3}{4}$.

OBJECTIVE

2 Dividing Mixed Numbers

To divide mixed numbers, rewrite them as improper fractions.

2 EXAMPLE Dividing Mixed Numbers

Measurement You have $9\frac{1}{2}$ in. of horizontal space for a row of photos on a poster board. Each photo is $2\frac{3}{4}$ in. wide. How many photos can you fit?

To find how many $2\frac{3}{4}$-in. photos will fit in a $9\frac{1}{2}$-in. space, divide $9\frac{1}{2}$ by $2\frac{3}{4}$.

$9\frac{1}{2} \div 2\frac{3}{4} = \frac{19}{2} \div \frac{11}{4}$ ← **Write the mixed numbers as improper fractions.**

$= \frac{19}{2} \cdot \frac{4}{11}$ ← **Multiply by the reciprocal of $\frac{11}{4}$, which is $\frac{4}{11}$.**

$= \frac{19}{{}_{1}\cancel{2}} \cdot \frac{\cancel{4}^{2}}{11}$ ← **Divide 4 and 2 by their GCF, which is 2.**

$= \frac{38}{11}$ ← **Multiply.**

$= 3\frac{5}{11}$ ← **Write as a mixed number.**

You can fit 3 photos in the space.

Check Understanding 2 **a.** Find $5\frac{3}{4} \div 3\frac{2}{3}$. **b.** Find $4\frac{1}{8} \div 5\frac{1}{2}$.

3 EXAMPLE Real-World Problem Solving

Meal Planning How many servings of the smaller cereal box are in the larger cereal box?

To find how many $1\frac{1}{2}$-oz servings are in $19\frac{1}{2}$ oz, divide $19\frac{1}{2}$ by $1\frac{1}{2}$.

Estimate $19\frac{1}{2} \div 1\frac{1}{2} \approx 20 \div 2$, or 10

$19\frac{1}{2} \div 1\frac{1}{2} = \frac{39}{2} \div \frac{3}{2}$ ← **Write the mixed numbers as improper fractions.**

$= \frac{39}{2} \cdot \frac{2}{3}$ ← **Multiply by the reciprocal of $\frac{3}{2}$, which is $\frac{2}{3}$.**

$= \frac{{}^{13}\cancel{39} \cdot \cancel{2}^{1}}{{}_{1}\cancel{2} \cdot \cancel{3}_{1}}$ ← **Divide 39 and 3 by their GCF, 3. Divide 2 by itself.**

$= \frac{13}{1} = 13$ ← **Simplify.**

There are thirteen $1\frac{1}{2}$-oz servings in the larger cereal box.

Check for Reasonableness The answer, 13, is close to the estimate, 10. The answer is reasonable.

3 **a.** Find $7\frac{3}{4} \div 1\frac{2}{3}$. **b.** Find $1\frac{3}{4} \div 4\frac{1}{8}$.

c. **Reasoning** Can you use the rule for multiplying by the reciprocal for whole numbers such as $10 \div 2$? Explain.

More Than One Way

You want to put 4 lb of raisins in bags so that each bag contains $\frac{2}{3}$ lb. How many bags do you need?

Kayla's Method

I can use mental math. I know that $\frac{2}{3}$ of 3 is 2. So $\frac{2}{3}$ of 6 must be 4.

I need 6 bags.

Will's Method

I can divide 4 by $\frac{2}{3}$.

$4 \div \frac{2}{3} = \frac{4}{1} \div \frac{2}{3}$ ← **Write the whole number as a fraction.**

$= \frac{4}{1} \cdot \frac{3}{2}$ ← **Multiply by the reciprocal of $\frac{2}{3}$.**

$= \frac{{}^{2}4 \cdot 3}{1 \cdot 2_{1}}$ ← **Divide 4 and 2 by their GCF, 2.**

$= \frac{6}{1}$ ← **Simplify.**

$= 6$

I need 6 bags.

Choose a Method

Suppose you want to bike 12 miles in $1\frac{1}{3}$ hours. What should your average speed be? Describe your method, and explain why you chose it.

EXERCISES

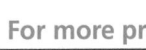

For more practice, see *Extra Practice*.

A Practice by Example

Find each quotient. Exercises 1 and 7 have been started for you.

Example 1 (page 207)

1. $\frac{1}{8} \div \frac{1}{2} = \frac{1}{8} \cdot \frac{2}{1}$
2. $\frac{4}{5} \div \frac{1}{4}$
3. $\frac{4}{5} \div \frac{1}{3}$
4. $\frac{5}{16} \div \frac{1}{2}$
5. $\frac{2}{7} \div \frac{1}{9}$
6. $\frac{1}{9} \div \frac{5}{6}$

Examples 2, 3 (page 208)

7. $1\frac{1}{2} \div 3\frac{1}{4} = \frac{3}{2} \div \frac{13}{4}$
8. $2\frac{1}{6} \div 3\frac{5}{6}$
9. $8\frac{1}{3} \div 2\frac{1}{2}$
10. $1\frac{5}{9} \div 2\frac{1}{3}$
11. $5\frac{1}{4} \div 3\frac{1}{2}$
12. $5\frac{1}{3} \div 4\frac{2}{3}$

Find each quotient.

13. $2\frac{2}{3} \div 5\frac{1}{9}$
14. $6\frac{2}{3} \div 1\frac{1}{4}$
15. $3\frac{3}{4} \div 4\frac{1}{2}$
16. $11\frac{1}{2} \div 3\frac{1}{2}$
17. $12\frac{3}{4} \div 4\frac{1}{2}$
18. $11\frac{1}{3} \div 4\frac{1}{2}$

19. **Planning** Telephone cable is being installed along a $6\frac{3}{4}$-mi long street. It takes a day to install $1\frac{1}{8}$ mi. How long will the project take?

B Apply Your Skills

20. You can run $\frac{1}{5}$ mi in 2 min. How long will it take you to run 2 mi?

21. **Geometry** The area of a rectangle is 117 ft^2. The length of the rectangle is $9\frac{3}{4}$ ft. What is the width of the rectangle?

Real-World Connection

Careers Marine biologists collect and analyze data on marine life.

22. **Biology** A manatee can swim 5 mi in $1\frac{1}{4}$ h. How far can the manatee swim in 1 h?

Find each quotient.

23. $16 \div \frac{2}{3}$
24. $\frac{1}{2} \div 3\frac{1}{4}$
25. $\frac{2}{3} \div 8$
26. $10\frac{1}{5} \div 11\frac{1}{5}$
27. $5\frac{1}{3} \div \frac{8}{15}$
28. $13\frac{1}{2} \div 15\frac{1}{4}$
29. $\frac{5}{8} \div 12\frac{1}{2}$
30. $7\frac{3}{4} \div 12\frac{1}{4}$
31. $10\frac{3}{4} \div 43$

Algebra **Evaluate each expression for $c = \frac{4}{5}$ and $d = 6\frac{2}{3}$.**

32. $\frac{9}{16} \div c$
33. $\frac{1}{5} \div d$
34. $1\frac{1}{4} \div d$
35. $d \div c$
36. $20 \div d$
37. $\frac{4}{5} \div c$
38. $16\frac{1}{2} \div d$
39. $28 \div c$
40. $d \div \frac{20}{3}$

41. **Error Analysis** Your friend wrote the reciprocal of $5\frac{3}{8}$ as $5\frac{8}{3}$. Explain why your friend is incorrect. What is the correct reciprocal?

42. **Number Sense** Without dividing, tell whether $\frac{4}{5} \div \frac{1}{3}$ is greater than or less than $\frac{4}{5} \div \frac{2}{3}$. Explain.

Patterns **Find the missing number in each sequence for Exercises 43–48.**

43. $5, 7\frac{2}{5}, ■, 12\frac{1}{5}, \ldots$
44. $■, 46\frac{1}{2}, 43, 39\frac{1}{2}, \ldots$
45. $\frac{3}{4}, ■, 3, 6, \ldots$
46. $82, ■, 83\frac{5}{7}, 84\frac{4}{7}, \ldots$
47. $16, 4, ■, \frac{1}{4}, \ldots$
48. $\frac{1}{3}, ■, 3, 9, \ldots$

49. **Writing in Math** Which positive number is its own reciprocal? Which number has no reciprocal? Explain.

50. Estimate $8\frac{2}{5} \div 3\frac{1}{2}$. Compare your estimate to the exact quotient.

51. **Calculator** You can use this key sequence to find $2\frac{1}{2} \div \frac{5}{6}$.

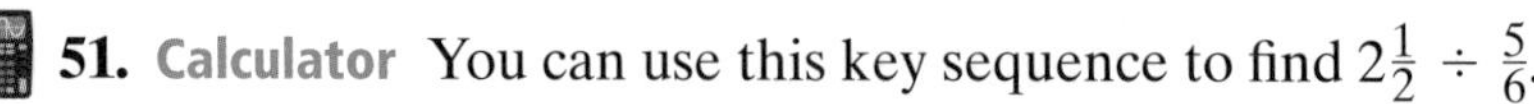

Write and use a key sequence to find $13\frac{7}{8} \div 6\frac{1}{6}$.

Challenge **Find each quotient.**

52. $20\frac{7}{10} \div 2\frac{1}{4}$ **53.** $\frac{33}{100} \div 1.1$ **54.** $0.56 \div 1\frac{2}{5}$

55. $8\frac{6}{8} \div 0.7$ **56.** $5\frac{1}{4} \div 3\frac{1}{2} \div 3$ **57.** $1\frac{3}{8} \div 2.75 \div 30$

58. If $\frac{1}{12} \div \frac{x}{6} = \frac{1}{10}$, what is the value of x? Explain.

59. **Stretch Your Thinking** What will row 10 of the pattern look like?

$$1 + 2 = 3$$
$$4 + 5 + 6 = 7 + 8$$
$$9 + 10 + 11 + 12 = 13 + 14 + 15$$
$$16 + 17 + 18 + 19 + 20 = 21 + 22 + 23 + 24$$

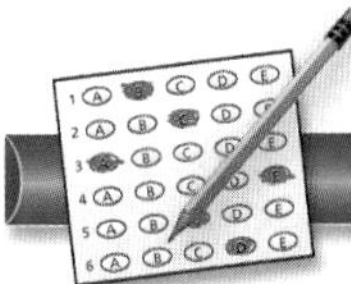

Test Prep

Multiple Choice

60. Which quotient does NOT equal 1?

A. $2\frac{3}{4} \div \frac{11}{4}$ **B.** $\frac{7}{8} \div \frac{7}{8}$ **C.** $\frac{7}{8} \div \frac{8}{7}$ **D.** $2 \div \frac{4}{2}$

61. A recipe calls for 3 lb of ground turkey. You have one package of ground turkey that weighs $1\frac{1}{4}$ lb, and another package that weighs $1\frac{5}{8}$ lb. How much more ground turkey do you need for the recipe?

F. $1\frac{1}{8}$ lb **G.** 1 lb **H.** $\frac{7}{8}$ lb **I.** $\frac{1}{8}$ lb

62. Choose the expression with the smallest quotient.

A. $8\frac{1}{2} \div \frac{1}{2}$ **B.** $8\frac{1}{2} \div 4\frac{1}{2}$ **C.** $8\frac{1}{2} \div \frac{1}{4}$ **D.** $8\frac{1}{2} \div 2$

Short Response

63. For an art project, you need to cut out squares that measure $1\frac{7}{8}$ inches on each side. You have a strip of paper that measures $10\frac{5}{8}$ inches by $1\frac{7}{8}$ inches.

a. How many whole squares can you cut from the paper?

b. From the paper than remains, can you cut a rectangle that measures $1\frac{7}{8}$ inches by $1\frac{3}{16}$ inches?

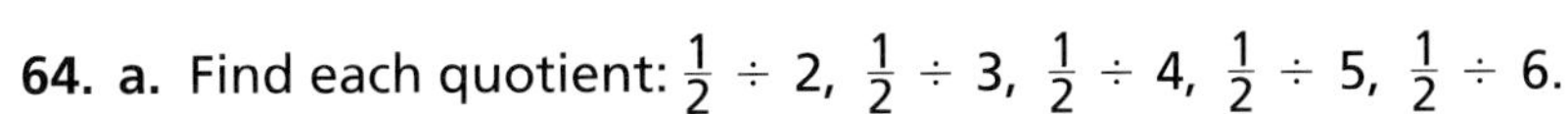

Take It to the NET
Online lesson quiz at
www.PHSchool.com
Web Code aba-0405

64. a. Find each quotient: $\frac{1}{2} \div 2$, $\frac{1}{2} \div 3$, $\frac{1}{2} \div 4$, $\frac{1}{2} \div 5$, $\frac{1}{2} \div 6$.

b. What happens to a quotient as the divisor increases in value?

Mixed Review

Lesson 3-6 **Compare each pair of fractions. Use <, >, or =.**

65. $\frac{7}{9}$ ■ $\frac{4}{5}$ **66.** $\frac{9}{27}$ ■ $\frac{1}{3}$ **67.** $\frac{5}{12}$ ■ $\frac{2}{6}$

Lesson 2-2 **Algebra** **Solve each equation using mental math.**

68. $w - 5 = 17$ **69.** $\frac{h}{7} = 6$ **70.** $28 = a - 12$

71. $5y = 35$ **72.** $p + 8 = 31$ **73.** $27 = 3z$

Technology

Using a Fraction Calculator

For Use With Lesson 4-5

You can use a fraction calculator to compute with fractions. A fraction calculator gives your result in fraction form.

1 EXAMPLE Adding Mixed Numbers

Find $3\frac{4}{5} + 2\frac{5}{8}$.

3 UNIT 4 / 5 + 2 UNIT 5 / 8 = 6⌴17/40

The sum is $6\frac{17}{40}$.

To simplify an answer, you may need to use SIMP = more than once.

2 EXAMPLE Multiplying Mixed Numbers

Find $9\frac{3}{8} \cdot 4\frac{2}{3}$.

9 UNIT 3 / 8 × 4 UNIT 2 / 3 =

43⌴18/24 SIMP = 43⌴9/12 SIMP = 43⌴3/4

The product is $43\frac{3}{4}$.

3 EXAMPLE Dividing Mixed Numbers

Find $5\frac{3}{4} \div 1\frac{7}{8}$.

5 UNIT 3 / 4 ÷ 1 UNIT 7 / 8 =

3⌴4/60 SIMP = 3⌴2/30 SIMP = 3⌴1/15

The quotient is $3\frac{1}{15}$.

EXERCISES

Find the value of each expression.

1. $8\frac{7}{10} + 9\frac{1}{5}$ **2.** $14\frac{5}{12} - 6\frac{5}{8}$ **3.** $11\frac{4}{5} + 8\frac{1}{4}$ **4.** $9\frac{3}{4} \cdot 4\frac{5}{6}$

5. $7\frac{2}{3} \cdot 10\frac{1}{4}$ **6.** $18\frac{3}{10} \div 10\frac{1}{2}$ **7.** $17\frac{11}{12} \cdot 21\frac{3}{8}$ **8.** $28\frac{7}{16} - 19\frac{5}{8}$

9. a. Error Analysis A student calculated $4\frac{2}{3} + 5\frac{3}{4}$. The student's answer was 17⌴11/12. Is this answer reasonable? Explain.

b. What error may the student have made when entering the fractions?

Algebra

4-6 Solving Equations With Fractions

What You'll Learn

To solve one-step equations

To solve two-step equations

. . . And Why

To solve currency problems, as in Example 2

Check Skills You'll Need

For help, go to Lesson 2-6.

Solve each equation. Check your answer.

1. $3x + 7 = 37$ **2.** $11j - 84 = 92$ **3.** $4q + 13 = 57$

4. $31 = 7w - 11$ **5.** $6r - 18 = 30$ **6.** $9 = 7a - 12$

7. Reasoning Name two properties of equality that you used to solve Question 6.

OBJECTIVE

Interactive lesson includes instant self-check, tutorials, and activities.

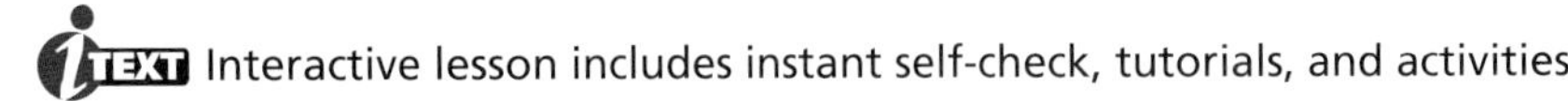

1 Solving One-Step Equations

Investigation: Modeling Equations With Fractions

1. Use the model to find the solution of each equation.

a. $x + \frac{1}{2} = \frac{11}{12}$ **b.** $x - \frac{3}{5} = \frac{3}{10}$

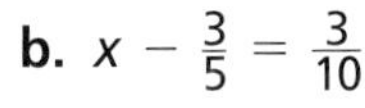

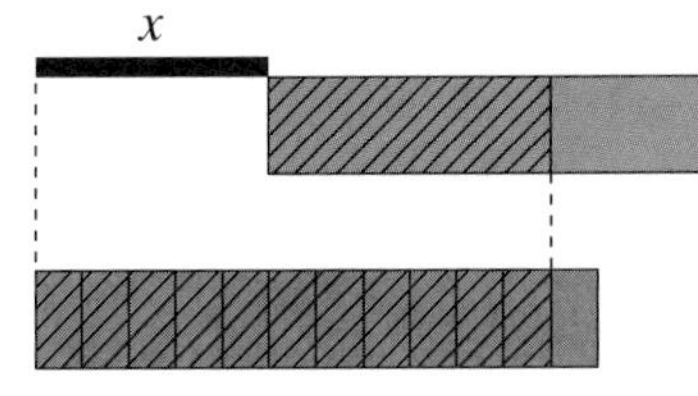

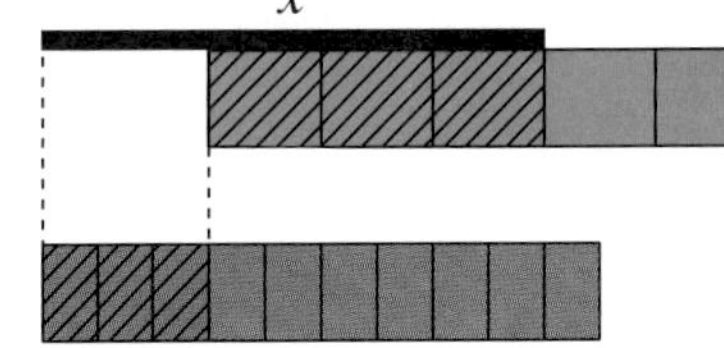

2. Write a rule for solving equations like the ones above.

Need Help?
To review solving equations by adding or subtracting, go to Lesson 2-3.

In Chapter 2, you solved equations using inverse operations. Use subtraction to undo addition, and use addition to undo subtraction.

1 EXAMPLE Solving by Adding or Subtracting

Solve $n - \frac{1}{2} = 4\frac{3}{4}$.

$n - \frac{1}{2} = 4\frac{3}{4}$

$n - \frac{1}{2} + \frac{1}{2} = 4\frac{3}{4} + \frac{1}{2}$ ← **Add $\frac{1}{2}$ to each side.**

$n = 4\frac{3}{4} + \frac{2}{4}$ ← **Find the LCD, which is 4.**

$n = 4\frac{5}{4} = 5\frac{1}{4}$ ← **Add the numerators. Write as a mixed number.**

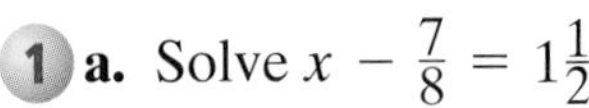

Check Understanding 1 **a.** Solve $x - \frac{7}{8} = 1\frac{1}{2}$. **b.** Solve $h + \frac{2}{5} = \frac{9}{10}$.

To solve equations involving multiplication and division, use inverse operations and the Multiplication and Division Properties of Equality. Use division to undo multiplication, and use multiplication to undo division.

2 EXAMPLE Solving by Multiplying or Dividing

Money Paper money is printed in sheets. Inspectors check about one fourth of the sheets. If 44 sheets are checked, how many sheets were printed?

Words one fourth of sheets printed equals sheets checked

Let s = number of sheets printed.

Equation $\frac{1}{4} \cdot s = 44$

$\frac{s}{4} = 44$ ← **Write $\frac{1}{4}s$ as $\frac{s}{4}$.**

$4 \cdot \frac{s}{4} = 4 \cdot 44$ ← **Since s is divided by 4, multiply each side by 4.**

$s = 176$ ← **Simplify.**

Check $\frac{1}{4}(176) = 44$ ✔

176 sheets were printed.

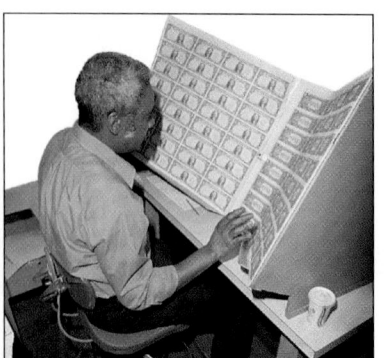

Real-World Connection

Money is printed in sheets of 32 bills.

Check Understanding 2 **a.** Solve $\frac{1}{3}s = 5$. **b.** Solve $\frac{t}{8} = 3$.

OBJECTIVE 2

Solving Two-Step Equations

One way to solve a two-step equation is to first undo addition or subtraction. Then, undo multiplication or division.

3 EXAMPLE Solving a Two-Step Equation

Solve $\frac{2}{3}n - 6 = 22$.

$\frac{2}{3}n - 6 = 22$

$\frac{2}{3}n - 6 + 6 = 22 + 6$ ← **Add 6 to each side.**

$\frac{2}{3}n = 28$ ← **Simplify.**

$\frac{3}{2} \cdot \frac{2}{3}n = \frac{3}{2} \cdot \frac{28}{1}$ ← **Multiply each side by $\frac{3}{2}$, the reciprocal of $\frac{2}{3}$. Simplify.**

$1n = \frac{42}{1}$ ← **Multiply.**

$n = 42$ ← **Simplify.**

Check $\frac{2}{3}(42) - 6 = 28 - 6 = 22$ ✔

Check Understanding 3 **a.** Solve $\frac{1}{4}x + 3 = 11$. **b.** Solve $\frac{3}{5}g - 5 = 7$.

c. Reasoning In part (b) above, would you get the correct answer if you multiplied 7 by $\frac{5}{3}$ before adding 5? Explain.

EXERCISES

For more practice, see *Extra Practice*.

A Practice by Example

Example 1 (page 213)

Solve. Exercise 1 has been started for you. Check your answer.

1. $h + \frac{1}{2} = 5\frac{1}{4}$; $h + \frac{1}{2} - \frac{1}{2} = 5\frac{1}{4} - \frac{1}{2}$

2. $10 = q - 4\frac{1}{2}$

3. $u - \frac{2}{3} = 3\frac{1}{3}$

4. $a - 3\frac{1}{8} = 7$

5. $\frac{2}{6} = c + \frac{1}{3}$

Example 2 (page 214)

6. $\frac{1}{2}s = 21$

7. $\frac{1}{5}u = 17$

8. $\frac{b}{7} = 7$

9. $11 = \frac{s}{10}$

10. $\frac{3}{4}t = 16$

11. $\frac{x}{4} = 25$

12. Business On a recent day, a store manager noted that 65 customers bought at least eight items. This was one fifth of the total number of customers that day. Write and solve an equation to find the total number of customers.

Example 3 (page 214)

Solve each equation.

13. $\frac{1}{2}x + 3 = 5$

14. $\frac{1}{4}x + 10 = 12$

15. $\frac{x}{6} - 7 = 3$

16. $\frac{1}{5}n + 2 = 8$

17. $6 = \frac{d}{11} + 1$

18. $5 = \frac{g}{9} - 5$

B Apply Your Skills

19. $10 = y + 2\frac{2}{3}$

20. $z - 1\frac{3}{4} = 4\frac{1}{2}$

21. $x + \frac{1}{2} = \frac{11}{12}$

22. $\frac{1}{5}s = 16$

23. $\frac{3}{4}b + 5 = 14$

24. $\frac{5}{14}n - 8 = 2$

Mental Math **Solve each equation.**

25. $k - \frac{3}{8} = \frac{5}{8}$

26. $4\frac{3}{4} = v - 1\frac{1}{2}$

27. $s - \frac{2}{9} = \frac{1}{3}$

Reading Math

For help with reading and solving Exercise 28, see p. 217.

28. Geography About two fifths of the total area of Michigan is covered by water. This is about 40,000 mi^2. What is the total area of Michigan? Write an equation and solve it.

29. Error Analysis A student solved the equation at the right. What error did the student make? What is the correct answer?

$$x - \left(-\frac{1}{2}\right) = 3$$
$$x - \left(-\frac{1}{2}\right) + \frac{1}{2} = 3 + \frac{1}{2}$$
$$x = 3\frac{1}{2}$$

30. Writing in Math Describe a pair of daily activities that are inverses of each other. Describe an activity that has no inverse.

C Challenge

Solve each equation.

31. $\frac{x}{10} + 1.5 = 3.8$

32. $4.5 = \frac{b}{5} - 2.1$

33. $\frac{m}{2} - 1.002 = 0.93$

34. $0.25n - 2 = \frac{3}{4}$

35. $\frac{3}{10}p + 4 = 0.5$

36. $\frac{3}{4} = 0.375d - 3$

37. Stretch Your Thinking One year, there were exactly four Tuesdays and four Saturdays in October. On what day did October 1 fall that year?

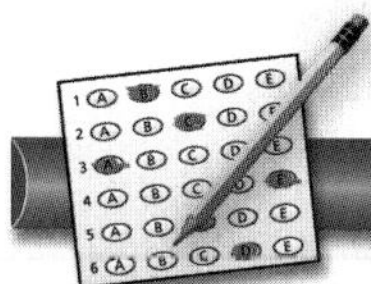

Test Prep

Multiple Choice

38. This year, $\frac{3}{4}$ of the students went on a class trip. There are a total of 240 students. How many students went on the trip?

A. 312 **B.** 240 **C.** 200 **D.** 180

39. For which equation is n less than 1?

F. $\frac{3}{4} + n = 1\frac{4}{5}$ **G.** $n + 1\frac{2}{7} = 1\frac{4}{9}$

H. $2\frac{3}{4} = 1\frac{3}{5} + n$ **I.** $n + \frac{2}{3} = 1\frac{4}{5}$

40. You buy a pair of rollerblades on sale for $64.99. This is $4.98 less than the original price. If g represents the original price, which equation CANNOT be used to find the original price?

A. $g - 4.98 = 64.99$ **B.** $64.99 + 4.98 = g$

C. $64.99 = g - 4.98$ **D.** $g + 4.98 = 64.99$

41. For which equation is b greater than 1?

F. $\frac{2}{3} - b = 3\frac{1}{3}$ **G.** $\frac{3}{4} - b = 1\frac{1}{8}$ **H.** $\frac{1}{3} = 2\frac{5}{6} - b$ **I.** $\frac{1}{4} - b = \frac{1}{2}$

Take It to the NET
Online lesson quiz at
www.PHSchool.com
Web Code aba-0406

42. A cycling route is 56 mi long. There is a water station every $3\frac{3}{4}$ mi. Which equation represents the total number of water stations w?

A. $56w = 3\frac{3}{4}$ **B.** $3\frac{3}{4}w = 56$

C. $3\frac{3}{4} - w = 56$ **D.** $w + 3\frac{3}{4} = 56$

Short Response

43. You spend q hours each week at softball practice and $2\frac{1}{2}$ times as long on your homework. You spend $7\frac{1}{2}$ hours on your homework.

a. Write an equation to find how many hours you spend each week at softball practice.

b. Solve your equation.

Mixed Review

Lesson 3-8

Write each improper fraction as a whole number or a mixed number in simplest form.

44. $\frac{61}{6}$ **45.** $\frac{59}{10}$ **46.** $\frac{26}{5}$ **47.** $\frac{77}{11}$ **48.** $\frac{50}{7}$

49. $\frac{89}{15}$ **50.** $\frac{64}{16}$ **51.** $\frac{35}{3}$ **52.** $\frac{82}{2}$ **53.** $\frac{73}{7}$

Lesson 2-9

Solve each inequality. Graph the solution.

54. $z + 9 > 21$ **55.** $p + 3 \geq 19$ **56.** $a - 5 \leq 25$

57. $d - 7 < 23$ **58.** $s + 10 > 32$ **59.** $y - 11 \geq 39$

Lesson 2-1

Algebra **Write an algebraic expression for each word phrase.**

60. 12 more than a **61.** one third of x **62.** 4 less than z

63. 8 times p **64.** 18 minus y **65.** p increases by 12

Reading Math — Understanding Word Problems

For Use With Page 215, Exercise 28

Read the problem below. Then follow along with Juan as he works through the problem. You can check your understanding with the exercises at the bottom of the page.

28. Geography About two fifths of the total area of Michigan is covered by water. This is about 40,000 mi^2. What is the total area of Michigan? Write an equation and solve it.

What Juan Thinks	What Juan Writes
Where do I start? First, I need to understand what is being asked.	Two fifths of a number is 40,000. What is the number?
Next, I need to write an equation. I know that "of" means times, and I know that "is" means equals. I'll let x stand for the total area.	$\frac{2}{5} \cdot x = 40{,}000$
Now I have to get x by itself. The inverse of multiplying by $\frac{2}{5}$ is dividing by $\frac{2}{5}$, which is the same as multiplying by its reciprocal. The reciprocal is $\frac{5}{2}$.	$\frac{\cancel{5}^{1}}{{}_{1}\cancel{2}} \cdot \frac{\cancel{2}^{1}}{\cancel{5}_{1}} \cdot x = \cancel{40{,}000}^{20{,}000} \cdot \frac{5}{\cancel{2}_{1}}$ $x = 20{,}000 \cdot 5$ $x = 100{,}000$
It looks like the answer is 100,000 mi^2, but I should check my answer in the original equation to be sure.	$\frac{2}{5} \cdot 100{,}000 \stackrel{?}{=} 40{,}000$ $\frac{2}{{}_{1}\cancel{5}} \cdot \cancel{100{,}000}^{20{,}000} \stackrel{?}{=} 40{,}000$ $2 \cdot 20{,}000 \stackrel{?}{=} 40{,}000$ $40{,}000 = 40{,}000$
I'm right! The last thing I'll do is write my answer, including the units.	The total area of Michigan is 100,000 mi^2.

EXERCISES

1. **Computers** Your old computer had $\frac{4}{5}$ of the memory of your new computer. Your old computer had 192 megabytes of memory. How much memory does your new computer have? Write an equation and solve it.

2. **Geography** The average area of a state in the United States is 75,500 mi^2. What is the total area of the United States? Write an equation and solve it.

Problem Solving

4-7 Try, Check, and Revise and Work Backward

What You'll Learn

OBJECTIVE 1 To solve a problem using two different methods

. . . And Why

To compare strategies in problem solving, as in Example 1

Check Skills You'll Need

For help, go to Lesson 4-2.

Find each sum.

1. $\frac{2}{3} + \frac{1}{9}$ **2.** $\frac{5}{7} + \frac{1}{3}$ **3.** $\frac{4}{11} + \frac{3}{4}$

4. $\frac{1}{2} + \frac{3}{4}$ **5.** $\frac{3}{6} + \frac{8}{16}$ **6.** $\frac{5}{3} + \frac{6}{10}$

7. Number Sense How is adding fractions with the same denominator similar to adding integers? How is it different?

OBJECTIVE

Interactive lesson includes instant self-check, tutorials, and activities.

1 Solving a Problem Using Two Different Methods

When to Use These Strategies You can ***try, check, and revise*** if you have an estimate that makes sense. ***Working backward*** can work well if a problem asks you to find an initial value. In this lesson, these strategies are used separately as two different methods.

1 EXAMPLE

Real-World Problem Solving

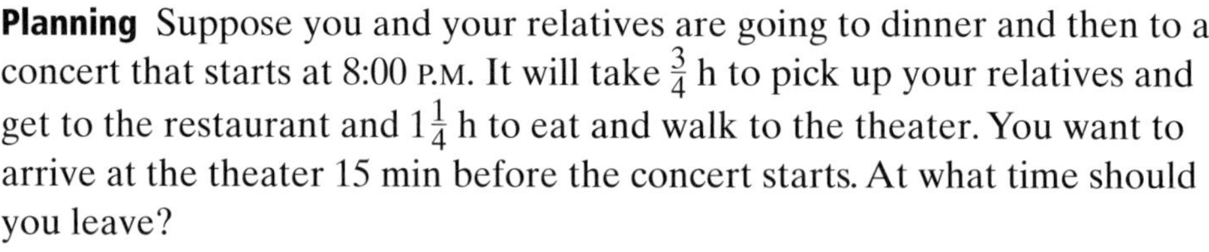

Planning Suppose you and your relatives are going to dinner and then to a concert that starts at 8:00 P.M. It will take $\frac{3}{4}$ h to pick up your relatives and get to the restaurant and $1\frac{1}{4}$ h to eat and walk to the theater. You want to arrive at the theater 15 min before the concert starts. At what time should you leave?

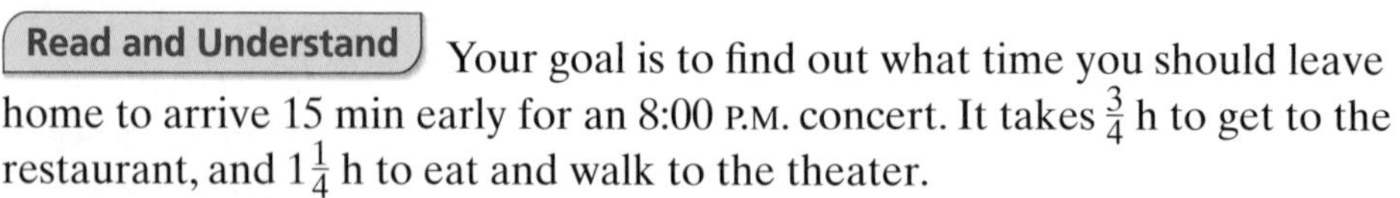

Read and Understand Your goal is to find out what time you should leave home to arrive 15 min early for an 8:00 P.M. concert. It takes $\frac{3}{4}$ h to get to the restaurant, and $1\frac{1}{4}$ h to eat and walk to the theater.

Plan and Solve

Method 1 Try, Check, and Revise

Choose a value that makes sense and then check it. If your first try is not a solution, use the results to revise your estimate.

Leave Home	Arrive at Restaurant	Arrive at Concert	Result
5:00 P.M.	5:45 P.M.	7:00 P.M.	45 min early

Leaving at 5:00 P.M. causes you to arrive 45 min earlier than intended. Therefore, by leaving 45 min later, at 5:45 P.M., you will arrive at 7:45 P.M., which is 15 min early for the concert.

Method 2 Work Backward

You know that the series of events must *end* at 8:00 P.M. It makes sense to work backward to find when you must leave your house.

Concert starts. 8:00 P.M.	Arrive at theater. 7:45 P.M.	Arrive at dinner. 6:30 P.M.	Leave home. 5:45 P.M.

Working backward shows that by leaving at 5:45 P.M. you will get to the concert 15 min early.

Look Back and Check It takes $\frac{3}{4}$ h to pick up your relatives and get to the restaurant, and $1\frac{1}{4}$ h to eat and walk to the theater. You want to arrive 15 min early, which is equal to $\frac{1}{4}$ h. Add these times to find the total time from when you leave your house to when the concert starts.

$$\frac{3}{4} + 1\frac{1}{4} + \frac{1}{4} = 2\frac{1}{4}\text{ h}$$

Subtract $2\frac{1}{4}$ h from 8:00 P.M and you find that you must leave home at 5:45 P.M. The answer checks.

1 Look back at Example 1. Suppose that the concert starts at 8:30 P.M., and it takes 20 min to pick up your relatives. At what time should you leave?

EXERCISES

For more practice, see *Extra Practice*.

Solve each problem by using either of the methods in the lesson. Check each answer in the original problem.

Example 1 (page 218)

1. Entertainment The new movie that opened yesterday was so boring that half of the people in the theater left after the first 45 min. In the next 15 min, half of the remaining people left. After 18 more people left, there were 35 people who were there at the start of the movie. How many people were there at the start of the movie?

2. Jobs You returned home from mowing lawns at 3:00 P.M. on Saturday. It took $1\frac{1}{2}$ h to mow the first lawn. The second lawn took twice as long to mow. After a half-hour lunch break, it took $1\frac{1}{4}$ h to mow one more lawn. At what time did you start?

3. Time After school today, you spent $1\frac{3}{4}$ h at practice and then a half hour in the library. It took you 15 min to get home at 6:00 P.M. What time did you start practice?

4. If you start with a number, add 5, and then multiply by 7, the result is 133. What was the original number?

Need Help?
- Reread the problem.
- Identify the key facts and details.
- Tell the problem in your own words.
- Try a different strategy.
- Check your work.

B Apply Your Skills

Use any strategy to solve each problem. Show your work.

Strategies

- Draw a Diagram
- Look for a Pattern
- Make a Graph
- Make an Organized List
- Make a Table
- Simulate a Problem
- Solve a Simpler Problem
- Try, Check, and Revise
- Use Logical Reasoning
- Work Backward
- Write an Equation

5. You have ten coins that have a total value of $.65. You have no pennies. None of the coins are greater than a quarter. What are the coins?

6. Money Your brother has saved $60 to spend on basketball cards. He plans to buy the cards at a sale. Single cards are $9, and if you buy three cards, you get a fourth for $7. If you buy five cards, the cost is $39.50. What is the greatest number of cards your brother can get for $60?

7. Sports A gymnast practices 28 h in one week. Each day the gymnast practices one hour more than the day before. How many hours does the gymnast practice on the fifth day?

8. Your friend spends one third of her money on lunch. At lunch, you give her $2.50 to repay a loan. Then your friend spends $4.00 for a movie ticket and $2.50 for a snack. She has $4.90 left. How much did she have before lunch?

9. Fund-Raising At a fund-raising event attended by 150 people, $4,000 was collected for charity. If 25 people gave nothing, what was the average donation from those who gave?

10. The stack consists of five rows of boxes that are all the same size.

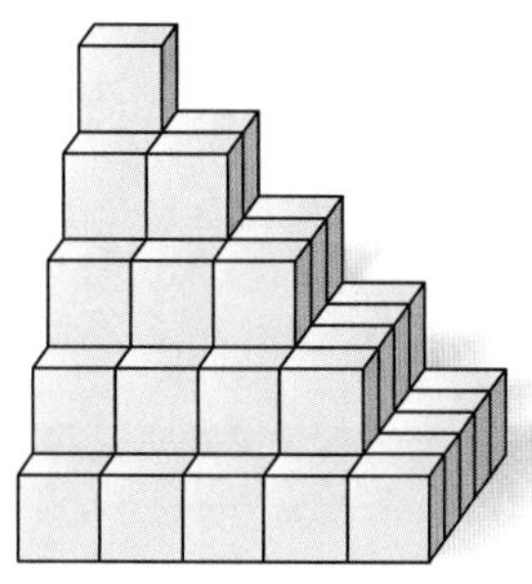

a. How many boxes are in the stack?
b. If another row is added to the bottom of the stack, how many boxes will be in that row?
c. How many boxes will be in the *n*th row?

11. Biology Baby crocodiles are about 12 in. long when they hatch and grow about 10 in. each year. How old is a crocodile that is 32 in. long?

12. Shopping Your friend goes shopping with $35. She buys a sweater that is on sale for half price and uses a coupon for $5 off the sale price. She has $10.50 left. What was the original price of the sweater?

13. Salary Your cousin and your brother start a new job on the same day. Your brother will earn a salary of $28,000 the first year. He will then receive a $4,000 raise each year that follows. Your cousin's salary for her first year is $41,000, followed by a $1,500 yearly raise. In what year will your brother's salary be more than your cousin's salary?

14. Show how to cut a round pizza into 11 slices with exactly 4 straight cuts.

Real-World Connection

In spring, a female crocodile lays 30 to 70 eggs. The eggs hatch after 90 days.

15. A science student has a balance scale and weights of 9 mg, 7 mg, 2 mg, and 5 mg. How can she use these weights to find out whether a piece of copper wire weighs 1 mg?

16. **Writing in Math** Is the use of inverse operations important when you work backward to solve a problem? Explain.

C Challenge

17. **Business** A manager of a department store plans to make an electronic game shop in a section of the store that is 12 ft wide and 20 ft long. Using the pattern shown at the right, the manager wants to cover the floor with tiles that measure 1 ft on each side. How many blue tiles will be needed? How many white tiles will be needed?

18. **Stretch Your Thinking** There are 8 square tables. One person can sit at each side of each table. The tables need to be arranged so that each table shares a side with at least one other table, and 18 people need to be seated. How can the tables be arranged? Find as many arrangements as you can.

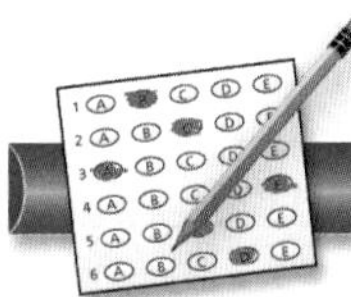

Test Prep

Multiple Choice

19. Which quotient is equal to 1?

A. $\frac{1}{2} \div 2$ B. $2\frac{1}{2} \div \frac{7}{2}$ C. $4\frac{1}{2} \div \frac{9}{2}$ D. $\frac{6}{2} \div 2$

20. What is the value of $2 \div \frac{2}{3} + 3 \div \frac{3}{4}$?

F. $\frac{7}{12}$ G. $\frac{8}{11}$ H. 3 I. 7

Take It to the NET
Online lesson quiz at
www.PHSchool.com
Web Code aba-0407

21. A rectangle is $1\frac{2}{5}$ in. by $2\frac{1}{2}$ in. What is the rectangle's perimeter?

A. $8\frac{3}{5}$ in. B. $7\frac{4}{5}$ in. C. $5\frac{3}{5}$ in. D. $4\frac{4}{5}$ in.

Short Response

22. In a CD collection, $\frac{1}{4}$ are dance CDs and $\frac{1}{3}$ are hip-hop CDs. **(a)** If there are 15 dance CDs, how many hip-hop CDs are in the collection? **(b)** Explain how you found your answer to part (a).

Mixed Review

Lesson 4-6

Algebra **Solve each equation.**

23. $a - \frac{1}{3} = 7$ 24. $m + \frac{2}{7} = \frac{11}{14}$ 25. $r - \frac{3}{8} = \frac{7}{8}$

26. $2\frac{3}{4} + x = 6$ 27. $s - 3\frac{1}{3} = 8\frac{1}{6}$ 28. $7\frac{1}{2} = n - \frac{5}{2}$

Lesson 3-9

Write each fraction as a decimal.

29. $\frac{3}{5}$ 30. $\frac{2}{3}$ 31. $\frac{7}{15}$

32. $\frac{5}{6}$ 33. $\frac{5}{2}$ 34. $\frac{1}{16}$

4-8 Changing Units in the Customary System

What You'll Learn

To change units of length and capacity

To change units of weight

. . . And Why

To find the weight of a bike, as in Example 3

Check Skills You'll Need

For help, go to Lesson 4-6.

Solve each equation.

1. $\frac{1}{4} + y = \frac{3}{4}$ **2.** $x - \frac{5}{8} = \frac{1}{8}$ **3.** $\frac{7}{10} = d + \frac{2}{5}$

4. $\frac{5}{12} + p = \frac{7}{3}$ **5.** $\frac{1}{2}h = 6$ **6.** $2k = \frac{4}{7}$

7. Reasoning Does $\frac{1}{2}s = 16$ have the same solution as $16 = \frac{1}{2}s$? Explain.

OBJECTIVE

Interactive lesson includes instant self-check, tutorials, and activities.

1 Changing Units of Length and Capacity

Most people in the United States use the customary system of measurements for length, capacity, and weight. You can use fractions and mixed numbers to change units in the system.

Reading Math

The customary system is sometimes called "the English system," even though it is no longer used in England.

Customary Units of Measure

Type	Length	Capacity	Weight
Unit	inch (in.) foot (ft) yard (yd) mile (mi)	fluid ounce (fl oz) cup (c) pint (pt) quart (qt) gallon (gal)	ounce (oz) pound (lb) ton (t)
Equivalents	1 ft = 12 in. 1 yd = 3 ft 1 mi = 5,280 ft	1 c = 8 fl oz 1 pt = 2 c 1 qt = 2 pt 1 gal = 4 qt	1 lb = 16 oz 1 t = 2,000 lb

1 EXAMPLE Changing Units of Length

Carpentry A carpenter has a board 10 ft long. A piece 5 ft 3 in. long is cut from the board. What is the length in feet of the remaining piece?

You need to subtract 5 ft 3 in. from 10 ft.

5 ft 3 in. $= 5\frac{3}{12}$ ft $= 5\frac{1}{4}$ ft ← **Write 3 in. as a fraction of a foot.**

$10 - 5\frac{1}{4} = 9\frac{4}{4} - 5\frac{1}{4} = 4\frac{3}{4}$ ← **Rename 10 as $9\frac{4}{4}$. Then subtract.**

The remaining piece is $4\frac{3}{4}$ ft long.

1 How much shorter than a 10-ft board is a board 8 ft 5 in. long?

To change from a smaller unit to a larger unit, you *divide*.

2 EXAMPLE Changing Units of Capacity

How many one-cup servings are in a 36-fl oz bottle of juice?

Think of the relationship between fluid ounces and cups. 8 fl oz = 1 c ($\div$ 8)

To change 36 fl oz to cups, divide 36 by 8.

$36 \div 8 = 4.5$

There are $4\frac{1}{2}$ one-cup servings in a 36-fl oz bottle.

Check Understanding 2 How many one-cup servings are in a 50-fl oz bottle?

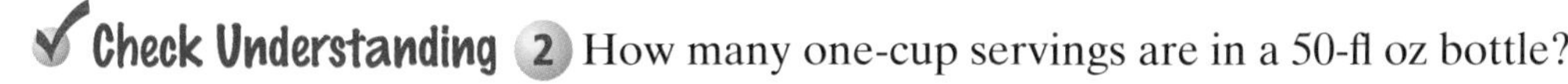

OBJECTIVE 2 Changing Units of Weight

To change from a larger unit to a smaller unit, you *multiply*.

3 EXAMPLE Real-World Problem Solving

Cycling The lighter the frame of a mountain bike, the easier it is to cycle. Which bike shown in the ad will be easier to cycle?

Think of the relationship between pounds and ounces. 1 lb = 16 oz ($\times$ 16)

To change $4\frac{1}{4}$ lb to ounces, multiply $4\frac{1}{4}$ by 16.

$4\frac{1}{4} \cdot 16 = \frac{17}{\cancel{4}_1} \cdot \frac{\cancel{16}^4}{1}$ ← **Write $4\frac{1}{4}$ as an improper fraction. Then multiply.**

$= 68$

The $4\frac{1}{4}$-lb bike weighs 68 oz. It is lighter than the 76-oz bike.

Check Understanding 3 **a.** Find the number of ounces in $4\frac{5}{8}$ lb.

b. **Number Sense** Explain why you multiply to change from a larger to a smaller unit, and divide to change from a smaller to a larger unit.

EXERCISES

For more practice, see *Extra Practice*.

A Practice by Example

Example 1 (page 222)

Complete. Exercise 1 has been started for you.

1. 4 ft 6 in. = ■ ft; $4\frac{6}{12}$ ft = ■ ft

2. 1 ft 9 in. = ■ ft

3. 60 in. = ■ ft

4. 4 ft = ■ in.

5. 26 in. = ■ ft

6. **Measurement** How many feet tall is a woman whose height is 66 in.?

Example 2 (page 223)

Complete.

7. 48 fl oz = ■ c
8. 64 fl oz = ■ c
9. 26 fl oz = ■ c
10. 4 c = ■ fl oz
11. 44 fl oz = ■ c
12. 9 c = ■ fl oz

Example 3 (page 223)

13. $\frac{3}{4}$ lb = ■ oz
14. $2\frac{1}{4}$ lb = ■ oz
15. $3\frac{3}{4}$ lb = ■ oz
16. 32 oz = ■ lb
17. 80 oz = ■ lb
18. 35 oz = ■ lb

B Apply Your Skills

Tell whether you would *multiply* or *divide* to change from one unit of measure to the other.

19. gallons to quarts
20. ounces to pounds
21. yards to feet
22. pints to cups
23. feet to miles
24. tons to pounds

25. Writing in Math Explain how fluid ounces and ounces differ.

26. **Geography** The length of the Amazon River in South America is about 4,000 mi. How many feet is this?

Real-World Connection
The Amazon River is the world's second longest river. Only the Nile River in Africa is longer.

Choose an appropriate unit of measure. Explain your choice.

27. length of your pencil
28. weight of your math book
29. capacity of a swimming pool
30. length of a sports field
31. capacity of a soda can
32. distance between two cities

Complete.

33. 500 lb = ■ t
34. $1\frac{1}{5}$ t = ■ lb
35. $5\frac{1}{4}$ gal = ■ qt
36. 7 pt = ■ qt
37. 4 yd 2 ft = ■ yd
38. 16 ft = ■ yd
39. $4\frac{1}{2}$ pt = ■ c
40. 9 lb = ■ oz
41. $2\frac{1}{2}$ qt = ■ c
42. 4 mi = ■ ft
43. 288 oz = ■ lb
44. 48 qt = ■ gal

45. **Error Analysis** Your friend claims that a quarter-pound hamburger is heavier than a six-ounce hamburger. Is your friend correct? Explain.

46. **Data File, p. 185** Find the length in feet of Kings Canyon.

C Challenge

Order each set of measurements from smallest to greatest.

47. $\frac{1}{10}$ mi, 50 yd, and 175 ft
48. 2 gal, 24 c, and 7 qt

49. **Measurement** Three students recorded their heights as 64 in., $5\frac{1}{6}$ ft, and $1\frac{2}{3}$ yd. Find the average height in feet of the three students.

50. **Hiking** You are hiking a 2-mi long trail. You pass by a sign showing that you have hiked 1,000 ft. How many feet do you have left to hike?

51. **Stretch Your Thinking** Place the digits 2, 4, 5, and 7 in the boxes to make the equation true. $\frac{3}{6} = \frac{9}{18} = \frac{■■}{■■}$

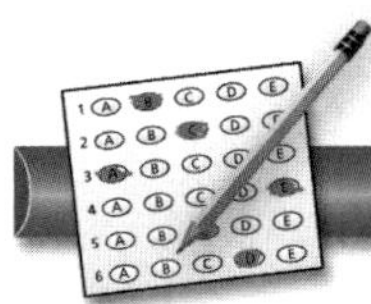

Test Prep

Reading Comprehension **Read the passage and answer the questions below.**

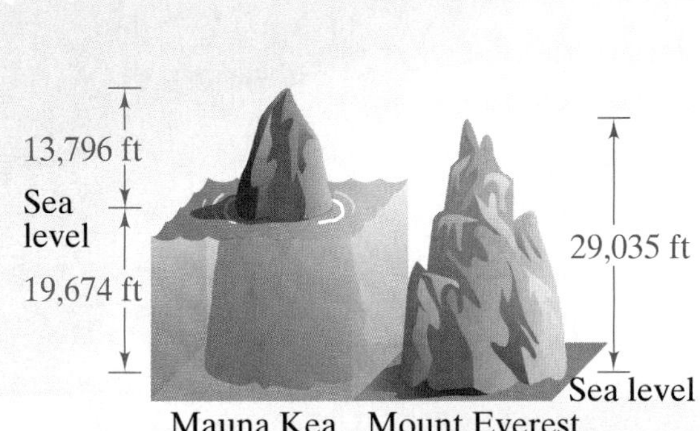

Climb or Dive?

What is the tallest mountain in the world? Mt. Everest has the highest elevation above sea level. However, Hawaii's Mauna Kea is truly the world's tallest mountain, though much of it is hidden in the Pacific Ocean. What is the lowest elevation on Earth? The Dead Sea is 1,345 ft below sea level. In the oceans, the lowest elevation is the Marianas Trench. It lies 36,198 ft below the surface of the Pacific Ocean.

Take It to the NET
Online lesson quiz at **www.PHSchool.com**
Web Code aba-0408

52. About how many miles high is Mauna Kea?

53. About how many miles taller is Mauna Kea than Mount Everest?

54. How many yards below sea level is the Dead Sea?

55. About what fraction of a mile below sea level is the Dead Sea?

Mixed Review

Lesson 2-7 **Algebra** **Write an equation for each sentence. Then solve the equation.**

56. The sum of a number and 5 is 27.

57. Ten less than a number is 15.

58. A number increased by 23 is 56.

59. Five times a number is 33.

Lesson 1-4 **Choose a reasonable estimate.**

60. capacity of a soda can 250 mL or 250 L

61. height of your desk 68 cm or 68 m

Checkpoint Quiz 2 Lessons 4-4 through 4-8

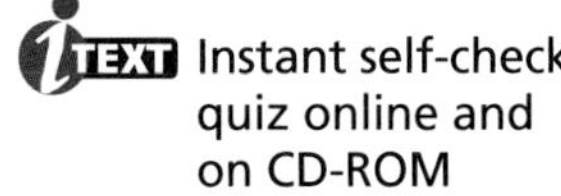

Instant self-check quiz online and on CD-ROM

Find each product or quotient.

1. $\frac{1}{3} \cdot \frac{6}{7}$

2. $\frac{5}{9} \div \frac{5}{6}$

3. $12\frac{1}{2} \div 1\frac{7}{8}$

4. $\frac{3}{4} \cdot 4\frac{1}{3}$

Algebra **Solve each equation.**

5. $\frac{1}{2}a - 4 = 6$

6. $28 = \frac{4}{5}z + 5$

7. $\frac{1}{4}t - 5 = -13$

Complete.

8. 28 in. = ■ ft

9. $6\frac{1}{4}$ gal = ■ qt

10. $\frac{3}{4}$ lb = ■ oz

Estimating in Different Systems

For Use With Lesson 4-8

Every day you see measurements in both the customary system and the metric system. You can use estimates to help you compare measurements across the two systems.

A liter is a little less than a quart.
A meter is a little more than a yard.
An inch is about 2.5 cm.
A kilometer is about 0.6 mi.
A kilogram is about 2.2 lb.

You may be more familiar with temperatures measured in Fahrenheit than in Celsius. You can use the table at the right to help you relate to Celsius temperatures.

Celsius Temperature	How It Feels
30°	hot
20°	nice
10°	cold
0°	ice

EXAMPLE

Which measurement is longer, 15 cm or 10 in.?

One inch is about 2.5 cm.

$= 10 \cdot 2.5$ ← **Multiply by 10 to find the number of centimeters in 10 in.**

$= 25$ ← **There are about 25 cm in 10 in.**

10 in. is longer than 15 cm.

EXERCISES

Which of the two measurements is greater?

1. 600 km or 200 mi
2. 0°C or 0°F
3. 80 L or 40 gal
4. 50 cm or 25 in.
5. 30 lb or 20 kg
6. 10°F or 20°C

7. Travel A sign says "Jacksonville, 200 km." About how many miles would you have to drive to get there?

8. Clothing A sign indicates that the temperature is 27°C. Would you be more comfortable in a short-sleeved shirt or in a ski parka?

9. An exchange student tells you that he is 175 cm tall and weighs 72 kg.
a. About how many feet tall is the exchange student?
b. About how many pounds does the exchange student weigh?

10. Hiking You are told to bring about a gallon of water for a long hike. Bottled water is sold in liter bottles. How many liter bottles should you buy?

4-9 Precision

What You'll Learn

To find and compare the precision of measurements

. . . And Why

To measure oven temperature, as in Example 1

✓ Check Skills You'll Need

For help, go to Lesson 1-1.

Estimate each sum or difference by rounding to the nearest half dollar.

1. \$9.13 − \$4.62

2. \$7.63 + \$5.49

3. \$12.13 − \$8.37

4. \$16.53 − \$2.75

5. \$18.50 + \$6.19

6. \$35.71 + \$18.29

New Vocabulary • precision

Interactive lesson includes instant self-check, tutorials, and activities.

OBJECTIVE

1 Using Precision

Investigation: Precision in Measurements

When you measure an object, you should measure in an appropriate unit. You would measure a stapler in inches, not in miles.

Number Sense Choose the more appropriate unit of measure.

1.	the capacity of a car's gas tank	ounces	gallons
2.	the length of a marathon road race	miles	feet
3.	the weight of a horse	kilograms	grams
4.	the length of an eyelash	meters	millimeters
5.	the weight of a baseball	ounces	pounds

6. Choose one of your answers from Questions 1–5. Explain why you chose that unit of measure.

You can estimate the length of the butterfly as about 5 cm. A more exact measurement is 48 mm.

The **precision** of a measurement refers to its degree of exactness. The marks on a scale or other instrument tell you the precision that is possible.

1 EXAMPLE Finding Precision

Cooking Oven thermometers measure cooking temperatures. What is the greatest precision possible with the thermometer shown?

Each mark represents 25°F. Measurements are precise to the nearest 25°F.

Check Understanding 1 What is the greatest precision possible with each ruler below?

a. (ruler: 0, 1, inches)

b.

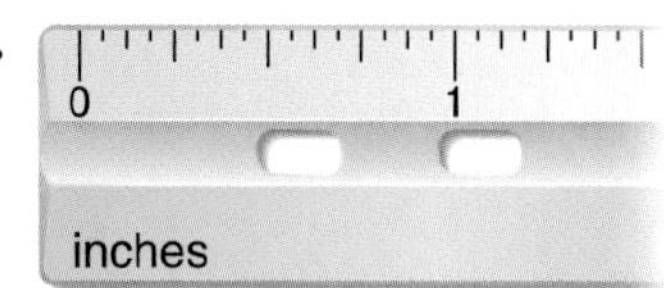

c. **Reasoning** Is the ruler in part (a) more precise than the ruler in part (b)? Explain.

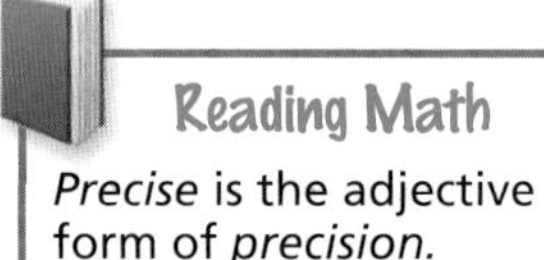

Reading Math

Precise is the adjective form of *precision.*

When you compare measurements, the more precise measurement is the one with the smaller unit of measure.

2 EXAMPLE Precision in Measurement

Choose the more precise measurement.

a. 12 fl oz, 2 c

Since fluid ounces are smaller than cups, the measurement 12 fl oz is more precise.

b. 3 L, 2.5 L

Since tenths of a liter are smaller than liters, the measurement 2.5 L is more precise.

c. 9.8 km, 7.87 km

Since hundredths of a kilometer are smaller than tenths of a kilometer, 7.87 km is more precise.

Check Understanding 2 Choose the more precise measurement.

a. 25.5 g, 11 g **b.** 2 ft, 13 in. **c.** 16.9 L, 13.25 L

d. **Reasoning** You know that 12 in. equals 1 ft. Does this mean that the two measurements are equally precise? Explain.

A calculation is only as precise as the least precise measurement used in the calculation. When you add or subtract measurements with the same unit, round your answer to match the least precise measurement.

3 EXAMPLE Precision and Rounding

Find each sum or difference. Round your answer appropriately.

a. 8.4 g + 5 g

8.4 + 5 = 13.4

Since 5 is less precise than 8.4, round to the nearest whole number. The sum is 13 g.

b. 9.97 cm − 5.9 cm

9.97 − 5.9 = 4.07

Since 5.9 is less precise than 9.97, round to the nearest tenth. The difference is 4.1 cm.

Check Understanding 3 Find each sum or difference. Round your answer appropriately.
a. 45 m − 0.9 m **b.** 11.4 g + 2.65 g **c.** 2 L + 1.75 L

EXERCISES

For more practice, see *Extra Practice.*

A Practice by Example

Example 1 (page 228)

Find the greatest precision possible for each scale shown.

1.
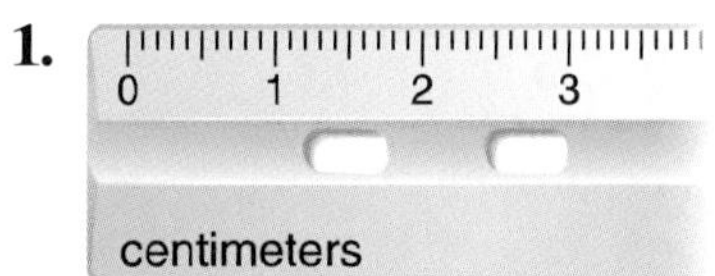

2.
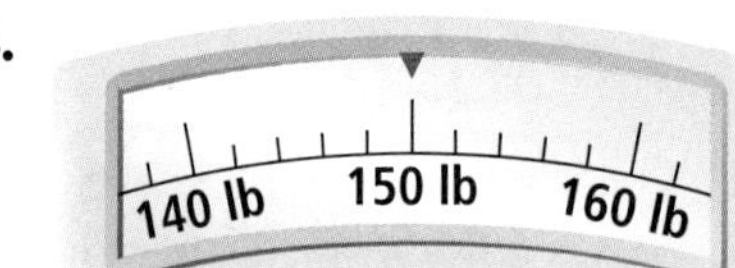

Example 2 (page 228)

Choose the more precise measurement.

3. 16 in., $11\frac{15}{16}$ in. **4.** 30 g, 2.5 kg **5.** 37 t, 56 lb

6. 25 qt, 38 pt **7.** 21 L, 35 mL **8.** 6.1 lb, 6.37 lb

9. 12 mo, 1 yr **10.** 0.25 g, 101 mg **11.** 12 days, 2 wk

Example 3 (page 229)

Find each sum or difference. Round your answer appropriately.

12. 6.53 oz + 2.4 oz **13.** 18 g − 3.8 g **14.** 6.52 in. − 5.8 in.

15. 4.2 yd + 6.84 yd **16.** 1.2 cm + 6.35 cm **17.** 8.23 m − 5 m

B Apply Your Skills

Find the length of each segment to the greatest precision possible.

18.

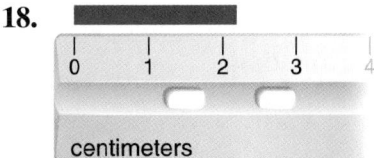

0 1 2 3 4
centimeters

19.
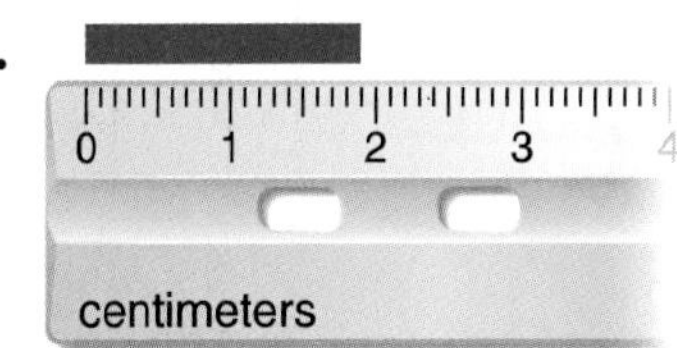

Choose the more precise unit of measure.

20. g, kg **21.** L, mL **22.** ft, mi **23.** oz, lb

24. qt, pt **25.** yd, ft **26.** m, km **27.** gal, qt

28. **Writing in Math** Your friend says that 5.25 kg is a more precise measurement than 6.2 g because a hundredths unit is smaller than a tenths unit. Do you agree? Explain.

Find each sum or difference. Round your answer appropriately.

29. 3.61 m + 7.445 m **30.** 12.125 g + 7.58 g **31.** $2\frac{3}{8}$ in. + $6\frac{1}{2}$ in.

32. 12.221 m − 7.4 m **33.** $6\frac{4}{8}$ yd − $2\frac{1}{4}$ yd **34.** $8\frac{5}{6}$ mi − $3\frac{3}{4}$ mi

35. Mountain Climbing A climber ascends 2,458.75 ft up a 3,000-ft mountainside. How much farther does the climber have to go to reach the top? Round your answer appropriately.

C Challenge

Choose the more precise unit of measure.

36. foot, meter **37.** gallon, liter **38.** centimeter, inch

39. deciliter, gallon **40.** kilometer, mile **41.** kilogram, pound

42. Stretch Your Thinking When a positive number is divided by its reciprocal, the result is $\frac{4}{9}$. What is the number?

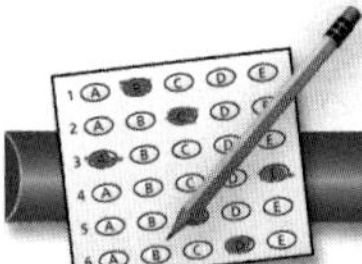

Test Prep

Multiple Choice

43. Which is more precise than 35 min?
A. $\frac{7}{12}$ h **B.** $35\frac{1}{2}$ min **C.** 60 min **D.** 1 h

44. Which unit is most appropriate for the amount of gasoline in a car?
F. mL **G.** mm **H.** L **I.** m

45. Find 43.87 m + 19.7 m. Round your answer.
A. 63.6 m **B.** 63.57 m **C.** 63 m **D.** 24.2 m

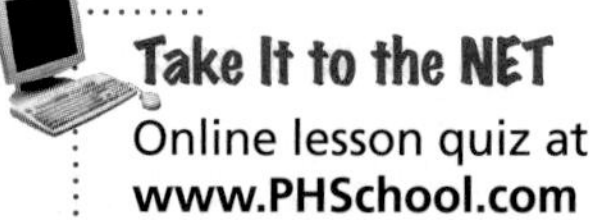

Take It to the NET
Online lesson quiz at
www.PHSchool.com
Web Code aba-0409

46. Which mixed number is closest in value to $5\frac{2}{3}$?
F. $6\frac{20}{27}$ **G.** $5\frac{9}{15}$ **H.** $5\frac{9}{18}$ **I.** $5\frac{7}{30}$

Mixed Review

Lesson 3-2 **Write in scientific notation.**

47. 5,000 **48.** 3,200 **49.** 160,000 **50.** 919.07

51. 4,700,000 **52.** 83 thousand **53.** 51 million **54.** 3 billion

Lesson 3-1 **Simplify.**

55. $8^2 + 11$ **56.** $5^3 - 7^2$ **57.** $(9 - 3)^2$

58. $(-5)^3$ **59.** -3^4 **60.** $(8^2 + 16) \div 2$

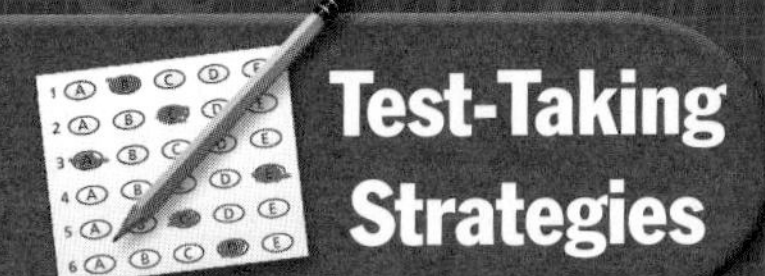

Test-Taking Strategies

Reading-Comprehension Questions

Reading-comprehension questions are based on a passage that gives you facts and information. First read the question carefully. Make sure you understand what is being asked. Then read the passage. Look for the information you need to answer the question.

EXAMPLE

Recycling Math The United States produces over 4 pounds of trash per person each day, and recycles about one fourth of it. Canada produces about $3\frac{1}{2}$ pounds of trash per person each day, and recycles about one tenth of it. Japan produces about $2\frac{1}{2}$ pounds of trash per person each day, and recycles about one fifth of it.

In one week, a family living in the United States produced 112 pounds of trash. About how many pounds of the trash will be recycled?

What is being asked? the number of pounds of trash that will be recycled

Identify the information you need. The United States recycles about one fourth of the trash it produces.

Solve the problem. Pounds of recycled trash $= \frac{1}{4} \cdot 112 = 28.$

About 28 pounds of trash will be recycled.

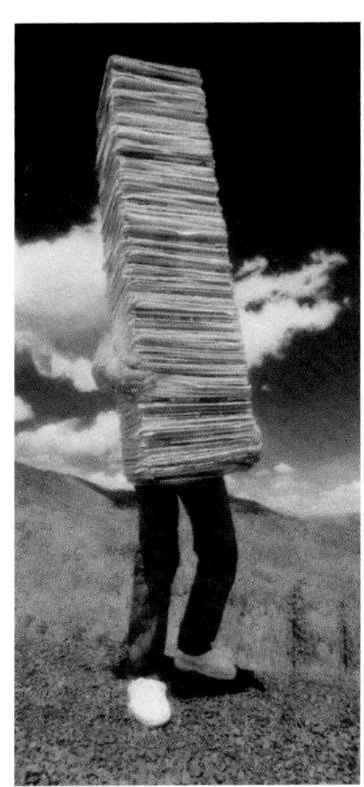

EXERCISES

Use the passage in the Example to complete Exercises 1–4.

1. **a.** About how many pounds of trash will a Canadian family of four produce in one week?
   b. About how many pounds of the trash will be recycled?
   c. Compare your answer in part (b) to the corresponding number for a U.S. family of four. About how many more pounds of trash will be recycled by a U.S. family?
2. In one week, a family living in Japan produces 85 pounds of trash. About how many pounds of trash will be recycled?
3. Suppose your family recycles one third of its trash. How much more trash does your family recycle compared to the average U.S. family?
4. Your school recycles two fifths of its paper. In one month, your school produced 25 pounds of paper. How many pounds were *not* recycled?

Chapter 4 Chapter Review

Vocabulary

benchmark (p. 187) **precision** (p. 227) **reciprocal** (p. 207)

Reading Math: Understanding Vocabulary

Choose the correct vocabulary term to complete each sentence.

1. The number $\frac{7}{8}$ is the __?__ of the number $\frac{8}{7}$.
2. A __?__ is a number used to replace fractions that are less than 1.
3. The __?__ of a measurement refers to its degree of exactness.
4. When you use a __?__ to estimate a sum, your answer has less __?__ than the exact answer.

Take It to the NET
Online vocabulary quiz at **www.PHSchool.com**
Web Code abj-0451

Skills and Concepts

4-1 Objectives

- To estimate sums and differences
- To estimate products and quotients

You can use the benchmarks $0, \frac{1}{2}$, and 1 to estimate sums and differences of fractions. To estimate sums, differences, products, and quotients of mixed numbers, round to the nearest whole number or use compatible numbers.

Estimate each answer.

5. $\frac{3}{4} + \frac{1}{5}$ **6.** $\frac{8}{9} - \frac{3}{8}$ **7.** $3\frac{1}{8} \cdot 9\frac{9}{10}$ **8.** $12\frac{2}{5} \div 3\frac{8}{9}$

9. Maps A map shows three trails of $2\frac{1}{2}$ mi, $1\frac{4}{5}$ mi, and $3\frac{3}{10}$ mi. You want to hike the entire length of each trail. Estimate the total distance.

4-2 and 4-3 Objectives

- To add fractions
- To subtract fractions
- To add mixed numbers
- To subtract mixed numbers

To add or subtract fractions, you first find a common denominator and then add or subtract the numerators. To add or subtract mixed numbers, you add or subtract the fractions, and then add or subtract the whole numbers. You may need to rename a mixed number before subtracting.

Find each sum or difference.

10. $\frac{3}{4} - \frac{1}{8}$ **11.** $2\frac{1}{3} + \frac{3}{4}$ **12.** $16\frac{2}{3} - 9\frac{4}{5}$ **13.** $8\frac{1}{6} + 7\frac{3}{12}$

4-4 and 4-5 Objectives

- To multiply fractions
- To multiply mixed numbers
- To divide fractions
- To divide mixed numbers

To multiply fractions, you multiply their numerators and multiply their denominators. To divide by a fraction, you multiply by its **reciprocal.**

Find each product or quotient.

14. $\frac{2}{3} \cdot \frac{3}{8}$ **15.** $\frac{3}{5} \cdot 1\frac{1}{2}$ **16.** $2\frac{2}{3} \cdot 3\frac{3}{8}$ **17.** $8\frac{5}{6} \cdot 10\frac{3}{4}$

18. $\frac{2}{3} \div \frac{4}{3}$ **19.** $5\frac{1}{4} \div \frac{7}{8}$ **20.** $4\frac{4}{5} \div 1\frac{1}{3}$ **21.** $1\frac{1}{3} \div 4\frac{4}{5}$

4-6 Objectives

- ▼ To solve one-step equations
- ▼ To solve two-step equations

Use inverse operations and the Properties of Equality to solve equations. Use addition to undo subtraction and subtraction to undo addition. Use multiplication to undo division and division to undo multiplication.

Solve each equation.

22. $a + \frac{2}{5} = 1\frac{1}{2}$ **23.** $q - 3\frac{1}{5} = 5\frac{3}{10}$ **24.** $\frac{1}{5}g = 10$

25. $\frac{1}{3}x + 8 = 17$ **26.** $3 = \frac{z}{9} - 7$ **27.** $\frac{3}{4} = \frac{3}{8}h - 3$

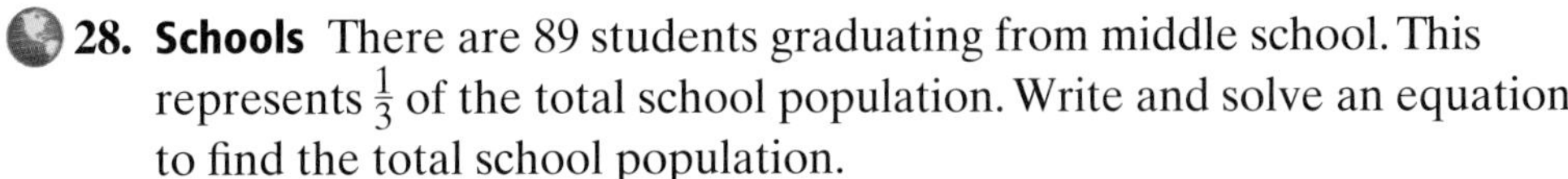

28. Schools There are 89 students graduating from middle school. This represents $\frac{1}{3}$ of the total school population. Write and solve an equation to find the total school population.

4-7 Objective

- ▼ To solve a problem using two different methods

To solve some problems, you may have to work backward. Working backward can work well if a problem asks you to find an initial value.

29. Shopping Suppose you buy a pair of shoes during a "$\frac{1}{4}$-off" sale. The original price is $34. After you pay for the shoes, you have $14.26 left. How much money did you start with? Check your answer in the original problem.

4-8 Objectives

- ▼ To change units of length and capacity
- ▼ To change units of weight

To change from a smaller unit to a larger unit, you *divide.* To change from a larger unit to a smaller unit, you *multiply.*

Complete.

30. 42 in. = ■ ft **31.** 12 fl oz = ■ c **32.** 80 oz = ■ lb

33. 10,560 ft = ■ mi **34.** 2 t = ■ lb **35.** $3\frac{1}{2}$ qt = ■ pt

4-9 Objective

- ▼ To find and compare the precision of measurements

The **precision** of a measurement refers to its degree of exactness. The smaller the units on a measuring instrument, the more precise the measurement. When you add or subtract measurements with the same unit, round your answer to match the precision of the least precise measurement.

Choose the more precise measurement.

36. 12 c, 8 pt **37.** 5.5 L, 2 L **38.** 8.5 m, 8.75 m

39. 1 d, 23 h **40.** 25 g, 3.5 kg **41.** $11\frac{3}{16}$ in., 5 in.

Find each sum or difference. Round your answer appropriately.

42. 17.3 g − 10 g **43.** $5\frac{1}{3}$ yd + 8 yd **44.** 7.75 cm + 3.8 cm

45. 5.25 lb + 15.75 lb **46.** 8 L − 3.005 L **47.** 12.175 m − 7.05 m

Chapter 4

Chapter Test

Take It to the NET
Online chapter test at
www.PHSchool.com
Web Code: aba-0452

Estimate each answer.

1. $\frac{7}{8} + \frac{15}{16}$
2. $\frac{3}{5} - \frac{1}{2}$
3. $7\frac{1}{8} + 2\frac{3}{4}$
4. $8\frac{3}{8} - 5\frac{1}{3}$
5. $4\frac{5}{8} \cdot 2\frac{1}{10}$
6. $43\frac{1}{2} \div 5\frac{1}{5}$
7. **Tutoring** You tutored for $2\frac{1}{2}$ h on Monday, $2\frac{1}{6}$ h on Wednesday, and $1\frac{3}{4}$ h on Friday. Estimate the total number of hours you tutored for the week.

Find each sum or difference.

8. $\frac{15}{16} - \frac{3}{16}$
9. $\frac{1}{4} + \frac{2}{3}$
10. $\frac{1}{2} - \frac{3}{8}$
11. $\frac{2}{3} + \frac{5}{6}$
12. $8\frac{2}{5} + 5\frac{3}{5}$
13. $1\frac{2}{3} - \frac{3}{4}$
14. $4\frac{3}{4} + 5\frac{1}{5}$
15. $9\frac{3}{8} - 5\frac{1}{4}$
16. At birth, a baby weighs $7\frac{3}{8}$ lb. The baby weighs $8\frac{13}{16}$ lb at the one-month checkup. How much weight did the baby gain?
17. You ride your bike $1\frac{3}{10}$ mi to school. At the end of the day, you stop at a park on the way home. The park is $\frac{2}{5}$ mi from school. How far is the park from your house?

Find each product or quotient.

18. $\frac{4}{5} \cdot \frac{1}{4}$
19. $\frac{4}{5} \div \frac{1}{4}$
20. $\frac{3}{4} \cdot \frac{2}{3}$
21. $\frac{1}{4} \div \frac{4}{5}$
22. $1\frac{2}{3} \cdot 1\frac{1}{4}$
23. $1\frac{2}{3} \div 1\frac{1}{4}$
24. $150 \div 2\frac{2}{3}$
25. $5\frac{3}{8} \cdot 3\frac{3}{4}$
26. **Masonry** A brick is $1\frac{7}{8}$ in. high. Mortar that is $\frac{3}{8}$ in. thick is spread on each row of bricks. How many rows of bricks are needed to reach the top of a $7\frac{1}{2}$-ft doorway?

Algebra **Solve.**

27. $10\frac{3}{4} = n - \frac{5}{8}$
28. $w + 4\frac{3}{5} = 6\frac{1}{2}$
29. $\frac{1}{4}m = 10$
30. $\frac{y}{12} = 2\frac{1}{2}$
31. $\frac{1}{4}x - 10 = 2$
32. $9 = \frac{d}{7} + 1$
33. $\frac{3}{10}k - 1 = \frac{1}{2}$
34. $7\frac{3}{4} = \frac{3}{8}h + 6$
35. **Earnings** You work $12\frac{1}{2}$ h at \$6.50 per hour and deposit your earnings in a savings account. You withdraw \$24 for a shirt. You then have \$89.23 in your account. How much money was in your account before you were paid?
36. **Discounts** You are an employee at a store that is having a "$\frac{1}{3}$-off" sale. Employees get an additional $\frac{1}{5}$ off the sale price. How much would you pay for a jacket that originally cost \$60?

Complete.

37. 38 in. = ■ ft
38. 60 oz = ■ lb
39. $3\frac{3}{4}$ qt = ■ c
40. $1\frac{2}{3}$ mi = ■ ft
41. $5\frac{1}{2}$ yd = ■ in.
42. 50 fl oz = ■ c
43. **Writing in Math** About how heavy should an object be before you start to measure the object in tons instead of pounds? Explain.
44. You have $1\frac{1}{2}$ lb of fish. How many 6-oz servings can you make?
45. You jog $8\frac{1}{2}$ times around the block. The distance around the block is 770 yd. About how many miles have you jogged? (1 mi = 1,760 yd)

Choose the more precise measurement.

46. 36 min, $1\frac{1}{4}$ h
47. 1 t, 500 lb
48. 100.5 mg, 10.67 g
49. 18 months, 1 year

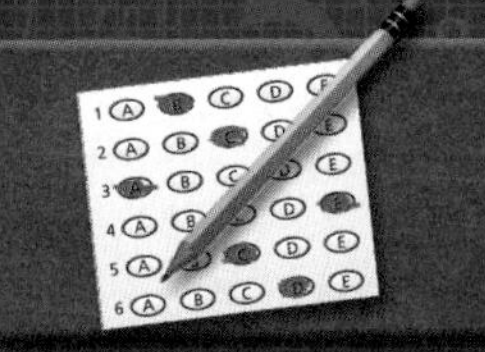

Test Prep

Multiple Choice

For Exercises 1–12, choose the correct letter.

1. Which pair of numbers has a product that is greater than its sum?
   A. −2, −5 B. −3, 3
   C. 4, −2 D. 0, 1

2. What are the prime factors of 136?
   F. 2, 2, 34 G. 2, 2, 2, 17
   H. 2, 2, 3, 17 I. 2, 3, 3, 15

3. What is the mean of the temperatures shown below?
   92° 87° 79° 85° 92°
   A. 87° B. 90° C. 92° D. 85°

4. You buy a package of socks for $4.89, a T-shirt for $7.75, and a pair of shorts for $14.95. Estimate to the nearest dollar the amount of change you will get back if you give the cashier $30.
   F. about $1 G. about $2
   H. about $3 I. about $4

5. What is the solution of $5y + 11 = 56$?
   A. 9 B. 8 C. 13 D. 10

6. Which list is in order from least to greatest?
   F. $\frac{1}{3}, \frac{3}{4}, \frac{1}{5}$ G. $5\frac{1}{8}, 5\frac{1}{4}, 5\frac{2}{3}$
   H. $\frac{13}{12}, \frac{4}{5}, \frac{3}{7}$ I. $\frac{8}{9}, \frac{2}{5}, \frac{1}{2}$

7. The average person drinks about 2.5 quarts of water each day. How many pints is this?
   A. 2 pt B. 3 pt C. 4 pt D. 5 pt

8. Which variable expression can be described by the word phrase "*r* increased by 2"?
   F. $2r$ G. $r - 2$
   H. $r + 2$ I. $r \cdot 2$

9. Which decimal is closest to $\frac{11}{16}$?
   A. 0.687 B. 0.69 C. 0.68 D. 0.7

10. Estimate $6\frac{3}{4} \cdot 3\frac{1}{5}$.
    F. 18 G. 21 H. 24 I. 27

11. Your friend divided 0.56 by 0.7 and got 8 for an answer. This answer is not correct. Which answer is correct?
    A. 0.08 B. 0.008 C. 0.8 D. 80

12. Which graph shows the solution of $d + 10 \leq 19$?
    F. 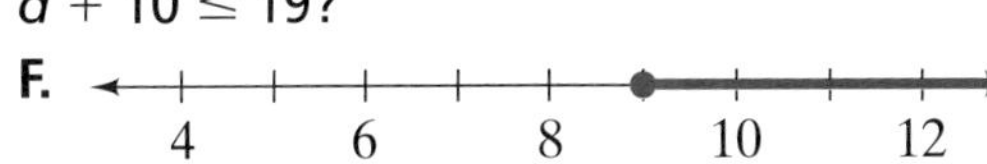
    G. 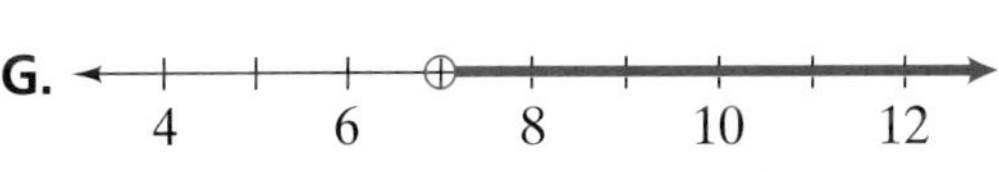
    H. 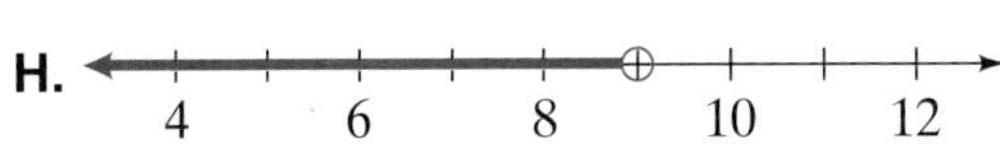
    I. 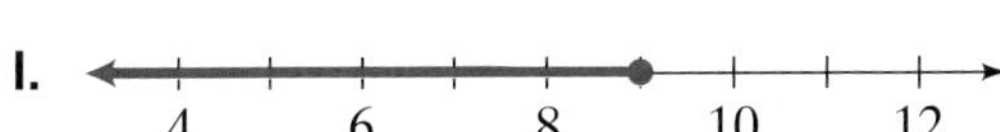

Gridded Response

13. During the summer, you work 27 hours per week. Each week, you earn $168.75. How many dollars do you earn per hour?

Short Response

14. Is 54.5 g or 54.5 kg a more reasonable estimate for a person's weight? Explain.

15. You and four friends are planning a surprise birthday party. Each of you contributes the same amount of money *m* for the food.
    a. Write a variable expression for the total amount of money contributed for food.
    b. Evaluate your expression for $m = \$7.75$.

Extended Response

16. One goaltender makes 72 saves on 78 shots. Another makes 52 saves on 56 shots.
    a. Write two fractions in simplest form to express the numbers of saves per shot.
    b. Which goaltender has the greater number of saves per shot?
    c. Explain how you found your answer to part (b).

Real-World Snapshots

Into the Earth With Integers

Applying Fractions Millions of people come to Arizona each year to stand at the edge of the Grand Canyon and look down at the Colorado River, a mile below. If you're one of them, you might decide to hike the winding trail to the canyon floor.

Collared Lizard

Adult collared lizards typically grow up to 10–13 in. long and can travel at speeds over 10 mi/h. To escape predators, they can run bipedally (on two legs).

Put It All Together

Materials 10 index cards, markers, two boxes

What You'll Need

- Number four of the index cards −2, −1, +1, and +2. Put them in one of the boxes and label it "numerators."
- Number the remaining index cards 3, 4, 5, 6, 7, and 8. Put them in the other box and label it "denominators."

How To Play

- The goal of the game is to move from the canyon rim (0) to the canyon floor (−1).
- Draw one card from each box. Write down the fraction it represents. (For example, −2 from the numerator box and 5 from the denominator box represent $-\frac{2}{5}$, or descending $\frac{2}{5}$ mi into the canyon.) *To leave the canyon rim, you must draw a negative numerator.*
- Replace the cards and draw again. Add the fractions. Repeat until one of the players reaches −1 (or beyond). If your total rises above 0, you are back on the rim. *Start again at 0!*

1. Write an equation to show how far you go toward the bottom in your first two moves. *Use zero for each positive move before your first negative move.*
2. a. **Reasoning** How would you calculate the total distance you hiked? Explain.
   b. How far did you hike?
3. a. **Writing in Math** Choose whichever numerator and whichever denominator you want for your first move. Explain your choice.
   b. **Reasoning** Suppose you can choose for each move, but you cannot use the same denominator twice. How many moves will it take for you to get to the bottom? Explain, using a fraction sentence.

Riding Down

Mules are one form of transportation in the Grand Canyon.

The Pinyon Jay

Pinyon jays live in the Grand Canyon, and among the Pinyon and Juniper pines throughout the southwest.

Take It to the NET For more information about canyons, go to **www.PHSchool.com.**
Web Code: abe-0453

CHAPTER 5

Ratios, Rates, and Proportions

Lessons

5-1 Ratios

5-2 Unit Rates and Proportional Reasoning

5-3 Problem Solving: Draw a Diagram and Solve a Simpler Problem

5-4 Proportions

5-5 Solving Proportions

5-6 Using Similar Figures

5-7 Maps and Scale Drawings

Key Vocabulary

- cross products (p. 257)
- equal ratios (p. 242)
- indirect measurement (p. 269)
- polygon (p. 268)
- proportion (p. 256)
- rate (p. 246)
- ratio (p. 241)
- scale (p. 275)
- scale drawing (p. 275)
- similar polygons (p. 268)
- unit price (p. 247)
- unit rate (p. 246)

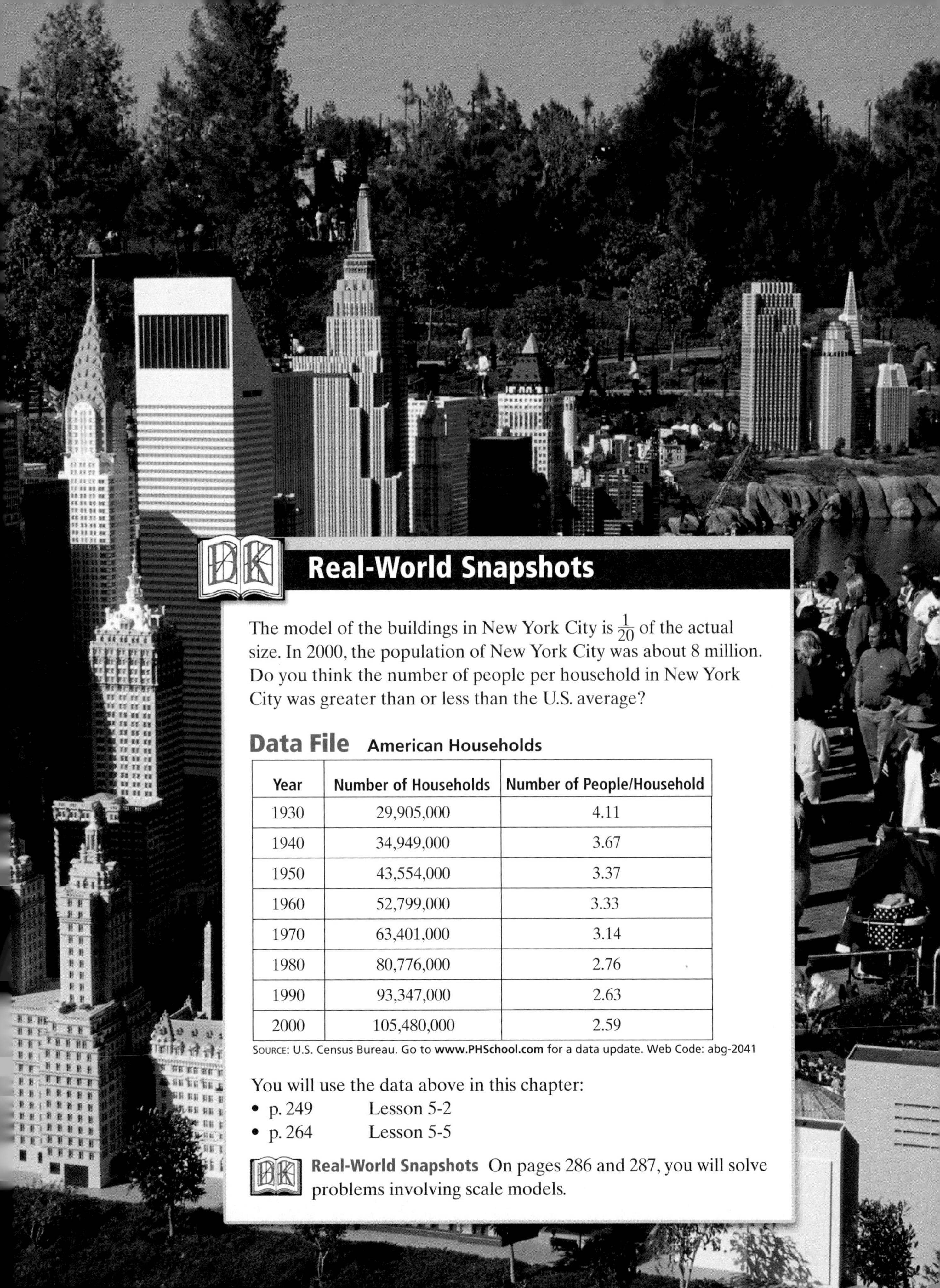

Real-World Snapshots

The model of the buildings in New York City is $\frac{1}{20}$ of the actual size. In 2000, the population of New York City was about 8 million. Do you think the number of people per household in New York City was greater than or less than the U.S. average?

Data File American Households

Year	Number of Households	Number of People/Household
1930	29,905,000	4.11
1940	34,949,000	3.67
1950	43,554,000	3.37
1960	52,799,000	3.33
1970	63,401,000	3.14
1980	80,776,000	2.76
1990	93,347,000	2.63
2000	105,480,000	2.59

SOURCE: U.S. Census Bureau. Go to **www.PHSchool.com** for a data update. Web Code: abg-2041

You will use the data above in this chapter:

- p. 249 Lesson 5-2
- p. 264 Lesson 5-5

Real-World Snapshots On pages 286 and 287, you will solve problems involving scale models.

Chapter 5 Preview

Where You've Been

- In Chapter 3, you learned to simplify and compare fractions. You learned to express fractions as decimals.
- In Chapter 4, you learned to add, subtract, multiply, and divide fractions and mixed numbers.

Where You're Going

- In Chapter 5, you will write ratios and unit rates. You will solve proportions and find values in similar figures, maps, and scale models.
- Applying what you learn, you will use a map to plan a trip. You will also find the scale of a model used by a special-effects artist.

Special-effects artists use scale models.

Instant self-check online and on CD-ROM

Diagnosing Readiness

 For help, go to the lesson in green.

Multiplying and Dividing Decimals (Lesson 1-3)

Find each product or quotient.

1. (3.6)(4) **2.** 14.2 ÷ 8 **3.** (15.9)(3) **4.** 44.46 ÷ 6

5. 23.73 ÷ 7 **6.** 95.32 ÷ 16 **7.** (12.74)(9) **8.** 52.6 ÷ 5

Solving Equations by Multiplying or Dividing (Lesson 2-4)

Algebra Solve.

9. $4n = 32$ **10.** $\frac{a}{6} = 10$ **11.** $18 = 9z$ **12.** $49k = 7$

13. $56j = 8$ **14.** $5m = 55$ **15.** $15 = \frac{p}{5}$ **16.** $72 = 3z$

Comparing and Ordering Fractions (Lesson 3-6)

Compare. Use <, >, or =.

17. $\frac{8}{9}$ ■ $\frac{3}{4}$ **18.** $\frac{7}{12}$ ■ $\frac{4}{5}$ **19.** $\frac{6}{3}$ ■ $\frac{24}{12}$

20. $\frac{1}{6}$ ■ $\frac{1}{7}$ **21.** $\frac{6}{9}$ ■ $\frac{2}{3}$ **22.** $\frac{1}{8}$ ■ $\frac{1}{2}$

Simplifying Fractions (Lesson 3-5)

Write each fraction in simplest form.

23. $\frac{12}{16}$ **24.** $\frac{15}{30}$ **25.** $\frac{42}{48}$ **26.** $\frac{27}{72}$

27. $\frac{19}{57}$ **28.** $\frac{25}{45}$ **29.** $\frac{34}{51}$ **30.** $\frac{16}{56}$

5-1 Ratios

What You'll Learn

To write ratios

To find equal ratios

. . . And Why

To compare weights, as in Example 4

✓ Check Skills You'll Need

For help, go to Lesson 3-5.

Write each fraction in simplest form.

1. $\frac{2}{4}$ **2.** $\frac{21}{27}$ **3.** $\frac{36}{63}$

4. $\frac{8}{24}$ **5.** $\frac{2}{16}$ **6.** $\frac{15}{21}$

New Vocabulary • ratio • equal ratios

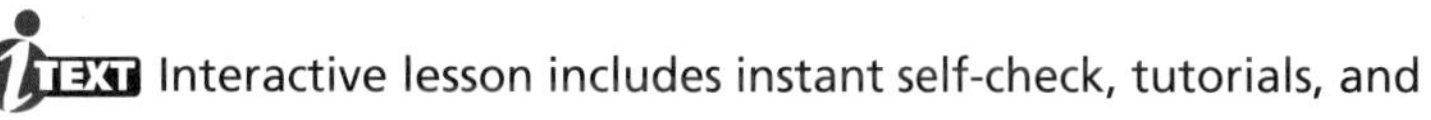

Interactive lesson includes instant self-check, tutorials, and activities.

OBJECTIVE 1

Writing Ratios

Investigation: A Survey of Birthday Data

1. Take a survey of your class. Find each person's birth month, as in the example at the right.
2. For each month, write the following fraction: $\frac{\text{number born in month}}{\text{number in class}}$
3. If there are the same number of birthdays in each month, each fraction will equal $\frac{1}{12}$. Find whether each of your fractions is greater than, less than, or equal to $\frac{1}{12}$.

Birthdays	
January	II
February	I
March	III
April	I
May	~~IIII~~

In a middle school class, 5 of the 24 students were born in August. You can compare the numbers 5 and 24 by dividing to form the ratio $\frac{5}{24}$.

Key Concepts **Ratio**

A **ratio** is a comparison of two quantities by division. You can write a ratio in three ways.

Arithmetic	Algebra
5 to 24 5 : 24 $\frac{5}{24}$	a to b $a : b$ $\frac{a}{b}$ where $b \neq 0$

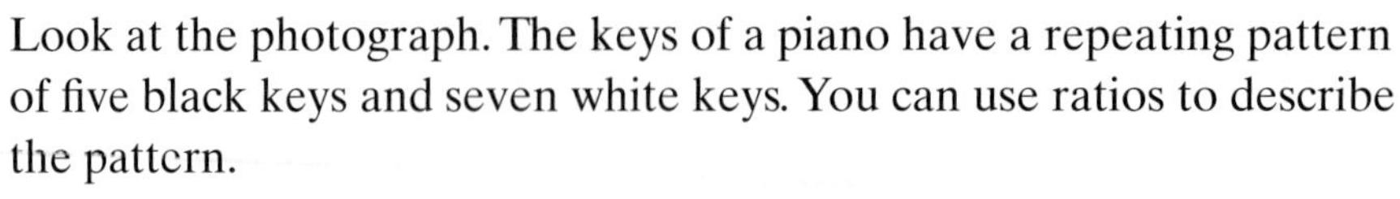

Look at the photograph. The keys of a piano have a repeating pattern of five black keys and seven white keys. You can use ratios to describe the pattern.

You can use a ratio to compare part to part. The ratio of black piano keys to white piano keys in the pattern is 5 : 7. You can also compare part to whole. The ratio of black keys to all keys in the pattern is 5 : 12.

5	7
12	

1 EXAMPLE **Writing Ratios** 

Music Using the pattern shown above, write the ratio of black keys to all keys in three ways.

black keys→ 5 to 12 ←all keys

black keys→ 5 : 12 ←all keys

$\frac{5}{12}$ ← black keys / ← all keys

Check Understanding 1 Write each ratio in three ways. Use the pattern of piano keys shown above.
a. white keys to all keys
b. black keys to white keys

You can use decimals to express and compare ratios.

2 EXAMPLE **Writing Ratios as Decimals** 

Social Studies An official U. S. flag has a length-to-width ratio of 19 : 10. The largest U. S. flag measures 505 ft by 255 ft. Is this an official U. S. flag?

official flag ↓ $\frac{19}{10}$ ← length → / ← width → largest flag ↓ $\frac{505}{255}$

$\frac{19}{10} = 1.9$ ← **Write as a decimal. Round if necessary.** → $\frac{505}{255} \approx 1.98$

Since 1.98 is not equal to 1.9, the largest flag is *not* an official United States flag.

Check Understanding 2 **a.** Write the ratio 7 : 3 as a decimal. Round to the nearest hundredth.
b. **Number Sense** When will a ratio equal a decimal between 0 and 1?

OBJECTIVE 2

Finding Equal Ratios

Two ratios that name the same number are **equal ratios.** Two students report the ratio of the number of girls in a class to the total number of students. One student says the ratio is $\frac{18}{30}$. The other says the ratio is $\frac{9}{15}$. The two ratios are equal ratios.

You can find equal ratios by writing a ratio as a fraction and finding equivalent fractions.

3 EXAMPLE Writing Equal Ratios

Find two ratios equal to $\frac{12}{15}$.

$\frac{12 \times 2}{15 \times 2} = \frac{24}{30}$ ← **Multiply the numerator and denominator by 2.**

$\frac{12 \div 3}{15 \div 3} = \frac{4}{5}$ ← **Divide the numerator and denominator by 3.**

Two ratios equal to $\frac{12}{15}$ are $\frac{24}{30}$ and $\frac{4}{5}$.

Check Understanding 3 Find two ratios equal to $\frac{10}{16}$.

To write a ratio in simplest form, divide the numerator and the denominator by the GCF.

Need Help?

For help finding the greatest common factor (GCF), go to Lesson 3-4.

4 EXAMPLE Writing a Ratio in Simplest Form

Biology A black bear weighs about 325 lb. A polar bear weighs about 1,000 lb. Write a ratio in simplest form to compare the weights of the bears.

$\frac{325}{1,000} = \frac{325 \div 25}{1,000 \div 25} = \frac{13}{40}$ ← **Divide the numerator and denominator by the GCF, 25.**

The ratio of the black bear's weight to the polar bear's weight is 13 to 40.

Check Understanding 4 **a.** Write the ratio of the polar bear's weight to the black bear's weight. Then write the ratio in simplest form.

b. **Reasoning** How can you tell whether a ratio is in simplest form?

EXERCISES

For more practice, see *Extra Practice*.

A Practice by Example

Example 1 (page 242)

Write a ratio in three ways, comparing the first quantity to the second.

1. A week has five school days and two weekend days.
2. About 24 out of 25 Californians live in a metropolitan area.
3. About one in every four people swims at least six times each year.

Example 2 (page 242)

Express each ratio as a decimal.

4. 7:8 5. 18 to 5 6. $\frac{267}{100}$ 7. 12:25

8. **Nutrition** The U.S. Department of Agriculture (USDA) recommends that no more than $\frac{3}{10}$ of your Calories come from fat. In a bowl of Tastycrunch cereal, 15 out of 120 Calories are from fat. Is this within the USDA recommendation? Explain.

Example 3 (page 243)

Find two ratios equal to each ratio.

9. $\frac{212}{100}$ **10.** $\frac{36}{18}$ **11.** $\frac{26}{54}$ **12.** $\frac{360}{180}$

Example 4 (page 243)

Write each ratio in simplest form.

13. $\frac{44}{12}$ **14.** $\frac{18}{8}$ **15.** $\frac{16}{56}$ **16.** $\frac{9}{72}$

17. Cars A jack for a car requires a force of 120 lb to lift a 3,000-lb car. In simplest form, what is the ratio of the car's weight to the force required to lift the car?

B Apply Your Skills

18. Cooking To make pancake batter, you need 2 cups of water for every 3 cups of flour. You plan to use 9 cups of flour. Write a ratio for the number of cups of water to the number of cups of flour you will use.

19. Writing in Math Explain to a friend how to write a ratio in simplest form. Give an example.

Compare the ratios below. Tell whether they are *equal* or *not equal.*

20. $\frac{18}{24}, \frac{3}{4}$ **21.** $\frac{12}{24}, \frac{50}{100}$ **22.** $\frac{22}{1}, \frac{1}{22}$

23. 16:3, 27:5 **24.** 2 to 3, 24 to 36 **25.** 6:7, 30:35

Real-World Connection

Careers Atmospheric scientists study the effects of chemicals on our environment.

26. Chemistry A chemical formula shows the ratio of atoms in a substance. The formula for carbon dioxide is CO_2. This means carbon dioxide has 1 atom of carbon (C) for every 2 atoms of oxygen (O). Write the ratio of hydrogen (H) atoms to oxygen atoms in the substances in parts (a) and (b) below.

a. water, H_2O **b.** disinfectant, H_2O_2

c. Reasoning Ammonia has a ratio of 1 atom of nitrogen (N) to 3 atoms of hydrogen. What is its chemical formula?

Use the table for Exercises 27 and 28.

	Room 101	Room 104	Room 107
Girls	12	9	9
Boys	16	20	12

27. In which two rooms is the ratio of girls to boys the same?

28. The students in Room 101 and Room 104 have one class together. Using simplest form, write the ratio of girls to boys for the combined class.

29. Sports A softball diamond measures 65 ft by 65 ft. A baseball diamond measures 90 ft by 90 ft. Write each ratio described in parts (a) and (b) below in simplest form.

a. the length of a side of a softball diamond to the length of a side of a baseball diamond

b. the area of a softball diamond to the area of a baseball diamond

c. Reasoning Explain why the ratio of the sides is not equal to the ratio of the areas.

30. **Error Analysis** Your math class includes 15 girls and 10 boys. Two new students, a girl and a boy, enroll in your class. Your friend says the ratio is the same as before. Explain why your friend is not correct.

31. **Cars** Antifreeze protects a car's radiator. One brand recommends mixing at least 2 parts antifreeze with every 1 part water for protection to $-82°F$.
 a. List all of the ratios in the table that provide that protection.
 b. **Reasoning** You want a car with a 15-qt radiator to be protected. You want to use the least amount of antifreeze. How much antifreeze and how much water should you use?

Mixing Antifreeze

Antifreeze (qt)	Water (qt)
8	4
7.5	3
12	8
3.5	1
9	18

Challenge

32. A bag contains red, blue, and yellow marbles. The ratio of red marbles to blue marbles is 1:4. The ratio of blue marbles to yellow marbles is 2:5. What is the ratio of red marbles to yellow marbles?

33. **Stretch Your Thinking** The pattern at the right uses nine toothpicks. How can you form five triangles by moving only three toothpicks?

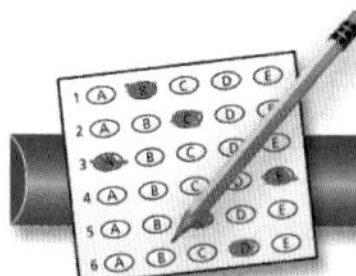

Test Prep

Multiple Choice

34. Which ratio is equal to the ratio $\frac{50}{12}$?
 A. 6 to 25 B. $\frac{12}{50}$ C. 25:6 D. $\frac{6}{25}$

35. Which of the following ratios is written in simplest form?
 F. $\frac{8}{52}$ G. $\frac{15}{65}$ H. $\frac{27}{81}$ I. $\frac{9}{14}$

Take It to the NET
Online lesson quiz at
www.PHSchool.com
Web Code: aba-0501

36. Which of the following ratios is NOT equal to the ratio $\frac{2}{5}$?
 A. $\frac{6}{10}$ B. $\frac{8}{20}$ C. $\frac{12}{30}$ D. $\frac{14}{35}$

Extended Response

37. A rectangle has a base of 9 cm and a height of 16 cm. A second rectangle's base and height are 3 times as large. Find the area of each rectangle. What is the ratio of the area of the second rectangle to the area of the first rectangle? Justify your answer.

Mixed Review

Lesson 2-4 **Algebra** **Solve each equation.**

38. $72 = 8x$ 39. $\frac{y}{3} = 15$ 40. $-5 = \frac{q}{7}$

Lesson 1-1 **Estimate.**

41. $412 \cdot 83$ 42. $23.5 + 23.1$ 43. $28.7 \div 5.4$

5-2 Unit Rates and Proportional Reasoning

What You'll Learn

 To find unit rates

 To use unit prices

. . . And Why

To find speed, as in Example 2

Check Skills You'll Need

For help, go to Lesson 5-1.

Write each ratio in simplest form.

1. $\frac{15}{25}$	**2.** $\frac{4}{36}$	**3.** $\frac{28}{49}$
4. $\frac{9}{12}$	**5.** $\frac{22}{16}$	**6.** $\frac{64}{72}$

New Vocabulary • rate • unit rate • unit price

 Interactive lesson includes instant self-check, tutorials, and activities.

OBJECTIVE 1 Finding Unit Rates

A **rate** is a ratio that compares two quantities measured in different units. Suppose you read 233 words in two minutes. Your reading rate is $\frac{233 \text{ words}}{2 \text{ minutes}}$.

The rate for one unit of a given quantity is the **unit rate.** To find a unit rate, divide the first quantity by the second quantity. For a reading rate of $\frac{233 \text{ words}}{2 \text{ minutes}}$, the unit rate is 116.5 words per minute.

1 EXAMPLE Finding a Unit Rate

A box of cereal contains 8 servings and has a total of 36 grams of fat. Find the unit rate of grams of fat per serving.

grams → $\frac{36}{8} = 4.5$ ← **Divide the first quantity by the second quantity.**
servings →

The unit rate is $\frac{4.5 \text{ grams}}{1 \text{ serving}}$, or 4.5 grams per serving.

Check Understanding 1 Find the unit rate for 210 heartbeats in 3 minutes.

The model below shows the relationships in Example 1.

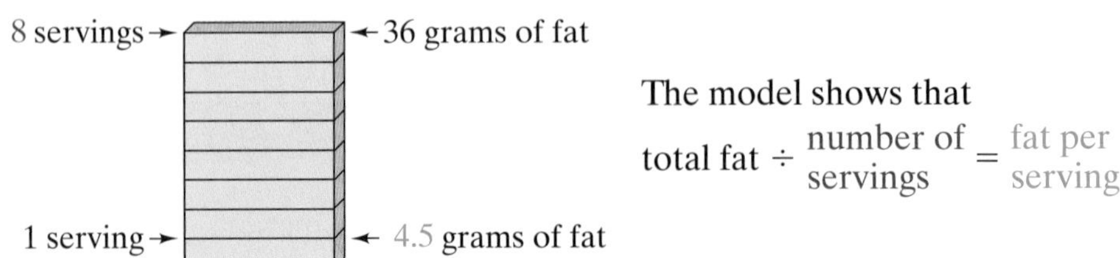

You can express speed as a unit rate involving a unit of time. Sometimes the time is given in more than one unit, such as minutes and seconds. Convert the time to a single unit, such as seconds, to find the speed.

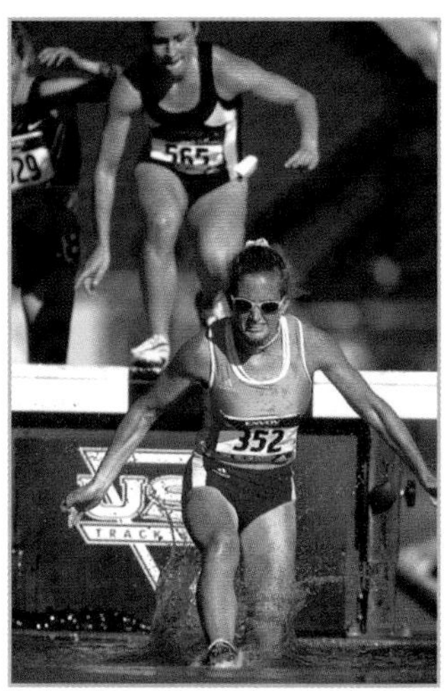

Real-World Connection

In a steeplechase, racers jump hurdles and run through puddles.

2 EXAMPLE **Real-World Problem Solving**

Sports Justyna Bak of Poland set a world record for the women's 3,000-m steeplechase. Her time was 9 min 25.31 s. What was her speed in meters per second? Round your answer to the nearest hundredth.

Step 1 Convert the time to a single unit.

9 min = 9 · 60 s ← **Convert 9 min to seconds.**

= 540 s

540 + 25.31 = 565.31 ← **Add the remaining seconds.**

Her time was 565.31 s.

Step 2 Write the ratio of meters to seconds. Use a calculator to divide.

meters → / seconds → $\frac{3,000}{565.31}$ = 3,000 ÷ 565.31 = 5.3068228

≈ 5.31 ← **Round to the nearest hundredth.**

Justyna Bak's speed was 5.31 m/s.

Check Understanding 2 **a.** Write the unit rate in words/min for typing 6,750 words in 2 h 30 min.
b. **Reasoning** How can you check your answer to part (a)?

OBJECTIVE

2 Using Unit Prices

A unit rate that gives the cost per unit is a **unit price.** Suppose the box of cereal mentioned earlier weighs 8 oz and has a unit price of $.31 per ounce. You want to find the total price of the box of cereal.

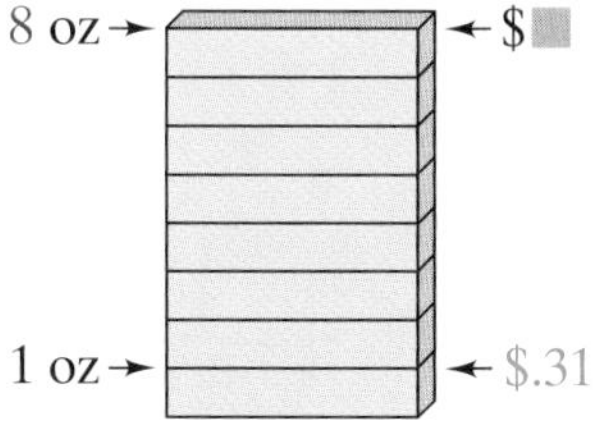

The model shows that
unit price · number of ounces = total price.

3 EXAMPLE **Using Unit Price to Find Total Price** 

Prices In the supermarket, the price tag is missing from a box of cereal. Use the information at the right to find the price of the box.

$.31 · 8 = $2.48 ← **unit price · number of units = total price**

The total price of the box of cereal is $2.48.

Check Understanding 3 **a.** The unit price for dog food is $.35/lb. How much does a 20-lb bag cost?
b. **Number Sense** If the unit price in part (a) drops to $.32/lb because of a sale, how much lower is the price for the 20-lb bag?

To find the unit price, divide the total price of the item by the size of the item or the number of units in the item.

4 EXAMPLE Using Unit Price to Compare

Smart Shopping Two sizes of shampoo bottles are shown. Which size is the better buy? Round to the nearest cent.

Divide to find the unit price of each size.

$\begin{matrix}\text{price} \rightarrow \\ \text{size} \rightarrow\end{matrix} \dfrac{\$3.99}{13.5 \text{ fl oz}} \approx \$.30/\text{fl oz}$

$\begin{matrix}\text{price} \rightarrow \\ \text{size} \rightarrow\end{matrix} \dfrac{\$6.19}{16 \text{ fl oz}} \approx \$.39/\text{fl oz}$

Since \$.30 < \$.39, the 13.5-fl-oz bottle is the better buy.

Check Understanding 4 Find each unit price. Then determine the better buy.

a. 48 fl oz of fruit juice for \$3.05, or 64 fl oz for \$3.59

b. 8.5 oz of mixed vegetables for \$.79, or 14.5 oz for \$1.09

EXERCISES

For more practice, see *Extra Practice*.

A Practice by Example

Find the unit rate for each situation. Round to the nearest hundredth, if necessary. Exercise 1 has been started for you.

Example 1 (page 246)

1. travel 1,200 mi in 4 h
$\dfrac{\text{miles} \rightarrow 1{,}200}{\text{hours} \rightarrow \quad 4}$

2. score 96 points in 6 games

3. earn \$145 in 25 h

4. write 11 pages in 2 h

5. skate 1,000 m in 200 s

6. solve 35 problems in 70 min

Example 2 (page 247)

7. run 400 m in 1 min 32 s

8. swim 500 yd in 3 min 20 s

9. drive 168 mi in 2 h 30 min

10. bike 23.25 km in 1 h 45 min

11. read 50 pages in 1 h 25 min

12. hike 5 mi in 2 h 10 min

Example 3 (page 247)

Find the total price using each unit price.

13. 5 ft at \$3 per foot

14. 15 yd^2 at \$2.25 per square yard

15. 10 gal at \$2.40 per gallon

16. 26 oz at \$.15 per ounce

17. 10 g at \$.24 per gram

18. 9 lb at \$1.29 per pound

Example 4 (page 248)

Find each unit price.

19. \$12 for 4 yd^2

20. \$3.45 for 3.7 oz

21. \$9.86 for 2.4 lb

22. \$9 for 5 L

Find each unit price. Then determine the better buy.

23. detergent: 32 fl oz for $1.99
50 fl oz for $2.49

24. crackers: 12 oz for $2.69
16 oz for $3.19

B Apply Your Skills

25. **a.** A school has 945 students and 35 teachers. What is the student-to-teacher ratio? Write your answer as a unit rate.
b. **Reasoning** If both the numbers of teachers and students increase by 5, does the unit rate remain the same? Explain.

26. **Data File, p. 239** Use the data for the number of people per household and the number of households to estimate the population of the United States in 1930 and in 1990. Round each population to the nearest million. Then write the ratio of the populations in simplest form.

The total price and unit price are given. Find the number of units.

27. $800 at $.16 per gallon

28. $76.84 at $4.52 per pound

Number of Persons per Square Mile in New Jersey

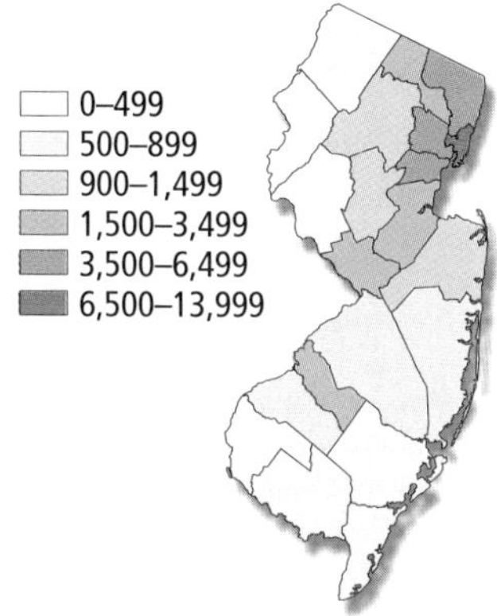

SOURCE: U.S. Census Bureau. Go to **www.PHSchool.com** for a data update. Web Code: abg-2041

Real-World Connection

A map like this one gives a visual representation of population density.

29. **Geography** Population density is the number of people per unit of area.
a. Alaska has the lowest population density of any state in the United States. It has 626,932 people in 570,374 mi^2. What is its population density? Round to the nearest person per square mile.
b. **Reasoning** New Jersey has 1,134.5 people/mi^2. It has the highest population density of any state. Can you conclude that 1,134.5 people live in every square mile of New Jersey? Explain.
c. **Writing in Math** Explain how you can find the population density of your city or town.

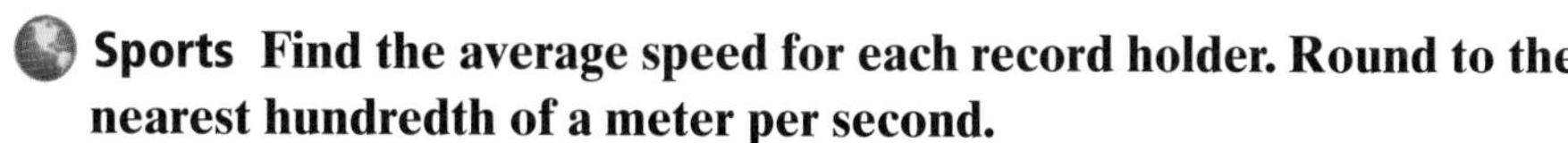

Sports Find the average speed for each record holder. Round to the nearest hundredth of a meter per second.

30. Florence Griffith-Joyner, USA, 100 m, 10.49 s

31. Michael Johnson, USA, 200 m, 19.32 s

32. Wilson Kipketer, Denmark, 800 m, 1 min 41.11 s

Find each unit price. Then determine the better buy.

33. ribbon: $.49 for 1 yd
$1.95 for 3 yd

34. walnuts: $3.49 for 1 lb
$2.49 for 10 oz

Find each unit price.

35. 36. 37. 38.

Challenge **Science** **The human heart beats an average of 2,956,575,000 times in 75 years. About how many times will the heart beat for each time period?**

39. one year **40.** one day **41.** one minute

42. **Stretch Your Thinking** Use one 2 and one 6 to write a numerical expression that equals 64.

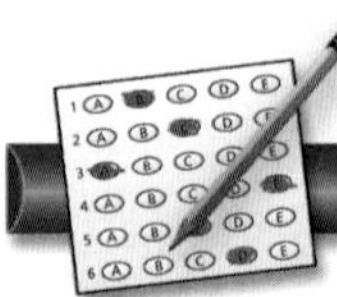

Test Prep

Multiple Choice

43. Which rate gives the best price for potatoes?

A. \$.69/lb **B.** $\frac{\$2.13}{3 \text{ lb}}$ **C.** $\frac{\$3.35}{5 \text{ lb}}$ **D.** $\frac{\$6.80}{10 \text{ lb}}$

44. Which rate gives the best price for oranges?

F. \$.95/lb **G.** $\frac{\$3.15}{3 \text{ lb}}$ **H.** $\frac{\$4.95}{5 \text{ lb}}$ **I.** $\frac{\$9.80}{10 \text{ lb}}$

45. A carpenter renovating a house is sanding the dining room floor. She sands 300 ft^2 of wood floor in 1 h 40 min. What is the unit rate in square feet per minute?

A. 0.3 **B.** 0.9 **C.** 3 **D.** 9

46. A farmer sells artichokes for \$1.54 each. How much will it cost to buy one artichoke each for seven people?

F. \$.22 **G.** \$1.54 **H.** \$7.28 **I.** \$10.78

Short Response

47. An airplane travels 1,824 mi in 4 h 45 min. Find the airplane's speed in miles per minute. Explain how you found your answer.

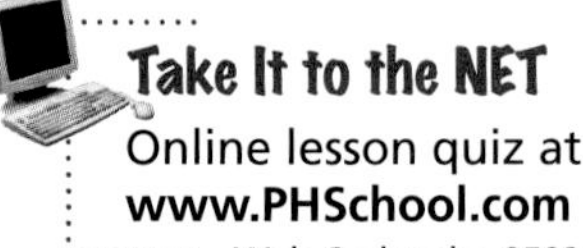

Take It to the NET
Online lesson quiz at
www.PHSchool.com
Web Code: aba-0502

48. You can buy a plain white T-shirt for \$6.25. After printing your school mascot on it, you can sell the T-shirt for \$9.50. If you sell 12 T-shirts at a basketball game, how much profit do you make?

Mixed Review

Lesson 3-1 **Use paper and pencil, mental math, or a calculator to simplify.**

49. 3^3 **50.** 9^4 **51.** 6^7 **52.** 10^8

53. 2^8 **54.** 5^4 **55.** 8^6 **56.** 3^9

Lesson 2-9 **Algebra** **Solve each inequality. Graph the solution.**

57. $a + 3 < 8$ **58.** $j - 12 \geq -5$ **59.** $x + 5 \leq -3$

60. $m - 6 \geq 5$ **61.** $w - 8 > -7$ **62.** $d + 4 < 18$

Lesson 1-1 **Estimate. Round to the nearest whole number before you add or subtract.**

63. 4.88 + 3.45 **64.** 26.125 − 12.324 **65.** 21.47 − 9.29

66. 231.26 + 18.83 **67.** 16.38 − 9.12 **68.** 2.56 + 7.98

Extension Dimensional Analysis

For Use With Lesson 5-2

Analyzing units of measure to decide how to convert from one unit to another is called dimensional analysis. For example, since 1 ft = 12 in. and $\frac{1\text{ ft}}{12\text{ in.}} = 1$, you can multiply by $\frac{1\text{ ft}}{12\text{ in.}}$ to convert from inches to feet. For unit conversion tables, see Lessons 1-4 and 4-8.

1 EXAMPLE Converting Units

Use dimensional analysis to convert 42 in. to feet.

$42\text{ in.} = \frac{42\text{ in.}}{1} \cdot \frac{1\text{ ft}}{12\text{ in.}}$ ← **Use a conversion factor that changes inches to feet.**

$= \frac{{}^{7}\cancel{42}\ \cancel{\text{in.}} \cdot 1\text{ ft}}{{}_{2}\cancel{12}\ \cancel{\text{in.}}}$ ← **Divide the common units.**

$= \frac{7}{2}\text{ ft}$ ← **Simplify.**

$= 3\frac{1}{2}\text{ ft}$ ← **Write as a mixed number.**

2 EXAMPLE Finding the Better Buy Real World

Shopping Brand A costs \$5.29 for 1 gal of cranberry juice. Brand B costs \$2.39 for 64 fl oz of cranberry juice. Which brand has the lower unit price?

Step 1 Convert units so both brands have the same unit of measure.

$64\text{ fl oz} = \frac{64\text{ fl oz}}{1} \cdot \frac{1\text{ gal}}{128\text{ fl oz}}$ ← **Use a conversion factor that changes fluid ounces to gallons.**

$= \frac{64\ \cancel{\text{fl oz}} \cdot 1\text{ gal}}{128\ \cancel{\text{fl oz}}}$ ← **Divide the common units.**

$= 0.5\text{ gal}$ ← **Simplify.**

Step 2 Find the unit price of each brand and compare.

$\frac{\$5.29}{1\text{ gal}} = \$5.29/\text{gal}$ ← **Brand A**

$\frac{\$2.39}{0.5\text{ gal}} = \$4.78/\text{gal}$ ← **Brand B**

Since \$4.78 < \$5.29, Brand B has the lower unit price.

EXERCISES

Use dimensional analysis to make each conversion.

1. 10 qt to gallons **2.** 38 cm to meters **3.** 6 kg to grams **4.** 5 mi to yards

5. 15 g to kilograms **6.** 1,056 ft to miles **7.** 137 oz to pounds **8.** 24 fl oz to cups

Use dimensional analysis to determine which item has the lower unit price.

9. 8 ft for \$3.29 or 5 yd for \$6.62 **10.** 16 pt for \$52.87 or 3 gal for \$69.60

11. 27 g for \$16.20 or 1.2 kg for \$320 **12.** 5 lb for \$8.23 or 60 oz for \$7.15

Problem Solving

5-3 Draw a Diagram and Solve a Simpler Problem

What You'll Learn

To solve a problem using two different methods

. . . And Why

To compare strategies in problem solving, as in Example 1

✓ Check Skills You'll Need

For help, go to Lesson 1-7.

Find each sum or difference.

1. $-10 - 2$ **2.** $7 + (-3)$ **3.** $-4 + (-5)$

4. $-9 + 14$ **5.** $-6 - 1$ **6.** $12 - (-8)$

7. Simplify $-10 + 2 - 1 + 2 - 1 + 2 - 1$.

OBJECTIVE 1

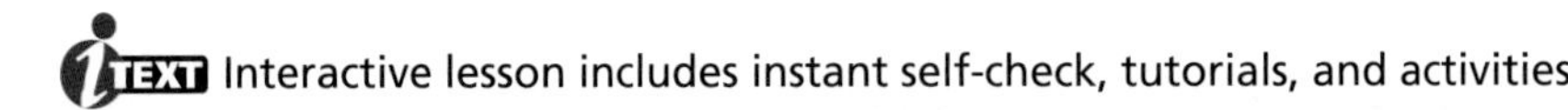

Solving a Problem Using Two Different Methods

When to Use These Strategies You can ***draw a diagram*** to show a problem visually. For problems that seem to have an overwhelming number of steps, you can ***solve a simpler problem*** that is similar. In this lesson, these strategies are used separately in two different methods.

1 EXAMPLE Using Strategies

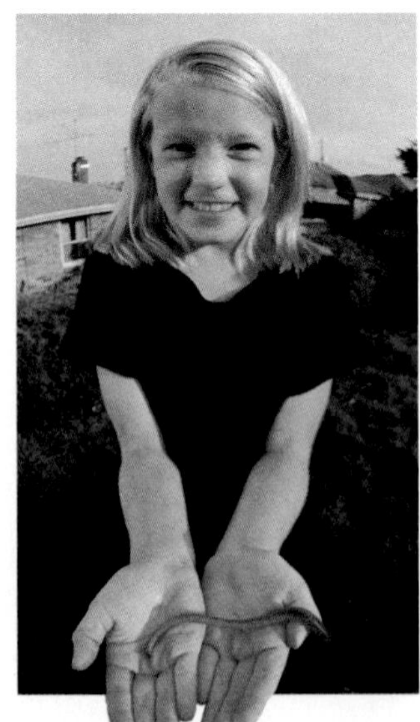

A worm is trying to escape from a well 10 ft deep. The worm climbs 2 ft per day, but each night it slides back 1 ft. How many days will the worm take to climb out of the well?

Read and Understand The total distance to travel is 10 ft. The worm gains 2 ft during the day, but loses 1 ft each night. The goal is to find out how many days the worm will take to get out of the well.

Plan and Solve

Method 1 Draw a Diagram Draw a diagram, such as the one at the right, that allows you to track the worm's position from day to day.

The worm reaches 10 ft and climbs out of the well at the end of the ninth day.

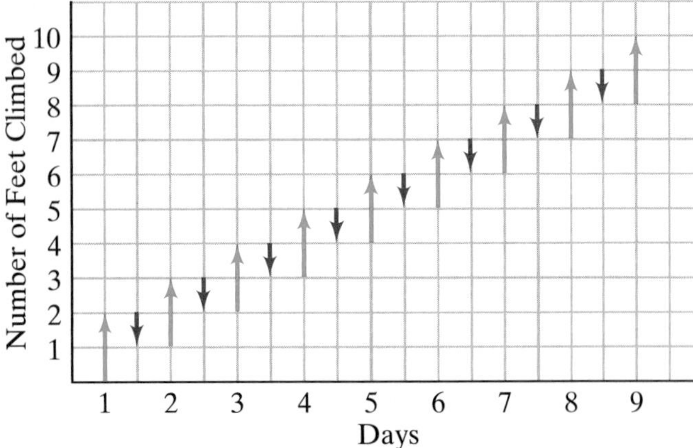

Method 2 Solve a Simpler Problem

Instead of solving the problem for a 10-ft well, change the problem to a simpler one based on a 3-ft well, and then on a 4-ft well.

Time	3-ft Well Distance From Bottom	4-ft Well Distance From Bottom
End of day 1	Up 2 ft	Up 2 ft
End of night 1	Up 1 ft	Up 1 ft
End of day 2	Up 3 ft	Up 3 ft
End of night 2		Up 2 ft
End of day 3		Up 4 ft

The worm will take 2 days to climb out of a 3-ft well and 3 days to climb out of a 4-ft well. So it would take 9 days to climb out of a 10-ft well.

Look Back and Check Your first thought might have been that the worm progresses 1 ft each day and therefore needs 10 days to escape. The worm does move a total of 1 ft each day, except on the ninth day. On the ninth day it climbs 2 ft and reaches the edge of the well.

Check Understanding

1 a. Look back at the two methods used to solve Example 1. Which method would you use? Why?

b. Suppose the worm works hard during the day and is able to climb 3 ft per day. Then it slides 2 ft per night. How many days will it take for the worm to climb out of the 10-ft well?

EXERCISES

For more practice, see *Extra Practice*.

A Practice by Example

Example 1 (page 252)

Solve each problem by either drawing a diagram or solving a simpler problem. Explain why you chose the method you used.

1. **Sports** You schedule the games for your basketball league's tournament. If a team loses a game, it is eliminated. There are 32 teams. How many games do you need to schedule to determine the league champion?

2. Each morning Jacob walks to school. At 8:20 A.M. he passes a stoplight that is two blocks from home. He walks another block and reaches the town library at 8:24 A.M. At this point he is three blocks from school and halfway there. If Jacob walks at the same pace all the way to school, when does he arrive at school?

3. At the first meeting of the Table Tennis Club, the seven members decide to have a tournament in which each player will play a game against each other player. How many games will there be?

4. There are 10 girls and 8 boys in a club. The club advisor can send one boy and one girl to a conference. How many different pairs of students can go to the conference?

Need Help?
- Reread the problem.
- Identify the key facts and details.
- Tell the problem in your own words.
- Try a different strategy.
- Check your work.

B Apply Your Skills

Strategies

- Draw a Diagram
- Look for a Pattern
- Make a Graph
- Make an Organized List
- Make a Table
- Simulate a Problem
- Solve a Simpler Problem
- Try, Check, and Revise
- Use Logical Reasoning
- Work Backward
- Write an Equation

Use any strategy to solve each problem. Show your work.

5. Writing in Math The Science Club treasurer finds that the bill for 18 sweatshirts has two digits blurred by water damage. The bill reads $■68.9■. The treasurer is sure that the first and last digits are the same. What do you think the total price is? Explain your choice.

6. **Jobs** Carla and Tanya are paid $135.00 for painting a fence. Carla works 6 h and Tanya works 9 h. If they are paid at the same rate, what is Tanya's share of the money?

7. **Money** Trevor has $8 in savings and adds $1 each week. Aretha has $12 in savings and adds $3 each week. After how many weeks will Aretha's account have twice as much as Trevor's account?

8. **Geometry** How many triangles are in the design?

9. You and two friends are out running. You pass a group of five other runners. Each person in each group greets each person in the other group. How many greetings are there?

10. A mother wants to give land to her three children. She gives $\frac{1}{2}$ of the land to the oldest child, $\frac{1}{3}$ of the land to her second child, and $\frac{1}{9}$ of the land to her youngest child. She keeps 1 acre for herself. How many acres of land does each child get?

11. A box contains the five disks shown. Suppose you draw three disks at random and add the numbers together. How many different totals are possible? What are they?

C Challenge

12. **Social Studies** At the beginning of every new term, each of the nine judges on the U. S. Supreme Court shakes hands with every other judge. How many handshakes take place?

13. **Stretch Your Thinking** A school has 1,000 students and 1,000 lockers. The lockers are numbered from 1 to 1,000. The students enter the school one at a time.

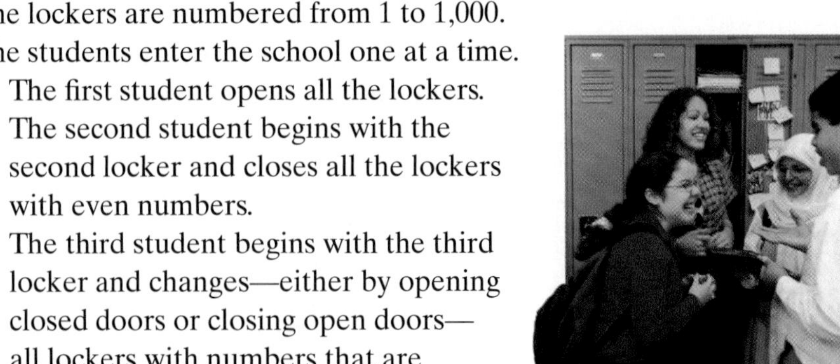

- The first student opens all the lockers.
- The second student begins with the second locker and closes all the lockers with even numbers.
- The third student begins with the third locker and changes—either by opening closed doors or closing open doors—all lockers with numbers that are multiples of 3.
- The fourth student begins with the fourth locker and changes all lockers with numbers that are multiples of 4.

Repeat this pattern until all the students walk past all the lockers. After the last student has gone by, which lockers are open?

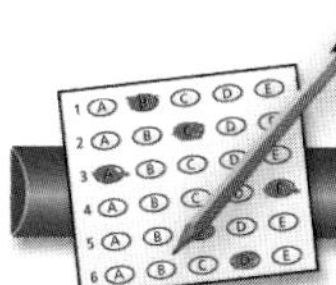

Test Prep

Multiple Choice

14. If $2m - 6 = 14$, what is the value of m?

A. 3 **B.** 7 **C.** 10 **D.** 21

15. Which equation has the same solution as $\frac{x}{2} - 3 = 11$?

F. $x - 3 = 22$ **G.** $\frac{x}{2} - 3 + 3 = 11 - 3$

H. $\frac{x}{2} - 3 + 3 = 11 + 3$ **I.** $\frac{x - 3}{2} = 11$

Take It to the NET
Online lesson quiz at
www.PHSchool.com
Web Code: aba-0503

16. Which equation does NOT have the solution -1.5?

A. $\frac{9}{w} = -6$ **B.** $-10w = 15$

C. $4 - 3w = 8.5$ **D.** $-1 - 2w = -4$

Short Response

17. Your parents just bought a refrigerator for $1,100. They made a down payment of $350 and will pay the rest of the cost in equal monthly payments over the next two years **(a)** Write an equation. **(b)** Solve your equation to determine the amount of each payment.

Mixed Review

Lesson 2-1

Algebra **Write each variable expression in words.**

18. $n + 3$ **19.** $x - 7$ **20.** $5z$ **21.** $\frac{y}{2}$

22. $2m - 3$ **23.** $7 + 4r$ **24.** $8 - \frac{1}{2}x$ **25.** $\frac{3}{4}s + 2r$

Lesson 1-7

Find each sum or difference.

26. $-7 - 3$ **27.** $-5 + 8$ **28.** $3 - (-5)$ **29.** $8 + (-2)$

Checkpoint Quiz 1 — Lessons 5-1 through 5-3

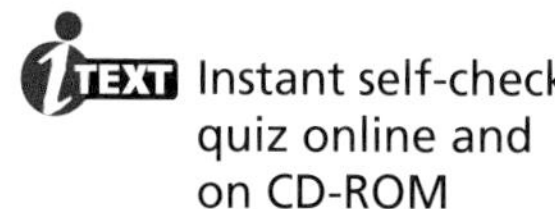

Instant self-check quiz online and on CD-ROM

1. Write the ratio 7:52 in two other ways.

Write each ratio in simplest form.

2. $\frac{4}{6}$ **3.** $\frac{16}{48}$ **4.** 24 to 14 **5.** 18:27

Write a unit rate for each situation.

6. type 126 words in 3 min **7.** score 45 points in 5 games

Find each unit price. Then determine the better buy.

8. 3 for $.79, 4 for $.99 **9.** 5 for $39, 7 for $46

10. The last time you bought pizza, 3 pizzas were just enough for 7 people. At this rate, how many pizzas should you buy for a party for 33 people?

5-4 Proportions

What You'll Learn

 To test if ratios can form a proportion

 To use cross products

. . . And Why

To compare answers to a survey, as in Example 1

Check Skills You'll Need

For help, go to Lesson 3-6.

Compare. Use <, >, or =.

1. $\frac{3}{4}$ ■ $\frac{5}{8}$ **2.** $\frac{3}{7}$ ■ $\frac{12}{28}$ **3.** $\frac{2}{3}$ ■ $\frac{11}{15}$

4. $\frac{1}{6}$ ■ $\frac{1}{12}$ **5.** $\frac{4}{11}$ ■ $\frac{4}{9}$ **6.** $\frac{7}{10}$ ■ $\frac{42}{60}$

New Vocabulary • proportion • cross products

OBJECTIVE

TEXT Interactive lesson includes instant self-check, tutorials, and activities.

1 Testing Ratios

You know that the ratios $\frac{6}{8}$ and $\frac{9}{12}$ are equal, since each ratio simplifies to $\frac{3}{4}$. You can write the equation $\frac{6}{8} = \frac{9}{12}$.

Key Concepts — Proportion

A **proportion** is an equation stating that two ratios are equal.

Arithmetic	Algebra
$\frac{6}{8} = \frac{9}{12}$	$\frac{a}{b} = \frac{c}{d}, b \neq 0, d \neq 0$

You can test a pair of ratios to determine whether they can form a proportion. One method of testing ratios is to write both ratios in simplest form and see if they are equal.

1 EXAMPLE Writing Ratios in Simplest Form

Did You See a Movie This Weekend?

Class	Yes	Total Number
A	10	24
B	25	60

Surveys For each class, look at the ratio of the number of students who saw a movie to the total number of students. Can the ratios form a proportion?

Class A: $\frac{10}{24} = \frac{10 \div 2}{24 \div 2} = \frac{5}{12}$ ← **Divide 10 and 24 by their GCF, which is 2.**

Class B: $\frac{25}{60} = \frac{25 \div 5}{60 \div 5} = \frac{5}{12}$ ← **Divide 25 and 60 by their GCF, which is 5.**

Since both ratios are equal to $\frac{5}{12}$, the ratios are proportional.

1 Determine whether the ratios in each pair can form a proportion.

a. $\frac{12}{18}, \frac{50}{75}$ **b.** $\frac{10}{12}, \frac{40}{56}$ **c.** $\frac{3}{5}, \frac{39}{65}$

Another way to show that two ratios can form a proportion is to show that a common multiplier connects their numerators and denominators.

2 EXAMPLE Finding a Common Multiplier

Determine whether the ratios in each pair can form a proportion by finding a common multiplier.

a. $\frac{4}{5}$ and $\frac{32}{40}$

$$\frac{4}{5} \stackrel{?}{=} \frac{32}{40} \quad (\times 8 \text{ numerators}, \times 8 \text{ denominators})$$

$\frac{4}{5}$ and $\frac{32}{40}$ can form a proportion.

b. $\frac{7}{21}$ and $\frac{28}{63}$

$$\frac{7}{21} \stackrel{?}{=} \frac{28}{63} \quad (\times 4 \text{ numerators}, \times 3 \text{ denominators})$$

$\frac{7}{21}$ and $\frac{28}{63}$ *cannot* form a proportion.

Check Understanding 2 Determine whether the ratios in each pair can form a proportion by finding a common multiplier.

a. $\frac{3}{11}, \frac{15}{55}$ **b.** $\frac{1}{2}, \frac{4}{10}$ **c.** $\frac{15}{60}, \frac{75}{300}$

d. **Reasoning** Show that the ratios in part (c) are equal by writing them in simplest form.

OBJECTIVE

2 Using Cross Products

You can use the properties of equality to discover another way to determine whether ratios can form a proportion.

$\frac{6}{8} = \frac{9}{12}$ ← **Use the ratios from the beginning of the lesson.**

$\frac{6}{8}\left(\frac{8}{1} \cdot \frac{12}{1}\right) = \frac{9}{12}\left(\frac{8}{1} \cdot \frac{12}{1}\right)$ ← **Use the Multiplication Property of Equality. Multiply each side by both denominators.**

$\frac{6}{{}_1\cancel{8}}\left(\frac{\cancel{8}^1}{1} \cdot \frac{12}{1}\right) = \frac{9}{{}_1\cancel{12}}\left(\frac{8}{1} \cdot \frac{\cancel{12}^1}{1}\right)$ ← **Divide numerators and denominators by their GCF.**

$6 \cdot 12 = 9 \cdot 8$

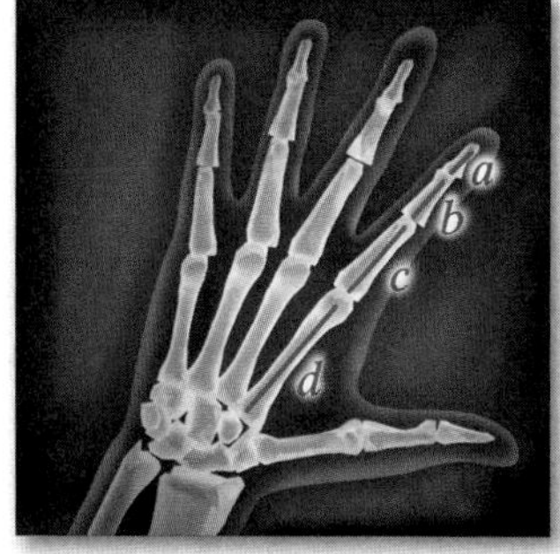

Real-World Connection

The lengths of the bones in your hand form a proportion.

SOURCE: *Fascinating Fibonaccis*

The products $6 \cdot 12$ and $9 \cdot 8$ are called cross products. For two ratios, the **cross products** are found by multiplying the denominator of one ratio by the numerator of the other ratio.

$6 \cdot 12$ 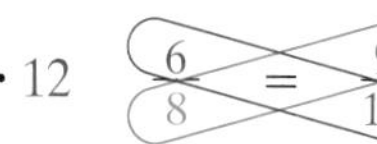 $8 \cdot 9$

Key Concepts **Cross-Products Property**

If two ratios form a proportion, the cross products are equal. If two ratios have equal cross products, they form a proportion.

Arithmetic	Algebra
$\frac{6}{8} = \frac{9}{12}$	$\frac{a}{b} = \frac{c}{d}$
$6 \cdot 12 = 8 \cdot 9$	$ad = bc$, where $b \neq 0$ and $d \neq 0$

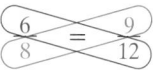

You can use the Cross-Products Property to determine whether ratios form a proportion.

3 EXAMPLE Using Cross Products

Do the ratios in each pair form a proportion?

a. $\frac{5}{9}, \frac{30}{54}$

$\frac{5}{9} \stackrel{?}{=} \frac{30}{54}$ ← Test each pair of ratios.

$5 \cdot 54 \stackrel{?}{=} 9 \cdot 30$ ← Write cross products.

$270 = 270$ ← Simplify.

Yes, $\frac{5}{9}$ and $\frac{30}{54}$ form a proportion.

b. $\frac{7}{8}, \frac{55}{65}$

$\frac{7}{8} \stackrel{?}{=} \frac{55}{65}$ ← Test each pair of ratios.

$7 \cdot 65 \stackrel{?}{=} 8 \cdot 55$ ← Write cross products.

$455 \neq 440$ ← Simplify.

No, $\frac{7}{8}$ and $\frac{55}{65}$ do *not* form a proportion.

3 Determine whether the ratios in each pair can form a proportion by using cross products.

a. $\frac{3}{8}, \frac{6}{16}$ **b.** $\frac{6}{9}, \frac{4}{6}$ **c.** $\frac{4}{8}, \frac{5}{9}$

EXERCISES

For more practice, see *Extra Practice*.

Example 1 (page 256)

Determine whether the ratios in each pair can form a proportion by writing each ratio in simplest form. Exercise 1 has been started for you.

1. $\frac{1}{2}, \frac{14}{28}$ **2.** $\frac{6}{8}, \frac{4}{3}$ **3.** $\frac{8}{18}, \frac{20}{45}$ **4.** $\frac{21}{24}, \frac{56}{64}$

$\frac{14}{28} = \frac{\cancel{14}^{1}}{_{2}\cancel{28}}$

5. $\frac{15}{45}, \frac{3}{15}$ **6.** $\frac{45}{9}, \frac{10}{2}$ **7.** $\frac{19}{76}, \frac{5}{20}$ **8.** $\frac{17}{34}, \frac{2}{3}$

Example 2 (page 257)

Determine whether the ratios in each pair can form a proportion by finding a common multiplier.

9. $\frac{2}{8}, \frac{18}{72}$ **10.** $\frac{5}{2}, \frac{65}{26}$ **11.** $\frac{40}{12}, \frac{160}{3}$ **12.** $\frac{7}{9}, \frac{35}{45}$

13. $\frac{11}{20}, \frac{3}{5}$ **14.** $\frac{45}{60}, \frac{3}{4}$ **15.** $\frac{16}{9}, \frac{96}{54}$ **16.** $\frac{3}{10}, \frac{15}{25}$

Example 3 (page 258)

Determine whether the ratios in each pair can form a proportion by using cross products.

17. $\frac{6}{10}, \frac{9}{15}$ **18.** $\frac{4}{5}, \frac{10}{13}$ **19.** $\frac{7}{8}, \frac{15}{24}$ **20.** $\frac{6}{14}, \frac{3}{7}$

21. $\frac{7}{22}, \frac{28}{77}$ **22.** $\frac{12}{15}, \frac{20}{25}$ **23.** $\frac{6}{10}, \frac{24}{42}$ **24.** $\frac{5}{9}, \frac{15}{27}$

B Apply Your Skills

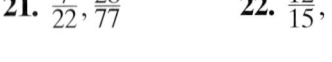

25. Decorating A certain shade of green paint requires 4 parts blue to 5 parts yellow. If you mix 16 quarts of blue paint with 25 quarts of yellow paint, will you get the desired shade of green? Explain.

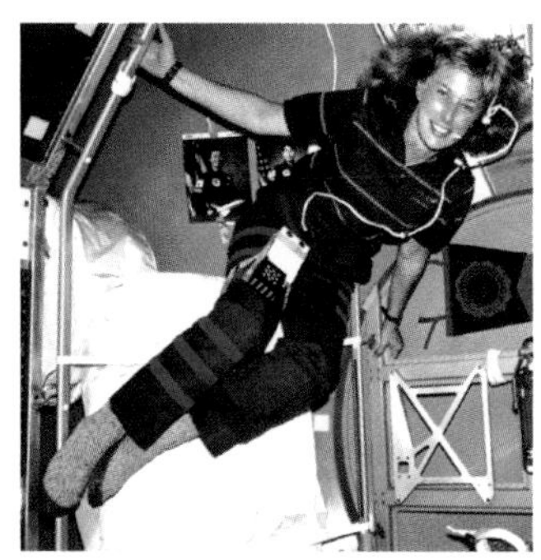

Real-World Connection

Astronauts conduct experiments while they are weightless.

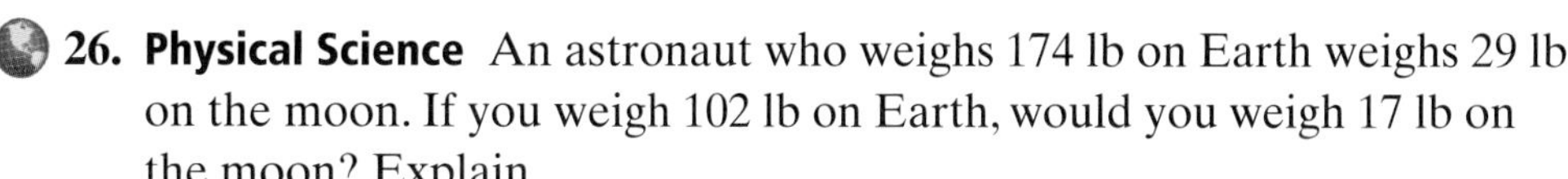

26. **Physical Science** An astronaut who weighs 174 lb on Earth weighs 29 lb on the moon. If you weigh 102 lb on Earth, would you weigh 17 lb on the moon? Explain.

Determine whether the ratios in each pair form a proportion.

27. $\frac{56}{2}, \frac{110}{3}$ 28. $\frac{18}{12}, \frac{4.8}{3.6}$ 29. $\frac{20}{1.5}, \frac{60}{4.5}$ 30. $\frac{3.5}{35}, \frac{2.04}{204}$

Geometry **Show that the ratio of b to h is the same in each pair of figures.**

31. 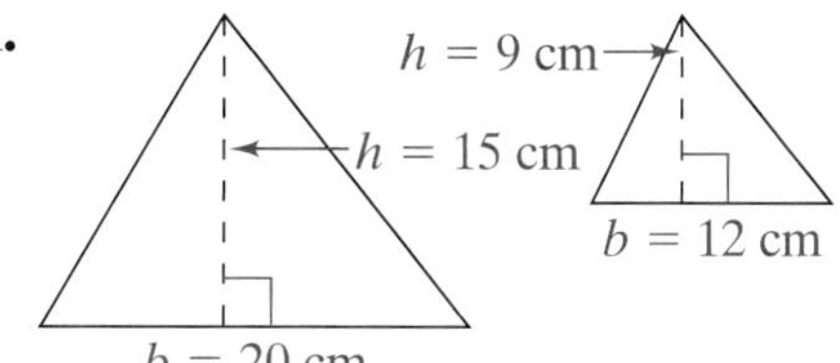

32. 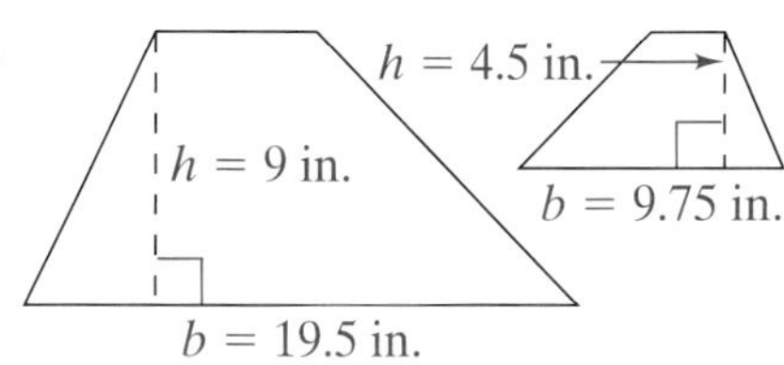

Challenge

33. Do $\frac{\text{length of side } s \text{ of square } ABCD}{\text{perimeter of square } ABCD}$ and $\frac{\text{length of side } x \text{ of square } EFGH}{\text{perimeter of square } EFGH}$ *always*, *sometimes*, or *never* form a proportion? Explain.

34. **Writing in Math** Explain why $\frac{a}{b}$ and $\frac{a+b}{b}$ can *never* form a proportion.

35. **Stretch Your Thinking** If it takes you one minute to cut one board, how long will it take you to cut a 10-ft board into 10 equal pieces?

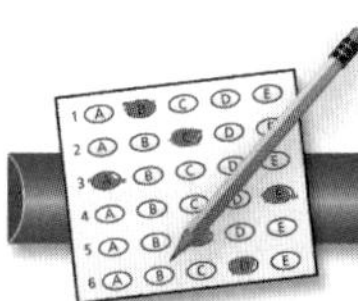

Test Prep

Multiple Choice

36. Which ratio can form a proportion with $\frac{3}{4}$?

A. $\frac{4}{3}$ B. $\frac{18}{20}$ C. $\frac{1}{2}$ D. $\frac{21}{28}$

37. Which ratio CANNOT form a proportion with $\frac{5}{8}$?

F. $\frac{20}{32}$ G. $\frac{100}{160}$ H. $\frac{45}{56}$ I. $\frac{10}{16}$

Take It to the NET
Online lesson quiz at
www.PHSchool.com
Web Code: aba-0504

38. Which ratio is NOT in simplest form?

A. $\frac{2}{5}$ B. $\frac{2}{7}$ C. $\frac{3}{7}$ D. $\frac{3}{9}$

Short Response

39. Explain in words how to determine whether $\frac{15}{25}$ and $\frac{3}{4}$ can form a proportion.

Mixed Review

Lesson 2-3

Algebra **Solve each equation.**

40. $y - 3 = 6$ 41. $m + 5 = 3$ 42. $b + 7 = 10$

Lesson 1-10

Find the mean and median of each set of data.

43. 14, 20, 5, 17, 15, 16, 17, 18 44. 8.2, 15.9, 7.25, 9.5, 10.4

Algebra

5-5 Solving Proportions

What You'll Learn

To use unit rates to solve proportions

To solve proportions involving variables

. . . And Why

To calculate a cost, as in Example 1

✓ Check Skills You'll Need

For help, go to Lesson 5-2.

Write the unit rate for each situation.

1. 192 km in 24 d
2. 240 ft in 15 s
3. 248 mi in 4 h
4. 50 push-ups in 2 min
5. 180 words in 3 min
6. 45 examples in 15 min
7. Draw a model to represent the unit rate for 100 calls in 5 h.

 Interactive lesson includes instant self-check, tutorials, and activities.

OBJECTIVE 1

Solving Proportions Using Unit Rates

Reading Math

Sometimes mi/gal is written as mpg.

Suppose you know that your car gets 29 mi/gal and you have 10 gal of gas. You estimate that you can go $29 \cdot 10$, or 290, miles before you run out of gas. You are using a unit rate and multiplying.

You can use unit rates to solve a proportion. First find the unit rate. Then multiply to solve the problem.

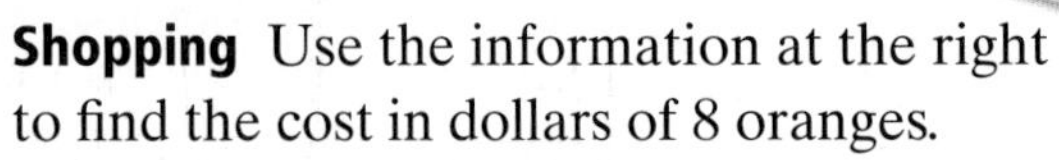

1 EXAMPLE Using Unit Rates

6 for $2.34

Shopping Use the information at the right to find the cost in dollars of 8 oranges.

Solve the proportion $\frac{2.34 \text{ dollars}}{6 \text{ oranges}} = \frac{x \text{ dollars}}{8 \text{ oranges}}$.

Step 1 Find the unit price.

$\frac{2.34 \text{ dollars}}{6 \text{ oranges}}$

$\$2.34 \div 6$ oranges ← **Divide to find the unit price.**

$.39/orange

Step 2 You know the cost of one orange. Multiply to find the cost of 8 oranges.

$\$.39 \cdot 8 = \$3.12$ ← **Multiply the unit rate by the number of oranges.**

The cost of 8 oranges is $3.12.

✓ Check Understanding 1

a. Postcards cost $2.45 for 5 cards. How much will 13 cards cost?

b. Swimming goggles cost $84.36 for a case of 12. At this rate, how much will it cost to get new goggles for 17 members of a swim team?

OBJECTIVE

2 Solving Proportions Involving Variables

You can use mental math to solve some proportions. When a proportion involves a variable, you solve the proportion by finding the value of the variable.

2 EXAMPLE Solving Using Mental Math (Algebra)

Solve each proportion using mental math.

a. $\frac{z}{12} = \frac{21}{36}$

$\frac{z}{12} = \frac{21}{36}$ (×3 on numerator and denominator) ← Since 12 × 3 = 36, find what number times 3 equals 21.

$z = 7$ ← Use mental math.

b. $\frac{8}{10} = \frac{n}{40}$

$\frac{8}{10} = \frac{n}{40}$ (×4 on numerator and denominator) ← Since 10 × 4 = 40, 8 × 4 = *n*.

$n = 32$ ← Use mental math.

Check Understanding 2 Solve each proportion using mental math.

a. $\frac{3}{8} = \frac{b}{24}$ **b.** $\frac{m}{5} = \frac{16}{40}$ **c.** $\frac{15}{30} = \frac{5}{p}$

d. **Reasoning** Why does a common factor make it easy to use mental math to solve proportions?

Many proportions cannot easily be solved with mental math. In these situations, you can use cross products to solve a proportion.

3 EXAMPLE Solving Using Cross Products (Algebra)

Solve $\frac{25}{38} = \frac{15}{x}$ using cross products.

$\frac{25}{38} = \frac{15}{x}$

$25x = 38(15)$ ← Write the cross products.

$25x = 570$ ← Simplify.

$\frac{25x}{25} = \frac{570}{25}$ ← Divide each side by 25.

$x = 22.8$ ← Simplify.

Check Understanding 3 Solve each proportion using cross products.

a. $\frac{12}{15} = \frac{x}{20}$ **b.** $\frac{16}{34} = \frac{d}{51}$ **c.** $\frac{22}{36} = \frac{110}{m}$

d. **Number Sense** Does the proportion $\frac{38}{25} = \frac{x}{15}$ have the same solution as the proportion in Example 3? Explain.

More Than One Way

Nature An oyster bed covers 36 m^2. Your class studies 4 m^2 of the oyster bed. In those 4 m^2, you count 96 oysters. Predict the number of oysters in the entire bed.

Carlos's Method

I will let x represent the number of oysters in the 36 m^2 bed.

$$\begin{matrix}\text{oysters} \rightarrow \\ \text{area} \rightarrow\end{matrix} \frac{96}{4} = \frac{x}{36} \begin{matrix}\leftarrow \text{oysters} \\ \leftarrow \text{area}\end{matrix} \quad \leftarrow \text{Write a proportion.}$$

$$96(36) = 4x \quad \leftarrow \text{Write the cross products.}$$

$$3{,}456 = 4x \quad \leftarrow \text{Simplify.}$$

$$\frac{3{,}456}{4} = \frac{4x}{4} \quad \leftarrow \text{Divide each side by 4.}$$

$$864 = x \quad \leftarrow \text{Simplify.}$$

There are about 864 oysters in the oyster bed.

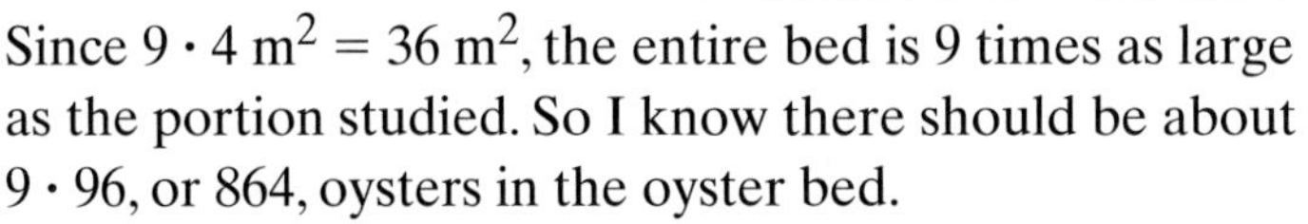

Brianna's Method

Since $9 \cdot 4\ m^2 = 36\ m^2$, the entire bed is 9 times as large as the portion studied. So I know there should be about $9 \cdot 96$, or 864, oysters in the oyster bed.

Choose a Method

You buy a bag of 400 marbles. In a handful of 20 marbles, you find 8 red marbles. About how many red marbles are in the bag? Explain why you chose the method you used.

EXERCISES

For more practice, see *Extra Practice*.

A Practice by Example

Example 1 (page 260)

Solve each problem by finding a unit rate and multiplying. Exercise 1 has been started for you.

1. If 5 fish cost \$6.45, what is the cost of 8 fish? $\frac{\$6.45}{5 \text{ fish}} = \$1.29/\text{fish}$
2. If 12 roses cost \$18.96, what is the cost of 5 roses?
3. If 3 onions weigh 0.75 lb, how much do 10 onions weigh?
4. If 13 key chains cost \$38.35, what is the cost of 20 key chains?
5. At a telethon, a volunteer can take 48 calls over a 4-hour shift. At this rate, how many calls can 12 volunteers take in a 4-hour shift?
6. **Small Business** You are selling packs of 12 pens for \$3.48. At this rate, how much should you charge for a pack of 20 pens?

Example 2
(page 261)

Solve each proportion using mental math.

7. $\frac{2}{7} = \frac{x}{21}$ **8.** $\frac{18}{32} = \frac{m}{16}$ **9.** $\frac{c}{10} = \frac{36}{60}$

10. $\frac{y}{13} = \frac{12}{39}$ **11.** $\frac{16}{38} = \frac{b}{19}$ **12.** $\frac{9}{w} = \frac{36}{20}$

13. $\frac{c}{35} = \frac{4}{7}$ **14.** $\frac{33}{55} = \frac{3}{n}$ **15.** $\frac{5}{p} = \frac{20}{24}$

Example 3
(page 261)

Solve each proportion using cross products.

16. $\frac{8}{12} = \frac{y}{30}$ **17.** $\frac{15}{33} = \frac{m}{22}$ **18.** $\frac{c}{28} = \frac{49}{16}$

19. $\frac{y}{18} = \frac{21}{63}$ **20.** $\frac{14}{34} = \frac{x}{51}$ **21.** $\frac{9}{30} = \frac{p}{16}$

22. $\frac{20}{w} = \frac{12}{3}$ **23.** $\frac{27}{20} = \frac{36}{v}$ **24.** $\frac{19}{r} = \frac{152}{4}$

B Apply Your Skills

25. There are 385 mosquitoes in 11 ft^3. Predict the number in 15 ft^3.

26. There are 144 tulips in 8 m^2. Predict the number in 25 m^2.

27. There are 240 ants in 5 ft^2. Predict the number in 13 ft^2.

28. There are 56 geese in 50 ft^2. Predict the number in 120 ft^2.

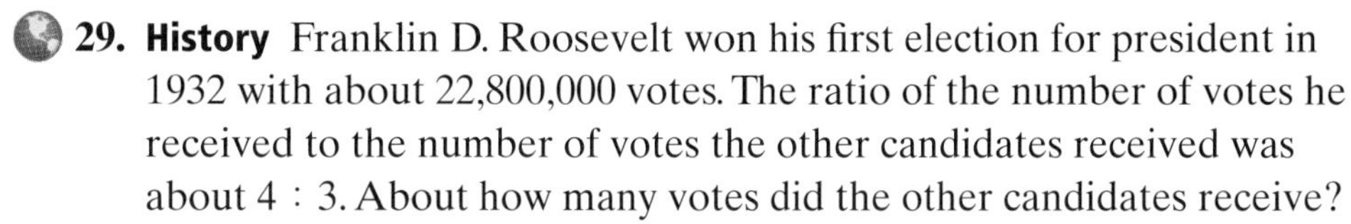

29. History Franklin D. Roosevelt won his first election for president in 1932 with about 22,800,000 votes. The ratio of the number of votes he received to the number of votes the other candidates received was about 4 : 3. About how many votes did the other candidates receive?

30. Reasoning How do the unit prices posted in a grocery store make it easy to solve a proportion problem?

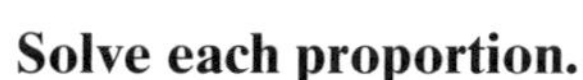

Solve each proportion.

31. $\frac{240 \text{ mi}}{15 \text{ gal}} = \frac{x \text{ mi}}{28 \text{ gal}}$ **32.** $\frac{30 \text{ ft}}{8 \text{ seconds}} = \frac{165 \text{ ft}}{t \text{ seconds}}$

33. $\frac{\$4.68}{16 \text{ in.}} = \frac{\$1.17}{m \text{ in.}}$ **34.** $\frac{8 \text{ cups}}{6 \text{ teaspoons}} = \frac{n \text{ cups}}{18 \text{ teaspoons}}$

35. $\frac{d \text{ mi}}{3 \text{ h}} = \frac{48 \text{ mi}}{9 \text{ h}}$ **36.** $\frac{\$3.06}{k \text{ oz}} = \frac{\$5.10}{64 \text{ oz}}$

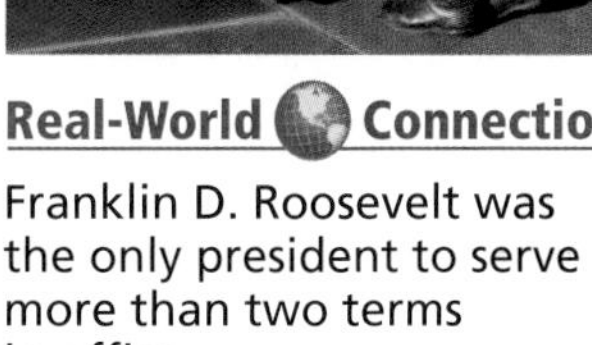

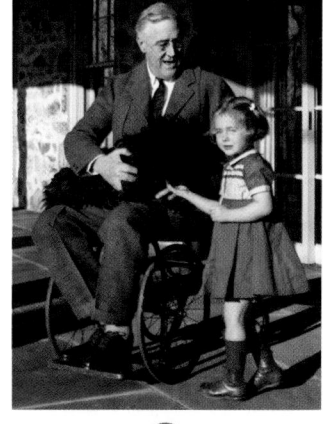

Real-World Connection

Franklin D. Roosevelt was the only president to serve more than two terms in office.

37. Travel A commercial jet takes $4\frac{3}{4}$ hours to fly 2,475 mi from New York City to Los Angeles. About how many hours will it take a jet flying at the same average rate to fly 5,470 mi from Los Angeles to Tokyo? Round to the nearest quarter of an hour.

38. Error Analysis A videocassette recorder uses 2 m of tape in 3 min when set on extended play. To determine how many minutes a tape that is 240 m long can record on extended play, one student wrote the proportion $\frac{2}{3} = \frac{n}{240}$. Explain why this proportion is incorrect. Then write a correct proportion.

Writing in Math

For help with writing to compare, as in Exercise 39, see p. 266.

39. Writing in Math You estimate that it will take you 75 min to bike 15 mi to a state park. After 30 min, you have traveled 5 mi. Compare your actual rate to your estimate. At your current rate, will you arrive sooner or later than your estimate? Explain.

Solve each proportion using cross products. Round to the nearest tenth, if necessary.

40. $\frac{1.7}{2.5} = \frac{3.4}{d}$ **41.** $\frac{y}{9.3} = \frac{12.6}{5.4}$ **42.** $\frac{33.1}{x} = \frac{6.2}{1.3}$ **43.** $\frac{16.9}{13.5} = \frac{t}{7.4}$

44. $\frac{r}{18.5} = \frac{6.2}{9.7}$ **45.** $\frac{1.5}{0.2} = \frac{w}{6.9}$ **46.** $\frac{12.3}{24.4} = \frac{6.1}{a}$ **47.** $\frac{5.8}{c} = \frac{17.2}{23.4}$

48. Wages Your friend receives \$57.04 for working 8 h.
 a. Find her hourly wage.
 b. How much does she receive for working 7 h?

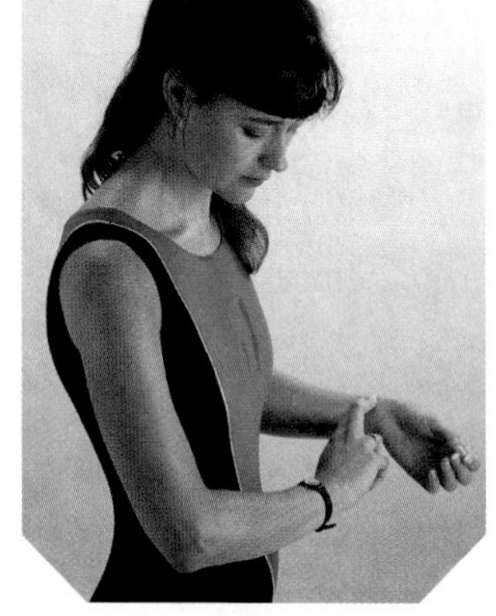

Real-World Connection

Your pulse tells you how hard your heart is working.

49. Health To find your pulse rate (number of heartbeats per minute), you place your index finger and middle finger of one hand over the underside of your opposite wrist. When you find a pulse, count the number of beats in 15 seconds and use a proportion.
 a. What is your pulse rate if you count 18 beats in 15 seconds?
 b. How many beats do you count in 15 seconds if your pulse rate is 96 beats/min?
 c. Reasoning Explain why this method of finding your pulse rate is only an estimate of your actual pulse rate.

50. A recipe for fruit salad serves 4 people. It calls for 2 oranges and 16 grapes. You want to serve 10 people. How many oranges and how many grapes will you need?

51. There are 450 students and 15 teachers in a school. The school hires 2 new teachers. To keep the student-to-teacher ratio the same, how many total students should attend the school?

52. a. **Data File, p. 239** Find the ten-year interval with the greatest difference in number of households.
 b. Find the difference in the population over this interval.

C Challenge

Algebra **Solve each proportion for *x*.**

53. $\frac{a}{x} = \frac{b}{c}$ **54.** $\frac{1}{4} = \frac{6}{x+1}$ **55.** $\frac{3}{\frac{1}{2}} = \frac{x}{7}$

56. Stretch Your Thinking There are fewer sixth-grade students than seventh-grade students in the Rice School. The ninth grade has more students than either the eighth grade or the seventh grade. The number of students in the fifth grade is less than the number in the sixth grade. Which grade has the most students?

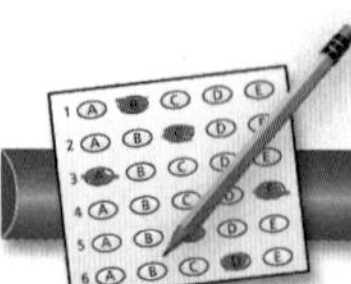

Test Prep

Gridded Response

57. What is the value of x in the proportion $\frac{5}{x} = \frac{15}{39}$?

58. Business partners A and B split their profits by a ratio of 3 : 2. If partner A receives \$27,000, how many dollars does partner B receive?

59. Mixing 3 oz of vinegar with 16 oz of water makes a cleaning solution. To make the same solution, how many ounces of vinegar should you mix with 128 oz of water?

60. The ratio of the width of a rectangle to its length is 5 : 8. What is the width in feet if the length is 12 ft?

Online lesson quiz at **www.PHSchool.com**
Web Code: aba-0505

61. You get paid \$9.50 for working 3 h. If you get paid at the same rate, how many dollars do you get paid for working 8 h?

62. You ran $4\frac{1}{8}$ mi at track practice one day and $3\frac{3}{4}$ mi the next day. Write the number of miles you ran in those two days as an improper fraction.

Mixed Review

Lesson 5-4 **Determine whether the ratios in each pair form a proportion.**

63. $\frac{4}{9}, \frac{24}{36}$ **64.** $\frac{25}{45}, \frac{55}{99}$ **65.** $\frac{18}{63}, \frac{26}{91}$

66. $\frac{28}{84}, \frac{30}{75}$ **67.** $\frac{18}{22}, \frac{27}{33}$ **68.** $\frac{3}{7}, \frac{123}{289}$

Lesson 5-1 **Write each ratio in two other ways.**

69. 17 to 9 **70.** 3 : 15 **71.** $\frac{16}{7}$

72. $\frac{29}{2}$ **73.** 25 to 33 **74.** 4 : 9

Lesson 1-6 **Order the numbers from least to greatest.**

75. $16, -12, 10, -3$ **76.** $-6, -3, 8, -2, 1$ **77.** $5, 0, -1, 2, -5$

78. $-8, 4, -10, 1, 0$ **79.** $2, 7, -1, -5, 3$ **80.** $8, -4, -1, -6, 5$

Math at Work

Amusement Park Designers

Amusement park designers consider the architecture and technology of the rides, the landscape of the park, the lighting, and the sound.

A designer wants to create safe, exciting rides and interesting, fun parks. To do this, designers use models similar to the attractions that they plan to build as they design the park.

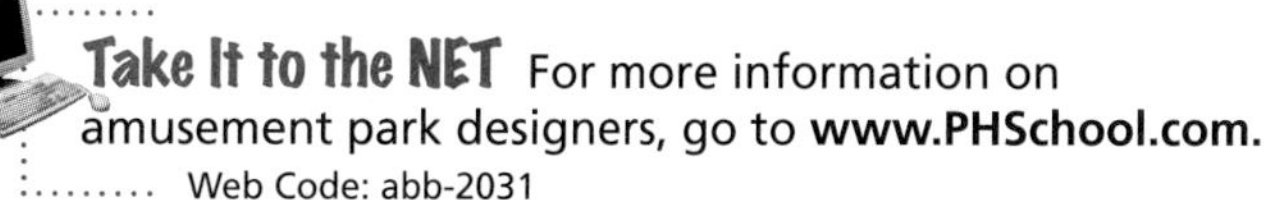

For more information on amusement park designers, go to **www.PHSchool.com.**
Web Code: abb-2031

Writing to Compare

For Use With Exercise 39, page 263

Sometimes you are asked to compare two or more quantities, methods, or concepts. When you are writing to compare two quantities, it is important to make sure that the quantities are similar.

On page 263, you will find the following exercise:

39. **Writing in Math** You estimate that it will take you 75 min to bike 15 mi to a state park. After 30 min, you have traveled 5 mi. Compare your actual rate to your estimate. At your current rate, will you arrive sooner or later than your estimate? Explain.

Here is one student's response.

My actual speed was $\frac{5 \text{ mi}}{30 \text{ min}}$, while my estimated speed was $\frac{15 \text{ mi}}{75 \text{ min}}$. Since the rates have different denominators, I cannot compare the numerators directly. I can set up a proportion to get a common denominator.

$$\frac{5 \text{ mi}}{30 \text{ min}} = \frac{x \text{ mi}}{75 \text{ min}}$$
$$30x = 5 \cdot 75$$
$$30x = 375$$
$$\frac{30x}{30} = \frac{375}{30}$$
$$x = 12.5$$

So, my actual speed is $\frac{12.5 \text{ mi}}{75 \text{ min}}$, which is less than the estimate. Since my actual speed is less than my estimated speed, I will arrive later than estimated.

EXERCISES

1. A 32-oz jar of jam costs \$1.99. An 18-oz jar of the same brand costs \$1.44. Compare the prices and determine which is the better buy. Explain your reasoning.

2. A cheetah can run at a top speed of about 100 km/h. The world record in the 100-m dash is 9.79 seconds. Use the data to compare the top speeds of cheetahs and humans.

3. In 1921 in Silver Lake, Colorado, $6\frac{1}{3}$ ft of snow fell in 24 h. In 1969 in Bessans, France, 68 in. of snow fell in 19 h. Compare the two snowfalls. Which was more intense? Explain.

5-6 Using Similar Figures

What You'll Learn

To identify similar figures

To find missing lengths in similar figures

. . . And Why

To measure distances indirectly, as in Example 3

Check Skills You'll Need

For help, go to Lesson 5-5.

Solve each proportion.

1. $\frac{x}{4} = \frac{12}{8}$ **2.** $\frac{n}{9} = \frac{10}{15}$ **3.** $\frac{a}{2} = \frac{36}{9}$

4. $\frac{4}{b} = \frac{16}{48}$ **5.** $\frac{84}{14} = \frac{g}{12}$ **6.** $\frac{38}{3} = \frac{19}{m}$

New Vocabulary

- polygon
- similar polygons
- indirect measurement

Interactive lesson includes instant self-check, tutorials, and activities.

OBJECTIVE 1

Identifying Similar Figures

Investigation: Exploring Similar Figures

1. Which pairs of figures have exactly the same shape but not necessarily the same size?

A.

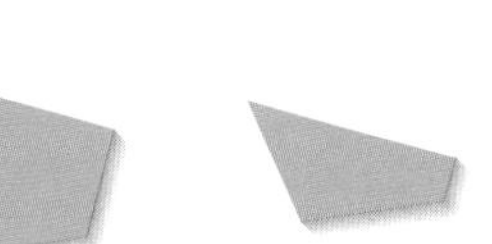

B.

C.

D.

2. What is true about the angles of the figures with the same shape?

When two figures have the same shape, but not necessarily the same size, they are *similar*. In the similar triangles below, corresponding angles have the same measure. Since $\frac{40}{60} = \frac{50}{75} = \frac{34}{51}$, the corresponding sides are proportional. You write $\triangle ABC \sim \triangle FGH$, where the symbol $\sim$ means "is similar to."

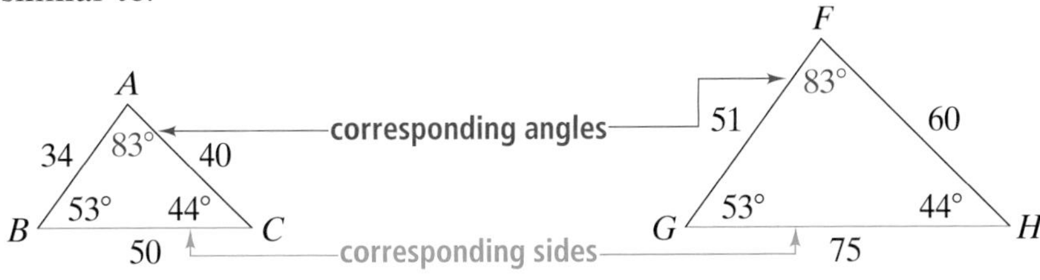

A **polygon** is a closed plane figure formed by three or more line segments that do not cross.

Key Concepts **Similar Polygons**

Two polygons are **similar polygons** if

- corresponding angles have the same measure, and
- the lengths of corresponding sides form equal ratios.

1 EXAMPLE Verifying That Figures Are Similar

Verify that the triangles are similar.

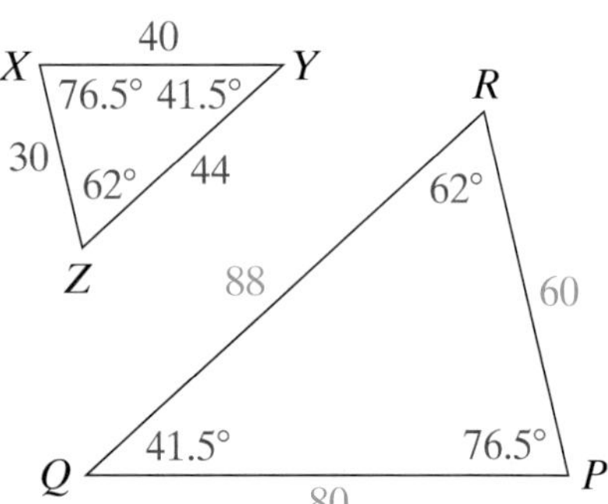

The measures of $\angle X$ and $\angle P$ are 76.5°.
The measures of $\angle Y$ and $\angle Q$ are 41.5°.
The measures of $\angle Z$ and $\angle R$ are 62°.
$\frac{40}{80} = \frac{1}{2}$, $\frac{44}{88} = \frac{1}{2}$, and $\frac{30}{60} = \frac{1}{2}$.

The measures of corresponding angles are equal. The lengths of corresponding sides form equal ratios. So $\triangle XYZ \sim \triangle PQR$.

Check Understanding 1 Are the trapezoids below similar? Explain.

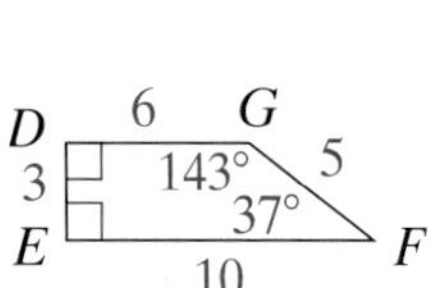

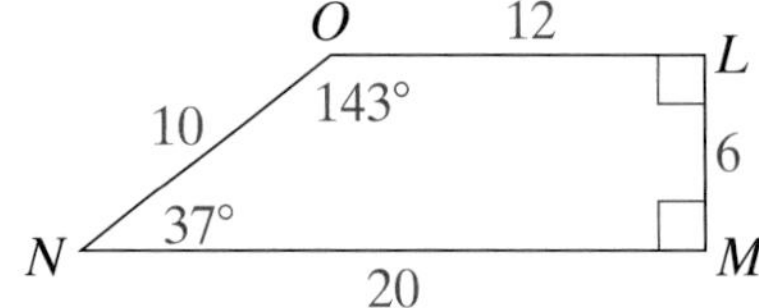

OBJECTIVE

2 Finding Missing Lengths

With similar figures, you can use proportions to find missing side lengths.

2 EXAMPLE Finding a Missing Measure Algebra

The two triangles at the right are similar. Find the value of x.

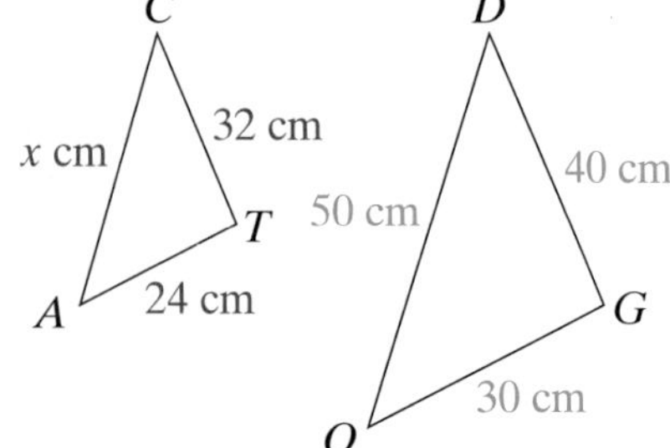

$\frac{x}{50} = \frac{24}{30}$ ← **Write a proportion.**

$30x = 50 \cdot 24$ ← **Write the cross products.**

$\frac{30x}{30} = \frac{1{,}200}{30}$ ← **Divide each side by 30.**

$x = 40$ ← **Solve for x.**

Check Understanding 2 **Reasoning** Find x in Example 2 using the ratio of the sides of lengths 32 cm and 40 cm. Explain why the answer should be the same.

You can use **indirect measurement** to measure distances that are difficult to measure directly. You can do this using proportions and similar triangles.

3 EXAMPLE **Real-World Problem Solving**

Indirect Measurement A 6-ft person standing near a flagpole has a shadow 4.5 ft long. The flagpole has a shadow 15 ft long. What is the height of the flagpole?

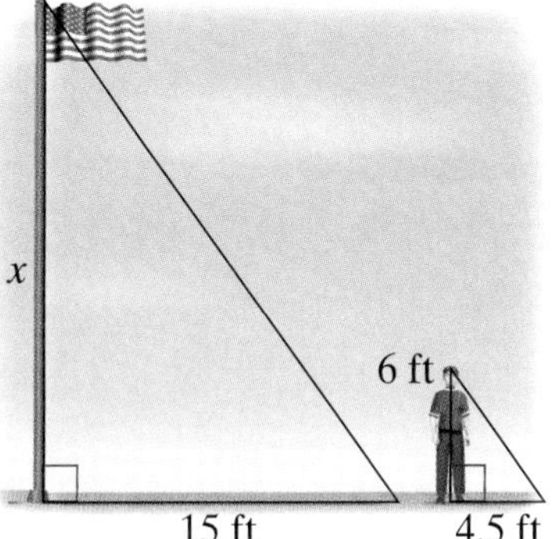

Draw a diagram like the one at the right. Let x represent the height of the flagpole.

$\frac{x}{6} = \frac{15}{4.5}$ ← **Write a proportion.**

$4.5x = 6 \cdot 15$ ← **Write the cross products.**

$\frac{4.5x}{4.5} = \frac{6 \cdot 15}{4.5}$ ← **Divide each side by 4.5.**

$x = 20$ ← **Simplify.**

The height of the flagpole is 20 ft.

Check Understanding 3 **a.** A 6-ft person has a shadow 5 ft long. A nearby tree has a shadow 30 ft long. What is the height of the tree?

b. A telephone pole has a 12-ft shadow. A nearby person is 5 ft tall and has a 3-ft shadow. How tall is the telephone pole?

EXERCISES

For more practice, see *Extra Practice.*

A Practice by Example

Example 1 (page 268)

Geometry **Determine whether each pair of figures is similar. Explain why or why not.**

1.

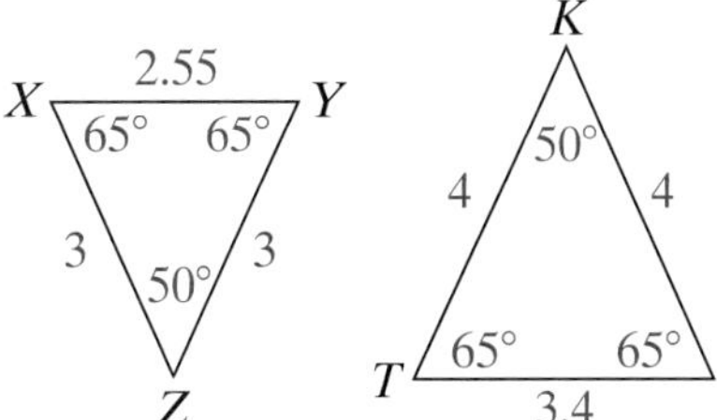

2.

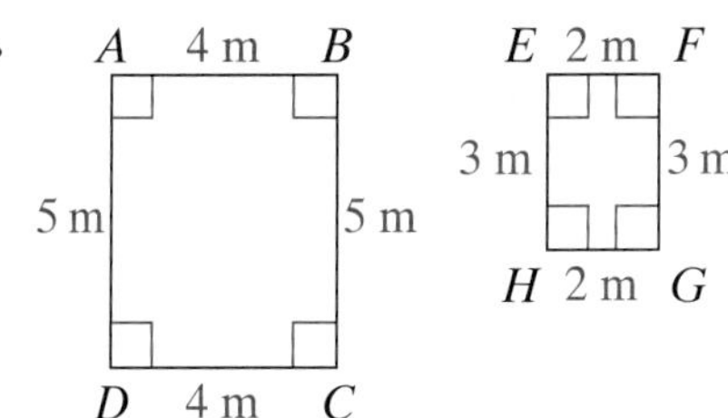

Example 2 (page 268)

Algebra **$\triangle ABC$ is similar to $\triangle PQR$. Find each measure.**

3. length of $\overline{AB}$

4. length of $\overline{RP}$

5. measure of $\angle A$

6. measure of $\angle Q$

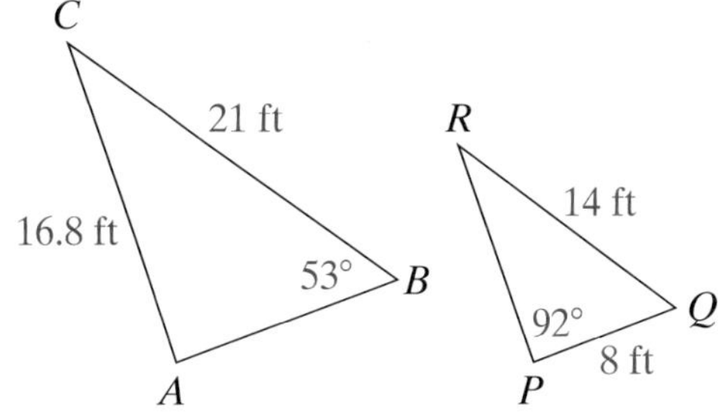

Example 3 (page 269)

7. **Indirect Measurement** A woman is 5 ft tall and her shadow is 4 ft long. A nearby tree has a shadow 30 ft long. How tall is the tree?

8. **Indirect Measurement** A man is standing near a totem pole. The man is 74 in. tall. His shadow is 4 ft long. The shadow of the totem pole is 6 ft long. How tall is the totem pole?

B Apply Your Skills

Geometry **Each pair of figures below is similar. Find the value of each variable.**

9. 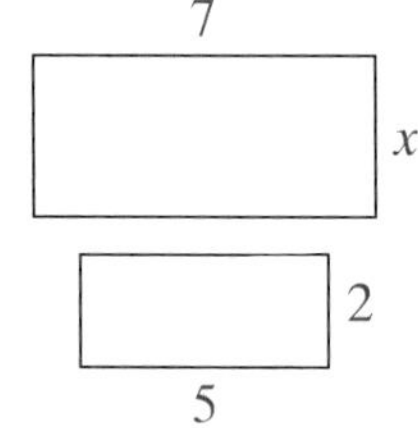

10. 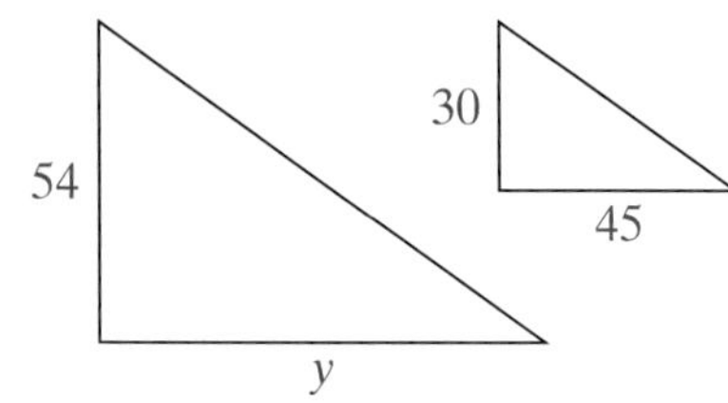

11. 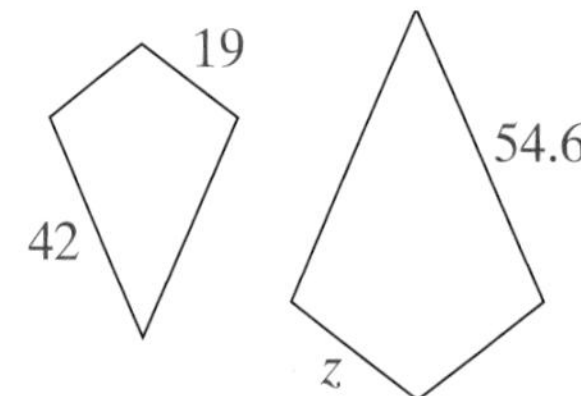

12. 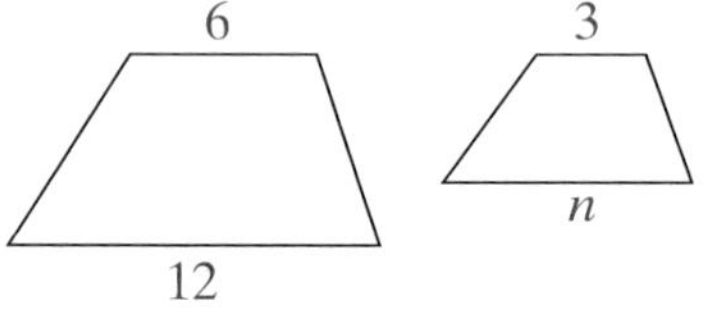

13. a. Reasoning In a pair of similar triangles, the ratio of the perimeters is equal to the ratio of a pair of corresponding sides. Explain why.
b. Is this true for any pair of similar figures? Explain.

14. Open-Ended Think of something that is difficult to measure directly. Explain how you would measure it indirectly.

15. **Surveying** Refer to the diagram at the right. Surveyors know that $\triangle PQR$ and $\triangle STR$ are similar. They want to determine the distance across the lake, but they cannot measure it directly.

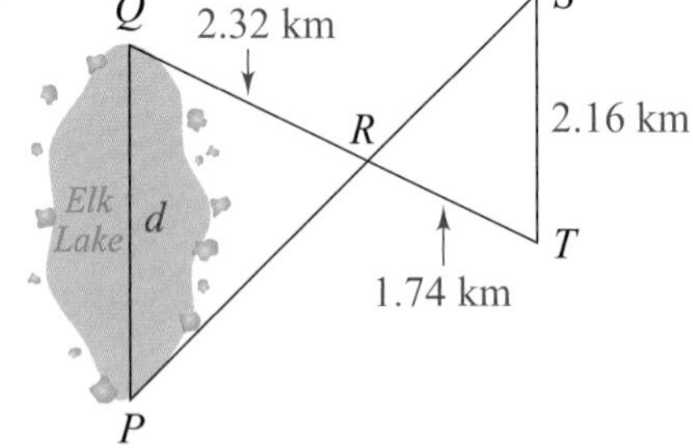

a. Write a proportion that relates the lengths of $\overline{PQ}$, $\overline{QR}$, $\overline{TR}$, and $\overline{ST}$.
b. Find d, the distance across the lake.
c. Reasoning If you know the lengths of $\overline{PR}$ and $\overline{SR}$ instead of $\overline{TR}$ and $\overline{QR}$, can you find d? Explain.
d. Reasoning If you know the length of $\overline{SR}$ instead of $\overline{TR}$, can you find d? Explain.

Real-World Connection

Careers Surveyors use similar figures to measure distances indirectly.

16. Writing in Math Give three examples of real-world objects that are similar. Explain why they are similar.

17. A rectangle with an area of 32 in.^{2} has one side measuring 4 in. A similar rectangle has an area of 288 in.^{2}. How long is the longer side in the larger rectangle?

18. **Flags** You want to enlarge a copy of the flag of the Philippines. The two flags will be similar. You want the longer side to measure 6 ft. How long should you make the shorter side?

$\triangle ABC \sim \triangle DEF$. The ratio of the lengths of corresponding sides is 2 : 5. The lengths of $\overline{AB}$, $\overline{DF}$, and $\overline{BC}$ are 6, 25, and 8, respectively. The measure of $\angle B$ is 90°. Find each measure.

19. $\overline{DE}$ 20. $\overline{AC}$ 21. $\overline{EF}$ 22. $\angle E$

23. The ratio of the corresponding sides of two similar triangles is 4 : 9. The sides of the smaller triangle are 10 cm, 16 cm, and 18 cm. Find the perimeter of the larger triangle.

For each ratio of a smaller triangle to a larger triangle in Exercises 24–27, find the perimeter of the larger if the sides of the smaller are 4, 9, and 11.

24. 2 : 3 25. 4 : 7 26. 6 : 11 27. 12 : 13

C Challenge

28. **Art** An artist has a painting that is 16 in. by 20 in. She wants a reproduction that is a similar rectangle 35 in. on its longer side.
   a. What is the length of the shorter side of the reproduction?
   b. The charge for the reproduction is $.60 per square inch. What is the total cost of the reproduction?

29. **Stretch Your Thinking** Two bricks have the same weight. The first brick is placed on one side of a scale. The second brick is cut into quarters. Three-fourths of the second brick and a $\frac{3}{4}$-lb weight are placed on the other side to balance the scale. How much does a whole brick weigh?

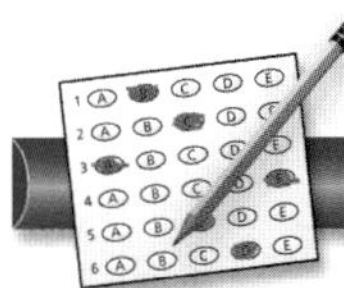

Test Prep

Multiple Choice

Use the diagram for Exercises 30–31. $\triangle LMN \sim \triangle TVU$.

30. Which of the following is NOT true?
   A. $\angle N$ corresponds to $\angle U$.
   B. $\angle V$ corresponds to $\angle L$.
   C. $\overline{LN}$ corresponds to $\overline{TU}$.
   D. $\overline{NM}$ corresponds to $\overline{UV}$.

T V U 12 m N 16 m 8 m L M

31. What is the length of $\overline{UT}$?
   F. 6 m G. 8 m H. 16 m I. 24 m

32. A 2.5-m stick casts a 3.2-m shadow. How tall is a nearby building that casts a shadow that is 19.2 m long?
   A. 12 m B. 15 m C. 25 m D. 38 m

33. What is the unit rate for walking 5 mi in 1 h 40 min?
   F. 0.04 mi/min G. 0.05 mi/min H. 0.4 mi/min I. 0.5 mi/min

Short Response

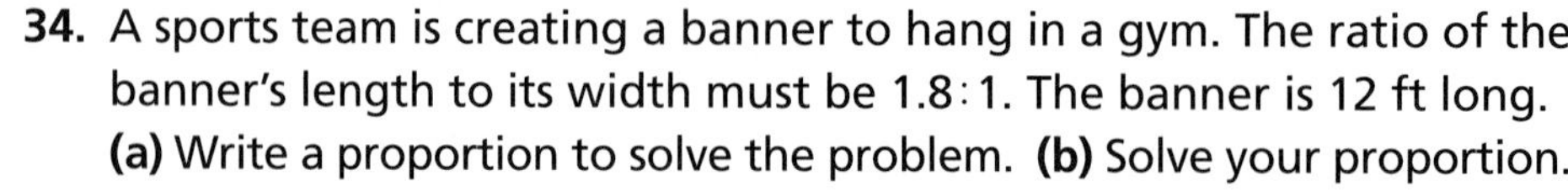

34. A sports team is creating a banner to hang in a gym. The ratio of the banner's length to its width must be 1.8 : 1. The banner is 12 ft long. **(a)** Write a proportion to solve the problem. **(b)** Solve your proportion.

Take It to the NET
Online lesson quiz at **www.PHSchool.com**
Web Code: aba-0506

35. You are making a chili recipe that calls for 56 oz of diced tomatoes and 2 large onions. You want to make as much chili as you can with 5 large onions. How many ounces of diced tomatoes should you use? **(a)** Explain how you would solve the problem. **(b)** Solve the problem.

Mixed Review

Lesson 4-9

Find each sum or difference. Round your answer to match the less precise measurement.

36. 5.1 cm − 2.32 cm **37.** 12.2 yd + 13 yd **38.** 10 g − 4.7 g

39. 16.26 in. + 3.8 in. **40.** 3.1 oz + 5.63 oz **41.** 10.75 m − 4.8 m

Lesson 3-8

Write each number as an improper fraction.

42. $3\frac{1}{5}$ **43.** $2\frac{3}{4}$ **44.** $3\frac{7}{8}$ **45.** $4\frac{5}{12}$

46. $2\frac{1}{6}$ **47.** $5\frac{2}{7}$ **48.** $8\frac{1}{4}$ **49.** $7\frac{5}{8}$

Lesson 2-3

Algebra **Solve each equation.**

50. $x - 4 = -12$ **51.** $-8 = y + 6$ **52.** $-5 + x = 12$

53. $11 = 17 + q$ **54.** $p - (-2) = 5$ **55.** $32 + n = 32$

Checkpoint Quiz 2 — Lessons 5-4 through 5-6

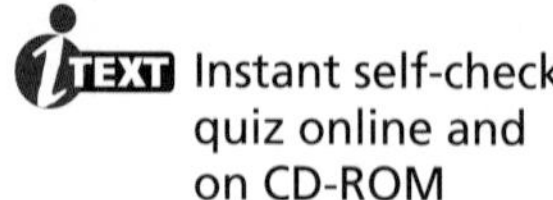

Instant self-check quiz online and on CD-ROM

Determine whether the ratios in each pair are proportional.

1. $\frac{5}{8}, \frac{12}{20}$ **2.** $\frac{4}{10}, \frac{2}{5}$ **3.** $\frac{24}{15}, \frac{4}{3}$ **4.** $\frac{8}{3}, \frac{48}{18}$

5. The last time you bought hamburgers for your friends, 5 hamburgers cost $5.25. At this rate, what is the cost of 8 hamburgers?

6. Seven movie tickets cost $57.75. What is the cost of two movie tickets?

$\triangle ABC$ is similar to $\triangle WXY$. Find each measure.

7. $\angle X$ **8.** $\angle C$

9. length of $\overline{AB}$ **10.** length of $\overline{WY}$

A, B, C; 18, 120°, 12
W, X, Y; 6, 26°, 8

Creating Similar Figures

For Use With Lesson 5-6

Using the computer is a great way to explore similar figures. For this activity you need geometry software.

Activity

Follow these steps to draw two similar triangles like those at the right.

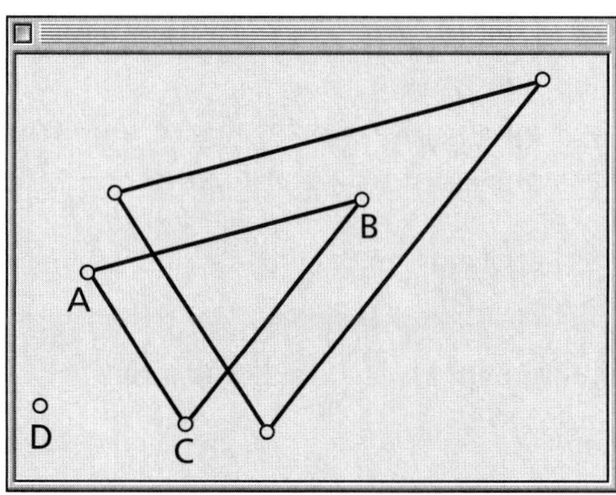

Step 1 Draw a triangle and label it ABC.

Step 2 Draw a point D not on the triangle.

Step 3 Create a triangle similar to $\triangle ABC$ using the *dilation* command. To use this command, you will need to enter a *scale factor* and name one point as the *center* of the dilation. Use 2 as a scale factor and name point D as the center.

EXERCISES

1. Change the shape of $\triangle ABC$ by dragging point A, B, or C. What happens to the larger triangle each time?

2. **Explore** Drag point D to different locations. Describe what happens in each case below.
   a. D is inside $\triangle ABC$.
   b. D is on $\overline{AB}$.
   c. D is on top of point C.

3. Use the software to draw $\overleftrightarrow{AD}$ (line AD), $\overleftrightarrow{BD}$, and $\overleftrightarrow{CD}$.
   a. What do you notice about the lines and the larger triangle?
   b. Why do you think that point D is called the center of the dilation?

4. Create a third triangle similar to $\triangle ABC$. This time use 0.5 as the scale factor. Keep D as the center. What do you notice about the new triangle?

5. a. **Open-Ended** Create more triangles similar to $\triangle ABC$ by choosing other scale factors. Again keep D as the center.
   b. **Writing in Math** Explain how your choice of scale factor affects the final figure.
   c. **Writing in Math** Use what you have learned to write a definition for scale factor.

Learning Vocabulary

For Use With Lesson 5-6

As you study mathematics this year, make your own mathematics dictionary of new vocabulary terms. Use the following guide for each new term.

- Write the vocabulary term and its definition. Include any symbols for the term.
- If possible, draw a diagram. Include details, using other related terms you know.
- Give one or more examples of the term.
- Give one or more "non-examples," and explain how they are different.

EXAMPLE

Write an entry for your dictionary for the term *rate*. Include the special term *unit rate*.

A rate is a ratio in which the numerator and denominator have different units. For a unit rate, the denominator is 1.

$\frac{20 \text{ people}}{5 \text{ cars}}$ is a rate because the numerator and denominator have different units. $\frac{4 \text{ people}}{1 \text{ car}}$ or $\frac{4 \text{ people}}{\text{car}}$ is the unit rate.

$\frac{20 \text{ people}}{5 \text{ people}}$ is a ratio, but it is not a rate because the numerator and denominator have the same unit.

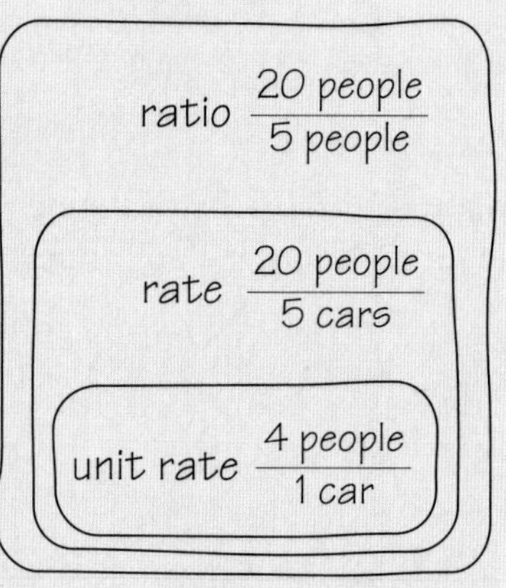

EXERCISES

Write an entry for your dictionary for each term.

1. proportion
2. similar figures
3. cross products
4. indirect measurement
5. equal ratios
6. divisible

Write an entry for the first term. Your entry should include the second term.

7. unit price, unit rate
8. exponent, power
9. LCM, multiple

Suppose you have written an entry for your dictionary for each term. What "non-example" might you also show? Explain.

10. proper fraction
11. repeating decimal
12. prime number

5-7 Maps and Scale Drawings

What You'll Learn

OBJECTIVE 1 To use proportions to solve problems involving scale

. . . And Why

To use maps, as in Example 2

Check Skills You'll Need

For help, go to Lesson 5-5.

Solve each proportion.

1. $\frac{2}{3} = \frac{x}{12}$ **2.** $\frac{9}{5} = \frac{27}{y}$ **3.** $\frac{15}{m} = \frac{25}{5}$

4. $\frac{3}{5} = \frac{c}{30}$ **5.** $\frac{t}{21} = \frac{6}{18}$ **6.** $\frac{13}{n} = \frac{52}{4}$

New Vocabulary

- scale drawing
- scale

Interactive lesson includes instant self-check, tutorials, and activities.

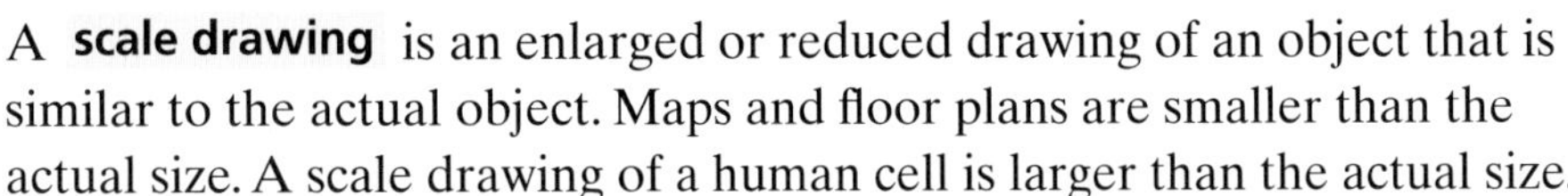

OBJECTIVE

1 Solving Problems Involving Scale

A **scale drawing** is an enlarged or reduced drawing of an object that is similar to the actual object. Maps and floor plans are smaller than the actual size. A scale drawing of a human cell is larger than the actual size.

> **Reading Math**
>
> On a map, the equal sign in 1 in. = 30 mi does not mean that the two quantities are equal, as it would in an equation.

A **scale** is the ratio that compares a length in a drawing to the corresponding length in the actual object. If a 30-mile road is 1 in. long on a map, you can write the scale of the map in these three ways:

1 in. : 30 mi $\qquad \frac{1 \text{ in.}}{30 \text{ mi}} \qquad$ 1 in. = 30 mi

↑ drawing ↑ actual

1 EXAMPLE Using a Scale Drawing (Algebra)

You have a scale drawing of a boat. The length of the boat on the drawing is 3 cm. What is the actual length of the boat?

Write the scale of the drawing, 1 cm = 1.5 m, as $\frac{1 \text{ cm}}{1.5 \text{ m}}$. Then write a proportion in which each ratio compares centimeters to meters.

Let n represent the actual length of the boat.

drawing (cm) → / actual (m) → $\frac{1}{1.5} = \frac{3}{n}$ ← drawing (cm) / ← actual (m)

$1n = 1.5(3)$ ← **Write cross products.**

$n = 4.5$ ← **Simplify.**

The actual length of the boat is 4.5 m.

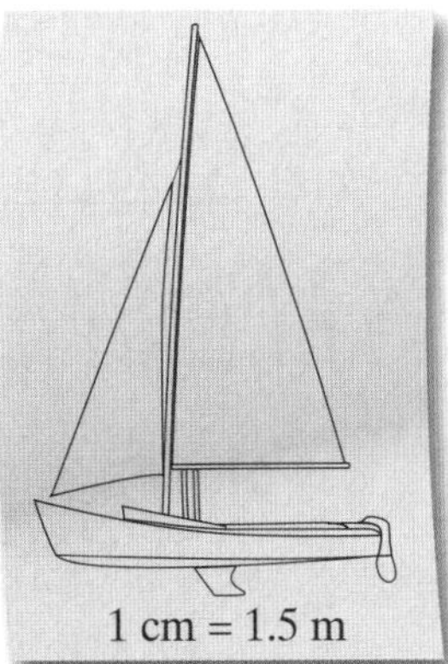

1 cm = 1.5 m

Check Understanding **1** **Estimation** If the mast of the boat in Example 1 is about 10 cm tall on the drawing, about how tall is the mast on the actual boat?

You can use proportions and a map's scale to find actual distances.

2 EXAMPLE Real-World Problem Solving

Test-Prep Tip

When writing a proportion, make sure each ratio compares the same types of quantities.

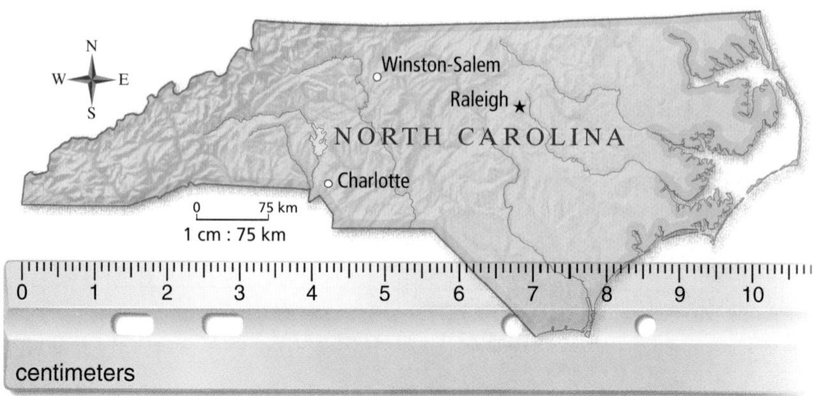

Geography Find the actual distance from Charlotte to Winston-Salem.

Step 1 Use a centimeter ruler to find the map distance from Charlotte to Winston-Salem. The map distance is about 1.6 cm.

Step 2 Use a proportion to find the actual distance. Let n represent the actual distance.

$$\frac{\text{map (cm)}}{\text{actual (km)}} \rightarrow \frac{1}{75} = \frac{1.6}{n} \leftarrow \frac{\text{map (cm)}}{\text{actual (km)}} \qquad \leftarrow \text{Write a proportion.}$$

$$1n = 75(1.6) \qquad \leftarrow \text{Write cross products.}$$

$$n = 120 \qquad \leftarrow \text{Simplify.}$$

The actual distance from Charlotte to Winston-Salem is about 120 km.

Check Understanding 2 Find the actual distance between each pair of cities.

a. Charlotte and Raleigh **b.** Raleigh and Winston-Salem

You can use the GCF of two numbers to find the scale of a drawing or a model.

3 EXAMPLE Finding the Scale

Models Refer to the model boxcar shown at the right. The actual length of a boxcar is 609 in. What is the scale of the model?

$$\frac{\text{scale length}}{\text{actual length}} \rightarrow \frac{7}{609} = \frac{1}{87} \qquad \leftarrow \text{Divide each measure by the GCF, 7.}$$

The scale is 1 in. : 87 in.

Check Understanding 3 The length of a room in an architectural drawing is 10 in. Its actual length is 15 ft. What is the scale of the drawing?

Investigation: Making a Scale Drawing

Make a scale drawing of your classroom.

1. Using a meter stick or yardstick, measure the classroom. Measure the length and width of the room and anything else you think you need.
2. Choose a scale large enough to produce a good drawing, but small enough to fit on your paper.
3. Complete your drawing. Include the scale.

EXERCISES

For more practice, see *Extra Practice*.

A Practice by Example

Example 1 (page 275)

Algebra A scale drawing has a scale of 3 in. : 10 ft. Find the actual length for each drawing length.

1. 21 in. **2.** 15 in. **3.** 6 in.

4. 45 in. **5.** 13.5 in. **6.** 1.5 in.

Example 2 (page 276)

Geography Find the actual distance between each pair of cities. Use a ruler to measure. Round to the nearest mile.

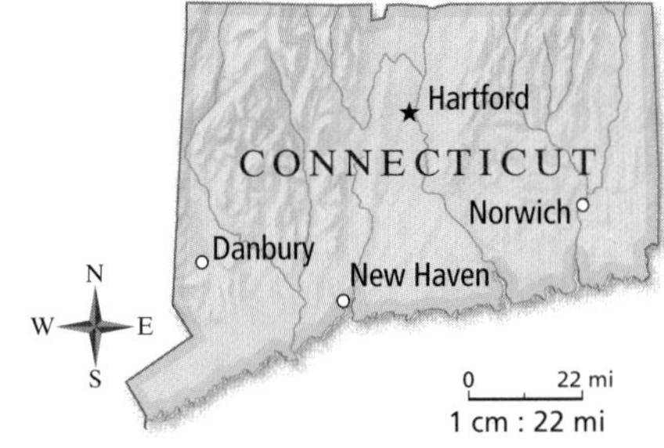

7. Hartford and Danbury

8. Norwich and Hartford

9. New Haven and Norwich

10. New Haven and Danbury

Example 3 (page 276)

11. Architecture The height of a building in an architectural drawing is 10 in. Its actual height is 150 ft. What is the scale of the drawing?

12. The width of the scale drawing of a sofa is 15 cm. The actual width of the sofa is 150 cm. What is the scale of the drawing?

B Apply Your Skills

The scale of a map is $\frac{1 \text{ cm}}{3.75 \text{ km}}$. Find the actual distance for each map distance.

13. 8 cm **14.** 20 cm **15.** 28 cm

16. 16 mm **17.** 24 mm **18.** 50 mm

19. Writing in Math You are making a scale drawing with a scale of 2 in. = 17 ft. Explain how you find the length of the drawing of an object that has an actual length of 51 ft.

20. **Reasoning** The scale of a drawing is 5 cm : 1 mm. Is the scale drawing larger or smaller than the actual figure? Explain.

21. **Architecture** The blueprint is a scale drawing of an apartment. The dimensions of the master bedroom are 12 ft × 20 ft.

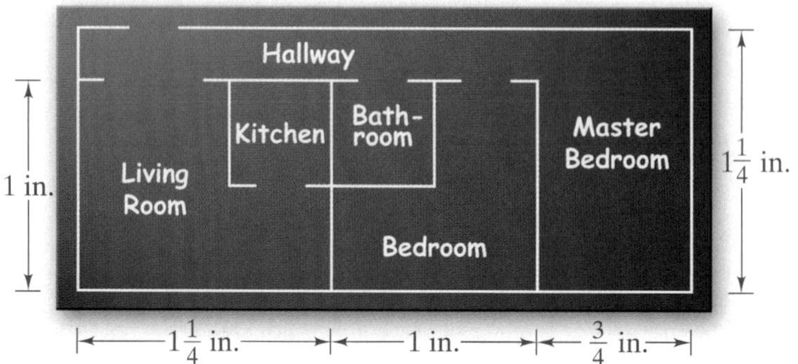

a. Complete: The scale is ■ : 4 ft.

b. Sketch a copy of the floor plan. Write the actual dimensions in place of the scale dimensions.

The scale of a map is 1 cm : 3.6 km. Find the actual distance for each map distance. Round your answer to the nearest tenth, if necessary.

22. 12 cm 23. 2 cm 24. 18 cm 25. 52 mm 26. 28 mm

Use a centimeter ruler to measure the length of the segment shown in each figure below. Find the scale of each drawing.

27. Peach Aphid

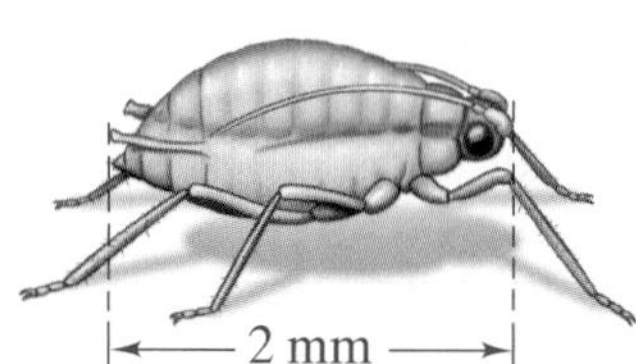

28. Killer Whale

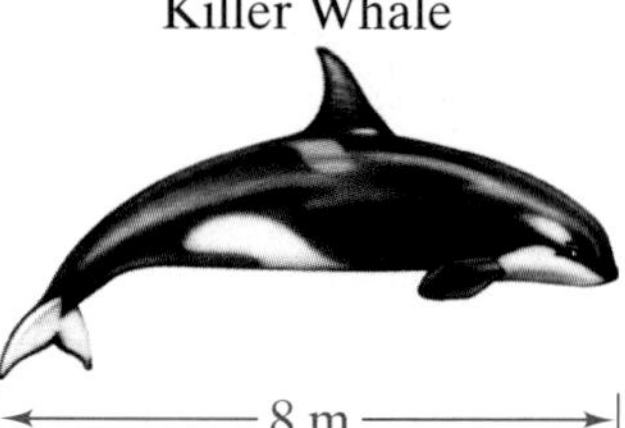

29. **Dinosaurs** Special-effects artists often use scale models. The actual height of a velociraptor is estimated to have been approximately 2 ft. An artist draws the dinosaur with a height of 4 in. on paper.

a. What would be an appropriate scale for a model of the velociraptor?

b. The same scale is used for a model of a tyrannosaurus, whose actual height was 16 ft. What is the height of the model?

C Challenge

The scale of a drawing is $\frac{1}{4}$ in. : 6 ft. Find the length on the drawing for each actual length.

30. 18 ft 31. 66 ft 32. 204 ft 33. 84 ft

34. A building is drawn with a scale of 1 in. : 3 ft. The height of the drawing is 1 ft 2 in. After a design change, the scale is modified to be 1 in. : 4 ft. What is the new height of the drawing?

35. **Stretch Your Thinking** Use the pattern in the equations below to find the sum of the first 100 odd numbers.

$1 = 1$

$1 + 3 = 4$

$1 + 3 + 5 = 9$

$1 + 3 + 5 + 7 = 16$

$1 + 3 + 5 + 7 + 9 = 25$

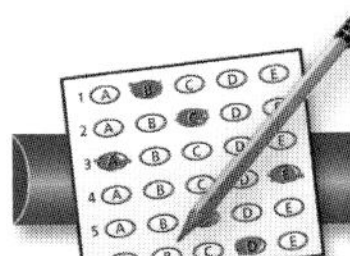

Test Prep

Reading Comprehension

Read the passage and answer the questions below.

Computer-Aided Spacesuit Design

Clothes designed for space must allow astronauts to move and breathe in an airless environment. An astronaut's suit must protect the astronaut from the sun's harsh rays. Computers help designers improve spacesuits for future space travelers. For a computer image in which each length is $\frac{1}{8}$ of the actual length, the designer knows that all dimensions will have the same ratio.

36. Suppose the computer image of the pants of a spacesuit is 5 in. long. How long are the actual pants?

37. An astronaut's arm is 32 in. long. Find the arm length in the computer image for a spacesuit.

Multiple Choice

38. The scale of a blueprint is 1 in. : 6.5 ft. What are the actual dimensions of a room if the blueprint's dimensions are 3 in. × 4 in.?
A. 19.5 ft × 26 ft **B.** 39 ft × 52 ft
C. 26 ft × 39 ft **D.** 6 ft × 8 ft

39. The scale of a map is 1 cm : 5 km. The distance between two cities is 112 km. How far apart are they on a map?
F. 11.2 cm **G.** 22.4 cm **H.** 56 cm **I.** 560 cm

Mixed Review

Lesson 5-6

40. Find the values of x and y in the similar triangles below.

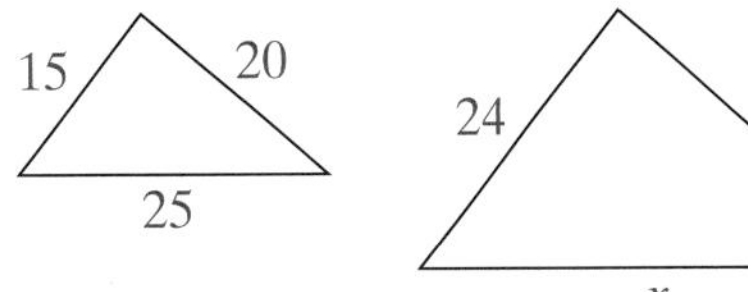

Lesson 2-6

Algebra **Solve each equation.**

41. $3x + 2 = 17$
42. $\frac{x}{5} + 5 = 21$
43. $2a - 4 = 8$

Plan a Trip

For Use With Lesson 5-7

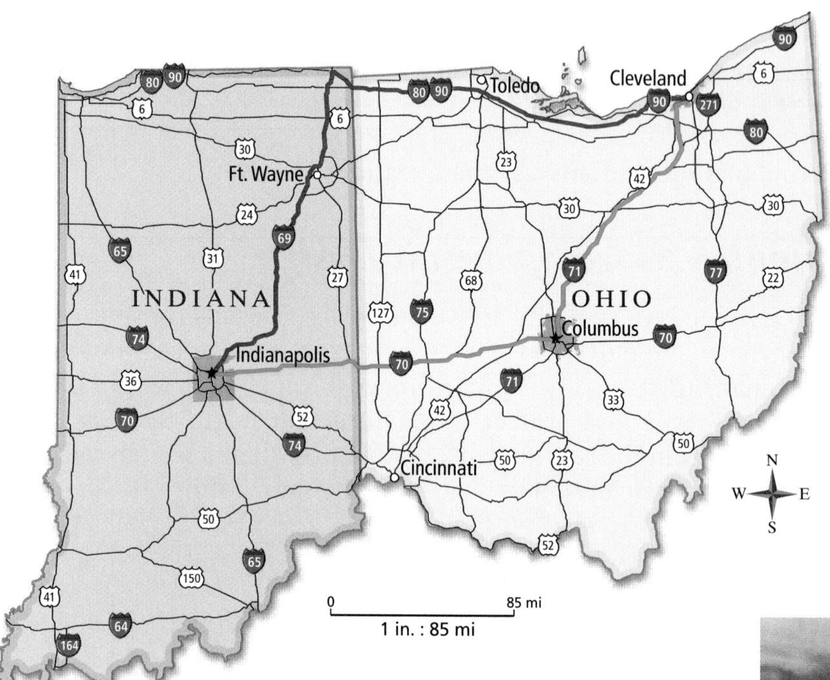

Located on the shore of Lake Erie, the 150,000-square-foot Rock and Roll Hall of Fame and Museum is a landmark for the city of Cleveland, Ohio.

Activity

Use the map above to plan a trip from Indianapolis to Cleveland.

1. Measure the distances on Routes 69 and 80/90 from Indianapolis to Fort Wayne, Fort Wayne to Toledo, and Toledo to Cleveland. Add them to get the total map distance.
2. Locate the scale on the map. Use the scale to convert the map distance into the actual distance for your trip.
3. Use an average speed of 50 mi/h. Find the time it will take to drive the total actual distance. If you plan to drive no more than 4 hours per day, how many days will your trip take?
4. Suppose you want to make the same trip, but you want to visit your friend in Columbus on the way. Plan your trip from Indianapolis to Cleveland going through Columbus. Compare this to the other trip.
5. **Research** Now suppose that you are planning a cross-country road trip from Trenton, New Jersey, to San Francisco, California. Locate a map of the United States and plan your trip. Decide which cities you would like to visit along the way. How long will your trip take you?

Test-Taking Strategies

Using a Variable

You can solve many problems by using a variable to represent an unknown quantity. Let the variable represent the quantity you are looking for. Then use the variable to write an equation or inequality.

EXAMPLE

Purple is a mixture of the primary colors red and blue. A certain shade of purple paint requires 6 parts red to 7 parts blue. If you have 16 quarts of red paint, how many quarts of blue paint do you need to make the desired shade of purple? How many quart cans of blue paint do you need to buy?

The problem is asking for the amount of blue paint needed to make a shade of purple. You can write and solve a proportion.

Let b represent the number of quarts of blue paint you need.

red paint → / blue paint → $\frac{6}{7} = \frac{16}{b}$ ← red paint / ← blue paint ← **Write a proportion.**

$6b = 112$ ← **Write the cross products and simplify.**

$\frac{6b}{6} = \frac{112}{6}$ ← **Divide each side by 6.**

$b = 18\frac{2}{3}$ ← **Simplify.**

You need $18\frac{2}{3}$ quarts of blue paint. You should buy 19 cans.

EXERCISES

1. **Party Planning** A party platter contains a variety of dried fruits. To serve 16 people, 96 pieces of fruit are needed. How many pieces of dried fruit are needed to serve 22 people?

2. A paper distributor is shipping poster tubes to an art gallery. The distributor has previously shipped 560 tubes in 16 boxes. At this rate, how many boxes would the distributor need to ship 112 poster tubes?

3. **Art** A class of 37 students is making origami boxes. Each box uses 8 pieces of origami paper. The class will split into groups of at most 3 students per group. If each group is going to make one box, what is the least number of pieces of paper needed by the class?

4. **Gas Mileage** A 4-cylinder car typically gets 21 miles for every gallon of gas. The odometer reading on a car is 22,050 miles. How many gallons of gas have been used since the car was purchased?

5. A recipe calls for 3 eggs per serving. Eggs come in cartons of 12. If you are going to make 14 servings, how many cartons of eggs do you need to buy?

Chapter Review

Vocabulary

cross products (p. 257)
equal ratios (p. 242)
indirect measurement (p. 269)
polygon (p. 268)
proportion (p. 256)
rate (p. 246)
ratio (p. 241)
scale (p. 275)
scale drawing (p. 275)
similar polygons (p. 268)
unit price (p. 247)
unit rate (p. 246)

Reading Math: Understanding Vocabulary

Choose the correct term to complete each sentence.

1. A street map is an example of (a scale drawing, cross products).
2. Knowing an (indirect measurement, unit price) is helpful for getting the best buy when you shop.
3. A speed limit of 40 mi/h is an example of a (rate, proportion).
4. A ratio that compares a length in a drawing to the actual length of an object is a (scale, proportion).
5. When two polygons have corresponding angles with equal measures and corresponding sides with proportional lengths, the polygons are (cross products, similar).

Take It to the NET
Online vocabulary quiz at **www.PHSchool.com**
Web Code: abj-0551

Skills and Concepts

5-1 Objectives
- To write ratios
- To find equal ratios

A **ratio** is a comparison of two quantities by division. You can write the same ratio in three ways. To find equal ratios, multiply or divide the numerator and denominator by the same nonzero number.

Write each ratio in simplest form.

6. $\frac{9}{30}$ **7.** $\frac{64}{20}$ **8.** 99 : 33 **9.** 75 to 20 **10.** $\frac{45}{180}$

11. Sports In the 2000 summer Olympics, the United States won 97 medals, including 39 gold medals. Write the ratio of gold medals to total medals in three ways.

5-2 and 5-3 Objectives
- To find unit rates
- To use unit prices
- To solve a problem using two different methods

A **rate** is a ratio that compares two quantities measured in different units. A **unit rate** has a denominator of 1. Find a **unit price** by dividing the price of an item by the size of the item.

You can use different strategies to solve the same problem.

Write the unit rate for each situation.

12. 282 passengers in 47 cars **13.** 600 Calories for 8 servings

14. Shopping A 10-oz box of cereal costs \$2.79. A 13-oz box of the same brand of cereal costs \$3.99. Find the unit price for each item and determine which is the better buy.

Use any strategy to solve each problem. Show your work.

15. Gymnastics A gymnast scores a total of 125 points in the first 4 meets of the season. At this rate, how many points will she score by the end of the 14-meet schedule?

16. Suppose you can peel 3 potatoes in 5 minutes. At this rate, how long will it take you to peel 10 potatoes?

5-4 and 5-5 Objectives

- To test if ratios can form a proportion
- To use cross products
- To use unit rates to solve proportions
- To solve proportions involving variables

A **proportion** is an equation stating that two ratios are equal. If two ratios form a proportion, the **cross products** are equal.

Solve each proportion.

17. $\frac{3}{7} = \frac{n}{28}$ **18.** $\frac{3}{5} = \frac{15}{x}$ **19.** $\frac{a}{18} = \frac{12}{72}$ **20.** $\frac{32}{c} = \frac{4}{17}$

21. Wood A local lumberyard sells a total of 250,000 board feet of hardwood each year. The ratio of softwood to hardwood is 5 : 3. Write and solve a proportion to find the amount of softwood sold each year. Round your answer to the nearest thousand.

5-6 Objectives

- To identify similar figures
- To find missing lengths in similar figures

Two polygons are **similar polygons** if corresponding angles have equal measure and the lengths of corresponding sides form equal ratios.

22. A fire hydrant is 30 in. tall and casts a shadow 8 in. long. How tall is a nearby tree that casts a shadow 4 ft long?

Each pair of figures is similar. Find each missing value.

23.

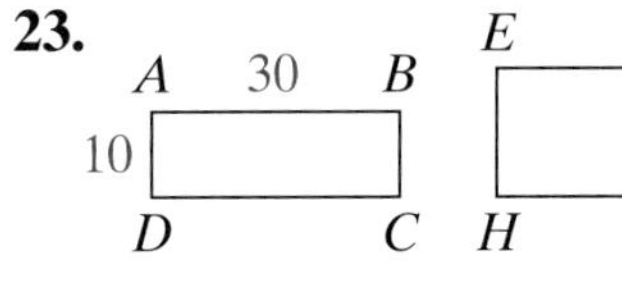

$BADC \sim EFGH$

24.

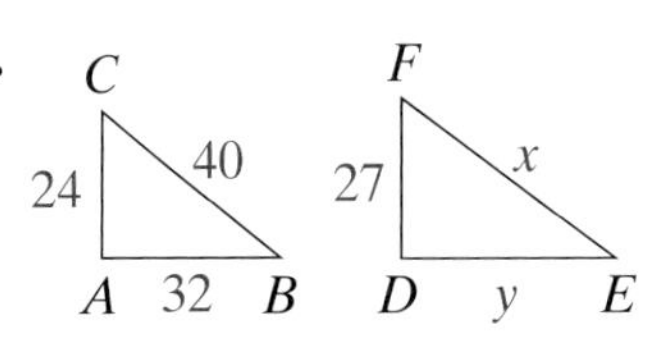

$\triangle ABC \sim \triangle DEF$

5-7 Objective

- To use proportions to solve problems involving scale

A **scale drawing** is an enlarged or reduced drawing of an object that is similar to the actual object. A **scale** is a ratio that compares a length in a drawing to the corresponding length in the actual object.

25. Maps The scale on a map is 1 in. : 333 mi. The map distance from Chicago to Tokyo is 12 in. Find the actual distance between the cities.

26. Architecture A drawing's scale is 0.5 in. : 10 ft. A room is 15 ft long. How long is the room on the drawing?

Chapter Test

Online chapter test at
www.PHSchool.com
Web Code: aba-0552

1. Write a ratio for this information in three ways: In the United States, 98 million out of 99.6 million homes have at least one television.

Write each ratio in two other ways.

2. $\frac{9}{7}$ **3.** 48 : 100 **4.** 33 to 9

5. 46 : 50 **6.** 19 to 91 **7.** 6 : 7

8. Gas Mileage Engineers test four cars to find their fuel efficiency. Use the information in the table below. Which car gets the most miles per gallon?

Car	Miles	Gallons Used
A	225	14
B	312	15
C	315	10
D	452	16

Find the unit rate for each situation.

9. run 2.3 km in 7 min

10. earn $36.00 in 4 h

11. Writing in Math You need to buy 10 lb of rice. A 2-lb bag costs $1.29. A 10-lb bag costs $6.99. You want to buy a 10-lb bag so you have fewer items to carry. Your friend thinks buying five 2-lb bags is a better deal because the unit rate is lower. Is your friend correct? Explain.

Solve each proportion.

12. $\frac{6}{5} = \frac{n}{7}$ **13.** $\frac{3}{7} = \frac{8}{x}$

14. $\frac{k}{4} = \frac{9}{32}$ **15.** $\frac{3.5}{d} = \frac{14}{15}$

16. $\frac{80}{35} = \frac{w}{7}$ **17.** $\frac{y}{18} = \frac{2.4}{15}$

18. The ratio of teachers to students in a middle school is 2 to 25. There are 350 students in the school. Find the number of teachers.

19. Maps A map with a scale of 1 in. : 175 mi shows two cities 5 in. apart. How many miles apart are the cities?

Write each ratio in simplest form.

20. $\frac{7}{49}$ **21.** $\frac{12}{4}$ **22.** $\frac{8}{2}$

23. $\frac{14}{18}$ **24.** $\frac{68}{100}$ **25.** $\frac{15}{95}$

26. In the figure below, $\triangle JKL \sim \triangle PQR$. Find x and y.

J 7.5 K 17.5 15 L   P 6 Q y x R

27. Utilities Last month, your electric bill was $25.32 for 450 kilowatt-hours of electricity. At that rate, what would be the bill for 240 kilowatt-hours?

28. A person who is 60 in. tall casts a shadow that is 15 in. long. How tall is a nearby lamppost that casts a shadow that is 40 in. long?

Use mental math to solve each proportion.

29. $\frac{14}{36} = \frac{7}{x}$ **30.** $\frac{40}{16} = \frac{x}{2}$

31. $\frac{x}{1} = \frac{24}{2}$ **32.** $\frac{4}{9} = \frac{12}{x}$

33. Suppose you are making a scale drawing of a giraffe that is 5.5 m tall. The drawing is 7 cm tall. What is the scale of the drawing?

34. Ballooning A hot-air balloon 2,100 ft above the ground can descend at the rate of 1.5 ft/s. The balloon is scheduled to land at 3:30 P.M. When should the balloonist start descending?

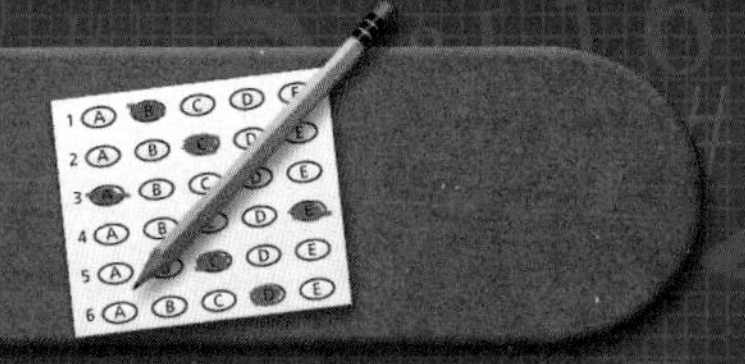

Test Prep

Reading Comprehension **Read each passage and answer the questions that follow.**

Europe Goes Euro Until recently, you needed different types of money (francs, marks, punts, etc.) to travel through Europe. Now all you need to get by in most European countries is the new European currency, the euro. One U.S. dollar buys about 1.1 euros. One French franc was worth about 0.15 euros, and an Irish punt was worth about 1.27 euros.

1. About how many euros were 20 French francs worth?
A. 0.15 euros **B.** 3.00 euros
C. 20.00 euros **D.** 150.00 euros

2. Hsio came home from a trip with currency worth 20 U.S. dollars. She had 10 euros and the rest in U.S. currency. About how many dollars did she have?
F. \$8.90 **G.** \$9.09
H. \$10.00 **I.** \$10.91

3. About how many U.S. dollars would you get if you exchanged 15 euros?
A. \$1.36 **B.** \$13.64
C. \$16.50 **D.** \$27.28

4. Which expression shows how many French francs you could get for one Irish punt?
F. 0.15×1.27 **G.** $\frac{0.15}{1.27}$
H. $0.15 + 1.27$ **I.** $\frac{1.27}{0.15}$

More Money Notes In the United States, paper money is all the same size: 2.61 inches wide by 6.14 inches long and 0.0043 inches thick. But did you know that American banknotes used to be bigger? Until 1929, they were 3.125 inches wide by 7.4218 inches long. By the way, it costs about 4.2 cents to produce one paper note.

5. What is the current ratio of length to width for U.S. paper money?
A. 0.43 : 1 **B.** 2.35 : 1
C. 2.61 : 1 **D.** 6.14 : 1

6. Suppose you make a stack of one thousand \$100 bills. How tall is the stack?
F. 0.043 in. **G.** 0.43 in.
H. 4.3 in. **I.** 43 in.

7. What is the best approximation of the ratio of the current length of U.S. notes to the length before 1929?
A. 1 : 2 **B.** 3 : 4
C. 5 : 6 **D.** 9 : 10

8. The government prints about 12 billion paper notes each year. What is the best estimate of how much this costs?
F. \$.5 million **G.** \$5 million
H. \$50 million **I.** \$500 million

A Matter of Scale

Applying Ratios Some movies are about people suddenly shrinking in size. They find themselves in environments both familiar and unfamiliar. A piece of furniture becomes a cliff to climb. Insects become beasts to fear. Although special-effects technicians create many of the visuals on computers, model makers provide scale models for some objects. Using a consistent scale for the models keeps the illusion believable.

Put It All Together

1. You have been sent on a mission to learn as much as you can about a giant and her home.
   a. **Research** Use the clues in the "Giant's World" caption. Research the sizes of things mentioned in the caption. Then find the scale of the giant's world to your world.
   b. Use your scale to find the dimensions of at least three items from the giant's kitchen. Sketch the items and label their dimensions.
   c. Find the height of the giant.
2. Your next trip has brought you to a home inhabited by tiny people.
   a. **Research** Use the clues in the "Miniature World" caption and your research to find the scale of the miniature room to your world.
   b. Use your scale to find the dimensions of at least three items in the miniature living room. Sketch these items and label their dimensions.
   c. Find the height of a person who lives in the tiny house.
3. **Reasoning** Suppose someone in your class is 5 ft 5 in. tall, and another person is 4 ft 10 in. tall. Will these two people get the same answers in Exercises 1 and 2? Explain.

Giant's World

When standing on your toes, you can just barely reach the top of a cereal box.

When stood on end, a teaspoon reaches to the bottom of your rib cage.

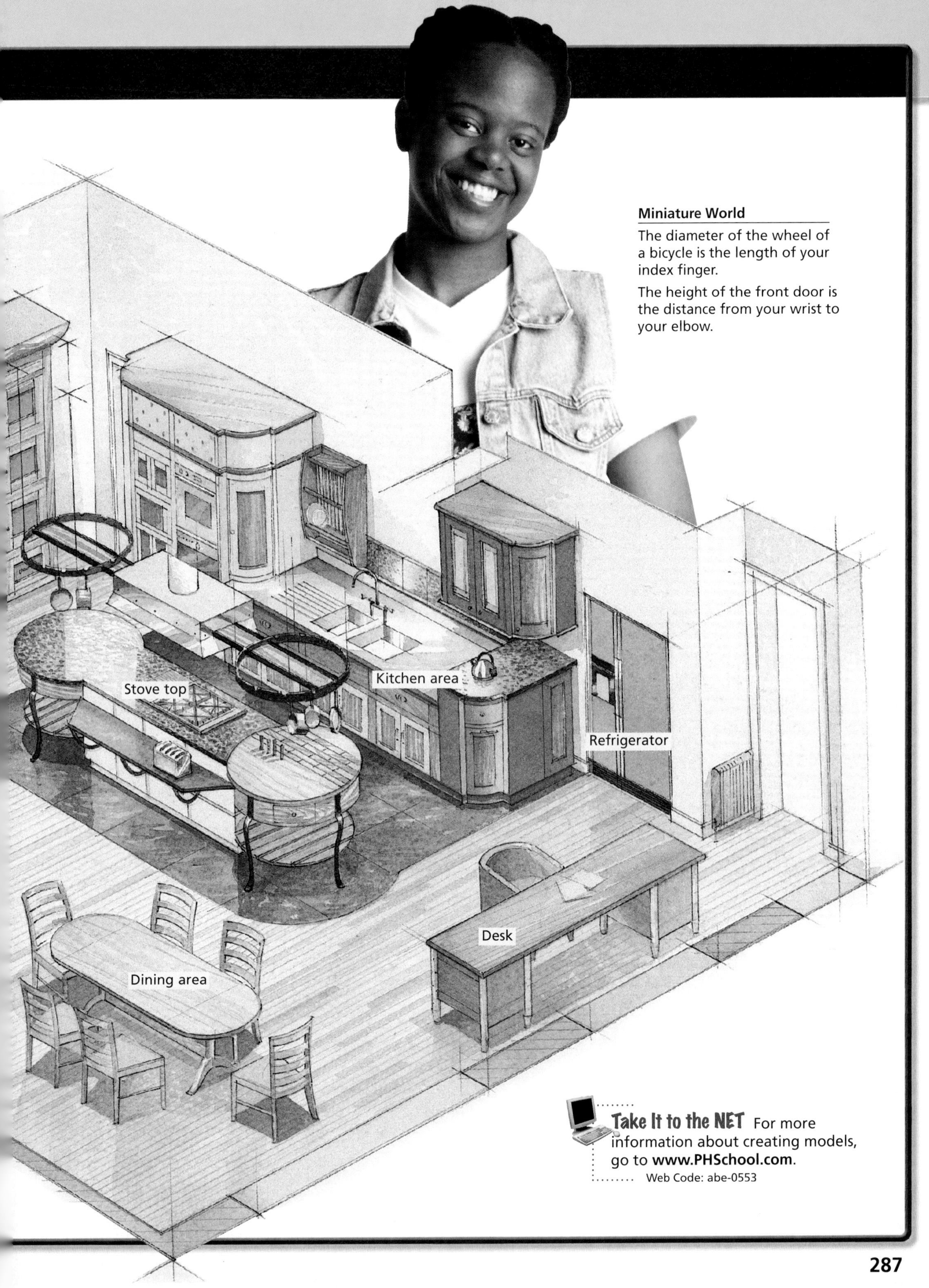

Miniature World

The diameter of the wheel of a bicycle is the length of your index finger.

The height of the front door is the distance from your wrist to your elbow.

Take It to the NET For more information about creating models, go to **www.PHSchool.com**.
Web Code: abe-0553

CHAPTER 6

Percents

Lessons

- **6-1** Understanding Percents
- **6-2** Percents, Fractions, and Decimals
- **6-3** Percents Greater Than 100% or Less Than 1%
- **6-4** Finding a Percent of a Number
- **6-5** Solving Percent Problems Using Proportions
- **6-6** Solving Percent Problems Using Equations
- **6-7** Applications of Percent
- **6-8** Finding Percent of Change
- **6-9** Problem Solving: Write an Equation

Key Vocabulary

- commission (p. 324)
- discount (p. 329)
- markup (p. 328)
- percent (p. 291)
- percent of change (p. 327)

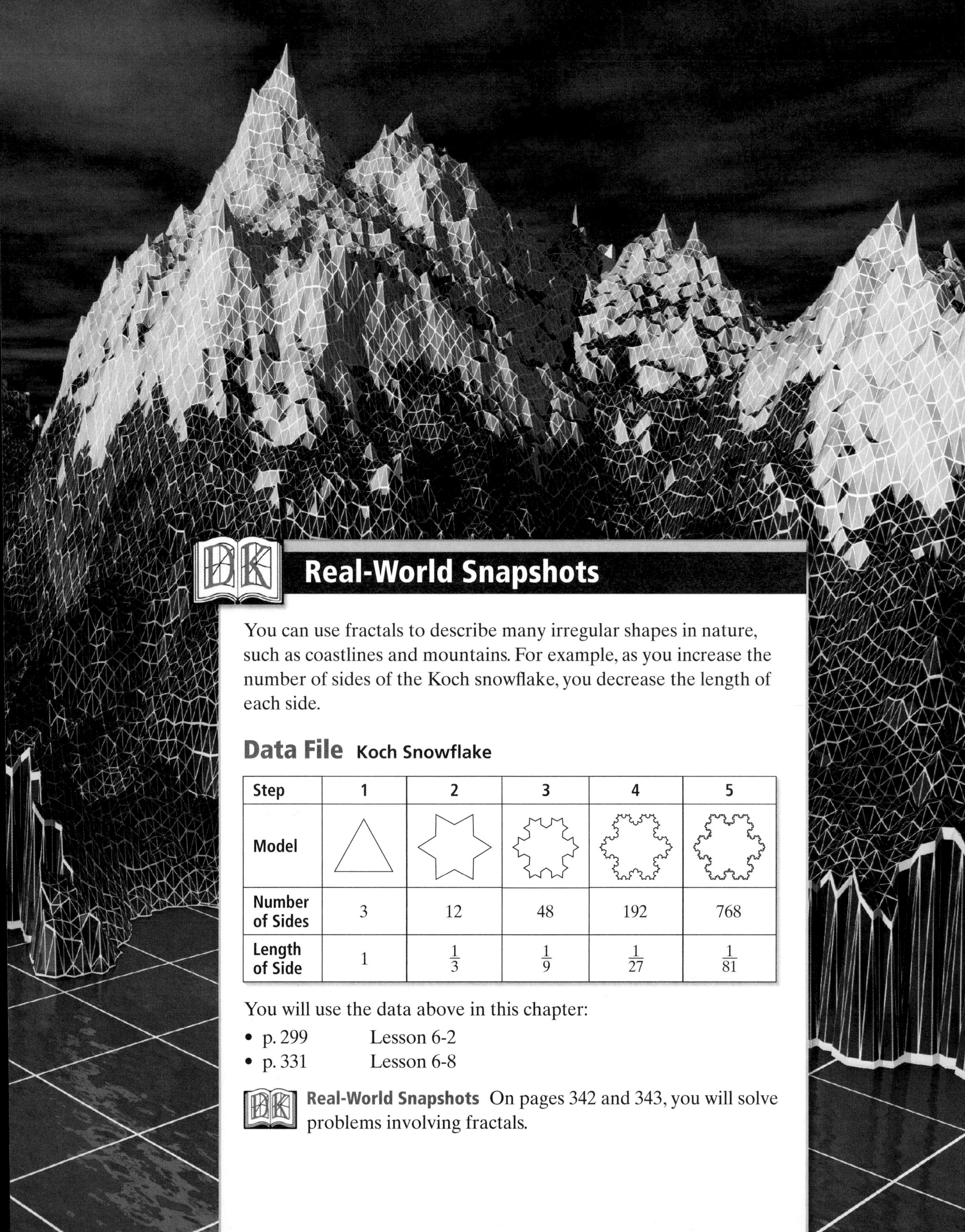

Real-World Snapshots

You can use fractals to describe many irregular shapes in nature, such as coastlines and mountains. For example, as you increase the number of sides of the Koch snowflake, you decrease the length of each side.

Data File Koch Snowflake

Step	1	2	3	4	5
Model					
Number of Sides	3	12	48	192	768
Length of Side	1	$\frac{1}{3}$	$\frac{1}{9}$	$\frac{1}{27}$	$\frac{1}{81}$

You will use the data above in this chapter:

- p. 299 Lesson 6-2
- p. 331 Lesson 6-8

Real-World Snapshots On pages 342 and 343, you will solve problems involving fractals.

Chapter 6 Preview

Where You've Been

- In Chapters 2 and 4, you learned to solve equations.
- In Chapter 5, you learned to write ratios and solve proportions.

Where You're Going

- In Chapter 6, you will compare percents with decimals and fractions and solve percent problems using proportions and equations.
- Applying what you learn, you will find an appropriate tip to give for a service that you receive.

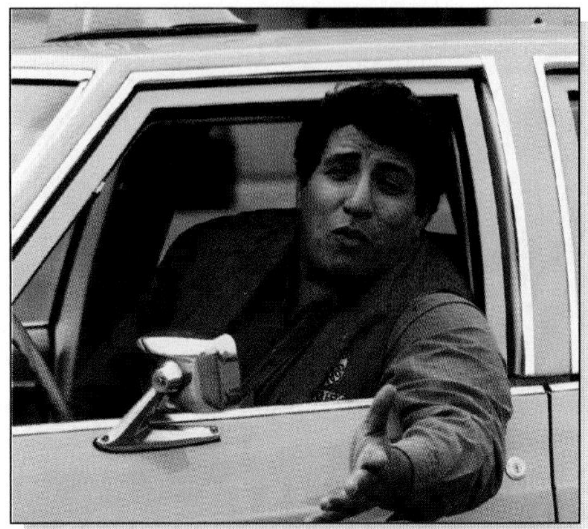

Many factors affect the fare for a taxi, but the passenger determines the tip.

Instant self-check online and on CD-ROM

Diagnosing Readiness

For help, go to the lesson in green.

Using Estimation Strategies (Lesson 1-1)

Use compatible numbers to estimate each quotient.

1. $74.89 \div 14.7$ **2.** $1{,}409 \div 102.4$ **3.** $495.89 \div 99.3$

Solving Equations by Multiplying or Dividing (Lesson 2-4)

Solve each equation.

4. $0.8t = 24$ **5.** $0.35w = 280$ **6.** $\frac{n}{0.6} = 14$ **7.** $\frac{z}{0.25} = 12$

Fractions and Decimals (Lesson 3-9)

Write each decimal as a fraction in simplest form.

8. 0.85 **9.** 0.4 **10.** 0.68 **11.** 1.25 **12.** 0.01

Solving Equations With Fractions (Lesson 4-6)

Solve each equation.

13. $\frac{2}{3}x = 8$ **14.** $\frac{1}{5}y = 11$ **15.** $\frac{3}{4}t = 15$

Using Proportional Reasoning (Lesson 5-5)

Solve each proportion using cross products.

16. $\frac{4}{5} = \frac{n}{100}$ **17.** $\frac{x}{8} = \frac{27}{100}$ **18.** $\frac{6}{a} = \frac{3}{100}$

6-1 Understanding Percents

What You'll Learn

 To model percents

 To write percents using equal ratios

. . . And Why

To find a percent grade on a quiz, as in Example 4

For help, go to Lesson 3-5.

Use multiples to write two fractions equivalent to each fraction.

1. $\frac{2}{5}$ **2.** $\frac{13}{50}$ **3.** $\frac{3}{25}$

4. $\frac{1}{10}$ **5.** $\frac{17}{20}$ **6.** $\frac{3}{4}$

New Vocabulary

- **percent**

 Interactive lesson includes instant self-check, tutorials, and activities.

1 Modeling Percents

A **percent** is a ratio that compares a number to 100. You can write the ratio $\frac{25}{100}$ as 25%.

1 EXAMPLE Finding Percents From a Model

> **Reading Math**
> Percent means "per hundred." The root *cent* appears in words such as century, centimeter, and centipede.

Decorating The floor plan shows a bedroom that is 10 ft × 10 ft. Write a ratio and a percent to represent the floor space needed for each piece of furniture in the room.

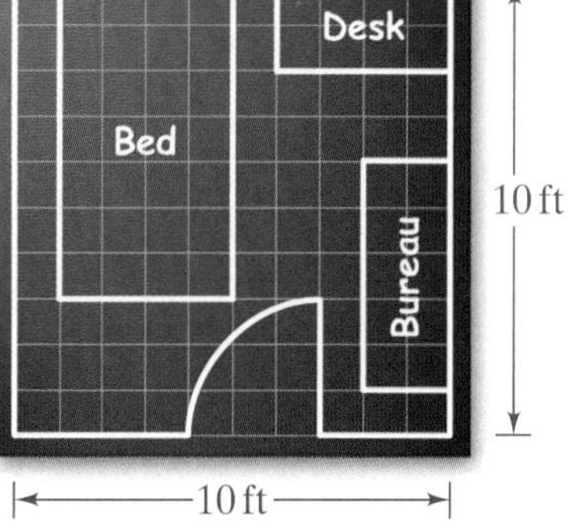

Count the number of grid spaces for each piece. Write as a ratio to the total number of grid spaces, 100. Then write as a percent.

bed $\frac{28}{100} = 28\%$ **bureau** $\frac{10}{100} = 10\%$

desk $\frac{8}{100} = 8\%$

Check Understanding 1 Write a ratio and a percent for the unused floor space.

You can model a percent using a 10 × 10 grid.

2 EXAMPLE Writing Percents as a Model

Model 25% on a 10 × 10 grid.

Shade 25 of the 100 grid spaces. →

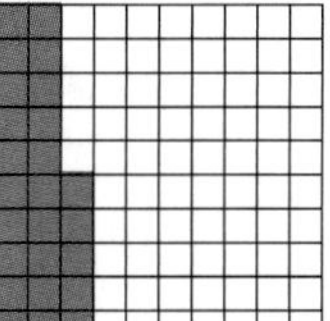

Check Understanding 2 Model each percent on a 10 × 10 grid.

a. 97% **b.** 4% **c.** 59.5%

OBJECTIVE 2

Writing Percents Using Equal Ratios

The factors of 100 are 1, 2, 4, 5, 10, 20, 25, 50, and 100. Ratios that have these numbers as their denominators are easy to write as percents by finding equal ratios.

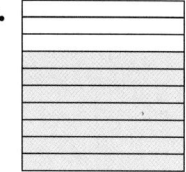

Need Help?
To find equal ratios, multiply the numerator and denominator of a ratio by the same nonzero number.
$\frac{a}{b} = \frac{a \cdot c}{b \cdot c}, c \neq 0$

3 EXAMPLE Finding Percents From Models

What percent does each shaded area represent?

a. 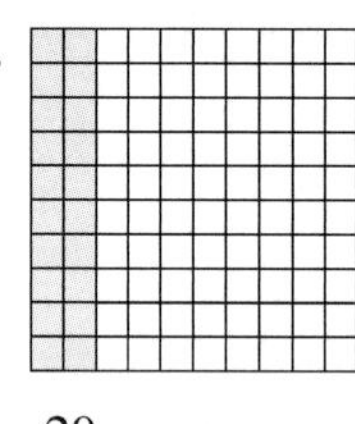

$\frac{20}{100} = 20\%$

b. 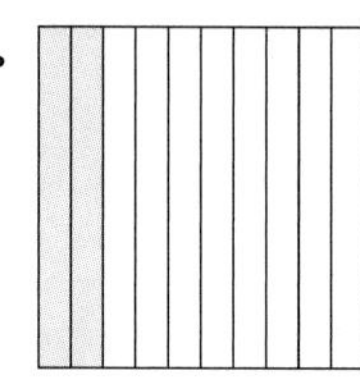

$\frac{2}{10} = \frac{20}{100} = 20\%$

c. 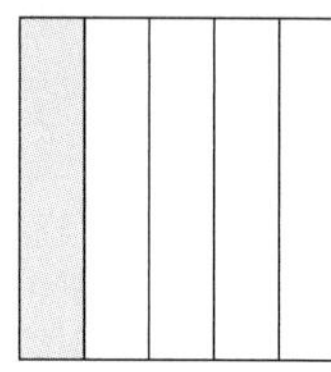

$\frac{1}{5} = \frac{20}{100} = 20\%$

Check Understanding 3 Write a ratio and a percent for each shaded area.

a. 

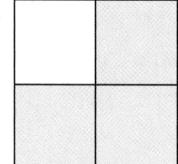

b. 

c. 

d. **Number Sense** You shade 4 squares in a grid. How many squares are there if the shaded portion represents 20% of the grid?

You can write ratios with different denominators as percents by writing an equal ratio with a denominator of 100.

4 EXAMPLE Using Equal Ratios

Grades You take a quiz that has 20 questions and get 17 correct answers. What is your percent grade on the quiz?

number of correct answers → / number of total answers → $\frac{17}{20}$ ← Write a ratio.

$\frac{17 \cdot 5}{20 \cdot 5}$ ← Since 20 · 5 is 100, multiply numerator and denominator by 5.

$\frac{85}{100}$ ← Simplify.

85% ← Write as a percent.

Your percent grade is 85%.

Check Understanding 4 Write each ratio as a percent.

a. $\frac{6}{25}$ **b.** $\frac{3}{4}$ **c.** $\frac{1}{50}$ **d.** $\frac{9}{20}$

e. **Reasoning** How can you use percents to compare two ratios with different denominators?

EXERCISES

For more practice, see *Extra Practice*.

A Practice by Example

Example 1 (page 291)

Write a ratio and a percent for each shaded figure.

1. 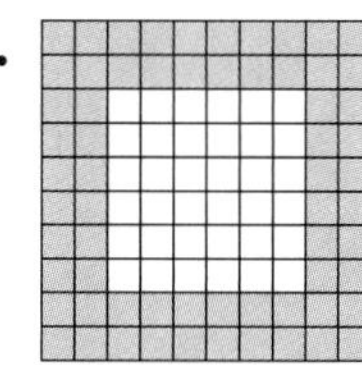

2. 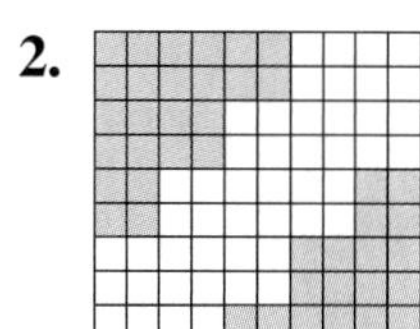

3. 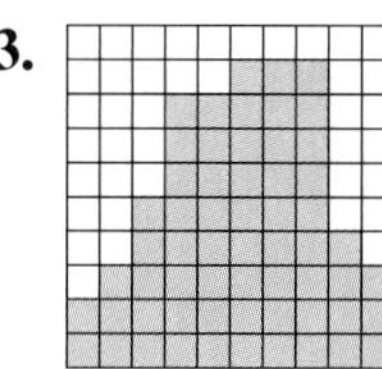

Example 2 (page 291)

Model each percent on a 10 × 10 grid.

4. 17% **5.** 35% **6.** 78% **7.** 10%

8. 8% **9.** 1.5% **10.** 90.5% **11.** 65%

Example 3 (page 292)

Write a ratio and a percent for each shaded area.

12.

13. 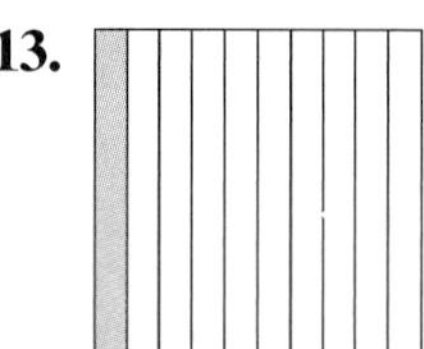

14. 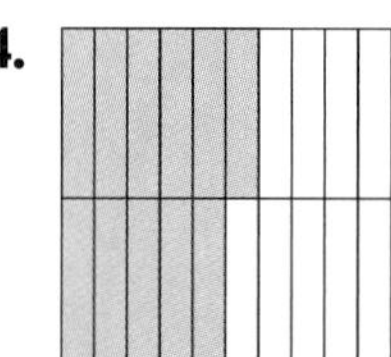

Example 4 (page 292)

Write each ratio as a percent. Exercise 15 has been started for you.

15. $\frac{3}{5} = \frac{60}{100}$ **16.** $\frac{1}{2}$ **17.** $\frac{21}{25}$ **18.** $\frac{9}{50}$

19. $\frac{11}{20}$ **20.** $\frac{1}{4}$ **21.** $\frac{3}{10}$ **22.** $\frac{24}{25}$ **23.** $\frac{1}{5}$

24. Clothing Six of your ten pairs of jeans are blue. What percent of your jeans are blue?

B Apply Your Skills

Find what percent of a dollar each set of coins makes.

25. 2 quarters and 2 dimes

26. 3 quarters, 1 dime, 3 pennies

27. 1 nickel and 4 pennies

28. 1 quarter, 4 nickels, 7 pennies

Social Studies Write each ratio as a percent.

29. Government An amendment to the U. S. Constitution must be ratified by at least three fourths of the states to become law.

30. Geography The area of Argentina is about three tenths the area of the United States.

31. History In the Battle of Tippecanoe, General William Harrison applauded his troops because nineteen twentieths of his soldiers had never before been in a battle.

32. Writing in Math Explain how to change $\frac{11}{25}$ into a percent.

Write a ratio and a percent for each shaded figure.

33. 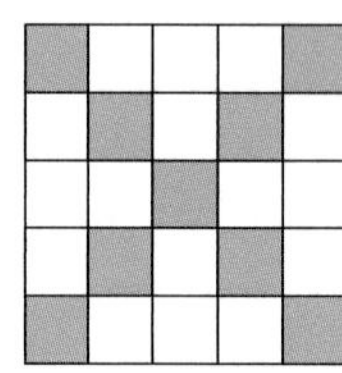

34. 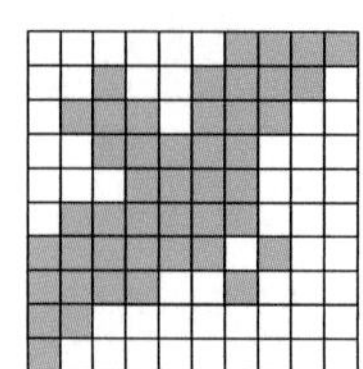

35. 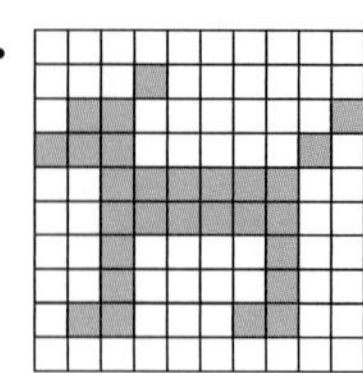

36. Open-Ended Draw and shade the first letter of your name on a 10×10 grid. Determine what percent of the grid is shaded.

Number Sense **Use percents to compare each pair of ratios. Use $<$, $>$, or $=$.**

37. $\frac{3}{5}$ and $\frac{7}{10}$

38. $\frac{3}{4}$ and $\frac{19}{25}$

39. $\frac{1}{2}$ and $\frac{23}{50}$

Estimate the percent of each figure that is shaded.

40. 

41. 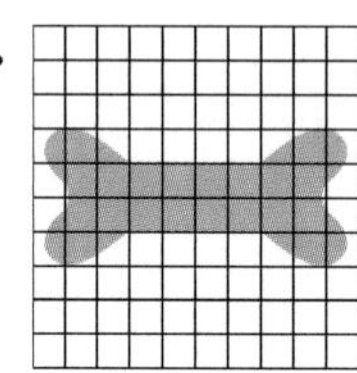

42. 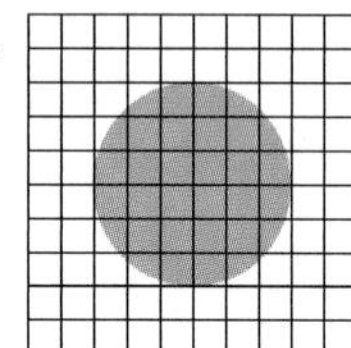

43. Stretch Your Thinking Andy has twice as many books as Kathi. Morey has one-third as many books as Kira. Kira has 4 more books than Andy. If Kathi has 16 books, how many books does Morey have?

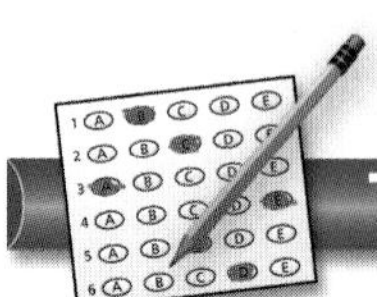

Test Prep

Gridded Response

Use the table at the right to find the percent of people surveyed who prefer each yogurt flavor.

44. strawberry

45. blueberry

46. vanilla

47. peach

Most Popular Yogurt Flavors

Personal Favorite	Ratio
Strawberry	$\frac{2}{5}$
Blueberry	$\frac{3}{25}$
Vanilla	$\frac{3}{50}$
Peach	$\frac{3}{100}$

Take It to the NET
Online lesson quiz at **www.PHSchool.com**
Web Code aba-0601

Mixed Review

Lesson 4-3 **Find each sum or difference.**

48. $7\frac{4}{5} + 9\frac{7}{10}$

49. $17\frac{2}{9} - 12\frac{1}{3}$

50. $9\frac{3}{11} - 8\frac{3}{8}$

51. $21\frac{2}{5} + 15\frac{1}{4}$

Lesson 3-9 **Write each fraction as a decimal.**

52. $\frac{8}{12}$

53. $\frac{3}{18}$

54. $\frac{7}{9}$

55. $\frac{5}{9}$

6-2 Percents, Fractions, and Decimals

What You'll Learn

 To connect percents and decimals

 To connect percents and fractions

. . . And Why

To find percent of fat content in food, as in Example 4

For help, go to Lesson 3-9.

Write each fraction as a decimal.

1. $\frac{5}{16}$ **2.** $\frac{1}{8}$ **3.** $\frac{11}{40}$

4. $\frac{5}{6}$ **5.** $\frac{4}{9}$ **6.** $\frac{2}{15}$

7. Reasoning Compare $\frac{1}{3}$ to $0.3\overline{3}$. Explain your reasoning.

 Interactive lesson includes instant self-check, tutorials, and activities.

OBJECTIVE 1

Percents and Decimals

Patterns Copy the table. Use the pattern you see in the first two columns to complete the table.

Fraction	$\frac{83}{100}$	$\frac{13}{100}$	$\frac{29}{100}$	■	■
Decimal	0.83	0.13	■	0.67	■
Percent	83%	13%	■	■	19%

1. Describe the pattern of writing the decimals in the table as percents.
2. Describe the pattern of writing the fractions in the table as percents.

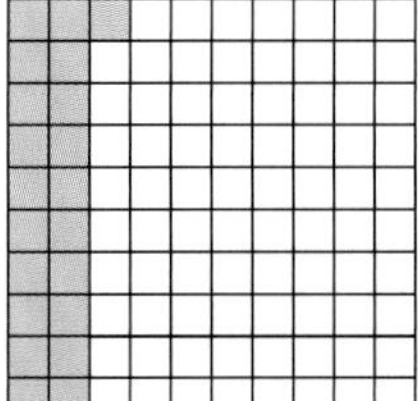

You can use a model to compare percents and decimals. From Lesson 6-1, you know that the shaded portion of the grid is 21 out of 100, or 21%.

Consider each square to be 0.01 of the whole.
The shaded portion is 21×0.01, or 0.21.
The model represents 0.21, or 21%.

To write a decimal as a percent, multiply the decimal by 100, or move the decimal point two places to the right. Then write a % sign.

$$0.45 \times 100 \rightarrow 0.45. \rightarrow 45\%$$

1 EXAMPLE Writing Decimals as Percents

Write each decimal as a percent.

a. 0.05 0.05. = 5%

b. 0.759 0.75.9 = 75.9%

c. 0.4 0.40. = 40%

← Move the decimal point two places to the right.

✔ Check Understanding 1 Write each decimal as a percent.

a. 0.07 **b.** 0.607 **c.** 0.9 **d.** 0.25

To write a percent as a decimal, divide it by 100, or move the decimal point two places to the left.

64.5% → .64.5 → 0.645

2 EXAMPLE Writing Percents as Decimals

Write each percent as a decimal.

a. 12% 0.12. → 0.12

b. 47.5% 0.47.5 → 0.475

c. 2% 0.02. → 0.02

← Move the decimal point two places to the left.

✔ Check Understanding 2 Write each percent as a decimal.

a. 35% **b.** 12.5% **c.** 9% **d.** 7.8%

You can order numbers by first writing each number as a decimal. Sometimes it is helpful to use a number line.

3 EXAMPLE Ordering Percents, Fractions, and Decimals

Order 0.52, 37%, 0.19, and $\frac{1}{4}$ from least to greatest. Use a number line.

Write all numbers as decimals. Then locate each on a number line.

0.52 ← This number is already in decimal form.

37% = 0.37 ← Move the decimal point two places to the left.

0.19 ← This number is already in decimal form.

$\frac{1}{4}$ = 0.25 ← Divide the numerator by the denominator.

Need Help?
For help converting a fraction to a decimal, see Lesson 3-9.

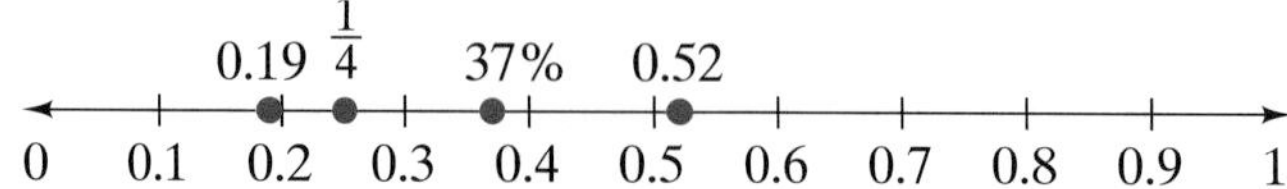

✔ Check Understanding 3 Order from least to greatest.

a. $\frac{3}{10}$, 0.74, 29%, $\frac{11}{25}$ **b.** 15%, $\frac{7}{20}$, 0.08, 50%

OBJECTIVE

2 Percents and Fractions

When the denominator of a fraction is a factor of 100, you can easily use equal ratios to convert the fraction to a percent. For fractions with other denominators, you can use a calculator to convert the fraction into a decimal, and then rewrite the decimal as a percent.

4 EXAMPLE Real-World Problem Solving

Nutrition In a slice of cheese pizza, 45 Calories are from fat. There are 158 total Calories in each slice. What percent of the Calories are from fat? Round to the nearest tenth of a percent.

Estimate $\frac{45}{158} \approx \frac{40}{160}$, which is $\frac{1}{4}$, or 25%.

Calories from fat → total Calories → $\frac{45}{158}$ ← Write the ratio.

45 ÷ 158 = 0.284810127 ← Use a calculator.

$= 28.4810127\%$ ← Write as a percent.

$\approx 28.5\%$ ← Round to the nearest tenth of a percent.

About 28.5% of the Calories are from fat.

Check for Reasonableness 28.5% is close to 25%, so the answer is reasonable.

4 Write each fraction as a percent. When necessary, round to the nearest tenth of a percent.

a. $\frac{3}{5}$ **b.** $\frac{9}{75}$ **c.** $\frac{21}{40}$ **d.** $\frac{11}{16}$

You can write a percent as a fraction. First write the percent as a fraction with a denominator of 100. Then simplify the fraction.

Real-World Connection

An elephant eats about 6% of its body weight in vegetation each day.

5 EXAMPLE Writing Percents as Fractions

Biology An elephant sleeps about 15% of each day. What fraction of each day does an elephant sleep?

$15\% = \frac{15}{100}$ ← Write 15% as a fraction with a denominator of 100.

$= \frac{15 \div 5}{100 \div 5}$ ← Divide the numerator and the denominator by the GCF, 5.

$= \frac{3}{20}$ ← Simplify the fraction.

An elephant sleeps about $\frac{3}{20}$ of each day.

5 Write each percent as a fraction in simplest form.

a. 95% **b.** 8% **c.** 79% **d.** 10%

e. **Number Sense** When you write a percent as a fraction with a denominator of 100, what are the only possibilities for the GCF of the numerator and the denominator of the fraction?

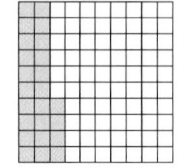

Key Concepts — Percent Summary

Model	Fraction	Decimal	Percent
[10×10 grid with 24 squares shaded]	$\frac{24}{100}$, or $\frac{6}{25}$	0.24	24%

Here is a table of frequently used fractions, decimals, and percents.

Fraction	$\frac{1}{8}$	$\frac{1}{4}$	$\frac{1}{3}$	$\frac{1}{2}$	$\frac{2}{3}$	$\frac{3}{4}$
Decimal	0.125	0.25	$0.33\overline{3}$	0.5	$0.66\overline{6}$	0.75
Percent	12.5%	25%	$33\frac{1}{3}\%$	50%	$66\frac{2}{3}\%$	75%

EXERCISES

For more practice, see *Extra Practice*.

A Practice by Example

Example 1 (page 296)

Write each decimal as a percent.

1. 0.52 **2.** 0.375 **3.** 0.09 **4.** 0.155 **5.** 0.6

Example 2 (page 296)

Write each percent as a decimal.

6. 32% **7.** 88% **8.** 19.1% **9.** 3% **10.** 1.25%

Example 3 (page 296)

Order from least to greatest.

11. $\frac{1}{2}$, 12%, 0.25 **12.** 68%, 0.37, $\frac{3}{10}$ **13.** 0.81, $\frac{4}{5}$, 90%

14. 72%, $\frac{3}{4}$, 0.68 **15.** $\frac{1}{8}$, 18%, 0.19 **16.** 0.52, 14%, $\frac{5}{8}$

Example 4 (page 297)

Write each fraction as a percent. When necessary, round to the nearest tenth of a percent. Exercise 17 has been started for you.

17. $\frac{45}{50} = 0.90$ **18.** $\frac{7}{8}$ **19.** $\frac{1}{12}$

20. $\frac{5}{6}$ **21.** $\frac{7}{9}$ **22.** $\frac{3}{11}$

23. In your class, 9 of the 26 students are in the chorus. What percent of your class is in the chorus? Round to the nearest tenth of a percent.

Example 5 (page 297)

Write each percent as a fraction in simplest form.

24. 12% **25.** 6% **26.** 20%

27. 45% **28.** 17% **29.** 30%

30. **Computers** A computer screen shows the print on a page at 75% of full size. Write 75% as a fraction.

B Apply Your Skills

Compare. Use <, >, or =.

31. $0.32 \;■\; 3.2\%$
32. $\frac{18}{36} \;■\; 50\%$
33. $80\% \;■\; \frac{7}{8}$
34. $53\% \;■\; 0.532$
35. $24\% \;■\; 0.24$
36. $\frac{1}{3} \;■\; 33\%$

Potato Facts

Nutrient	RDA
Magnesium	14%
Iron	34%
Vitamin B6	35%

SOURCE: National Institutes of Health

37. **Nutrition** The table at the left shows the percent of the Recommended Daily Allowance for some of the nutrients in a 6-oz baked potato.
    a. Write each percent as a fraction and as a decimal.
    b. Suppose you eat a 6-oz baked potato. What percent of each nutrient do you still need to meet the Recommended Daily Allowance?

38. **Grades** Your teacher uses different methods of grading quizzes. You have had six quizzes with grades of 85%, $\frac{9}{10}$, $\frac{16}{20}$, 92%, $\frac{21}{25}$, and 79%.
    a. Write your grades in order from least to greatest.
    b. Find the average percent grade of your six quizzes.

39. **Data File, p. 289** Find the difference in the length of the sides from Step 1 to Step 2. Write your answer as a percent.

Number Sense **To write percents containing mixed numbers as fractions, you multiply the mixed number by $\frac{1}{100}$. Simplify where possible. Write each percent as a fraction.**

Sample $33\frac{1}{3}\% = 33\frac{1}{3} \times \frac{1}{100} = \frac{100}{3} \times \frac{1}{100} = \frac{1}{3}$

40. $62\frac{1}{2}\%$
41. $16\frac{2}{3}\%$
42. $6\frac{1}{4}\%$
43. $2\frac{1}{2}\%$
44. $3\frac{1}{3}\%$
45. $13\frac{1}{3}\%$

Math in the Media **Use the cartoon for Exercises 46–48.**

46. a. Write the percent of the pizza with olives as a fraction.
    b. How many slices of pizza will have olives?

47. a. Find the percent of the pizza that is plain.
    b. How many slices of the pizza will be plain?

48. What percent of the pizza will have onions and green peppers?

49. **Writing in Math** Does 0.4 equal 0.4%? Explain.

Match each percent with an equal fraction or decimal.

50. 3%	**51.** 30%	**52.** $33\frac{1}{3}$%	**53.** 3.3%	**54.** 33%
A. $\frac{1}{3}$	**B.** 0.033	**C.** 0.33	**D.** $\frac{3}{10}$	**E.** 0.03

Challenge

Write each percent as a fraction. Simplify where possible.

55. 19.1% **56.** 1.25% **57.** 67.8% **58.** 3.75%

Macaroni & Cheese

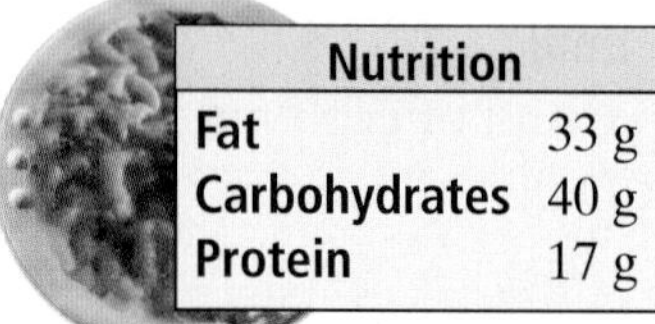

Nutrition	
Fat	33 g
Carbohydrates	40 g
Protein	17 g

Spaghetti & Meat Sauce

Nutrition	
Fat	12 g
Carbohydrates	39 g
Protein	19 g

59. Nutrition Before a race, runners usually eat foods high in carbohydrates. A gram of fat has 9 Calories. A gram of protein and a gram of carbohydrates each has 4 Calories.

a. How many Calories does one serving of macaroni and cheese have?

b. How many Calories does one serving of spaghetti and meat sauce have?

c. What percent of the Calories in each meal is from carbohydrates? Round to the nearest percent.

d. Reasoning Which meal is the better choice for a runner? Why?

60. Stretch Your Thinking Use a whole number, a fraction, and one plus sign to make four 2's add to 23.

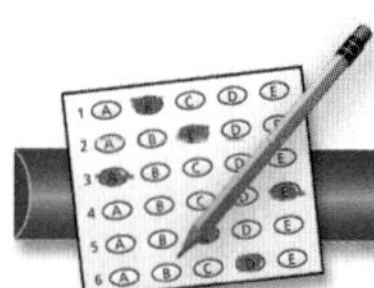

Test Prep

Multiple Choice

61. Which fraction equals $66\frac{2}{3}$%?

A. $\frac{66}{100}$ B. $\frac{200}{3}$ C. $\frac{68}{3}$ D. $\frac{18}{27}$

Take It to the NET
Online lesson quiz at
www.PHSchool.com
Web Code aba-0602

62. Which decimal equals $6\frac{1}{4}$%?

F. 0.00625 G. 0.0625 H. 0.625 I. 6.25

63. Which quantity has the least value?

A. $\frac{3}{8}$ B. 0.38 C. 3.9% D. 3.7

Short Response

64. Explain how to rewrite a fraction as a percent. Give an example.

Mixed Review

Lesson 3-9

Write each decimal as a fraction or mixed number in simplest form.

65. 1.8 **66.** 2.25 **67.** 0.004 **68.** 0.7

69. 2.3 **70.** 1.04 **71.** 0.35 **72.** 0.005

Lesson 1-3

Find each product.

73. 0.35×80 **74.** 0.05×42 **75.** 1.02×0.9 **76.** 2.4×0.7

6-3 Percents Greater Than 100% or Less Than 1%

What You'll Learn

To use percents greater than 100% or less than 1%

. . . And Why

To find a percent in the U.S. House, as in Example 4

Check Skills You'll Need

For help, go to Lesson 6-1.

Model each percent.

1. 40% **2.** 1% **3.** 100%

Write each ratio as a percent.

4. $\frac{1}{100}$ **5.** $\frac{49}{50}$ **6.** $\frac{19}{20}$ **7.** $\frac{2}{25}$

OBJECTIVE

Interactive lesson includes instant self-check, tutorials, and activities.

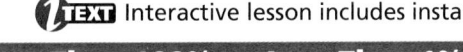

1 Using Percents Greater Than 100% or Less Than 1%

A percent is a ratio that compares a number to 100. If the number compared to 100 is greater than 100, the percent is greater than 100%. If the number compared to 100 is less than 1, the percent is less than 1%.

1 EXAMPLE Rewriting Percents Greater Than 100

Real World

Nutrition You get 110% of the Recommended Daily Allowance of vitamin C from one half of a grapefruit. Write 110% as a decimal and as a fraction.

$110\% = 1.10$ ←To write as a decimal, move the decimal point two places to the left.

$110\% = \frac{110}{100}$ ←To write as a fraction, use the definition of percent.

$= \frac{11}{10}$, or $1\frac{1}{10}$ ←Simplify the fraction.

110% equals 1.10 in decimal form and $1\frac{1}{10}$ in fraction form.

Check Understanding 1 Write 125% as a decimal and as a fraction in simplest form.

2 EXAMPLE Rewriting Percents Less Than 1

Write 0.7% as a decimal and a fraction.

$0.7\% = 0.007$ ←To write as a decimal, move the decimal point two places to the left.

$0.7\% = \frac{0.7}{100}$ ←To write as a fraction, use the definition of percent.

$= \frac{0.7 \cdot 10}{100 \cdot 10}$ ←Multiply numerator and denominator by 10.

$= \frac{7}{1{,}000}$ ←Simplify as a fraction with a whole number numerator.

0.7% equals 0.007 in decimal form and $\frac{7}{1{,}000}$ in fraction form.

Check Understanding 2 Write 0.35% as a decimal and as a fraction in simplest form.

A mixed number represents a percent greater than 100%.

3 EXAMPLE Writing Mixed Numbers as Percents

Entertainment You want to see a movie. The cost of admission to a movie is $1\frac{7}{8}$ times the cost of renting a video. Write this mixed number as a percent.

$1\frac{7}{8}$ = 1 [+] 7 [÷] 8 [=] 1.875 ←Use a calculator.

= 1.87.5 = 187.5% ←Move the decimal point two places to the right.

The cost of admission to a movie is 187.5% of the cost of renting a video.

Check Understanding 3 Write each mixed number or decimal as a percent. When necessary, round to the nearest hundredth of a percent.

a. $3\frac{5}{12}$ **b.** $2\frac{4}{5}$ **c.** 1.71 **d.** 4.005

A proper fraction represents a percent less than 100%.

4 EXAMPLE Real-World Problem Solving

Government West Virginia has 3 members in the U.S. House of Representatives. There are a total of 435 representatives. What percent of the representatives are from West Virginia? Round to the nearest hundredth of a percent.

$\frac{\text{West Virginia representatives}}{\text{total number of representatives}} = \frac{3}{435}$ ←Write the fraction.

= 0.0068965517 ←Use a calculator.

≈ 0.69% ←Write as a percent, and round.

About 0.69% of the representatives are from West Virginia.

Check Understanding 4 Idaho has two members in the U.S. House of Representatives. Find the percent of the representatives that are from Idaho. Round to the nearest hundredth of a percent.

EXERCISES

For more practice, see *Extra Practice*.

A Practice by Example

Write each percent as a decimal and as a fraction in simplest form.

Example 1 (page 301)

1. 180% **2.** 130% **3.** 175%

4. 345% **5.** 240% **6.** 452%

Example 2 (page 301)

7. 0.1% **8.** 0.75% **9.** 0.09%

10. 0.16% **11.** 0.5% **12.** 0.05%

Write each number as a percent. When necessary, round to the nearest hundredth of a percent.

Example 3 (page 302)

13. $4\frac{3}{4}$ **14.** $1\frac{3}{5}$ **15.** $1\frac{1}{100}$

16. $2\frac{29}{50}$ **17.** $3\frac{7}{20}$ **18.** $2\frac{3}{8}$

19. 1.034 **20.** 2.65 **21.** 4.81

Example 4 (page 302)

22. $\frac{7}{1,000}$ **23.** $\frac{1}{400}$ **24.** $\frac{3}{500}$

25. $\frac{7}{998}$ **26.** $\frac{5}{684}$ **27.** $\frac{2}{329}$

28. 0.00675 **29.** 0.0028 **30.** 0.0001

31. Reading A library finds that borrowing reference books between libraries is $1\frac{9}{10}$ of what it was 15 years ago. Write this fraction as a percent.

B Apply Your Skills

Write each percent as a decimal and a fraction.

32. Sales Jewelry sales in December were 166% of sales in November.

33. Weather On March 1, the snowpack in the Northern Great Basin of Nevada was 126% of the average snowpack.

34. Environment Some studies indicate that the desert shrublands could increase as much as 185% in the next century due to global warming.

Real-World Connection

Shrubs are the leading plant form in places where there is little rainfall.

Model each percent using one or more 10 × 10 grids.

35. 175% **36.** 120% **37.** 0.5%

Write each number as a percent.

38. $\frac{6}{5}$ **39.** 1.55 **40.** $\frac{51}{25}$ **41.** $1\frac{3}{4}$ **42.** $\frac{15}{8}$

Decide whether each percent is reasonable. Explain why or why not.

43. Buttermilk is 105% milk fat.

44. Rainfall in Oklahoma this year is reported to be 120% of the average.

45. A scientific study concluded that 0.5% of the seeds will not grow.

46. The addition raised the school's value to 0.7% of its previous value.

47. Writing in Math What does it mean to reach 120% of a savings goal?

C Challenge

Write each percent as a decimal.

48. $152\frac{1}{8}\%$ **49.** $114\frac{3}{16}\%$ **50.** $190\frac{5}{7}\%$ **51.** $210\frac{7}{40}\%$

52. Auctions Recently, a near-mint copy of the Baltimore Orioles 1966 Yearbook was auctioned for $15. The yearbook cost $.50 in 1966. Write a ratio of the auction price to the original price. Find the percent.

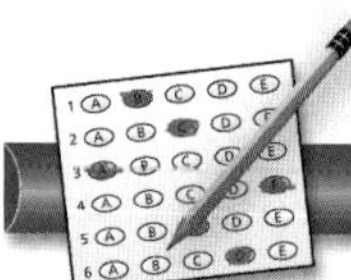

Test Prep

Multiple Choice

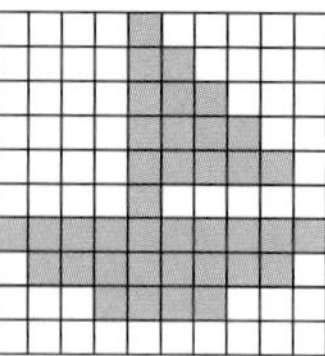

53. Which set of numbers represents the shaded area of the figure at the right?

A. 0.38%, $\frac{38}{100}$, 0.038 **B.** 3.8%, $\frac{38}{100}$, 0.38

C. 38%, $\frac{38}{100}$, 0.038 **D.** 38%, $\frac{38}{100}$, 0.38

Take It to the NET
Online lesson quiz at
www.PHSchool.com
Web Code aba-0603

54. The fraction $\frac{9}{1,000}$ is equal to which set of numbers?

F. 0.9%, 0.009 **G.** 0.9%, 90 **H.** 9%, 0.9 **I.** 90%, 0.90

55. One hour is what percent of one week? Round to the nearest tenth.

A. 0.5% **B.** 0.6% **C.** 5.9% **D.** 6.0%

Short Response

56. You miss 1 day of school out of 180 days in the school year.
a. Explain how to express 1 day out of school as a percent.
b. Round to the nearest tenth of a percent.

Mixed Review

Lesson 6-2

Write each percent as a fraction in simplest form.

57. 28% **58.** 37.5% **59.** 80% **60.** 74%

61. 19% **62.** 10% **63.** 95% **64.** 3%

Lesson 4-4

Find each product.

65. $\frac{3}{5} \cdot 40$ **66.** $\frac{5}{9} \cdot 144$ **67.** $\frac{7}{8} \cdot 280$ **68.** $\frac{1}{6} \cdot 423$

Practice Game

Order, Please!

What You'll Need

- 30 pieces of construction paper, each with a fraction, decimal, or a percent written on it. Include mixed numbers or the equivalent decimals and percents.

How to Play

- Select two teams of five players. Each player receives one piece of construction paper.
- When play begins, team members must order themselves from the least to the greatest numbers.
- The first team to order their numbers correctly is the winner.

6-4 Finding a Percent of a Number

What You'll Learn

To use a percent to find part of a whole

To use mental math and estimation with percents

. . . And Why

To find the number of students, as in Example 2

Check Skills You'll Need

For help, go to Lesson 1-9.

Find each product using the Distributive Property and mental math.

1. $80 \cdot 15$
2. $61 \cdot 15$
3. $75 \cdot 18$
4. $42 \cdot 1.5$
5. $78 \cdot 0.9$
6. $27 \cdot 1.1$
7. Explain how you could use the Distributive Property to find \$38 $\times$ 15 using mental math.

OBJECTIVE

Interactive lesson includes instant self-check, tutorials, and activities.

1 Using a Percent to Find Part of a Whole

Investigation: Using Percent Data From a Graph

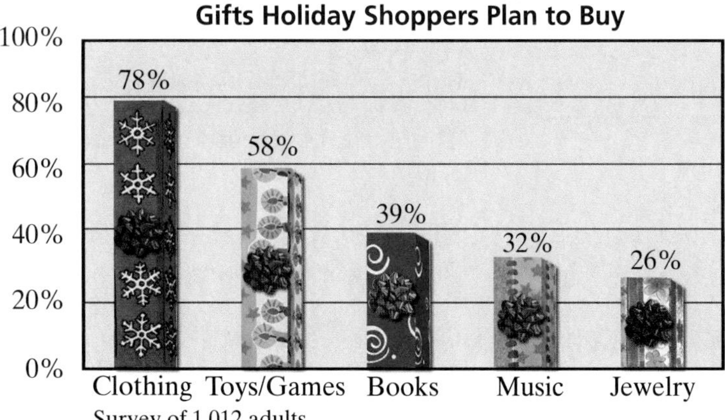

1. What do most people have on their gift list?
2. How many people answered the survey?
3. a. What do about $\frac{1}{3}$ of the people have on their lists?
   b. About how many people does that represent?
4. a. What do about $\frac{1}{4}$ of the people have on their lists?
   b. About how many people does that represent?
5. Why do you think the sum of the percents is greater than 100%?

To find 25% of 44, you can write 25% either as a decimal or a fraction and then multiply by 44.

1 EXAMPLE Finding a Percent of a Whole

Find 25% of 44.

Method 1 Write 25% as a fraction and multiply.

$25\% = \frac{25}{100} = \frac{1}{4}$ ← **Write the percent as a fraction in simplest form.**

$\frac{1}{4} \cdot 44 = 11$ ← **Multiply.**

Method 2 Write 25% as a decimal and multiply.

$25\% = 0.25$ ← **Write the percent as a decimal.**

$0.25 \cdot 44 = 11$ ← **Multiply.**

Check Understanding 1 **a.** Find 45% of 130.

b. **Reasoning** When would you use a decimal to find a percent? When would you use a fraction to find a percent?

2 EXAMPLE Real-World Problem Solving

Sports There are 75 students at tryouts for the basketball team. Of this number, 64% are in the seventh grade. How many seventh-grade students are trying out for the team?

> **Need Help?**
> For help in writing a percent as a fraction, go to Lesson 6-2.

Estimate 64% of 75 $\approx \frac{2}{3} \cdot 75$, or 50

$64\% = 0.64$ ← **Change the percent to a decimal.**

$0.64 \cdot 75 = 48$ ← **Multiply.**

There are 48 seventh-grade students attending tryouts for the basketball team.

Check for Reasonableness The answer 48 is close to the estimate 50. The answer is reasonable.

Check Understanding 2 Of the seventh-grade students who tried out, 37.5% made the team. How many seventh-grade students made the team?

OBJECTIVE 2 Using Mental Math and Estimation With Percents

You can use mental math to find percents of numbers involving percents such as 100%, 50%, 10%, and 1%.

- 100% of a number is the number itself. 100% of 190 = 190
- 50% of a number is $\frac{1}{2}$ of the number. 50% of 190 = 95
- 10% of a number is 0.1 of the number. 10% of 190 = 19.0.
- 1% of a number is 0.01 of the number. 1% of 190 = 1.90.

3 EXAMPLE Using Mental Math

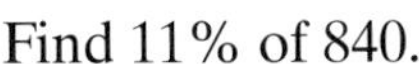

Find 11% of 840.

What you think
11% is 10% + 1%.
10% of 840 is 0.1 · 840, or 84.
1% of 840 is 0.01 · 840, or 8.4.
So 84 + 8.4 = 92.4.

Why it works

$0.11 \cdot 840$ ← **Write 11% as a decimal.**
$(0.10 + 0.01) \cdot 840$ ← **Substitute 0.10 + 0.01 for 0.11.**
$(0.10 \cdot 840) + (0.01 \cdot 840)$ ← **Use the Distributive Property.**
$84 + 8.4$ ← **Multiply.**
92.4 ← **Simplify.**

✓ Check Understanding 3 Use mental math to find each percent of 2,400.
a. 40% **b.** 99% **c.** 9% **d.** 61%

Need Help?
For help using compatible numbers, go to Lesson 1-1.

You can use compatible numbers to estimate a percent.

4 EXAMPLE Estimating a Percent

Estimate 32% of 912.

32% · 912 ← **Write an expression.**
↓ ↓
$\frac{1}{3} \cdot 900 = 300$ ← **Use compatible numbers such as $\frac{1}{3}$ and 900.**

Check for Reasonableness 32% of 912 is 0.32 · 912, or 291.84, which is close to the estimate 300. The answer is reasonable.

✓ Check Understanding 4 Estimate each answer.
a. 24% of 238 **b.** 19% of 473 **c.** 82% of 747 **d.** 63% of 810

EXERCISES

For more practice, see *Extra Practice*.

A Practice by Example

Examples 1, 2 (page 306)

Find each answer. Exercise 1 has been started for you.

1. 6% of 90
6% of 90 = 0.06 · 90

2. 125% of 64

3. 12.5% of 56

4. 12% of 230

5. 75% of 240

6. 15% of 45

7. 3% of 12

8. 150% of 17

9. 7% of 300

10. 27% of 120

11. 60% of 120

12. 20% of 80

13. Four hundred students attended a school dance. If 35% of the students were boys, how many boys attended the dance?

14. Of 90 coins in a bank, 20% are quarters. Find the number of quarters in the bank.

Example 3 (page 307)

Mental Math **Find each answer using mental math.**

15. 11% of 536	**16.** 9% of 780	**17.** 50% of 948
18. 40% of 216	**19.** 51% of 840	**20.** 30% of 714
21. 60% of 520	**22.** 49% of 150	**23.** 90% of 345

Example 4 (page 307)

Estimate each answer.

24. 27% of 162	**25.** 33% of 88	**26.** 53% of 721
27. 19% of 399	**28.** 98% of 65	**29.** 73% of 522
30. 66% of 243	**31.** 48% of 658	**32.** 13% of 326

33. **Number Sense** Is 32% of 96 the same value as 96% of 32? Explain your reasoning.

34. a. **Books** A large bookcase contains 75 books. If 64% of the books are novels, how many novels are in the bookcase?
    b. Robert Louis Stevenson wrote 12.5% of the novels in part (a). How many Stevenson novels are in the bookcase?

ON SALE NOW!
30% off
Calico originally $5.68/yd.
Cotton Knit originally $5.98/yd.
50% off
Patterns originally $4.98
25% off
Scissors originally $12.98
Thread 65% off originally $1.49
Hurry in! Sale Ends Saturday!

Sewing **Use the advertisement at the left for Exercises 35–38.**

35. a. What percent of the original price of the calico fabric is the sale price?
    b. What is the sale price?

36. What is the sale price of the patterns?

37. Find the sale price of the scissors.

38. Which costs less on sale, the calico or the cotton knit fabric? How much less?

Find each answer.

39. Find 37.5% of 12.	**40.** What is 8% of 25?	**41.** Find 30% of 40.
42. What is 25% of 95?	**43.** Find 190% of 13.	**44.** What is 20% of 20?
45. What is 120% of 34?	**46.** Find 12% of 33.	**47.** Find 30% of 120.

48. **Sales** The regular price of a calculator is $15.40. Today only, you can buy it for 70% of the regular price. If you buy the calculator today, how much will you pay for it?

49. **Salary** A nurse earning an annual salary of $39,235 gets a 4% raise. What is the amount of the raise?

Real-World Connection

Helicopters drop water, foam, or fire retardant to prevent fires from spreading.

50. Forestry Russia had 17,000 forest fires in 2001. Aircraft extinguished 40% of the fires. How many of the fires were put out by aircraft?

51. Sales Suppose you want to buy a $450 stereo. With a down payment of 30%, the store will charge no interest and will let you make payments of $35 per month. How many months will it take you to buy the stereo?

Find each answer by estimating.

52. Find 40.5% of 321.

53. What is 13% of 475?

54. What is 63% of 123?

55. Find 59.7% of 91.

56. What is 110% of 478?

57. Find 120% of 850.

58. Data Analysis At a high school, 150 students are surveyed about their foreign language classes. The graph below shows their responses.

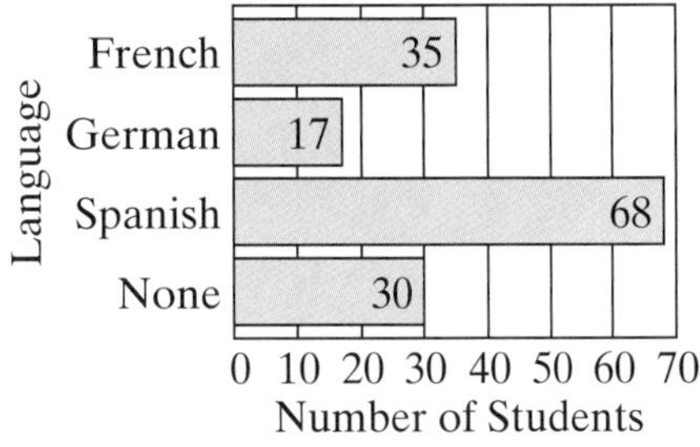

a. How many students take French? What percent of the 150 students surveyed take French?

b. Find the percent of students taking each of the other languages.

c. **Estimation** The high school population is 2,500. Use the percents that you found in parts (a) and (b). Estimate the number of students at the school taking each language.

59. Grades You take a test with 25 questions on it. Your grade on the test is 84%. How many questions do you get right?

60. Writing in Math Explain how you would find 99% of 800.

C Challenge

Find each amount.

61. $\frac{1}{2}$% of $32,000

62. $\frac{1}{4}$% of $65,000

63. $\frac{3}{4}$% of $41,000

64. a. Reasoning The number of students in this year's seventh-grade class is 110% of the number in last year's class. When you write 110% as a ratio, what number is in the denominator? Why?

b. Are there more or fewer students in this year's class? Why?

c. There were 260 students in last year's class. How many students are in this year's class?

65. Stretch Your Thinking I am a 2-digit number. I am the difference of two numbers whose sum is 36. The larger of these numbers is twice the smaller. What number am I?

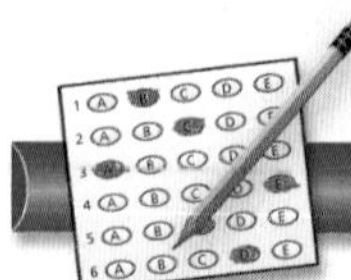

Test Prep

Multiple Choice

66. Find 0.1% of 560.

A. 0.056 **B.** 0.56 **C.** 5.6 **D.** 56

67. Which expression provides the best estimate for 37% of 621?

F. 40% of 600 **G.** $33\frac{1}{3}\%$ of 600

H. $33\frac{1}{3}\%$ of 630 **I.** 35% of 700

Take It to the NET
Online lesson quiz at
www.PHSchool.com
Web Code aba-0604

68. At a sale where everything is 70% of the original price, you find a jacket originally priced at \$58.90 and a pair of jeans originally priced at \$29.95. Estimate the total cost.

A. \$30 **B.** \$60 **C.** \$90 **D.** \$120

Extended Response

69. A woman with a salary of \$41,820 gets a raise of 4%. Her expenses have increased by \$1,800. Explain whether she now has enough money to pay her expenses.

Mixed Review

Lesson 6-2 **Write each decimal as a percent.**

70. 0.04 **71.** 0.92 **72.** 0.45

Lesson 5-5 **Algebra** **Solve each proportion using cross products.**

73. $\frac{13}{39} = \frac{n}{60}$ **74.** $\frac{7}{15} = \frac{28}{m}$ **75.** $\frac{21}{x} = \frac{5}{8}$

Lesson 4-6 **Algebra** **Solve each equation.**

76. $y + \frac{1}{2} = \frac{7}{8}$ **77.** $x - \frac{3}{10} = 6$ **78.** $a - \frac{3}{4} = \frac{1}{2}$

Checkpoint Quiz 1 — Lessons 6-1 through 6-4

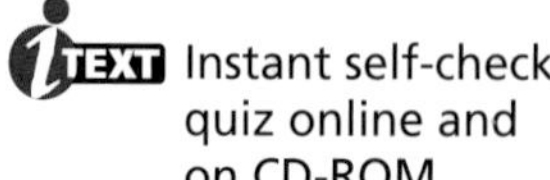

Instant self-check quiz online and on CD-ROM

Write each percent as a decimal and as a fraction in simplest terms.

1. 45% **2.** 135% **3.** 0.98%

Write each fraction as a percent.

4. $\frac{14}{25}$ **5.** $\frac{3}{15}$ **6.** $\frac{1}{250}$

Find each answer.

7. What is 29% of 58? **8.** Find 190% of 16. **9.** Find 0.5% of 48.

10. A club has 100 members. Each of the five officers gets six other members to help decorate for a club party. What percent of the club members help decorate?

Algebra

6-5 Solving Percent Problems Using Proportions

What You'll Learn

To find the percent using proportions

To find the whole using proportions

. . . And Why

To find total earnings, as in Example 4

Check Skills You'll Need

For help, go to Lesson 5-5.

Solve each proportion using cross products.

1. $\frac{n}{32} = \frac{1}{4}$
2. $\frac{6}{n} = \frac{2}{5}$
3. $\frac{7}{8} = \frac{n}{100}$
4. $\frac{7}{20} = \frac{35}{n}$
5. $\frac{42}{n} = \frac{3}{4}$
6. $\frac{9}{25} = \frac{n}{100}$
7. Explain how you would solve the proportion $\frac{n}{60} = \frac{75}{100}$.

Interactive lesson includes instant self-check, tutorials, and activities.

OBJECTIVE 1

Finding the Percent Using Proportions

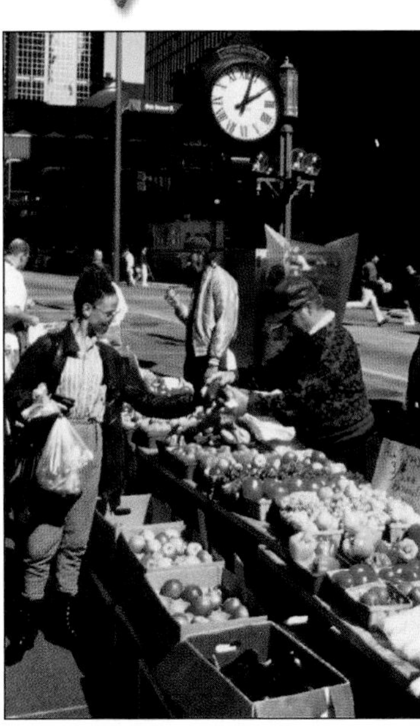

Many growers sell their produce at markets in nearby cities.

In a market, 44 of the 80 types of vegetables are grown locally. What percent of the vegetables are grown locally? You can use a model to help find this percent.

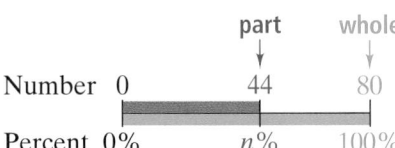

		part	whole
Number	0	44	80
Percent	0%	n%	100%

$\frac{44}{80} = \frac{n}{100}$ ← **The part, 44, corresponds to *n* in the model.** ← **The whole, 80, corresponds to 100.**

1 EXAMPLE Finding a Percent

What percent of 80 is 44?

Using the model above, you can write a proportion and find the percent.

$\frac{44}{80} = \frac{n}{100}$ ← **Write a proportion.**

$80n = 44(100)$ ← **Write the cross products.**

$\frac{80n}{80} = \frac{44(100)}{80}$ ← **Divide each side by 80.**

$n = 55$ ← **Simplify.**

44 is 55% of 80.

Check Understanding 1 Use a proportion to solve.

a. What percent of 92 is 23?
b. 36 is what percent of 125?
c. **Number Sense** Is the answer to "What percent of 44 is 80?" the same as the answer to Example 1? Explain.

2 EXAMPLE Real-World Problem Solving

Real-World Connection

The brass instruments are trumpet, trombone, French horn, and tuba.

Music In a school band of 24 students, 9 students play brass instruments. What percent of the band members play brass instruments?

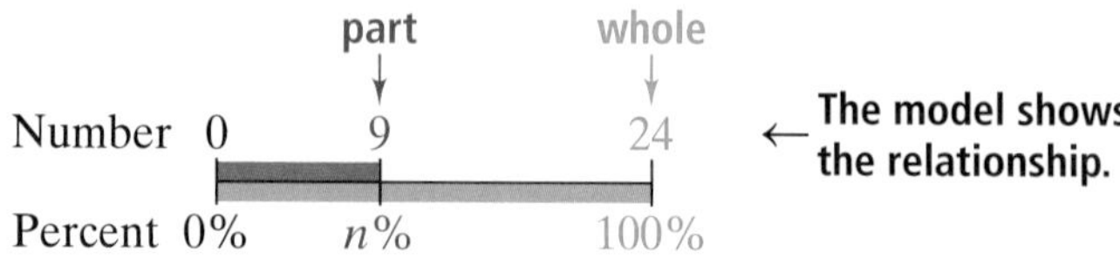

← The model shows the relationship.

$$\frac{9}{24} = \frac{n}{100}$$ ← Write a proportion.

$$24n = 9(100)$$ ← Write the cross products.

$$\frac{24n}{24} = \frac{9(100)}{24}$$ ← Divide each side by 24.

$$n = 37.5$$ ← Simplify.

37.5% of the band members play brass instruments.

Check Understanding 2 **a.** Reasoning In Example 2, how do you know to use $\frac{9}{24}$ and not $\frac{24}{9}$?

b. In Example 2, 3 of the 9 students are girls. What percent of the band is made up of girls who play brass instruments?

OBJECTIVE 2

Finding the Whole Using Proportions

You can use the same proportion model to show other relationships between a number, a percent, and the whole.

3 EXAMPLE Finding the Whole

54 is 20% of what number?

		part	whole
Number	0	54	n
Percent	0%	20%	100%

← The model shows the relationship.

$$\frac{54}{n} = \frac{20}{100}$$ ← Write the proportion.

$$20n = 54(100)$$ ← Write the cross products.

$$\frac{20n}{20} = \frac{54(100)}{20}$$ ← Divide each side by 20.

$$n = 270$$ ← Simplify.

54 is 20% of 270.

Check Understanding 3 Use a proportion to solve.

a. 42 is 56% of what number?

b. 65% of what number is 39?

c. Number Sense Is the answer to "70 is 125% of what number?" greater than or less than 70? Explain.

You can find the whole if you know a percent and the amount that the percent represents.

4 EXAMPLE Real-World Problem Solving

Budgeting Suppose you have a part-time summer job. You decide that 30% of your earnings can be spent on entertainment. You plan a movie and pizza night with friends that will cost you $10.50. How much will you need to earn at your job in order to stay within your budget?

Model the relationship.

	part	whole	
Number 0	$10.50	n	← The model shows the relationship.
Percent 0%	30%	100%	

$\frac{10.50}{n} = \frac{30}{100}$ ← Write the proportion.

$30n = 10.50(100)$ ← Write the cross products.

$\frac{30n}{30} = \frac{10.50(100)}{30}$ ← Divide each side by 30.

$n = 35$ ← Simplify.

You need to earn $35 to stay within your budget.

Check 30% of 35 = 0.30 · 35 = 10.50 ✔

✔ Check Understanding 4 Use a proportion to solve.

a. 60 is 24% of what number?

b. 40% of what number is 96?

c. **Reasoning** Is it reasonable to budget 30% for entertainment, 50% for savings, and 25% for clothes? Why or why not?

Percent problems involve a part, a percent, and a whole. If you know two of the three pieces, you can find the missing piece. The easiest piece to identify is the percent. The word *of* is usually followed by the whole.

Here is a summary of what you have learned.

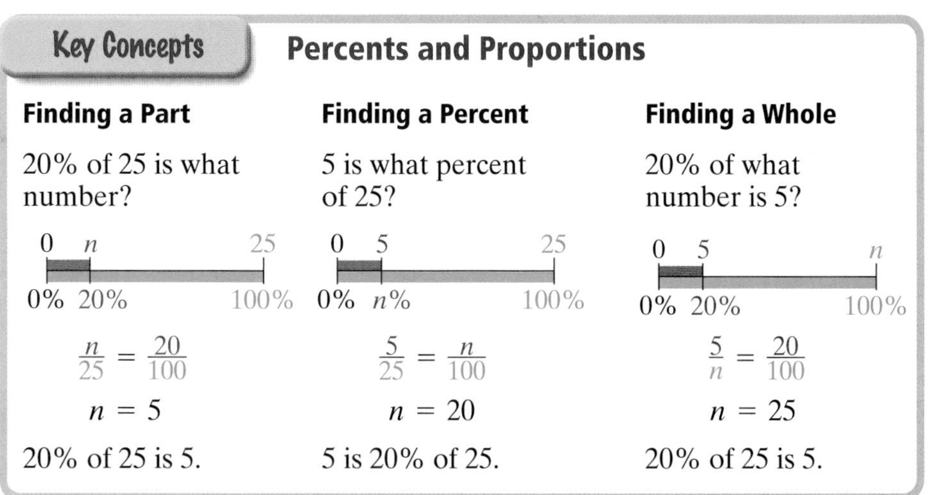

Key Concepts — Percents and Proportions

Finding a Part

20% of 25 is what number?

0, n, 25; 0%, 20%, 100%

$\frac{n}{25} = \frac{20}{100}$

$n = 5$

20% of 25 is 5.

Finding a Percent

5 is what percent of 25?

0, 5, 25; 0%, n%, 100%

$\frac{5}{25} = \frac{n}{100}$

$n = 20$

5 is 20% of 25.

Finding a Whole

20% of what number is 5?

0, 5, n; 0%, 20%, 100%

$\frac{5}{n} = \frac{20}{100}$

$n = 25$

20% of 25 is 5.

For more practice, see *Extra Practice*.

A Practice by Example

Example 1 (page 311)

Use a proportion to solve.

1. 24 is what percent of 32?
2. What percent of 230 is 23?
3. What percent of 25 is 23?
4. What percent of 400 is 8?
5. 21 is what percent of 168?
6. 246 is what percent of 656?
7. 364 is what percent of 455?
8. What percent of 600 is 84?

Example 2 (page 312)

9. **Time** A school holds classes from 8:00 A.M. to 2:00 P.M. For what percent of a 24-h day does this school hold classes?
10. **Government** Based on the 2000 census, Arizona gained 2 seats in the U.S. House of Representatives. Arizona had 6 seats. What percent of the representatives from Arizona was gained in 2000?
11. **Work** You have a paper route with 40 customers. What percent of the paper route have you completed when you have delivered 28 papers?

Example 3 (page 312)

Use a proportion to solve.

12. 80% of what number is 15?
13. 68% of what number is 51?
14. 42 is 12% of what number?
15. 21 is 84% of what number?
16. 108 is 225% of what number?
17. 342 is 36% of what number?
18. 36 is 72% of what number?
19. 28 is 35% of what number?

Example 4 (page 313)

20. **Sales** A sweater is on sale for $33. This is 75% of the original price. Find the original price.
21. **Tax** You purchase a telescope in a state with a 5% sales tax. You pay $12.45 in tax. What is the price of the telescope?
22. **School** You have answered 12 questions on a homework assignment and are now 60% done. How many questions are in the assignment?

B Apply Your Skills

Write a proportion for each model. Solve for *n*.

23. 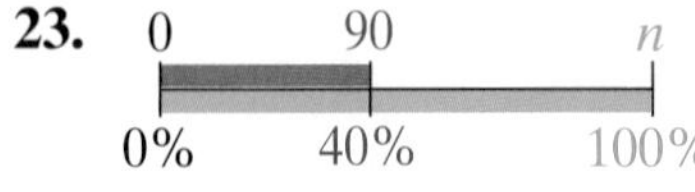

24. 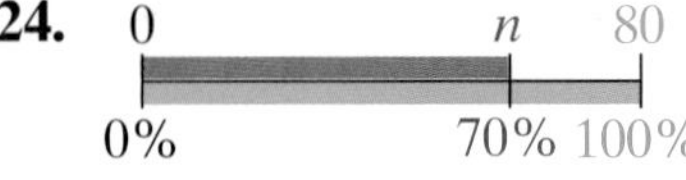

25. 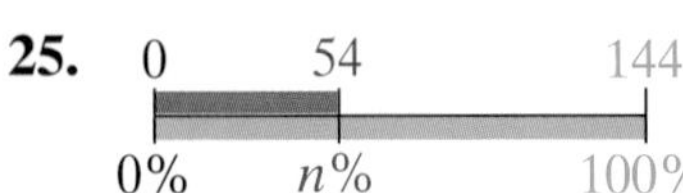

26. 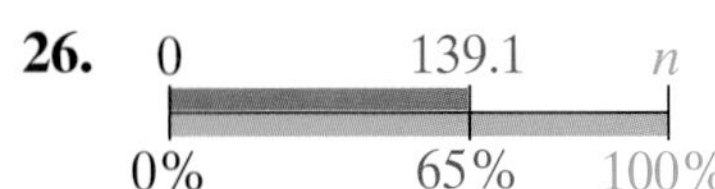

27. **a.** 50 is what percent of 75? **b.** 75 is what percent of 50?
    c. Which results in a percent greater than 100%—your answer to part (a) or your answer to part (b)? Why?

Real-World Connection

Some schools award ribbons for outstanding academic performance.

28. **Awards** An awards banquet is attended by 120 people. Ribbons are awarded for first, second, and third place in each of 25 categories. No one gets more than one ribbon. What percent of the people attending the banquet receives a ribbon?

29. **Sports** At a track meet, there are 8 runners for each of 6 qualifying runs. The top 25% of the field will qualify for a regional race. How many of the runners at the meet will qualify for the regional race?

30. **Open-Ended** Write a percent problem that compares the number of boys to the number of girls in your class.

Match each question with the proportion you could use to solve it.

31. What is 40% of 15? **A.** $\frac{15}{40} = \frac{n}{100}$

32. 15 is what percent of 40? **B.** $\frac{15}{n} = \frac{40}{100}$

33. 40% of what number is 15? **C.** $\frac{n}{15} = \frac{40}{100}$

Use a proportion to solve.

34. What percent of 128 is 6.4?

35. 272 is 80% of what number?

36. 72.5% of what number is 29?

37. 2.5 is what percent of 20?

38. 74% of what number is 29.6?

39. What percent of 1,800 is 972?

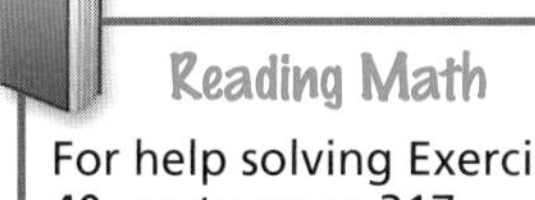

Reading Math

For help solving Exercise 40, go to page 317.

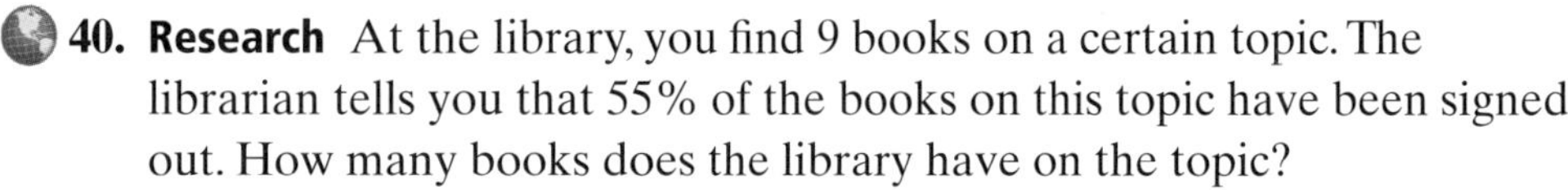

40. **Research** At the library, you find 9 books on a certain topic. The librarian tells you that 55% of the books on this topic have been signed out. How many books does the library have on the topic?

41. **Error Analysis** Your friend solves, "32 is 15% of what number?" by solving the proportion $\frac{n}{32} = \frac{15}{100}$. Explain why your friend is not correct.

42. **Writing in Math** In every percent proportion, there are four quantities. One of the four is always the same quantity. Explain why.

Challenge

Use a proportion to solve.

43. 29 is $16\frac{2}{3}$% of what number?

44. $66\frac{2}{3}$% of what number is 13?

45. **Number Sense** What percent of the numbers from 1 to 20 is prime?

46. **Supplies** Your school orders 210 boxes of chalk, which is 70% of last year's order. Find the decrease in the number of boxes of chalk.

47. **Automobiles** A car dealer advertises "All cars 19% off sticker price!" A buyer pays $10,930.95 for a car. What is the sticker price?

48. **Stretch Your Thinking** How many different squares are shown in the figure at the right?

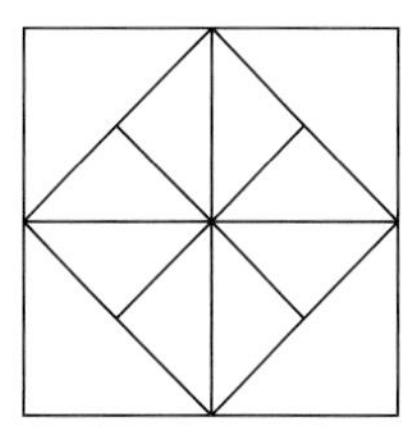

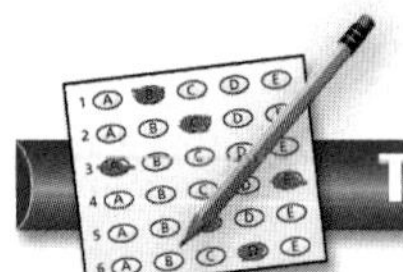

Test Prep

Multiple Choice

49. Which proportion can you use to find what percent 13 is of 20?

A. $\frac{13}{20} = \frac{n}{100}$ **B.** $\frac{n}{20} = \frac{13}{100}$ **C.** $\frac{13}{n} = \frac{100}{20}$ **D.** $\frac{n}{13} = \frac{20}{100}$

50. Use the table. Of the 129 people who responded to the survey, how many say that lizards or snakes are their favorite pets?

Favorite Pet	
Amphibians	3%
Lizards	48%
Snakes	28%
Turtles	11%
Can't choose	3%
Other	7%

SOURCE: www.tkreptiles.com

Take It to the NET
Online lesson quiz at **www.PHSchool.com**
Web Code aba-0605

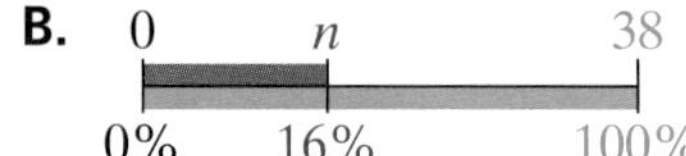

F. 26 **G.** 76 **H.** 98 **I.** 100

51. Which of the following models can you use to answer the question, "16 is 38% of what number?"

A. 0 38 n / 0% 16% 100%

B. 0 n 38 / 0% 16% 100%

C. 0 16 38 / 0% n% 100%

D. 0 16 n / 0% 38% 100%

Short Response

52. You participate in a 50-mi fund-raising walk. You walk 40% of the distance the first day and $\frac{1}{3}$ of the remaining distance on the second day. How many more miles do you have to walk? Explain.

Mixed Review

Lesson 6-4

Find each answer.

53. 56% of 144 **54.** 81% of 63 **55.** 43% of 92

56. 3% of 200 **57.** 17% of 360 **58.** 22% of 84

Lesson 3-5

Write each fraction in simplest form.

59. $\frac{8}{10}$ **60.** $\frac{4}{12}$ **61.** $\frac{5}{100}$ **62.** $\frac{16}{24}$ **63.** $\frac{18}{54}$

Lesson 2-5

Algebra **Write an equation for each sentence. Then solve.**

64. The product of 3 and a number is equal to −48.

65. Two more than 5 times a number is 37.

66. The sum of 6 times a number and 7 is the same as 91.

Reading Math — Understanding Word Problems

For Use With Exercise 40, Page 315

Read through the problem below and then follow along with what Karen thinks as she solves the problem. Check your understanding with the exercise at the bottom of the page.

40. Research At the library, you find 9 books on a certain topic. The librarian tells you that 55% of the books on this topic have been signed out. How many books does the library have on the topic?

What Karen Thinks	What Karen Writes
What information is given? I'll copy and underline the important information.	You find 9 books on a shelf. 55% of the books have been signed out.
What am I trying to find out? I'll write the question.	How many books does the library have on this topic?
If 55% of the books have been signed out, what percent is on the shelf?	100% − 55% = 45%
I know that 9 is the part and 45 is the percent. I can write a proportion to find the whole.	$\frac{9}{n} = \frac{45}{100}$
To solve the proportion, I find the cross products.	$45n = 900$
To solve for n, I divide both sides by 45.	$\frac{45n}{45} = \frac{900}{45}$
Is 20 books a reasonable answer? The number of books on the shelf is about half the number of books on the topic. Yes, my answer is reasonable.	$n = 20$ The library has 20 books on this topic.

EXERCISE

1. There are 144 students in a school one day. Four percent of the students are absent. How many students go to this school?

Algebra

6-6 Solving Percent Problems Using Equations

What You'll Learn

To write and solve percent equations

. . . And Why

To find a percent in a survey, as in Example 3

✓ Check Skills You'll Need

For help, go to Lesson 2-4.

Write an equation for each sentence. Then solve the equation.

1. Three times a number is 51.
2. A number divided by 4 is 12.
3. Seventy is 5 times a number.
4. Five is a number divided by 11.
5. One hundred times a number is 33.
6. A number divided by 10 is 6.

OBJECTIVE

iTEXT Interactive lesson includes instant self-check, tutorials, and activities.

1 Writing and Solving Percent Equations

You can translate percent problems into equations.

1 EXAMPLE Finding the Part

Need Help?

This model shows that n is 39% of 377.

What number is 39% of 377?

Words	A number	is	39%	of	377.
	Let n = the number.				
Equation	n	=	0.39	·	377

$n = 0.39 \cdot 377 = 147.03$ ← **Simplify.**

✓ Check Understanding 1 27% of 60 is what number?

When you know the percent and the part, you can find the whole.

2 EXAMPLE Finding the Whole

Real World

Skiing In New Hampshire, a ski resort is able to open 60% of its runs to skiers. There are 27 runs open. How many runs are there at this resort?

Words	60%	of	the number of ski runs	is	27.
	Let x = the number of ski runs at the resort.				
Equation	0.60	·	x	=	27

$0.60x = 27$

$\frac{0.60x}{0.60} = \frac{27}{0.60}$ ← **Divide each side by 0.60.**

$x = 45$ ← **Simplify.**

There are 45 ski runs at the resort.

Check Understanding 2 Use an equation to solve: 54% of what number is 81?

When you know the part and the whole, you can find the percent.

3 EXAMPLE Finding the Percent 

Recreation Of 3,072 teens surveyed, 2,212 say they read for fun. What percent of the teens say they read for fun?

Words A percent of 3,072 is 2,212 .

Let p = the percent.

Equation $p \cdot 3{,}072 = 2{,}212$

$$p \cdot 3{,}072 = 2{,}212$$

$$3{,}072p = 2{,}212 \quad \leftarrow \text{Simplify.}$$

$$\frac{3{,}072p}{3{,}072} = \frac{2{,}212}{3{,}072} \quad \leftarrow \text{Divide each side by 3,072.}$$

$$p = 0.7200520833 \quad \leftarrow \text{Use a calculator.}$$

$$p \approx 72\% \quad \leftarrow \text{Write the decimal as a percent.}$$

Of the teens surveyed, 72% say they read for fun.

Check Understanding 3 Use an equation to solve: What percent of 325 is 65?

EXERCISES

For more practice, see *Extra Practice*.

A Practice by Example

Example 1 (page 318)

Write and solve an equation to find the part of a whole.

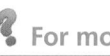

1. 18% of 90 is what number?
2. What number is 41% of 800?
3. What number is 5% of 522?
4. 70% of 279 is what number?
5. What number is 90% of 13?
6. 9% of 351 is what number?
7. 36% of 95 is what number?
8. What number is 56% of 48?
9. **Food** A person is on a 1,500-Calorie eating plan of which 24% of the Calories are from protein. How many Calories are from protein?

Example 2 (page 318)

Write and solve an equation to find the whole.

10. 96% of what number is 24?
11. 40% of what number is 30?
12. 50.4 is 36% of what number?
13. 48% of what number is 216?
14. 12% of what number is 72?
15. 12.8 is 32% of what number?
16. 684 is 95% of what number?
17. 72% of what number is 630?

18. Sports The school basketball team won 24 games. This is 60% of the games played. How many games has the team played?

19. Climate Today's high temperature is 45°F. This is 90% of the normal high temperature for this day. What is the normal high temperature?

Example 3 (page 319)

Write and solve an equation to find the percent.

20. What percent of 496 is 124?

21. What percent of 625 is 550?

22. 39 is what percent of 260?

23. 18 is what percent of 48?

24. What percent of 1,120 is 56?

25. What percent of 620 is 372?

26. 140 is what percent of 224?

27. What percent of 400 is 41?

28. Grades You take a 25-question test and answer 22 questions correctly. What percent of the questions do you answer correctly?

B Apply Your Skills

29. Singing Of the 60 students who belong to a chorus, 30% sing alto and 45% sing soprano. What number of students sings alto or soprano?

30. Food You make 72 cookies for a bake sale. This number is 20% of the cookies at the bake sale. How many cookies are at the bake sale?

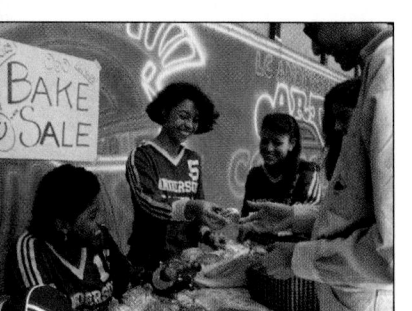

Real-World Connection
Many schools fund extracurricular activites through bake sales.

Match each question with its answer.

31. What is 36% of 90? **A.** 125

32. What is 48% of 60? **B.** 40%

33. What percent of 90 is 36? **C.** 40

34. What percent of 36 is 90? **D.** 32.4

35. 90% of what number is 36? **E.** 28.8

36. 48% of what number is 60? **F.** 250%

37. Writing in Math Write and solve a problem that involves a percent and a number of students.

38. Education The average daily attendance of one school is about 92% of the school's enrollment. The average daily attendance is 422 students. How many students are enrolled in this school?

Use the table. Find the percent of a 365-day year that are school days in each country.

39. China **40.** Israel **41.** Russia

42. What percent of the number of school days in Scotland is the number of school days in the United States?

Length of School Year

Country	Days
China	251
Israel	215
Russia	210
Scotland	200
United States	180

Source: *The Top 10 of Everything*

43. a. Your club has a "name the mascot" contest. Of the 28 votes submitted, Nanook is the winning name with 12 votes. Did more than half of the voting members select the name Nanook?

b. What percent of the votes submitted are for Nanook?

44. Theater The attendance at the school play on Friday night was 95% of the attendance on Saturday night. If 300 people attended on Saturday night, how many attended on Friday night?

45. Gardening You plant 40 pots with seedlings. Eight of the pots contain tomato plants. What percent of your seedlings are tomato plants?

Write an equation for each question. Then solve the equation.

46. What is 29% of 1,974?

47. What percent of 840 is 546?

48. 606.9 is 85% of what number?

49. What is 77% of 413?

50. What percent of 950 is 399?

51. 24.3 is 18% of what number?

Challenge

52. What number is 80% of $3\frac{1}{8}$?

53. $2\frac{1}{10}$ is what percent of $2\frac{4}{5}$?

54. What percent of $4x$ is x?

55. What percent of $12n$ is $36n$?

56. Stretch Your Thinking A substance doubles in volume every minute. At 9:00 A.M., a small amount is placed in a container. At 10:00 A.M., the container is just full. At what time was the container one-quarter full?

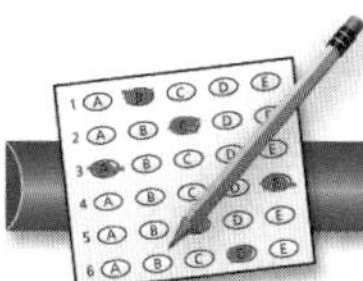

Test Prep

Multiple Choice

57. Which expression can be used to find 6% of 92?
A. 6 · 92 **B.** 0.6 · 92 **C.** 0.06 · 92 **D.** 92 ÷ 0.06

58. 36 is approximately what percent of 33?
F. 1.09% **G.** 12% **H.** 92% **I.** 109%

Take It to the NET
Online lesson quiz at www.PHSchool.com
Web Code aba-0606

59. Which expression can be used to solve: 45 is 30% of what number?
A. 45 · 0.30 **B.** 45 · 30 **C.** 0.30 ÷ 45 **D.** 45 ÷ 0.30

Short Response

60. Twenty-nine out of 40 students go on a field trip. What percent of the students do NOT go on the trip? Show your work.

Mixed Review

Lesson 4-8

Complete.

61. 6 ft 3 in. = ■ ft

62. 4 lb 2 oz = ■ oz

63. $5\frac{1}{2}$ c = ■ fl oz

Lesson 3-4

Find all the factors of each number.

64. 48

65. 75

66. 140

Algebra

6-7 Applications of Percent

What You'll Learn

To find tax and tips

To find commissions

. . . And Why

To find cost including sales tax, as in Example 1

For help, go to Lesson 6-3.

Write each percent as a decimal and as a fraction in simplest form.

1. 105% **2.** 118%
3. 250% **4.** 0.5%
5. 0.3% **6.** 0.8%

New Vocabulary • commission

Interactive lesson includes instant self-check, tutorials, and activities.

OBJECTIVE 1

Finding Tax and Tips

In many states, you pay a sales tax on items you buy. The sales tax is a percent of the purchase price. A tax percent is also called a tax rate.

sales tax = tax rate · purchase price

1 EXAMPLE Finding Sales Tax

Real World

Shopping A desk you plan to buy costs \$159.99. In the state where you are shopping, the sales tax rate is 6%. What will you pay for the desk?

$0.06 \cdot 159.99 = 9.60$ ← **Find the sales tax. Round to the nearest cent.**

$159.99 + 9.60 = 169.59$ ← **Add the purchase price to the sales tax.**

You will pay \$169.59 for the desk.

Check Understanding 1 **a.** The store has a bigger desk that costs \$182.99. You have only \$200 to spend. Do you have enough money for the bigger desk?

b. Find the payment for a purchase of \$37.50 with a sales tax rate of 4%.

A tip is a percent of a bill that you give to the person providing a service. Often 15% is considered to be a reasonable percent for good service. You can find 15% using estimation and mental math.

Step 1 Round the bill to the nearest dollar.

Step 2 Find 10% of the bill by moving the decimal point one place to the left.

Step 3 Find 5% of the bill by taking one half of the result of Step 2.

Step 4 Add the amounts of Step 2 and Step 3 together to find 15%.

2 EXAMPLE Estimating a Tip 

Consumer Your family takes a taxi to the train. The taxi fare is \$17.85. Find the amount of a 15% tip for the taxi driver.

$17.85 \approx 18$ ← **Round to the nearest dollar.**

$0.1 \cdot 18 = 1.8$ ← **Find 10% of the bill.**

$\frac{1}{2} \cdot 1.8 = 0.9$ ← **Find 5% of the bill. 5% is $\frac{1}{2}$ of the 10% amount.**

$1.8 + 0.9 = 2.7$ ← **Add 10% amount and 5% amount to get 15%.**

For a \$17.85 taxi fare, a 15% tip is about \$2.70.

Check Understanding 2 Estimate a 15% tip for each amount.

a. \$58.20 **b.** \$61.80 **c.** \$49.75 **d.** \$29.59

e. **Reasoning** How could you estimate a 20% tip for exceptional service?

In some real-world situations, you must add both the tax and the tip.

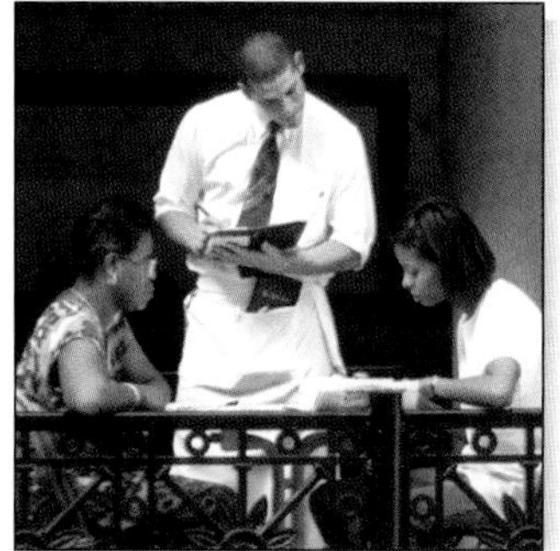

Real-World Connection

Careers Waiters and waitresses use arithmetic skills to total bills without a calculator.

3 EXAMPLE Real-World Problem Solving

Restaurants Suppose you treat a friend to lunch. The total cost of the food items is \$9.68. A 7% sales tax will be added and you want to give a tip of 20% for excellent service. How much will you pay for lunch?

Step 1 Find the sales tax.

$$0.07 \cdot 9.68 = 0.68$$

The sales tax is \$.68.

Step 2 Find the tip.

$9.68 \approx 10$ ← **Round to the nearest dollar.**

$0.2 \cdot 10 = 2$ ← **Find 20% of the bill.**

The tip is \$2.

Step 3 Add the tax and tip to the bill to find the total.

$$\begin{aligned} \text{total} &= \text{food bill} + \text{tax} + \text{tip} \\ &= 9.68 + 0.68 + 2.00 \\ &= 12.36 \end{aligned}$$

You will pay \$12.36 for lunch.

Check Understanding 3 **a.** **Reasoning** Find 127% of \$9.68. Is your answer the same as the answer to Example 3? Explain.

b. You order a pizza for home delivery. There is a 5% delivery fee, and you want to give the driver a 20% tip. If the pizza costs \$12.60, how much should you pay the driver?

OBJECTIVE

2 Finding Commissions

Some sales jobs pay you a percent of the amount you sell. This percent is called a commission. A commission may be paid in addition to a salary.

commission = commission rate · sales

4 EXAMPLE Finding a Commission

Find the commission on a \$500 sale, with a commission rate of 12.5%.

$0.125 \cdot 500$ ← **Change 12.5% to 0.125.**

62.5 ← **Simplify.**

The commission is \$62.50 for a \$500 sale.

✓ Check Understanding 4 Find the commission on a \$3,200 sale when the commission rate is 6%.

5 EXAMPLE Real-World  Problem Solving

Earnings A salesperson receives a salary of \$650 each week, plus a commission of 4% of all sales. In one week, his sales are \$1,250. What does the salesperson earn that week?

Words total earnings = salary + commission

Let t = total earnings.

Equation $t = 650 + 0.04 \cdot 1{,}250$

$t = 650 + 0.04 \cdot 1{,}250$ ← **Write the equation.**

$= 650 + 50$ ← **Multiply.**

$= 700$ ← **Simplify.**

The salesperson earns \$700.

✓ Check Understanding 5 A salesperson has a weekly salary of \$800 and a commission rate of 3.5% of sales. Find the salesperson's earnings for a week when sales are \$1,400.

EXERCISES

For more practice, see *Extra Practice*.

A Practice by Example

Example 1 (page 322)

Find each total.

1. \$35.99 with a 5% sales tax
2. \$72.75 with a 6% sales tax
3. \$81 with a 5.5% sales tax
4. \$258 with a 5.7% sales tax
5. **Shopping** The price of a coat is \$114 before sales tax. The sales tax is 7%. Find the total cost of the coat.

Example 2 (page 323)

Estimate a 15% tip for each amount.

6. $68.50 **7.** $30.80 **8.** $9.89 **9.** $27.59

10. Grooming You go to a stylist for a haircut. The cost of the haircut is $12.50. Find the amount of a 15% tip for the stylist.

Example 3 (page 323)

Find the total payment, given the cost, tax rate, and tip rate.

11. $35.75, 5% tax, 15% tip **12.** $51.80, 6.7% tax, 20% tip

13. Shopping You buy a book for $12.99 in a store that has a city tax of 0.5% and a state tax of 6.25%. How much will you pay for the book?

Example 4 (page 324)

Find each commission, given the sale and the commission rate.

14. $800, 12% **15.** $2,500, 8% **16.** $2,000, 7.5% **17.** $600, 4.5%

Example 5 (page 324)

Find total earnings, given the salary, commission rate, and sales.

18. $2,500 plus 4% on sales of $1,500 **19.** $750 plus 6.5% on sales of $600

20. $800 plus 2.5% on sales of $1,000 **21.** $400 plus 5% on sales of $1,800

B Apply Your Skills

Find the sales tax rate for each purchase.

22. purchase, $25.79; tax, $1.29 **23.** purchase, $312; tax, $9.36

24. Shopping You select four packages of modeling clay and a set of tools for a craft project. If there is a 6% sales tax, how much money will you need to buy these supplies?

25. A real estate agent earns a weekly salary of $200. This week, he sells one home for $120,000 and is paid a commission rate of 5%. Find his total earnings for the week.

26. Sales A company pays commissions of 6% on the first $500 in sales and 8% on sales over $500. What is the commission on an $800 sale?

27. Writing in Math Explain how you can estimate the tax on a sale of $2,500 when the tax rate is 5.9%.

Find the cost of each service, given the percent and the amount of the tip.

28. 15% tip; $11.10 **29.** 20% tip; $19.70 **30.** 15% tip; $20.04

C Challenge

Find the commission rate.

31. Total earnings are $515 including a salary of $200 and sales of $3,000.

32. Total earnings are $970 including a salary of $350 and sales of $12,400.

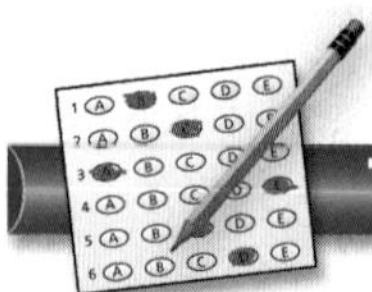

Test Prep

Reading Comprehension

Read the passage and answer the questions below.

To Insure Proper Service

You can say that TIPS are given *To Insure Proper Service.* When you read "Gratuity Not Included," you want to give an appropriate tip for the type of service you receive. A good tip for taxi drivers or hairstylists is 15%. Restaurant and laundry workers can expect between 15% and 20%.

Take It to the NET Online lesson quiz at **www.PHSchool.com** Web Code aba-0607

33. What is the cost of a haircut if the tip is \$4.50?

34. How much should you offer in order to give the maximum tip for a laundry service of \$11.50?

35. What percent is a tip of \$6 for a taxi fare of \$20? How does this tip compare to the recommended tip for a \$20 taxi ride?

Short Response

36. A salesperson earns a salary of \$150 plus 8% commission on all sales. How much will he earn if his sales are \$2,990? Show your work.

Mixed Review

Lesson 5-2

Write each unit rate.

37. 408 mi on 12 gal of gasoline

38. \$16.45 for 7 lb of fish

Lesson 2-4

Algebra **Solve.**

39. $-13t = 52$

40. $-5x = -30$

41. $-2 = \frac{x}{24}$

42. $\frac{g}{-17} = -51$

Checkpoint Quiz 2

Lessons 6-5 through 6-7

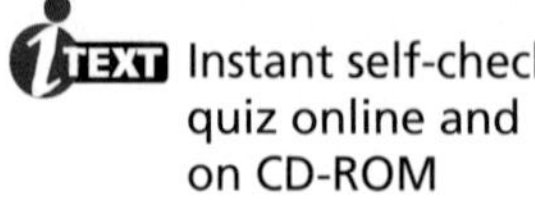

Instant self-check quiz online and on CD-ROM

Find each answer using a proportion.

1. 35 is what percent of 60?

2. 14.4 is 90% of what number?

3. What percent of 75 is 63?

4. 56% of what number is 75.6?

Find each answer using an equation.

5. What percent of 120 is 54?

6. What is 72% of 95?

7. What is 120% of 185?

8. 459 is 85% of what number?

9. Sales Find the commission for a rate of 5.5% and \$1,400 in sales.

10. Shopping Find the total for items costing \$56.72 with a sales tax of 7%.

6-8 Finding Percent of Change

What You'll Learn

To find percent of increase

To find percent of decrease

. . . And Why

To find a percent of discount, as in Example 3

✓ Check Skills You'll Need

For help, go to Lesson 6-5.

Use a proportion to solve.

1. 18 is 36% of what number?
2. 120 is 160% of what number?
3. What percent of 64 is 52?
4. What percent of 105 is 42?
5. 46% of what number is 36.8?
6. 33 is what percent of 55?

New Vocabulary • percent of change • markup • discount

OBJECTIVE

Interactive lesson includes instant self-check, tutorials, and activities.

1 Finding Percent of Increase

Investigation: Exploring Percent of Change

1. Find the change in population from 1990 to 2000 for each state.
2. Which state had the greater change in population?
3. Write the ratio $\frac{\text{change in population}}{\text{1990 population}}$ for each state. Then write each ratio as a percent.
4. Compare the two percents. Which state had the greater population change in terms of percent?

Populations of Two States

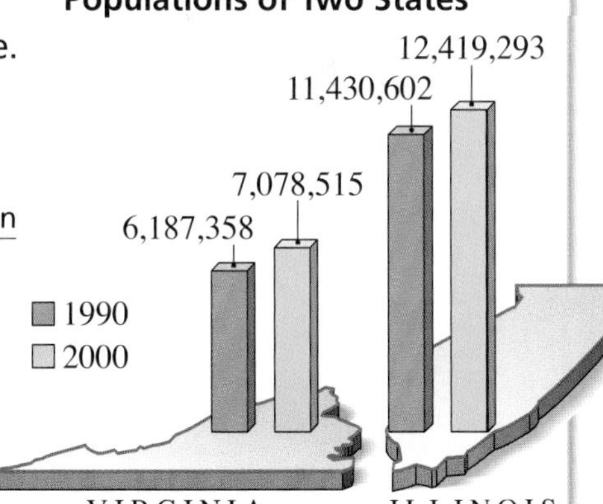

SOURCE: U.S. Census Bureau.
Go to **www.PHSchool.com** for a data update.
Web Code abg-2041

The number of representatives that your state sends to Washington, D.C. depends on the population of your state. Every ten years, the number of representatives may change, based on your state's population. You can find the percent of change for representatives.

The **percent of change** is the percent a quantity increases or decreases from its original amount. To find a percent of change, use these two steps.

Step 1 Subtract to find the amount of change.

Step 2 Use the proportion $\frac{\text{amount of change}}{\text{original amount}} = \frac{\text{percent of change}}{100}$.

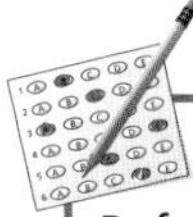

Test-Prep Tip

Before you find the percent of change, decide whether the change is an increase or a decrease.

1 EXAMPLE Finding a Percent of Increase

Government North Carolina had 12 seats in the U.S. House of Representatives in the 1990s. After the 2000 census, North Carolina had 13 seats. Find the percent of increase in the number of representatives.

$13 - 12 = 1$ ← **Find the amount of change.**

$\frac{1}{12} = \frac{n}{100}$ ← **Write a proportion.**

$12n = 1(100)$ ← **Find the cross products.**

$\frac{12n}{12} = \frac{1(100)}{12}$ ← **Divide each side by 12.**

$n = 8.\overline{3}$ ← **Simplify.**

The number of representatives from North Carolina increased by 8.3%.

Check Understanding 1 **a.** In 2000, California went from 52 to 53 representatives. Find the percent of increase for California.

b. **Reasoning** The amount of increase is the same for North Carolina and California. The percent of increase is different. Why?

To make a profit, stores charge more for merchandise than they pay for it. The difference between the selling price and the original cost, or the store's cost, of an item is called the **markup.** The percent of increase is the percent of markup.

Markup = selling price − original cost.

To find a percent of markup, you use the proportion below.

$$\frac{\text{amount of markup}}{\text{original cost}} = \frac{\text{percent of markup}}{100}$$

2 EXAMPLE Finding a Percent of Markup

Shopping An electronics store orders sets of walkie-talkies for \$14.85 each. The store sells each set for \$19.90. What is the percent of markup?

$19.90 - 14.85 = 5.05$ ← **Find the amount of markup.**

$\frac{5.05}{14.85} = \frac{n}{100}$ ← **Write the proportion.**

$14.85n = 5.05(100)$ ← **Find the cross products.**

$\frac{14.85n}{14.85} = \frac{5.05(100)}{14.85}$ ← **Divide each side by 14.85.**

$n \approx 34$ ← **Simplify.**

The percent of markup is 34%.

Check Understanding 2 **a.** Find the percent of markup for a headset that a store buys for \$17.95 and sells for \$35.79.

b. Find the percent of markup for a model boat that costs you \$14.80 and you sell for \$20.

c. **Reasoning** Is it possible to have a markup of 200%? Explain. Include an example.

OBJECTIVE

2 Finding Percent of Decrease

The difference between the original price and the sale price of an item is called a **discount.** The percent of decrease is the percent of discount.

3 EXAMPLE Finding a Percent of Discount

Music During a clearance sale, a keyboard that normally sells for \$49.99 is discounted to \$34.99. What is the percent of discount?

$49.99 - 34.99 = 15.00$ ← **Find the amount of discount.**

$\frac{15}{49.99} = \frac{n}{100}$ ← **Write the proportion.**

$49.99n = 15(100)$ ← **Find the cross products.**

$\frac{49.99n}{49.99} = \frac{15(100)}{49.99}$ ← **Divide each side by 49.99.**

$n \approx 30$ ← **Simplify.**

The percent of discount for the keyboard is 30%.

Check Understanding 3 Find the percent of discount of a \$24.95 novel that is discounted to \$14.97.

More Than One Way

A jacket goes on sale with a discount of 40% off the original price. The original price of the jacket was \$42.95. What is the sale price of the jacket?

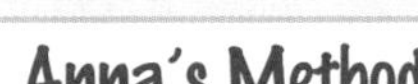

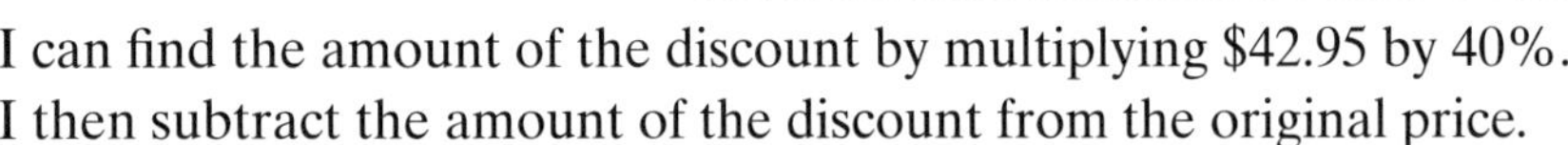

I can find the amount of the discount by multiplying \$42.95 by 40%. I then subtract the amount of the discount from the original price.

$42.95 \cdot 0.40 = 17.18$ ← **Find the amount of the discount.**

$42.95 - 17.18 = 25.77$ ← **Subtract the discount from the original price.**

The jacket costs \$25.77 on sale.

Since 40% is discounted, I will still have to pay 60% of the original price. I multiply the original price of \$42.95 by the percent I need to pay.

$42.95 \cdot 0.60 = 25.77$ ← **Find the discounted price.**

The jacket costs \$25.77 on sale.

Choose a Method

You get a discount of 20% on a \$27.50 ticket. How much will your ticket cost? Describe your method, and explain why you chose it.

EXERCISES

For more practice, see *Extra Practice*.

A Practice by Example

Example 1 (page 328)

Find each percent of increase. Round to the nearest tenth of a percent.

1. 60 to 75 **2.** 88 to 99 **3.** 120 to 240 **4.** 15 to 35

5. 2 to 7 **6.** 12 to 63 **7.** 135 to 200 **8.** 12 to 18

9. Business A restaurant worker earning \$5.15/h receives a raise. He now earns \$6/h. Find the percent of increase in his hourly rate of pay.

10. Groceries If the cost of a dozen eggs rises from \$.99 to \$1.34, what is the percent of the increase?

Example 2 (page 328)

Find each percent of markup. Round to the nearest tenth of a percent.

11. original cost \$22; selling price \$33

12. original cost \$15; selling price \$60

13. original cost \$10; selling price \$22

14. original cost \$13.50; selling price \$25

15. original cost \$40; selling price \$59.75

16. Find the percent of markup for a pillow that a store buys for \$3.25 and sells for \$7.50.

Example 3 (page 329)

Find each percent of discount. Round to the nearest tenth of a percent.

17. original price \$70; sale price \$63 **18.** original price \$9; sale price \$4

19. original price \$110; sale price \$88 **20.** original price \$10; sale price \$7

21. original price \$480; sale price \$300 **22.** original price \$29; sale price \$25

23. Crafts One package of poster boards usually sells for \$8.40. This week, the package is on sale for \$6.30. What is the percent of the discount?

B Apply Your Skills

Find each percent of change. Round to the nearest tenth of a percent. State whether the change is an increase or a decrease.

24. 56 to 78 **25.** 6 to 9 **26.** 150 to 147 **27.** 60 to 54

28. 30 to 16 **29.** 27 to 20 **30.** 16 to 54 **31.** 12.5 to 8.4

32. Sports A football player gained 1,200 yd last season and 900 yd this season. Find the percent of change. State whether the change is an increase or a decrease.

33. Entertainment A television is on sale for \$449.95. This is \$30 off the original price. Find the percent of the discount.

34. **Fund-Raising** You pay $9.68 for supplies to make three cakes for a bake sale. Each cake sells for $4. What is the percent of the markup?

35. **Business** A toy store opened five years ago. The owner uses a computer to track yearly income. She uses a program that prints @@@ in some cells instead of numbers. Copy and complete the spreadsheet.

	A	B	C	D
1	Year	Sales ($)	Change From Last Year ($)	Change From Last Year (%)
2	1	200,000	(not open last year)	(not open last year)
3	2	240,000	40,000	@@@
4	3	300,000	@@@	@@@
5	4	330,000	@@@	@@@

A percent of depreciation in value for property is a percent of decrease. Find the percent of depreciation for Exercises 36–38.

36. **Consumer** You bought a new mountain bike for $525 one year ago. That same bike is now worth $472.50.

37. **Clothing** One year ago, your coat cost $70. This coat is now worth $59.

38. **Music** A new stereo costs $425. The one-year-old stereo costs $382.50.

39. a. **Data File, p. 289** Find the percent of increase in the number of sides between each step and the following step.
    b. **Patterns** How many sides does the snowflake have at Step 6?

Find the price of each item.

40. originally $36.75; 65% markup

41. originally $82; 35% discount

42. originally $942; 28% discount

43. originally $91; 120% markup

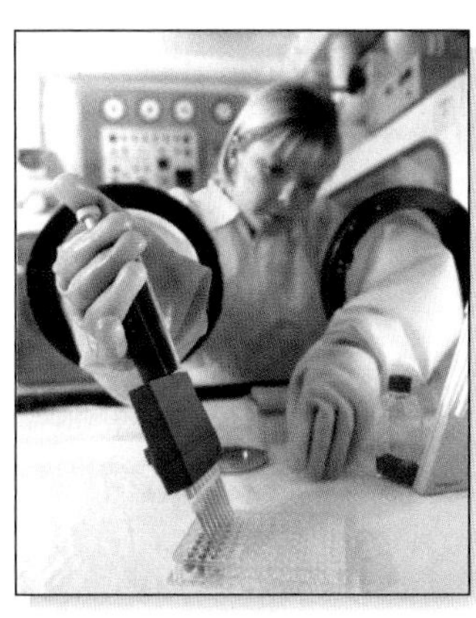

Real-World Connection
Careers Biological scientists develop new vaccines and medical treatments.

44. **Salary** A biological scientist earning an annual salary of $49,239 gets a 4% raise. What is the new annual salary for this scientist?

45. **Occupations** According to the U.S. Department of Labor, the fastest growing occupation is computer engineer. In 1998, there were 299,000 jobs in this field. By 2008, there should be 622,000 jobs. Find the percent of increase.

46. a. **Business** A seasonal store buys 5 doz T-shirts for $4.29 each. The store owner decides to sell the T-shirts for $6.59 each. What is the percent of increase in the price of the T-shirts?
    b. After a month, the remaining 2 doz T-shirts go on sale for $4.59 each. What is the percent of decrease in the price of the T-shirts?

47. **Writing in Math** Describe how you can find the percent of change in the number of students in your school from last year to this year.

C Challenge

48. **a.** Increase \$34.95 by 20%, then decrease the result by 30%.
    b. Decrease \$34.95 by 30%, then increase the result by 20%.
    c. **Reasoning** Is your answer to part (a) the same as your answer to part (b)? Why or why not?

49. The cost of renting a movie increases 10% every year for three years. Find the percent of change at the end of the three-year period.

50. **a.** **Stationery** A storeowner buys a case of 144 pens for \$28.80. Tax and shipping costs him an additional \$8.64. He sells the pens for \$.59 each. How much will he collect if he sells all of the pens?
    b. What is the amount of the markup per pen?
    c. What is the percent of the markup?

51. **Stretch Your Thinking** Fill in the boxes with the numbers 1 through 10 so the number below any two numbers is the difference between those numbers. The order in which the numbers are subtracted does not have to be the same in each case.

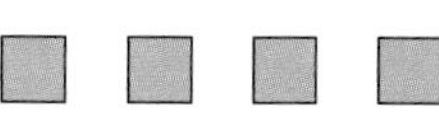

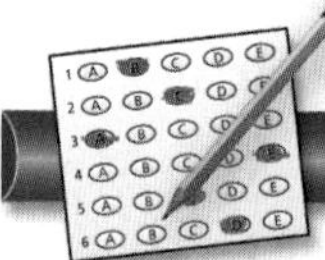

Test Prep

Multiple Choice

52. Which of the following does NOT represent a 20% decrease?
A. 75 to 60 **B.** 2.5 to 2 **C.** 50 to 30 **D.** 150 to 120

53. Which equation can you use to find the percent of increase for a \$25 ticket to the ball game that is now \$32?
F. $\frac{25}{32} = \frac{n}{100}$ **G.** $\frac{32}{25} = \frac{n}{100}$ **H.** $\frac{7}{32} = \frac{n}{100}$ **I.** $\frac{7}{25} = \frac{n}{100}$

Online lesson quiz at www.PHSchool.com
Web Code aba-0608

54. What is the percent of increase from 40 to 100?
A. 250% **B.** 150% **C.** 60% **D.** 40%

Short Response

55. A \$79 CD player is discounted 30%. **(a)** Explain how to find the discounted price. **(b)** Find the discounted price.

Mixed Review

Lesson 6-7 **Algebra** **Find each payment.**

56. \$218 with a 6.25% sales tax 57. \$451 with a 4.5% sales tax

Lesson 3-9 **Write each fraction as a decimal.**

58. $\frac{19}{25}$ 59. $\frac{8}{12}$ 60. $\frac{3}{18}$ 61. $\frac{7}{9}$ 62. $\frac{4}{6}$

Lesson 2-1 **Algebra** **Evaluate for $m = 8$ and $n = -2$.**

63. $6m + 8 + 5n$ 64. $18 - 3(m + n)$ 65. $-mn + 2$

6-9 Write an Equation

What You'll Learn

1. To solve problems by writing equations

. . . And Why

To solve a percent problem, as in Example 1

✓ Check Skills You'll Need

For help, go to Lesson 6-4.

Find each answer.

1. 60% of 32 **2.** 120% of 250

3. 37% of 74 **4.** 26.5% of 95

5. 0.05% of 8 **6.** 345% of 1,226

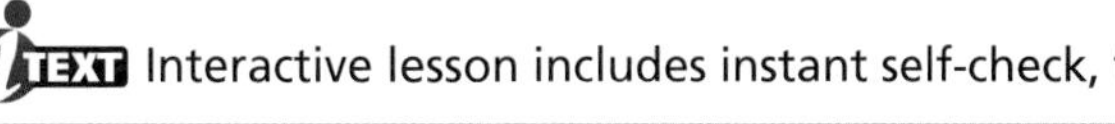

Interactive lesson includes instant self-check, tutorials, and activities.

OBJECTIVE 1 Solving Problems by Writing Equations

Finding a discount or markup is not always a one-step process.

1 EXAMPLE Real-World Problem Solving

Clothing A coat was originally \$140, but then it was discounted 60%. At the register, a second discount was given for an unknown percent. The receipt says the final price is \$33.60. What was the second discount?

Reading Math

Discounts that are taken one after another are called "successive discounts."

Read and Understand The coat originally cost \$140 and was discounted by 60%. Given that the final cost of the coat was \$33.60, your goal is to find the second discount.

Plan and Solve First, find the price after the first discount. As a result of the 60% discount, the cost was 40% of the original price.

$$0.40 \cdot \$140 = \$56$$

The cost of the coat after the first discount was \$56. Subtracting \$33.60 from \$56 gives you \$22.40, the amount of the second discount.

Words	Percent of second discount	of	\$56	is	\$22.40 .
↓	Let d = the second percent of discount.				
Equation	d	$\cdot$	56	=	22.40

$56d = 22.40$

$\frac{56d}{56} = \frac{22.4}{56}$ ← **Divide each side by 56.**

$d = 0.4$ ← **Simplify.**

$= 40\%$ ← **Change to percent.**

The second discount was 40%.

Look Back and Check To check, confirm that the second discount of 40% does give the final price of \$33.60. Forty percent of \$56 is \$22.40 and \$56 − \$22.40 is \$33.60. So the answer checks.

✔ Check Understanding **1** During a 25% off sale, a furniture store sells a couch for \$450. Another store sells the same couch for \$750. Find the percent of discount for the original price of the couch compared to the price of the couch at the second store.

2 EXAMPLE Real-World Problem Solving

Real-World Connection

A diamond cutter uses a lens to get the best view of the diamond.

Jewelry A jewelry store buys a pair of diamond earrings for \$90 and sells the pair for \$315. What is the maximum percent of discount the jewelry store can give and still make \$60 in profit from the earrings?

Read and Understand The store pays \$90 for earrings that are sold at \$315. Your goal is to find the maximum percent of discount the store can give and still make \$60 in profit.

Plan and Solve To make at least \$60, the store will have to sell the earrings for at least \$90 + \$60, or \$150. So the discount will be \$315 − \$150, or \$165.

Words	Maximum percent of discount	of	\$315	is	\$165.
↓	Let d = maximum percent of discount.				
Equation	d	$\cdot$	315	=	165

$315d = 165$

$\frac{315d}{315} = \frac{165}{315}$ ← **Divide each side by 315.**

$d = 0.5238095238$ ← **Use a calculator.**

$d \approx 52\%$ ← **Change decimal to percent.**

The maximum percent of discount the store can offer is 52%.

Look Back and Check You can ***try, check, and revise*** different percents. The price of the earrings has to be at least \$150 for the store to earn \$60.

Percent Discount	Percent Paid by Customer	Cost of Earrings	Result
51%	49%	49% · \$315 = \$154.35	✔
52%	48%	48% · \$315 = \$151.20	✔
53%	47%	47% · \$315 = \$148.05	Too low
54%	46%	46% · \$315 = \$144.90	Too low

The answer checks.

2 **a.** In Example 2, what is the percent of markup on the earrings?

b. What would be the maximum percent of discount the jewelry store could give and still make a \$75 profit on the earrings?

EXERCISES

For more practice, see *Extra Practice.*

A Practice by Example

Solve each problem by writing an equation. Check each answer in the original problem.

Example 1 (page 333)

Need Help?
- Reread the problem.
- Identify the key facts and details.
- Tell the problem in your own words.
- Try a different strategy.
- Check your work.

1. A store has a frequent shopper program. Depending on the number of items purchased in the previous month, you get an additional 10%, 20%, or 30% off. During a 15% off sale, you paid $37.40 for a $55 item. Which frequent shopper discount did you receive?

2. A comic book store gives a discount that depends on the number of comics you buy. If you buy from 1 to 5 books, your discount is 5%. If you buy from 6 to 10 books, your discount is 10%. If you buy more than 10 books, your discount is 20%. Your friend pays $15.29 for comics originally priced at $16.99. What is the least number of books that your friend bought?

Example 2 (page 334)

3. A candle maker pays $1.35 for supplies to make each candle. The candle maker normally makes a profit of $.85 on each one. What is the maximum percent of discount that the candle maker can offer while making a profit of $.35 on each candle?

4. A bookstore pays $12.75 for hardcover books and charges $29.95. What is the maximum percent of discount that it can offer while still making a profit of $5 on each book?

B Apply Your Skills

Use any strategy to solve each problem. Show your work.

Strategies
- Draw a Diagram
- Look for a Pattern
- Make a Graph
- Make an Organized List
- Make a Table
- Simulate a Problem
- Solve a Simpler Problem
- Try, Check, and Revise
- Use Logical Reasoning
- Work Backward
- Write an Equation

5. **Writing in Math** Your brother finds that the bill for 18 sweatshirts ordered by his club has two digits blurred by water damage. He is sure that the first and last digits are the same. What do you think the total price is? Explain your reasoning.
   $■69.9■

6. **Patterns** Examine the list at the right and look for a pattern.
   a. Write the sixth row.
   b. What is the last number in the 11th row? In the 23rd row?
   c. What is the sum of the numbers in the 4th row? In the 10th row?
   d. **Reasoning** How can you find the sum of any row when you know the row number?

Row 1	1
Row 2	1 3
Row 3	1 3 5
Row 4	1 3 5 7
Row 5	1 3 5 7 9
Row 6	■

7. **Geometry** The length of a rectangle is twice the width. The perimeter of the rectangle is 42 cm. Find the length and width.

8. **Cooking** A recipe that makes 2 doz raisin bars calls for $\frac{3}{4}$ c of flour. How much flour will be needed to make five dozen?

Challenge

9. **Population Growth** The population of a town increases at the rate of 1% each year. Today the town's population is 10,500. What will the population be in five years?

10. **Stretch Your Thinking** In the number array at the right, in which column will 1,000 appear?

	2 →	3 →	4 →	5 ↴
↵ 9 ←	8 ←	7 ←	6 ←	
	→ 10	11	12	13
17	16	15	14	
	18	19	20	21
25	24	23	22	

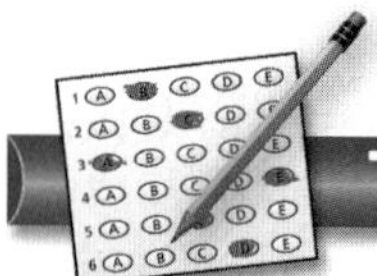

Test Prep

Multiple Choice

11. Team A wins 70% of the 20 games it plays. Team B plays 15 games and wins 80% of them. What is the greatest number of games won by either team?
A. 16 **B.** 14 **C.** 12 **D.** 10

12. About 12% of an iceberg's mass is above water. If the mass above water is 9,000,000 kg, what is the mass of the entire iceberg?
F. 108,000 kg **G.** 1,080,000 kg
H. 75,000,000 kg **I.** 120,000,000 kg

Take It to the NET
Online lesson quiz at
www.PHSchool.com
Web Code aba-0609

13. The retail price of an item is $6.99. What is the total cost of the item with 6.5% sales tax?
A. $6.92 **B.** $7.41 **C.** $7.44 **D.** $7.83

14. The total cost of an item, including sales tax, is $26.74. The percent of sales tax is 7%. What is the price of the item before sales tax?
F. $26 **G.** $25 **H.** $23 **I.** $21

Short Response

15. The retail price of an item is $13.99, and with sales tax, the total cost is $15.11. What is the percent of sales tax? Show your work.

Mixed Review

Lesson 6-8

Find each percent of change. Round to the nearest tenth of a percent. State whether the change is an increase or a decrease.

16. 125 to 251 **17.** 22 to 13 **18.** 21 to 63

19. 31 to 35 **20.** 5 to 11 **21.** 159 to 145

Lesson 6-4

Find each answer. Round to the nearest tenth of a percent.

22. 17% of 56 **23.** 22% of 3,000 **24.** 200% of 72

25. 175% of 120 **26.** 20% of 60 **27.** 3% of 47

Test-Taking Strategies

Work Backward

A useful problem-solving strategy for answering multiple-choice questions is to ***work backward.*** Check to see which choice results in a correct answer by substituting the answers into the problem.

EXAMPLE

In a pile of dimes and quarters, there are twice as many dimes as quarters. The total value of the coins is \$9.45. How many quarters are in the pile?

A. 11 **B.** 18 **C.** 21 **D.** 24

Check each answer to see whether it works.

A. 11 quarters = 2.75	22 dimes = 2.20	2.75 + 2.20 = 4.95	✘
B. 18 quarters = 4.50	36 dimes = 3.60	4.50 + 3.60 = 8.10	✘
C. 21 quarters = 5.25	42 dimes = 4.20	5.25 + 4.20 = 9.45	✔

Choice C is the only answer that works.

EXERCISES

Solve each problem by working backward.

1. You have some stamps worth 4¢ and 5¢. The total value of the stamps is \$1. There are 22 stamps in all. How many 5¢ stamps do you have?
   A. 3 **B.** 6 **C.** 9 **D.** 12

2. If $3x - 14 = 127$, what is the value of x?
   F. 47 **G.** 43 **H.** 41 **I.** 37

3. What is the greatest number of movie tickets you can buy if you have \$33.48 and each movie ticket costs \$6.75?
   A. 3 **B.** 4 **C.** 5 **D.** 6

4. Your grades on four math tests are 97, 88, 79, and 92. What grade do you need on the fifth test to reach an average of 90?
   F. 90 **G.** 92 **H.** 94 **I.** 96

5. If you start with a number, add 5, and then multiply by 7, the result is 133. What is the number?
   A. 12 **B.** 14 **C.** 15 **D.** 21

6. For your birthday, you receive \$48 and a \$15 gift certificate to a department store. The store is having a sale that takes 40% off the price of all items. What is the total value of the merchandise you can buy and still have \$7.50 left for lunch?
   F. \$70.50 **G.** \$88.20 **H.** \$92.50 **I.** \$100

Chapter 6 Chapter Review

Vocabulary

commission (p. 324)
discount (p. 329)
markup (p. 328)
percent (p. 291)
percent of change (p. 327)

Reading Math: Understanding Vocabulary

Choose the vocabulary term from the column on the right that best completes each sentence.

1. The difference between the selling price and the store's cost is the _?_.
2. A _?_ can be either an increase or a decrease.
3. To write a _?_ as a decimal, divide it by 100.
4. The difference between the original price and the sale price is the _?_.
5. A _?_ is a percent of the sales made by a salesperson.

A. commission
B. discount
C. markup
D. percent
E. percent of change

Take It to the NET
Online vocabulary quiz at **www.PHSchool.com**
Web Code abj-0651

Skills and Concepts

6-1 and 6-2 Objectives

- To model percents
- To write percents using equal ratios
- To connect percents and decimals
- To connect percents and fractions

A **percent** is a ratio that compares a number to 100.

To write a decimal as a percent, multiply the decimal by 100, or move the decimal point two places to the right. To write a percent as a decimal, divide by 100, or move the decimal point two places to the left.

To write a fraction as a percent, convert the fraction into a decimal first. To write a percent as a fraction, write the percent with a denominator of 100 and simplify.

Write each percent as a decimal and as a fraction in simplest form.

6. 65% **7.** 2% **8.** 1.8% **9.** $62\frac{1}{2}\%$

Write each number as a percent.

10. $\frac{3}{8}$ **11.** 0.16 **12.** 0.03 **13.** $\frac{17}{40}$

6-3 and 6-4 Objectives

- To use percents greater than 100% or less than 1%
- To use a percent to find part of a whole
- To use mental math and estimation with percents

A mixed number represents a percent greater than 100%.

To find a percent of a whole, write the percent as a decimal or a fraction and then multiply.

Write each number as a percent.

14. 1.43 **15.** $\frac{7}{500}$ **16.** $2\frac{3}{4}$ **17.** 0.008

Find each answer.

18. Find 82% of 54. **19.** What is 41% of 16? **20.** Find 135% of 72.

6-5 and 6-6 Objectives

- To find the percent using proportions
- To find the whole using proportions
- To write and solve percent equations

Percent problems are solved by using a proportion or an equation.

Use a proportion or an equation to solve.

21. What percent of 40 is 28? **22.** 38 is 80% of what number?

23. What is 60% of 420? **24.** 80% of 15 is what number?

25. 0 54 n / 0% 75% 100%

26. 0 36 180 / 0% n% 100%

27. Technology The price of a new version of a computer game is 120% of the price of the original version. The original version cost $48. What is the cost of the new version?

6-7 Objectives

- To find tax and tips
- To find commissions

A tip is a percent of a bill that you give to the person providing a service. A **commission** is a percent of a sale.

28. Restaurants You go to dinner at a restaurant with four other people. The total for the food you ordered is $43.85. There is a 5% food tax. You want to give a 15% tip. You decide to share the bill equally. Estimate how much you will pay.

29. Find the commission on a $6,700 sale when commission is paid at 4%.

30. Insurance An insurance company pays its agents 40% commission on the first-year's premium and 5% on the second-year's premium for life insurance policies. If the premiums are $500 per year, what is the total commission that will be paid during the two years?

6-8 and 6-9 Objectives

- To find percent of increase
- To find percent of decrease
- To solve problems by writing equations

A **percent of change** is the percent a quantity increases or decreases from its original amount. Use the proportion $\frac{\text{amount of change}}{\text{original amount}} = \frac{\text{percent of change}}{100}$.

Markup is an example of a percent of increase. **Discount** is an example of a percent of decrease.

Find each percent of change. Round to the nearest percent. State whether the change is an increase or a decrease.

31. $90 to $75 **32.** 3.5 ft to 4.2 ft **33.** 120 lb to 138 lb

34. Shopping The sale price of a game is $24.95. Its original price was $36. Find the percent of change. Round to the nearest percent.

35. Writing in Math When you find a percent of change, how do you know whether the percent of change is an increase or a decrease?

Chapter Test

1. Write each decimal as a percent and write each percent as a decimal.
   a. 5% **b.** 0.3 **c.** 125%
   d. 0.0045 **e.** 0.39% **f.** 3.4

2. Write each fraction as a percent and each percent as a fraction.
   a. 35% **b.** $\frac{3}{4}$ **c.** 2%
   d. $\frac{7}{8}$ **e.** 125% **f.** $\frac{6}{5}$

3. According to the census, 0.98% of females in the United States in 1990 were named Barbara. Express this percent as a fraction.

4. Model each percent on 10 × 10 grids.
   a. 34% **b.** 285% **c.** $12\frac{1}{2}$%

5. During the summer, you work 20 h per week at a grocery. Sixty percent of your job is restocking the shelves. How many hours per week do you spend restocking the shelves?

6. Draw a model and write a proportion to find the answer to "25% of what number is 30?"

7. Use a proportion to solve.
   a.
   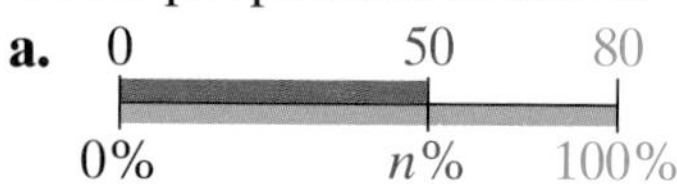

   b.
   0 60 n
   0% 80% 100%

   c. What is 225% of 15?
   d. 6 is 0.15% of what number?

8. Write an equation for each question. Then solve the equation.
   a. What percent of 82 is 10.25?
   b. 108% of 47 is what number?
   c. 99 is 72% of what number?
   d. 12 is what percent of 1,920?
   e. What is 62% of 128?
   f. 168% of what number is 714?

9. There are 6 sets of twins among 250 students. What percent of the students have a twin?

10. **Shopping** You buy a sweater for $18.75, which is 25% off the original price. What was the original price?

11. Your swimming coach requires you to swim 8 lengths. You swim 10 lengths. What percent of the required practice did you swim?

Find each percent of change. Round to the nearest tenth of a percent. State whether the change is an increase or a decrease.

12. 4.15 to 4.55 **13.** 379 to 302 **14.** 72 to 102

15. **Jobs** According to the U.S. Department of Labor, total employment is expected to increase from 146 million in 2000 to 168 million in 2010. Find the percent of increase.

16. **Recreation** A summer camp has 15 cabins that sleep 8 campers each and 5 cabins that sleep 6 campers each. Due to renovations within the camp, two of the smaller cabins will not be used this summer. Find the percent of decrease in the number of campers who can attend the camp this summer.

17. **a. Restaurants** You order items from a menu that total $7.85. Your bill comes to $8.30, including the tax. What is the percent of the tax? Round to the nearest tenth.
    b. Estimate a 15% tip for this order before the tax.

18. A salesperson receives a salary of $300 per week and a 6% commission on all sales. How much does this salesperson earn in a week with $2,540 in sales?

19. A bicycle helmet costs a store $29.62. The store sells the helmet for $39.99. Find the percent of markup.

20. **Writing in Math** Explain how to determine whether you are finding a percent of increase or a percent of decrease between two values.

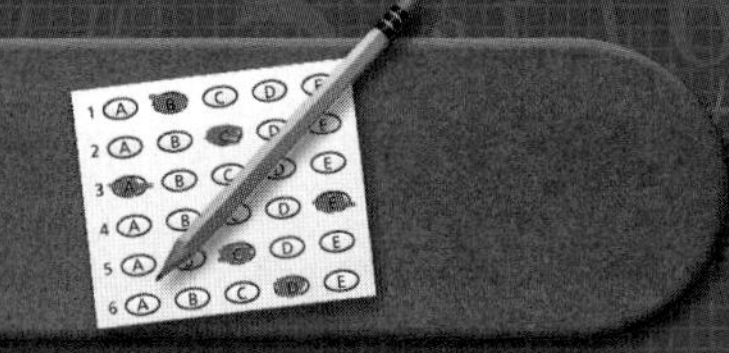

Test Prep

Multiple Choice

1. Which number is closest to 35% of 1,291?
A. 400 **B.** 450 **C.** 500 **D.** 550

2. Which equation is NOT equivalent to $2x - 3 = 5$?
F. $2x = 8$ **G.** $4x - 3 = 10$
H. $2x - 4 = 4$ **I.** $x - 1.5 = 2.5$

3. Which expression equals $3 \times 3 \times 3 \times 3$?
A. 3^4 **B.** 4^3 **C.** 4×3 **D.** 3^3

4. In which set of numbers is 9 a factor of all the numbers?
F. 36, 18, 21 **G.** 108, 252, 45
H. 98, 81, 450 **I.** 120, 180, 267

5. Which point on the number line shows the product $\left(1\frac{7}{8}\right)\left(2\frac{1}{5}\right)$?

A B C D
0 1 2 3 4 5

6. Which fraction is closest in value to 0.46?
F. $\frac{19}{50}$ **G.** $\frac{22}{50}$ **H.** $\frac{25}{50}$ **I.** $\frac{28}{50}$

7. You buy a sandwich for \$3.45, a salad for \$2.25, and a drink for \$.89. How much change do you receive from a \$10 bill?
A. \$16.59 **B.** \$4.30 **C.** \$3.41 **D.** \$2.59

8. Which statement is NOT true?
F. $\frac{12}{16} = \frac{9}{12}$ **G.** $\frac{12 + 16}{16} = \frac{9 + 12}{12}$
H. $\frac{12}{9} = \frac{16}{12}$ **I.** $\frac{12 + 1}{16} = \frac{9 + 1}{12}$

9. What is $\frac{5}{8}$ written as a percent?
A. 625% **B.** 160% **C.** $62\frac{1}{2}$% **D.** 16%

10. Write the numbers 0.361×10^7, 4.22×10^7, and 13.5×10^6 in order from least to greatest.
F. $13.5 \times 10^6, 0.361 \times 10^7, 4.22 \times 10^7$
G. $4.22 \times 10^7, 13.5 \times 10^6, 0.361 \times 10^7$
H. $0.361 \times 10^7, 13.5 \times 10^6, 4.22 \times 10^7$
I. $13.5 \times 10^6, 4.22 \times 10^7, 0.361 \times 10^7$

11. Find the value of $\frac{2m}{m + 2n}$ when $m = -4$ and $n = 3$.
A. -8 **B.** -4 **C.** 0 **D.** 4

12. Which is the best estimate of $92.56 \cdot 37.1$?
F. 2,700 **G.** 3,600 **H.** 4,000 **I.** 4,500

13. Which expression has the greatest value?
A. $32 - (-12)$ **B.** $32 - |-12|$
C. $-32 - (-12)$ **D.** $|-32 - (-12)|$

14. The mean of six numbers is 9. Five of the numbers are 4, 7, 9, 10, and 11. What is the sixth number?
F. 6 **G.** 9 **H.** 12 **I.** 13

Gridded Response

15. A map's scale is 1 in. : 15 mi. Two towns are 3.5 in. apart on the map. How many miles apart are the two towns?

16. A video store charges \$.75 per day for overdue videos. Your friend has a video that was due on Sunday. She returns it on the following Friday. How much does she owe?

Short Response

17. Eighteen students in a class of 25 students plan to go on a hiking trip. What percent of the students plan to go on the trip? Show your work.

18. A blue shark swims about 2.26 mi in 10 min. What is the speed of the shark in **(a)** miles per minute **(b)** miles per hour?

Extended Response

19. A movie theater charges \$6 for admission and \$4.50 for a bucket of popcorn. Write an expression for the total cost for a group of friends to see a movie and split one bucket of popcorn. Then evaluate your expression for five friends.

Fractal Facts

Applying Percents A fractal is a design that repeats itself at smaller and smaller levels. Fractals give us beautiful, intricate pictures of things like ferns and rivers. They also provide a practical way to increase surface area. For example, the circulatory system branches from arteries into smaller and smaller blood vessels called capillaries. Because there are so many of them, capillaries have a much greater surface area than arteries and can absorb nutrients more effectively.

The activity models how the length of a "blood vessel" increases as it branches out into smaller capillaries.

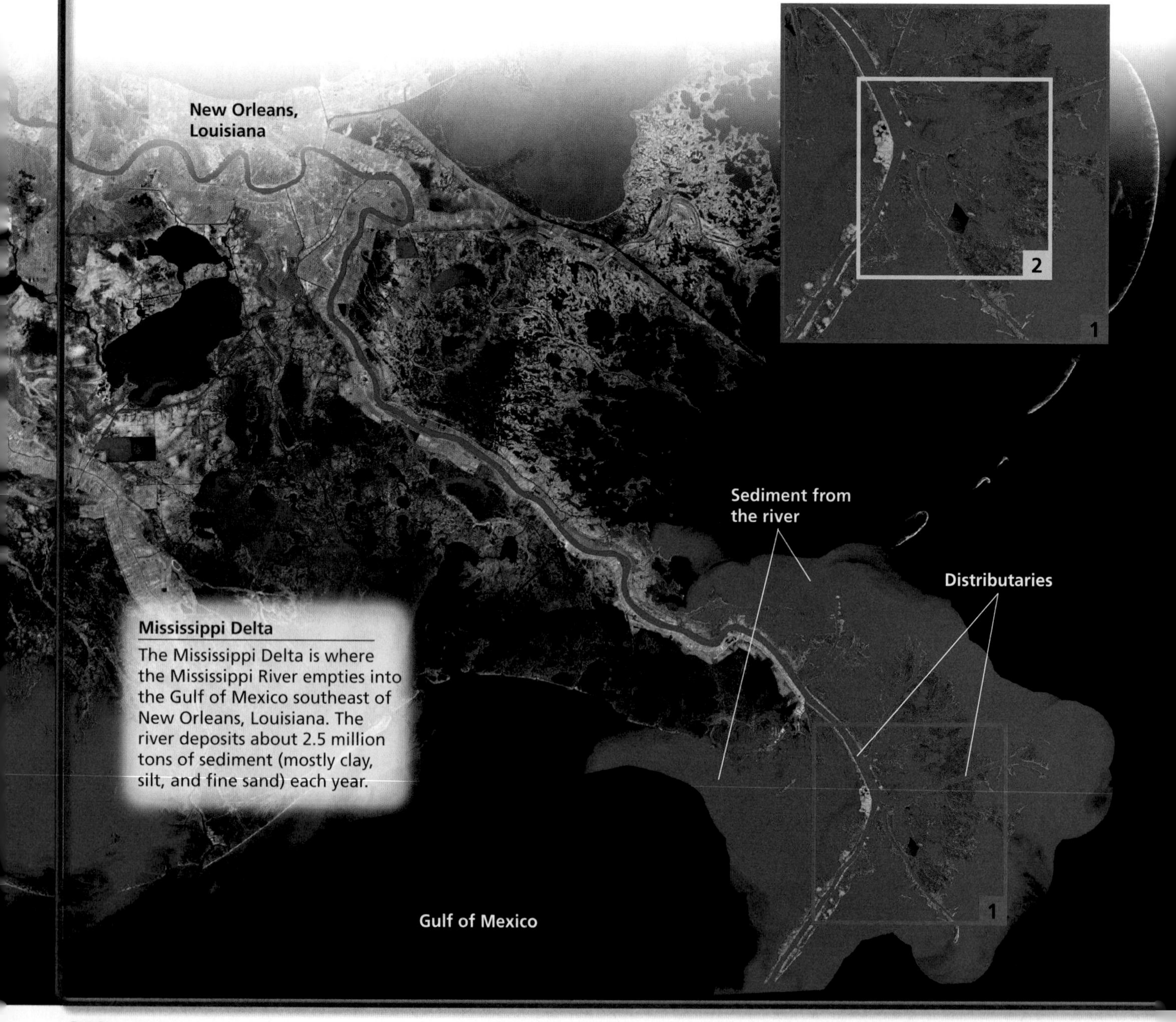

Mississippi Delta

The Mississippi Delta is where the Mississippi River empties into the Gulf of Mexico southeast of New Orleans, Louisiana. The river deposits about 2.5 million tons of sediment (mostly clay, silt, and fine sand) each year.

Fractals in Nature

Each fern leaf (called a "frond") has many small fronds along its main vein. Each of the small fronds also has many even smaller fronds.

Main vein

Fern frond

Smaller fronds

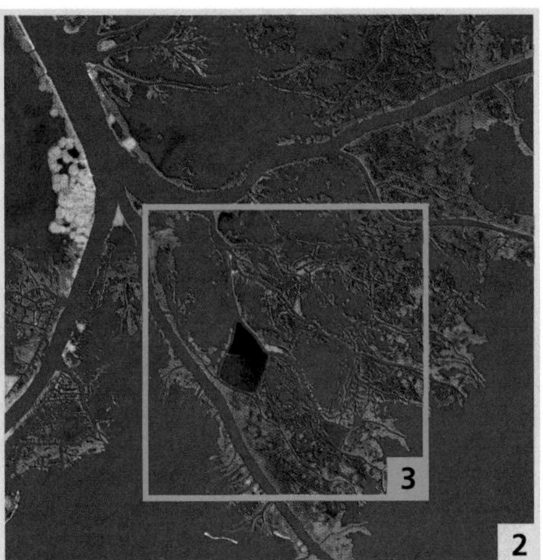

Fractal Structure

At the delta, the Mississippi River splits into distributaries, or branches. Many of the distributaries split into smaller branches. The smallest branches of the river look the same as the larger ones.

Put It All Together

Materials ruler, scissors, tape

1. Cut four thin strips of paper of equal length. Choose a length that is easy to divide into thirds. Use one strip to model a simple blood vessel. Mark it to show three equal segments.

a. How long is your blood vessel?

b. Fold an unmarked strip into thirds and tape it to form a triangle. Attach this triangle to the center segment of your blood vessel. Measure the total length of the paper blood vessel after you add the triangle. How much did the length increase?

length

c. Use your answers to parts (a) and (b). Find the percent of increase.

2. Use the last two strips to make four new triangles with sides that are $\frac{1}{9}$ the length of the marked strip. Attach each triangle to the center of each of the the four segments of your blood vessel.

a. How long is the blood vessel after you add the four smaller triangles? How much did the length increase?

b. What is the percent increase?

3. Patterns Describe the pattern as a percent increase from one step to the next. Predict the total length if you repeat the pattern one more time.

4. Find the percent increase in length of the blood vessel from the first step to the last step.

Take It to the NET For more information about fractals, go to **www.PHSchool.com**.

Web Code: abe-0653

CHAPTER 7

Geometry

Lessons

7-1 Lines and Planes

7-2 Measuring and Classifying Angles

7-3 Constructing Bisectors

7-4 Triangles

7-5 Quadrilaterals and Other Polygons

7-6 Problem Solving: Draw a Diagram and Look for a Pattern

7-7 Congruent Figures

7-8 Circles

7-9 Circle Graphs

Key Vocabulary

- acute angle (p. 352)
- adjacent angles (p. 353)
- angle bisector (p. 358)
- central angle (p. 383)
- chord (p. 383)
- equilateral triangle (p. 363)
- isosceles triangle (p. 363)
- obtuse angle (p. 352)
- perpendicular bisector (p. 357)
- polygon (p. 369)
- regular polygon (p. 370)
- right angle (p. 352)
- scalene triangle (p. 363)
- skew lines (p. 348)
- straight angle (p. 352)
- vertical angles (p. 353)

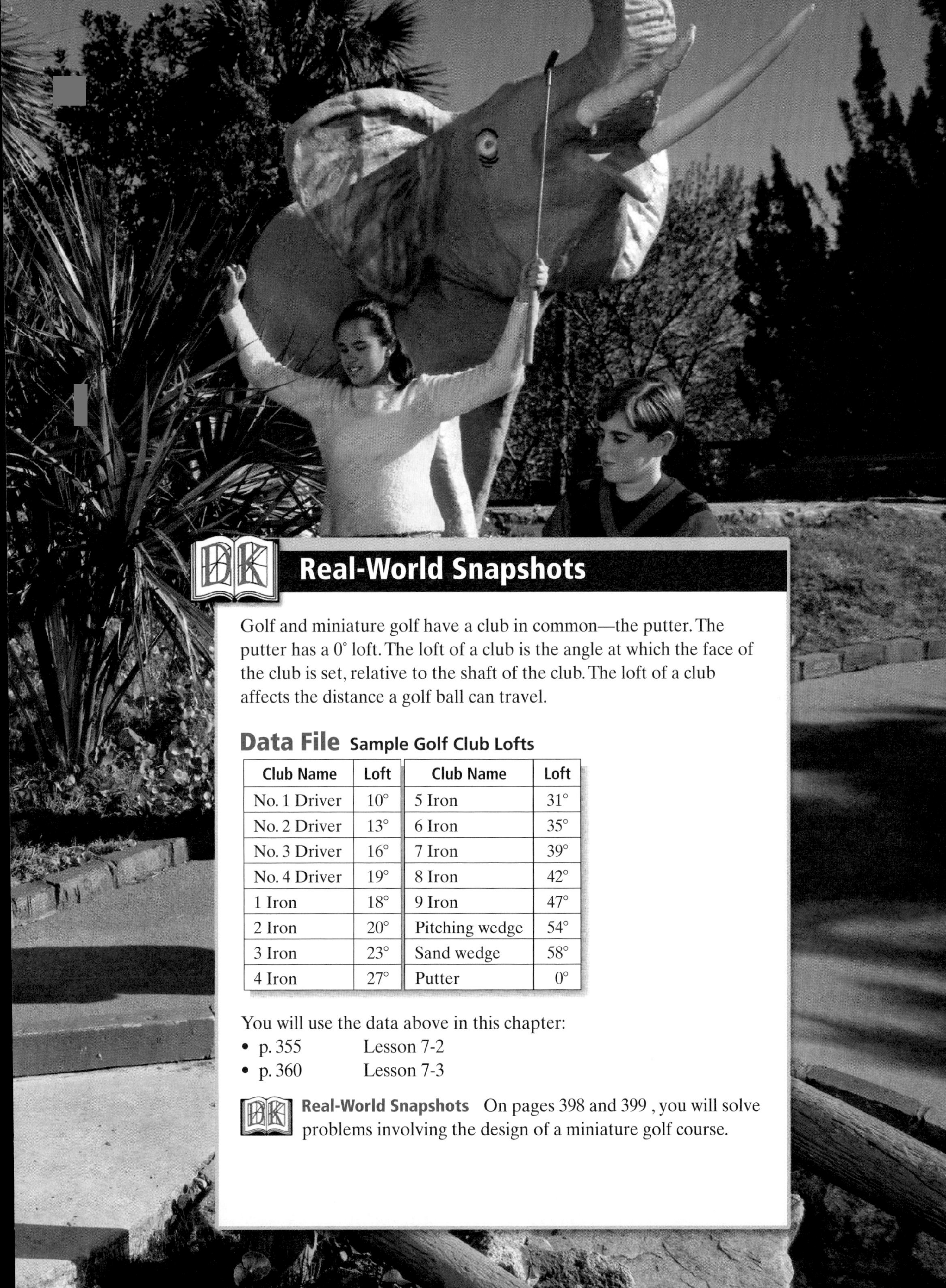

Real-World Snapshots

Golf and miniature golf have a club in common—the putter. The putter has a 0° loft. The loft of a club is the angle at which the face of the club is set, relative to the shaft of the club. The loft of a club affects the distance a golf ball can travel.

Data File Sample Golf Club Lofts

Club Name	Loft	Club Name	Loft
No. 1 Driver	10°	5 Iron	31°
No. 2 Driver	13°	6 Iron	35°
No. 3 Driver	16°	7 Iron	39°
No. 4 Driver	19°	8 Iron	42°
1 Iron	18°	9 Iron	47°
2 Iron	20°	Pitching wedge	54°
3 Iron	23°	Sand wedge	58°
4 Iron	27°	Putter	0°

You will use the data above in this chapter:

- p. 355 Lesson 7-2
- p. 360 Lesson 7-3

Real-World Snapshots On pages 398 and 399 , you will solve problems involving the design of a miniature golf course.

Chapter 7 Preview

Where You've Been

- In Chapter 5, you learned how to write ratios and rates, and how to use proportions to solve problems involving similar figures and maps.
- In Chapter 6, you learned how to model percents, how to find and estimate the percent of a number, and how to solve percent problems using proportions and equations.

Where You're Going

- In Chapter 7, you will learn how to classify angles, triangles, and quadrilaterals, and determine if geometric shapes are congruent.
- You will learn to interpret circle graphs and to use data to construct a circle graph.
- Applying what you have learned, you will classify the angle in a tool that a physical therapist uses.

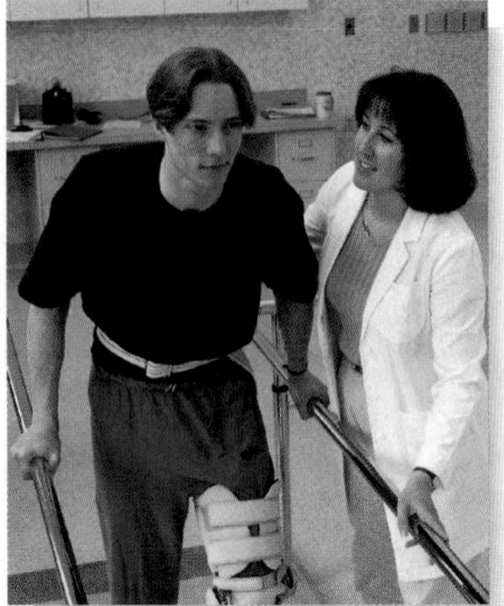

Physical therapists use mathematics in developing therapies for patients.

iTEXT Instant self-check online and on CD-ROM

Diagnosing Readiness

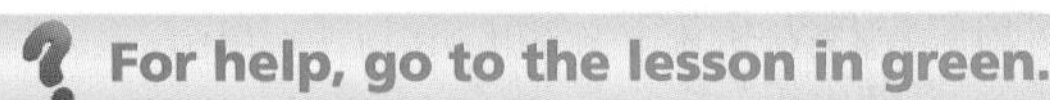

For help, go to the lesson in green.

Comparing Integers (Lesson 1-6)

Compare. Use <, >, or =.

1. 83 ■ 90 **2.** 120 ■ 99 **3.** 0 ■ 47 **4.** 21 ■ 11

Solving One-Step Equations (Lesson 2-3)

Solve each equation.

5. $d + 17 = 19$ **6.** $m - 12 = 3$ **7.** $j - 5 = 7$

8. $m - 15 = 90$ **9.** $58 + n = 63$ **10.** $y + 86 = 180$

Solving Proportions (Lesson 5-5)

Solve each proportion.

11. $\frac{5}{16} = \frac{25}{w}$ **12.** $\frac{n}{12} = \frac{20}{15}$ **13.** $\frac{18}{k} = \frac{6}{37}$ **14.** $\frac{23}{12} = \frac{x}{24}$

Finding a Percent of a Number (Lesson 6-4)

Find each answer.

15. 30% of 360 **16.** 24% of 360 **17.** 4.5% of 360 **18.** 18% of 360

7-1 Lines and Planes

What You'll Learn

OBJECTIVE 1 To identify segments, rays, and lines

. . . And Why

To identify segments in architecture, as in Example 2

✓ Check Skills You'll Need

For help, go to Lesson 2-8.

Graph the solution of each inequality.

1. $x \leq -3$ **2.** $x < -1$ **3.** $x \leq 2$

4. $x \geq 5$ **5.** $x > -1$ **6.** $x < 4$

New Vocabulary

- point
- line
- ray
- segment
- plane
- intersecting lines
- parallel lines
- skew lines

 Interactive lesson includes instant self-check, tutorials, and activities.

OBJECTIVE

1 Identifying Segments, Rays, and Lines

A **point** indicates location. A point has no size. You name a point by a capital letter.

A B

point A point B

A **line** is a series of points that extend in two opposite directions without end. You name a line by any two points on the line or a lowercase letter.

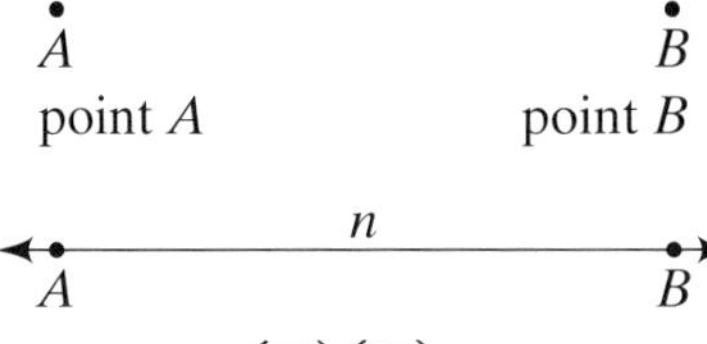

$\overleftrightarrow{AB}$, $\overleftrightarrow{BA}$, n

A **ray** is part of a line with one endpoint and all the points of the line on one side of the endpoint. You name a ray using two points, starting with the endpoint.

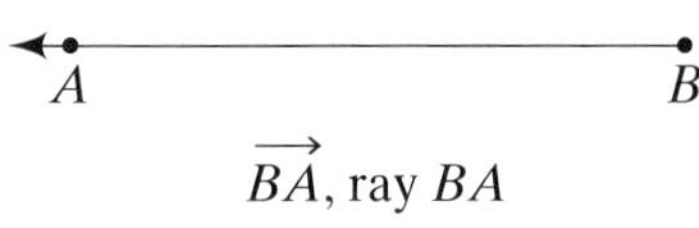

$\overrightarrow{BA}$, ray BA

A **segment** is part of a line with two endpoints and all points in between. You name a segment by its endpoints. AB indicates the length of $\overline{AB}$.

A B

$\overline{AB}$, $\overline{BA}$

1 EXAMPLE Naming Segments, Rays, and Lines

Use the points in each diagram to name the figure shown.

a. X Y

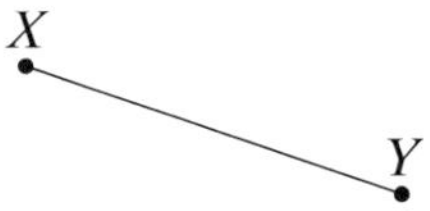

$\overline{XY}$

b.

$\overrightarrow{JT}$

c.

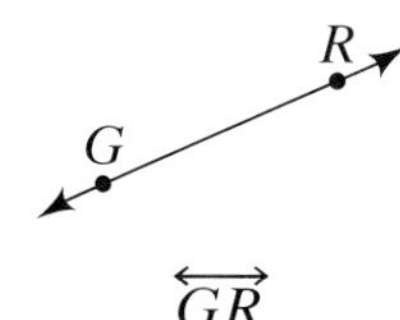

$\overleftrightarrow{GR}$

✓ **Check Understanding** **1** Use the points in each diagram to name the figure shown.

a. P D **b.** R S **c.** A V

A **plane** is a flat surface that extends indefinitely in all directions and has no thickness. There are two planes in the diagram at the right.

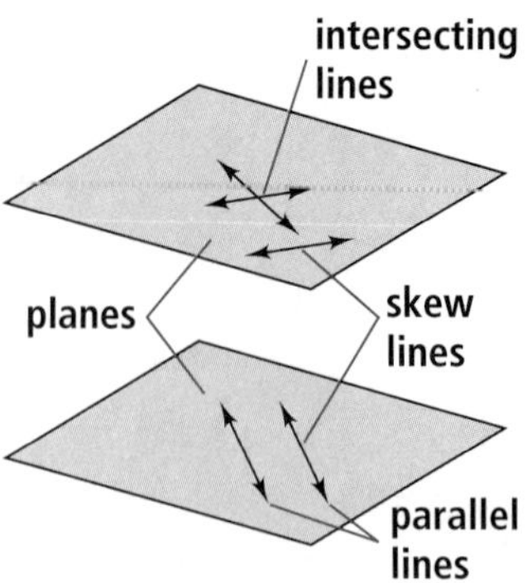

Intersecting and parallel lines lie in the same plane. **Intersecting lines** have exactly one point in common. **Parallel lines** are lines in the same plane that never intersect. Parallel segments and rays lie in parallel lines.

Skew lines lie in different planes. They are neither parallel nor intersecting.

2 EXAMPLE Intersecting, Parallel, and Skew

Architecture Use the information in the photograph to name a segment with the given description.

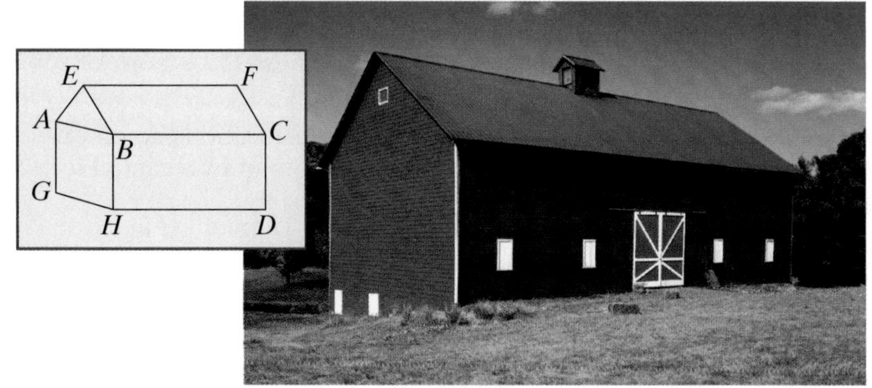

a. parallel to $\overline{AB}$
$\overline{GH}$ is parallel to $\overline{AB}$.

b. skew to $\overline{AB}$
$\overline{EF}$ is skew to $\overline{AB}$.

Check Understanding 2 Name all the segments in the photograph above that have each of the following characteristics.

a. parallel to $\overline{BC}$ **b.** intersect $\overline{BH}$ **c.** skew to $\overline{AG}$

d. **Reasoning** $\overline{CD}$ and $\overline{AG}$ do not intersect. Are they skew? Explain.

EXERCISES

For more practice, see *Extra Practice*.

A Practice by Example

Example 1 (page 347)

Use the points in each diagram to name the figure shown.

1.  L C
2. 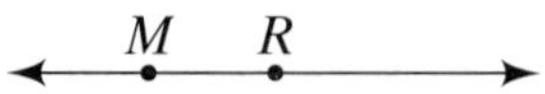 M R
3.  K E
4.  O D
5.  Y T
6.  W A
7.  Z V
8. 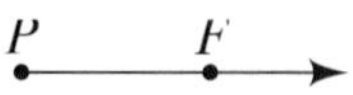 P F
9.  Q S

Example 2 (page 348)

Buildings **Use the diagram below for Exercises 10–14.**

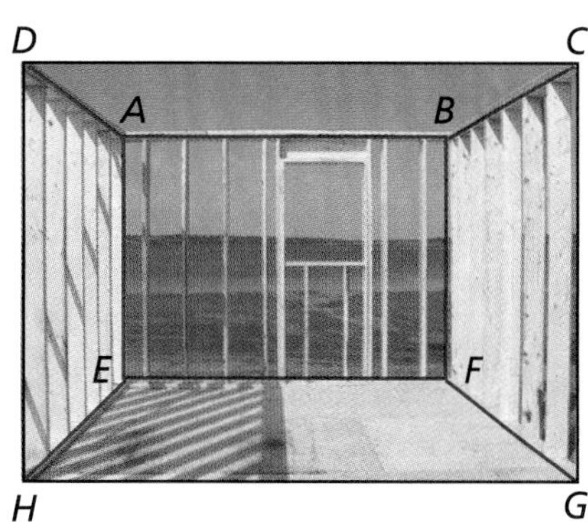

10. Name all the segments parallel to $\overline{AD}$.

11. Name all the segments intersecting $\overline{FG}$.

12. Name all the segments skew to $\overline{BC}$.

13. Name all the segments intersecting $\overline{AD}$.

14. Name all the segments parallel to $\overline{EH}$.

B Apply Your Skills

Draw each figure.

15. $\overleftrightarrow{AD}$

16. $\overline{NB}$

17. $\overrightarrow{QW}$

18. $\overleftrightarrow{PR}$

19. $\overrightarrow{AB}$, with $\overline{AC}$ on $\overrightarrow{AB}$

20. $\overline{FG}$ intersecting $\overleftrightarrow{TU}$

21. points C and D on the same line

22. $\overrightarrow{TB}$ and $\overrightarrow{TA}$ on the same line

23. **Carpentry** Are the rungs on a stepladder parallel, intersecting, or skew?

24. **Error Analysis** Jim says that in the box shown at the right $\overleftrightarrow{EF}$ and $\overleftrightarrow{GH}$ are parallel, since they do not intersect. Why is Jim incorrect?

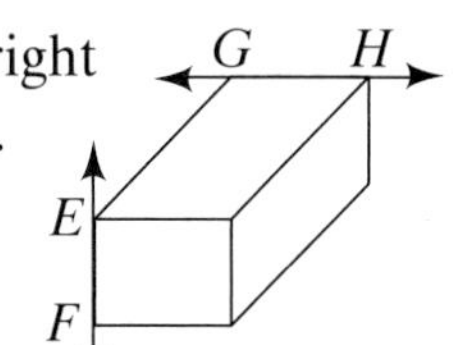

25. **Writing in Math** Describe examples of parallel, intersecting, and skew lines in your classroom.

C Challenge

26. Name each segment, ray, and line in the figure below.

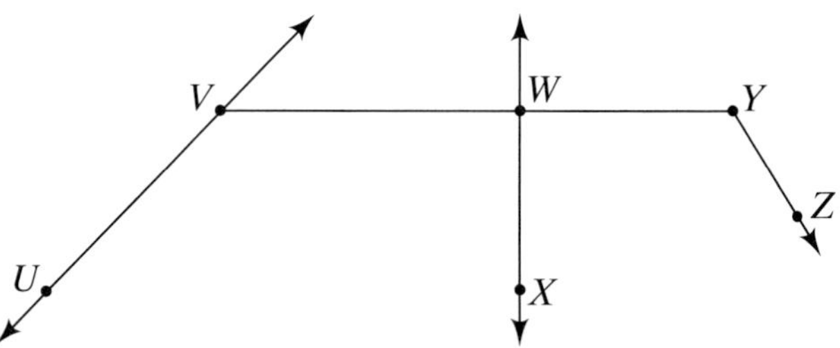

27. **Stretch Your Thinking** I am a three-digit number. My digits are 3, 5, and 7. I am divisible by 3, 5, and 7. What number am I?

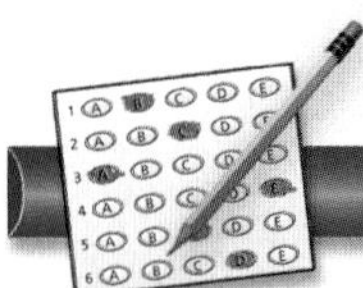

Test Prep

Multiple Choice

28. Which is NOT a name for the figure at the right?

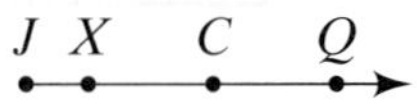

J X C Q

A. $\overrightarrow{JQ}$ **B.** $\overrightarrow{CQ}$ **C.** $\overrightarrow{JC}$ **D.** $\overrightarrow{JX}$

29. Which statement could be true?

F. $\overleftrightarrow{MN}$ is parallel to $\overleftrightarrow{LM}$.

G. $\overleftrightarrow{PR}$ is parallel to and skew to $\overleftrightarrow{ST}$.

H. $\overleftrightarrow{CD}$ intersects and is skew to $\overleftrightarrow{DE}$.

I. $\overleftrightarrow{WX}$ intersects $\overleftrightarrow{YZ}$.

Take It to the NET Online lesson quiz at **www.PHSchool.com** Web Code aba-0701

30. W, X, Y, and Z all lie on the same line. $\overline{WX}$ and $\overline{YZ}$ do not intersect. $\overline{ZW}$ and $\overline{XW}$ intersect at only one point. $\overline{YZ}$ and $\overline{ZW}$ intersect at only one point. Which is a correct order for the points?

A. W, X, Y, Z **B.** X, Y, W, Z **C.** Z, W, X, Y **D.** Y, Z, W, X

Short Response

31. $\overleftrightarrow{AB}$ and $\overleftrightarrow{CD}$ are parallel. $\overleftrightarrow{CD}$ and $\overrightarrow{EF}$ intersect. Do you know whether $\overleftrightarrow{AB}$ and $\overrightarrow{EF}$ intersect? Explain.

Mixed Review

Lesson 6-8

Algebra **Find the percent of change. State whether the change is an increase or a decrease. Round to the nearest percent.**

32. old: \$5.75; new: \$6.25

33. old: 380 ft; new: 320 ft

34. old: 3.95 lb; new: 4.25 lb

35. old: 28.3 gal; new: 25.1 gal

Lesson 5-5

Solve each proportion.

36. $\frac{16}{x} = \frac{38}{19}$

37. $\frac{19}{3} = \frac{c}{15}$

38. $\frac{48}{20} = \frac{w}{5}$

Math at Work

Architect

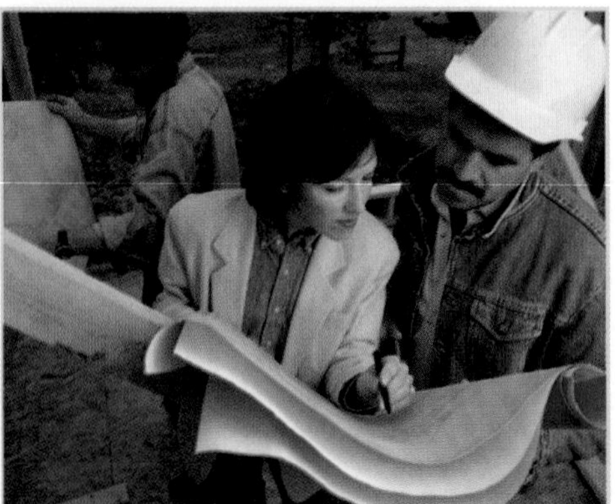

Do you have an eye for design? Then architecture could be a career for you. An architect uses creativity, math, science, and art to plan a building that is beautiful, functional, safe, and economical.

An architect must understand spatial relationships and be able to manage, supervise, and communicate complex ideas.

Take It to the NET For more information on architects, visit **www.PHSchool.com**. Web Code abb-2031

7-2 Measuring and Classifying Angles

What You'll Learn

OBJECTIVE 1 To measure and describe angles

OBJECTIVE 2 To work with pairs of angles

. . . And Why

To classify angles in architecture, as in Example 2

✓ Check Skills You'll Need

For help, go to Lesson 2-2.

Use mental math to solve each equation.

1. $k + 12 = 15$ **2.** $\ell + 20 = 90$ **3.** $m + 5 = 28$

4. $n + 40 = 180$ **5.** $p + 16 = 90$ **6.** $s + 22 = 30$

New Vocabulary • angle • vertex • acute angle • right angle • obtuse angle • straight angle • complementary • supplementary • adjacent angles • vertical angles • congruent angles

Interactive lesson includes instant self-check, tutorials, and activities.

OBJECTIVE 1 Measuring and Describing Angles

An **angle** ($\angle$)is formed by two rays with a common endpoint. You can call the angle at the right $\angle DCE$, $\angle ECD$, $\angle C$, or $\angle 1$.

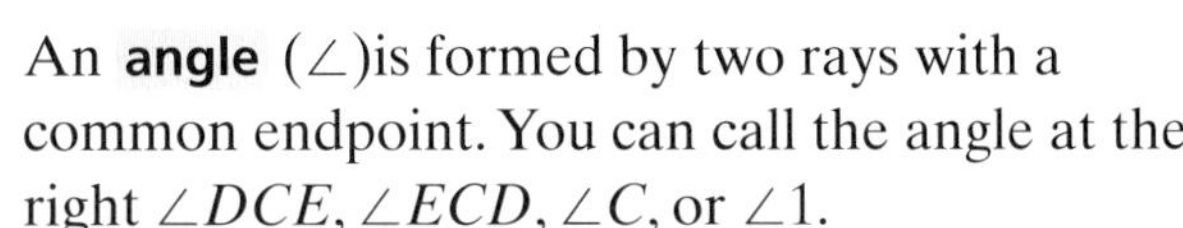

A **vertex** is the point of intersection of two sides of an angle or figure. Point *C* is the vertex of the angle at the right. The plural of *vertex* is *vertices*.

You can use a protractor to measure angles. Write "the measure of $\angle C$" as $m\angle C$.

1 EXAMPLE Measuring Angles

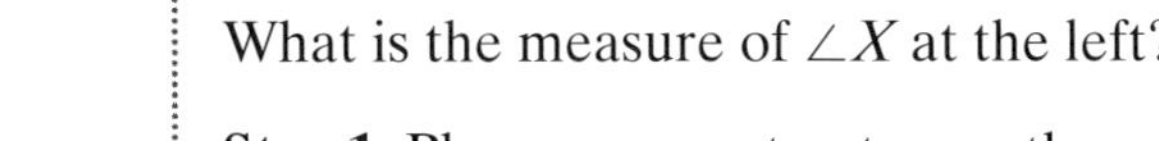

What is the measure of $\angle X$ at the left?

Step 1 Place your protractor on the vertex of the angle, as shown.

Step 2 Make sure that one side of the angle passes through zero on one of the protractor's scales.

Step 3 Read the same scale where it intersects the second side of the angle.

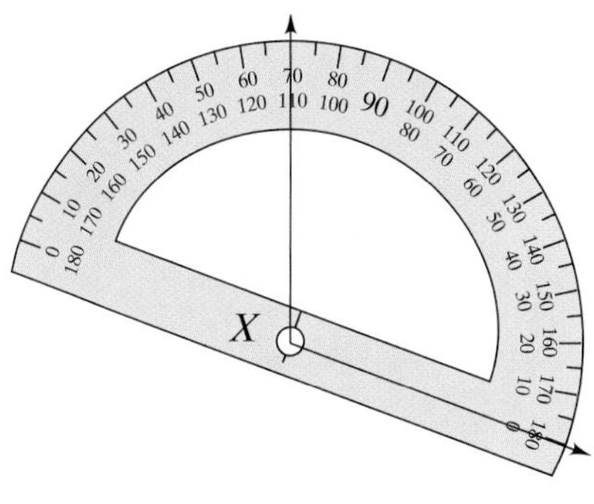

$m\angle X = 110°$

✓ Check Understanding 1 Measure $\angle G$ using a protractor.

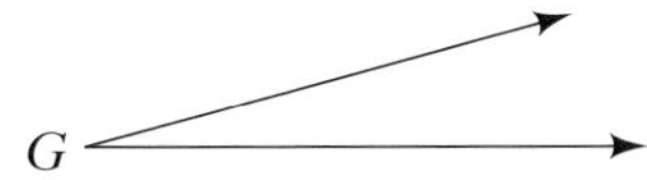

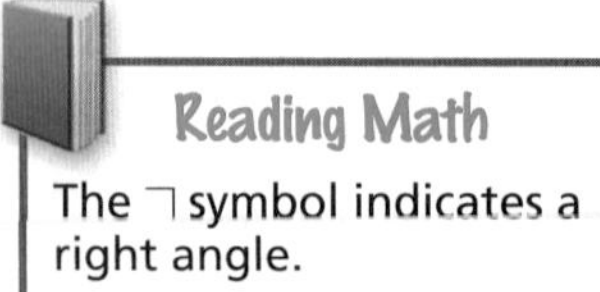

You can classify angles by their measures.

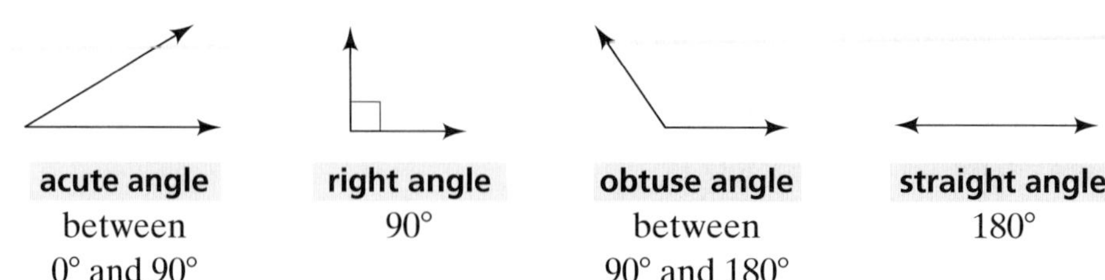

acute angle between 0° and 90°

right angle 90°

obtuse angle between 90° and 180°

straight angle 180°

Notice that a straight angle is a line.

2 EXAMPLE Identifying Angles — Real World

Architecture A geodesic dome, a building system invented by R. Buckminster Fuller, is pictured below. Identify three acute angles and three obtuse angles.

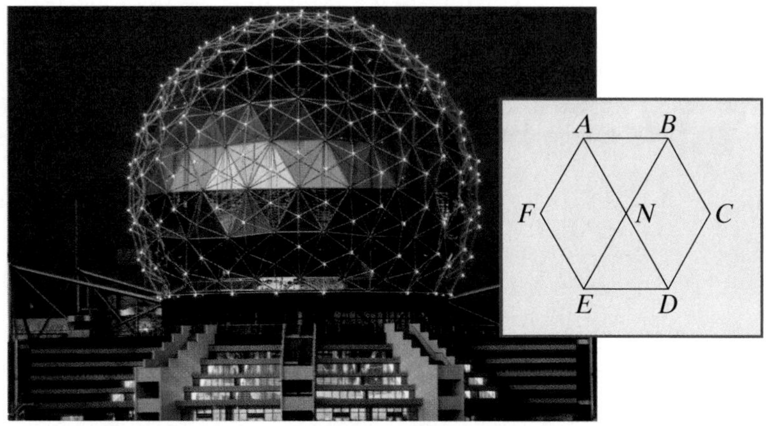

acute angles: $\angle FAN$, $\angle NAB$, and $\angle DNE$

obtuse angles: $\angle F$, $\angle C$, and $\angle FAB$

Check Understanding 2 Classify each angle as *acute*, *right*, *obtuse*, or *straight*.

a. 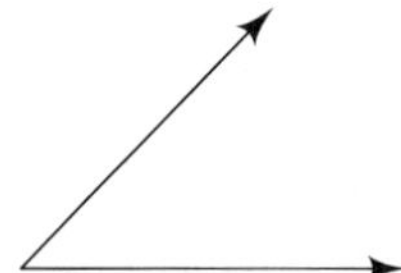 **b.** **c.** 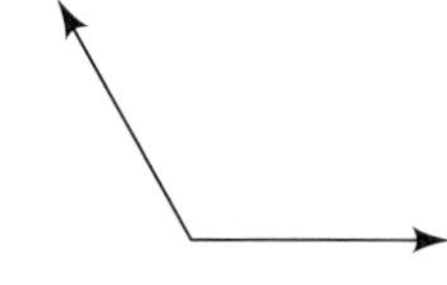

OBJECTIVE

2 Working With Pairs of Angles

If the sum of the measures of two angles is 90°, the angles are **complementary.** If the sum is 180°, the angles are **supplementary.**

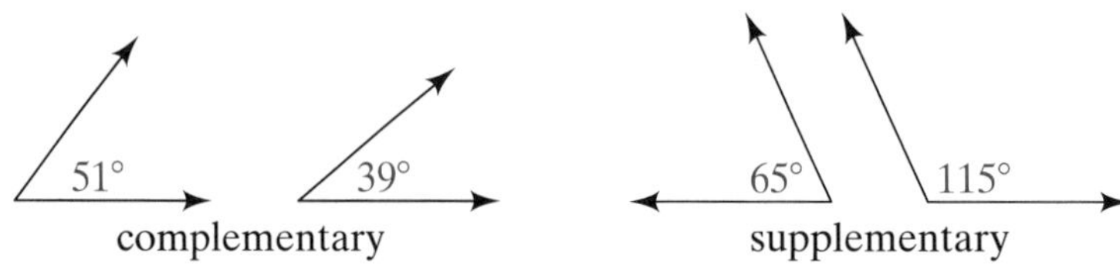

Suppose you know that two angles are supplementary, and you know the measure of one of the angles. You can use an equation to find the measure of the other angle.

3 EXAMPLE Finding Complements and Supplements (Algebra)

The measure of $\angle A$ is 37°. Find the measure of its supplement.

Let x = the measure of the supplement of $\angle A$.

$x + m\angle A = 180°$ ← **The angles are supplementary.**

$x + 37° = 180°$ ← **Substitute 37° for $m\angle A$.**

$x + 37° - 37° = 180° - 37°$ ← **Subtract 37° from each side.**

$x = 143°$ ← **Simplify.**

The measure of the supplement of $\angle A$ is 143°.

Check Understanding 3
a. Find the measure of the complement of $\angle A$ in Example 3.
b. **Reasoning** Is the supplement of an angle always greater than its complement? Explain.

Adjacent angles share a vertex and a side but have no interior points in common. Angles 1 and 2 below are adjacent angles. Adjacent angles formed by two intersecting lines are supplementary.

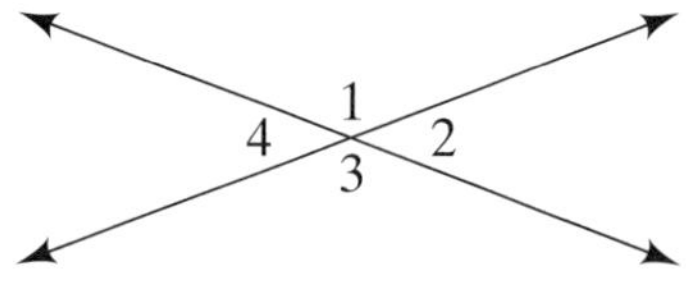

> **Need Help?**
> *Congruent* means having the same size and shape.

Angles 1 and 3 above are vertical angles. **Vertical angles** are formed by two intersecting lines and are opposite each other. Vertical angles have equal measures. Angles with equal measures are **congruent angles.**

4 EXAMPLE Finding Angle Measures (Algebra)

Find the measures of $\angle 1$, $\angle 2$, and $\angle 3$, if $m\angle 4 = 128°$.

$m\angle 1 + 128° = 180°$ ← **$\angle 1$ and $\angle 4$ are supplementary.**

$m\angle 1 + 128° - 128° = 180° - 128°$

$m\angle 1 = 52°$

$m\angle 2 = 128°$ ← **$\angle 2$ and $\angle 4$ are vertical angles.**

$m\angle 3 = 52°$ ← **$\angle 1$ and $\angle 3$ are vertical angles.**

Check Understanding 4
a. Find the measures of $\angle 5$, $\angle 6$, and $\angle 7$, if $m\angle 8 = 72°$.
b. **Reasoning** For Example 4 and part (a), what is the sum of the measures of the angles formed by two intersecting lines?

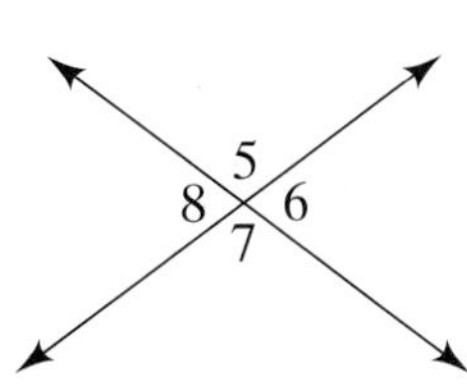

More Than One Way

If $m\angle 1 = 140°$ and $m\angle 2 = 40°$, what is $m\angle 3$?

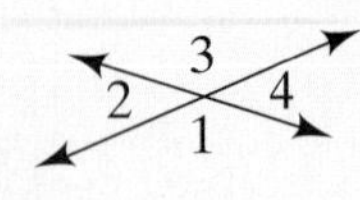

Carlos's Method

Since $\angle 3$ and $\angle 1$ are across from each other, they are vertical angles. Since vertical angles have the same measure, $m\angle 3 = m\angle 1$. So $m\angle 3 = 140°$.

Kayla's Method

$\angle 2$ and $\angle 3$ together form a straight angle, so their measures add up to 180°. This means that they are supplementary angles.

$$40° + m\angle 3 = 180°$$

$$40° - 40° + m\angle 3 = 180° - 40° \quad \leftarrow \text{Subtract 40° from each side.}$$

$$m\angle 3 = 140° \quad \leftarrow \text{Simplify.}$$

So $m\angle 3$ is 140°.

Choose a Method

In the figure at the right, $m\angle BEC = 25°$ and $m\angle CED = 155°$. Find the $m\angle AEB$. Explain why you chose the method you used.

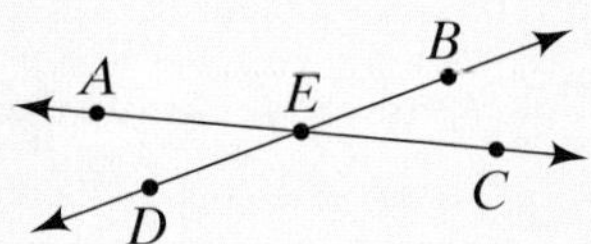

EXERCISES

For more practice, see *Extra Practice.*

A Practice by Example

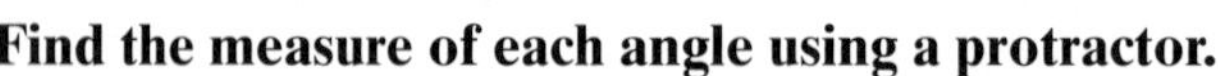

Find the measure of each angle using a protractor.

Example 1 (page 351)

1.

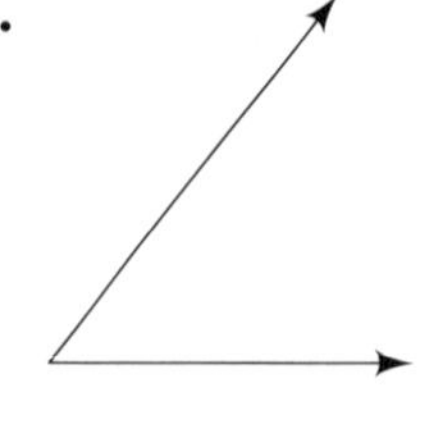

2.

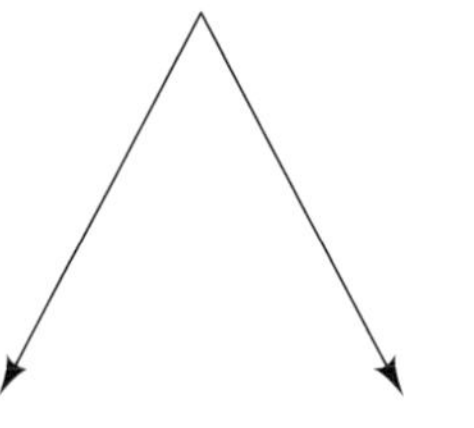

3.

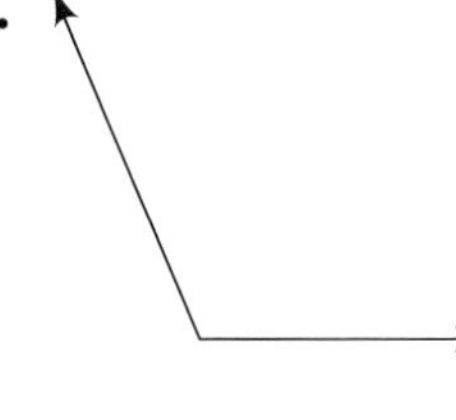

Test-Prep Tip

Estimate the angle measure first. If the angle is larger than a corner of this page, its measure will be greater than 90°.

4.

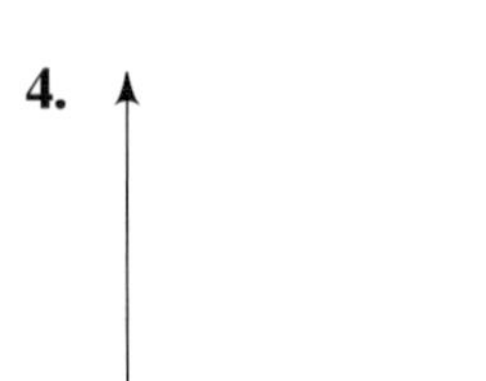

5.

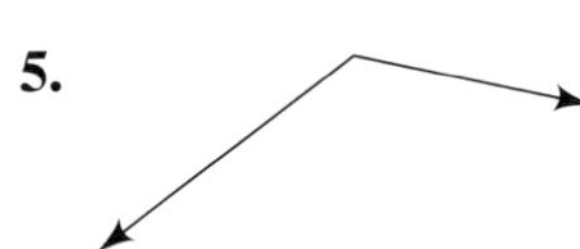

6.

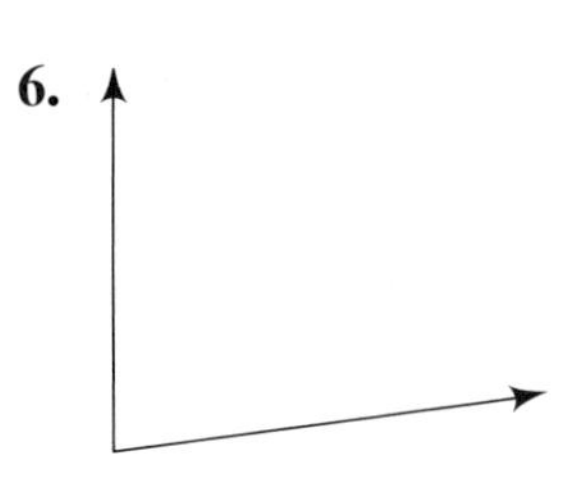

Example 2 (page 352)

Classify each angle as *acute*, *right*, *obtuse*, or *straight*.

7. 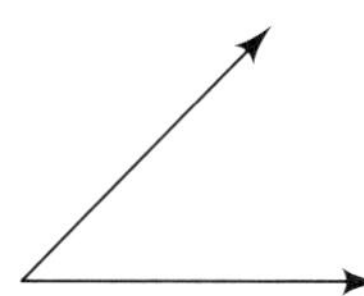

8. 

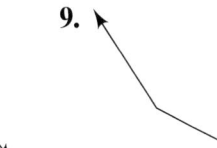

9.

10. 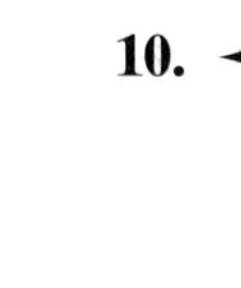

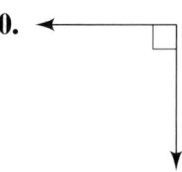

11. **City Planning** Engineers are planning to put in a new road that will make an angle of 120° with an existing road. Classify the angle as *acute*, *right*, *obtuse*, or *straight*.

Example 3 (page 353)

Algebra **Find the measures of the complement and supplement of each angle.**

12. $m\angle A = 45°$
13. $m\angle B = 5°$
14. $m\angle C = 76°$
15. $m\angle D = 50°$
16. $m\angle E = 79°$
17. $m\angle F = 67°$
18. $m\angle G = 12°$
19. $m\angle H = 36°$

Example 4 (page 353)

Algebra **In the diagram at the right, $m\angle 2 = 123°$. Find the measure of each of the following angles.**

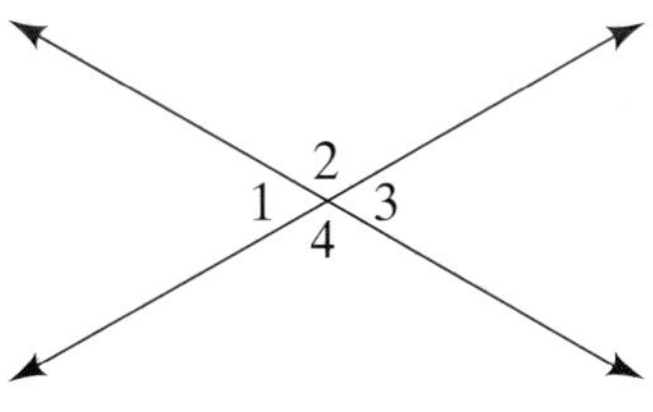

20. $m\angle 1$
21. $m\angle 3$
22. $m\angle 4$

B Apply Your Skills

Algebra **Find the measures of the complement and supplement of each angle.**

23. $m\angle A = 23.5°$
24. $m\angle B = 37.6°$
25. $m\angle C = 47.9°$
26. $m\angle D = 56.4°$
27. $m\angle E = 75.1°$
28. $m\angle F = 82.2°$

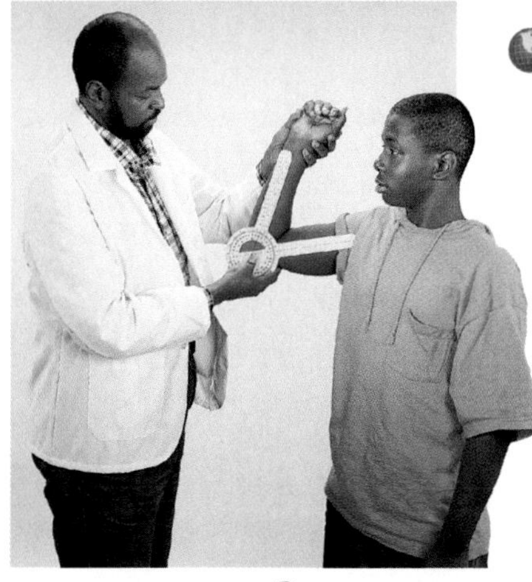

Real-World Connection

Careers Physical therapists help people regain mobility after an accident.

29. **Physical Therapy** Physical therapists use goniometers to measure the amount of motion a person has in a joint, like an elbow or a knee. Estimate the measure of the angle in the photograph.

Use the figure at the right to name the following.

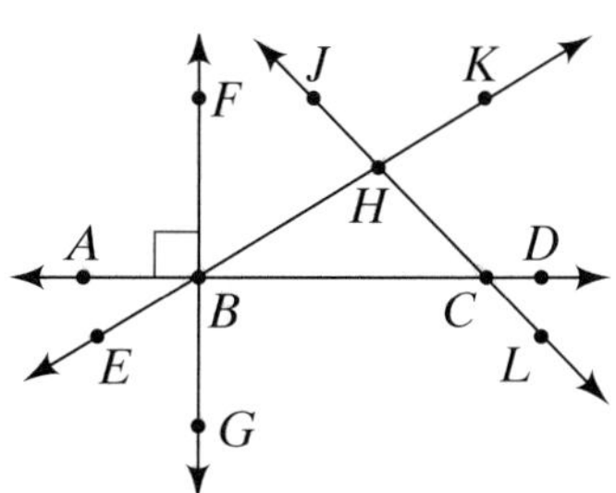

30. two pairs of adjacent supplementary angles
31. four right angles
32. two pairs of obtuse vertical angles
33. two pairs of complementary angles

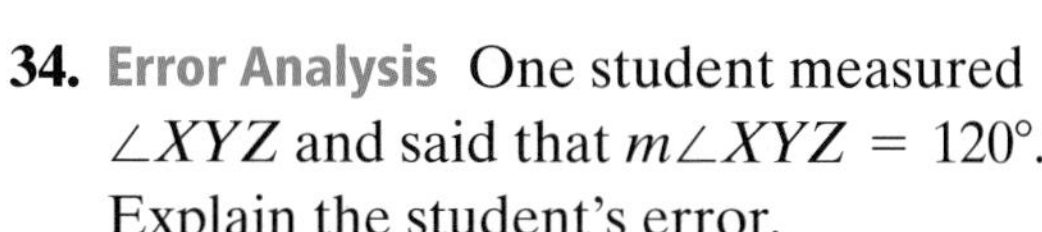

34. **Error Analysis** One student measured $\angle XYZ$ and said that $m\angle XYZ = 120°$. Explain the student's error.

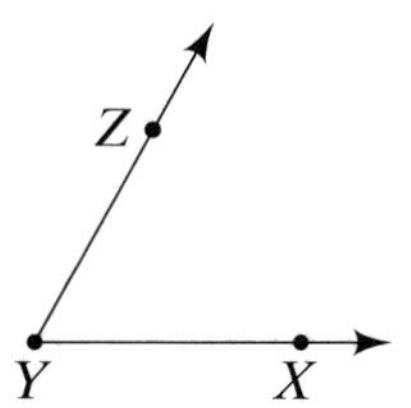

35. **Data File, p. 345** Classify the loft angle of a No. 4 driver.

36. **Writing in Math** Can an angle ever have the same measure as its complement? Explain.

C Challenge

37. You know that $\angle B$ is the complement of $\angle A$ and $m\angle B = 51°$, and $m\angle A = (3x - 12)°$. Find x.

38. **Stretch Your Thinking** I am a three-digit number. When you reverse my digits, a greater number is formed. The product of the new number and me is 65,125. What number am I?

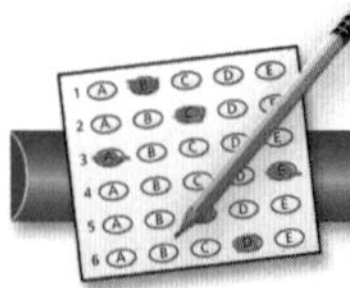

Test Prep

Reading Comprehension **Read the passage and answer Exercises 39 and 40 below.**

Identifying Ivory

Ivory smugglers try to slip illegal ivory from elephant tusks into the United States by labeling the elephant tusks as mammoth tusks. Ed Espinoza of the United States Fish and Wildlife Service found that the markings on photocopied tusks have different angles. Markings on mammoth tusks create angles that measure 90° or less. Markings on elephant tusks create angles that measure 115° or more.

39. Tell whether each photocopy comes from a mammoth or an elephant.

a. 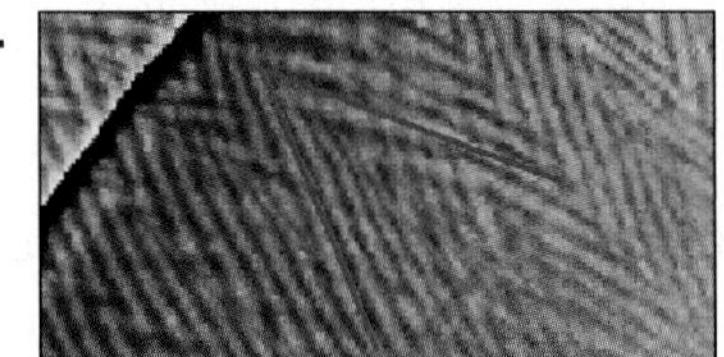

b. 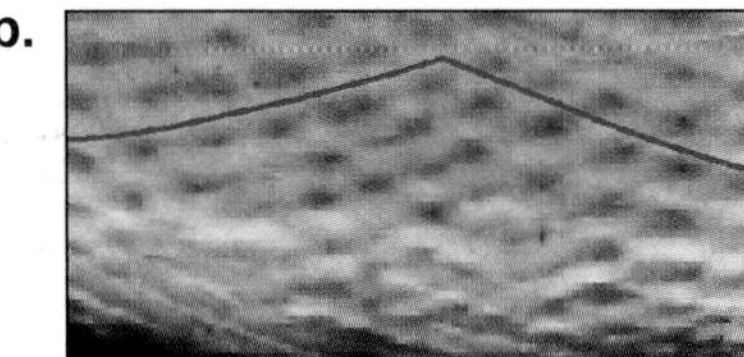

Take It to the NET
Online lesson quiz at
www.PHSchool.com
Web Code aba-0702

40. Suppose two tusks from the same type of animal have angles that are complementary. Would the animal be a mammoth or an elephant?

Multiple Choice

41. What is the measure of the complement of a 48° angle?
A. 32° **B.** 42° **C.** 132° **D.** 142°

42. The supplement of which angle is NOT acute?
F. 85° **G.** 91° **H.** 102° **I.** 131°

Mixed Review

Lesson 6-7 **43.** **Dining** You add a 15% tip to your bill of \$37. How much do you pay?

Lesson 5-7 **For a scale of 1 cm : 12 km, find the actual length for each drawing length.**

44. 0.5 cm **45.** 1.2 cm **46.** 1.7 cm **47.** 2 cm

7-3 Constructing Bisectors

What You'll Learn

To construct segment bisectors

To construct angle bisectors

. . . And Why

To fold origami, as in Exercise 19

✓ Check Skills You'll Need

For help, go to Lesson 7-1.

Use the points in each diagram to name the figure shown.

1. 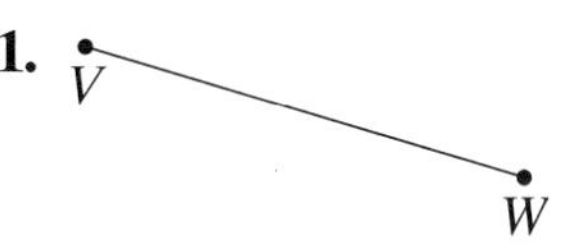

2.

3. 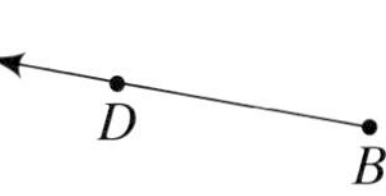

4. 

5. 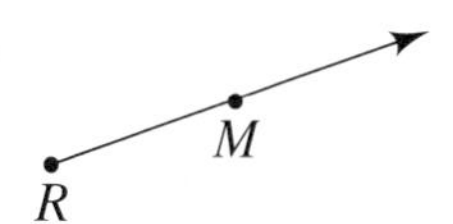

6. 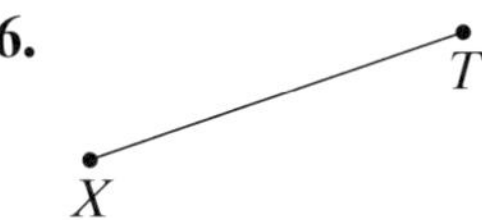

New Vocabulary • midpoint • segment bisector • perpendicular lines • perpendicular bisector • compass • arc • angle bisector

OBJECTIVE 1

Constructing Segment Bisectors

Interactive lesson includes instant self-check, tutorials, and activities.

Investigation: Folding Bisectors

- Draw a segment on tracing paper. Label the endpoints *A* and *B*.
- Fold the paper so that point *A* lies on point *B*.
- Unfold the paper and label the intersection of $\overline{AB}$ and the fold line as point *M*.

1. What is the relationship between $\overline{AM}$ and $\overline{MB}$?

2. What kind of angles does the fold line make with $\overline{AB}$?

The **midpoint** of a segment is the point that divides the segment into two segments of equal length. A **segment bisector** is a line, segment, or ray that goes through the midpoint of a segment.

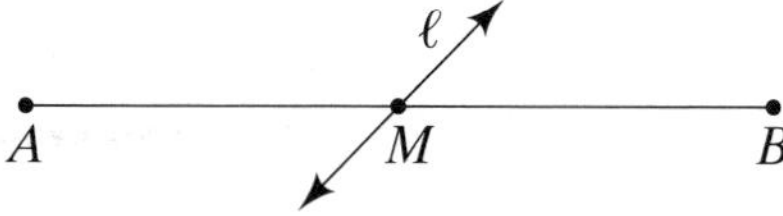

$\overline{AM}$ is congruent to $\overline{MB}$.
M is the midpoint of $\overline{AB}$.
Line ℓ is a segment bisector of $\overline{AB}$.

Perpendicular lines intersect to form right angles. A segment bisector that is perpendicular to a segment is the **perpendicular bisector** of the segment.

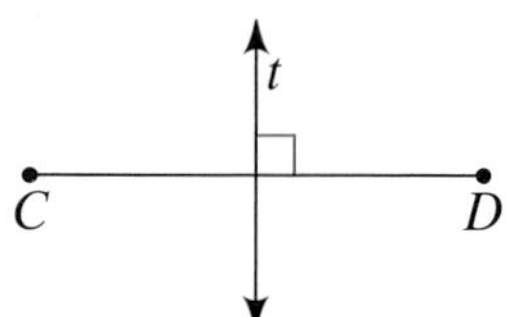

A **compass** is a geometric tool used to draw circles and arcs. An **arc** is a part of a circle.

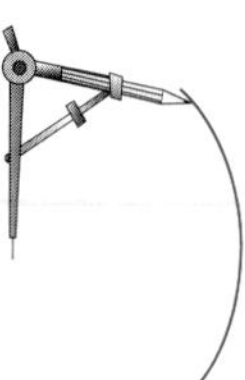

You can use a compass and straightedge (an unmarked ruler) to construct the perpendicular bisector of a given segment.

1 EXAMPLE Constructing a Perpendicular Bisector

Construct the perpendicular bisector of $\overline{AB}$.

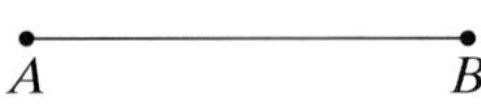

Step 1 Set the compass to more than half the length of $\overline{AB}$. Put the tip of the compass at A and draw an arc intersecting $\overline{AB}$.

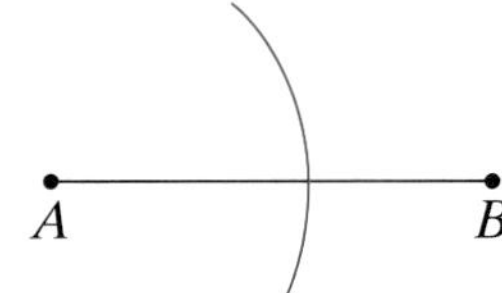

Step 2 Keeping the compass set at the same width, put the tip at B and draw another arc intersecting $\overline{AB}$. Points C and D are where the arcs intersect.

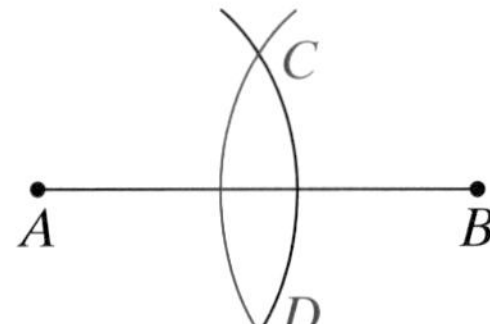

Step 3 Draw $\overleftrightarrow{CD}$. The intersection of $\overline{AB}$ and $\overleftrightarrow{CD}$ is point M. $\overleftrightarrow{CD}$ is the perpendicular bisector of $\overline{AB}$. Point M is the midpoint of $\overline{AB}$.

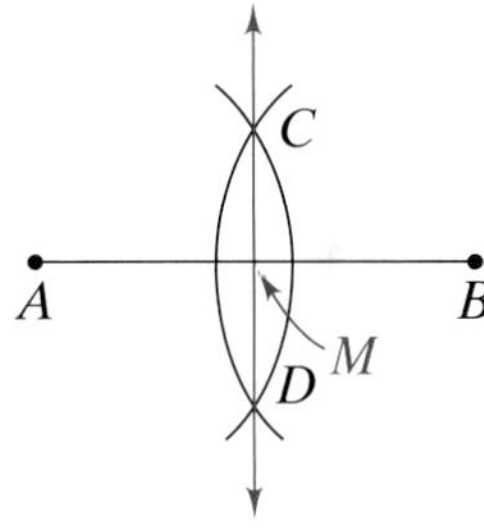

Real-World Connection

This 1482 edition of Euclid's *Elements of Geometry* was the first math book produced on a printing press.

SOURCE: Wellesley College Library Special Collections

Check Understanding 1

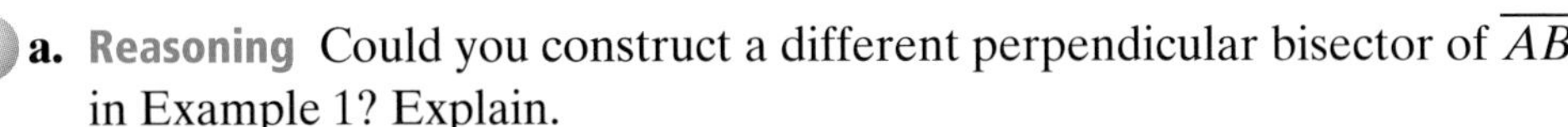

a. Reasoning Could you construct a different perpendicular bisector of $\overline{AB}$ in Example 1? Explain.

b. Draw a segment 3 in. long. Label the segment $\overline{XY}$. Construct the perpendicular bisector of $\overline{XY}$.

OBJECTIVE

2 Constructing Angle Bisectors

An **angle bisector** is a ray that divides an angle into two congruent angles.

In the diagram at the right, $\overrightarrow{BT}$ bisects $\angle ABC$. $\angle ABT$ is congruent to $\angle TBC$. So $m\angle ABT = m\angle TBC$.

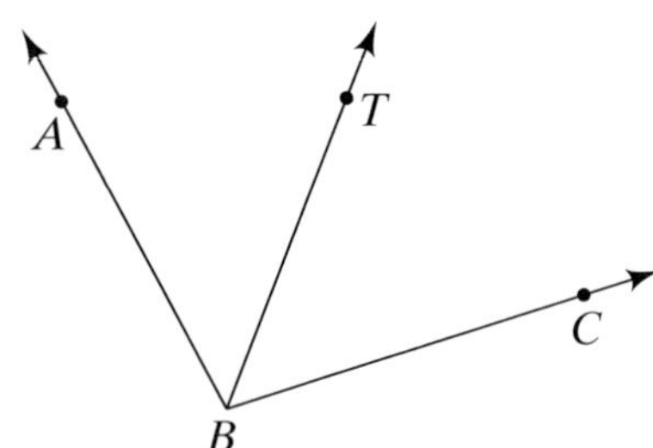

You can construct the bisector of an angle using a compass and a straightedge.

2 EXAMPLE Constructing an Angle Bisector

Construct the angle bisector of $\angle P$.

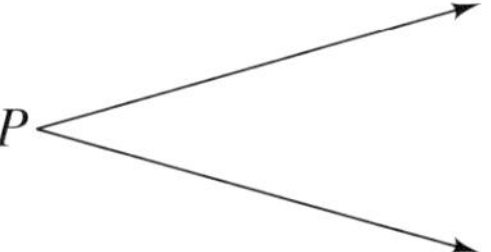

Step 1 Put the tip of the compass at P and draw an arc that intersects the sides of $\angle P$. The points of intersection are S and T.

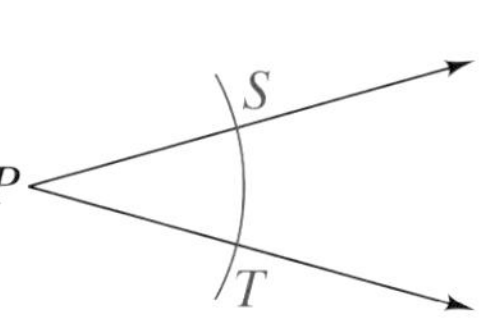

Step 2 Using the same compass opening, place the compass tip at S and then at T, and draw intersecting arcs. Point X is where the arcs intersect.

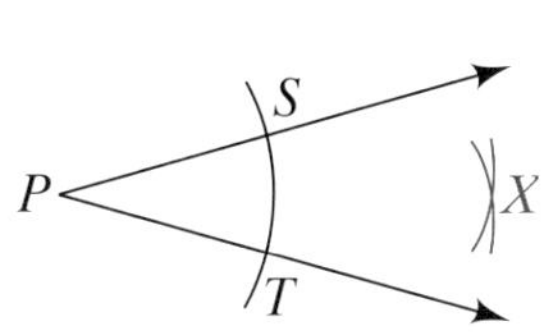

Step 3 Draw $\overrightarrow{PX}$. $\overrightarrow{PX}$ is the bisector of $\angle SPT$.

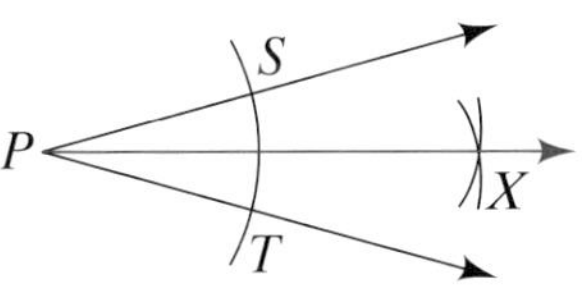

Check Understanding 2 **a.** Draw an obtuse angle. Construct its angle bisector.
b. The bisector of $\angle JKL$ is $\overrightarrow{KN}$. If $m\angle JKL$ is 66°, what is $m\angle JKN$?

EXERCISES

For more practice, see *Extra Practice*.

A Practice by Example

Example 1 (page 358)

Copy each segment. Then construct its perpendicular bisector.

1. C ———————— D **2.** K ———————— L

3. Draw a segment between 2 in. and 3 in. long. Label the segment $\overline{GH}$. Construct the perpendicular bisector of $\overline{GH}$.

4. Draw a segment greater than 4 in. long. Label the segment $\overline{MN}$. Construct the perpendicular bisector of $\overline{MN}$.

Example 2 (page 359)

Trace each angle. Then construct its angle bisector.

5.

6.

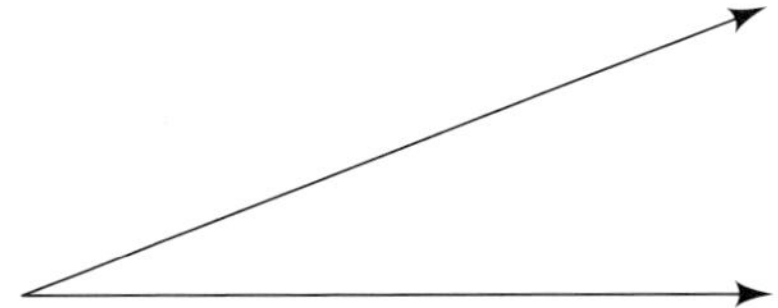

7. The bisector of $\angle LMN$ is $\overrightarrow{MR}$. If $m\angle LMN$ is 48°, what is $m\angle LMR$?

8. The bisector of $\angle CDE$ is $\overrightarrow{DN}$. If $m\angle CDE$ is 162°, what is $m\angle NDE$?

Apply Your Skills

Need Help?
AB means the length of $\overline{AB}$.

Point B is the midpoint of $\overline{AC}$. Complete.

9. $AB = 4$ in., $AC = ■$

10. $AC = 9$ cm, $AB = ■$

11. $BC = 5$ ft, $AB = ■$

12. $AB = 17$ mm, $AC = ■$

13. $AC = 3$ in., $BC = ■$

14. $BC = 75$ cm, $AC = ■$

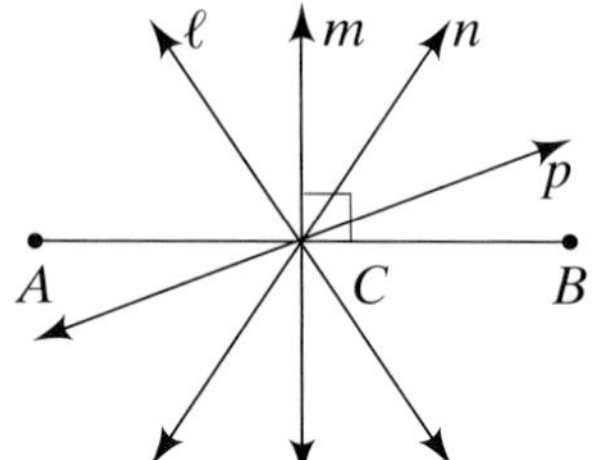

15. In the figure at the right, C is the midpoint of $\overline{AB}$. Which of the segment bisectors is the perpendicular bisector of $\overline{AB}$?

16. **Reasoning** How many segment bisectors can a segment have? Explain.

17. Draw $\overline{CD}$ at least 3 in. long. Then construct and label the following segments.

a. a segment half as long as $\overline{CD}$

b. a segment one fourth as long as $\overline{CD}$

18. Draw an obtuse angle, $\angle ABC$.

a. Construct an angle one fourth the measure of $\angle ABC$.

b. **Reasoning** How could you construct an angle three fourths the measure of $\angle ABC$?

19. **Origami** To make an origami crane like the ones below, you make folds that bisect $\angle ABC$ twice to get $\angle ABE$. What is the measure of $\angle ABE$?

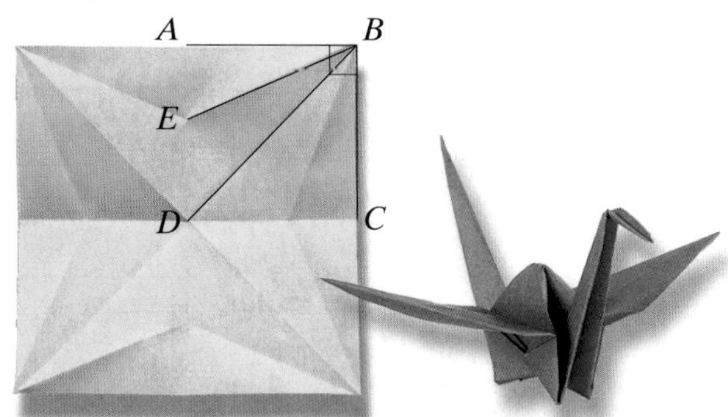

20. **Writing in Math** How is creating an angle bisector similar to creating a segment bisector?

21. **Bridge** A support for a certain section of a bridge looks like the diagram at the right. $\overline{JR}$ bisects $\angle PJT$, $\overline{JQ}$ bisects $\angle PJR$, and $\overline{JS}$ bisects $\angle RJT$. If $m\angle PJT = 80°$, what is $m\angle QJT$?

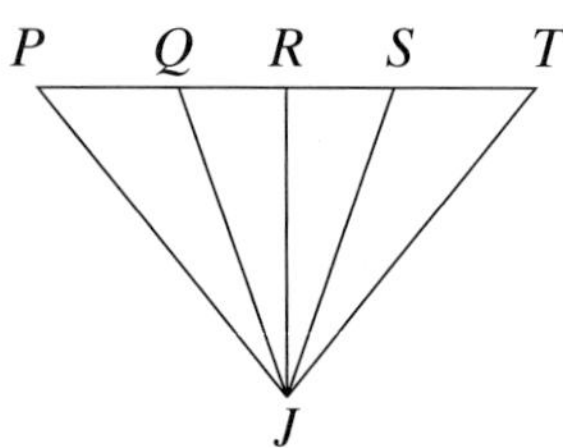

22. **a.** Construct a 90° angle.

b. Construct a 45° angle.

23. **Data File, p. 345** Draw an angle with the same measure as the loft angle of a pitching wedge. Bisect that angle. Which club has a loft angle equal to the measure of the new angle?

The angle bisector of $\angle MNO$ is $\overrightarrow{NP}$. Complete.

24. $m\angle MNO = 56°, m\angle MNP = \blacksquare$ **25.** $m\angle PNO = 56°, m\angle ONM = \blacksquare$

26. $m\angle ONP = 74°, m\angle MNO = \blacksquare$ **27.** $m\angle MNO = 74°, m\angle PNM = \blacksquare$

C Challenge

28. What is the supplement of the angle formed by $\overrightarrow{BA}$ and the bisector of $\angle ABC$, if $m\angle ABC = 56°$?

29. What is the complement of the angle formed by $\overrightarrow{RT}$ and the bisector of $\angle TRS$, if $m\angle TRS = 118°$?

30. Point A is the midpoint of $\overline{XY}$. Point Y is the midpoint of $\overline{XZ}$. Point Z is the midpoint of $\overline{AB}$. $\overline{XA}$ is 2 cm long. How long is $\overline{XB}$?

31. **Stretch Your Thinking** How would you divide the figure shown at the right into two parts with the same size and shape?

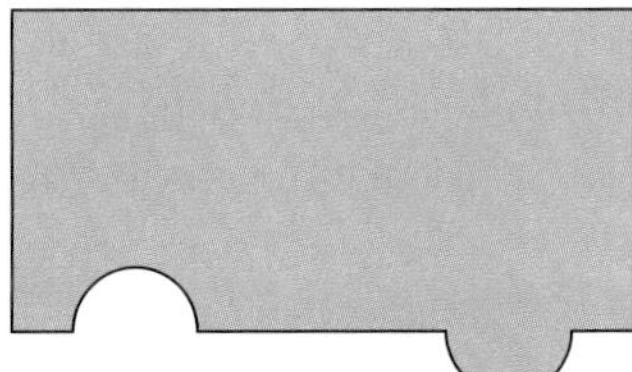

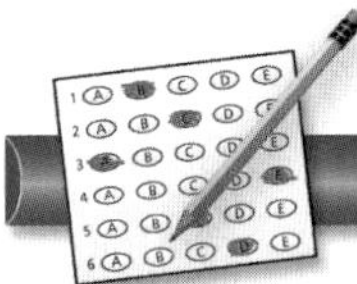

Test Prep

Multiple Choice

32. The bisector of $\angle PQR$ is $\overrightarrow{QS}$. The measure of $\angle PQS$ is 48°. What is the measure of $\angle PQR$?

A. 24° **B.** 48° **C.** 72° **D.** 96°

33. The bisector of $\angle ACB$ is $\overrightarrow{CD}$. The measure of $\angle ACB$ is 54°. What is the measure of $\angle DCB$?

F. 27° **G.** 54° **H.** 81° **I.** 108°

34. Point G is the midpoint of $\overline{FH}$. GF is 4 cm. Find FH.

A. 2 cm **B.** 4 cm **C.** 6 cm **D.** 8 cm

Short Response

35. $AB = BC = 3$ ft. Do you know that B is the midpoint of $\overline{AC}$? Explain.

36. Suppose you bisect a straight angle, and then bisect one of the resulting angles. You continue this process until you have an angle that measures 11.25°. How many angles would you need to bisect? Show your work.

Take It to the NET
Online lesson quiz at
www.PHSchool.com
Web Code aba-0703

Mixed Review

Lesson 6-7

37. **Dining** You are eating dinner in a restaurant. You leave a 15% tip of \$4.89. What is the price of the meal without the tip?

Lesson 5-1

Write each ratio in two other ways.

38. 5 to 7 **39.** 6 : 13 **40.** $\frac{9}{4}$ **41.** $\frac{16}{25}$

Extension Angles and Parallel Lines

For Use With Lesson 7-3

You can use a compass and straightedge to construct an angle congruent to a given angle. Example 1 shows how to construct an angle congruent to $\angle A$ shown at the right.

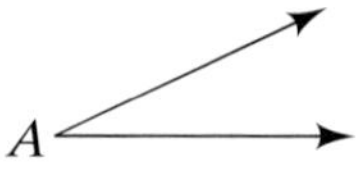

1 EXAMPLE Constructing a Congruent Angle

Construct $\angle B$ congruent to $\angle A$.

Step 1 Draw a ray with endpoint B.

Step 2 Place the tip of the compass at A. Make an arc that intersects the sides of $\angle A$. The points of intersection are C and D.

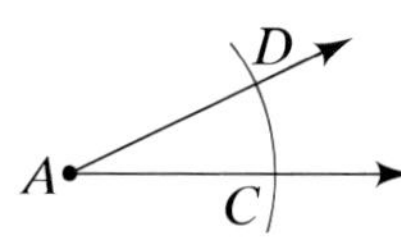

Step 3 With the same compass opening, place the tip of the compass at B and draw an arc that intersects the ray at E.

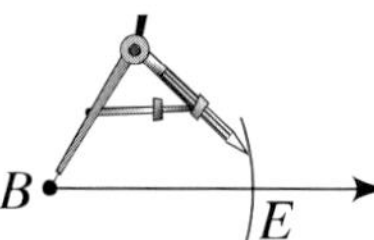

Step 4 Change the compass opening to the length from C to D. Using this compass opening, place the tip of the compass at E. Draw an arc to determine point F. Draw $\overrightarrow{BF}$.

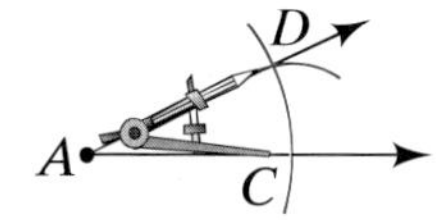

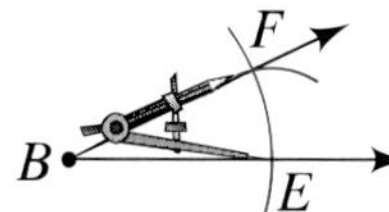

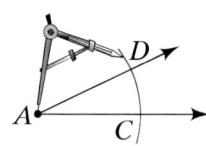

$m\angle B = m\angle A$.

When a line intersects two parallel lines, congruent angles are formed. You can use the construction of congruent angles to construct parallel lines.

2 EXAMPLE Constructing Parallel Lines

Draw a line parallel to n.

Step 1 Draw line m intersecting line n at A. Then label point B on line m.

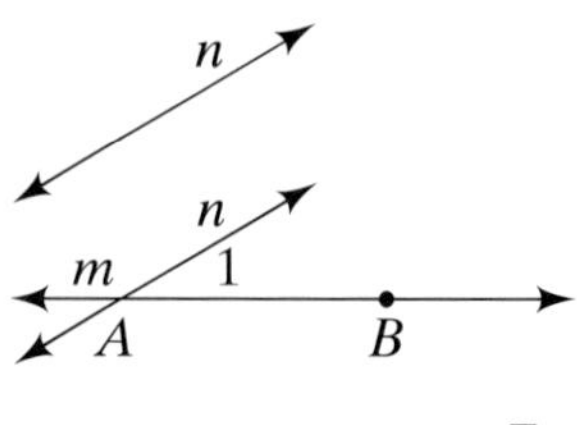

Step 2 Follow the instructions in Example 1 above to copy $\angle 1$ at B.

$\overrightarrow{BF}$ is parallel to line n.

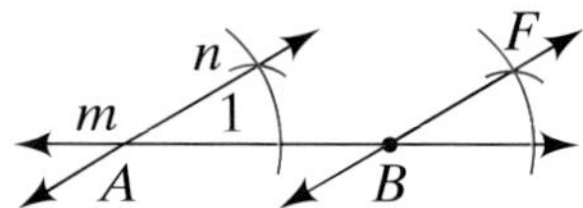

EXERCISES

1. Draw an obtuse angle, $\angle JKL$. Construct an angle congruent to $\angle JKL$.
2. Draw line d. Construct a line parallel to line d.

7-4 Triangles

What You'll Learn

To classify triangles by sides and angles

To find angle measures of a triangle

. . . And Why

To classify triangles in building architecture, as in Example 1

For help, go to Lesson 7-2.

Classify each angle as *acute*, *right*, *obtuse*, or *straight*.

1.

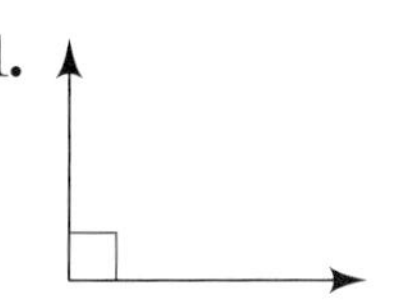

2.

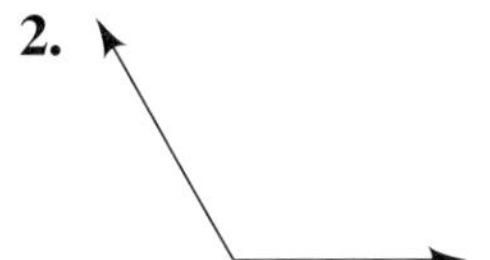

3.

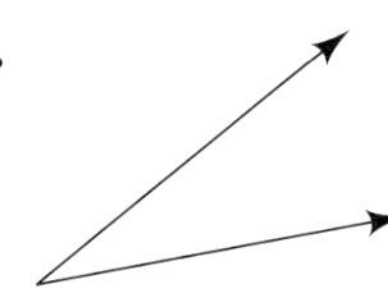

New Vocabulary

- congruent sides
- scalene triangle
- isosceles triangle
- equilateral triangle
- right triangle
- acute triangle
- obtuse triangle

OBJECTIVE

Interactive lesson includes instant self-check, tutorials, and activities.

1 Classifying Triangles

Congruent sides have the same length. You can classify a triangle by the number of congruent sides it has.

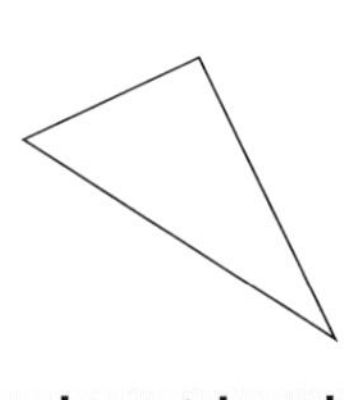

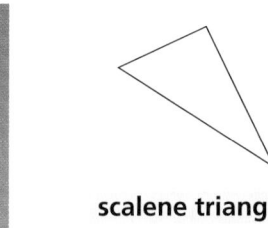

scalene triangle
no congruent sides

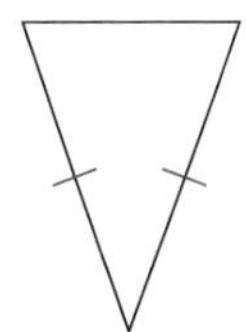

isosceles triangle
at least two congruent sides

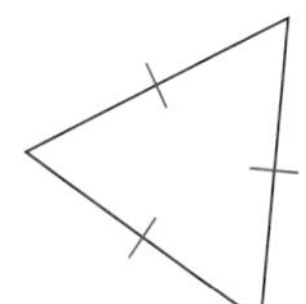

equilateral triangle
three congruent sides

Tick marks are used to indicate congruent sides of a figure. Notice the tick marks on the isosceles and equilateral triangles.

1 EXAMPLE Classifying Triangles by Sides

Architecture At the left is the Transamerica Building in San Francisco. Classify the front of the building by its sides.

The front of the Transamerica Building is an isosceles triangle.

Check Understanding 1 Classify each triangle by its sides.

a.

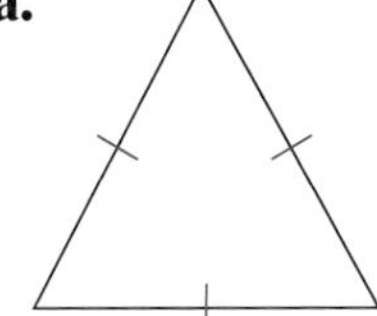

b.

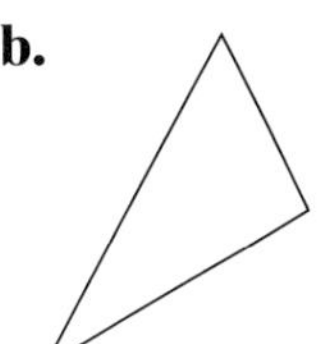

c.

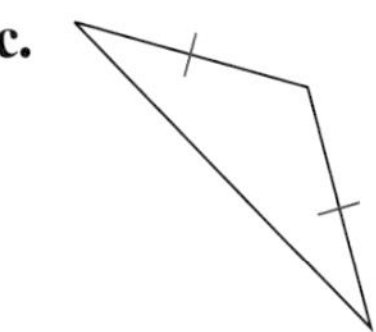

You can also classify a triangle by its angle measures.

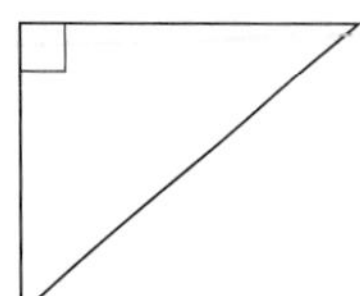

right triangle
one right angle

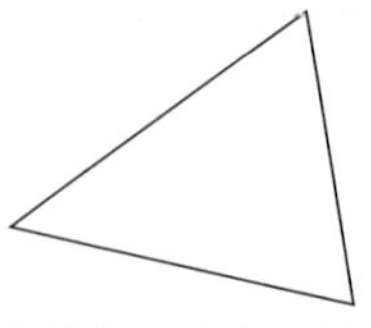

acute triangle
three acute angles

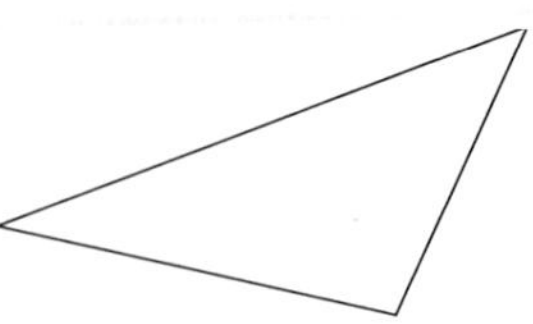

obtuse triangle
one obtuse angle

2 EXAMPLE Classifying Triangles by Angles

Classify the triangle shown below by its angle measures.

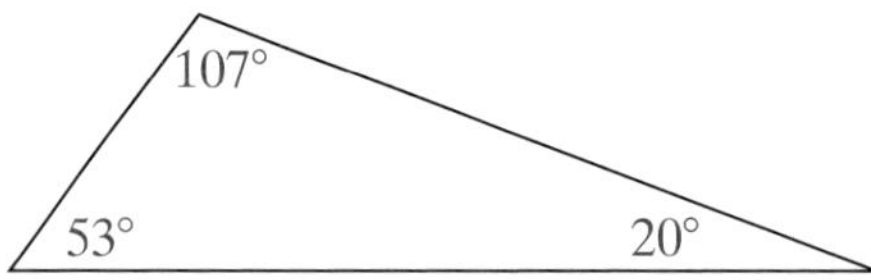

The triangle has one obtuse angle, so it is an obtuse triangle.

Check Understanding 2 Classify each triangle by its angle measures.

a.

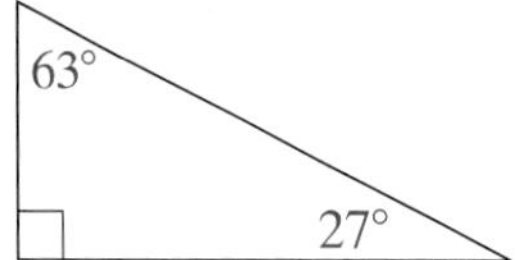

b.

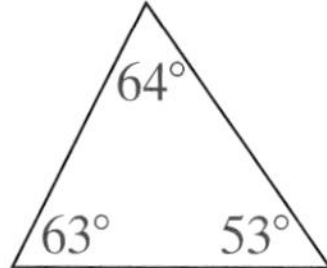

OBJECTIVE

2 Finding Measures of Angles in a Triangle

Investigation: Angles of a Triangle

- Cut out a paper triangle.
- Number the angles of the triangle and tear them off the triangle.
- Place the three angles side-by-side to form adjacent angles with no angles overlapping.

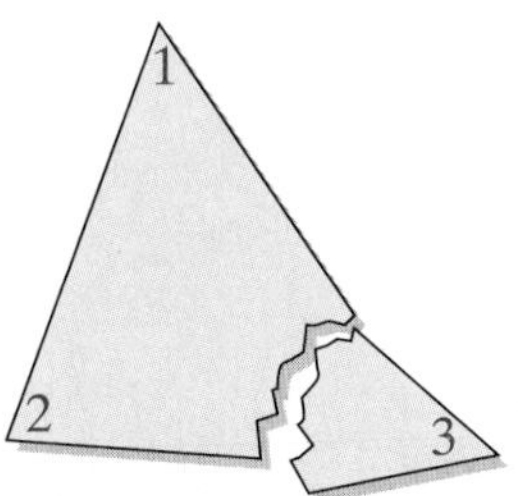

1. a. Make a conjecture about the sum of the angle measures of your triangle.
   b. Compare your results with other students. What seems to be true?

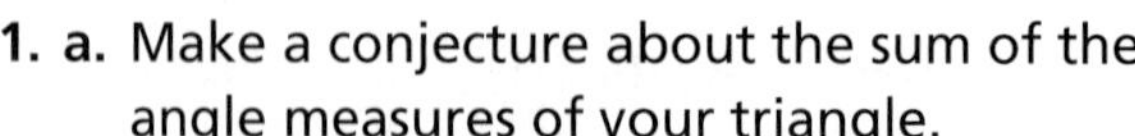

The sum of the measures of the angles of every triangle is the same.

Key Concepts **Angle Sum of a Triangle**

The sum of the measures of the angles of a triangle is 180°.

Suppose you know the measures of two of the angles of a triangle. You can write and solve an equation to find the measure of the third angle.

3 EXAMPLE Finding an Angle Measure (Algebra)

Need Help? For help solving equations, go to Lesson 2-3.

Find the value of x in the triangle at the right.

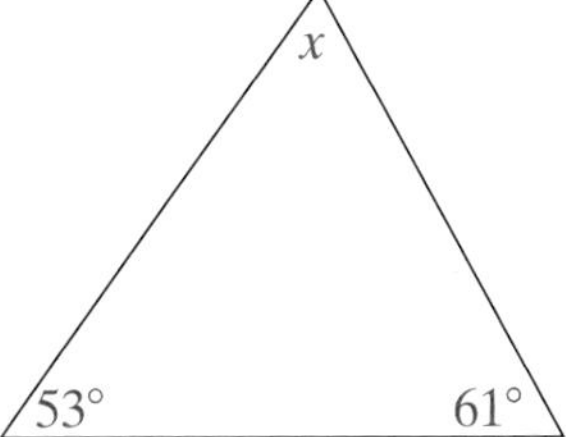

$$x + 53° + 61° = 180°$$
$$x + 114° = 180°$$
$$x + 114° - 114° = 180° - 114°$$
$$x = 66°$$

Check Understanding 3 Find the value of x in each triangle.

a.
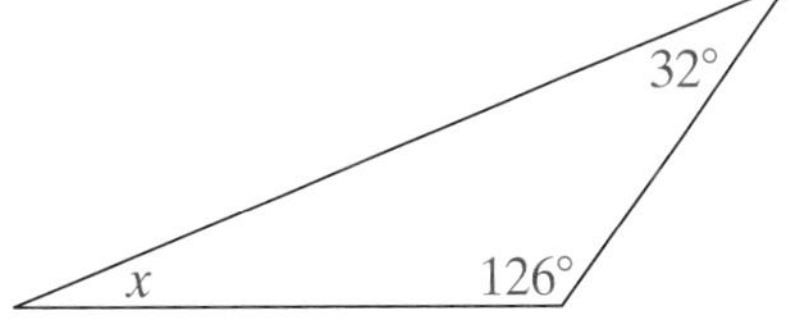

b.
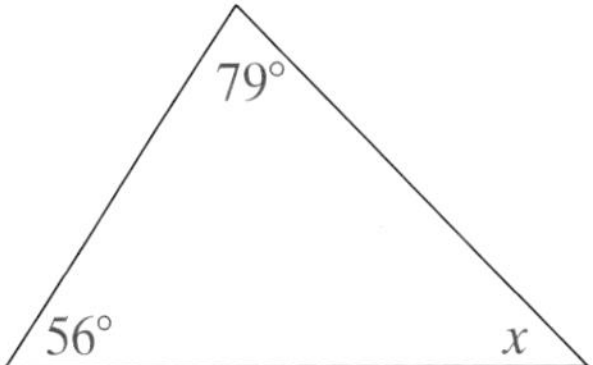

EXERCISES

For more practice, see *Extra Practice*.

A Practice by Example

Example 1 (page 363)

Classify each triangle by its sides.

1. 

2. 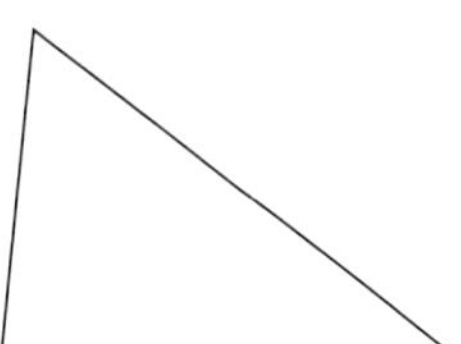

3. 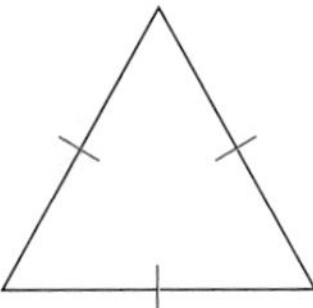

4. 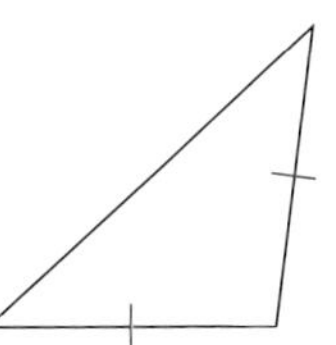

5. 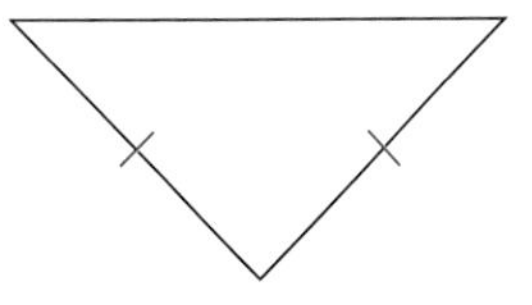

6. 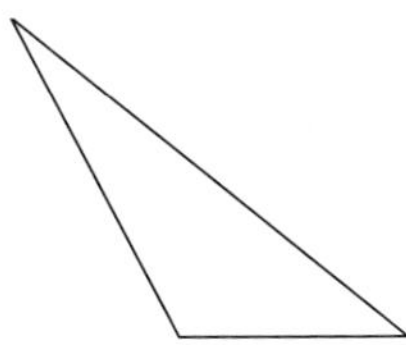

Example 2 (page 364)

Classify each triangle by its angle measures.

7. 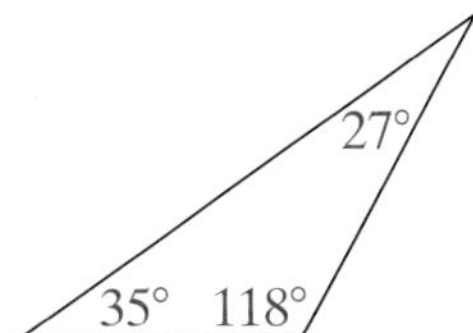

8. 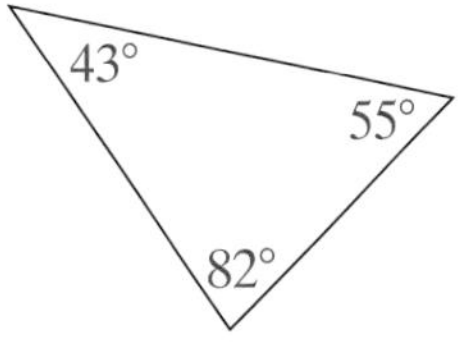

9. 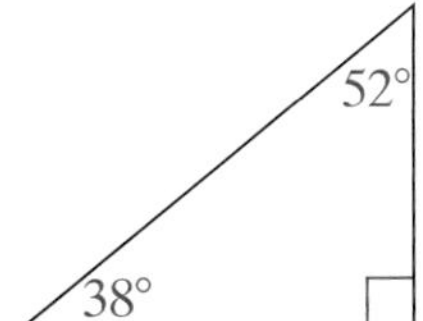

10. 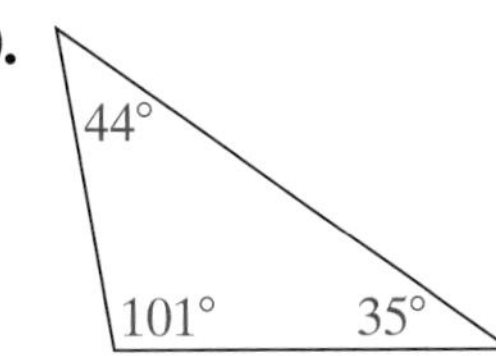

11. 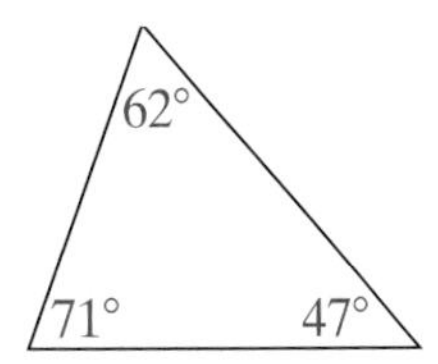

12. 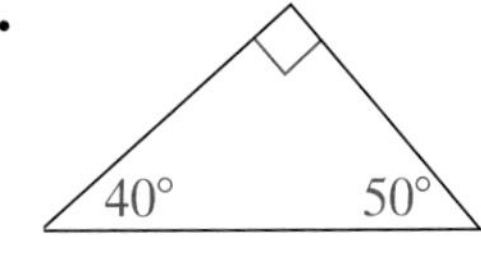

Example 3
(page 365)

Algebra **Find the value of x in each triangle.**

13.
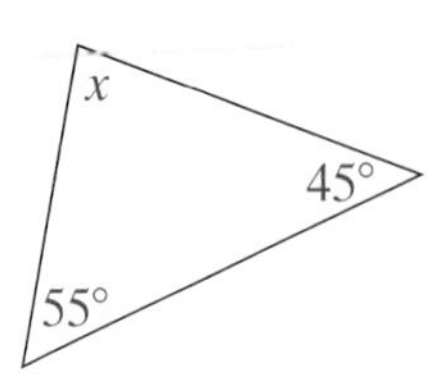

14.
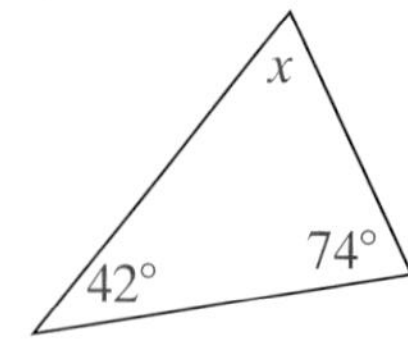

15.
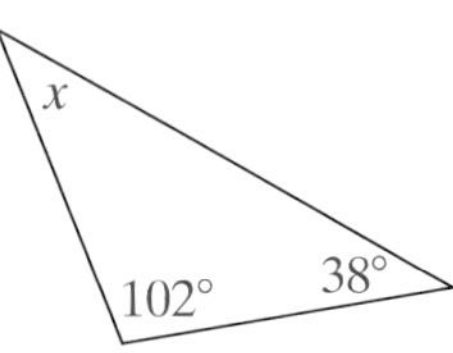

16.
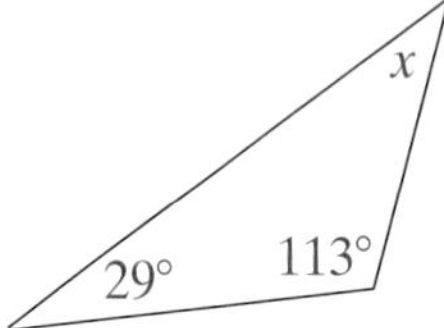

17.
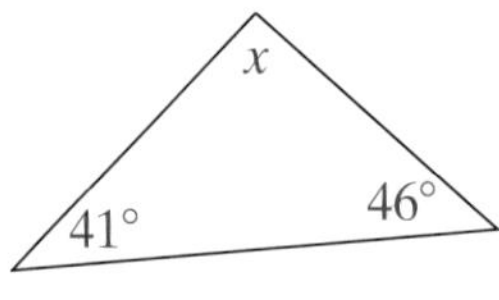

18.
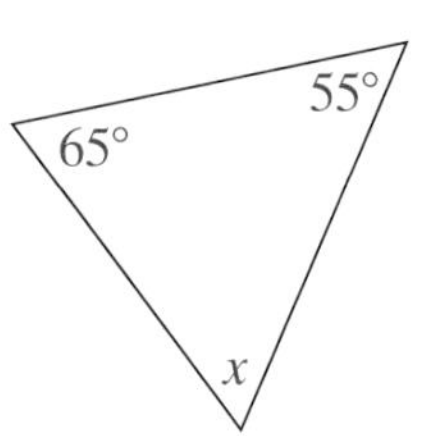

B Apply Your Skills

Classify each triangle by its angle measures.

19.
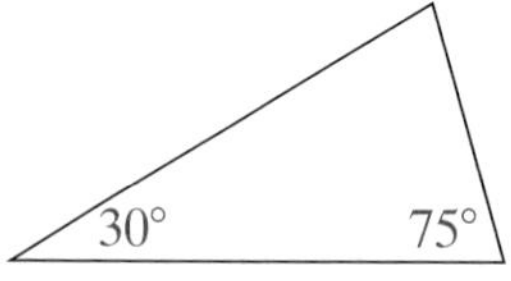

20.
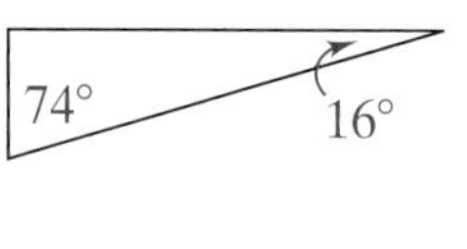

21.
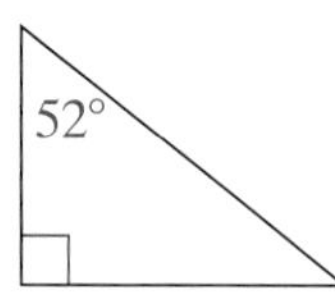

22. **Writing in Math** In the figure at the right, what is the measure of $\angle E$? Show your work and justify your steps.

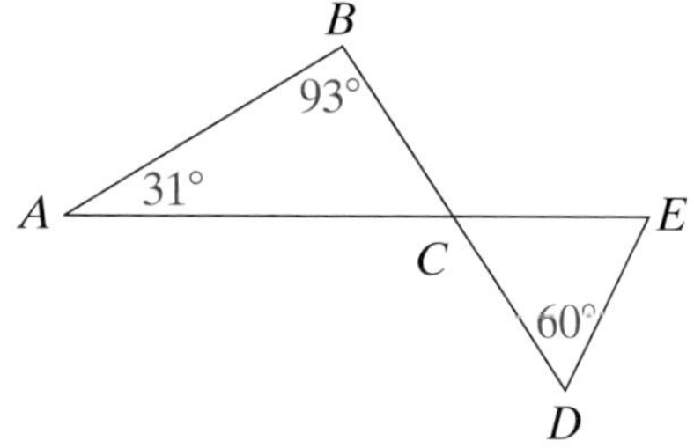

23. **Traffic** The traffic sign at the left is used in Norway. Classify the shape of the sign by its sides.

Algebra **Suppose the sides of a triangle have each of the given measures. Classify each triangle by its sides.**

24. j, j, j

25. $2a, 2a, 2a$

26. $3w, 4w, 8w$

27. $p, 1.5p, 1.5p$

28. $3x, 3x, 5x$

29. $2k, 3k, 4k$

30. The triangles shown are right triangles.
  a. What is the sum of the measures of the two acute angles in each triangle?
  b. What appears to be the relationship of the two acute angles in these triangles?
  c. **Reasoning** Is this true for all right triangles? Explain.

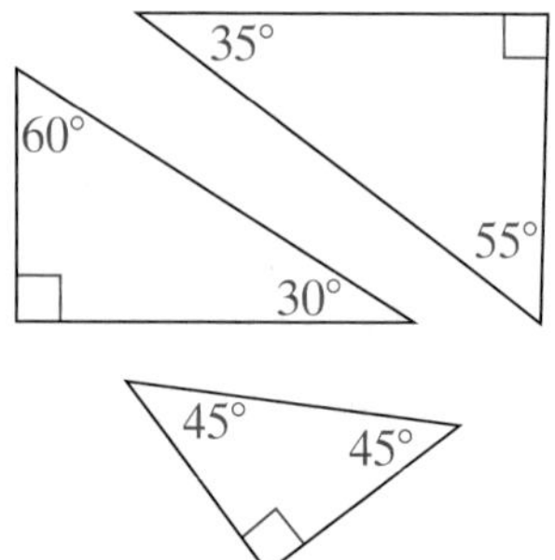

C Challenge

31. a. Trace the equilateral triangle shown on page 363. Fold the triangle so that each side is bisected. What do you notice about the angles of the equilateral triangle?
  b. What appears to be true of the measures of the three angles of an equilateral triangle?

32. **Reasoning** Two sides of an isosceles triangle are 6 in. and 2 in. What is the length of the third side? Why?

33. **Stretch Your Thinking** I am a two-digit odd number. My cube is a five-digit odd number. The digits in my cube are all different and are also different from my digits. What number am I?

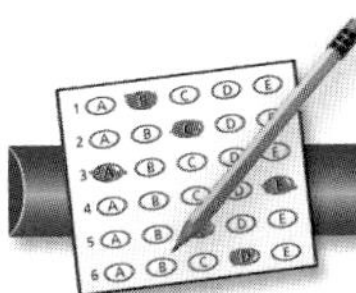

Test Prep

Multiple Choice

34. Two angles of a triangle are 102° and 48°. What is the measure of the third angle?
A. 20° B. 30° C. 40° D. 50°

Take It to the NET
Online lesson quiz at **www.PHSchool.com**
Web Code aba-0704

35. A triangle has two angles that measure 37°. What is the measure of the third angle?
F. 53° G. 106° H. 137° I. 143°

36. Which word could NOT describe a triangle with two congruent sides?
A. equilateral B. obtuse C. scalene D. isosceles

Short Response

37. A right triangle has one angle that measures 36°. **(a)** Write an equation to find the measure of the other acute angle. **(b)** Solve your equation.

Mixed Review

Lesson 6-3

Write each percent as a decimal and as a fraction in simplest form.

38. 116% 39. 137% 40. 155% 41. 175%

Lesson 3-9

Write each quotient as a decimal. Use a bar to show repeating decimals.

42. 5 ÷ 3 43. 7 ÷ 16 44. 15 ÷ 18 45. 10 ÷ 6

Checkpoint Quiz 1 Lessons 7-1 through 7-4

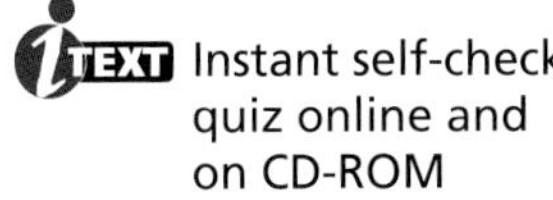

Instant self-check quiz online and on CD-ROM

Use the points in each diagram to name the figure shown.

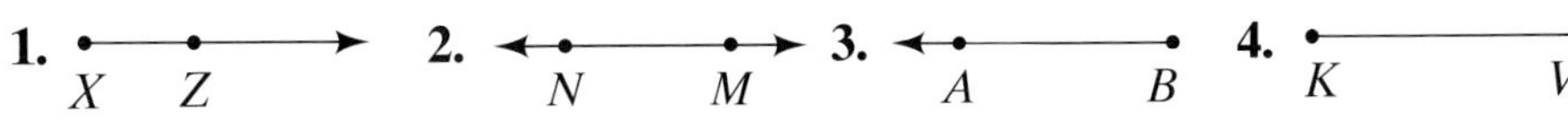

Find the measures of the complement and supplement of each angle.

5. $m\angle T = 12°$ 6. $m\angle R = 47°$ 7. $m\angle U = 65°$ 8. $m\angle E = 83°$

9. A triangle has angles that measure 63° and 47°. What is the measure of the third angle?

10. Draw an acute angle and label it *CDE*. Construct its bisector.

Writing to Justify

For Use With Exercise 22, Page 366

When you are asked to justify your steps, you first need to show all of your work. Then write a reason for each step.

On page 366, you will find the following exercise:

22. **Writing in Math** In the figure at the right, what is the measure of $\angle E$? Show your work and justify your steps.

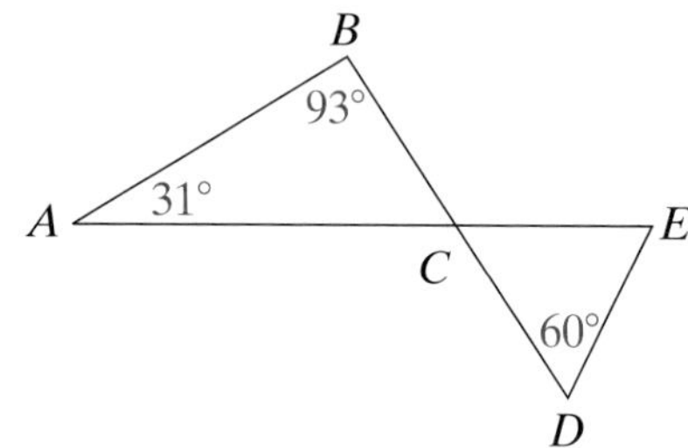

Here are one student's steps and reasons for each step.

Step	Reason
$m\angle ACB + 31° + 93° = 180°$	The sum of the angles of a triangle is 180°.
$m\angle ACB + 124° = 180°$	Add: 31 + 93 = 124.
$m\angle ACB + 124° - 124° = 180° - 124°$	Subtraction Property of Equality
$m\angle ACB = 56°$	Subtract: 180 − 124 = 56.
$m\angle ECD = 56°$	Vertical angles are congruent.
$m\angle E + 56° + 60° = 180°$	The sum of the angles of a triangle is 180°.
$m\angle E + 116° = 180°$	Add: 56 + 60 = 116.
$m\angle E + 116° - 116° = 180° - 116°$	Subtraction Property of Equality
$m\angle E = 64°$	Subtract: 180 − 116 = 64.

EXERCISES

1. In the figure, $\overleftrightarrow{CD}$ is the perpendicular bisector of $\overline{AB}$. If $m\angle B = 27°$, what is $m\angle DCB$? Show your work and justify your steps.

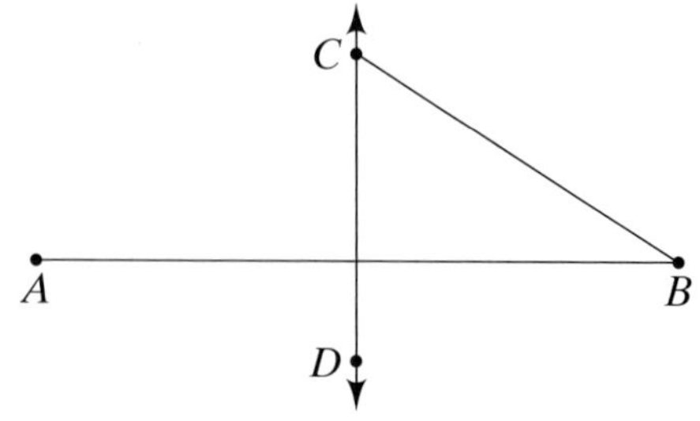

2. One angle of a right triangle measures 64°. What are the measures of the other two angles? Show your work and justify your steps.

3. In a triangle, the measure of $\angle X$ is 12° more than three times the measure of $\angle Y$. The measure of $\angle X$ is 93°. Classify $\angle Y$. Show your work and justify your steps.

7-5 Quadrilaterals and Other Polygons

What You'll Learn

 To classify polygons

 To identify special quadrilaterals

. . . And Why

To identify polygons in architecture, as in Example 2

For help, go to Lesson 7-4.

Classify each triangle by its sides.

1. 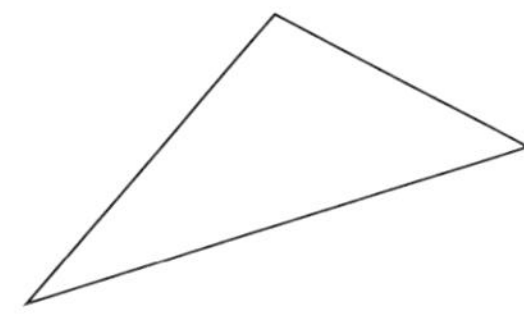

2. 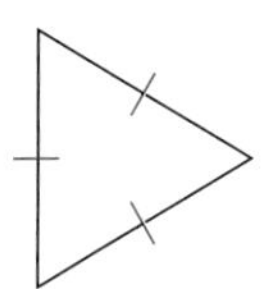

3. 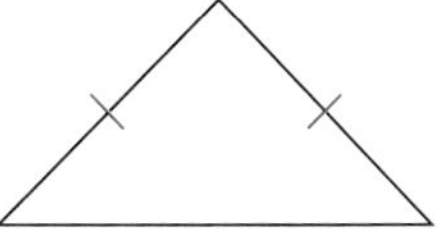

4. 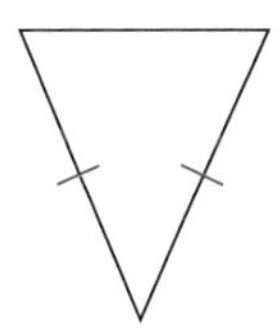

5. 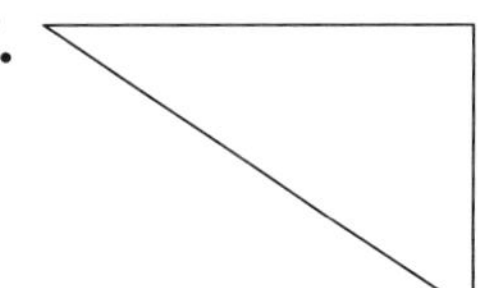

6. 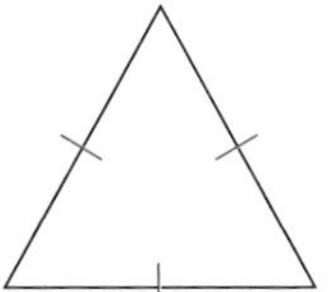

New Vocabulary
- polygon
- quadrilateral
- pentagon
- hexagon
- octagon
- decagon
- regular polygon
- irregular polygon
- trapezoid
- parallelogram
- rectangle
- rhombus
- square

OBJECTIVE 1

 Interactive lesson includes instant self-check, tutorials, and activities.

Classifying Polygons

Road signs, chalkboards, and flags are all examples of polygons. A **polygon** is a closed plane figure with sides formed by three or more line segments. The sides meet only at their endpoints.

You classify polygons by their number of sides.

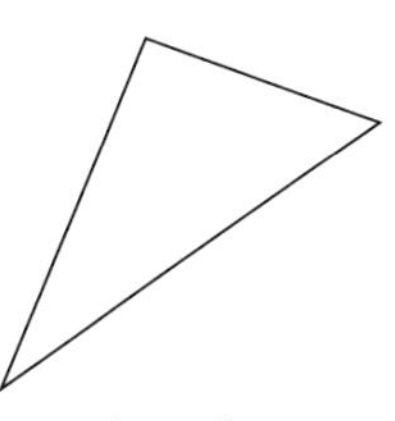

triangle
3 sides

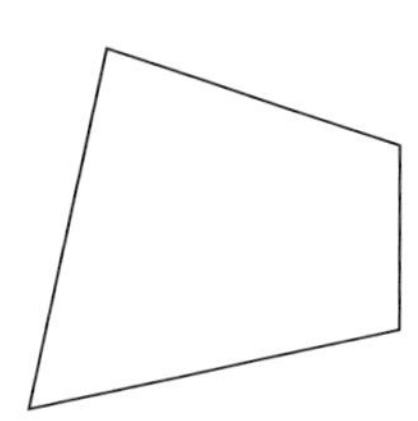

quadrilateral
4 sides

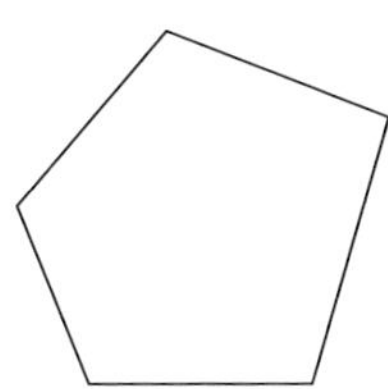

pentagon
5 sides

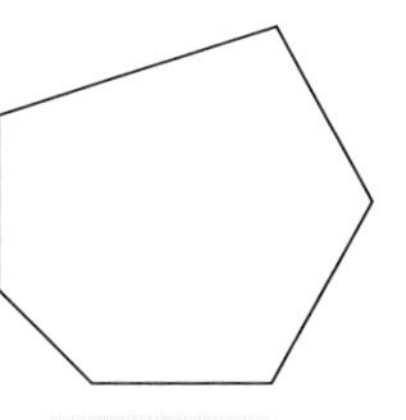

hexagon
6 sides

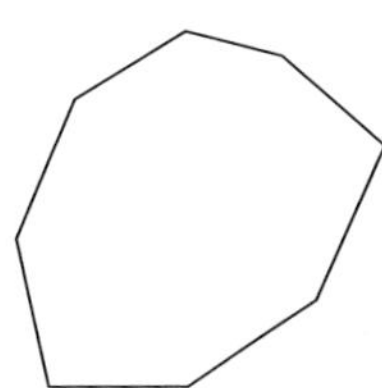

octagon
8 sides

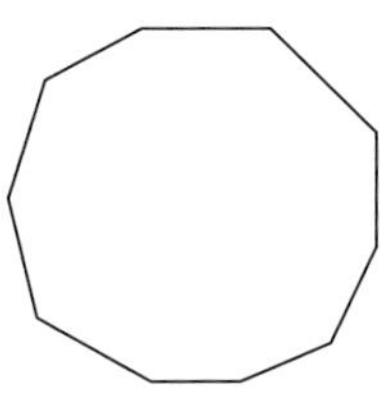

decagon
10 sides

A **regular polygon** is a polygon with all sides congruent and all angles congruent. An **irregular polygon** is a polygon with sides that are not all congruent and/or angles that are not all congruent.

1 EXAMPLE Identifying Regular Polygons

Identify each polygon and classify it as *regular* or *irregular*.

a.

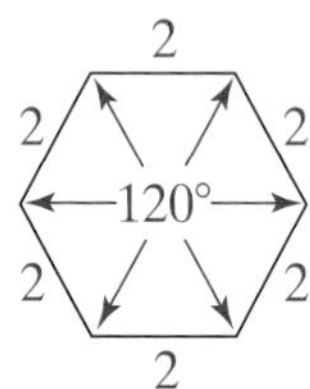

The hexagon is regular.

b.

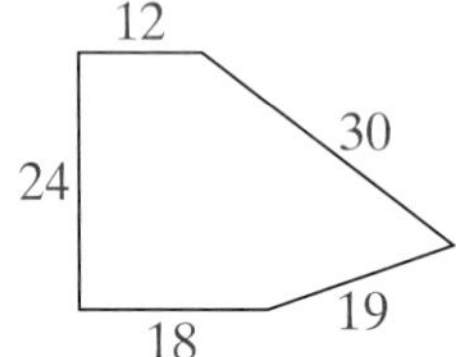

The pentagon is irregular.

Check Understanding 1 Identify each polygon and classify it as *regular* or *irregular*.

a.

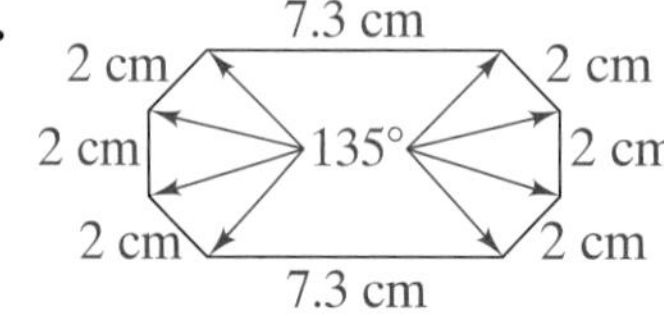

b.

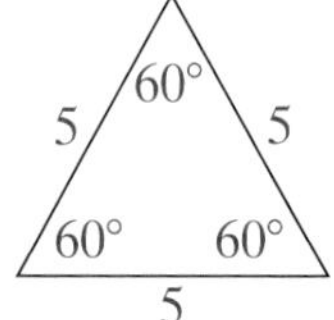

OBJECTIVE

2 Identifying Special Quadrilaterals

Some quadrilaterals have special names. A **trapezoid** is a quadrilateral with exactly one pair of parallel sides. The arrows on a drawing indicate parallel sides.

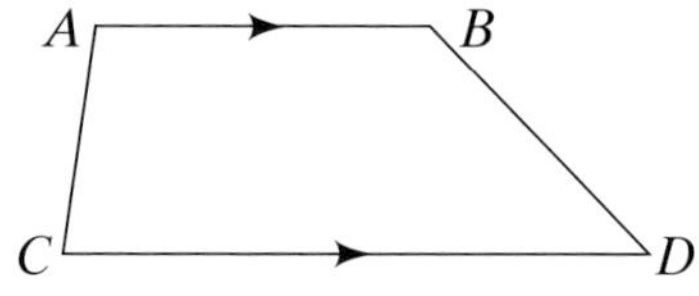

$\overline{AB}$ is parallel to $\overline{CD}$.

A **parallelogram** is a quadrilateral with both pairs of opposite sides parallel. There are three special types of parallelograms.

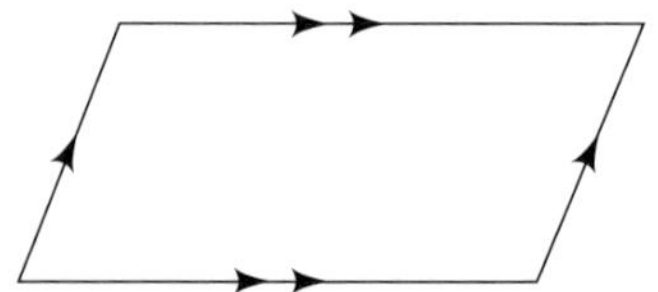

A **rectangle** is a parallelogram with four right angles.

A **rhombus** is a parallelogram with four congruent sides.

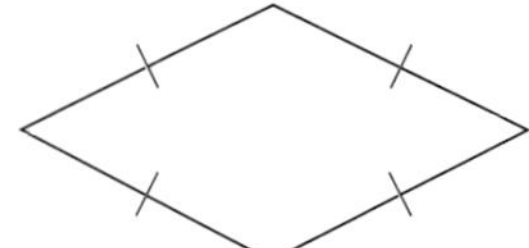

A **square** is a parallelogram with four right angles and four congruent sides.

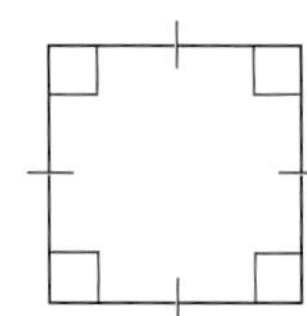

2 EXAMPLE Classifying Polygons

Architecture Use the best names to identify the polygons in the window shown at the right.

The outside frame is an octagon. Inside the frame there are triangles, rectangles, trapezoids, and a square.

Check Understanding 2 Use the best names to identify the polygons in each pattern.

a. 

b.  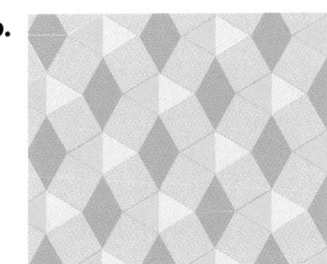

You can use dot paper or graph paper to draw special quadrilaterals.

3 EXAMPLE Drawing Quadrilaterals

Draw each of the following figures on dot paper.

a. a parallelogram that is not a rectangle or a rhombus

b. a rhombus that is not a square

Check Understanding 3 **a.** Use dot paper or graph paper to draw a trapezoid with a pair of opposite sides congruent.

b. **Reasoning** Can you draw a square that is not a rhombus? Explain.

EXERCISES

For more practice, see *Extra Practice*.

A Practice by Example

Example 1
(page 370)

Identify each polygon and classify it as *regular* or *irregular*. Explain.

1. 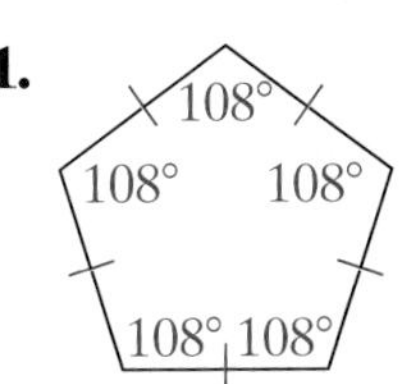

2. 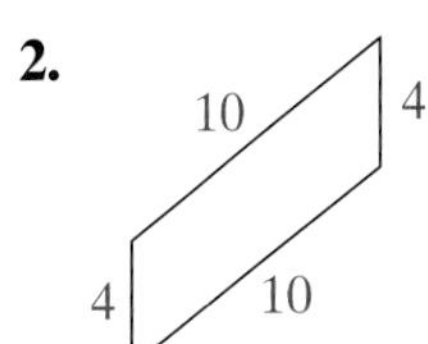

3. 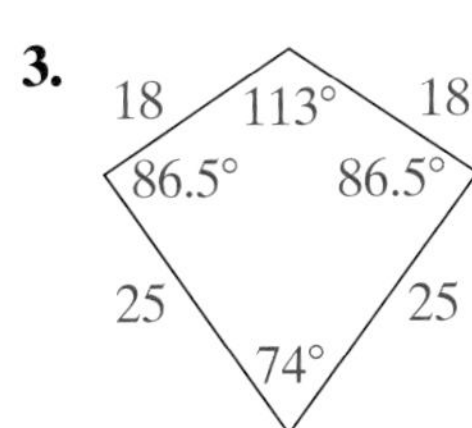

Use the best names to identify the polygons in each pattern.

Example 2 (page 371)

4. 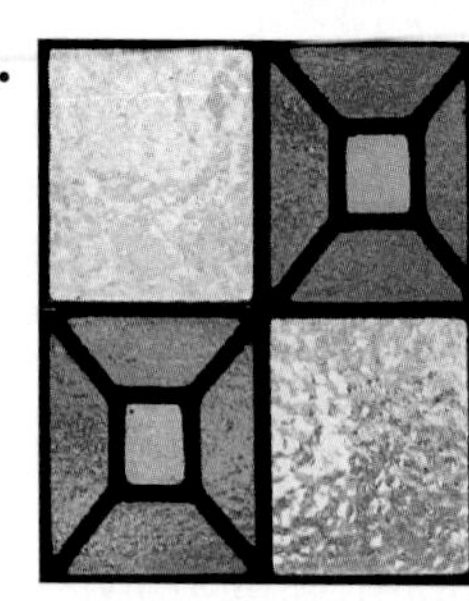

5. 

6. 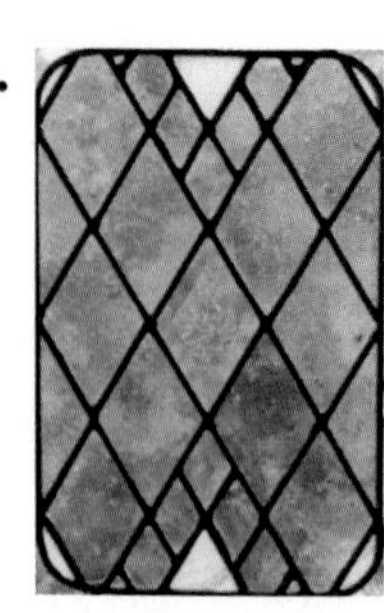

Example 3 (page 371)

Use dot paper or graph paper to draw each quadrilateral.

7. a trapezoid with vertical sides parallel

8. two squares such that the second has twice the perimeter of the first

B Apply Your Skills

Judging by appearance, classify each quadrilateral. Then name the parallel sides.

9. 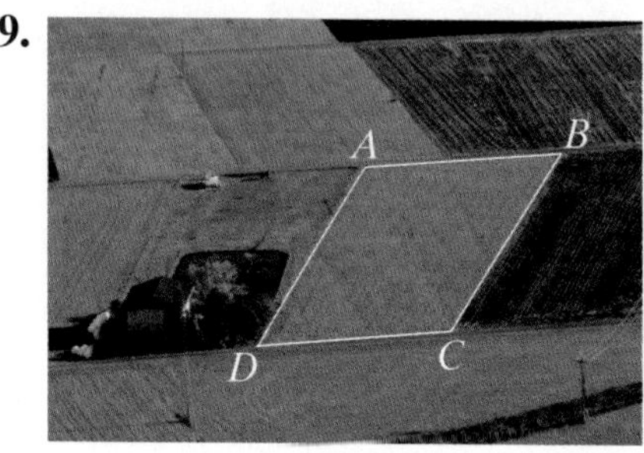

10. 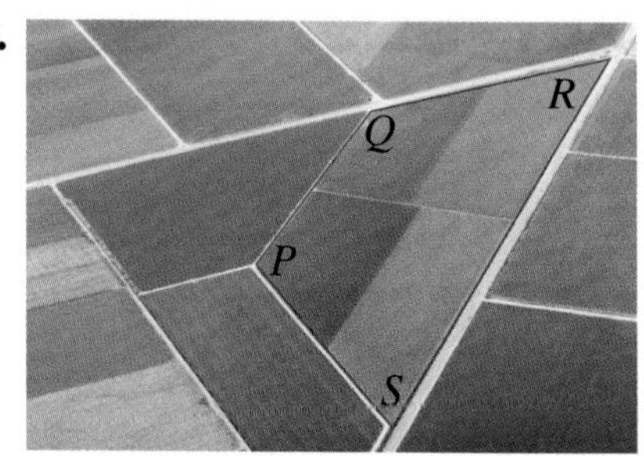

Sketch each polygon.

11. pentagon

12. octagon

13. regular quadrilateral

14. a. Sketch a rhombus with four congruent angles. What is another name for the figure that you sketched?

 b. Sketch a rectangle with four congruent sides. What is another name for the figure that you sketched?

 c. Writing in Math Can a quadrilateral be both a rhombus and a rectangle? Explain.

15. Math in the Media Read the cartoon and answer the questions below.

LET'S ASK SQUARE... HE ALWAYS HAS THE RIGHT ANGLE ON THINGS.

 a. Sketch a pentagon that has one right angle.

 b. Reasoning Can a trapezoid have three right angles? Draw a diagram to support your answer.

16. **a.** Use a ruler to draw a trapezoid with opposite sides congruent.
b. A *diagonal* joins two vertices that are not endpoints of the same side of a polygon. Draw and measure the diagonals of the figure you drew in part (a). What do you notice?

17. Draw a quadrilateral with exactly one pair of congruent opposite angles.

C Challenge

List all additional side lengths and angle measures you can find for each quadrilateral.

18. parallelogram $ABCD, AB = 6$ cm, $m\angle A = 65°$

19. rhombus $WXYZ, WX = 4$ cm

20. rectangle $JKLN, KL = 5$ in.

21. trapezoid $PQRS, QR = 10$ cm, $m\angle Q = 65°$

22. **Stretch Your Thinking** I am a seven-digit number. My first five digits are 2, 1, 3, 5, and 8 in that order. I am divisible by 99. What are my last two digits?

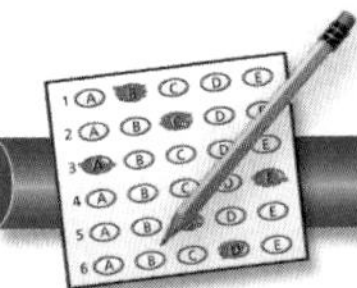

Test Prep

Multiple Choice

23. What is a name for the figure at the right?
A. quadrilateral B. decagon
C. pentagon D. octagon

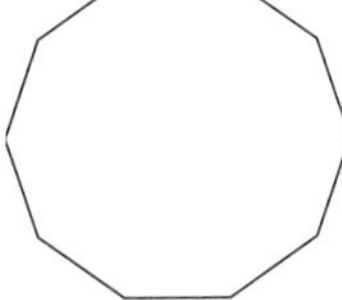

24. What is NOT a name for the figure at the right?
F. rectangle G. parallelogram
H. quadrilateral I. rhombus

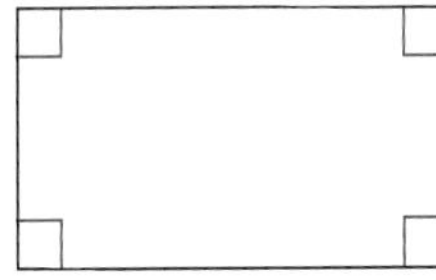

25. How many congruent sides does a rhombus have?
A. 1 B. 2 C. 3 D. 4

Short Response

26. Write four names for a quadrilateral with four congruent sides and four congruent angles. Which is the best name?

Mixed Review

Lesson 4-1

Estimate each answer.

27. $12\frac{1}{8} - 5\frac{2}{3}$ 28. $16\frac{3}{4} \div 4\frac{3}{4}$ 29. $\frac{1}{5} + \frac{5}{12}$

Lesson 3-4

State whether each number is *prime* or *composite*. If composite, write its prime factorization.

30. 15 31. 29 32. 333 33. 6,453

Problem Solving

7-6 Draw a Diagram and Look for a Pattern

What You'll Learn

OBJECTIVE 1 To solve a problem by combining strategies

. . . And Why

To find measures for polygons with many sides, as in Example 1

Check Skills You'll Need

For help, go to Lesson 7-2.

Find the measures of the complement and supplement of each angle.

1. $m\angle 1 = 27°$ **2.** $m\angle 2 = 83°$ **3.** $m\angle 3 = 13°$

4. $m\angle 4 = 42°$ **5.** $m\angle 5 = 34°$ **6.** $m\angle 6 = 7°$

OBJECTIVE

Interactive lesson includes instant self-check, tutorials, and activities.

1 Solving a Problem by Combining Strategies

When to Use These Strategies You can combine the strategies ***Draw a Diagram*** and ***Look for a Pattern*** to solve many geometry problems.

1 EXAMPLE Exploring Patterns in Geometry

Real-World Connection

Understanding geometry helps artists draw realistic figures.

What is the sum of the measures of the angles of a 12-sided polygon?

Read and Understand The goal is to find the sum of the measures of the angles of a 12-sided polygon.

Plan and Solve The diagram below shows all the possible diagonals that can be drawn from one vertex of each polygon shown. The diagonals divide the polygons into triangles. Remember that the sum of the measures of the angles of a triangle is 180°.

3 sides
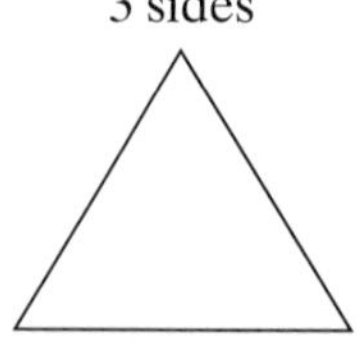

4 sides
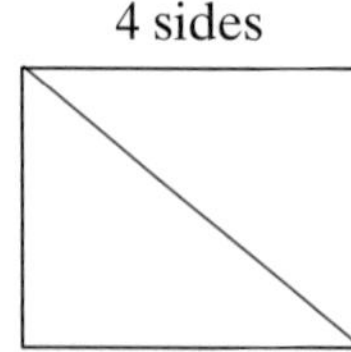

5 sides
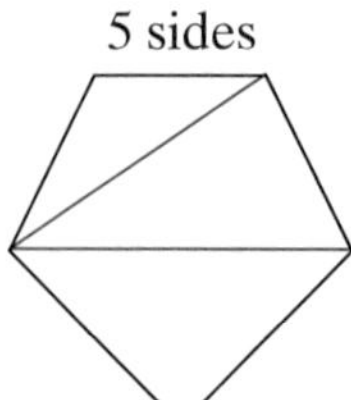

6 sides
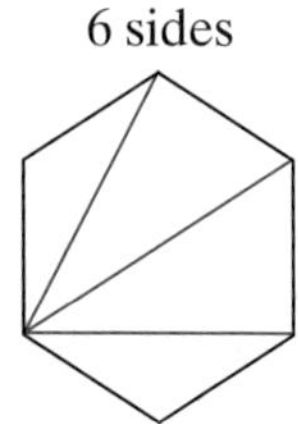

Make a table to organize the information from the diagram. Include a column for finding the sum of the measures of the angles of each polygon.

Sides	Triangles	Sum of Angles
3	1	$1 \cdot 180° = 180°$
4	2	$2 \cdot 180° = 360°$
5	3	$3 \cdot 180° = 540°$

The data in the table indicates the following patterns.

- The number of triangles formed is two less than the number of sides of a polygon.
- The sum of the measures of the angles of each polygon is the number of triangles times 180°.

For a 12-sided polygon, the number of triangles is $12 - 2 = 10$. The sum of the measures of the angles is $10 \cdot 180 = 1{,}800°$.

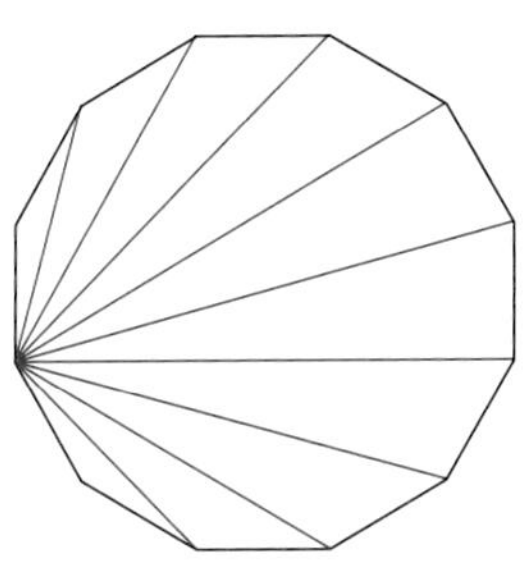

Look Back and Check To check that a 12-sided polygon has exactly ten triangles when a diagonal is drawn from one vertex, draw a diagram.

For a 12-sided polygon, there are 10 triangles formed, which is the same number of triangles predicted using the pattern. So, 1,800° is the sum of the measures of the angles of a 12-sided polygon.

Check Understanding **1** From the pattern, find the number of blocks in a figure with 12 rows.

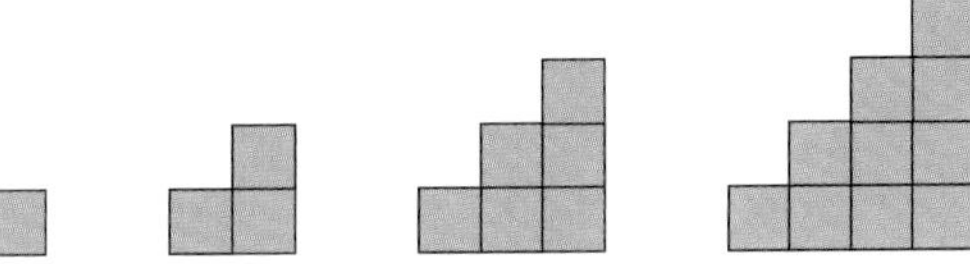

EXERCISES

For more practice, see *Extra Practice.*

A Practice by Example

Example 1 (page 374)

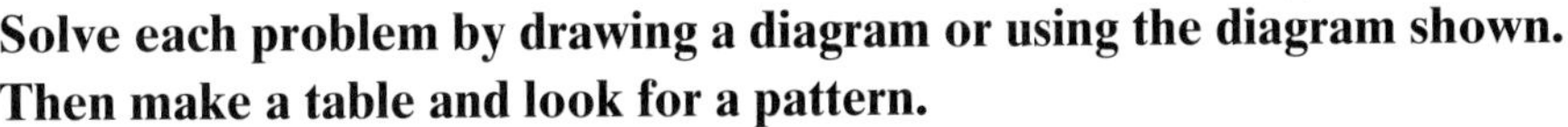

Solve each problem by drawing a diagram or using the diagram shown. Then make a table and look for a pattern.

Need Help?
- Reread the problem.
- Identify the key facts and details.
- Tell the problem in your own words.
- Try a different strategy.
- Check your work.

1. The figure at the right shows a pattern created by black and white tiles. How many black tiles will be needed for nine rows?

2. The figure at the right has four rows that contain small triangles. How many small triangles will there be if there are eight rows?

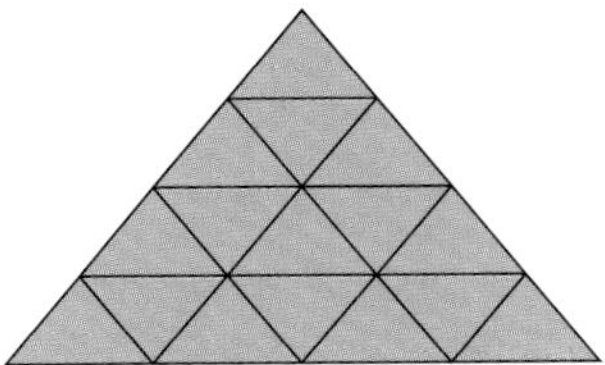

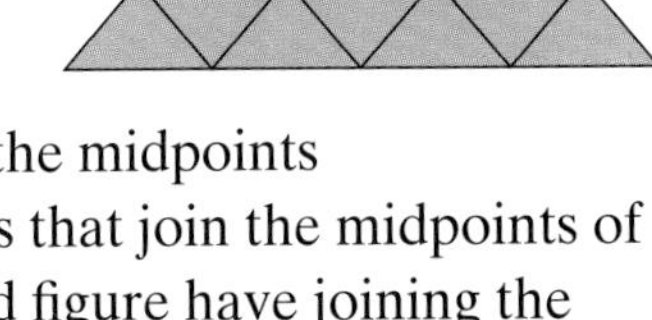

3. The triangle below has 3 segments that join the midpoints of the sides. The quadrilateral has 6 segments that join the midpoints of the sides. How many segments does a 7-sided figure have joining the midpoints of the sides?

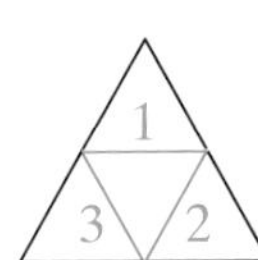

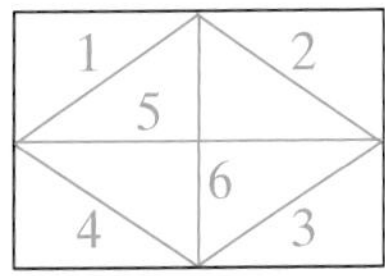

B Apply Your Skills

Strategies

- Draw a Diagram
- Look for a Pattern
- Make a Graph
- Make an Organized List
- Make a Table
- Simulate a Problem
- Solve a Simpler Problem
- Try, Check, and Revise
- Use Logical Reasoning
- Work Backward
- Write an Equation

Use any strategy to solve each problem. Show your work.

4. **Travel** You take a trip to visit your cousin. By 10:15 A.M. the train has traveled 20 mi. By 10:30 A.M. the train has traveled an additional 15 mi. You are now halfway to your cousin's town.
   a. If the train's rate is constant, what is its rate?
   b. At what time will you reach your cousin's town?

5. **Money** You have $1.55 in dimes and quarters. Find all the possible combinations of coins that you might have.

6. **Writing in Math** Use what you know about triangles and straight angles to explain the relationship between the measure of $\angle ABD$ and the measures of $\angle BDC$ and $\angle DCB$.

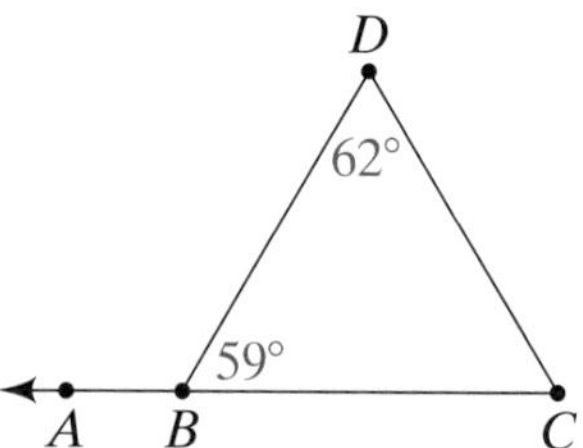

7. Find the number of diagonals in a 14-sided polygon.

8. Andrew, Bret, and Carl work as an artist, a banker, and a conductor. Andrew and the artist play tennis together. The conductor helps Carl plant his garden. Bret is not the conductor, and he does not know Andrew. What does each person do for a living?

9. A library has 8 tables and 42 chairs. There are several small tables with 4 chairs each and some large tables with 6 chairs each. How many tables of each type are in the library?

10. **Jobs** Carla and Marie are paid $75 for painting a fence. Carla works 6 h, and Marie works 9 h. How much is Carla's share of the money?

11. Rosa, Alberto, and Lewis are in a band together. They play guitar, piano, and drums. Alberto is the cousin of the guitar player. Rosa lives next door to the drummer and two blocks from the guitar player. Who plays which instrument?

12. **Carpentry** A furniture maker is designing a table for a customer who likes furniture that has unusual shapes. The furniture maker plans a tabletop that is a triangle with two congruent angles. The third noncongruent angle of the tabletop is 30°. What are the measures of the other two angles?

13. The diagram at the right shows part of a design made by using toothpicks to form triangles. The top row uses three toothpicks to form triangles. The second row uses six more toothpicks, and the third row uses nine more toothpicks.

   a. If you continue the design so that it has seven rows, how many toothpicks do you need altogether?
   b. Which row will use 24 toothpicks?

14. Suppose you buy several pencils at a discount store. All the pencils are the same price, and you buy as many pencils as the cost (in cents) of each pencil. The pencils cost a total of $1.44. How many pencils do you buy?

15. **Stretch Your Thinking** I am an acute angle. My supplement and my complement are supplementary angles. What's my measure?

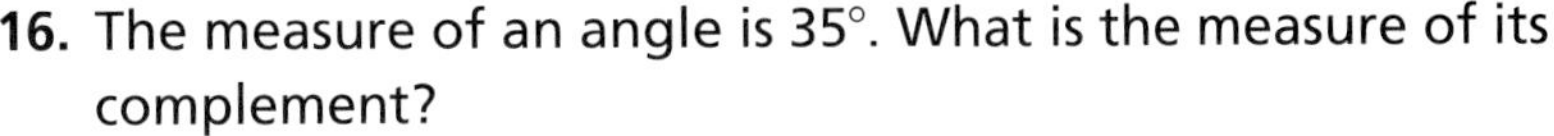

Test Prep

Multiple Choice

16. The measure of an angle is 35°. What is the measure of its complement?
   A. 35° B. 55° C. 145° D. 325°

Take It to the NET
Online lesson quiz at www.PHSchool.com
Web Code aba-0706

17. The measure of an angle is 67°. What is the measure of its supplement?
   F. 23° G. 67° H. 113° I. 293°

18. Two adjacent angles are formed by intersecting lines. The measure of one of the angles is 24°. What is the measure of the other angle?
   A. 24° B. 66° C. 156° D. 336°

Extended Response

19. $\overleftrightarrow{AB}$ intersects $\overleftrightarrow{CD}$ at point E. The measure of $\angle AEC$ is 40°. Use this information to find the measures of $\angle AED$, $\angle DEB$, and $\angle BEC$. Draw a diagram and justify your steps.

Mixed Review

Lesson 7-3 **Draw each figure. Construct its perpendicular bisector or angle bisector.**

20. acute $\angle ACE$ 21. obtuse $\angle KLM$ 22. $\overline{HJ}$

Lesson 6-8 **Find each percent of markup. Round to the nearest tenth of a percent.**

23. original cost: $45; selling price: $72

24. original cost: $29; selling price: $50

25. original cost: $125; selling price: $267

26. original cost: $1,023; selling price: $1,790.25

7-7 Congruent Figures

What You'll Learn

To identify and work with congruent figures

. . . And Why

To verify that manufactured parts are congruent, as in Example 2

✓ Check Skills You'll Need

For help, go to Lesson 7-4.

Find the value of x in each triangle.

1. 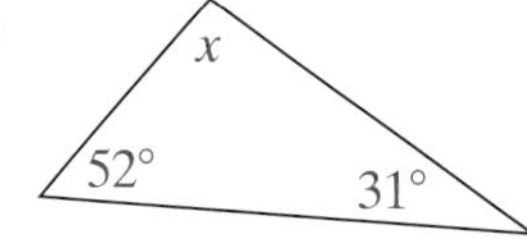

2. 60° x

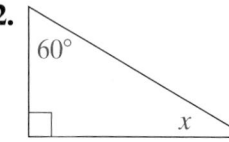

3. x 53° 63°

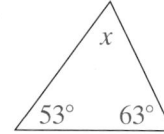

New Vocabulary • congruent polygons

OBJECTIVE

Interactive lesson includes instant self-check, tutorials, and activities.

1 Identifying and Working With Congruent Figures

Investigation: Exploring Congruent Figures

1. Match the figures with the same size and shape.

a. b. c. d.

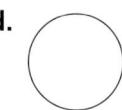

e.  f.  g.  h.

2. How could you check that the figures you matched above are really the same size and shape?
3. Suppose you trace a polygon and match your tracing with another polygon that has the same size and shape. What would be true of the matching angles and segments?

Congruent polygons are polygons with the same size and shape. The corresponding parts (sides and angles) of congruent polygons are congruent. The symbol $\cong$ means "is congruent to."

$\overline{AB} \cong \overline{ED}$ $\quad \overline{BC} \cong \overline{DF}$ $\quad \overline{CA} \cong \overline{FE}$

$\angle A \cong \angle E$ $\quad \angle B \cong \angle D$ $\quad \angle C \cong \angle F$

$$\triangle ABC \cong \triangle EDF$$

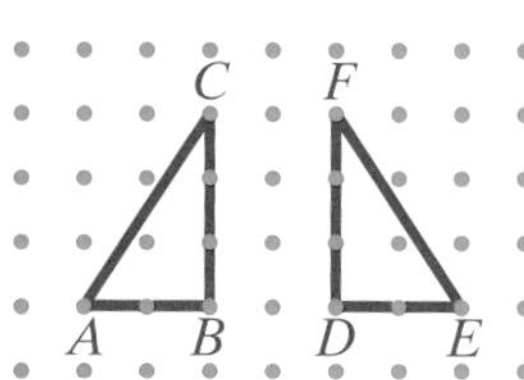

Notice that the vertices of the congruent triangles are written in corresponding order.

1 EXAMPLE Identifying Congruent Figures

Are the figures *congruent* or *not congruent*? Explain.

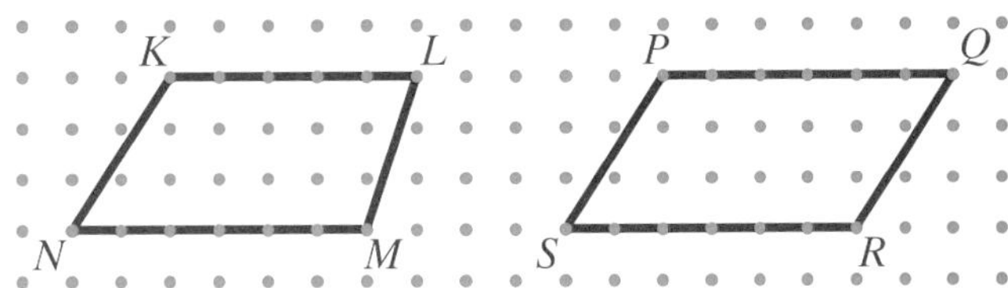

$\overline{KN} \cong \overline{PS}$ and $\overline{NM} \cong \overline{SR}$, but $\overline{LM}$ is not congruent to $\overline{QR}$.

The figures are *not congruent*.

Check Understanding 1 Are the figures below *congruent* or *not congruent*? Explain.

To make products consistently the same, manufacturers assemble them from congruent components.

Real-World Connection

Congruent parts for a product are usually created on an assembly line.

2 EXAMPLE Real-World Problem Solving

Manufacturing Assembly-line workers must make sure that the same parts for a product manufactured on an assembly line are all congruent. To do this, they compare each part to a sample part. Is $\triangle UVW$ congruent to the sample triangle, $\triangle RST$?

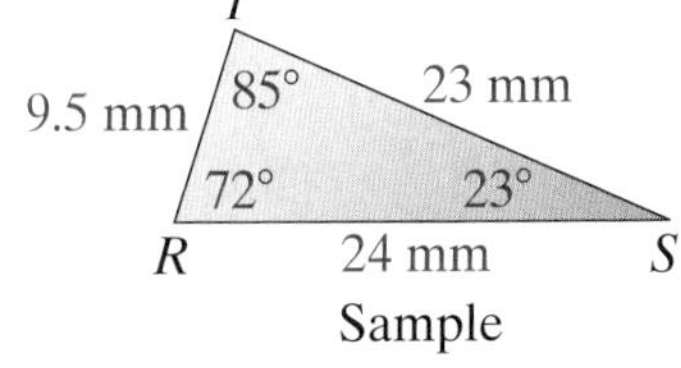

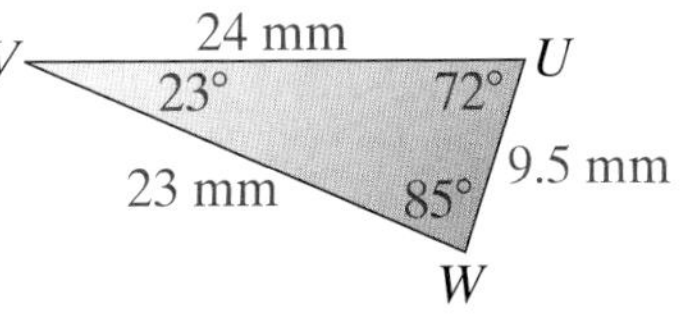

$\overline{UV} \cong \overline{RS}, \overline{VW} \cong \overline{ST}, \overline{WU} \cong \overline{TR}$,
$\angle U \cong \angle R, \angle V \cong \angle S$, and $\angle W \cong \angle T$.

$\triangle UVW \cong \triangle RST$; so the triangle and the sample triangle are congruent.

Check Understanding 2 Is the right figure congruent to the sample figure? Explain.

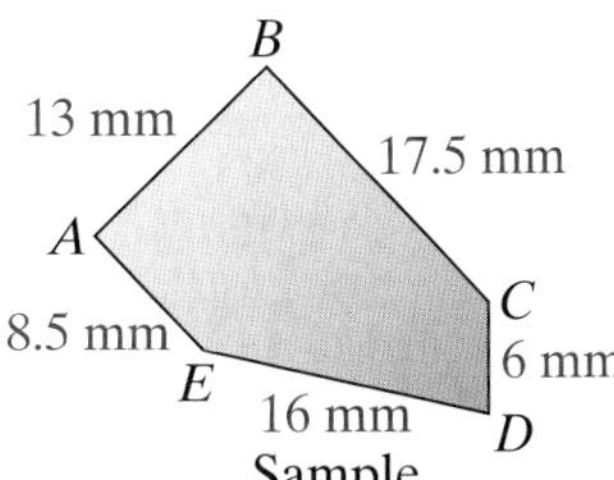

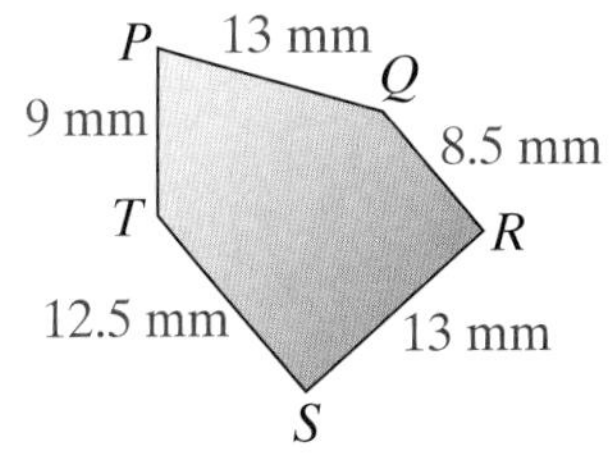

If you know that figures are congruent, you can use information about one to find information about the other.

3 EXAMPLE Working With Congruent Figures

The triangles at the right are congruent.

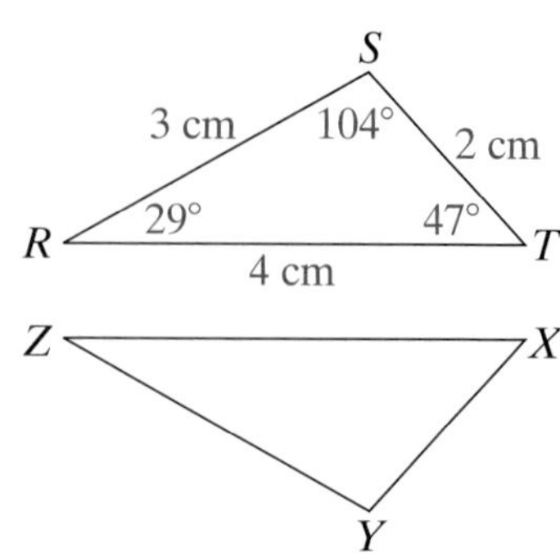

a. Write six congruences involving corresponding parts of the triangles.

$\angle X \cong \angle T$ $\quad \angle Y \cong \angle S$ $\quad \angle Z \cong \angle R$

$\overline{XY} \cong \overline{TS}$ $\quad \overline{ZY} \cong \overline{RS}$ $\quad \overline{ZX} \cong \overline{RT}$

b. Find ZY and $m\angle X$.

$ZY = 3$ cm $\leftarrow$ $\overline{ZY} \cong \overline{RS}$, so $ZY = RS$.

$m\angle X = 47°$ $\leftarrow$ $\angle X \cong \angle T$, so $m\angle X = m\angle T$.

Check Understanding **3** The quadrilaterals at the right are congruent.

a. Write the congruences for the corresponding parts.

b. Find AD and $m\angle G$.

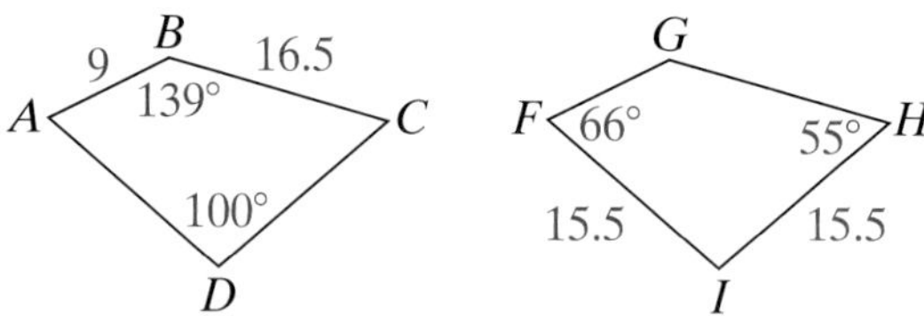

EXERCISES

For more practice, see *Extra Practice.*

A Practice by Example

Example 1 (page 379)

Identify each pair of figures as *congruent* or *not congruent*. Explain.

1.

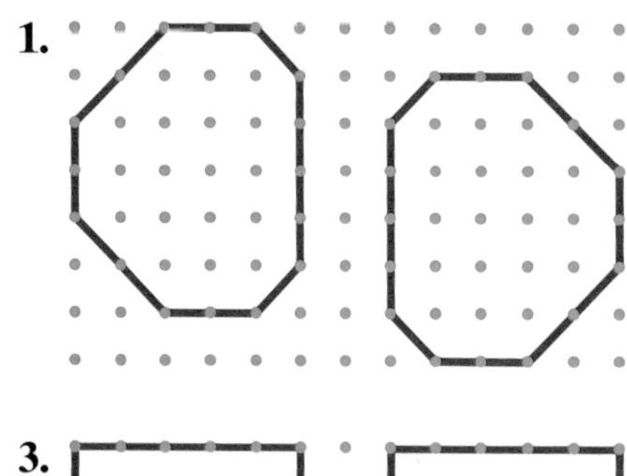

2.

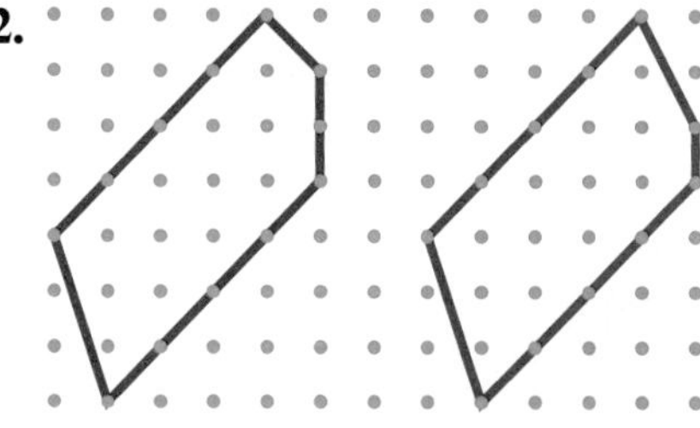

3.

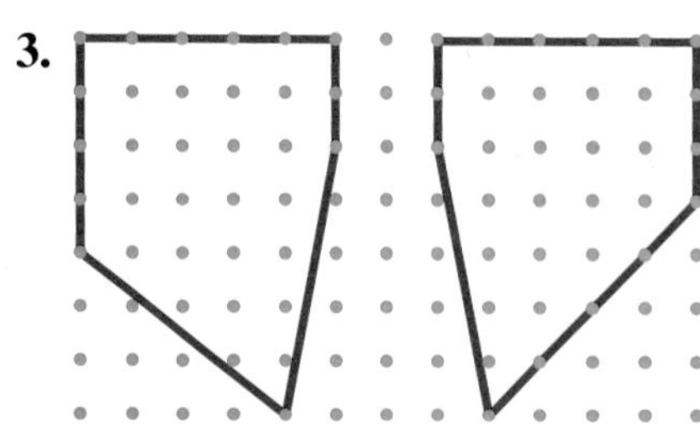

4.

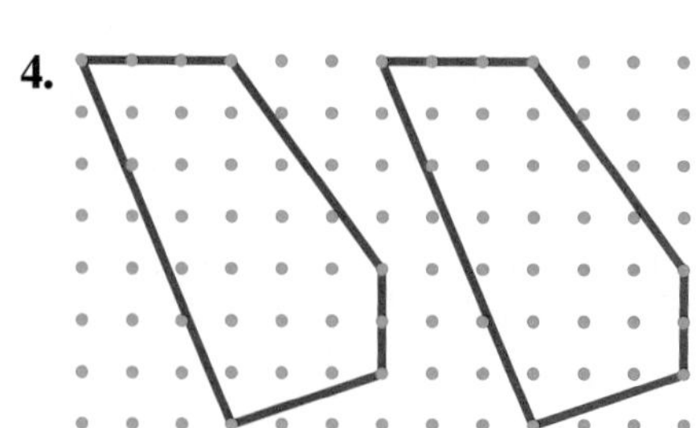

Example 2 (page 379)

In each exercise, is the right figure congruent to the sample figure?

5. 15 cm, 59°, 68°, 17.5 cm, 16 cm, 53°
Sample
16 cm, 53°, 17.5 cm, 68°, 59°, 15 cm

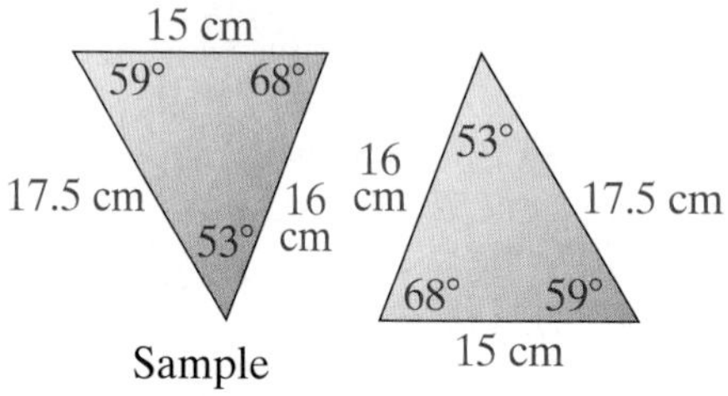

6. A, 4 cm, B, 6 cm, D, C
Sample
P, 8 cm, Q, 4 cm, S, R

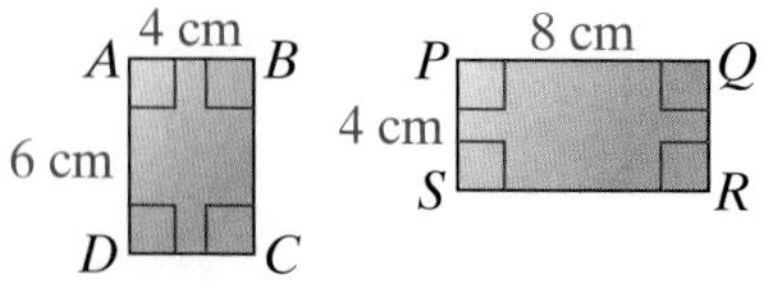

Example 3 (page 380)

Each pair of figures is congruent.

a. Write the congruences for the corresponding parts of the figures.

b. Find the missing side lengths and angle measures.

7.

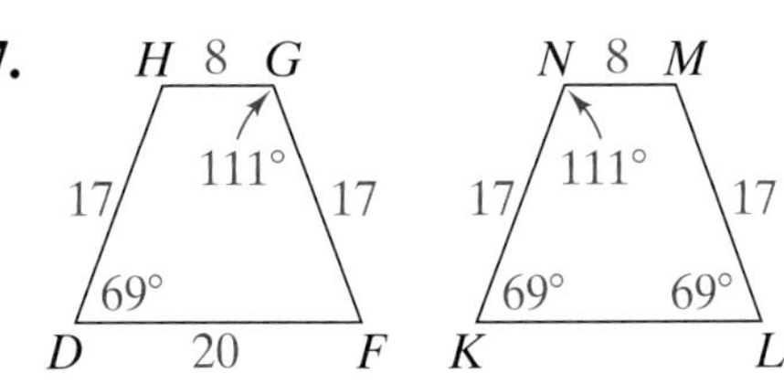

8.

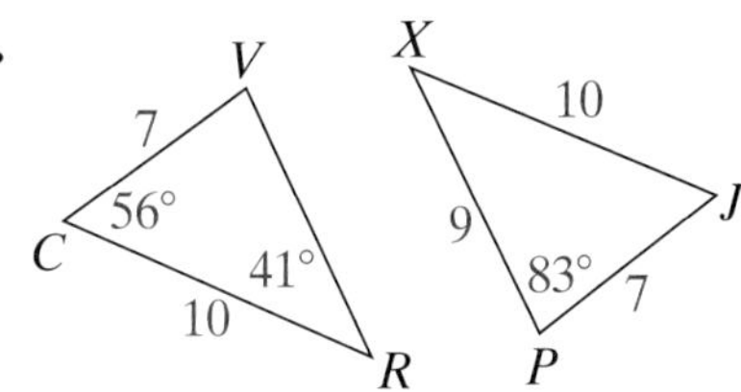

9.

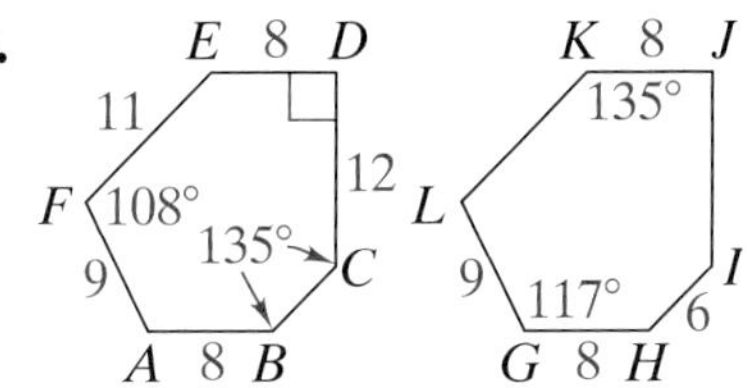

10.

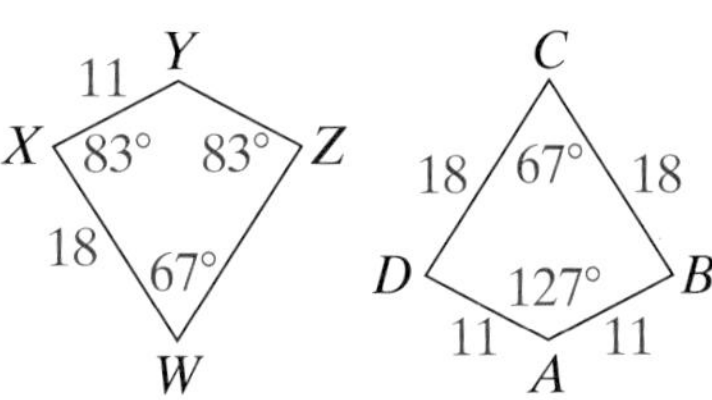

11.

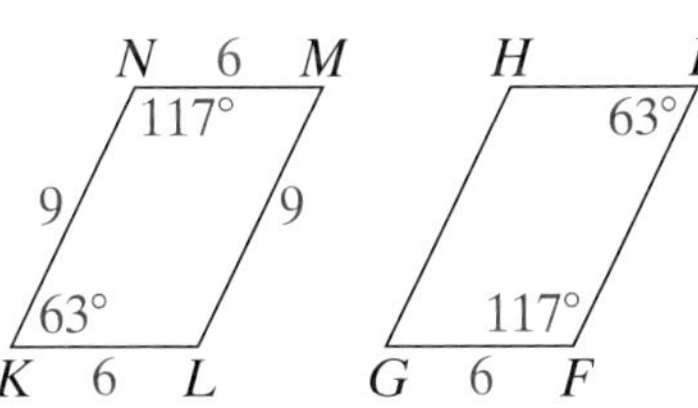

12.

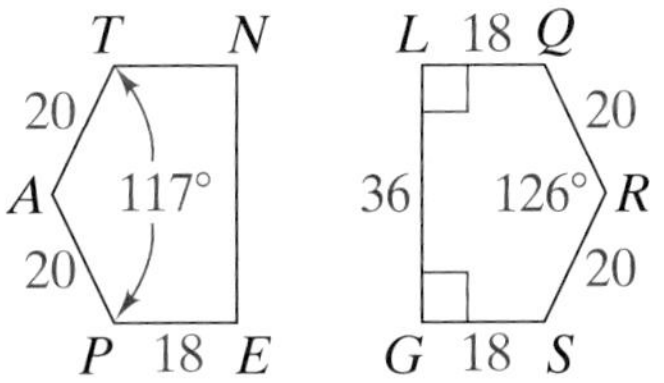

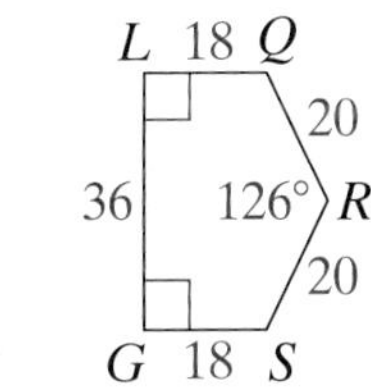

B Apply Your Skills

Complete each congruence statement.

13. $\triangle ABC \cong$ ■

14. $\triangle ABC \cong$ ■

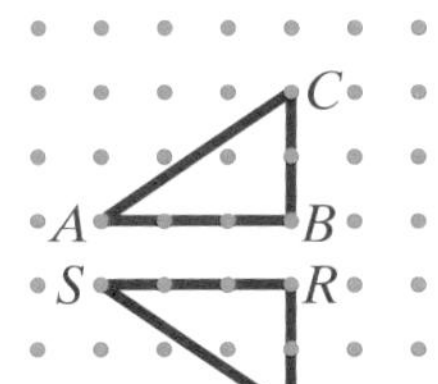

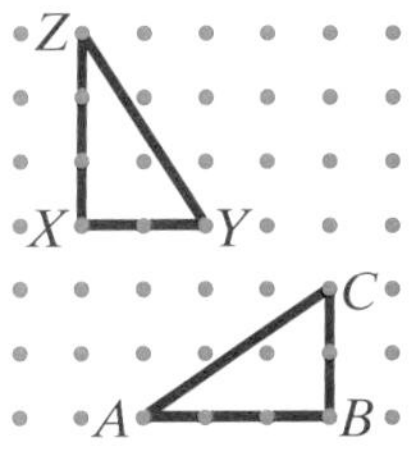

15. $\triangle ABC \cong$ ■

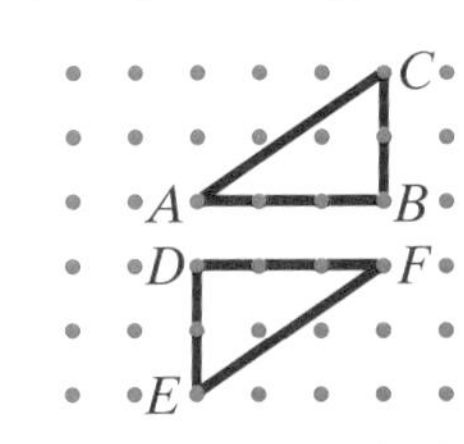

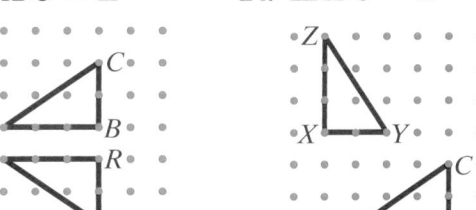

16. **Writing in Math** If you know that corresponding angles in triangles GHI and JKL are congruent, do you know that the triangles are congruent? Explain.

Buildings A truss like the one shown is a basic support for the roof line of many homes. Complete each congruence statement. $\triangle ABC \cong \triangle ABD$.

17. $\angle D \cong$ ■

18. $\angle CAB \cong$ ■

19. $\angle ABC \cong$ ■

20. $\overline{AC} \cong$ ■

21. $\overline{BC} \cong$ ■

22. $\overline{AB} \cong$ ■

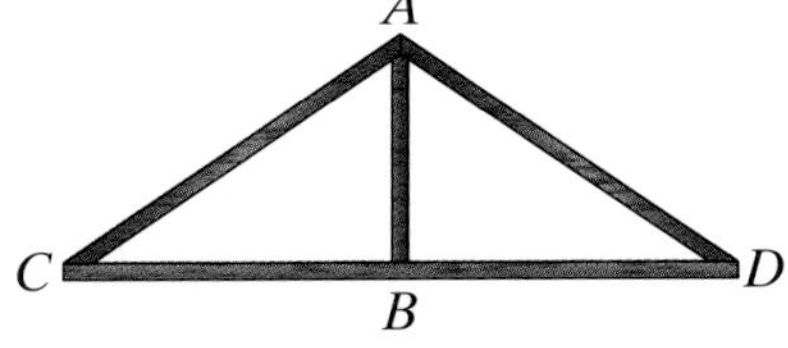

C Challenge

23. **Reasoning** Does the statement $\triangle JKL \cong \triangle MNO$ say the same thing as the statement $\triangle JKL \cong \triangle NOM$? Explain.

24. **Stretch Your Thinking** Points W, X, Y, and Z all lie on the same line. Z is the point farthest to the left. XY is 5 units, XZ is 2 units, and XW is 6 units. Find YW.

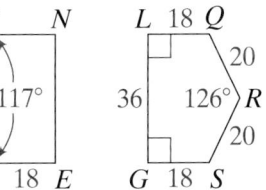

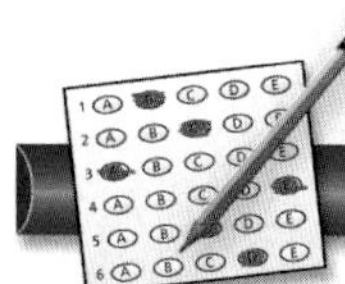

Test Prep

Multiple Choice

$\triangle PQR \cong \triangle STR$. Use the triangles for Exercises 25–27.

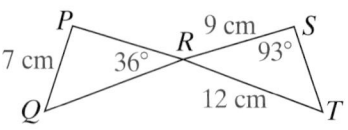

25. Find $m\angle P$.
    A. 36° **B.** 51° **C.** 93° **D.** 144°

26. What is the perimeter of $\triangle RST$?
    F. 19 cm **G.** 21 cm **H.** 28 cm **I.** 56 cm

27. Find $m\angle Q$.
    A. 144° **B.** 93° **C.** 51° **D.** 36°

Take It to the NET
Online lesson quiz at
www.PHSchool.com
Web Code aba-0707

Extended Response

28. *ABCD* is a rectangle. Is $\triangle ABD \cong \triangle CDB$? Justify your answer.

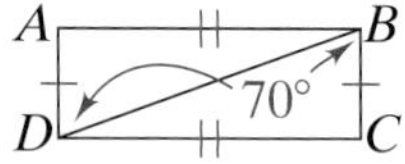

Mixed Review

Lesson 7-2

Classify each angle as *acute*, *right*, *obtuse*, or *straight*.

29. $m\angle G = 48°$
30. $m\angle X = 95°$
31. $m\angle T = 125°$
32. $m\angle K = 90°$

Lesson 1-10

Find the mean of each data set.

33. 1 1 3 3 5 6 7 10
34. 11 25 27 27 36 42 49

Checkpoint Quiz 2 — Lessons 7-5 through 7-7

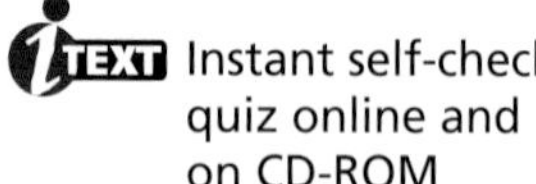

Instant self-check quiz online and on CD-ROM

Use dot paper or graph paper to draw each figure.

1. a square
2. a parallelogram
3. a trapezoid
4. Identify the pair of figures as *congruent* or *not congruent*. Explain.

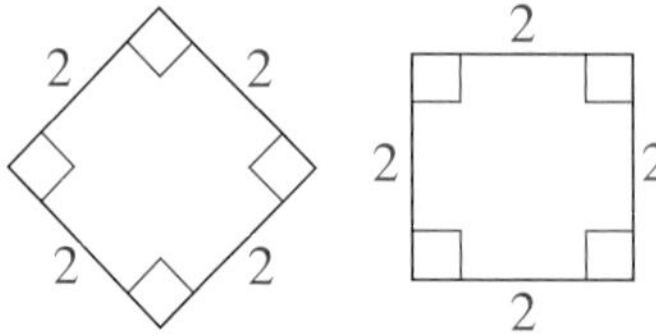

5. Shana climbed a set of stairs and stopped on the middle step. She then walked down 2 steps, up 4 steps, and down 3 steps. Finally she walked up 5 steps and was at the top of the stairs. How many steps are in the set of stairs? Show your work.

7-8 Circles

What You'll Learn

To identify parts of a circle

. . . And Why

To name arcs on a Ferris wheel, as in Example 3

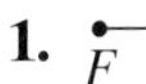

Check Skills You'll Need

For help, go to Lesson 7-1.

Use the points in each diagram to name the figure shown.

1.  F R
2.  Z J
3.  N K

4. Of the three figures in Questions 1–3, which could you name in more than one way? Explain.

New Vocabulary • circle • radius • diameter • central angle • chord • semicircle

Interactive lesson includes instant self-check, tutorials, and activities.

OBJECTIVE 1 Identifying Parts of a Circle

A **circle** is the set of points in a plane that are all the same distance from a given point, called the center. You name a circle by its center. Circle O is shown at the right.

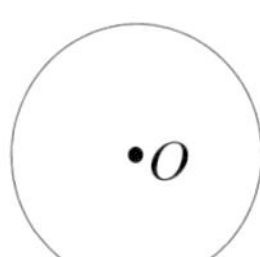

A **radius** is a segment that connects the center of a circle to the circle.

$\overline{OB}$ is a radius of circle O.

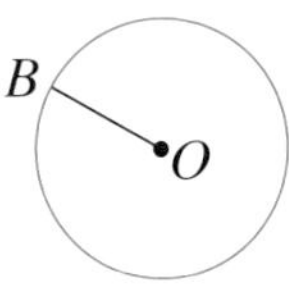

A **diameter** is a segment that passes through the center of a circle and has both endpoints on the circle.

$\overline{AC}$ is a diameter of circle O.

C
O
A

A **central angle** is an angle with its vertex at the center of a circle. $\angle AOB$ is a central angle of circle O.

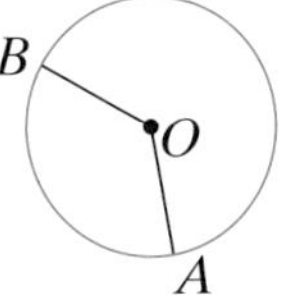

A **chord** is a segment that has both endpoints on the circle. $\overline{AD}$ is a chord of circle O.

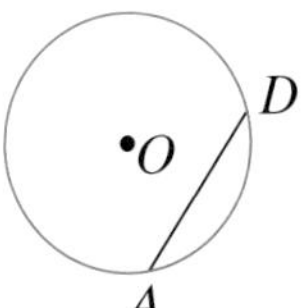

Real-World Connection

Any two hands of a clock form central angles on the circular face of the clock.

Notice that a central angle is formed by two radii. Two radii lying on the same line form a diameter of a circle. So a radius is half a diameter.

1 EXAMPLE Naming Parts Inside a Circle

Reading Math

The plural of *radius* is *radii* (RAY-dee-eye).

Name all the radii, diameters, central angles, and chords shown for circle O.

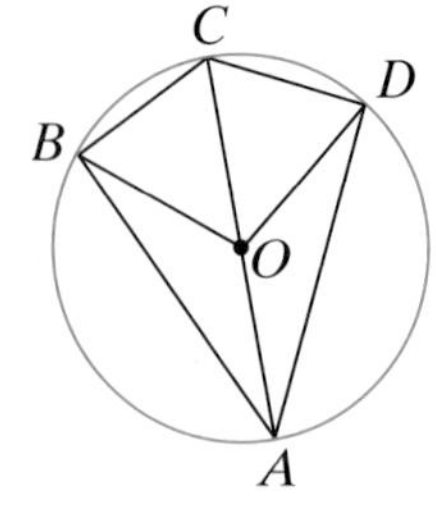

radii: $\overline{OA}$, $\overline{OB}$, $\overline{OC}$, and $\overline{OD}$

diameter: $\overline{AC}$

chords: $\overline{AB}$, $\overline{BC}$, $\overline{CD}$, $\overline{DA}$, and $\overline{AC}$

central angles: $\angle AOB$, $\angle AOC$, $\angle AOD$, $\angle BOC$, $\angle BOD$, and $\angle COD$

Check Understanding 1 a. Name all the radii, diameters, chords, and central angles shown in circle P.

b. **Reasoning** Must a diameter also be a chord? Explain.

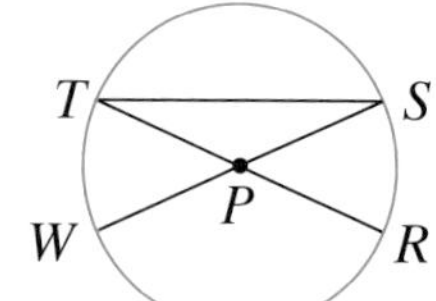

Recall that an arc is part of a circle. A **semicircle** is an arc that is half of the circumference of a circle. In circle D, $\overset{\frown}{AB}$ and $\overset{\frown}{CA}$ are arcs less than the length of a semicircle. $\overset{\frown}{CAB}$ is a semicircle. Three letters are used to name a semicircle or an arc longer than a semicircle.

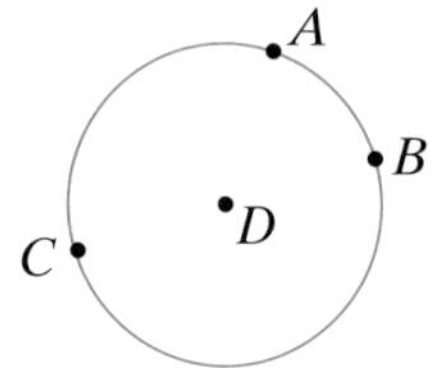

2 EXAMPLE Naming Arcs

Name three of the arcs in circle O.

Three arcs are $\overset{\frown}{XZ}$, $\overset{\frown}{XY}$, and $\overset{\frown}{ZXY}$.

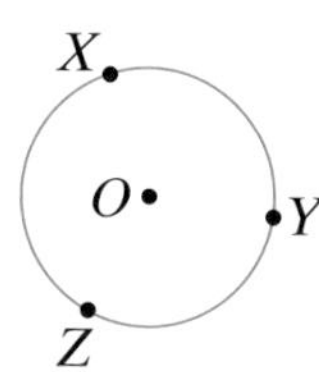

Check Understanding 2 Name three arcs in circle O not mentioned above.

You can use arcs to describe real-world situations involving distances around circles.

3 EXAMPLE Real-World Problem Solving

Amusement Parks You are in the red car of a Ferris wheel. Your friend is in the green car. Name two different arcs between you and your friend.

The shorter arc is $\overset{\frown}{DE}$.
The longer arc is $\overset{\frown}{DCE}$.

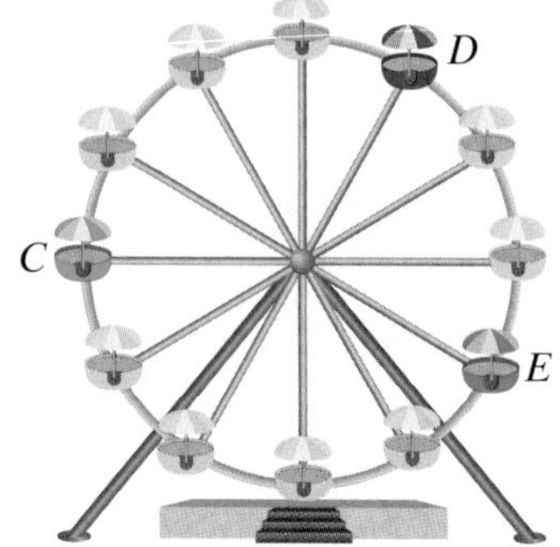

3 Name two different arcs from the blue car to the green car.

EXERCISES

For more practice, see *Extra Practice*.

A Practice by Example

Example 1 (page 384)

Name each of the following for circle *M*.

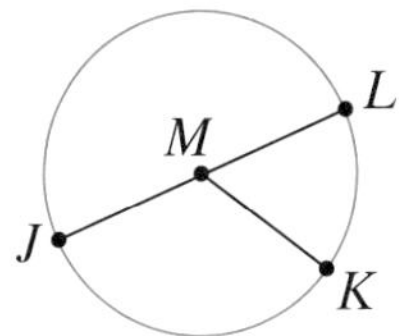

1. center **2.** radii **3.** chords

4. diameter **5.** central angles

Name each of the following for circle *O*.

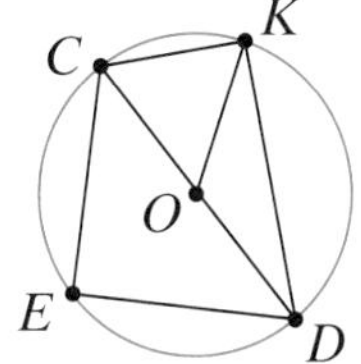

6. center **7.** radii **8.** chords

9. diameter **10.** central angles

Examples 2 and 3 (page 384)

Name the following arcs for circle *Q*.

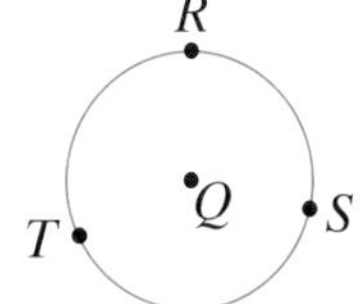

11. all arcs shorter than a semicircle

12. all arcs longer than a semicircle

Name the following arcs for circle *A*.

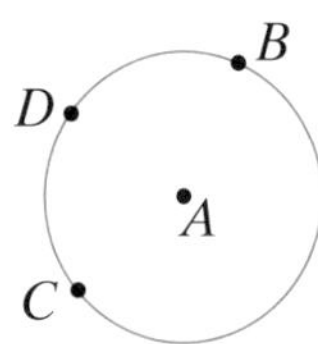

13. all arcs shorter than a semicircle

14. all arcs longer than a semicircle

B Apply Your Skills

Name each of the following for circle *D*.

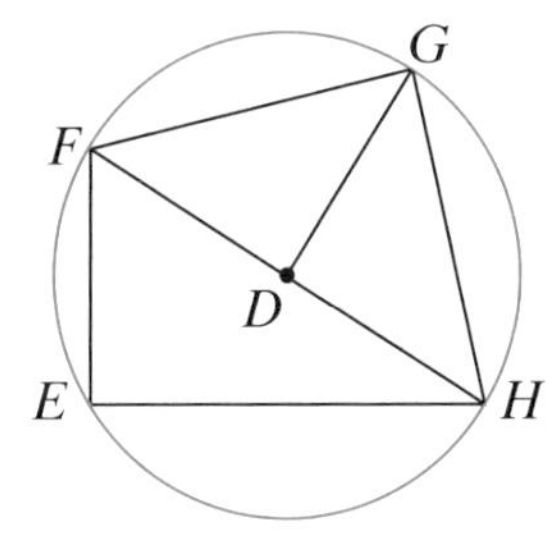

15. two chords **16.** two central angles

17. a diameter **18.** five arcs

19. an isosceles triangle **20.** the longest chord

21. In circle *D* at the above right, if the measure of $\angle FDG = 90°$, what is the measure of $\angle HDG$?

22. Reasoning Can a radius also be a chord? Explain.

Real-World Connection

Careers Fabric designers use geometric shapes, including circles, to create beautiful fabrics.

23. **a.** Open-Ended Draw a design that includes a quadrilateral inside a circle with vertices on the circle.

b. Writing in Math Describe your design so someone can draw it without looking at your drawing.

C Challenge

Reasoning **Draw several diagrams that fit each description. Then make a conjecture.**

24. a quadrilateral whose vertices are the endpoints of two diameters

25. a triangle that has all endpoints on a circle and one of its sides is a diameter of the circle

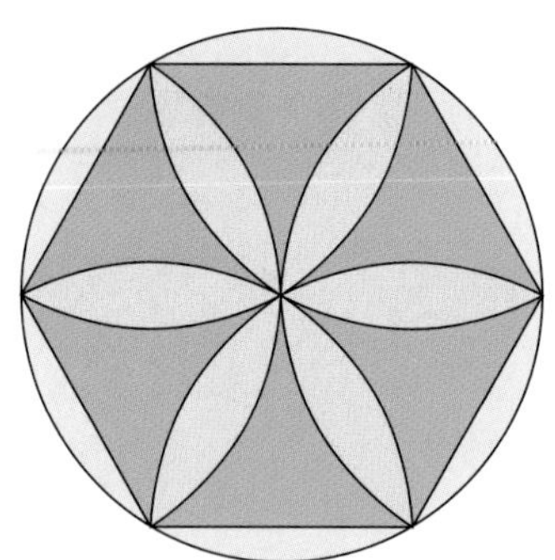

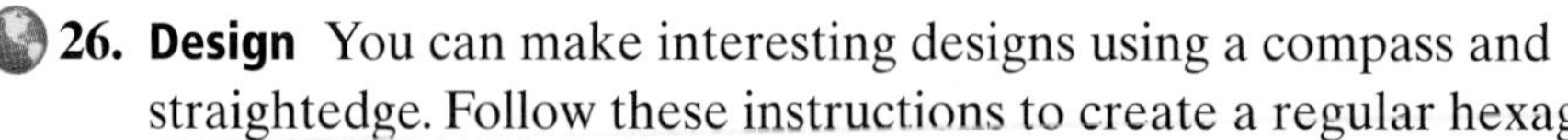

26. **Design** You can make interesting designs using a compass and straightedge. Follow these instructions to create a regular hexagon.
   a. Use a compass to draw a circle twice.
   b. Keeping the compass set to the same width, put the tip on the circle and make a small arc that intersects the circle twice.
   c. Move the tip of the compass to an intersection. Make another arc. Continue around the circle.
   d. Draw a chord between each pair of consecutive arcs.

27. **Stretch Your Thinking** Angie and Tim draw different angles. The measure of Angie's angle is 2° more than 3 times the measure of Tim's angle. The measure of Angie's angle is 26° greater than the measure of a right angle. What is the measure of Tim's angle?

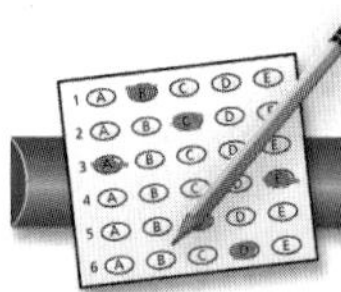

Test Prep

Multiple Choice

Use circle *D* at the right for Exercises 28–30.

28. Which is NOT an arc of the circle?
   A. $\overset{\frown}{JP}$ B. $\overset{\frown}{LDR}$
   C. $\overset{\frown}{MRJ}$ D. $\overset{\frown}{LPJ}$

29. How many chords have *L* as an endpoint?
   F. 1 G. 2
   H. 3 I. 4

Take It to the NET
Online lesson quiz at
www.PHSchool.com
Web Code aba-0708

30. $\overline{RL}$ is a diameter of circle D. What is the measure of $\angle RDL$?
   A. 45° B. 90° C. 135° D. 180°

Short Response

31. Circle *K* has points *A*, *B*, *C*, *D*, and *E* on it, in that order. (a) Sketch circle *K*. Sketch chords $\overline{AB}$, $\overline{BC}$, $\overline{CD}$, $\overline{DE}$, and $\overline{EA}$. (b) What kind of figure is *ABCDE*?

Mixed Review

Lesson 7-2

Find the measure of each angle using a protractor.

32. 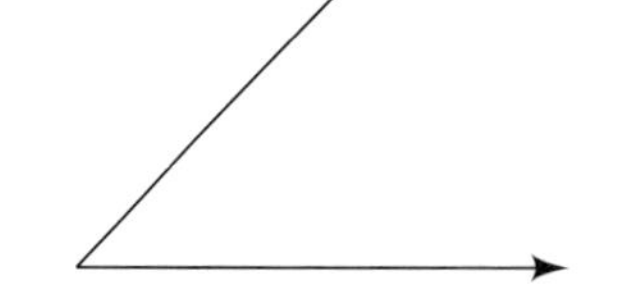

33. 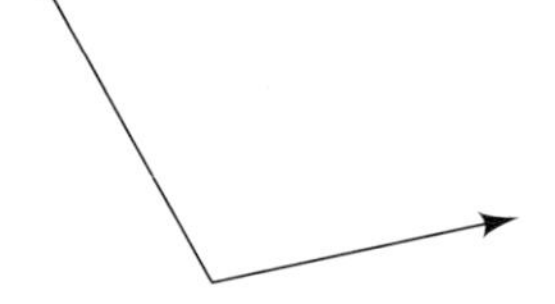

34. 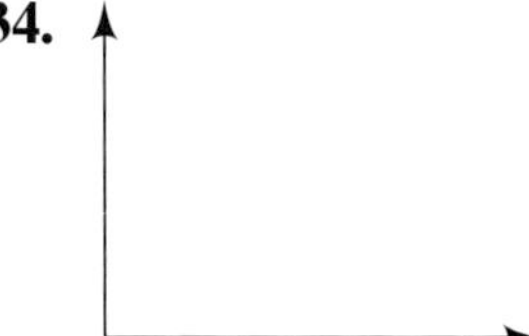

Lesson 4-6

Algebra **Solve each equation.**

35. $p - \frac{4}{7} = 5\frac{1}{14}$

36. $3\frac{1}{2} = x - 1\frac{3}{4}$

37. $\frac{1}{2} = w + 4\frac{5}{12}$

Reading Math

Learning Vocabulary

In Chapter 5, you learned to make your own mathematics dictionary for new words and symbols. Here are some additional strategies for learning new vocabulary.

Strategy 1 Break words apart into prefixes and roots. Then combine the meaning of the two parts. For example, *bisector* has the prefix *bi* and the root *sector*. Bi means "two" and *sector* means "section," so *bisector* means "two sections."

Here are some common prefixes and roots that you have used in this chapter.

deca (ten)	*octa* (eight)
dia (through)	*para* (beside)
equi (equal)	*penta* (five)
gon (angle)	*poly* (many)
hexa (six)	*quadr* (four)
mid (middle)	*tri* (three)

Strategy 2 Think about common meanings of words. For example, an acute pain is a sharp pain. Connecting the word *acute* with the word *sharp* will help you remember that an acute angle is less than 90°.

EXERCISES

For Exercises 1–6, break each word into a prefix and a root. Then combine the meaning of both parts. Does the meaning you wrote make sense given the definition of the word? Explain.

1. hexagon

2. parallel

3. midpoint

4. decagon

5. polygon

6. triangle

For Exercises 7–9, tell how the common word can help you remember the mathematical term.

	Common word	Mathematical term
7.	straight (as in *stand straight*)	straight angle
8.	intersection (as in *a street intersection*)	intersecting lines
9.	adjacent (as in *adjacent neighbor*)	adjacent angle

10. How does the prefix *dia* connect to the words *diagonal* and *diameter*?

7-9 Circle Graphs

What You'll Learn

To analyze circle graphs

To construct circle graphs

. . . And Why

To display information, as in Example 2

Check Skills You'll Need

For help, go to Lesson 6-4.

Find each answer.

1. 25% of 360 **2.** 60% of 360 **3.** 72% of 360

4. 18% of 360 **5.** 95% of 360 **6.** 54% of 360

New Vocabulary • circle graph

OBJECTIVE 1

Interactive lesson includes instant self-check, tutorials, and activities.

Analyzing Circle Graphs

A **circle graph** is a graph of data where a circle represents the whole. Each wedge, or sector, in the circle is part of the whole. The total must be 100%.

1 EXAMPLE Analyzing a Circle Graph

Music In 2001, consumers spent \$13.7 billion on music recordings. Use the information in the circle graph below to answer each question.

Music That People Buy

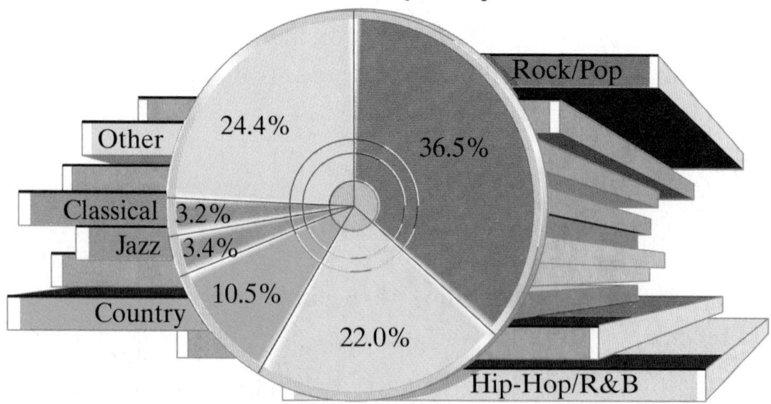

SOURCE: Recording Industry Association of America

a. Which category of music was bought the most?
Rock/pop music was bought the most.

b. Approximately how much money was spent on country music?
10.5% of \$13.7 billion $= 0.105 \cdot \$13.7$ billion $\approx \$1.4$ billion

Check Understanding **1** Approximately how much money was spent on jazz music?

OBJECTIVE

2 Constructing Circle Graphs

A circle graph is divided into sectors. Each sector is determined by a central angle. The sum of the measures of the central angles is 360°.

2 EXAMPLE Constructing a Circle Graph

Real-World Connection

Launching a shuttle requires about 64,000 gallons of fuel each minute.

Science Use the information in the table below to make a circle graph.

NASA Space Shuttle Expenditures

Category	Cost (millions of dollars)
Orbiter	698.8
Propulsion	1,053.1
Operations	738.8
Upgrades	488.8

SOURCE: *Statistical Abstract of the United States*
Go to **www.PHSchool.com** for a data update.
Web Code abg-2041

Step 1 Add to find the total space shuttle expenditures.

$698.8 + 1{,}053.1 + 738.8 + 488.8 = 2{,}979.5$ (million dollars)

Step 2 For each central angle, set up a proportion to find the angle measure. Use a calculator to solve.

$\frac{698.8}{2{,}979.5} = \frac{a}{360}$ $\quad$ $\frac{1{,}053.1}{2{,}979.5} = \frac{b}{360}$ $\quad$ $\frac{738.8}{2{,}979.5} = \frac{c}{360}$ $\quad$ $\frac{488.8}{2{,}979.5} = \frac{d}{360}$

$a \approx 84.4°$ $\quad$ $b \approx 127.2°$ $\quad$ $c \approx 89.3°$ $\quad$ $d \approx 59.1°$

Step 3 Draw a circle. Draw the central angles using the measures found in Step 2. Label each section. Include a title and a key.

NASA Space Shuttle Expenditures (millions of dollars)

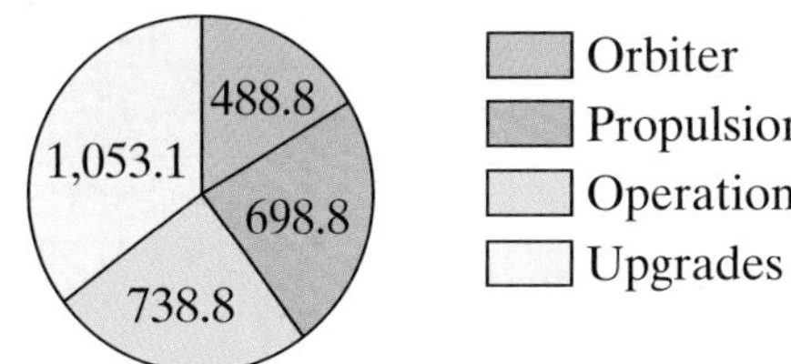

Check Understanding 2 **a.** Find the measure of the central angle that you would draw to represent blood type A.

b. Use the information in the table at the right to make a circle graph.

Human Blood Types

Blood Type	Percent
A	40%
B	11%
AB	4%
O	45%

SOURCE: American Association of Blood Banks

EXERCISES

For more practice, see *Extra Practice*.

A Practice by Example

Example 1 (page 388)

Use the circle graph below for Exercises 1–4.

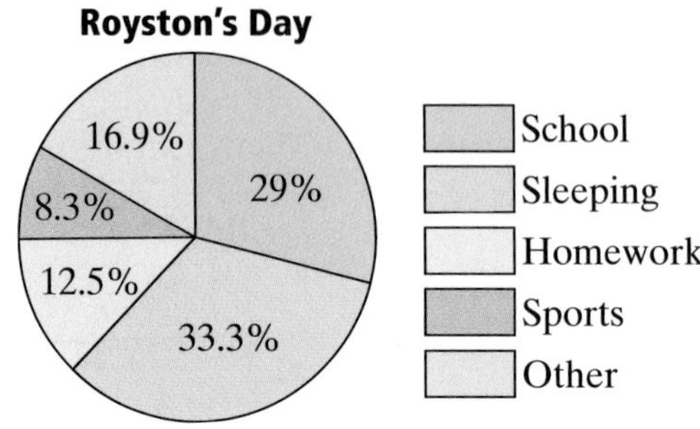

1. What takes up the most time of Royston's day?

2. What percent of Royston's day is typically spent doing homework?

3. What percent of Royston's day is spent outside of school?

4. How much time does Royston spend sleeping?

Example 2 (page 389)

Find the measure of the central angle that you would draw to represent each percent in a circle graph. Round to the nearest degree.

5. 11% **6.** 30% **7.** 34% **8.** 25%

9. 28% **10.** 39% **11.** 12.5% **12.** 14.5%

Use the information in each table to make a circle graph.

13. **Frozen Yogurt Sales**

Flavor	Scoops
Vanilla	84
Chocolate	107
Strawberry	43

14. **Movie Rentals**

Type	Number
Action	7
Comedy	9
Other	5

B Apply Your Skills

Travel **Use the circle graph for Exercises 15–18.**

15. What country or region is most visited by United States travelers?

16. **Reasoning** Can you tell what country is least visited by United States travelers? Explain.

17. Approximately how many people travel to Europe from the United States each year?

18. **Reasoning** Why use *Europe* rather than list every country individually?

U.S. Foreign Travel (millions of people per year)

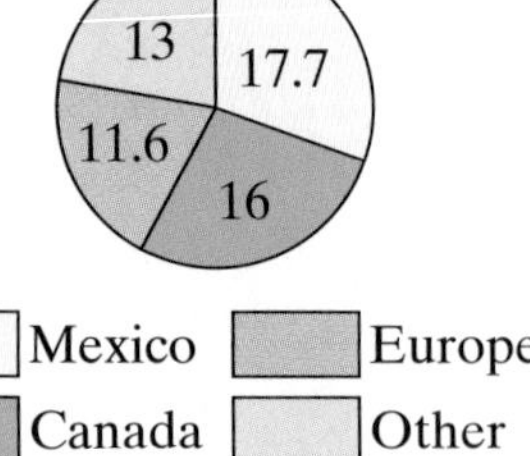

SOURCE: Statistical Abstract of the United States
Go to **www.PHSchool.com** for a data update. Web Code abg-2041

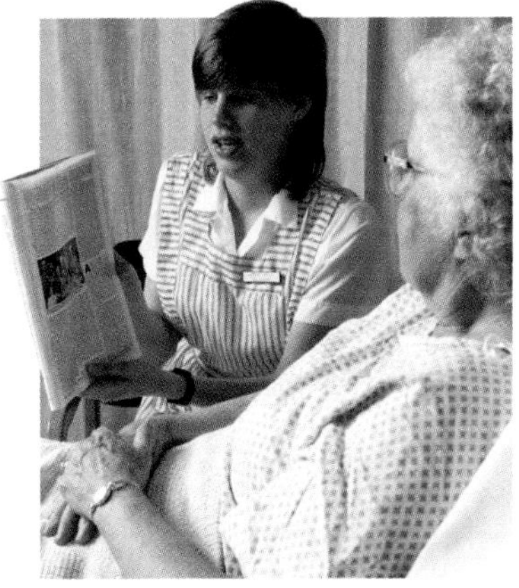

Real-World Connection

Student volunteers are important assets for many community centers and hospitals.

19. **Volunteering** You are coordinating your class's volunteer efforts at your community hospital. You want to show how many days each week students are volunteering. Use the table to make a circle graph.

Days	1	2	3	4	5
Students	11	5	5	2	2

20. **City Planning** An engineer is making a presentation on how many commuters use each method of transportation. Use the information in the table to make a circle graph.

Method of Transportation	Percent of Commuters
Personal Vehicle (1 passenger)	45%
Personal Vehicle (2 or more passengers)	15%
Public Transportation	30%
Bicycle	6%
Other	4%

Number Sense **Find the missing values for each graph.**

21. 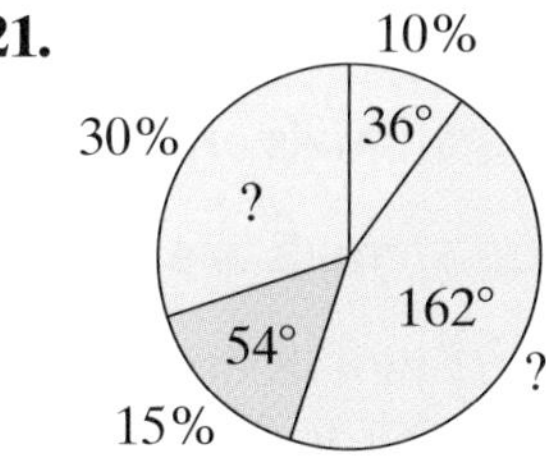

22. 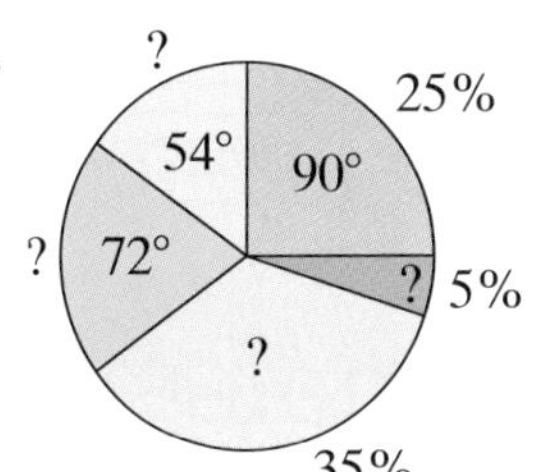

23. 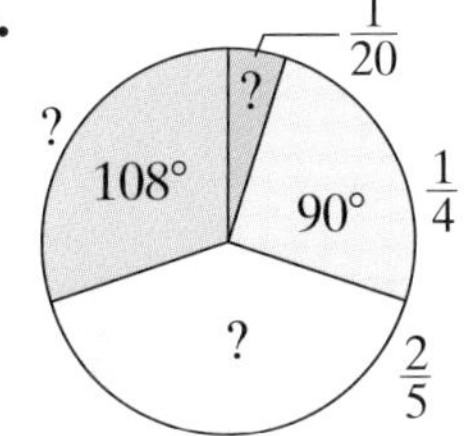

24. a. **Survey** The data below show the results of a survey on the preferred day for grocery shopping. Use the data to draw a circle graph.

Day	Percent	Day	Percent
Monday	4	Friday	17
Tuesday	5	Saturday	29
Wednesday	12	Sunday	7
Thursday	13	No preference	13

b. If 1,200 people were interviewed for the survey, how many people gave each response?

25. **Writing in Math** In a survey on the most important car safety features, people gave more than one response. In a second survey, people gave only one response. Which survey results can you show in a circle graph? Why?

26. Use the data at the right to draw a circle graph.

Transportation Mode	Walk	Bicycle	Bus	Car
Number of Students	252	135	432	81

C Challenge

27. **Budgets** The Miller family wants to buy a new car. Mr. Miller makes a graph of how his family spends its monthly income of \$2,400.

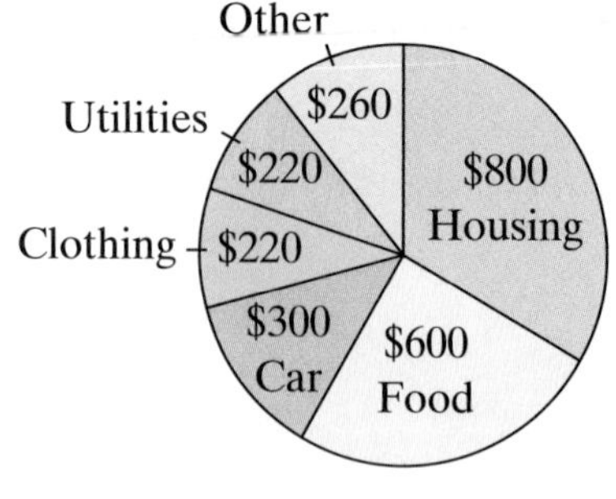

   a. What percent of the budget is for car expenses?
   b. Mr. Miller estimates that payments on a new car will increase the monthly car expenses to \$840. What percent of the monthly budget will car expenses be if the family buys a new car?
   c. **Reasoning** What changes do you think the Miller family should make in the budget so that they can buy a new car? Make a circle graph that shows the changes you suggest.

28. **Stretch Your Thinking** Use three segments to divide an equilateral triangle into four congruent triangles.

Test Prep

Gridded Response

Use the circle graph for Exercises 29–33. There are 150 animals in the store.

Sal's Pet Store

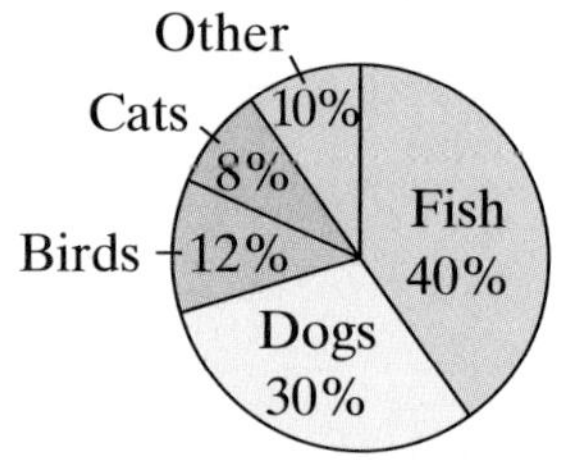

29. What number of the animals are dogs?
30. What number of the animals are cats?
31. What number of the animals are something other than birds and fish?
32. What is the number of degrees in the central angle for the dogs' sector?
33. What is the number of degrees in the central angle for the birds' sector?

Online lesson quiz at **www.PHSchool.com**
Web Code aba-0709

Mixed Review

Lesson 6-2 **Write each number as a percent.**

34. 0.07 35. 3.5 36. $\frac{3}{8}$ 37. $\frac{9}{20}$

Lesson 4-3 **Find each sum or difference.**

38. $\frac{2}{3} + \frac{3}{8}$ 39. $4\frac{1}{6} + 6\frac{2}{9}$ 40. $7\frac{3}{4} + \frac{11}{16}$ 41. $\frac{7}{8} - \frac{1}{4}$

42. $\frac{5}{6} + \frac{4}{9}$ 43. $5\frac{2}{5} + 9\frac{1}{10}$ 44. $6\frac{3}{8} - 2\frac{1}{4}$ 45. $14\frac{5}{8} - 6\frac{5}{12}$

Test-Taking Strategies

Drawing a Diagram

Sometimes a diagram is not supplied with a problem. You can ***draw a diagram*** to help you solve the problem. Make sure your diagram is large enough for you to label all of the parts.

EXAMPLE

$\triangle CRT \cong \triangle POV$. The measure of $\angle C$ is 41°, and the measure of $\angle T$ is 104°. What is the measure of $\angle O$?

Draw and label triangles CRT and POV. Label angles C and T. Label the corresponding angles in $\triangle POV$. Write an equation to find the measure of $\angle O$.

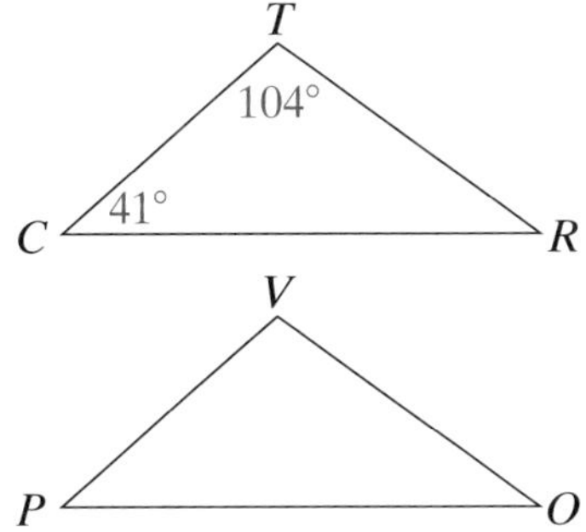

Let $x = m\angle O = m\angle R$.

$$x + 41° + 104° = 180°$$
$$x + 145° = 180°$$
$$x + 145° - 145° = 180° - 145°$$
$$x = 35°$$

The measure of $\angle O$ is 35°.

EXERCISES

Draw a diagram to solve each problem.

1. $\overleftrightarrow{QR}$ intersects $\overleftrightarrow{ST}$ at point U. If the measure of $\angle QUT$ is 123° and the measure of $\angle TUR$ is 57°, what is the measure of $\angle SUR$?
2. A right triangle has one angle that measures 16°. What are the measures of the other two angles?
3. The angle bisector of one angle of a triangle forms two angles that measure 27°. The angle bisector of another angle forms two angles that measure 34°. What is the measure of the third angle of the triangle?
4. Rectangle $ABCD$ shares $\overline{BC}$ with equilateral triangle BCE. The length of $\overline{CD}$ is 4 cm, and the length of $\overline{DA}$ is 3 cm. What is the length of $\overline{BE}$?
5. Circle J has a radius of 6 in. Radii $\overline{JK}$ and $\overline{JL}$ form an angle that is not a straight angle. The length of $\overline{KL}$ is not 6 in. Classify $\triangle JKL$ according to its sides.

Chapter Review

Vocabulary

acute angle (p. 352)
acute triangle (p. 364)
adjacent angles (p. 353)
angle (p. 351)
angle bisector (p. 358)
arc (p. 358)
central angle (p. 383)
chord (p. 383)
circle (p. 383)
circle graph (p. 388)
compass (p. 358)
complementary (p. 352)
congruent angles (p. 353)
congruent polygons (p. 378)
congruent sides (p. 363)
decagon (p. 369)
diameter (p. 383)
equilateral triangle (p. 363)
hexagon (p. 369)
intersecting lines (p. 348)
irregular polygon (p. 370)
isosceles triangle (p. 363)
line (p. 347)
midpoint (p. 357)
obtuse angle (p. 352)
obtuse triangle (p. 364)
octagon (p. 369)
parallel lines (p. 348)
parallelogram (p. 370)
pentagon (p. 369)
perpendicular bisector (p. 357)
perpendicular lines (p. 357)
plane (p. 348)
point (p. 347)
polygon (p. 369)
quadrilateral (p. 369)
radius (p. 383)
ray (p. 347)
rectangle (p. 370)
regular polygon (p. 370)
rhombus (p. 370)
right angle (p. 352)
right triangle (p. 364)
scalene triangle (p. 363)
segment (p. 347)
segment bisector (p. 357)
semicircle (p. 384)
skew lines (p. 348)
straight angle (p. 352)
square (p. 370)
supplementary (p. 352)
trapezoid (p. 370)
vertex (p. 351)
vertical angles (p. 353)

Reading Math: Understanding Vocabulary

Take It to the NET
Online vocabulary quiz at **www.PHSchool.com**
Web Code abj-0751

Choose the correct term to complete each sentence.

1. (Parallel, Skew) lines lie in the same plane.

2. A (decagon, pentagon) is a polygon with five sides.

3. Angles whose sum is 90° are (complementary, supplementary) angles.

4. A(n) (isosceles, scalene) triangle has no congruent sides.

5. An (acute, obtuse) angle measures less than 90°.

Skills and Concepts

7-1 and 7-2 Objectives

- To identify segments, rays, and lines
- To measure and describe angles
- To work with pairs of angles

Parallel lines are lines that lie in the same plane and have no points in common. **Skew lines** do not lie in the same plane. The sum of two **complementary** angles is 90°. The sum of two **supplementary** angles is 180°.

Find the measures of the complement and supplement of each angle.

6. $m\angle A = 55°$ **7.** $m\angle B = 27°$ **8.** $m\angle C = 87°$ **9.** $m\angle D = 12°$

7-3 Objectives

- To construct segment bisectors and angle bisectors

You can use a **compass** to construct **segment bisectors** and **angle bisectors.**

10. Draw a segment. Construct its perpendicular bisector.

11. Draw an acute angle. Construct its angle bisector.

7-4 and 7-5 Objectives

- To classify triangles by sides and angles
- To find angle measures of a triangle
- To classify polygons
- To identify special quadrilaterals

You can classify a triangle by the measures of its sides or the measures of its angles. The sum of the measures of the angles of any triangle is 180°. A **polygon** is classified by the number of sides it has. A **regular polygon** has congruent sides and congruent angles.

Find the value of *x*. Then classify each triangle by its sides and by its angles.

12.
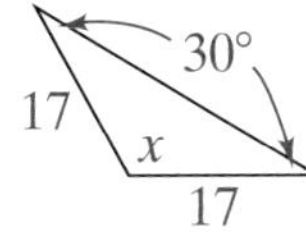

13.
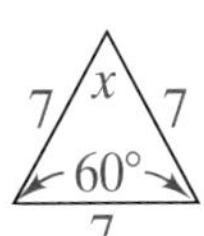

14.
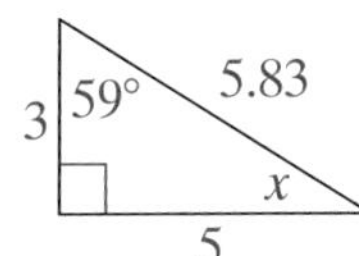

Classify each polygon by its sides. Then classify it as *regular* or *irregular*.

15.
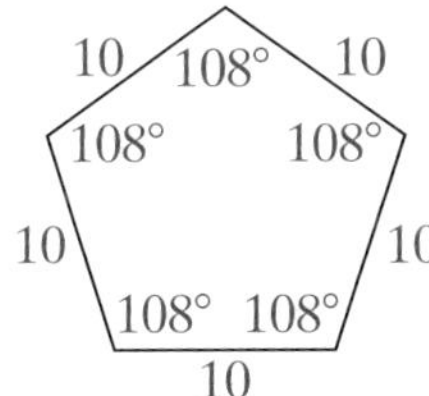

16.
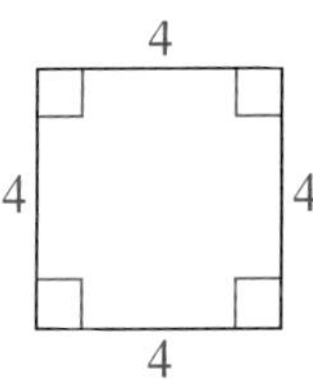

17.
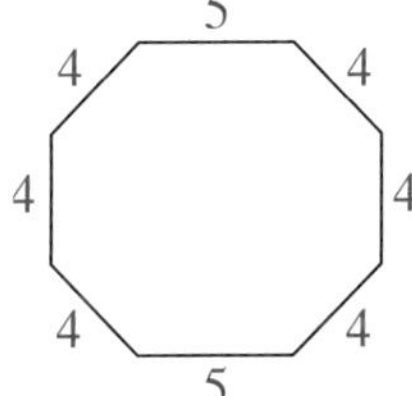

7-6 Objective

- To solve a problem by combining strategies

You can solve problems by drawing a diagram and looking for a pattern.

18. The figure shows a pattern created by black and white triangles. How many white triangles will be needed for 12 rows?

7-7 Objective

- To identify and work with congruent figures

Congruent polygons have the same size and shape. Corresponding parts of congruent polygons are congruent.

19. a. Write the congruencies for the corresponding parts of the congruent figures.

b. Find the missing side lengths and angle measures of the congruent figures.

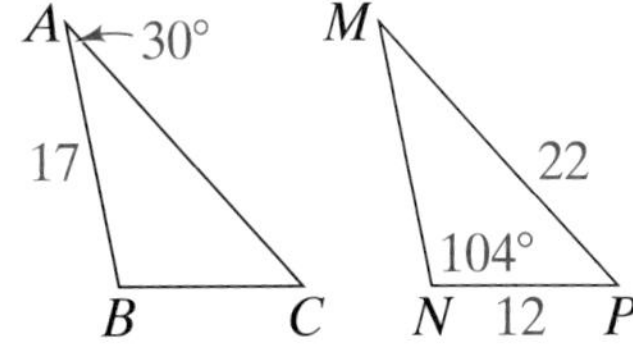

7-8 and 7-9 Objectives

- To identify parts of a circle
- To analyze and construct circle graphs

A **circle** is the set of points in a plane that are all the same distance from the center. A circle can have **radii, diameters, central angles, chords,** and **arcs.**

Circle graphs present data as percents or fractions of a total.

Name each of the following parts in circle *T*.

20. radii **21.** diameters **22.** center

23. chords **24.** arcs longer than a semicircle

Chapter Test

Use the diagram for Exercises 1–3.

1. Name all the segments parallel to $\overline{AB}$.
2. Name all the segments intersecting $\overline{FG}$.
3. Name all the segments skew to $\overline{DH}$.

Use a protractor to measure each angle.

4. 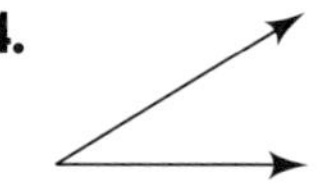

5. 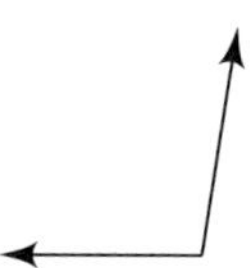

Find the measures of the complement and supplement of each angle.

6. $m\angle H = 45°$
7. $m\angle R = 7°$
8. $m\angle K = 89°$
9. $m\angle P = 25°$
10. What is the supplement of a 102° angle?
11. Does a 98° angle have a complement? Explain.
12. Draw a segment. Construct its bisector.
13. Draw an obtuse angle. Construct its bisector.

Find the value of *x* in each triangle. Classify each triangle by its side lengths and angle measures.

14. 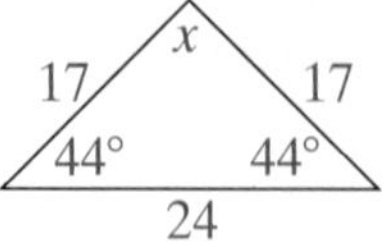

15. 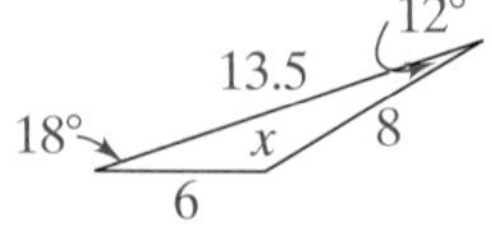

Identify each polygon.

16. 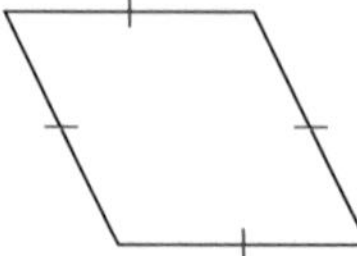

17. 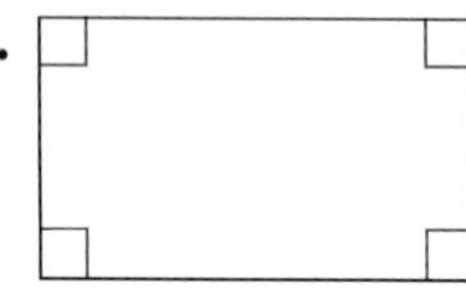

18. Find the number of diagonals in a decagon.
19. Draw two figures that continue the pattern.

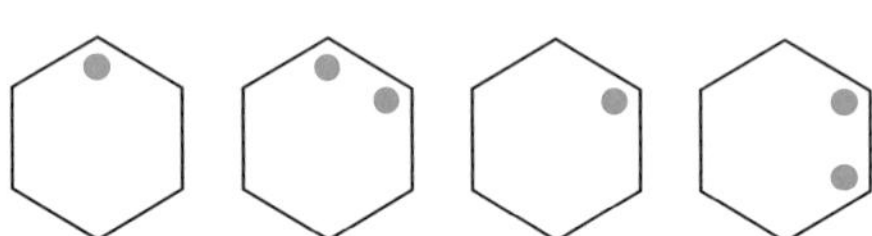

In the diagram, $\triangle ABC \cong \triangle MNP$. Complete each statement.

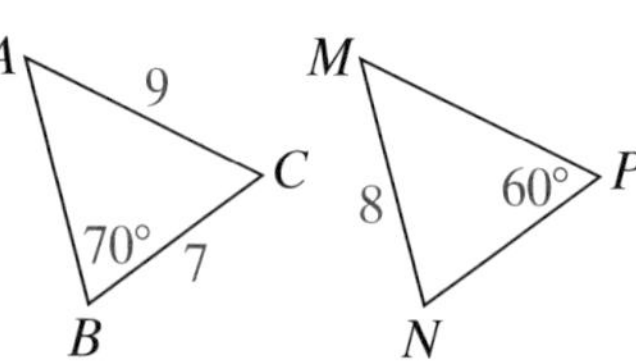

20. $\overline{AC} \cong$ ■
21. ■ $\cong \overline{PN}$
22. $\angle B \cong$ ■
23. ■ $\cong \angle M$
24. $AB =$ ■
25. $m\angle N =$ ■
26. $MP =$ ■

Name each of the following for circle *W*.

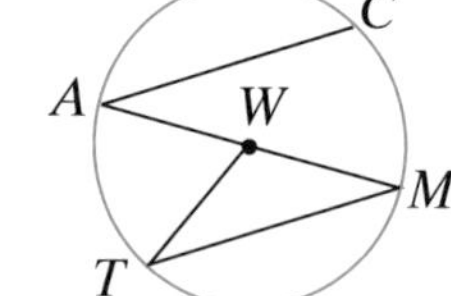

27. three radii
28. two chords
29. two central angles
30. one diameter
31. three arcs shorter than half the circle
32. **Class Trip** Students earned the following amounts of money to pay the transportation costs of a class trip. Make a circle graph for the data.

Fund Raiser	Money
Car wash	\$150
Paper drive	\$75
Book sale	\$225
Food stand	\$378

33. **Writing in Math** Briefly explain the differences and similarities among a rectangle, a rhombus, and a square.

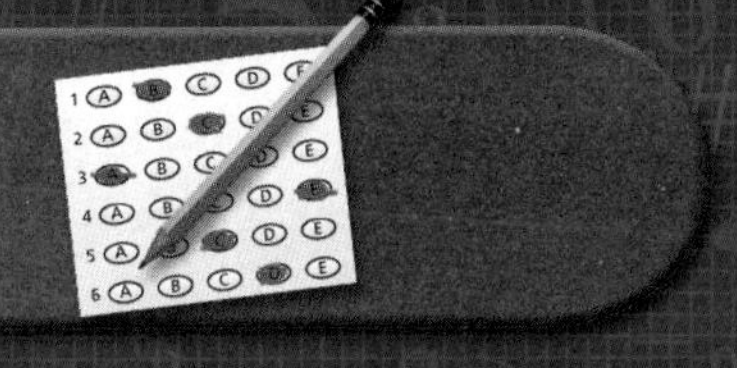

Test Prep

Reading Comprehension **Read each passage and answer the questions that follow.**

Energetic Math The amount of energy that Americans use each year varies greatly from state to state. People in Alaska use the most, 1,143.7 BTU (British Thermal Units). People in Hawaii use the least, 200.9 BTU. People in Texas, Ohio, Vermont, and New York use 587.8 BTU, 370.2 BTU, 283.8 BTU, and 225.5 BTU, respectively.

1. Energy consumption in Hawaii is, on average, about what percent of the energy consumption in Alaska?
A. 18% **B.** 21% **C.** 25% **D.** 550%

2. Energy consumption in Texas is, on average, about what percent of the consumption in Vermont?
F. 50% **G.** 100% **H.** 150% **I.** 200%

3. People moving from New York to Ohio might expect their energy consumption to increase by about what percent?
A. 40% **B.** 61% **C.** 64% **D.** 164%

4. For the states mentioned in the passage, what is the median energy consumption?
F. 320 BTU **G.** 327 BTU
H. 389 BTU **I.** 469 BTU

The Value of Education People with more education generally earn more money. On average, college graduates make about $21 per hour. If you have some college, but don't finish, you can expect an average of about $13 per hour. High school graduates with no college earn about $11 per hour, and those who don't finish high school average about $8 per hour.

5. For the average earnings for high school students compared to earnings of college graduates, which expression could you use to find the percent of increase?
A. $\frac{(21 - 8)}{8}$ **B.** $\frac{(13 - 11)}{11}$
C. $\frac{(21 - 11)}{11}$ **D.** $\frac{(21 - 11)}{21}$

6. Which is the best estimate of how much the average college graduate earns in a year? (Use 8 hours per day, 5 days per week.)
F. $8,400 **G.** $21,000
H. $42,000 **I.** $68,000

7. A person who drops out of high school will earn, on average, about what percent of the earnings of someone who completes high school but does not go to college?
A. 40% **B.** 62% **C.** 73% **D.** 138%

8. A job pays $546 for 40 hours of work in one week. What percent is this of the average wage for a person who started college but didn't finish?
F. 95% **G.** 105% **H.** 155% **I.** 215%

Real-World Snapshots

Golf Course Math

Applying Geometry A good miniature golf course should be challenging and creative. The best courses have some clever twist to delight even the most experienced players. For example, consider a course where you tee off right next to the hole and have to go all the way around, avoiding obstacles, to finish where you started.

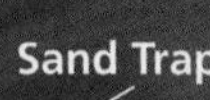

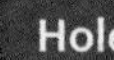

Put It All Together

Materials ruler, protractor

1. Design a hole for a miniature golf course so that the tee (start) and the hole (finish) are right next to each other, and you end where you began. Shape the hole and arrange obstacles so it takes 5 strokes to play.
2. On your hole diagram, use a ruler to draw the path the ball might travel from the tee around the obstacles and back to the hole. Mark the starting (and ending) point A and label the others B, C, D, and E. What is the name of the polygon you drew?

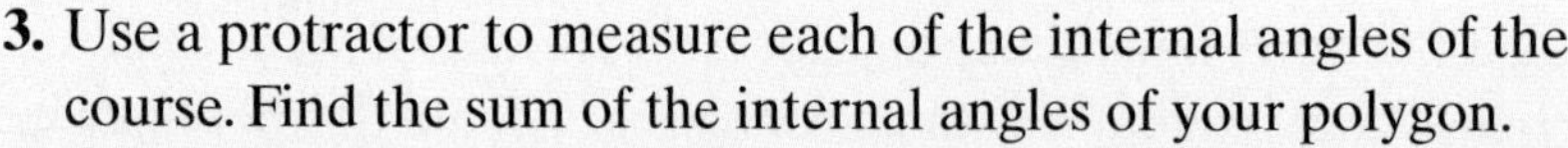

3. Use a protractor to measure each of the internal angles of the course. Find the sum of the internal angles of your polygon.
4. Draw a different five-stroke path that the ball could follow. Find the sum of the internal angles. How does your answer compare with the first total? How does it compare with the totals that other students in your class are getting for their courses?
5. **a.** Draw two lines from one of the vertices to the two other non-adjacent vertices (for example, by connecting B to D and B to E). Make sure your lines stay inside the polygon. How many triangles did you make?

   b. Recall that the sum of the measures of the interior angles of one triangle is 180°. Calculate the sum of the measures of the interior angles of your polygon.

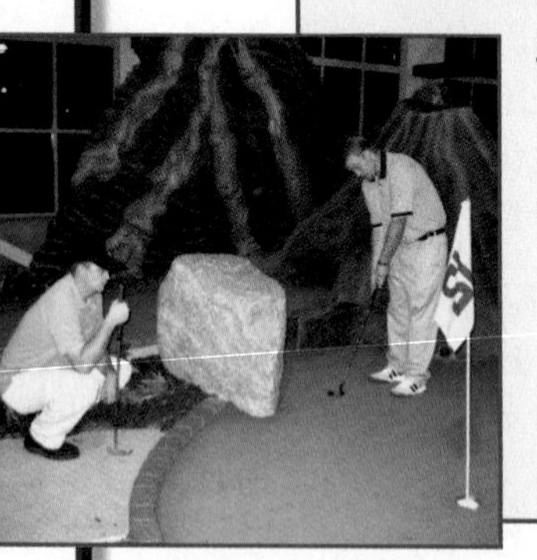

Miniature Golfing

There are about 150 professional miniature golfers in the United States.

Miniature Golf in America

Americans play about 11,550,000 rounds of miniature golf each year at an average cost of $4.25 per round.

Take It to the NET For more information about miniature golf, go to **www.PHSchool.com**.
Web Code: abe-0753

CHAPTER 8

Geometry and Measurement

Lessons

8-1 Estimating Length and Area

8-2 Areas of Parallelograms and Triangles

8-3 Areas of Other Figures

8-4 Circumferences and Areas of Circles

8-5 Square Roots and Irrational Numbers

8-6 The Pythagorean Theorem

8-7 Three-Dimensional Figures

8-8 Surface Areas of Prisms and Cylinders

8-9 Volumes of Rectangular Prisms and Cylinders

8-10 Problem Solving: Try, Check, and Revise and Write an Equation

Key Vocabulary

- area (p. 404)
- circumference (p. 419)
- cylinder (p. 438)
- hypotenuse (p. 432)
- irrational number (p. 428)
- net (p. 442)
- prism (p. 437)
- Pythagorean Theorem (p. 432)
- square root (p. 426)
- surface area (p. 443)
- volume (p. 449)

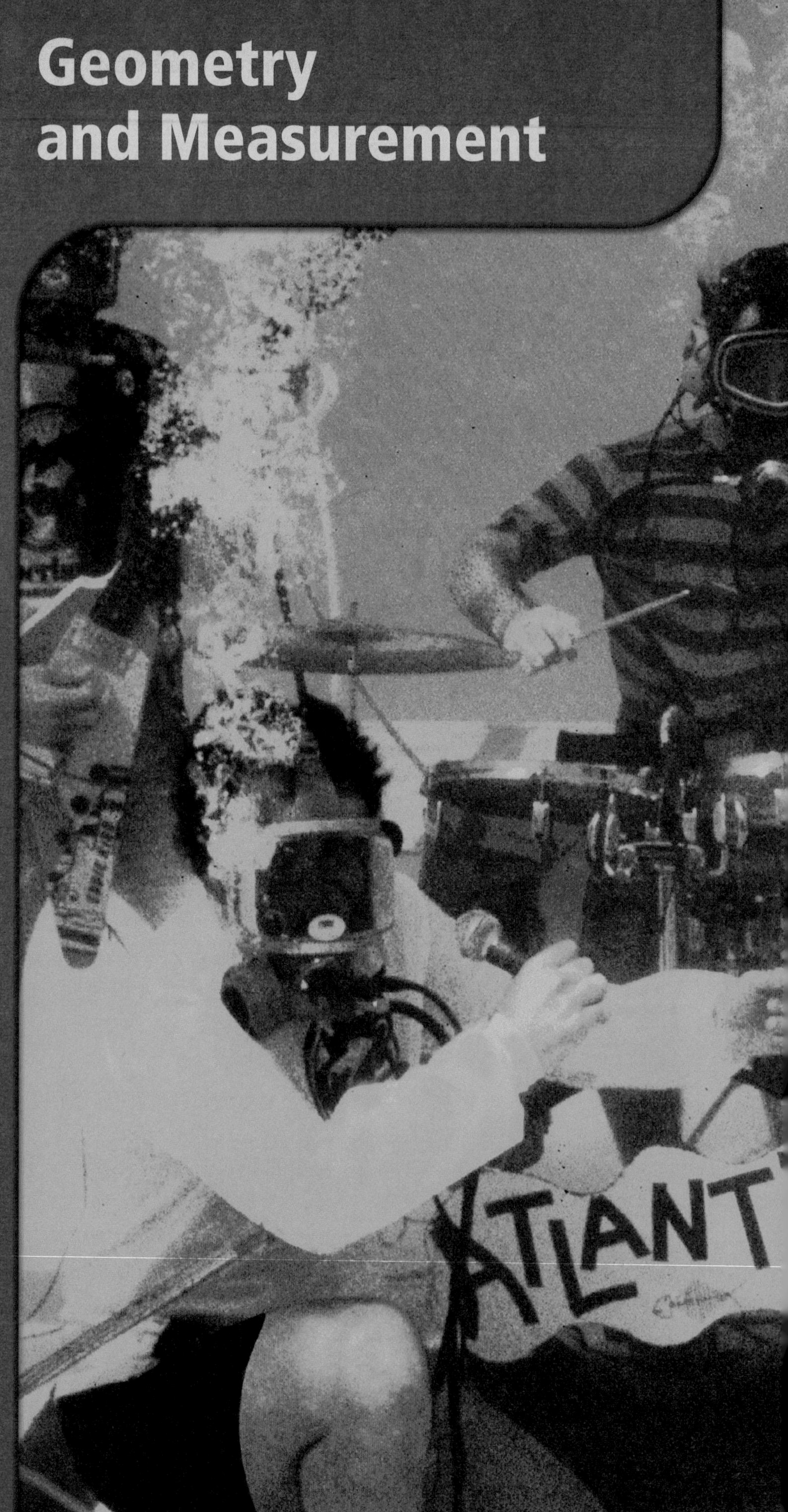

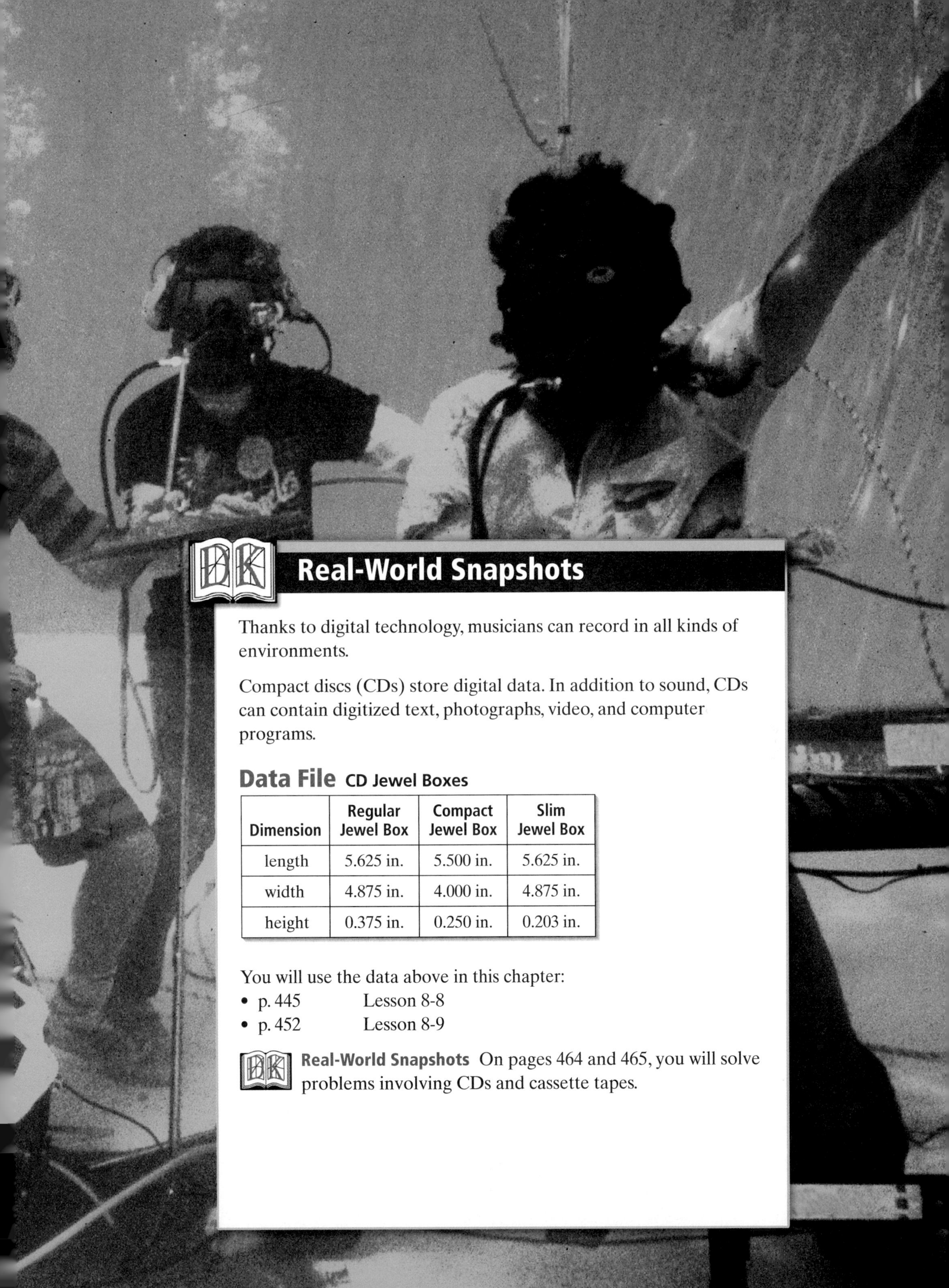

Real-World Snapshots

Thanks to digital technology, musicians can record in all kinds of environments.

Compact discs (CDs) store digital data. In addition to sound, CDs can contain digitized text, photographs, video, and computer programs.

Data File CD Jewel Boxes

Dimension	Regular Jewel Box	Compact Jewel Box	Slim Jewel Box
length	5.625 in.	5.500 in.	5.625 in.
width	4.875 in.	4.000 in.	4.875 in.
height	0.375 in.	0.250 in.	0.203 in.

You will use the data above in this chapter:

- p. 445 Lesson 8-8
- p. 452 Lesson 8-9

Real-World Snapshots On pages 464 and 465, you will solve problems involving CDs and cassette tapes.

Chapter 8 Preview

Where You've Been

- In Chapter 7, you learned to classify polygons and special quadrilaterals. You also learned to identify the parts of a circle.

Where You're Going

- In Chapter 8, you will find the areas of polygons and circles. You will solve problems involving square roots and the Pythagorean Theorem.
- You will identify three-dimensional figures. You will also find the surface area and volume of three-dimensional figures.
- Applying what you learn, you will calculate the volume of an aquarium.

The thickness of the glass of an aquarium is determined by the tank's dimensions and the depth of the water.

Instant self-check online and on CD-ROM

Diagnosing Readiness

For help, go to the lesson in green.

Multiplying Decimals (Lesson 1-3)

Find each product.

1. $0.25 \cdot 3.14 \cdot 4$ **2.** $3 \cdot 20.5 \cdot 2$ **3.** $1.57 \cdot 0.5 \cdot 4$ **4.** $100 \cdot 3.14 \cdot 10$

Order of Operations (Lesson 3-1)

Simplify.

5. $3^3 \cdot (8 - 6)^2$ **6.** $(2^3 \cdot 5) - 6^2$ **7.** $6^2 \cdot 2 + 5^2$

Changing Units in the Customary System (Lesson 4-8)

Complete.

8. 3 c = ■ fl oz **9.** 12 ft = ■ in. **10.** 48 oz = ■ lb **11.** 108 in. = ■ ft

Finding the Measures of Angles in Triangles (Lesson 7-4)

Algebra Find the value of x in each triangle.

12.

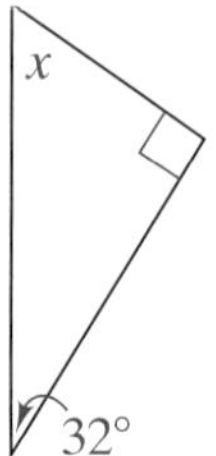

13.

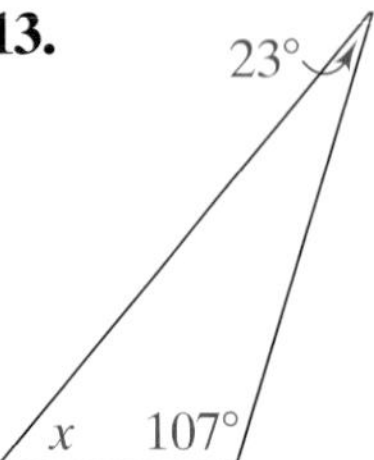

14.

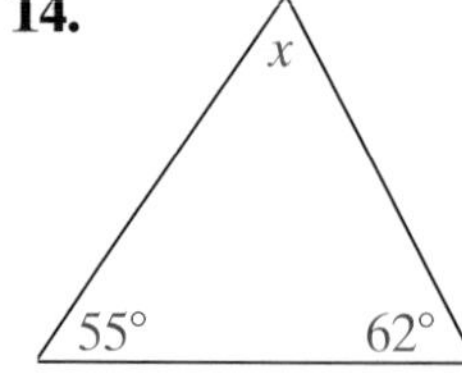

15.

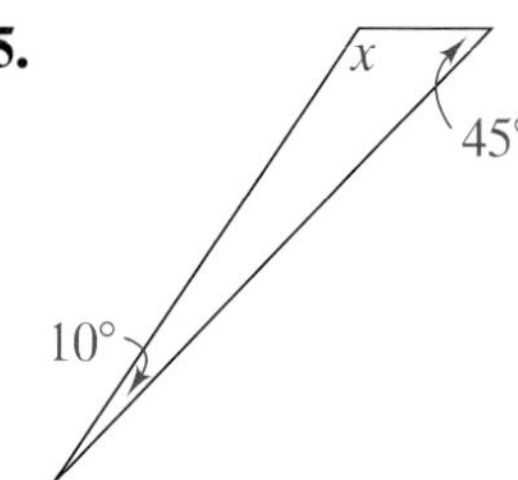

8-1 Estimating Length and Area

What You'll Learn

 To estimate length

 To estimate area

. . . And Why

To estimate map areas, as in Example 3

Check Skills You'll Need

For help, go to Lesson 4-8.

Complete.

1. 6 ft = ■ in.
2. 48 in. = ■ ft
3. 17 ft = ■ in.
4. 60 in. = ■ ft
5. 26 in. = ■ ft
6. 4 ft = ■ in.

New Vocabulary • area

OBJECTIVE

 Interactive lesson includes instant self-check, tutorials, and activities.

1 Estimating Length

A measurement must include a unit of measure to make sense. If you are not given a unit of measure, you must choose an appropriate one. Knowing the approximate size of an object helps you choose. Your need for precision is also an important factor to consider.

Need Help?
For a reference table for estimating length go to p. 222.

1 EXAMPLE Choosing Appropriate Units of Measure

Choose an appropriate customary unit of length you might use to estimate each measurement.

a. length of a moving truck

An appropriate measure is feet. ← **A moving truck is used to move large objects. If you are moving, you only need to know if a truck is big enough to fit all of your things.**

b. width of a picture frame

An appropriate measure is inches. ← **You want a picture frame to fit the picture you put in it, so you need a measure that has a high degree of precision.**

Check Understanding 1 Choose an appropriate customary unit of length for estimating each measurement.

a. length of a stepladder
b. wingspan of a butterfly
c. length of a spoon
d. height of a house

Longer distances, like driving distances, are measured in miles. Shorter distances are measured in feet or inches.

2 EXAMPLE Choosing Reasonable Estimates

Choose a reasonable estimate. Explain your choice.

a. the length of a new pencil: 7 in. or 7 ft

The length of a new pencil is a little more than the width of your hand with your fingers stretched out. So 7 in. is the better estimate.

b. the height of a flagpole: 30 in. or 30 ft

The height of a flagpole is about the height of a two-story building. So 30 ft is the better estimate.

Check Understanding 2 Choose a reasonable estimate for the length of a shirt sleeve: 18 in. or 18 ft. Explain your choice.

OBJECTIVE

2 Estimating Area

The **area** of a figure is the number of square units a figure encloses.

3 EXAMPLE Estimating Area Real World

Geography Estimate the area of Lake Superior. Each square below represents 900 mi^2.

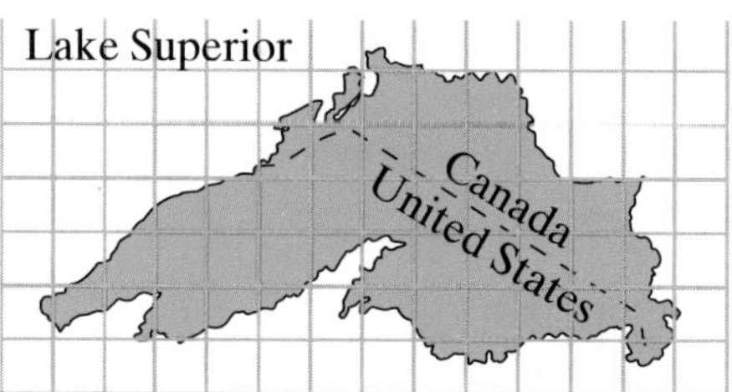

Count the number of squares filled or almost filled. Then count the number of squares that are about half-filled.

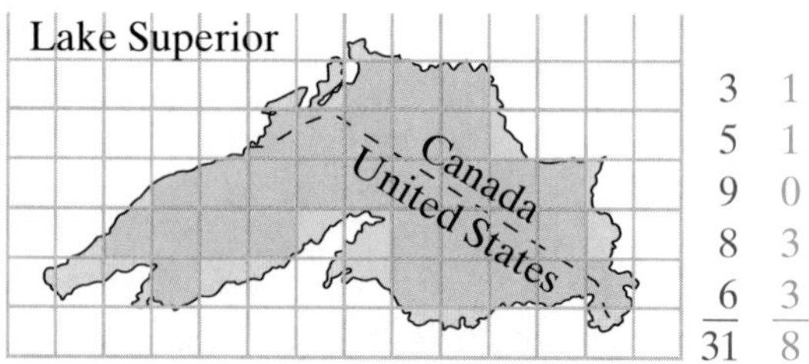

Estimate the number of squares filled by adding the filled squares plus the half-filled squares, which is $31 + \frac{1}{2}(8)$, or 35. Multiply 35 by 900 mi^2. The area is about 31,500 mi^2.

Check Understanding 3 **a.** Estimate the area of the shaded region. Each square represents 4 yd^2.

b. Reasoning How could you estimate the perimeter of the shaded region?

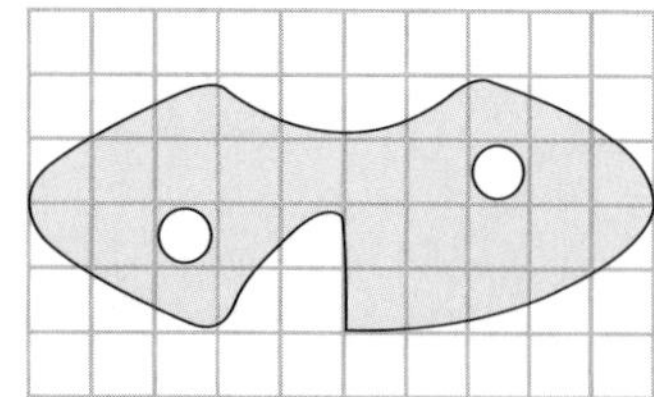

EXERCISES

For more practice, see *Extra Practice.*

A Practice by Example

Example 1 (page 403)

Choose an appropriate customary unit of length for estimating each measurement.

1. the width of your fingernail
2. the perimeter of a football field
3. the height of a volleyball net
4. the height of a basketball rim
5. the size of an ant
6. the perimeter of a classroom

Example 2 (page 404)

Choose a reasonable estimate. Explain your choice.

7. width of your hand: 6 in. or 6 ft
8. depth of an in-ground swimming pool: 10 in. or 10 ft
9. length of a mouse's tail: 2 in. or 2 yd
10. perimeter of a school building: 600 ft or 600 yd

Example 3 (page 404)

Estimate the area of each shaded region. Each square represents 25 mi^2.

11. 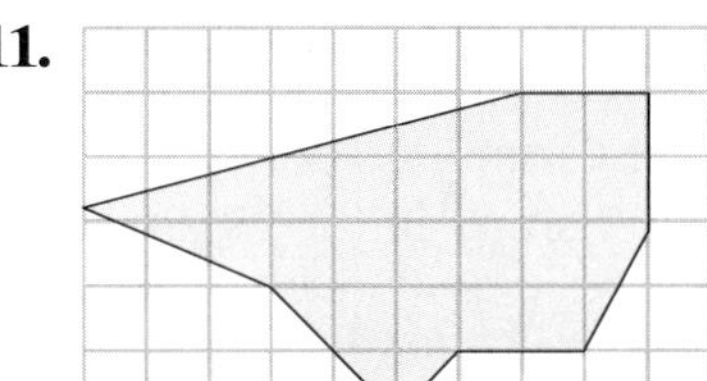

12. 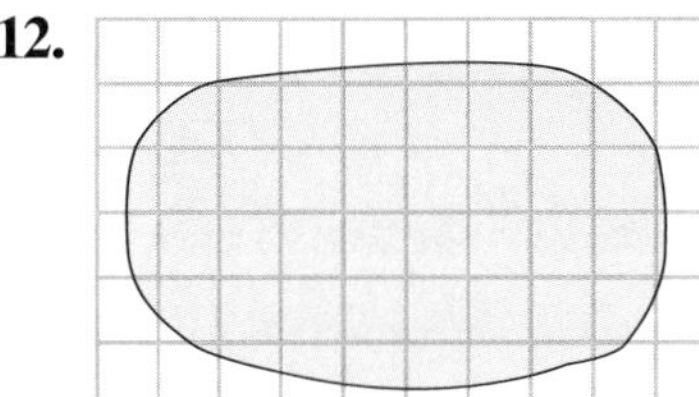

B Apply Your Skills

Estimate each length in centimeters. (1 cm)

13.
14.
15.
16.

17. **Writing in Math** How could you use a piece of string to estimate the perimeter of the puzzle piece at the right?

Need Help?
For help with metric units of length, go to Skills Handbook page 709.

Choose the metric unit of measure listed that you would use to estimate the given length or area.

18. the height of a telephone pole: mm, cm, m, km
19. the perimeter of a playground: mm, cm, m, km
20. the length of a nail: mm, cm, m, km
21. the area of a farmer's field: mm^2, cm^2, m^2, km^2

Estimate each length in inches. (1 in.)

22.
23.
24.
25.

C Challenge

26. **Geography** Estimate the area of Florida. Each square represents 5,575 mi^2.

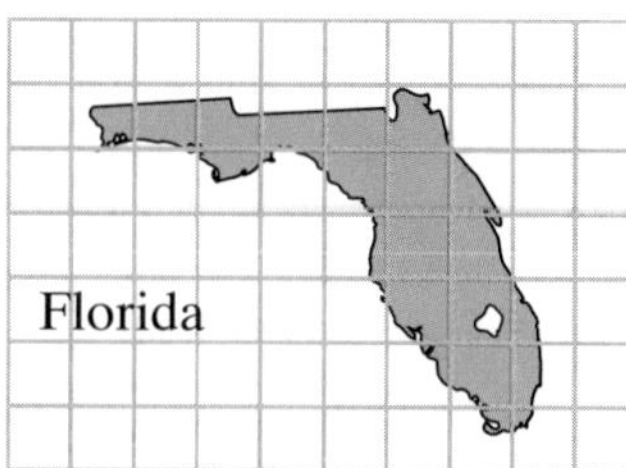

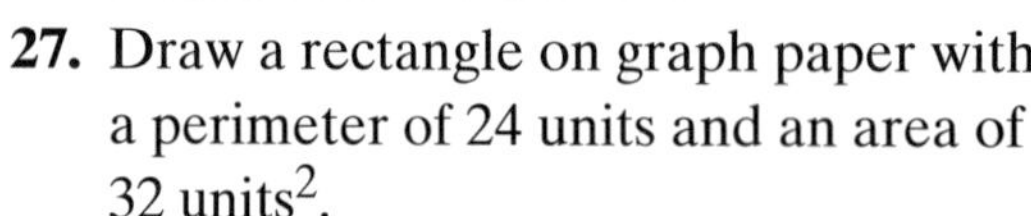

27. Draw a rectangle on graph paper with a perimeter of 24 units and an area of 32 $units^2$.

28. **Stretch Your Thinking** Jena, Sally, Jack, and Gary have seats next to each other at a school play. Jack sits next to Sally but not next to Gary. Gary is not sitting next to Jena. Who is sitting next to Jena?

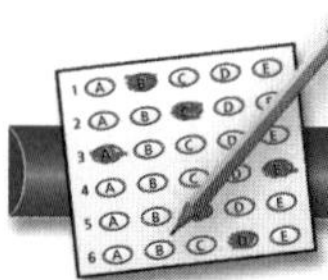

Test Prep

Reading Comprehension **Read the passage and answer the questions below.**

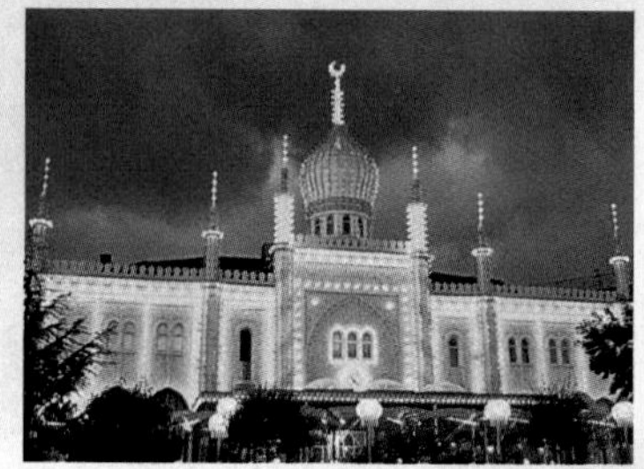

A Tale of Inspiration

Tivoli Gardens in Copenhagen, Denmark, was founded in 1833 and is the world's oldest amusement park. The park covers about 20 acres and has 25 attractions.

The park features animated scenes from Hans Christian Andersen's fairy tales. After visiting in the 1950s, Walt Disney began his plans for Disneyland.

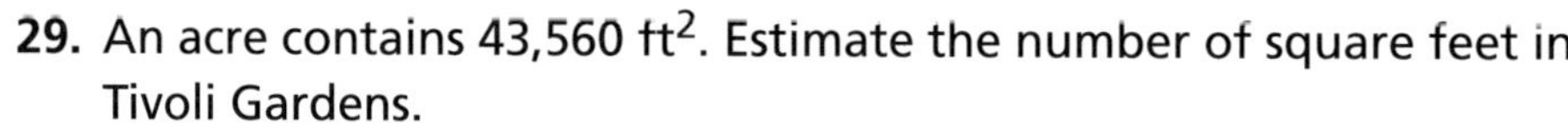

29. An acre contains 43,560 ft^2. Estimate the number of square feet in Tivoli Gardens.

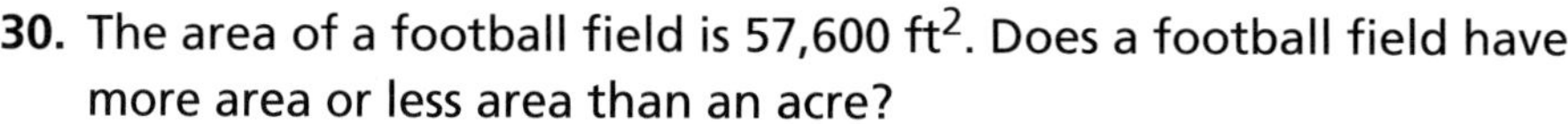

30. The area of a football field is 57,600 ft^2. Does a football field have more area or less area than an acre?

Take It to the NET
Online lesson quiz at
www.PHSchool.com
Web Code: aba-0801

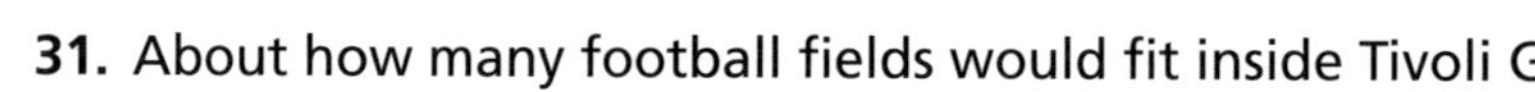

31. About how many football fields would fit inside Tivoli Gardens?

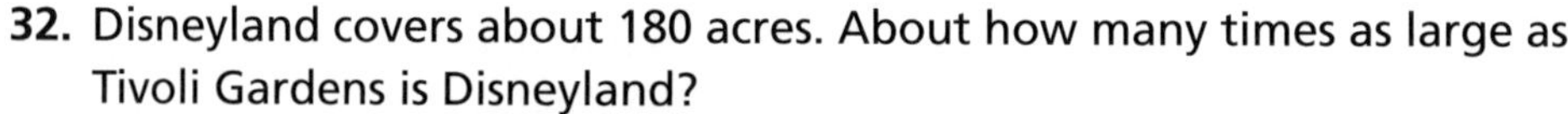

32. Disneyland covers about 180 acres. About how many times as large as Tivoli Gardens is Disneyland?

Mixed Review

Lesson 6-8

Algebra **Find each percent of increase or decrease. Round to the nearest tenth.**

33. 20 to 50
34. 32 to 8
35. 99 to 55
36. 75 to 110
37. 60 to 24
38. 45 to 135

Lesson 5-5

Algebra **Solve each proportion using mental math.**

39. $\frac{m}{35} = \frac{4}{5}$
40. $\frac{55}{99} = \frac{5}{x}$
41. $\frac{9}{p} = \frac{180}{200}$

8-2 Areas of Parallelograms and Triangles

What You'll Learn

 To find the area of a parallelogram

 To find the area of a triangle

. . . And Why

To find the area of a quilt piece, as in Example 3

Check Skills You'll Need

For help, go to Lesson 4-4.

Find each product.

1. $\frac{1}{2} \cdot 12$
2. $20 \cdot \frac{1}{2}$
3. $\frac{1}{2} \cdot 4$
4. $\frac{1}{2} \cdot 16$
5. $15 \cdot \frac{1}{2}$
6. $\frac{1}{2} \cdot 9$

New Vocabulary • height of a parallelogram • base of a parallelogram • base of a triangle • height of a triangle

OBJECTIVE

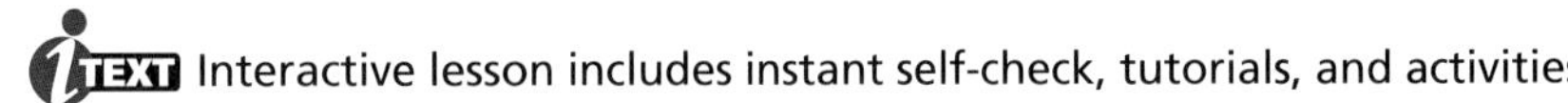

Interactive lesson includes instant self-check, tutorials, and activities.

1 Finding the Area of a Parallelogram

Investigation: Area of a Parallelogram

1. Using graph paper, draw a parallelogram like the one at the right. What figures are formed by the perpendicular segment?

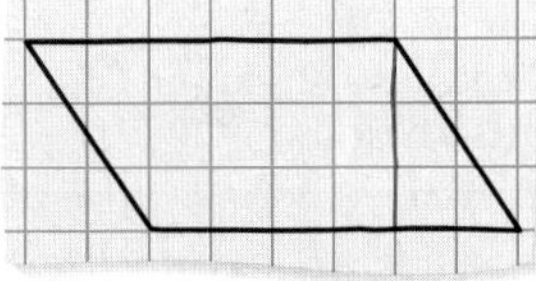

2. Cut out the parallelogram and then cut along the perpendicular segment. Rearrange the pieces to form a rectangle.
   a. What is the area of the rectangle?
   b. What was the area of the parallelogram?

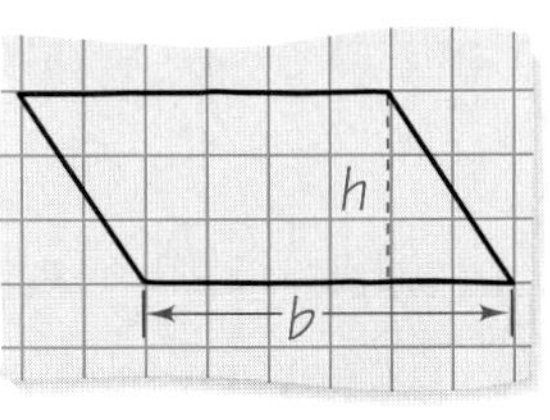

3. **Reasoning** How do b and h relate to the length and width of the rectangle?

Need Help?
A parallelogram is a quadrilateral with parallel opposite sides.

The **height of a parallelogram** is the perpendicular distance from one **base of a parallelogram** to the other.

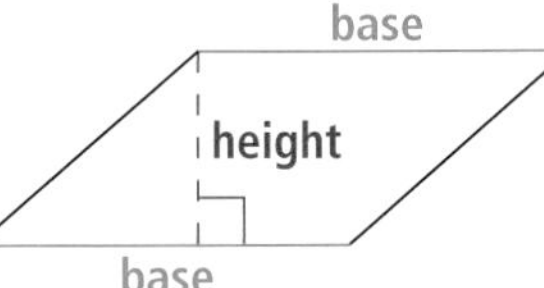

A rectangle is a special kind of parallelogram. The diagram below relates the formula for the area of a parallelogram to the formula for the area of a rectangle.

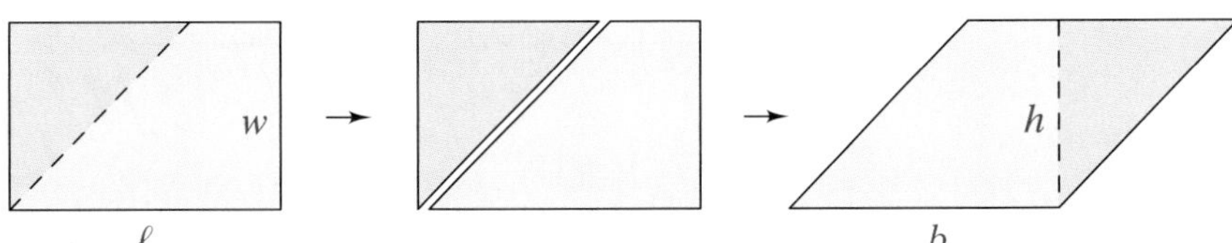

Area of a rectangle = ℓw　　**Area of a parallelogram = bh**

Key Concepts — Area of a Parallelogram

The area of a parallelogram is equal to the product of any base b and the corresponding height h.

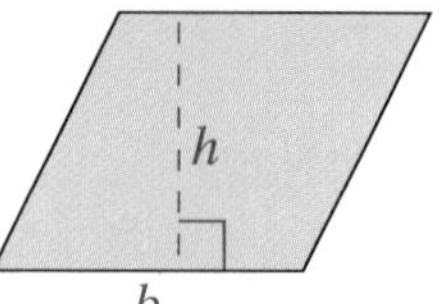

$\leftarrow A = bh \rightarrow$

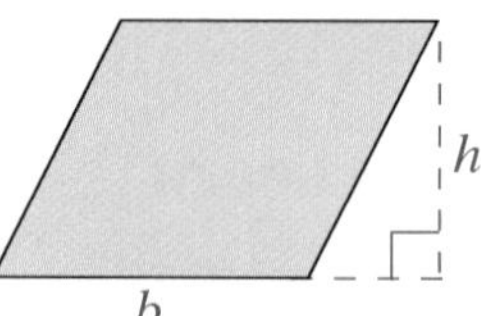

1 EXAMPLE Finding Areas of Parallelograms

Find the area of each parallelogram.

a.

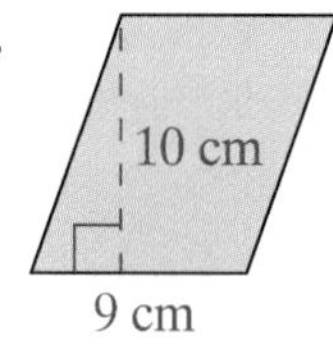

b.

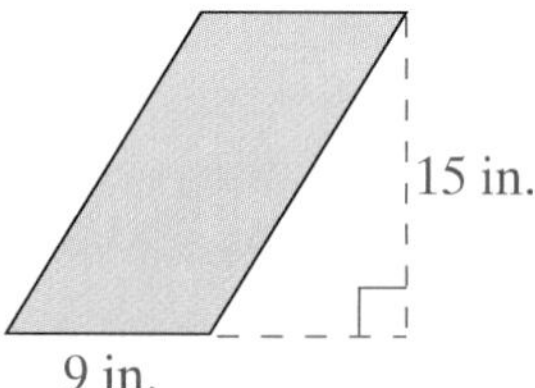

a.		b.
$A = bh$	← **Use the area formula.** →	$A = bh$
$= (9)(10)$	← **Substitute.** →	$= (9)(15)$
$= 90$	← **Simplify.** →	$= 135$

The area is 90 cm^2.

The area is 135 $in.^2$.

Need Help?
Areas are always in square units.

Check Understanding 1 Find the area of each parallelogram.

a.

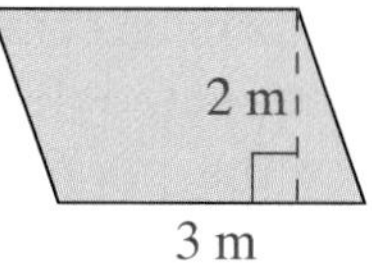

b.

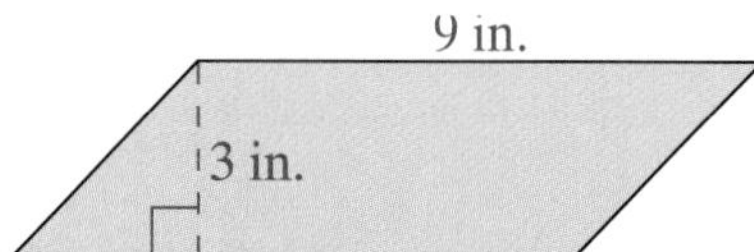

OBJECTIVE

2 Finding the Area of a Triangle

Any side of a triangle can be considered the **base of a triangle.** The **height of a triangle** is the length of the perpendicular segment from a vertex to the base opposite the vertex.

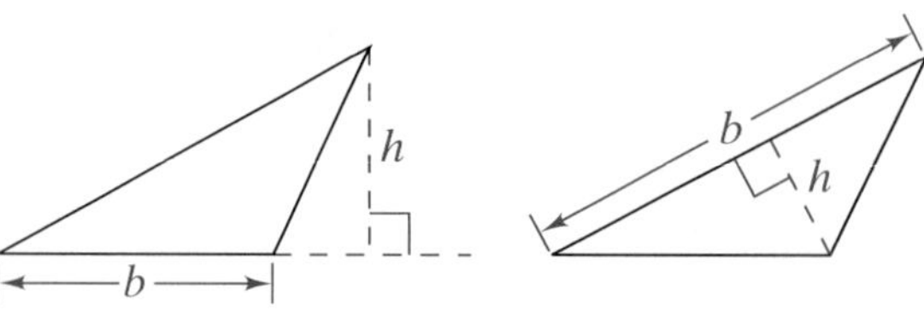

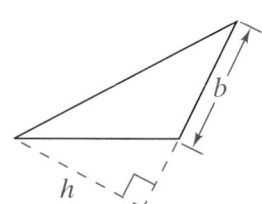

In the obtuse triangles on the left and right above, the base is extended so the height can be measured.

The formula for the area of a triangle follows from the area of a parallelogram.

The area of a parallelogram = *bh*. ↓

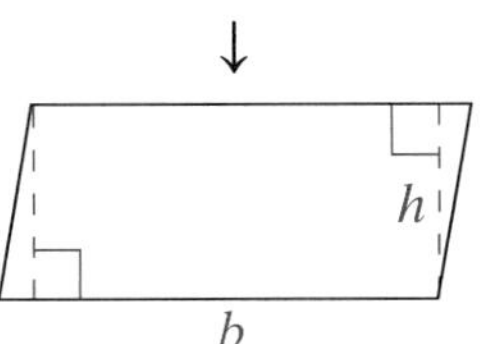

Draw one diagonal. ↓

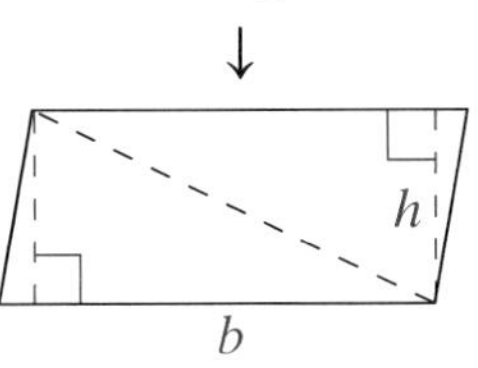

Break the parallelogram into two triangles. ↓

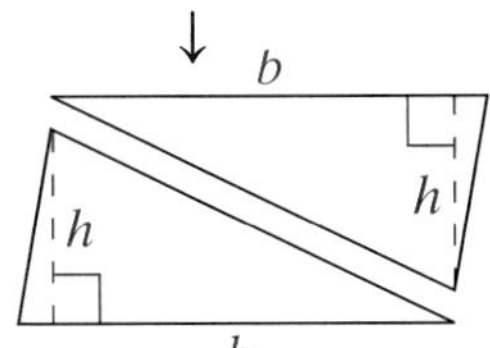

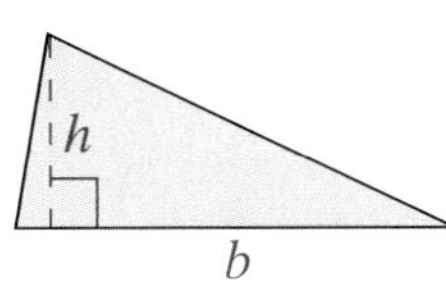

← **The area of a triangle is half the area of a parallelogram.**

Key Concepts — Area of a Triangle

The area of a triangle is equal to half the product of any base and the corresponding height.

$$A = \frac{1}{2}bh$$

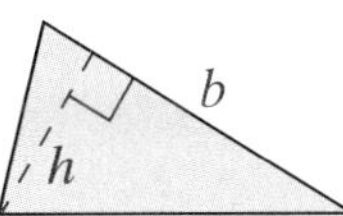

Need Help?
Perpendicular segments intersect to form right angles.

When finding the area of a triangle, remember that the height must be perpendicular to the base. Sometimes you are given more information than you need to solve the problem.

2 EXAMPLE Finding Areas of Triangles

Find the area of each triangle.

a.

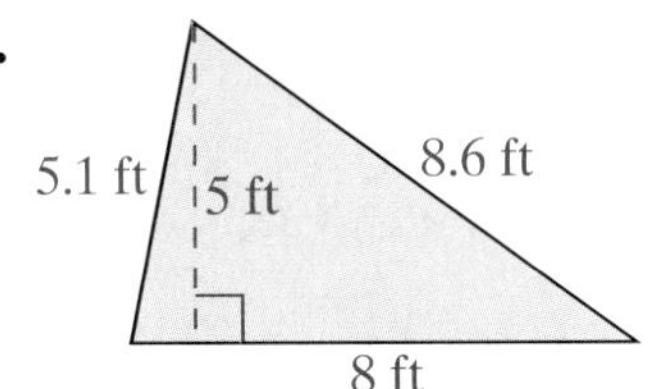

b.

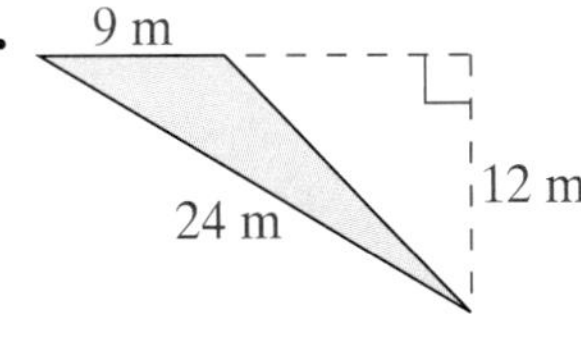

a.
$A = \frac{1}{2}bh$ ← **Use the area formula.** →
$= \frac{1}{2}(8)(5)$ ← **Substitute.** →
$= 20$ ← **Simplify.** →

The area is 20 ft^2.

b.
$A = \frac{1}{2}bh$
$= \frac{1}{2}(9)(12)$
$= 54$

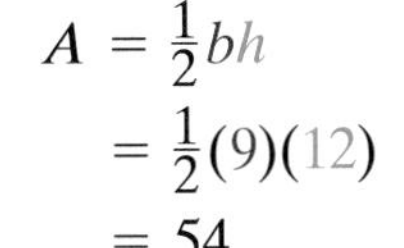

The area is 54 m^2.

✔ Check Understanding 2 Find the area of each triangle.

a.

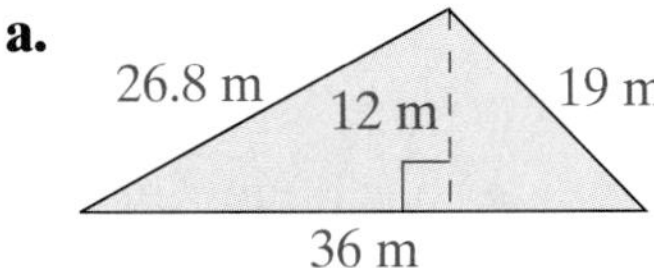

b.

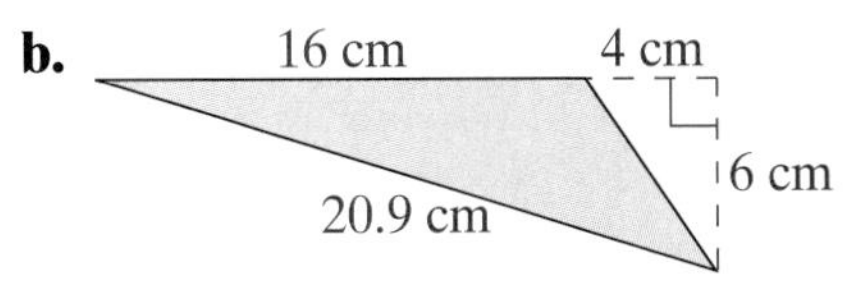

3 EXAMPLE Real-World Problem Solving

Quilting How much fabric do you need for each triangular piece of fabric on the quilt?

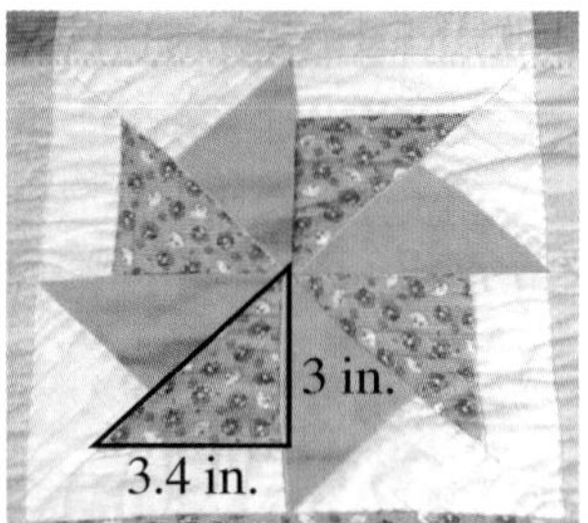

$A = \frac{1}{2}bh$ ← Use the area formula.

$= \frac{1}{2}(3.4)(3)$ ← Substitute.

$= 5.1$ ← Simplify.

You need 5.1 in.^2 of fabric.

Check Understanding 3 **Mental Math** How much fabric do you need for a triangular quilt piece with a base of 5 cm and a height of 6 cm?

EXERCISES

A Practice by Example

Example 1 (page 408)

Find the area of each parallelogram. Exercise 1 has been started for you.

1.

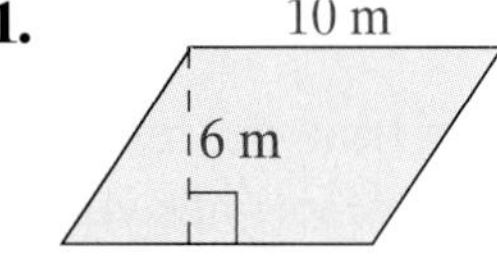

$A = bh = (10)(6)$

2. 5 m; 5 m

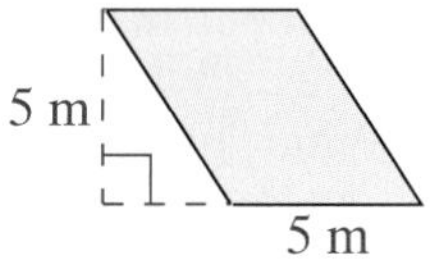

3.

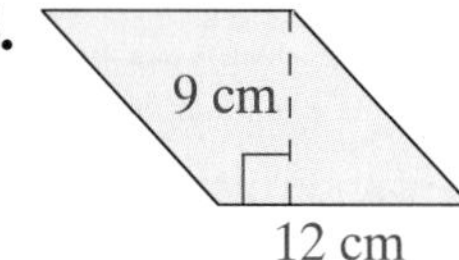

4.

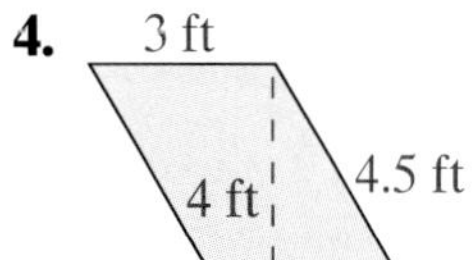

5.

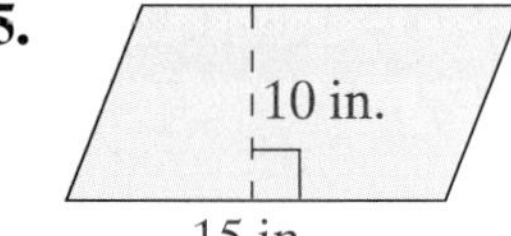

6.

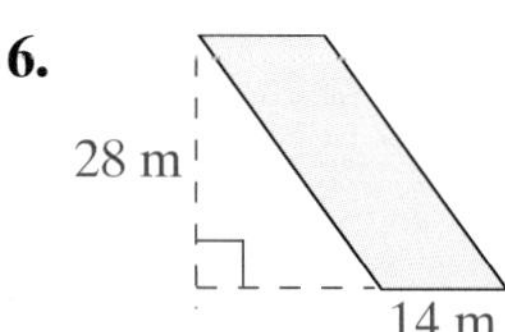

Example 2 (page 409)

Find the area of each triangle. Exercise 7 has been started for you.

7. 8 cm; 14 cm

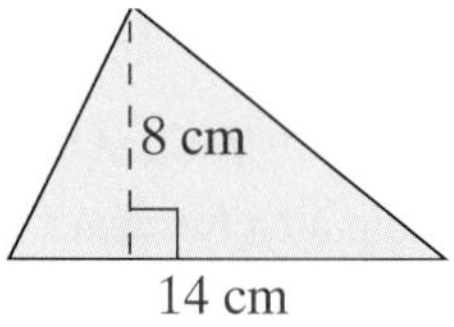

$A = \frac{1}{2}bh = \frac{1}{2}(14)(8)$

8.

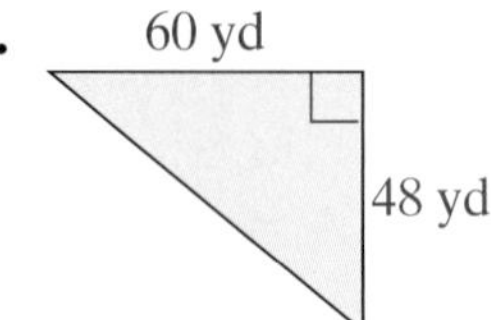

9.

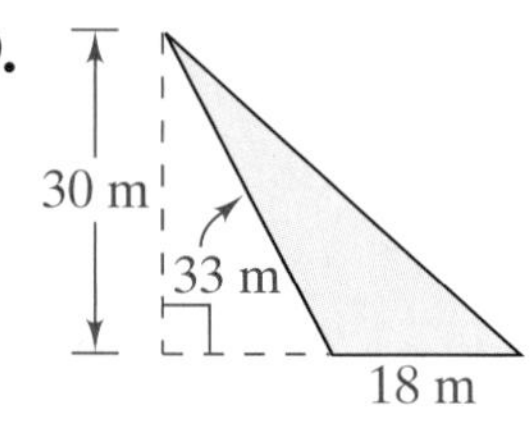

10. 12 km; 26.8 km; 12 km

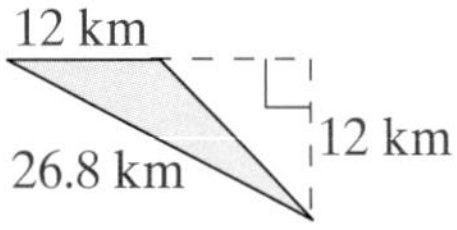

11.

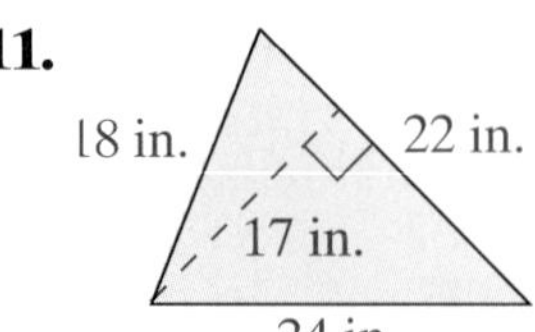

12. 28 m; 21 m; 35 m

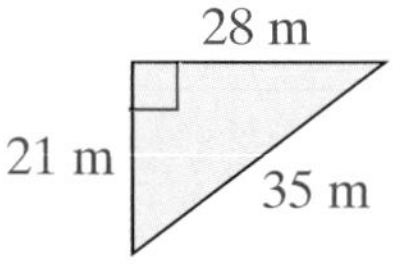

Example 3 (page 410)

13. Carpentry A carpenter has blueprints for a wooden triangular patio. The base is 5 m and the height is 7 m. What is the area of the patio?

14. **Conservation** A conservation group plans to buy a triangular plot of land. Use the diagram below. What is the area of the plot of land?

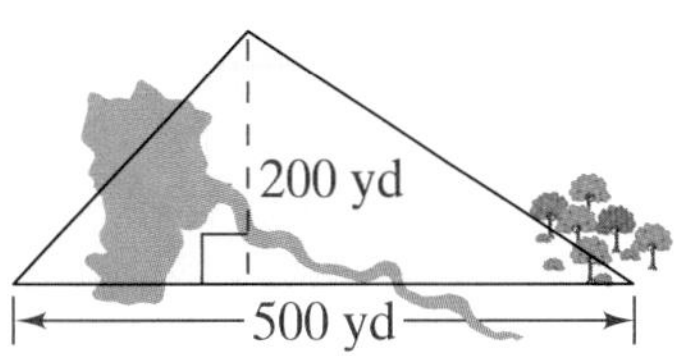

B Apply Your Skills

Find each area for base b and height h of a parallelogram.

15. $b = 14$ in. $h = 6$ in.

16. $b = 25$ mi $h = 25$ mi

17. $h = 40$ cm $b = 0.5$ cm

18. $h = 1{,}000$ m $b = 20$ m

Find each area for base b and height h of a triangle.

19. $b = 4$ in. $h = 6$ in.

20. $b = 12$ m $h = 17$ m

21. $h = 6.2$ ft $b = 2.5$ ft

22. $h = 100$ km $b = 200$ km

23. **Geography** The shape of the state of Tennessee is similar to a parallelogram. Estimate the area of Tennessee.

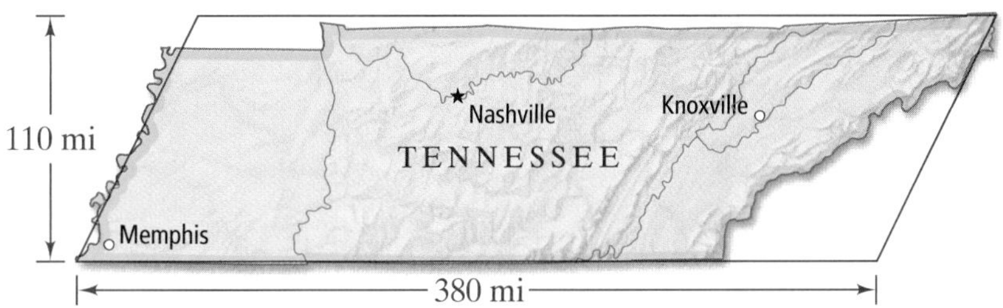

24. **Reasoning** The rectangle and the parallelogram at the right have the same perimeter. Why is the area of the rectangle greater than the area of the parallelogram?

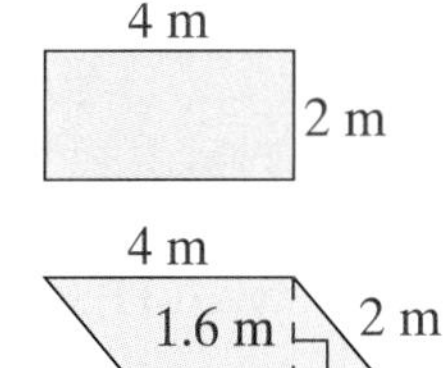

25. **Writing in Math** The base of a triangle is doubled and the height remains the same. How does the area change? Explain using examples.

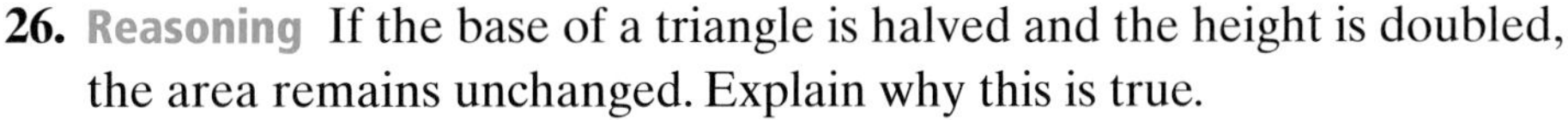

26. **Reasoning** If the base of a triangle is halved and the height is doubled, the area remains unchanged. Explain why this is true.

Real-World Connection

Careers Rescue swimmer is one of the jobs offered in the coast guard.

27. **Rescue** A coast guard rescue helicopter receives a distress call from a ship out at sea. The diagram at the right displays the search pattern the helicopter will use. Each pass from a central point forms an equilateral triangle. What is the area of one of the triangular regions?

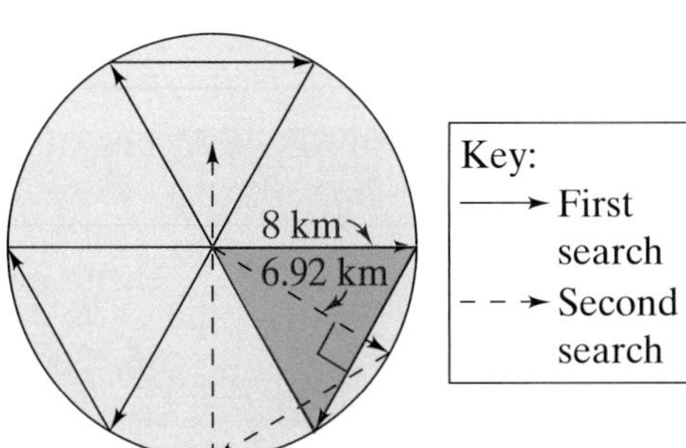

28. a. Copy and complete the table by finding the perimeter and area of each rectangle.

ℓ	w	P	A
3 in.	1 in.	■	■
6 in.	2 in.	■	■
9 in.	3 in.	■	■
12 in.	4 in.	■	■

b. **Number Sense** What happens to the perimeter of a rectangle when you double, triple, or quadruple the dimensions?

c. **Number Sense** What happens to the area of a rectangle when you double, triple, or quadruple the dimensions?

C Challenge

29. Find the area and perimeter of the figure at the right.

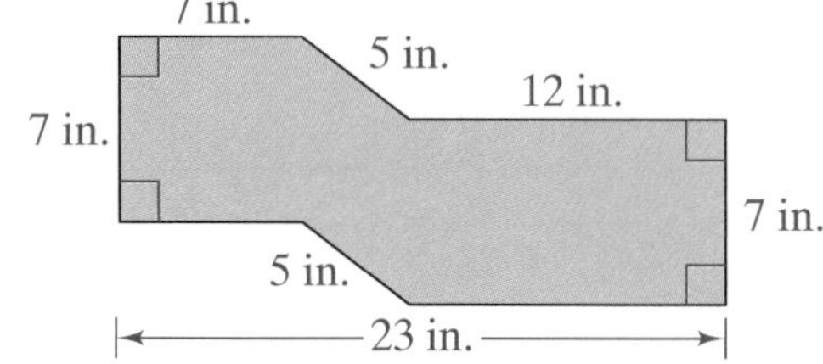

30. **Reasoning** The bases of two parallelograms are the same length. The height of the first parallelogram is half the height of the second. What is the ratio of the area of the first parallelogram to the area of the second? Justify your answer.

31. **Stretch Your Thinking** The area of an isosceles right triangle is 72 ft^2. What is the length of the two equal sides?

Test Prep

Multiple Choice

32. What is the area of a triangle with base 10 cm and height 25 cm?
A. 35 cm^2 **B.** 62.5 cm^2 **C.** 125 cm^2 **D.** 250 cm^2

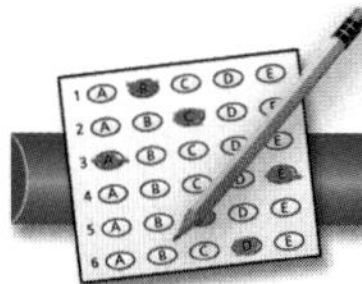

Take It to the NET
Online lesson quiz at **www.PHSchool.com**
Web Code: aba-0802

33. What is the area of a parallelogram with base 30 ft and height 25 ft?
F. 55 ft^2 **G.** 187.5 ft^2 **H.** 375 ft^2 **I.** 750 ft^2

34. Square *MNOP* has perimeter *x* ft. What is its area in terms of *x*?
A. $\frac{x^2}{16}$ **B.** $4x^2$ **C.** $\frac{x^2}{4}$ **D.** $\frac{x}{16}$

Short Response

35. A triangular lot in a state park has a base of 4 mi and a height of 6 mi **(a)** If the base and height are doubled, what is the area of the new lot? **(b)** By how many times will the area increase?

Mixed Review

Lesson 6-3

Write each percent as a decimal and as a fraction in simplest form.

36. 200% **37.** 135% **38.** 152% **39.** 0.03% **40.** 0.45%

Lesson 4-2

Find each sum.

41. $\frac{2}{7} + \frac{4}{21}$ **42.** $\frac{7}{9} + \frac{1}{3}$ **43.** $\frac{3}{10} + \frac{3}{15}$ **44.** $\frac{1}{10} + \frac{3}{4}$

8-3 Areas of Other Figures

What You'll Learn

To find the area of a trapezoid

To find the areas of irregular figures

. . . And Why

To estimate the area of a state, as in Example 1

For help, go to Lesson 8-2.

Find the area of each figure.

1.

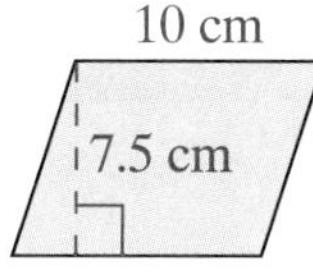

2.

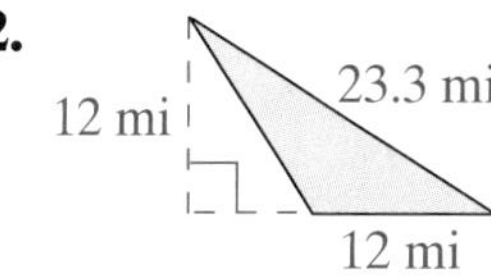

3.

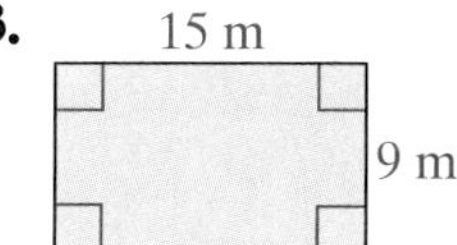

New Vocabulary • **bases of a trapezoid** • **height of a trapezoid**

OBJECTIVE 1

Interactive lesson includes instant self-check, tutorials, and activities.

Finding the Area of a Trapezoid

Need Help?
A trapezoid is a quadrilateral that has exactly one pair of parallel sides.

- Fold a piece of lined paper in half along one of the lines.
- On one side, draw two segments of different lengths on two of the lines.
- Connect the endpoints of the segments to form a trapezoid.
- Cut out the trapezoid, cutting through both layers of the folded paper. You now have two congruent trapezoids.
- Label bases b_1 and b_2 and height h for each trapezoid.
- Arrange the trapezoids to form a parallelogram.

1. a. Write an expression for the length of the base of the parallelogram.
   b. Write an expression for the area of the parallelogram using b_2, b_1, and h.
2. **Reasoning** How does the area of each trapezoid compare to the area of the parallelogram?
3. Write a formula for the area of a trapezoid.

The formula for the area of a trapezoid follows from the formula for the area of a parallelogram.

The two parallel sides of a trapezoid are the **bases** with lengths b_1 and b_2. The **height** h is the length of a perpendicular segment connecting the bases.

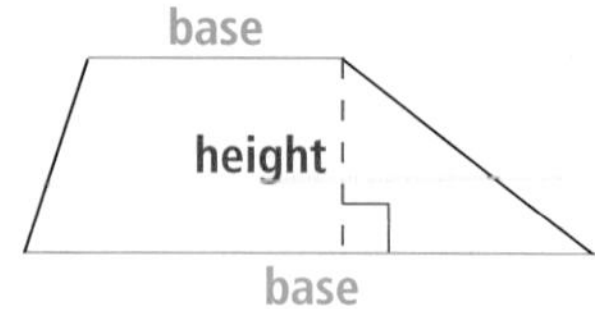

Reading Math

Read b_1 as "base 1" and b_2 as "base 2."

If you put two identical trapezoids together, you get a parallelogram. The area of the parallelogram is $(b_1 + b_2)h$. The area of one trapezoid equals $\frac{1}{2}(b_1 + b_2)h$.

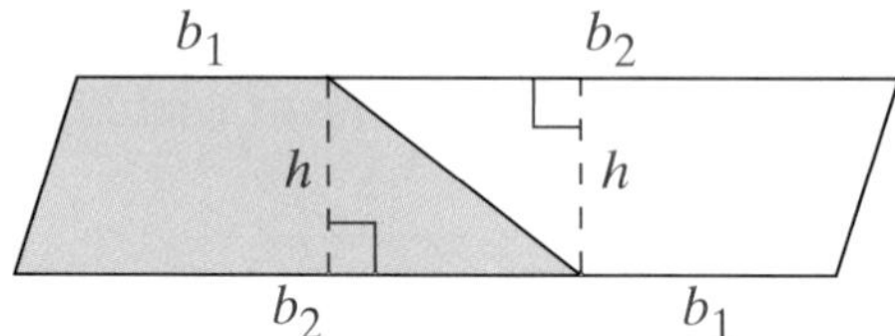

Key Concepts **Area of a Trapezoid**

The area of a trapezoid is one half the product of the height and the sum of the lengths of the bases.

$$A = \frac{1}{2}h(b_1 + b_2)$$

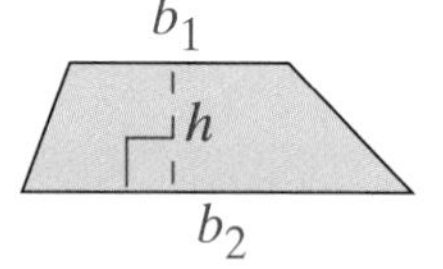

Real-World Connection

At Crater of Diamonds State Park in Arkansas, visitors can search for and keep diamonds and other gems.

You can estimate the area of states shaped like trapezoids.

1 EXAMPLE Finding the Area of a Trapezoid

Real World

Geography Estimate the area of Arkansas by finding the area of the trapezoid shown.

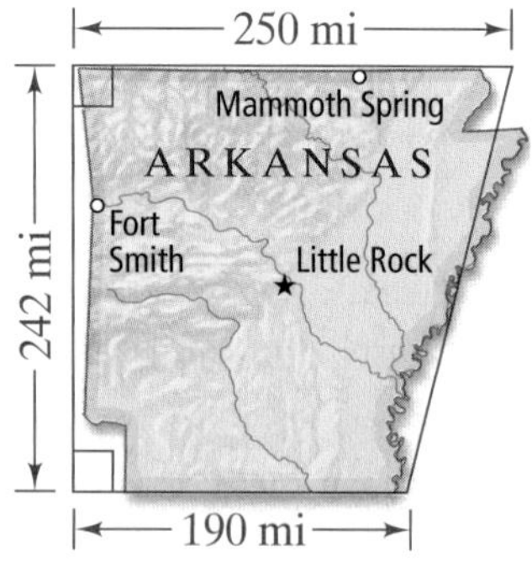

$A = \frac{1}{2}h(b_1 + b_2)$ ← **Use the area formula for a trapezoid.**

$= \frac{1}{2}(242)(250 + 190)$ ← **Substitute for h, b_1, and b_2.**

$= \frac{1}{2}(242)(440)$ ← **Add.**

$= 53{,}240$ ← **Multiply.**

The area of Arkansas is about 53,240 mi^2.

Check Understanding 1 Find the area of each trapezoid.

a.

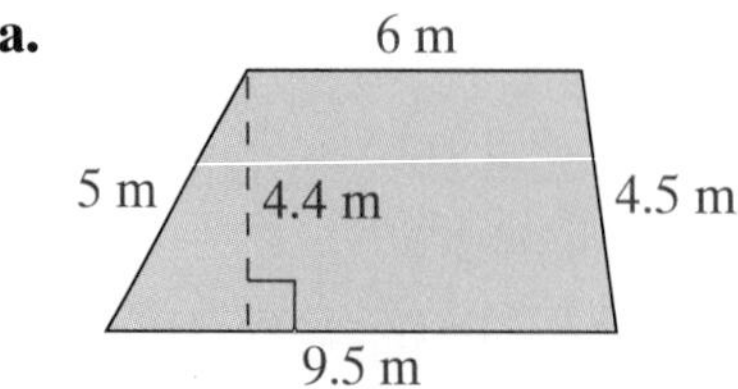

b.

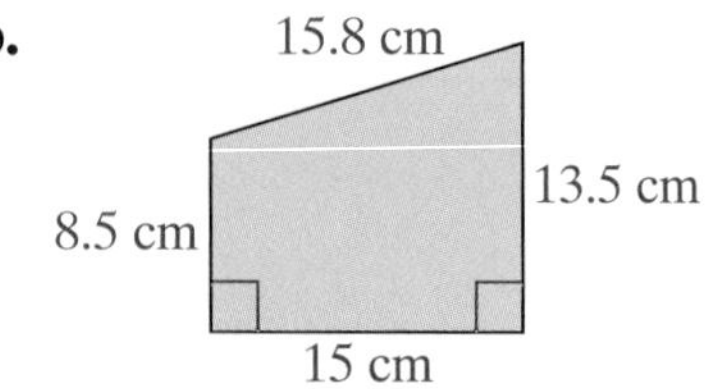

c. **Reasoning** How can you find the area of a trapezoid without using the formula for the area of a trapezoid?

OBJECTIVE 2

Finding the Areas of Irregular Figures

You can find the area of an irregular figure by separating it into familiar figures, finding the area of each piece, and adding the areas together.

2 EXAMPLE Finding the Area of an Irregular Figure

Find the area of the irregular figure.

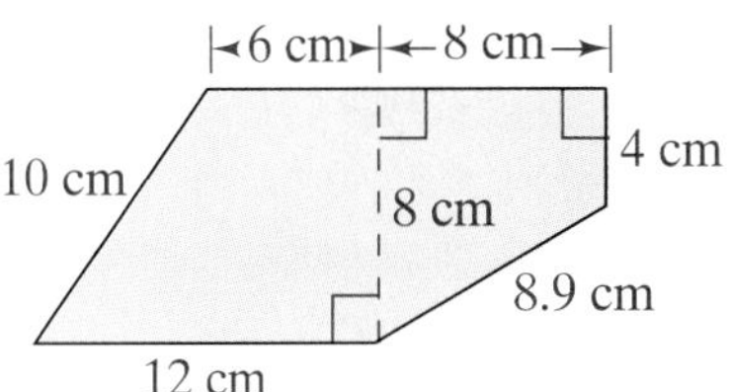

Step 1 Separate the irregular figure into familiar figures.

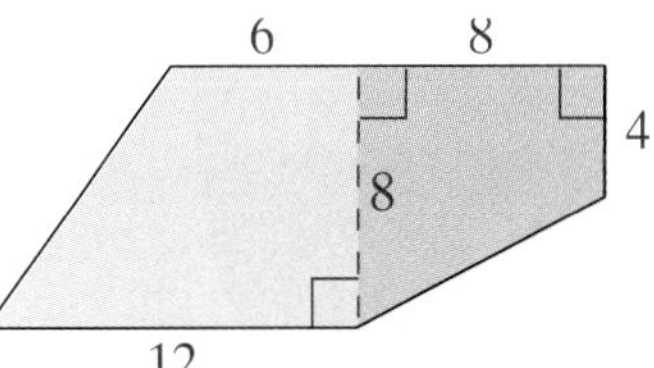

Step 2 Find the area of each smaller figure.

Area of the blue trapezoid:

$A = \frac{1}{2}h(b_1 + b_2)$ ← **Use the area formula for a trapezoid.**

$= \frac{1}{2}(8)(6 + 12)$ ← **Substitute for h, b_1, and b_2.**

$= \frac{1}{2}(8)(18)$ ← **Add.**

$= 72$ ← **Multiply.**

Area of the green trapezoid:

$A = \frac{1}{2}h(b_1 + b_2)$ ← **Use the area formula for a trapezoid.**

$= \frac{1}{2}(8)(4 + 8)$ ← **Substitute for h, b_1, and b_2.**

$= \frac{1}{2}(8)(12)$ ← **Add.**

$= 48$ ← **Multiply.**

Step 3 Add to find the total area.

$72 + 48 = 120$

The area of the irregular figure is 120 cm^2.

Check Understanding 2 Find the area of the irregular figure.

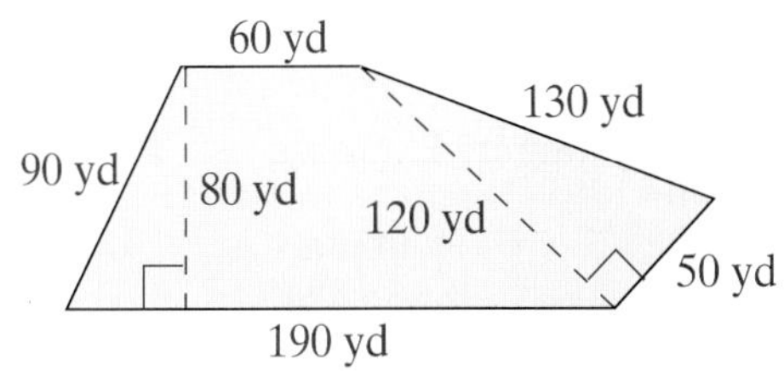

More Than One Way

Anna and Ryan are helping their friends build a large wooden deck. What is the area of the deck?

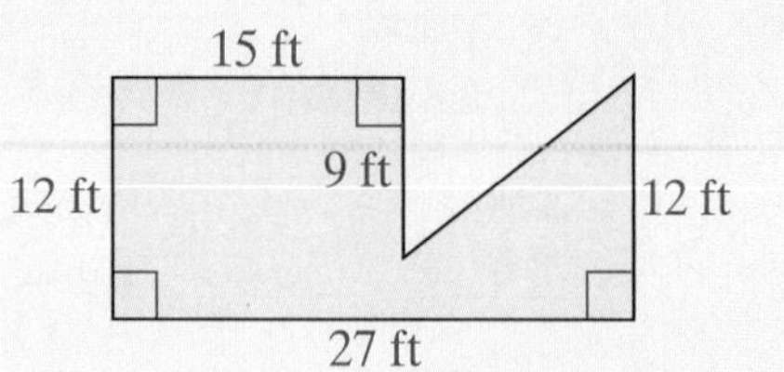

Anna's Method

I'll subtract the area of the triangle from the area of the rectangle.

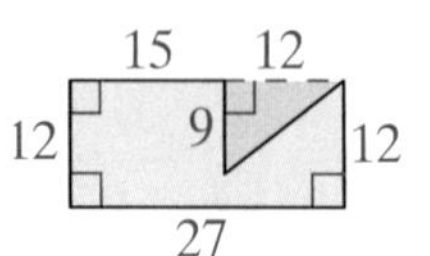

Area of the rectangle:

$A = bh$

$= (27)(12) = 324$

Area of the triangle:

$A = \frac{1}{2}bh$

$= \frac{1}{2}(12)(9) = 54$

$A = 324 - 54 = 270$

The area of the deck is 270 ft^2.

Ryan's Method

I'll add the areas of the rectangle and the trapezoid.

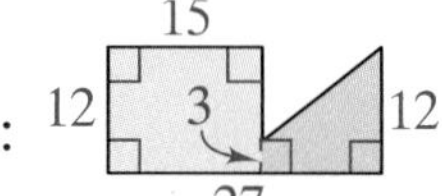

Area of the rectangle:

$A = bh$

$= (15)(12)$

$= 180$

Area of the trapezoid:

$A = \frac{1}{2}h(b_1 + b_2)$

$= \frac{1}{2}(12)(3 + 12)$

$= 90$

$A = 180 + 90 = 270$

The area of the deck is 270 ft^2.

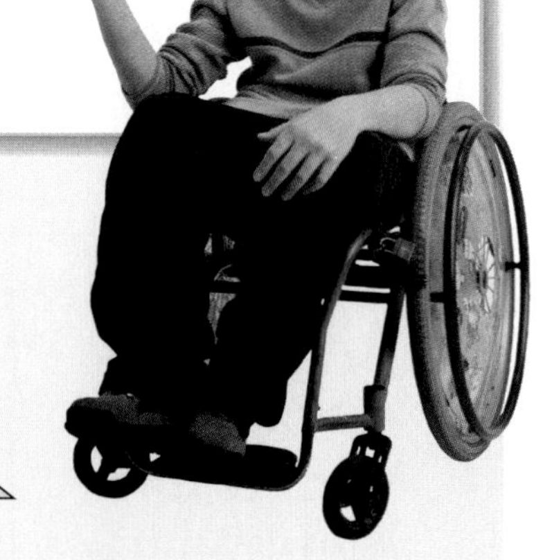

Choose a Method

Find the area of the figure.

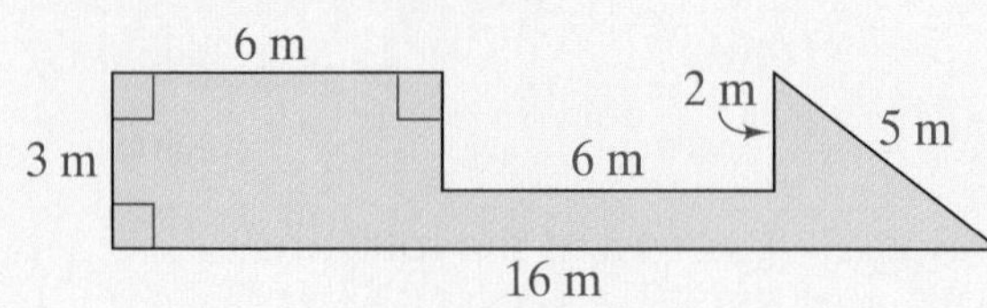

EXERCISES

For more practice, see *Extra Practice.*

A Practice by Example

Example 1 (page 414)

Find the area of each trapezoid.

1.

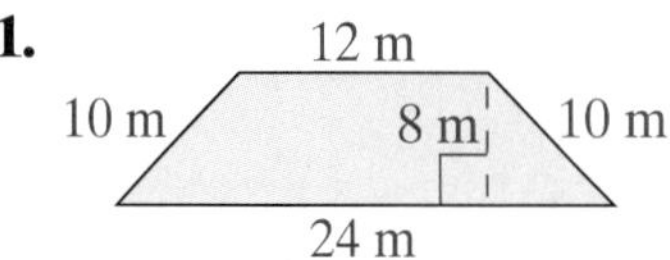

2.

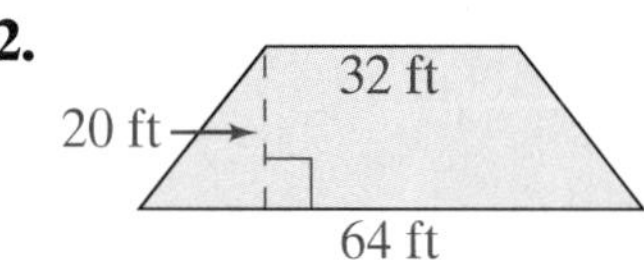

3. **Geography** Estimate the area of Nevada by finding the area of the trapezoid shown at the right.

4. **Engineering** When the Erie Canal opened in 1825, it was hailed as an engineering marvel. Find the area of the trapezoidal cross section of the Erie Canal below.

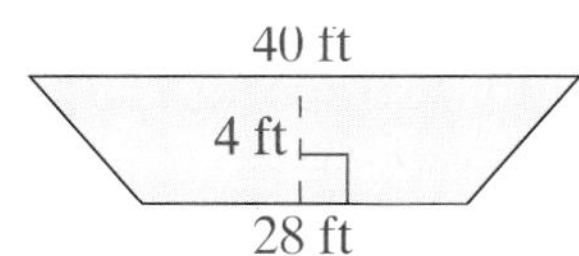

Example 2 (page 415)

Use familiar figures to find the area of each irregular figure.

5.

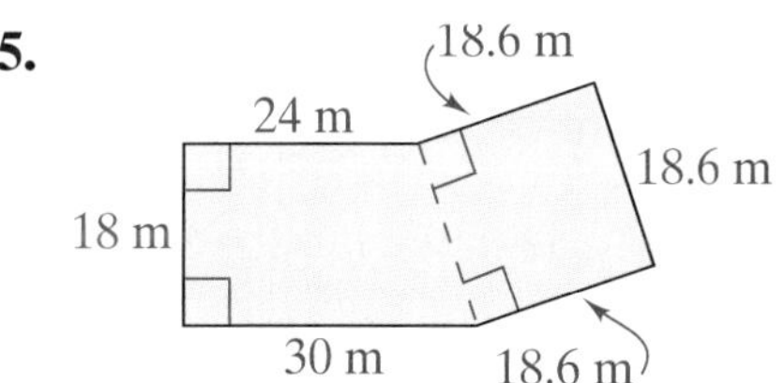

6.

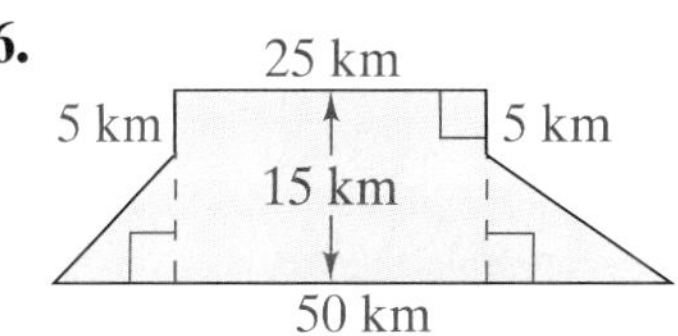

7.

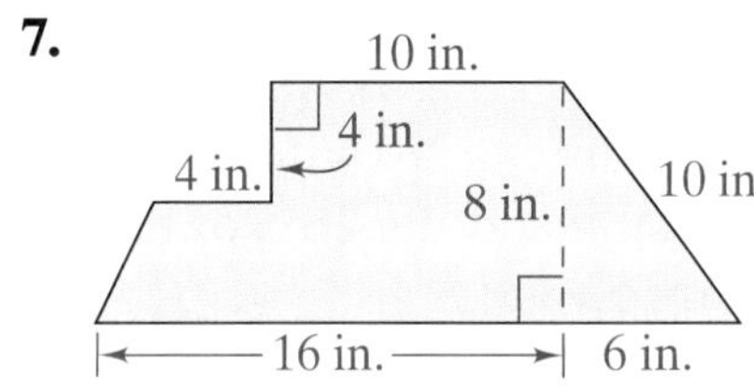

8.

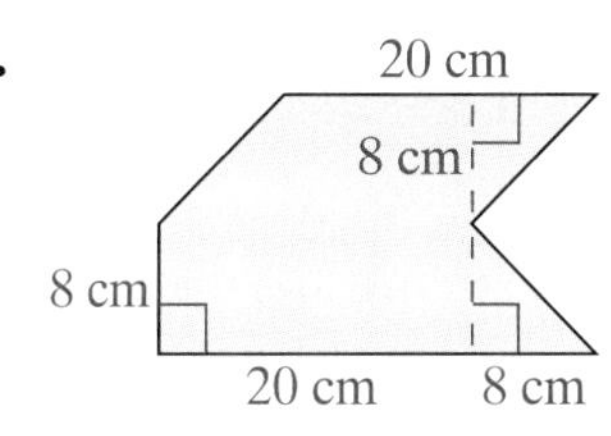

9.

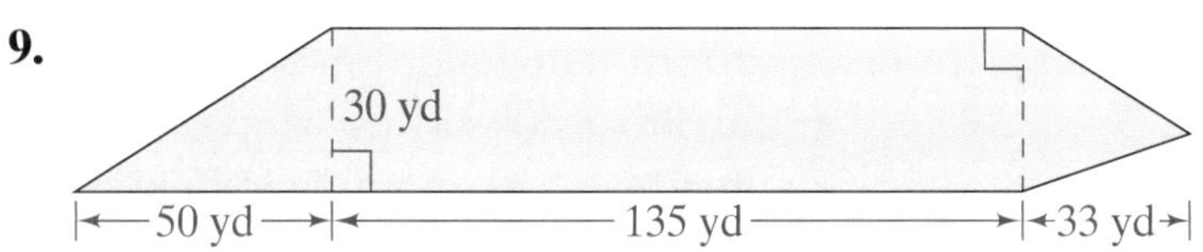

B Apply Your Skills

Find the area of each trapezoid given the bases b_1 and b_2 and height h.

10. $b_1 = 3$ m, $b_2 = 7$ m, $h = 3$ m

11. $b_1 = 11$ in., $b_2 = 16$ in., $h = 9$ in.

12. $b_1 = 5.6$ cm, $b_2 = 8.5$ cm, $h = 6$ cm

13. $b_1 = 3\frac{1}{2}$ ft, $b_2 = 2\frac{1}{4}$ ft, $h = 2$ ft

14. **Music** A hammered dulcimer is shaped like a trapezoid. The top edge is 17 in. long, and the bottom edge is 39 in. long. The distance from the top edge to the bottom edge is 16 in. What is the area of the dulcimer?

15. **Interior Design** You plan to replace the carpeting in the room shown at the right. What is the area of the room?

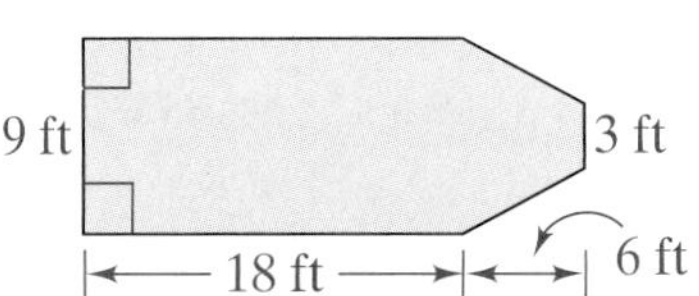

16. a. What are the whole-number possibilities for the lengths of its bases if a trapezoid has an area of 3 m^2 and a height of 1 m?

b. **Writing in Math** Explain how you found the lengths in part (a).

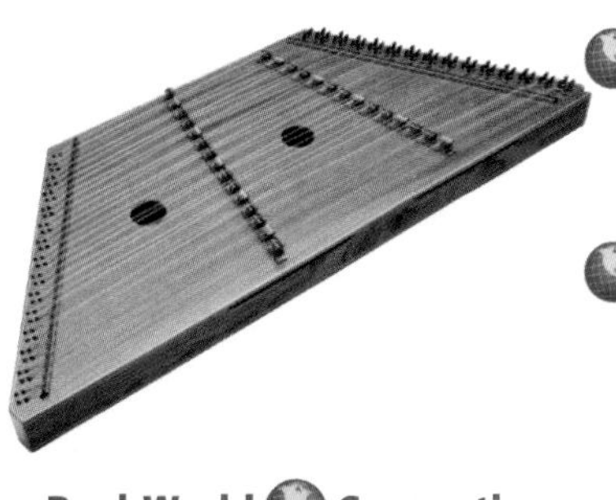

Real-World Connection

You play the hammered dulcimer by striking the strings with small hammers.

Use familiar figures to find the area and perimeter of each figure.

17.

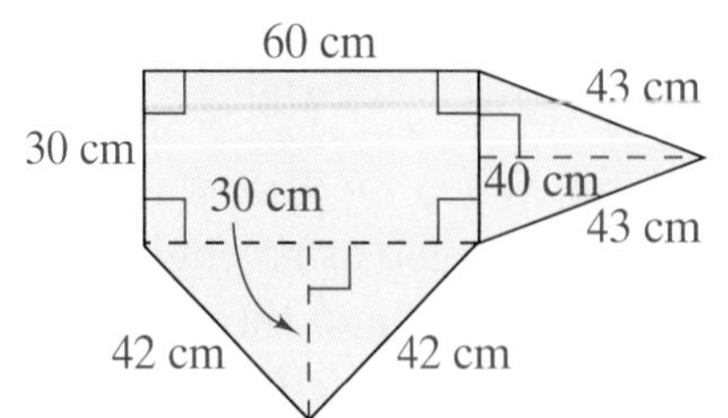

18.

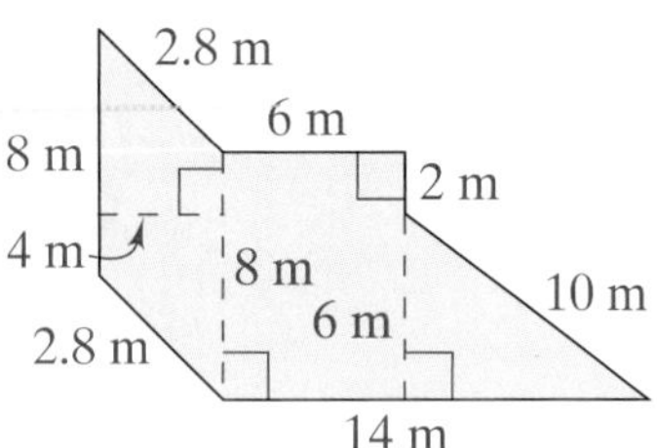

C Challenge

19. **Algebra** A trapezoid has an area of 184 in.^{2}. The height is 8 in. and one base is 16 in. Write and solve an equation to find the length of the other base of the trapezoid.

20. **Stretch Your Thinking** One of the players on the Fairview High School football team tells his friend that all of the numbers on the football jerseys are prime numbers less than 100. What is the greatest number of players that can be on the team?

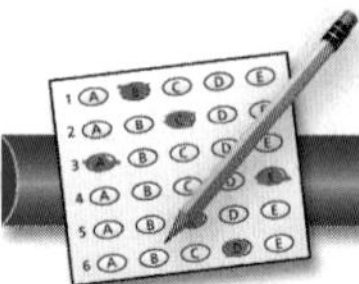

Test Prep

Gridded Response

21. What is the difference in square feet between the area of the international free-throw lane and the area of the NBA free-throw lane?

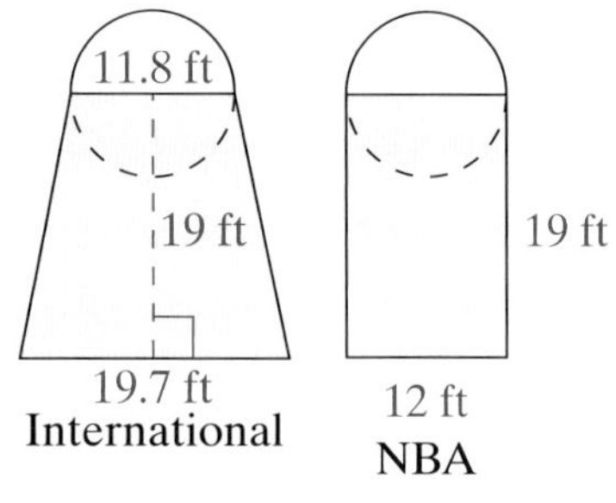

22. A trapezoid has bases that measure 8 ft and 11 ft. The height measures 14 ft. If the dimensions of the trapezoid are doubled, by how many times will the area increase?

23. What is the area, in square meters, of the figure at the right?

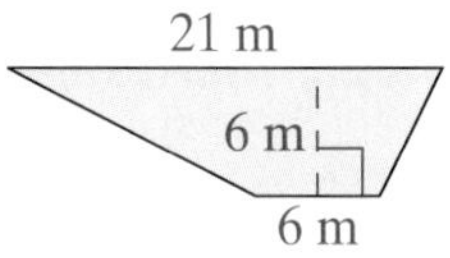

21 m

6 m

6 m

Take It to the NET
Online lesson quiz at **www.PHSchool.com**
Web Code: aba-0803

24. A homeowner is building a trapezoidal brick patio and needs to determine its total area. The bases measure 14 ft and 20 ft. The distance between the bases is 12 ft. What is the area of the patio in square feet?

Mixed Review

Lesson 6-7 **Find each payment.**

25. \$453 with a 6% sales tax

26. \$49.95 with a 5.5% sales tax

Lesson 4-6 **Algebra** **Solve each equation.**

27. $\frac{1}{5}x - 3 = 8$

28. $10 = \frac{m}{7} + 3$

29. $\frac{n}{9} - 5 = -3$

8-4 Circumferences and Areas of Circles

What You'll Learn

To find the circumference of a circle

To find the area of a circle

. . . And Why

To find areas of circus rings, as in Example 3

Check Skills You'll Need

For help, go to Lesson 3-1.

Simplify.

1. 1^2 **2.** 9^2 **3.** 11^2

4. $2 \cdot 3^2$ **5.** $4 \cdot 6^2$ **6.** $5 \cdot 8^2$

New Vocabulary • circumference • pi

Interactive lesson includes instant self-check, tutorials, and activities.

OBJECTIVE 1 Finding the Circumference of a Circle

In the picture below, a Sacagawea dollar rolls on end in stages until it makes one complete revolution. The distance the dollar rolls is the same as the distance around the edge of the dollar. This distance is the dollar's circumference. **Circumference** is the distance around a circle.

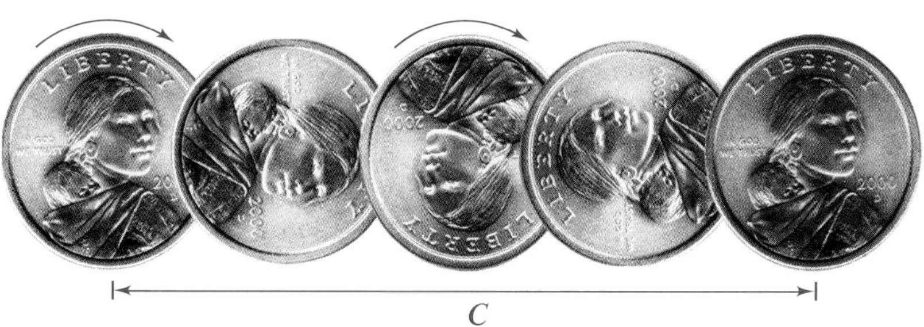

Pi is the ratio of a circle's circumference C to its diameter d. Use the symbol π for this ratio. So, $\pi = \frac{C}{d}$. The formula for the circumference comes from this ratio.

Need Help?

$d = 2r$

$r = \frac{d}{2}$

Key Concepts **Circumference of a Circle**

The circumference of a circle is π times the diameter.

$$C = \pi d = 2\pi r$$

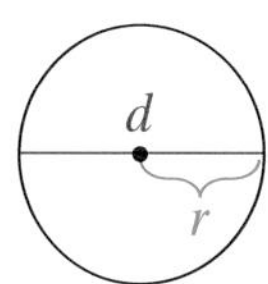

Pi is a nonterminating and nonrepeating decimal. Both $\frac{22}{7}$ and 3.14 are good approximations for π. Many calculators have a key for π and display it to nine decimal places. Your results will vary slightly, depending on which value for π you use.

1 EXAMPLE Finding the Circumference of a Circle

a. Find the circumference of the circle using 3.14 for π.

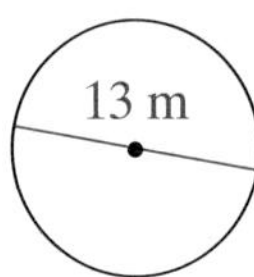

b. Find the circumference of the circle using a calculator's π key.

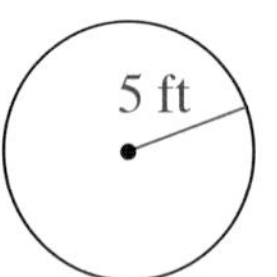

a.		b.
$C = \pi d$	← Use the formula for circumference →	$C = 2\pi r$
$\approx 3.14(13)$	← Substitute. →	$= 2\pi(5)$
$= 40.82$	Use a calculator. →	$\approx$ 31.41592654

The circumference is approximately 40.8 m.

The circumference is approximately 31.4 ft.

Check Understanding 1 Find the circumference of each circle. Round to the nearest tenth.

a.

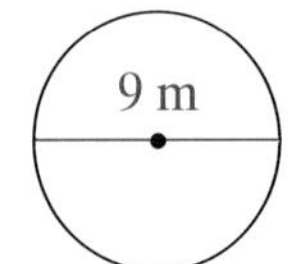

b.

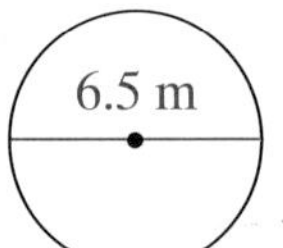

c.

OBJECTIVE

2 Finding the Area of a Circle

Investigation: Relating the Area of a Circle to the Radius

Answer Questions 1–3 for each circle. Then answer Question 4.

a.

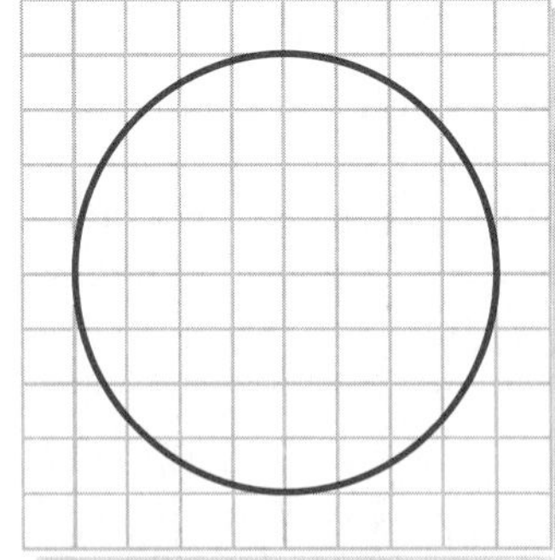

b.

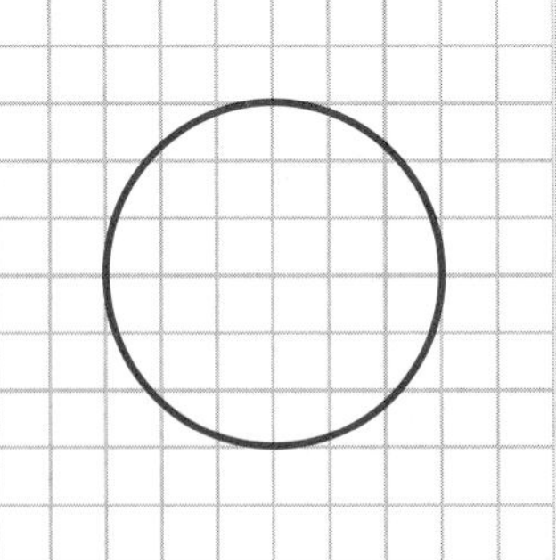

1. What is the radius?
2. Estimate the area of the circle.
3. Use a calculator to find the ratio $\frac{A}{r^2}$.
4. **Writing in Math** Write a conjecture relating the area of a circle to the square of its radius.

The ratio of every circle's area A to the square of its radius r is always the same. In fact, the quotient equals π. So $\frac{A}{r^2} = \pi$.

Key Concepts **Area of a Circle**

The area of a circle is the product of π and the square of the radius r.

$$A = \pi r^2$$

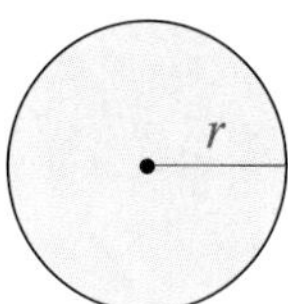

2 EXAMPLE Finding the Area of a Circle

Find the area of the circle to the nearest unit.

11.5 cm

$A = \pi r^2$ ← **Use the formula for the area of a circle.**

$= \pi(11.5)^2$ ← **Substitute 11.5 for the radius.**

$= 415.47562$ ← **Use a calculator.**

≈ 415 ← **Round to the nearest unit.**

The area of the circle is about 415 cm^2.

2 Find the area of each circle. Round to the nearest unit.

a. 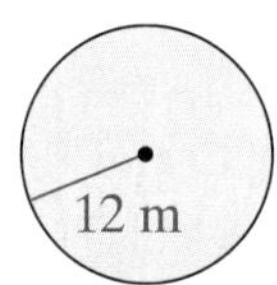

b. 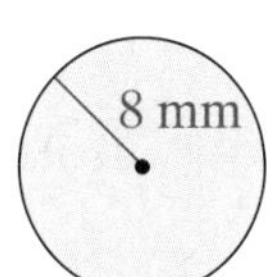

c. 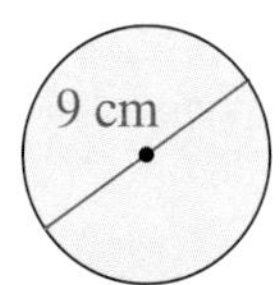

d. Reasoning Explain how you find the area of a circle if you know its diameter.

You can find the area of circles in real-world situations.

3 EXAMPLE Real-World Problem Solving

Circus A standard circus ring has a diameter of 13 m. What is the area of the ring? Round to the nearest tenth.

> **Reading Math**
> *Circus* is the Latin word for *circle*.

$r = \frac{13}{2} = 6.5$ ← **The radius is half of the diameter.**

$A = \pi r^2$ ← **Use the formula for the area of a circle.**

$= \pi(6.5)^2$ ← **Substitute 6.5 for the radius.**

$= 132.73228$ ← **Use a calculator.**

≈ 132.7 ← **Round to the nearest tenth.**

The area of a standard circus ring is approximately 132.7 m^2.

Check Understanding **3** The diameter of the center circle on a professional hockey rink is 30 ft. What is the area of the center circle? Round to the nearest tenth.

EXERCISES

For more practice, see *Extra Practice*.

Practice by Example

Example 1 (page 420)

Find the circumference of each circle. Round to the nearest tenth. Exercise 1 has been started for you.

1. 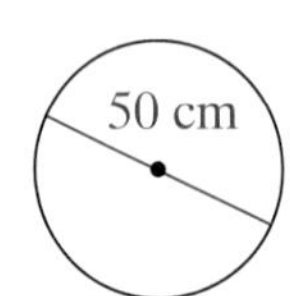

$C = \pi d = \pi(50)$

2. 17 mm

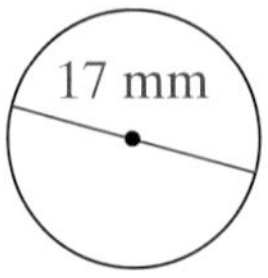

3. 27 m

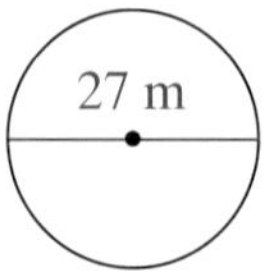

4. 40 in.

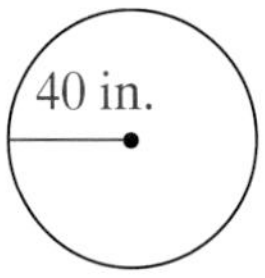

5. 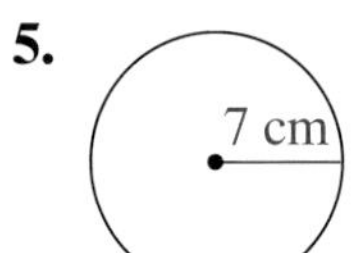

6. 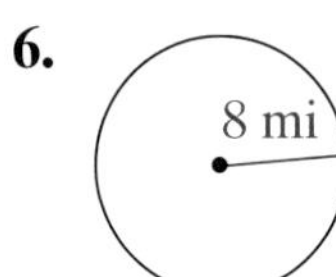

Example 2 (page 421)

Find the area of each circle. Round to the nearest unit.

7. 6 in.

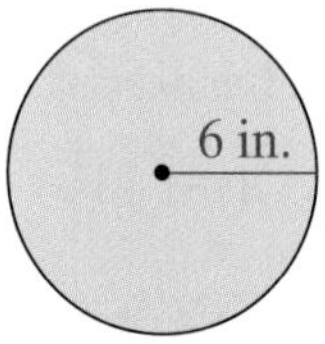

8. 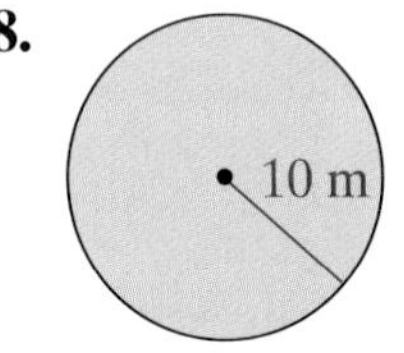

9. 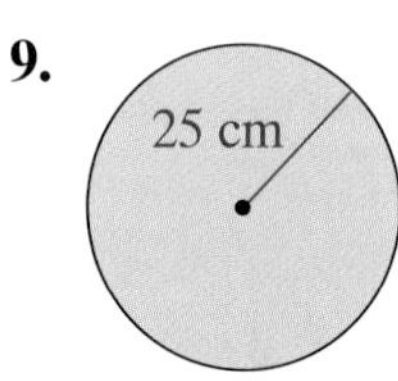

10. 3 yd

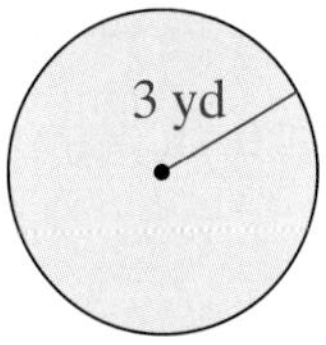

11. 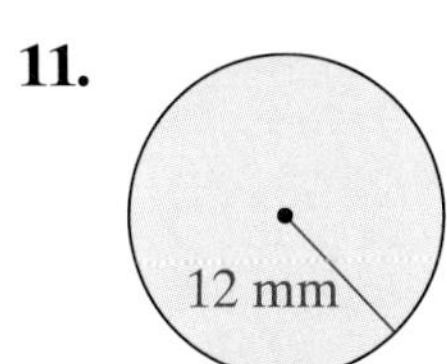

12. 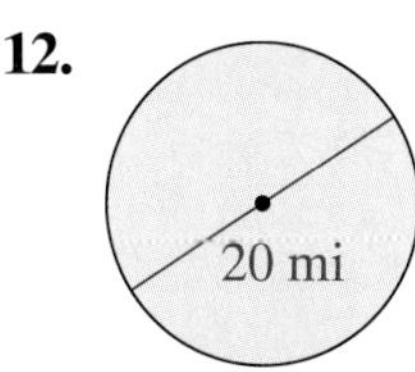

13. 30 ft

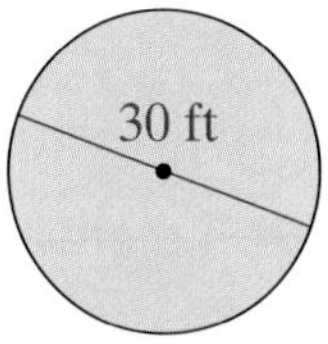

14. 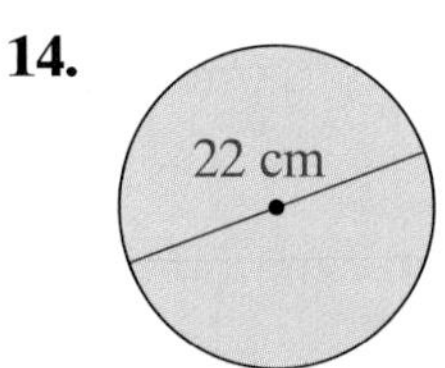

15. 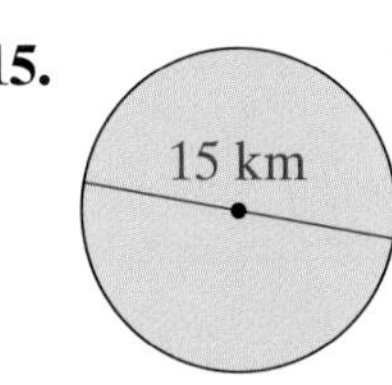

Example 3 (page 421)

16. Social Studies The circular base of the tipis of the Sioux and Cheyenne tribes have a diameter of about 15 ft. What is the area of the base? Round to the nearest unit.

17. a. Pools A circular pool has a diameter of 20 ft. You want to purchase a cover for the pool. What area needs to be covered? Round to the nearest foot.

b. The cover in part (a) is made with a diameter of 22 ft so it overhangs the pool. What is the area of the cover rounded to the nearest foot?

18. Technology Airport Surveillance Radar (ASR) tracks planes in a circular region around an airport. What is the area covered by the radar if the diameter of the circular region is 120 nautical miles? Round to the nearest unit.

B Apply Your Skills

19. **History** To celebrate the new millennium, the Millennium Ferris wheel was constructed in London, England. The diameter of the wheel is 135 m. What is the circumference? Round to the nearest unit.

Use $\pi \approx \frac{22}{7}$ to estimate the circumference and area for each circle. Where necessary, round to the nearest tenth.

20. $r = 14$ m
21. $r = \frac{7}{10}$ cm
22. $d = 22$ in.
23. $d = 12$ ft

Real-World Connection

Stonehenge was built about 3000–1600 BC near Salisbury, England. No one knows for sure the purpose of the site.

24. **Archaeology** The large stones of Stonehenge are arranged in a circle about 30 m in diameter. Find the area of the circle.

25. **Bicycles** The front wheel of a high-wheel bicycle from the late 1800s was larger than the rear wheel to increase the bicycle's overall speed. The front wheel measured in height up to 60 in. Find the circumference and area of the front wheel of a high-wheel bicycle.

26. **Reasoning** Which has a greater area—three circles each with a radius of 1 m, or one circle with a radius of 3 m? Explain.

Estimate the diameter of each circle with the given circumference.

27. $C = 31.4$ m
28. $C = 22$ mm
29. $C = 50$ ft
30. $C = 157$ in.
31. $C = 30.78$ m
32. $C = 78.5$ yd

33. a. Use the π key to calculate the area of the circle at the right to the nearest hundredth.
    b. Use 3.14 for π to calculate the area of the circle to the nearest hundredth.
    c.  **Writing in Math** Kenny says the area of the circle is about 99 m^2. Lynn says the area is about 98 m^2. Whose is the better estimate? Explain.

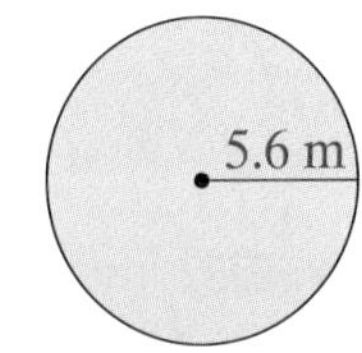

34. Estimate the area of the figure below to the nearest hundredth.

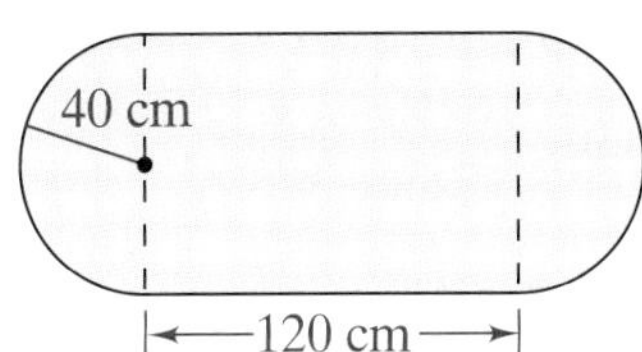

C Challenge

Find the area of each circle with the given circumference. Use $\frac{22}{7}$ for π.

35. $C = 22$ m
36. $C = 11$ ft
37. $C = 99$ in.

38. The diameter of the large circle at the right is 2.6 cm. The diameter of each small circle is 0.6 cm. Find the area of the shaded region to the nearest tenth of a centimeter.

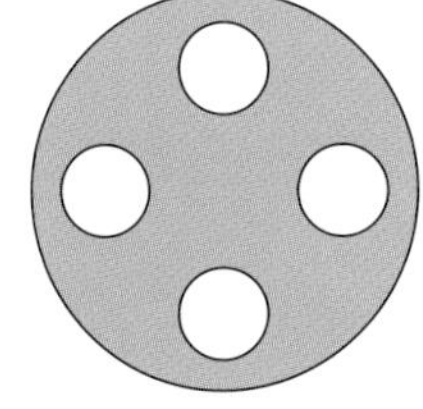

39. **Stretch Your Thinking** One fourth of one third is the same as one half of what fraction?

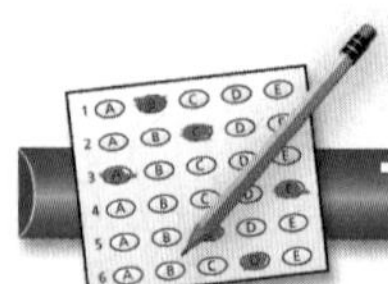

Test Prep

Multiple Choice

40. What is the area of a circle with a diameter of 6 m? Use 3.14 for π.
A. 18.84 m^2 **B.** 28.26 m^2 **C.** 37.68 m^2 **D.** 113.04 m^2

41. What is the circumference of a circle with a 16-yd radius? Use 3 for π.
F. 48 yd **G.** 96 yd **H.** 192 yd **I.** 768 yd

42. If you double the radius of a circle, what happens to the area?
A. It remains the same. **B.** It doubles.
C. It triples. **D.** It quadruples.

Take It to the NET
Online lesson quiz at
www.PHSchool.com
Web Code: aba-0804

Extended Response

43. The diameter of a small drum's surface is 5.5 in. Find the circumference and area of the drum to the nearest tenth. Show your work.

Mixed Review

Lesson 7-7

$\triangle CAT \cong \triangle DOG$. Complete each congruence statement.

44. $\angle A \cong$ ■ **45.** $\angle G \cong$ ■ **46.** $\overline{CT} \cong$ ■

Lesson 7-2

Find the measure of the supplement of each angle.

47. $m\angle A = 150°$ **48.** $m\angle B = 35°$ **49.** $m\angle C = 61°$

Checkpoint Quiz 1 — Lessons 8-1 through 8-4

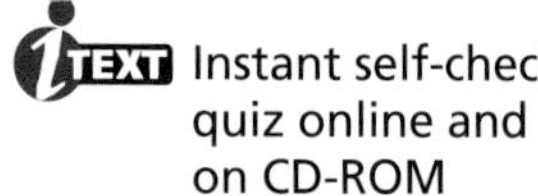

Instant self-check quiz online and on CD-ROM

Each square below represents 20 km^2. Estimate the area of each region.

1. 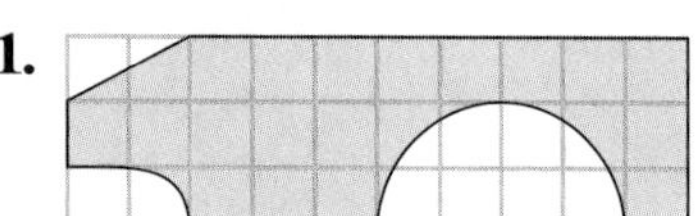

2. 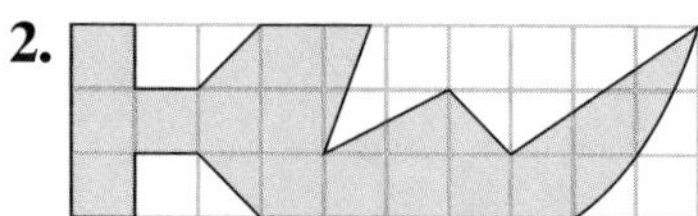

Find the area of each figure. Where necessary, use familiar figures.

3.

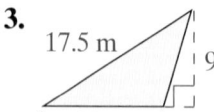

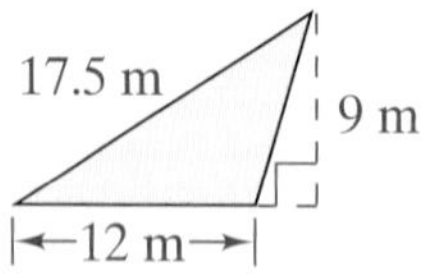

4. 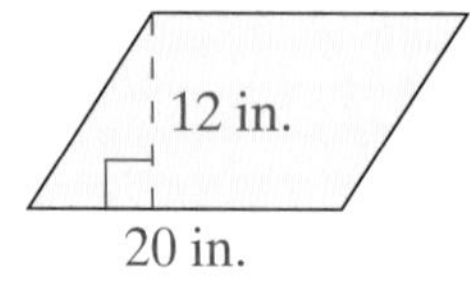

5. 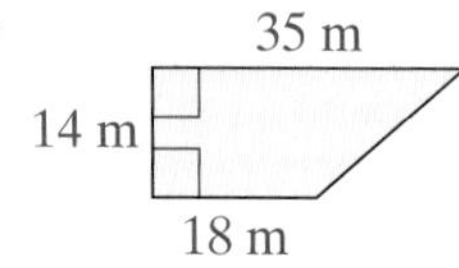

6. 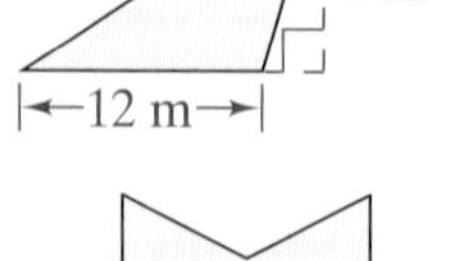

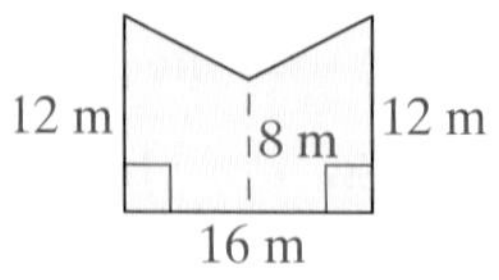

7. 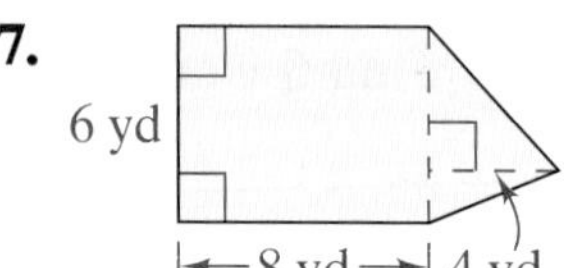

8. 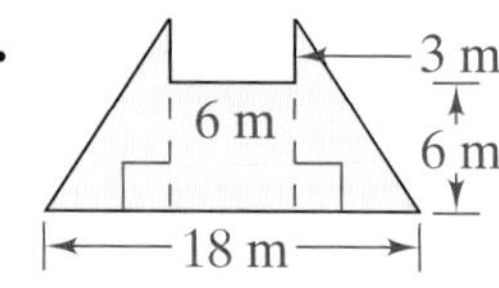

Find the circumference and area. Use 3.14 for π. Round to the nearest tenth.

9. 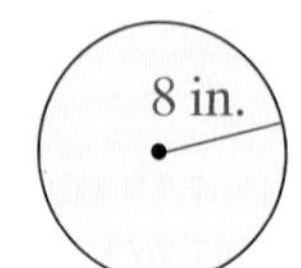

10. 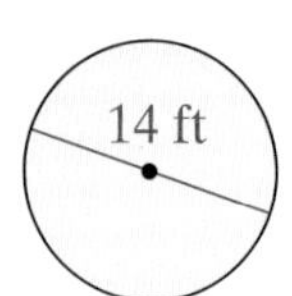

Making a Concept Map

For Use With Lesson 8-4

As you learn new concepts, it helps to think about how they connect to each other. One way to do this is to create a concept map. A concept map is a diagram with lines that connect related things.

Use the terms *parallelogram, polygon, quadrilateral, rectangle, rhombus, square,* and *trapezoid* to make a concept map.

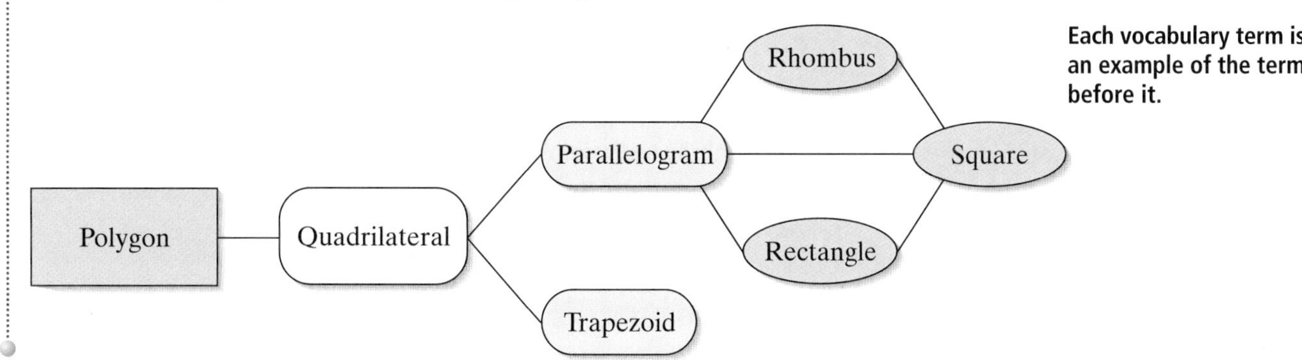

Each vocabulary term is an example of the term before it.

EXERCISES

1. Use the concept map above and the terms *pentagon, hexagon, octagon,* and *decagon* to make a larger concept map.
2. An incomplete concept map for *triangle* is below. Fill in the ovals using terms from the Chapter 7 vocabulary list on page 394.

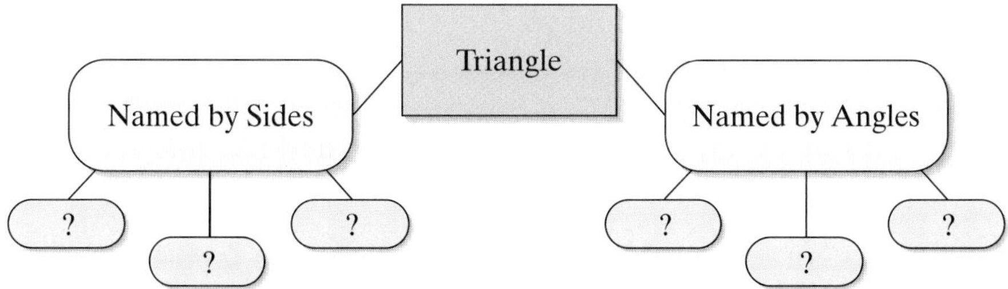

3. Use the list below to make a concept map for *area*.

parallelogram	trapezoid
height (parallelogram)	height (trapezoid)
base (parallelogram)	base_1
triangle	base_2
height (triangle)	circle
base (triangle)	radius

8-5 Square Roots and Irrational Numbers

What You'll Learn

To find square roots of numbers

To classify numbers

. . . And Why

To find the side length of a square pedestal, as in Example 3

Check Skills You'll Need

For help, go to Lesson 3-1.

Simplify.

1. 8^2
2. 12^2
3. 2^2
4. 7^2
5. 4^2
6. 5^2
7. Explain how to find the square of any number.

New Vocabulary • perfect square • square root • irrational number

Interactive lesson includes instant self-check, tutorials, and activities.

OBJECTIVE 1 Finding Square Roots

Investigation: Squares and Square Roots

Use tiles or grid paper to construct a square with an area of 25 units^2.

1. What is the length of each side of the square?

Attempt to construct squares with areas 16, 12, 9, and 4 square units.

2. a. Which of the areas can you construct?
   b. What is the length of each side of the squares that you can construct?
3. Which of the areas could you not construct? Explain why not.

A number that is the square of an integer is a **perfect square.** For example, the square of 2 is 4, so 4 is a perfect square.

The inverse of squaring a number is finding a **square root.** The symbol $\sqrt{}$ indicates the nonnegative square root of a number. The square roots in this book are the positive square roots of numbers.

Reading Math

Read $\sqrt{9}$ as "the square root of 9."

1 EXAMPLE Finding Square Roots of Perfect Squares

Simplify $\sqrt{49}$.

$\sqrt{49} = 7 \quad \leftarrow 49 = 7^2$

Check Understanding 1 Simplify $\sqrt{64}$.

2 EXAMPLE Applying Square Roots

Whirlpools The area of a square cover for a whirlpool is 144 ft^2. What is the length of each side of the cover?

$A = s^2$ ← Use the formula for the area of a square.

$144 = s^2$ ← Substitute 144 for the area.

$\sqrt{144} = \sqrt{s^2}$ ← Take the square root of each side.

$12 = s$ ← Simplify.

The length of each side of the square whirlpool cover is 12 ft.

Check Understanding 2 A square sheet of aluminum has an area of 36 ft^2. How long is each side of the aluminum sheet?

When a number is not a perfect square, you can estimate its square root.

$\sqrt{25}$ $\sqrt{33}$ $\sqrt{36}$ 5 6 ← $\sqrt{25} < \sqrt{33} < \sqrt{36}$

$\sqrt{33}$ is between 5 and 6.

Real-World Connection

Careers A sculptor models, carves, and fashions three-dimensional representations.

3 EXAMPLE Estimating Square Roots

Sculpting An artist plans to place her sculpture on a square pedestal in a local park. The pedestal has an area of 40 ft^2. Estimate the length of each side of the pedestal.

$A = s^2$ ← Use the formula for the area of a square.

$40 = s^2$ ← Substitute 40 for the area.

$\sqrt{40} = \sqrt{s^2}$ ← Take the square root of each side.

$\sqrt{40} = s$ ← Simplify.

$\sqrt{36} < \sqrt{40} < \sqrt{49}$ ← Find perfect squares close to 40.

$6 < \sqrt{40} < 7$ ← Simplify.

$\sqrt{40}$ is between 6 and 7. Since 40 is closer to 36 than it is to 49, $\sqrt{40} \approx 6$. Therefore, each side of the pedestal measures about 6 ft.

Check Understanding 3 **a.** Number Sense If the artist wants a pedestal with half the area above, should the artist make each side half as long? Explain.

b. Estimate the value of $\sqrt{70}$.

OBJECTIVE

2 Classifying Numbers

You learned in Lesson 3-10 that a rational number is the ratio of two integers $\frac{a}{b}$, where $b \neq 0$. Rational numbers in decimal form either terminate or repeat.

An **irrational number** is a number that cannot be written as a ratio of two integers. As decimals, irrational numbers neither terminate nor repeat.

This diagram summarizes the relationship among the numbers with which you are now familiar.

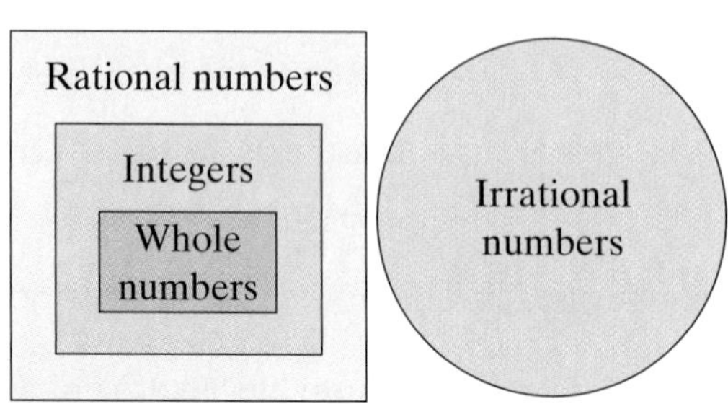

If a positive integer is not a perfect square, its square root is irrational.

Rational $\rightarrow \sqrt{4}, \sqrt{9}, \sqrt{16}$

Irrational $\rightarrow \sqrt{2}, \sqrt{3}, \sqrt{27}$

4 EXAMPLE Classifying Numbers

Identify each number as rational or irrational.

a. $\sqrt{14}$ irrational ← **14 is not a perfect square.**

b. $\sqrt{100}$ rational ← **100 is a perfect square.**

c. 0.323223222 . . . irrational ← **The decimal neither terminates nor repeats.**

d. -0.98 rational ← **It is a terminating decimal.**

e. 0.2323 . . . rational ← **It is a repeating decimal.**

4 Identify each number as rational or irrational.

a. $\sqrt{2}$ **b.** $\sqrt{81}$ **c.** $0.\overline{6}$ **d.** $1\frac{2}{7}$

EXERCISES

Example 1 (page 426)

Simplify each square root.

1. $\sqrt{16}$ **2.** $\sqrt{100}$ **3.** $\sqrt{36}$ **4.** $\sqrt{25}$ **5.** $\sqrt{81}$

6. $\sqrt{169}$ **7.** $\sqrt{144}$ **8.** $\sqrt{121}$ **9.** $\sqrt{1}$ **10.** $\sqrt{9}$

Example 2 (page 427)

11. A fence surrounds a square plot of land. The area of the land is 400 yd^2. Find the length of each side of the fence.

12. Industrial Arts A square piece of plywood covers an area of 64 ft^2. What is the length of each side of the plywood?

Example 3 (page 427)

Estimate the value of each square root.

13. $\sqrt{18}$ **14.** $\sqrt{5}$ **15.** $\sqrt{41}$ **16.** $\sqrt{54}$ **17.** $\sqrt{75}$

18. the length of the side of a square deck with an area of 98 ft^2

Example 4 (page 428)

Identify each number as rational or irrational.

19. $\sqrt{99}$ **20.** $\sqrt{41}$ **21.** $\sqrt{49}$ **22.** -0.4744 **23.** $-\frac{3}{2}$

24. $-0.666666\ldots$ **25.** $0.12122122212222\ldots$ **26.** $0.\overline{35}$

B Apply Your Skills

For each number, write all the sets to which it belongs. Choose from *rational number, irrational number, whole number,* and *integer.*

27. $\frac{3}{5}$ **28.** $0.\overline{23}$ **29.** $\sqrt{36}$ **30.** 4.5 **31.** $\frac{22}{7}$

32. $\sqrt{100}$ **33.** $5.121231234\ldots$ **34.** $\sqrt{35}$

35. **Open-Ended** Write three irrational numbers between 4 and 5.

Math in the Media **Use the cartoon below for Exercises 36 and 37.**

FOXTROT ***by Bill Amend.***

36. Does the cartoon suggest that π is *rational* or *irrational*?

37. What are some rational numbers that you can use to approximate π?

38. **a.** What is the square root of $\frac{1}{4}$? What is the square root of $\frac{4}{9}$?

b. **Writing in Math** Write a method of finding the square root of a fraction.

Find the length of the side of a square with the given area.

39. 64 km^2 **40.** 81 m^2 **41.** 121 ft^2 **42.** 4 mi^2

43. 225 $in.^2$ **44.** 196 yd^2 **45.** 169 cm^2 **46.** 400 mm^2

C Challenge

47. **Science** When an object falls, the distance that it falls is given by the formula $d = 16t^2$, where d is the distance in feet and t is the time in seconds.

a. A stone that falls from the top of a cliff takes 7 s to reach the ground. How high is the cliff?

b. Another stone falls from a bridge 1,600 ft above the water. How long does it take for the stone to reach the water?

48. **Stretch Your Thinking** If Lori gives Cameron 5 eggs, he will have three times as many eggs as Lori. If Cameron gives Lori 5 eggs, they will have the same number of eggs. How many eggs do they each have?

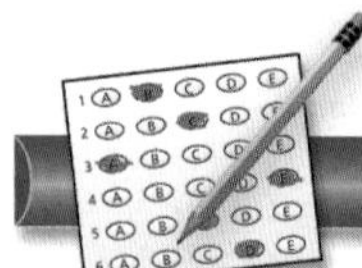

Test Prep

Multiple Choice

49. Which of the following simplifies to 8?
A. $\sqrt{4}$ **B.** $\sqrt{16}$ **C.** $\sqrt{32}$ **D.** $\sqrt{64}$

50. Which of the following is an irrational number?
F. $\sqrt{25}$ **G.** $\sqrt{49}$ **H.** $\sqrt{81}$ **I.** $\sqrt{109}$

Take It to the NET
Online lesson quiz at
www.PHSchool.com
Web Code: aba-0805

51. The area of a square piece of tile is 144 cm^2. How long is each side of the square tile?
A. 12 cm **B.** 36 cm **C.** 72 cm **D.** 20,736 cm

Extended Response

52. The area of a square plot of land is 5,625 m^2. A fence is built around the plot of land. What is the perimeter of the fence? Show your work.

Mixed Review

Lesson 6-4

Find each answer.

53. 5% of 40 **54.** 60% of 90 **55.** 75% of 15 **56.** 30% of 120

Lesson 5-5

Algebra **Solve each proportion using cross products.**

57. $\frac{4}{5} = \frac{m}{35}$ **58.** $\frac{10}{16} = \frac{15}{p}$ **59.** $\frac{k}{21} = \frac{14}{49}$ **60.** $\frac{8}{w} = \frac{6}{54}$

Practice Game

SQUARE ROOT BINGO

What You'll Need

- 20 index cards. On each card write one of the first 20 perfect squares (not including 0) under the square root symbol.

8	20	11	3
2	12	6	10
14	4	1	9
17	15	7	5

How to Play

- All players draw a 16-square playing board. In each square, they write a number from 1–20 without repeats. See the sample at the right.
- One player shuffles the index cards and places them face down.
- The player to the right chooses the top card and places it face up. Players with the matching square root on their board place a mark over the appropriate square.
- Play continues with the player to the right choosing the next card.
- The winner is the first player who has four marks diagonally, horizontally, or vertically.

Investigation

Exploring the Pythagorean Theorem

For Use With Lesson 8-6

You will learn about the Pythagorean Theorem in Lesson 8-6. The activity and exercises below will help you understand why the theorem works.

Activity

Step 1 Use centimeter graph paper to draw a right triangle with the right angle included between sides that are 3 cm and 4 cm long.

Step 2 Draw squares that have the horizontal and vertical sides of the right triangle as sides.

Step 3 Use another piece of the graph paper to make a square on the side opposite the right angle, as shown at the right.

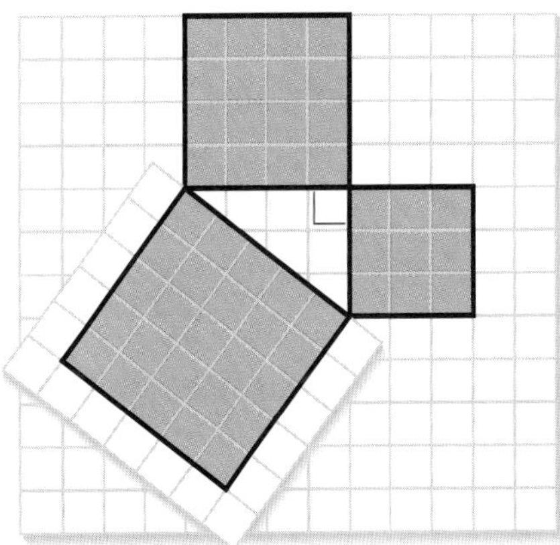

EXERCISES

1. What is the length of the side of the square opposite the right angle?

2. What is the area of each of the three squares?

3. Draw a right triangle on centimeter graph paper with the right angle included between sides that are 8 cm and 15 cm long. Repeat Steps 2 and 3 above.

a. What is the length of each side of the square made on the side opposite the right angle?

b. What is the area of each of the three squares?

4. Use the triangle at the right. What are the areas of the three squares made on the sides of the right triangle?

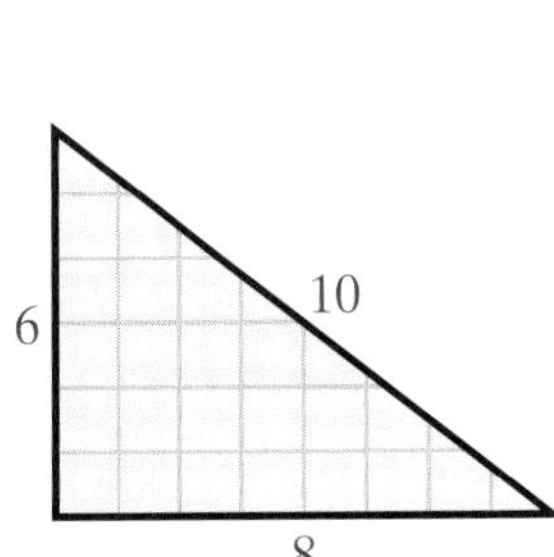

5. a. Reasoning Look for a pattern. What seems to be the relationship of the areas of the smaller two squares and the third square made on the sides of a right triangle?

b. Write an equation for each triangle that compares the areas of its squares.

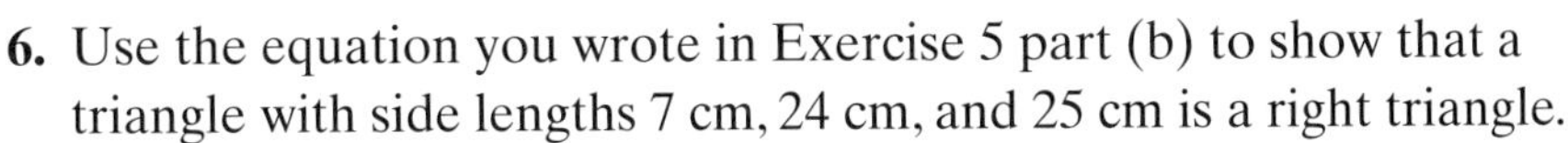

6. Use the equation you wrote in Exercise 5 part (b) to show that a triangle with side lengths 7 cm, 24 cm, and 25 cm is a right triangle.

7. Writing in Math A triangle has side lengths 6 cm, 10 cm, and 12 cm. Explain why this triangle is not a right triangle.

8-6 The Pythagorean Theorem

What You'll Learn

To use the Pythagorean Theorem

. . . And Why

To find the length of a water slide, as in Example 3

Check Skills You'll Need

For help, go to Lesson 8-5.

Simplify each square root.

1. $\sqrt{4}$
2. $\sqrt{16}$
3. $\sqrt{36}$
4. $\sqrt{49}$
5. $\sqrt{100}$
6. $\sqrt{64}$

New Vocabulary • legs • hypotenuse • Pythagorean Theorem

Interactive lesson includes instant self-check, tutorials, and activities.

OBJECTIVE

1 Using the Pythagorean Theorem

In a right triangle, the two shortest sides are **legs.** The side opposite the right angle is the **hypotenuse.**

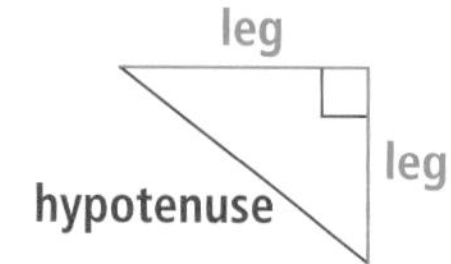

The Pythagorean Theorem shows how the legs and hypotenuse of a right triangle are related.

Key Concepts — Pythagorean Theorem

The **Pythagorean Theorem** states that in any right triangle, the sum of the squares of the lengths of the legs is equal to the square of the length of the hypotenuse.

$$a^2 + b^2 = c^2$$

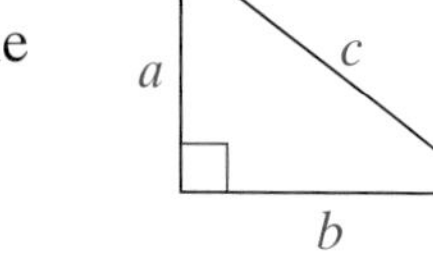

You can find the length of a hypotenuse of a right triangle using this theorem.

1 EXAMPLE Finding the Length of a Hypotenuse

Find the length of the hypotenuse of the triangle.

12 ft
9 ft
c

$c^2 = a^2 + b^2$ ← Pythagorean Theorem

$c^2 = 9^2 + 12^2$ ← Substitute.

$c^2 = 81 + 144$ ← Simplify.

$c^2 = 225$

$\sqrt{c^2} = \sqrt{225}$ ← Take the square root of each side.

$c = 15$

The length of the hypotenuse is 15 ft.

Test-Prep Tip

Recognizing whole numbers that work in the Pythagorean Theorem, like 9, 12, and 15, can save you time.

Check Understanding **1** Find the length of the hypotenuse in the triangle at the right.

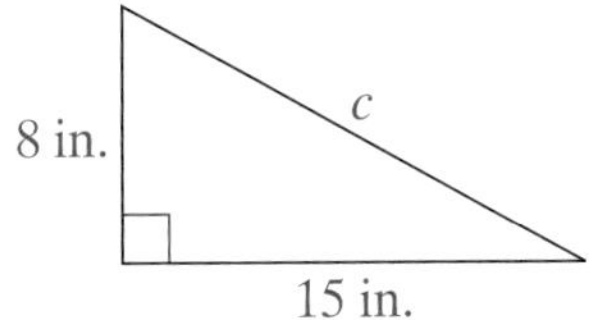

You can use the Pythagorean Theorem to find the length of a leg of a right triangle.

2 EXAMPLE Finding the Length of a Leg

Find the length of the missing leg of the triangle.

$a^2 + b^2 = c^2$ ← **Pythagorean Theorem**

$a^2 + 8^2 = 10^2$ ← **Substitute.**

$a^2 + 64 = 100$ ← **Simplify.**

$a^2 + 64 - 64 = 100 - 64$ ← **Subtract 64 from each side.**

$a^2 = 36$ ← **Simplify.**

$\sqrt{a^2} = \sqrt{36}$ ← **Take the square root of each side.**

$a = 6$

The length of the leg is 6 m.

Check Understanding **2** **a. Number Sense** If the hypotenuse above is increased to 12 m and the 8 m leg is unchanged, will the length of a increase to 8 m? Explain.

b. Find the missing length at the right.

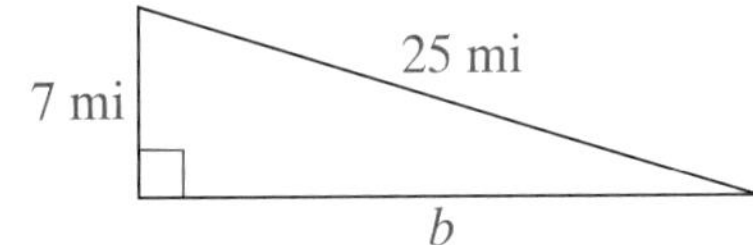

Real-World Connection

Some water slides are straight, while others have curves.

3 EXAMPLE Real-World Problem Solving

Recreation A water slide starts 6 m above the water and extends 11 m horizontally. What is the length of the slide to the nearest tenth of a meter?

Draw a diagram to illustrate the problem.

Use the Pythagorean Theorem.

$c^2 = a^2 + b^2$ ← **Use the Pythagorean Theorem.**

$c^2 = 6^2 + 11^2$ ← **Substitute.**

$c^2 = 36 + 121$ ← **Square 6 and 11.**

$c^2 = 157$ ← **Add.**

$\sqrt{c^2} = \sqrt{157}$ ← **Take the square root of each side.**

$c \approx 12.529964$ ← **Use a calculator.**

The length of the slide is about 12.5 m long.

Check Understanding **3** A support wire is attached to the top of a 60-m tower. It meets the ground 25 m from the base of the tower. How long is the support wire?

For more practice, see *Extra Practice.*

A Practice by Example

Example 1 (page 432)

Find the length of the hypotenuse of each triangle. Round to the nearest tenth of a unit, if necessary. Exercise 1 has been started for you.

1.

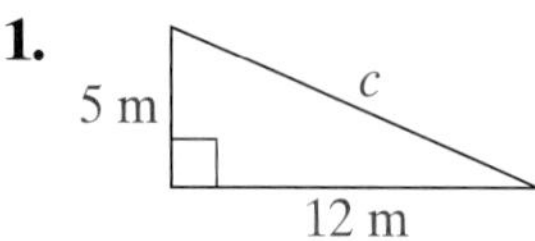

$$a^2 + b^2 = c^2$$
$$5^2 + 12^2 = c^2$$

2.

c
9 m
15 m

3.

15 m
8 m
x

4.

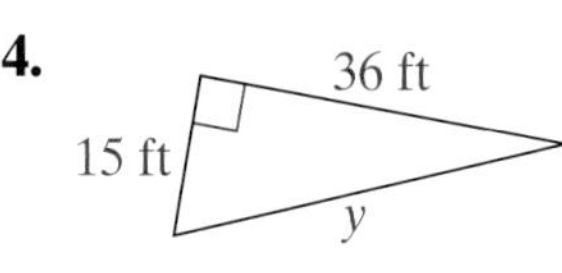

5.

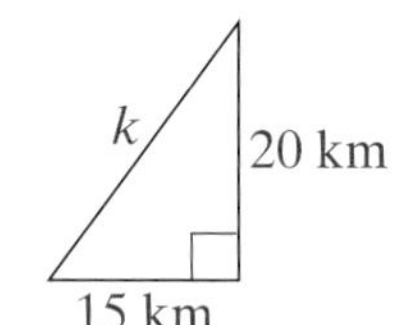

6.

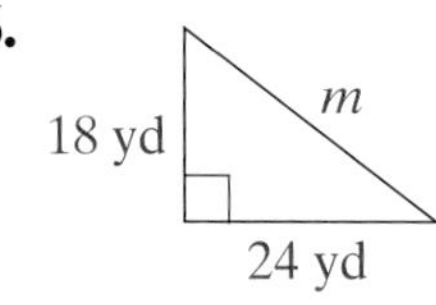

7.

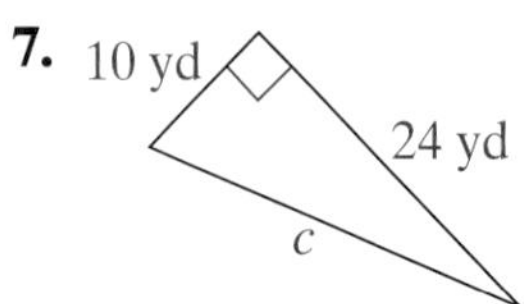

8.

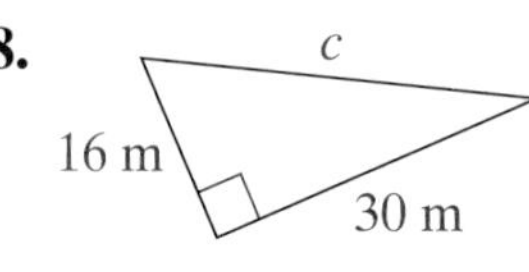

9.

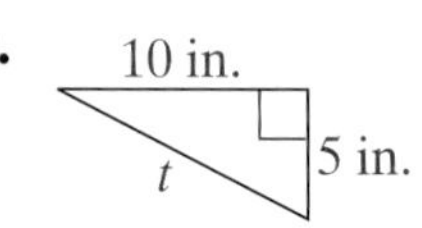

Example 2 (page 433)

Find each missing length. Round to the nearest tenth of a unit, if necessary.

10.

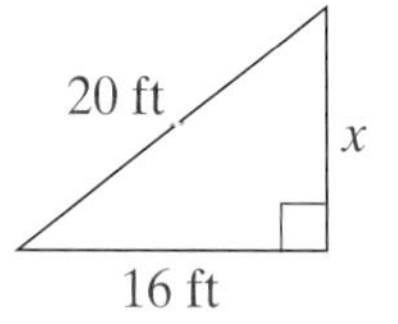

11.

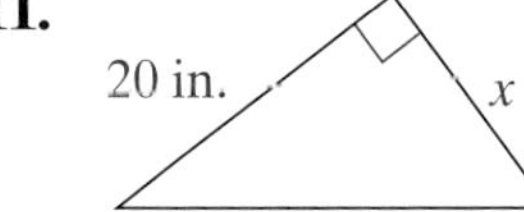

12.

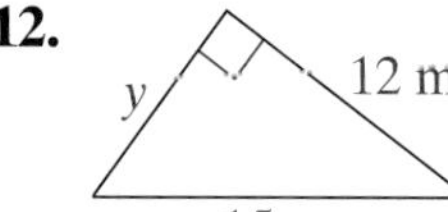

13.

50 cm
14 cm
c

14.

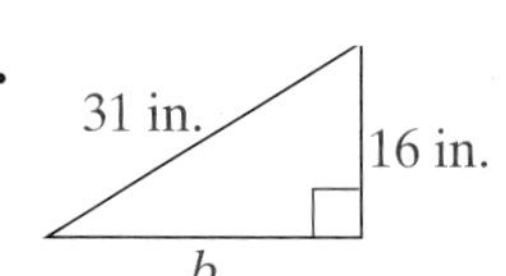

15.

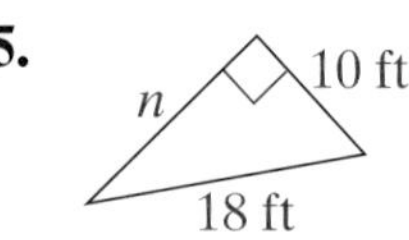

16.

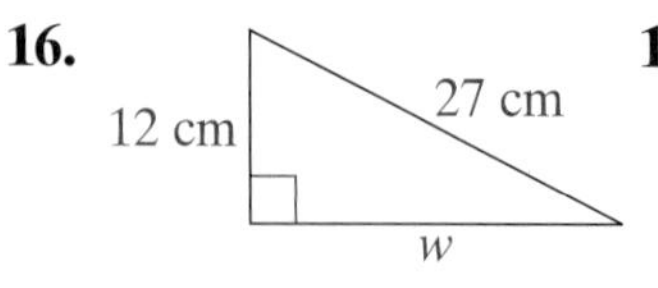

17.

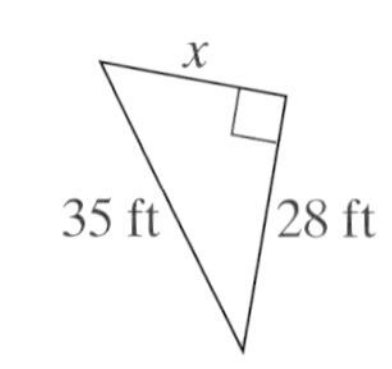

18.

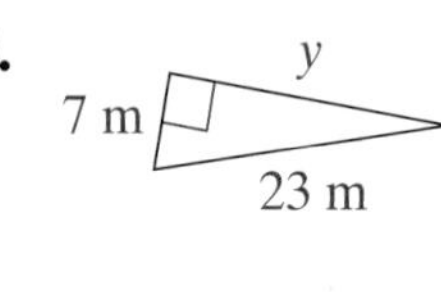

Example 3 (page 433)

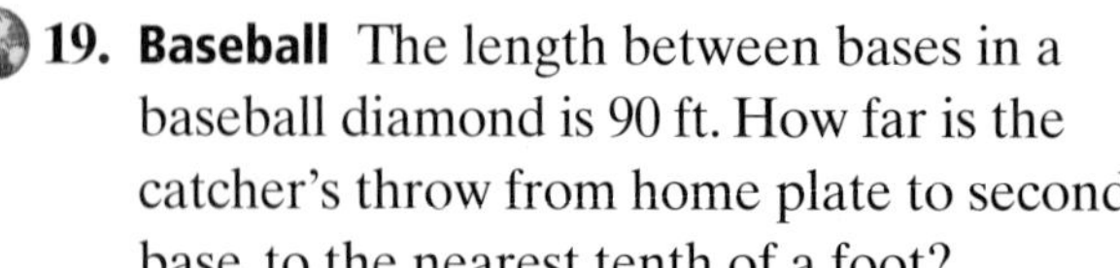

19. Baseball The length between bases in a baseball diamond is 90 ft. How far is the catcher's throw from home plate to second base, to the nearest tenth of a foot?

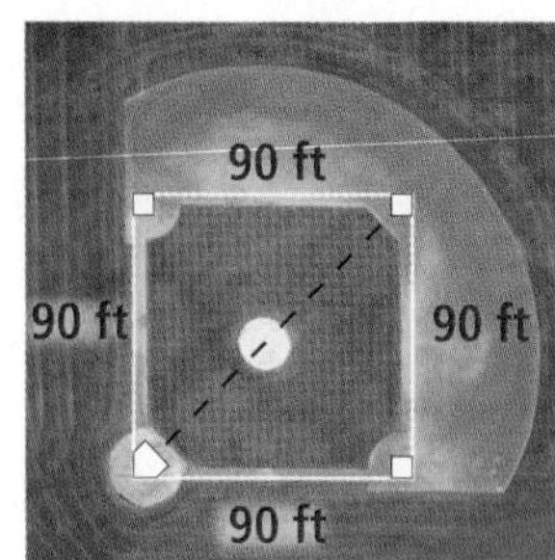

20. A rectangular park is 600 m long and 300 m wide. You walk diagonally across the park from corner to corner. How far do you walk, to the nearest meter?

21. **Construction** The rectangular section of wood fencing below is reinforced with a piece of wood nailed across the diagonal of the rectangle. What is the length of the diagonal?

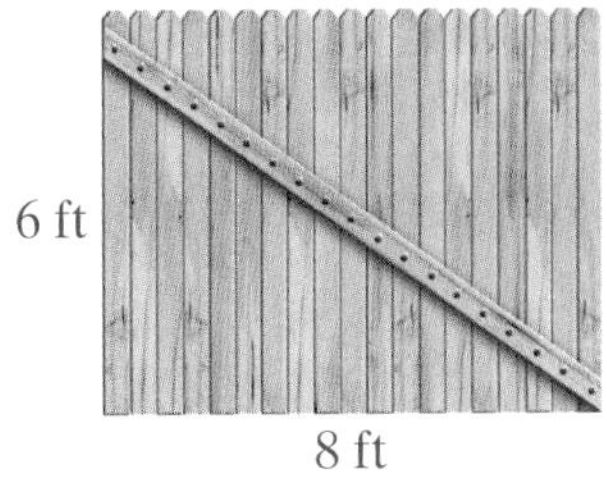

22. **Tennis** A tennis court measures 78 ft long and 27 ft wide. To the nearest foot, what is the length of the diagonal of the court?

B Apply Your Skills

The lengths of two sides of a right triangle are given. Find the length of the third side to the nearest tenth.

23. legs 8 m and 11 m
24. legs 10 cm and 14 cm
25. legs 12 ft and 20 ft
26. leg 25 in. and hypotenuse 35 in.
27. leg 18 yd and hypotenuse 28 yd
28. leg 6 m and hypotenuse 12 m

29. a. $\overline{AC}$ is the diameter of circle O. Find $\overline{AC}$.
b. Find the circumference and area of the circle. Round to the nearest tenth.

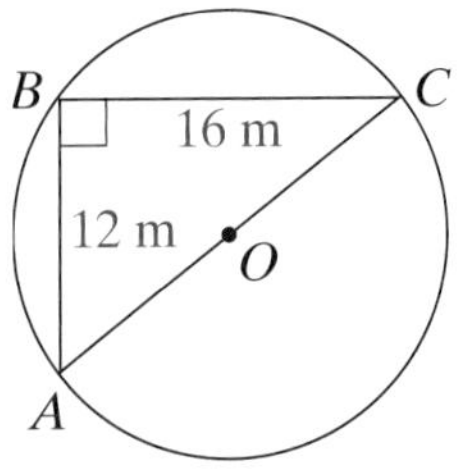

30. **Camping** A large tent has an adjustable center pole. A rope 26 ft long connects the top of the pole to a peg 24 ft from the bottom of the pole. What is the height of the pole? Round to the nearest hundredth if necessary.

Find the perimeter of each triangle to the nearest tenth.

31.

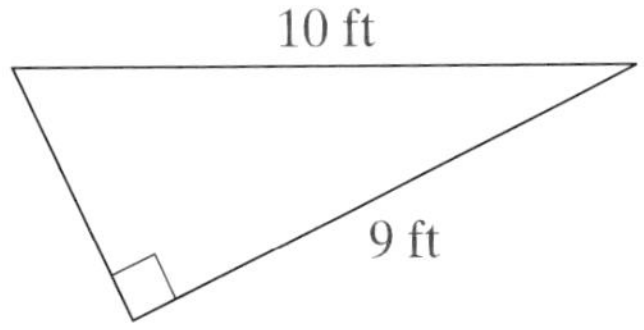

32.

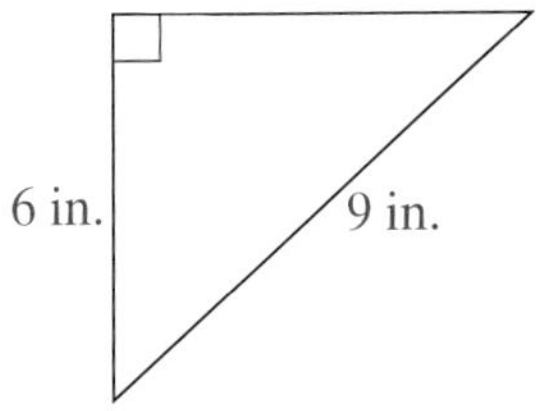

Real-World Connection

Lighthouses warn ships of dangerous locations and guide them to harbors.

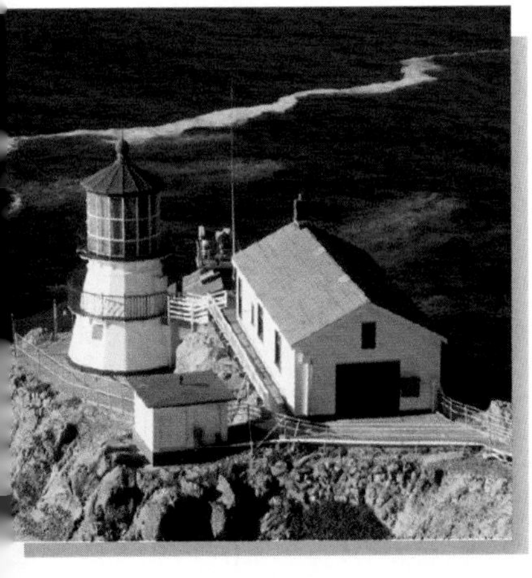

33. **Navigation** A dock is located 24 km directly east of a lighthouse. A sailboat is directly north of the lighthouse. The sailboat is 25 km from the dock. How far away is the sailboat from the lighthouse?

34. A ladder is 6 m long. How much farther up a wall does the ladder reach when the base of the ladder is 2 m from the wall than when it is 3 m from the wall? Give the answer to the nearest tenth of a meter.

35. **Writing in Math** A triangle has side lengths measuring 10 m, 24 m, and 26 m. Explain how to use the Pythagorean Theorem to determine whether or not the triangle is a right triangle.

Challenge

36. **Reasoning** The length of two sides of a right triangle are 9 cm and 14 cm. What are the two possible lengths for the third side? Round to the nearest tenth of a centimeter.

Find the perimeter and area of each triangle to the nearest tenth.

37. 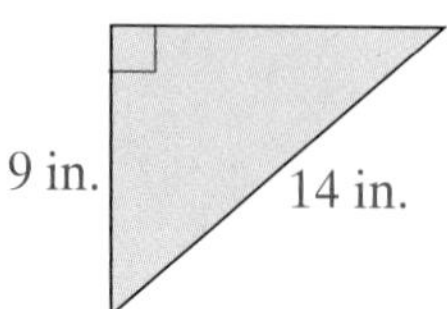

38. 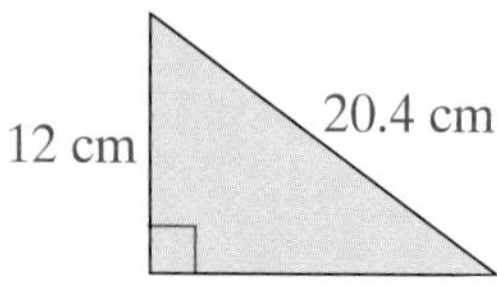

39. 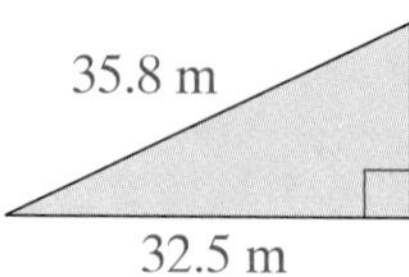

40. **Stretch Your Thinking** Find x.

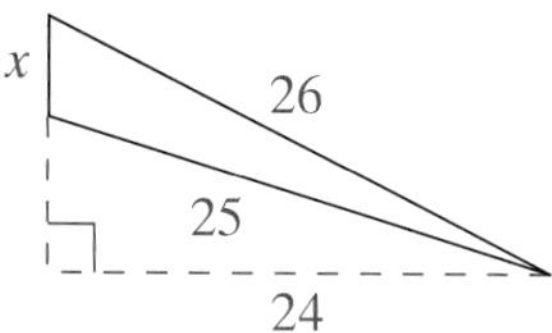

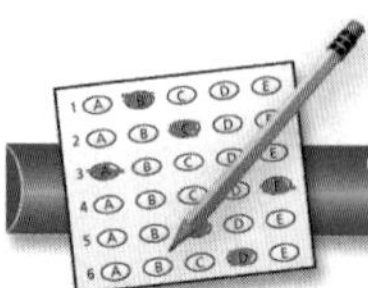

Test Prep

Multiple Choice

41. What is the length of the hypotenuse if the legs of a right triangle are 7 m and 24 m?

    A. 5.6 m B. 22.9 m C. 25 m D. 625 m

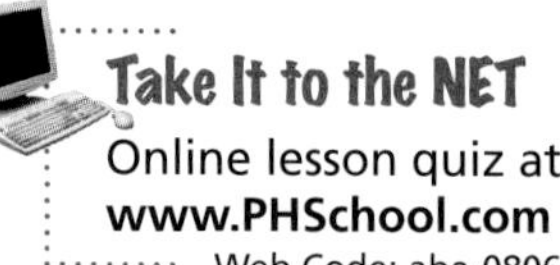

Online lesson quiz at **www.PHSchool.com** Web Code: aba-0806

42. The hypotenuse of a right triangle is 3.5 cm and one leg is 2.1 cm. What is the area of the triangle, rounded to the nearest tenth?

    F. 1.8 cm^2 G. 2.1 cm^2 H. 2.9 cm^2 I. 7.8 cm^2

43. Estimate the width of the lake.

    A. 10 km B. 331.7 km
    C. 781 km D. 1,100 km

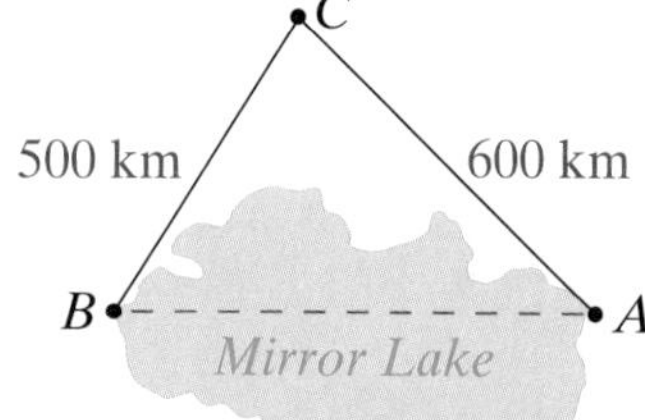

Extended Response

44. A square pool has sides 30 yd long. Is a 45-yd rope long enough to span across the pool diagonally? Show your work.

Mixed Review

Lesson 8-5

Simplify each square root.

45. $\sqrt{25}$ 46. $\sqrt{36}$ 47. $\sqrt{4}$ 48. $\sqrt{81}$ 49. $\sqrt{64}$

Lesson 6-6

Algebra **Write and solve an equation to find the part of a whole.**

50. What number is 5% of 225? 51. What number is 60% of 40?

52. The amount of paper a company uses Tuesday is 85% of the amount of paper used on Monday. If 5,000 sheets of paper were used on Monday, how much paper was used on Tuesday?

8-7 Three-Dimensional Figures

What You'll Learn

OBJECTIVE 1 To identify and draw three-dimensional figures

. . . And Why

To name three-dimensional shapes, as in Example 2

Check Skills You'll Need

For help, go to Lesson 7-5.

Use dot paper to draw each figure.

1. rhombus
2. trapezoid
3. rectangle
4. square

New Vocabulary

• three-dimensional figure • face • edge • prism • bases of a prism • height of a prism • cube • cylinder • bases of a cylinder • height of a cylinder • pyramid • vertex of a pyramid • base of a pyramid • cone • base of a cone • vertex of a cone • sphere • center of a sphere

TEXT Interactive lesson includes instant self-check, tutorials, and activities.

OBJECTIVE 1 Identifying and Drawing Three-Dimensional Figures

Real-World Connection

A glass prism can refract, or bend, light.

Many of the figures that surround you are three-dimensional. A **three-dimensional figure,** or solid, is a figure that does not lie in a plane.

Some three-dimensional figures have only flat surfaces. A flat surface shaped like a polygon is called a **face.** Each segment formed by the intersection of two faces is an **edge.**

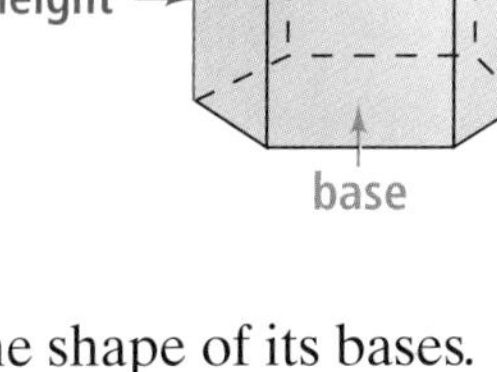

A **prism** is a three-dimensional figure with two parallel and congruent polygonal faces, called **bases.** The other faces are rectangles. The **height** of a prism is the length of a perpendicular segment that joins the bases. A prism is named for the shape of its bases.

A **cube** is a rectangular prism with faces that are squares.

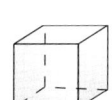

EXAMPLE 1 Identifying Prisms

Describe the base and name the prism.

The bases are triangles, so the figure is a triangular prism.

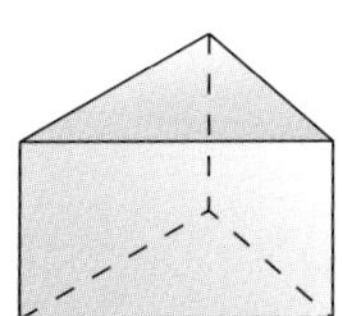

Check Understanding 1 Describe the base and name the prism.

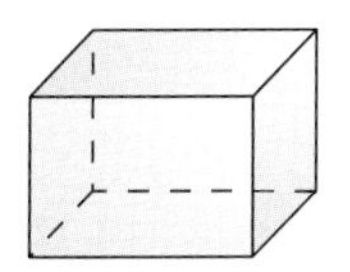

A **cylinder** has two congruent parallel **bases** that are circles. The **height** of a cylinder is the length of a perpendicular segment that joins the bases.

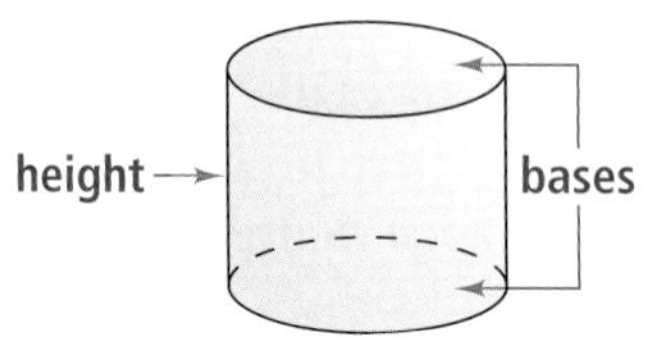

A **pyramid** is a three-dimensional figure with triangular faces that meet at one point, a **vertex,** and a **base** that is a polygon. A pyramid is named for the shape of its base.

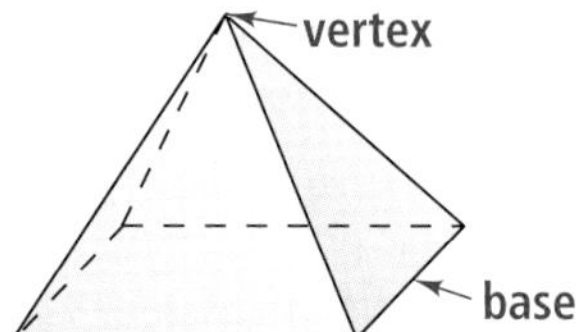

A **cone** has one circular **base** and one **vertex.**

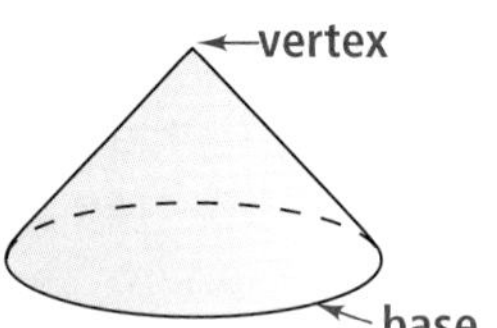

A **sphere** is the set of all points in space that are the same distance from a **center** point.

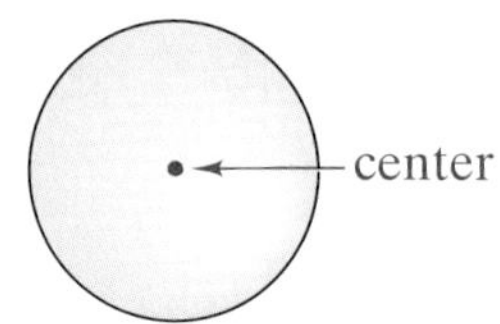

2 EXAMPLE Naming Figures

Architecture Look at the architectural blocks at the right. Name Figure 3.

Figure 3 is a cylinder.

2 **a.** Name Figure 1.
b. Name Figure 2.

You can use graph paper to draw three-dimensional figures.

3 EXAMPLE Drawing Three-Dimensional Figures

Draw a hexagonal prism.

Step 1 Draw a hexagon.

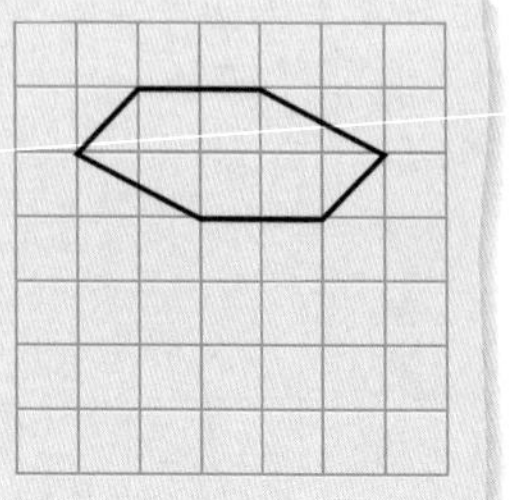

Step 2 Draw a second hexagon congruent to the first.

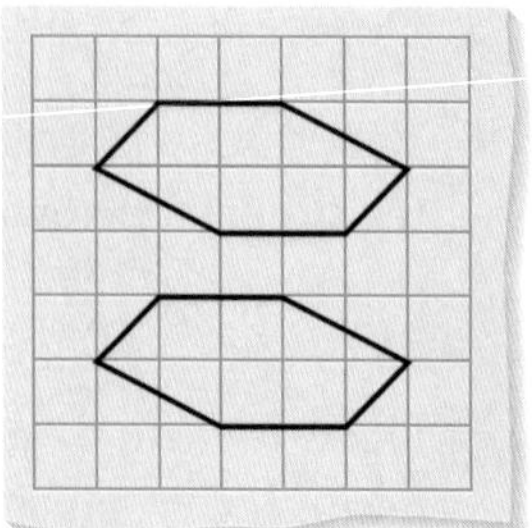

Step 3 Connect the vertices. Use dashed lines for hidden edges.

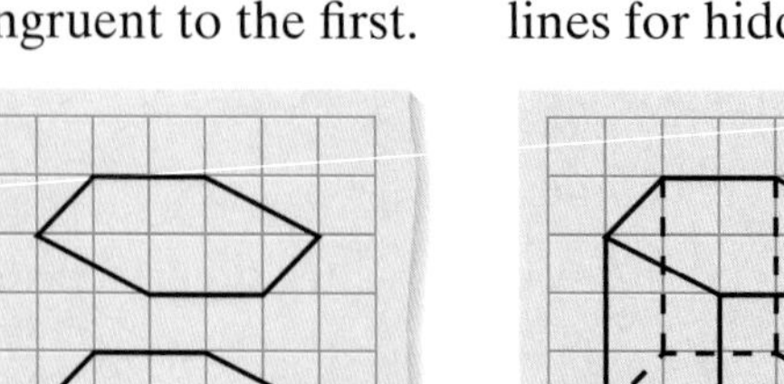

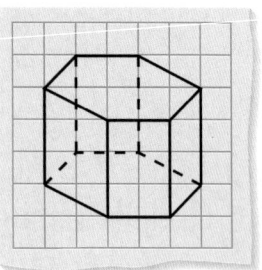

Check Understanding 3 Use graph paper to draw a triangular prism.

EXERCISES

For more practice, see *Extra Practice*.

Practice by Example

Example 1 (page 437)

Describe each base and name each prism.

1. 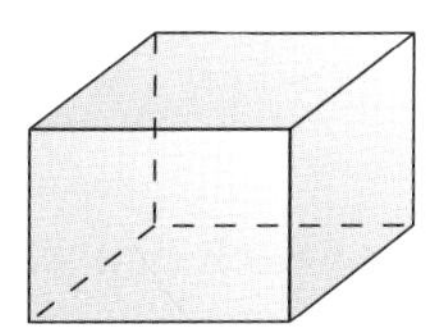

2. 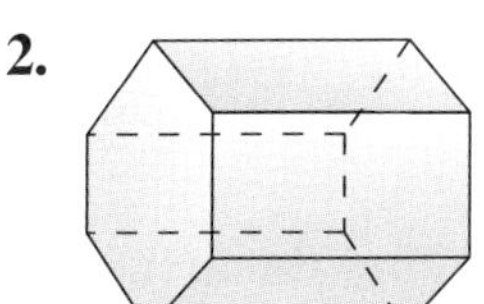

3. 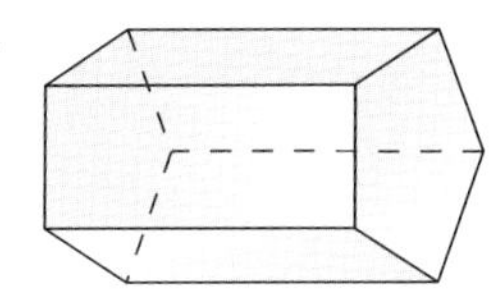

4. 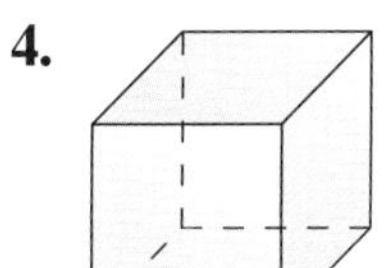

5. 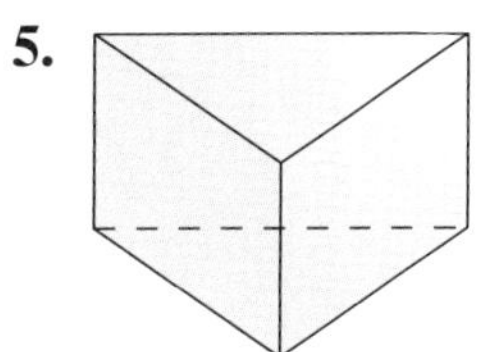

6. 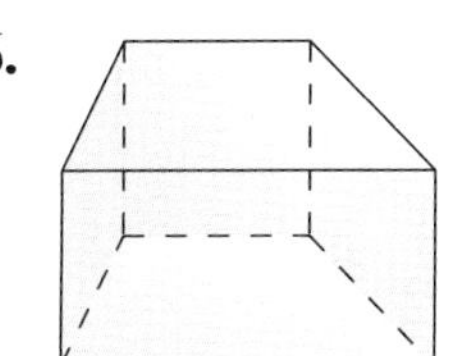

Example 2 (page 438)

Name each figure.

7. 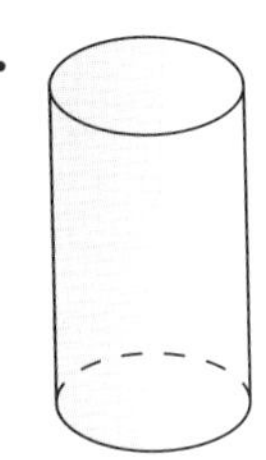

8. 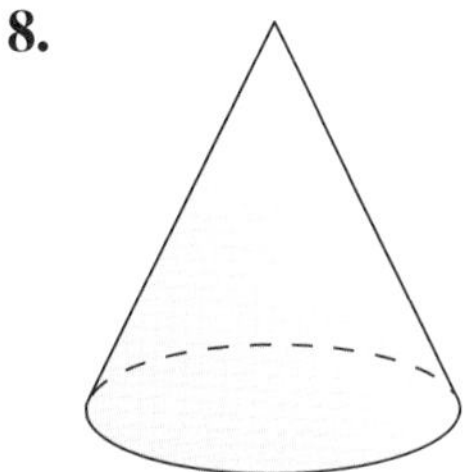

9. 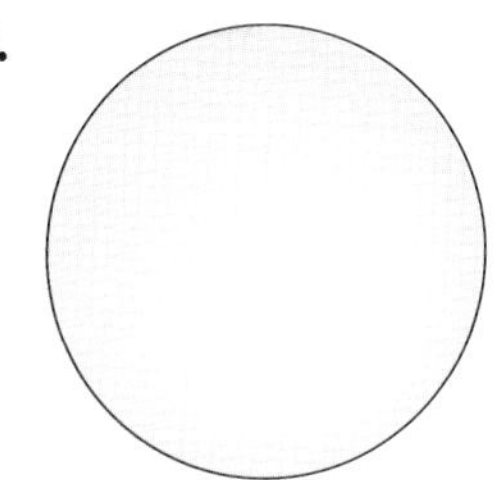

10.

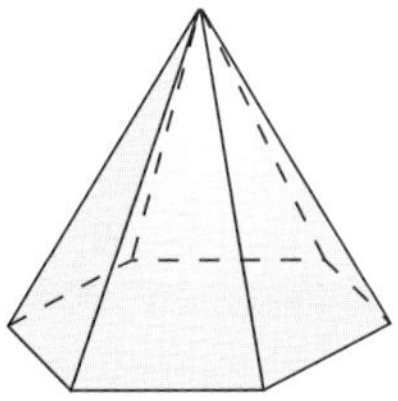

11. 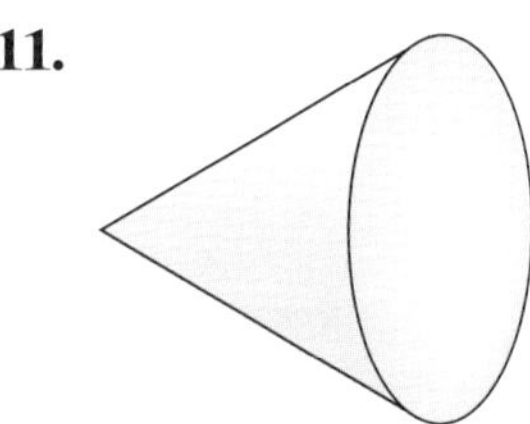

12. 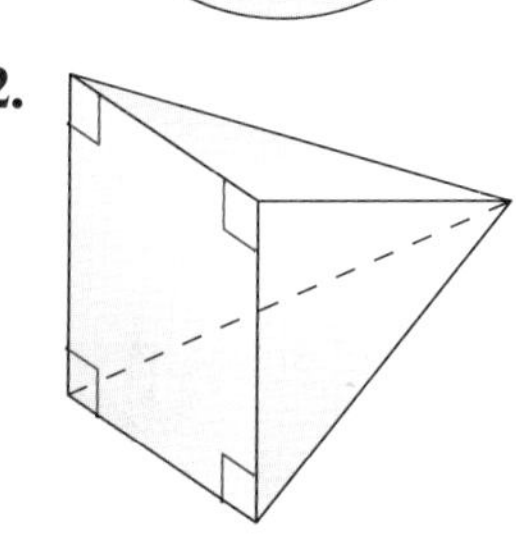

Example 3 (page 438)

Use graph paper to draw each figure.

13. rectangular prism

14. cube

15. cylinder

16. pentagonal prism

17. triangular pyramid

18. square pyramid

B Apply Your Skills

Name the three-dimensional figure in each photograph.

19. 

20. 

21. 

22. **Writing in Math** Are the edges of a cube congruent? Explain.

Use the pentagonal pyramid at the right.

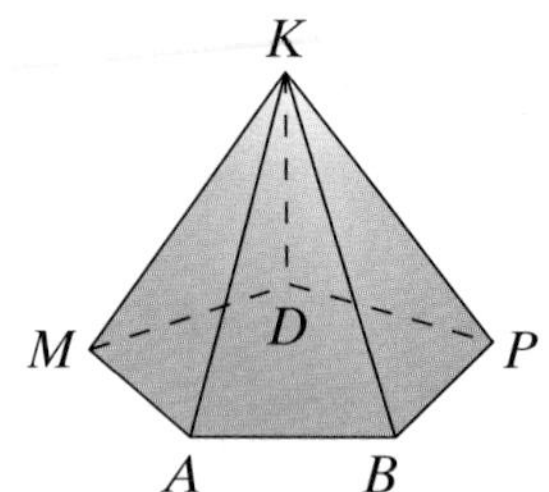

23. Name four edges that intersect $\overline{AB}$.

24. Name any edges that are parallel to $\overline{AB}$.

25. Name the five edges that are *not* parallel to $\overline{AB}$ and do *not* intersect $\overline{AB}$.

Find the areas of the faces of each figure.

26. 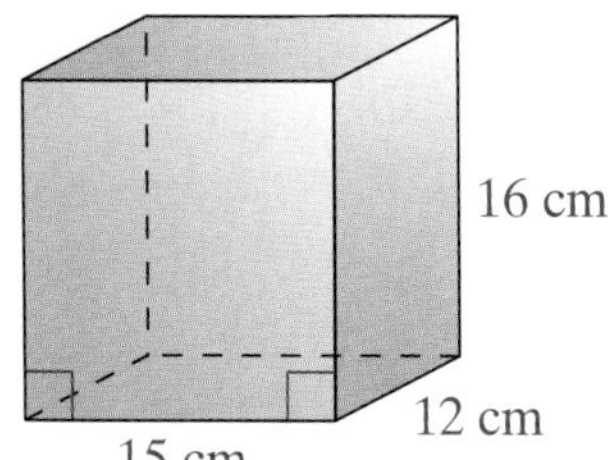

27. 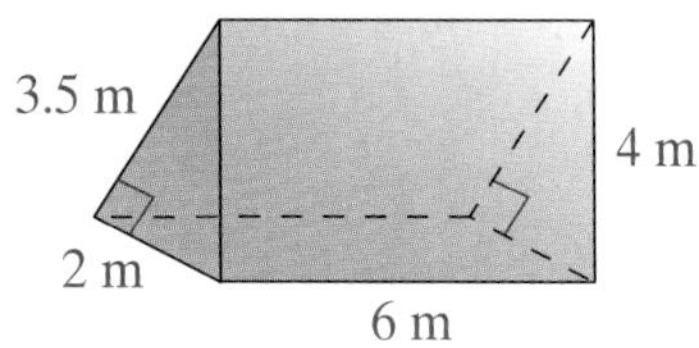

Challenge

Identify the number of faces, edges, and vertices each figure has.

28. square pyramid

29. hexagonal pyramid

30. pentagonal prism

31. cube

32. **Stretch Your Thinking** The students in Miss Kirk's dance class stand evenly spaced in a circle. The students count off by 1's. The student who counts 6 is directly across from the student who counts 19. How many students are in Miss Kirk's class?

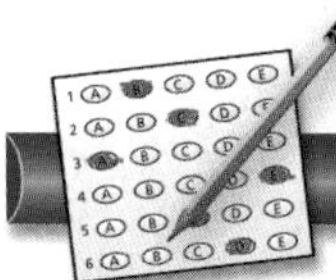

Test Prep

Multiple Choice

33. Which three-dimensional figure does NOT have a base?
A. cone B. prism C. pyramid D. sphere

34. What is the shape of the base of a cylinder?
F. hexagon G. square H. circle I. triangle

35. Which three-dimensional figure has only squares as faces?
A. pyramid B. cube C. cone D. cylinder

Take It to the NET
Online lesson quiz at
www.PHSchool.com
Web Code: aba-0807

Short Response

36. Explain the similarities and differences between cones and pyramids.

Mixed Review

Lesson 8-6

37. The hypotenuse of a right triangle is 61 m long. One leg is 60 m long. What is the length of the third side?

Lesson 8-2

38. The area of a parallelogram is 45 in.^{2}. The perpendicular distance between the bases is 9 in. What is the length of the base?

Three Views of an Object

For Use With Lesson 8-7

Three-dimensional objects can be drawn to show that they have length, width, and height. Alternatively, you can make three drawings that each show only one view of the blocks at a time. The views the drawings show are the *top view,* the *front view,* and the *right side view.*

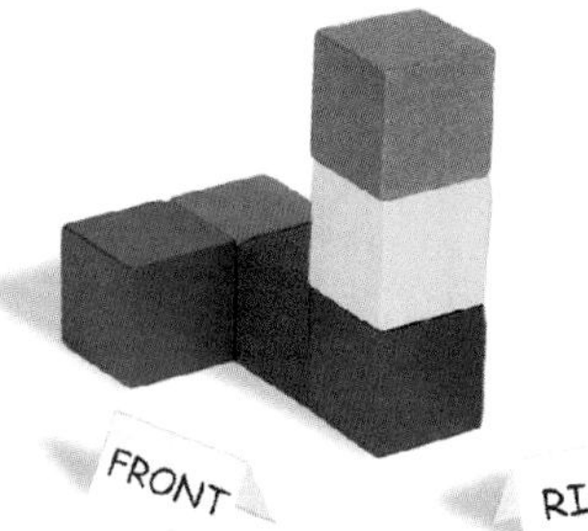

EXAMPLE Drawing Three Views

Draw the top, front, and right side views of each figure.

Draw the top view as if you are looking down on the blocks.

Draw the front view as if you are in front of the blocks.

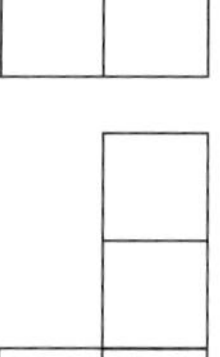

Draw the right side view as if you are on the right side of the blocks.

EXERCISES

Draw the top, front, and right side views of each figure.

1.

2.

3.

Use the top, front, and right side views to draw a three-dimensional figure.

4. Top Front Right

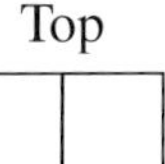

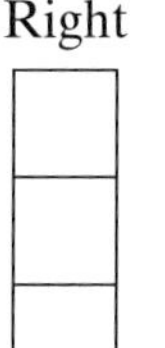

5. Top Front Right

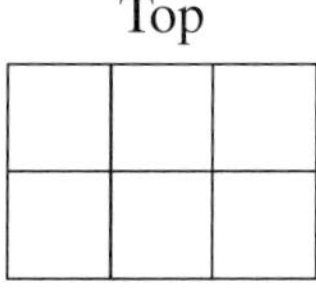

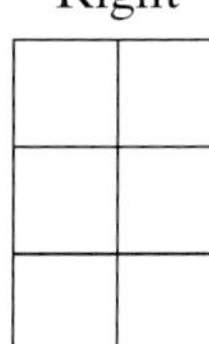

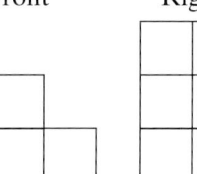

8-8 Surface Areas of Prisms and Cylinders

What You'll Learn

To draw a net

To find the surface areas of prisms and cylinders using nets

. . . And Why

To find the surface area of a birthday present, as in Example 3

✓ Check Skills You'll Need

For help, go to Lesson 8-2.

Find the area of each triangle.

1. 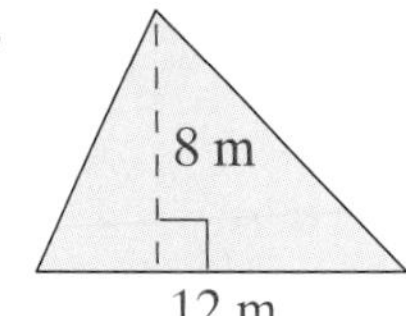

2.

3. 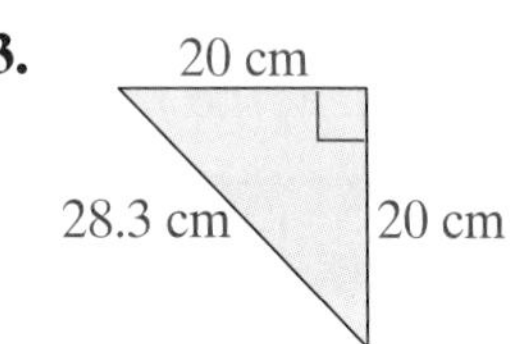

New Vocabulary • net • surface area

Interactive lesson includes instant self-check, tutorials, and activities.

OBJECTIVE 1 Drawing a Net

A **net** is a two-dimensional pattern that you can fold to form a three-dimensional figure. Packagers use nets to design boxes.

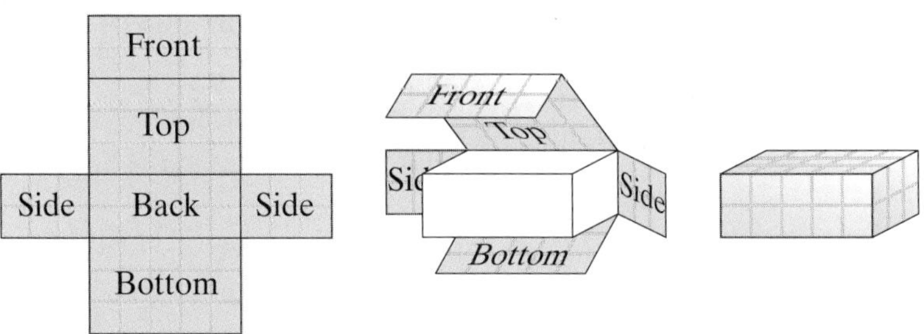

You can draw many different nets for a three-dimensional figure.

1 EXAMPLE Drawing a Net

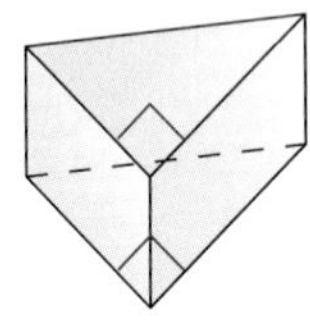

Draw a net for the triangular prism at the left.

Back
Top
Left
Right
Bottom

← **Begin by labeling the bases and faces.**

First draw one base. Then draw one face that connects both bases. Next, draw the other base. Draw the remaining faces. →

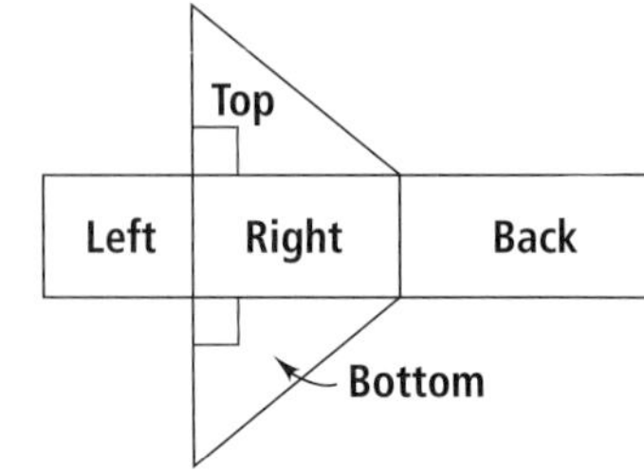

✓ Check Understanding 1 Draw a different net for the right triangular prism in Example 1.

OBJECTIVE

2 Finding Surface Areas Using Nets

The **surface area** of a prism is the sum of the areas of its faces. You measure surface area of a prism in square units. One way to find the surface area is to find the area of its net.

2 EXAMPLE Surface Area of a Prism

Find the surface area of the triangular prism.

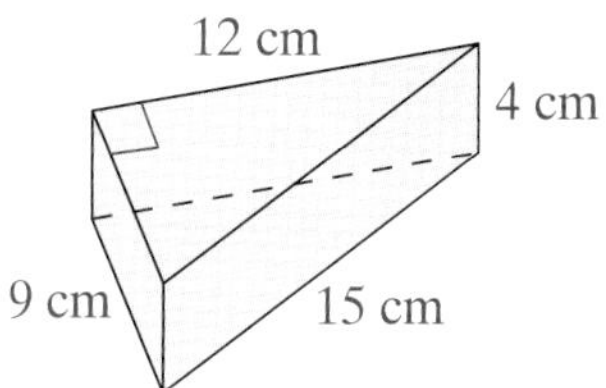

First draw a net for the prism.

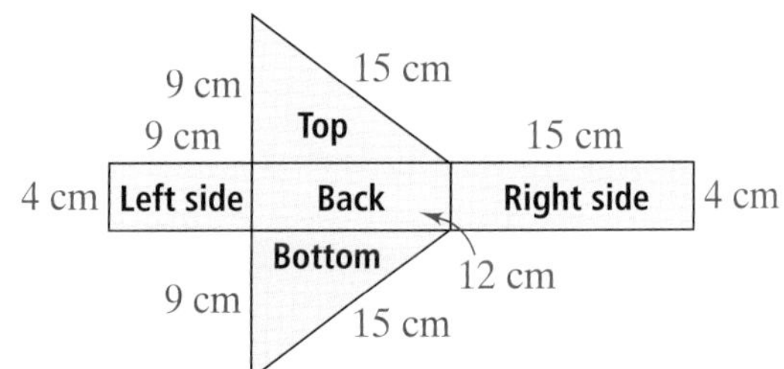

Then find the total area of the five faces.

left side back right side top bottom

$$4(9) + 4(12) + 4(15) + \frac{1}{2}(12)(9) + \frac{1}{2}(12)(9) = 252$$

The surface area of the triangular prism is 252 cm^2.

Check Understanding 2 Find the surface area of the rectangular prism.

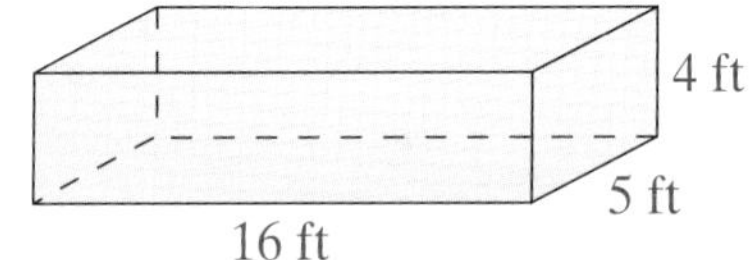

If you cut a label from a can, you will see that the label is a rectangle. The height of the rectangle is about the height of the can. The base length of the rectangle is the circumference of the can.

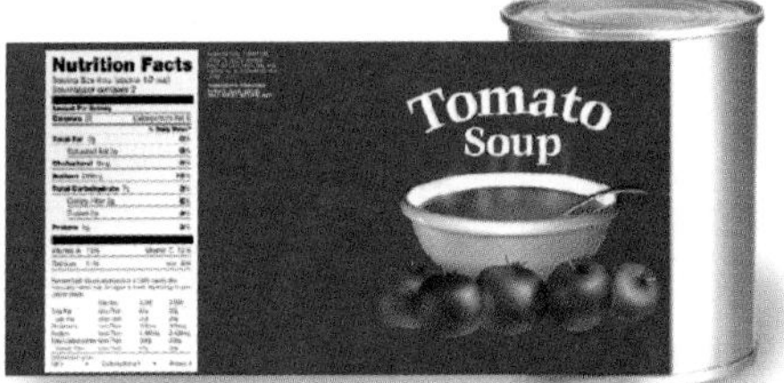

Similarly, if you cut up a cylinder you get a rectangle and two circles.

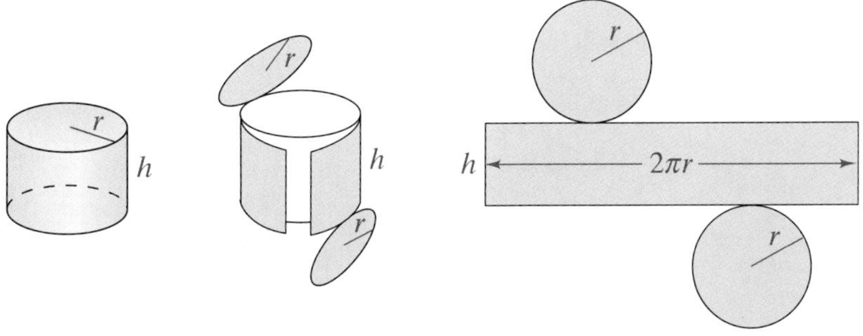

You can use a net of a cylinder to find its surface area.

3 EXAMPLE Surface Area of a Cylinder

Crafts You plan to make a custom birthday present for your sister. The first step is to cover a coffee can with construction paper. How much construction paper do you need?

Step 1 Draw a net.

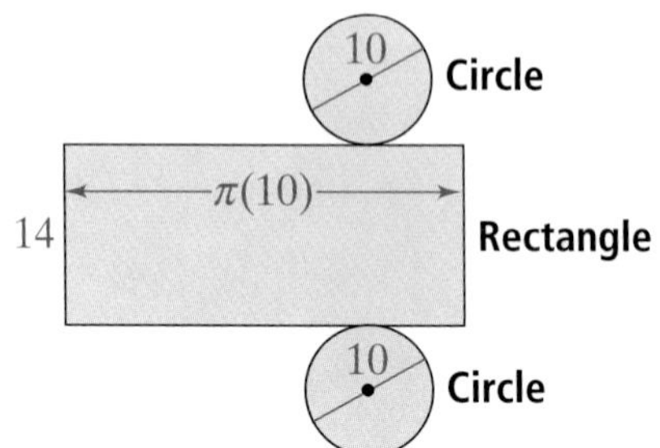

Step 2 Find the area of one circle.

$$A = \pi r^2$$
$$= \pi(5)^2$$
$$= \pi(25)$$
$$\approx 78.54 \text{ cm}^2$$

Step 3 Find the area of the rectangle.

$$(\pi d)h = \pi(10)(14)$$
$$= 140\pi$$
$$\approx 439.82 \text{ cm}^2$$

Step 4 Add the areas of the two circles and the rectangle.

$$\text{Surface area} = 78.54 + 78.54 + 439.82$$
$$= 596.9 \text{ cm}^2$$

The amount of construction paper needed is about 597 cm^2.

Check Understanding 3

a. What is the surface area of the cylinder at the right? Round to the nearest tenth.

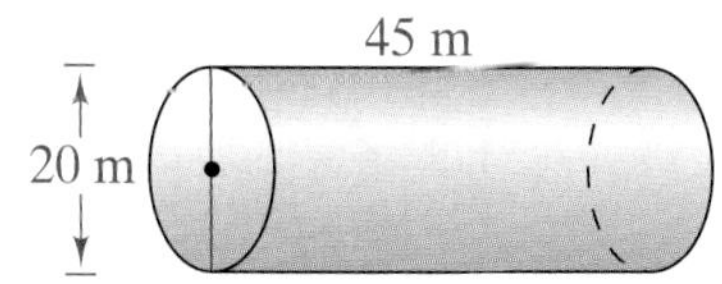

b. **Reasoning** What are the similarities and differences of nets of different cylinders?

EXERCISES

For more practice, see *Extra Practice*.

Example 1 (page 442)

Draw a net for each three-dimensional figure.

1.

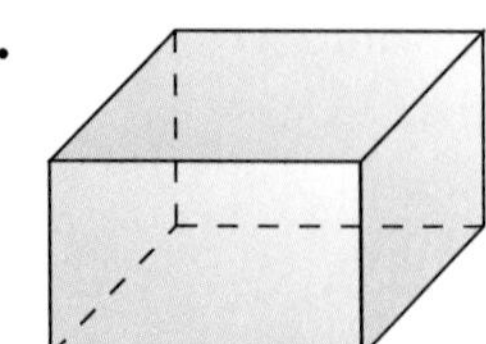

2.

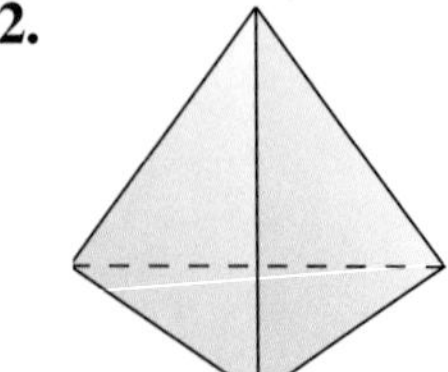

3.

4.

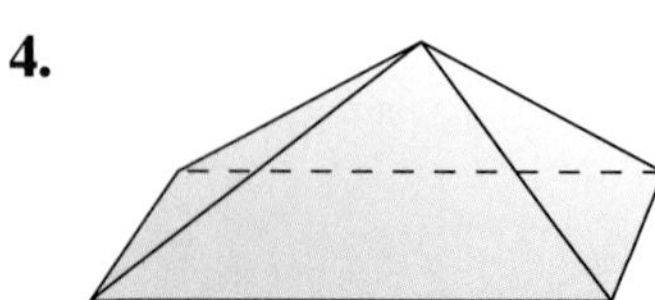

Example 2 (page 443)

Find the surface area of each prism.

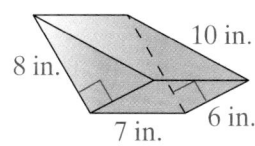

5.

9 m
6 m
10 m
8 m

6.

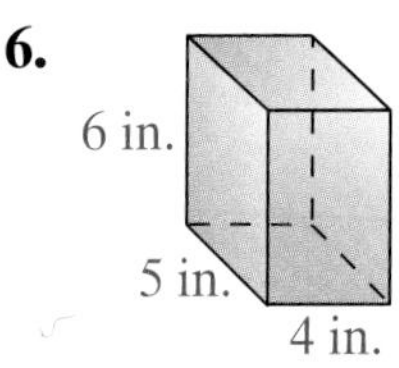

7.

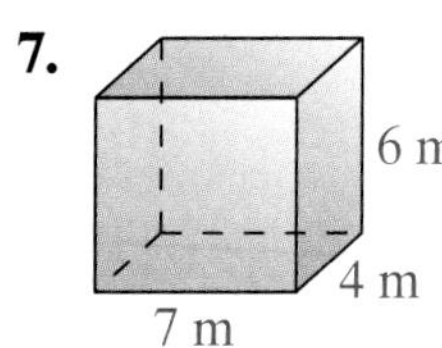

8.

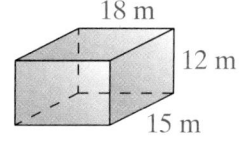

10 in.
8 in.
7 in.
6 in.

9.

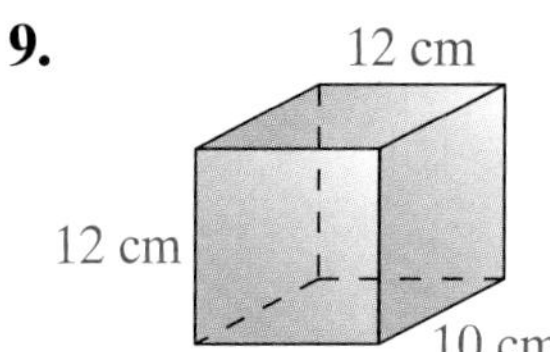

10.

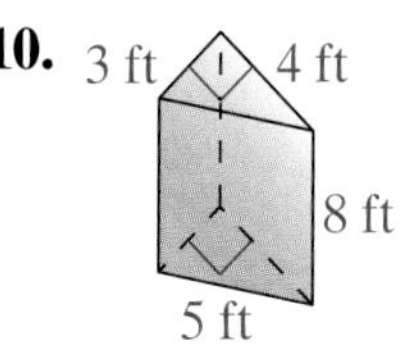

11.

18 m
12 m
15 m

12.

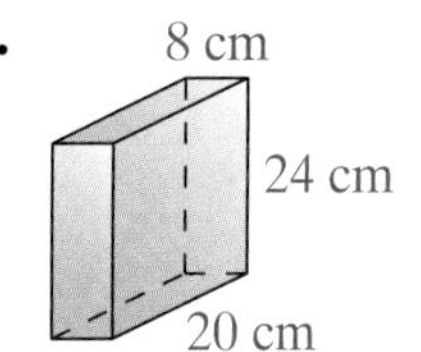

13.

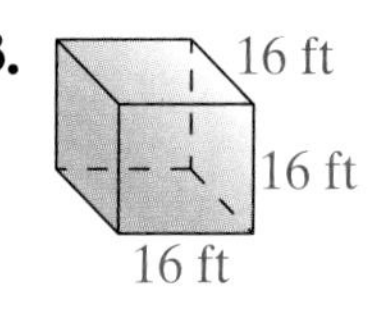

Example 3 (page 444)

Find the surface area of each cylinder. Round to the nearest tenth.

14.

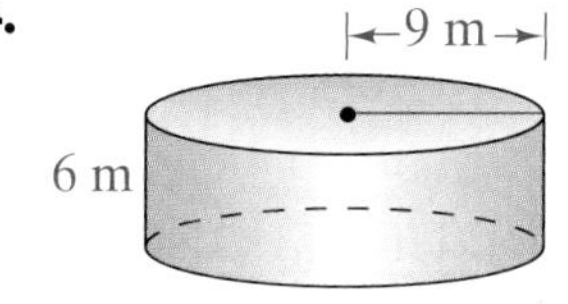

15.

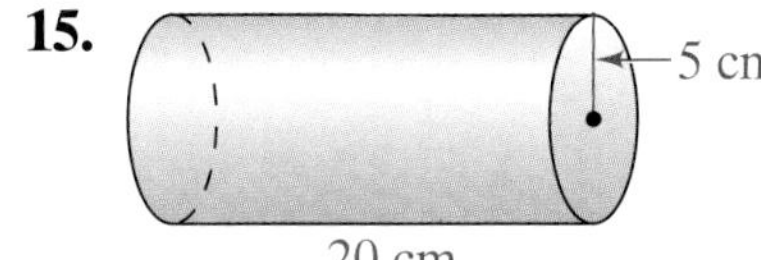

16.

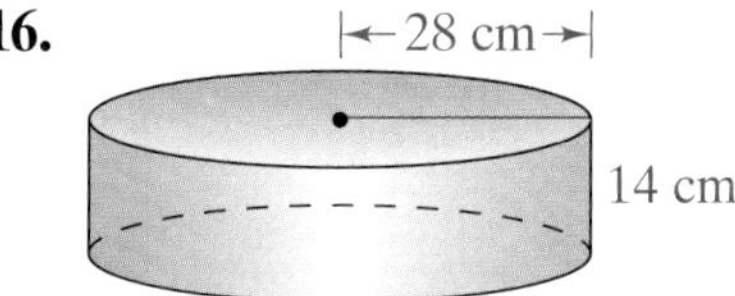

17.

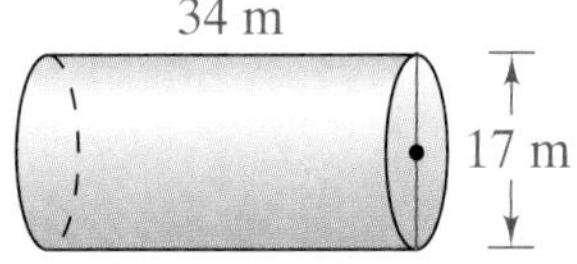

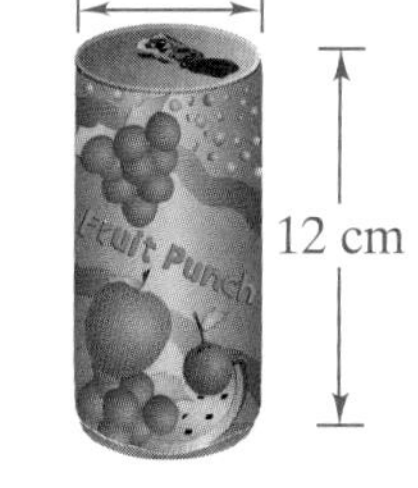

18. Manufacturing Aluminum cans are cut from a large sheet of metal. Find the amount of aluminum needed to make a can similar to the one at the left. Round to the nearest tenth of a centimeter.

B Apply Your Skills

Identify the figure formed by each net. Then find its surface area.

19.

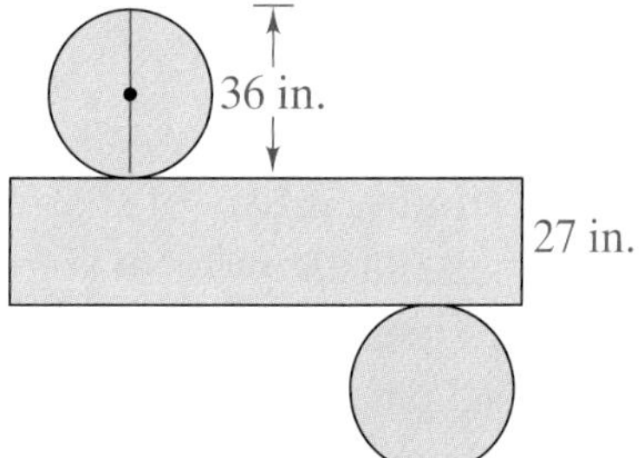

20.

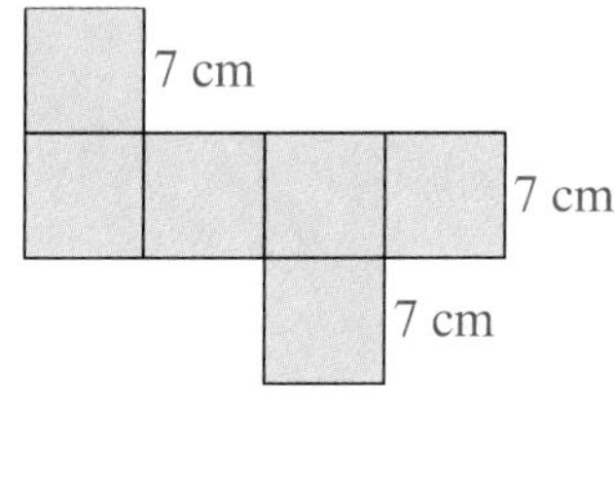

21. Writing in Math Which has a greater effect on the surface area of a cylinder—doubling the radius or doubling the height? Explain.

22. Data File, p. 401 You have purchased a CD in a regular jewel box for a present. Find the surface area of the jewel box to plan how much wrapping paper you will need.

23. **Music** Suppose you wish to make a cylindrical case for the bass drum at the left so that the drum fits exactly in the case. What is the surface area of the case to the nearest tenth?

24. **Open-Ended** Draw a net for a prism that has a surface area of 72 cm^2.

25. **Reasoning** Which has a greater surface area—a cylinder with a 2-m diameter and 4-m height, or a cylinder with a 4-m diameter and 2-m height? Explain.

26. **Packaging** The diameter of the base of a large can of peanuts is 4 in. The height of the can is $6\frac{1}{2}$ in. Find the surface area of the can. Round to the nearest tenth of an inch.

Find the surface area of each cylinder given the base radius and height of the cylinder. Round to the nearest square unit.

27. $r = 3$ cm $h = 10$ cm	**28.** $r = 7$ ft $h = 25$ ft	**29.** $r = 12$ m $h = 16$ m	**30.** $r = 10$ in. $h = 3$ ft

31. **Error Analysis** A student says the two cylinders below have the same surface area. Explain the student's error.

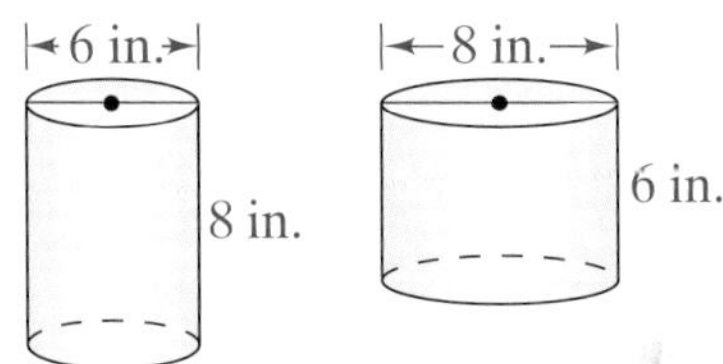

32. **Camping** Polyester is a popular material used for tents like the one at the right. The tent is similar to a triangular prism. Calculate the surface area of the tent to find the amount of polyester needed to make it.

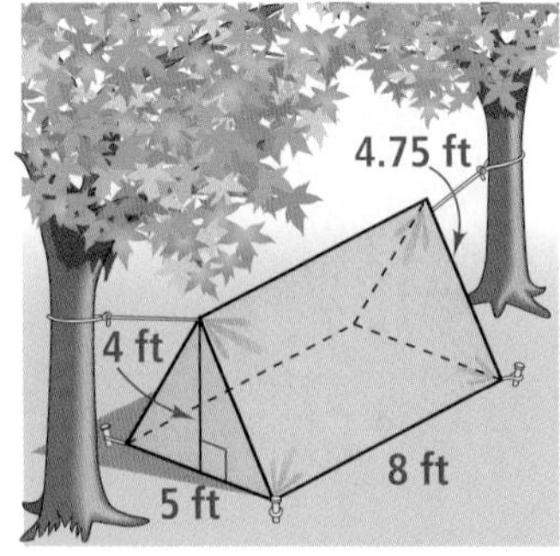

33. **Industry** A cosmetics company that makes small cylindrical bars of soap wraps the bars in plastic prior to shipping. Find the surface area of a bar of soap if the diameter is 5 cm and the height is 2 cm. Round to the nearest tenth of a centimeter.

34. You have to purchase wrapping paper to cover a gift. Calculate the surface area of the box to find how much wrapping paper you will need.

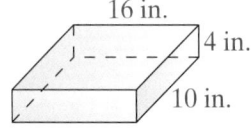

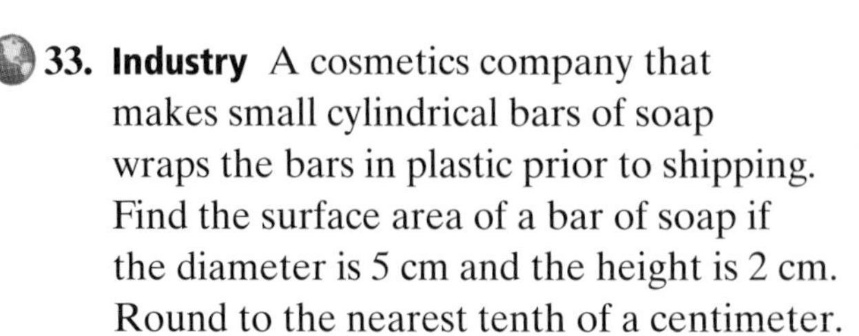

C Challenge

Find the surface area of each figure. Round to the nearest tenth.

35.
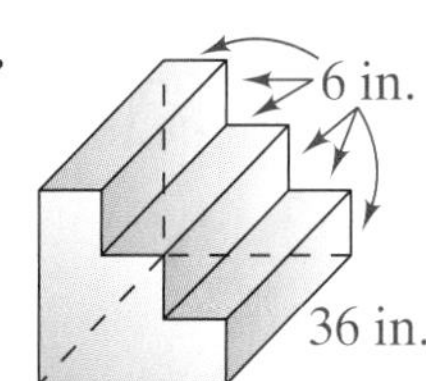

36.
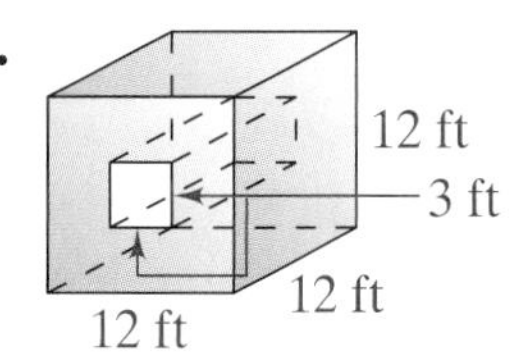

37.
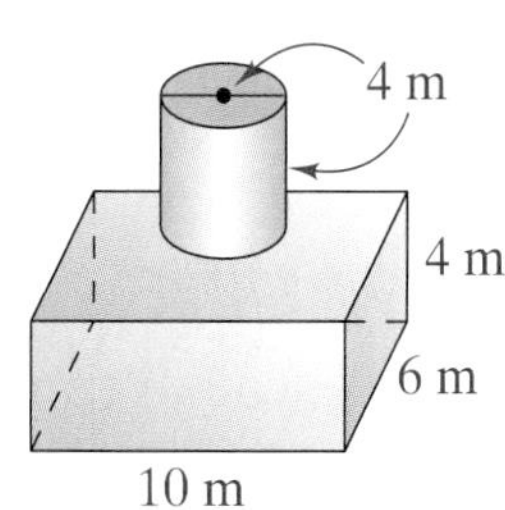

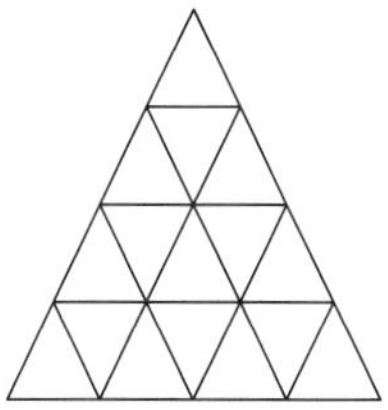

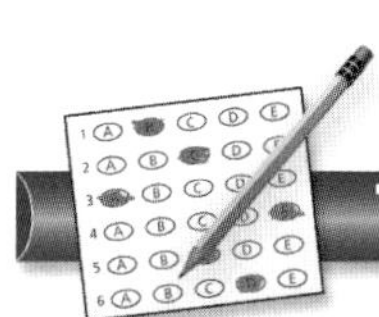

38. Stretch Your Thinking What is the total number of triangles in the figure at the left?

Test Prep

Multiple Choice

39. Find the surface area of the cylinder to the nearest square unit.

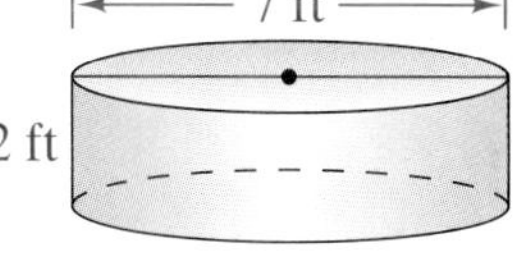

A. 57 ft^2 B. 113 ft^2
C. 121 ft^2 D. 242 ft^2

40. Find the surface area of the prism to the nearest square unit.

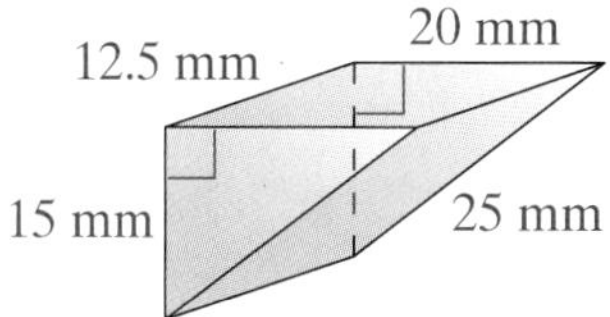

F. 1,350 mm^2 G. 1,050 mm^2
H. 862 mm^2 I. 750 mm^2

Take It to the NET
Online lesson quiz at
www.PHSchool.com
Web Code: aba-0808

41. What is the sum of the surface areas of the two figures to the nearest square unit?

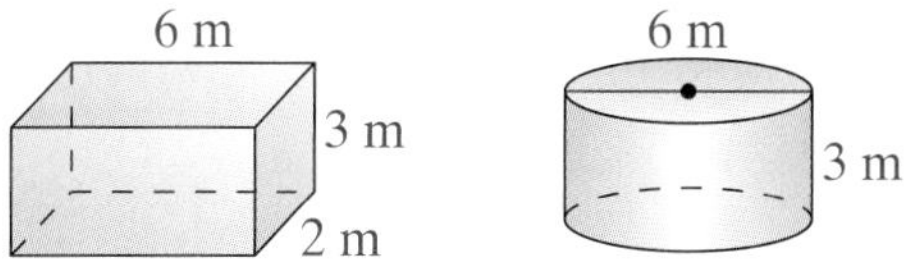

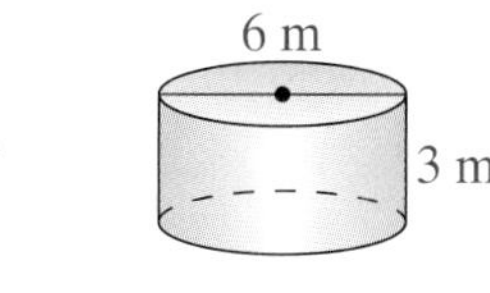

A. 162 m^2 B. 185 m^2
C. 197 m^2 D. 411 m^2

Short Response

42. Suppose the lengths of the sides of a cube are doubled. What effect does this have on the surface area of the cube? Explain.

Mixed Review

Lesson 8-7

Use graph paper to draw each figure.

43. triangular prism **44.** square pyramid **45.** cone

Lesson 7-8

Name each of the following for circle *O*.

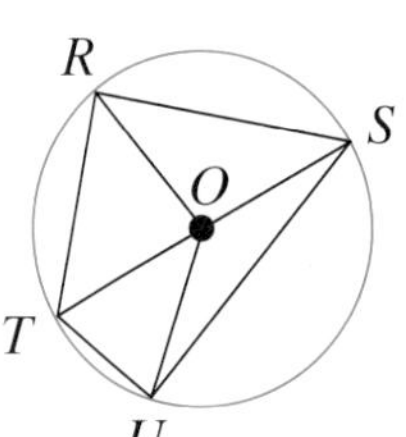

46. two chords

47. a diameter

48. four radii

49. an isosceles triangle

Extension

Patterns in 3-Dimensional Figures

For Use With Lesson 8-8

You can explore number patterns using unit cubes.

Suppose you use unit cubes to make a larger cube. You paint the outside of the larger cube formed with two unit cubes on an edge.

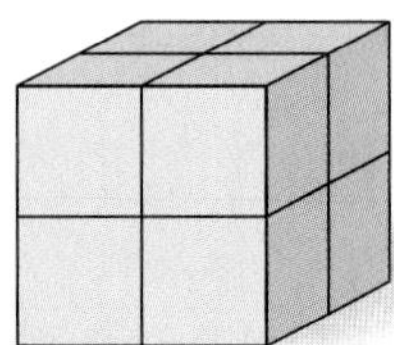

You need eight unit cubes to form the larger cube. Each cube has three sides painted.

EXERCISES

Use the table for Exercises 1–3.

Number of Unit Cubes on an Edge	Total Number of Unit Cubes	Total Number Expressed as a Power	Number of Unit Cubes With Given Number of Sides Painted			
			0	1	2	3
2	8	2^3	0	0	0	8
3	■	■	■	■	■	■
4	■	■	■	■	■	■
5	■	■	■	■	■	■
6	■	■	■	■	■	■
7	■	■	■	■	■	■

1. Copy and complete a table like the one above for cubes formed by the given number of unit cubes on an edge. Use the figure at the right to help you fill in the row for 3 unit cubes on an edge.

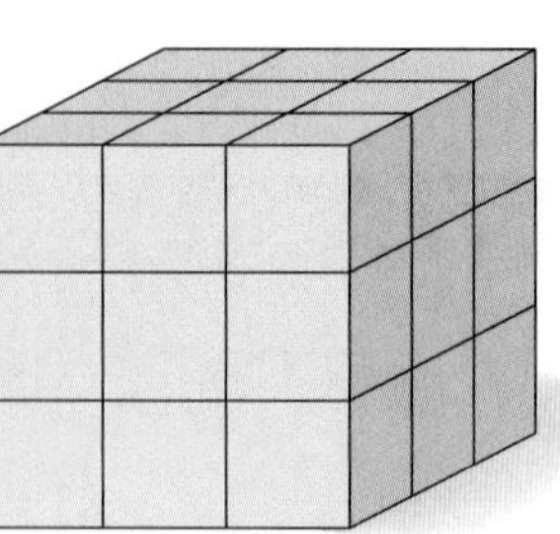

2. a. **Patterns** Describe the number pattern you see in each of the last four columns of your table.
   b. Use the number patterns and extend the table for 8 number cubes on an edge.

3. a. **Number Sense** What is the total number of unit cubes in a cube with 10 unit cubes on an edge?
   b. If there are 15 unit cubes on an edge, how many unit cubes will have no sides painted? One side painted? Two sides painted?
   c. **Reasoning** If 144 unit cubes have two sides painted, how many unit cubes are on one edge of the cube?

8-9 Volumes of Rectangular Prisms and Cylinders

What You'll Learn

To find the volume of a prism

To find the volume of a cylinder

. . . And Why

To find the volume of a paint can, as in Example 3

For help, go to Lesson 8-4.

Find the area of each circle. Round to the nearest square unit.

1.
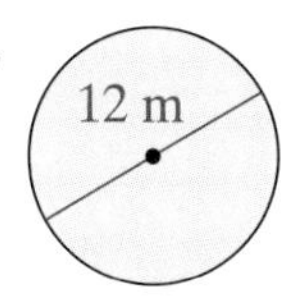

2.
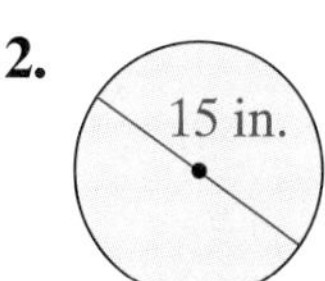

3.
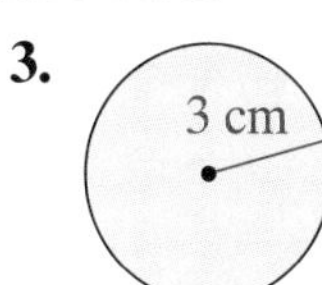

New Vocabulary • volume • cubic unit

Interactive lesson includes instant self-check, tutorials, and activities.

OBJECTIVE 1

Finding the Volume of a Prism

one cubic centimeter (1 cm^3)

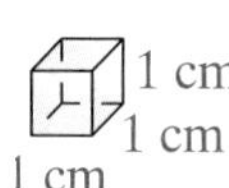

The **volume** of a three-dimensional figure is the number of cubic units needed to fill the space inside the figure. A **cubic unit** is a cube with edges one unit long.

Consider filling the rectangular prism at the right with cubic centimeters.

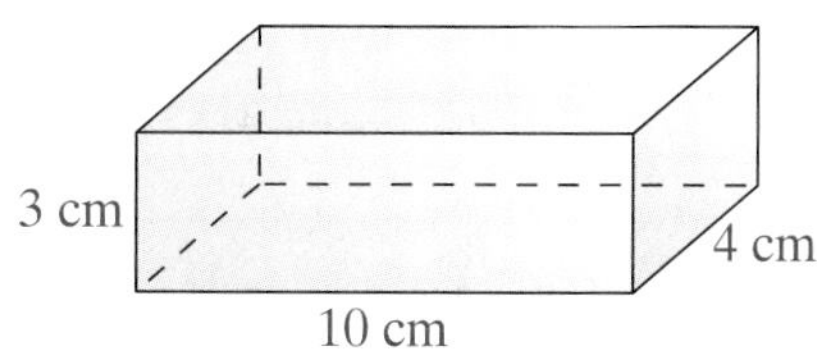

The bottom layer of the prism contains $10 \cdot 4$, or 40, cubes.

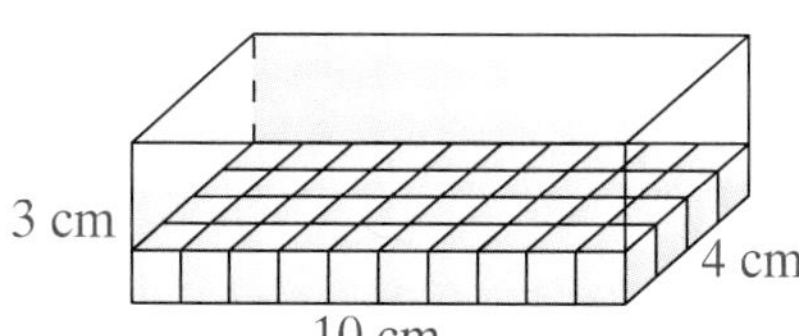

Three layers of 40 cubes fit in the prism.
$3 \cdot 40 = 120$

The volume of the prism is 120 cm^3.

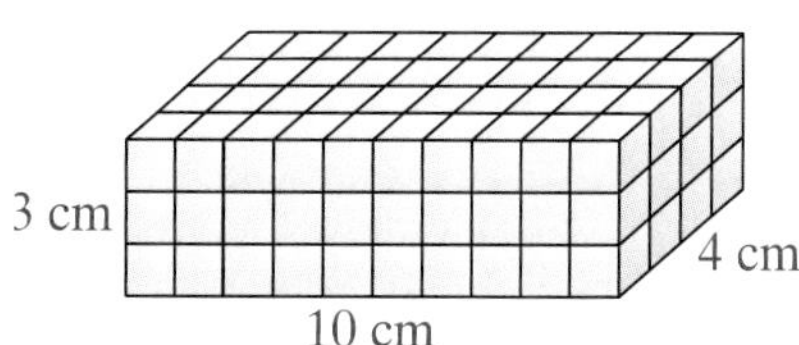

The calculation of volume above suggests the following formula.

Key Concepts — **Volume of a Rectangular Prism**

$$V = \text{area of base} \cdot \text{height} = Bh = \ell wh$$

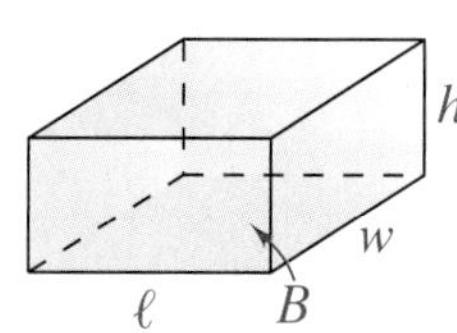

1 EXAMPLE Finding the Volume of a Rectangular Prism

Find the volume of the rectangular prism.

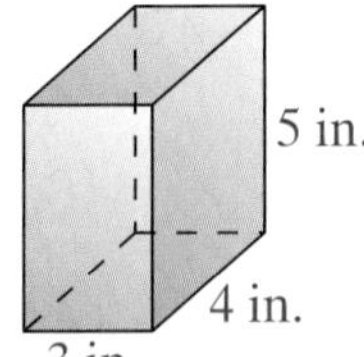

$V = \ell wh$ ← **Use the formula.**

$= (3)(4)(5)$ ← **Substitute.**

$= 60$ ← **Multiply.**

The volume of the rectangular prism is 60 in.^{3}.

Check Understanding 1 Find the volume of each rectangular prism.

a.

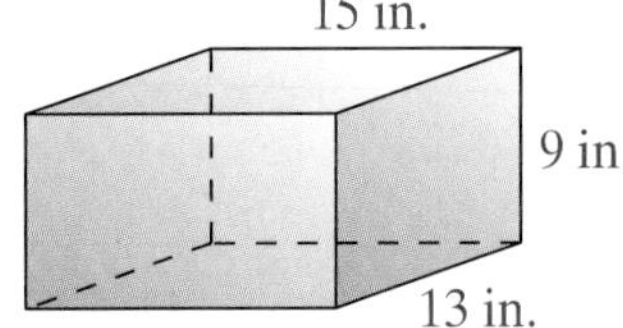

b.

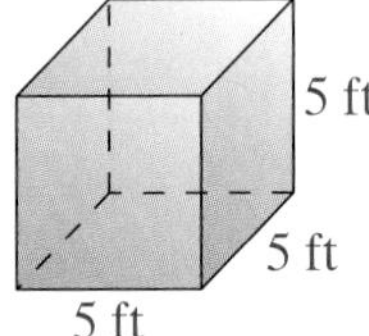

OBJECTIVE

2 Finding the Volume of a Cylinder

The volume formulas for prisms and cylinders are similar.

Key Concepts **Volume of a Cylinder**

$V = \text{area of base} \cdot \text{height}$

$= Bh$

$= \pi r^2 h$

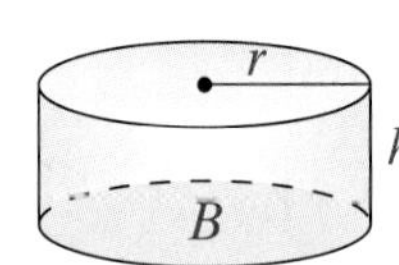

2 EXAMPLE Finding the Volume of a Cylinder

Find the volume of the cylinder. Round to the nearest cubic centimeter.

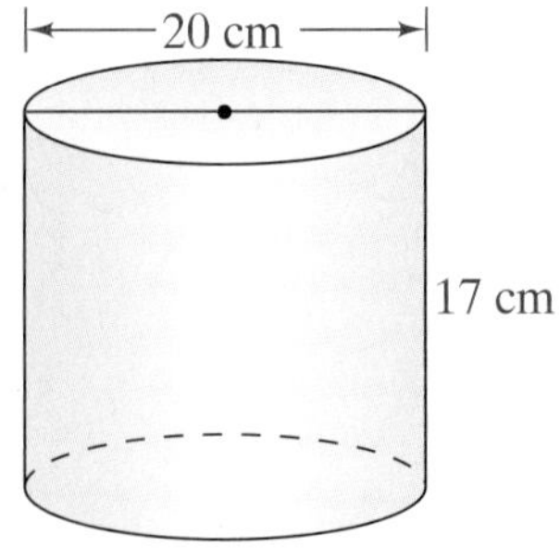

$V = \pi r^2 h$ ← **Use the formula.**

$= (\pi)(10)^2(17)$ ← **Substitute.**

≈ 5340.7075 ← **Use a calculator.**

The volume of the cylinder is about 5,341 cm^3.

Check Understanding 2 Find the volume of the cylinder. Round to the nearest cubic meter.

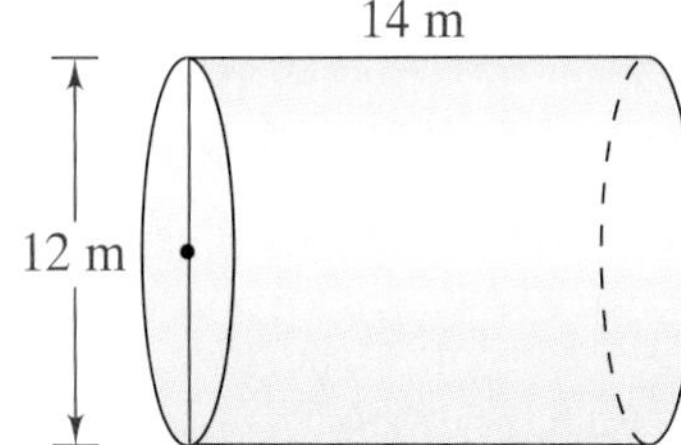

3 EXAMPLE — Real-World Problem Solving

Painting Estimate the volume of the cylindrical paint can. Then find the volume to the nearest cubic unit.

Estimate:

$V = \pi r^2 h$ ← **Use the formula.**

$\approx (3)(4)^2(9)$ ← **Use 3 to estimate π.**

$\approx (50)(9)$ ← **Use 50 to estimate 48 (3 · 16).**

≈ 450

The estimated volume is 450 cm^3.

Actual volume:

$V = (\pi)(4)^2(9) \approx 452.38934$

The actual volume is about 452 cm^3.

Check Understanding 3

a. Estimate the volume of the cylinder. Then find the volume to the nearest cubic centimeter.

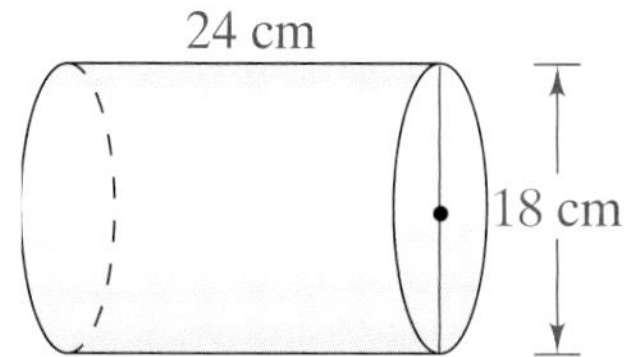

b. **Reasoning** Suppose you estimate using 20 for 4^2 instead of 16 in Example 3. Will your estimate be reasonable?

EXERCISES

For more practice, see *Extra Practice*.

A Practice by Example

Example 1 (page 450)

Find the volume of each rectangular prism.

1.

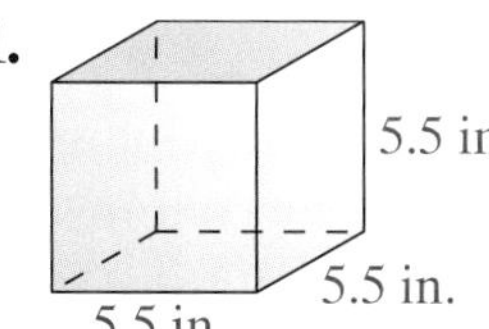

2.

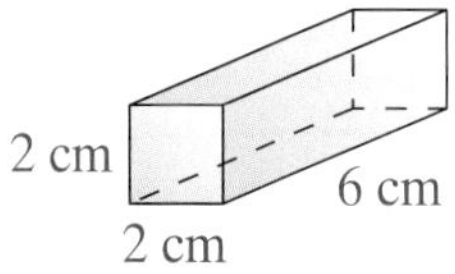

2 cm
6 cm
2 cm

3.

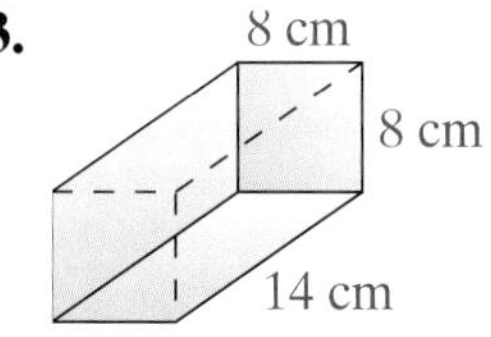

4.

9 in.
14 in.
10.5 in.

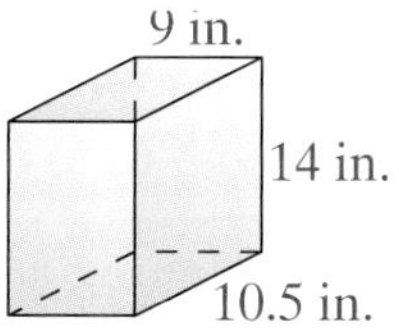

5.

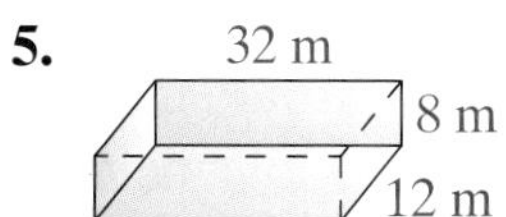

6.

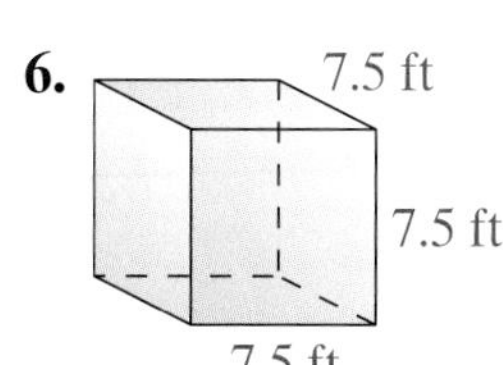

Example 2 (page 450)

Find the volume of each cylinder. Round to the nearest cubic unit.

7.

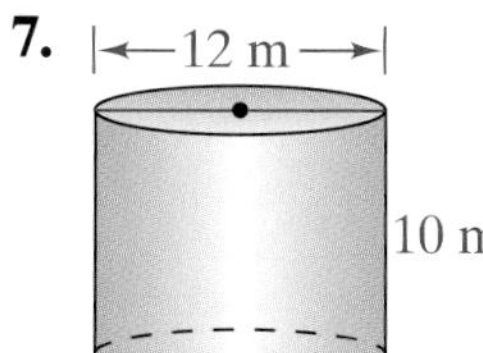

8.

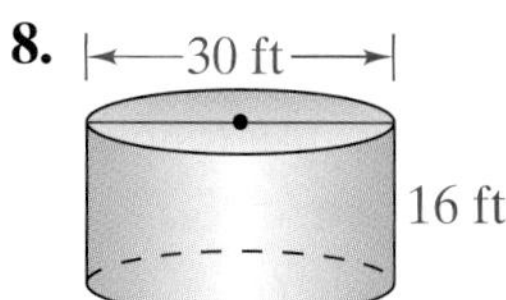

9.

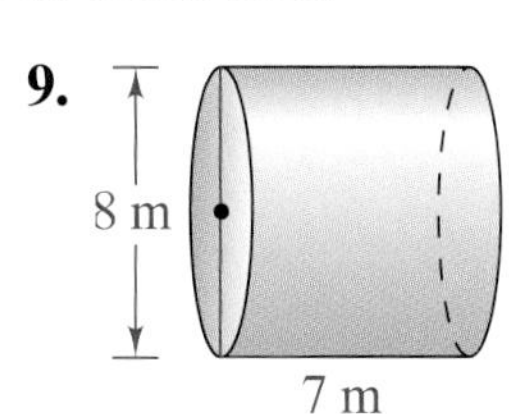

Find the volume of each cylinder. Round to the nearest cubic unit.

10. 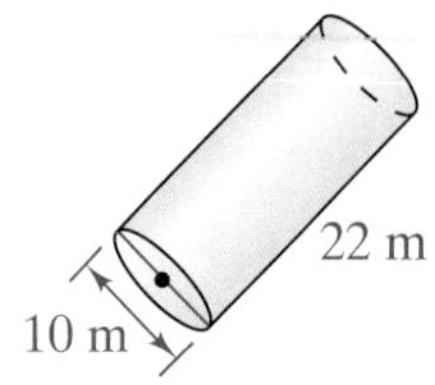

11. 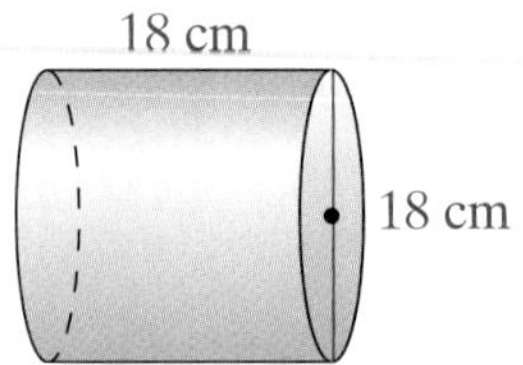

12. 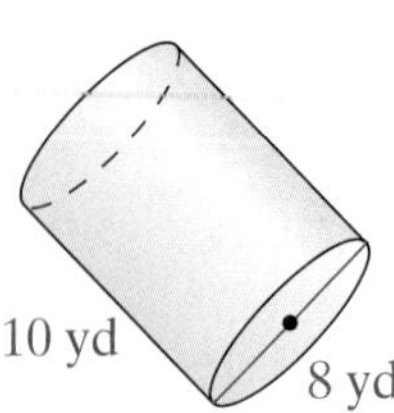

Example 3 (page 451)

Packaging Estimate the volume of each cylinder. Then find the volume to the nearest cubic unit.

13. 

14. 

15. 

16. 

B Apply Your Skills

Find the height of each rectangular prism given the volume, length, and width.

17. $V = 455 \text{ cm}^3$
$\ell = 10$ cm
$w = 7$ cm

18. $V = 525 \text{ m}^3$
$\ell = 7.5$ m
$w = 3.5$ m

19. $V = 5{,}832 \text{ in.}^3$
$\ell = 18$ in.
$w = 18$ in.

20. a. Compare the volumes of the figures.
b. Reasoning Why are their volumes different?

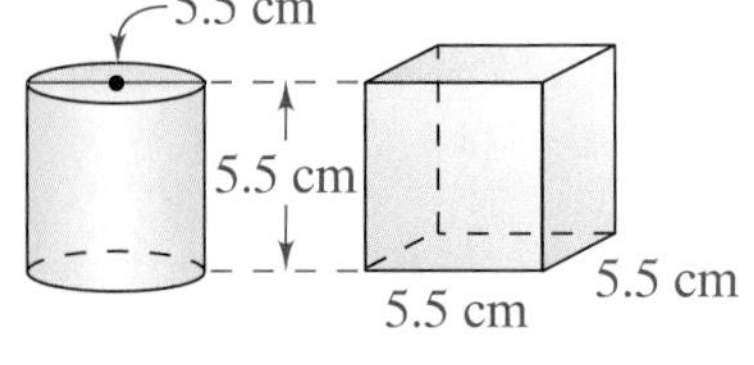

21. Writing in Math Explain how you would find the radius of a cylinder with a height of 10 in. and a volume of 385 in.^{3}. (Use $\pi = 3.14$.)

22. Data File, p. 401 You are designing a shelf to hold CDs. Find the difference in volume of a stack of 50 CDs in regular jewel boxes versus a stack of 50 CDs in slim jewel boxes, if the CDs are stacked height to height. Give your answer to the nearest cubic inch.

Find the length of the radius of each cylinder given the volume and height. Use $\pi = 3.14$.

23. $V = 314 \text{ ft}^3$
$h = 25$ ft

24. $V = 15{,}700 \text{ cm}^3$
$h = 50$ cm

25. $V = 1{,}356.48 \text{ cm}^3$
$h = 12$ cm

Real-World  **Connection**

Some aquariums are cylinders, making it possible to view the fish from all directions.

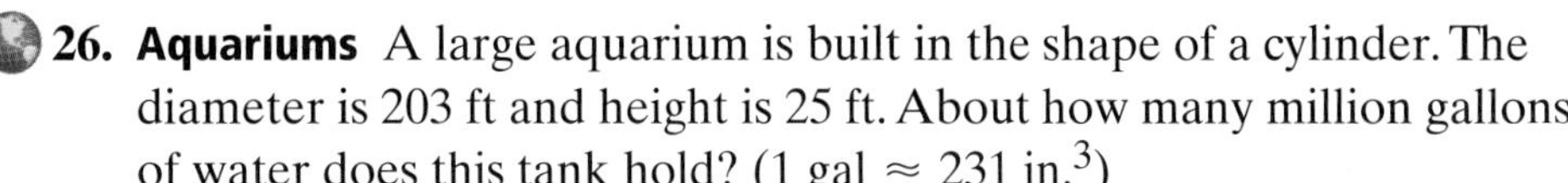

26. Aquariums A large aquarium is built in the shape of a cylinder. The diameter is 203 ft and height is 25 ft. About how many million gallons of water does this tank hold? (1 gal ≈ 231 in.^3)

27. a. The triangular prism at the right was formed by cutting a rectangular prism in half. Find the volume of the rectangular prism.
b. Use your answer to part (a) to find the volume of the triangular prism.
c. Show that the volume of the triangular prism is the area of its base times its height.

28. Find the volume of a rectangular prism with length 11 ft, width 5 ft, and height 6 ft.

C Challenge

Find the volume of each figure to the nearest cubic unit.

29.

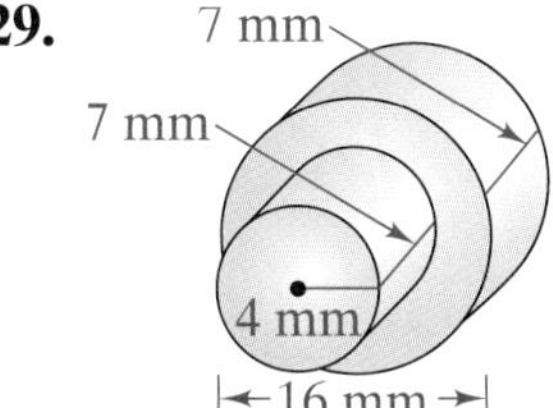

30.

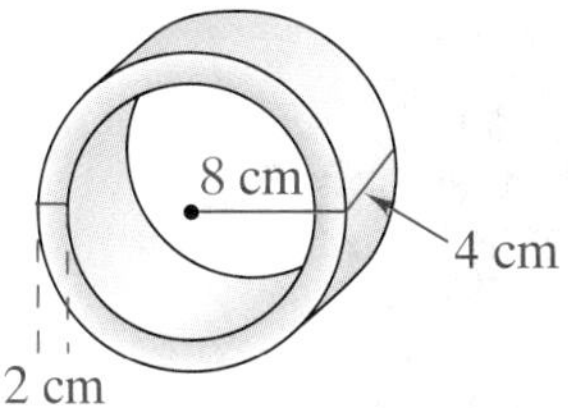

31. Find the volume of the prism at the right.

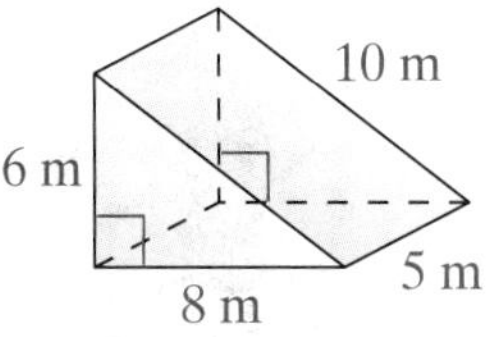

32. A normal duck has two legs. A lame duck has one leg. A sitting duck has no legs. Betty has 33 ducks. She has two more normal ducks than lame ducks and two more lame ducks than sitting ducks. How many legs in all do the 33 ducks have?

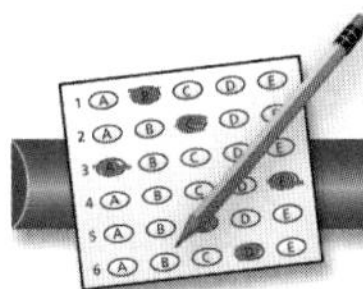

Test Prep

Multiple Choice

33. A rectangular prism has a volume of 180 cm^3. The length is 5 cm and the height is 6 cm. What is the width of the prism?

A. 1 cm **B.** 6 cm **C.** 30 cm **D.** 36 cm

34. How does the volume of a cylinder change if the base radius of the cylinder is doubled?

F. no change **G.** It doubles.
H. It triples. **I.** It quadruples.

35. How does the volume of a cylinder change if the height is doubled?

A. no change **B.** It doubles.
C. It triples. **D.** It quadruples.

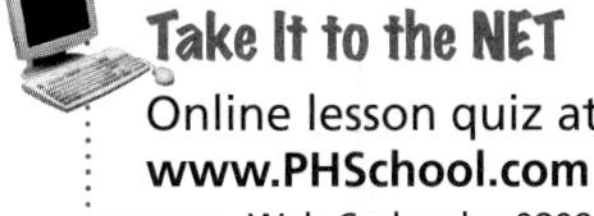

Take It to the NET
Online lesson quiz at **www.PHSchool.com**
Web Code: aba-0809

Short Response

36. A cylinder has a base radius 20 ft and height 10 ft.
a. Draw and label a diagram of the cylinder.
b. What is the volume of the cylinder, to the nearest cubic foot.

Mixed Review

Lesson 8-3 **Find the area of each irregular figure.**

37.

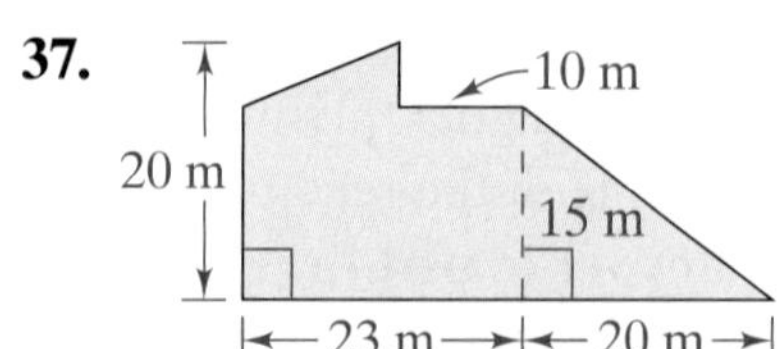

38.

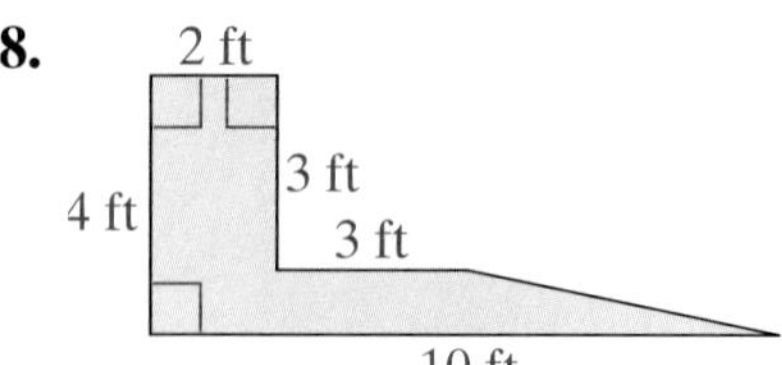

Lesson 7-2 **Find the measures of the complement and supplement of each angle.**

39. $m\angle A = 40°$ **40.** $m\angle B = 65°$ **41.** $m\angle C = 37°$ **42.** $m\angle D = 5°$

43. $m\angle E = 55°$ **44.** $m\angle F = 30°$ **45.** $m\angle G = 88°$ **46.** $m\angle H = 20°$

Checkpoint Quiz 2 — Lessons 8-5 through 8-9

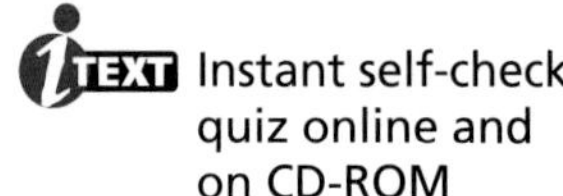

Instant self-check quiz online and on CD-ROM

1. Find two consecutive whole numbers that $\sqrt{77}$ falls between.

Find each missing length.

2. 15 cm, x, 36 cm

3.

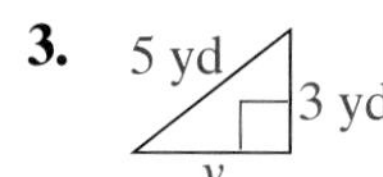

4.

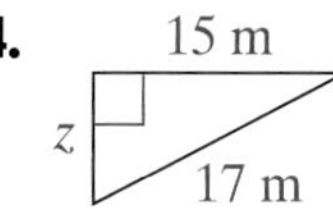

Name each figure.

5.

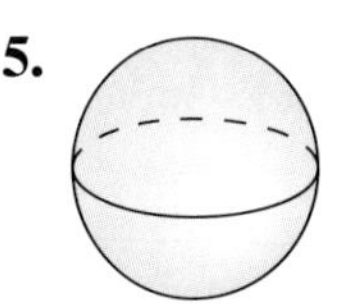

6.

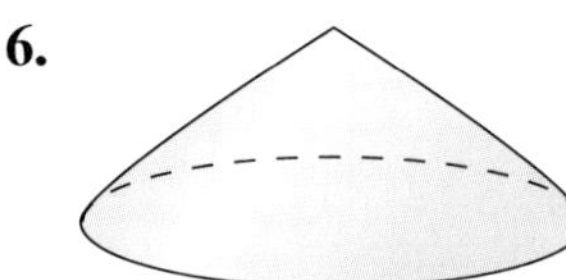

Find the surface area of each figure. Round to the nearest tenth, if necessary.

7.

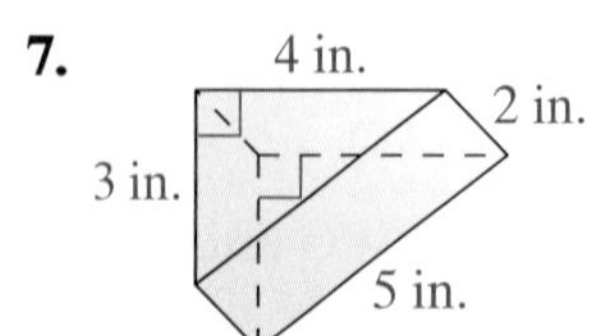

8.

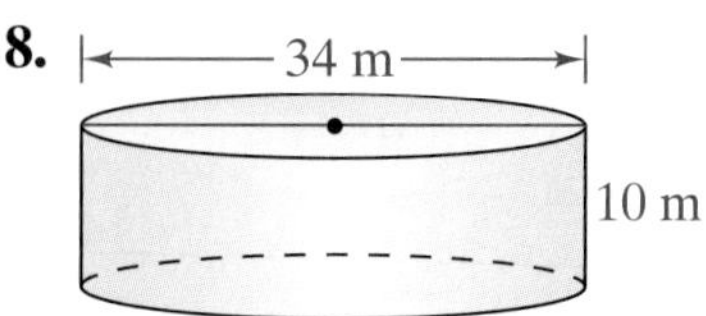

Find the volume of the rectangular prism and the cylinder. Round to the nearest cubic unit if necessary.

9.

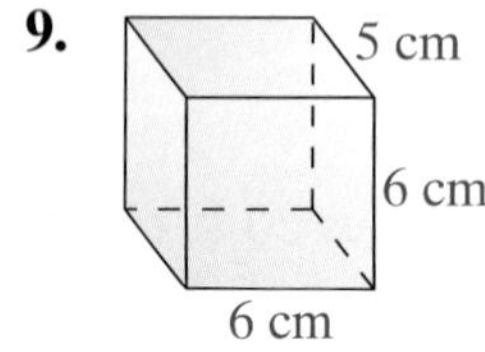

10.

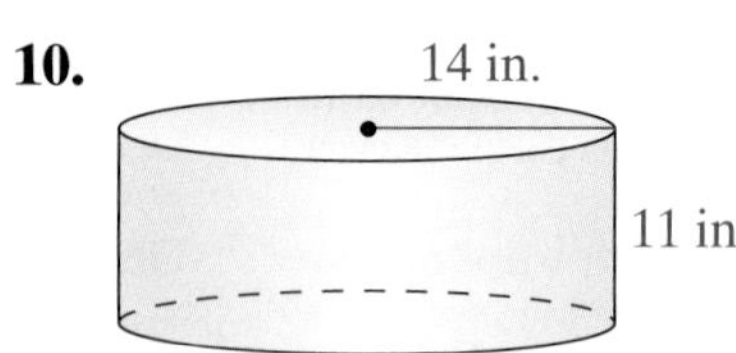

Problem Solving

8-10 Try, Check, and Revise and Write an Equation

What You'll Learn

OBJECTIVE 1 To solve a problem using two different methods

. . . And Why

To compare strategies in solving measurement problems, as in Example 1

Check Skills You'll Need

For help, go to Lesson 4-6.

Solve each equation.

1. $\frac{1}{3}x = 5$
2. $12 = \frac{b}{3}$
3. $\frac{1}{4}r + 6 = 26$
4. $\frac{2}{5}m - 4 = 4$
5. $\frac{5}{8}w - \frac{1}{2} = 6$
6. $\frac{2}{4} = c + \frac{1}{6}$

OBJECTIVE

iTEXT Interactive lesson includes instant self-check, tutorials, and activities.

1 Solving a Problem Using Two Different Methods

When to Use These Strategies If you are sure the solutions of a problem are whole numbers, then ***try, check, and revise***. If you are not sure, then ***write an equation***. These strategies are used as separate methods in Example 1.

1 EXAMPLE Real-World Problem Solving

Boat Building A group of students is building a sailboat. They have 48 ft^2 of material to make a sail. They design the sail as shown at the left. Find the length of the base and the height.

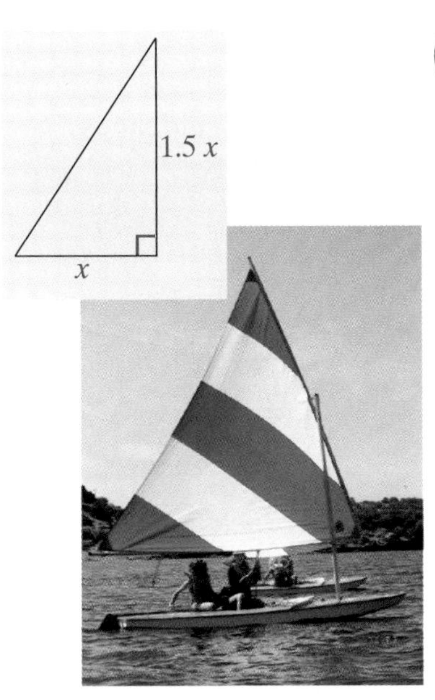

Real-World Connection

Sail makers work with boat designers to construct sails shaped for a particular boat's design.

Read and Understand The maximum area the sail material can cover is 48 ft^2. You need to find the length of the base and the height, given that the height is 1.5 times the length of the base.

Method 1 Try, Check, and Revise

Plan and Solve You know there is a relationship between the height and base. Use that to test possible dimensions of the triangle formed by the boom (base), the mast (height), and the sail and see if they produce the desired area. Organize the test results in a table.

Boom	Mast	Area	Conclusion
6	9	$\frac{1}{2} \cdot 6 \cdot 9 = 27$	Too low
10	15	$\frac{1}{2} \cdot 10 \cdot 15 = 75$	Too high
8	12	$\frac{1}{2} \cdot 8 \cdot 12 = 48$	✔

The length of the base is 8 ft. The height is 12 ft.

Method 2 Write an Equation

Another way to solve this problem is to use the formula for the area of a triangle to write an equation.

1.5 x

x

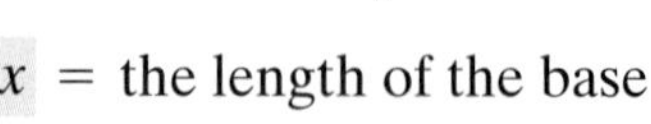

x = the length of the base

$1.5x$ = the height

The formula for the area of a triangle is $A = \frac{1}{2}bh$. You know the area of sail material is 48 ft^2.

$$\frac{1}{2} \cdot b \cdot h = A \quad \leftarrow \text{Use the area formula.}$$

$$\frac{1}{2} \cdot x \cdot 1.5x = 48 \quad \leftarrow \text{Substitute.}$$

$$\frac{1}{2} \cdot 1.5x^2 = 48 \quad \leftarrow \text{Multiply } x \text{ and } 1.5x.$$

$$\frac{3}{4}x^2 = 48 \quad \leftarrow \text{Simplify.}$$

$$\frac{4}{3} \cdot \frac{3}{4}x^2 = 48 \cdot \frac{4}{3} \quad \leftarrow \text{Multiply each side by } \tfrac{4}{3}.$$

$$x^2 = 64 \quad \leftarrow \text{Simplify.}$$

$$\sqrt{x^2} = \sqrt{64} \quad \leftarrow \text{Take the square root of each side.}$$

$$x = 8 \quad \leftarrow \text{Simplify.}$$

$$1.5x = 1.5(8) \quad \leftarrow \text{Substitute 8 into the expression for the height.}$$

$$= 12 \quad \leftarrow \text{Multiply.}$$

The height of the sail is 12 ft and the length of the base is 8 ft.

Look Back and Check To check the answer you can look at the guidelines given for the length of the base and the height. The height has to be 1.5 times as long as the base.

$1.5 \cdot 8 = 12$

Also the area has to equal 48 ft^2.

$\frac{1}{2} \cdot 8 \cdot 12 = 48$

The answer checks.

Check Understanding **1** **a.** Look back at the two methods used to solve Example 1. Which method would you use? Why?

b. A neighborhood group is putting up fencing around a rectangular garden with the dimensions shown at the right. The members know they need an area of 2,450 ft^2 for the garden. How much fencing material will they need?

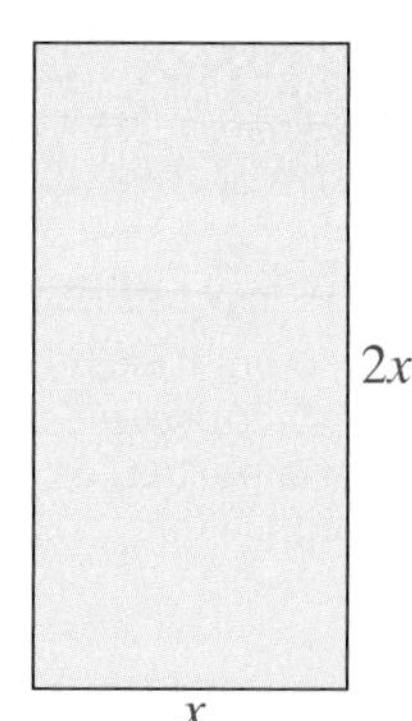

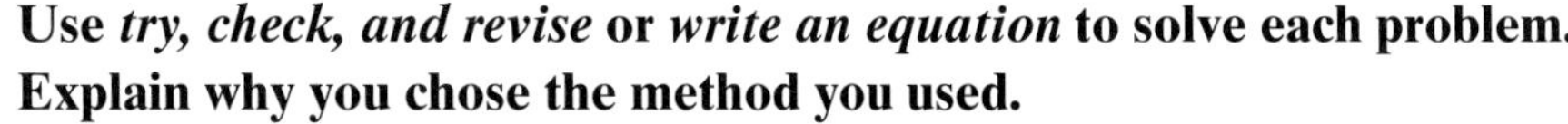

EXERCISES

For more practice, see *Extra Practice*.

A Practice by Example

Use *try, check, and revise* or *write an equation* to solve each problem. Explain why you chose the method you used.

Example 1 (page 455)

1. **Measurement** A square dance floor has an area of 1,444 ft^2. What are its dimensions?

2. **Carpentry** You are building a tabletop for a workbench. The length is 8 ft and the area of the top that you want is 24 ft^2. How wide should the tabletop be?

Need Help?
- Reread the problem.
- Identify the key facts and details.
- Tell the problem in your own words.
- Try a different strategy.
- Check your work.

3. In the triangle $\overline{AB} \cong \overline{AC}$. The area of the triangle is 100 cm^2. What is the length of the third side?

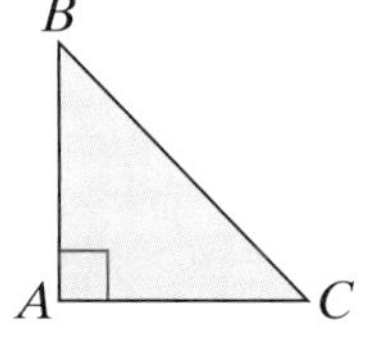

4. **Measurement** The width of a rectangle is 4 cm less than its length. The area of the rectangle is 96 cm^2. Find the length and width of the rectangle.

5. One leg of a right triangle measures 10 cm. The hypotenuse measures 26 cm. Find the length of the other leg.

B Apply Your Skills

Use any strategy to solve each problem. Show your work.

6. Find the next two numbers in the pattern below.
   100, 25, 50, 12.5, 25, ■, ■

7. a. What is the longest segment shown in the rectangular prism?
   b. What measurements do you need to find x? To find y?
   c. Find x and y.

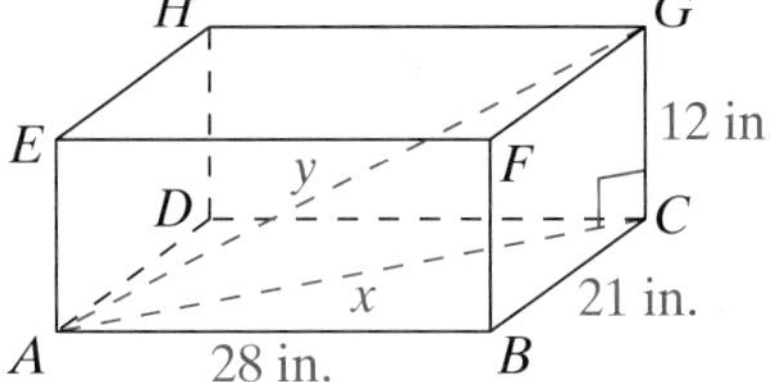

8. a. **Measurement** The mass of 8 cm^3 of aluminum is about 22 g. Name two sets of dimensions possible for an 8 cm^3 rectangular prism.
   b. **Reasoning** What information in part (a) is not necessary? Explain.

9. **Pets** You and your friend each make a purchase at the pet store. You buy the lizard and frogs at the left below for \$15.35. Your friend buys the lizards and frog at the right for \$15.85. How much does one lizard cost?

Strategies

- Draw a Diagram
- Look for a Pattern
- Make a Graph
- Make an Organized List
- Make a Table
- Simulate a Problem
- Solve a Simpler Problem
- Try, Check, and Revise
- Use Logical Reasoning
- Work Backward
- Write an Equation

10. **a.** Use a calculator to find the following products.

$15 \cdot 15$ $25 \cdot 25$ $35 \cdot 35$ $45 \cdot 45$

b. 

Describe any patterns that you find in part (a).

c. Use the patterns you found in part (b) to write each of the following products without multiplying the given numbers.

$55 \cdot 55$ $65 \cdot 65$ $75 \cdot 75$ $85 \cdot 85$

C Challenge

11. Tom has cartons measuring 3 ft × 2 ft × 6 in. He wishes to store them in a space 15 ft × 9 ft × 24 ft. He can stack the cartons on top of each other, but not inside each other. How many cartons can he store?

12. **Stretch Your Thinking** The diagonal of a rectangle has a length of $\sqrt{40}$ m. The area of the rectangle is 12 m^2. What is the perimeter of the rectangle?

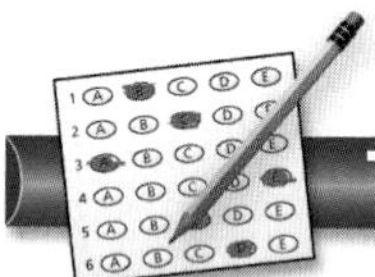

Test Prep

Multiple Choice

Refer to the diagram at the right for Exercises 13–15.

13. Kevin's yard measures 60 ft by 40 ft. Kevin will plant shrubs at the front of his yard as shown. He will plant grass in the rest of his yard. How many square feet of grass will Kevin need?

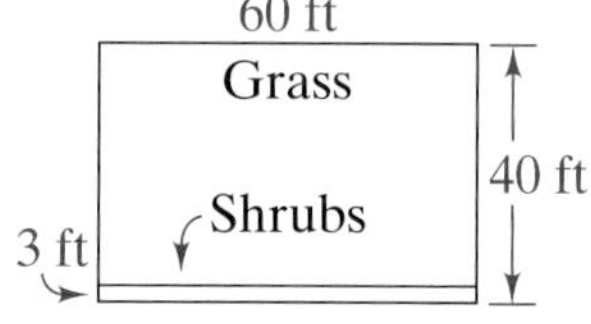

A. 180 ft^2 B. 2,220 ft^2 C. 2,400 ft^2 D. 2,580 ft^2

Online lesson quiz at **www.PHSchool.com**
Web Code: aba-0810

14. How many square feet of shrubs will Kevin need?

F. 180 ft^2 G. 2,220 ft^2 H. 2,400 ft^2 I. 2,580 ft^2

15. Kevin wants to place a small circular fountain in the middle of the yard. Its diameter is 6 ft. About how many square feet of grass will he now need? Use 3.14 for π.

A. 2,000 ft^2 B. 2,192 ft^2 C. 2,220 ft^2 D. 2,372 ft^2

Short Response

16. Square *ABCD* has perimeter *s* units. What is its area in terms of *s*? Show your work.

Mixed Review

Lesson 7-2

Classify each angle as *acute*, *right*, *obtuse*, or *straight*.

17. $m\angle A = 56°$ **18.** $m\angle B = 177°$ **19.** $m\angle C = 89°$

20. $m\angle D = 180°$ **21.** $m\angle E = 90°$ **22.** $m\angle F = 13°$

Lesson 3-2

Write in standard form.

23. 6.5×10^5 **24.** 2.3×10^2 **25.** 5.26×10^7 **26.** 9.45×10^9

Test-Taking Strategies: Finding Multiple Correct Answers

Some questions have more than one correct answer. Test each answer. Then choose the statement that includes only the correct answers.

EXAMPLE

The perimeter of a rectangle is 42 in. Which of the following could be true?

I. The area of the rectangle is 90 in.^2.
II. The length of one side of the rectangle is 21 in.
III. The length of the diagonal of the rectangle is 15 in.

A. I and II only **B.** II and III only **C.** I and III only **D.** I, II, and III

Test each answer to see whether it could be true for a rectangle with a perimeter of 42 in.

Answer I is possible for a rectangle with dimensions 6 in. by 15 in.

Answer II is not possible. If the length of one side of the rectangle is 21 in., then its opposite side would also measure 21 in. The lengths of the two sides would total 42 in., leaving zero inches of the length for the other two sides.

Answer III is possible for a rectangle with dimensions 9 in. by 12 in.

Only answers I and III could be true. The correct choice is C.

EXERCISES

1. To which sets of numbers does $\sqrt{100}$ belong?

I. rational numbers
II. integers
III. whole numbers

A. I and II only **B.** II and III only **C.** I and III only **D.** I, II, and III

2. Which set(s) of side lengths of a triangle can form a right triangle?

I. 7 m, 24 m, 25 m
II. 24 cm, 45 cm, 51 cm
III. 10 km, 24 km, 28 km

F. I and II only **G.** II and III only **H.** I and III only **I.** I, II, and III

3. The area of a rectangle is 98 m^2. Which of the following could be true?

I. The perimeter of the rectangle is 42 m.
II. The length of one side of the rectangle is 196 m.
III. The length is twice the width.

A. I and II only **B.** II and III only **C.** I and III only **D.** I, II, and III

Chapter Review

Vocabulary

area (p. 404)
base(s) (pp. 407, 408, 414, 437, 438)
center of a sphere (p. 438)
circumference (p. 419)
cone (p. 438)
cube (p. 437)
cubic unit (p. 449)
cylinder (p. 438)
edge (p. 437)
face (p. 437)
height (pp. 407, 408, 414, 437, 438)
hypotenuse (p. 432)
irrational number (p. 428)
legs (p. 432)
net (p. 442)
perfect square (p. 426)
pi (p. 419)
prism (p. 437)
pyramid (p. 438)
Pythagorean Theorem (p. 432)
sphere (p. 438)
square root (p. 426)
surface area (p. 443)
three-dimensional figure (p. 437)
vertex (p. 438)
volume (p. 449)

Reading Math: Understanding Vocabulary

Take It to the NET Online vocabulary quiz at **www.PHSchool.com** Web Code: abj-0851

Choose the correct term to complete each sentence.

1. A(n) (edge, vertex) is the intersection of two faces.
2. The longest side of a right triangle is the (hypotenuse, leg).
3. A (prism, pyramid) has two parallel and congruent bases.
4. The perimeter of a circle is the (area, circumference) of the circle.
5. A (cone, cylinder) has one circular base and one vertex.

Skills and Concepts

8-1 Objectives

- To estimate length
- To estimate area

The **area** of a figure is the number of square units it encloses.

6. Estimate the area of the shaded region. Each square represents 20 in.^{2}.

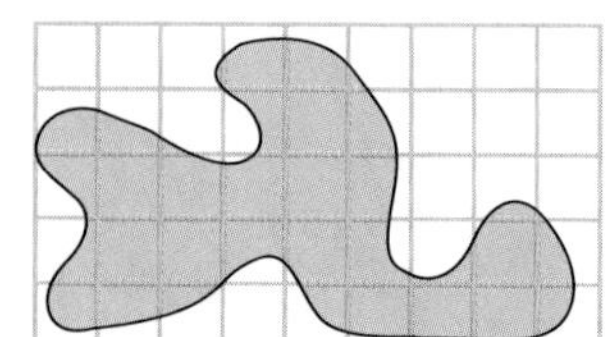

7. Choose a reasonable estimate for the width of a book—7 in. or 7 ft. Explain your choice.

8-2 and 8-3 Objectives

- To find the areas of parallelograms, triangles, trapezoids, and irregular figures

To find the area of an irregular figure, separate it into familiar figures and find the area of each piece using the formulas below. Then add the areas.

parallelogram	triangle	trapezoid
$A = bh$	$A = \frac{1}{2}bh$	$A = \frac{1}{2}h(b_1 + b_2)$

Use familiar figures to find the area of each figure.

8.

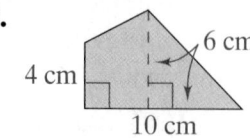

9. 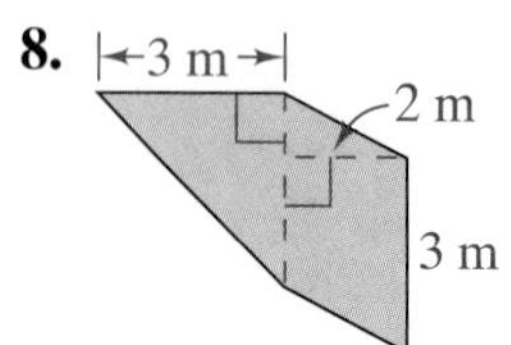

10. 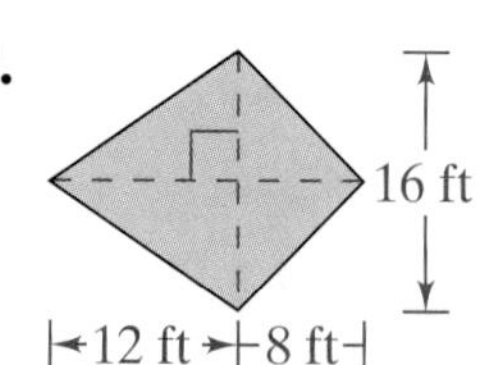

8-4 Objectives

- To find the circumference and area of a circle

To find the **circumference** of a circle, use the formula $C = \pi d = 2\pi r$. To find the area of a circle, use the formula $A = \pi r^2$.

Find the circumference and area of each circle. Round your answers to the nearest unit.

11. 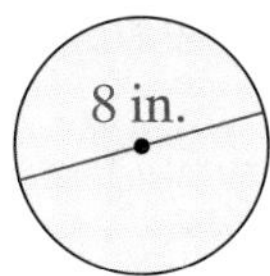

12. 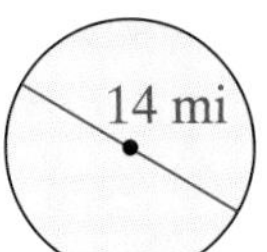

13. 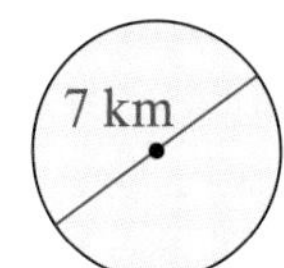

8-5 and 8-6 Objectives

- To find square roots of numbers
- To classify numbers
- To use the Pythagorean Theorem

A **perfect square** is a square of an integer. The opposite of squaring a number is finding its **square root.** Many of the square roots that exist are **irrational numbers,** or numbers that cannot be written as the ratio of two integers.

The **Pythagorean Theorem,** $a^2 + b^2 = c^2$, relates the lengths of the **legs** of a right triangle to the length of its **hypotenuse.**

14. Art A square piece of glass in a picture frame covers an area of 36 in.^{2}. What is the length of each side of the glass?

15. Find two consecutive whole numbers that $\sqrt{45}$ falls between.

16. A pipeline is placed diagonally across a rectangular field that is 25 yd wide and 30 yd long. How long is the pipeline, to the nearest yard?

8-7 to 8-9 Objectives

- To identify and draw three-dimensional figures
- To draw a net
- To find the surface areas and volumes of prisms and cylinders

To find the **surface area** of a prism and cylinder, draw a **net** and find the area of the net.

To find the **volume** of a prism, use the formula $V = \ell wh$. To find the volume of a cylinder, use the formula $V = \pi r^2 h$.

A cone has one circular base and one **vertex**.

Find the surface area and volume. Round to the nearest tenth.

17. 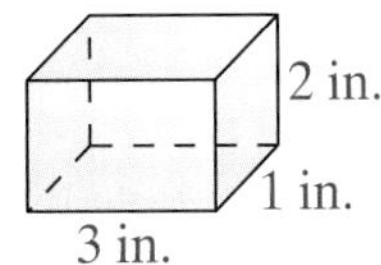

18. 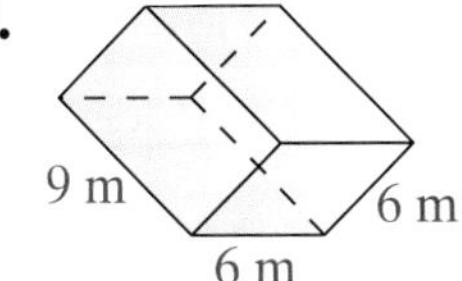

19. 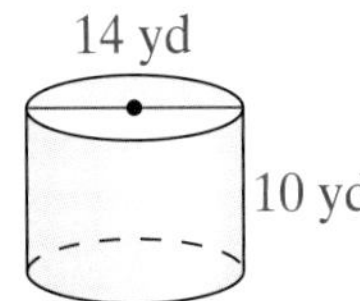

8-10 Objective

- To solve a problem using two different methods

20. Construction The area of a window is 18 ft^2. The length of the window will be two times the width of the window. What are the dimensions of the window?

21. Measurement The volume of a rectangular prism is 2,058 cm^3. The length of the prism is three times the width. The height is 14 cm. Find the other dimensions.

Chapter 8 Chapter Test

Estimate the area of each shaded region. Each square represents 50 in.^{2}.

1. 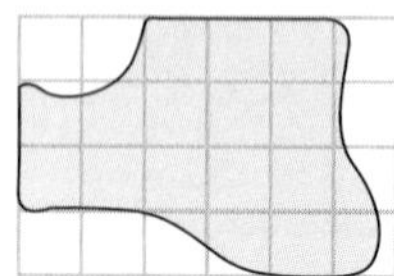

2. 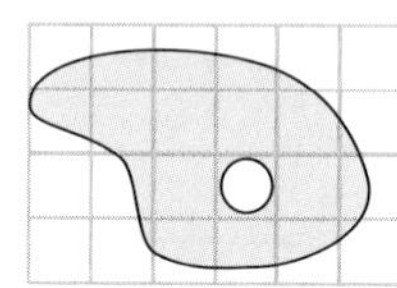

Find the area of each figure.

3. 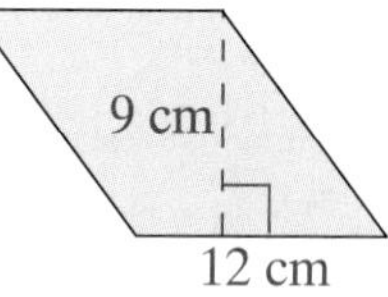

4. 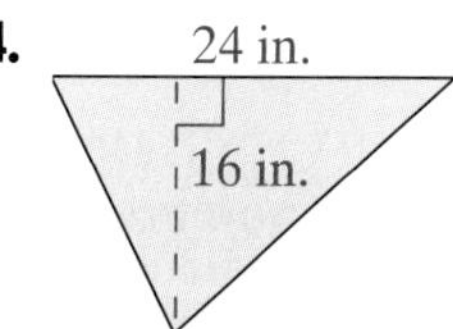

5. 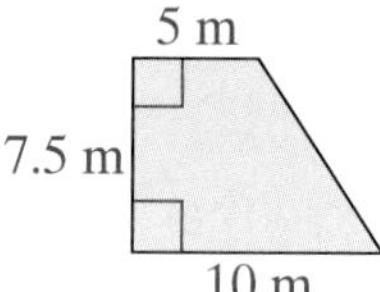

6. 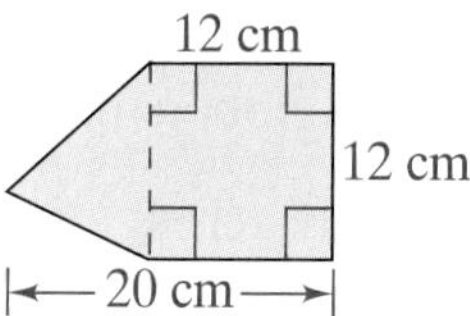

Find the circumference and area of each circle. Round to the nearest tenth.

7. 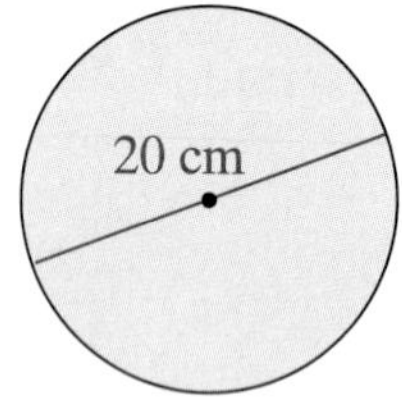

8. 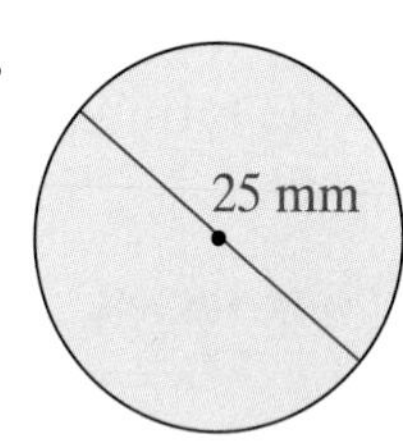

Simplify each square root.

9. $\sqrt{9}$ **10.** $\sqrt{25}$ **11.** $\sqrt{49}$ **12.** $\sqrt{100}$

13. $\sqrt{121}$ **14.** $\sqrt{1}$ **15.** $\sqrt{64}$ **16.** $\sqrt{81}$

17. A square plot of land has an area of 100 m^2. What is the perimeter of the plot?

Find two consecutive whole numbers that each number falls between. Then estimate the number's value.

18. $\sqrt{55}$ **19.** $\sqrt{63}$ **20.** $\sqrt{8}$ **21.** $\sqrt{45}$

Find each missing length to the nearest tenth.

22. 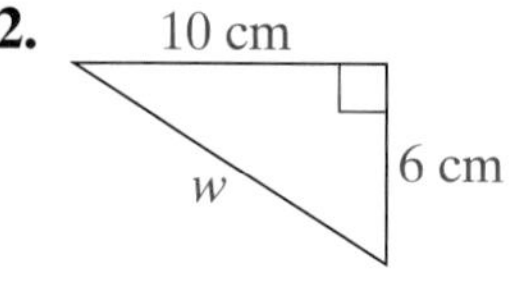

23. 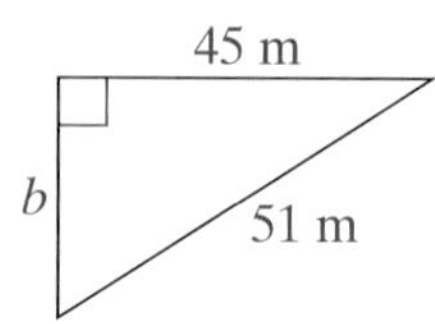

24. Ladders A ladder 26 ft long is placed 10 ft from the base of a house. How high up the side of the house does the ladder reach?

25. Support Cables A support cable connects the top of a 30-m pole to an anchor 20 m from the base of the pole. How long is the support cable, to the nearest tenth of a meter?

Identify each number as *rational* or *irrational*.

26. $\sqrt{30}$ **27.** $3.\overline{7}$ **28.** $\frac{22}{7}$ **29.** π

Find the surface area to the nearest whole unit.

30. 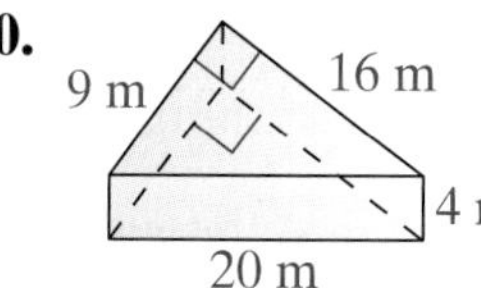

31. 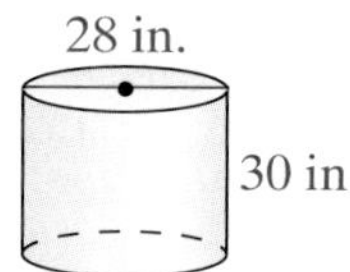

Find the volume to the nearest whole unit.

32. 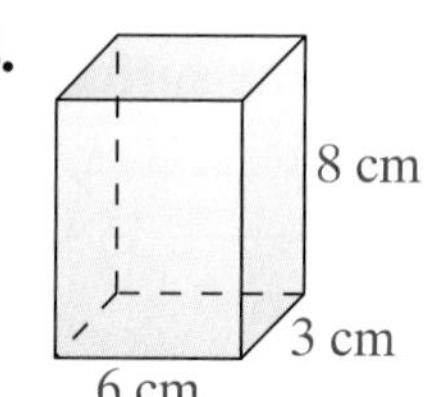

33. 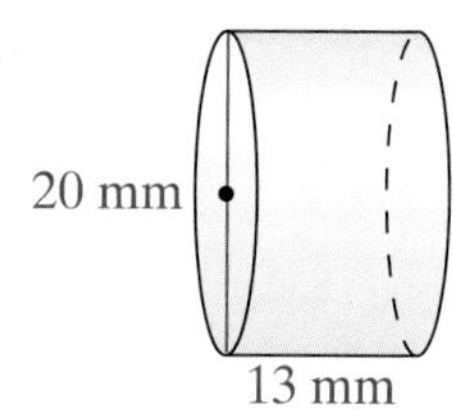

34. The area of a rectangular playground is 1,800 yd^2. The width is twice the length. What are the dimensions of the playground?

35. Writing in Math Explain how you would show that a triangle with side lengths 7 in., 24 in., and 25 in. is a right triangle.

Test Prep

Multiple Choice

For Exercises 1–10, choose the correct letter.

1. Which number has the greatest value?
   A. 2^5 **B.** 3^3 **C.** 5^2 **D.** 20^1

2. Rectangle *ABCD* has dimensions 3 in. × 4 in. What is the area and perimeter of *ABCD*?
   F. $A = 12$ in.^{2}, $P = 12$ in.
   G. $A = 12$ in.^{2}, $P = 14$ in.
   H. $A = 6$ in.^{2}, $P = 12$ in.
   I. $A = 12$ in.^{2}, $P = 7$ in.

3. The rectangles are similar. Which proportion could NOT be used to find the value of *x*?

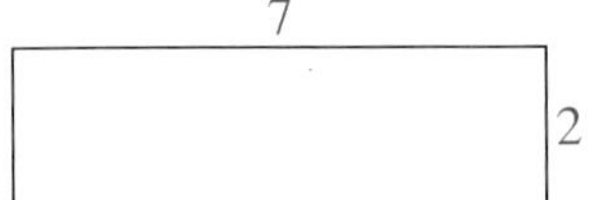

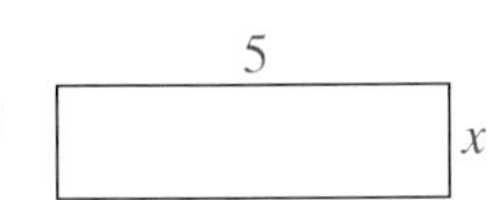

   A. $\frac{7}{5} = \frac{2}{x}$ **B.** $\frac{x}{2} = \frac{7}{5}$
   C. $\frac{x}{5} = \frac{2}{7}$ **D.** $\frac{2}{7} = \frac{x}{5}$

4. Which of the following could NOT be the length of the sides of a right triangle?
   F. 8, 15, 17 **G.** 10, 24, 26
   H. 15, 35, 40 **I.** 12, 16, 20

5. Which expression could you use to find the area of the cylinder's base?
   A. $2 \cdot \pi \cdot 5$
   B. $\pi \cdot 2.5 \cdot 2.5$
   C. $\pi \cdot 5 \cdot 5$
   D. $2 \cdot \pi \cdot 2.5 \cdot 6$

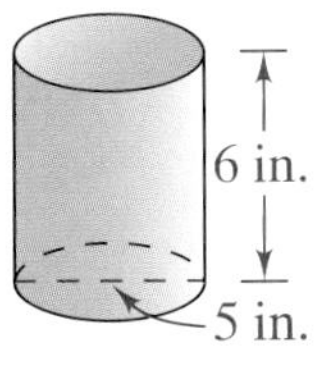

6. Which figure has the greatest volume?

   F.
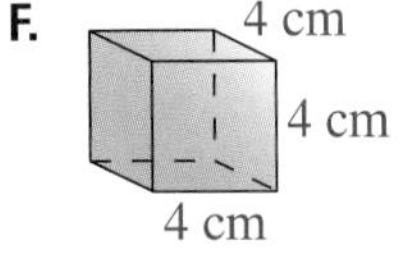

   G.
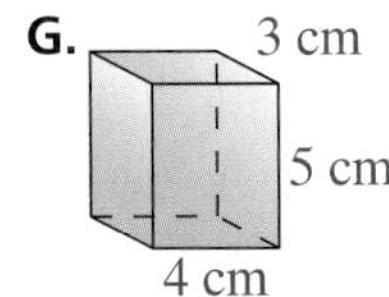

   H.
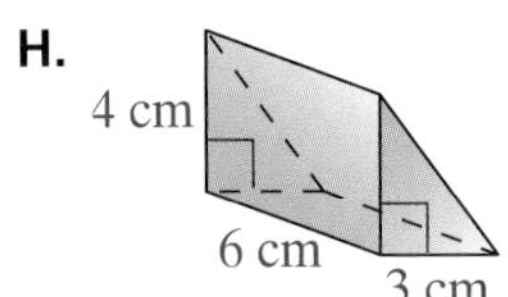

   I.
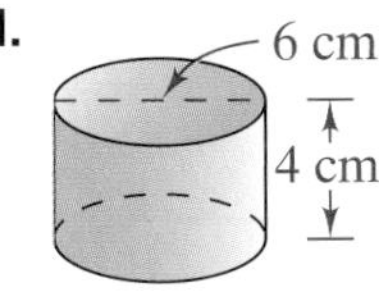

7. Which equation can you use to represent the following? Five more than half of the people (*p*) on the bus are students (*s*).
   A. $\frac{p}{2} + 5 = s$ **B.** $(p - 5) \div 2 = s$
   C. $\frac{p}{2} - 5 = s$ **D.** $(p + 5) \div 2 = s$

8. What is the value of *x* to the nearest tenth?
   F. 17.0 **G.** 12.7
   H. 8.5 **I.** 7

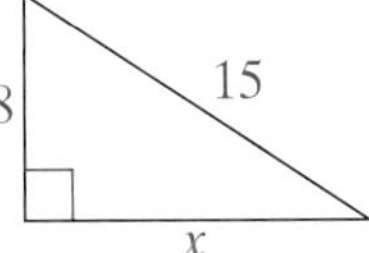

9. Which expression does NOT equal 12?
   A. $\sqrt{144}$ **B.** $\sqrt{36} + \sqrt{36}$
   C. $\sqrt{4} + \sqrt{64}$ **D.** $\sqrt{81} + \sqrt{9}$

10. What number is 75% of 150?
    F. 11.25 **G.** 20
    H. 112.5 **I.** 11,250

Gridded Response

11. A triangle has a height of 8 ft and a base of 15 ft. Find the triangle's area in square feet.

12. **Sewing** You sew 34 squares for a quilt. This is 5% of the squares used in the quilt. How many squares are there to sew altogether?

Short Response

13. Define a variable and write an inequality to model "To qualify for the long-jump finals, I need to jump at least 14 ft."

14. The area of a circular rug is 113.04 ft^2. What is the diameter of the rug? Use $\pi = 3.14$. Show your work.

Extended Response

15. The ratio of the corresponding sides of two similar triangles is 3 : 5. The sides of the smaller triangle are 9 m, 12 m, and 18 m. Find the perimeter of the larger triangle. Show your work.

Real-World Snapshots

Musical Shapes

Applying Volume Today's music comes in many forms. You're probably most familiar with compact discs (CDs) and cassette tapes. Maybe you've also seen older vinyl records or the newer mini-discs. These forms of music look and play differently, but you may have noticed that the recorded areas all have the same geometric shape.

Put It All Together

Materials centimeter ruler, cassette tape, CDs

1. Wind the tape in a cassette completely around one of the spools, making a cylinder.

- **a.** Measure the diameter of the cylinder of tape and the height of the tape. Because the tape is inside a plastic cover, you may have to approximate these measurements.
- **b.** Find the volume of the cylinder.
- **c.** Notice that the center of the cylinder is a spool. Measure the diameter of the spool. Find its volume.
- **d.** Subtract the volume of the spool from the total volume. What is the volume of the magnetic tape?

Cassette tape

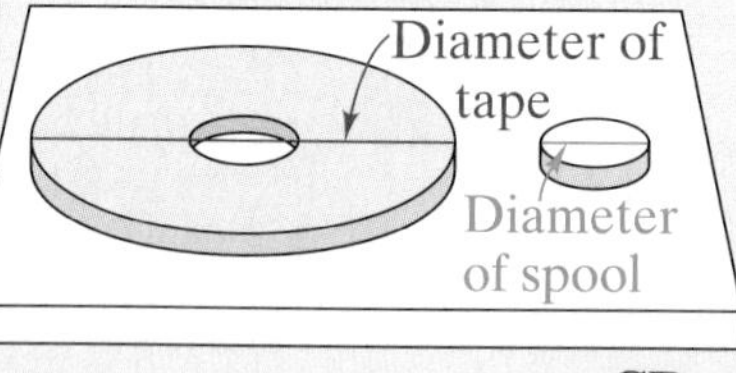

2. a. Measure the radius of a CD.

- **b.** Find the height of the CD. (*Hint:* Stack several CDs, measure their combined height, and divide by the number of discs.)
- **c.** Find the volume of the CD.
- **d.** Measure the radius from the center of the CD to the beginning of the music area. (See the photo at the right.) This section contains no music. Find its volume.
- **e.** Subtract your answer to part (d) from your answer to part (c) to find the volume used for music.

CD

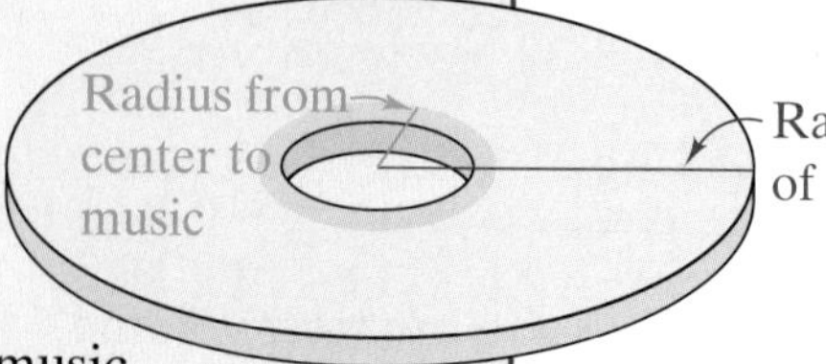

3. a. How many minutes of music are on the tape? How many minutes are stored in each cubic centimeter of volume?

- **b.** How many minutes of music are on the CD? How many minutes are stored in each cubic centimeter of volume?
- **c.** **Writing in Math** Which format stores music more efficiently, a cassette or a CD? Explain.

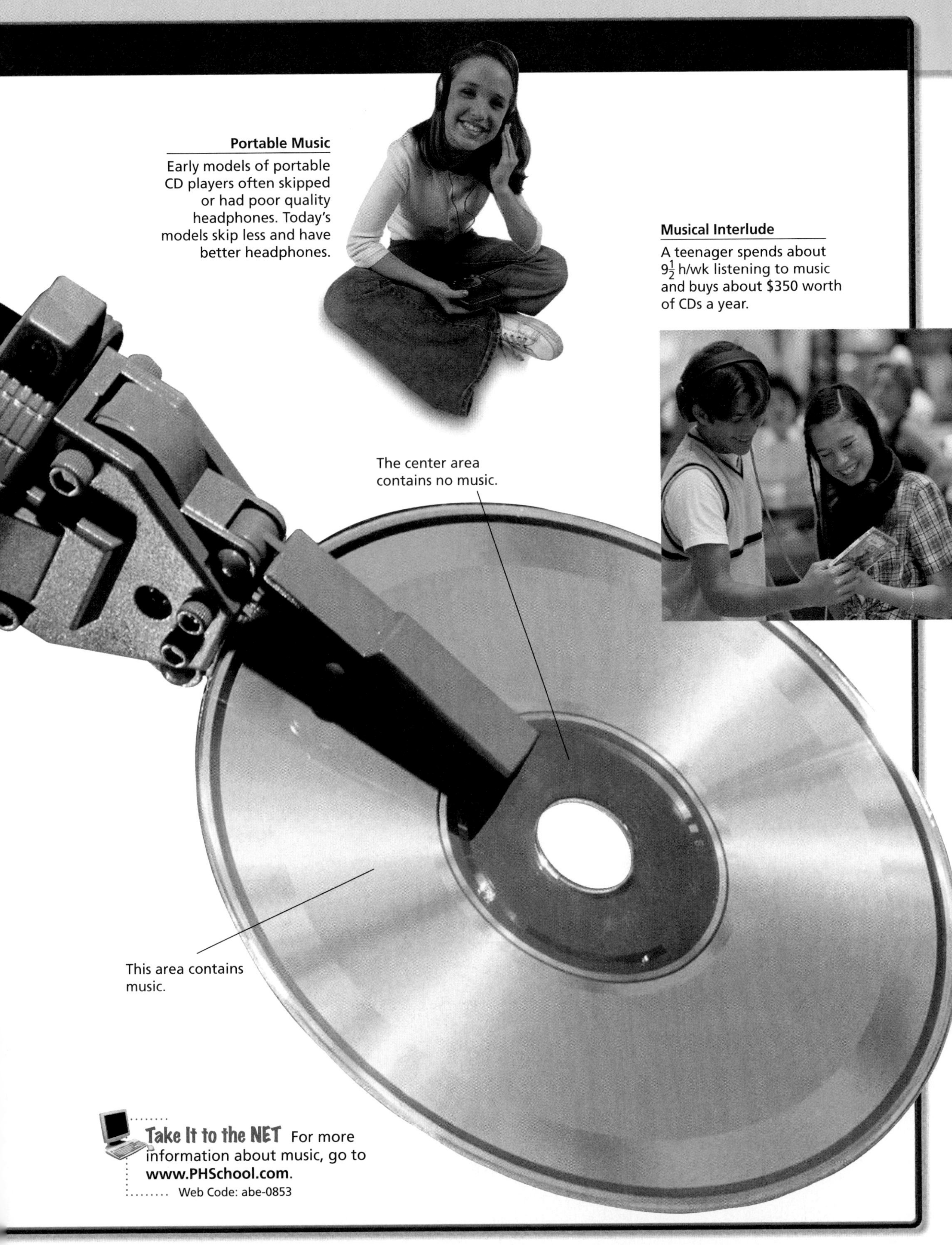
Portable Music
Early models of portable CD players often skipped or had poor quality headphones. Today's models skip less and have better headphones.
Musical Interlude
A teenager spends about $9\frac{1}{2}$ h/wk listening to music and buys about $350 worth of CDs a year.
The center area contains no music.
This area contains music.
Take It to the NET For more information about music, go to **www.PHSchool.com**.
Web Code: abe-0853

Algebra

CHAPTER 9

Patterns and Rules

Lessons

9-1 Patterns and Graphs

9-2 Number Sequences

9-3 Patterns and Tables

9-4 Function Rules

9-5 Using Tables, Rules, and Graphs

9-6 Interpreting Graphs

9-7 Simple and Compound Interest

9-8 Problem Solving: Write an Equation

9-9 Transforming Formulas

Key Vocabulary

- arithmetic sequence (p. 474)
- balance (p. 500)
- compound interest (p. 500)
- conjecture (p. 475)
- formula (p. 507)
- function (p. 484)
- geometric sequence (p. 475)
- principal (p. 499)
- sequence (p. 474)
- simple interest (p. 499)

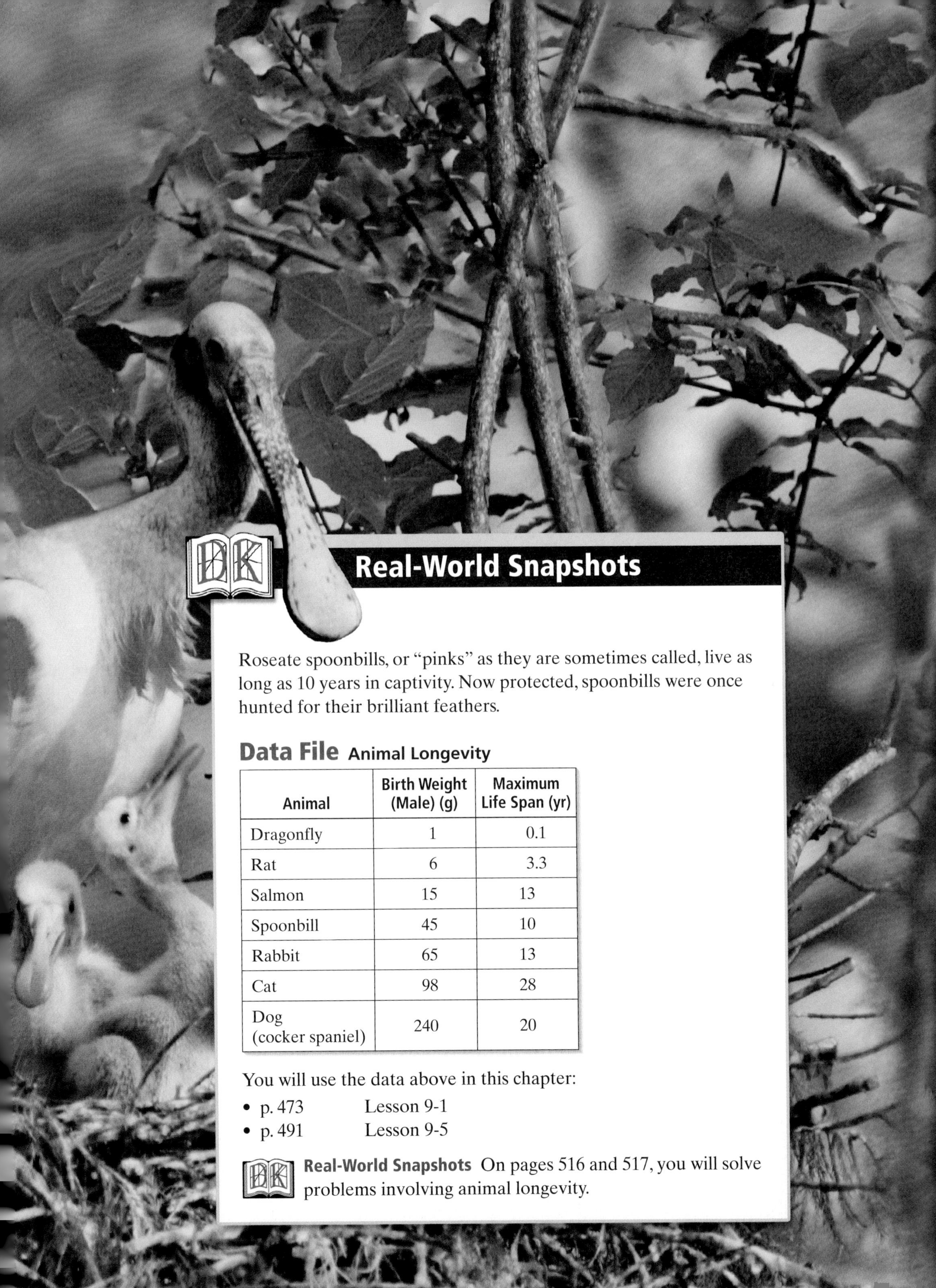

Real-World Snapshots

Roseate spoonbills, or "pinks" as they are sometimes called, live as long as 10 years in captivity. Now protected, spoonbills were once hunted for their brilliant feathers.

Data File Animal Longevity

Animal	Birth Weight (Male) (g)	Maximum Life Span (yr)
Dragonfly	1	0.1
Rat	6	3.3
Salmon	15	13
Spoonbill	45	10
Rabbit	65	13
Cat	98	28
Dog (cocker spaniel)	240	20

You will use the data above in this chapter:

- p. 473 Lesson 9-1
- p. 491 Lesson 9-5

Real-World Snapshots On pages 516 and 517, you will solve problems involving animal longevity.

Chapter 9 Preview

Where You've Been

- In Chapter 2, you wrote algebraic expressions and equations to represent patterns and real-world situations. You also solved equations.
- In Chapter 5, you used proportions to represent patterns.

Where You're Going

- In Chapter 9, you will represent patterns by using function tables, writing rules, and drawing graphs.
- Applying what you learn, you will write and graph a function rule to find distance traveled over time.

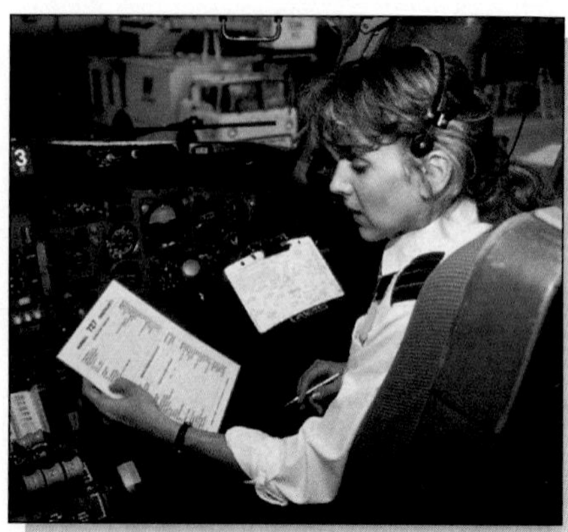

Pilots use functions to plan flights.

Instant self-check online and on CD-ROM

Diagnosing Readiness

For help, go to the lesson in green.

Evaluating and Writing Algebraic Expressions (Lesson 2-1)

Evaluate each expression using $r = 4, s = -2$, and $t = 5.1$.

1. $3r - t$ **2.** rst **3.** $8s^2 + rt$ **4.** $1.5(1 + s)^r$

Solving Two-Step Equations (Lesson 2-6)

Solve each equation.

5. $3x - 1 = 14$ **6.** $10 + 3n = 25$ **7.** $4(b - 3) = 7$ **8.** $-5x = 3x - 22$

Exponents and Order of Operations (Lesson 3-1)

Simplify.

9. $2^3 \cdot 2 - 4^2$ **10.** $2^3 \cdot (2 - 4)^2$ **11.** $(3 - 2)^2 - 2^2$ **12.** $4^3 + 4 \div 4^2$

Solving Equations With Fractions (Lesson 4-6)

Solve each equation.

13. $\frac{2}{3}n - 10 = 14$ **14.** $\frac{x}{7} = 49$ **15.** $1.5 + \frac{4}{5}a = 21$ **16.** $\frac{1}{2}p + \frac{1}{6} = 1\frac{1}{2}$

Percents, Fractions, and Decimals (Lesson 6-2)

Write each percent as a decimal.

17. 4% **18.** 12% **19.** 3.58% **20.** 4.05% **21.** 10.3%

9-1 Patterns and Graphs

What You'll Learn

To make graphs

To use graphs to make estimates

. . . And Why

To find the cost of a phone call, as in Example 3

For help, go to Lesson 3-10.

Draw a number line from 0 to 10. Graph and label each point.

1. 7 **2.** 9.5 **3.** $3\frac{1}{2}$

4. 2.3 **5.** 0.8 **6.** $4\frac{3}{4}$

7. Order from least to greatest.
$-5.6, 3\frac{1}{3}, -\frac{5}{6}, 2.98, -5.\overline{5}$

OBJECTIVE 1

 Interactive lesson includes instant self-check, tutorials, and activities.

Making Graphs

Graphs can help you see patterns in data. A graph includes two *scales*, or rulers—the horizontal axis and the vertical axis. An *interval* is the difference between the values on a scale.

1 EXAMPLE Choosing Scales and Intervals

Interest on Savings

Amount Saved ($)	Interest Earned ($)
200	8
350	14
500	20
750	30
900	36

Graph the data in the table at the left.

Step 1 Choose the scales and intervals.

Use the horizontal scale of the graph for the data in the first column. Use the vertical scale for the data in the second column. Start both scales at 0.

- Choose the interval for the horizontal scale. The greatest amount saved is \$900. If each interval is \$100, then the number of intervals is 900 ÷ 100, or 9.
- Choose the interval for the vertical scale. The greatest interest earned is \$36. If each interval is \$4, then the number of intervals is 36 ÷ 4, or 9.

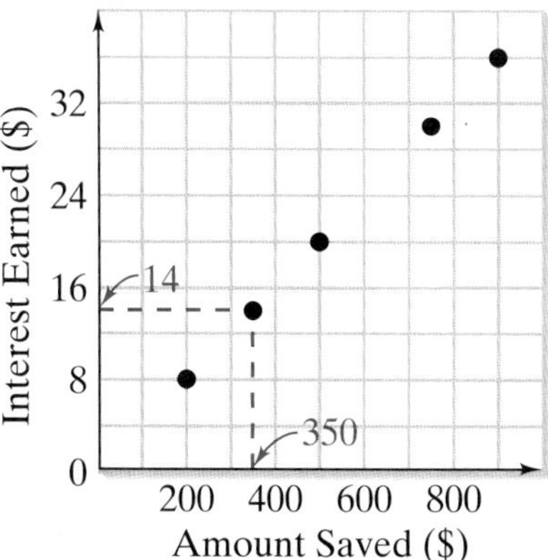

Step 2 Use points to represent the data. The red dashes show how to plot the point representing Interest Earned of \$14 on an Amount Saved of \$350.

Check Understanding 1 **a.** Graph the data in Example 1 using a vertical interval of \$5.
b. Reasoning Which interval is easier to graph—\$4 or \$5? Explain.

Graphs having from 6 to 10 intervals are easy to read.

2 EXAMPLE Real-World Problem Solving

Stuffed Animals

Number	Cost ($)
100	40
200	67
300	94
400	121
500	148

Toys A toy manufacturer produces stuffed animals. Graph the manufacturing costs.

The pattern in the first column of data suggests a horizontal interval of 100.

The greatest value in the second column is $148.

$148 ÷ 10 intervals, or $14.80 per interval
$148 ÷ 6 intervals, or $24.67 per interval

Choose a vertical interval that is between $14.80 and $24.67. An interval of $20 is easy to use.

Use points to represent the data.

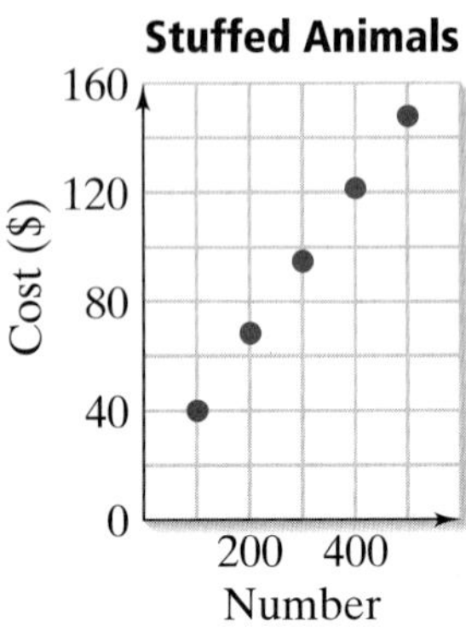

Check Understanding 2 Graph the data in the table at the right.

Yogurt Costs

Yogurt (pt)	Price ($)
50	26
100	49
150	72
200	95

OBJECTIVE

2 Using Graphs to Make Estimates

You can use a graph to make estimates between data points.

3 EXAMPLE Estimating on a Graph Real World

Cellular Phones The graph below shows the costs of different cell phone calls. The points are connected because the phone company charges for the exact amount of time a call takes. How much does a call of $3\frac{1}{2}$ min cost?

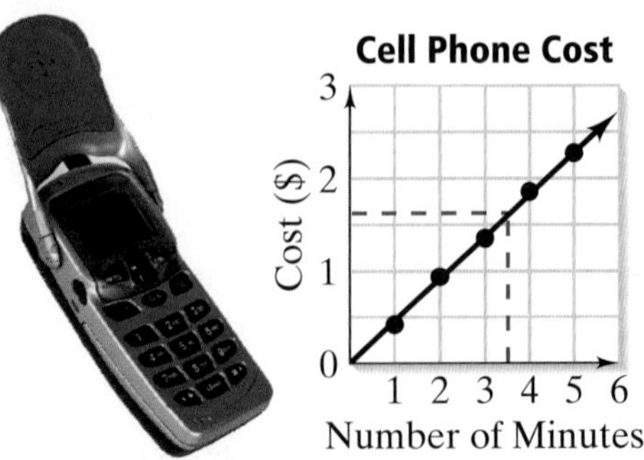

Draw lines to locate the value on the vertical axis that corresponds to $3\frac{1}{2}$ on the horizontal axis.

The cost is greater than $1.50, but less than halfway between $1.50 and $2.00, or $1.75. Estimate the answer as $1.60.

The cost of a $3\frac{1}{2}$-min call is about $1.60.

Check Understanding 3 Use the graph in Example 3 to estimate the cost of a $4\frac{1}{2}$-min call.

You can use a graph to make a prediction. Extend the graph and find a corresponding value on the appropriate axis.

Real-World Connection
The U.S. Department of Agriculture recommends cooking beef to 160°F.

4 EXAMPLE Extending a Graph

The graph shows the relationship between Celsius and Fahrenheit temperatures. Estimate the Celsius temperature for 160°F.

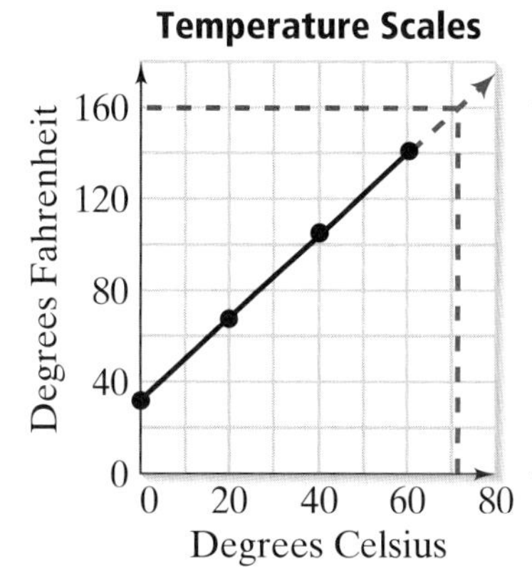

← Extend the graph as shown.

For 160°F, the Celsius temperature ← is slightly more than 70°. Estimate the answer.

A temperature of 160°F is about 71°C.

Check Understanding 4 **a.** Estimate the Fahrenheit temperature for 80°C.
b. Reasoning For what type of data would you need to extend the graph in the opposite direction?

EXERCISES

For more practice, see *Extra Practice.*

A Practice by Example

Example 1 (page 469)

Graph the data in each table.

1. **Shoveling Snow**

Hours Worked	Salary ($)
2	18
4	36
5	45
6	54

2. **A Cow's Weight**

Age (months)	Weight (lb)
1	15
2	28
3	40
4	54
5	66

3. Use a different interval for the vertical axis to graph the data from Exercise 2.

Example 2 (page 470)

Graph the data in each table.

4. **Plant Growth**

Age (yr)	Height (cm)
5	90
7	95
9	102
11	110

5. **Used Dirt Bike Prices**

Age (yr)	Price ($)
2	43
4	37
6	30

Example 3 (page 470)

Estimate using your graphs from Exercises 4 and 5.

6. the height of an 8-year-old plant

7. the plant's age when it was 105 cm tall

8. the price of a used bike that is 5 years old

9. the age of a bike that is being sold for $40

Example 4 (page 471)

Estimate using the graph at the right.

10. the cost of 85 h of electricity

11. the cost of 100 h of electricity

12. How many hours cost $6.50?

Electricity Charges

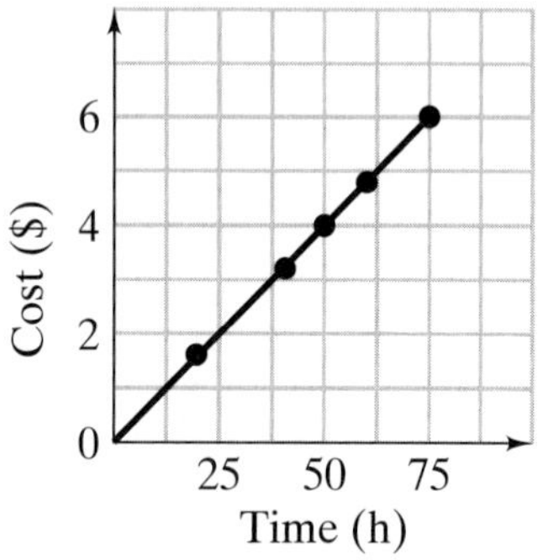

Cost ($): 0, 2, 4, 6
Time (h): 25, 50, 75

Apply Your Skills

13. a. Geometry Graph the perimeters of squares with side lengths of 1, 2, 3, 4, and 5 in.

b. Estimate the side length of a square with perimeter 9.6 in.

c. Estimate the perimeter of a square with side length 3.5 in.

d. Calculator Test your estimates with a calculator. Were your estimates correct?

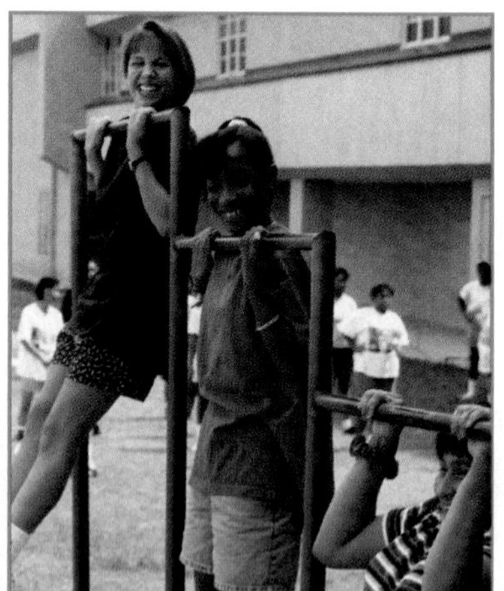

Real-World Connection

The Presidential Physical Fitness Challenge consists of five fitness tests, including pull-ups.

14. Physical Fitness To qualify for the Presidential Physical Fitness Award, girls between the ages of 11 and 14 must be able to run one mile within the times listed.

a. Graph the data.

b. Estimate the time for a 17-year-old girl.

c. Error Analysis Why might your estimate be inaccurate?

Age (yr)	Time (mins)
11	9.03
12	8.38
13	8.22
14	7.98

Graph the data in each table. Use your graph to estimate the missing value.

15.

Hours of Sleep	Math Test Score
9	93
8	85
7	74
6	n

16.

Age (yr)	Weight (lb)
1	3.5
2	n
4	8
5	9.5

17.

Time (h)	Temp. (°C)
1	12
2	15
5	24
8	n

18.

Time (s)	Distance (mi)
10	15
15	22.5
25	37.5
n	48

19. Writing in Math Describe what a graph looks like when both sets of values increase.

20. **Data file, p. 467** Draw a graph of the animal longevity data. Place Life Span on the vertical axis and Birth Weight on the horizontal axis.

Challenge

21. **Books** The table shows costs to print books.
   a. Estimate the cost of 2,500 books.
   b. Estimate the cost of 7,500 books.
   c. Find the unit costs to print 5,000 and 10,000 books. Why does the unit cost depend on the size of the order?

Number of Books	Cost ($)
5,000	175,000
10,000	290,000

22. **Work** Suppose a neighbor will pay you $10 per week to wash windows. Another neighbor will give you $40 and then pay $7 per week.
   a. Make two tables, one for each neighbor, showing the amount you receive from each neighbor for 1, 2, 3, 4, and 5 weeks of work.
   b. Graph both sets of data on the same axes.
   c. How much will you receive from each neighbor after 10 weeks?
   d. **Reasoning** Which method of payment do you prefer? Explain.

23. **Stretch Your Thinking** How many ways can you arrange 10 blocks in 3 containers so that the number of blocks in each container is even?

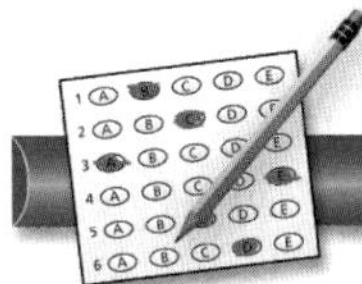

Test Prep

Multiple Choice

For Exercises 24 and 25, graph the data at the right.

x	y
−1	3
0	4
2	6
4	8

24. Estimate the value of y when $x = 12$.
   A. 12 B. 16 C. 24 D. 30

25. Estimate the value of x when $y = 18$.
   F. 10 G. 14 H. 28 I. 30

Extended Response

26. a. Graph the data for bacteria growth.
   b. When the environment changes, the growth rate changes. Use your graph to estimate when a change in the environment occurred.
   c. Estimate the time at which there were 12 bacteria.

Bacteria Growth

Time (min)	Number of Bacteria
0	5
20	10
40	15
60	20
80	60

Online lesson quiz at www.PHSchool.com
Web Code: aba-0901

Mixed Review

Lesson 6-2 **Write each percent as a decimal.**

27. 38% 28. 5% 29. 150% 30. 6.2%

Lesson 1-7 **Find each sum or difference.**

31. $-4 + 7$ 32. $-4 - 7$ 33. $-4 + (-7)$ 34. $-4 - (-7)$

9-2 Number Sequences

What You'll Learn

 To use arithmetic sequences

 To use geometric and other sequences

. . . And Why

To identify types of patterns, as in Example 3

Check Skills You'll Need

For help, go to Lesson 1-7.

Add.

1. $-3 + 3$ **2.** $-3 + 2$

3. $-3 + 1$ **4.** $-3 + 0$

5. $-3 + (-1)$ **6.** $-3 + (-2)$

New Vocabulary • sequence • arithmetic sequence • geometric sequence • conjecture

Interactive lesson includes instant self-check, tutorials, and activities.

OBJECTIVE 1

Using Arithmetic Sequences

Investigation: Finding a Pattern

Use pattern blocks or draw diagrams.

1. Make the next two figures in the pattern below.

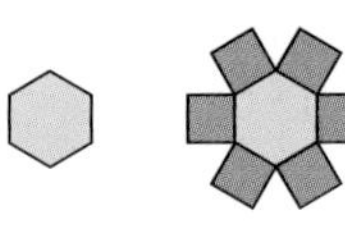
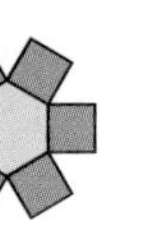
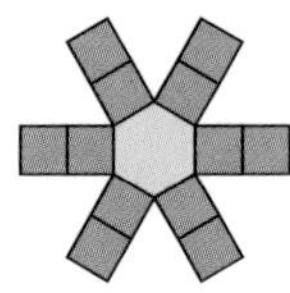

Figure 1 Figure 2 Figure 3

2. How many blocks do you add to each figure to make the next figure in the pattern?

3. Copy and complete the table below.

Figure	1	2	3	4	5	6	7	8
Total Blocks in Figure	1	■	■	■	■	■	■	■

4. Describe any patterns that you notice in your table.

The set of numbers 1, 3, 5, 7, 9, . . . has a pattern. If you add 2 to any number, you get the next number in the set.

A **sequence** is a set of numbers that follow a pattern. Each number in a sequence is a *term*. You can find each term of an **arithmetic sequence** by adding a fixed number (called the common difference) to the previous term.

Reading Math

You pronounce *arithmetic sequence* as "ar-ith-MEH-tik SEE-kwens."

1 EXAMPLE Rules for Arithmetic Sequences

Write a rule to describe the sequence 12, 7, 2, −3, ... Then find the next three terms in the sequence.

$$\begin{array}{ccccccc} 12 & & 7 & & 2 & & -3 \\ \searrow & \nearrow & \searrow & \nearrow & \searrow & \nearrow & \\ & +(-5) & & +(-5) & & +(-5) & \end{array}$$

← **Find the common difference.**

The rule is *Start with 12 and add −5 repeatedly.*

The next three terms are −8, −13, and −18.

Check Understanding 1 **a.** Write a rule for the sequence 44, 35, 26, 17, ... Find the next three terms.

b. **Reasoning** The rule for a sequence is *Start with 21 and subtract 11 repeatedly.* Is it an arithmetic sequence? Explain.

OBJECTIVE

2 Using Geometric and Other Sequences

In a **geometric sequence,** you find each term by multiplying the previous term by a fixed number (called the common ratio).

2 EXAMPLE Rules for Geometric Sequences

Write a rule for the sequence 27, 9, 3, 1, ... Find the next three terms.

$$\begin{array}{ccccccc} 27 & & 9 & & 3 & & 1 \\ \searrow & \nearrow & \searrow & \nearrow & \searrow & \nearrow & \\ & \cdot\frac{1}{3} & & \cdot\frac{1}{3} & & \cdot\frac{1}{3} & \end{array}$$

← **Find the common ratio.**

The rule is *Start with 27 and multiply by $\frac{1}{3}$ repeatedly.*

$$\left.\begin{aligned} 1 \cdot \tfrac{1}{3} &= \tfrac{1}{3} \\ \tfrac{1}{3} \cdot \tfrac{1}{3} &= \tfrac{1}{9} \\ \tfrac{1}{9} \cdot \tfrac{1}{3} &= \tfrac{1}{27} \end{aligned}\right\}$$

← **Find the next three terms.**

Need Help?

Dividing is the same as multiplying by a reciprocal.

The next three terms are $\frac{1}{3}$, $\frac{1}{9}$, and $\frac{1}{27}$.

Check Understanding 2 **a.** Write a rule for the sequence 1,000; 100; 10; . . . . Find the next three terms.

b. **Reasoning** The rule for a sequence is *Start with 12 and divide by −4 repeatedly.* Is it a geometric sequence? Explain.

A sequence can be arithmetic, geometric, both, or neither. It is neither arithmetic nor geometric if you cannot find a common difference or a common ratio.

A **conjecture** is a prediction that suggests what you expect will happen. When you look for a pattern and write a rule to describe the pattern in a sequence, you are using *inductive reasoning.* The conjectures you make may not always be true. Check your results whenever possible.

3 EXAMPLE Real-World Problem Solving

Geometry Write a rule to find the number of circles in each figure. Is the sequence *arithmetic*, *geometric*, *both*, or *neither*?

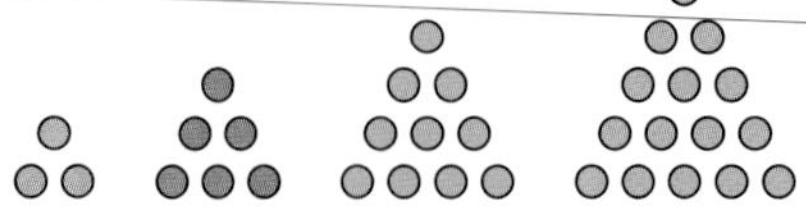

3 6 10 15 . . . ← number of circles in each figure

+ 3 + 4 + 5 ← Look for a common difference or a common ratio.

The rule is *Start with 3 and add consecutive integers. First add 3, then add 4, and so on.*

The sequence is neither arithmetic nor geometric. ← conjecture

Look Back and Check Is there a common ratio?

3 6 10 15

$\cdot 2$ $\cdot 1\frac{2}{3}$ $\cdot 1\frac{1}{2}$

← You cannot multiply by or add the same number to each term to find the next term. The sequence is neither arithmetic nor geometric. The conjecture is correct.

Check Understanding 3 Identify each sequence as *arithmetic*, *geometric*, *both*, or *neither*.

a. 1, 2, 6, 24, . . . **b.** 2, 3, 6, 11, . . . **c.** 10, 9, 8, 7, . . .

EXERCISES

For more practice, see *Extra Practice*.

A Practice by Example

Write a rule for each sequence. Then find the next three terms.

Example 1 (page 475)

1. 5, 10, 15, 20, . . .
2. 3, 7, 11, 15, . . .
3. 34, 29, 24, 19, . . .
4. 25, 21, 17, 13, . . .
5. 63, 54, 45, 36, . . .
6. −8, −1, 6, 13, . . .

Example 2 (page 475)

7. 1, 2, 4, 8, . . .
8. 2, −6, 18, −54, . . .
9. 600, −300, 150, . . .
10. $\frac{1}{2}, \frac{1}{4}, \frac{1}{8}, \frac{1}{16}, \ldots$
11. −2, 4, −8, 16, . . .
12. $\frac{1}{4}, \frac{1}{12}, \frac{1}{36}, \frac{1}{108}, \ldots$

Example 3 (page 476)

Identify each sequence as *arithmetic, geometric, both,* or *neither*.

13. 2, 5, 10, 17, 26, . . .
14. 1, 4, 9, 16, 25, . . .
15. 7, 14, 28, 56, . . .
16. −2, −2, −2, . . .
17. 300, 60, 12, 2.4, . . .
18. 84, 63, 42, 21, . . .
19. **Employment** Suppose an employer pays new employees \$8/h the first year, \$9/h the second year, \$10/h the third year, and \$15/h the fourth year. Is the pattern *arithmetic*, *geometric*, *both*, or *neither*?

B Apply Your Skills

20. **Running** Mario can run a mile in 9 min. After 4 months of training for a marathon, he hopes to run a mile in 8 min. His time decreases 15 s each month. What would you tell Mario about his conjecture?

Real-World Connection

The queen bee lays her eggs in the cells of the hive.

21. Science A female bee has two biological parents—a female and a male. A male bee has only one parent, a female.

a. Make a family tree that shows seven generations of ancestors of a male bee. Find the number of ancestors in each.

b. The numbers of ancestors form a number sequence. Is it *arithmetic*, *geometric*, *both*, or *neither*?

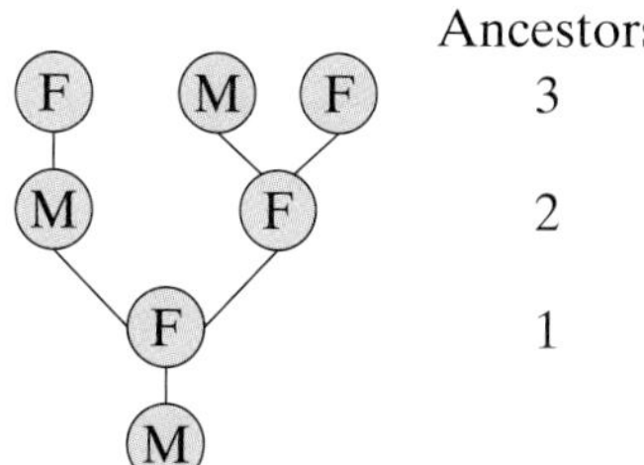

Write a rule for each sequence. Then find the next three terms.

22. 2, 4, 8, 16, . . .

23. 4, −8, 16, −32 . . .

24. 2, −4, 8, −16, . . .

25. −2, −4, −8, −16, . . .

26. $\frac{1}{3}, \frac{1}{6}, \frac{1}{9}, \frac{1}{12}, \ldots$

27. −5, −1, 3, 7, . . .

28. 1, 5, 14, 30, 55, . . .

29. 1, 5, 13, 29, . . .

30. −1, 1, −2, 2, . . .

31. For Exercises 26–30, tell whether each sequence is *arithmetic*, *geometric*, *both*, or *neither*.

32. a. How many blue tiles will be in the ninth figure of the pattern? How many yellow tiles?

b. Write a rule to describe the pattern.

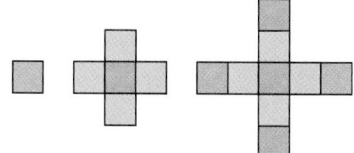

33. Pattern the pattern below and make a conjecture about the next term in the sequence. Test your conjecture with a calculator.

$123 \times 9 = 1{,}107$ $\quad$ $1{,}234 \times 9 = 11{,}106$ $\quad$ $12{,}345 \times 9 = 111{,}105$

34. Nature The Fibonacci sequence 1, 1, 2, 3, 5, 8, . . . occurs in nature.

a. Is the Fibonacci sequence *arithmetic*, *geometric*, *both*, or *neither*?

b. Find the ninth and tenth terms in the Fibonacci sequence.

c. Reasoning Is the sequence in Exercise 21 a Fibonacci sequence?

Write a rule for each sequence.

35. 1, 1.5, 2, 2.5, . . .

36. 0.4, 0.8, 1.2, 1.6, . . .

37. 10, 9.3, 8.6, 7.9, . . .

38. 0.1, 0.3, 0.9, 2.7, . . .

39. 0.5, 1.5, 4.5, 13.5, . . .

40. 0.2, 0.4, 0.6, 0.8, . . .

41. the even integers greater than 12

42. the negative odd integers

Reading Math

For help reading and solving Exercise 43, go to page 479.

43. a. Geometry Find the area of the rectangle.

b. Double the dimensions and find the new area.

c. Make a conjecture about how the area changes as the dimensions are doubled.

d. Test your conjecture with a different rectangle.

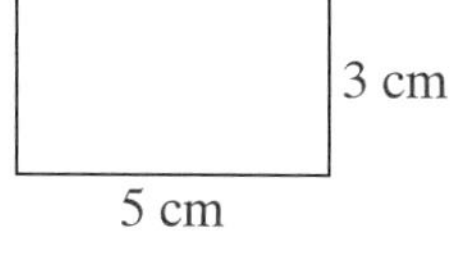

44. Writing in Math Every term of a sequence is 1. Is it *arithmetic*, *geometric*, *both*, or *neither*? Explain.

45. **a.** List rows 4, 5, 6, and 7 in the pattern.
b. Find the sum of each row.
c. Write a rule for finding the sum of the numbers in each row.
d. **Reasoning** Predict the sum of the numbers in the twentieth row.

row 1	1
row 2	1 2 1
row 3	1 2 3 2 1

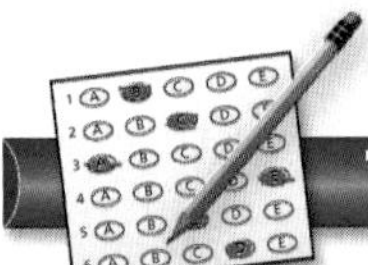

Calculator **Make a conjecture about the next term in each sequence. Test your conjecture with a calculator.**

46. $2^4 = 16$
$2^3 = 8$
$2^2 = 4$
$2^1 = 2$
$2^0 = \blacksquare$

47. $3^4 = 81$
$3^3 = 27$
$3^2 = 9$
$3^1 = 3$
$3^0 = \blacksquare$

48. $4^4 = 256$
$4^3 = 64$
$4^2 = 16$
$4^1 = 4$
$4^0 = \blacksquare$

C Challenge

49. Make a conjecture about the next term in the sequence, and find it.
$1, 4, -1, 6, -3, 8, -5, 10, -7, 12, \ldots$

50. **Geometry** How does the volume of a rectangular solid change when its dimensions are doubled? Make a conjecture and test it.

51. **Stretch Your Thinking** When you draw either one of two diagonals in a polygon, it is divided into two congruent triangles. What is the polygon?

Test Prep

Multiple Choice

52. What are the next two terms in the sequence 1, 64, 2, 32, 4, 16, . . . ?
A. 16, 8 **B.** 8, 16 **C.** 8, 8 **D.** 32, 64

53. A rectangular ranch is 2 mi long by 6 mi wide. If its dimensions are doubled, by how many times will its area increase?
F. 2 **G.** 3 **H.** 4 **I.** 8

Take It to the NET
Online lesson quiz at
www.PHSchool.com
Web Code: aba-0902

54. What is the next term in the sequence $1, -2, 4, -5, 7, -8, \ldots$?
A. -10 **B.** 9 **C.** 10 **D.** 11

Short Response

55. The sum of two numbers is always greater than each of the numbers. Show why you think this statement is true or prove that it is false.

Mixed Review

Lesson 5-7

The scale on a map is 2 in. : 50 mi. Find the actual distance for each map distance. Round your answer to the nearest tenth.

56. 3 in. **57.** $\frac{1}{2}$ in. **58.** $1\frac{3}{4}$ in. **59.** 5 in.

Lesson 5-1

Write each ratio in simplest form.

60. $\frac{200}{550}$ **61.** $\frac{270}{45}$ **62.** $\frac{18}{60}$ **63.** $\frac{24}{120}$

Reading Math: Understanding Word Problems

For Use With Page 477, Exercise 43

Read through the problem below. Then follow what Jacob thinks as he solves the problem. Check your understanding with the exercise at the bottom of the page.

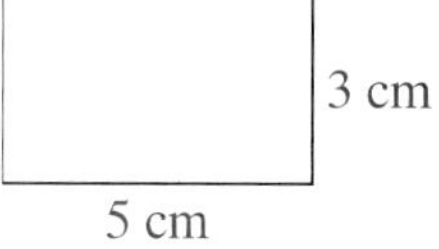

a. Geometry Find the area of the rectangle.
b. Double the dimensions and find the new area.
c. Make a conjecture about how the area changes as the dimensions are doubled.
d. Test your conjecture with a different rectangle.

What Jacob Thinks / What Jacob Writes

Thinks: I'll write what I know from the diagram.

Writes: Length = 5 cm   Width = 3 cm

Thinks: To find area, I can use the length and width.

Writes: a. $A = \ell w = 5 \cdot 3 = 15$
The area of the rectangle is 15 cm^2.

Thinks: Doubling the dimensions means doubling the length and width. Then I can find the area of the new rectangle.

Writes: b. New length $= 2 \cdot 5 = 10$ cm
New width $= 2 \cdot 3 = 6$ cm

$A = 10 \cdot 6 = 60$ The new area is 60 cm^2.

Thinks: To write a conjecture, I need to see a pattern. Sometimes a table helps me see a pattern in a set of numbers. I'll make a table.

Writes: c.

	w	Area
5	3	15
↓ · 2	↓ · 2	↓ · ?
10	6	60

← $15 \cdot 4 = 60$

Thinks: I see the pattern. The new area is 4 times the original area. I can write a conjecture now.

Writes: Conjecture: When a rectangle's dimensions are doubled, its area is multiplied by 4.

Thinks: To test my conjecture, I'll try a new rectangle by doubling the dimensions again.

Writes: d.

10	6	60
↓ · 2	↓ · 2	↓ · 4
20	12	240

← $60 \cdot 4 \stackrel{?}{=} 240$ ✔

Thinks: So, my conjecture does work! The new area is four times the area of my original rectangle.

Writes: The area of the new rectangle is 4 times the area of the original rectangle. The conjecture works.

EXERCISES

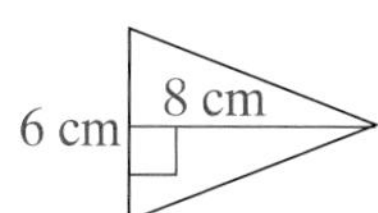

1. **a.** Find the area of the triangle at the right.
   b. Find the area of a triangle with dimensions $\frac{1}{2}$ of those at the right.
   c. Make a conjecture about how the area changes as the dimensions are halved, and then test your conjecture with a new triangle.

9-3 Patterns and Tables

What You'll Learn

To represent patterns in tables

To write rules using tables

. . . And Why

To find gasoline mileage, as in Example 1

✔ Check Skills You'll Need

For help, go to Lessons 2-3 and 2-4.

Solve each equation.

1. $x + 4 = -6$

2. $7t = 112$

3. $5y = -135$

4. $a + (-3) = 17$

5. $36 + p = 118$

6. $-18r = -18$

7. Reasoning Complete the equation with one operation followed by one number. $2 \blacksquare \blacksquare = 12$

Interactive lesson includes instant self-check, tutorials, and activities.

OBJECTIVE 1 Representing Patterns in Tables

You can use a table to represent a number pattern.

1 EXAMPLE Representing a Pattern

Real World

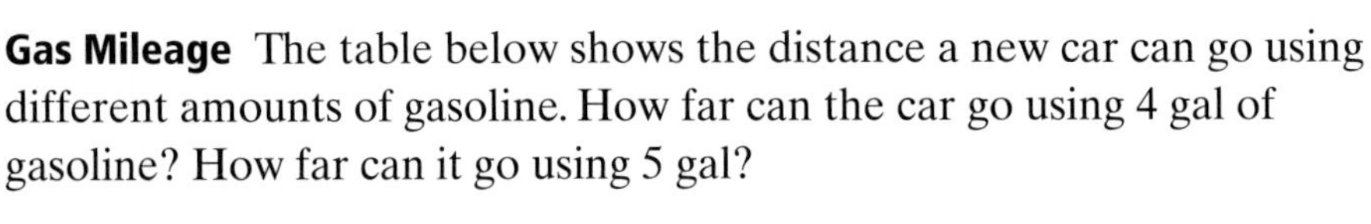

Gas Mileage The table below shows the distance a new car can go using different amounts of gasoline. How far can the car go using 4 gal of gasoline? How far can it go using 5 gal?

Gas (gal)	Miles Driven
1	18.1
2	36.2
3	54.3
4	■
5	■

= 1 × 18.1
= 2 × 18.1
= 3 × 18.1

The values in the second column are 18.1 times the values in the first column.

$4(18.1) = 72.4$ and $5(18.1) = 90.5$

The car can go 72.4 mi using 4 gal and 90.5 mi using 5 gal.

Real-World Connection

Hybrid cars improve fuel efficiency by using both gasoline and electricity.

✔ Check Understanding 1

a. Copy and complete the table.

b. Find the cost of 20 lb of fresh fish.

c. Reasoning The relationship between values is the same for each row of the table in Example 1. Explain why this helps you find the pattern.

Fresh Fish (lb)	Price ($)
1	6.50
2	13.00
3	19.50
4	■
5	■

You can use the relationship between values in the rows of a table to find missing values.

2 EXAMPLE Finding the Values of Variables

Find the values of p and q in the table at the right.

A	B
1	18
4	72
7	p
12	216
q	270

What are the possible relationships between the quantities in a row?

First row: $1 + 17 = 18$ or $1 \cdot 18 = 18$
Second row: $4 + 68 = 72$ or $4 \cdot 18 = 72$

The rule that works for both rows is *Multiply by 18.*

$7 \cdot 18 = p$ $\quad q \cdot 18 = 270$ ← **Find p and q using the rule.**
$126 = p$ $\quad q = 15$

Check You can check your rule by testing another row of values.
$12 \cdot 18 = 216$ ✔ ← **The answer checks.**

Check Understanding 2 Find the values of the variables in the table at the right.

C	3	5	x	9	11
D	66	110	132	198	y

OBJECTIVE

2 Writing Rules Using Tables

A table can help you write a variable expression that describes a sequence.

3 EXAMPLE Using a Table With a Sequence

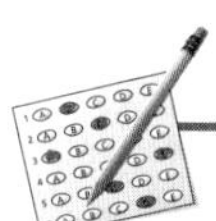

Test-Prep Tip
Using a rule to find any term in a sequence is often referred to as "finding the *n*th term."

Write an expression to describe the rule for the sequence 8, 16, 24, 32, ... Then find the 100th term in the sequence.

8	16	24	32	. . .
↑	↑	↑	↑	
Term 1	**Term 2**	**Term 3**	**Term 4**	**and so on**

Make a table that pairs the term numbers and the values in the sequence.

Term Number	1	2	3	4	. . .	n
	↓ · 8	↓ · 8	↓ · 8	↓ · 8	↓ · 8	↓ · 8
Value of Sequence	8	16	24	32	. . .	■

In words, the rule is *Multiply the term number by 8.*
If you let n = the term number, you can write this rule as $n \cdot 8$, or $8n$.

$n \cdot 8$ ← **Write an expression for the rule.**
$100 \cdot 8 = 800$ ← **Use $n = 100$ to find the 100th term.**

Check Understanding 3 **a.** Write an expression for the rule for −8, −7, −6, −5, ... Find the 100th term in the sequence.

b. **Mental Math** The rule for a sequence is $100n$, where n is the term number. Find the 100th term.

EXERCISES

For more practice, see *Extra Practice*.

A Practice by Example

Example 1 (page 480)

Copy and complete each table.

1.

Cans of Soup	Number of Servings
3	9
4	12
5	15
6	■
7	■

2.

Beads (dozen)	Cost ($)
1	0.48
2	0.96
3	1.44
4	■
5	■

3.

Change in a Parking Meter ($)	Time Allowed to Park (h)
0.25	0.5
0.50	1
0.75	■
1.25	■

4.

Miles	Time (h)
10	0.4
20	0.8
30	1.2
40	■
50	■

Example 2 (page 481)

Find the values of the variables in each table.

5.

A	B
7	84
9	108
11	132
15	m
n	240

6.

C	D
25	−5
50	−10
75	−15
p	−18
120	q

7.

E	F
32	40
96	120
112	s
144	180
t	230

Example 3 (page 481)

Write a variable expression to describe the rule for each sequence. Then find the 100th term.

8. 11, 22, 33, 44, . . .

9. −19, −18, −17, −16, . . .

10. $\frac{1}{2}, 1, 1\frac{1}{2}, 2, \ldots$

11. −3, −6, −9, −12, . . .

12. −18, −36, −54, −72, . . .

13. 100, 200, 300, 400, . . .

B Apply Your Skills

14. Gasoline One month's average price for regular unleaded gasoline is $1.20 per gallon. Using this relationship, make a table that shows the price for 5, 10, 15, and 25 gallons of regular unleaded gasoline.

15. Music The table shows costs for violin lessons. Copy and complete the table.

Time (h)	0.5	1	1.5	2
Cost ($)	12.50	■	■	■

16. Measurement There are 36 inches in 1 yard. Make a table that shows the number of yards in 72 inches, 180 inches, and 288 inches.

17. a. Copy and complete the table.

b. Writing in Math Write a rule in words to find y when you know x.

x	0	1	2	3	4	■
y	−1	2	5	8	■	14

18. Temperature The relationship between Kelvin (K) and Celsius (C) temperatures is $K = 273 + C$. Make a table of Kelvin temperatures for Celsius temperatures of 0°, 10°, 20°, 40°, 80°, and 120°.

Real-World Connection

The freezing point of water is 0°C, or 273 K.

Find the values of the variables in each table.

19.

A	0	10	100	1,000	y
B	0	0.05	x	5	50

20.

C	$\frac{1}{2}$	$\frac{1}{3}$	$\frac{1}{4}$	n	$\frac{1}{6}$
D	$\frac{1}{3}$	m	$\frac{1}{6}$	$\frac{2}{15}$	$\frac{1}{9}$

21. Geometry Use the relationship between side length and area to make a table for the areas of squares with sides of 2, 3, 5, 8, 10, and 12 in.

22. a. Patterns Make a table that shows the number of blue and yellow squares for each group.

b. How many blue squares will be in group 10?

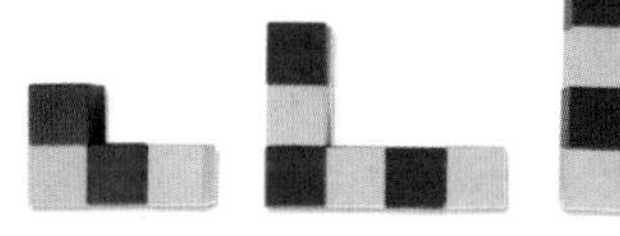

Challenge

23. Use the relationship $y = \frac{3}{2}x$.

a. Make a table that shows the values of y for $x = -2, -4, 2,$ and 4.

b. Find the value of x for $y = 0$.

24. One $cm^3 = 1$ mL. Use this relationship to make a table showing the number of liters in 3 cm^3, 300 cm^3, and 3,000 cm^3.

25. Stretch Your Thinking Using only addition and subtraction and just three operation signs, write an expression that equals 100 using the digits shown. Do not change the order of the digits. 1 2 3 4 5 6 7 8 9

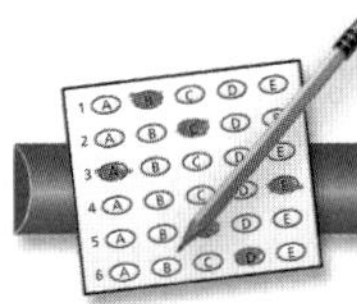

Test Prep

Gridded Response

Use the table. Find the value of *y* for each value of *x*.

x	y
0	3
2	5
4	7

26. −2

27. 0.2

28. 5

29. 7

30. 20

31. 100

Take It to the NET
Online lesson quiz at www.PHSchool.com
Web Code aba-0903

Mixed Review

Lesson 4-4 **Find each product.**

32. $\frac{1}{4}$ of 28

33. $\frac{3}{5} \cdot 25$

34. $\frac{2}{7} \cdot \frac{21}{50}$

35. $4\frac{2}{3} \cdot 4\frac{1}{2}$

Lesson 1-8 **Find each product.**

36. $-4 \cdot (-4)$

37. $20 \cdot (-9)$

38. $250 \cdot (-5)$

39. $-11 \cdot (-11)$

9-4 Function Rules

What You'll Learn

To write function rules

To evaluate functions

. . . And Why

To find a rule for driving distance, as in Example 1

Check Skills You'll Need

For help, go to Lesson 2-1.

Evaluate $-4x + 1$ for each value of x.

1. -2 **2.** 0 **3.** $\frac{1}{2}$

4. -1 **5.** $\frac{1}{4}$ **6.** $-\frac{1}{4}$

7. Mental Math Evaluate $5x - 1$ for $x = 0$.

New Vocabulary

- function

Interactive lesson includes instant self-check, tutorials, and activities.

OBJECTIVE 1 Writing Function Rules

Suppose you are riding in a car at an average speed of 50 mi/h. You can expect to travel 100 mi in 2 h, since $2 \cdot 50 = 100$.

The distance you travel depends on the driving time. The "function machine" at the right shows the relationship between time (input) and distance (output).

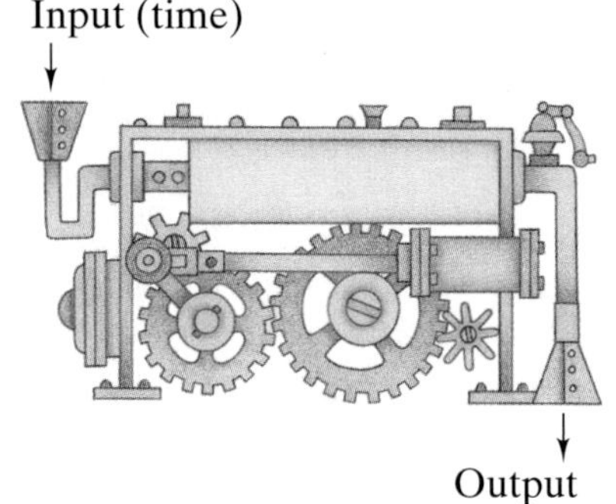

A **function** is a relationship that assigns exactly one output value for each input value.

1 EXAMPLE Real-World Problem Solving

Travel You are traveling in a car at an average speed of 55 mi/h. Write a function rule for the relationship between the time and distance you travel.

You can ***make a table*** to solve this problem.

Input: time (h)	1	2	3	4
Output: distance (mi)	55	110	165	220

distance in miles = $55 \cdot$ time in hours ← **Write the function rule in words.**

$d = 55t$ ← **Use variables *d* for distance and *t* for time.**

Reading Math

An output is a function of the input.

Check Understanding 1

a. Write a function rule for the relationship between time and distance for an average speed of 62 mi/h.

b. Reasoning What type of sequence do the outputs in Example 1 form?

The variables x and y are often used to represent input and output. You can describe the relationship between the values in the table in three ways.

Input	Output
1	4
2	5
3	6
4	7

Each output is 3 greater than the input.

Output = Input + 3

$$y = x + 3$$

You can write a function rule by looking for patterns in a function table.

2 EXAMPLE Writing Function Rules

Write a rule for the function represented by each table.

a.

x	y
0	0
1	−4
2	−8
3	−12

When $x = 0$, $y = 0$. Each y equals −4 times x.

The function rule is $y = -4x + 0$, or $y = -4x$.

b.

x	y
0	−3
1	−1
2	1
3	3

When $x = 0$, $y = -3$. Each y equals 2 times x, plus −3.

The function rule is $y = 2x + (-3)$, or $y = 2x - 3$.

Check Understanding 2 Write a rule for the function represented by the table at the right.

x	0	1	2	3
y	1	5	9	13

OBJECTIVE

2 Evaluating Functions

Given a function rule, you can evaluate the function for any input value.

3 EXAMPLE Finding Input/Output Pairs

Use the function $y = -3x + 5$. Find y for $x = 0, 1, 2,$ and 3. Then make a table for the function.

$y = -3(0) + 5 = 5$ ← **Substitute 0, 1, 2, and 3 for x.**

$y = -3(1) + 5 = 2$

$y = -3(2) + 5 = -1$ **List the values in a table.** →

$y = -3(3) + 5 = -4$

x	$y = 3x + 5$
0	5
1	2
2	−1
3	−4

Check Understanding 3 Use the function rule $y = 2x - 4$. Find y for $x = 0, 1, 2,$ and 3. Then make a table for the function.

EXERCISES

For more practice, see *Extra Practice*.

A Practice by Example

Example 1 (page 484)

Write a function rule that represents each relationship.

1. the time t and the distance d you travel at an average speed of 30 mi/h
2. the number n of words you type and the time t it takes, at a typing rate of 32 words/min
3. the amount c of energy you burn and the time t you spend exercising, burning Calories at a rate of 12 Cal/min

Example 2 (page 485)

Write a rule for the function represented by each table.

4.

x	y
0	0
1	5
2	10
3	15

5.

x	y
0	4
1	5
2	6
3	7

6.

x	y
0	5
1	8
2	11
3	14

7.

x	y
0	1
1	−8
2	−17
3	−26

8.

x	y
0	−2
1	0
2	2
3	4

9.

x	y
0	0
1	−8
2	−16
3	−24

Example 3 (page 485)

Use each function rule. Find y for $x = 0, 1, 2$, and 3. Then make a table for the function.

10. $y = x + 2$
11. $y = 12 - 2x$
12. $y = 4x$
13. $y = x \div 2$
14. $y = 9 - x$
15. $y = -3x$
16. $y = 2x + 1$
17. $y = 4x - 2$
18. $y = x^2 + 1$

B Apply Your Skills

19. **Writing in Math** Choose one of the tables from Exercises 4–9. Explain what patterns you noticed and how you found the rule.

20. **a.** **Measurement** Write a rule for the number of inches n in f feet.
    b. Use your function rule to find the number of inches in 7 ft.

Need Help?
Remember that a function has only one output for each input.

Explain whether each situation represents a function.

21. Input: the number of pounds a turkey weighs
    Output: the number of $\frac{1}{4}$-lb servings

22. Input: the number of days in a month
    Output: the number of Tuesdays in the month

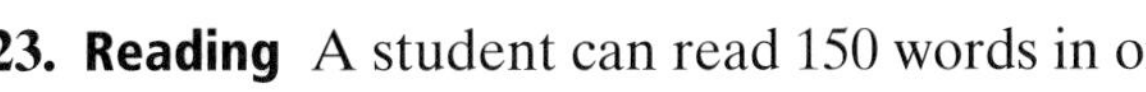

Real-World Connection

The ability to read is a fundamental skill in all modern societies.

23. **Reading** A student can read 150 words in one minute.
 a. Write a function rule to represent the relationship between the number of words and the time in which they are read.
 b. How many words can the student read in 8 minutes?
 c. How long would it take the student to read 2,850 words?
 d. **Reasoning** Is your answer to part (c) an input or an output? Why?

Use the function rule $y = \frac{2}{x}$. Evaluate the function for each value of x.

24. -2 **25.** -1 **26.** 10 **27.** -3

28. **Money** Suppose you put \$.50 in your piggy bank on July 1, \$1.00 on July 2, \$1.50 on July 3, and so on. Use n to represent the date. Write a function rule for the amount you put in for any date in July.

Write a rule for the function represented by each table.

29.

x	y
0	0
1	$\frac{1}{2}$
2	1
3	$1\frac{1}{2}$

30.

x	y
0	$-\frac{1}{2}$
1	$1\frac{1}{2}$
2	$3\frac{1}{2}$
3	$5\frac{1}{2}$

31.

x	y
0	1
1	$1\frac{1}{2}$
2	2
3	$2\frac{1}{2}$

32.

Laundry Loads	Cost (\$)
1	2.75
2	5.50
3	8.25
4	11.00

33.

Time (h)	Kangaroo's Distance (km)
2	96
4	192
6	288

C Challenge

Use the function rule $y = x^2 + 2x$. Evaluate the function for each value of x.

34. -0.25 **35.** $-\frac{1}{2}$ **36.** $1\frac{1}{4}$ **37.** -0.2

38. Use the function machine.
 a. Make an input/output table for integer inputs from -5 to 5.
 b. Which two input values result in an output of 22?
 c. **Reasoning** If two input values produce the same output, is the rule a function? Explain.

Input

$x^2 + x + 2$

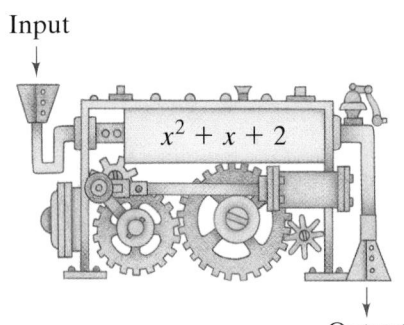

Output

39. **Stretch Your Thinking** When 4 is subtracted from a certain mixed number less than 10, the result is the same as the quotient of that mixed number and 4. What is the mixed number?

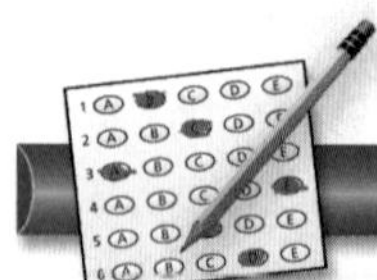

Test Prep

Multiple Choice

40. Which function rule describes the number of feet f as a function of the number of yards y?
A. $f = \frac{1}{3}y$ **B.** $f = 3y$ **C.** $f = 6y$ **D.** $f = 12y$

41. Use the function rule $y = 6x - 1$. Find the value of y for $x = 1$.
F. -7 **G.** -5 **H.** 5 **I.** 7

Take It to the NET
Online lesson quiz at **www.PHSchool.com**
Web Code aba-0904

42. Which rule represents the function in the table below?
A. $s = 6.5h$ **B.** $h = 6.5 + s$ **C.** $h = 13s$ **D.** $s = 13h$

Hours Worked	1	2	3	4
Salary ($)	6.50	13.00	19.50	26.00

Short Response

43. a. Write a rule for the function that represents the total cost of an item with a 5% sales tax.
b. Use your rule to find the total cost of a $15 item.

Mixed Review

Lesson 6-7 **Find each percent of decrease. Round to the nearest tenth of a percent.**

44. 100 to 80 **45.** 7 to 3 **46.** 400 to 250

Lesson 6-4 **Find each answer.**

47. 8% of 12 **48.** 70% of 150 **49.** 120% of 60

Checkpoint Quiz 1 — Lessons 9-1 through 9-4

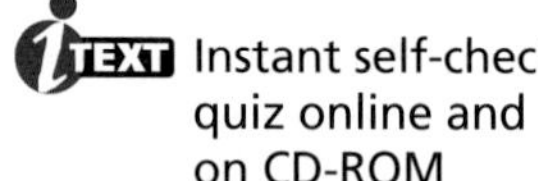
Instant self-check quiz online and on CD-ROM

Write a rule for each sequence. Then find the next three terms.

1. 7, 14, 21, 28, . . . **2.** 250, 220, 190, 160, . . .

3. 2, 5, 11, 23, . . . **4.** −4, 12, −36, 108, . . .

5. Identify each sequence in Exercises 1–4 as *arithmetic*, *geometric*, *both*, or *neither*.

For Exercises 6–10, use the table at the right.

6. Find the values of m and n.

7. Graph the values in the table.

8. Use the graph to estimate the value of x for $y = 10$.

9. Write a rule for the function.

10. Find the value of y for $x = 11$.

x	y
2	7
4	13
5	m
7	22
n	28

Algebra

9-5 Using Tables, Rules, and Graphs

What You'll Learn

To graph functions

. . . And Why

To find plant growth, as in Example 2

✔ Check Skills You'll Need

For help, go to Lesson 9-4.

Make a table of values for each function. Use inputs of 0, 1, 2, and 3.

1. $y = 2x$
2. $y = -x$
3. $y = 4x - 2$
4. $y = x + 5$
5. $y = \frac{1}{2}x$
6. $y = -3x$

Interactive lesson includes instant self-check, tutorials, and activities.

OBJECTIVE

1 Graphing Functions

Investigation: Graphing a Function

1. Count the number of times you breathe in one minute. Repeat four times and record your results. Find the mean of your results.
2. Copy and complete the table, using your mean.

t (min)	1	2	3	4	5	6
Number of Breaths	■	■	■	■	■	■

3. Write a function rule.
4. Draw a graph of your data. Put the number of minutes on the horizontal scale and the number of breaths on the vertical scale.

The graph of a function shows the relationship between inputs and outputs.

1 EXAMPLE Graphing Using a Function Table

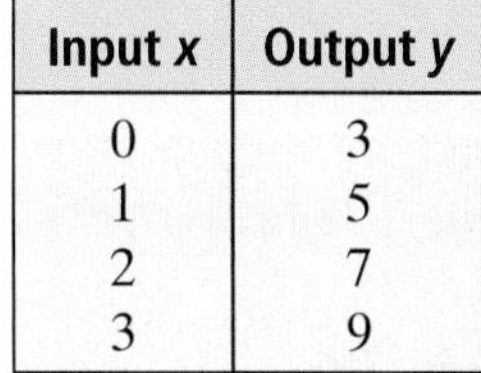

Input x	Output y
0	3
1	5
2	7
3	9

Graph the function represented by the table at the left.

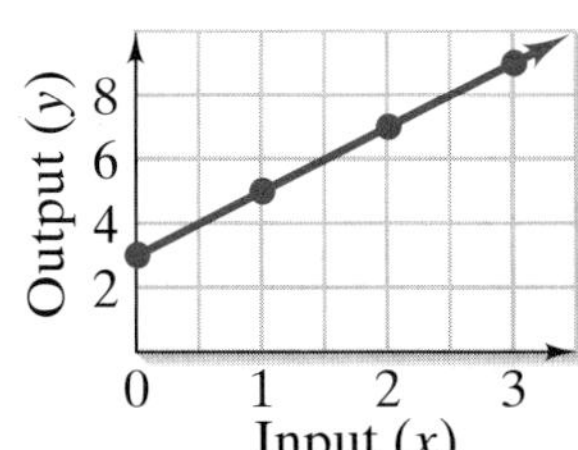

Graph input x on the horizontal axis and output y on the vertical axis.

Draw a line through the points.

✔ Check Understanding 1 Graph the function represented by the table at the right.

Input x	0	1	2	3
Output y	5	8	11	14

You can also graph a function using its function rule.

2 EXAMPLE Real-World Problem Solving

Plants A plant grows 1.38 cm for each hour of sunlight it receives. Write and evaluate a function rule to find the growth of the plant when it receives 15 h of sunlight. Then graph the function.

Real-World Connection

Careers Botanists study the life and growth of plants.

Step 1 Write a function rule.

Words Growth equals 1.38 times hours of sunlight

Let g = growth in centimeters. Let s = hours of sunlight.

Equation $g = 1.38 \cdot s$

Step 2 Evaluate the function.

$g = 1.38 \cdot 15 = 20.7$ ← **Substitute 15 for *s*.**

The plant grows 20.7 cm when it receives 15 h of sunlight.

Step 3 Make a table of values and graph the function.

Hours of Sunlight (s)	Centimeters of Growth (g)
1	1.38
2	2.76
3	4.14
4	5.52

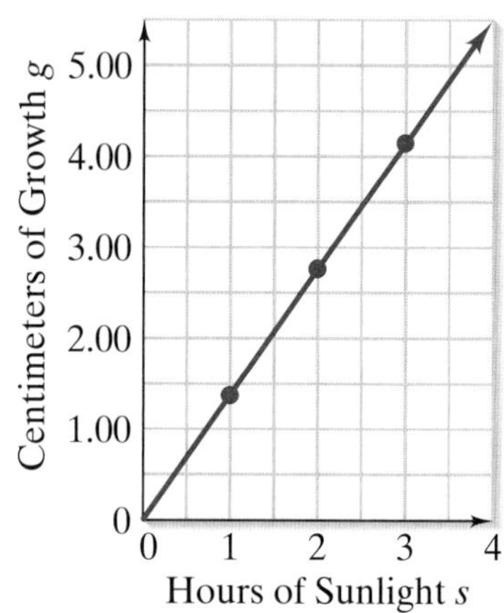

Check Understanding 2

a. The cost of a long distance telephone call is a function of time in minutes. A state-to-state call costs 13¢/min. Write and evaluate a function to find the cost of a 15-min call. Then graph the function.

b. **Reasoning** Does every function have an output of 0 for an input value of 0? Explain.

EXERCISES

For more practice, see *Extra Practice*.

A Practice by Example

Example 1 (page 489)

Graph the function represented by each table.

1.

Input x	Output y
0	1
1	4
2	7
3	10

2.

Input x	Output y
0	0
1	12
2	24
3	36

Example 2 (page 490)

Write and evaluate a function to find the output for an input of 10 h. Then graph the function.

3. **Employment** Total salary S is a function of the number t of hours worked. Your salary is \$6/h.

4. **Calories** Total Calories c burned by walking is a function of the number t of hours spent walking. You burn an average of 300 Cal/h.

5. **Air Travel** Total distance d is a function of the number t of hours traveled. Airplane speed averages 320 mi/h.

B Apply Your Skills

Graph each function. Use input values of 1, 2, 3, 4, and 5.

6. $y = 5x$

7. $y = 2x + 1$

8. $y = x \div 2$

9. **Open-Ended** Choose one function rule from Exercises 6–8. Describe a situation that could represent the function.

Real-World Connection

In 1928, Amelia Earhart became the first woman to fly across the Atlantic Ocean.

10. **Flight** Amelia Earhart once held the record for the fastest transcontinental flight speed. The table shows the relationship between distance and time for her flight.
    a. Write a rule for the function represented by the table.
    b. Find Amelia Earhart's average speed. Justify your answer.
    c. Estimate the number of hours it took her to fly 1,890 mi.
    d. Graph the function.

Amelia Earhart's Flight

Time (h)	Distance (mi)
2	362
4	724
6	1,086
8	1,448

Match each graph with a function rule.

11.

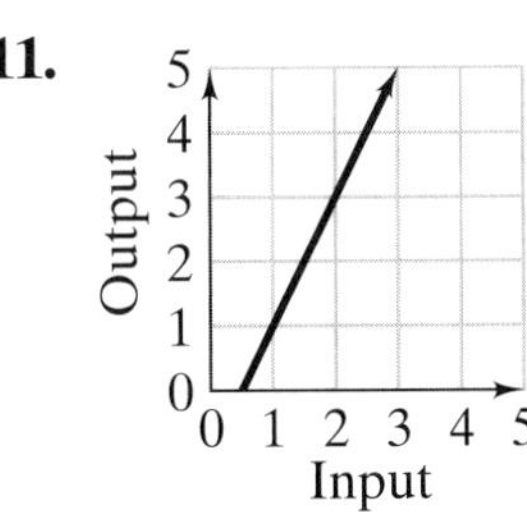

12.

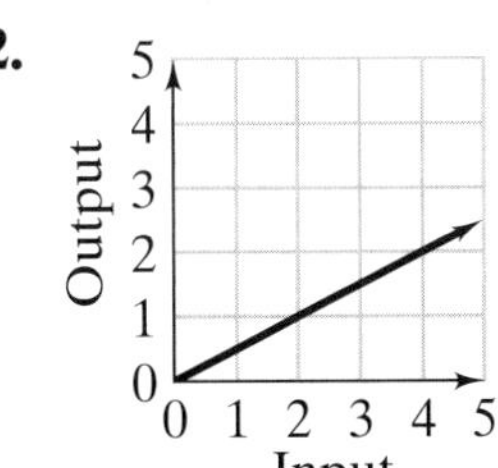

13.

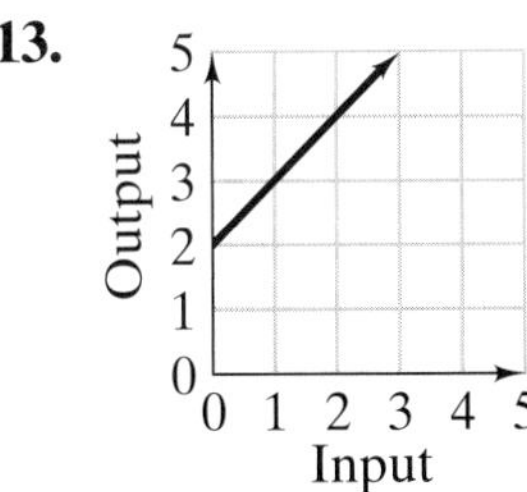

A. Output = $\frac{1}{2} \cdot$ Input

B. Output = Input + 2

C. Output = $2 \cdot$ Input − 1

14. **Writing in Math** For each situation, which would best represent a function—a table, a rule, or a graph? Explain your choice.
    a. You only have a few values or you do not know the rule.
    b. You have many input and output values.
    c. You want to see the relationship between the values.

15. a. **Data File, p. 467** It costs \$380 per year to feed a cat. Write a function rule for the cost c of feeding a cat during its lifetime y.
    b. Evaluate the function to find the cost of feeding a cat that lives to the maximum life span.

16. **a.** Make a function table for the graph.
b. Write a rule for the function.

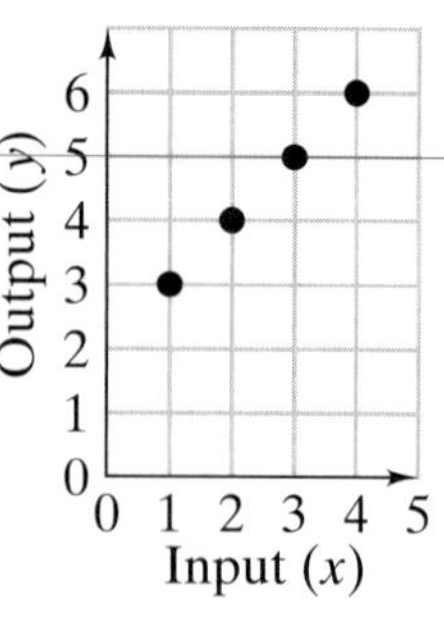

Evaluate $y = 2x^2 - 8$ for each value of x.

17. 3
18. 0
19. -2
20. -3
21. 2
22. $\frac{1}{2}$

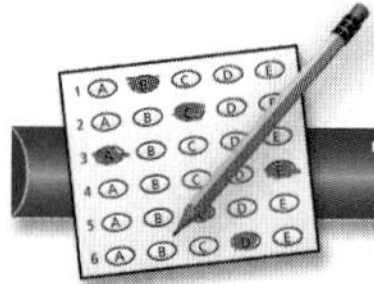

Challenge

23. **Geometry** The area of a square is a function of the length of a side. Write a rule and graph the function. Describe the shape of your graph.

24. **Stretch Your Thinking** You have a total of 12 cards in 4 different colors. The probability of drawing a green card is the same as the probability of drawing a yellow card. The probability of drawing a red card is $\frac{1}{4}$ and of drawing a blue card is $\frac{1}{12}$. How many green cards are in the box?

Test Prep

Multiple Choice

25. Which number can be an output for the function $y = 2x - 1$ if only whole numbers are used as inputs?
A. 6 **B.** 8 **C.** 11 **D.** 14

26. Which output value would NOT be on the graph of the function $y = -4x + 20$ for input values of 0, 1, 2, 3?
F. 0 **G.** 8 **H.** 12 **I.** 16

27. Which situation CANNOT be modeled by $y = 4x$?
A. the cost of a call at 4¢/min
B. the perimeter of a trapezoid
C. your pay after working 4 h
D. the number of stamps in 4 packs

Extended Response

Take It to the NET
Online lesson quiz at
www.PHSchool.com
Web Code: aba-0905

28. You ride a bicycle at 12 mi/h. The distance you ride is a function of time.
a. Copy and complete the table.
b. Graph the function.
c. How many miles do you ride in 3.5 h?

Time (h)	Distance (mi)
1	12
1.5	18
2	*a*
2.5	*b*

Mixed Review

Lesson 3-6

Compare. Use <, >, or =.

29. $\frac{7}{9}$ ■ $\frac{3}{4}$
30. $\frac{5}{14}$ ■ $\frac{2}{6}$
31. $\frac{7}{30}$ ■ $\frac{1}{3}$
32. $\frac{8}{24}$ ■ $\frac{2}{6}$

Lesson 1-3

Find the value of each expression.

33. (95.26)(110)
34. (0.23)(8.45)
35. $0.384 \div 9.6$
36. $19.563 \div 6$

Technology Three Views of a Function

For Use With Lesson 9-5

When you input a function rule in a graphing calculator, you can view the graph of the function or a table of values.

EXAMPLE

Graph $y = 9 - x$ and make a table of values.

Step 1 Use WINDOW to set the range.

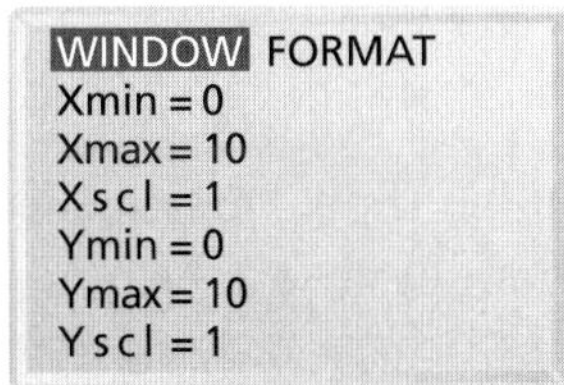

Step 2 Use Y= to enter the function.

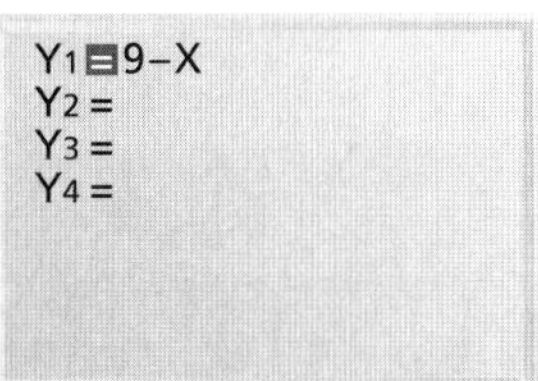

Step 3 Use the GRAPH feature to view the graph.

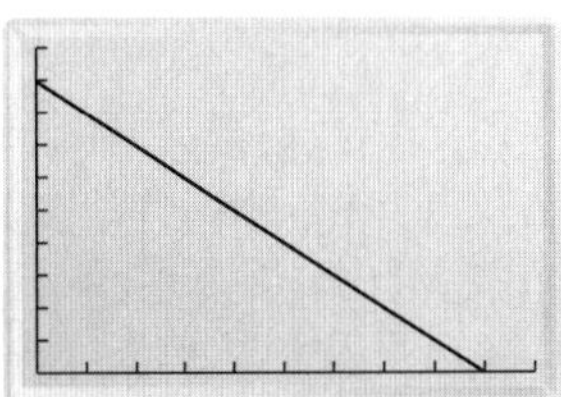

Step 4 Use the TABLE feature to make a table of values.

X	Y1
0	9
1	8
2	7
3	6
4	5
5	4
6	3

X=0

Step 5 Sketch the graph and copy the table of values.

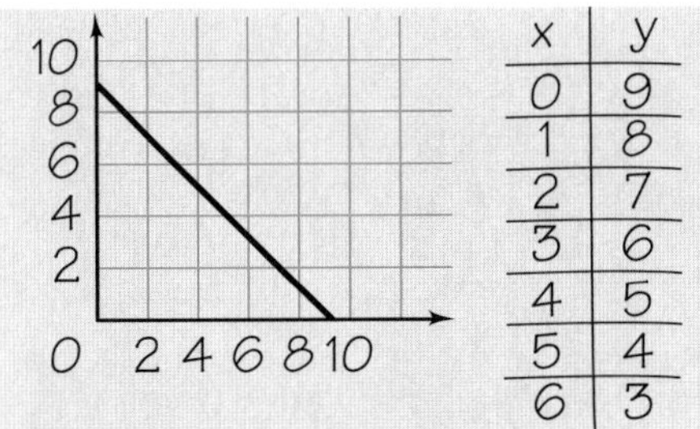

x	y
0	9
1	8
2	7
3	6
4	5
5	4
6	3

EXERCISES

Use a graphing calculator to graph each function and make a table of values. Sketch the graph and copy the table of values.

1. $y = 2x$

2. $y = x - 3$

3. $y = 13 - 2x$

4. $y = x + 1$

5. $y = 3x - 4$

6. $y = 0.5x + 6$

7. $y = 7$

8. $y = x^2$

9. $y = x^2 - 8x + 16$

9-6 Interpreting Graphs

What You'll Learn

OBJECTIVE 1 To describe a graph

OBJECTIVE 2 To sketch a graph from a description

. . . And Why

To graph a trip to school and back, as in Example 2

Check Skills You'll Need

For help, go to Lesson 9-4.

Find the distance for the following times. Use $d = rt$ with $r = 40$ mi/h.

1. 2 h **2.** 2.5 h **3.** 5 h

4. 3.5 h **5.** $\frac{1}{4}$ h **6.** $\frac{1}{2}$ h

7. **Reasoning** What does the graph of the function $d = 40t$ look like?

OBJECTIVE 1

Describing Graphs

Interactive lesson includes instant self-check, tutorials, and activities.

When you graph a function rule, you can see how one quantity changes compared to another.

1 EXAMPLE Describing a Graph

Real World

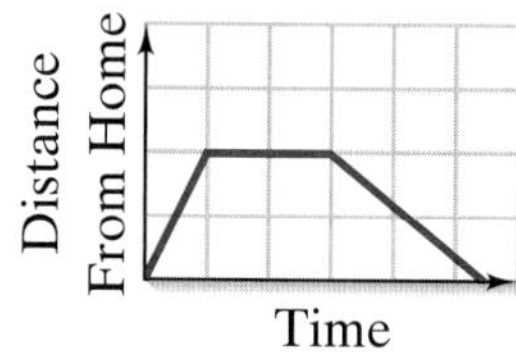

Shopping You ride your bike to the supermarket and shop. The graph at the left relates time and your distance from home. Describe what you can tell about the trip from the steepness of the lines.

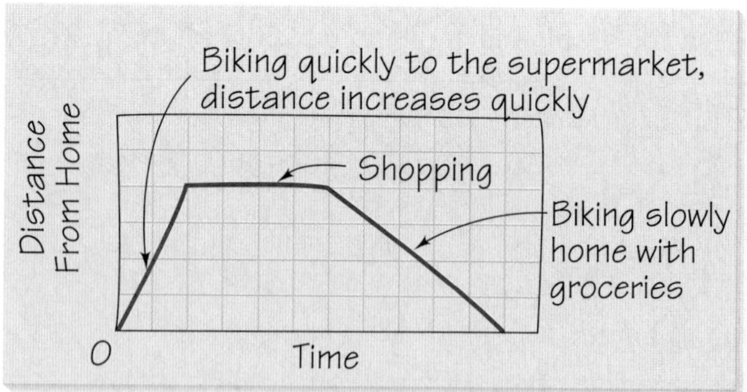

A steeper line on the graph shows faster speed. A horizontal line represents a period of no change in distance from home.

Check Understanding

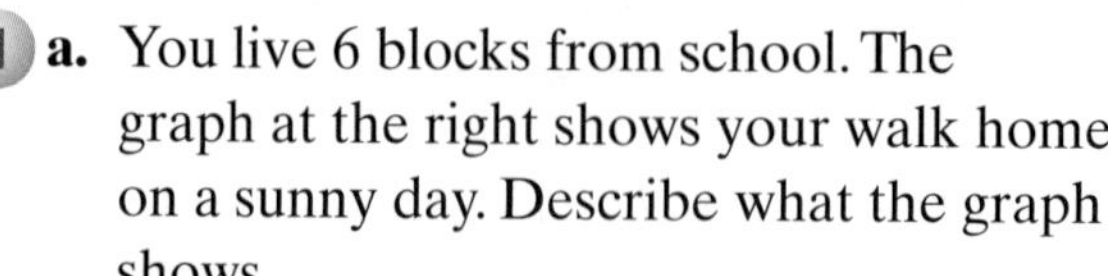

1 **a.** You live 6 blocks from school. The graph at the right shows your walk home on a sunny day. Describe what the graph shows.

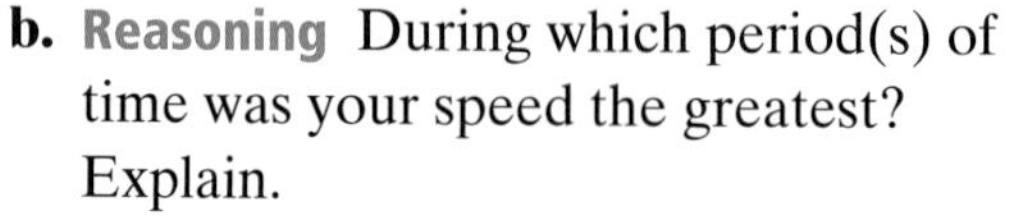

b. **Reasoning** During which period(s) of time was your speed the greatest? Explain.

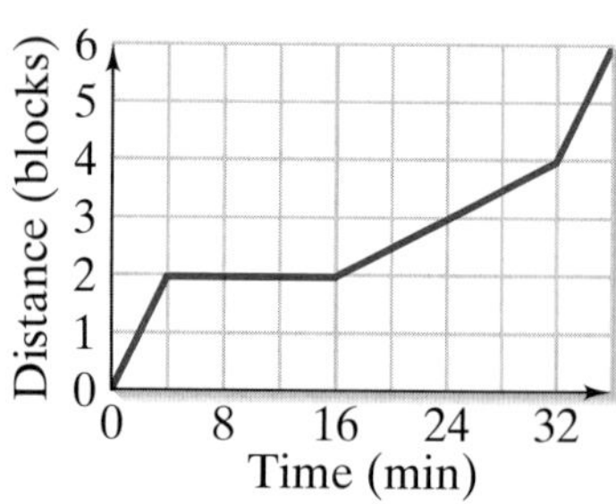

OBJECTIVE

2 Sketching Graphs

You can sketch a graph to describe a real-world situation.

2 EXAMPLE Sketching a Graph

Transportation Ciara's mom drove her part of the way to school. Ciara waited for a friend and walked the rest of the way to school. She took a bus home. Sketch a graph to show the distance Ciara traveled compared to time.

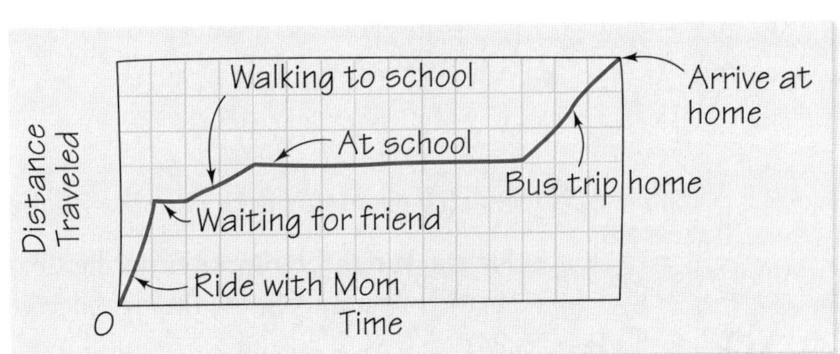

Check Understanding 2 **a.** Sketch a graph of the situation in Example 2 using *Distance from Home* instead of *Distance Traveled* for the vertical axis.

b. Reasoning How is your graph different from the one in Example 2?

When you draw a graph, you may need to consider what is reasonable in a real-world context.

3 EXAMPLE Real-World Problem Solving

Games The cost to play games at an arcade is given in the table. Make a graph of the cost to play 1, 2, 3, and 4 games at the arcade.

Step 1 Make a table.

Number of Games	Cost ($)
1	2.00
2	3.50
3	5.00
4	6.50

Step 2 Graph. Do not connect the points.

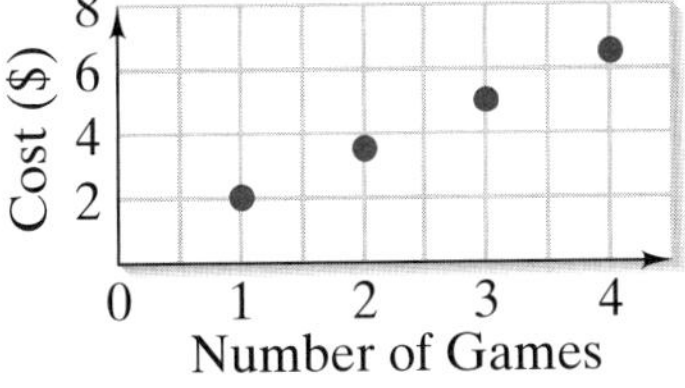

Check for Reasonableness Each cost is for playing an entire game. You cannot pay for a part of a game. It is reasonable not to connect the points.

Check Understanding 3 **a.** The table shows the number of cans in the cafeteria juice machine over time. Graph the data.

b. Does it make sense to connect the points in this graph? Explain.

Time	Number of Cans
8 A.M.	30
9 A.M.	20
10 A.M.	19
11 A.M.	19

EXERCISES

For more practice, see *Extra Practice*.

A Practice by Example

Example 1 (page 494)

Describe what each graph shows.

1.

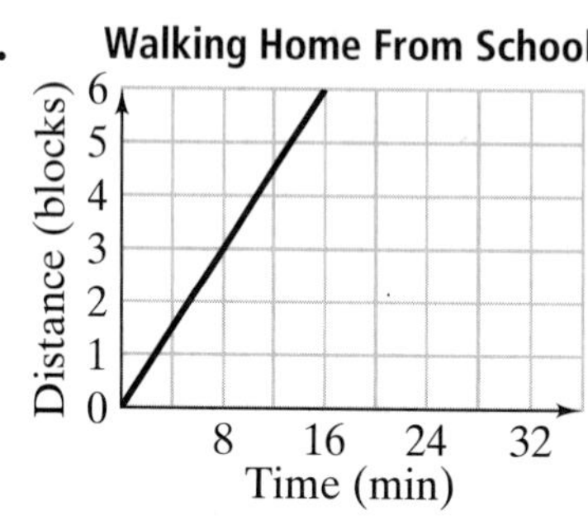

2.

Distance From Home

Distance (mi)
0
5
10
15
20
25
0
1
2
3
4
Time (h)

Example 2 (page 495)

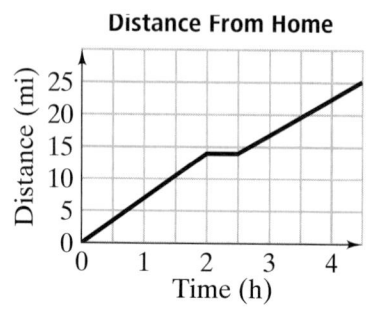

Sketch a graph for each situation. Label each section and each axis.

3. You run three blocks from the library and then walk five more blocks to your home. Show the distance you travel on the vertical axis.

4. You ride your bike slowly up a steep hill, and then quickly down the other side. Show your speed on the vertical axis.

5. You climb a jungle gym and then slide down the slide. Show the distance from the ground on the vertical axis.

6. You cycle 2 mi, stop at a traffic light, and then proceed at your original speed for another mile. Show the distance you travel on the vertical axis.

Example 3 (page 495)

Graph the data. Should you connect the points on each graph? Explain.

7. Lemonade Sales

Cups Sold	Income ($)
1	0.75
2	1.50
3	2.25
4	3.00
5	3.75

8. Miles From Home

Time (h)	Miles
1	60
2	85
3	120
4	180

B Apply Your Skills

9. Library You pay a 5-cent fine for each day a library book is overdue.
a. Graph the cost of fines for a book overdue by 1, 2, 3, 4, and 5 days.
b. Did you connect the points on your graph? Explain.

10. Suppose you are steadily pouring sand into the bowl at the left. Which graph below better shows the relationship of the height of the sand with the amount you have poured? Why?

A.

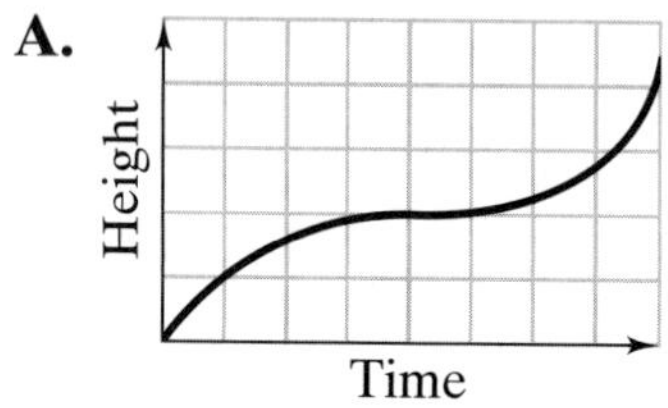

B.

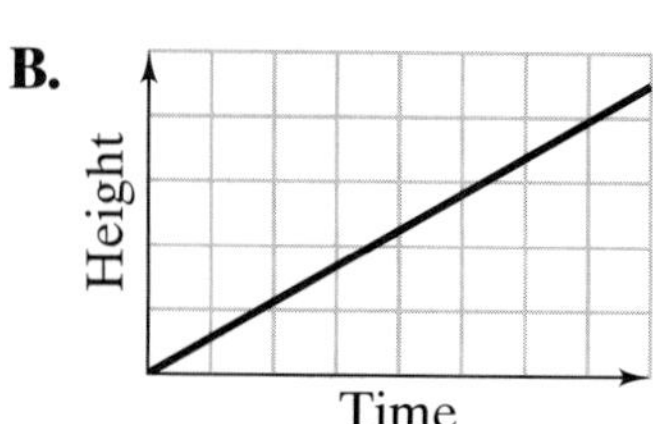

Real-World Connection Girls from birth to age 2 grow about 15 times as fast as teens ages 14–20.

Match each graph with the situation that describes it.

11. 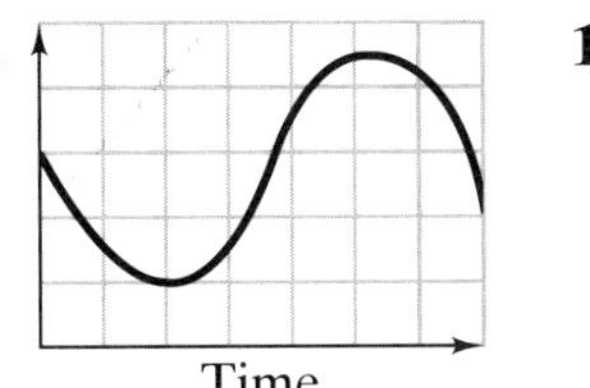

12. 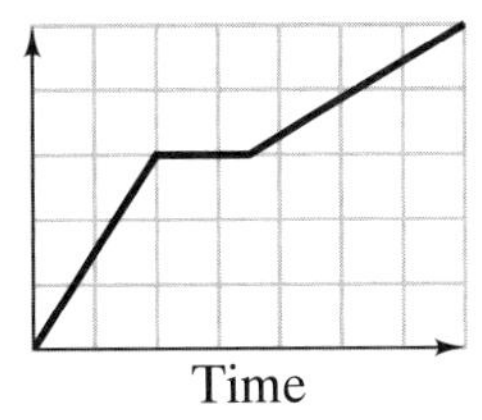

13. 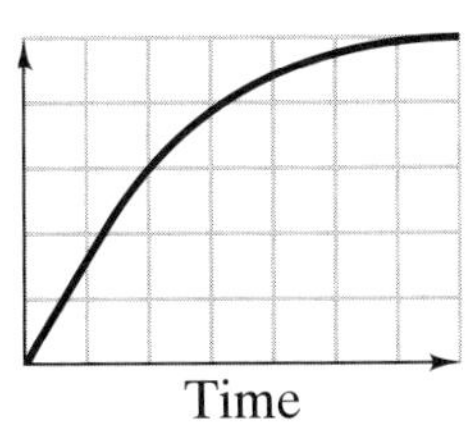

A. height of a person from birth to age 20

B. air temperature in a 24-hour period starting at midnight

C. distance raced with a fall over a hurdle

14. Sports The graph shows a 100-m race. One student starts 5 s after the other.

a. Describe what the graph shows.

b. Who wins the race?

c. **Reasoning** If the lines were parallel, what would the graph tell you about who wins the race?

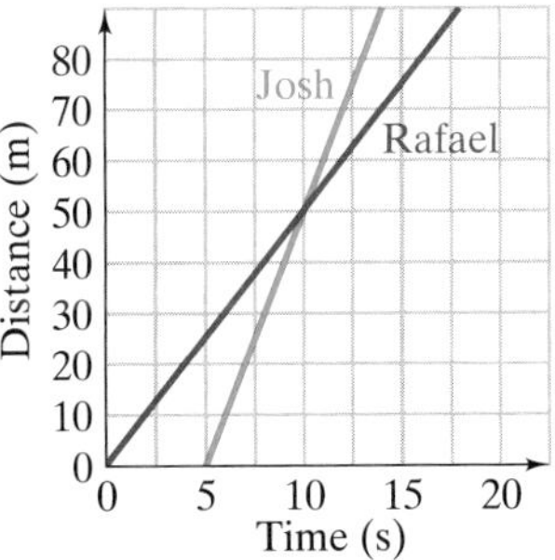

Sketch a graph for each situation.

15. A flag is raised on a flagpole.

16. Judy takes a walk to the mall. She stops to visit a friend. Judy continues walking to the mall, shops for a while, and then runs home for dinner.

17. **Writing in Math** Lee, Paulo, and Mary each walk their dogs six times around the block. Who walks the fastest? Justify your answer.

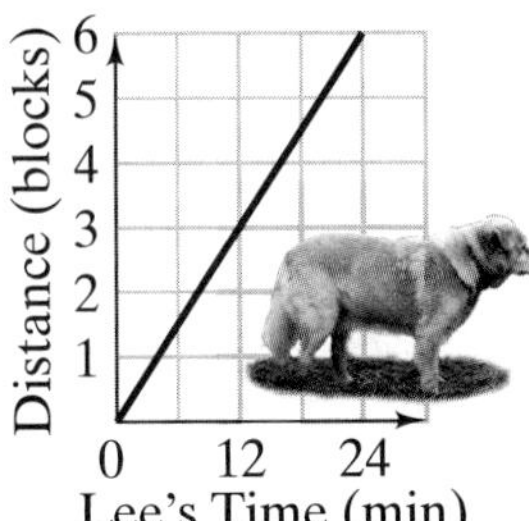

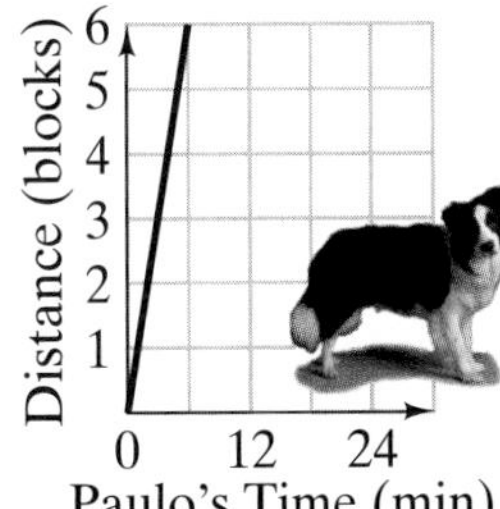

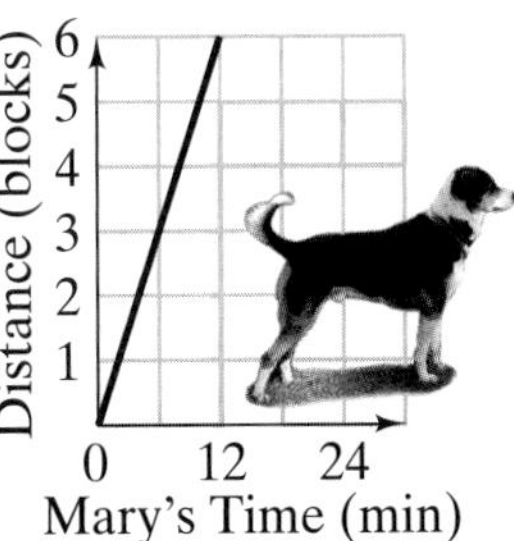

Sketch a graph for each situation. Label the axes.

18. **Geometry** As a square's dimensions increase, its perimeter increases.

19. **Nutrition** The more crackers you eat, the more Calories you consume.

20. **Reasoning** A driver sets a car's cruise control to 50 mi/h. Which graph shows the car's speed? Which shows the distance traveled? Explain.

A. 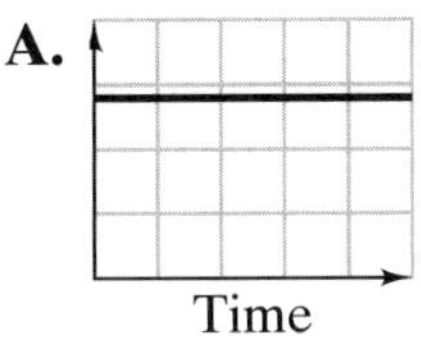

B. 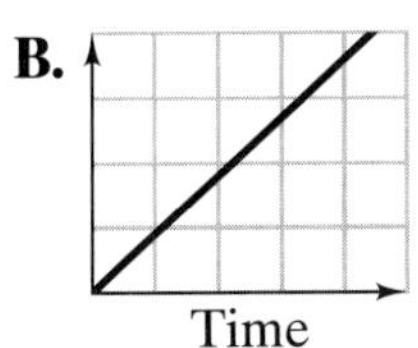

Ⓒ Challenge

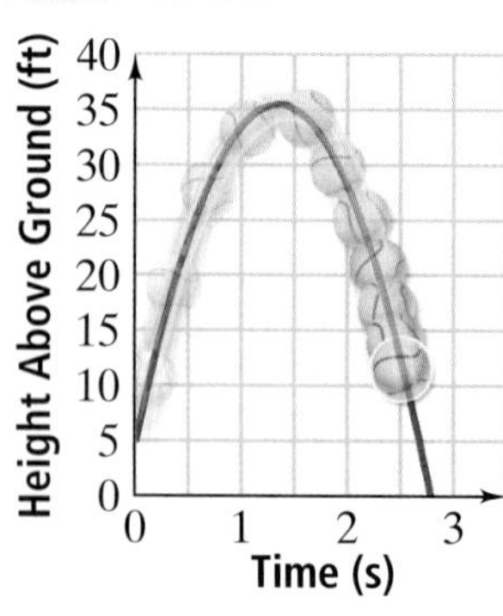

Estimation **Refer to the graph at the left. It shows what happens when a ball is thrown in the air.**

21. When does the ball hit the ground?

22. Why are there two times when the ball's height is 20 ft? What are they?

23. When the time is 0, the height of the ball is *not* 0. Why?

24. **Stretch Your Thinking** The last digit of a four-digit number is twice the first. The second is three less than the third. The third is the sum of the first and last. Each digit is different and none is 0. What number is it?

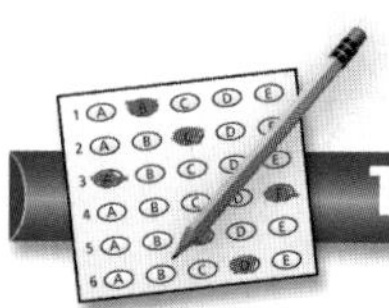

Test Prep

Reading Comprehension **Read the passage and answer the questions below.**

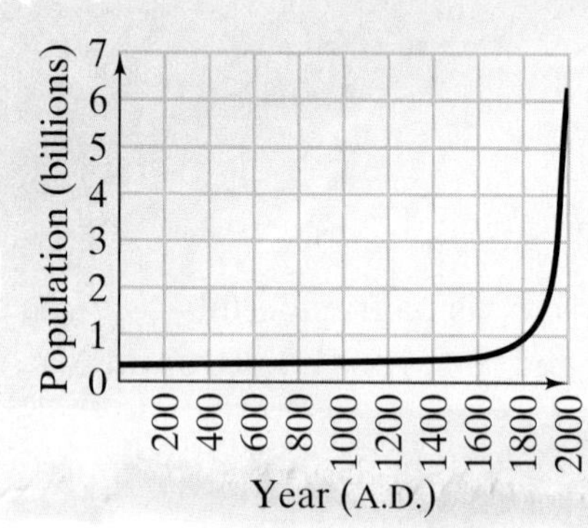

The Population Explosion

From A.D. 1 to 1650, the world population grew by 300 million. The average growth was just 180,000 people per year, or about 21 people per hour. Today twelve babies are born every three seconds, but only five people die. This means that the population is growing by about 8,400 people per hour, or about 73.6 million per year.

25. Which is a function rule for converting population growth from per hour to per year?
    A. $y = 60 \cdot 24 \cdot 12 \cdot x$ B. $y = 24 \cdot 12 \cdot 12 \cdot x$
    C. $y = 52 \cdot 24 \cdot x$ D. $y = 24 \cdot 365 \cdot x$

Take It to the NET
Online lesson quiz at
www.PHSchool.com
Web Code: aba-0906

26. What is the approximate daily population growth today?
    F. 6.1 million G. 3.1 million H. 201,600 I. 8,400

27. Explain how the graph illustrates the data in the article.

Mixed Review

Lesson 8-2

Find the area of a triangle with the given base and height.

28. 5 m, 2 m 29. 10 ft, 3 ft 30. 18 cm, 6 cm 31. 19 in., 6 in.

Lesson 6-5

Algebra **Solve.**

32. What is 2% of 12?
33. What percent of 150 is 50?
34. What percent of 60 is 12?
35. What is 120% of 25?

9-7

Simple and Compound Interest

What You'll Learn

To find simple interest

To find compound interest

. . . And Why

To find the balance in an account, as in Example 3

Check Skills You'll Need

For help, go to Lesson 6-2.

Change each percent to a decimal.

1. 4%	**2.** 9%	**3.** 2.0%
4. 6.5%	**5.** 5.09%	**6.** 18.21%

New Vocabulary • principal • simple interest • compound interest • balance

Interactive lesson includes instant self-check, tutorials, and activities.

OBJECTIVE 1 Finding Simple Interest

Money does not grow on trees, but it does grow in a bank. When you deposit money, you earn money, called "interest." When you borrow, you pay interest.

The original amount you deposit or borrow is the **principal.** Interest calculated only on the principal is **simple interest.**

You can use a formula to calculate simple interest.

Key Concepts **Simple Interest Formula**

$$I = prt$$

I is interest, p is principal, r is annual rate of interest, and t is time in years.

1 EXAMPLE Finding Simple Interest

Find the simple interest on \$300 borrowed for 3 years at an annual interest rate of 4%.

$I = prt$ ← **Write the formula.**

$I = (300)(0.04)(3)$ ← **Substitute. Use 0.04 for 4%.**

$= 36$ ← **Simplify.**

The interest is \$36.

Check Understanding 1 **a.** Find the simple interest on a \$220 loan at a 5% annual rate for 4 years.
b. **Reasoning** Of what quantities is interest a function?

A graph of simple interest shows the increase in interest earned over time.

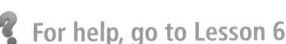

2 EXAMPLE Graphing Simple Interest

You have \$500 in an account at an annual rate of 5.1%. Interest is paid and withdrawn at the end of each year. Graph the total interest you earn after 1, 2, 3, and 4 years.

Step 1 Make a table. Let t = time.

Time (yr)	Interest (\$)
1	25.50
2	51.00
3	76.50
4	102.00

Step 2 Draw a graph.

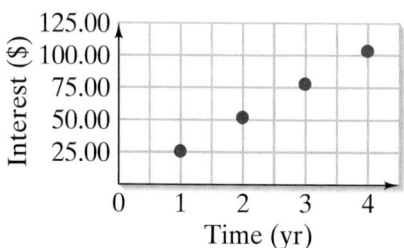

Interest (\$): 125.00, 100.00, 75.00, 50.00, 25.00
0 1 2 3 4
Time (yr)

Check Understanding 2 Graph the simple interest you earn on \$950 at an annual rate of 4.2%.

OBJECTIVE 2

Finding Compound Interest

Compound interest is interest that is paid on the original principal and on any interest that has been left in the account. The **balance** of an account is the principal plus the interest earned.

Key Concepts **Compound Interest Formula**

$$B = p(1 + r)^t$$

B is balance, p is principal, r is annual interest rate, and t is time in years.

3 EXAMPLE Real-World Problem Solving

Banking Suppose you deposit \$5,000 in a bank account that pays 3.75% interest compounded annually. What is your balance after 9 years?

$B = p(1 + r)^t$	← Write the formula.
$= 5{,}000(1 + 0.0375)^9$	← Substitute. Use 0.0375 for 3.75%.
$\approx 5{,}000(1.392813439)$	← Use a calculator to simplify the power.
$= 6{,}964.07$	← Round to the nearest cent.

The balance after 9 years is \$6,964.07.

Check for Reasonableness The compound interest is \$6,964.07 − \$5,000, or about \$1,964. Simple interest would be I = (\$5,000)(0.0375)(9), or about \$1,688. Since compound interest is greater, the answer is reasonable.

Need Help?
For help using the Order of Operations with exponents, go to Lesson 3-1.

Check Understanding 3 You deposit \$3,000 in a bank account that pays 4.25% interest compounded annually. What is your balance after 12 years?

EXERCISES

For more practice, see *Extra Practice*.

A Practice by Example

Example 1 (page 499)

Find the simple interest on a $340 loan at each rate.

1. 7% annual interest, 3 years
2. 12% annual interest, 5 years
3. 15% annual interest, 1 year
4. 6% annual interest, 6 years

Example 2 (page 500)

Graph the total simple interest earned for each amount over 4 years.

5. $500 at 4.5%
6. $1,200 at 6.5%
7. $375 at 5.75%
8. $200 at 5.0%
9. $2,000 at 10%
10. $2,000 at 0.5%

Example 3 (page 500)

Find the balance in each compound interest account.

11. $1,400 after 3 years at 5.5%
12. $1,800 after 11 years at 6.0%
13. $900 after 10 years at 4.62%
14. $2,500 after 50 years at 2.2%

B Apply Your Skills

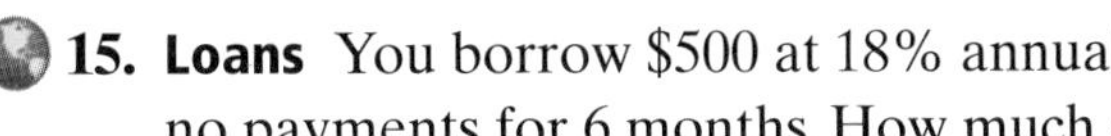

15. Loans You borrow $500 at 18% annual compound interest. You make no payments for 6 months. How much do you owe after 6 months?

16. a. Estimation Suppose you invest $2,000 for 5 years at 4% compounded annually. Which would increase your balance in 5 years the most? Explain.

A. doubling the starting amount from $2,000 to $4,000
B. doubling the interest rate to 8% annual interest
C. doubling the time from 5 years to 10 years

b. Calculator Check your answer to part (a). Were you correct?

Real-World Connection

Banks offer savings accounts that earn compound interest at a variety of rates.

Find the simple interest earned in each account.

17. $1,000 at 5% for 9 months
18. $4,500 at 4% for 8 months
19. $2,000 at 3.6% for 3 months
20. $500 at 1.75% for 180 days

The spreadsheet shows calculations using the compound interest formula. Use it for Exercises 21 and 22.

	A	B	C	D	E
1	Year	Balance at Start of Year	Rate	Interest	Balance at End of Year
2	1st	$3,000.00	0.04	$120.00	$3,120.00
3	2nd	$3,120.00	0.04	$124.80	$3,244.80
4	3rd	$3,244.80	0.04	$129.79	$3,374.59

21. State which column corresponds to each variable in the formula.

a. p **b.** r **c.** t **d.** B

22. Show how to calculate the amount in cell E4.

23. **Writing in Math** Certificates of Deposit (CDs) allow you to save money at fixed compound interest rates, provided that you do not withdraw your money before the end of the term. What advantages do longer term CDs have? Disadvantages?

LOANS CDs BILLS ACCOUNT

Certificate of Deposit

Term	Interest Rate
3 month	2.72%
6 month	2.77%
12 month	2.96%
24 month	3.93%
36 month	3.64%
60 month	4.22%

C Challenge

24. **Reasoning** You invest \$2,000 in a simple interest account. The balance in 8 years is \$2,720. What is the interest rate?

25. **Stretch Your Thinking** Three friends are guessing the number of buttons in a jar. They guess 495, 514, and 537. One guess is off by 8, another by 15, and another by 27. How many buttons are in the jar?

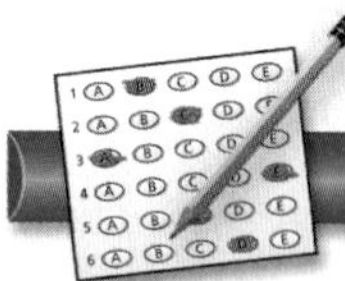

Test Prep

Multiple Choice

26. Which expression would you use to find the balance for \$200 invested for 6 years at a 5% interest rate compounded annually?
A. $200(1.06)^5$ **B.** 200(0.06)(5) **C.** $200(1.05)^6$ **D.** 200(0.05)(6)

Take It to the NET
Online lesson quiz at **www.PHSchool.com**
Web Code: aba-0907

27. You borrow \$200 at a 3% simple interest rate. About how much interest will you owe in 18 months?
F. \$6 **G.** \$9 **H.** \$12 **I.** \$108

Short Response

28. You invest \$100 for 5 years. Which will yield a greater balance, an account with a 3% simple interest rate or one with a 3% rate compounded annually? How much greater? Show your work.

Mixed Review

Algebra **Solve each equation.**

Lesson 2-6
29. $-3t - 10 = 11$
30. $\frac{1}{2}x - 5 = 7$
31. $\frac{p}{2} + 12 = 5$

Lesson 2-3
32. $5 + n = -4$
33. $-10 = x - 15$
34. $-12 + c = -1$

Checkpoint Quiz 2 — Lessons 9-5 through 9-7

Instant self-check quiz online and on CD-ROM

1. Graph $y = 2x - 4$.
2. Graph $d = rt$ for a 35 mi/h rate.
3. You walk for 3 h, eat lunch for 1 h, bike for 1 h, and then do homework for 2 h. Sketch a graph that describes your speed.
4. Graph the total simple interest earned over 4 years on \$850 invested at an annual rate of 4.4%.
5. If you save \$850 at an interest rate of 3.5% compounded annually, how much money would you have in the account after 5 years?

9-8 Write an Equation

What You'll Learn

To solve problems by writing equations

. . . And Why

To solve a problem using a function, as in Example 1

Check Skills You'll Need

For help, go to Lesson 2-1.

Evaluate each expression using the values $r = 3, s = 4$, and $t = -2$.

1. $4r$
2. $5s + t$
3. $-3r - s$
4. $\frac{1}{2}t + s$
5. $rs + t$
6. $2st - r$

OBJECTIVE

1 Solving Problems by Writing Equations

Interactive lesson includes instant self-check, tutorials, and activities.

Writing a function rule in the form of an equation can help you solve a problem. Use variables for values that are unknown or subject to change.

1 EXAMPLE Real-World Problem Solving

Materials to make a toboggan cost \$8 each. A craftsman budgets \$2,000 this year and \$3,000 next year. How many toboggans can he make each year?

Read and Understand Your goal is to find the number of toboggans the craftsman can make each year using his budget and the cost of materials.

Plan and Solve Write a function rule for the number of toboggans.

 **Words**	amount budgeted	divided by	cost of materials	is the	number of toboggans
	Let b = amount budgeted. Let n = number of toboggans.				
Equation	b	$\div$	\$8	$=$	n

$$\frac{b}{8} = n$$

$\frac{2{,}000}{8} = n$ $\quad$ $\frac{3{,}000}{8} = n$ $\quad$ ← **Substitute b = 2,000 and b = 3,000.**

$250 = n$ $\quad$ $375 = n$ $\quad$ ← **Solve for n.**

The craftsman can make 250 toboggans this year and 375 next year.

Look Back and Check Multiply each number of toboggans by the cost.

$250 \cdot 8 = 2{,}000$ ✓ $\quad$ $375 \cdot 8 = 3{,}000$ ✓ $\quad$ ← **Both answers check.**

Real-World Connection

A toboggan is a wooden sled.

Check Understanding 1 A 150-lb woman burns about 131 Cal/mi running 6 mi/h. She ran 40 mi this week and 35 mi last week. How many Calories did she burn each week?

2 EXAMPLE Real-World  Problem Solving

Mountain bikes are designed for rough terrain. Freestyle bikes are designed for roads.

Consumer Decisions You plan to purchase a mountain bike for \$267 or a freestyle bike for \$183. You have \$90 and will save \$7 each week. How long will it take to save enough for each bike?

Read and Understand Your goal is to find how many weeks it will take to save enough for each bike.

Plan and Solve Set up a function rule to represent the situation.

Words	total saved	is	savings	plus	amount saved each week	times	number of weeks

Let s = total amount saved. Let n = number of weeks.

Equation	s	$=$	\$90	$+$	\$7	$\cdot$	n

Mountain bike		Freestyle bike
$267 = 90 + 7n$	← **Substitute 267 and 183 for *s*.** →	$183 = 90 + 7n$
$177 = 7n$	← **Solve for *n*.** →	$93 = 7n$
$25.3 \approx n$		$13.3 \approx n$

It will take 26 weeks to save enough for the mountain bike and 14 weeks for the freestyle bike.

Look Back and Check Use the number of weeks and the function rule to find how much was saved during each period.

$s = 90 + 7n$

$= 90 + 7(26) = 272$ ← **The amount saved for the mountain bike.**

$= 90 + 7(14) = 188$ ← **The amount saved for the freestyle bike.**

The mountain bike costs \$267. The freestyle bike costs \$183. You have saved enough to purchase either bike. Both answers are reasonable.

Check Understanding 2 Family membership at a science museum costs \$89 per year. In addition, omnitheatre shows cost \$22.50 per family each visit. How many omnitheatre shows could a family see if its yearly budget is \$300?

EXERCISES

 For more practice, see *Extra Practice*.

Examples 1, 2 (pages 503, 504)

Use a function rule to solve each problem. Check your answer.

1. **Travel** Suppose your family's car gets 23 mi/gal. Your family plans two trips. The first will be 540 mi and the second will be 270 mi. To the nearest gallon, how many gallons of gas will each trip require?

Need Help?
- Reread the problem.
- Identify the key facts and details.
- Tell the problem in your own words.
- Try a different strategy.
- Check your work.

2. Sales A company's new product is sold for $16.50 per unit. About how many units does it sell altogether in the United States and Europe?

Product Sales

United States $400,000

Europe $230,000

3. Business The operating costs of a swimsuit distributor are $120,000 per year plus $23 per swimsuit. The current partners have $500,000 to spend and are considering a new partner who has $150,000. How many swimsuits can they produce with and without the new partner?

Use any strategy or a combination of strategies to solve each problem.

4. Saving You are saving $5 each week to attend a summer program that costs $300. You already have $84. You have also received a $50 scholarship for the program. How many weeks of saving do you need?

- Draw a Diagram
- Look for a Pattern
- Make a Graph
- Make an Organized List
- Make a Table
- Simulate a Problem
- Solve a Simpler Problem
- Try, Check, and Revise
- Use Logical Reasoning
- Work Backward
- Write an Equation

5. Measurement Using a balance scale and three weights, you can weigh any whole number of pounds from 1 lb to 13 lb. What are the weights?

6. Zoo The table below describes costs for admission to the zoo.

a. What is the cost of admission for an adult? For a child?

b. The cost of admission for a group of four people is $14. How many adults and how many children are in the group?

Children	Adults	Cost
0	4	$20
1	3	$18

7. Geometry How many diagonals does a regular 8-sided figure have?

8. Writing in Math During a sale, a store manager reduces a sweater's price by 30%. After the sale, the manager increases the price by 30%. Are the prices before and after the sale equal? Explain.

9. Five sand pails aligned side by side contain a total of 100 shells. Each bucket contains two shells fewer than the bucket to its left. How many shells are in each bucket?

10. Stretch Your Thinking Copy the diagram at the right. Write the numbers 1 through 10 inside the rectangles so that the sum of the numbers along any side is 18.

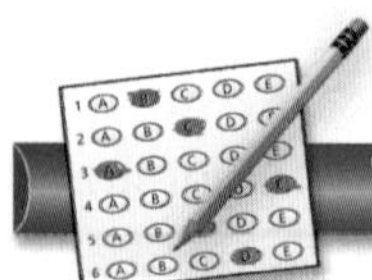

Test Prep

Multiple Choice

11. Five pounds of potatoes cost \$3.45. How much do 2 lb cost?
A. \$.89 **B.** \$1.38 **C.** \$1.73 **D.** \$2.14

12. On Monday $\frac{4}{7}$ of the students at school bought a hot lunch. About what percent of the students did NOT buy a hot lunch?
F. 37% **G.** 43% **H.** 57% **I.** 62%

Take It to the NET
Online lesson quiz at
www.PHSchool.com
Web Code: aba-0908

13. All items in a store are 30% off. When you open a store charge card, you receive an additional 15% off your first purchase. Which expression represents the final price of an item that costs n dollars?
A. $0.3n - 0.15$ **B.** $0.7n - 0.85n$
C. $(0.7)(0.85)n$ **D.** $(0.7)(0.15)n$

Short Response

14. A survey of 1,500 users shows that 850 are extremely happy with an Internet service provider. If there are a total of 30,000 users, about how many are extremely happy? Show your work.

Mixed Review

Lesson 9-4

Algebra **Use the function rule $y = 3x - 3$. Find y for each input value.**

15. 3 **16.** 5 **17.** -4 **18.** $\frac{5}{6}$

19. 3.5 **20.** -7 **21.** -0.6 **22.** 0

23. $\frac{2}{3}$ **24.** 7.2 **25.** -2.8 **26.** $\frac{7}{6}$

Lesson 9-2

Write a rule for each arithmetic sequence. Then find the next three terms.

27. 15, 22, 29, 36, . . . **28.** 9, 11.3, 13.6, 15.9, . . . **29.** $\frac{1}{2}, \frac{3}{4}, 1, \frac{5}{4}, \ldots$

Math at Work

Artist

Artists use a variety of materials to create images—oils, watercolors, plaster, clay, or even computers. Graphic artists work for businesses. Fine artists display their works in galleries or museums.

Artists use angles and lines to draw in perspective, an important skill for any aspiring artist.

Take It to the NET For more information about artists, go to **www.PHSchool.com.**
Web Code abb-2031

Algebra

9-9 Transforming Formulas

What You'll Learn

OBJECTIVE 1 To solve for a variable

. . . And Why

To save for new clothes, as in Example 2

Check Skills You'll Need

For help, go to Lessons 2-3 and 2-4.

Solve each equation.

1. $a - 5 = 9$
2. $10 = -5x$
3. $12 = 4.5t$
4. $y + 8 = -12$
5. $\frac{p}{4} = -8$
6. $-3 + m = 1.2$

New Vocabulary

- formula

Interactive lesson includes instant self-check, tutorials, and activities.

OBJECTIVE 1

Solving for a Variable

A **formula** is a rule that shows the relationship between two or more quantities. You can use the properties of equality to transform a formula and solve for a variable.

1 EXAMPLE Transforming a Formula

Reading Math

Transform and *formula* share the same root word, *form*.

Solve the formula for the perimeter of a rectangle $P = 2\ell + 2w$ for ℓ.

$P = 2\ell + 2w$ ← **Write the formula.**

$P - 2w = 2\ell$ ← **Subtraction Property of Equality**

$\frac{P - 2w}{2} = \frac{2\ell}{2}$ ← **Division Property of Equality**

$\frac{P - 2w}{2} = \ell$ ← **Simplify.**

Check for Reasonableness Use $P = 10$ ft, $\ell = 3$ ft, and $w = 2$ ft to check your answer.

$P = 2\ell + 2w$	$\ell = \frac{P - 2w}{2}$	
$10 = 2(3) + 2(2)$	$3 = \frac{10 - 2(2)}{2}$	← **Substitute.**
$10 = 10$ ✔	$3 = 3$ ✔	

Check Understanding 1

a. Solve $y = 2x - 4$ for x.

b. Check your answer for part (a) using $y = 20$ and $x = 12$.

c. **Reasoning** By what property do you notice that solving $y = 2(x - 2)$ for x will give the same result as your answer to part (a)?

You can transform formulas to solve real-world problems. First solve for the desired variable. Then substitute the values you know.

2 EXAMPLE Using a Transformed Formula

Savings Your bank account has an annual interest rate of 5.7%. You plan to withdraw the interest at the end of each year to buy new clothes. How much should you invest in order to have \$100 to spend?

$I = prt$ ← **You plan to withdraw interest, so use the simple interest formula.**

$\frac{I}{rt} = p$ ← **Solve for *p*.**

$\frac{100}{(0.057)(1)} = p$ ← **Substitute 100 for *I*, 0.057 for *r*, and 1 for *t*.**

$1{,}754.39 \approx p$

You should invest about \$1,755.

Check Understanding 2 Find the interest rate that yields \$120 interest each year on \$2,000.

More Than One Way

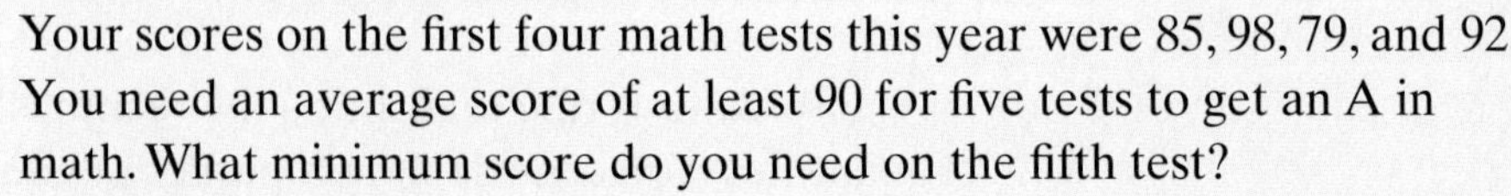

Your scores on the first four math tests this year were 85, 98, 79, and 92. You need an average score of at least 90 for five tests to get an A in math. What minimum score do you need on the fifth test?

Will's Method

I can set up a formula for finding the mean and solve for the missing grade. I'll use a variable for each score. Let z = missing score.

Formula for mean → $90 = \frac{v + w + x + y + z}{5}$

Mult. Prop. of Equality → $5(90) = v + w + x + y + z$

$5(90) - (v + w + x + y) = z$ ← **Subtraction Prop. of Equality**

$5(90) - (85 + 98 + 79 + 92) = z = 96$ ← **Substitute and simplify.**

I need a minimum score of 96 on the fifth test.

Sarah's Method

I'll write an equation and work backward. The sum s of all the scores divided by the number of scores should be 90.

$s \div 5 = 90$ ← **Write an equation.**

$s = 450$ ← **Solve for *s*.**

The sum of the current scores is 85 + 98 + 79 + 92, or 354. So, for a total of 450, I need a score on the fifth test of 450 − 354, or 96.

Choose a Method

Your scores on three tests are 95, 89, and 75. You can replace your lowest score with the mean of the score and a retest. For an average score of 90, what is the minimum you must score on the retest?

EXERCISES

For more practice, see *Extra Practice.*

A Practice by Example

Solve each equation for the variable in red.

Example 1 (page 507)

1. $x = yz$ **2.** $t = \frac{u + v}{2}$ **3.** $p = 3r - 5$

4. $P = 4s$ **5.** $q = \frac{p}{r}$ **6.** $p = s - c$

7. $A = \frac{1}{2}bh$ **8.** $h = \frac{k}{j}$ **9.** $I = prt$

Example 2 (page 508)

10. How long would it take to earn \$6,000 in interest on a principal of \$9,000 at an annual simple interest rate of 4.1%?

11. You earn \$1,400 simple interest on a principal of \$12,500 in 4 years. What is the interest rate on the account?

12. Suppose you borrow money for a year at a simple interest rate of 7.2%. You pay \$86.40 in interest. How much did you borrow?

B Apply Your Skills

13. a. Real Estate A real estate agent earns 7% commission on the sale of a house. Write a formula for commission c. Let s = selling price.

b. The agent's commission is \$8,400. Find the selling price of the house.

Real-World Connection

Careers Bricklayers are skilled in the craft of building walls, fireplaces, and other structures.

14. Construction Bricklayers use the formula $N = 7\ell h$ to estimate the number of bricks needed to cover a wall. N is the number of bricks, ℓ is the length of the wall in feet, and h is the height. If 980 bricks are used to build a wall 20 ft long, how high is the wall?

Solve each formula for the variable in red.

15. $V = \ell wh$ **16.** $r = \frac{d}{t}$

17. $F = \frac{9}{5}C + 32$ **18.** $V = \pi r^2 h$

19. **Writing in Math** Choose a formula from Exercises 15–18. Write and solve a problem involving the transformed version of the formula.

20. Sales You can use the formula $p = s - c$ to find the profit p with selling price s and cost c of an item. Find the selling price of an item that costs a seller \$4.50 if she needs to make a profit of \$.90.

Solve each equation for the variable in red.

21. $x = 3y + 6$ **22.** $t = \frac{1}{2}r$

23. $w = 3n + 5m$ **24.** $s = 0.5k - j$

25. $\frac{1}{2}b = d - 2$ **26.** $y = mx + b$

27. Baseball The formula for batting average a is $a = \frac{h}{n}$, where h is the number of hits and n is the number of times at bat. The highest major league lifetime batting average was .366 by Ty Cobb, who had 4,191 hits. About how many times at bat did he have?

Need Help?
For help finding the circumference of a circle, go to Lesson 8-4.

28. Geometry Find the radius of the circle. Use 3.14 for π.

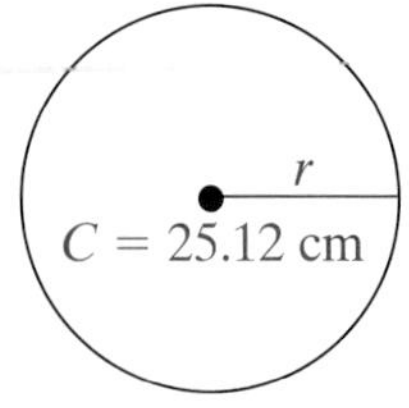

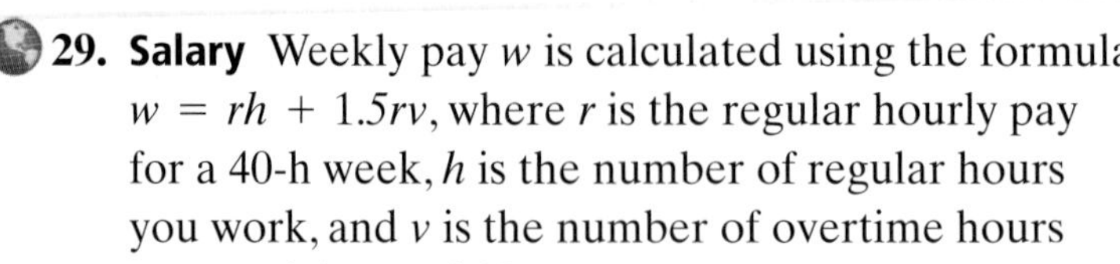

29. Salary Weekly pay w is calculated using the formula $w = rh + 1.5rv$, where r is the regular hourly pay for a 40-h week, h is the number of regular hours you work, and v is the number of overtime hours you work beyond 40.

a. Find the amount of your weekly paycheck for 40 h at a regular hourly pay of \$9 per hour and 5 extra hours at the overtime rate.

b. Find the number of extra hours you work at the overtime rate if the amount of your total weekly paycheck is \$468.

C Challenge

Solve each equation for the variable in red.

30. $a^2 + b^2 = c^2$

31. $\frac{2}{3}m - 4 = p$

32. $V = \frac{1}{3}\pi r^2 h$

33. $A = \frac{1}{2}h(b_1 + b_2)$

34. Geometry The surface area S of a cube with side length e is $S = 6e^2$. Find the side length of a cube with a surface area of 150 cm^2.

35. Stretch Your Thinking What whole number, when added to 1,000,000, gives a greater result than 1,000,000 multiplied by the same number?

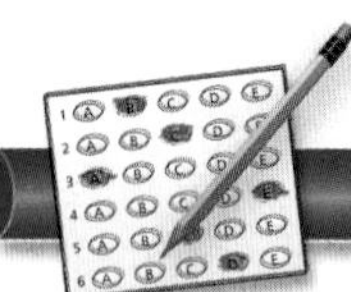

Test Prep

Multiple Choice

36. Solve for s in the equation $p = st$.

A. $s = \frac{t}{p}$ **B.** $s = \frac{p}{t}$ **C.** $s = pt$ **D.** $s = p - t$

37. Solve for x in the function $y = 3x - 5$.

F. $x = \frac{y + 3}{5}$ **G.** $x = \frac{y + 5}{3}$ **H.** $x = y + \frac{3}{5}$ **I.** $x = y + \frac{5}{3}$

38. Solve for a in the equation $\frac{1}{2}a - b = c$.

A. $a = \frac{c + b}{2}$ **B.** $a = \frac{c - b}{2}$ **C.** $a = 2(c + b)$ **D.** $a = \frac{1}{2}bc$

Take It to the NET
Online lesson quiz at www.PHSchool.com
Web Code: aba-0909

Mixed Review

Lesson 8-6 **Find the missing side length. Round your answer to the nearest tenth of a unit.**

39.

8 m
c
12 m

40.

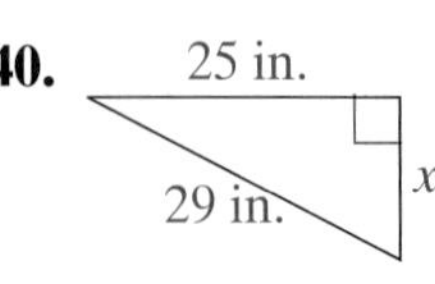

Lesson 7-2 **Classify each angle as *acute*, *obtuse*, *right*, or *straight*.**

41. $m\angle A = 55^\circ$ **42.** $m\angle A = 180^\circ$ **43.** $m\angle C = 99^\circ$

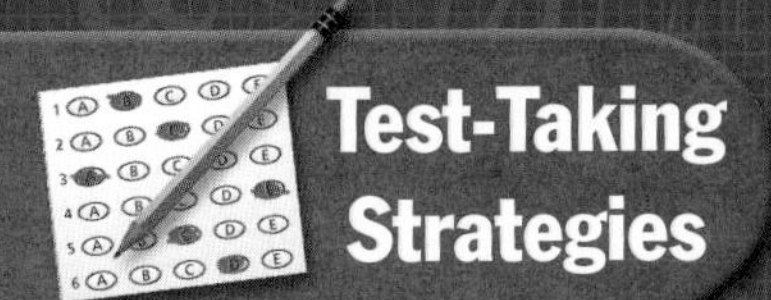

Test-Taking Strategies

Using Estimation

Using estimation can help you find an answer, check an answer, or eliminate one or more answer choices.

1 EXAMPLE

A store is having a 30% off sale on all of its cross-training sneakers. What is the sale price on a pair of sneakers that costs $84.99?

A. $25.50 **B.** $51.99 **C.** $59.49 **D.** $79.99

You can estimate by changing $84.99 to a number that is easy to multiply in your head, such as $90.

A 30% discount will result in a sale price that is 70% of the regular price.

$s = 0.7c$ ← **Write a function rule for sale price. Let s = sale price. Let c = regular cost.**

$\approx 0.7(90)$ ← **Substitute the estimated value.**

$= 63$ ← **Use mental math.**

The sale price will be a little less than $63. The correct answer is C.

2 EXAMPLE

The formula for converting Celsius temperatures to Fahrenheit temperatures is $F = \frac{9}{5}C + 32$. Sterling silver melts at approximately 893°C. What is the Fahrenheit temperature?

F. 998°F **G.** 1,422°F **H.** 1,639°F **I.** 1,995°F

$F = \frac{9}{5}(893) + 32$ ← **Substitute into the formula.**

$\approx 2(900) + 32$ ← **Estimate. $\frac{9}{5} \approx \frac{10}{5}$, or 2, and $893 \approx 900$.**

$= 1{,}832$ ← **This is an overestimate, since $900 > 893$ and $2 > \frac{9}{5}$.**

According to your estimate, the answer is between choices C and D. So, you can eliminate choices A and B.

EXERCISES

1. A salon is offering a 20% discount on all hairstyles. What is the discount price for a style that regularly costs $23.50?

   A. $12.50 **B.** $14.75 **C.** $18.80 **D.** $22.00

2. The melting point of pure gold is 1,945°F. Convert this temperature to Celsius using the formula $C = \frac{5}{9}(F - 32)$.

   F. 1,063°C **G.** 1,159°C **H.** 1,205°C **I.** 1,495°C

Chapter Review

Vocabulary

arithmetic sequence (p. 474)
balance (p. 500)
compound interest (p. 500)
conjecture (p. 475)
formula (p. 507)
function (p. 484)
geometric sequence (p. 475)
principal (p. 499)
sequence (p. 474)
simple interest (p. 499)

Reading Math: Understanding Vocabulary

Choose the correct term to complete each sentence.

1. A sequence is (arithmetic, geometric) if each term is found by adding the same number to the previous term.
2. A (formula, function) has only one output value for each input value.
3. (Balance, Principal) is an amount deposited or borrowed.
4. Interest paid on an original deposit and on any interest that has been left in an account is (compound, simple) interest.
5. A (conjecture, formula) is a prediction.

Take It to the NET
Online vocabulary quiz at **www.PHSchool.com**
Web Code: abj-0951

Skills and Concepts

9-1 Objectives
- To make graphs
- To use graphs to make estimates

Graphs can help you visualize the relationship between data. Graphs have horizontal and vertical scales. Each scale is divided into intervals.

Graph the data in each table.

6.

Servings	1	2	3
Calories	280	560	840

7.

Time (days)	2	4	6
Pay ($)	15	30	45

8. Use your graph from Exercise 7 to estimate the pay for 11 work days.

9-2 and 9-3 Objectives
- To use arithmetic sequences
- To use geometric and other sequences
- To represent patterns in tables
- To write rules using tables

A **sequence** is a set of numbers that follow a pattern. You find each term of an **arithmetic sequence** by adding a common difference to the previous term, and of a **geometric sequence** by multiplying each term by a common ratio. Use a table to show a pattern, find a relationship, and find unknown quantities.

Identify each sequence as *arithmetic, geometric, both,* or *neither.* Write a rule for the sequence. Then find the next three terms.

9. $2, 10, 18, 26, \ldots$
10. $48, 4, \frac{1}{3}, \ldots$
11. $0, 1, 4, 13, 40, \ldots$

12. a. Make a table to represent the sequence $-6, -12, -18, -24, \ldots$.
    b. Write a variable expression for the rule. Then find the 100th term.

9-4 and 9-5 Objectives

- To write function rules
- To evaluate functions
- To graph functions

A **function** is a relationship that assigns exactly one output value for each input value. You can write a function rule by looking for patterns in a table. The graph of a function shows the relationship between inputs and outputs.

13. a. Make a function table for the graph.
    b. Write a function rule.

14. a. Write a rule for the function represented by the table.
    b. Graph the function.

15. Evaluate the function $y = -2x + 5$ for x-values of $-1, 0, 1, 2,$ and 3.

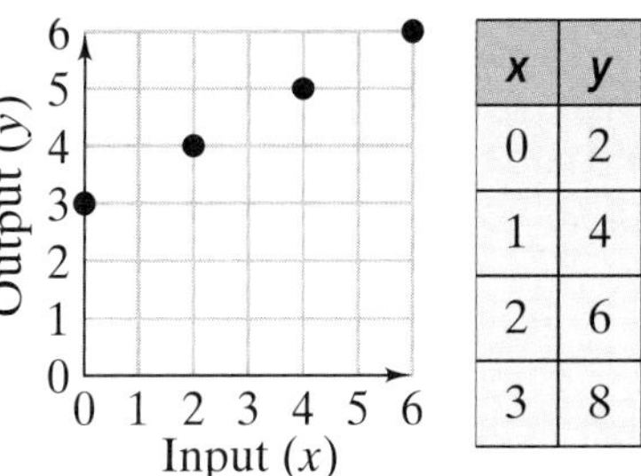

x	y
0	2
1	4
2	6
3	8

9-6 Objectives

- To describe a graph
- To sketch a graph from a description

The graph of a function shows how one quantity changes relative to another. In a real-world context, you need to consider what is reasonable.

16. Describe a situation that the graph at the right might represent.

17. **Jogging** You jog at a rate of 3 mi/h. You jog for 3 h. You stop and spend 1 h eating lunch. Then you jog at 3 mi/h for an hour. Sketch a graph that represents the total distance you have traveled.

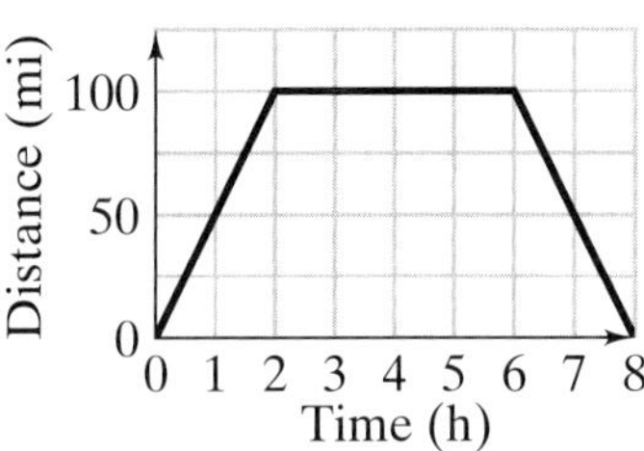

9-7 Objectives

- To find simple interest
- To find compound interest

You use the formula $I = prt$ to find **simple interest**. You use the formula $B = p(1 + r)^t$ to find the **balance** of an account with **compound interest**.

18. Explain the difference between simple interest and compound interest.

19. You deposit $1,500 in an account earning 6% simple interest. How much interest do you earn in five years?

20. You deposit $2,500 in an account that pays 5.7% interest compounded annually. What is the balance after five years?

9-8 and 9-9 Objectives

- To solve problems by writing equations
- To solve for a variable

Writing an equation or a function rule can help you solve a problem. A **formula** is a rule that shows the relationship between two or more quantities. Use properties of equality to solve for any variable in a formula.

21. **Fund-Raising** Suppose 250 people bought tickets to attend your school's annual world cultures festival. The international club spent $180 on preparations and made a $695 profit. How much did each ticket cost?

Solve each formula for x.

22. $z = 3x + y$

23. $k = -4xyz$

24. $\frac{1}{9}x - 4 = \frac{z}{3}$

Chapter Test

Write a rule for each sequence. Find the next three terms.

1. 1, 3, 9, 27, . . .
2. 4, 9, 14, 19, . . .
3. 3, 4, 6, 9, . . .
4. 10, 8, 6, 4, . . .
5. −23, −19, −15, . . .
6. 6, 3, 1.5, 0.75, . . .

7. Identify each sequence in Exercises 1–6 as *arithmetic*, *geometric*, *both*, or *neither*.

8. a. Graph the data.
b. Estimate the framed width for a photo that is 9.5 in. wide.
c. Estimate the framed width for an 18-in. photo.

Picture Framing

Photo Width (in.)	Framed Width (in.)
5	4.17
8	6.67
12	10

Make a function table for each function.

9. the cost for 1 to 5 books at \$2.95 each

10. the perimeter of a square with sides of 5, 6, 7, 8, and 9 in.

Write a function rule for each table.

11.

x	y
0	−2
1	−7
2	−12
3	−17

12.

x	y
0	1
1	3
2	5
3	7

13.

x	y
0	0
1	3
2	6
3	9

14. Graph the functions in Exercises 12 and 13.

Evaluate each function for $x = -2, 0,$ and 5.

15. $y = x - 5$
16. $y = 9 + x$
17. $y = 2x + 1$
18. $y = x^2 - 1$

19. Which is *not* an output for $y = 2x^2 - 5$?
A. −3 **B.** 45 **C.** 27 **D.** −8

20. a. Make a function table for the graph.
b. Write a rule for the function.
c. How much is saved when \$100 is earned?

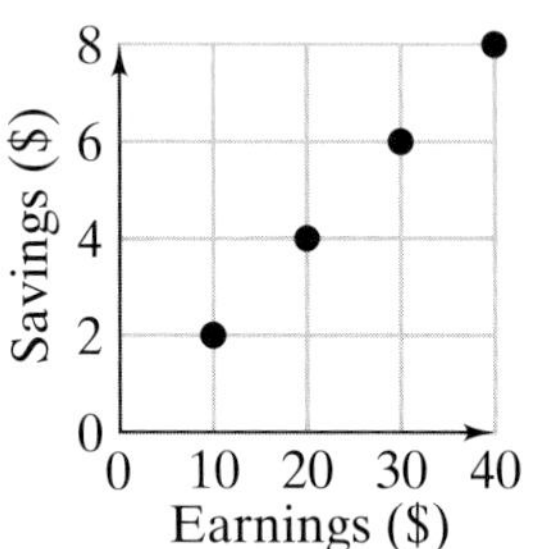

21. Sports You dribble a basketball five times, pause briefly, and then shoot it into the hoop. Sketch a graph that describes the ball's height as a function of time.

22. Writing in Math Describe what the graph shows.

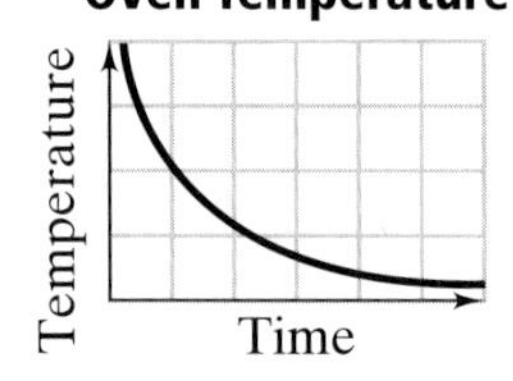

23. Suppose you borrow \$500 from a bank that charges 14.5% interest compounded annually. What is the balance you owe after 4 years?

Solve each formula for *n*.

24. $3n - p = 6m$
25. $PV = nRT$
26. $s = (n - 2)180$
27. $(m + 1)n = b$

28. Home Repairs A plumber charges a customer \$185 for repairs. The cost of parts is \$65 and the plumber charges \$30 per hour for labor. Write and solve an equation to find the number *t* of hours the plumber worked.

29. Science Density is found using the formula $D = \frac{m}{V}$, where *m* is mass in grams (g) and *V* is volume in cubic centimeters (cm^3). What is the volume of a pearl with a density of 2.72 g/cm^3 and a mass of 1.768 g?

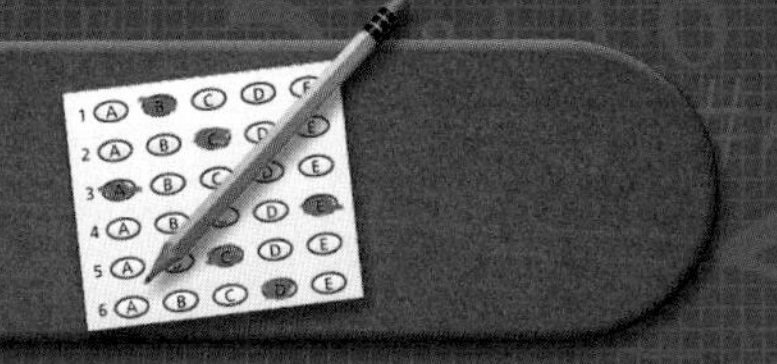

Test Prep

Reading Comprehension **Read each passage and answer the questions that follow.**

Grade A To calculate grades for report cards, Ms. Sammler uses students' test scores during the semester. She also gives credit for class participation. First, she finds the mean test score for each student, which she calls "T." She then adds in the "P" factor— zero, three, or five points for class participation. She adds those items to get "G," the grade.

1. Hari's test scores are 80, 85, and 90. He never contributes in class, so he gets zero for participation. What will his grade "G" be?
   A. 83 **B.** 85 **C.** 88 **D.** 90

2. Ms. Sammler writes on the board and says, "Here is a mathematical equation that describes my system." What does she write?
   F. $G = \frac{1}{3}T + P$ **G.** $G = T + P$
   H. $3G = T + P$ **I.** $T = G + P$

3. Jennifer knows her test average is 88, so she is pleasantly surprised when she gets a 93 on her report card. What is her "P" factor?
   A. 0 **B.** 3 **C.** 5 **D.** 6

4. Jaime gets five points for class participation and receives an 85 on his report card. Which set could NOT have been his test scores?
   F. 60, 80, 100 **G.** 70, 70, 100
   H. 79, 80, 81 **I.** 80, 81, 83

Archaeology Archaeologists find the age of materials like bone, cloth, and wood using "Carbon-14 (C-14) dating." A tiny fraction (about one out of a trillion) of carbon atoms are radioactive and decay over time. Scientists measure the amount of C-14 left in an object to calculate its age. C-14 has a half-life of 5,700 years. This means that half of it remains after 5,700 years. In another 5,700 years, half of the remaining half will remain, and so on.

5. A 5,700-year-old bone has 10^{13} C-14 atoms. How many C-14 atoms did it have originally?
   A. 10^{13} **B.** 2×10^{13}
   C. 10^{14} **D.** 10^{26}

6. A wood fragment is about 11,000 years old. About what portion of its C-14 has decayed?
   F. 0.25 **G.** 0.50 **H.** 0.75 **I.** 1.0

7. How old would an object be if only $\frac{1}{8}$ of its original carbon-14 atoms remained?
   A. $2 \times 5{,}700$ years **B.** $3 \times 5{,}700$ years
   C. $4 \times 5{,}700$ years **D.** $8 \times 5{,}700$ years

8. Radioactive Potassium-40 (K-40) is found naturally in the human body. Its half-life is 1.3 billion years. After 1.3 billion years, how would the remaining percent of K-40 compare to the remaining percent of C-14?

   F. The percent of K-40 would be greater.
   G. The percent of C-14 would be greater.
   H. The same percent of each would remain.
   I. There would be more K-40 atoms than C-14 atoms.

Through the Ages

Applying Graphs Different animals have different life expectancies, which means they live different lengths of time. Reptiles, such as turtles, can live for more than a hundred years. Some insects, such as dragonflies, may live only a year or two.

You may know the saying that one dog year is like seven human years. That's because, on average, people live about seven times as long as dogs. But how do other animals compare? How old is a five-year-old cat or horse in human years? You can use graphs to make these comparisons.

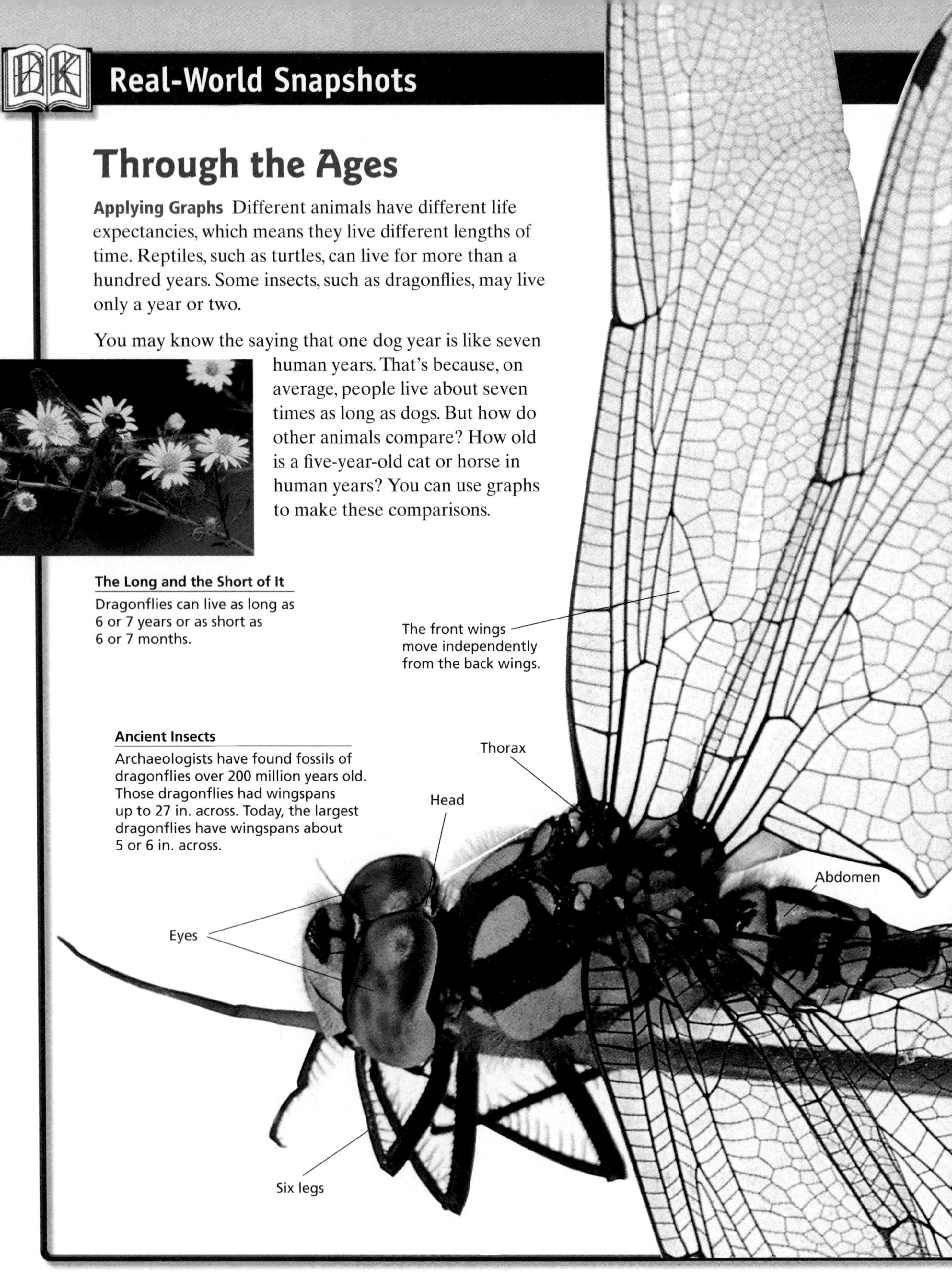

The Long and the Short of It

Dragonflies can live as long as 6 or 7 years or as short as 6 or 7 months.

Ancient Insects

Archaeologists have found fossils of dragonflies over 200 million years old. Those dragonflies had wingspans up to 27 in. across. Today, the largest dragonflies have wingspans about 5 or 6 in. across.

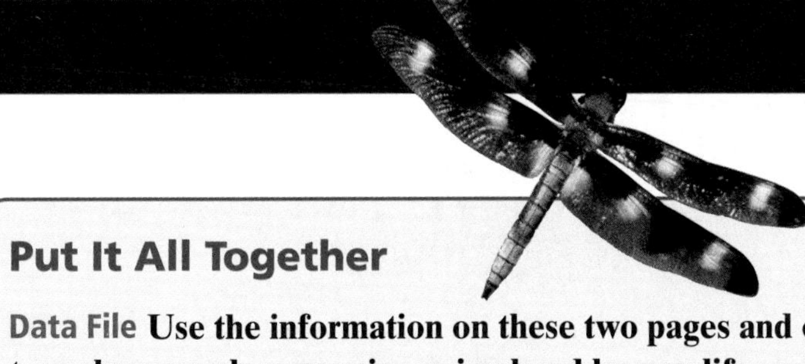

Put It All Together

Data File Use the information on these two pages and on page 467 to make a graph comparing animal and human life expectancies.

1. **a.** Start your graph by labeling the x-axis "Animal Age" and labeling the y-axis "Human Age." Use a scale up to 100 on each axis.
   b. Graph the point $(1, 7)$ to show that 1 dog year is equivalent to 7 human years. Draw a line through the origin and this point.
   c. Use the line you graphed to find the "human age" of an 8-year-old dog.
   d. Use the line you graphed to find your age in "dog years."
2. Use your graph from Question 1. Choose at least three animals. Plot a point that compares the animal's maximum life span to a human's maximum life span of 100 years. Use the points and the origin to draw lines for each animal.
3. Pick one of the animals from your graph. Compare the animal's life to a human's life. At what age would the animal be likely to start kindergarten? At what age would it graduate from high school? Mark those points on your graph.
4. Suppose you get a newborn kitten when you are 32 years old. How old will you be when you and the cat are the same age in human years?
5. **Reasoning** Many animals mature more quickly than people. They learn to walk a few hours after birth, and they are able to care for themselves in less than a year. How would you change the shape of a human–animal age graph to show this more rapid development?

Take It to the NET For more information about dragonflies, go to **www.PHSchool.com**.
Web Code: abe-0953

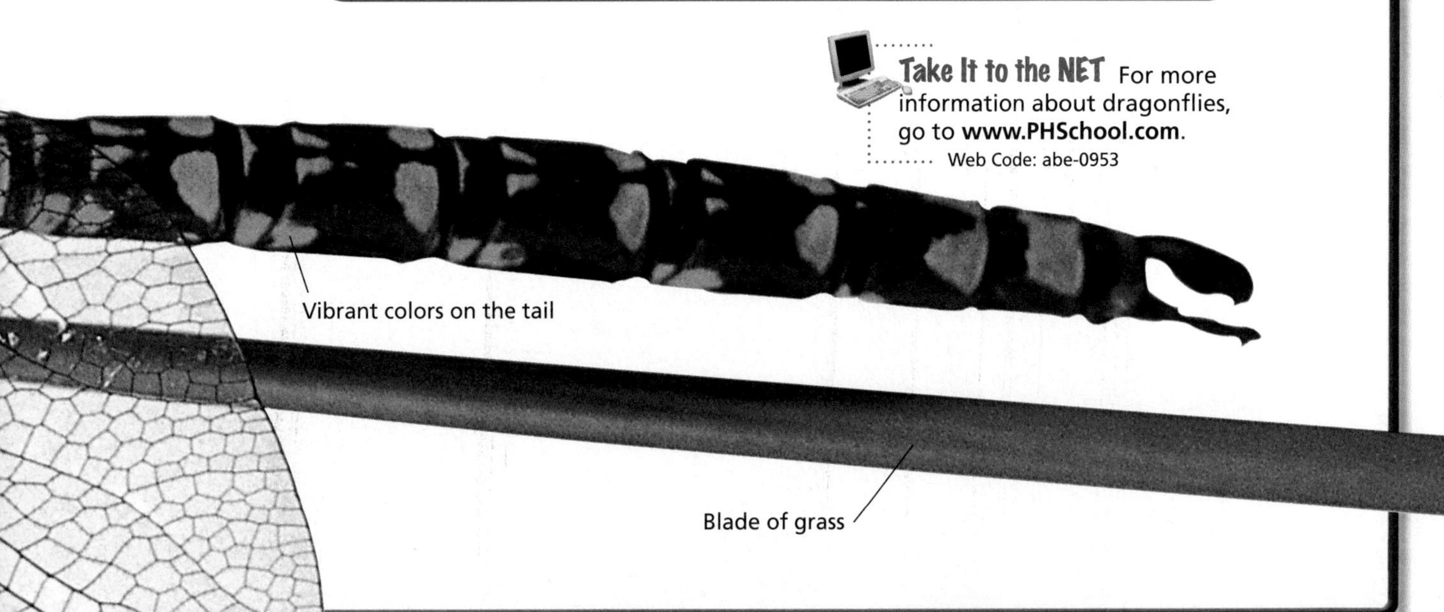

Algebra

CHAPTER 10

Graphing in the Coordinate Plane

Lessons

10-1 Graphing Points in Four Quadrants

10-2 Graphing Linear Equations

10-3 Finding the Slope of a Line

10-4 Exploring Nonlinear Relationships

10-5 Problem Solving: Make a Table and Make a Graph

10-6 Translations

10-7 Symmetry and Reflections

10-8 Rotations

Key Vocabulary

- angle of rotation (p. 560)
- coordinate plane (p. 521)
- image (p. 549)
- linear equation (p. 528)
- line symmetry (p. 554)
- nonlinear equation (p. 540)
- ordered pair (*x*, *y*) (p. 521)
- reflection (p. 555)
- rotation (p. 559)
- rotational symmetry (p. 559)
- slope (p. 533)
- transformation (p. 549)
- translation (p. 549)
- *x*-axis (p. 521)
- *x*-coordinate (p. 521)
- *y*-axis (p. 521)
- *y*-coordinate (p. 521)

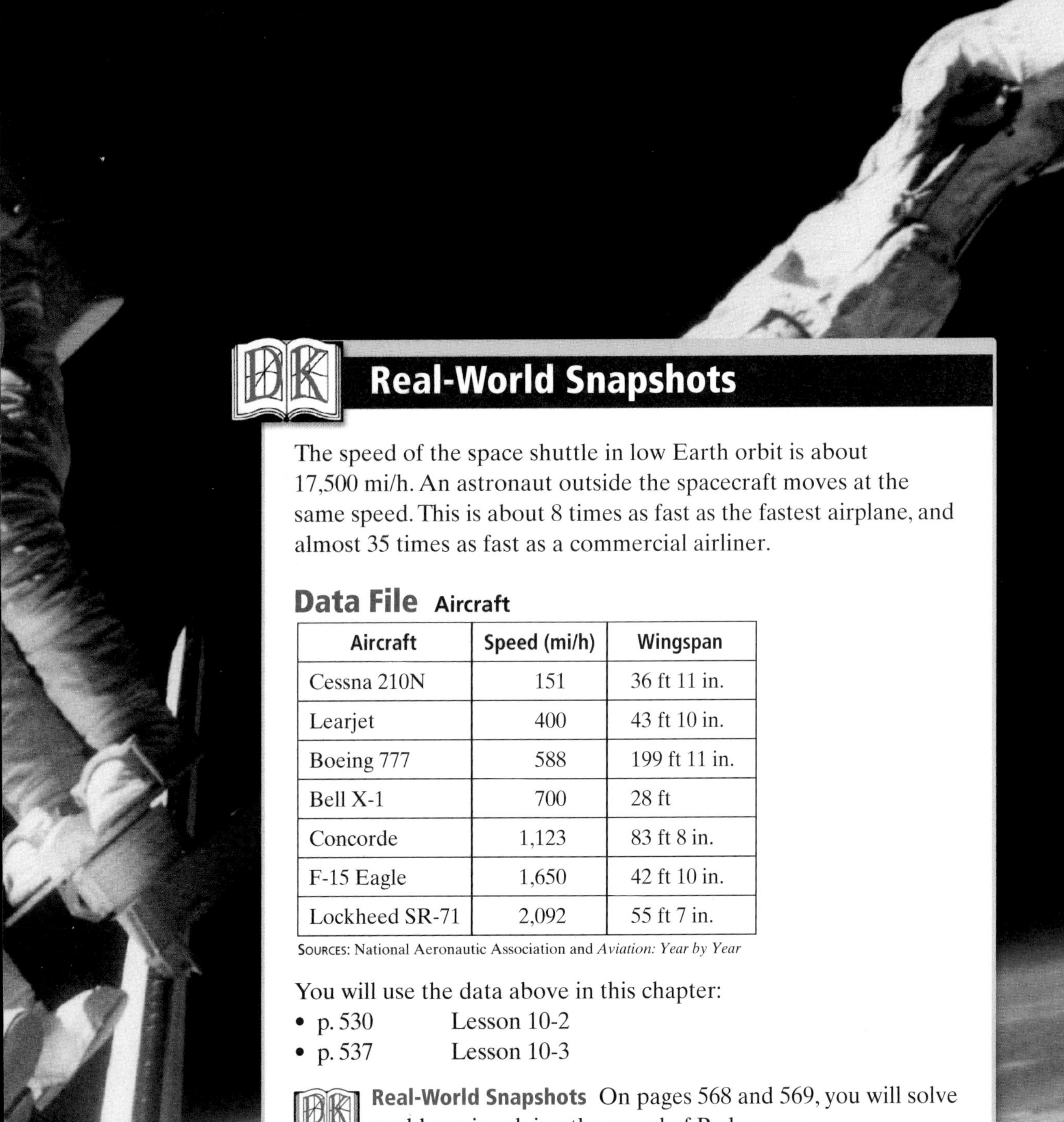

Real-World Snapshots

The speed of the space shuttle in low Earth orbit is about 17,500 mi/h. An astronaut outside the spacecraft moves at the same speed. This is about 8 times as fast as the fastest airplane, and almost 35 times as fast as a commercial airliner.

Data File Aircraft

Aircraft	Speed (mi/h)	Wingspan
Cessna 210N	151	36 ft 11 in.
Learjet	400	43 ft 10 in.
Boeing 777	588	199 ft 11 in.
Bell X-1	700	28 ft
Concorde	1,123	83 ft 8 in.
F-15 Eagle	1,650	42 ft 10 in.
Lockheed SR-71	2,092	55 ft 7 in.

SOURCES: National Aeronautic Association and *Aviation: Year by Year*

You will use the data above in this chapter:

- p. 530 Lesson 10-2
- p. 537 Lesson 10-3

Real-World Snapshots On pages 568 and 569, you will solve problems involving the speed of Pod-racers.

Chapter 10 Preview

Where You've Been

- In Chapter 9, you represented functions using tables, rules, and graphs. You also described real-world situations using graphs.

Where You're Going

- In Chapter 10, you will learn about the coordinate plane and how to find the slope of a line. You will also work with transformations.
- Applying what you learn, you will find the slopes of ski trails.

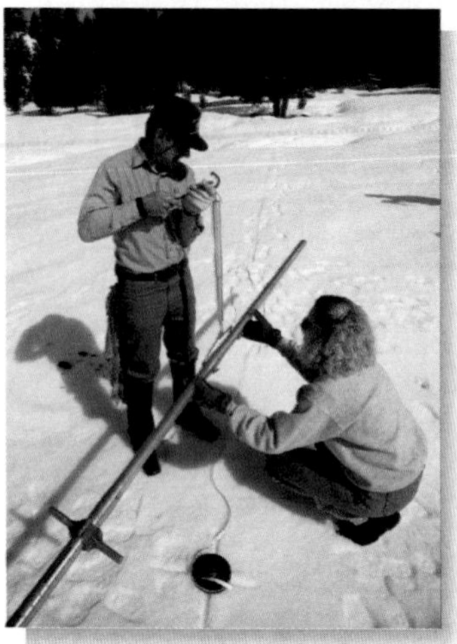

Avalanche forecasters use algebra in their work.

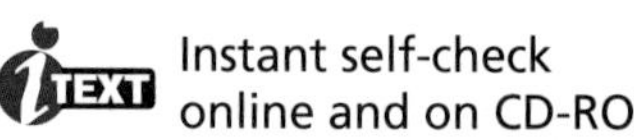

Instant self-check online and on CD-ROM

Diagnosing Readiness

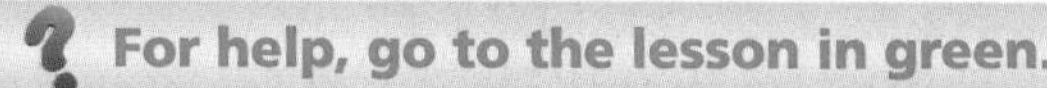

For help, go to the lesson in green.

Graphing Integers (Lesson 1-6)

Algebra Graph each integer and its opposite on a number line.

1. 7 **2.** -5 **3.** -3 **4.** 6

Evaluating Algebraic Expressions (Lesson 2-1)

Algebra Evaluate each expression using the values $a = 5$, $c = 2$, and $g = 7$.

5. $9g$ **6.** $-2a$ **7.** $8c - 10$ **8.** $2a - 5c$

9. ac **10.** $3g - c$ **11.** $2c + a$ **12.** $3a - 4g$

Using Exponents (Lesson 3-1)

Simplify each expression.

13. 5^3 **14.** $(-2)^6$ **15.** 11^3 **16.** $(-10)^4$

Simplifying Fractions (Lesson 3-5)

Write each fraction in simplest form.

17. $\frac{12}{14}$ **18.** $\frac{35}{42}$ **19.** $\frac{20}{36}$ **20.** $\frac{50}{95}$

Classifying Angles (Lesson 7-2)

Classify each angle as *acute*, *right*, *obtuse*, or *straight*.

21. $m\angle A = 43°$ **22.** $m\angle B = 90°$ **23.** $m\angle C = 148°$

24. $m\angle D = 180°$ **25.** $m\angle E = 167°$ **26.** $m\angle F = 79°$

10-1 Graphing Points in Four Quadrants

What You'll Learn

OBJECTIVE 1 To graph points on the coordinate plane

. . . And Why

To locate points on a plane, as in Example 1

✓ Check Skills You'll Need

For help, go to Lesson 1-6.

Graph each number and its opposite on a number line.

1. 5 **2.** −3 **3.** 1

4. −10 **5.** 12 **6.** 8

New Vocabulary

• coordinate plane • *x*-axis • *y*-axis • origin • ordered pair (*x*, *y*) • *x*-coordinate • *y*-coordinate • quadrants • horizontal • vertical

Interactive lesson includes instant self-check, tutorials, and activities.

OBJECTIVE

1 Graphing Points on the Coordinate Plane

Rene Descartes (1596–1650) was a French mathematician and philosopher. An old legend says that he looked up at the ceiling one day and noticed a fly crawling across it. Descartes began thinking about how to describe the exact position of the fly on the ceiling. His thoughts led to the development of the coordinate plane system.

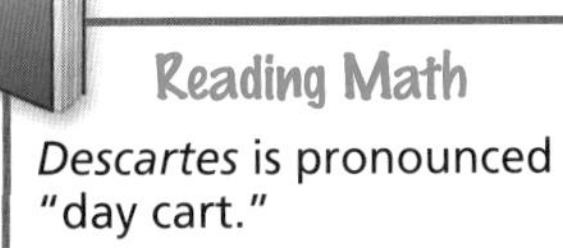

Reading Math

Descartes is pronounced "day cart."

A **coordinate plane** is a grid formed by a horizontal number line called the ***x*-axis** and a vertical number line called the ***y*-axis.**

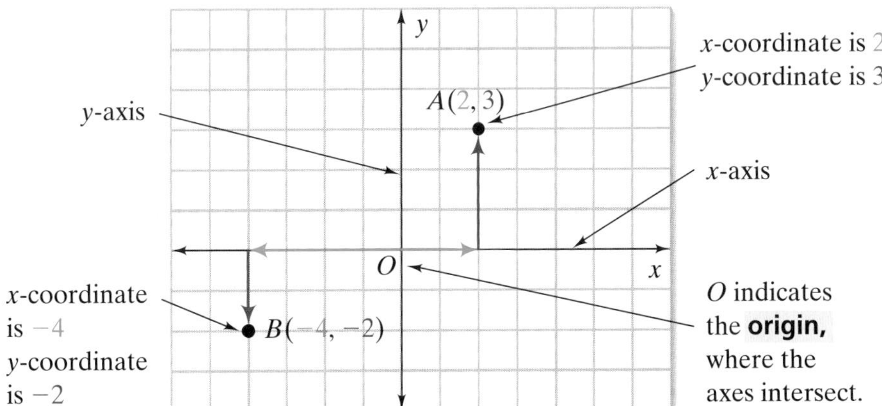

An **ordered pair (*x*, *y*)** gives the coordinates of the location of a point. The ordered pair (0, 0) indicates the origin O. The ordered pair (2, 3) identifies point A.

The first number in an ordered pair is the ***x*-coordinate.** It tells the number of horizontal units a point is from O. The second number is the ***y*-coordinate.** It tells the number of vertical units a point is from O.

1 EXAMPLE Writing Coordinates

Position Use coordinates to define the position of the fly on the ceiling, as legend says Rene Descartes did.

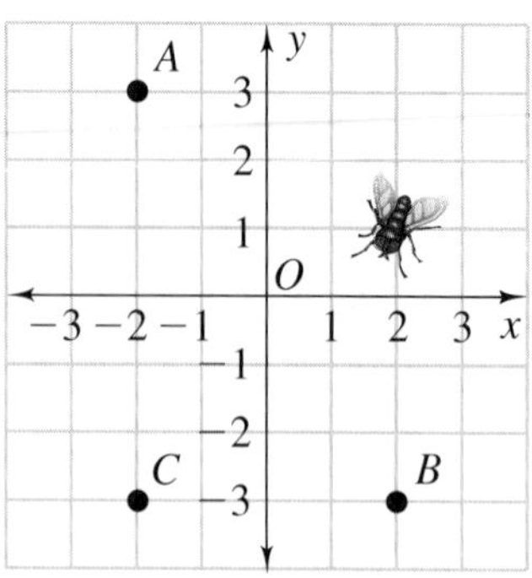

The fly is 2 units to the right of the y-axis. So the x-coordinate is 2.

The fly is 1 unit above the x-axis. So the y-coordinate is 1.

The ordered pair for the location of the fly is (2, 1).

Need Help?
You can remember that x is the first coordinate in an ordered pair because x comes before y in the alphabet.

Check Understanding 1
a. Write the coordinates of points A, B, and C.
b. What are the coordinates of the origin?

The x- and y-axes divide the coordinate plane into four **quadrants.**

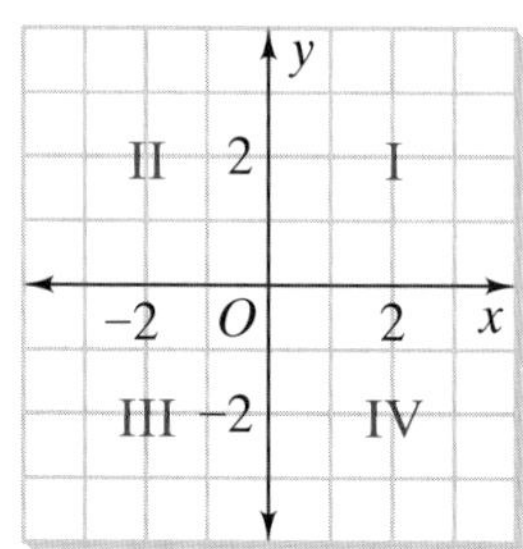

You can use an ordered pair to graph a point on a plane.

2 EXAMPLE Graphing a Point

Graph point $A(3, -5)$ on a coordinate plane.

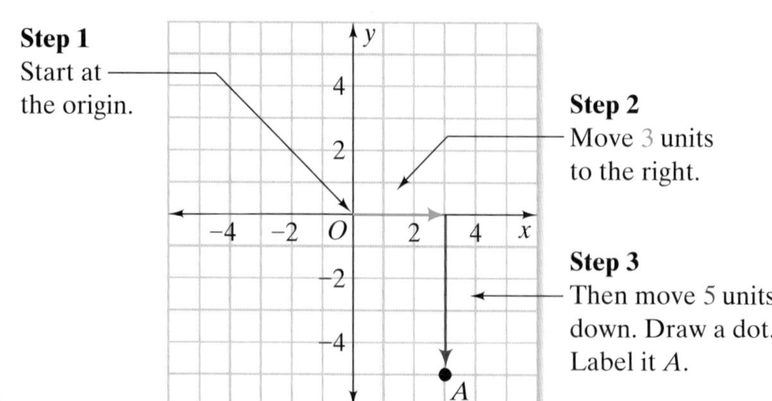

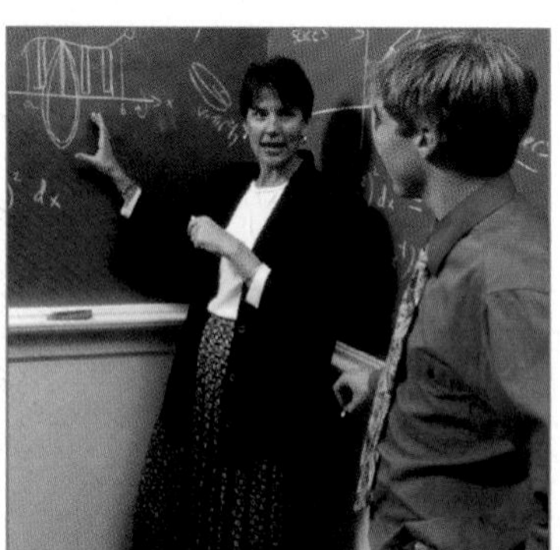

Real-World Connection
Careers Math teachers must know how to graph all types of functions.

Check Understanding 2 Graph each point on the same coordinate plane.
a. $P(3, 5)$ **b.** $Q(-3, -5)$ **c.** $R(-3, 5)$
d. In which quadrant is each point located?

In a coordinate plane, lines that are parallel to the x-axis are **horizontal.** Lines that are parallel to the y-axis are **vertical.**

3 EXAMPLE Identifying Horizontal and Vertical Lines

> **Reading Math**
> To remember which lines are horizontal, think of a line formed by the horizon.

Graph the line containing $(-3, 3)$ and $(-3, -2)$. Then graph the line containing $(3, 2)$ and $(-1, 2)$. Identify each line as horizontal or vertical.

Graph $(-3, 3)$ and $(-3, -2)$. Draw a line through the points.

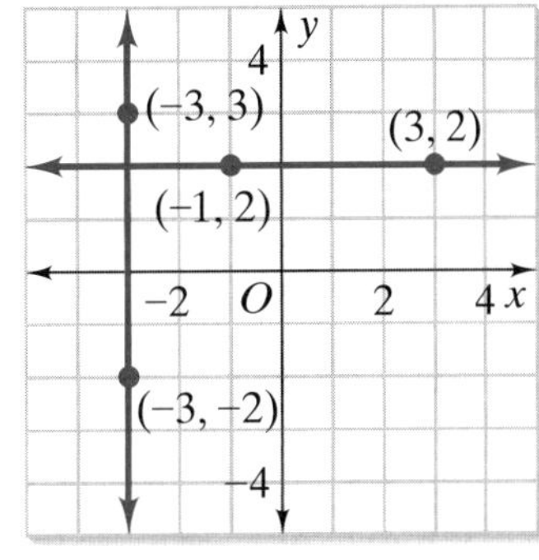

Graph $(3, 2)$ and $(-1, 2)$. Draw a line through the points.

The line containing $(-3, 3)$ and $(-3, -2)$ is vertical. The line containing $(3, 2)$ and $(-1, 2)$ is horizontal.

Check Understanding 3 Graph the line containing each pair of points. Identify the line as horizontal or vertical.

a. $(-6, -4), (3, -4)$ **b.** $(2, -1), (2, 4)$

c. **Reasoning** What do you notice about the y-coordinate of any point on a horizontal line? What do you notice about the x-coordinate of any point on a vertical line?

Investigation: Exploring Patterns in the Coordinate Plane

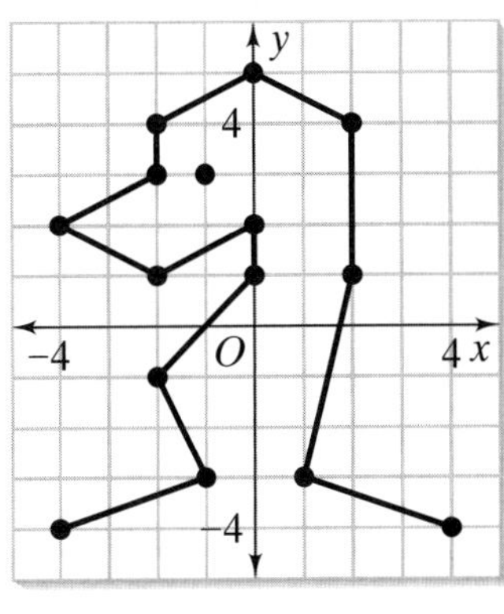

1. Graph a dot-to-dot drawing like the one at the right. Use all quadrants.
2. Organize the ordered pairs for each dot into four groups based on quadrants. Ignore any dots that are on either the x- or y-axes.
3. Look at all of the ordered pairs in the first quadrant. What do you notice about the signs of the x- and y-coordinates?
4. Repeat step 3 for the other three quadrants.
5. Using what you discovered in steps 3 and 4, write a rule that relates the signs of the x- and y-coordinates of an ordered pair to the quadrant in which the point is located.

EXERCISES

For more practice, see *Extra Practice*.

A Practice by Example

Example 1 (page 522)

Write the coordinates of each point.

1. A 2. B
3. C 4. D
5. E 6. F

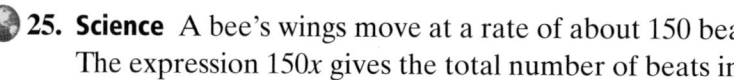

Example 2 (page 522)

Graph each point on the same coordinate plane.

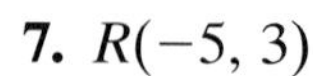

7. $R(-5, 3)$ 8. $S(-3, -2)$
9. $T(-6, 2)$ 10. $U(5, -3)$
11. $V(2, 6)$ 12. $W(6, 2)$

Example 3 (page 523)

Graph the line containing each pair of points. Identify the line as horizontal or vertical.

13. $(-6, 5), (-6, -5)$ 14. $(-3, -2), (4, -2)$ 15. $(9, 4), (5, 4)$
16. $(6, 0), (-1, 0)$ 17. $(2, -1), (2, 3)$ 18. $(0, 3), (0, -2)$

B Apply Your Skills

Without graphing, tell whether the line containing each pair of points is horizontal, vertical, or neither.

19. $(4, 4), (-1, 4)$ 20. $(-7, 8), (7, -8)$ 21. $(0, 0), (-4, 0)$
22. $(-5, 8), (6, -8)$ 23. $(-1, 0), (-1, 9)$ 24. $(8, 7), (2, -1)$

25. **Science** A bee's wings move at a rate of about 150 beats per second. The expression $150x$ gives the total number of beats in x seconds.
 a. Evaluate the expression for 1, 3, and 5 seconds.
 b. Graph the ordered pairs.

Real-World Connection
The wings of a bee move at a very fast rate. This allows the bee to fly in any direction or even hover in one place.

26. a. List the coordinates of three points that are on the red line.
 b. **Reasoning** If the x-coordinate of a point on the line is 37, what is the y-coordinate? Explain.

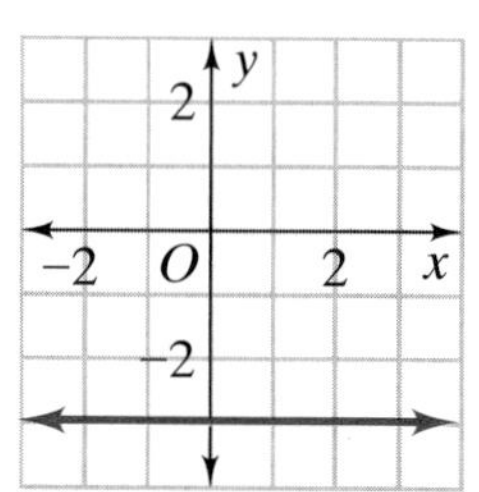

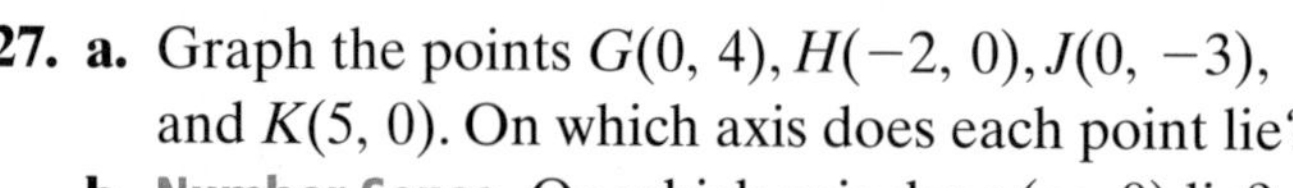

27. a. Graph the points $G(0, 4)$, $H(-2, 0)$, $J(0, -3)$, and $K(5, 0)$. On which axis does each point lie?
 b. **Number Sense** On which axis does $(m, 0)$ lie? On which axis does $(0, n)$ lie?

28. **Writing in Math** Explain how you can tell what quadrant an ordered pair is in by looking at the signs of its x- and y-coordinates.

Without graphing, identify the quadrant in which each point lies.

29. (x, y) if $x < 0$ and $y < 0$ 30. (x, y) if $x < 0$ and $y > 0$

C Challenge

Open-Ended **Draw and label each quadrilateral on a coordinate plane so that each vertex is in a different quadrant.**

31. square **32.** parallelogram **33.** trapezoid

34. **Robotics** A robot arm must move the black peg in the diagram onto the white square. The peg must be moved around—not over—the red walls. List the coordinates of the vertices of a path the robot arm might follow to move the peg.

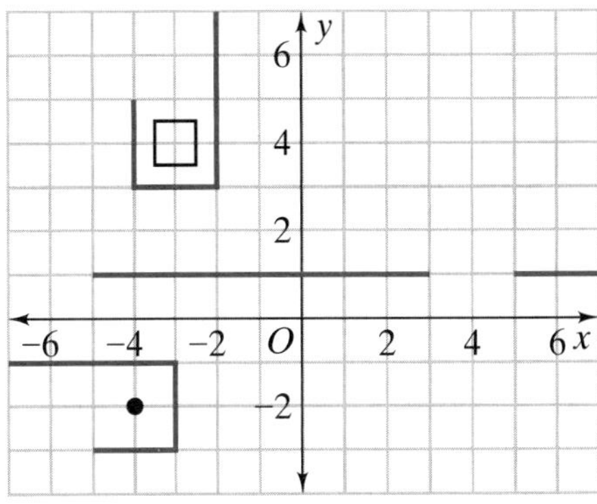

35. **Stretch Your Thinking** Judy lists a fifth integer with the set 3, 6, 7, and 10. The number she lists makes the mean of the five numbers equal to their median. What number does Judy list with the data?

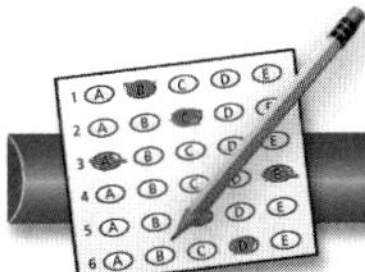

Test Prep

Multiple Choice

36. A vertical line goes through (2, −5). Which of the following points lies on the line?

A. (5, 3) **B.** (0, 0) **C.** (−4, −5) **D.** (2, 0)

37. In which quadrant is the *x*-coordinate of a point positive and the *y*-coordinate negative?

F. I **G.** II **H.** III **I.** IV

Take It to the NET
Online lesson quiz at **www.PHSchool.com**
Web Code: aba-1001

38. Name a point on the *y*-axis that is the same distance from the origin as (0, 7).

A. (−7, 0) **B.** (7, 0) **C.** (0, −7) **D.** (7, 7)

Short Response

39. After being moved 6 units down and 4 units to the left, a point is at (−2, −2). What were the original coordinates of the point?

Mixed Review

Lesson 8-5

Simplify each square root.

40. $\sqrt{36}$ **41.** $\sqrt{121}$ **42.** $\sqrt{9}$ **43.** $\sqrt{400}$ **44.** $\sqrt{64}$

Lesson 6-8

Algebra **Find each percent of discount. Round to the nearest tenth.**

45. original price \$6, sale price \$5

46. original price \$15, sale price \$9

47. original price \$29, sale price \$26

48. original price \$50, sale price \$43

49. original price \$34, sale price \$25

50. original price \$79, sale price \$70

Extension Geometry in the Coordinate Plane

For Use With Lesson 10-1

Graphing a geometric figure on a coordinate plane can help you find the length of a side or the area of the figure.

1 EXAMPLE Triangles

Connect the points $L(-3, -2)$, $M(-1, 3)$, and $N(4, -2)$ to form $\triangle LMN$. Find the area of the triangle using the formula $A = \frac{1}{2}bh$.

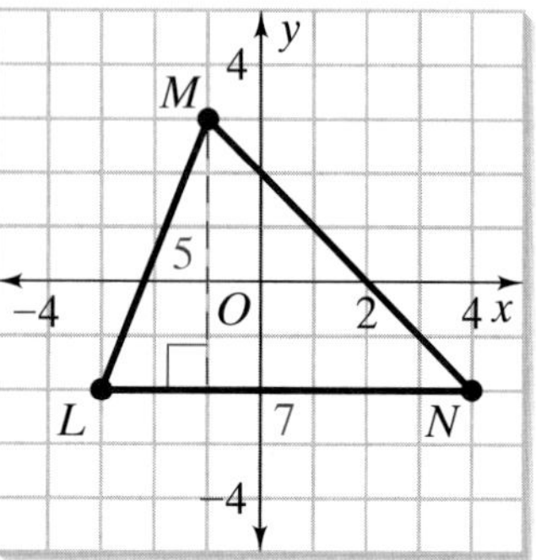

The base of the triangle is 7 units. There are 5 units between point M and the base, so the height of the triangle is 5 units.

$A = \frac{1}{2}bh$

$= \frac{1}{2} \cdot 7 \cdot 5$ ← **Substitute.**

$= 17.5$ ← **Simplify.**

The area of the triangle is 17.5 units^2.

2 EXAMPLE Length of the Hypotenuse

Connect the points $H(-1, -3)$, $I(5, -3)$, and $J(5, 5)$ to form right $\triangle HIJ$. Find the length of the hypotenuse.

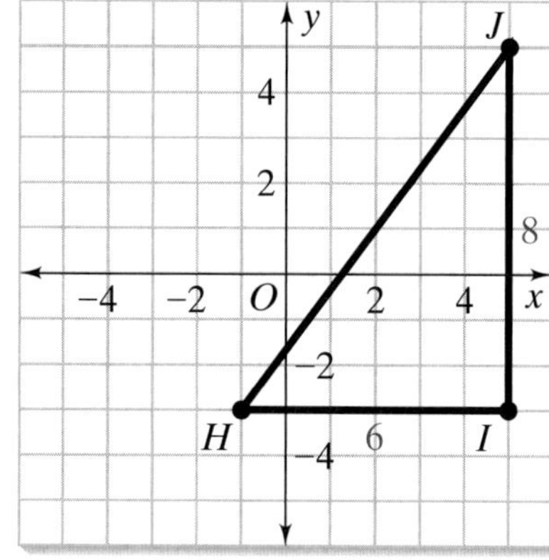

You can see from the graph that the lengths of the legs are 6 units and 8 units.

$a^2 + b^2 = c^2$ ← **Use the Pythagorean Theorem.**

$6^2 + 8^2 = c^2$ ← **Substitute.**

$36 + 64 = c^2$ ← **Simplify.**

$100 = c^2$ ← **Simplify.**

$\sqrt{100} = c$ ← **Find the value of c.**

$10 = c$ ← **10 is the square root of 100.**

The length of the hypotenuse is 10 units.

EXERCISES

1. Connect the points $A(4, -4)$, $B(4, 4)$, and $C(-2, 3)$ to form $\triangle ABC$. Find the area of the triangle.
2. Connect the points $Q(-5, 4)$, $R(3, 4)$, and $S(3, -7)$ to form right $\triangle QRS$. Find the length of the hypotenuse. Round to the nearest tenth.
3. Connect the points $E(-3, 4)$, $F(-3, -9)$, $G(6, -4)$, and $H(6, 9)$ to form a parallelogram. Find the area of the parallelogram.

Algebra

10-2 Graphing Linear Equations

What You'll Learn

To find ordered pairs that are solutions of linear equations

To graph linear equations

. . . And Why

To find the amount of money saved, as in Exercise 40

Check Skills You'll Need

For help, go to Lesson 2-1.

Evaluate each expression. Use the values $p = 2, n = 3$, and $s = 4$.

1. $p + 7$ **2.** $12 + n$ **3.** $s + s$

4. $12 - p$ **5.** $2(n - 1)$ **6.** $n + s - p$

7. Number Sense In Exercise 6, does it matter whether you add or subtract first? Explain.

New Vocabulary • graph of an equation • linear equation

Interactive lesson includes instant self-check, tutorials, and activities.

OBJECTIVE 1

Finding Ordered Pairs

To make a tire swing, you need enough rope to reach the tree branch, plus another 5 ft for tying the rope. You can model the swing using the equation $y = x + 5$, where x is the number of feet the tire hangs below the branch, and y is the number of feet of rope you need.

Any ordered pair that makes an equation true is a solution of the equation. The ordered pair (6, 11) is a solution of $y = x + 5$, because $11 = 6 + 5$. In the swing problem, the solution tells you that you need 11 ft of rope to hang the tire 6 ft below the branch.

1 EXAMPLE Testing Ordered Pairs

Determine whether each ordered pair is a solution of $y = x + 5$.

a. (40, 45)

$y = x + 5$

$45 \stackrel{?}{=} 40 + 5$ ← Substitute for x and y in the equation.

$45 = 45$ ✔

(40, 45) is a solution of the equation.

b. (21, 27)

$y = x + 5$

$27 \stackrel{?}{=} 21 + 5$

$27 \neq 26$

(21, 27) is not a solution of the equation.

Check Understanding 1 Determine whether each ordered pair is a solution of $y = 3x - 1$.

a. (4, 11) **b.** (7, 12) **c.** (17, 23)

You can find solutions of an equation by making a table. Choose different values for x and substitute them into the equation.

2 EXAMPLE Making a Table of Values

Find three solutions of $y = x - 4$.

Choose three values for x. Then make a table.

x	$x - 4$	y	(x, y)
−2	−2 − 4	−6	(−2, −6)
0	0 − 4	−4	(0, −4)
4	4 − 4	0	(4, 0)

Three solutions of $y = x - 4$ are $(-2, -6)$, $(0, -4)$, and $(4, 0)$.

Need Help?
When choosing x-values, select values that include zero, positive numbers, and negative numbers.

Check Understanding 2 Find three solutions of each equation.

a. $y = x - 2$ **b.** $y = x + 5$ **c.** $y = -3x$

OBJECTIVE

2 Graphing Linear Equations

The **graph of an equation** is the graph of all the points with coordinates that are solutions of the equation. An equation is a **linear equation** when the graph of its solutions is a line.

3 EXAMPLE Graphing a Linear Equation

Graph the linear equation $y = x + 1$.

Step 1 Choose values for x. Make a table of the values.

x	$x + 1$	y	(x, y)
−4	−4 + 1	−3	(−4, −3)
−2	−2 + 1	−1	(−2, −1)
0	0 + 1	1	(0, 1)
1	1 + 1	2	(1, 2)
3	3 + 1	4	(3, 4)

Step 2 Graph the points. Draw a line through the points.

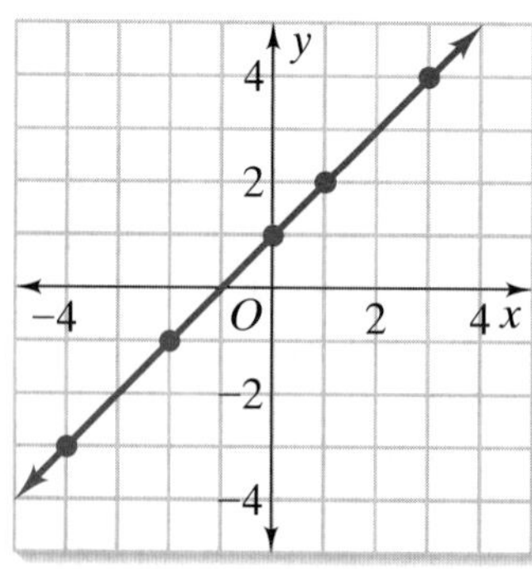

Check Understanding 3 **a.** Using the graph, find two more solutions of $y = x + 1$.

b. Graph the linear equation $y = 2x$.

c. **Reasoning** How many solutions does a linear equation have? Explain your reasoning.

EXERCISES

For more practice, see *Extra Practice.*

A Practice by Example

Example 1 (page 527)

Determine whether each ordered pair is a solution of $y = x + 12$.

1. $(-12, 24)$ 2. $(12, 24)$ 3. $(0, -12)$ 4. $(-12, 0)$

5. $(24, 12)$ 6. $(7, 19)$ 7. $(6, 15)$ 8. $(9, 21)$

Example 2 (page 528)

Find three solutions of each equation.

9. $y = x + 2$ 10. $y = x + 9$ 11. $y = x - 8$ 12. $y = -2x + 4$

13. $y = 5x$ 14. $y = 3x - 1$ 15. $y = -8x$ 16. $y = 4x - 5$

Example 3 (page 528)

Graph each linear equation.

17. $y = x - 1$ 18. $y = x - 3$ 19. $y = 3x$ 20. $y = 5 + x$

21. $y = x + 4$ 22. $y = -5x$ 23. $y = 2 - x$ 24. $y = 4 - x$

25. $y = -x - 5$ 26. $y = \frac{1}{3}x$ 27. $y = 2x - 1$ 28. $y = \frac{1}{2}x + 4$

B Apply Your Skills

29. a. Copy and complete the table to find three solutions of $y = x - 7$.
    b. Graph the ordered pairs and connect them to form a line.

x	x − 7	y	(x, y)
0	■	■	■
−3	■	■	■
10	■	■	■

30. **Error Analysis** A student says that $(-1, -5)$ is a solution of $y = -3x - 2$. What error do you think the student made?

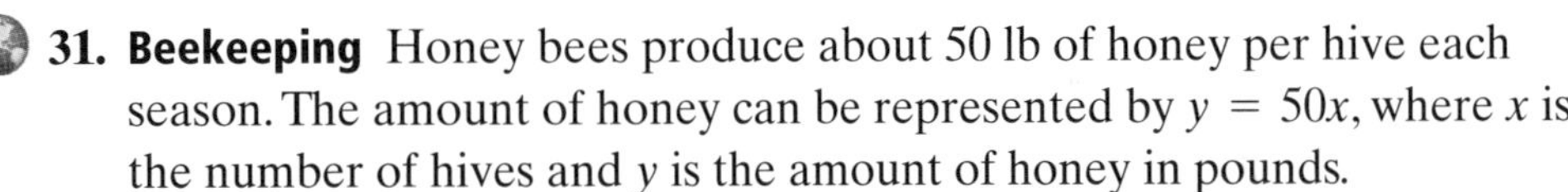

31. **Beekeeping** Honey bees produce about 50 lb of honey per hive each season. The amount of honey can be represented by $y = 50x$, where x is the number of hives and y is the amount of honey in pounds.
    a. **Number Sense** What numbers would not be appropriate for a table of values for this equation? Explain.
    b. Make a table of values for $y = 50x$, and graph the equation.

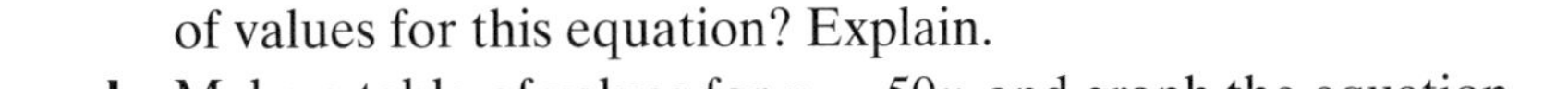

On which of the following lines does each point lie? A point may lie on more than one line.

I. $y = x + 6$ II. $y = x - 6$ III. $y = 2x + 3$

32. $(-3, -3)$ 33. $(0, -6)$ 34. $(-2, -1)$

35. $(0, 0)$ 36. $(3, 9)$ 37. $(0, 3)$

Real-World Connection

Beekeepers provide their bees with hives, which include sections where bees build their honeycombs.

38. **Gardening** A gardener is building a fence around a square garden. The formula for the amount of fencing is $P = 4s$, where P is the perimeter of the garden and s is the length of a side.
    a. Use a table of values to graph the equation $P = 4s$.
    b. If the perimeter is 48 units, what is the length of each side?

39. **Writing in Math** Why is it a good idea to plot at least three points when you graph a linear equation?

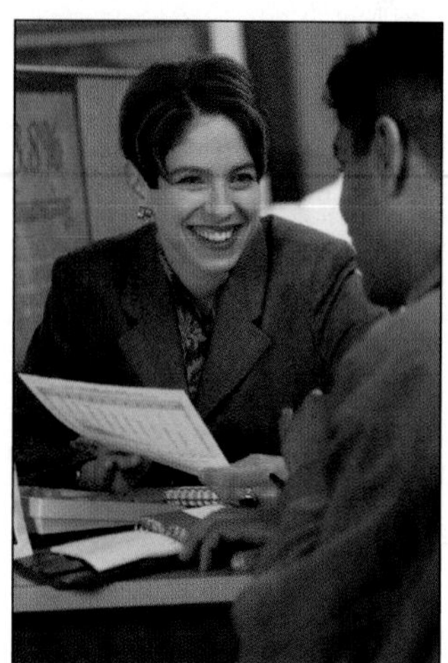

Real-World Connection

Careers Financial planners help people budget and save money.

40. **Money** You have \$35 saved at the beginning of the year. You plan to save \$5 each week. Your savings plan can be modeled with the equation $y = 5x + 35$.
   a. Use a table of values to graph the equation in the first quadrant of the coordinate plane.
   b. How much money will you have saved after 8 weeks?
   c. In how many weeks will you save \$60?

Use the graph for Exercises 41 and 42.

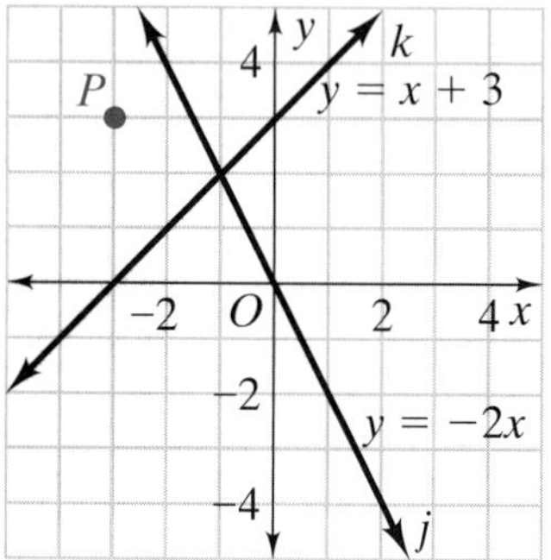

41. Use point P and the equations for lines j and k to show that point P is not a solution of either equation.

42. What are the coordinates of the point that is a solution of the equations of both lines j and k?

Graph each linear equation.

43. $2y + 10 = 2x$ 44. $y = 2x - 4$ 45. $-y = x$

Match each equation with a line on the graph.

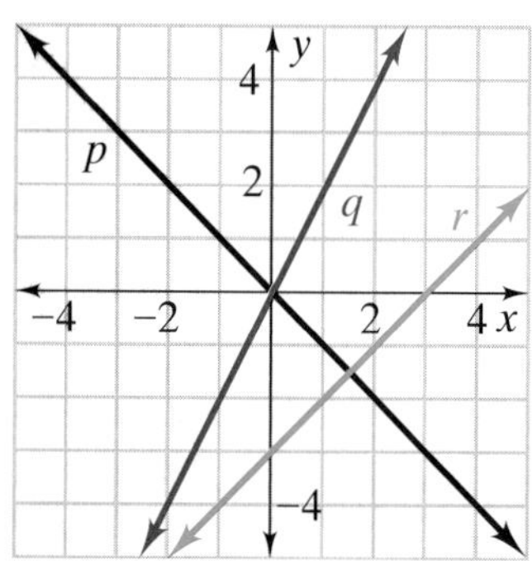

46. $y = x - 3$

47. $y = 2x$

48. $y = -x$

49. **Data File, p. 519** In the linear equation $y = \frac{1}{2}x$, x is the speed of each aircraft, and y is the number of miles traveled $\frac{1}{2}$ hour after it reaches that speed. Use the data to make a table of values for $y = \frac{1}{2}x$. Graph the equation.

Challenge

50. a. Graph $y = x$ and $y = -x$ on the same coordinate plane.
   b. Find the ordered pair that is a solution to both equations.
   c. **Geometry** Do these lines appear to be perpendicular or parallel?

For each equation, tell whether its graph passes through the second quadrant. Explain how you know.

51. $y = x - 5$ 52. $y = 2x$ 53. $y = x + 3$ 54. $y = x$

55. **Stretch Your Thinking** Kerri and Sam run laps every day. Kerri runs $\frac{1}{5}$ of a lap per minute, and Sam runs $\frac{1}{4}$ of a lap per minute. They start running at the same place and agree to run until they reach the starting point at the same time. How many laps does each person run?

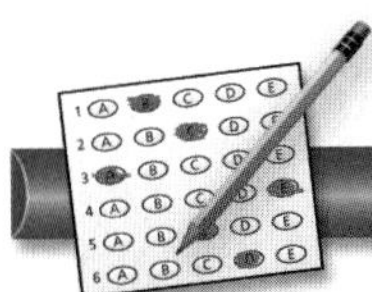

Test Prep

Reading Comprehension **Read the passage and answer the questions below.**

Cushions of Corn

The Popcorn Institute reports that sales of popcorn have increased recently. One reason is that many companies now use popcorn instead of plastic foam to cushion packages. Environmentally friendly popcorn is easy to produce. A hot-air popper about the size of a microwave oven can make about $\frac{1}{2}$ pound of popcorn in 1 minute, or about 30 pounds in 1 hour.

56. **a.** Let x represent the number of minutes the popper is on. Let y represent the popper's output in pounds. The equation $y = \frac{1}{2}x$ describes the relationship between x and y. Make a table of values for the equation. Find three solutions.

b. Use the points from your table to graph the equation.

Take It to the NET
Online lesson quiz at
www.PHSchool.com
Web Code: aba-1002

57. Does it make sense to extend your line in Exercise 56 into the third quadrant? Explain.

58. If the popper is on for five minutes, how many pounds of popcorn will you have? Show your work.

59. If the popper makes 8 lb of popcorn, how long is it on? Show your work.

Mixed Review

Lesson 8-6

Find each missing length. Round to the nearest tenth, if necessary.

60.

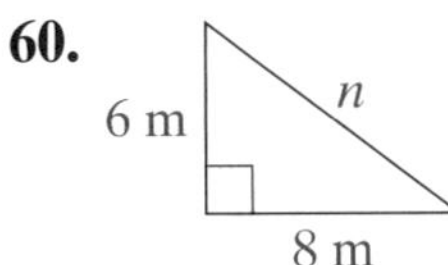

61.

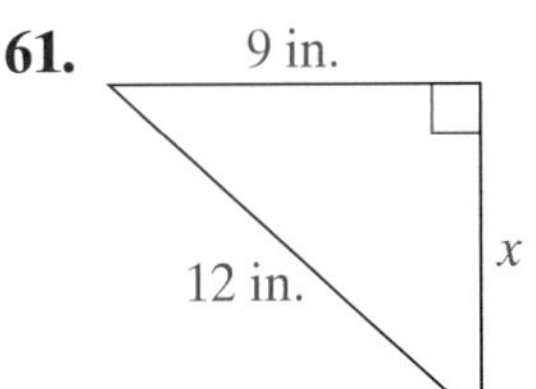

62.

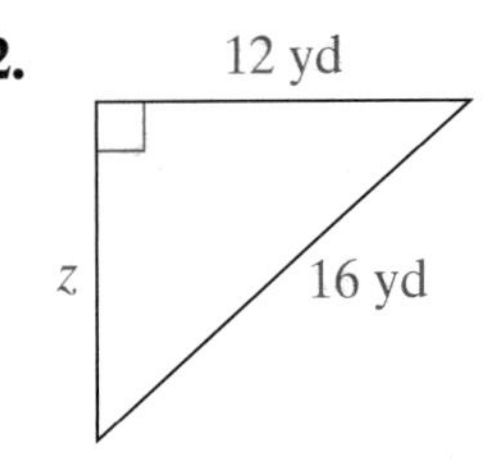

Lesson 7-2

Classify each angle as *acute*, *right*, *obtuse*, or *straight*.

63. $m\angle A = 150°$

64. $m\angle B = 45°$

65. $m\angle C = 180°$

66.

67.

68.

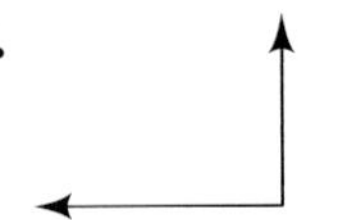

Reading Math

Learning Vocabulary

For Use With Lesson 10-2

Some math concepts are based on ideas that you learned earlier. When learning new vocabulary words, you can compare them to other ideas you already know.

EXAMPLE

For each vocabulary word, state how it is like a word or concept that you have already learned. Then state how it is different.

	It's like a...	But different because it...
integer	whole number	also includes the opposite
mixed number	fraction	includes a whole number
rate	ratio	has units
cube	square	is three-dimensional
radius	diameter	has one of its endpoints at the center
rhombus	square	has no right angles

EXERCISES

For each geometry vocabulary word, state how it is like a word or concept that you have already learned. Then state how it is different.

1. edge **2.** sphere **3.** circumference

4. square **5.** diameter **6.** surface area

For each algebra vocabulary word, state how it is like a word or concept that you have already learned. Then state how it is different.

7. unit rate **8.** function **9.** percent

10. inequality **11.** Multiplication Property of Inequality

12. Refer to Lesson 10-1. Using the vocabulary list, choose a word. Describe how the vocabulary word is like another word or concept that you learned previously. Then state how it is different.

13. **Open-Ended** Think about different words that you use every day. Choose a word and explain how it is like another word. Then explain how it is different.

10-3 Finding the Slope of a Line

What You'll Learn

To find and use the slope of a line

. . . And Why

To find the slope of a ski trail, as in Example 2

Check Skills You'll Need

For help, go to Lesson 3-5.

Write each fraction in simplest form.

1. $\frac{6}{8}$ **2.** $\frac{8}{10}$ **3.** $\frac{8}{-12}$ **4.** $\frac{-4}{-12}$ **5.** $\frac{-15}{3}$

New Vocabulary

• slope • rise • run

OBJECTIVE 1

Interactive lesson includes instant self-check, tutorials, and activities.

1 Finding and Using the Slope of a Line

Investigation: Exploring Slope

1. Draw the first quadrant of a coordinate plane. Label the x- and y-axes.
2. Begin at the origin. Roll a number cube to determine the number of units you should move to the right. For example, right 2.
3. Roll the number cube again. Move up the number of units rolled. For example, up 3. Plot a point where you end up.
4. From your point, move the same number of units to the right as you did in step 2. Now move the same number of units up as you did in step 3 and plot a second point.
5. Repeat what you did in step 4 two more times. Connect the points in the order that you graphed them.
6. Repeat the Investigation using new values for moving right and up.
7. What can you conclude about the graph formed when you plot points by moving the same number of units horizontally and vertically?

Reading Math

Skiers use the word *slope* to refer to the side of a mountain.

Slope is a ratio that describes the steepness of a line. For any line, slope compares the vertical change, called the **rise,** to the horizontal change, called the **run.**

$$\text{slope} = \frac{\text{rise}}{\text{run}}$$

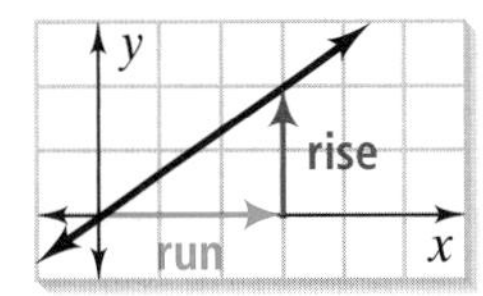

When a line goes upward from left to right, it has a positive slope. When a line goes downward from left to right, it has a negative slope.

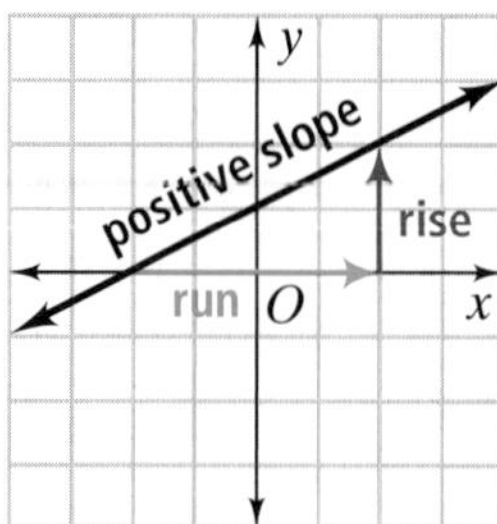

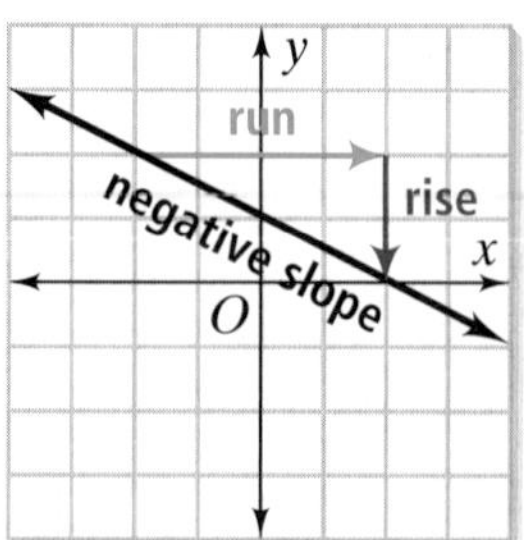

1 EXAMPLE Finding Slope

Find the slope of the line.

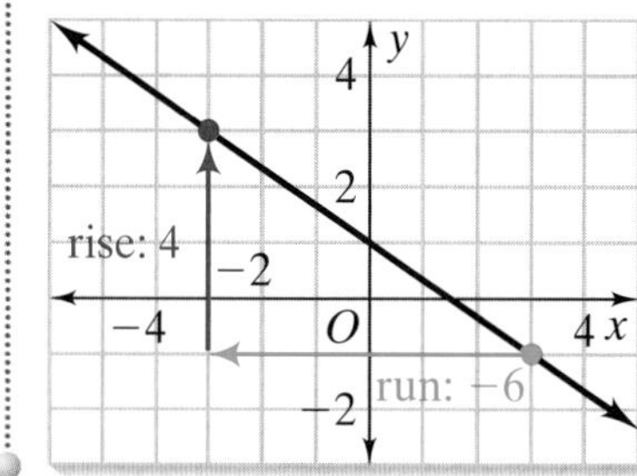

$$\text{slope} = \frac{\text{rise}}{\text{run}}$$

$$= \frac{4}{-6} \leftarrow \textbf{rise divided by run}$$

$$= -\frac{2}{3} \leftarrow \textbf{Simplify.}$$

Check Understanding 1 **a.** Find the slope of the line using points A and D.
b. Use two other points, B and C, to find the slope. How does using different points affect the slope?

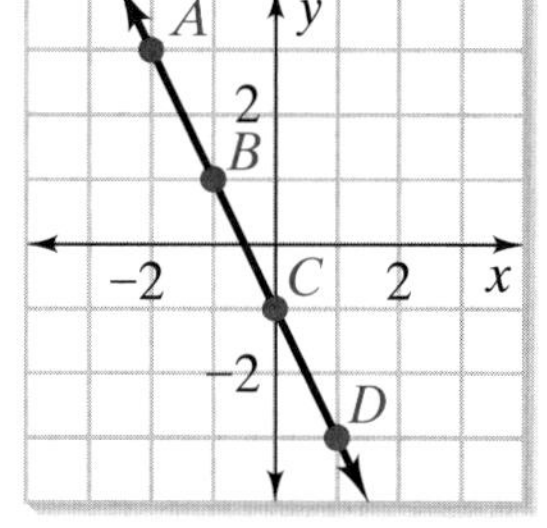

Reading Math
Constant means "remaining the same."

The graph of any linear equation has a constant slope. If you pick any two points on a line, the ratio of rise to run is always the same.

In real-world situations, the slope describes the steepness of a line. As the absolute value of the slope increases, so does the steepness of the line. The steepness decreases as the absolute value of the slope gets closer to zero.

2 EXAMPLE Real-World Problem Solving

Avalanches Avalanches are more likely to occur on trails where the absolute value of the slope is between 0.5 and 1. Find the slope of the trail and determine whether an avalanche is likely.

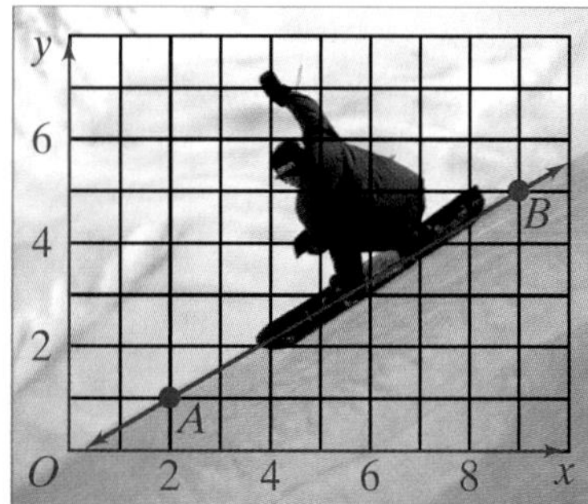

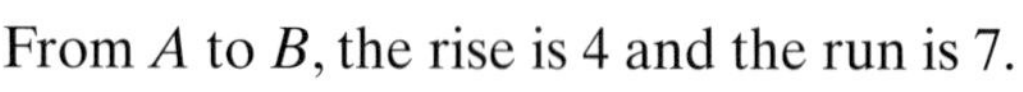

From A to B, the rise is 4 and the run is 7.

$\text{slope} = \frac{4}{7} \approx 0.57$

The slope is about 0.57, so an avalanche is likely.

Check Understanding 2 a. Find the slope of the roof.

b. Slope is used to find the pitch, or steepness, of a roof. Roof A has a 3-12 pitch, which means it rises 3 in. for every 12 in. of run. Roof B has a 10-12 pitch, which means it rises 10 in. for every 12 in. of run. Which roof is steeper? Explain.

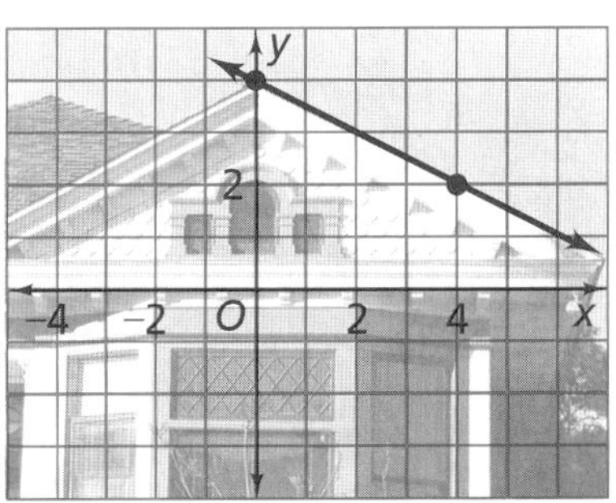

You can use slope to graph a line if you know a point on the line.

3 EXAMPLE Graphing a Line

Need Help?
Slopes of $-\frac{1}{2}$, $\frac{-1}{2}$, and $\frac{1}{-2}$ are all equivalent.

Draw a line through the origin with a slope of $-\frac{3}{2}$.

Step 1 Graph a point at (0, 0).

Step 2 Move 3 units down and then 2 units to the right. Graph a second point.

Step 3 Connect the points to form a line.

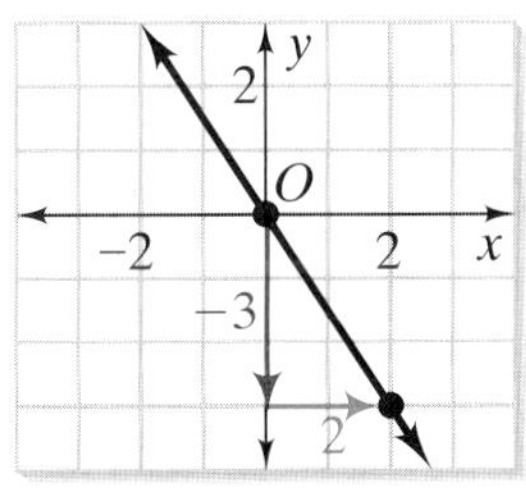

Check Understanding 3 a. **Reasoning** Start at (0, 0) and go up 3 units and left 2 units. Connect the points to form a line. Is this line the same as in Example 3? Explain.

b. Draw a line through $P(2, 1)$ with a slope of $\frac{4}{3}$.

EXERCISES

For more practice, see *Extra Practice*.

A Practice by Example

Example 1 (page 534)

Find the slope of each line.

1.

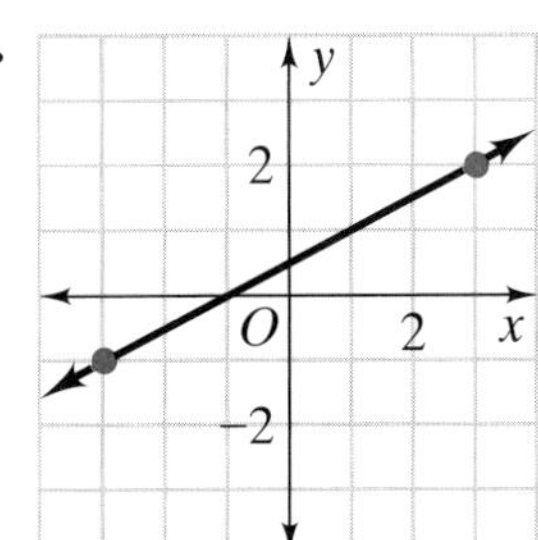

2.

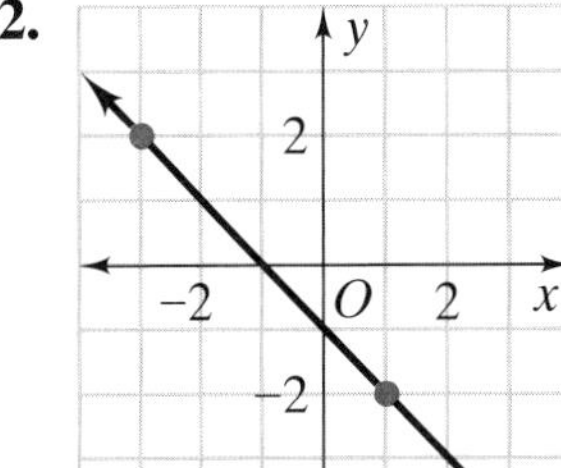

3.

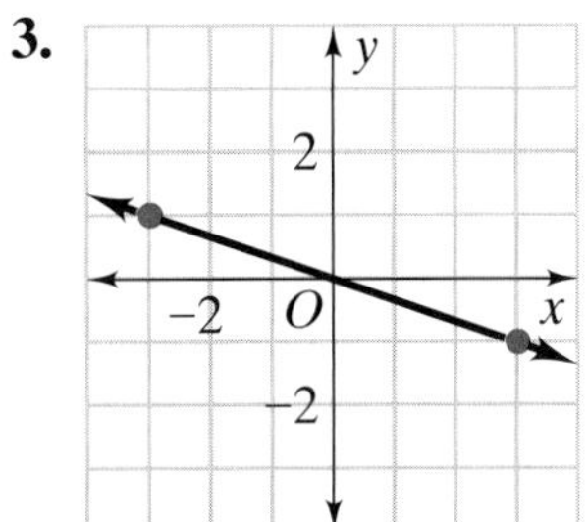

4.

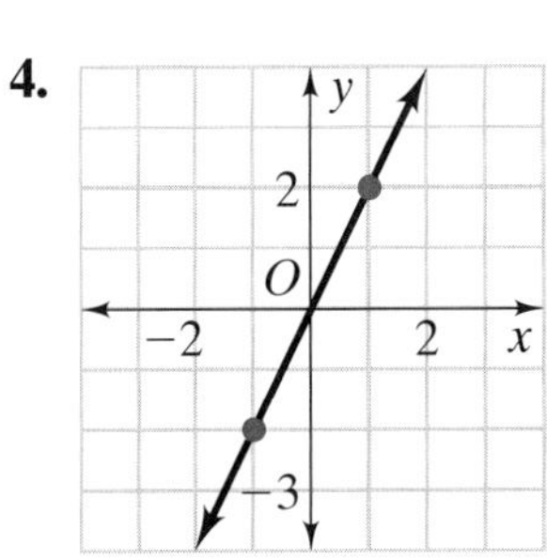

Example 2 (page 534)

Find the slope of each incline.

5.

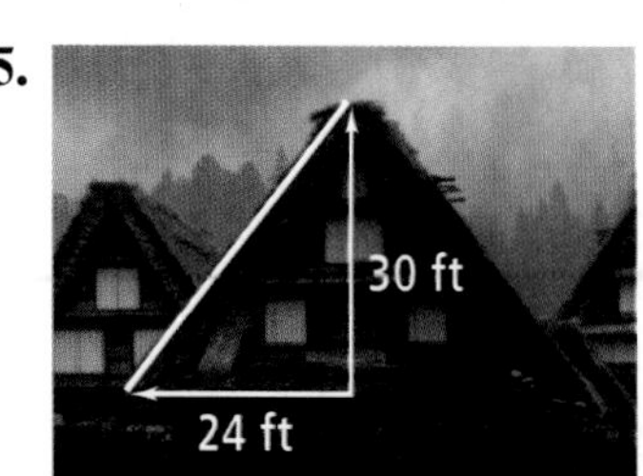

6.

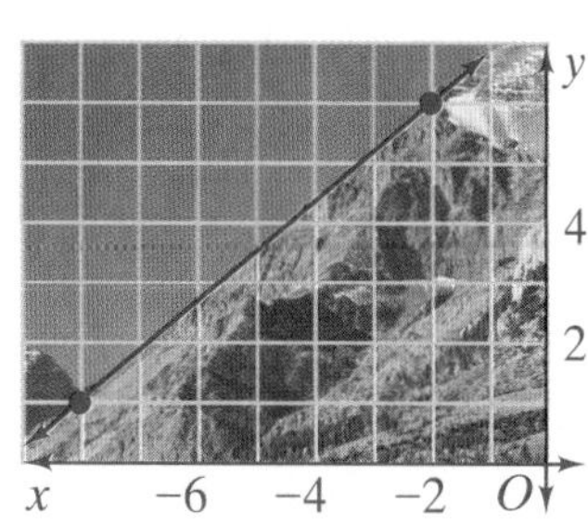

Example 3 (page 535)

Draw a line with the given slope through the given point.

7. $P(0, 0)$, slope $= 2$

8. $M(1, 3)$, slope $= \frac{1}{2}$

9. $R(6, 6)$, slope $= \frac{5}{2}$

10. $A(5, -5)$, slope $= -\frac{2}{3}$

11. $Q(3, 1)$, slope $= -\frac{1}{4}$

12. $B(5, 3)$, slope $= -1$

B Apply Your Skills

13. a. In the graph at the right, which line has a negative slope?

b. Find the slopes of lines j and k.

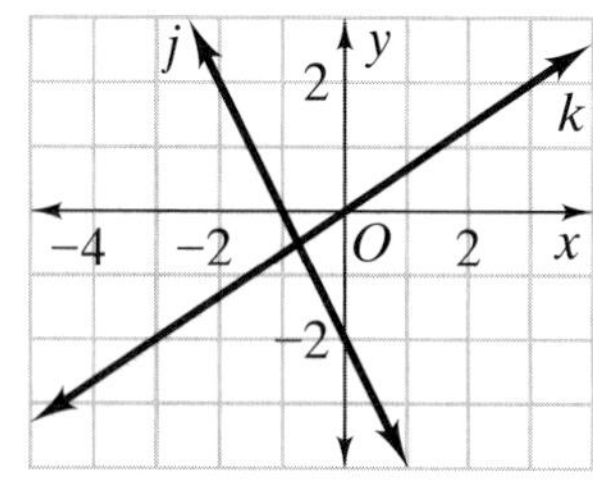

14. Error Analysis Your classmate graphs a line through $(4, 2)$ and $(5, -1)$ and finds the slope of the line to be 3. Explain why your classmate is incorrect.

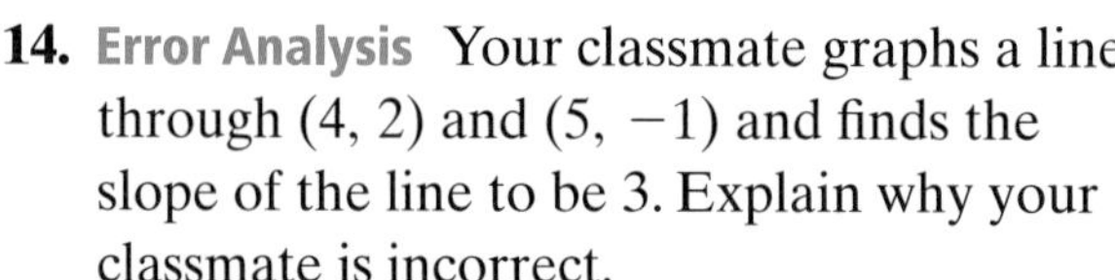

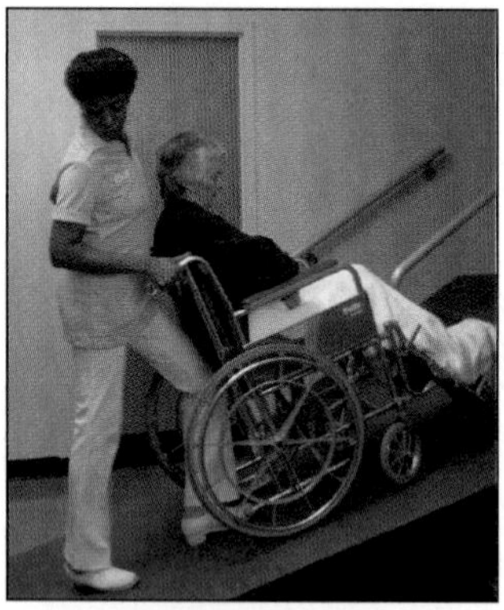

15. Ramps Guidelines for a wheelchair ramp allow a maximum of 1 in. of rise for every 12 in. of run. The ramp at the left runs 6 ft 8 in. and rises 2 ft 9 in. Does the ramp meet the guidelines? Explain.

Real-World Connection

Ramps make buildings accessible to everyone.

Graph the given points. Find the slope of the line through the points.

16. $(4, 8), (5, 10)$

17. $(4, -1), (-4, 1)$

18. $(2, 7), (3, -1)$

19. $(2, -5), (-5, 0)$

20. $(5, 1), (-3, -3)$

21. $(-6, -5), (2, 6)$

22. Land The slope of a piece of land is its grade. If the grade of a piece of land is 12%, then what is its slope?

23. Cars The graph shows the value of a car for the first seven years of ownership.

a. What was the value of the car when it was new?

b. What is the slope of the graph?

c. What does the slope tell you about the relationship between the age of the car and its value?

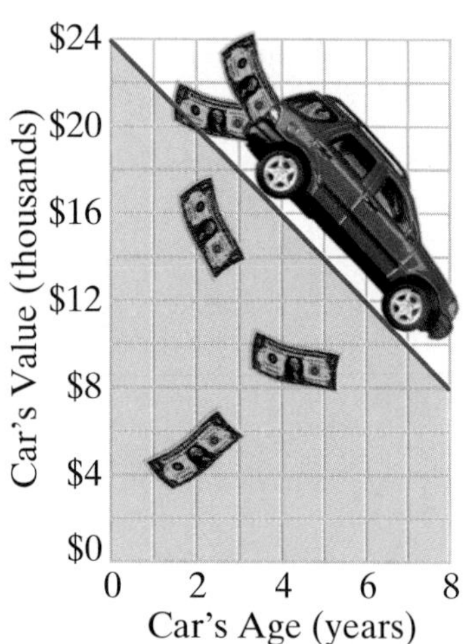

24. Writing in Math Explain why it is more difficult to run up a hill with a slope of $\frac{1}{2}$ than a hill with a slope of $\frac{1}{6}$.

25. **Math in the Media** How many sections of the graph in the cartoon have a positive slope? How many have a negative slope? Explain.

...and here's a chart that shows what you might see if you looked at a mountain range through a tennis racket.
WWW.VDGI.COM/BIZARRO
Dist. by Universal Press Synd. © DAN PIRARO 1997

26. **Data File, p. 519** Let y represent the distance traveled by the aircraft. Let x represent the number of hours at speed r.
   a. Choose three of the aircraft. Graph $y = rx$ for each aircraft on the same coordinate plane.
   b. For each aircraft find the distance traveled after 3 h.
   c. **Number Sense** Describe the connection between the slope of each line and the speed of the aircraft.

Graph the line through the given point with the given slope.

27. (1, 1), slope $= -5$

28. origin, slope $= -\frac{4}{2}$

29. a point on the y-axis at $y = -3$, slope $= \frac{-1}{-6}$

C Challenge

30. Graph each line and find its slope.
   a. line r through points (0, 4) and (3, −3)
   b. line s through points (1, 7) and (4, 0)
   c. What do you notice about the slopes of lines r and s? How is this reflected in the graph?

31. **Stretch Your Thinking** You are thinking about starting your own newspaper delivery route to earn extra money. You have 250 customers signed up for 7 days a week. The distributor charges you $.45 for the daily paper and $1.50 for the Sunday paper. You wish to earn at least $20,000 per year. How much should you charge each customer per week?

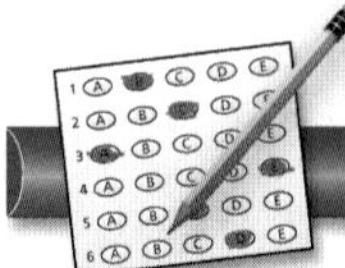

Test Prep

Multiple Choice

32. Which could be the slope of a line going upward from left to right?

A. -1 B. $\frac{3}{5}$ C. $-\frac{6}{2}$ D. $-\frac{1}{4}$

33. What is the slope of the line that includes (−6, 0) and (0, 2)?

F. $-\frac{3}{10}$ G. $\frac{3}{10}$ H. $\frac{1}{3}$ I. $\frac{9}{5}$

34. The point (2, −3) lies on a line with a positive slope. Through which quadrant can this line NOT pass?

A. I B. II C. III D. IV

Take It to the NET
Online lesson quiz at **www.PHSchool.com**
Web Code: aba-1003

Extended Response

35. a. Find the slope of the line through points P and Q.
    b. Find the slope of the line through points P and R.
    c. Are lines ℓ and m perpendicular?
    d. What is the product of the slopes of lines ℓ and m?

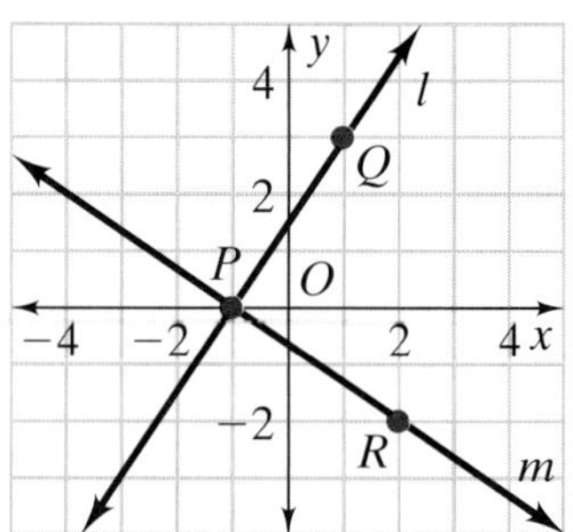

Mixed Review

Lesson 6-2

Order from least to greatest.

36. $60\%, \frac{3}{4}, 0.3$ **37.** $\frac{7}{9}, 75\%, 0.78$ **38.** $37.5\%, \frac{13}{20}, 0.225$

39. **Pets** Aquarium fish are the most popular pets in America. About one out of every eight households keeps fish for pets. Express the fish-owning households as a fraction, a decimal, and a percent.

Lesson 5-6

$\triangle ABC \sim \triangle PQR$.
Find each measure.

40. length of $\overline{PR}$

41. length of $\overline{AB}$

42. measure of $\angle R$

43. measure of $\angle A$

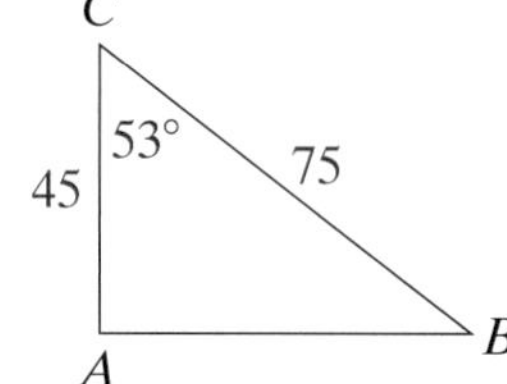

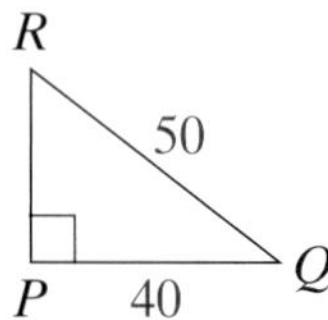

Checkpoint Quiz 1 — Lessons 10-1 through 10-3

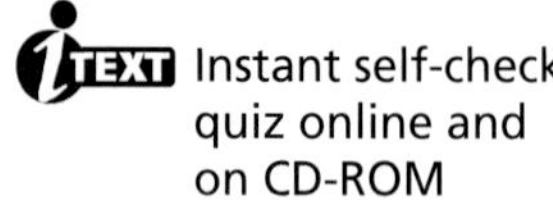

Graph the line containing each pair of points. Identify the line as vertical or horizontal.

1. $(-2, 3), (-2, -5)$ **2.** $(-3, 4), (1, 4)$ **3.** $(2, -4), (2, 5)$

Graph each linear equation.

4. $y = x + 7$ **5.** $y = -3x + 2$ **6.** $y = x - 3$

7. Find the slope of the line at the right.

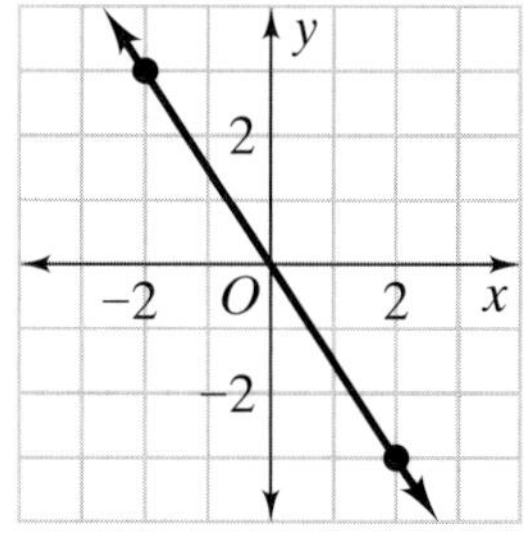

Draw a line with the given slope through the given point.

8. $P(-2, 0)$, slope $= 3$

9. $A(0, -3)$, slope $= \frac{1}{2}$

10. $M(1, -4)$, slope $= -\frac{4}{3}$

Technology

Exploring Slope

For Use After Lesson 10-3

You can use a graphing calculator to help you explore the relationship between an equation and the slope of the equation's graph.

EXAMPLE

Use a graphing calculator to find the slope of $y = 2x + 1$.

Step 1 Use Y= to enter the equation.

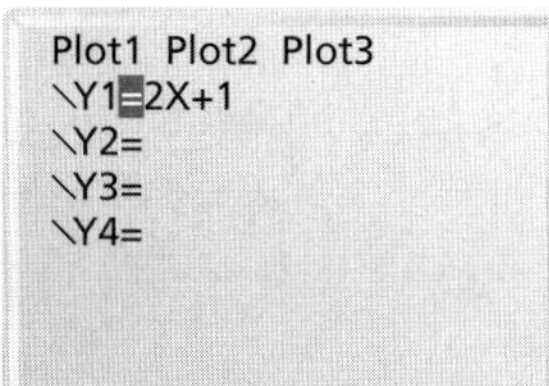

Step 2 Press ZOOM 0 ▶ ENTER for the integer mode.

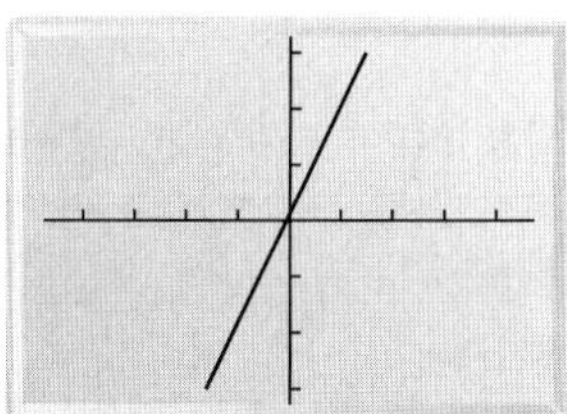

Step 3 Press TRACE. The x-coordinate is 0, and the y-coordinate is 1.

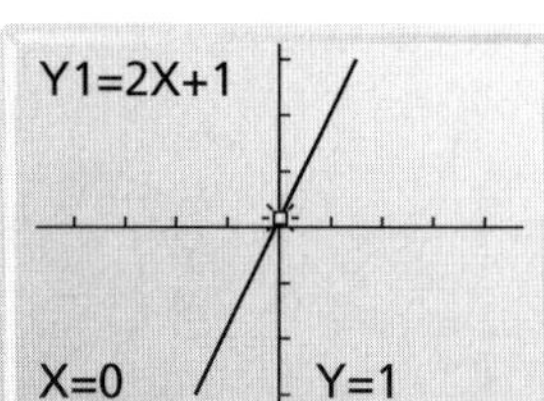

Step 4 Use ▶ to move the cursor to the right 1 unit.

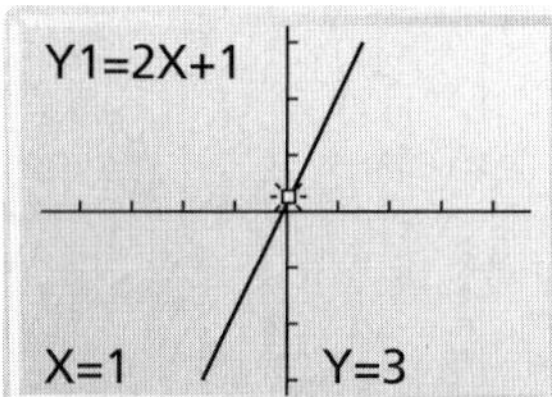

Step 5 Repeat step 4 and examine how the coordinates change. As the x-coordinate increases 1 unit, the y-coordinate increases 2 units. Another way to say this is that for every 1 unit of run, there are 2 units of rise.

slope $= \frac{\text{rise}}{\text{run}} = \frac{2}{1}$, or 2

EXERCISES

Use a graphing calculator to find the slope of each equation.

1. $y = 2x - 3$ **2.** $y = x + 3$ **3.** $y = \frac{1}{3}x + 2$ **4.** $y = -3x$

5. Reasoning Look at each slope you found. How is the slope of a line represented in each equation?

Without graphing, find the slope of each line.

6. $y = 8x + 3$ **7.** $y = -x - 1$ **8.** $y = -\frac{1}{2}x + 9$ **9.** $y = \frac{5}{2}x - 3$

10-4 Exploring Nonlinear Relationships

What You'll Learn

OBJECTIVE 1 To graph nonlinear equations

. . . And Why

To find the distance an object falls, as in Exercise 25

Check Skills You'll Need

For help, go to Lesson 10-2.

Find three solutions of each equation.

1. $y = x + 12$
2. $y = x - 20$
3. $y = 15x$
4. $y = 3x - 2$
5. $y = 4 - x$
6. $y = 5x + 2$

New Vocabulary • nonlinear equation

Interactive lesson includes instant self-check, tutorials, and activities.

OBJECTIVE 1 Graphing Nonlinear Equations

You know that the graph of a linear equation is a straight line. A **nonlinear equation** is an equation with a graph that is not a straight line. The graph of the equation $y = -x^2$ is an example of a curve called a parabola. When you throw or kick a ball in the air, the path the ball follows is a parabola.

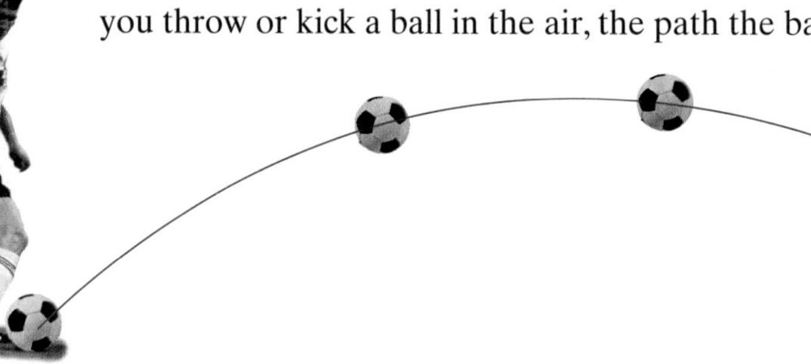

1 EXAMPLE Graphing a Parabola

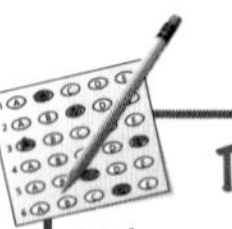

Test-Prep Tip
When substituting a value for x in $-x^2$, make sure you square the value *before* finding its opposite.

Graph $y = -x^2$ using integer values of x from -3 to 3.

x	$-x^2$	y	(x, y)
-3	$-(-3)^2$	-9	$(-3, -9)$
-2	$-(-2)^2$	-4	$(-2, -4)$
-1	$-(-1)^2$	-1	$(-1, -1)$
0	$-(0)^2$	0	$(0, 0)$
1	$-(1)^2$	-1	$(1, -1)$
2	$-(2)^2$	-4	$(2, -4)$
3	$-(3)^2$	-9	$(3, -9)$

← Make a table of values.

Graph the ordered pairs. Then connect the points. →

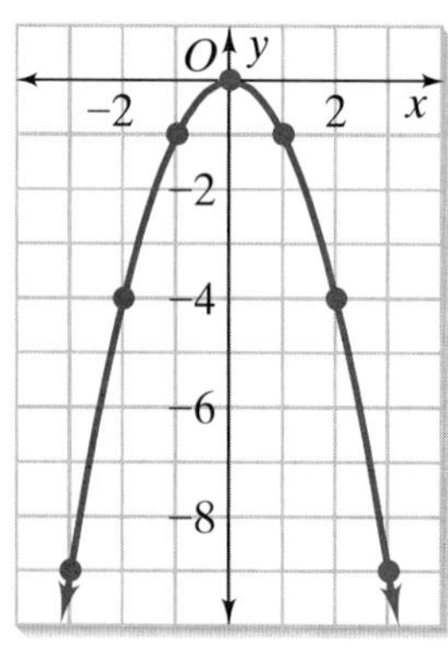

Check Understanding 1 **a.** Graph $y = 2x^2$ using integer values of x from -3 to 3.
b. Number Sense Why is the graph of $y = 2x^2$ only in Quadrants I and II?

The equation $y = |x|$ is an absolute value equation with two variables. The graphs of absolute value equations are V-shaped.

2 EXAMPLE Graphing Absolute Value Equations

Graph $y = |x|$ using integer values of x from -2 to 2.

x	$\lvert x \rvert$	y	(x, y)
-2	$\lvert -2 \rvert$	2	$(-2, 2)$
-1	$\lvert -1 \rvert$	1	$(-1, 1)$
0	$\lvert 0 \rvert$	0	$(0, 0)$
1	$\lvert 1 \rvert$	1	$(1, 1)$
2	$\lvert 2 \rvert$	2	$(2, 2)$

← **Make a table of values.**

Graph the ordered pairs. Then connect the points. →

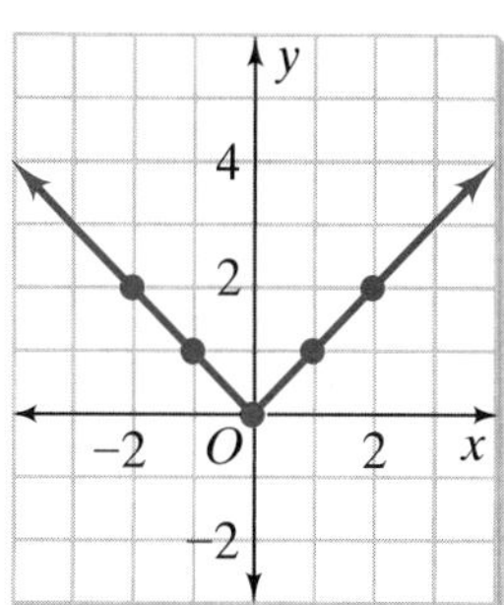

Check Understanding 2 Graph $y = 2|x|$ using integer values of x from -2 to 2.

More Than One Way

Determine whether $(-3, 10)$ is a solution of $y = x^2 + 2$.

Sarah's Method

I can tell by using my graphing calculator. I press Y= and enter $y = x^2 + 2$. Then I select the integer mode under ZOOM. I can use the TRACE feature to get the screen at the right.

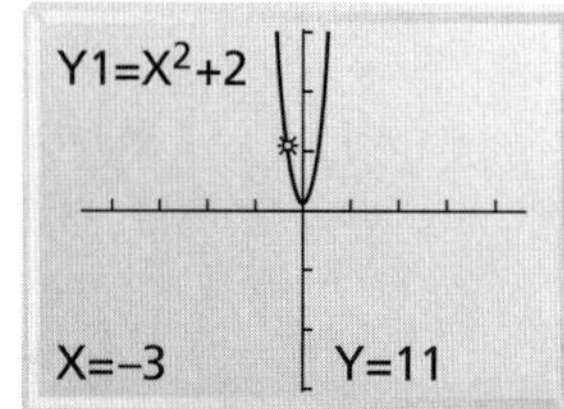

At $x = -3, y = 11$, so $(-3, 10)$ is not a solution of $y = x^2 + 2$.

Will's Method

I can tell by substituting -3 for x and 10 for y in the equation.

$y = x^2 + 2$

$10 \stackrel{?}{=} (-3)^2 + 2$ ← **Substitute.**

$10 \stackrel{?}{=} 9 + 2$ ← **Multiply.**

$10 \neq 11$ ← **Add.**

The equation is not true, so $(-3, 10)$ is not a solution of $y = x^2 + 2$.

Choose a Method

Determine whether $(5, 20)$ is a solution of $y = x^2 - 5$. Describe your method, and explain why you chose it.

EXERCISES

For more practice, see *Extra Practice*.

A Practice by Example

Make a table of values for each equation. Use integer values of x from -3 to 3. Then graph the equation.

Example 1 (page 540)

1. $y = x^2$ **2.** $y = -2x^2$ **3.** $y = x^2 + 2$

4. $y = x^2 - 2$ **5.** $y = 4x^2$ **6.** $y = x^2 - 3$

7. $y = -5x^2$ **8.** $y = -x^2 + 3$ **9.** $y = -x^2 - 4$

Example 2 (page 541)

10. $y = 3|x|$ **11.** $y = \frac{1}{2}|x|$ **12.** $y = |x| + 1$

13. $y = |x| - 1$ **14.** $y = 2|x|$ **15.** $y = |x| - 5$

16. $y = \frac{1}{3}|x|$ **17.** $y = |x| + 3$ **18.** $y = 5|x|$

B Apply Your Skills

Without graphing, tell whether the graph of each equation will be a line, a parabola, or the graph of an absolute value equation.

19. $y = 5x^2$ **20.** $y = 5x - 2$ **21.** $y = 3|x|$

22. $y = \frac{1}{10}x$ **23.** $y = \frac{1}{3}x^2 + 8$ **24.** $y = 10|x|$

25. Science To prove that two objects of different sizes fall at the same rate, Galileo dropped two objects of different sizes from the Tower of Pisa. The equation $d = 16t^2$ can be used to find the distance, in feet, that the objects fall in t seconds.

a. Make a table of values to find out how far the objects fall after 0, 1, 3, and 5 seconds.

b. Use the table of values to graph the equation.

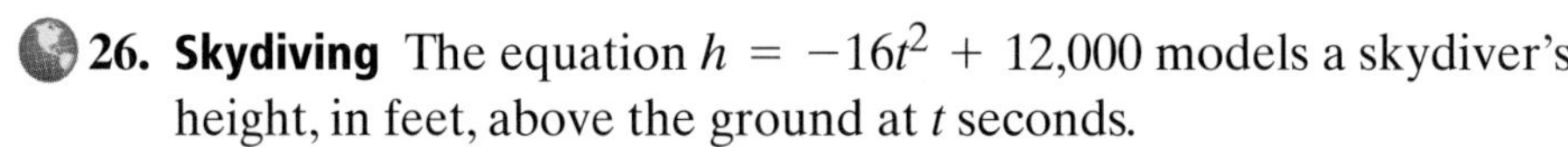

Real-World Connection

Jump altitudes for skydivers range from 7,500 ft to 15,000 ft.

26. Skydiving The equation $h = -16t^2 + 12{,}000$ models a skydiver's height, in feet, above the ground at t seconds.

a. Make a table of values to find the skydiver's height at 0, 5, 10, and 20 seconds.

b. Graph the equation.

c. Use the graph to find the height of the skydiver at 12 s.

Match each graph with an equation.

27.

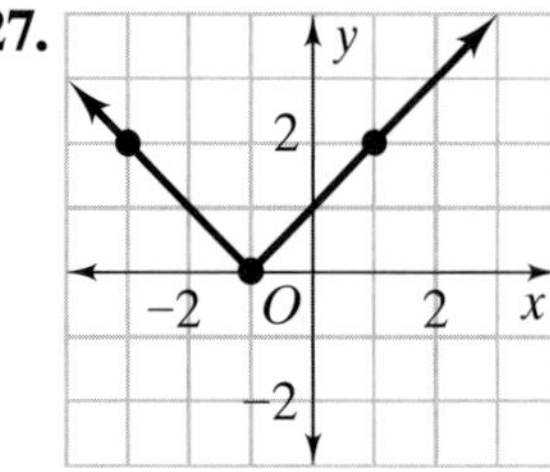

28.

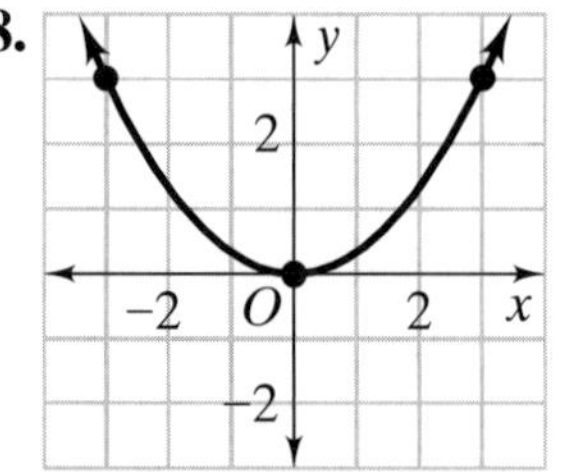

29.

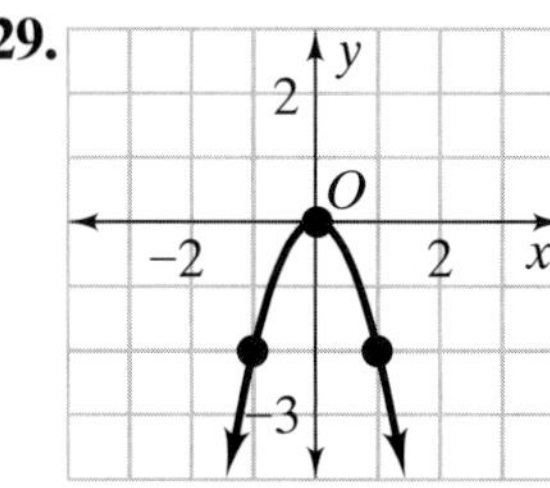

A. $y = |x + 1|$ **B.** $y = |x| - 1$ **C.** $y = \frac{1}{2}x^2$

D. $y = \frac{1}{3}x^2$ **E.** $y = x^2 - 8$ **F.** $y = -2x^2$

Use integer values of x from -3 to 3 to graph each equation.

30. $y = 2x^2 - 4$ **31.** $y = -x^2 - 3$ **32.** $y = 3|x| + 5$

33. $y = -x^2 - 6$ **34.** $y = -|x| + 1$ **35.** $y = -2|x| - 2$

36. **Writing in Math** Does the slope of a parabola and an absolute value equation stay the same between any two points on their graphs? Explain.

37. **a.** Make a table of values for $y = -|x|$. Draw a graph of the equation.
b. Number Sense Will the graph of $y = -|x|$ ever have points in Quadrants I and II? Explain.

Use integer values of x from -3 to 3 to graph each equation.

38. $y = |x - 1|$ **39.** $y = |x + 1|$ **40.** $y = 2|x + 1|$

41. $y = (x + 1)^2$ **42.** $y = (x - 1)^2$ **43.** $y = \left(\frac{1}{2}x - 1\right)^2$

44. Stretch Your Thinking You are making 160 hamburgers for a school fair. Rolls come in packages of 16, 24, and 36. How many different combinations of packages can be used so that there are no leftovers?

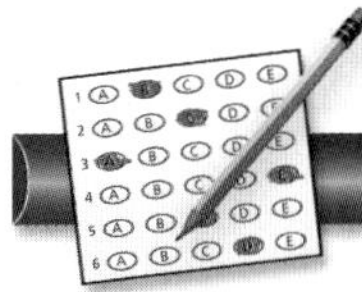

Test Prep

Gridded Response

45. For the equation graphed at the right, what is the value of y when $x = -2$?

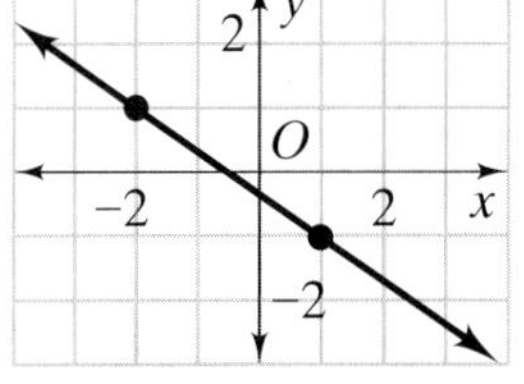

46. For the linear equation $y = 3x - 4$, what is the value of y when $x = 8$?

47. For the absolute value equation $y = |x| - 7$, what is the value of y when $x = -9$?

48. For the nonlinear equation $y = x^2 + 10$, what is the value of y when $x = 6$?

Mixed Review

Lesson 7-8 **Name all the given parts that are in the circle.**

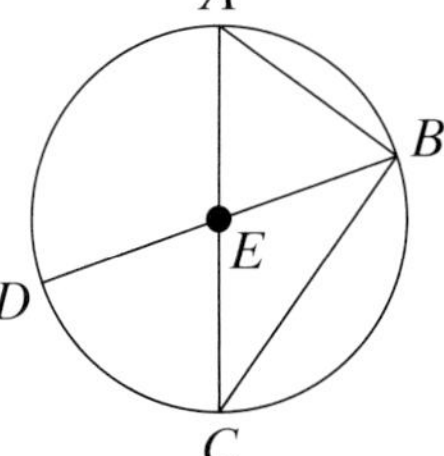

49. chords **50.** diameters

51. radii **52.** central angles

Lesson 4-9

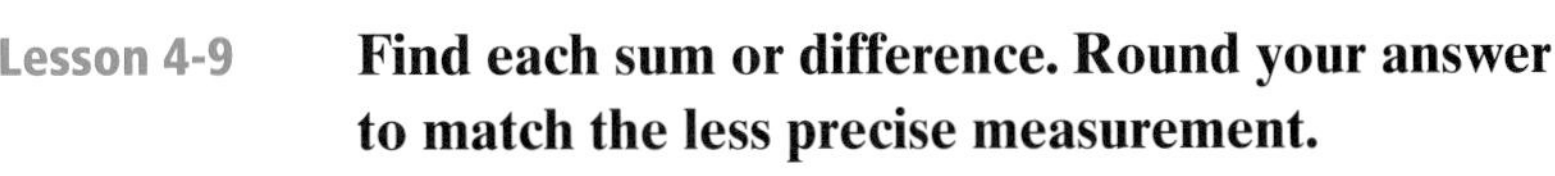

Find each sum or difference. Round your answer to match the less precise measurement.

53. 2.5 mm + 2.54 mm **54.** 41 ft − 26.8 ft **55.** 17.06 m − 8.31 m

56. 8.23 g − 7.8 g **57.** 8.29 gal + 25.9 gal **58.** 32.06 mL + 9.3 mL

Make a Table and Make a Graph

What You'll Learn

To solve a problem by combining strategies

. . . And Why

To make population predictions, as in Example 1

✓ Check Skills You'll Need

For help, go to Lesson 10-2.

Graph each linear equation.

1. $y = x + 4$
2. $y = x - 1$
3. $y = -3x - 2$
4. $y = 5x$
5. $y = -2x + 3$
6. $y = 4x + 1$
7. $y = -x + 1$
8. $y = \frac{1}{2}x + 2$
9. $y = x - 3$

Interactive lesson includes instant self-check, tutorials, and activities.

OBJECTIVE 1

Solving a Problem by Combining Strategies

When to Use These Strategies A real-world problem may ask you to examine a set of data and draw a conclusion. In such a problem, ***make a table*** to organize the data. Using the data, ***make a graph*** to look for a relationship.

Real-World Connection

Wolves live in family groups called packs. A typical pack has 8 members, but some have more than 20.

1 EXAMPLE Real-World Problem Solving

Wildlife Population A wildlife preserve surveyed its wolf population in 1996 and counted 56 wolves. Four years later there were 40 wolves. In 2002 there were 32 wolves in the preserve. If the wolf population changes at a constant rate, in what year will there be fewer than 15 wolves?

Read and Understand Given the wolf population in 1996, 2000, and 2002, you are to find the year in which there will be fewer than 15 wolves.

Plan and Solve *Make a table* to organize the information in the problem. Then *make a graph* to predict when the wolf population will be below 15.

Let x equal the number of years since the first survey. For 1996, $x = 0$. Let y equal the wolf population.

Year	x	Wolves (y)	(x, y)
1996	0	56	(0, 56)
2000	4	40	(4, 40)
2002	6	32	(6, 32)

Now that you have three points, you can use them to make a graph. Choose the scale of the graph. Since the maximum y-value is 56, use an interval of 5 on the y-axis. Use 1 for the interval on the x-axis.

Step 1 Graph the points (0, 56), (4, 40), and (6, 32).

Step 2 The points form a line. Connect the points and extend the line.

Step 3 Find the x-value at which the wolf population is 15. This occurs at $x \approx 10.25$.

About 10 years after 1996, in 2006, there will be fewer than 15 wolves.

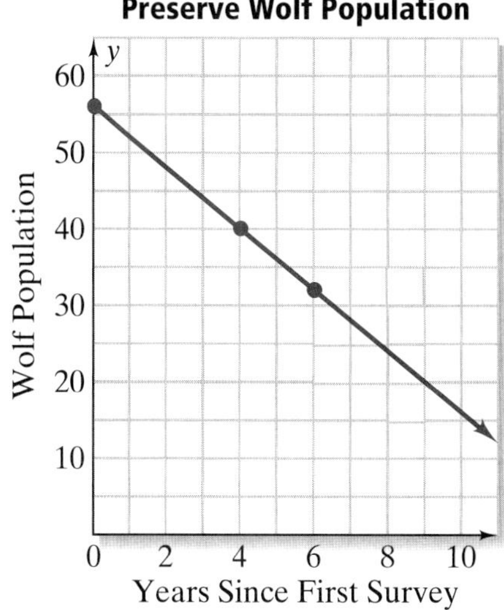

Look Back and Check From 2000 to 2002, the wolf population decreased by 8. Since the rate of decrease is constant, you can say that every 2 years the population decreases by 8.

Year	Wolves
2000	40
2002	$40 - 8 = 32$
2004	$32 - 8 = 24$
2006	$24 - 8 = 16$

In the beginning of 2006, there will be about 16 wolves. So the answer that there will be fewer than 15 in 2006 is reasonable.

Check Understanding 1 You purchase a plant 3 in. tall. After the second week it is 4 in. tall. Four weeks later it is 6 in. tall. About how tall is the plant after the seventh week?

EXERCISES

For more practice, see *Extra Practice*.

A Practice by Example

Example 1 (page 544)

Solve each problem by making a table and then making a graph.

1. **Business** You are starting a business selling lemonade. You know that it costs \$6 to make 20 c of lemonade and \$7 to make 30 c of lemonade. How much will it cost to make 50 c of lemonade?

2. **Driving** A driver of a car slows to a stop. The decrease in speed is constant. When the driver first applies the brakes, the car is going 50 mi/h. After 5 s the car is traveling 30 mi/h. About how long does it take the car to stop?

3. **Savings** You have \$10 saved and plan to save an additional \$2 each week. How much will you have after 7 weeks?

Need Help?
- Reread the problem.
- Identify the key facts and details.
- Tell the problem in your own words.
- Try a different strategy.
- Check your work.

4. Animals A baby hamster weighs 4 g when it is born. It weighs 28 g at 4 wk and 52 g at 8 wk. Assuming a constant rate of increase, how much will the hamster weigh at 14 wk?

B Apply Your Skills

Choose a strategy or a combination of strategies to solve each problem.

Strategies

- Draw a Diagram
- Look for a Pattern
- Make a Graph
- Make an Organized List
- Make a Table
- Simulate a Problem
- Solve a Simpler Problem
- Try, Check, and Revise
- Use Logical Reasoning
- Work Backward
- Write an Equation

5. Writing in Math In Exercise 4, is it reasonable to assume that the hamster will continue to grow at the same rate? Why or why not?

6. Fund-Raising A booster club sells $\frac{3}{4}$ of the tickets to the club's fashion show. It has 175 tickets left. How many tickets were printed?

7. Home Improvement A diagram of a kitchen is below. Suppose you want to tile the floor using square ceramic tiles that are 6 in. on each side. How many tiles do you need?

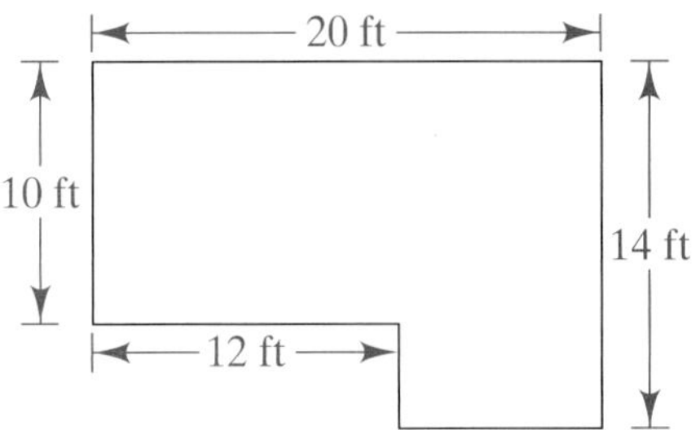

8. Money With $8.75 in your pocket, you decide to treat yourself to lunch. How much can you spend on lunch and still have enough to leave a 15% tip?

9. Geometry The area of the square below is 64 square units. Point C is the midpoint of $\overline{AD}$. Point B is the midpoint of $\overline{AC}$. What fraction of the square is shaded?

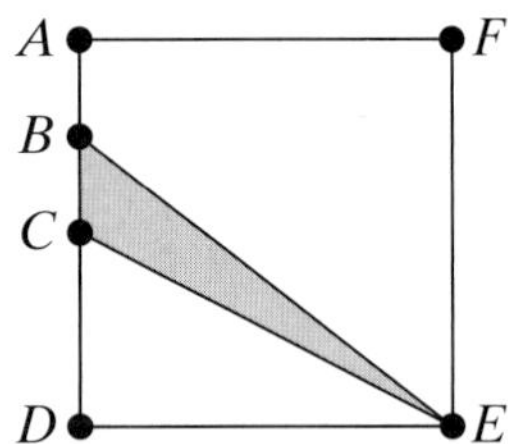

10. Museums A museum collects $250 for admission on a Saturday. An adult ticket costs $10, while a child's ticket is $5. What are three possible combinations for the number of adults and the number of children that are at the museum on the Saturday?

C Challenge

11. Hobbies A pet store has 362 tropical fish and 15 large fish tanks. The store charges $3.50 per fish and $55 for a large fish tank. How much money can the store earn from its current stock?

12. Stretch Your Thinking A survey of 40 shoppers found that 12 like Crunchy Cereal and 23 like Wheat Cereal. Twice as many dislike both brands as like both brands. How many shoppers like both brands?

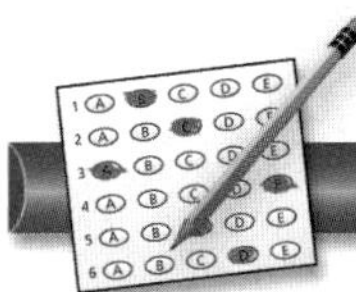

Test Prep

Multiple Choice

13. Which point is in the same quadrant as (2, −4)?
A. (1, 2) **B.** (−3, 4) **C.** (−4, −2) **D.** (1, −10)

14. Which ordered pair is a solution to both $y = 2x - 2$ and $y = -x + 4$?
F. (0, −2) **G.** (2, 2) **H.** (1, 3) **I.** (2, 3)

Take It to the NET
Online lesson quiz at
www.PHSchool.com
Web Code: aba-1005

15. Which ordered pair is NOT a solution to $y = 2x + 5$?
A. (2, 9) **B.** (5, 15) **C.** (3, 12) **D.** (4, 13)

16. Which equation has a slope that is the same as the slope of $y = 3x + 5$?
F. $y = \frac{21}{7}x + 5$ **G.** $y = -\frac{6}{2}x + 5$ **H.** $y = \frac{1}{3}x + 5$ **I.** $y = -3x$

Short Response

17. What are two solutions of $y = -x - 1$? Show your work.

Mixed Review

Lesson 10-2

Algebra **Find three solutions of each equation.**

18. $y = 4x - 2$ **19.** $y = -3x - 6$ **20.** $y = 5x + 4$

21. $y = 10x$ **22.** $y = 3x + 7$ **23.** $y = x - 7$

Lesson 9-7

Find the simple interest earned by each account.

24. \$1,100 principal
3% annual interest rate
2 years

25. \$3,000 principal
7.5% annual interest rate
10 years

Practice Game

Hide and Seek

What You'll Need

- 2 players, two sheets of graph paper

How to Play

- Using graph paper, draw the first quadrant of the coordinate plane. Label the x- and y-axes from 0 to 10.
- Draw a triangle or rectangle on your graph. The ordered pairs for each vertex consist of whole numbers.
- You and your opponent take turns trying to locate each vertex of your opponent's shape by calling out ordered pairs that are whole numbers.
- If your opponent's guess falls inside your figure, you say "inside." If it falls outside your figure, you say "outside." If it is on the border, you say "border." If the guess falls on a vertex, you must say "bingo."
- The first player to name each vertex of the opponent's figure wins.

Investigation: Exploring Slides, Flips, and Turns

For Use With Lesson 10-6

To change the position of a geometric figure, you can use *slides*, *flips*, and *turns*.

A *slide* moves a figure so that every point moves the same direction and the same distance.

A *flip* reflects a figure over a line.

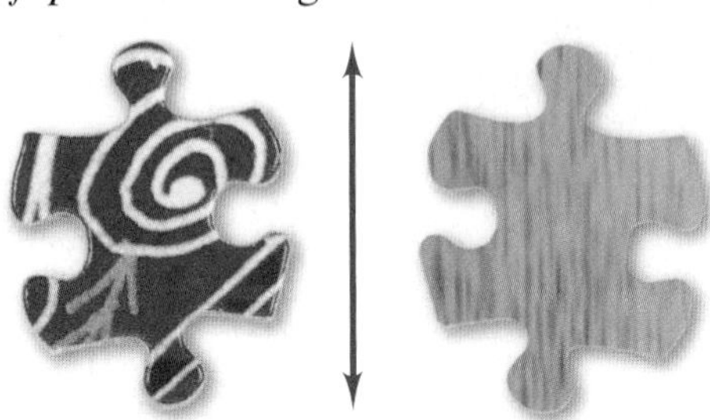

A *turn* rotates a figure around a point.

EXERCISES

Describe each transformation as a *slide*, *flip*, or *turn*.

1.

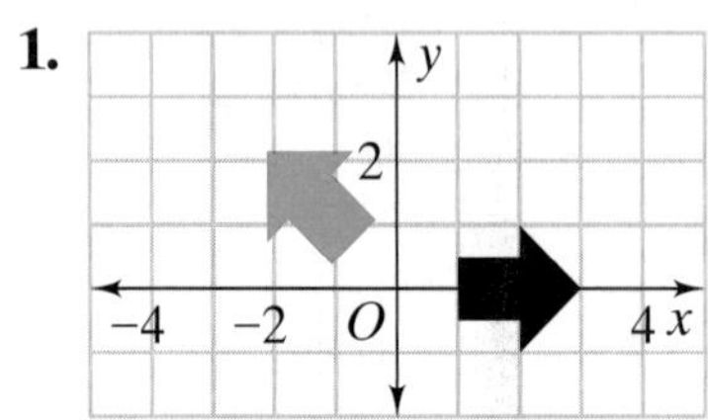

2.

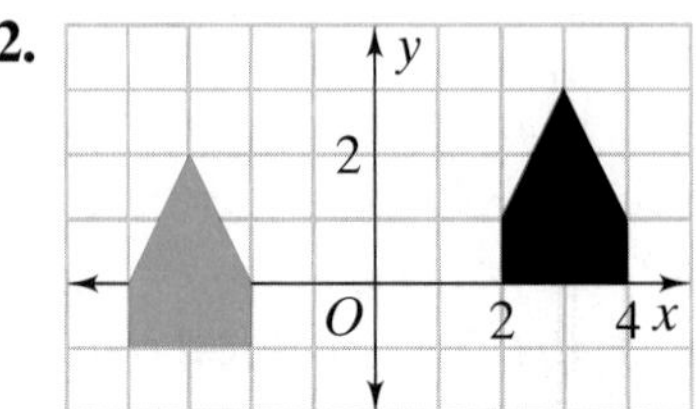

3.

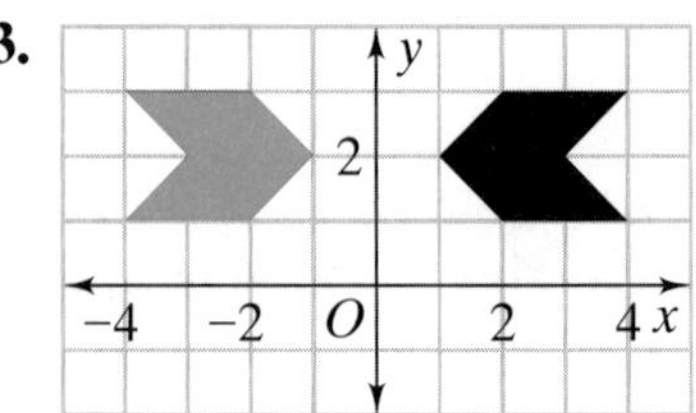

4. **Writing in Math** Describe how two flips can have the same effect as one slide. Include a drawing to illustrate your example.

5. **Open-Ended** Give a real-world example that involves a slide, a flip, or a turn.

10-6 Translations

What You'll Learn

To graph translations

To write rules for translations

. . . And Why

To translate, or slide, computer images, as in Example 4

Check Skills You'll Need

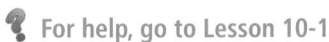

For help, go to Lesson 10-1.

Graph each point on the same coordinate plane.

1. $E(3, 1)$
2. $R(1, 0)$
3. $G(-3, -1)$
4. $S(2, -2)$
5. **Reasoning** Why do you need two coordinates to locate a point on the coordinate plane?

New Vocabulary

- transformation
- translation
- image
- prime notation (A')

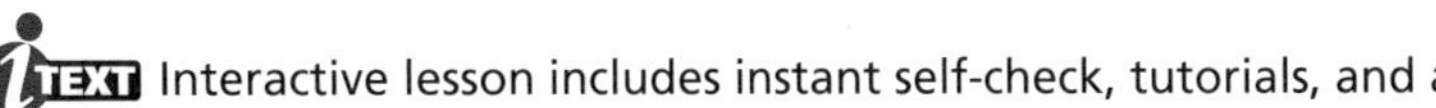

Interactive lesson includes instant self-check, tutorials, and activities.

OBJECTIVE 1 Graphing Translations

A **transformation** is a change of the position, shape, or size of a figure. Three types of transformations that change position only are slides, flips, and turns. Another name for a slide is a translation. A **translation** is a transformation that moves every point of a figure the same distance and in the same direction.

The figure you get after a transformation is the **image** of the original. You use **prime notation** (A') to identify an image point. You read A' as "A prime."

> **Reading Math**
>
> In prime notation, A'' represents a point that has been moved twice. Read A'' as "A double prime."

1 EXAMPLE Translating a Point

Translate point $F(4, 1)$ up 2 units and left 3 units. What are the coordinates of the image F'?

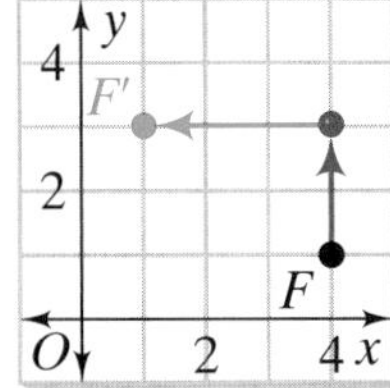

← Count up 2 units from point F and 3 units to the left. Graph point F'.

The coordinates of F' are (1, 3).

Check Understanding 1

a. Translate point $G(-4, 1)$ right 1 unit and down 4 units. What are the coordinates of the image G'?

b. Which coordinate doesn't change when you translate a point horizontally? Vertically?

To show a translation, you can use arrow notation. For the translation of F to F' in Example 1, you can write $F(4, 1) \rightarrow F'(1, 3)$.

To translate a geometric figure, first translate each vertex of the figure. Connect the image points to finish the translation. When a geometric figure is translated, the image is congruent to the original figure.

2 EXAMPLE Translating a Figure

Reading Math
You read $F \to F'$ as "point F maps onto point F'."

The vertices of $\triangle ABC$ are $A(-4, 3)$, $B(-1, 4)$, and $C(-3, 1)$. Translate $\triangle ABC$ right 2 units and down 4 units. Use arrow notation to show the translation.

Step 1
Graph and label the vertices of $\triangle ABC$. →
Connect the points.

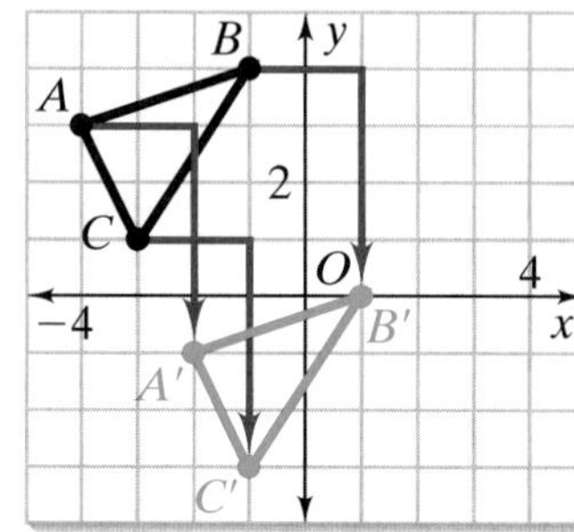

Step 2
Translate each vertex
← 2 units to the right and 4 units down.

Step 3
Label the new vertices
← A', B', and C'.
Connect the points.

$A(-4, 3) \to A'(-2, -1)$, $B(-1, 4) \to B'(1, 0)$, $C(-3, 1) \to C'(-1, -3)$.

Check Understanding 2 Graph $\triangle ABC$ from Example 2. Translate it left 3 units and up 1 unit. Use arrow notation to show the translation.

OBJECTIVE

2 Writing Rules for Translations

To find the coordinates of a translated image, add or subtract the number of units moved from the coordinates of the original figure.

3 EXAMPLE Writing a Rule

Write a rule for the translation of $\triangle MNP$. Use arrow notation.

The horizontal change from N to N' is 4 units to the right, so $x \to x + 4$.

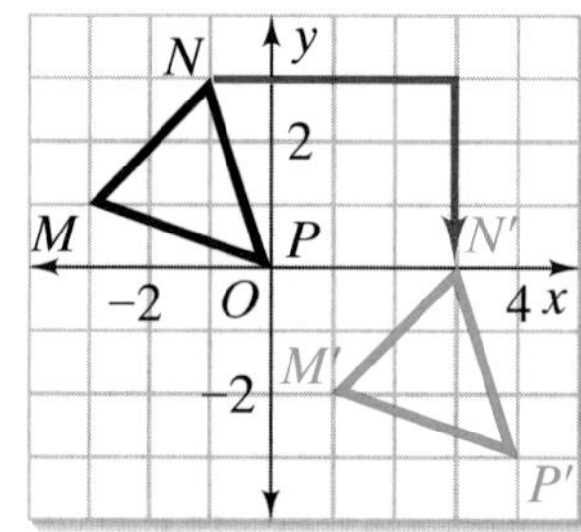

The vertical change from N to N' is 3 units down, so $y \to y - 3$.

The rule for the translation is $(x, y) \to (x + 4, y - 3)$.

Check Understanding 3 **a.** Write a rule for the translation of $\triangle PRQ$.
b. **Number Sense** A figure is translated to the left 2 units and up 6 units. Complete the general rule to show how to find the image: $(x, y) \to (x + \blacksquare, y + \blacksquare)$.

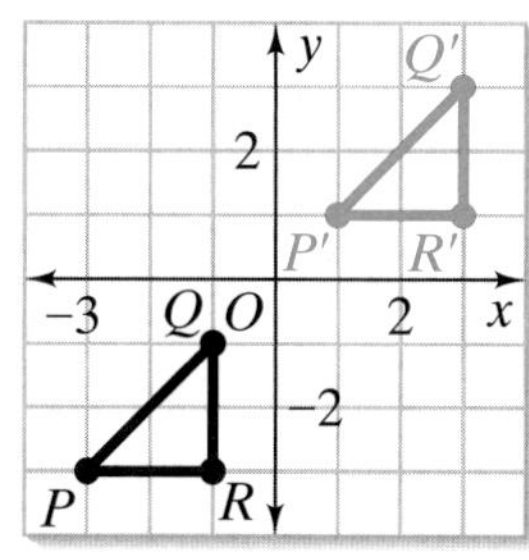

4 EXAMPLE Real-World Problem Solving

Computer Animation Computer animators use translation to move objects across a computer screen. Write a rule for the translation of spaceship A that a computer could apply to the other spaceships.

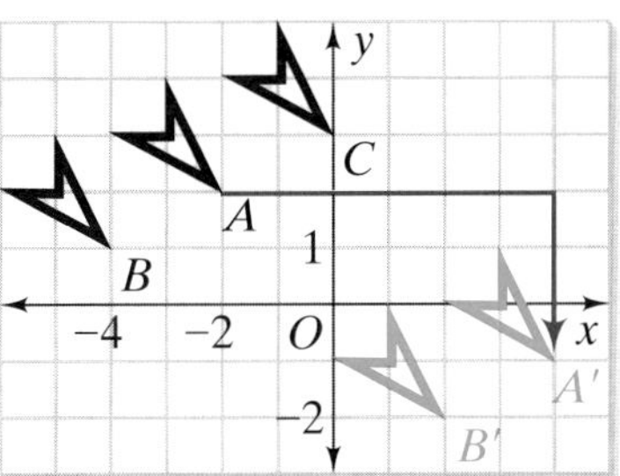

To translate A to A', move 6 units to the right and 3 units down.

The rule for the translation is $(x, y) \rightarrow (x + 6, y - 3)$.

Look Back and Check To check the rule, apply it to point B.

$$(x, y) \rightarrow (x + 6, y - 3)$$
$$B(-4, 1) \rightarrow B'(-4 + 6, 1 - 3) = B'(2, -2) \checkmark$$

Check Understanding 4 Write a rule for the translation of spaceship A to (4, 3).

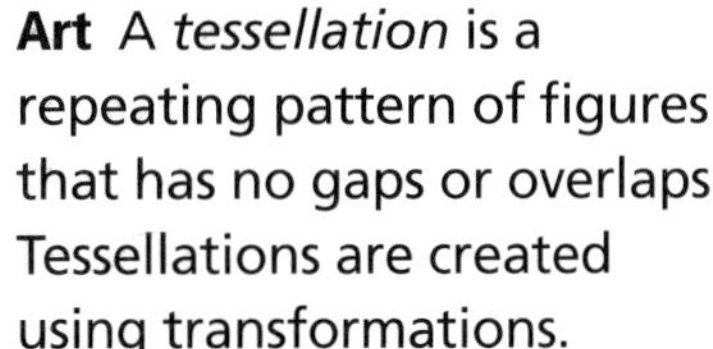

Investigation: Exploring Tessellations

Art A *tessellation* is a repeating pattern of figures that has no gaps or overlaps. Tessellations are created using transformations.

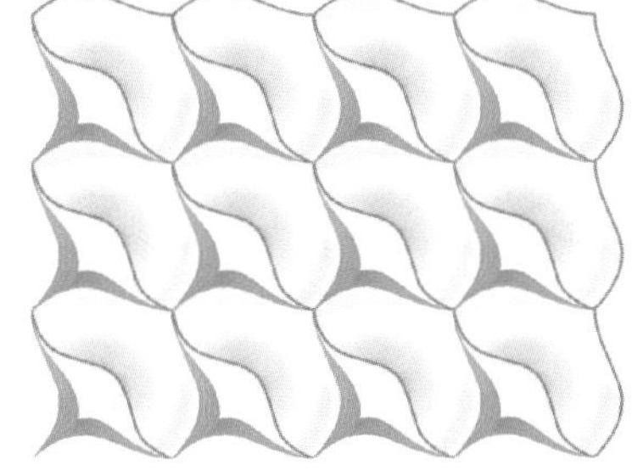

Start with a square cut out of a piece of cardboard.

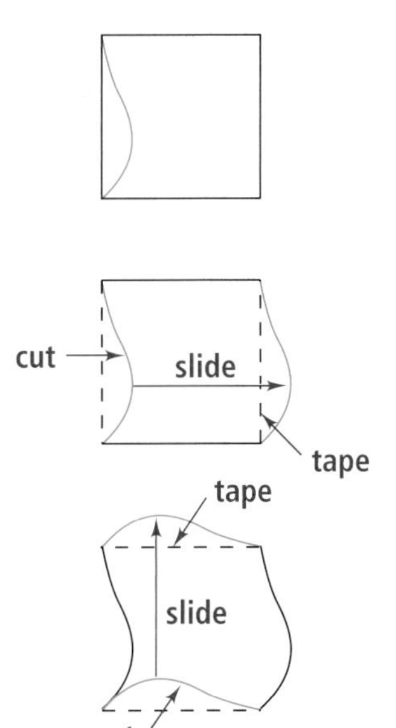

- As shown at the left, draw a curve from one vertex of the square to a neighboring vertex.
- Cut along the curve you drew. Translate the cut-out piece to the opposite side of the square and tape it down.
- Draw the same curve on the bottom and repeat the process.
- Trace around your figure on a piece of paper. Carefully translate the figure to the right so that the edges touch.
- After you have covered a row, translate your figure downward to start a new row. Continue tracing until you have covered the paper.

1. How much space was wasted on the paper? Explain why a regular hexagon is better than a regular pentagon for a bee's honeycomb.

For more practice, see *Extra Practice*.

A Practice by Example

Example 1 (page 549)

Translate each point left 2 units and down 5 units. Give the coordinates of the image point.

1. (3, 3) **2.** (0, 0) **3.** (−3, 2) **4.** (−6, −1) **5.** (6, −1)

Example 2 (page 550)

Graph each translation of $\triangle ABC$. Use arrow notation to show the translation.

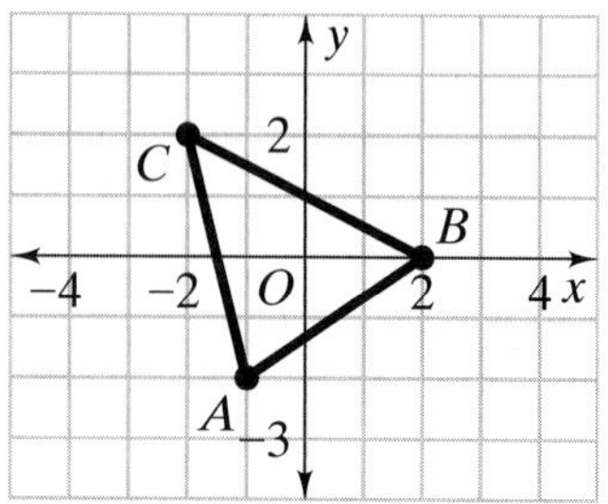

6. left 3 units **7.** up 2 units

8. down 2 units **9.** left 4 units

10. right 5 units

11. left 3 units, up 1 unit

Example 3, 4 (pages 550, 551)

Write a rule for the translation shown in each graph.

12.

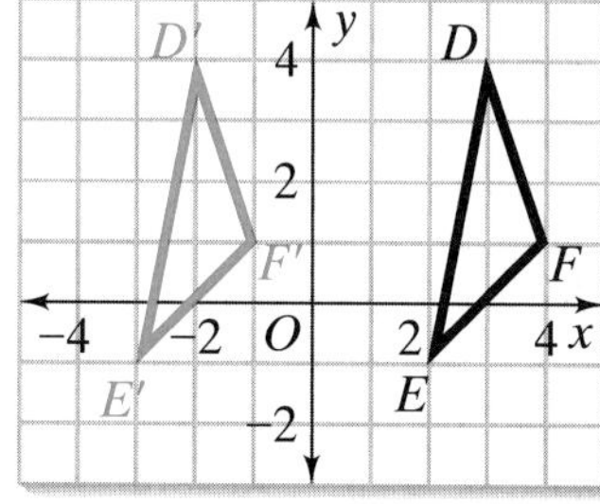

13.

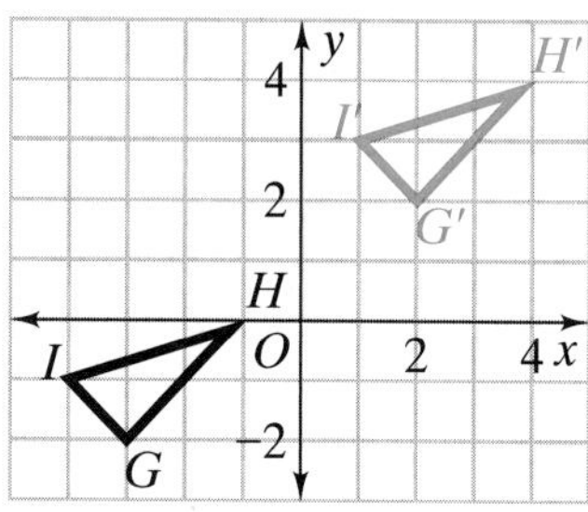

B Apply Your Skills

14. **Mental Math** Translate point $L(2, 4)$ right 2 units and up 6 units. Translate its image, point L', left 4 units and down 5 units. What are the coordinates of the image of point L'?

15. **Aviation** Three airplanes are flying in a triangular formation. After 1 min, airplane P moves to P'. Give the new coordinates of each airplane and write a rule to describe the direction that the airplanes move.

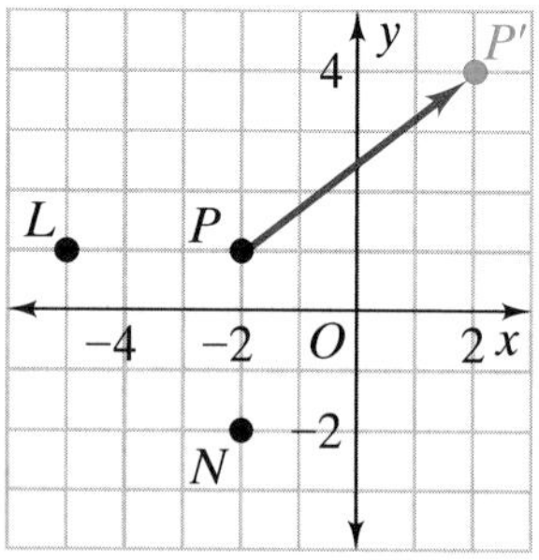

16. **Writing in Math** Why is it helpful to describe a translation by stating the horizontal change first?

Real-World Connection

It is not easy for pilots to fly in a formation. They must remain the same distance apart and keep the same speed from point to point.

Graph each point and its image. Write a rule to describe the translation.

17. $M(3, 5)$; right 3 units, down 1 unit

18. $T(-1, 6)$; right 4 units, up 1 unit

19. $C(-2, -5)$; right 1 unit, up 2 units

20. $H(4, 0)$; left 1 unit, up 4 units

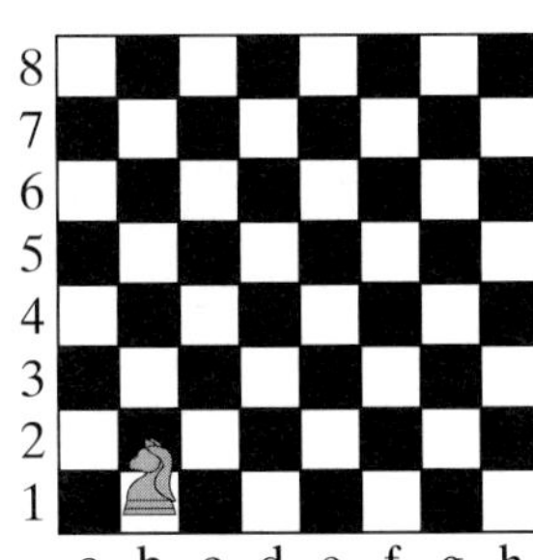

21. **Chess** In chess, translations are used to move the pieces across the board. A knight moves in an L shape: two vertical spaces and one horizontal space, or two horizontal spaces and one vertical space.
   a. The knight is at b1. What translation will move the knight to c3?
   b. What series of translations will move the knight from c3 to h7?

Find the horizontal change and the vertical change for each translation.

22. $P(4, -6) \rightarrow P'(0, 8)$ 23. $A(-1, 3) \rightarrow A'(2, 4)$ 24. $F(2, 2) \rightarrow F'(1, -7)$

Challenge

$\triangle CAT$ has vertices $C(4, 6)$, $A(0, 8)$, and $T(-6, -4)$. Graph $\triangle CAT$ and its image for each transformation.

25. $(x, y) \rightarrow \left(\frac{1}{2}x, \frac{1}{2}y\right)$

26. $(x, y) \rightarrow (2x, 2y)$

27. **Stretch Your Thinking** You made 12 of 30 shots in the first 3 games of the basketball season. In the next game, you took 10 shots and raised your season average to 50%. How many of the 10 shots did you make?

Test Prep

Multiple Choice

28. Which is a translation of $K(-1, 5)$ to the left 5 units and down 2 units?
   A. $K'(4, 3)$ B. $K'(-6, 3)$ C. $K'(-6, 7)$ D. $K'(-3, 0)$

29. Point $C(x, y)$ is translated left 2 units and up 4 units. What rule describes the translation?
   F. $(x, y) \rightarrow (x + 2, y + 4)$ G. $(x, y) \rightarrow (x + 2, y - 4)$
   H. $(x, y) \rightarrow (x - 2, y + 4)$ I. $(x, y) \rightarrow (x + 4, y - 2)$

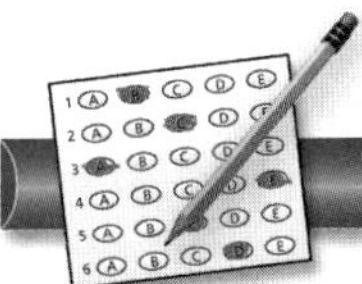

Take It to the NET
Online lesson quiz at
www.PHSchool.com
Web Code: aba-1006

30. Which triangle is a translation image of $\triangle XYZ$?
   A. $\triangle ABC$ B. $\triangle JKL$
   C. $\triangle RST$ D. $\triangle PQR$

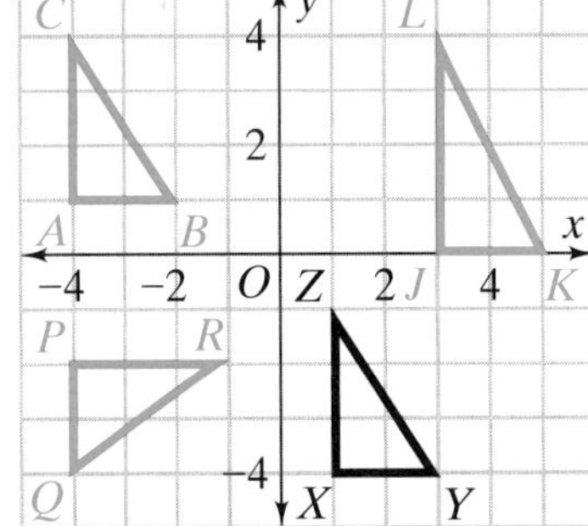

Short Response

31. $\triangle RST$ has vertices $R(2, -5)$, $S(1, 1)$, and $T(-3, -1)$. Find the coordinates of S' and T', given $R(2, -5) \rightarrow R'(5, -7)$.

Mixed Review

Lesson 9-4

Algebra **Use each function rule. Find y for $x = 0, 1, 2,$ and 3.**

32. $y = 3x + 2$ 33. $y = -x + 4$ 34. $y = -2x - 1$

Lesson 5-4

Determine whether the ratios in each pair can form a proportion.

35. $\frac{6}{12}, \frac{12}{14}$ 36. $\frac{3}{20}, \frac{2}{10}$ 37. $\frac{4}{10}, \frac{20}{45}$ 38. $\frac{27}{6}, \frac{36}{8}$ 39. $\frac{1}{4}, \frac{3}{15}$

10-7 Symmetry and Reflections

What You'll Learn

To identify lines of symmetry

To graph reflections

. . . And Why

To identify lines of symmetry in art and nature, as in Example 1

✓ Check Skills You'll Need

For help, go to Lesson 10-6.

Translate each point left 4 units and up 3 units.

1. $J(3, -2)$ **2.** $W(-1, -4)$ **3.** $B(-2, 2)$ **4.** $P(-4, 1)$

5. Mental Math Suppose $P(0, -3) \rightarrow P'(-2, -5)$. What is the horizontal change? What is the vertical change?

New Vocabulary • line symmetry • line of symmetry • reflection • line of reflection

 Interactive lesson includes instant self-check, tutorials, and activities.

OBJECTIVE 1 Identifying Lines of Symmetry

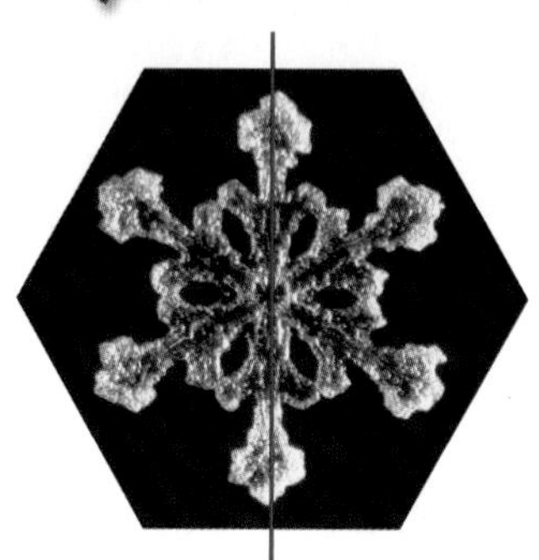

Snowflakes form when water vapor freezes. Snowflakes are symmetrical.

A figure has **line symmetry** if a line can be drawn through the figure so that one side is a mirror image of the other. A **line of symmetry,** such as the red line drawn through the snowflake, divides a figure into mirror images. If you fold along the red line, one side of the snowflake fits exactly onto the other side of the snowflake. Some objects have more than one line of symmetry.

1 EXAMPLE Lines of Symmetry

Photography Line symmetry can be found in works of art and in nature. Identify the lines of symmetry in each photograph.

a.

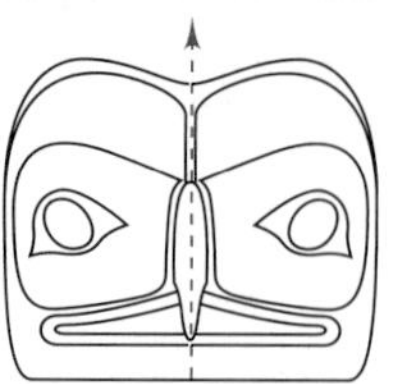

one line of symmetry

b.

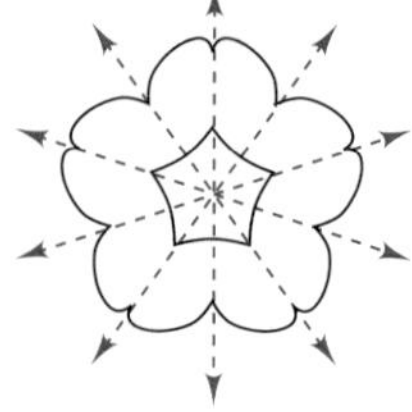

five lines of symmetry

✔ Check Understanding **1** Trace the figure and draw the line(s) of symmetry. If there are no lines of symmetry, write *none*.

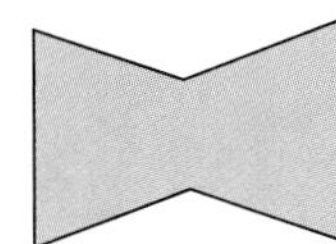

OBJECTIVE

2 Graphing Reflections

A **reflection** is a transformation that flips a figure over a line called a **line of reflection.** When a figure is reflected, the image is congruent to the original.

2 EXAMPLE Reflecting a Point

Graph the point $A(2, -3)$ and its reflection over the indicated axis. Write the coordinates of the reflected point.

a. y-axis **b.** x-axis

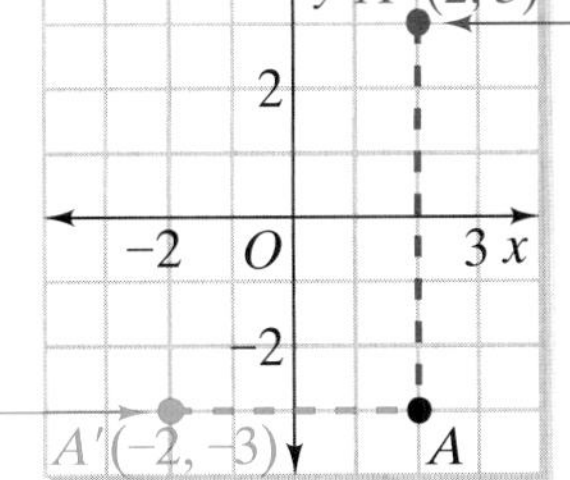

b. A is 3 units below the x-axis, so A'' is 3 units above the x-axis.

a. A is 2 units to the right of the y-axis, so A' is 2 units to the left of the y-axis.

✔ Check Understanding **2** Graph $C(-1, 2)$ and its reflection over the indicated axis. Write the coordinates of the reflected point.

a. x-axis **b.** y-axis

3 EXAMPLE Graphing a Reflection

Graph the reflection of $\triangle ABC$ over the y-axis. Use arrow notation to describe the original triangle and its reflection.

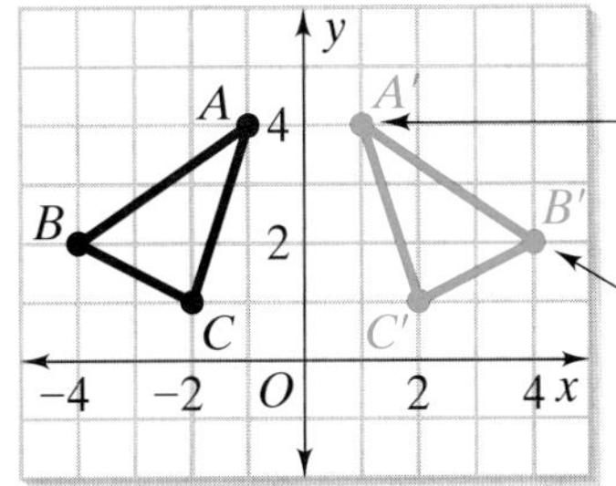

Since A is 1 unit to the left of the y-axis A' is 1 unit to the right of the y-axis.

Reflect the other vertices. Draw $\triangle A'B'C'$.

$A(-1, 4), B(-4, 2), C(-2, 1) \rightarrow A'(1, 4), B'(4, 2), C'(2, 1)$

✔ Check Understanding **3** **a.** Graph $\triangle ABC$ and its reflection over the x-axis. Use arrow notation to describe the original triangle and its reflection.

b. **Number Sense** What do you notice about the x- and y-coordinates of each vertex of $\triangle ABC$ and its reflected image?

EXERCISES

For more practice, see *Extra Practice*.

A Practice by Example

Example 1 (page 554)

Trace each figure and draw the line(s) of symmetry. If there are no lines of symmetry, write *none*.

1. **2.**  **3.** **4.**

Example 2 (page 555)

Graph each point and its reflection over the indicated axis. Write the coordinates of the reflected point.

5. (3, 8), x-axis

6. (−5, 7), y-axis

7. (−3, −6), x-axis

8. (5, −3), y-axis

9. (9, 3), y-axis

10. (−7, −1), x-axis

11. (2, 0), y-axis

12. (0, −4), x-axis

13. (−4, 3), x-axis

14. (2, −6), y-axis

Example 3 (page 555)

$\triangle A'B'C'$ is a reflection of $\triangle ABC$ over the y-axis. Complete each statement.

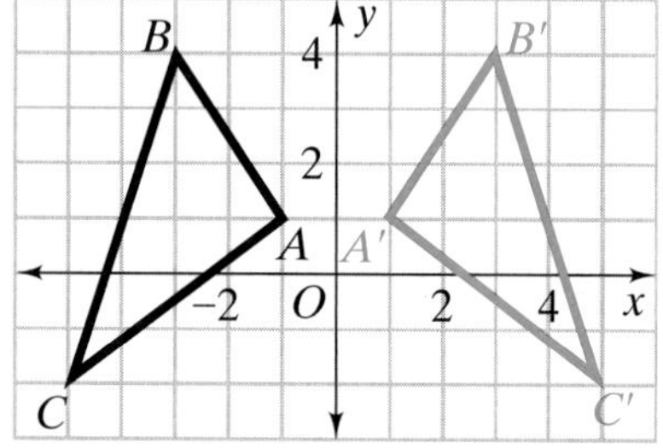

15. $A(-1, 1) \rightarrow A'(■, ■)$

16. $B(-3, 4) \rightarrow B'(■, ■)$

17. $C(-5, -2) \rightarrow C'(■, ■)$

18. Graph $\triangle ABC$ from Exercises 15–17. Then graph its reflection over the x-axis. Use arrow notation to describe the original triangle and its reflection.

19. The graph of $\square ABCD$ has vertices at $A(-3, 3)$, $B(-1, 3)$, $C(-1, -1)$, and $D(-3, -1)$. Graph $\square ABCD$ and its reflection over the y-axis. Use arrow notation to describe the original rectangle and its reflection.

B Apply Your Skills

20. **Writing in Math** $\triangle WXY$ has vertices $W(-4, -2)$, $X(4, 2)$, and $Y(1, -4)$. Its image $\triangle W'X'Y'$ has vertices $W'(-4, 2)$, $X'(4, -2)$, and $Y'(1, 4)$. Over which axis is $\triangle WXY$ reflected? Explain.

21. **Open-Ended** Name four capital letters of the alphabet that are symmetrical. Write the letters and show the line(s) of symmetry.

Use the graph at the left for Exercises 22–24.

22. For which two points is the x-axis the line of reflection?

23. For which two points is the y-axis the line of reflection?

24. Point C is *not* the reflection of point E over the x-axis. Explain why.

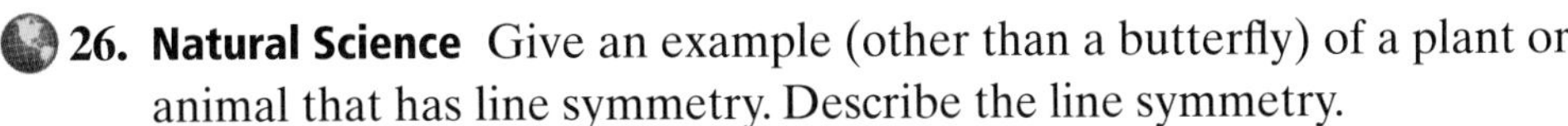

25. **Error Analysis** Your friend says that reflecting a point across the y-axis means multiplying its y-coordinate by -1 and keeping its x-coordinate the same. Explain why your friend is wrong.

Real-World Connection

Animals with symmetry usually have external body parts that repeat on either side of the body.

26. **Natural Science** Give an example (other than a butterfly) of a plant or animal that has line symmetry. Describe the line symmetry.

Tell whether the graph shows a reflection or a translation. Name the line of reflection or describe the translation using arrow notation.

27.

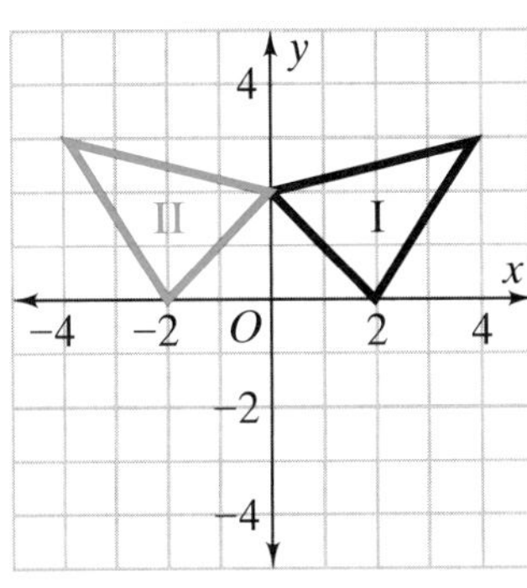

28.

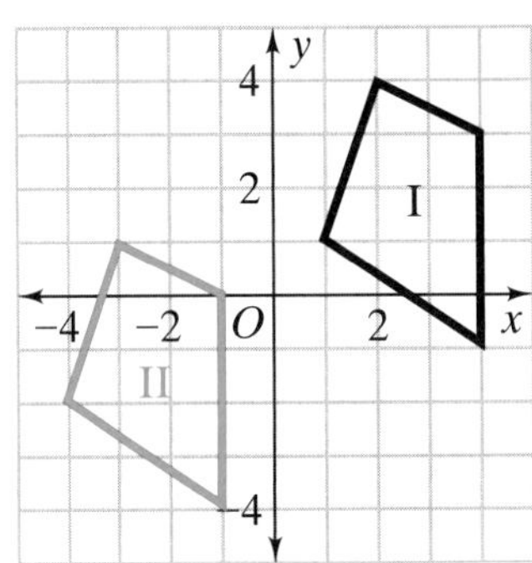

29.

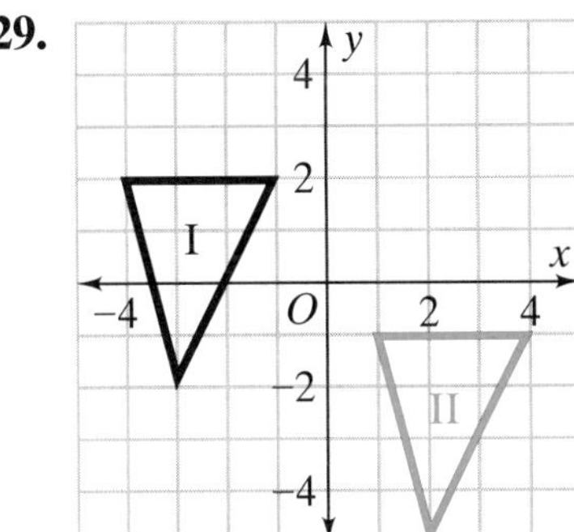

30.

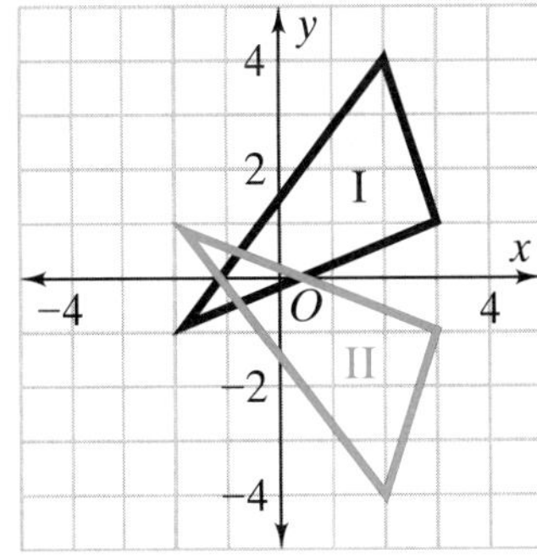

Mental Math **Without graphing, name the coordinates of the point's image after it is reflected over the x- and y-axes.**

31. $(3, -1)$ **32.** $(-3, -4)$ **33.** $(2, 1)$ **34.** $(7, 2)$

35. $(0, -2)$ **36.** $(3, 0)$ **37.** $(-4, -3)$ **38.** $(-5, 4)$

C Challenge

39. **a.** The vertices of $\triangle LMN$ are $L(0, 0)$, $M(0, 5)$, and $N(4, 0)$. Graph $\triangle LMN$ on a coordinate plane.
b. Graph the reflection of $\triangle LMN$ over the x-axis.
c. Use $\triangle LMN$ and its image. Reflect both triangles over the y-axis.
d. Outline the perimeter of the figure formed by the four triangles. What type of polygon is formed?

40. **a.** Graph the line $y = -2x$ and its reflection over the y-axis.
b. What is the slope of the image line? How is it related to the slope of the original line?

41. **Stretch Your Thinking** You arrange the numbers 2, 3, 4, and 5, one plus sign, and one equal sign into a true equation. What is your equation?

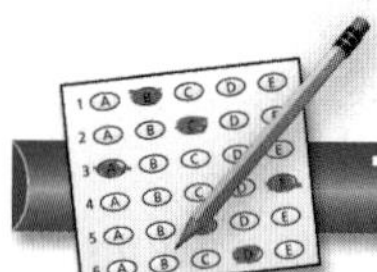

Test Prep

Multiple Choice

42. Which word has a line of symmetry?
A. CODE **B.** BOY **C.** EXIT **D.** FOOD

43. What are the coordinates of the image point when (7, −5) is reflected across the *y*-axis?
F. (−7, 5) **G.** (−7, −5) **H.** (7, 5) **I.** (7, −5)

Take It to the NET
Online lesson quiz at **www.PHSchool.com**
Web Code: aba-1007

44. How many lines of symmetry does a square have?
A. 3 **B.** 4 **C.** 5 **D.** 6

Extended Response

45. $\triangle BCD$ has vertices $B(-4, -3)$, $C(6, -3)$, and $D(-1, 4)$. Graph $\triangle BCD$ and its reflection over the *y*-axis. Then find the areas of $\triangle BCD$ and its image.

Mixed Review

Lesson 4-6

Algebra **Solve each equation.**

46. $p - 5\frac{3}{4} = 10$ **47.** $\frac{1}{2}x - 11 = 19$ **48.** $\frac{3}{5}s = 20$

49. $4 + \frac{1}{2}b = 11$ **50.** $m + 4\frac{2}{3} = 15$ **51.** $\frac{8}{2}x = 12$

Lesson 2-9

Algebra **Solve each inequality. Graph the solution.**

52. $7 + x \geq 9$ **53.** $-5 \leq x - 6$ **54.** $0 \geq z + 12$

Checkpoint Quiz 2 — Lessons 10-4 through 10-7

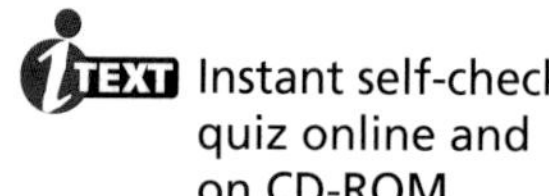

Instant self-check quiz online and on CD-ROM

Graph each equation.

1. $y = 3x^2$ **2.** $y = |x| - 2$ **3.** $y = 2x^2 + 3$

4. Money For your birthday you are given \$150. After three weeks you have \$120. Two weeks after that, you have \$100. If the amount that you spend each week remains constant, how much will you have 10 weeks after your birthday?

Translate each point right 3 units and up 7 units. Give the coordinates of the image point.

5. (−6, 2) **6.** (9, −1) **7.** (0, −7) **8.** (−2, −3)

Graph each point and its reflection across the indicated axis. Write the coordinates of the reflected point.

9. (−3, 1) across the *y*-axis **10.** (6, −4) across the *x*-axis

10-8 Rotations

What You'll Learn

 To identify rotational symmetry

 To rotate a figure about a point

. . . And Why

To identify symmetry in designs, as in Example 2

For help, go to Lesson 7-2.

Draw an angle for each measure. Then classify each angle as *acute*, *right*, *obtuse*, or *straight*.

1. 60°   **2.** 120°   **3.** 90°   **4.** 180°

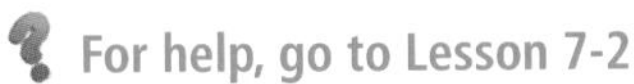

New Vocabulary • rotation • center of rotation • rotational symmetry • angle of rotation

OBJECTIVE

Interactive lesson includes instant self-check, tutorials, and activities.

1 Identifying Rotational Symmetry

Reading Math

Counterclockwise means the opposite of the direction a clock's hands move.

The blades of this windmill revolve counterclockwise. One full turn of 360° brings a blade back to its original position.

A **rotation** is a transformation that turns a figure about a fixed point called the **center of rotation.** In this book, all rotations are counterclockwise. If you rotate point A about point O, the image is A' for a 90° rotation, A'' for a 180° rotation, and A''' for a 270° rotation.

A figure has **rotational symmetry** if it can be rotated 180° or less and match the original figure. In the photo, the windmill blades show rotational symmetry of 90° and 180°.

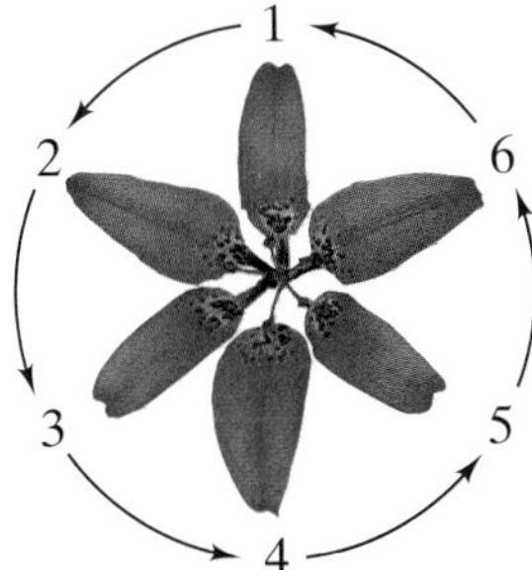

1 EXAMPLE Rotational Symmetry

Nature Does the flower have rotational symmetry?

To determine whether the flower has rotational symmetry, rotate petal 1 to the position of each of the other petals.

The flower looks the same at each position, so it has rotational symmetry.

Check Understanding **1** Does each figure have rotational symmetry? Explain.

a.

b.

When a figure has rotational symmetry, the angle measure that it rotates is the **angle of rotation.**

2 EXAMPLE Real-World Problem Solving

Design Does the wheel have rotational symmetry? If so, find the angle of rotation.

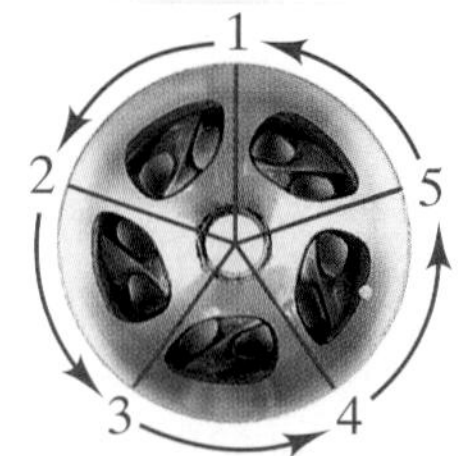

The wheel matches itself in 5 positions, so it has rotational symmetry. The angle of rotation is $360° \div 5$, or $72°$.

Check Understanding 2 **a.** Does the figure have rotational symmetry? If it does, find the angle of rotation.

b. Error Analysis Your friend believes that if the size of the wheel in Example 2 is doubled, then the angle of rotation also doubles. Explain why your friend is incorrect.

OBJECTIVE

2 Rotating a Figure About a Point

In the figure, $\triangle RSO$ has rotated $90°$ about point O. The center of rotation is point O. The image of $\triangle RSO$ is $\triangle R'S'O'$.

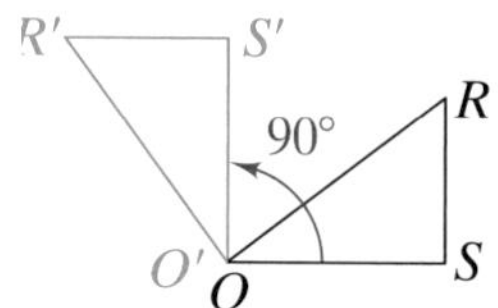

3 EXAMPLE Drawing Rotated Images

Draw the image of $\triangle RSO$ after each rotation.

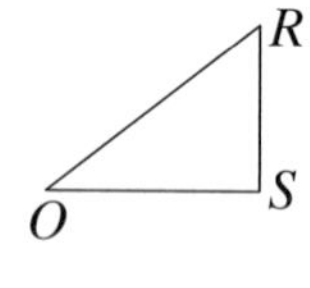

a. $180°$ about O

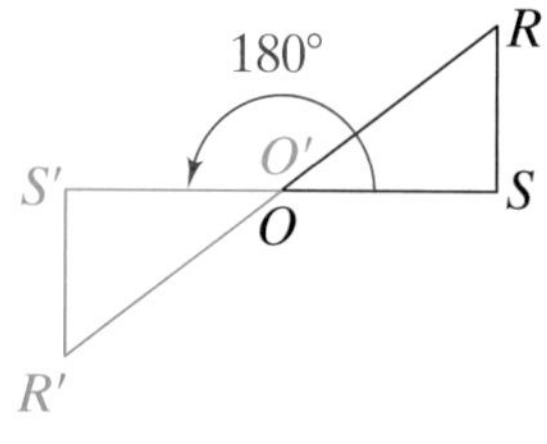

b. $270°$ about O

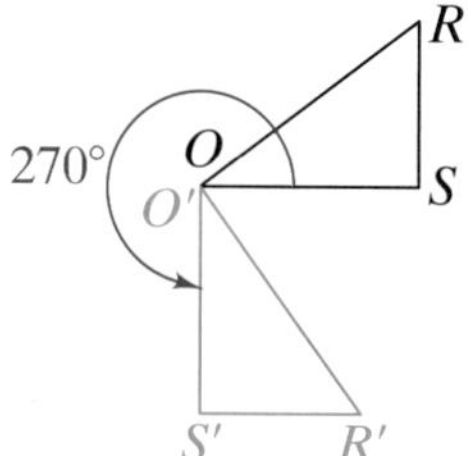

Check Understanding 3 **a.** Copy the figure at the right. Draw its image after a rotation of $90°$ about point O.

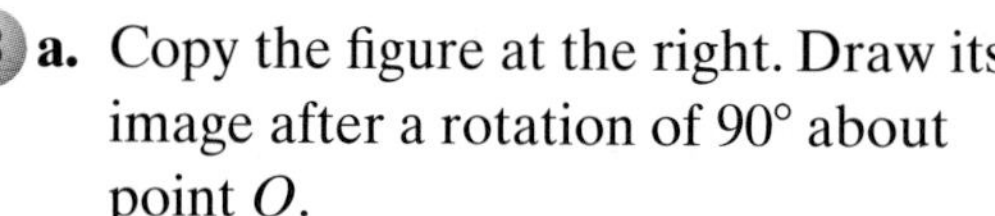

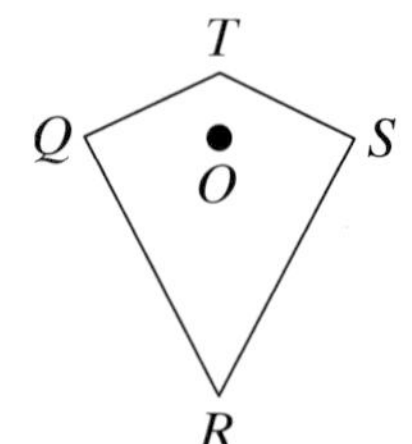

b. Number Sense What degree rotation would rotate the figure so that it is upside down? So that it returns to its original position?

EXERCISES

For more practice, see *Extra Practice*.

Practice by Example

Example 1 (page 559)

Does each figure have rotational symmetry?

1. 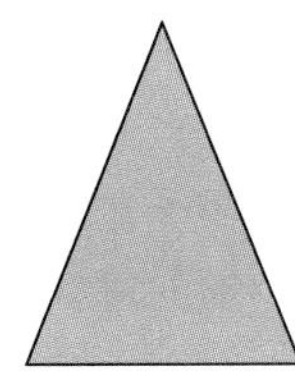

2. 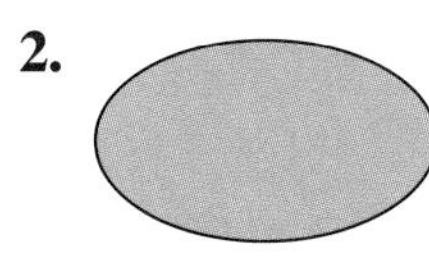

3. 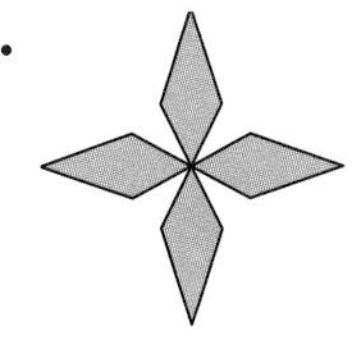

Example 2 (page 560)

Does each figure have rotational symmetry? If it does, find the angle of rotation.

4. 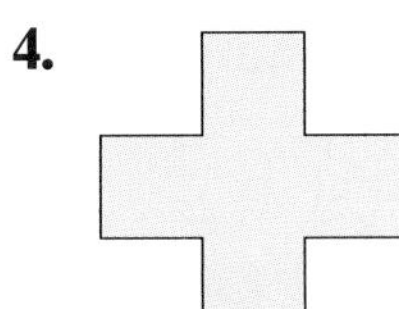

5. 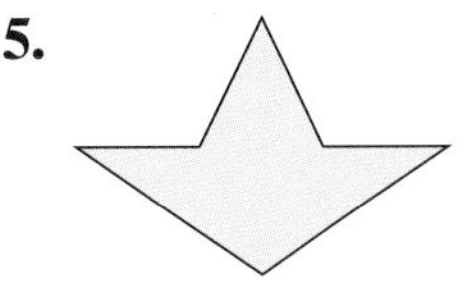

6. 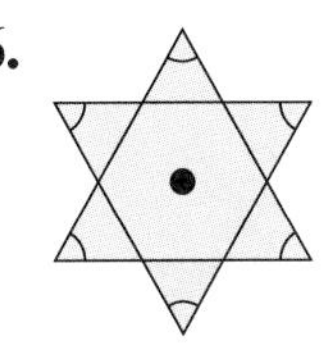

Example 3 (page 560)

Copy each figure. Draw the image of each figure after rotations of 90°, 180°, and 270° about point O.

7. 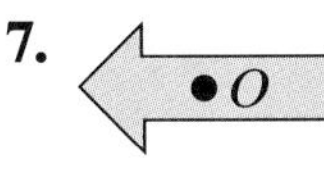

8. 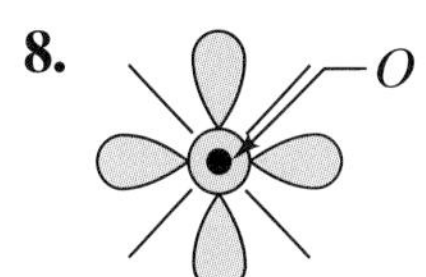

9. 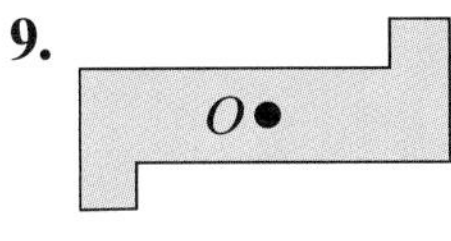

B Apply Your Skills

10. Draw rectangle $ABCD$ with vertices at $A(0, 0)$, $B(0, 2)$, $C(4, 2)$, and $D(4, 0)$. Then draw three images formed by rotating the rectangle 90°, 180°, and 270° about the rectangle's center.

11. Writing in Math Describe an object in your classroom that has rotational symmetry. Explain how it shows rotational symmetry.

12. **Clocks** The second hand of a clock makes a full revolution once every minute. What is its angle of rotation after 20 seconds? After 45 seconds?

Figure II is an image of Figure I. Identify each transformation as a translation, a reflection, or a rotation.

13. 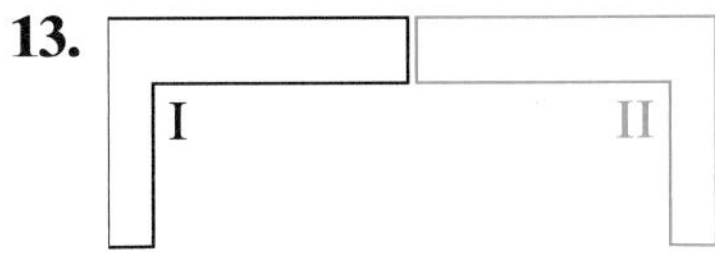

14. 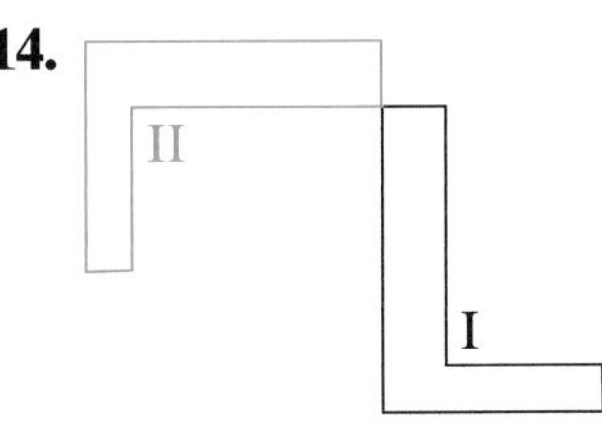

Mental Math **A triangle lies entirely in Quadrant I. In which quadrant will the triangle lie after each rotation about (0, 0)?**

15. 270°

16. 90°

17. 180°

18. a. What rotation will move point A to point B? Point A to point C? Point A to point D?
b. Does the square have rotational symmetry? Explain.

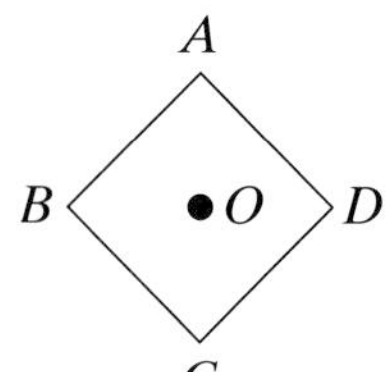

19. **Open-Ended** Draw a capital letter of the alphabet that has rotational symmetry. Indicate the center of rotation.

Graph each point. Then rotate it the given number of degrees about the origin. Give the coordinates of the image.

20. $E(-6, -2)$; 180° 21. $F(-2, 0)$; 270° 22. $G(6, 5)$; 90°

23. **Stretch Your Thinking** A car has wheels with a diameter of 3 ft. About how many miles per hour is the car traveling if the wheels are turning about 600 revolutions per minute?

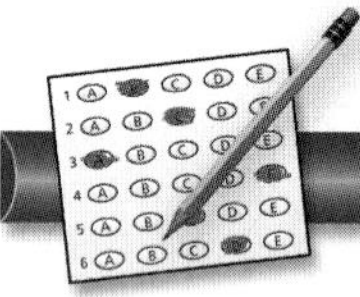

Test Prep

Multiple Choice

24. Which letter does NOT have 180° rotational symmetry?
A. M B. H C. I D. X

25. Which figure is NOT a rotation of the other figures?
F. 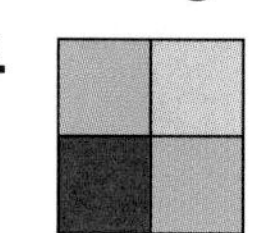 G. 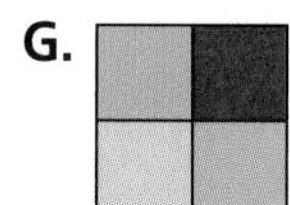 H. 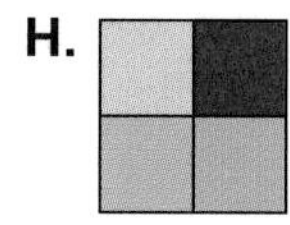 I. 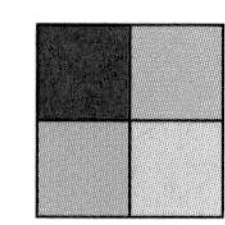

Take It to the NET
Online lesson quiz at
www.PHSchool.com
Web Code: aba-1008

26. Which of the following movements describes a figure that has been moved 270° counterclockwise about a point?
A. translation B. symmetry C. reflection D. rotation

Extended Response

27. $P(5, 6)$ is rotated 90°, 180°, and 270° about the origin. Give the coordinates of each image. Show your work.

Mixed Review

Lesson 6-6

Algebra **Write and solve an equation to find the part of a whole.**

28. 78% of 40 is what number?
29. What is 80% of 20?
30. What number is 40% of 60?
31. 25% of 110 is what number?
32. 62% of 200 is what number?
33. What is 90% of 1,000?

Lesson 1-3

Find each product.

34. $3.7 \cdot 19.8$ 35. $2.9 \cdot 13.82$ 36. $12.14 \cdot 8$ 37. $3.0 \cdot 5.18$
38. $0.25 \cdot 1.5$ 39. $3.56 \cdot 2.5$ 40. $10.2 \cdot 20.1$ 41. $0.75 \cdot 10$

Answering True/False Questions

True/false questions give statements that must be entirely true. Otherwise, the statement is false. When words such as *all*, *always*, *none*, and *never* are used, the statement may be true for many cases, and false for just one.

1 EXAMPLE

True or false? The graphs of $y = 2x - 1$ and $y = -x + 3$ never intersect.

For the statement to be true, the graphs of the equations would have to be parallel. Draw the graphs.

y = 2x − 1

x	y
−1	−3
0	−1
1	1

y = −x + 3

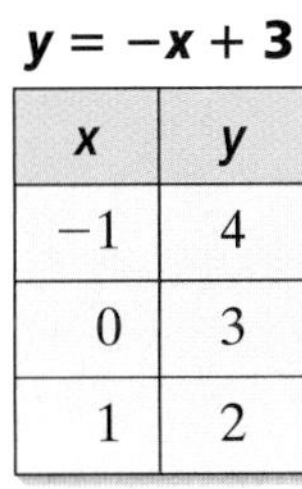

x	y
−1	4
0	3
1	2

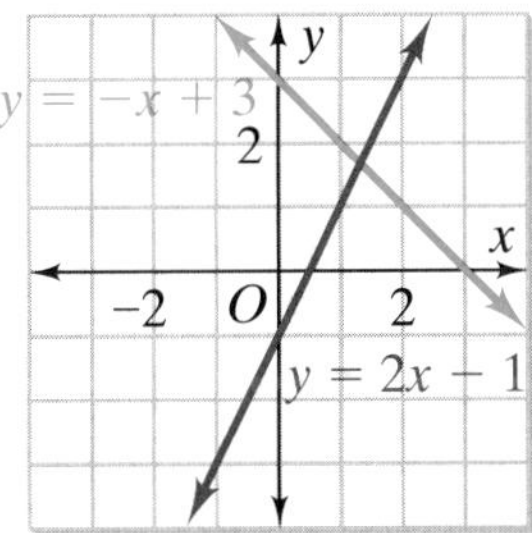

The graphs do intersect at one point. Since the statement uses the word *never,* it is false.

2 EXAMPLE

True or false? The reflection of any point with the coordinates (a, b) over the x-axis and then the y-axis is $(-a, -b)$.

Since the statement uses the word *any*, you should try a few different test values, for example, $A(-2, 1)$, $B(3, 2)$, and $C(-4, -4)$.

$A(-2, 1) \rightarrow A'(-2, -1) \rightarrow A''(2, -1)$

$B(3, 2) \rightarrow B'(3, -2) \rightarrow B''(-3, -2)$

$C(-4, -4) \rightarrow C'(-4, 4) \rightarrow C''(4, 4)$.

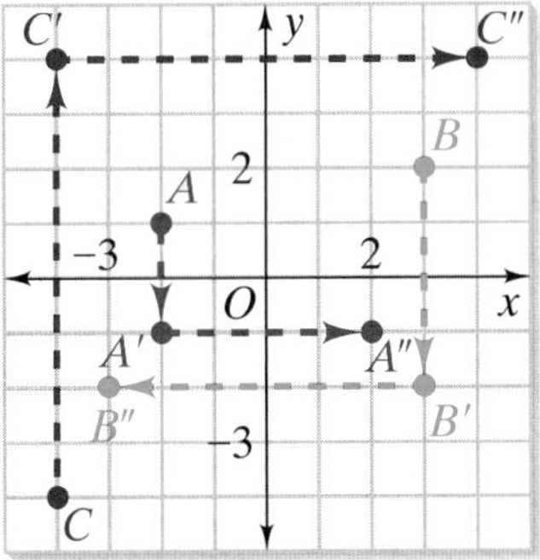

For each value $(a, b) \rightarrow (-a, -b)$. According to the test values, the statement is true.

EXERCISES

Determine whether each statement is *true* or *false*. Explain your reasoning.

1. None of the points on the graph of $y = x^2$ are in Quadrants III or IV.
2. The graphs of $y = 2x - 3$ and $y = 2x + 7$ intersect.
3. The graph of $y = |x|$ always has a slope of 1.

Chapter Review

Vocabulary

angle of rotation (p. 560)
center of rotation (p. 559)
coordinate plane (p. 521)
graph of an equation (p. 528)
horizontal (p. 523)
image (p. 549)
line of reflection (p. 555)
line of symmetry (p. 554)
linear equation (p. 528)
line symmetry (p. 554)
nonlinear equation (p. 540)
ordered pair (*x*, *y*) (p. 521)
origin (p. 521)
prime notation (p. 549)
quadrants (p. 522)
reflection (p. 555)
rise (p. 533)
rotation (p. 559)
rotational symmetry (p. 559)
run (p.533)
slope (p. 533)
transformation (p. 549)
translation (p. 549)
vertical (p. 523)
***x*-axis** (p. 521)
***x*-coordinate** (p. 521)
***y*-axis** (p. 521)
***y*-coordinate** (p. 521)

Reading Math: Understanding Vocabulary

Choose the correct term to complete each sentence.

1. A flip over a line is a (translation, reflection).
2. A rotation turns a figure about a fixed point called the (center of rotation, angle of rotation).
3. Slope compares the vertical change, called the (rise, run), to the horizontal change, called the (rise, run).
4. The second number in a(n) (coordinate plane, ordered pair) is the y-coordinate.
5. If a graph of the solutions of an equation is a line, then the equation is a (linear equation, nonlinear equation).

Take It to the NET
Online vocabulary quiz at **www.PHSchool.com**
Web Code: abj-1051

Skills and Concepts

10-1 and 10-2
Objectives

- To graph points on the coordinate plane
- To find ordered pairs that are solutions of linear equations
- To graph linear equations

An **ordered pair (x, y)** gives the coordinates of a point. Any ordered pair that makes an equation true is a solution of the equation. The **graph of an equation** is the graph of all the points with coordinates that are solutions of the equation.

Graph the line containing each pair of points. Identify the line as horizontal or vertical.

6. $(5, 0), (-2, 0)$ **7.** $(-2, 5), (-2, -5)$ **8.** $(0, 3), (-2, 3)$

Find three solutions of each equation.

9. $y = x + 3$ **10.** $y = x - 5$ **11.** $y = 2x + 1$ **12.** $y = -x - 2$

Graph each linear equation.

13. $y = 4x + 2$ **14.** $y = -2x + 3$ **15.** $y = 3x - 1$ **16.** $y = \frac{1}{2}x + 2$

10-3, 10-4 and 10-5 Objectives

- To find and use the slope of a line
- To graph nonlinear equations
- To solve a problem by combining strategies

Slope is a ratio that describes the steepness of a line.

$$\text{slope} = \frac{\text{rise}}{\text{run}}$$

A **nonlinear equation** is an equation with a graph that is not a straight line.

Draw a line with the given slope through the given point.

17. $B(2, 4)$, slope $= 2$ **18.** $R(-1, 2)$, slope $= \frac{1}{3}$ **19.** $P(0, -3)$, slope $= 1$

Make a table of values for each equation. Use integer values of x from -3 to 3. Then graph the equation.

20. $y = x^2 - 1$ **21.** $y = |x| + 1$ **22.** $y = 2x^2 - 2$ **23.** $y = 4|x|$

24. Sports You are training for the cross-country team. The coach recommends that you run 20 mi the first week and 24 mi the third week. By the tenth week, you should be running 38 mi each week. If the number of miles you are running each week increases at a constant rate, how many miles will you run during the sixth week?

10-6, 10-7, and 10-8 Objectives

- To graph translations
- To write rules for translations
- To identify lines of symmetry
- To graph reflections
- To identify rotational symmetry
- To rotate a figure about a point

A **transformation** is the change of the position, shape, or size of a figure. A **translation** is a transformation that moves every point of a figure the same distance and in the same direction.

A figure has **line symmetry** when one side of the figure is a mirror image of the other side. A **reflection** is a transformation that flips a figure over a line.

A **rotation** is a transformation that turns a figure about a fixed point.

Graph each transformation of $\triangle ABC$. Use arrow notation to show the translation.

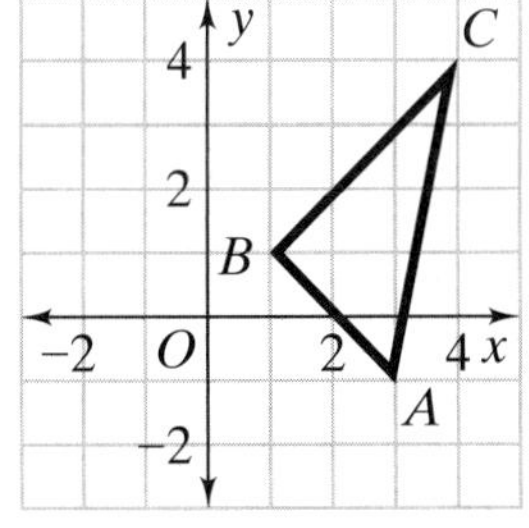

25. down 2 units **26.** left 3 units

27. right 3 units and down 5 units

28. Graph $\triangle ABC$ from Exercises 25–27. Then graph its reflection over the x-axis. Use arrow notation to describe the transformation.

Does each figure have rotational symmetry? If it does, find the angle of rotation.

29.

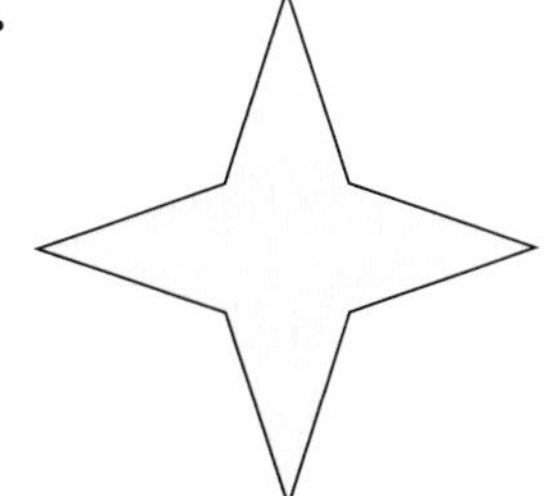

30.

Chapter 10

Chapter Test

Take It to the NET
Online chapter test at
www.PHSchool.com
Web Code: aba-1052

Graph each point on the same coordinate plane.

1. $A(1, 4)$
2. $B(-2, -1)$
3. $C(3, -2)$
4. $D(-3, 2)$

Graph the line containing each pair of points. Identify the line as vertical or horizontal.

5. $(2, -1), (-3, -1)$
6. $(2, 5), (2, -5)$

Determine whether each ordered pair is a solution of $y = -2x + 5$.

7. $(3, -5)$
8. $(2.5, 0)$
9. $(4, -3)$
10. $(0, 5)$

Graph each linear equation.

11. $y = x - 3$
12. $y = 3x + 1$
13. $y = -x + 2$
14. $y = 2x - 4$

Graph each pair of points. Determine the slope of the line through the points.

15. $E(7, 1), F(-3, 3)$
16. $G(-2, 6), H(0, 0)$
17. $L(-4, 0), M(0, 2)$
18. $S(8, 5), T(1, -1)$

Draw a line with the given slope through the given point.

19. $P(-2, -1)$, slope $\frac{1}{4}$
20. $R(2, 4)$, slope $-\frac{2}{3}$

Graph each equation for integer values of x from -3 to 3.

21. $y = x^2 - 2$
22. $y = 2|x| + 1$

23. **Advertising** To advertise in the classifieds of a local paper costs \$2 plus \$.25 for each word. Make a table to graph the equation $y = 0.25x + 2$, where x is the number of words and y is the total cost.

24. Draw the images of the triangle after rotations of 90°, 180°, and 270° about O.

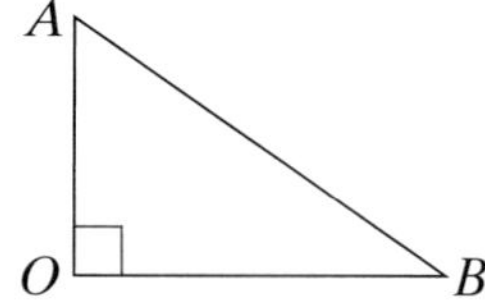

The graph of $\triangle ABC$ has vertices at $A(1, 3)$, $B(5, 8)$, and $C(7, 1)$. Graph each image of $\triangle ABC$ for the transformation described. Use arrow notation to show the transformation.

25. translated right 1 unit and down 3 units
26. translated left 3 units and up 2 units
27. reflected over the y-axis

Write a rule for the translation shown in each graph.

28. 

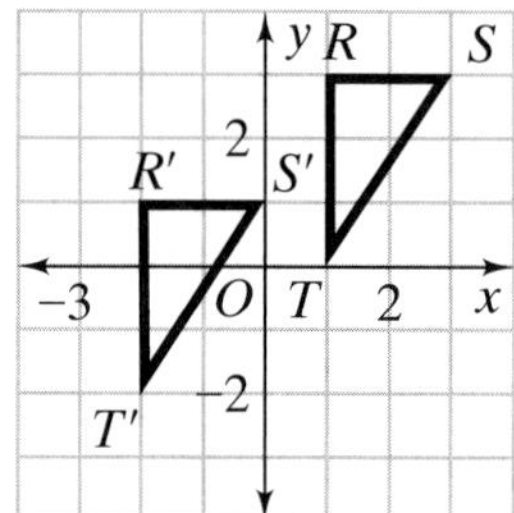

29. 

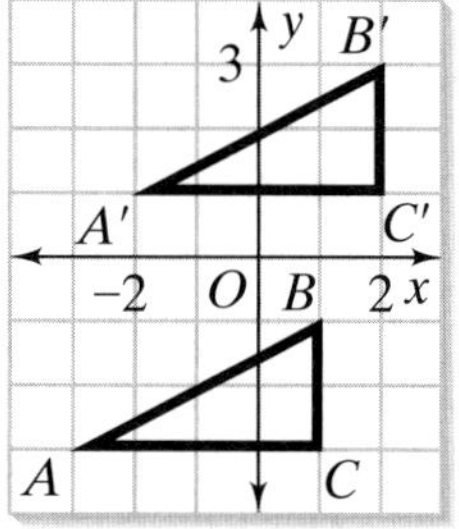

Use the two figures below for Exercises 30 and 31.

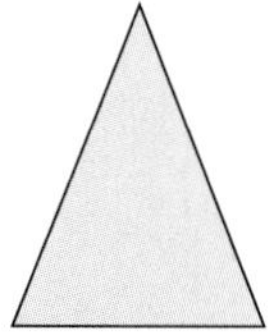

30. Trace each figure and draw the line(s) of symmetry. If there are no lines of symmetry, write *none*.

31. Does each figure have rotational symmetry? If it does, what is the angle of rotation?

32. **Writing in Math** Give an example of a rotation, a reflection, and a translation you might see in the real world.

Test Prep

CUMULATIVE REVIEW
CHAPTERS 1–10

Multiple Choice

Choose the correct letter.

1. Which rule best describes the function in the table?

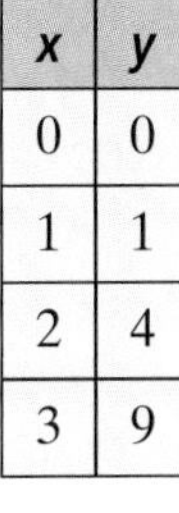

x	y
0	0
1	1
2	4
3	9

A. $y = x + 2$
B. $y = x$
C. $y = 2x$
D. $y = x^2$

2. A bus company charges $10.50 per ticket. It costs the company $200 to run the bus. Which equation describes this situation?
F. $P = 10.5x + 200$
G. $P = 10.5x - 200$
H. $P = 200x + 10.5$
I. $P = 10.5 + x - 200$

3. A muffin recipe calls for $2\frac{1}{4}$ c of flour and makes 12 muffins. How many muffins can you make with 6 c of flour?
A. 24 **B.** 30 **C.** 32 **D.** 45

4. What is the ones digit of 7^{23}?
F. 3 **G.** 5 **H.** 7 **I.** 9

5. For which linear equation is $(-3, 0.5)$ NOT a solution?
A. $x - 2y = 4$ **B.** $4y = 3x + 11$
C. $x = -6y$ **D.** $x + 6y = 0$

6. A bag of 15 lemons costs $2.30. What is the approximate unit price of a lemon?
F. $.075 **G.** $.13
H. $.15 **I.** $.30

7. Which translation moves $\triangle ABC$ to $\triangle A'B'C'$?

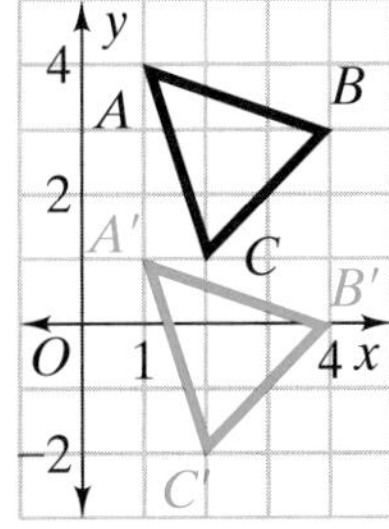

A. $(x, y) \rightarrow (x - 3, y)$
B. $(x, y) \rightarrow (x + 3, y)$
C. $(x, y) \rightarrow (x, y - 3)$
D. $(x, y) \rightarrow (x, y + 3)$

8. Order the numbers 0.361×10^7, 4.22×10^7, and 13.5×10^6 from least to greatest.
F. 13.5×10^6, 0.361×10^7, 4.22×10^7
G. 4.22×10^7, 13.5×10^6, 0.361×10^7
H. 0.361×10^7, 13.5×10^6, 4.22×10^7
I. 13.5×10^6, 4.22×10^7, 0.361×10^7

9. Of 26 letters in the alphabet, 5 are vowels. What percent are vowels?
A. about 19% **B.** about 21%
C. about 30% **D.** about 33%

10. Which expression has the greatest value?
F. $\frac{3}{4}(8)$ **G.** $2 \cdot 3.3$ **H.** 23 **I.** $\frac{2}{3} \cdot \frac{6}{5}$

11. A map of a city has a scale of 2 in. : $\frac{1}{2}$ mi. The distance on the map from the school to your house is $5\frac{1}{2}$ in. What is the actual distance?
A. $13\frac{3}{4}$ mi **B.** 11 mi **C.** $5\frac{1}{2}$ mi **D.** $1\frac{3}{8}$ mi

Gridded Response

12. What is the next term in this pattern?
500, 250, 125, . . .

13. Find the circumference in centimeters of a circle with a radius of 5 cm. Use 3.14 for π.

Short Response

14. A right triangle has legs of 12 ft and 16 ft. Find the longest side of the triangle.

15. A rectangular yard has a perimeter of 96 ft. To support a fence, 12 posts will be placed at equal intervals. How far apart are the posts?

Extended Response

16. You paid $385 for car repairs. The garage charged $125 for parts and $65 per hour for labor. Write and solve an equation to find the number of hours the mechanic worked on your car. Show your work.

Real-World Snapshots

On Your Mark!

Applying Coordinates Do you remember the great pod-racing scene in *Star Wars Episode 1*? The racers built their own Pod-racers, so each one looked and flew differently. Some Pod-racers got off to a fast start, but couldn't maintain their speed. Others started out slowly, then sped up. To build a winning Pod-racer, you'd want to know the length of the race, so you could choose the best engine.

Anakin Skywalker's control pod with cockpit computer

The ring rotates for stability, keeping the pod upright.

Put It All Together

Suppose you are designing a pod for the big race. You have four engines to choose from. Each performs differently. The table shows test results for each engine recorded at ten checkpoints around the track.

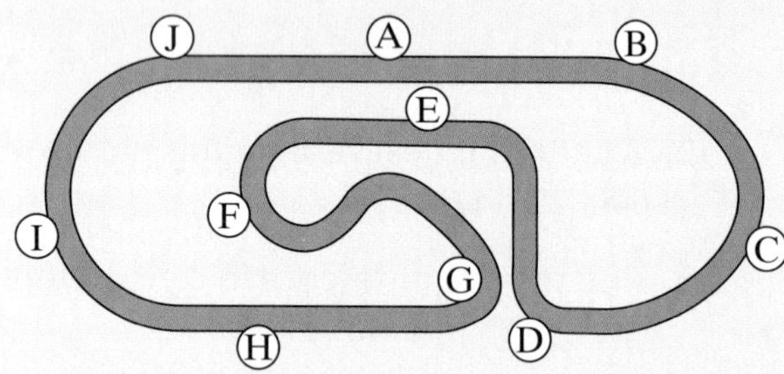

1. Make a graph, labeling the x-axis from 0 to 900 s, and the y-axis from 0 to 4,000 m. Plot the time–distance points for each of the four engines. (*Hint:* Use a different color for each engine.)
2. **a.** Connect the points for each engine.
   b. How are the graphs for the engines similar? How are they different?
3. **a.** Which engine starts a pod at the fastest speed?
   b. Which engine starts a pod at the slowest speed?
   c. Which two engines move the pod at a constant speed?
   d. Which engines speed up or slow down during the race?
   e. Which engine makes the pod go fastest at the end of 4,000 m?
4. **Reasoning** Suppose the big race is 2,000 m long. Which engine would you choose to complete the course the fastest? Would your answer change if the race were 3,000 m? Explain.

Anakin's fuel atomizer and distribution system make his engines perform better than some larger engines.

Anakin's Pod-racer

Each of the two Radon-Ulzer 620C racing engines, modified by Anakin Skywalker, is 7 m long. The estimated top speed of the Pod-racer is 947 km/h.

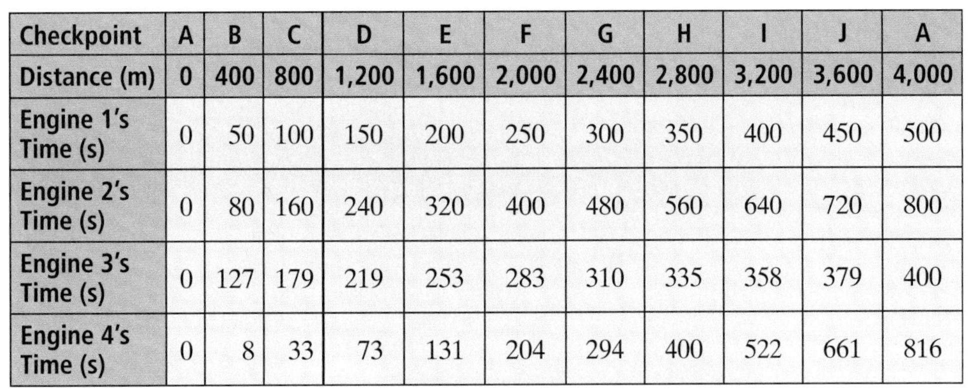

Checkpoint	A	B	C	D	E	F	G	H	I	J	A
Distance (m)	0	400	800	1,200	1,600	2,000	2,400	2,800	3,200	3,600	4,000
Engine 1's Time (s)	0	50	100	150	200	250	300	350	400	450	500
Engine 2's Time (s)	0	80	160	240	320	400	480	560	640	720	800
Engine 3's Time (s)	0	127	179	219	253	283	310	335	358	379	400
Engine 4's Time (s)	0	8	33	73	131	204	294	400	522	661	816

Take It to the NET For more information about flight, go to **www.PHSchool.com**.
Web Code: abe-1053

Energy binder arc

Anakin salvaged and rebuilt the engines.

Triple air scoops, or brakes, make it easier to control the Pod-racer around corners.

CHAPTER 11

Displaying and Analyzing Data

Lessons

11-1 Reporting Frequency

11-2 Spreadsheets and Data Displays

11-3 Other Displays

11-4 Problem Solving: Make a Table and Use Logical Reasoning

11-5 Random Samples and Surveys

11-6 Estimating Population Size

11-7 Using Data to Persuade

11-8 Exploring Scatter Plots

Key Vocabulary

- biased question (p. 597)
- box-and-whisker plot (p. 586)
- cell (p. 579)
- double bar graph (p. 580)
- double line graph (p. 580)
- frequency table (p. 573)
- histogram (p. 574)
- legend (p. 580)
- line plot (p. 573)
- negative trend (p. 614)
- no trend (p. 614)
- population (p. 596)
- positive trend (p. 614)
- random sample (p. 596)
- scatter plot (p. 613)
- spreadsheet (p. 579)

Real-World Snapshots

The bicycle is said to be the most efficient way yet devised to convert human energy into propulsion. In many countries, bicycles are a primary mode of transportation.

Data File Percent of Trips by Travel Mode

Country	Bicycle	Walking	Public Transit	Car	Other
Netherlands	30	18	5	45	2
Denmark	20	21	14	42	3
Switzerland	10	29	20	38	1
Sweden	10	39	11	36	4
Austria	9	31	13	39	8
Italy	5	28	16	42	9
Canada	1	10	14	74	1
United States	1	9	3	84	3

You will use the data above in this chapter:

- p. 588 Lesson 11-3
- p. 610 Lesson 11-7

Real-World Snapshots On pages 624 and 625, you will solve problems involving bicycles.

Chapter 11 Preview

Where You've Been

- In Chapter 1, you learned to calculate the mean, median, and mode of a set of data.
- In Chapter 10, you learned to graph points in the coordinate plane.

Where You're Going

- In Chapter 11, you will graph data using frequency tables, histograms, scatter plots, stem-and-leaf plots, and box-and-whisker plots. You will learn to interpret double bar graphs and double line graphs.
- You will learn to identify a random sample and write survey questions. You will learn to identify misleading graphs and statistics.
- Applying what you learn, you will identify biased survey questions.

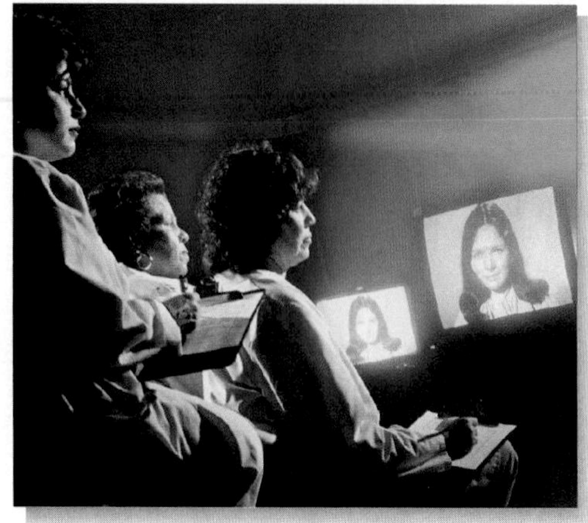

Television networks often renew or cancel series based on viewers' opinions.

Instant self-check online and on CD-ROM

Diagnosing Readiness

For help, go to the lesson in green.

Comparing Numbers (Lesson 1-6)

List the data in order from least to greatest.

1. 32, 31, 34, 30, 13, 33

2. 121, 119, 137, 125, 129

3. 11.1, 10.9, 11.3, 11.5, 10.2

4. $-4, -5, 0, -1, 2, -3$

Finding the Median of a Data Set (Lesson 1-10)

Find the median of each set of data.

5. 15, 9, 16, 12, 8, 10, 13

6. 27, 35, 24, 56, 29, 37

7. 55, 69, 112, 67, 32, 123, 45

8. 8.9, 8.5, 7.6, 8.4, 9.1, 8.5

Solving Proportions (Lesson 5-5)

Algebra Solve each proportion.

9. $\frac{3}{4} = \frac{a}{24}$

10. $\frac{2}{b} = \frac{3}{21}$

11. $\frac{n}{52} = \frac{17}{13}$

12. $\frac{12}{5} = \frac{a}{45}$

Graphing Points (Lesson 10-1)

Graph each point on the same coordinate plane.

13. $(-4, 7)$

14. $(0, -5)$

15. $(6, 3)$

16. $(2, 0)$

11-1 Reporting Frequency

What You'll Learn

To make a frequency table or line plot

To draw a histogram

. . . And Why

To show the distribution of data, as in Example 1

For help, go to Lesson 1-6.

List the data in order from least to greatest.

1. 23, 45, 61, 87, 91, 16, 22, 52
2. 4.1, 4.2, 4.13, 4.15, 4.3
3. 132, 116, 108, 191, 125, 132
4. 7.25, 7.3, 7.08, 7.9, 7.62

New Vocabulary • frequency table • line plot • histogram

OBJECTIVE 1

Interactive lesson includes instant self-check, tutorials, and activities.

Making a Frequency Table or Line Plot

A **frequency table** is a table that lists each item in a data set with the number of times the item occurs.

1 EXAMPLE Making a Frequency Table

Real-World Connection

For more information on the U.S. Constitution, go to **www.PHSchool.com**.
Web Code: abg-2041

Social Studies The Preamble to the U.S. Constitution begins: "We the People of the United States, in Order to form a more perfect Union . . ." The number of letters in each word of the Preamble is below.

2 3 6 2 3 6 6 2 5 2 4 1 4 7 5 9 7 6 8 11 7 3 3 6 7 7
3 7 7 3 6 3 9 2 7 2 9 3 3 9 2 6 3 9 4 12 3 3 6 6 2 7

Make a frequency table of the data.

Number of Letters in the Words of the Preamble

Number	1	2	3	4	5	6	7	8	9	10	11	12
Tally	/	~~////~~ ///	~~////~~ ~~////~~ //	///	//	~~////~~ ////	~~////~~ ////	/	~~////~~		/	/
Frequency	1	8	12	3	2	9	9	1	5	0	1	1

Check Understanding 1 The data below give the number of U. S. Representatives for 22 states. Make a frequency table of the data.

4 3 1 2 1 5 4 1 7 2 8 1 3 8 5 9 3 5 7 3 1 9

A **line plot** is a graph that shows the shape of a data set by stacking X's above each data value on a number line.

2 EXAMPLE Making a Line Plot

Make a line plot of the data in Example 1.

Number of Letters in Words of the Preamb e

1	2	3	4	5	6	7	8	9	10	11	12
X	XXXXXXXX	XXXXXXXXXXXX	XXX	XX	XXXXXXXXX	XXXXXXXXX	X	XXXXX		X	X

Write an *x* for each word above the number of letters in that word.

Draw a number line from the least to the greatest data item.

Check Understanding 2 **Reasoning** Use the line plot in Example 2 to find the mode of the data. How many words have this number of letters? Explain how you can tell.

OBJECTIVE 2

Drawing a Histogram

Reading Math

The *histo* in histogram is short for *history.*

A **histogram** is a bar graph with no spaces between the bars. The height of each bar shows the frequency of data within that interval. The intervals of a histogram are of equal size and do not overlap.

3 EXAMPLE Making a Histogram

Real World

Hobbies Make a histogram of the data in the frequency table.

How Many Baseball Cards Do You Have?

Number	15	16	17	18	19	20	21	22	23	24
Tally	~~IIII~~ I	I	III		II	IIII	I	IIII	~~IIII~~	III

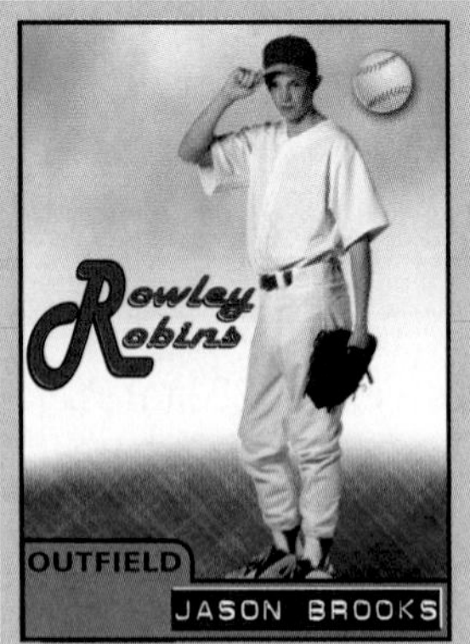

How Many Baseball Cards Do You Have? ← **Add a title.**

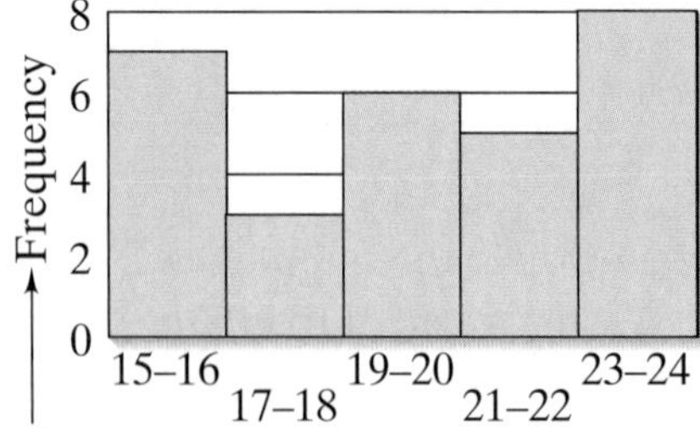

Label each axis. → Number of Baseball Cards

✓ Check Understanding **3** Find the difference between the greatest frequency and the least frequency in the histogram in Example 3.

More Than One Way

Use the table to make a data display.

Voting-Age Population Registered to Vote (percent)

State	Calif.	Fla.	Ga.	Ind.	Nev.	N.C.	Ore.	Tex.	Va.
Voters	52	59	62	62	47	63	66	59	60

Anna's Method

I can make a line plot. I'll use six intervals of 4.

Voting-Age Popu ation Registered to Vote (percent)

```
                 X     X
                 X     X
X     X          X     X     X
-----------------------------------
45–48    53–56    61–64
    49–52    57–60    65–68
```

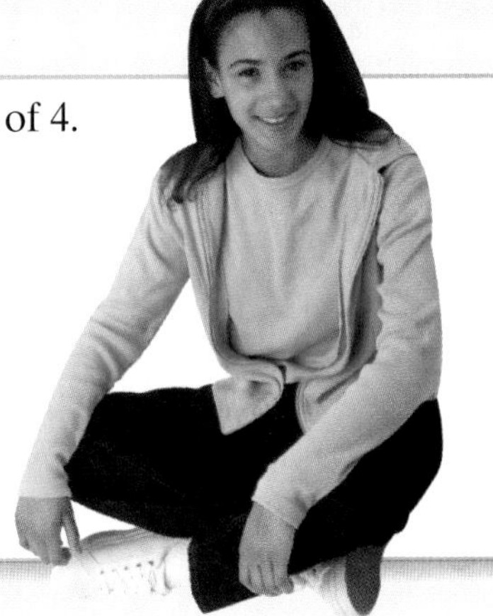

Chris's Method

I can make a histogram. I'll use five intervals of 5.

Voting-Age Population Registered to Vote (percent)

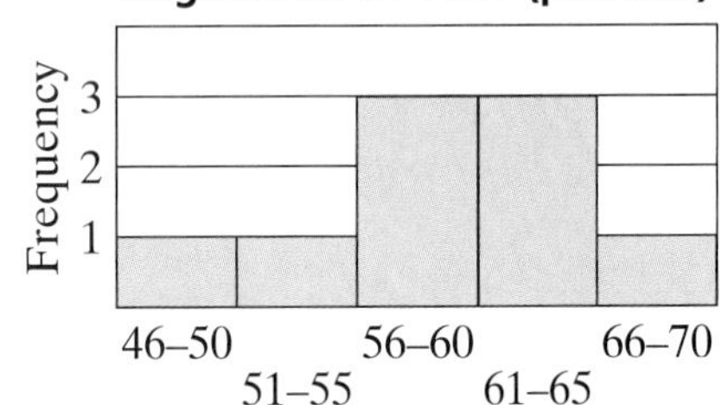

Choose a Method

Display the data in the table. Explain your choice of data display.

Number of Hours Worked per Week

Number	35	36	37	38	39	40	41	42	43	44
Tally	𝍸	|||	𝍸 ||	𝍸 ||	𝍸 |	𝍸 𝍸	|||	𝍸		|

Investigation: Collecting Data

1. **Survey** Ask each person in your class to select their favorite superhero from a list of ten. Use a table to record the responses.
2. Choose a method to display your results.

EXERCISES

For more practice, see *Extra Practice*.

A Practice by Example

Example 1 (page 573)

Make a frequency table of each set of data.

1. tickets sold per day
   45 48 51 53 50 46 46 50
   51 48 46 45 50 49 46
2. number of TVs per household
   1 3 2 2 1 4 1 2 2
   1 3 1 3 3 2 2 3 1
3. ages of students
   13 12 14 12 11 12 13 14 13 13 14 11 12 12 13 11 11
4. temperature in °F in June
   82 81 88 88 87 92 91 85 92 83 82 84 86 89 90
   87 86 84 83 84 87 86 90 91 87 86 80 84 91 90

Example 2 (page 574)

Make a line plot of each set of data.

5. number of plants sold per person
   5 10 11 8 7 11 9 8
   6 7 12 10 10 9 8 7 6
6. miles from home to shopping center
   2 4 10 5 4 6 7 9
   5 5 3 1 10 8 6 4 3
7. number of brothers and sisters
   1 3 4 2 2 1 3 1 0 2 0 1 3 4 2 1 0 1 2 0 3 4 2 5 2 6
8. blocks walked from home to school
   2 8 10 1 2 9 8 7 6 8 4 3 8 9 1 3 10 12 6 4 8

Example 3 (page 574)

Use each table to make a histogram.

9. **How Many Amusement Parks Did You Visit Last Year?**

Number of Parks	0–2	3–5	6–8	9–11
Frequency	10	4	3	1

10. **How Many Hours Do You Sleep Each Night?**

Number of Hours	5–6	7–8	9–10	11–12
Frequency	4	12	9	1

11. **How Many Meals Did You Eat Out Last Month?**

Number of Meals	0–3	4–7	8–11	12–15
Frequency	8	12	3	7

12. **How Many Pencils/Pens Are in Your Backpack?**

Number of Pencils/Pens	0–4	5–9	10–14	15–19
Frequency	6	13	7	4

B Apply Your Skills

13. **Books** The line plot shows the number of books each bookstore customer bought. How many customers bought more than three books?

14. Open-Ended Choose a nursery rhyme. Write the number of letters in each word. Make a line plot of the data.

Number of Books Purchased

5:30	6:45	5:45	6:15
6:25	6:20	7:15	7:45
8:00	7:00	8:00	7:30
6:00	7:10	7:50	6:10

15. **Health** The data at the left show when 16 people get up in the morning.
    a. Make a frequency table and a histogram. Use half-hour intervals such as 6:00–6:29 and 6:30–6:59.
    b. Which half-hour interval is the most common?

Entertainment Use the histogram for Exercises 16–20.

16. About how many people surveyed saw fewer than two movies last summer?

17. Which interval has the greatest number of responses? How many responses are in this interval?

18. About how many more people saw 4–5 movies than 8–9 movies?

19. About how many people answered the survey?

20. Reasoning Can you tell how many people saw exactly 7 movies? Explain.

How Many Movies Did You See in a Theater Last Summer?

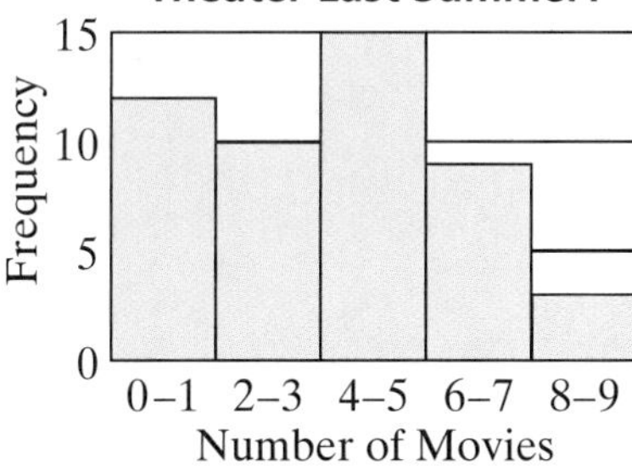

The line plot at the right shows responses to a survey.

21. What do the numbers in the line plot represent?

22. How many people answered the survey?

How Many Times Have You Flown in an Airplane?

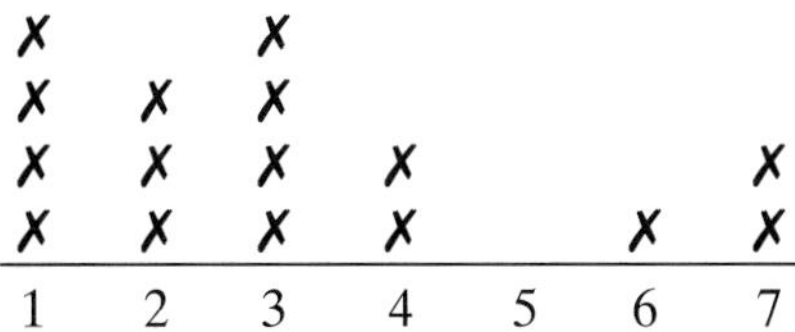

23. **Writing in Math** What is an advantage and a disadvantage of displaying information in a histogram? What is an advantage and a disadvantage of displaying information in a line plot?

C Challenge

24. **Real Estate** The table shows the prices of homes in a community.

\$129,000	\$132,000	\$121,000	\$115,000
\$138,000	\$152,000	\$147,000	\$136,000
\$137,000	\$148,000	\$175,000	\$127,000
\$192,000	\$133,000	\$167,000	\$154,000

a. Draw a histogram with 4 intervals of \$19,000 starting at \$115,000.

b. Draw a histogram with 8 intervals of \$9,000 starting at \$115,000.

c. **Reasoning** With an average home price of about \$144,000, which histogram better represents the data? Explain your choice.

25. **Stretch Your Thinking** Replace the ■s with the digits 2, 4, 5, 6, and 9 to make the least possible difference. Use each digit once.

$$\begin{array}{r} \blacksquare\blacksquare\blacksquare \\ -\ \blacksquare\blacksquare \\ \hline \end{array}$$

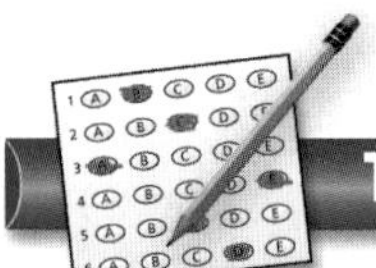

Test Prep

Gridded Response

Use the histogram at the right.

26. How many parents have fewer than six days of vacation?

27. How many parents have more than 15 days of vacation?

28. How many more parents have 16–20 vacation days than 6–10 vacation days?

29. How many parents are represented in the survey?

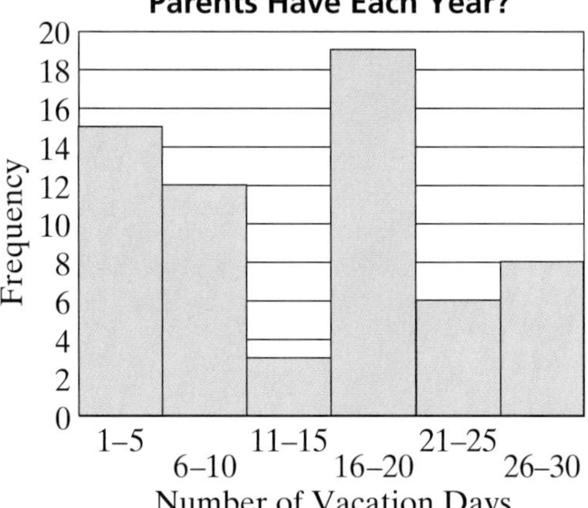

Online lesson quiz at **www.PHSchool.com**
Web Code: aba-1101

Mixed Review

Lesson 10-4

Algebra **Make a table of values for each equation. Use integer values of x from -3 to 3. Then graph each parabola.**

30. $y = x^2 - 1$

31. $y = 3x^2$

32. $y = -3x^2$

Lesson 9-7

Find the simple interest earned by each account.

33. \$1,000 principal
3% annual interest rate
4 years

34. \$3,000 principal
6% annual interest rate
2 years

11-2 Spreadsheets and Data Displays

What You'll Learn

To use a spreadsheet

To interpret double bar and double line graphs

. . . And Why

To compare numbers of households with VCRs and cable TV, as in Example 3

Check Skills You'll Need

For help, go to Lesson 9-1.

Graph the data in each table. Connect the points on the graph.

1.

a	1	2	3	4	5	6
b	2	3	4	5	6	7

2.

a	6	5	4	3	2	0
b	2	3	4	2	1	4

New Vocabulary

- spreadsheet
- cell
- double bar graph
- legend
- double line graph

Interactive lesson includes instant self-check, tutorials, and activities.

OBJECTIVE 1

Using a Spreadsheet

A **spreadsheet** is a tool for organizing and analyzing data. Spreadsheets are arranged in lettered columns and numbered rows. A **cell** is a box where a column and row meet.

1 EXAMPLE Using a Spreadsheet

Real World

Television Find the value in cell C3. What does it represent? How many households had VCRs in 2000?

Households with VCRs and Households with Cable TV (millions)

	A	B	C
1	Year	VCRs	Cable TV
2	1992	70.3	57.2
3	1994	72.8	59.7
4	1996	78.8	64.0
5	1998	84.1	67.1
6	2000	88.1	69.5

column; ← cell C3 ← row

SOURCE: MPAA and Nielsen Media Research

The value in cell C3 is 59.7. It represents the number of households, in millions, with cable TV in 1994. In 2000, 88.1 million households had VCRs.

Check Understanding 1

a. Find the value in cell B4. What does it represent?
b. Which cell has a value of 72.8 million?

OBJECTIVE 2

Interpreting Double Bar and Double Line Graphs

A **double bar graph** uses bars to compare two sets of data. The **legend,** or key, identifies the data that are compared.

Technology Hint

Using a spreadsheet, you can choose the data to graph, and then choose the type of graph you want.

2 EXAMPLE Interpreting a Double Bar Graph

Television In which years did the number of households with VCRs exceed 60 million? In which years did the number with cable TV exceed 60 million?

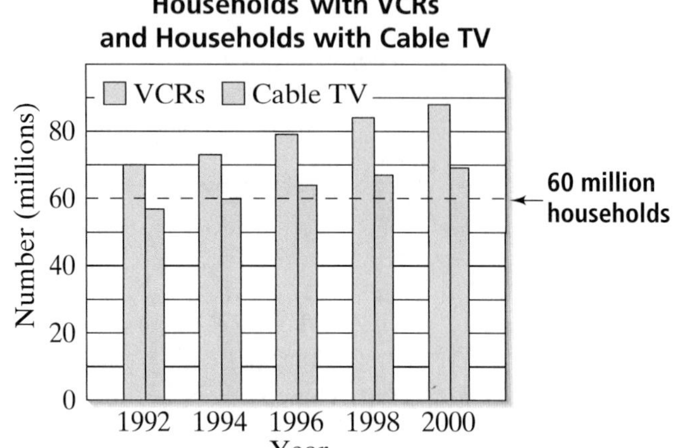

The number of households with VCRs exceeded 60 million in all years from 1992 through 2000. The number with cable TV exceeded 60 million in 1996, 1998, and 2000.

Check Understanding 2 In which years did the number of households with VCRs exceed 70 million?

A **double line graph** compares changes in two sets of data over time.

3 EXAMPLE Interpreting a Double Line Graph

Television Compare the VCR and cable TV data shown in the graph.

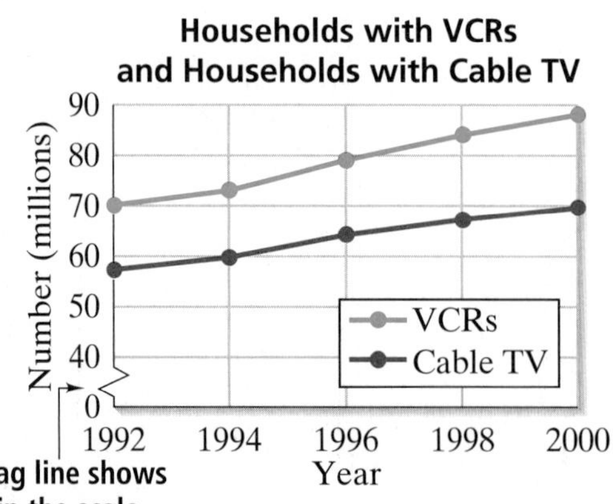

The zigzag line shows a break in the scale.

The number of households with VCRs is consistently greater than the number of households with cable TV.

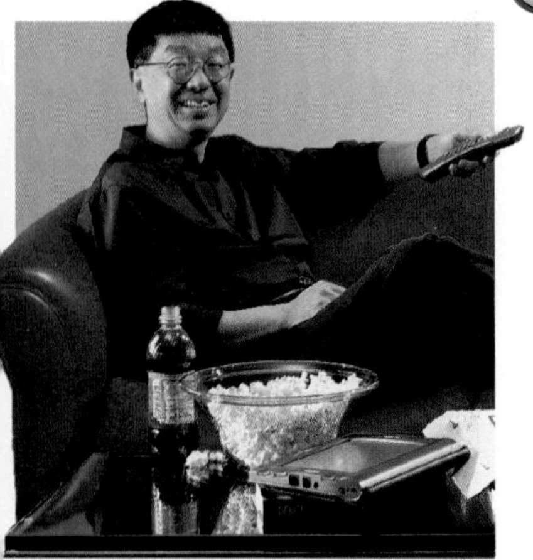

Real-World Connection

Henry C. Yuen developed a VCR that made recording TV programs easier.

✓ Check Understanding **3** Use the double line graph in Example 3.

a. Between which two years did the number of households with cable TV increase the most?

b. **Reasoning** When would you use a double line graph to present the data? When would you use a double bar graph?

Investigation: Making Graphs

1. **Data Collection** Find data about the number of students in each grade of your school five years ago. Find data about the number of students in each grade of your school this year.
2. Record your data in a spreadsheet.
3. Graph your data in a double bar graph. Remember to include a legend and a title.
4. Write a question that could be answered using your data.
5. Explain why a double bar graph is better than a double line graph to display your data.

EXERCISES

Example 1 (page 579)

Use the spreadsheet below for Exercises 1–10.

Recommended Nutrition in Dog and Cat Foods (Calories per 100 Calories)

	A	B	C	D
1	Animal	Fat	Carbohydrates	Protein
2	Dog	37	37	26
3	Cat	46	26	28

Give the value or content of each cell.

1. A2 **2.** D2 **3.** B3 **4.** B1 **5.** C2

6. In which cell is the word *Protein*? **7.** In which cell is the value 28?

8. In which cell is the word *Animal*? **9.** In which cell is the value 46?

10. How many more Calories from fat are recommended for cat food than for dog food?

Example 2 (page 580)

Libraries Use the bar graph for Exercises 11–16.

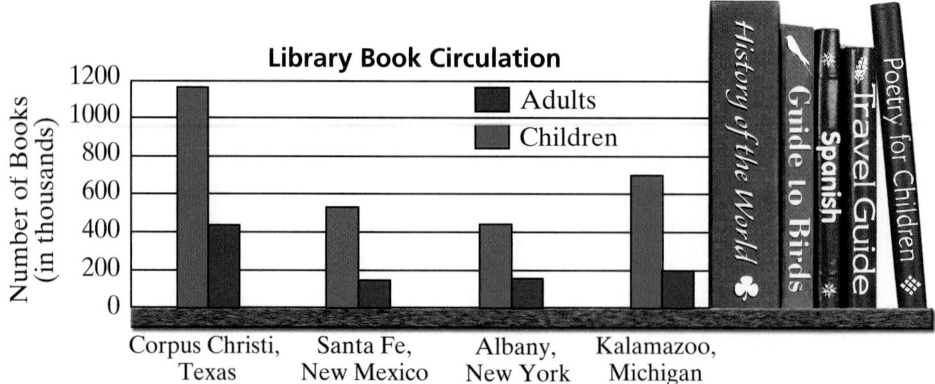

11. Which library circulated the most children's books? Adult books?

12. Which library had the greatest total circulation?

13. Find two libraries with about the same circulation of children's books.

14. Which libraries had a circulation of less than 600,000 children's books?

15. Which library had a circulation of more than 200,000 adult books?

16. Which library had the greatest difference between the numbers of adult books and children's books circulated?

Example 3 (page 581)

Industry Use the line graph for Exercises 17–21.

17. In which years did bicycle production exceed 64 million?

18. In which years did automobile production exceed 23 million?

19. Did bicycle production increase more between 1950 and 1970 or between 1970 and 1990?

20. Estimation About what year are the two lines closest together?

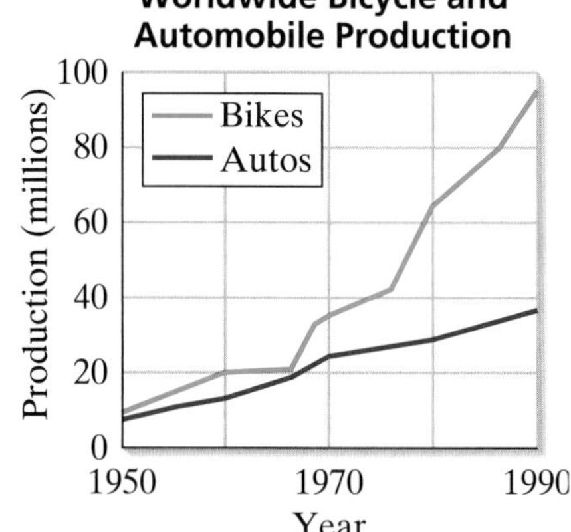

SOURCE: Worldwatch Institute

B Apply Your Skills

21. Reasoning The two lines begin to separate widely after the year they are closest together. Why might this be?

Population Use the graph at the right for Exercises 22 and 23.

22. Writing in Math Which state had the greatest growth between 1990 and 2000? Explain.

23. Estimation By about how much did the total population of the four states increase?

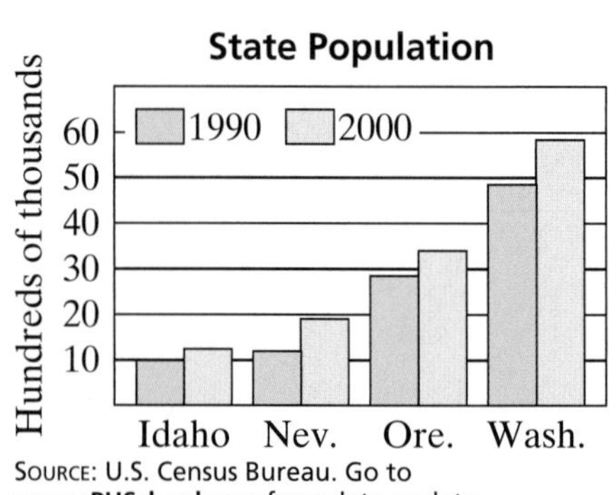

SOURCE: U.S. Census Bureau. Go to **www.PHSchool.com** for a data update. Web Code: abg-2041

Real-World Connection

Careers A costume designer makes costumes for television, theater, or films.

Entertainment Use the graph.

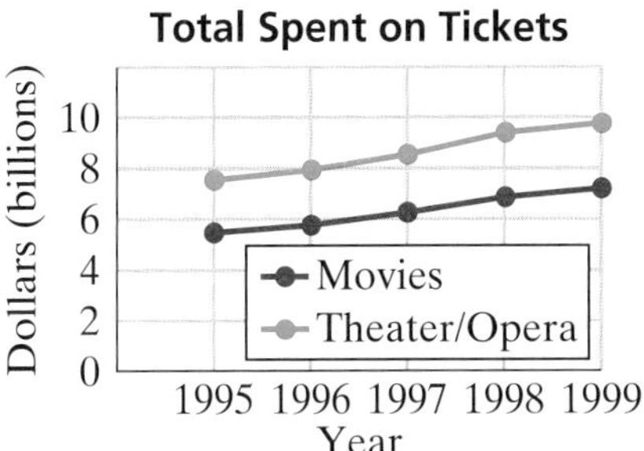

SOURCE: U.S. Census Bureau of Economic Analysis

24. Between which years did spending on theater/opera increase most? Explain how you can tell by looking at the graph.

25. **Estimation** About what year did spending on theater/opera tickets most exceed spending on movie tickets?

26. **Writing in Math** Recommended nutrition for humans in 100 Calories of food is 30 Calories of fat, 10 Calories of protein, and 60 Calories of carbohydrates. Compare this with the recommended nutrition for cats and dogs in the spreadsheet for Exercises 1–10.

27. **Estimation** In the double bar graph with Exercises 11–16, about how many adult books did the library in Kalamazoo, Michigan, circulate?

28. **Reasoning** Explain why a double line graph needs a legend.

Food Use the graph for Exercises 29–33.

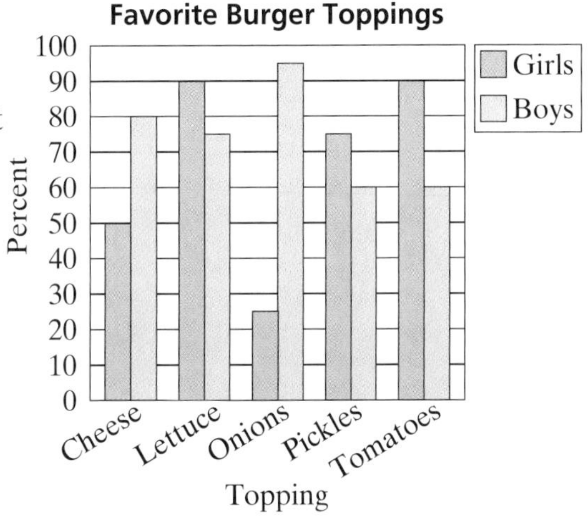

29. Which topping is the least favorite for girls?

30. Which toppings are the least favorite for boys?

31. Which topping is liked by about 75% of the girls?

32. **Business** A fast-food chain plans to introduce a new burger. Which topping should it offer to appeal to the most boys? Explain.

C Challenge

33. Suppose 380 boys are surveyed. About how many boys would you expect to choose tomatoes as their favorite burger topping?

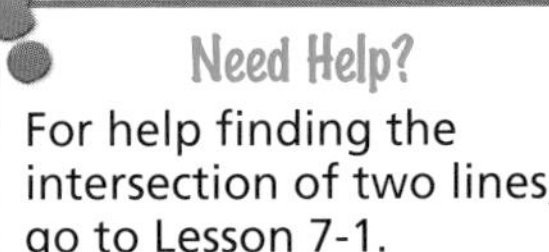

Need Help?

For help finding the intersection of two lines, go to Lesson 7-1.

Algebra Use the spreadsheet at the right for Exercises 34–36.

	A	B	C	D
1	x_1	y_1	x_2	y_2
2	0	1	0	4
3	1	?	1	5
4	2	?	2	?
5	3	10	3	?
6	4	13	4	8
7	5	16	5	9
8	6	19	6	10

34. Draw a double line graph. From the graph, find the missing y-values in the spreadsheet.

35. **Estimation** Estimate the coordinates of the intersection of the two lines.

36. Find a rule for each function.

37. **Stretch Your Thinking** Place one X in as many small squares as possible without forming a line of three X's in a vertical, horizontal, or diagonal row. What is the greatest number of X's for which you can do this?

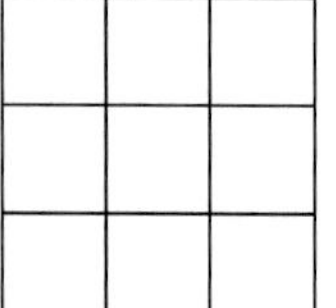

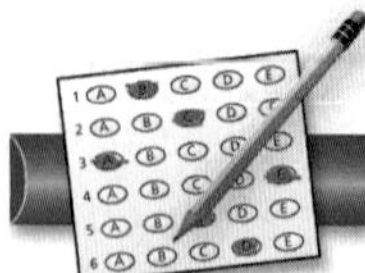

Test Prep

Multiple Choice

Use the line graph below for Exercises 38–41.

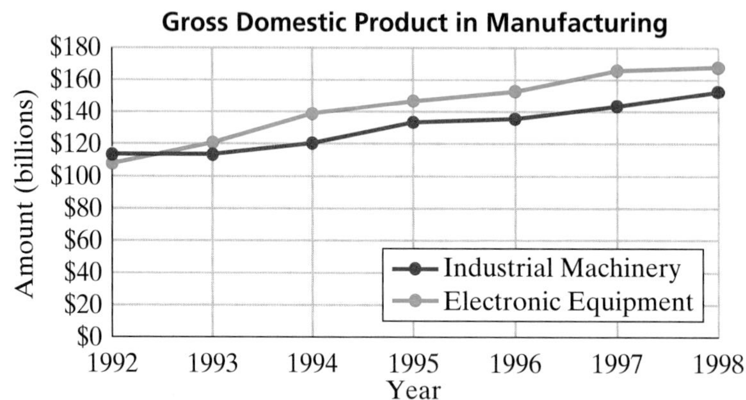

SOURCE: U.S. Census Bureau. Go to **www.PHSchool.com** for a data update. Web Code: abg-2041

38. What was the gross domestic product for electronic equipment in 1994?
   A. \$120 billion　**B.** \$130 billion
   C. \$140 billion　**D.** \$150 billion

Take It to the NET
Online lesson quiz at
www.PHSchool.com
Web Code: aba-1102

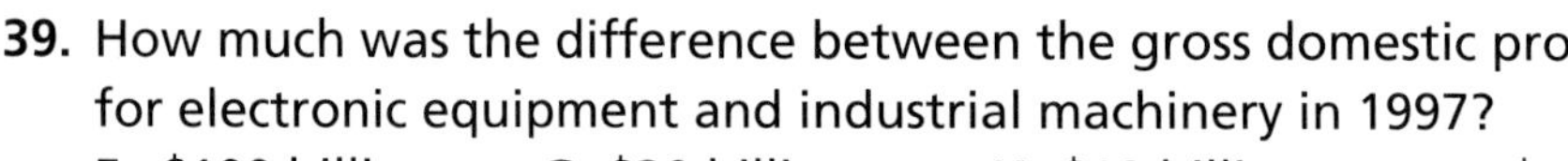

39. How much was the difference between the gross domestic products for electronic equipment and industrial machinery in 1997?
   F. \$100 billion　**G.** \$20 billion　**H.** \$10 billion　**I.** \$1 billion

40. In what year did the gross domestic product for electronic equipment first exceed the gross domestic product for industrial machinery?
   A. 1996　**B.** 1995　**C.** 1994　**D.** 1993

Short Response

41. In which intervals did the gross domestic product for electronic equipment NOT increase faster than the gross domestic product for industrial machinery? Explain your answer.

Mixed Review

Lesson 10-7

Graph each point and its reflection across the indicated axis. Write the coordinates of each reflected point.

42. $(-3, 8)$ across the y-axis　**43.** $(7, -4)$ across the y-axis

Lesson 9-5

Algebra **Use the function rule $y = -2x + 3$. Find y for each value of x.**

44. 4　**45.** 0　**46.** -3　**47.** 5.5　**48.** 0.5

11-3 Other Displays

What You'll Learn

 To make a stem-and-leaf plot

 To make a box-and-whisker plot

. . . And Why

To show the number of computer users, as in Example 3

Check Skills You'll Need

For help, go to Lesson 1-10.

Find the median of each set of data.

1. 24, 42, 51, 25, 63
2. 38, 30, 26, 20, 32, 48
3. 2.1, 3.2, 4.8, 5.6, 3.1, 2.6
4. 5.8, 6.9, 7.4, 3.9, 6.4
5. 110, 120, 130, 125
6. 225, 212, 231, 295, 264

New Vocabulary • stem-and-leaf plot • box-and-whisker plot

 Interactive lesson includes instant self-check, tutorials, and activities.

OBJECTIVE 1

Making a Stem-and-Leaf Plot

A **stem-and-leaf plot** is a graph that uses the digits of each number to show the shape of the data. Each data value is broken into a "stem" (digit or digits on the left) and a "leaf" (digit or digits on the right).

1 EXAMPLE Making a Stem-and-Leaf Plot (Real World)

Iron in Three Ounces of High-Protein Foods

Food	Iron (mg)
Clams	2.6
Crab meat	1.1
Salmon	0.7
Tuna	1.6
Ground beef	2.1
Steak	2.6
Lamb	1.4
Ham	0.7
Chicken	0.9
Turkey	1.5

SOURCE: *Home and Garden Bulletin, No. 72*

Nutrition Use the table at the left. Draw a stem-and-leaf plot of the data.

Step 1 Choose the stems. For these data, stems are made using the values in the ones place. Draw a vertical line to the right of the stems.

```
0 |   ← stems
1 |
2 |
```

Step 2 Find the leaves. For these data, the leaves are the values in the tenths place.

```
0 | 7 7 9    ← leaves
1 | 1 6 4 5
2 | 6 1 6
```

Step 3 Order the leaves from least to greatest. A key explains what your stems and leaves represent. Add a title.

Iron in Three Ounces of High-Protein Foods (mg)

```
0 | 7 7 9
1 | 1 4 5 6
2 | 1 6 6
```

key → **Key:** 0 | 7 means 0.7

Check Understanding 1 Make a stem-and-leaf plot of the wind speeds (in miles per hour) recorded during a storm: 9, 14, 30, 16, 18, 25, 29, 25, 38, 34, 33.

A back-to-back stem-and-leaf plot uses two sets of data. The side-by-side display makes the data easy to compare. Beginning from the stem, the leaves increase in value in each direction.

2 EXAMPLE **Real-World Problem Solving**

Weather Compare the two sets of data in the stem-and-leaf plot below. How many times did each city receive 3.5 in. of precipitation in a month?

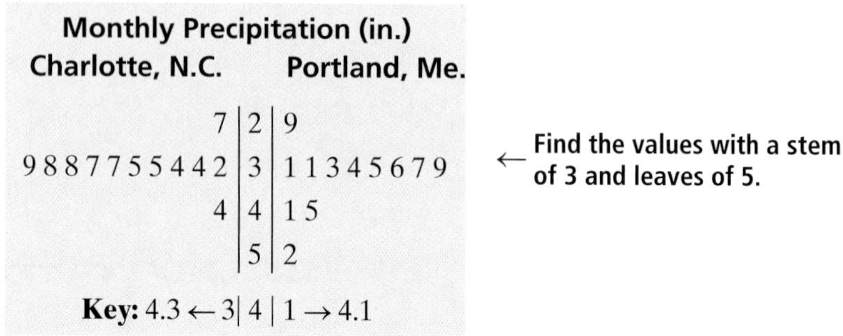

Monthly Precipitation (in.)

Charlotte, N.C.		Portland, Me.
7	2	9
9 8 8 7 7 5 5 4 4 2	3	1 1 3 4 5 6 7 9
4	4	1 5
	5	2

Key: 4.3 ← 3| 4 | 1 → 4.1

← **Find the values with a stem of 3 and leaves of 5.**

Charlotte twice received 3.5 in. of precipitation in a month. Portland received 3.5 in. only once.

Check Understanding 2

a. Which city had the month with the least precipitation? The most?

b. **Reasoning** Find the range of each set of data in Example 2.

c. **Number Sense** Which city had a higher median monthly precipitation? Explain.

OBJECTIVE 2

Making a Box-and-Whisker Plot

A **box-and-whisker plot** is a graph that summarizes a data set along a number line. There is a box in the middle, and whiskers at either side.

The least value of the data set determines the left whisker. The greatest value of the data set determines the right whisker.

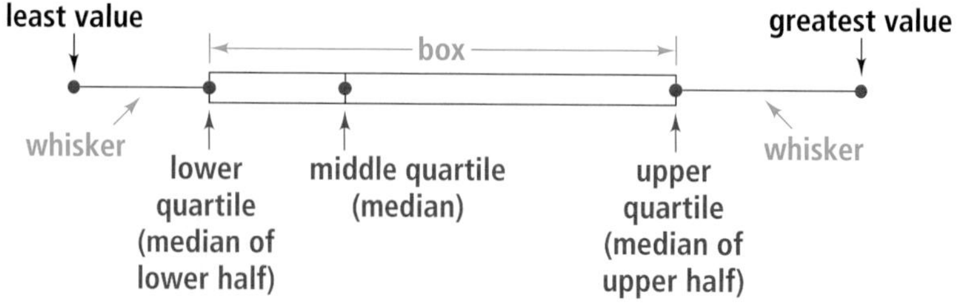

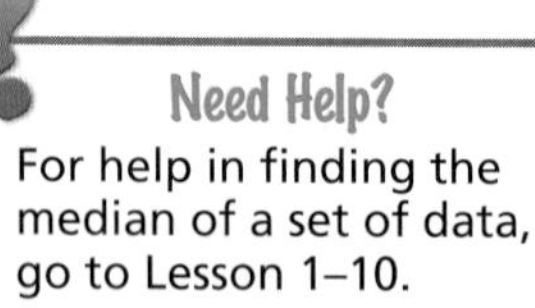

Need Help?
For help in finding the median of a set of data, go to Lesson 1–10.

You form the box using quartiles. Quartiles divide the data into four equal parts. Follow these steps to find the quartile values.

- Order the data from least to greatest.
- Find the middle quartile by finding the median of the entire data set. The median divides the data into two parts.
- Find the lower quartile by finding the median of the lower parts.
- Find the upper quartile by finding the median of the upper parts.

 Making a Box-and-Whisker Plot 

Computer Center The director of a computer center records the number of users each hour for one day. The results are 13, 14, 22, 25, 30, 29, 27, 18, 19, 14, 18, and 19. Make a box-and-whisker plot of the data.

13 14 14 18 18 19 19 22 25 27 29 30 ← **List the data in order.**

13 14 14 18 18 19 19 22 25 27 29 30 ← **Find the middle quartile.**

The median is 19.

13 14 14 18 18 19 19 22 25 27 29 30 ← **Find the lower and upper quartiles.**

The lower quartile is 16. **The upper quartile is 26.**

Use a number line to draw the box-and-whisker plot.

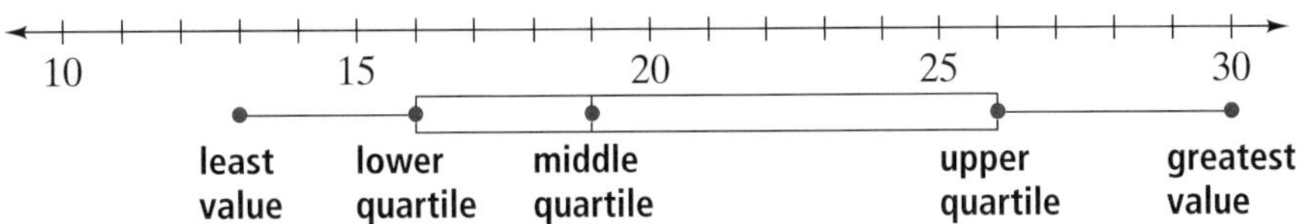

Check Understanding 3 **a.** Draw a box-and-whisker plot of the number of users each hour of another day. The results are 12, 16, 9, 11, 15, 12, 14, 16, 14, 12, 10, and 15.

b. **Reasoning** In Example 3 and Question 3a, is the middle quartile in the middle of the box? Explain.

EXERCISES

For more practice, see *Extra Practice.*

Practice by Example

Draw a stem-and-leaf plot for each set of data.

Example 1 (page 585)

1. sales of twelve companies (millions of dollars)
1.3 1.4 2.3 1.4 2.4 2.5 3.9 1.4 1.3 2.5 3.6 1.4

2. heights of giant sunflowers (in inches)
98 99 94 87 83 74 69 88 78 99 100 87 77

3. high temperatures (°F) in the desert
99 113 112 98 100 103 101 111 104 108 109 112 113 118

4. heights of ceilings in older homes (in feet)
9.7 12.3 10.2 11.5 14.1 9.6 13.7 14.4 11.5 9.7 11.6 11.5

Example 2 (page 586)

Height Use the stem-and-leaf plot at the right for Exercises 5–7.

Student Height (in.)

Female		Male
7 4 3 1 0 0	5	6 7
8 5 4 1 0	6	2 3 5 5 6 7 9
0	7	1 2 3 4 6

Key: 61 ← 1 | 6 | 3 → 63

5. How many females are 65 in. tall? How many males?

6. What is the height of the shortest male?

7. What is the height of the tallest female?

Example 3 (page 587)

Make a box-and-whisker plot for each set of data.

8. number of customers at a coffee house (30-minute intervals)
2 5 3 7 7 8 10 8 14 15 14 15 12 10 10 8 9 7 8 5 2 5 4 3

9. height of new tree (in inches)
32 42 54 36 40 34 42 42 56 54 34 46 38 39 41 40 38 35

10. number of consecutive days of overcast skies in December
24 11 14 16 14 11 16 22 13 17 19 16 8 21 15 19 17 11 23

11. average temperature (°F) in the northwest
62 55 60 85 62 65 68 70 55 60 65 62 58 60 62 68 65

B Apply Your Skills

Geography Use the map at the right.

12. Make a box-and-whisker plot.

13. What is the range of the data?

14. Which part has the greatest range?

Number of Counties in Western States

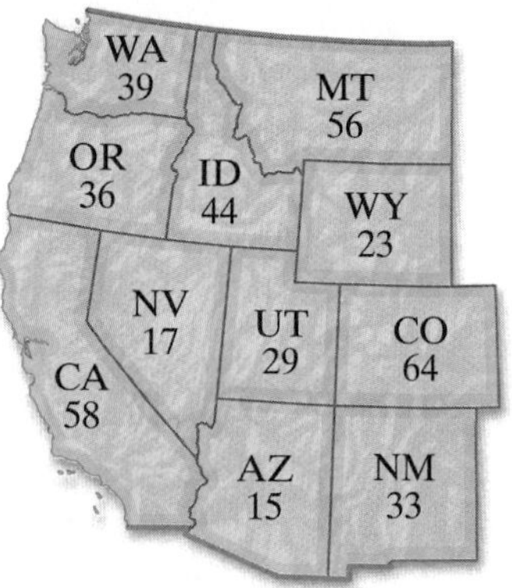

SOURCE: National Association of Counties

4	3 6 7
5	1 2
6	1 7
7	1 8
8	2 6 8

Key: 8 | 2 means 82

Use the stem-and-leaf plot at the left for Exercises 15–18.

15. How many data items are there?

16. What is the least value? The greatest value?

17. How many values are greater than 65?

18. Make a box-and-whisker plot.

Fund-Raising Use the stem-and-leaf plot for Exercises 19–23.

Distances Walked by Fund-Raisers (km)

16	1 1 2 3 5 5
17	0 2 2
18	4 5 8 9
19	3 6 7 9 9 9

Key: 19 | 3 means 19.3

19. What place values are the leaves?

20. How many data items are there?

21. How many people walked more than 19 km?

22. Find the range.

23. a. Writing in Math How would you find the median?

b. Reasoning How can you find the mode of a data set displayed in a stem-and-leaf plot?

24. **Data File, p. 571** Make a box-and-whisker plot of the percent of trips by bicycle for the countries in the table.

25. The *interquartile range* is the difference between the third and first quartiles. Find the interquartile range for the data below.
304 288 195 311 172 264 202 181 200 239 213

Challenge

26. **Data Collection** Measure the width of the hands of at least 10 people. Measure using metric units.
    a. Make a stem-and-leaf plot of the data you collect.
    b. Make a box-and-whisker plot of the data you collect.
    c. Find the range.
    d. Which graph is easier to use to find the median of the data? Explain.

27. **Algebra** The median for the set of data below is 48. What is the value of the missing data item?
    23 34 42 ■ 62 67

28. **Stretch Your Thinking** Holland Middle School is in a ten-team conference. During basketball season, each basketball team plays every other team at home. How many conference basketball games are played in a season?

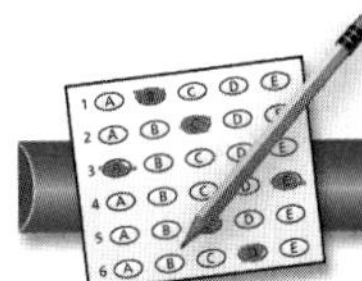

Test Prep

Reading Comprehension

Read the passage and answer the questions below.

Winning Careers

Kathy Whitworth won a total of 88 golf tournaments during her career. This made her the leader in career wins for women golfers. She was followed by Mickey Wright with 82 wins, Patty Berg with 60 wins, Louise Suggs with 58 wins, Betsy Rawls with 55 wins, Nancy Lopez with 48 wins, JoAnne Carner with 43 wins, Sandra Haynie with 42 wins, Babe Zaharias with 41 wins, Carol Mann with 38 wins, and Patty Sheehan with 35 wins.

29. What is the range of the data? Show your work.

30. Suppose you make a stem-and-leaf plot of the data. How many leaves does the stem 4 have?

Multiple Choice

Use the box-and-whisker plot for Exercises 31 and 32.

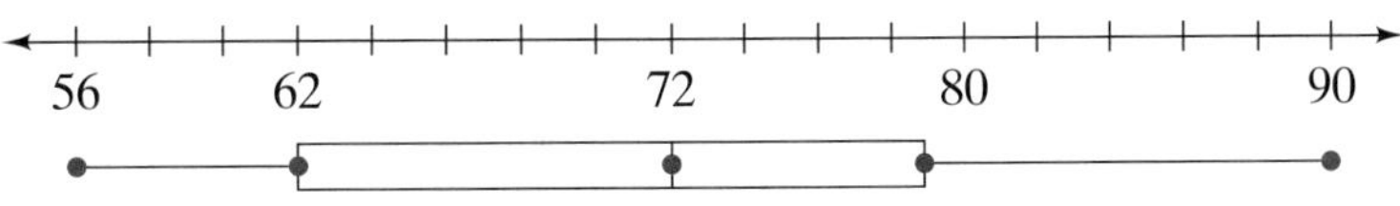

31. What is the middle quartile?
    A. 56 B. 62 C. 72 D. 79

32. What is the greatest value?
    F. 62 G. 72 H. 79 I. 90

Take It to the NET
Online lesson quiz at
www.PHSchool.com
Web Code: aba-1103

Mixed Review

Lesson 11-1 **Money** **Use the frequency table below for Exercises 33 and 34.**

Pocket Change

Number of Pennies	Frequency	Number of Pennies	Frequency
1–5	12	21–25	5
6–10	6	26–30	6
11–15	10	31–35	0
16–20	7	36–40	4

33. Can you tell from the table how many people had fewer than 17 pennies in their pockets? Explain.

34. Make a histogram of the data.

Lesson 10-6 **Geometry** **Use graph paper to graph each image of $\triangle ABC$ under the translation described. Give the coordinates of A', B', and C'.**

35. left 2 units

36. up 3 units

37. right 4 units

38. left 2 units, up 3 units

39. right 3 units, down 1 unit

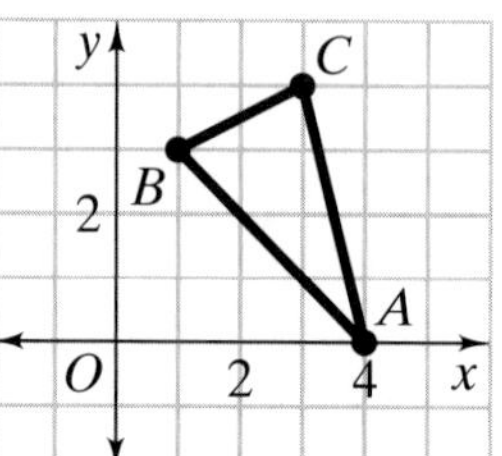

Checkpoint Quiz 1

Lessons 11-1 through 11-3

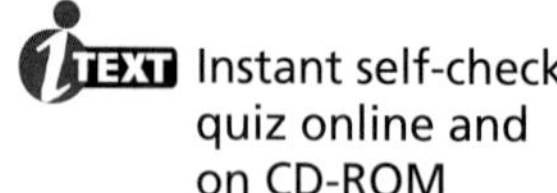
Instant self-check quiz online and on CD-ROM

1. Make a frequency table and a line plot of the data below.
5 7 8 3 5 4 6 7 8 9 1 2 5 4 2 1 3

2. Graph the data below. Explain why you chose the graph you drew.

Art Show Attendance

Day	Sun.	Mon.	Tue.	Wed.	Thur.	Fri.	Sat.
Number of Adults	54	29	22	28	12	15	49
Number of Children	32	21	16	20	8	10	36

3. Make a stem-and-leaf plot of the golf scores for 18-hole games.
120 112 130 128 124 117 118 117 121 113

4. Make a box-and-whisker plot of the average miles per gallon for different cars.
25 28 23 27 21 22 25 24 25 27 28 29 22 24

5. What is the range of the data in Exercise 3? Exercise 4?

Venn Diagrams

For Use With Lesson 11-3

A Venn diagram shows relationships between sets of items. Each set is represented separately. Items that belong to both sets are represented by the intersection in the diagram.

EXAMPLE Using a Venn Diagram

Geography There are 22 states that are all or partly in the eastern time zone, and 15 states that are all or partly in the central time zone. This includes the 5 states that are in both the eastern and central time zones. How many states are in either or both of the two time zones?

Draw a Venn diagram.

Eastern Time Zone States $22 - 5 = 17$

5

Central Time Zone States $15 - 5 = 10$

There are $17 + 5 + 10$, or 32 states in either or both the eastern and central time zones.

EXERCISES

1. **Geography** There are 10 states that are completely in the central time zone, and 7 states that are completely in the mountain time zone. There are 22 states that are in either or both time zones. Use a Venn diagram to find how many states are in both time zones.

2. a. **Pets** Suppose forty students in your class have pets. Thirty-two students have cats or dogs or both, but no birds. Eight students have birds. One student has all three kinds of pets. Copy and complete the Venn diagram below.

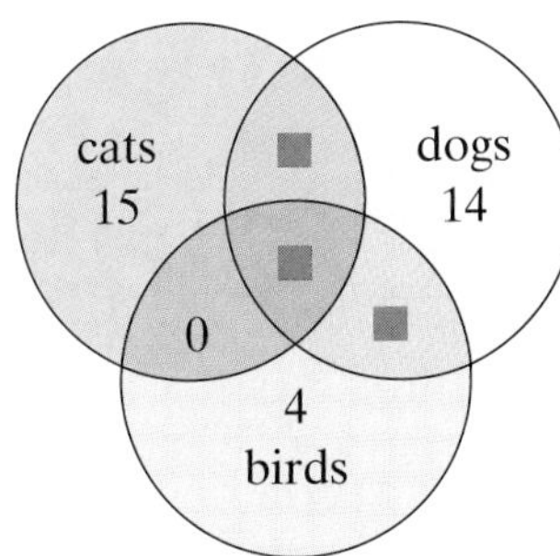

b. How many students have dogs and birds? Dogs and cats?

c. **Reasoning** A new student who has fish and no other pets joins the class. How many of the existing sets would this new set overlap?

3. **Data Collection** Conduct a survey of your class. Ask students whether they have brothers, sisters, both, or neither. Use a Venn diagram to display the results.

Problem Solving

11-4 Make a Table and Use Logical Reasoning

What You'll Learn

OBJECTIVE 1 To solve a problem by combining strategies

. . . And Why

To use multiple strategies of problem solving, as in Example 1

Check Skills You'll Need

For help, go to Lesson 11-1.

Make a frequency table and line plot for each set of data.

1. heights of students in inches
   52 55 56 56 57 58 53 56 55 53 58 60 52 57 56 55 59 52 56 57
2. ages of grandparents
   62 63 62 65 64 63 68 69 65 63 69 71 65 58 63 64 65 62 68 67

OBJECTIVE

iTEXT Interactive lesson includes instant self-check, tutorials, and activities.

1 Solving a Problem by Combining Strategies

When to Use These Strategies You can ***make a table*** to organize information. You can ***use logical reasoning*** to solve many puzzle-like problems. You can combine these strategies to solve problems.

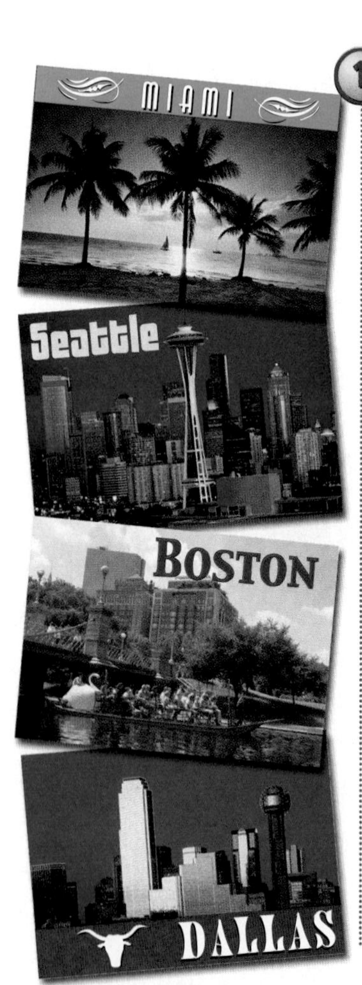

1 EXAMPLE Solving Puzzles

Reasoning Antoine, Bill, Carlos, and David live in Dallas, Seattle, Boston, and Miami. Bill is the brother of the man who lives in Seattle. David is not Bill's brother and does not live in Miami. Either Antoine or Carlos lives in Dallas. Antoine is an only child. Which person lives in which city?

Read and Understand The goal is to find which person lives in which city, given the four facts about where each person lives.

Plan and Solve Use a table to organize the information. After examining each fact, write *no* for choices that you can eliminate.

Fact 1 "Bill is the brother of the man who lives in Seattle." This means that Bill does not live in Seattle.

Fact 2 "David is not Bill's brother and does not live in Miami." This means that David does not live in Seattle or Miami.

	Dallas	Seattle	Boston	Miami
Antoine	■	■	■	■
Bill	■	no	■	■
Carlos	■	■	■	■
David	■	no	■	no

Fact 3 "Either Antoine or Carlos lives in Dallas." This means Bill and David do not live in Dallas. Now you know that David lives in Boston. Write *yes* for David and *no* for the others in the Boston column. Now you know that Bill lives in Miami. Fill in the Miami column.

	Dallas	Seattle	Boston	Miami
Antoine	■	■	no	no
Bill	no	no	no	yes
Carlos	■	■	no	no
David	no	no	yes	no

Fact 4 "Antoine is an only child." This means he is not Bill's brother, so he does not live in Seattle. He must live in Dallas. So Carlos lives in Seattle.

	Dallas	Seattle	Boston	Miami
Antoine	yes	no	no	no
Bill	no	no	no	yes
Carlos	no	yes	no	no
David	no	no	yes	no

Look Back and Check Use the table to check your answers in the original problem. Make sure there are no contradictions.

1 The top four runners cross the finish line as follows: Susan comes in after Mary. Donna comes in before Susan but does not win the race. Genevieve finishes last. What is the order of the runners?

EXERCISES

For more practice, see *Extra Practice*.

Example 1 (page 592)

Need Help?
- Reread the problem.
- Identify the key facts and details.
- Tell the problem in your own words.
- Try a different strategy.
- Check your work.

Use the strategies *Make a Table* and *Use Logical Reasoning* to solve each problem.

1. **Sports** Three lockers contain basketballs, footballs, and soccer balls. Each locker contains only one type of ball, and all the labels are incorrect. The locker marked "footballs" has basketballs. Which balls are in the lockers labeled "basketballs" and "soccer balls"?

2. Xiao, Gina, and Dena each like one of the following subjects: math, history, and art. Dena dislikes art. Gina knows the students who like art and math best. Match the students with their favorite subject.

3. **Fund-Raising** A class sells calendars to raise money for a field trip. The top four sellers are Joan, Amalie, Mandela, and Scott. Joan sells more calendars than Amalie, but fewer than Mandela. Scott also sells more than Amalie, but fewer than Joan. Who sells the most calendars?

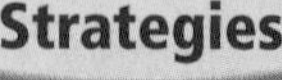

Apply Your Skills

Use any strategy or combination of strategies to solve each problem.

Strategies

Draw a Diagram
Look for a Pattern
Make a Graph
Make an Organized List
Make a Table
Simulate a Problem
Solve a Simpler Problem
Try, Check, and Revise
Use Logical Reasoning
Work Backward
Write an Equation

4. **Kites** A kite and its tail are 27 ft long. The tail is five times as long as the body. How long is the kite's tail?

5. **Languages** Who studies which language?
   - Keesha does not study German or Italian.
   - Frieda and Pascal do not study Chinese, but one of them studies French.
   - Keesha, Frieda, and Jared ride to classes together. One studies German, one studies Spanish, and one studies Italian.
   - The woman studying Italian is not Mika.

6. **Jobs** Match each person with his/her job. Ann is the sister of the teacher. Miguel has never met the teacher or the miner.

Carla	Writer
Miguel	Miner
Ann	Teacher

7. **Geology** Mount Whitney is about twice as tall as Harney Peak. Mount Davis is about 4,020 ft shorter than Harney Peak and 4 times as tall as Woodall Mountain, which is 806 ft. About how tall is Mount Whitney?

8. **Measurement** Six piglets in a litter have a mean weight of 8 lb. Find two possibilities for the weight of each piglet.

9. Of 50 students, how many have no cats, dogs, or gerbils?
   - Thirty have cats and 25 have dogs.
   - Sixteen have both cats and dogs, but no gerbils.
   - Five have only gerbils. Four have both dogs and gerbils. Two have both cats and gerbils.
   - Only one student has all three pets.

10. a. **Geography** Dornville is 15 mi south of Chester. Topson is 12 mi north of Dornville. Ludberg is 4.5 mi north of Topson. Order the towns from north to south.
    b. What is the distance from Dornville to Ludberg?

11. a. A grocer stacks oranges in the shape of a square pyramid. One side of the base has 6 oranges. How many oranges will the grocer use?
    b. **Writing in Math** Which problem-solving strategy did you use in part (a)? Explain your choice.

12. Martin has 10 loose identical red socks and 10 loose identical blue socks in a drawer. What is the least number of socks he would have to choose to be sure he finds a matching pair?

13. a. A fenced-in rectangular area has a perimeter of 40 ft. The fence has a post every 4 ft. How many posts are there?
    b. Each corner has a post. Can the field measure 10 ft by 10 ft?
    c. **Reasoning** What are the possible dimensions of the field? Explain.

C Challenge

14. **Number Sense** Theodore works for Mr. Jones. Mr. Jones agrees to start Theodore at $.01 the first day, $.02 the second day, $.04 the third day, $.08 the fourth day, and so on.
    a. How much does Theodore earn in fifteen days?
    b. Suppose Theodore can start at $10 the first day, $10.75 the second day, $11.50 the third day, $12.25 the fourth day, and so on. Would he earn more in fifteen days than he does in part (a)? Explain.

15. **Stretch Your Thinking** How many whole numbers between 100 and 400 contain the digit 2?

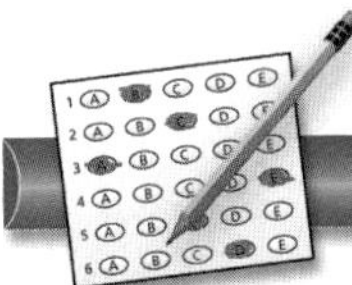

Test Prep

Multiple Choice

16. Which number is 345% expressed as a decimal?
A. 34.5 B. 3.45 C. 0.345 D. 0.0345

17. Add 20% of a number to the number itself. What percent of the result would you have to subtract to get the original number?
F. 25% G. 20% H. $16\frac{2}{3}$% I. 12.5%

Take It to the NET
Online lesson quiz at
www.PHSchool.com
Web Code: aba-1104

18. What is a good estimate of a 15% tip for a bill of $28.93?
A. $3.00 B. $4.50 C. $6.00 D. $43.00

Short Response

19. The cost of a computer before sales tax is $1,350, and the cost after sales tax is $1,431. What is the sales tax rate? Show your work.

Mixed Review

Lesson 10-2

Algebra **Graph each equation.**

20. $y = x + 2$
21. $y = -2x$
22. $y = \frac{1}{2}x + 3$
23. $y = 3x - 4$
24. $y = x - 7$
25. $2y = 4x + 6$

Lesson 5-4

Algebra **Solve each proportion.**

26. $\frac{36}{4} = \frac{x}{2}$
27. $\frac{m}{6} = \frac{5}{3}$
28. $\frac{4}{9} = \frac{12}{f}$
29. $\frac{9}{r} = \frac{3}{1}$
30. $\frac{14}{18} = \frac{y}{20}$
31. $\frac{22}{7} = \frac{11}{s}$
32. $\frac{80}{45} = \frac{16}{t}$
33. $\frac{3}{4} = \frac{15}{b}$

11-5 Random Samples and Surveys

What You'll Learn

OBJECTIVE 1 To identify a random sample

OBJECTIVE 2 To write a survey question

. . . And Why

To identify biased survey questions, as in Example 2

Check Skills You'll Need

For help, go to Lesson 6-2.

Write each ratio as a percent. Round your answer to the nearest tenth, where necessary.

1. 4 out of 5
2. 10 out of 40
3. 140 out of 200
4. 6 out of 18
5. 999 out of 1,000
6. 56 out of 56

New Vocabulary

- population
- sample
- random sample
- biased question

Interactive lesson includes instant self-check, tutorials, and activities.

OBJECTIVE 1 Identifying a Random Sample

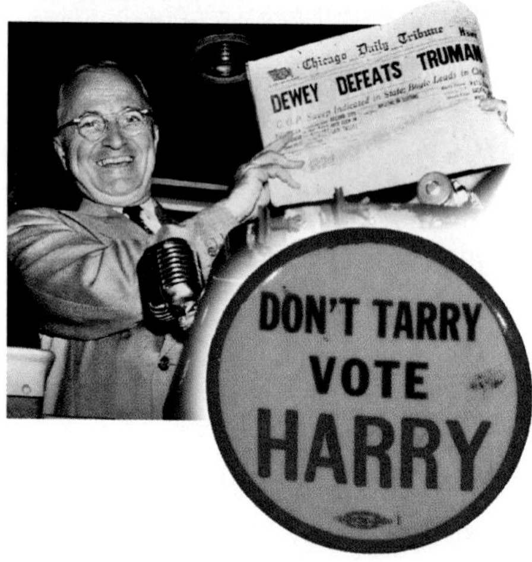

Real-World Connection

President Truman celebrated his victory by showing a headline written before the vote was counted.

In the 1948 United States presidential election, the candidates were Thomas Dewey and Harry Truman. Before the election, pollsters predicted that Dewey would win. When the actual votes were counted, however, Truman won.

A **population** is a group of objects or people. The population of an election is all the people who vote in that election. It is impractical to ask all the voters how they expect to vote. Pollsters select a **sample,** or a part of the population. In a **random sample,** each member of a population has an equal chance of being selected for the sample.

The pollsters who predicted that Dewey would win in 1948 did not use a random sample. They relied on a poll taken two weeks before the election, when many were undecided.

1 EXAMPLE Identifying a Random Sample

Suppose you are surveying customers at a mall to find which stores they shop at the most. Which sample is more likely to be random? Explain.

a. You survey shoppers at one entrance to the mall.

Customers entering at one entrance may be shopping at only the stores near that entrance. This sample is not random.

b. You walk around the mall and survey shoppers.

By walking around, you give everyone in the mall an equal chance of being surveyed. This sample is more likely to be random.

✓ Check Understanding 1 Suppose you are surveying a store's customers to find why they chose that store. Which sample is more likely to be random? Explain.

a. You survey 20 people outside the entrance from 5:00 P.M. to 8:00 P.M.
b. You survey 20 people outside the entrance between opening and closing.
c. Reasoning How would you take a random sample of a whole town?

OBJECTIVE 2

Writing a Survey Question

When you do a survey, you want to ask questions that do not influence the answer. A **biased question** is a question that makes an unjustified assumption, or makes one answer appear better than another.

Reading Math

Bias means "slant." A biased question slants the answers in one direction.

2 EXAMPLE Identifying Biased Questions

Music Is each question *biased* or *fair*? Explain.

a. "Do you think that soothing classical music is more pleasing than the loud, obnoxious pop music that teenagers listen to?"

This question is biased. It implies that all pop music is loud and that only teenagers listen to it. The adjectives "soothing" and "obnoxious" may also influence responses.

b. "Which do you think is the most common age group of people who like pop music?"

This question is fair. It does not assume that listeners of pop music fall into only one age group.

c. "Do you prefer classical music or pop music?"

This question is fair. It does not make any assumptions about classical music, pop music, or about people who listen to either kind.

✓ Check Understanding 2 Is each question *biased* or *fair*? Explain.

a. Do you prefer slimy anchovies or healthy vegetables on your pizza?
b. Which pizza topping do you like best?

Investigation: Writing Unbiased Questions

1. Choose a topic about which you would like people's opinions. Write five unbiased survey questions.
2. Data Collection Conduct the survey. Display the results of your survey in a graph.
3. Consider the results of your survey. Do you still think your questions were unbiased? If not, how would you change them?

EXERCISES

For more practice, see *Extra Practice.*

A Practice by Example

Example 1 (page 596)

Which sample is more likely to be random? Explain.

1. You want to survey teens about their snacking habits.
  a. You ask everyone at a party to name their favorite snack.
  b. You ask several teens entering a grocery store.

2. You want to survey seventh-grade students about their computer use.
  a. You ask seventh-graders leaving the cafeteria after lunch.
  b. You ask the seventh-graders entering a local library on Friday night.

3. You want to know the most popular book among students at your school.
  a. You ask students from different grades at your school.
  b. You ask a group of your friends.

4. You want to know which baseball team is considered to be the best.
  a. You ask everyone seated in your section of the ballpark.
  b. You ask several visitors at a tourist attraction.

Example 2 (page 597)

Is each question *biased* or *fair*? Explain.

5. Do you prefer getting invigorating exercise or being a couch potato?

6. Do you prefer to exercise or watch television?

7. Do you prefer rock music or jazz?

8. Do you prefer harsh rock music or soothing jazz?

9. Do you prefer unhealthy snacks or nutritious snacks?

10. What type of snack do you prefer?

B Apply Your Skills

11. Reasoning Suppose you are studying eating habits of college students. What question should you ask Joe Smith to help you decide whether he is a member of the population you are studying?

Clothes A manufacturer is conducting a survey to decide the price of a sweatsuit for women ages 18–35. Explain whether each method involves a random sample.

12. Randomly select names from a national telephone directory. Call these people and survey whoever answers.

13. Stand outside sporting goods stores and survey every woman aged 18–35 who enters.

14. Select names from a national telephone directory. Call these people and survey any woman 18–35 who answers.

15. Writing in Math Describe how you would sample the students in your school to get a random sample.

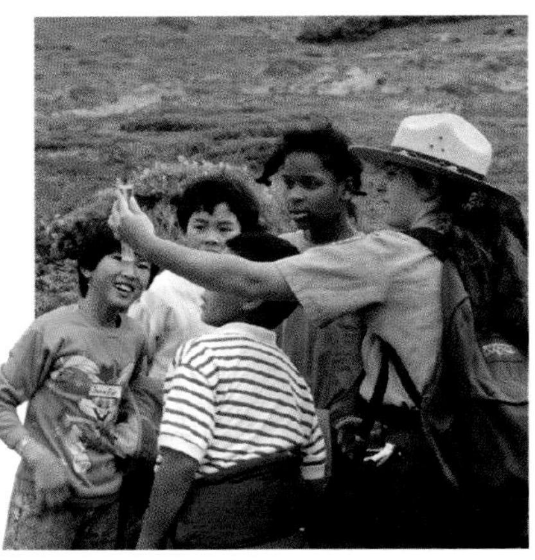

Real-World Connection

Careers A park ranger has a college degree related to park management, natural history, forestry, or outdoor recreation.

16. Parks Suppose you are gathering information about visitors to Yosemite National Park. You survey every tenth person entering the park. Would you get a random sample of visitors? Why or why not?

17. Public Transportation An urban planner wants to know how bus drivers are affected by work crews in the streets. How can the planner survey a random sample of bus drivers?

18. You want to survey teenage girls about their favorite sport.
 a. Write a survey question that is fair.
 b. How can you get a random sample?

19. Writing in Math How can you tell whether a survey question is biased? Explain.

20. Open-Ended Write a fair survey question. Rewrite your question in two different ways to make it biased.

21. Which survey would you use to determine attitudes about carnivals? Explain.

Survey	Question	Yes	No	Don't Know
A	Do you like going to noisy, overpriced carnivals?	53%	46%	1%
B	Do you like going to carnivals?	72%	27%	1%

C Challenge

22. a. Politics In a recent survey, 52% of voters favored a certain candidate. The survey had a margin of error of $\pm 2.5\%$. What is the greatest percent of voters in favor of the candidate? The least?
 b. Reasoning Explain the term *margin of error.*

23. A newspaper wants to survey 1 out of every 100 people of voting age in a local community. The community has 38,592 people of voting age. How many people should the newspaper survey?

24. Stretch Your Thinking Nine copies of a newsletter cost less than \$10. Ten copies of the same newsletter at the same price cost more than \$11. What is the cost of one newsletter?

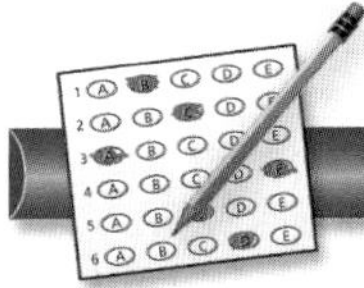

Test Prep

Multiple Choice

25. Which question is NOT biased?
 A. Do you prefer long biographical movies or funny movies?
 B. Do you prefer interesting biographical movies or movies that make you laugh?
 C. Do you prefer movies about people who have lived successful lives or movies based on sheer fantasy?
 D. Do you prefer biographical movies or comedy movies?

26. A manufacturer wants to know which color teenagers prefer for tennis shoes. Which survey more likely represents a random sample?
   F. asking 100 teenagers chosen at random in one state
   G. surveying teenagers selected from a list of all middle school and high school students nationwide
   H. surveying teenagers selected from a list of all athletes
   I. surveying boys across the country who take part in after-school sports

Short Response

27. Graph the data below. What can you conclude from the graph?

Take It to the NET
Online lesson quiz at
www.PHSchool.com
Web Code: aba-1105

Horse Show Attendance

Week	1	2	3	4	5
Number of Adults	1,258	1,397	2,058	2,193	1,873
Number of Children	524	648	1,852	2,358	2,145

Mixed Review

Lesson 11-1

The results of a survey about the number of books read over the summer are at the right.

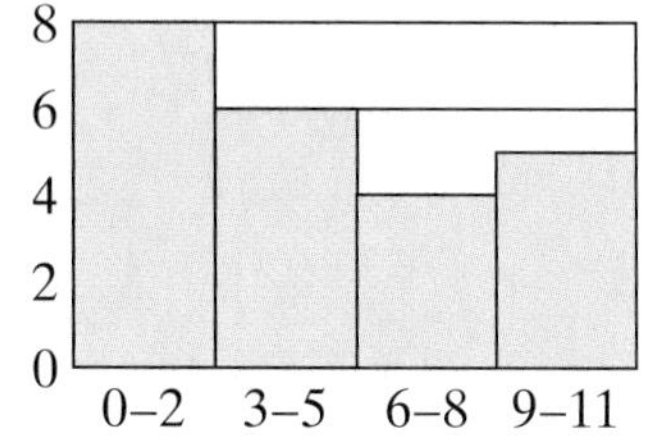

28. What should be the label of each axis?

29. How many people answered the survey?

30. How many people read fewer than 6 books?

Lesson 10-11

Graph the line containing each pair of points.

31. $(-2, 5), (-2, -5)$ 32. $(-4, -3), (-7, -3)$ 33. $(2, 4), (-5, 4)$

Lesson 9-9

Algebra **Solve for the variable indicated in red.**

34. $v = t + w$ 35. $P = 2w + 2\ell$ 36. $m = \frac{s + q}{r}$

Math at Work

Pollster

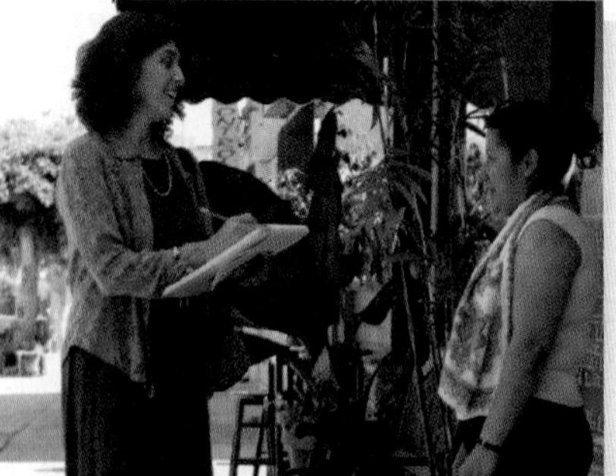

Pollsters interview people to find out their opinions and their preferences. Pollsters use math to analyze the data they collect by finding the mean, median, mode, and range of the data. This gives them an overall view of the collected data. They often graph data to display their findings.

Take It to the NET For more information about pollsters, visit the Prentice Hall Web site: **www.PHSchool.com.**
Web Code: abb-2031

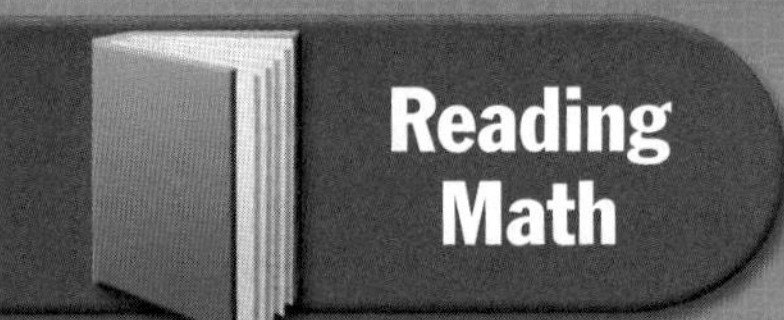

Understanding Word Problems

For Use With Lesson 11-5

Some problems contain too little information. You can use the problem-solving plan to decide if you have enough information to solve the problem. Ask yourself, "What do I know?" and "What do I need to find out?"

1 EXAMPLE

Identify the information you need to solve the following problem.
You buy three shirts for $39. How much do you spend on each shirt?

Read and Understand Read for understanding. Summarize the problem.

"What do I know?"	"What do I need to find out?"
I buy three shirts. I spend $39.	the price of the first shirt the price of the second shirt the price of the third shirt

The problem contains too little information. Since you cannot assume that the prices of the shirts are equal, you need to know the prices of two shirts before you can find the price of the third.

2 EXAMPLE

Identify the information you need to solve the following problem.
Find the circumference of a basketball.

Read and Understand Read for understanding. Summarize the problem.

"What do I know?"	"What do I need to find out?"
the formula for circumference: $C = \pi d$	the circumference of a basketball the diameter of a basketball

You need to find the diameter of a basketball before you can find the circumference.

EXERCISES

For each problem, write answers for "What do I know?" and "What do I need to find out?" Then state what information is missing.

1. You have a set of five numbers. Three of the numbers are 7, 9, and 11. The other two numbers are equal. What is the mean of the set?

2. You jog 4 mi every day. How far will you jog in a month?

Algebra

11-6 Estimating Population Size

What You'll Learn

To use the capture/recapture method

. . . And Why

To estimate a deer population, as in Example 1

Check Skills You'll Need

For help, go to Lesson 5-5.

Solve each proportion. Round your answers to the nearest tenth.

1. $\frac{2}{3} = \frac{a}{15}$
2. $\frac{3}{b} = \frac{21}{20}$
3. $\frac{n}{36} = \frac{11}{9}$
4. $\frac{0.2}{5} = \frac{a}{45}$
5. $\frac{4.2}{63} = \frac{0.6}{n}$
6. $\frac{n}{7} = \frac{24}{21}$
7. $\frac{5}{14} = \frac{n}{7}$
8. $\frac{2.3}{t} = \frac{9.2}{4}$

OBJECTIVE

Interactive lesson includes instant self-check, tutorials, and activities.

1 Using the Capture/Recapture Method

A method of estimating an animal population is the *capture/recapture method*. Researches collect, mark, and release animals. Then another group of animals is captured. The number of marked animals in the second group indicates the population size.

For several years, the mule deer population of Montana was declining. Researchers estimated the deer population, using the proportion below.

$$\frac{\text{number of marked deer counted}}{\text{total number of deer counted}} = \frac{\text{total number of marked deer}}{\text{estimate of deer population}}$$

1 EXAMPLE Using the Capture/Recapture Method

Real World

Deer Population Researchers know there are 105 marked deer in an area. On a flight over the area, they count 48 marked deer and a total of 638 deer. Estimate the deer population.

Use the capture/recapture method.

$$\frac{\text{number of marked deer counted}}{\text{total number of deer counted}} = \frac{\text{total number of marked deer}}{\text{estimate of deer population}}$$

$\frac{48}{638} = \frac{105}{x}$ ← **Write a proportion.**

$48x = 105 \cdot 638$ ← **Write cross products.**

$48x = 66{,}990$ ← **Multiply.**

$\frac{48x}{48} = \frac{66{,}990}{48}$ ← **Divide each side by 48.**

$x = 66{,}990$ ÷ 48 = 1395.625 ← **Use a calculator.**

$x \approx 1{,}396$ ← **Round to the nearest integer.**

There are about 1,396 deer in the area.

Real-World Connection

The mule deer is named for its mule-like ears.

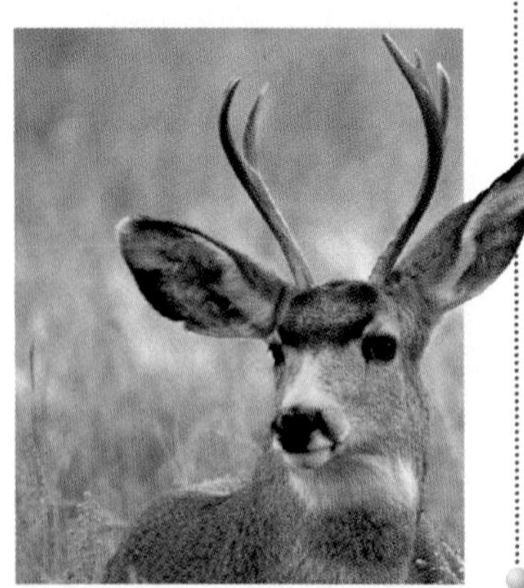

Check Understanding 1 **a.** Suppose the researchers of Example 1 count only 35 marked deer. Estimate the population.
b. Suppose the researchers of Example 1 count a total of 857 deer. Estimate the deer population.

EXERCISES

For more practice, see *Extra Practice*.

A Practice by Example

Example 1 (page 602)

Use a proportion to estimate the total deer population for each year.

	Year	Total Deer Counted	Marked Deer Counted	Total Marked Deer
1.	1	1,173	65	101
2.	2	1,017	42	83
3.	3	1,212	32	60
4.	4	1,707	30	36
5.	5	1,612	68	89
6.	6	1,590	37	59
7.	7	1,417	42	54
8.	8	1,608	85	110
9.	9	1,469	52	83

Need Help?
For help solving proportions, go to Lesson 5-4.

Use a proportion to estimate each animal population.

10. total trout counted: 2,985
tagged trout counted: 452
total tagged trout: 1,956

11. total bass counted: 3,102
tagged bass counted: 198
total tagged bass: 872

12. total black bears counted: 218
marked black bears counted: 25
total marked black bears: 35

13. total penguins counted: 7,234
marked penguins counted: 3,921
total marked penguins: 4,958

14. total wild horses counted: 1,583
marked wild horses counted: 496
total marked wild horses: 1,213

15. total rabbits counted: 5,804
marked rabbits counted: 3,214
total marked rabbits: 5,398

16. Otters There are 20 marked sea otters in a costal region. In a survey, marine biologists counted 42 sea otters, of which 12 were marked. About how many sea otters are in the area?

17. In a study, a fish and game department worker catches, tags, and frees 124 catfish. A few weeks later, he catches and frees 140 catfish. Thirty-five have tags. Estimate the number of catfish in the lake.

B Apply Your Skills

18. Data Analysis Use your answers to Exercises 1–9 on p. 603. Describe how the deer population changed over time.

19. Some researchers calculate the ratio of marked deer counted to the number of marked deer.
   a. Calculate this ratio for each year, using the data in Exercises 1–9. Write each ratio as a decimal rounded to the nearest thousandth.
   b. Writing in Math Explain how counting a high percent of the marked deer might affect the estimate of the deer population.

Real-World Connection

The eyes of hammerhead sharks are on the outer edges of their heads.

20. **Sharks** A biologist is studying the shark population off the Florida coast. He captures, tags, and sets free 38 sharks. A week later, of 25 sharks captured, 8 have tags. He uses the proportion $\frac{25}{8} = \frac{38}{x}$ to make an estimate. He estimates the population to be about 12.
   a. Find the error in the biologist's proportion.
   b. Estimate the shark population.

21. Reasoning Suppose the number of captured, tagged, and released animals of a population is small.
   a. If only a few animals are recaptured, would you expect most of the recaptured animals to have tags? Explain.
   b. If most animals are recaptured, would you expect most of the tagged animals to be recaptured? Explain.

22. **Alligators** A biologist spilled juice on the report at the right. Find the number of alligators that were caught, tagged, and set free.

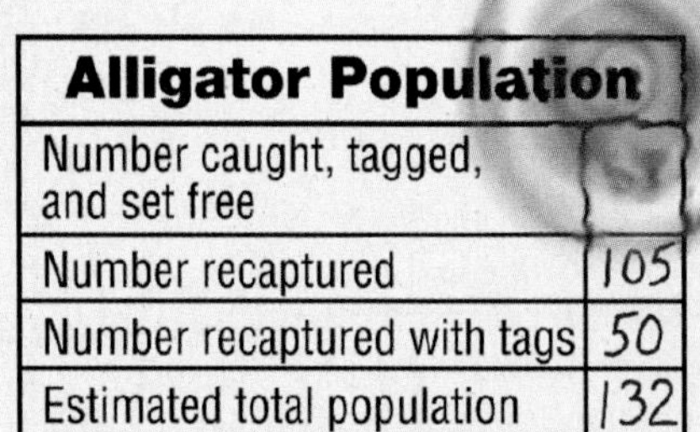

Alligator Population	
Number caught, tagged, and set free	
Number recaptured	105
Number recaptured with tags	50
Estimated total population	132

23. **Ecology** An ecology class is helping determine the squirrel population in a park. The students capture, tag, and free 68 squirrels. A week later, of 84 squirrels captured, 16 have tags.
   a. Estimate the number of squirrels in the park.
   b. Reasoning Suppose some squirrels lose their tags. How will this affect your estimate of the squirrel population?

C Challenge

24. **Fish** A fishery biologist captures, tags, and sets free 100 lake trout. Later, she captures 70 lake trout, of which 32 have tags. The biologist tags all the untagged fish and sets them free.
   a. Estimate the population.
   b. A week later, the biologist captures 123 lake trout, of which 74 have tags. Estimate the population.
   c. How does the second capture affect the estimate of the lake trout population? Explain.
   d. Which estimate do you think is more accurate? Explain.

25. In a capture/recapture program, 30% of the animals recaptured have tags. Suppose 70 animals were originally captured, tagged, and released. Estimate the population.

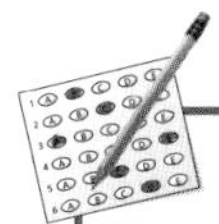

Test-Prep Tip

You can check your answer to a proportion by checking that the cross products are equal.

26. A local lake is stocked with 400 bass, and x of them are tagged. One week later, of x bass captured and released, 4 have tags. How many bass are captured and released?

27. **Stretch Your Thinking** I am the set of whole numbers between 100 and 400 containing at least one of the digits 4 and 5. How many whole numbers are in the set?

Test Prep

Multiple Choice

28. What is the solution of $\frac{7}{10} = \frac{21}{x}$?
A. 3 **B.** 3.3 **C.** 14.7 **D.** 30

29. There are 35 marked seals in a coastal region. Biologists count 36 seals, of which 8 are marked. About how many seals are in the region?
F. 10,080 seals **G.** 1,260 seals
H. 280 seals **I.** 158 seals

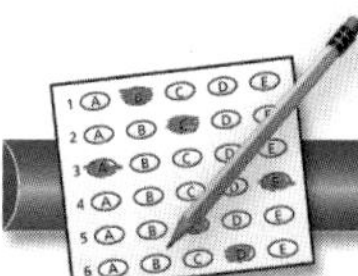

Take It to the NET

Online lesson quiz at **www.PHSchool.com**

Web Code: aba-1106

30. In a study of lake fish, a biologist catches, tags, and sets free 62 fish. A few weeks later, of 60 fish caught and released, 15 have tags. Estimate the number of fish in the lake.
A. 930 fish **B.** 248 fish **C.** 240 fish **D.** 16 fish

Extended Response

31. You are studying a raccoon population. You catch, tag, and set free 21 raccoons. After one month, you catch 32 raccoons, of which 14 have tags. After two months, you catch 28 raccoons, of which 13 have tags. After three months, you catch 36 raccoons, of which 18 have tags. Find an estimate for the population after each month. Display your results in a line graph and a bar graph. Explain which graph you would use to show the population trend.

Mixed Review

Lesson 10-1

Algebra **Graph each point on the same coordinate plane.**

32. (3, 4) **33.** (0, 0) **34.** (−5, −2) **35.** (−1, −2) **36.** (4, −3)

Lesson 9-2

Write a rule for each sequence. Then find the next three terms.

37. 3, 8, 13, 18, . . . **38.** −2, 1, 4, 7, . . . **39.** 27, 16, 5, −6, . . .

Lesson 7-7

40. **Geometry** $\triangle PQR \cong \triangle XYZ$. Find the angle measurements and side lengths of $\triangle XYZ$.

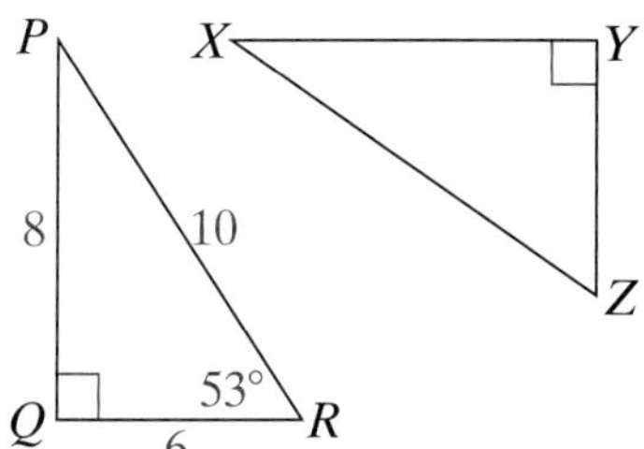

11-7 Using Data to Persuade

What You'll Learn

To identify misleading graphs

To identify misleading statistics

. . . And Why

To recognize misleading ads, as in Example 4

Check Skills You'll Need

For help, go to Lesson 1-10.

Find the mean, median, and mode of each set of data.

1. 122, 114, 113, 116, 120, 123, 119, 117, 123, 111
2. 54, 99, 50, 49, 55, 50, 49, 50, 58, 47, 55
3. 1.2, 3.4, 2.7, 0.9, 2.2, 3.1, 3.4, 1.7, 2.8, 1.9, 2.0
4. 29, 67, 39, 51, 169, 85, 30, 18, 64, 39, 41, 52

OBJECTIVE 1

iTEXT Interactive lesson includes instant self-check, tutorials, and activities.

Identifying Misleading Graphs

A graph can be a powerful way of presenting data. How a graph is drawn can affect the impression it gives about the data.

1 EXAMPLE Starting at Zero

a. The graph at the right shows the average amount of time 4th, 5th, 6th, and 7th graders spend on homework. How is this graph misleading?

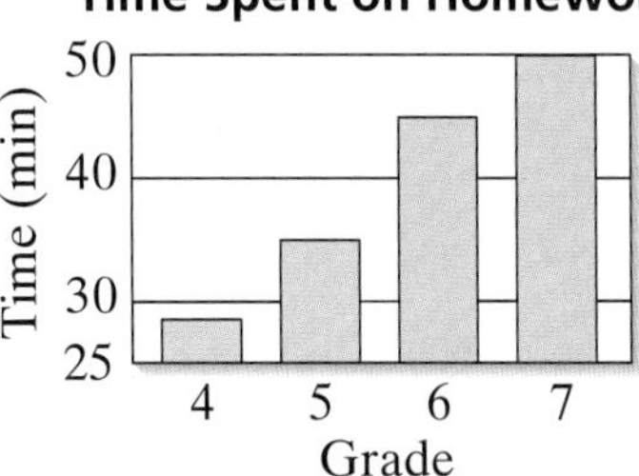

The graph starts at 25 on the vertical scale, rather than 0. This makes it seem that 4th graders spend almost no time doing homework.

b. Redraw the graph so it is not misleading.

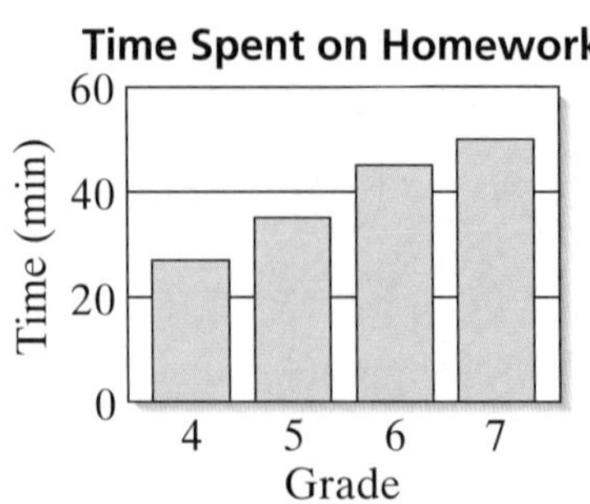

← **You can fix the graph by drawing it so the vertical scale starts at 0.**

Check Understanding **1** **Reasoning** Which graph would you use to try to convince your parents that your homework increased drastically from 5th grade to 7th grade? Explain.

Placing a break in a graph is useful when space is limited, or when you want to focus on change over a narrow range. However, breaks can also mislead.

The graph at the right shows another version of the graph from Example 1. It includes a break in the vertical scale and in the bars. The breaks alert you that the heights of the bars are not proportional to the data values.

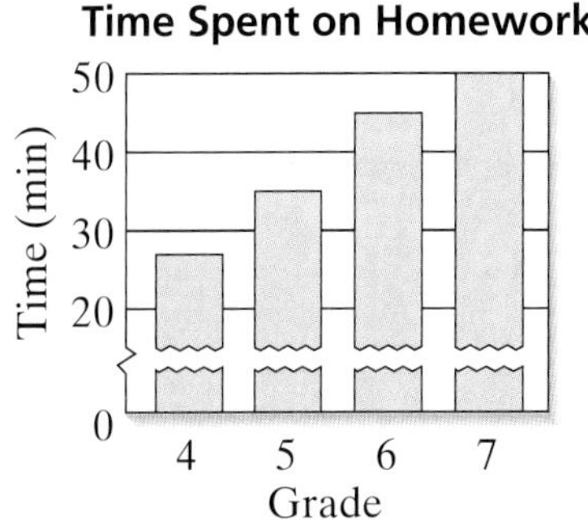

Graphs can also mislead if the vertical or horizontal axes have unequal or very large intervals.

2 EXAMPLE Misleading Intervals

Profit A company uses the graph below to show investors that annual profits are increasing steadily. Explain how the graph is misleading.

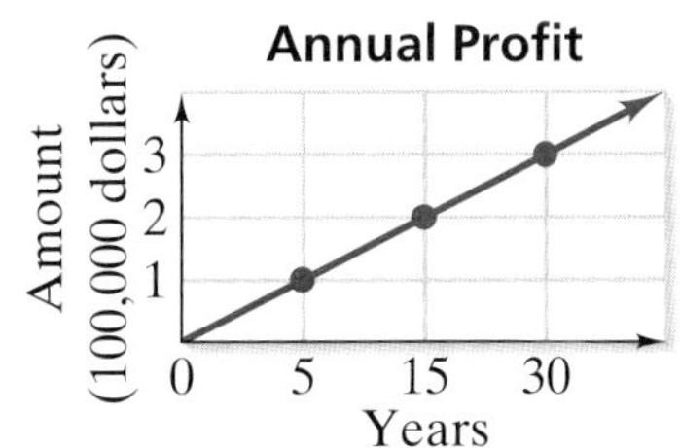

The intervals of the horizontal axis are unequal.

Annual profits increase $10,000 over the first 5 years and then another $10,000 over the next 10 years. Annual profits are increasing more slowly.

2 a. Reasoning Which interval actually has the least growth in profits?
b. Redraw the graph using equal intervals on both axes.

OBJECTIVE

2 Identifying Misleading Statistics

Using the mean, median, or mode of a set of data can inform or mislead.

3 EXAMPLE Misleading Use of the Mean

You survey students in your class to find the number of pets per student. The results are shown at the right. You want to convince your parents to let you have four pets by saying, "The mean number of pets my classmates have is four." How is this misleading?

How Many Pets Do You Have?

0, 0, 0, 1, 1, 1,
1, 1, 1, 2, 2, 2,
3, 4, 7, 15, 27

The mean is not a good measure of the typical number of pets. Two students have a large number of pets, which distorts the results.

3 a. Find the median and the mode of the data.
b. Reasoning Which of the three measures gives the best sense of the typical number of pets? Explain.

The mean, median, and mode use all the data in a set. You can mislead by presenting only part of the data or by leaving out important facts.

4 EXAMPLE **Real-World Problem Solving**

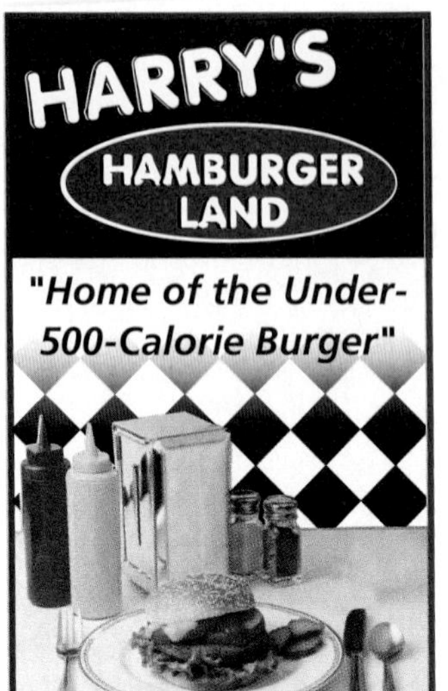

Advertising The poster is part of an ad campaign for Harry's Hamburger Land. Below are data about Harry's hamburgers. Is the advertisement misleading?

Item	Calories	Fat (g)	Average Number Sold Daily
Kiddie Burger	480	35	80
Hamburger Plus	575	42	68
Health Burger	580	40	65
Golden Fries Hamburger	660	57	43
Burger Deluxe	700	55	75

Since all but one of the hamburgers have more than 500 Calories, the advertisement is misleading.

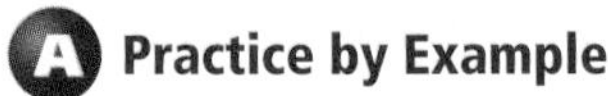

4 **a.** What is the mean number of Calories for the five types of hamburgers?
b. What is the mean number of grams of fat for the five types of hamburgers?
c. **Reasoning** How could you change the ad to better reflect the data?

EXERCISES

For more practice, see *Extra Practice*.

A Practice by Example

Examples 1, 2 (pages 606, 607)

For Exercises 1–4, complete the following.
(a) Tell what impression the graph makes.
(b) Tell how the graph makes this impression.
(c) Use the data to draw a graph that does not mislead.

1.

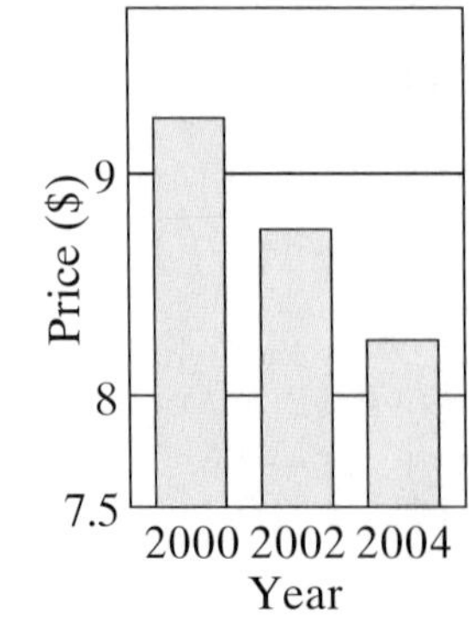

2.

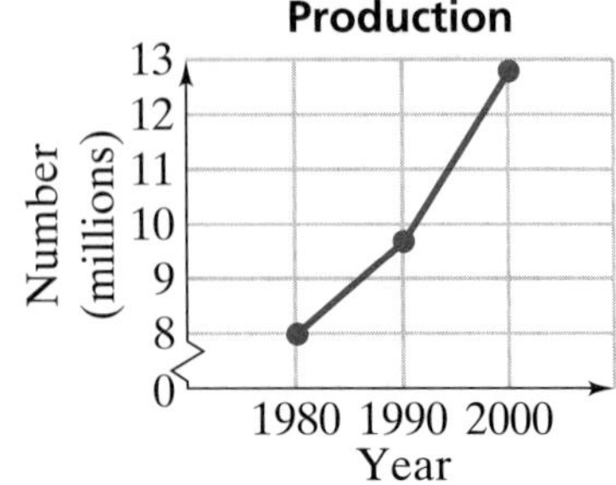

3.

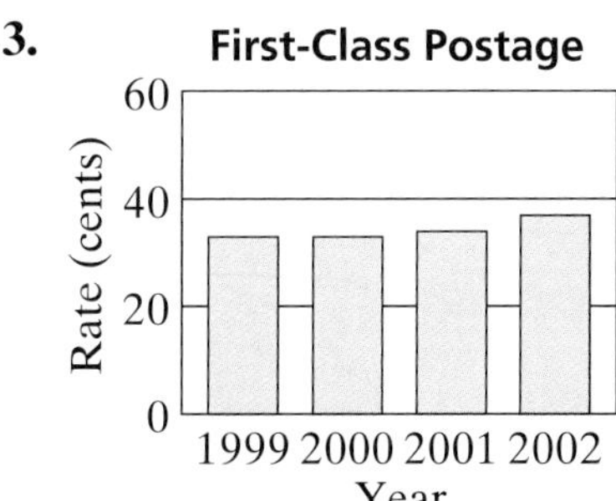

4.

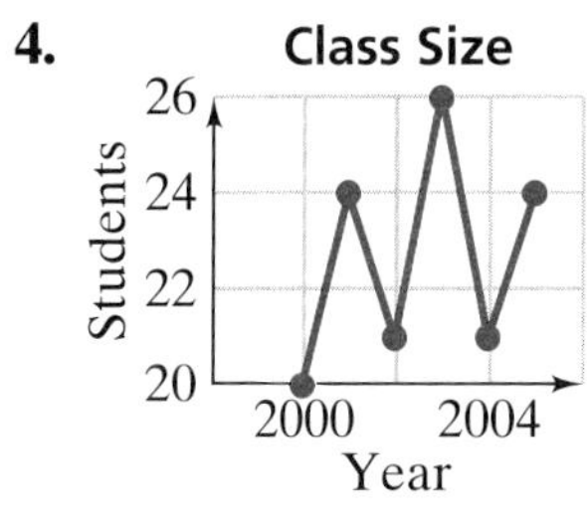

Examples 3, 4 (pages 607, 608)

5. Suppose you score 93, 83, 76, 92, and 76 on your social studies exams.
   a. You want to show your parents how well you are doing in class. Should you use the mean, median, or mode? Explain.
   b. If your teacher wants to influence you to work harder, which measure should your teacher use? Explain.

6. **Reasoning** Suppose you want to buy a bike. The prices are $119, $139, $149, $179, $189, $199, and $209. You want the bike that costs $189. Should you use the mean, median, or mode to convince your parents? Explain.

7. **Bowling** Kisha and Bill compete in a three-game bowling match. The table shows their scores.
   a. Bill says he won the match because he has a higher average. Is he correct?
   b. Kisha says she won the match. How can she justify this statement?

Bowling Scores

Game	1	2	3
Kisha	81	60	93
Bill	78	95	91

8. **Reasoning** To raise money for charity, your class holds a car wash. You pay $15 for washing materials and collect $128 in donations. Can you say you raised $128 for charity? Explain.

B Apply Your Skills

9. **Nutrition** Farnaz asks students at her school, "What's your favorite fruit?" She draws the graph below. Why is it misleading?

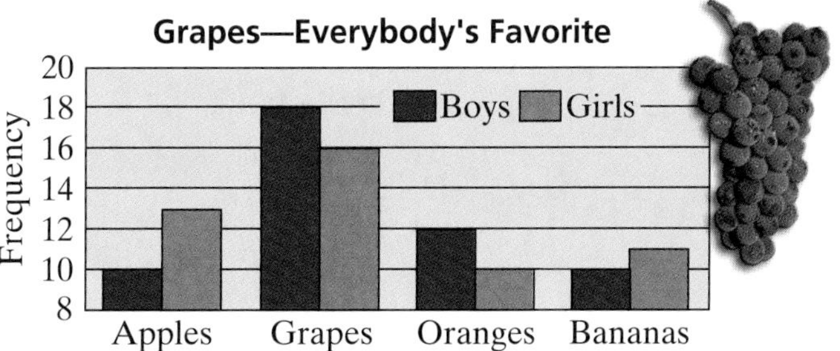

Men's Olympic 100-Meter Winners

Year	Time (s)
1988	9.92
1992	9.96
1996	9.84
2000	9.87

SOURCE: *Sports Almanac*

10. **Track and Field** The data show the winning times for the men's Olympic 100-meter event.
    a. Make a line graph that gives the impression that there has been great change in the winning times.
    b. Make a line graph that gives the impression that there has been little change in the winning times.
    c. **Reasoning** Which graph better represents the data? Explain.

For each graph, do the following. (a) Tell what impression the graph makes. (b) Tell how the graph makes this impression. (c) Use the data to draw a graph that does not mislead.

11.

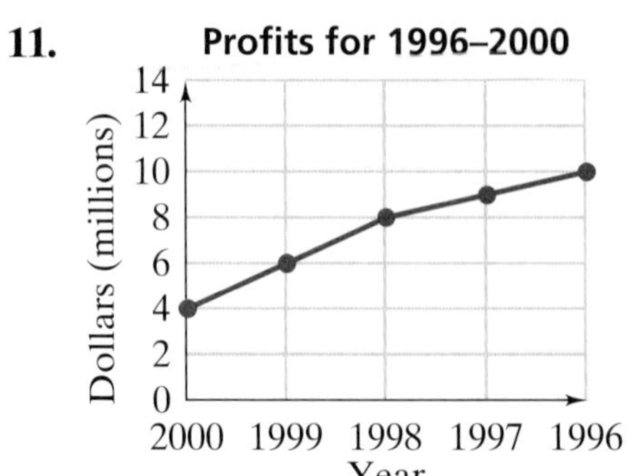

12.

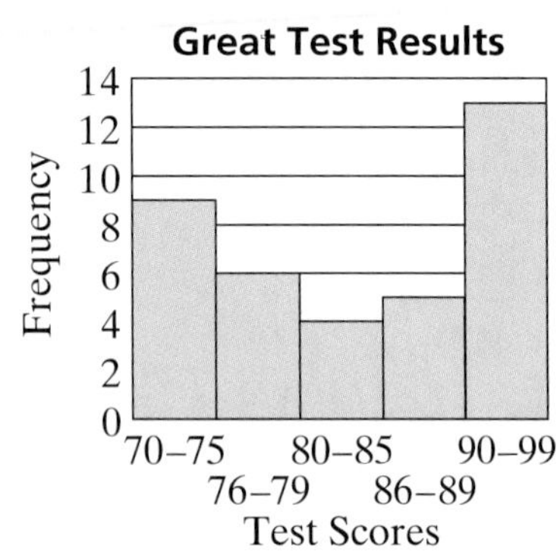

13. **Writing in Math** Spotless Cleaners sends out 200 customer surveys. The company gets 100 replies with 97 customers saying they are satisfied. In an ad, Spotless Cleaners says that 97% of their customers are satisfied. Is this statement misleading? Explain.

Measles Cases Reported in the United States

Year	Number of Cases (thousands)
1989	18.2
1990	27.8
1991	9.6
1992	2.2
1993	0.3
1994	1.0
1995	0.3
1996	0.5
1997	0.1
1998	0.1
1999	0.1

SOURCE: U.S. Centers for Disease Control and Prevention

14. Medicine The data and graph show measles cases in the United States.

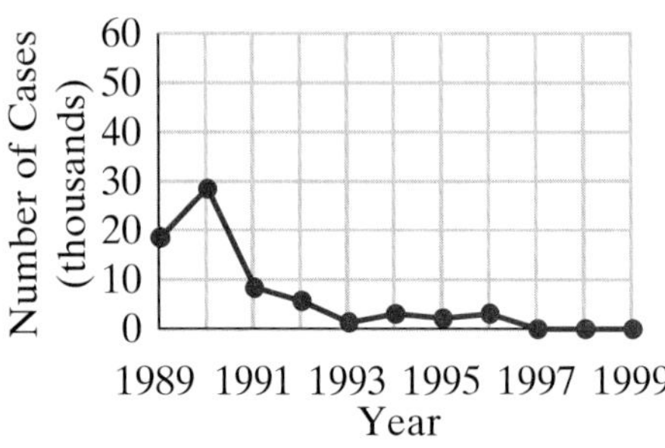

a. **Reasoning** What does the graph suggest about the outbreak of measles in 1990?

b. How was the graph drawn to give this impression?

c. Draw a better graph. Give your graph a title.

15. Wildlife The graph below shows the population of bald eagle pairs.

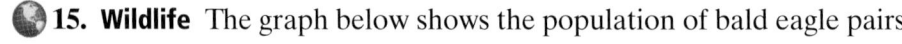

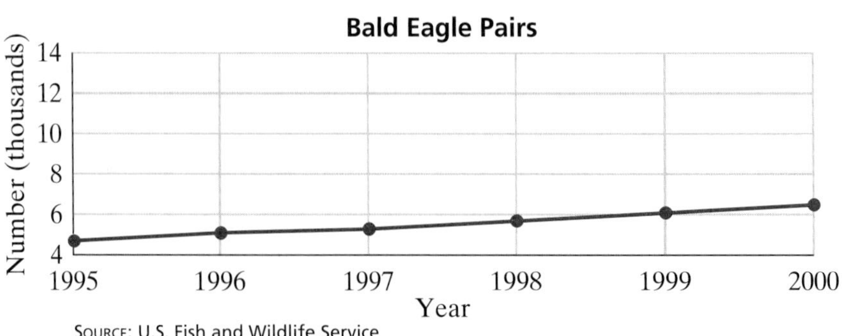

a. What impression does the graph create?

b. What was done to the graph to make this impression?

c. Use the data to draw a graph that does not mislead.

16. **Data File, p. 571** Use the data to make a graph that suggests that people in Switzerland walk twice as frequently as they use public transit.

C Challenge

17. a. Open-Ended Find a graph in a newspaper or magazine. Describe the data presented.
    b. Is the graph trying to influence you? Explain.

18. Stretch Your Thinking When you multiply 2,178 by four, the product is 8,712. Notice that the digits in the product are the reverse of the digits in 2,178. Find the four-digit number whose digits are reversed when multiplied by nine.

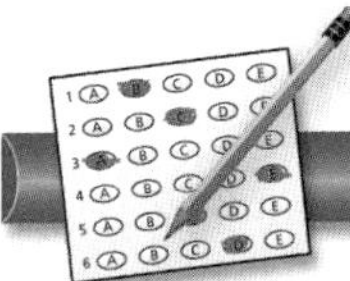

Test Prep

Multiple Choice

19. The point (−1, 5) is in which quadrant?
    A. I B. II C. III D. IV

20. What is the slope of a line through (1, 3) and (−2, −5)?
    F. −2 G. −0.5 H. 0.5 I. 2

Take It to the NET
Online lesson quiz at
www.PHSchool.com
Web Code: aba-1107

21. Which point is on a line with slope −3 passing through (−2, −5)?
    A. (−5, −4) B. (1, −4) C. (−1, −2) D. (−3, −2)

22. Simplify −42 ÷ 6.
    F. −48 G. −42
    H. −7 I. 7

Short Response

23. a. What happens to the population of the town between 2000 and 2010?
    b. Explain why the graph is misleading.

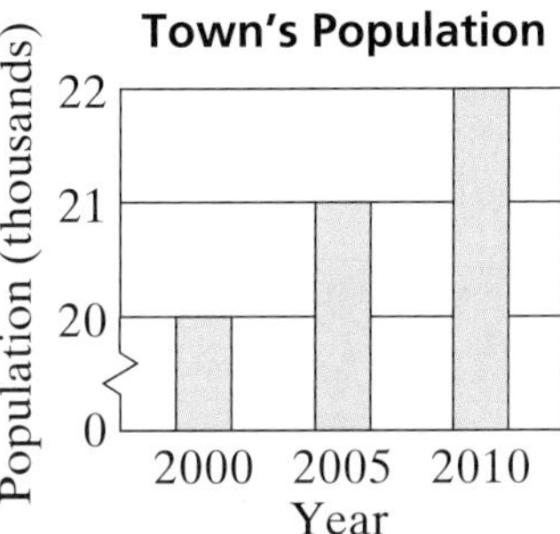

Mixed Review

Lesson 11-1 **Make a frequency table for each set of data.**

24. 4, 5, 5, 8, 3, 5, 7, 7, 10
25. 15, 16, 12, 17, 16, 12, 11, 27
26. 1.1, 1.4, 1.6, 1.3, 1.1, 1.4, 1.8
27. 62, 61, 63, 64, 66, 62, 63, 63, 67

Lesson 10-3 Algebra **Draw a line through the given point P with the given slope.**

28. $P(-1, 0)$, slope $= 2$
29. $P(0, 2)$, slope $= -3$
30. $P(5, 3)$, slope $= \frac{4}{3}$
31. $P(7, -1)$, slope $= -\frac{1}{2}$

Lesson 9-4 Algebra **Evaluate the function $y = \frac{x}{3}$ for each value of x.**

32. −3
33. −1
34. 12
35. −6
36. 0.18
37. 2.4
38. 0.9
39. 4.2

Writing to Persuade

For Use With Lesson 11-7

When you present information to persuade someone, you should:

- Identify your audience and your goal.
- Summarize the mathematics you used to reach your final answer.
- Make a graph or other visual display to reinforce your point.

EXAMPLE

Your parents choose full service over self service at the gas station. They say that \$.08/gal is not a big difference. You do not agree. Show how you could convince your parents.

Identify your audience and your goal Your audience is your parents. Your goal is to convince them that the extra money spent on full-service gasoline adds up over time.

Summarize the math Show the facts and steps used to reach your answer.

- *Our family fills the 25-gal tank once per week. The self service lane would save us \$.08/gal.*
- *One week's savings: 25 gal at \$.08/gal is 25 × \$.08 = \$2*
- *One month's savings: 4 × \$2 = \$8*

Make a graph A picture—or in this case, a graph—is worth a thousand words. Let x = the number of of months and y = total dollars saved. The equation $y = 8x$ models the amount your family could save. Graph the equation for 12 months to show the savings for a year.

EXERCISES

1. **Food Prices** Your family eats two boxes of cereal each week. Your parents buy a name-brand cereal that costs \$1.25 more per box than the store brand. Present the information and a graph to persuade your family to save money by buying the store-brand cereal.

2. Find another way that your family could change its spending habits to save money. Present information and a graph to persuade your family.

11-8 Exploring Scatter Plots

What You'll Learn

 To draw scatter plots

 To interpret scatter plots

. . . And Why

To describe trends in data, as in Example 2

Check Skills You'll Need

For help, go to Lesson 10-1.

Graph each point on the same coordinate plane.

1. (4, 0)
2. (2, 5)
3. (0, 3)
4. (1, 4)
5. (2, 3)
6. (0, 0)

New Vocabulary • scatter plot • positive trend • negative trend • no trend

OBJECTIVE 1

Interactive lesson includes instant self-check, tutorials, and activities.

Drawing Scatter Plots

A **scatter plot** is a graph that relates two sets of data. To make a scatter plot, plot the two sets of data as ordered pairs.

1 EXAMPLE Drawing Scatter Plots

Real World

Books Graph the data at the right in a scatter plot.

Each row in the table represents a point on the scatter plot.

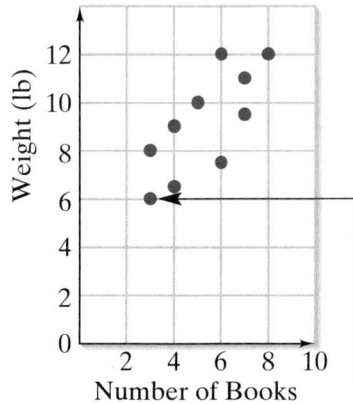

Book Bag Weights

Number of Books	Weight (lb)
3	6
3	8
4	6.5
4	9
5	10
6	7.5
6	12
7	9.5
7	11
8	12

Book Bag Weights

Weight (lb): 0, 2, 4, 6, 8, 10, 12

Number of Books: 2, 4, 6, 8, 10

This point is for the book bag that holds 3 books and weighs 6 lb.

Check Understanding 1

a. Copy the scatter plot. Graph this additional data in the scatter plot: 4 books in a book bag weighing 8 lb; 5 books in a book bag weighing 9.5 lb; and 6 books in a book bag weighing 10 lb.

b. Estimate the number of books in a book bag weighing 7 lb.

c. How much do you think a book bag with 10 books weighs? Explain.

OBJECTIVE

2 Interpreting Scatter Plots

You can use scatter plots to look for *trends*, or relationships. In Example 1, the scatter plot shows there is a relationship between the number of books in a bag and its weight. As the number of books increases, the weight of the bag generally increases.

You can examine a scatter plot to see whether there is a trend and what kind of trend is shown.

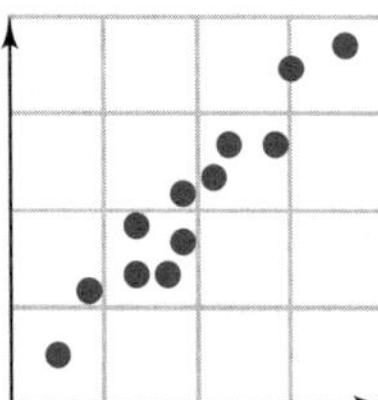

Positive trend

As one set of values increases, the other set tends to increase.

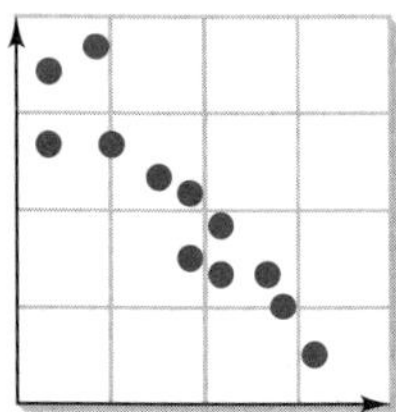

Negative trend

As one set of values increases, the other set tends to decrease.

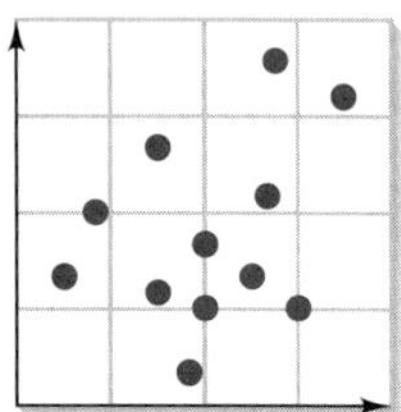

No trend

The points show no relationship.

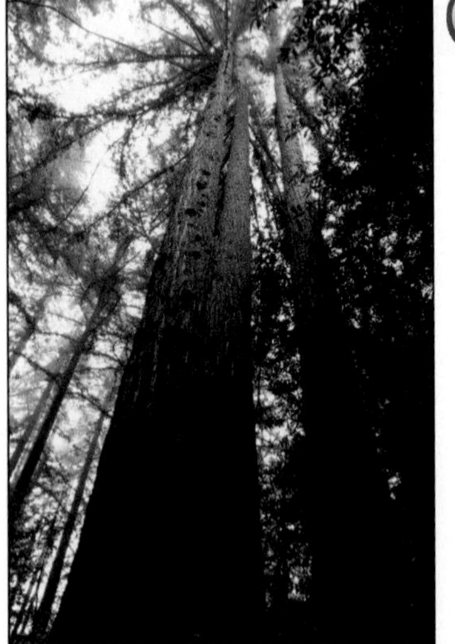

Real-World Connection

The average redwood tree is about 500 yr old and has a diameter of about 25 ft.

2 EXAMPLE Describing Trends in Scatter Plots

Trees Describe the trend in the scatter plot.

Age and Diameter of Trees

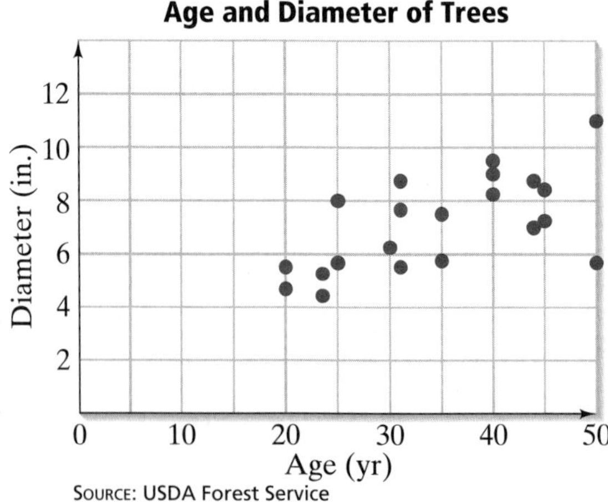

Source: USDA Forest Service

As the age increases, the diameter tends to increase. The scatter plot shows a positive trend.

Check Understanding 2 **Reasoning** A scatter plot has the horizontal scale "Number of Leaves on a Tree" and the vertical scale "Amount of Sunlight Beneath the Tree." Would you expect a positive trend, a negative trend, or no trend? Explain.

EXERCISES

For more practice, see *Extra Practice*.

A Practice by Example

Example 1 (page 613)

Graph each set of data in a scatter plot.

1.

Number of Letters	Number of Syllables
2	1
3	1
4	2
5	1
5	2
5	3
6	2
6	3
7	1
7	3

2.

Hours Studying	Test Grade
0.5	68
0.75	70
1	82
1	78
1.25	78
1.25	86
1.25	94
1.5	82
1.75	90
2	88

3.

Temperature (°F)	Weight of Clothing (lb)
60	5.5
58	5.2
50	6.2
42	6.8
36	7.8
32	7.4
30	8.4
26	9.9
22	10.9
20	12

4.

Height (in.)	Arm Span (in.)
58	57.5
64.5	64
67.5	68.5
65.5	66
63.5	62.5
64	66
71	72
62.5	63
66.5	67.5
69	70

5.

Height (in.)	55	56	54	56	60	56	58	55	55	54	60	59	54
Quiz Grade	32	36	34	32	32	40	42	36	40	28	30	32	44

Example 2 (page 614)

Describe the trend in each scatter plot.

6. 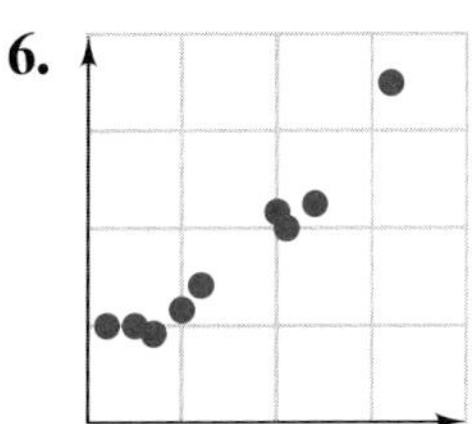

7. 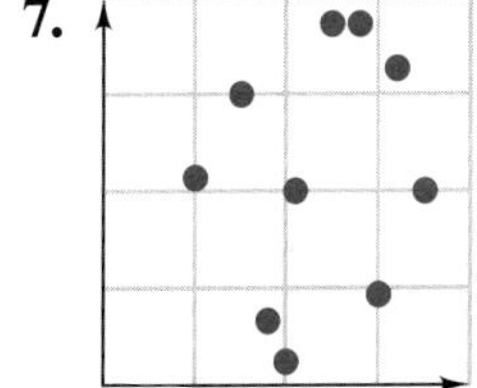

8. 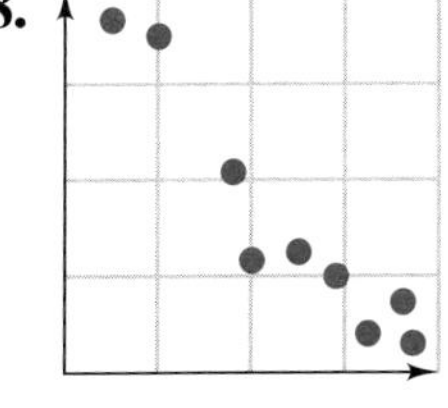

9. 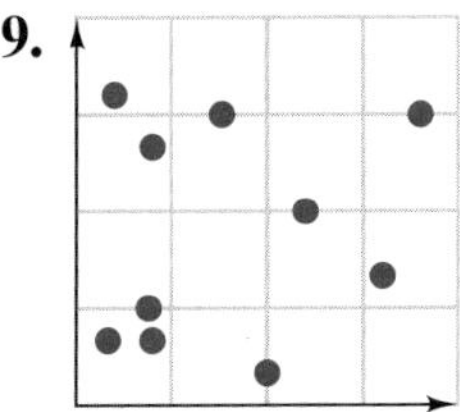

10. 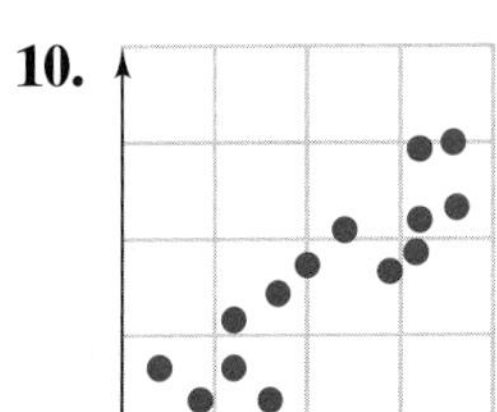

11. 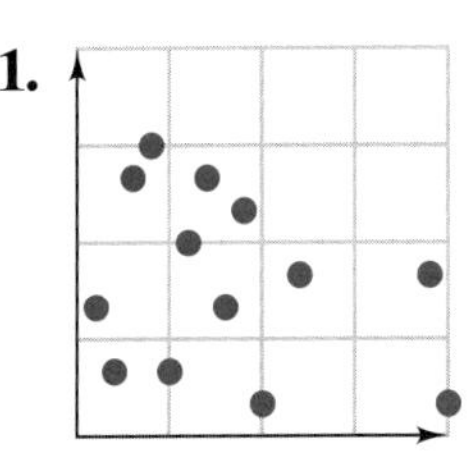

B Apply Your Skills **Movie Prices Use the table for Exercises 12–15.**

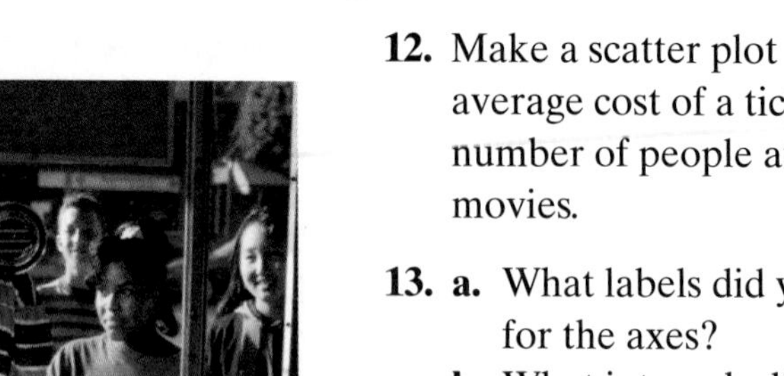

Real-World Connection

Teens make up 16 percent of the population, yet buy 26 percent of movie tickets.

12. Make a scatter plot using the average cost of a ticket and the number of people attending movies.

13. a. What labels did you choose for the axes?

b. What intervals did you choose for the axes?

14. Data Analysis What sort of trend do you see? Explain.

15. Reasoning How would the scatter plot change if you exchanged the two axes? Would the trend change? Explain.

Movie Attendance

Year	Average Ticket Cost (dollars)	Admissions (millions)
1994	4.18	1,292
1995	4.35	1,263
1996	4.42	1,339
1997	4.59	1,388
1998	4.69	1,481
1999	5.08	1,465
2000	5.39	1,421
2001	5.66	1,487

SOURCE: Motion Picture Association of America

Tell what trend you might expect to see in scatter plots using the sets of data in Exercises 16–19. Explain your reasoning.

16. horizontal axis: the number of children in a family; vertical axis: the number of pets

17. horizontal axis: hours spent watching television; vertical axis: hours spent studying

18. horizontal axis: area of a state; vertical axis: the number of governors the state has had

19. horizontal axis: the number of wins for a football team; vertical axis: the number of coaches the team has had in the last five years

20. Carmella made a scatter plot comparing the daily temperature and the number of people at a beach. Which of the three scatter plots below most likely represents the data? Explain your choice.

A.

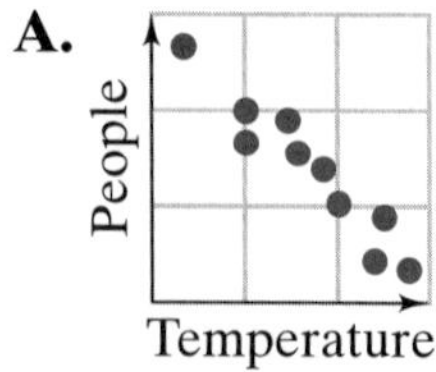

B.

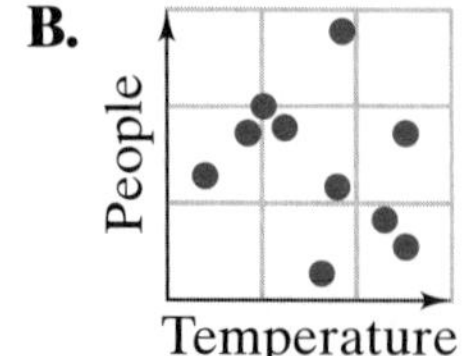

C.

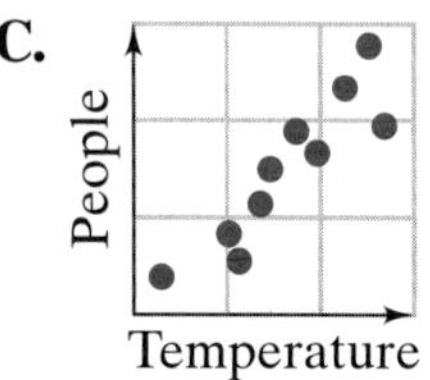

21. Reasoning A scatter plot shows a positive trend. Does this necessarily mean that the scatter plot is the graph of a function? Explain.

22. Writing in Math How is graphing on a scatter plot like graphing in the coordinate plane?

C Challenge **Animal Populations** **Use the data for Exercises 23–26.**

23. Can you see a pattern in the wolf population? In the moose population?

24. Make a scatter plot with the wolf population on the horizontal scale and the moose population on the vertical scale.

25. **Data Analysis** Do you see a relationship between the two populations? Explain.

Moose and Wolf Populations on Isle Royale, Michigan

Year	Wolf	Moose	Year	Wolf	Moose
1985	22	1,115	**1994**	17	1,770
1986	20	1,192	**1995**	16	2,422
1987	16	1,268	**1996**	22	1,163
1988	12	1,335	**1997**	24	500
1989	12	1,397	**1998**	14	699
1990	15	1,216	**1999**	25	750
1991	12	1,313	**2000**	29	850
1992	12	1,590	**2001**	19	900
1993	13	1,879	**2002**	17	1,100

SOURCE: National Park Service

26. **Reasoning** Could you make a double line graph of the data? Explain.

27. **Stretch Your Thinking** You ask 100 students if they like rock or country music. Ninety students say they like rock, 57 say they like country, and 7 say they like neither. How many students like both kinds of music?

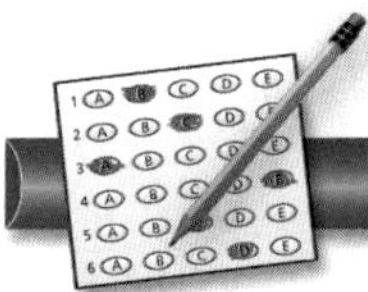

Test Prep

Multiple Choice

28. Describe the trend in the scatter plot.

A. positive trend **B.** negative trend
C. no trend **D.** opposite trend

Take It to the NET
Online lesson quiz at
www.PHSchool.com
Web Code: aba-1108

29. What trend might you see in a scatter plot with a horizontal scale of outdoor temperatures and a vertical scale of electricity used for air conditioning?

F. positive trend **G.** negative trend
H. no trend **I.** opposite trend

30. Describe the trend in the scatter plot.

A. positive trend **B.** negative trend
C. no trend **D.** opposite trend

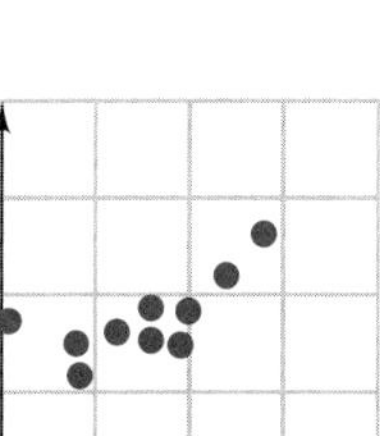

Short Response

31. **a.** Draw a scatter plot that has the horizontal scale "Number of Spelling Words" and the vertical scale "Quiz Grade."

b. Explain what the point (25, 84) represents.

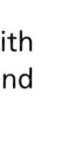

Extended Response **32.** Make a scatter plot of the data. Describe any trend in the data.

Monthly Electrical Use

Average Temperature (°F)	77	72	68	45	39	50	35	30	47
Electricity Use (kWh)	170	143	168	236	260	196	244	309	266

Mixed Review

Lesson 11-5

33. Is the question "Do you prefer summer or fall?" biased? Explain.

Lesson 11-3

Make a stem-and-leaf plot for each set of data.

34. number of students per teacher

27 29 34 24 29 19 30 19 25 22 27 15

35. depths at different levels in a pond (ft)

3.7 9.6 9.4 8.4 8.6 7.5 6.8 8.8 7.9 9.2 10.3 10.1 7.8

Lesson 10-2

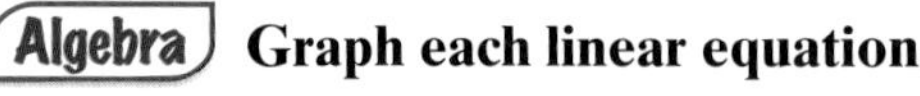

Algebra **Graph each linear equation.**

36. $y = x + 2$ **37.** $y = x - 4$ **38.** $y = 2x$ **39.** $y = -1 + x$

Checkpoint Quiz 2 — Lessons 11-4 through 11-8

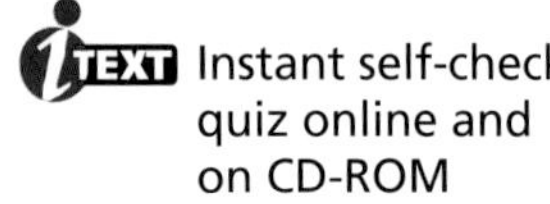

Instant self-check quiz online and on CD-ROM

1. Elsa, Anna, and LaToya go to the beach. Each girl carries a towel and a second item. One girl carries a green towel and a beach ball. Another carries iced tea and a red towel. Anna carries sandwiches. Elsa carries neither iced tea nor a blue towel. Which item does each girl carry?

2. For the data at the right, make a graph that would persuade movie makers to make more movies in Georgia.

Movies Filmed in Georgia

Year	Number
1995	9
1996	10
1997	9
1998	5
1999	3
2000	3
2001	4

SOURCE: Georgia Film Commission

3. Open-Ended Choose a survey topic and write a biased question and a fair question.

4. There are 108 marked turtles in a coastal region. In a survey, biologists count 51 turtles, of which 32 are marked. About how many turtles are in the region?

5. Which is the best way to survey a random sample of students from your school about their favorite radio station?

A. Survey 5 students in each first-period class.
B. Survey 12 band students.
C. Call 25 friends.
D. Survey each student in your math class.

Test-Taking Strategies

Answering the Question Asked

When answering a question, be sure to answer the question that is asked. Read the question carefully and identify the information you need to find. Eliminate answer choices that are not related to the question that is asked.

EXAMPLE

Use the stem-and-leaf plot.
What is the mode of the data?

A. 4 **B.** 20
C. 24 **D.** 25

Hair Dryer Prices

1	5 7
2	0 4 4 6
3	0 1 3 5

Key: 1 | 7 means $17.

The question asks for the mode, which is the number that appears the most. Choice A is the mode of the leaves, not of the data. Choice B is the range of the data, while choice D is the median. The correct answer is C.

EXERCISES

Use the double bar graph. Answers are given in metric tons.

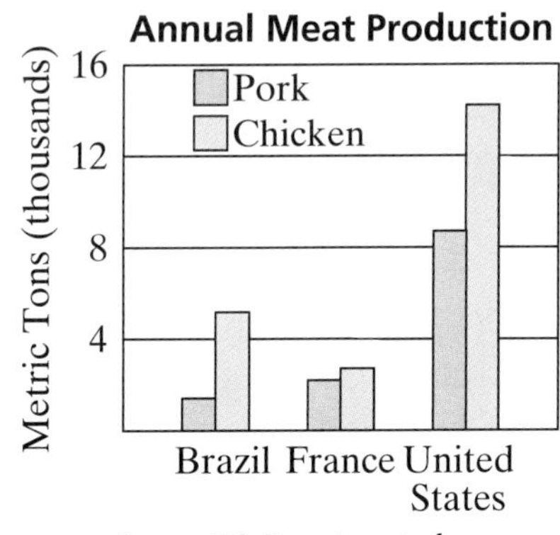

Source: U.S. Department of Agriculture

1. What is the approximate range of chicken produced?
   A. 5,000 **B.** 7,000 **C.** 11,000 **D.** 13,000

2. About how much pork and chicken does Brazil produce in a year?
   F. 2,000 **G.** 3,000 **H.** 5,000 **I.** 7,000

3. What is the approximate median of pork produced?
   A. 1,500 **B.** 2,000 **C.** 4,000 **D.** 7,000

Chapter 11 Chapter Review

Vocabulary

biased question (p. 597)
box-and-whisker plot (p. 586)
cell (p. 579)
double bar graph (p. 580)
double line graph (p. 580)
frequency table (p. 573)
histogram (p. 574)
legend (p. 580)
line plot (p. 573)
negative trend (p. 614)
no trend (p. 614)
population (p. 596)
positive trend (p. 614)
random sample (p. 596)
sample (p. 596)
scatter plot (p. 613)
spreadsheet (p. 579)
stem-and-leaf plot (p. 585)

Reading Math: Understanding Vocabulary

Choose the correct term to complete each sentence.

1. A (box-and-whisker, stem-and-leaf) plot uses the digits of the data.
2. A (negative, positive) trend involves a set of values that increases as another set of values decreases.
3. A (cell, legend) identifies the data being compared.
4. A (line plot, scatter plot) shows data by stacking X's above data values.
5. A (population, random sample) is a whole group.

Take It to the NET
Online vocabulary quiz at **www.PHSchool.com**
Web Code: abj-1151

Skills and Concepts

11-1 and 11-2
Objectives

- To make a frequency table or line plot
- To draw a histogram
- To use a spreadsheet
- To interpret double bar and double line graphs

A **frequency table** lists data items with the number of times each item occurs. A **line plot** shows data by stacking X's above data values on a number line. A **histogram** is a bar graph with no spaces between the bars.

A **double bar graph** compares two sets of data. A **double line graph** compares changes over time of two sets of data.

6. Make a frequency table and a line plot for the number of hours of TV watched per person per week: 5, 7, 9, 5, 3, 6, 8, 6, 5, 7, 6, 8, 7, 7, 6, 5, 4, 4, 5, 6.
7. a. **Education** According to the bar graph, which skill did most children have in 1999?

   b. Which skill improved the most from 1993 to 1999?

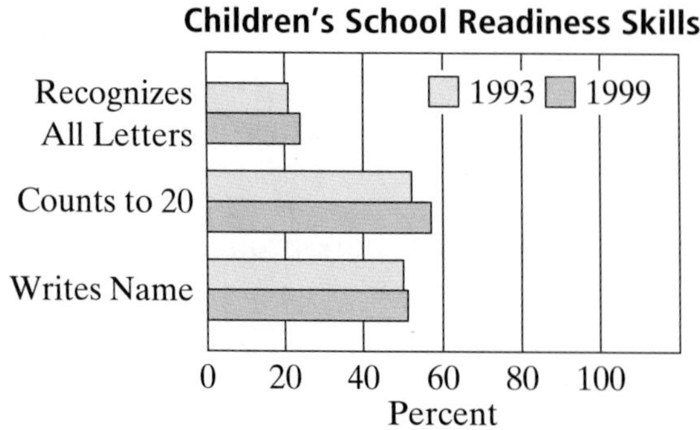

11-3 Objectives

- To make a stem-and-leaf plot
- To make a box-and-whisker plot

A **stem-and-leaf plot** uses the digits of each number to show the shape of the data. A **box-and-whisker plot** summarizes data using a number line.

8. Draw a stem-and-leaf plot for the temperatures below.

48 54 45 60 50 70 66 69 40 61 50 60 58
47 40 27 23 60 47 40 29 16 55 36 19 27

11-4 Objective

- To use multiple strategies to solve problems

You can solve problems by using logical reasoning and making a table.

9. Antonia, Becca, and Corwin each has a pet. One has a fish, one has a turtle, and one has a parrot. Antonia talked to the person with the parrot. Corwin doesn't like fish or parrots. Which person has each pet?

11-5 and 11-6 Objectives

- To identify a random sample
- To write a survey question
- To use the capture/recapture method

A **biased question** makes an unjustified assumption, or makes one answer appear better than another.

Biologists use the capture/recapture method to estimate a population size, using this proportion:

$$\frac{\text{number of marked animals counted}}{\text{total number of animals counted}} = \frac{\text{number of marked animals}}{\text{estimate of animal population}}$$

Tell whether each question is *biased* or *fair*. Explain.

10. What is your favorite activity after school?

11. Do you like the calm, peaceful ocean?

12. **Biology** Researchers know that there are 53 marked wolves in an area. On a flight over the area, they count 18 marked wolves and a total of 125 wolves. Estimate the wolf population.

11-7 and 11-8 Objectives

- To identify misleading graphs
- To identify misleading statistics
- To draw scatter plots
- To interpret scatter plots

Graphs present data visually. However, graphs can mislead if they use unequal intervals or improper breaks on the axes.

A **scatter plot** relates two sets of data, showing whether the data have a **positive trend,** a **negative trend,** or **no trend.**

13. How is the graph at the right misleading?

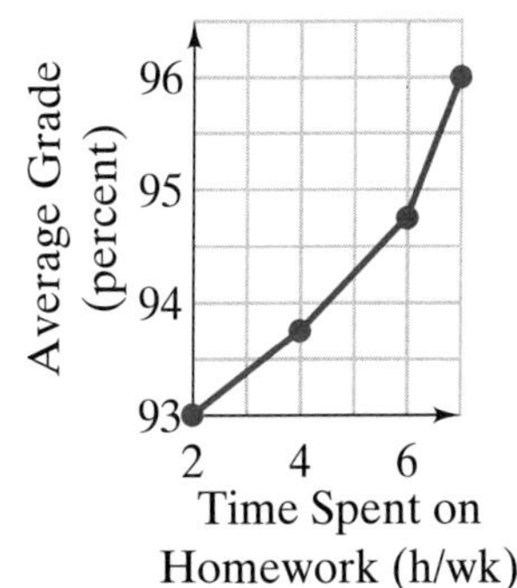

Describe the trend in each scatter plot.

14.

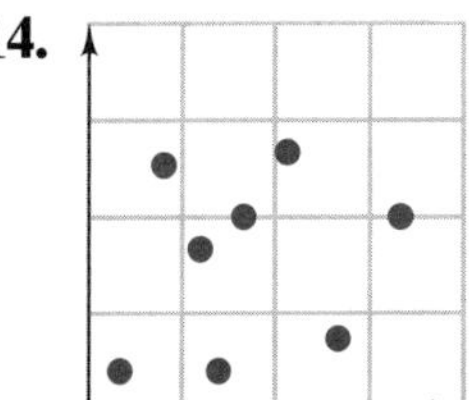

15.

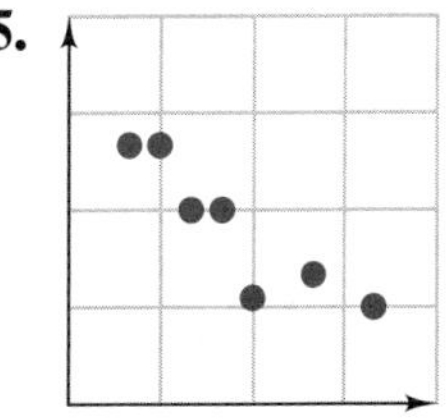

Chapter Test

A pollster asks 20 people how many hours they sleep each night. Use the data to draw each display in Exercises 1–5.

8 7.5 9 7 8 7.5 6 6.5 9.5 7.5
8 7.5 8 7 8 6.5 8 8.5 8.5 7.5

1. frequency table
2. line plot
3. histogram
4. stem-and-leaf plot
5. a. Make a box-and-whisker plot of the data.
   b. **Reasoning** Explain how the box-and-whisker plot of the data would change if the person who said 9 had said 12.

Use the spreadsheet below for Exercises 6–9.

	A	B	C	D
1	Student	Test 1	Test 2	Quiz
2	Alice	86	85	8
3	Xavier	91	89	9
4	Timotheo	79	84	8

6. What is the content of cell A3?
7. What is the content of cell C2?
8. In which cell is the word *Quiz*?
9. In which cell is the value 79?

Is each question *biased* or *fair*? Explain.

10. Do you prefer watching comedies or dramas?
11. Do you like watching violent sports or informational documentaries on TV?
12. Do you like sunny summers or dark winters?
13. Which season do you like best?
14. **Writing in Math** Explain how you could get a random sample of the people who use the town library.

Sales Use the double line graph below.

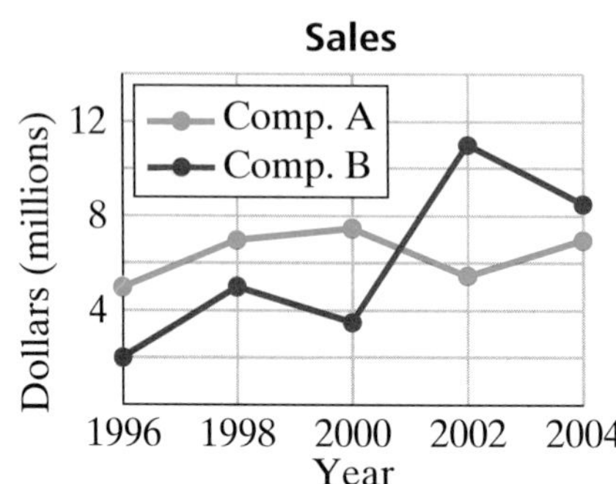

15. Estimate the year in which the sales were equal.
16. In which year were sales lowest for each company?
17. Redraw the graph to emphasize the highest sales for each company.
18. **Wages** Five students work at a store. Their hourly earnings are \$8, \$7.50, \$12, \$8.50, and \$8. One student earning \$8 wants a raise. Should the student use the mean, median, or mode to convince the boss?

Use a proportion to estimate each population.

19. total counted: 102
    tagged counted: 38
    total tagged: 56
20. total counted: 958
    tagged counted: 210
    total tagged: 305
21. LaTonya, Marco, and Anya are a designer, an architect, and a pharmacist, though not necessarily in that order. Anya knows the architect. Marco has never met the architect or the designer. Which person has each job?
22. a. Make a scatter plot of the data in the table.

Students' Ages and Heights

Age	12	13	12	14	14	13
Height (in.)	57	60	56	63	65	61

   b. Describe the trend in the scatter plot.

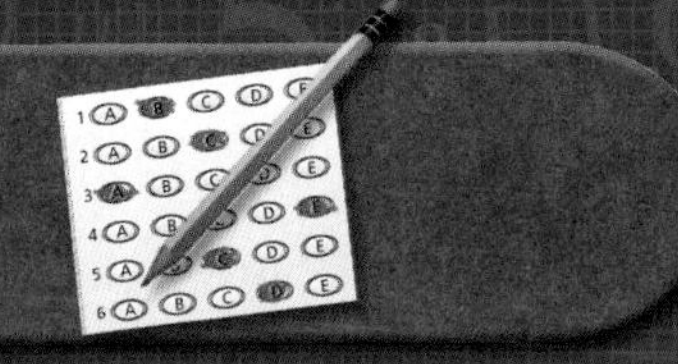

Test Prep

Reading Comprehension **Read each passage and answer the questions that follow.**

Baker Coordinates Mr. Baker, a math teacher, experimented with points on a coordinate plane. He invented an operation that he named after himself. To "bake" the point (x, y), make a new point with an x-coordinate that is the square of the original x-coordinate and with a y-coordinate that is the original y-coordinate.

1. If you "bake" the point (x, y), what ordered pair describes the coordinates of the new point?

A. (x, y) **B.** (x^2, y)
C. (x, y^2) **D.** (x^2, y^2)

2. If you "bake" a point in the second quadrant, in which quadrant is the new point located?

F. I **G.** II **H.** III **I.** IV

3. If you "bake" a point in the third quadrant, in which quadrant is the new point located?

A. I **B.** II **C.** III **D.** IV

4. If a point not on an axis has been "baked," in which quadrants could the new point be located?

F. either the first or second
G. either the first or third
H. either the first or fourth
I. either the second or third

Capital Geometry In 1790, George Washington hired Pierre L'Enfant to design a capital city. L'Enfant created an orderly grid. Streets that run north and south are numbered, and streets running east and west have letter names. Numbers and letters begin at the Capitol and run in both directions, so there are two 10th Streets and two K Streets. When you give an address, you also have to state its quadrant. The quadrants correspond to the four quadrants on a coordinate plane, but people call them by their compass directions: NE, SE, NW, and SW.

5. Ford's Theatre, where President Lincoln was shot, is located at 511 10th St., NW. In what quadrant is this?

A. I **B.** II **C.** III **D.** IV

6. Which word describes the location of the Capitol on the street grid of Washington, D.C.?

F. intercept **G.** origin
H. perimeter **I.** vertex

7. How many points are there where a 4th Street intersects an I Street?

A. one **B.** two **C.** four **D.** eight

8. A race is run along K Street. It starts at the intersection of 6th Street in NW, and goes to where K Street meets 6th Street in NE. What distance does the race cover?

F. 4 blocks **G.** 8 blocks
H. 12 blocks **I.** 24 blocks

Real-World Snapshots

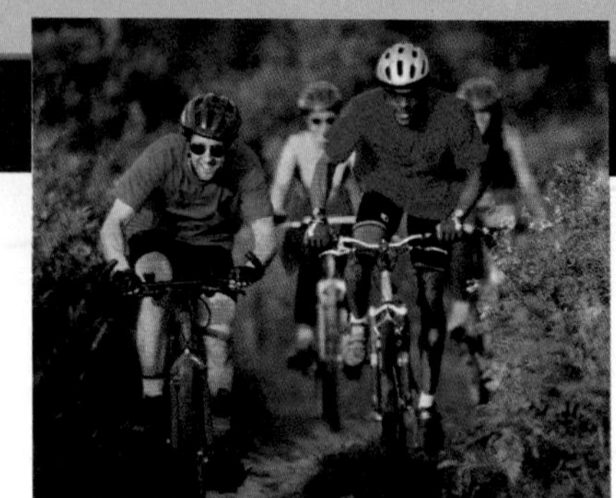

Bicycle Business

Applying Data Analysis Line graphs can communicate information more quickly than data tables because plots show how the data points are related. But line graphs can also be misleading. They can make a downward slide seem slight or an upward spike seem like a significant trend. You have to look critically at line graphs to see whether you're being informed … or misinformed.

Put It All Together

Materials graph paper

1. The table shows sales data for three bicycle companies. Pick one of the bicycle companies and activities on page 625. In each case, put the year on the horizontal axis and the sales on the vertical axis.
2. **Writing in Math** Compare your two line graphs. Which gives the more accurate view of the company's actual performance? Explain.
3. **Research** Find a graph in the newspaper. Is the graph a fair representation of the data? How could you change the graph to give a different impression?

Annual Sales for Three Bicycle Manufacturers (thousands of dollars)

Year	Better Bikes	Deals on Wheels	Super Cycles
1996	\$2,520	\$2,920	\$3,210
1997	\$2,369	\$3,008	\$3,082
1998	\$2,298	\$2,978	\$2,958
1999	\$2,160	\$2,978	\$3,106
2000	\$2,073	\$3,007	\$2,920
2001	\$1,991	\$3,158	\$2,832
2002	\$1,871	\$3,316	\$2,889
2003	\$1,778	\$3,448	\$3,062

Better Bikes

Sales have gone down since 1996.

A. Draw an optimistic line graph for the next stockholders' meeting.

B. Draw another line graph for the president of the company. Make the drop in sales look very serious.

Deals on Wheels

Sales have generally gone up over the last eight years.

A. Draw a line graph that will help convince the bank to give the company a big loan.

B. Draw a line graph showing employees why they can't have big raises this year.

Super Cycles

Although sales have gone up and down over the last eight years, sales rose from 2001 to 2003.

A. Draw a line graph that makes Super Cycles look incredibly successful by the year 2010. Use a dashed line to extend the graph.

B. Draw a line graph that a possible buyer of the company might use.

Take It to the NET For more information about bicycles, go to **www.PHSchool.com**.
Web Code: abe-1153

CHAPTER 12

Using Probability

Lessons

12-1 Probability

12-2 Experimental Probability

12-3 Problem Solving: Make an Organized List and Simulate a Problem

12-4 Sample Spaces

12-5 Compound Events

12-6 Permutations

12-7 Combinations

Key Vocabulary

- combination (p. 664)
- complement (p. 630)
- compound event (p. 653)
- counting principle (p. 648)
- dependent events (p. 655)
- event (p. 629)
- experimental probability (p. 636)
- factorial (p. 661)
- independent events (p. 654)
- odds against (p. 631)
- odds in favor (p. 631)
- outcome (p. 629)
- permutation (p. 660)
- sample space (p. 647)
- theoretical probability (p. 629)

Real-World Snapshots

There are five seconds left in a basketball game. The score is tied. Do you let the player who has made 2 out of 10 baskets attempt the winning basket? Or do you give the ball to the player who has made 8 out of 11 baskets? Probability based on past results can help you make decisions.

Data File Basketball Wins and Losses

Name of School	Location	Wins	Losses
Lincoln	Dallas, Texas	40	0
Rice	Manhattan, New York	29	2
Brookhaven	Columbus, Ohio	27	1
Lakewood	St. Petersburg, Florida	34	2
Westinghouse	Chicago, Illinois	30	5
Martin Luther King	Riverside, California	31	4
Northern	Pontiac, Michigan	23	4

SOURCE: HoopsUSA.com

You will use the data above in this chapter:

- p. 639 Lesson 12-2
- p. 657 Lesson 12-5

Real-World Snapshots On pages 676 and 677, you will solve problems involving basketball.

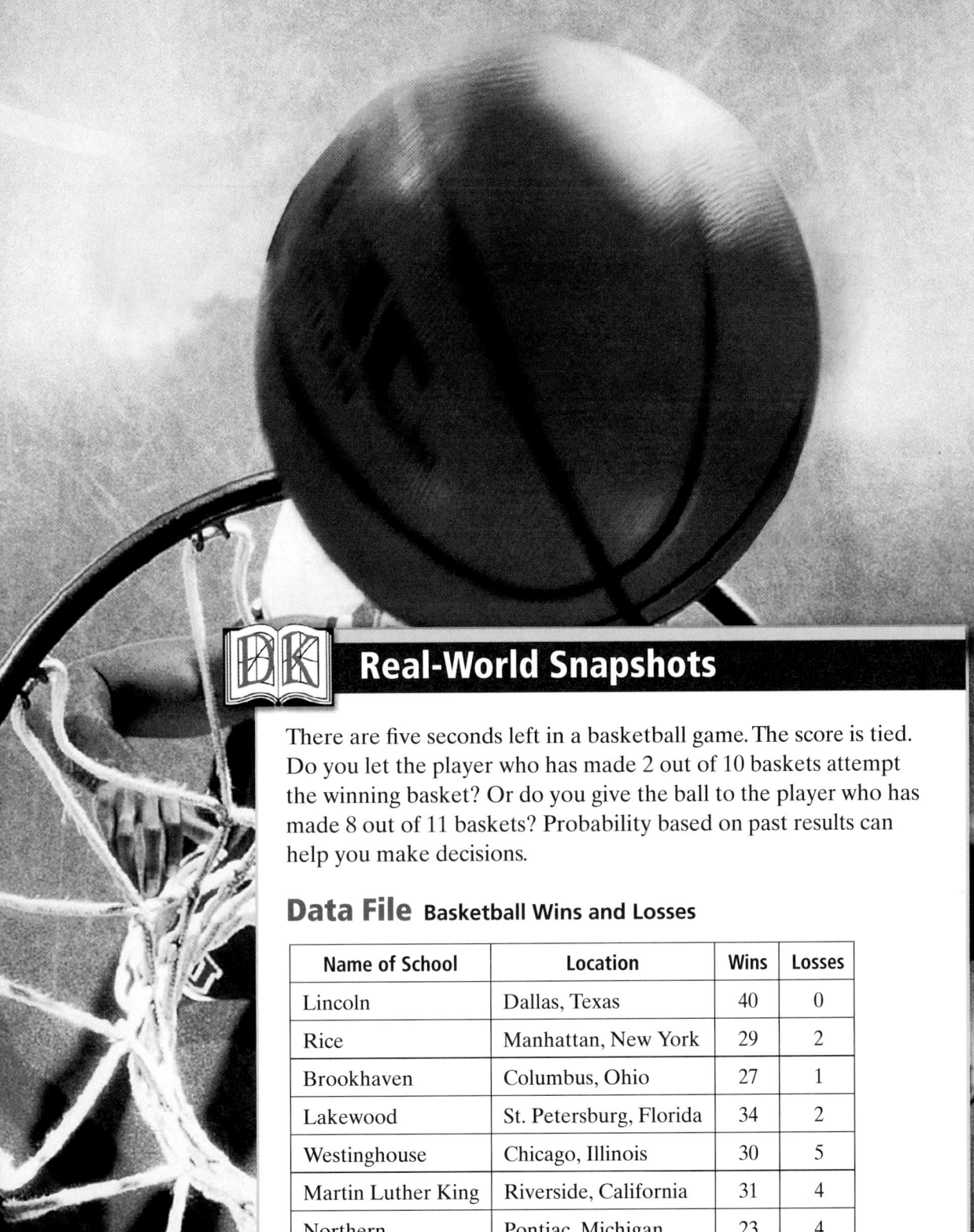

Chapter 12 Preview

Where You've Been

- In Chapter 5, you learned to write ratios and proportions.
- In Chapter 6, you learned to compare percents with decimals and fractions.

Where You're Going

- In Chapter 12, you will find the probability and odds of events. You will also learn to solve a problem by simulating the problem.
- Applying what you learn, you will use probability in real-world problems, such as predicting the number of defective bicycles made in a bicycle factory.

Quality control at a bicycle factory

Instant self-check online and on CD-ROM

Diagnosing Readiness

For help, go to the lesson in green.

Ratios (Lesson 5-1)

Write each ratio in simplest form.

1. $\frac{9}{24}$ 2. $\frac{20}{54}$ 3. $\frac{15}{65}$ 4. $\frac{28}{70}$

5. $\frac{16}{22}$ 6. $\frac{21}{84}$ 7. $\frac{18}{42}$ 8. $\frac{32}{72}$

Using Proportional Reasoning (Lesson 5-5)

Algebra Solve each proportion.

9. $\frac{3}{10} = \frac{x}{30}$ 10. $\frac{n}{14} = \frac{25}{8}$ 11. $\frac{22}{c} = \frac{66}{15}$

12. $\frac{16}{35} = \frac{20}{y}$ 13. $\frac{a}{24} = \frac{24}{9}$ 14. $\frac{19}{38} = \frac{f}{21}$

Percents, Fractions, and Decimals (Lesson 6-2)

Write each decimal as a percent.

15. 0.46 16. 0.265 17. 0.07

18. 0.256 19. 0.82 20. 0.02

Write each fraction as a percent. When necessary, round to the nearest tenth of a percent.

21. $\frac{4}{5}$ 22. $\frac{5}{11}$ 23. $\frac{8}{14}$

24. $\frac{12}{30}$ 25. $\frac{15}{32}$ 26. $\frac{18}{45}$

12-1 Probability

What You'll Learn

To find the probability of an event

To find the complements and the odds of events

. . . And Why

To find the probability of selecting a color, as in Example 2

Check Skills You'll Need

For help, go to Lesson 6-2.

Write each fraction as a decimal and a percent. Round to the nearest tenth of a percent, if necessary.

1. $\frac{31}{50}$ **2.** $\frac{19}{20}$ **3.** $\frac{11}{40}$ **4.** $\frac{11}{10}$

5. Explain how to write a percent as a decimal.

New Vocabulary

- outcome
- event
- theoretical probability
- complement
- odds in favor
- odds against

OBJECTIVE

iTEXT Interactive lesson includes instant self-check, tutorials, and activities.

1 Finding the Probability of an Event

An **outcome** is the result of an action. For example, rolling a 6 is a possible outcome of rolling a number cube once.

An **event** is an outcome or a group of outcomes. If all the outcomes are equally likely, you can use a formula to find the theoretical probability.

Key Concepts — Theoretical Probability

theoretical probability $= P(\text{event}) = \frac{\text{number of favorable outcomes}}{\text{total number of possible outcomes}}$

You can express probability as a fraction, a decimal, or a percent.

1 EXAMPLE Finding Probability

> **Reading Math**
>
> You read P(vowel) as "the probability of a vowel."

Suppose you select a letter at random from the letters shown at the right. Find the probability that you select a vowel. Express the probability as a fraction, a decimal, and a percent.

The event *vowel* has two outcomes, *A* and *E*, out of five possible outcomes.

$P(\text{vowel}) = \frac{2}{5}$ ← number of favorable outcomes ← total number of possible outcomes

$P(\text{vowel}) = \frac{2}{5} = 0.4 = 40\%$ ← Write as a fraction, decimal, and percent.

Check Understanding **1** Find P(consonant) for the letters in Example 1. Express the probability as a fraction, a decimal, and a percent.

All probabilities range from 0 to 1. The probability of rolling a 7 on a standard number cube is 0, so that is an *impossible* event. The probability of rolling a positive integer less than 7 is 1, so that is a *certain* event.

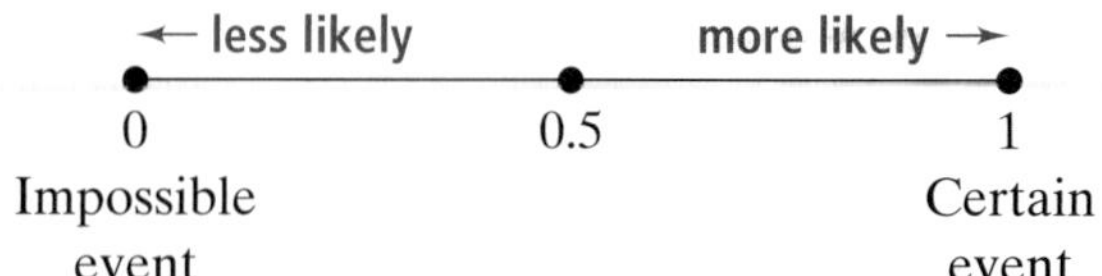

2 EXAMPLE Finding Probabilities From 0 to 1

Clothes The diagram below shows the jeans in Juanita's closet. Juanita selects a pair of jeans with her eyes shut. Find each probability.

a. P(dark-colored jeans)

There are 8 possible outcomes. Since there are 3 black pairs and 2 blue pairs, the event *dark-colored jeans* has 5 favorable outcomes.

$P(\text{dark-colored jeans}) = \frac{5}{8}$ ← number of favorable outcomes ← total number of possible outcomes

b. P(red jeans)

The event *red jeans* has no favorable outcome.

$P(\text{red jeans}) = \frac{0}{8} = 0$ ← number of favorable outcomes ← total number of possible outcomes

Check Understanding 2 You roll a standard number cube once.

a. Find P(multiple of 3). **b.** Find P(multiple of 8).

c. **Reasoning** Describe an event with a probability of $\frac{6}{6}$.

OBJECTIVE

2 Finding the Complements and the Odds of Events

The **complement** of an event is the collection of outcomes not contained in the event. The probability of the complement of an event is written P(not event). For example, $P(\text{rain}) + P(\text{not rain}) = 1$.

Key Concepts **Complement of an Event**

For any event A, the complement is *not* A.

$P(A) + P(\text{not } A) = 1 \qquad P(\text{not } A) = 1 - P(A)$

3 EXAMPLE Finding the Complement of an Event

Government The U.S. Senate has 100 members. There are two members representing each state. The probability that a member selected at random is from Kansas is 2%. Find *P*(not Kansas) as a decimal, a fraction, and a percent.

$P(\text{Kansas}) + P(\text{not Kansas}) = 1$ ← Write the formula.

$0.02 + P(\text{not Kansas}) = 1$ ← Substitute 0.02 for *P*(Kansas).

$0.02 - 0.02 + P(\text{not Kansas}) = 1 - 0.02$ ← Subtract 0.02 from each side.

$P(\text{not Kansas}) = 0.98 = \frac{98}{100} = 98\%$

Check Understanding 3 You roll a standard number cube once. Find each probability as a fraction, a decimal, and a percent.

a. *P*(not 6)   **b.** *P*(not 1, 2, 3, or 4)

The probability ratio compares favorable outcomes and total outcomes. You can also write ratios, called *odds*, that compare favorable outcomes and unfavorable outcomes.

Key Concepts — Odds

Odds in favor of an event = the ratio of the number of favorable outcomes to the number of unfavorable outcomes

Odds against an event = the ratio of the number of unfavorable outcomes to the number of favorable outcomes

4 EXAMPLE Finding Odds

Coins The reverse sides of five quarters are shown below. Find the odds that a quarter chosen at random shows at least one musical instrument.

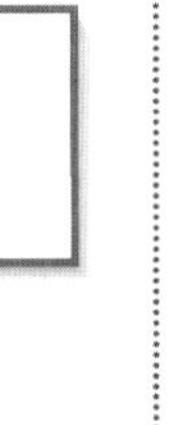

Reading Math

The odds 1 to 8 can be written as 1 : 8.

odds in favor = 2 to 3 or 2 : 3 ← Two have an instrument. Three do not.

The odds that a quarter shows at least one instrument are 2 to 3 in favor.

Check Understanding 4 Find the odds that a quarter chosen at random shows a race car.

EXERCISES

For more practice, see *Extra Practice.*

A Practice by Example

Example 1 (page 629)

You mix the letters A, C, Q, U, A, I, N, T, A, N, C, and E thoroughly. Without looking, you draw one letter. Find the probability of each event as a fraction, a decimal, and a percent.

1. $P(T)$ **2.** $P(A)$ **3.** $P(\text{vowel})$

4. $P(\text{consonant})$ **5.** $P(N)$ **6.** $P(Q \text{ or } C)$

7. You write the letters M, I, S, S, I, S, S, I, P, P, I on cards and mix them thoroughly in a hat. You select one card without looking. Find $P(\text{I})$.

Example 2 (page 630)

Suppose you spin the spinner once. Find each probability.

8. $P(12)$ **9.** $P(2 \text{ or } 4)$

10. $P(\text{multiple of } 3)$ **11.** $P(\text{even})$

12. $P(\text{multiple of } 5)$ **13.** $P(\text{number less than } 11)$

14. $P(\text{factor of } 10)$ **15.** $P(\text{number less than } 5)$

Example 3 (page 631)

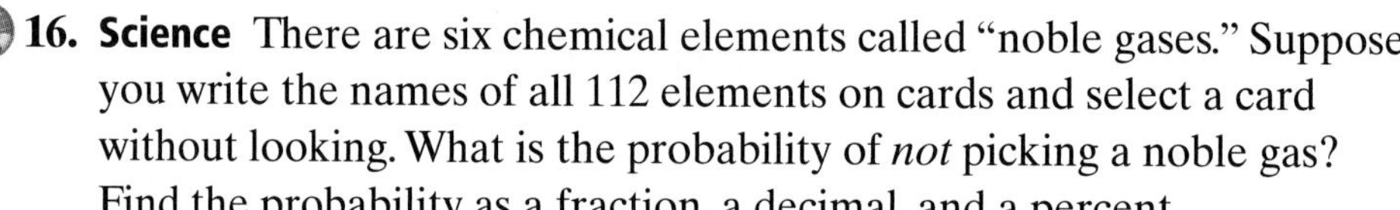

16. Science There are six chemical elements called "noble gases." Suppose you write the names of all 112 elements on cards and select a card without looking. What is the probability of *not* picking a noble gas? Find the probability as a fraction, a decimal, and a percent.

Example 4 (page 631)

You roll a standard number cube once. Find the odds in favor of each outcome.

17. rolling a 5 **18.** rolling a 3 **19.** rolling an odd number

B Apply Your Skills

Suppose you spin the spinner once. Find each probability.

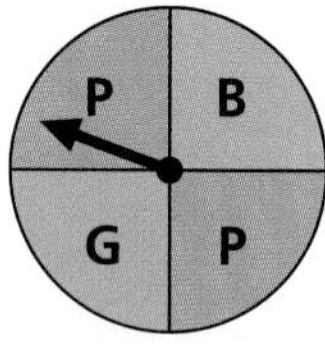

20. $P(\text{not green})$ **21.** $P(\text{purple or blue})$

22. $P(\text{white})$ **23.** $P(\text{not purple})$

24. Open-Ended One student from your class is selected at random.
  a. What is the probability that you are selected?
  b. What is the probability that a girl is *not* selected?
  c. Find $P(\text{girl or boy is selected})$.

25. a. Suppose $P(E) = 0.3$. Find $P(\text{not } E)$.
  b. Suppose $P(\text{not } E) = 65\%$. Find $P(E)$.

26. Calculate the odds for and against each event.
  a. Spin a spinner with equal sections lettered A–Z once; the spinner lands on the first letter of your name.
  b. Roll a standard number cube once; the number is a multiple of 3.

Real-World  Connection

Each year, the President delivers the State of the Union address before the members of Congress.

Government **The U.S. House of Representatives has 435 members. Suppose each member's name is put into a hat and one name is chosen at random. Find each probability as a decimal to the nearest hundredth.**

27. P(Florida)

28. P(Texas)

29. P(Illinois)

30. P(Pennsylvania)

31. P(Missouri)

32. P(Colorado)

U.S. House of Representatives

State	Number	State	Number
Florida	25	Missouri	9
Pennsylvania	19	Illinois	19
Colorado	7	Texas	32

SOURCE: U.S. Census Bureau. Go to **www.PHSchool.com** for a data update. Web Code aag-2041

Suppose you draw a marble at random from the bag.

33. Find each probability.
a. P(red)
b. P(blue)
c. P(red) + P(blue)
d. P(red or blue)

34. **a.** Complete: P(not red) = P(_?_).
b. Complete: P(not blue) = P(_?_).

C Challenge

35. Reasoning A bag contains an unknown number of marbles. You know that $P(\text{red}) = \frac{1}{4}$ and $P(\text{green}) = \frac{1}{4}$.
a. Are all the marbles red or green? Explain how you know.
b. How many marbles of each color might be in the bag? Are there other correct answers? Explain.

36. Writing in Math Suppose you have 3 nickels, 3 dimes, and 3 quarters in your pocket. Does the probability of drawing a dime from your pocket equal the probability of drawing a quarter? Explain.

37. Algebra The odds in favor of an event are 5 to a. What is the probability of the event in terms of a?

38. Stretch Your Thinking Shauna is half as old as Tatum. In twelve years, Shauna will be $\frac{5}{8}$ as old as Tatum. How old is Tatum now?

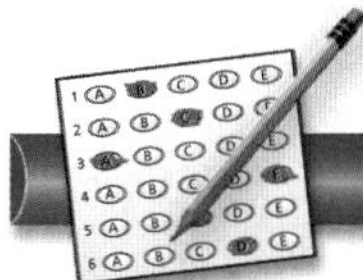

Test Prep

Gridded Response

39. Your ticket to the variety show qualifies you for the door-prize drawing. One ticket will be drawn from a box of 200 tickets. What is the probability of your ticket being drawn? Write your answer as a fraction.

40. A bag contains cards lettered A through G. You select a card at random from the bag. What is the probability that you select a vowel? Write your answer as a decimal, to the nearest hundredth.

41. What is the probability of rolling a number divisible by 4 on a standard number cube? Write your answer as a decimal, to the nearest thousandth.

Take It to the NET
Online lesson quiz at
www.PHSchool.com
Web Code aba-1201

42. The table at the right shows a group of people with different hair colors. A person is selected at random from the group. What is the probability that the person has black hair? Write your answer as a decimal, to the nearest thousandth.

Hair Color

Color	Number
Blond	58
Brown	64
Black	97

Mixed Review

Lesson 11-8

Describe the trend in each scatter plot.

43. 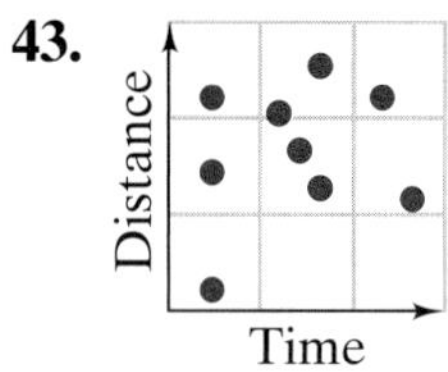

44. 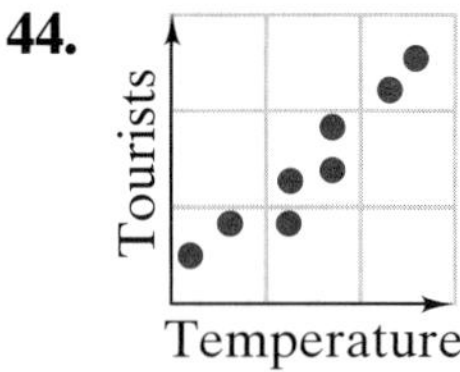

45. 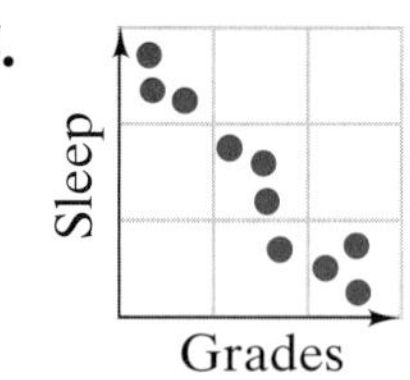

Lesson 11-5

Tell whether each question is *biased* or *fair*. Explain.

46. Do you prefer harsh contact sports or light aerobic exercise?

47. What type of books do you read?

Lesson 9-3

Evaluate each function rule for $x = -4$.

48. $y = x + 1$

49. $y = 3x$

50. $y = x \div 2$

51. $y = 2 - x$

52. $y = -5x$

53. $y = 2x + 5$

54. $y = 4 - 2x$

55. $y = x^2 + 1$

Practice Game

Products of Winners

What You'll Need

- Two standard number cubes

How to Play

- Take turns rolling two number cubes. Find the product of the two numbers. If the product is even, Player A scores a point. If the product is odd, Player B scores a point.

  After 15 rolls each, the player with more points wins.

  Who would you rather be, Player A or Player B?

Product Chart

	1	2	3	4	5	6
1	1	2	3	■	■	■
2	2	4	■	■	■	■
3	■	■	■	■	■	■
4	■	■	■	■	■	■
5	■	■	■	■	■	■
6	■	■	■	■	■	■

Exploring Experimental Probability

For Use With Lesson 12-2

If you flip one coin 100 times, you might expect to get heads and tails about the same number of times. What happens when you toss *two* coins 100 times?

EXAMPLE

Toss two coins 10 times. Record the results. Using the results, determine which event is most likely: two heads (HH), two tails (TT), or one head and onc tail (HT).

The table below shows one set of results for the experiment.

Toss	1	2	3	4	5	6	7	8	9	10
Result	HH	HT	HT	TT	HH	HT	TT	HT	HH	HT

In all, there are three outcomes of HH, two outcomes of TT, and five outcomes of HT.

According to these results, one head and one tail is the most likely event.

Activity

1. Conduct the following experiment.
   - Use two different coins, such as a penny and a nickel. Place them in a small paper cup. Cover the top, and shake the cup before each coin toss.
   - Toss both coins 100 times. Make a table to record each result as 2 heads (HH), 2 tails (TT), or 1 head and 1 tail (HT).

   a. Compare your results with other class members. Are they similar? Explain.

   b. **Reasoning** Do you think the three outcomes are equally likely? Or is one outcome more likely to occur than the others? Explain your reasoning.

GAME RULES

1. Player A receives 1 point if two heads (HH) are tossed.
2. Player B receives 1 point if two tails (TT) are tossed.
3. Player C receives 1 point if one head and one tail (HT) are tossed.

2. Three students play a coin-tossing game with the rules shown at the right.

   a. Do you think a game with these rules would be fair? Why or why not?

   b. **Open-Ended** How might you change the rules to make the game fair?

   c. Conduct an experiment to test your new game. Do you still think your game is fair? Explain.

12-2 Experimental Probability

What You'll Learn

To find experimental probability

To use simulations

. . . And Why

To predict bicycle defects, as in Example 2

Check Skills You'll Need

For help, go to Lesson 12-1.

You roll a standard number cube once. Find the probability of each event as a fraction, a decimal, and a percent.

1. $P(4)$ **2.** $P(\text{multiple of } 2)$ **3.** $P(8)$

4. Explain the difference between an event and an outcome.

New Vocabulary • **experimental probability**

Interactive lesson includes instant self-check, tutorials, and activities.

OBJECTIVE 1 Finding Experimental Probability

Investigation: Experimenting With Probability

Find the theoretical probability of getting a 3 when you roll a standard number cube once.

- Roll a number cube 10 times. Record the results.
- Write the ratio of the number of 3's rolled to the total number of rolls: $\frac{\blacksquare}{10}$
- Roll another 20 times and record the results.
- Write the ratio of the number of 3's rolled in all 30 rolls: $\frac{\blacksquare}{30}$

1. Compare the theoretical probability of rolling a 3 with each ratio above.
2. Did increasing the number of rolls affect your ratio? Explain.

Suppose you play a game that includes tossing a coin and rolling a number cube. Below are the results of eight turns.

Coin	Heads	Heads	Tails	Heads	Tails	Heads	Tails	Heads
Cube	2	5	1	2	3	2	3	5

Probability based on experimental data or observations is called **experimental probability.** In the table above, the event *heads and a 2* occurs three times out of eight trials.

Key Concepts **Experimental Probability**

$$P(\text{event}) = \frac{\text{number of times an event occurs}}{\text{total number of trials}}$$

1 EXAMPLE Finding Experimental Probability

Sports Suppose you attempt 16 free throws in a basketball game. Your results are at the right. Find the experimental probability of making a free throw.

Results of Free Throw Attempts

0 = miss				1 = make			
0	0	1	1	1	0	1	0
0	1	0	1	1	0	0	1

$P(\text{free throw}) = \frac{8}{16}$ ← number of throws made / ← total number of attempted free throws

$= \frac{1}{2}$ ← Simplify.

The experimental probability of making a free throw is $\frac{1}{2}$.

Check Understanding 1 In 60 coin tosses, 25 are tails. Find the experimental probability.

Businesses use experimental probability to test the quality of products.

2 EXAMPLE Real-World Problem Solving

Manufacturing A bicycle manufacturing company makes random checks of its products. Of 400 bikes, 12 are found to be defective.

a. What is the experimental probability that a bike is defective?

$P(\text{bikes}) = \frac{12}{400}$ ← number of defective bikes / ← total number of bikes checked

$= \frac{3}{100}$ ← Simplify.

The experimental probability is $\frac{3}{100}$.

b. Predict the number of defective bikes in a batch of 1,300.

Let x represent the predicted number of defective bikes.

defective bikes → / total bikes → $\frac{3}{100} = \frac{x}{1{,}300}$ ← defective bikes / ← total bikes ← Write a proportion.

$3(1{,}300) = 100x$ ← Write the cross products.

$3{,}900 = 100x$ ← Simplify.

$\frac{3{,}900}{100} = \frac{100x}{100}$ ← Divide each side by 100.

$39 = x$ ← Simplify.

You can predict 39 bikes out of 1,300 to be defective.

Real-World Connection

Bicycle manufacturing involves the careful assembling of many parts.

2 **a. Reasoning** Would you expect 39 defects in every batch of 1,300? Explain.
b. Predict the number of defective bikes in a batch of 3,500.

OBJECTIVE

2 Using Simulations

Some experiments are too difficult or time-consuming to perform. You can simulate, or model, problems to find experimental probabilities.

3 EXAMPLE Simulating an Event

Real World

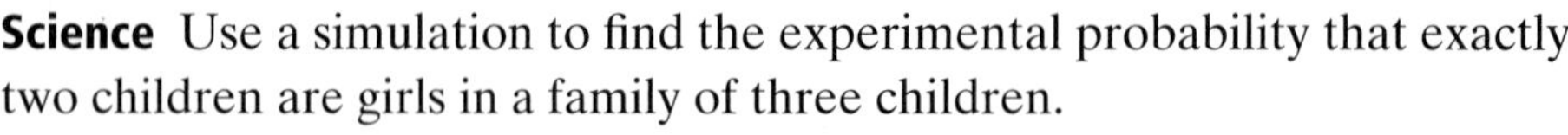

Science Use a simulation to find the experimental probability that exactly two children are girls in a family of three children.

Simulate the problem by tossing three coins at the same time. Assume that girls and boys are equally likely. Let "heads" represent a girl and "tails" represent a boy. A sample of 18 tosses is shown below.

Trial	Girl	Boy	Trial	Girl	Boy	Trial	Girl	Boy
1	✓✓	✓	7		✓✓✓	13	✓✓	✓
2	✓	✓✓	8	✓✓	✓	14	✓	✓✓
3	✓✓	✓	9	✓	✓✓	15		✓✓✓
4	✓✓	✓	10	✓✓✓		16	✓	✓✓
5	✓	✓✓	11	✓✓✓		17	✓✓	✓
6	✓	✓✓	12		✓✓✓	18	✓✓✓	

$P(\text{exactly two girls}) = \frac{6}{18}$ ← number of times *two heads* occur / ← total number of tosses

$= \frac{1}{3}$ ← Simplify.

According to this simulation, the experimental probability that exactly two of three children are girls is $\frac{1}{3}$.

✓Check Understanding 3 **a.** Use the data in Example 3. What is the experimental probability that all three children are boys?

b. Number Sense Suppose you want to find the probability that three out of five babies are boys. You decide to flip coins to simulate the problem. How many coins would you use? Explain.

EXERCISES

For more practice, see *Extra Practice*.

A Practice by Example

Example 1 (page 637)

Find each experimental probability.

1. tosses, 80; tails, 40; $P(\text{tails}) = \underline{\ ?\ }$

2. tosses, 120; tails, 75; $P(\text{tails}) = \underline{\ ?\ }$

3. tosses, 250; heads, 180; $P(\text{heads}) = \underline{\ ?\ }$

4. tosses, 500; heads, 210; $P(\text{heads}) = \underline{\ ?\ }$

5. You roll a number cube 100 times and get fifteen 5's. What is $P(5)$?

6. You spin a spinner 225 times and get red 30 times. What is $P(\text{red})$?

Example 2 (page 637)

Appliances A manufacturer checked washers at four plants and recorded the number of defective washers. Find each experimental probability.

	Plant	Number of Washers	Number Defective	P(Defective)
7.	1	2,940	588	■
8.	2	1,860	93	■
9.	3	640	26	■
10.	4	3,048	54	■

11. a. **Manufacturing** The quality-control engineer of Top Notch Tool Company finds flaws in 8 of 60 wrenches examined. What is the experimental probability that any wrench has a flaw?
    b. Suppose the company produces 2,400 wrenches a day. How many would you expect to have flaws?

Example 3 (page 638)

Baseball A baseball team averages one win to every one loss. Run a simulation to find each experimental probability for three games.

12. P(exactly three wins)

13. P(exactly 1 win and 2 losses)

14. P(exactly 2 wins and 1 loss)

15. P(exactly three losses)

B Apply Your Skills

16. a. A group has an equal number of boys and girls. A name is called out at random five times. Use a simulation to find the experimental probability that three of the five names called are boys.
    b. **Writing in Math** Would you prefer to toss one coin five times or five coins five times to simulate the problem? Explain.

17. a. **Data File, p. 627** The experimental probability of winning for a team that has 3 wins and 2 losses is $\frac{3}{5}$. Find the experimental probability of winning for each team in the table.
    b. Which team has $P(\text{win})$ equivalent to $\frac{6}{7}$?

Data Analysis **Use the data in the line plot. Find each experimental probability as a fraction in simplest form.**

18. P(Sunday)

19. P(Monday)

20. P(Tuesday)

21. P(Friday)

22. P(weekday)

23. P(weekend)

Students' Birthdays

Su	M	Tu	W	Th	F	Sa
✗✗✗	✗✗✗✗✗✗	✗✗✗✗✗	✗✗	✗✗✗	✗✗	✗✗✗✗

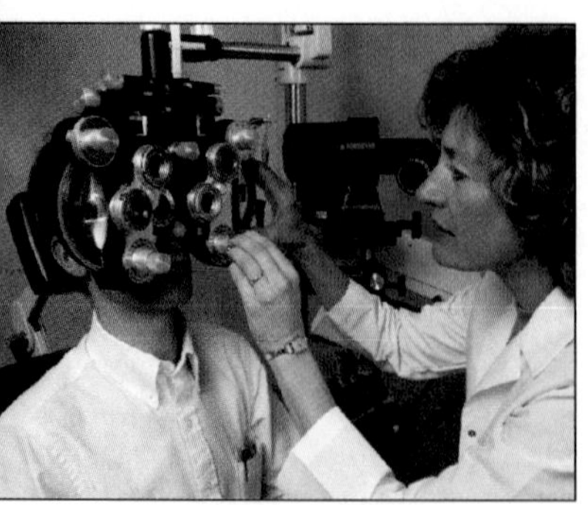

Real-World Connection

Color vision involves the use of special cells, called cones, located in the retina of the eye.

24. **a.** **Science** The probability that a male is colorblind is 8%. Suppose you interview 1,000 males. About how many would you expect to be colorblind?

b. **Reasoning** Will you get exactly this number? Explain.

Match each problem in Exercises 25–27 with an appropriate simulation. Justify your choice.

25. To win a game, you must guess two whole numbers from 1 to 6. What is the probability that you will guess both numbers?

26. The Golden Hen Egg Company packs eggs in groups of six per carton. The probability that an egg is cracked is $\frac{1}{6}$. What is the probability that an egg carton will contain exactly two cracked eggs?

27. A student guesses the answers on six true/false quiz questions. What is the probability that the student will guess exactly two answers correctly?

A. Roll six number cubes 30 times.

B. Toss six coins 10 times.

C. Choose two cards from a group of cards numbered 1 to 6. Repeat 40 times.

You select shirts at random from a shirt rack at a store. The results are shown. Find each experimental probability.

28. P(green)

29. P(orange)

30. P(gray)

31. P(blue or gray)

32. P(blue)

33. P(purple)

C Challenge

34. **a.** **Algebra** Knob Company estimates that on any day it makes x defective doorknobs. On Monday the total number of doorknobs is 252. Express the experimental probability of defective doorknobs on Monday in terms of x.

b. If the experimental probability is $\frac{1}{42}$, what is x?

35. **a.** **Stretch Your Thinking** A class of 22 students wants to break into small groups of different sizes. No two groups can have the same number of students. Each group has to have at least 2 students. What is the greatest number of groups the students can form?

b. What are the sizes of these groups?

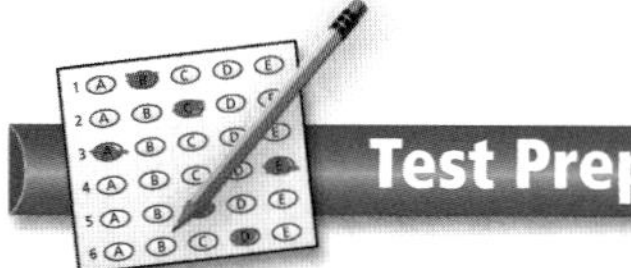

Test Prep

Reading Comprehension

Read the passage and answer the questions below.

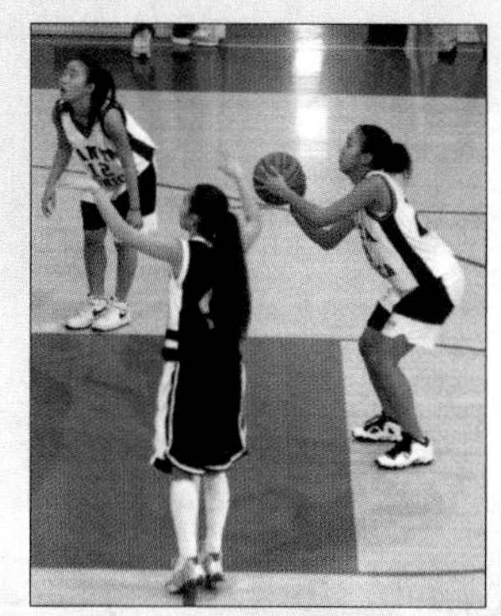

Shooting Stars

Basketball players keep track of how many free throws they shoot and how many they make. They use this information to chart their success from game to game. A player makes 25 free throws and misses 25 free throws in 50 shots. So the experimental probability of making a free throw is $\frac{1}{2}$. To simulate the results of her next 10 free throws, she tosses a coin 10 times. "Heads" represents making the basket and "tails" represents missing the basket. The results are H, T, H, H, H, T, T, H, T, and H.

36. According to the simulation, what is the experimental probability of her making a free throw?

37. According to the simulation, what is the experimental probability of her NOT making a free throw?

Multiple Choice

38. A hockey player makes 3 goals in 9 shots in a game. If you see one of the shots, what are the odds in favor of you seeing the player make the shot?

A. 1 to 3 **B.** 1 to 2 **C.** 2 to 1 **D.** 3 to 1

39. A quality-control inspector finds 30 defective mechanical pencils out of 1,000 that he checks. What is the percent of defective pencils?

F. 0.3% **G.** 3% **H.** 30% **I.** 300%

Take It to the NET
Online lesson quiz at **www.PHSchool.com**
Web Code aba-1202

40. The results of tossing a coin are given below. Which result has an experimental probability of getting heads equivalent to 40%?

A. heads, heads, tails, tails, heads **B.** tails, heads, heads, tails, tails
C. tails, heads, tails, tails, tails **D.** heads, tails, heads, heads, tails

Mixed Review

Lesson 12-1

The spinner is spun once. Find each probability.

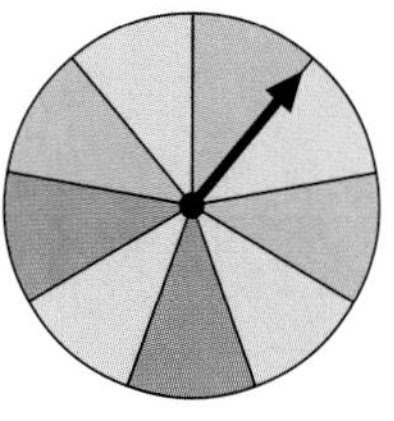

41. P(purple) **42.** P(blue)

43. P(blue or yellow) **44.** P(not yellow)

Lesson 11-3

Make a stem-and-leaf plot for each set of data.

45. number of field goals in a season:
20, 18, 16, 10, 25, 20, 16, 22, 30, 24, 15, 21, 26, 12

46. heights of buildings in Miami (in meters):
146, 240, 190, 137, 172, 160, 156, 172, 148, 233, 146, 148

Technology: Random Numbers

For Use With Lesson 12-2

You can use a random number table to simulate some problems. Graphing calculators and computer programs can generate random number tables.

	A	B	C	D
1	2260	1927	7807	0912
2	8879	6235	5897	8068
3	8121	4646	8368	1613
4	0821	8911	3022	0307
5	9393	5403	4930	4898

To generate a random number table in a spreadsheet, follow these steps.

Step 1 Highlight the group of cells you want for your table.

Step 2 Select the "Format Cells" menu.

Step 3 Choose the category "Custom" and enter "0000." Click "OK."

Step 4 Use the formula RAND()*10,000. This will make groups of 4 digits in each cell of a spreadsheet. (*Note:* Each time you generate a random number table, you will get a different group of digits.)

EXAMPLE

A rare lily bulb has a 50% chance of growing. You plant four bulbs. What is the experimental probability that all four will grow?

Use the random number table. Let even digits represent *grows*, and let odd digits represent *doesn't grow*. Then a 4-digit number of all even digits represents the event *all four grow*.

Of the 20 groups, 3 consist entirely of even digits. So the experimental probability of four bulbs growing is $\frac{3}{20}$, or 15%.

2260	1927	7807	0912
8879	6235	5897	8068
8121	4646	8368	1613
0821	8911	3022	0307
9393	5403	4930	4898

← **Any group of 4 even digits represents *all four grow.***

EXERCISES

Use the random number table above or generate your own to simulate each problem.

1. Use the information in the Example. Find the experimental probability that exactly three out of four bulbs will grow.
2. **a.** Suppose there is a 30% probability of being stopped by a red light at each of four stoplights. What is the experimental probability of being stopped by at least two red lights? Let 0, 1, and 2 represent red lights.
   b. **Reasoning** Suppose there is a 60% chance of a red light at each stop light. How many digits would you use to represent getting a red light? Explain.
3. **Writing in Math** Write a probability problem you can solve using a random number table. Solve your problem.

12-3 Make an Organized List and Simulate a Problem

Problem Solving

What You'll Learn

To solve a problem using two different methods

. . . And Why

To compare strategies in problem solving, as in Example 1

Check Skills You'll Need

For help, go to Lesson 12-2.

Suppose you roll a number cube 100 times. Find each experimental probability as a fraction in simplest form.

1. If you get twenty-five 5's, what is $P(5)$?
2. If you get an even number 48 times, what is $P(\text{even})$?
3. If you get 76 numbers less than four, what is $P(\text{less than } 4)$?

OBJECTIVE

Interactive lesson includes instant self-check, tutorials, and activities.

1 Solving a Problem Using Two Different Methods

When to Use These Strategies You can ***make an organized list*** to help you find theoretical probability. You can ***simulate a problem*** to find experimental probability. These strategies are used separately as two different methods in Example 1.

1 EXAMPLE Using Strategies

Pets A cat is expecting a litter of four kittens. The probabilities of male and female kittens are equal. What is the probability that the litter contains three females and one male?

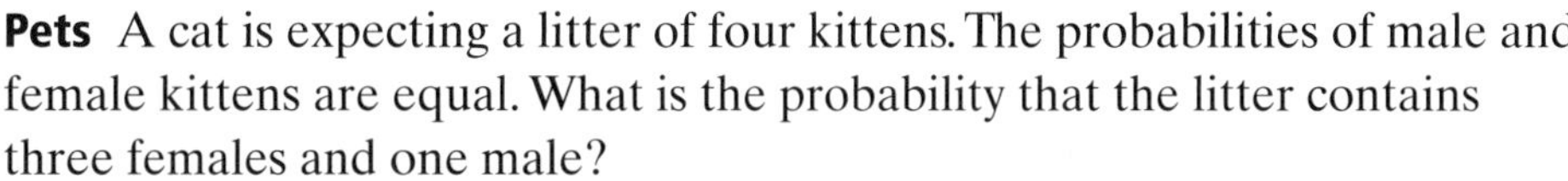

Read and Understand Your goal is to find the probability that the litter contains three females and one male, given there are four kittens and that the probabilities of males and females are equal.

Plan and Solve

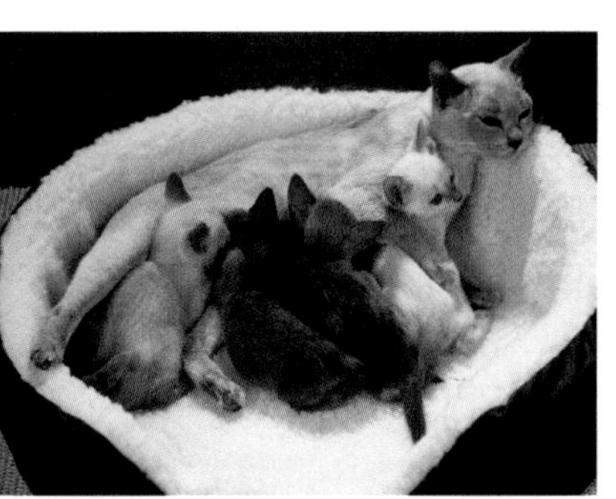

Real-World Connection

Cats average four kittens per litter. The range of the number of kittens in a litter is usually 1 to 8.

Method 1 Make an Organized List

Make an organized list to find the total number of possible outcomes and the number of favorable outcomes.

M M M M	M F M M	F M M M	F F M M
M M M F	M F M F	F M M F	(F F M F)
M M F M	M F F M	F M F M	(F F F M)
M M F F	(M F F F)	(F M F F)	F F F F

There are a total of 16 possible outcomes. Of those, 4 outcomes include three females and one male. So the theoretical probability of three females and one male in a litter of four kittens is $\frac{4}{16}$, or 0.25.

Method 2 Simulate the Problem

To simulate a problem, first design a model. Each kitten is either male or female. The two probabilities are equal. Tossing a coin makes sense since it has two outcomes, heads or tails, and each outcome is equally likely.

T T H H T T H H
H H T T T H T T
T H H H H T T T
H H H T T T T H
H T H T T T T T
H T H H H H T T
T H T H T H H T
T H H T H T T T
T H T T H T H H
H H H H H T H H
T H T H H H H H
H T H T H H H H
T T T H

Let "heads" represent a male and "tails" represent a female. Toss the coin 100 times. At the left are the results of one simulation. Separate the results into groups of 4, since there are 4 kittens in a litter. You now have 25 "litters" of 4.

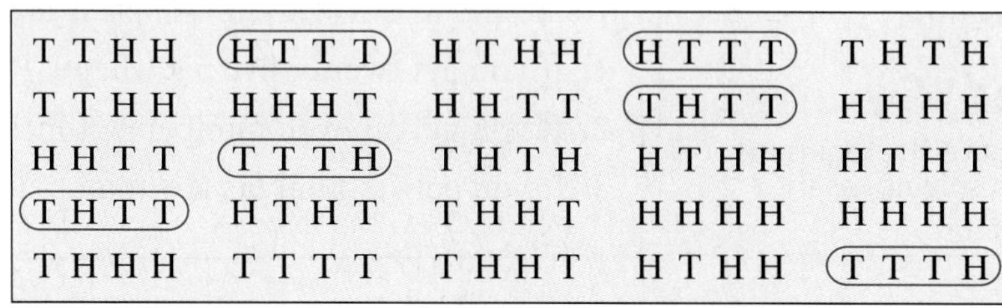

T T H H	H T T T	H T H H	H T T T	T H T H
T T H H	H H H T	H H T T	T H T T	H H H H
H H T T	T T T H	T H T H	H T H H	H T H T
T H T T	H T H T	T H H T	H H H H	H H H H
T H H H	T T T T	T H H T	H T H H	T T T H

Now you can find the experimental probability. Note that six groups contain three females and one male.

$$P(3 \text{ females and } 1 \text{ male}) = \frac{\text{number of times an event occurs}}{\text{total number of trials}} = \frac{6}{25} = 0.24$$

The experimental probability of a litter with 3 female kittens and 1 male kitten is 0.24.

Look Back and Check In Method 1, you found the theoretical probability. In Method 2, you found one value for the experimental probability, which is slightly less than the theoretical probability.

Repeating the simulation may result in a different experimental probability. The more trials you conduct, the more likely it is that the experimental probability will be close to the theoretical probability.

Check Understanding 1 **a.** Look back at the two methods in Example 1. Which method do you prefer? Why?

b. You are taking a 4-question true-false quiz. Find the probability of guessing exactly 4 out of 4 questions correctly.

EXERCISES

For more practice, see *Extra Practice*.

A Practice by Example

Solve each problem by either making an organized list or by simulating the problem. Explain why you chose the method you did.

Example 1 (page 643)

1. **Prizes** One of the letters in WIN appears under each bottle cap for Sparky Juice. To win a prize, you must collect all three letters. You are equally likely to get any of the three letters with each bottle. What is the probability that you will win after buying exactly three bottles?

Need Help?

- Reread the problem.
- Identify the key facts and details.
- Tell the problem in your own words.
- Try a different strategy.
- Check your work.

2. You are taking a 4-question true-false quiz and you don't know any of the answers. What is the probability that you guess exactly 3 out of 4 answers correctly?

3. A license plate contains three numerals. Even and odd digits are equally likely. What is the probability that all three numerals are even?

4. What is the probability that exactly three children in a family of five children will be boys? Assume that the probability of a boy is equal to the probability of a girl.

Apply Your Skills

Use any strategy to solve each problem. Show your work.

Strategies

Draw a Diagram
Look for a Pattern
Make a Graph
Make an Organized List
Make a Table
Simulate a Problem
Solve a Simpler Problem
Try, Check, and Revise
Use Logical Reasoning
Work Backward
Write an Equation

5. **Money** The Booster Club hires a band for a fund-raiser. The club guarantees the band a fee of $1,500 plus $4.50 for each ticket sold. There are 1,150 seats in the auditorium.
   a. What is the greatest amount of money the band can earn?
   b. The auditorium is 18% empty. How much does the band earn?

6. a. **Patterns** What is the side length of the fourth square in the pattern below?
   b. What would be the length of a side of the square that comes before the first square in the pattern?

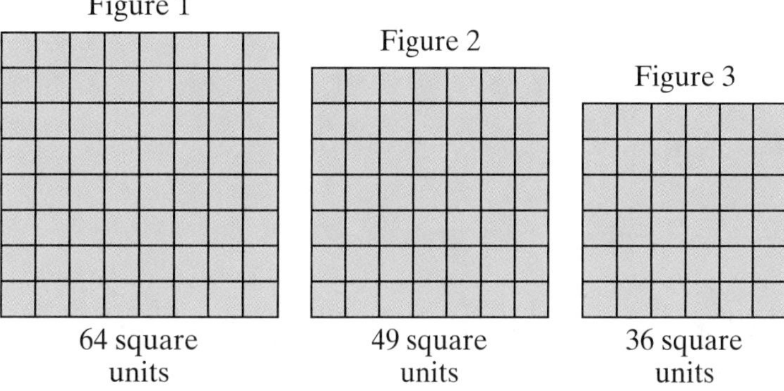

7. **Writing in Math** During a sale, a store manager reduces a jacket's price by 40%. After the sale, the manager increases the price by 40%. Are the prices before and after the sale the same? Explain.

8. **Weather** The temperature at 6:00 A.M. is 48°F. At 9:00 A.M. it is 60°F. The temperature climbs at the same rate from 9:00 A.M. to 11:00 A.M. What is the temperature at 10:00 A.M.?

9. **Model Cars** A restaurant gives away a model car with each meal. You are equally likely to get any of the five cars. What is the probability that you will get two of the same car after two meals?

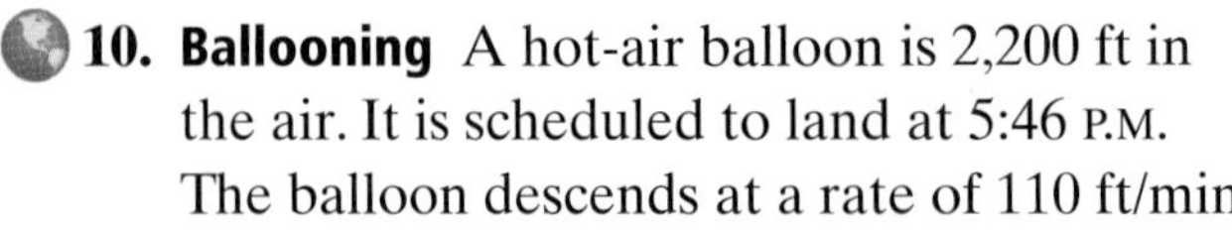

10. **Ballooning** A hot-air balloon is 2,200 ft in the air. It is scheduled to land at 5:46 P.M. The balloon descends at a rate of 110 ft/min. At what time should the descent begin?

11. Sixty students are standing in a circle. The students are spaced evenly and numbered consecutively from 1 to 60. You are number 7. Your friend is standing directly opposite you. What is your friend's number?

12. **Stretch Your Thinking** A cook uses one half of his flour to make bran muffins and one third of the remaining flour to make corn muffins. He has $1\frac{1}{2}$ c of flour left. How much flour did he start with?

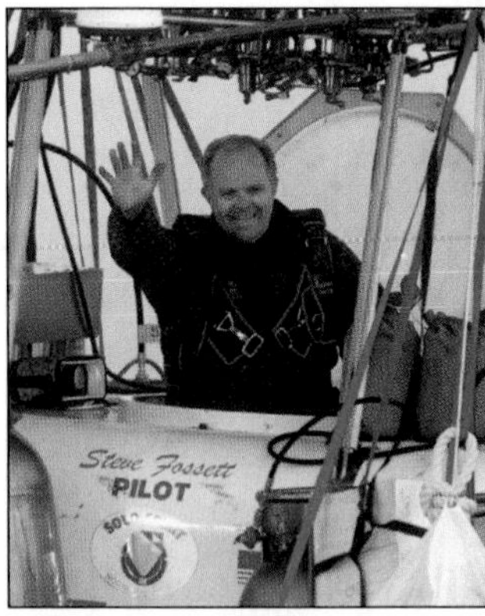

Real-World Connection

Steve Fossett was the first person to fly a hot-air balloon around the world.

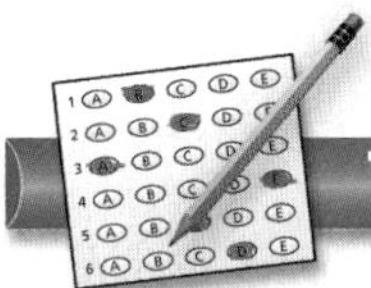

Test Prep

Multiple Choice

13. A bag contains 5 oranges, 5 golden apples, and 10 red apples. What is the probability that a piece of fruit selected at random is an apple?
    A. $\frac{1}{4}$ B. $\frac{1}{3}$ C. $\frac{1}{2}$ D. $\frac{3}{4}$

14. You flip a coin three times. What is the probability that you do NOT flip any heads?
    F. $\frac{1}{2}$ G. $\frac{1}{4}$ H. $\frac{1}{6}$ I. $\frac{1}{8}$

Take It to the NET
Online lesson quiz at **www.PHSchool.com**
Web Code aba-1203

15. All of the letters of the alphabet are in a bag. What is the probability of pulling one of the vowels a,e,i,o, or u from the bag?
    A. $\frac{2}{13}$ B. $\frac{5}{26}$ C. $\frac{4}{13}$ D. $\frac{21}{26}$

Short Response

16. Make an organized list of all possible outcomes for rolling two standard number cubes and finding their sum.

Mixed Review

Lesson 12-1

A number from 1 through 8 is selected at random. Find each probability as a fraction, a decimal, and a percent.

17. $P(4)$ 18. $P(7)$ 19. $P(\text{even})$

Lesson 10-6

Using graph paper, translate each point down 3 units. Give the coordinates of each image point.

20. (4, 5) 21. (−2, 0) 22. (2, −3)

12-4 Sample Spaces

What You'll Learn

 To find a sample space

 To use the counting principle

. . . And Why

To see all the outcomes of an experiment, as in Example 1

✓ Check Skills You'll Need

For help, go to Lesson 3-4.

Write the prime factorization of each number. Use exponents where possible.

1. 12 **2.** 14 **3.** 20 **4.** 72

5. Explain why a factor tree is useful in showing the prime factorization of 150.

New Vocabulary • sample space • counting principle

OBJECTIVE 1 Finding a Sample Space

Interactive lesson includes instant self-check, tutorials, and activities.

You win a prize if you choose the correct two letters from A, B, C, D, and E. What are the possible choices?

A, B A, C A, D A, E B, C B, D B, E C, D C, E D, E

The collection of all possible outcomes in an experiment is the **sample space.** You can use the sample space to find the probability of an event.

1 EXAMPLE Finding a Sample Space

Need Help?
For help using ordered pairs, see Lesson 10-1.

a. Make a table to find the sample space for rolling two number cubes colored red and blue. Write the outcomes as ordered pairs.

	1	2	3	4	5	6
1	(1, 1)	(2, 1)	(3, 1)	(4, 1)	(5, 1)	(6, 1)
2	(1, 2)	(2, 2)	(3, 2)	(4, 2)	(5, 2)	(6, 2)
3	(1, 3)	(2, 3)	(3, 3)	(4, 3)	(5, 3)	(6, 3)
4	(1, 4)	(2, 4)	(3, 4)	(4, 4)	(5, 4)	(6, 4)
5	(1, 5)	(2, 5)	(3, 5)	(4, 5)	(5, 5)	(6, 5)
6	(1, 6)	(2, 6)	(3, 6)	(4, 6)	(5, 6)	(6, 6)

← There are 36 possible outcomes.

b. Find the probability of rolling at least one "3."

There are 11 outcomes with at least one "3." There are 36 possible outcomes. So the probability of rolling a "3" is $\frac{11}{36}$.

✓ Check Understanding **1** Give the sample space for tossing two coins. Find the probability of tossing two heads.

Another way to show a sample space is by using a tree diagram. Each branch of the tree represents one choice.

2 EXAMPLE Using a Tree Diagram

River Travel Suppose you are going to travel on a river. You have two choices of boats—a kayak or a rowboat. The river splits into three smaller streams going north, northwest, and northeast.

a. What is the sample space for your journey?

Make a tree diagram for the outcomes.

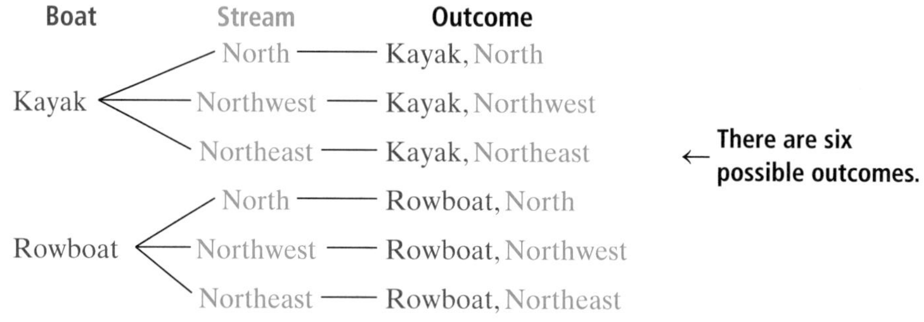

← There are six possible outcomes.

b. Suppose you select a trip at random. What is the probability of selecting a kayak and going north?

There is one favorable outcome (kayak, north) out of six possible outcomes. The probability is $\frac{1}{6}$.

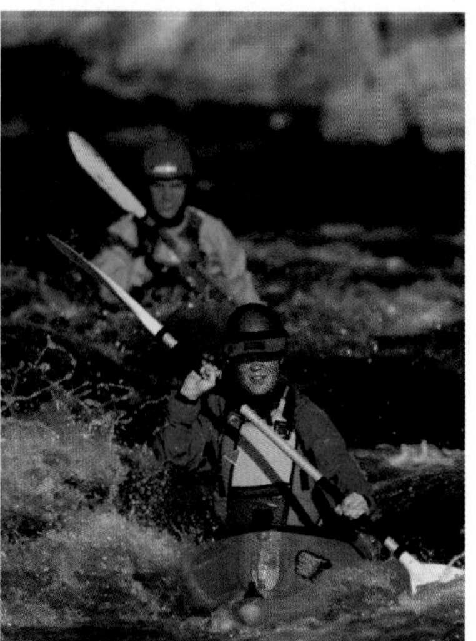

Kayaks originated with the Eskimos of Greenland. Now they are used worldwide.

Check Understanding 2 **a.** Suppose a canoe is added as another choice of boats in Example 2. Draw a tree diagram to show the sample space.
b. Find the probability of randomly selecting a canoe for your journey.

OBJECTIVE 2 Using the Counting Principle

In Example 2 above, there are 2 choices of boats and 3 choices of direction. There are 2×3, or 6, total possible choices. This suggests a simple way to find the number of outcomes, by using the **counting principle.**

Key Concepts The Counting Principle

Suppose there are m ways of making one choice and n ways of making a second choice. Then there are $m \times n$ ways to make the first choice followed by the second choice.

Example

If you can choose a shirt in 5 sizes and 7 colors, then you can choose 5×7, or 35, shirts.

3 EXAMPLE Using the Counting Principle

Food Suppose you order a sandwich by choosing one bread and one meat from the menu. How many different sandwiches are available?

THE
DELI COUNTER
SANDWICHES
FRESH BREADS
Rye
Wheat
White
Pita
Wrap
DELI MEATS
Roast Beef
Turkey
Ham
Pastrami
Salami
Liverwurst

Use the counting principle.

Bread		Meat	
number of choices	×	number of choices	
5	×	6	= 30

There are 30 different sandwiches available.

3 a. The manager of the Deli Counter decides to add tuna salad to the list of meat choices. How many different sandwiches are now available?

b. Suppose you select a sandwich from the menu at random. What is the probability of selecting a sandwich on rye bread?

EXERCISES

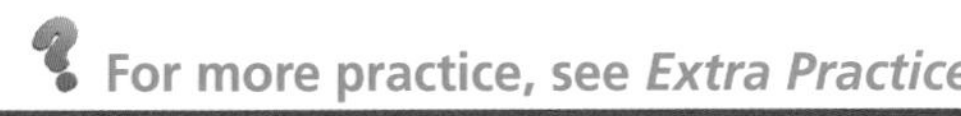

Example 1 (page 647)

Make a table to show the sample space for each situation and find the number of outcomes. Then find the probability.

1. You toss two coins. What is the probability of tossing one tail and one head?
2. You roll a standard number cube once. What is the probability of rolling a number less than 4?
3. You toss a coin and spin a spinner. The spinner has four equal sections numbered from 1 to 4. Find the probability of tossing tails and spinning 4.

Example 2 (page 648)

Make a tree diagram for each situation. Then find the probability of each event.

4. A spinner is half red and half blue. You spin it twice and get red both times.
5. You choose one letter at random from each of two sets of letters: A, B, C and W, X, Y, Z. You get A and W.
6. You choose at random from the letters A, B, C, and D, and you roll a standard number cube once. You get A and 5.
7. **Tours** A traveler chooses a tour of Baltimore, Maryland, at random from buses D, E, and F. After the bus tour, she chooses a harbor tour at random from boats 1, 2, and 3. She takes a tour with bus D and boat 2.

Example 3 (page 649)

Use the counting principle.

8. **Cooking** You are making a recipe with herbs and spices for a party at a friend's house. There are four types of herbs in your kitchen—basil, bay leaves, chives, and dill. You also have three types of seasoning—salt, pepper, and garlic powder. How many different recipes with one herb and one spice can you make?

9. **Education** There are four art teachers, three music teachers, and eight history teachers. How many ways can a student be assigned an art teacher, a music teacher, and a history teacher?

B Apply Your Skills

A spinner with four equal sections numbered from 1 to 4 is spun twice. Use the sample space below to find each probability.

Second Spin

First Spin	1	2	3	4
1	(1, 1)	(1, 2)	(1, 3)	(1, 4)
2	(2, 1)	(2, 2)	(2, 3)	(2, 4)
3	(3, 1)	(3, 2)	(3, 3)	(3, 4)
4	(4, 1)	(4, 2)	(4, 3)	(4, 4)

10. $P(1, 2)$
11. $P(1, \text{odd})$
12. $P(\text{even}, \text{odd})$
13. $P(6, 1)$
14. $P(\text{prime number}, 4)$
15. $P(4, \text{even})$

Find the number of outcomes for each situation.

16. Roll three standard number cubes once each.
17. Spin a spinner with three equal sections, numbered 1 to 3, four times.
18. Pick one of 7 boys and one of 12 girls.
19. Toss five coins once each.

20. a. **Clothes** Ardell has four suit jackets (white, blue, green, and tan) and four dress shirts in the same colors. How many different jacket-shirt outfits does Ardell have?
    b. Suppose he grabs a suit jacket and a dress shirt without looking. What is the probability that they will *not* be the same color?

Find each probability for rolling two standard number cubes.

21. $P(\text{two even numbers})$
22. $P(\text{sum of } 4)$
23. $P(\text{first number is odd})$
24. $P(\text{sum of } 1)$

Real-World Connection

Careers Tailors fit designer clothes for important events.

25. a. **Writing in Math** Explain how to use the counting principle to find the number of outcomes in a sample space.
    b. **Reasoning** Why is it sometimes helpful to use the counting principle instead of finding the sample space to find the number of outcomes of an event?

Use the menu for Exercises 26–29.

CITY CINEMA
POPCORN
small $3.00
medium . .$4.00
large $5.00
FRUIT PUNCH or LEMONADE
small $2.75
medium . .$3.00
large $3.25
jumbo . . . $3.75

26. List all the possible beverage orders.

27. You order lemonade and popcorn. Draw a tree diagram to show the sample space.

28. How many orders are possible for popcorn and a beverage?

29. **Reasoning** The theater manager uses the counting principle to find P(small popcorn, medium lemonade) $= \frac{1}{24}$. Do you agree? Explain.

Challenge

Use the table for Exercises 30–31.

Voting for Student Council

Number of Nominees	Number of Positions
7	3

30. How many people are eligible for the first position?

31. How many people are eligible for the second position once the first person has been selected? For the third position once the first two have been selected?

32. **Stretch Your Thinking** A certain percent has three digits with a decimal. The sum of its digits is 15. The percent is less than 100%. When the percent is written as a fraction in simplest form, it has a denominator that is a multiple of 4 and is less than 10. Find the percent.

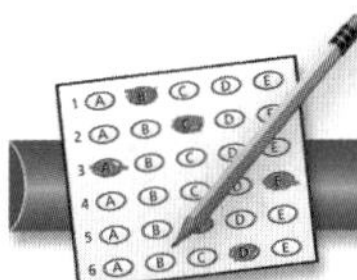

Test Prep

The sample space shows the possible results of tossing three coins once.

HHH	TTT
HHT	TTH
HTH	THT
HTT	THH

Multiple Choice

33. What is the probability of tossing three tails?
A. $\frac{3}{4}$ **B.** $\frac{1}{2}$ **C.** $\frac{1}{4}$ **D.** $\frac{1}{8}$

34. What is the probability of tossing heads exactly once?
F. $\frac{1}{4}$ **G.** $\frac{3}{8}$ **H.** $\frac{1}{2}$ **I.** $\frac{3}{4}$

35. What is the probability of NOT tossing any tails?
A. $\frac{3}{4}$ **B.** $\frac{5}{8}$ **C.** $\frac{1}{2}$ **D.** $\frac{1}{8}$

Take It to the NET
Online lesson quiz at
www.PHSchool.com
Web Code aba-1204

Extended Response

36. **a.** You roll a standard number cube once and spin a spinner with three equal sections numbered 1 through 3 once. Make a table to show the sample space.
b. Suppose you multiply the roll times the spin. Which event has a greater probability—an even product or an odd product? Explain.

Mixed Review

Lesson 11-1 **Make a frequency table and a line plot of each set of data.**

37. files downloaded from the Internet:
8 2 12 10 4 6 7 3 14 9 0 11 9 13 6 10 12 6 4 10

38. test scores:
80 92 78 100 75 90 86 87 92 83 93 79 76 80 95 85

Lesson 7-4 **Algebra** **Find the value of *x* in each triangle.**

39. 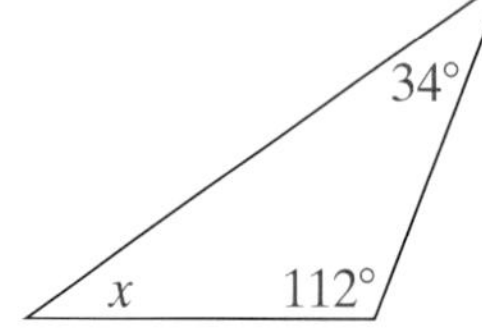

40. 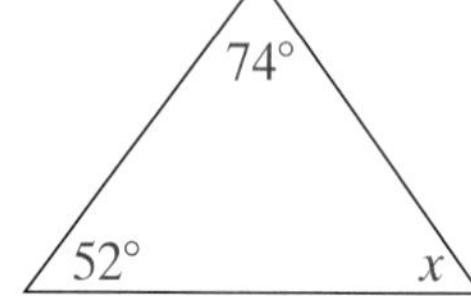

41. 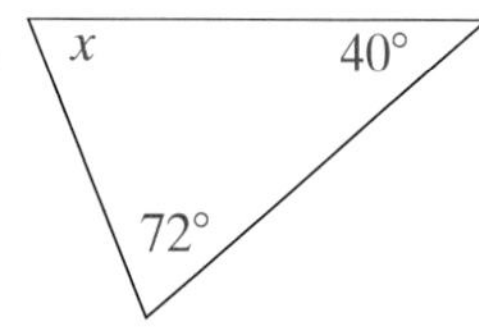

Checkpoint Quiz 1 — Lessons 12-1 through 12-4

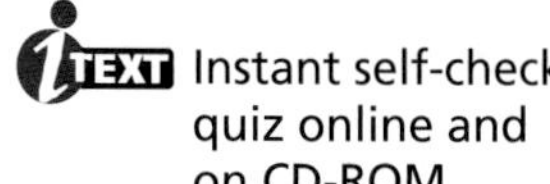

Suppose you spin the spinner at the right once. Write each probability as a fraction, a decimal, and a percent.

1. P(2 or 3)
2. P(not 4)

3. **Forestry** The table below shows a sample of the number of spruce trees counted in a forest area. Find the experimental probability of selecting a Serbian spruce.

Spruce Trees

Tree Type	Number
Norway spruce	32
Serbian spruce	20
Colorado spruce	67

4. **a.** A true-false quiz has 5 questions. Use a simulation or make an organized list. Find the probability of guessing at random and getting exactly 3 correct answers.
   b. 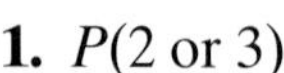 **Reasoning** Which strategy represents theoretical probability? Which strategy represents experimental probability? Explain.

5. **a.** You spin the spinner at the right twice. Give the sample space.
   b. Find the probability of spinning green twice.
   c. Find the probability of spinning purple, then blue.

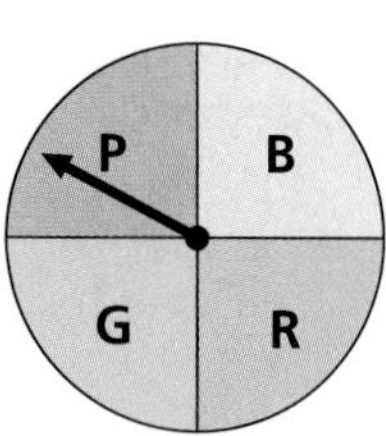

12-5 Compound Events

What You'll Learn

To find the probability of independent events

To find the probability of dependent events

. . . And Why

To analyze the probability of games, as in Example 2

✓ Check Skills You'll Need

For help, go to Lesson 4-4.

Find each product.

1. $\frac{3}{4} \cdot \frac{3}{4}$ **2.** $\frac{2}{5} \cdot \frac{3}{5}$ **3.** $\frac{1}{5} \cdot \frac{1}{4}$ **4.** $\frac{3}{7} \cdot \frac{2}{7}$

Simplify before finding each product.

5. $\frac{2}{3} \cdot \frac{3}{4}$ **6.** $\frac{1}{6} \cdot \frac{3}{5}$ **7.** $\frac{2}{3} \cdot \frac{1}{2}$ **8.** $\frac{2}{5} \cdot \frac{10}{11}$

New Vocabulary

- **compound event**
- **independent events**
- **dependent events**

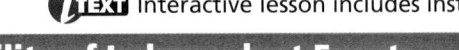

OBJECTIVE

Interactive lesson includes instant self-check, tutorials, and activities.

1 Finding the Probability of Independent Events

Investigation: Exploring Multiple Events

Suppose you want to select beads for a necklace as shown at the right, and you select the first bead without looking. You put the bead back and make another selection at random.

1. Give the sample space for the colors of the two beads. Write the outcomes as ordered pairs.
2. What is the probability of drawing a red bead for your first draw?
3. What is the probability of drawing red beads twice?
4. Suppose now that you draw a red bead and do not replace it. How many beads of each color are left?
5. Does the probability of drawing red on the second draw depend on whether you replace the first bead? Explain.

Suppose you select a bead from the beads shown above. You then select another bead. The selection of two beads involves two events. A **compound event** consists of two or more events.

A compound event consists of events that either do or do not depend on each other. Suppose a family has two children. The gender of the second child is independent of the gender of the first child.

Two events are **independent events** if the occurrence of one event does not affect the probability of the occurrence of the other.

Key Concepts **Probability of Independent Events**

If A and B are independent events, then $P(A, \text{then } B) = P(A) \times P(B)$.

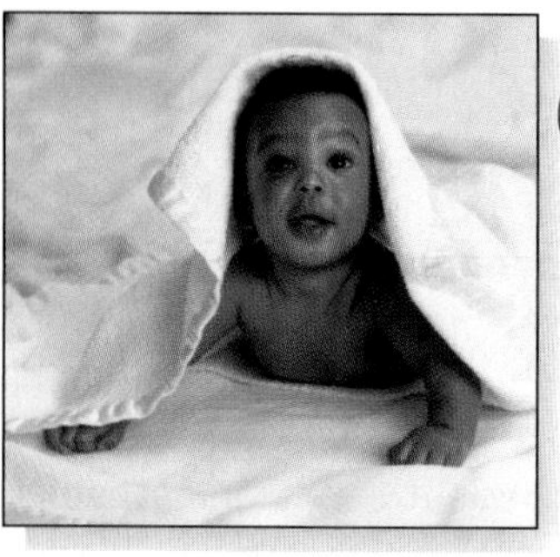

Real-World Connection

The probability that a child born is a girl is $\frac{100}{205}$, a little less than $\frac{1}{2}$.

1 EXAMPLE Probability of Independent Events

Real World

Families A family wants to have two children. What is the probability that both children will be girls?

Assume the probability of having a girl is $\frac{1}{2}$.

$P(\text{girl, then girl}) = P(\text{girl}) \times P(\text{girl})$ ← **Having a girl is the first and second event.**

$= \frac{1}{2} \times \frac{1}{2}$ ← **Substitute.**

$= \frac{1}{4}$ ← **Multiply.**

The probability that both children will be girls is $\frac{1}{4}$.

Check Understanding 1 Find $P(\text{girl, then boy})$.

You can use the formula for the probability of independent events to analyze games.

2 EXAMPLE Analyzing Games

Real World

Games "Spin Your Initials" uses a wheel lettered with equal sections A–Z. Suppose you spin it twice. Find $P(B, \text{then } Z)$.

The two events are independent. There are 26 letters in the alphabet.

$P(B, \text{then } Z) = P(B) \times P(Z)$ ← **Selecting B is the first event. Selecting Z is the second event.**

$= \frac{1}{26} \times \frac{1}{26}$ ← **Substitute.**

$= \frac{1}{676}$ ← **Multiply.**

The probability is $\frac{1}{676}$.

Check Understanding 2 **a.** A standard number cube is rolled twice. Find $P(6, \text{then } 6)$.

b. Mental Math If two independent events A and B each have a probability of $\frac{1}{3}$, what is $P(A, \text{then } B)$?

OBJECTIVE

2 Finding the Probability of Dependent Events

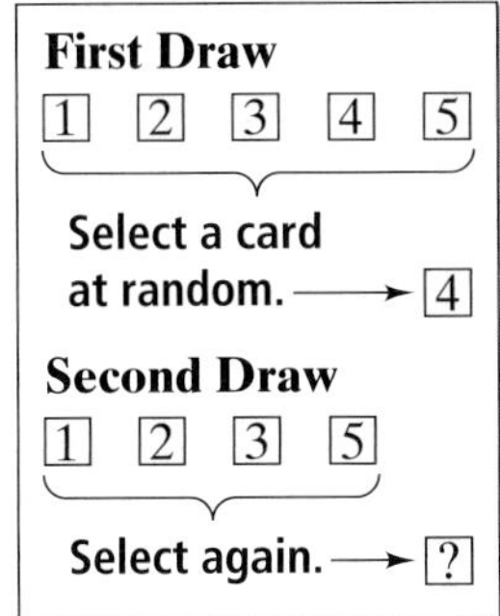

Suppose you play a game with cards numbered 1–5. You draw two cards at random. You draw the first card and do not replace it. The probability in the second draw *depends* on the result of the first draw.

Two events are **dependent events** if the occurrence of one event affects the probability of the occurrence of the other event.

3 EXAMPLE Probability of a Dependent Event

You select a card at random from those below. The card has the letter M. Without replacing the M card, you select a second card. Find the probability of selecting a card with the letter A after selecting M.

M	A	T	H	E	M	A	T	I	C	S

There are 10 cards remaining after selecting an M card.

$P(A) = \frac{2}{10}$ ← number of cards with the letter A / ← number of cards remaining

$P(A) = \frac{1}{5}$ ← Simplify.

The probability of selecting an A for the second card is $\frac{1}{5}$.

Check Understanding 3 Use the cards in Example 3. You select a card at random, and it has the letter T. Without replacing that T card, you select a second card. Find $P(S)$.

You can use a formula to find the probability of dependent events.

Key Concepts **Probability of Dependent Events**

If event B depends on event A, then $P(A, \text{then } B) = P(A) \times P(B \text{ after } A)$.

4 EXAMPLE Probability of Dependent Events

Games To play "Draw Your Initials," you draw a card from a bucket that contains cards lettered A–Z. Without replacing the first card, you draw a second one. Find the probability of winning if your initials are C and M.

The two events are dependent. After the first selection, there are 25 letters.

$P(C, \text{then } M) = P(C) \times P(M \text{ after } C)$ ← Use the formula for dependent events.

$= \frac{1}{26} \times \frac{1}{25}$ ← Substitute.

$= \frac{1}{650}$ ← Multiply.

The probability of winning is $\frac{1}{650}$.

Check Understanding 4 **Reasoning** Explain why the probability of selecting M second is $\frac{1}{25}$.

More Than One Way

You toss a coin three times. What is the probability of getting heads three times in a row?

Brianna's Method

Each toss of a coin is an independent event. The probability of getting heads for one coin toss is $\frac{1}{2}$. I can find the product of the probabilities of the three coin tosses.

$P(\text{three heads in a row}) = \frac{1}{2} \times \frac{1}{2} \times \frac{1}{2} = \frac{1}{8}$

The probability of three heads is $\frac{1}{8}$.

Chris's Method

I can make a tree diagram for the first, second, and third tosses of the coin. A favorable outcome is one with three heads. I will compare the number of favorable outcomes to the number of possible outcomes.

Toss 1	Toss 2	Toss 3	Outcome
H	H	H	HHH
		T	HHT
	T	H	HTH
		T	HTT
T	H	H	THH
		T	THT
	T	H	TTH
		T	TTT

The tree diagram shows 1 favorable outcome out of 8 possible outcomes. The probability of three heads is $\frac{1}{8}$.

Choose a Method

You toss a coin four times. What is the probability of getting tails all four times? Describe your method and explain why you chose it.

EXERCISES

For more practice, see *Extra Practice*.

Practice by Example

Examples 1, 2 (page 654)

You roll a standard number cube twice. Find each probability.

1. P(1, then 2)
2. P(3, then even)
3. P(less than 4, then 1)
4. P(odd, then even)
5. P(divisible by 2, then 5)
6. P(greater than 2, then odd)

Row	Student			
A	1	2	3	4
B	5	6	7	8

An arrangement of 8 students is shown at the left. The names of all the students are in a basket. The teacher draws one name and replaces it. Then the teacher draws a second name. Find each probability.

7. P(student 1, then student 8)

8. P(a student in row A, then a student in row B)

9. P(student 10, then a student in row B)

10. P(a student in row A, then student 6, 7, or 8)

Example 3 (page 655)

You draw the letter A from the group at the right. Without replacing the A, you draw a second letter. Find each probability.

11. $P(Z)$

12. P(vowel)

13. P(red)

14. P(blue)

15. Number Sense Which is greater, $P(A$, then red) or $P(A$, then blue)?

Example 4 (page 655)

A box contains 20 cards numbered 1–20. You draw a card. Without replacing the first card, you draw a second card. Find each probability.

16. P(1, then 20)

17. P(3, then even)

18. P(even, then 7)

Apply Your Skills

A bag contains 3 blue marbles, 4 red marbles, and 2 white marbles. Three times you draw a marble and return it. Find each probability.

19. P(red, then white, then blue)

20. P(red, then white, then white).

21. P(blue, then red, then blue)

22. P(all white)

23. Writing in Math When you draw marbles without replacing them, are the events *independent* or *dependent*? Explain.

24. Events with no outcomes in common are *disjoint events*. To find the probability of disjoint events, add the probabilities of the individual events. Suppose you select a number from 21 to 30 at random. What is the probability of selecting a number that is even or prime?

25. Geometry Two coins are dropped at random into the boxes shown at the right. What is the probability that both coins fall into a shaded box?

26. **Broadcasting** Five girls and seven boys want to be the two broadcasters for a school variety show. To be fair, a teacher puts the names of the students in a hat and draws two. Find P(girl, then boy).

Reading Math

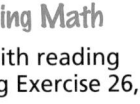

For help with reading and solving Exercise 26, see p. 659.

27. **Data File, p. 627** The basketball coach of Martin Luther King School has 35 stat sheets summarizing each game of the season. The coach selects two sheets at random. Find P(win, then loss) without replacement.

C Challenge

28. **Reasoning** Are the two events *independent* or *dependent*?
    a. You toss a nickel and then you toss a dime.
    b. You draw a card and then you draw another, without replacement.
    c. You grab a sock from the dryer without replacing it, and then grab another sock from the dryer.

29. You have two spinners with colors on them. The probability of spinning "green" on both spinners is $\frac{5}{21}$. The probability of spinning "green" on the first spinner alone is $\frac{1}{3}$. What is the probability of spinning "green" on the second spinner alone?

30. **Stretch Your Thinking** What is the relationship between the radius of each circle and the sides of the rectangle?

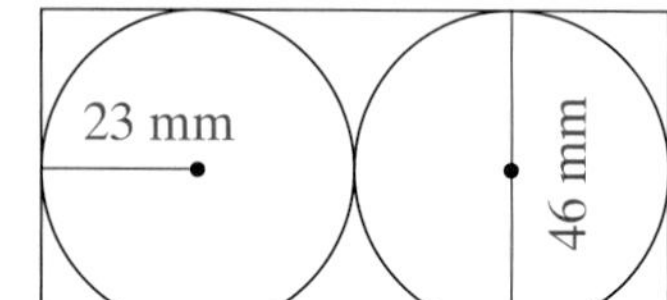

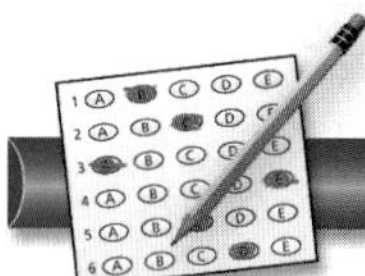

Test Prep

Multiple Choice

31. A wheel is evenly divided into sections numbered 1 to 4. You spin it twice. What is the probability of spinning a 3, then a 4?

    A. $\frac{1}{16}$ B. $\frac{1}{8}$ C. $\frac{1}{4}$ D. $\frac{1}{2}$

32. A bag contains one red marble, two blue marbles, and one green marble. You draw a marble at random and replace it. Then you draw a second marble. What is the probability of selecting a red marble, then a green marble?

    F. $\frac{1}{4}$ G. $\frac{1}{8}$ H. $\frac{1}{16}$ I. $\frac{1}{32}$

Take It to the NET
Online lesson quiz at
www.PHSchool.com
Web Code aba-1205

33. A wheel is evenly divided into sections labeled A to C. You spin it twice. What is the probability of spinning an A, then an A?

    A. $\frac{1}{9}$ B. $\frac{1}{3}$ C. $\frac{2}{3}$ D. $\frac{3}{4}$

Short Response

34. In a drawer containing 6 loose socks, 2 are blue, and 4 are black. You select a sock at random from the drawer. Without replacing the first sock, you select another sock. Find *P*(blue, then blue). Show your work.

Mixed Review

Lesson 12-4

35. Make a table to show the sample space for one spin of a spinner with equal sections numbered from 1 to 3 and one toss of a coin.

Lesson 7-9

Find the measure of the central angle you would draw to represent each percent in a circle graph. Round to the nearest degree.

36. 10% 37. 35% 38. 14% 39. 22%

40. 88% 41. 49% 42. 33.3% 43. 4.5%

Understanding Word Problems

For Use With Exercise 26, Page 657

Read through the problem below. Then follow along with what Maria thinks as she solves the problem. Check your understanding with the exercises at the bottom of the page.

26. Broadcasting Five girls and seven boys want to be the two broadcasters for a school variety show. To be fair, a teacher puts the names of the students in a hat and draws two. Find P(girl, then boy).

What Maria Thinks	What Maria Writes
I'll write the information I'm given in my own words.	There are 5 girls and 7 boys. There are 12 names placed in the hat.
It makes sense that the teacher would not replace the first name drawn. I'll write the probability of selecting a girl. Then I'll write the probability of selecting a boy without replacement.	$P(\text{girl}) = \frac{\text{number of girl's names}}{\text{total number of names}} = \frac{5}{12}$ $P(\text{boy}) = \frac{\text{number of boy's names}}{\text{total number of names left}} = \frac{7}{11}$
Now I can find the probability of the two dependent events.	$P(\text{girl, then boy}) = P(\text{girl}) \times P(\text{boy after girl})$
I'll substitute and multiply the probabilities.	$P(\text{girl, then boy}) = \frac{5}{12} \times \frac{7}{11} = \frac{35}{132}$
I can write my answer in a sentence now.	P(girl, then boy) is $\frac{35}{132}$.

EXERCISES

1. A bowl contains seven slips of paper, each with a different day of the week. You select two slips of paper at random without replacement. Find P(Monday, then Tuesday).

2. There are 4 discolored oranges in a bag of 30 oranges. You select one orange at random from the bag and do not replace it. You then select another orange. Find P(not discolored, then discolored).

3. **Travel** A tourist wants to visit two countries out of eight favorites. Six border an ocean. He puts the names of the countries in a box and draws two at random without replacement. Find P(ocean, then ocean).

12-6 Permutations

What You'll Learn

To find permutations

. . . And Why

To count the number of different arrangements, as in Example 2

Check Skills You'll Need

For help, go to Lesson 1-8.

Find each product.

1. $12 \cdot 11$ **2.** $20 \cdot 19$ **3.** $10 \cdot 9$ **4.** $13 \cdot 12$

5. $8 \cdot 7 \cdot 6$ **6.** $10 \cdot 9 \cdot 8$ **7.** $5 \cdot 4 \cdot 3$ **8.** $6 \cdot 5 \cdot 4$

New Vocabulary • permutation • factorial

OBJECTIVE 1

Interactive lesson includes instant self-check, tutorials, and activities.

Finding Permutations

Investigation: Exploring Arrangements

In one minute, write as many arrangements as you can, using each letter in the word STOP exactly once.

1. Did you use a strategy to make sure that you looked at every possible arrangement? Explain.
2. Is there another way to list every possible arrangement? Which way is easier? Explain.
3. How many of the arrangements are real words that are in the dictionary?

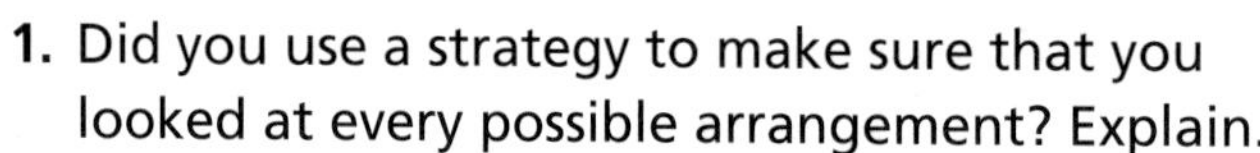

Reading Math

Permutation comes from a Latin word meaning "to change completely."

A **permutation** is an arrangement of objects in a particular order. The permutation STOP is different from the permutation POTS because the order of the letters is different.

1 EXAMPLE Finding Permutations

Find the number of permutations of the letters L, I, K, and E.

4	×	3	×	2	×	1	= 24	← Use the counting principle.
↑		↑		↑		↑		
first letter		second letter		third letter		fourth letter		

There are 24 different permutations.

Check Understanding 1 Find the number of permutations of the letters H, A, N, D, L, and E.

There are $4 \times 3 \times 2 \times 1$ permutations of the letters M, O, T, and H. The product of all positive integers less than or equal to a number is the **factorial** for that number. You write 4 factorial as 4!.

$4! = 4 \times 3 \times 2 \times 1$

2 EXAMPLE Finding Permutations Using Factorials

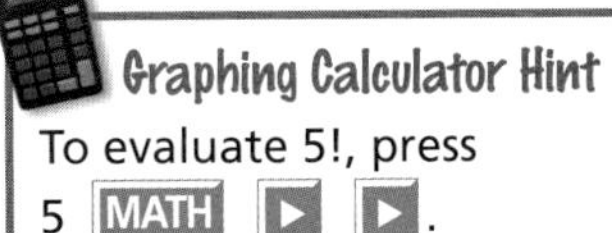

To evaluate 5!, press 5 MATH ▶ ▶. Scroll down to option 5—"!". Press ENTER twice.

Hobbies You attend an after-school activity where you learn to tie five different kinds of knots. You want to display them beside each other in a row. How many different arrangements of the knots can you make?

5!	=	5	×	4	×	3	×	2	×	1	= 120
↑		↑		↑		↑		↑		↑	
ways to place knots		first knot		second knot		third knot		fourth knot		fifth knot	

You can make 120 different arrangements of the knots.

Check Understanding 2 **a.** Write the number of permutations for the letters G, R, A, V, I, E, and S in factorial form. Then multiply.

b. **Reasoning** Does $3! + 2! = 5!$? Explain.

The sample space below shows the two-letter permutations of the 4 letters in STOP. There are 4 possible choices for the first letter, and 3 possible choices for the second letter. The number of permutations is $4 \times 3 = 12$.

ST	OP	TP	TS	PO	PT
TO	PS	OS	OT	SP	SO

3 EXAMPLE Real-World Problem Solving

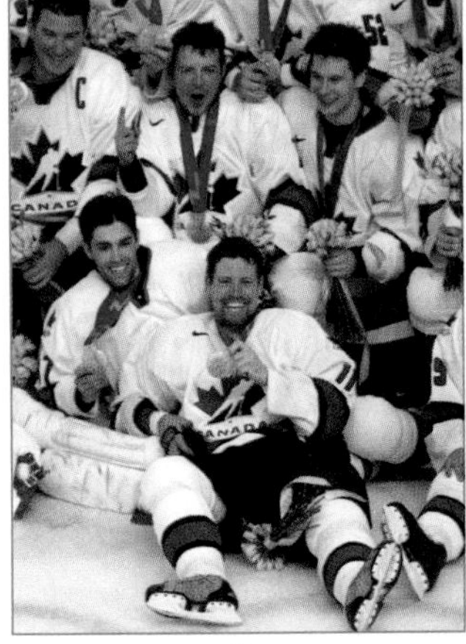

The Canadian team won the gold medal for men's ice hockey in the 2002 Olympics.

Sports There were 16 teams that competed in men's ice hockey at the Salt Lake City Olympics of 2002. Find the number of different ways that teams can win the gold, silver, and bronze medals.

There are 16 possible teams that can win the gold medal. After that, there are 15 teams that can win the silver medal. Finally, there are 14 teams that can win the bronze medal.

16	×	15	×	14	= 3,360	← Use the counting principle.
↑		↑		↑		
gold medal		silver medal		bronze medal		

There are 3,360 different ways that teams can win the three medals.

Check Understanding 3 **Reasoning** In Example 3, the number of permutations is not found by finding 16!. Explain why.

EXERCISES

For more practice, see *Extra Practice*.

A Practice by Example

Example 1 (page 660)

Find the number of permutations of each group of letters.

1. W, O, R, L, D **2.** H, U, M, A, N **3.** T, O, Y

4. P, I, C, K, L, E **5.** L, U, N, C, H, E, S **6.** M, A, R, S

Example 2 (page 661)

Write the number of permutations in factorial form. Then simplify.

7. C, A, T **8.** R, A, T, E, S **9.** P, A, C, K

10. D, E, P, A, R, T **11.** I, N, C, L, U, D, E **12.** L, U, C, K, Y

13. Planning Suppose you plan to shop, call a friend, study, and exercise on a weekend day. How many arrangements of activities can you plan?

Example 3 (page 661)

Find the number of two-letter permutations of the letters.

14. R, E, P, S **15.** Q, I, E, R, T, Y, U **16.** G, D, X, Z, C

17. A, E, I, O, U, Y **18.** M, A, P, L, E **19.** L, A, P

B Apply Your Skills

20. Soccer The table below shows the team names and uniform colors for a soccer league.

Team Names	Uniform Colors
Scorers	Blue
Defenders	Green
Passers	Red

a. Show the sample space of the different name-color possibilities.
b. Use the counting principle to support your answer to part (a).

21. Tourism The owner of a tour boat business has 15 employees. There are three different jobs—driving the boat, checking the boat for safety, and managing the money. In how many different ways can the jobs be assigned to three different people?

22. Suppose you scramble the letters P, A, and N.
a. Make an organized list of the sample space.
b. How many of the groups form real words? What are they?

Find the value of each factorial expression.

23. 4! **24.** 6! **25.** 7! **26.** 8! **27.** 10!

28. Two sisters and their brother are in line for movie tickets.
a. Make a list to show the sample space.
b. What is the probability that they will line up boy-girl-girl?

Real-World Connection

Careers Tour boat drivers show passengers around city harbors and rivers.

29. The password to a school computer has 3 letters of the alphabet. You don't have your password. Suppose you try different arrangements. If you are as unlucky as possible, how many will you have to try before you have access to the computer?

Find the value of each expresion.

30. 5! ÷ 2! **31.** 4! ÷ 3! **32.** 6! ÷ 4!

33. 7! ÷ 3! **34.** 5! ÷ 4! **35.** 8! ÷ 4!

36. Writing in Math Describe two different ways you can use a calculator to find the value of 6!.

Challenge

Algebra **Write an algebraic expression to show how many two-letter permutations are possible.**

37. n different letters **38.** $(n - 2)$ different letters

39. Stretch Your Thinking Kahil, Juan, Waylan, and Ricki all bought identical calculators. Kahil paid 10% more than Juan. Juan paid one fourth of what Waylan paid. Ricki paid 50% less than Waylan. Who paid the most? Who paid the least?

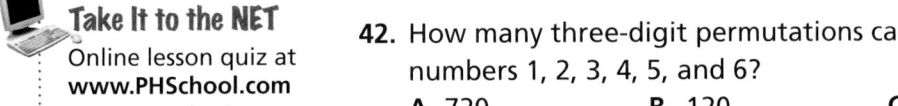

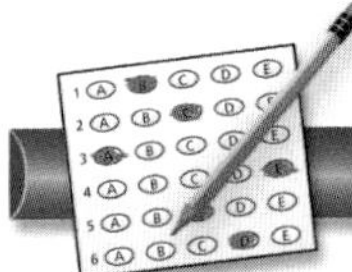

Test Prep

Multiple Choice

40. How many permutations are there of the letters J, U, L, and Y?
A. 1 **B.** 4 **C.** 10 **D.** 24

41. What is the value of 5!?
F. 120 **G.** 60 **H.** 24 **I.** 5

Take It to the NET
Online lesson quiz at
www.PHSchool.com
Web Code: aba-1206

42. How many three-digit permutations can be formed from the numbers 1, 2, 3, 4, 5, and 6?
A. 720 **B.** 120 **C.** 30 **D.** 6

Short Response

43. Suppose you scramble the letters A, B, C, D, and E in a box. Find the number of three-letter permutations. Show your work.

Mixed Review

Lesson 12-5

You have a set of 16 cards numbered 1–16. You select a card and put it back into the set. Then you select another card. Find each probability.

44. P(2, then 6) **45.** P(even, then odd) **46.** P(16, then odd)

Lesson 12-1

You roll a number cube. Find the odds in favor of each outcome.

47. rolling a 5 or 6 **48.** rolling an odd number

12-7 Combinations

What You'll Learn

To find combinations

. . . And Why

To know how many choices you have, as in Example 2

✓ Check Skills You'll Need

For help, go to Lesson 12-6.

Find the number of permutations of the letters.

1. G, I, R, L **2.** B, O, Y **3.** H, I, K, E, R, S

4. Why are the arrangements of letters important in the examples above?

New Vocabulary • combination

OBJECTIVE

Interactive lesson includes instant self-check, tutorials, and activities.

1 Finding Combinations

Whether you say "salt and pepper" or "pepper and salt," you still have the same two seasonings. A **combination** is a grouping of objects in which the order of the objects does not matter.

1 EXAMPLE Real-World Problem Solving

Clothing Suppose you are packing for a hiking trip. The colors of five caps are listed at the right. You decide to pack two caps. How many different combinations of two caps are possible?

Color	Letter
Blue	b
Yellow	y
Green	g
Red	r
Purple	p

Step 1 Let letters represent the five caps. Make an organized list of all possible permutations.

(b, y) (y, b) (g, b) (r, b) (p, b)
(b, g) (y, g) (g, y) (r, y) (p, y)
(b, r) (y, r) (g, r) (r, g) (p, g)
(b, p) (y, p) (g, p) (r, p) (p, r)

Step 2 Cross out the groups containing the same letters.

(b, y) ~~(y, b)~~ (g, b) (r, b) (p, b)
~~(b, g)~~ ~~(y, g)~~ (g, y) (r, y) (p, y)
~~(b, r)~~ ~~(y, r)~~ (g, r) ~~(r, g)~~ (p, g)
~~(b, p)~~ ~~(y, p)~~ ~~(g, p)~~ (r, p) ~~(p, r)~~

Ten different combinations of two caps are possible.

✓ Check Understanding **1** Suppose you have three caps and decide to pack two. How many different combinations of two caps are possible?

In Example 1, the total number of permutations for five caps taken two at a time is 5×4. The number of permutations of the smaller group, two caps, is 2×1. You can find the number of combinations by dividing the total number of permutations by the number of permutations for the smaller group.

$$\text{combinations} = \frac{\text{total number of permutations}}{\text{number of permutations of smaller group}} = \frac{5 \times 4}{2 \times 1} = 10$$

2 EXAMPLE Finding Combinations

Real World

Careers The school committee is planning a career day at your school. The committee invites a sportswriter, a physician, a business manager, a restaurant owner, a college professor, and a retail buyer. You plan to attend three presentations. How many different combinations of presentations are available to you?

Need Help? For help with permutations, go to Lesson 12-6.

Step 1 Find the total number of permutations.

$6 \times 5 \times 4 = 120$ permutations ← **Use the counting principle.**

(6 ↑ first choice; 5 ↑ second choice; 4 ↑ third choice)

Step 2 Find the number of permutations of the smaller group.

$3 \times 2 \times 1 = 6$ permutations ← **Use the counting principle.**

Step 3 Find the number of combinations.

$$\frac{\text{total number of permutations}}{\text{number of permutations of smaller group}} = \frac{120}{6} \quad \leftarrow \textbf{Divide.}$$

$$= 20 \quad \leftarrow \textbf{Simplify.}$$

There are 20 combinations of presentations available.

Check Understanding 2 **Number Sense** If you choose five presentations, how many different combinations of presentations are available to you?

EXERCISES

For more practice, see *Extra Practice.*

Practice by Example

A Practice by Example

Example 1 (page 664)

For Exercises 1 and 2, use the table to make an organized list.

1. **Swimming** The four swimmers listed at the right are trying out for the swim team. Two will make the team. How many different combinations of two swimmers are possible?

2. Suppose three of the swimmers will make the team. How many different combinations of three swimmers are possible?

Swimmer	Letter
Noah	N
Olivia	O
Kevin	K
Chloe	C

Test-Prep Tip

When you list combinations, be sure to eliminate all the duplicates.

3. How many different combinations of two seashells can you make from three seashells?

4. Dylan, Emma, Jorge, Lauren, and Julia want to go on a hiking trip. A camp counselor will choose three of them. How many different combinations of three hikers are possible?

Example 2 (page 665)

Find the number of combinations.

5. Choose two people from three.
6. Choose three people from five.
7. Choose two people from six.
8. Choose four people from six.

Track and Field **Use the poster for Exercises 9–12. Find the number of combinations for each situation.**

9. participate in 2 track events
10. participate in 2 games
11. participate in 2 field events
12. participate in 3 track events

TRACK AND FIELD DAY

Track Events
- 50-m run
- 100-m relay
- 100-m hurdles
- 200-m run

Field Events
- high jump
- long jump
- disc throw

Games
- baseball throw
- run the bases relay

B Apply Your Skills

Evaluate each expression.

13. $\frac{4!}{3!}$
14. $\frac{5!}{2!}$
15. $\frac{6!}{4!}$
16. $\frac{7!}{3!}$

Use the letters B, E, O, P, R, and W. Make a list of all of the combinations.

17. 2 vowels
18. 3 consonants
19. any 3 letters
20. any 4 letters
21. 4 consonants
22. any 5 letters

Determine whether each situation involves a combination or a permutation. Then answer the question.

23. You select three books from a bookshelf that holds eight books. How many different sets of books can you choose?

24. You have six toppings to use for a pizza. How many different three-topping pizzas can you make?

25. Four students stand beside each other for a photograph. How many different orders are possible?

26. **Reasoning** To open a combination lock, you must dial the numbers in the right order. Explain why "permutation lock" might be more appropriate than "combination lock" as a name for the lock shown at the left.

27. **Writing in Math** Use your own words and an example to explain the difference between a permutation and a combination.

28. **Paints** You want to mix some of the paint colors shown below.

a. How many different combinations of two paints are possible?
b. Suppose you choose two colors at random. Find P(blue and green).

29. **Music** You have 5 different CDs to play. Your CD player can hold 3 CDs. How many different combinations of 3 CDs can you select?

C Challenge

30. A club of 50 people wants to select 4 members to represent them. How many different combinations of 4 people are possible?

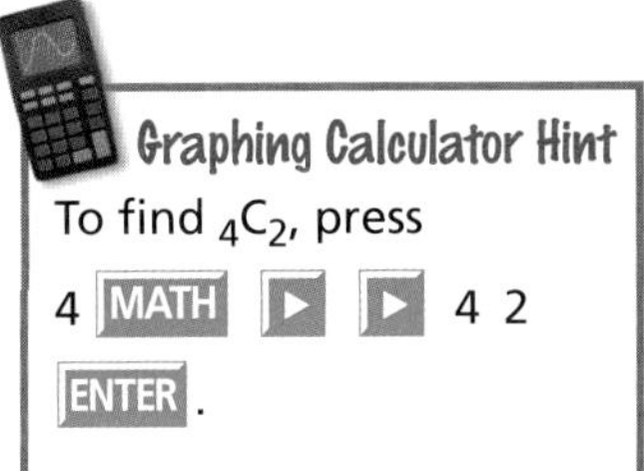

Graphing Calculator Hint
To find ${}_4C_2$, press
4 MATH ▶ ▶ 4 2
ENTER.

You can use a graphing calculator to find the number of combinations. Use ${}_nC_r$, where n is the total number of items and r is the number of items in a grouping. Use a graphing calculator to evaluate each combination.

31. ${}_7C_3$
32. ${}_6C_3$
33. ${}_8C_5$

34. **Stretch Your Thinking** Find three different fractions with one as a numerator. All three fractions must add up to 1.

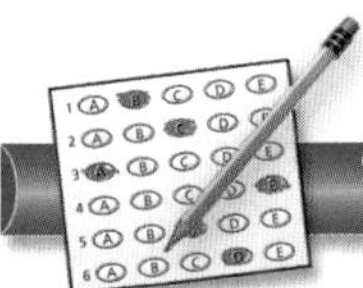

Test Prep

Multiple Choice

35. How many different groups of three people can you select from six people?
A. 120 B. 30 C. 20 D. 10

36. How many combinations of four numbers can you select from the numbers 1, 2, 3, and 4?
F. 1 G. 4 H. 12 I. 24

37. You want to pick a four-player golf team. There are eight players to choose from. How many different teams can you form?
A. 1,680 B. 336 C. 70 D. 48

Take It to the NET
Online lesson quiz at
www.PHSchool.com
Web Code aba-1207

38. You want to work two jobs in the summer. You have 12 job offers. How many different combinations of jobs can you choose?
F. 120 G. 110 H. 90 I. 66

Short Response

39. Andrea plans to buy a bicycle, a helmet, a water bottle, and a lock. Today she will buy some of the accessories. How many different sets of two accessories can she select? Show your work.

Mixed Review

Lesson 12-6 **Express the number of permutations in factorial form. Then simplify.**

40. D, O, G **41.** S, H, O, E **42.** D, R, U, M, S

43. S, P, R, I, N, G **44.** E, N, G, L, I, S, H **45.** M, I, L, K

Lesson 11-8 **Graph each set of data in a scatter plot.**

46. **Area and Population**

Area (square miles)	Population (thousands)
8	30
19	38
23	56
30	71
46	78
55	82

47. **Weights of Books**

Number of Pages	Weight of Book (oz)
575	36.0
585	32.0
725	42.0
860	49.0
920	75.0
1,000	82.0

48. Describe the trend in the scatter plot for Exercise 46.

Checkpoint Quiz 2 — Lessons 12-5 through 12-7

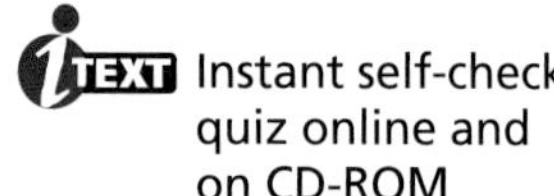

You draw a letter from the group at the right. After drawing the first letter, you replace it and draw another letter. Find each probability.

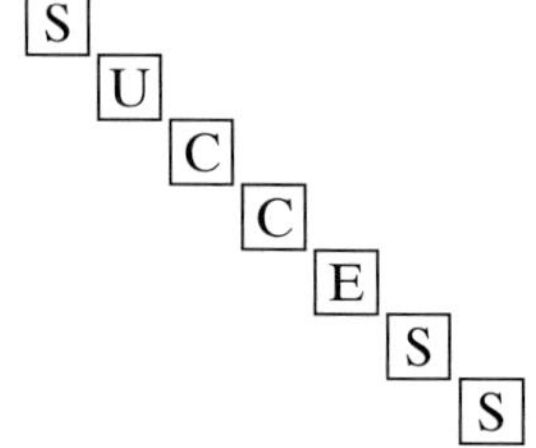

1. *P*(vowel, then S) **2.** *P*(C, then E)

3. *P*(U, then consonant) **4.** *P*(vowel, then C)

You have 4 blue cards, 1 red card, and 3 green cards. You draw a card, do not replace it, and draw a second card. Find each probability.

5. *P*(green, then red) **6.** *P*(blue, then green) **7.** *P*(red, then blue)

8. You decide to put the pictures of six friends in a row on a bulletin board. In how many ways can you arrange the pictures?

9. Flowers How many different combinations of four flowers can you make from six different flowers?

10. a. Schools A, B, C, and D have different dance themes in a cheerleading contest. Make a list of all permutations of the schools.

b. Two of the four schools will perform the opening cheers. How many combinations of two schools are possible?

Eliminating Answers

Before you try to answer a multiple-choice question, you may be able to save time by eliminating some answer choices. Then you can choose your answer carefully from the remaining choices.

1 EXAMPLE

A bag contains 10 blue, 6 red, and 4 green rubber balls. If you select a ball at random from the bag, what is the probability of *not* choosing a green ball?

A. $\frac{1}{5}$ **B.** $\frac{4}{5}$ **C.** $\frac{5}{6}$ **D.** $\frac{9}{10}$

Look at the denominator of each answer. The total number of outcomes is $10 + 6 + 4$, or 20. The denominator of the answer will be 20 or a factor of 20. Eliminate choice C because it has a 6 as the denominator.

Estimate the magnitude of the answer. Since most of the balls in the bag are not green, the probability of *not* choosing a green ball will be a fraction greater than $\frac{1}{2}$. Since choice A is less than $\frac{1}{2}$, you can eliminate choice A.

The correct answer is either B or D.

2 EXAMPLE

There are 1,060 students in a school. Use the results of the survey to predict the number of students in the school who have produced computer art.

Students Surveyed	Students Who Produced Computer Art
40	24

F. 260 students **G.** 480 students **H.** 636 students **I.** 790 students

The ratio 24 out of 40 is greater than $\frac{1}{2}$. Since $\frac{1}{2}$ of 1,060 is more than 500, you can eliminate choices F and G because they are less than 500.

The correct answer is either H or I.

EXERCISES

1. Explain why it is reasonable to eliminate choice D in Example 1.
2. Consider the following multiple-choice question.

   A friend hides 12 yellow eggs and 16 purple eggs for you to find in an egg hunt. What is *P*(yellow) for the first egg you find?

   A. $\frac{1}{4}$ **B.** $\frac{1}{3}$ **C.** $\frac{3}{8}$ **D.** $\frac{3}{7}$

   a. Explain why you can eliminate choices B and C in Exercise 2.
   b. What is the correct answer to the question?

Chapter Review

Vocabulary

combination (p. 664)	**event** (p. 629)	**odds in favor** (p. 631)
complement (p. 630)	**experimental probability** (p. 636)	**outcome** (p. 629)
compound event (p. 653)	**factorial** (p. 661)	**permutation** (p. 660)
counting principle (p. 648)	**independent events** (p. 654)	**sample space** (p. 647)
dependent events (p. 655)	**odds against** (p. 631)	**theoretical probability** (p. 629)

Reading Math: Understanding Vocabulary

Choose the correct term to complete each sentence.

1. A (combination, permutation) is a grouping of objects in which the order of the objects does not matter.
2. An outcome or a group of outcomes is a(n) (event, factorial).
3. Two events are (dependent, independent) if the occurrence of one event does not affect the probability of the occurrence of the other.
4. The (odds, theoretical probability) for an event equals the ratio of the number of favorable outcomes to the number of unfavorable outcomes.
5. (Theoretical, Experimental) probability is based on observations.

Take It to the NET
Online vocabulary quiz at **www.PHSchool.com**
Web Code abj-1251

Skills and Concepts

12-1 Objectives

- To find the probability of an event
- To find the complements and the odds of events

If all outcomes are equally likely, you can find the **theoretical probability** of an event using this formula:

$$P(\text{event}) = \frac{\text{number of favorable outcomes}}{\text{total number of possible outcomes}}$$

A card is drawn at random from the cards shown at the right. Find each probability.

T	R	U	M	P	E	T

6. $P(P)$
7. $P(T)$
8. $P(\text{not } P)$
9. $P(U)$
10. $P(\text{consonant})$
11. $P(\text{vowel})$

12-2 Objectives

- To find experimental probability
- To use simulations

You can find the **experimental probability** of an event using this formula:

$$P(\text{event}) = \frac{\text{number of times an event occurs}}{\text{total number of trials}}$$

12. a. **Games** A computer game company makes random checks of its games. Of 200 games, 4 are found to be defective. Find $P(\text{defective})$.
    b. Predict the number of defective games in a batch of 1,600.
13. What is the probability that the last four digits of a nine-digit social security number are all odd? Use a simulation.

12-3 Objective

▼ To solve a problem using two different methods

You can *make an organized list* to help you find the theoretical probability of an event. You can *simulate a problem* to help you find the experimental probability of the same event.

14. Nutrition You choose a piece of fruit, a flavor of yogurt, and a sandwich at random from the table. You want to find the probability of choosing an orange, strawberry yogurt, and a chicken sandwich.

Fruit	Yogurt	Sandwich
Orange	Strawberry	Chicken
Apple	Banana	Tuna

a. Make an organized list and use it to find the theoretical probability.
b. Use a simulation to find the experimental probability.

12-4 Objectives

▼ To find a sample space
▼ To use the counting principle

The collection of all possible outcomes in a probability experiment is called a **sample space.** You can use the **counting principle** to find the number of outcomes of an event.

Use the menu below for Exercises 15 and 16.

15. a. At the China Panda, if you order the Family Dinner, you choose one appetizer, one soup, and one main dish from the menu at the right. Draw a tree diagram to show the sample space.

b. Suppose you ask the restaurant to choose the meal for you. What is the probability of getting the egg roll, won-ton, and almond chicken for your meal?

Appetizers	**Soups**
Egg Rolls	Won-ton
Fried Won-tons	Sizzling Rice

Main Dishes
Almond Chicken
Sweet & Sour Pork
Beef with Broccoli

16. Use the counting principle to find the number of possible dinners.

12-5 Objectives

▼ To find the probability of independent events
▼ To find the probability of dependent events

Two events are **dependent events** if the occurrence of one event affects the probability of the occurrence of the other event.

A hat contains the names of eight girls and six boys. You draw two names from the hat without replacing the first name. Find each probability.

17. *P*(boy, then boy) **18.** *P*(girl, then boy) **19.** *P*(girl, then girl)

12-6 and 12-7 Objectives

▼ To find permutations
▼ To find combinations

A **permutation** is an arrangement of objects in a particular order. A **combination** is a grouping of objects in which the order of the objects does not matter.

20. Five students compete on a relay team. Only four of them can race at a time. How many different teams are possible?

21. Four students are selected for a relay team. In how many ways can they line up for the race?

Chapter Test

1. Use the data at the right. Find the experimental probability of each event as a fraction, a decimal, and a percent.

Marker Color	Frequency
Purple	6
Green	2
White	3
Black	5

a. P(purple)
b. P(green)
c. P(orange)

2. a. Quality Control Factory workers test 80 batteries. Four batteries are defective. What is the experimental probability that a battery is defective?
b. Predict the number of defective batteries in a batch of 1,600.

There are six open containers arranged as shown. A ball is tossed and falls into one of the containers. Find the probability of each event.

3. $P(4)$

4. P(even number)

5. P(a number greater than 4)

6. $P(7)$

1
2 3
4 5 6

Suppose you have a bag that contains six blue marbles, two green marbles, three red marbles, and one white marble. You select a marble at random. Find each probability.

7. P(blue) **8.** P(white)

9. P(blue or white) **10.** P(red)

11. P(blue, then white when blue is not replaced)

12. Each of the letters D E T E R M I N E D is written on a card. You mix the cards thoroughly. What is the probability of selecting an E, then an M? The first card is replaced before selecting the second card.

13. Writing in Math Suppose you flip a coin several times and record the results. Out of 20 trials, you get tails 9 times. What is the experimental probability of getting tails? Explain why this may differ from the theoretical probability.

14. A car comes in the colors and models listed in the table. Assume there is an equally likely chance of selecting any color or model.

Colors	Models
Silver	Hatchback
Gray	Coupe
Black	Sedan

a. Find the sample space of different car selections.
b. Find the probability that a car selected at random is a silver hatchback.
c. Find the probability that a car selected at random is a yellow coupe.

15. a. Find the number of two-letter permutations of the letters M, A, T, H.
b. Find the number of two-letter combinations of the letters M, A, T, H.

16. You are equally likely to get one of four prizes when you buy Good Morning Cereal. You want to use a simulation to find the probability of getting all four prizes when you buy four boxes of cereal. Which of the following is *not* a true statement? Choose A, B, C, or D.
A. You can simulate the problem by using a spinner divided into four equal sections.
B. A possible answer is four boxes.
C. The more trials you perform, the better your results should be.
D. The result of your simulation is an experimental probability.

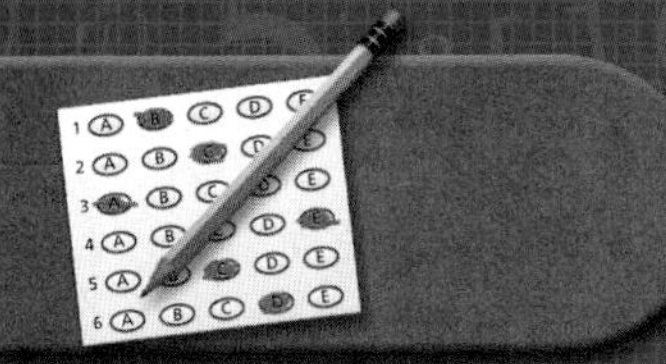

Test Prep

CUMULATIVE REVIEW

CHAPTERS 1–12

Take It to the NET

Online end-of-course test at **www.PHSchool.com**

Web Code aba-1254

Multiple Choice

For Exercises 1–24, choose the correct letter.

1. Use rounding to estimate. Determine which sum is between 21 and 22.
   A. 13.71 + 1.5 + 8.2
   B. 6.75 + 9.02 + 5.838
   C. 5.99 + 2.69 + 15.49
   D. 3.772 + 12.04 + 4.009

2. Which expression CANNOT be rewritten using the Distributive Property?
   F. 3(2 + 8) **G.** 5(2 · 3)
   H. (18 − 9)7 **I.** 9(14 − 6)

3. What is the solution of the equation $-15 = m - 9$?
   A. −24 **B.** −6 **C.** 6 **D.** 24

4. Which jar of peanut butter is the best buy?
   F. an 18-oz jar for $1.69
   G. a 30-oz jar for $2.59
   H. a 32-oz jar for $2.89
   I. a 24-oz jar for $2.09

5. Sarah bought a remnant of fabric $5\frac{1}{8}$ yd long to make pennants for the school contest. How many pennants can she make if $\frac{3}{4}$ yd is needed for each pennant?
   A. 5 **B.** 6 **C.** 7 **D.** 8

6. Which choice does NOT equal the others?
   F. 4% of 3,000 **G.** 40% of 30
   H. 40% of 300 **I.** 30% of 400

7. Suppose you spin the spinners once. What is the probability that the sum of the numbers is 10?
   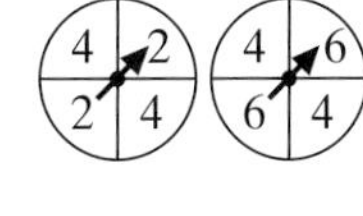

   A. 0 **B.** $\frac{1}{4}$ **C.** $\frac{1}{2}$ **D.** $\frac{3}{4}$

8. What is the volume of a rectangular prism that has dimensions 1 in., 2 in., and 3 in.?
   F. 6 in.^{3} **G.** 18 in.^{3}
   H. 22 in.^{3} **I.** 27 in.^{3}

9. How can 64 be written using exponents?
   A. 2^6 **B.** 4^3 **C.** 8^2
   D. All of the above are correct.

10. In the diagram at the right, which two angles are adjacent angles?
    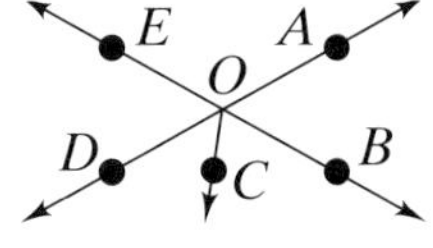

    F. ∠EOD, ∠DOC **G.** ∠BOC, ∠BOD
    H. ∠AOE, ∠BOC **I.** ∠AOB, ∠EOD

11. A circle has circumference 56.52 ft. What is its area? Use 3.14 for π.
    A. 28.26 ft^2 **B.** 56.52 ft^2
    C. 254.34 ft^2 **D.** 1,017.36 ft^2

12. What is the solution of the inequality $-4p < 36$?
    F. $p > 9$ **G.** $p < -9$
    H. $p > -9$ **I.** $p < 9$

13. If the area of the shaded region is 4 in.^{2}, what is the best estimate for the area of the unshaded region?
    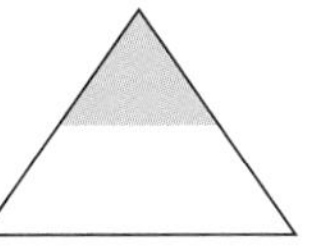
    A. 4 in.^{2} **B.** 8 in.^{2}
    C. 12 in.^{2} **D.** 16 in.^{2}

14. What percent of the letters of the alphabet are the vowels a, e, i, o, and u?
    F. about 15% **G.** about 19%
    H. about 30% **I.** about 33%

15. Order the numbers from least to greatest.
    $\frac{1}{8}, -0.18, 0.2, -\frac{2}{13}$
    A. $-\frac{2}{13}, -0.18, \frac{1}{8}, 0.2$
    B. $-0.18, -\frac{2}{13}, 0.2, \frac{1}{8}$
    C. $-0.18, -\frac{2}{13}, \frac{1}{8}, 0.2$
    D. $-\frac{2}{13}, 0.2, \frac{1}{8}, -0.18$

16. What is the solution of $\frac{x}{6} = \frac{20}{32}$?
    F. 3 **G.** 3.75 **H.** 4.8 **I.** 5

17. Which equation has the solution 4?

A. $k + 3 = -7$ B. $5 + x = 9$

C. $y - 8 = 12$ D. $1 + a = 3$

18. Find the slope of the line.

F. $-\frac{3}{2}$

G. $\frac{1}{3}$

H. $\frac{1}{2}$

I. 2

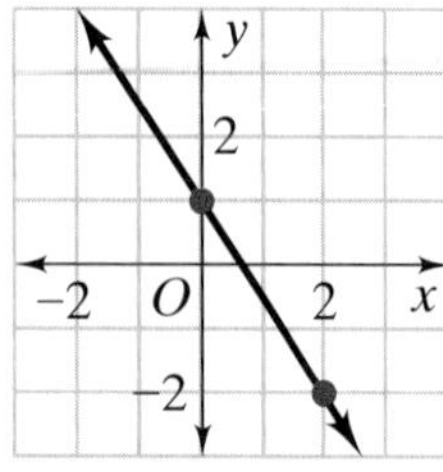

19. You plan to build a set of steps for an attic stairway. The steps must reach a height of $8\frac{1}{2}$ ft. Each step can be no more than $7\frac{3}{4}$ in. high. What is the least number of steps you need to build?

A. 11 B. 12 C. 13 D. 14

20. Rectangle *ABCD* and rectangle *AXYZ* are similar. How long is $\overline{XY}$?

F. 2.5 cm G. 2 cm

H. 1.6 cm I. 1.5 cm

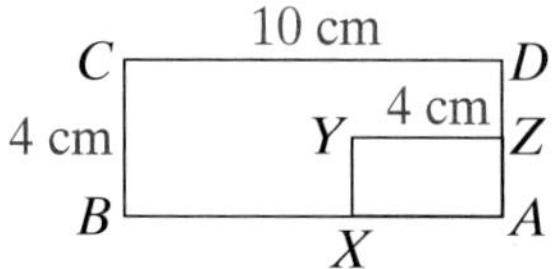

21. How many two-letter permutations of the letters C, A, R contain the letter R?

A. 2 B. 3

C. 4 D. 6

22. Which rule best describes the function in the table?

F. $y(x) = x + 2$

G. $y(x) = x$

H. $y(x) = 2x$

I. $y(x) = x^2$

x	y
0	0
1	1
2	4
3	9

23. Which expression shows the prime factorization of 120?

A. $2 \cdot 3 \cdot 4 \cdot 5$ B. $2 \cdot 3 \cdot 20$

C. $2^3 \cdot 3 \cdot 5$ D. $3^2 \cdot 13$

24. Find *x* in the triangle shown.

F. 23°

G. 27°

H. 33°

I. 53°

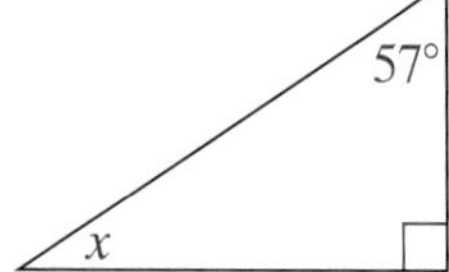

Gridded Response

Use the bar graph below for Exercises 25–27.

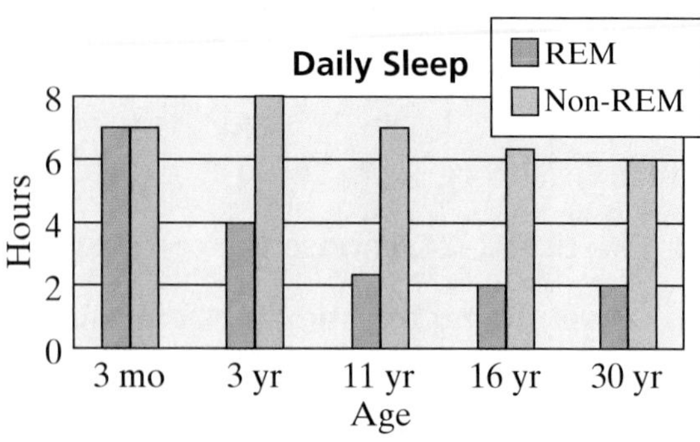

25. About how many hours per day does an 11-year-old spend in non-REM sleep?

26. About how many more hours does a 3-month-old spend in REM sleep than a 30-year-old?

27. About how many fewer hours does an 11-year-old spend in non-REM sleep than a 3-year-old?

For Exercises 28–30, refer to the graph below. The graph shows the height of an object over time.

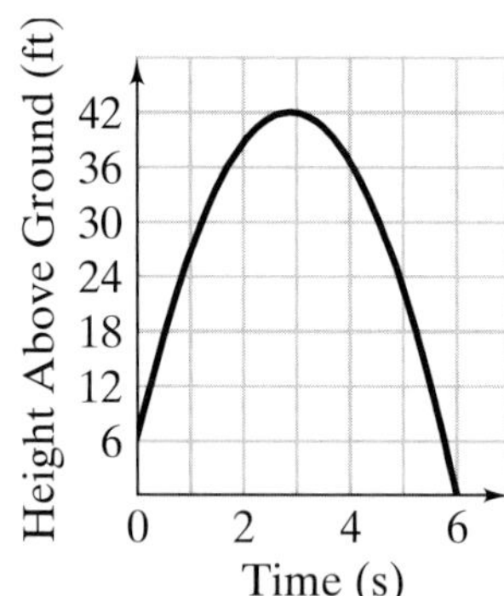

28. How many feet is the greatest height the object reaches?

29. How many seconds does it take the object to hit the ground?

30. How many feet is the initial height of the object?

31. Write 7.8×10^2 in standard form.

Short Response

32. Write a problem that $\frac{x}{3} + 11 = 16$ will solve.

33. Cards A through G are placed in a hat. You select a card from the hat at random. You select a second card without replacing the first card. What is the probability that both cards are vowels? Show your work.

34. The triangles at the right are congruent. Write six congruencies involving corresponding parts of the triangles.

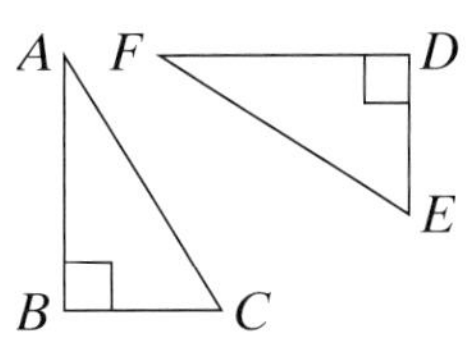

35. a. Write 0.9% as a decimal.
    b. Write 0.9% as a fraction.

36. Find the number of pounds in 72 ounces. Show your work.

Tell whether each graph shows a reflection or a translation. Name the line of symmetry or write a rule for the translation.

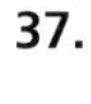

37.

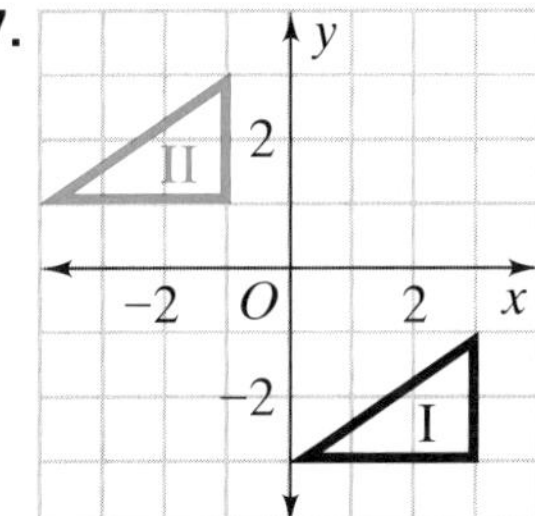

38.

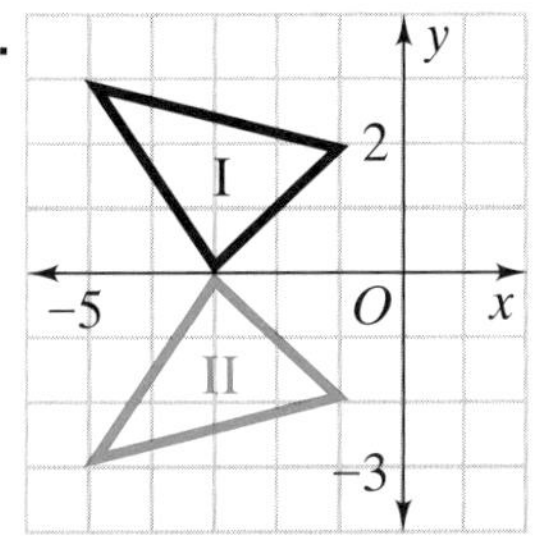

39. A map with the scale 2 in. : 250 mi shows two ponds to be 4 in. apart. How many miles apart are the ponds? Show your work.

40. Find the product 8(89) using the Distributive Property. Show your work.

41. Find the area of each triangle below.

a.

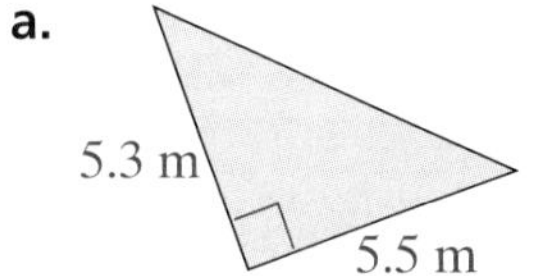

b.

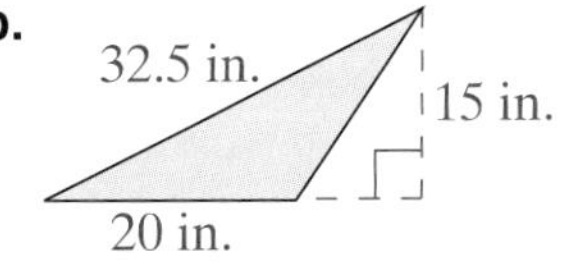

42. Find the length of the hypotenuse of the triangle to the nearest tenth. Show your work.

c
20 m
70 m

Extended Response

43. Find the mean, median, and mode of the data in the stem-and-leaf plot. Show your work.

7	0 0 5 8
8	1 5 6 9 9
9	4

Key: 7 | 0 means 70

44. You have \$50 saved at the beginning of the month. You plan to save \$25 each month. Your savings plan can be modeled with the equation $y = 25x + 50$.
    a. Graph this equation in the first quadrant of the coordinate plane.
    b. How much will you have saved in 6 months?
    c. In how many months will you have saved \$150?

45. St. Francis, Torrey Pines, and Marina schools all compete for the championship in field hockey.
    a. Make a table to find the sample space of possible outcomes of first, second, and third place.
    b. In how many outcomes does St. Francis win the championship with Marina in second place?
    c. In how many outcomes does Torrey Pines or Marina win the championship?

46. a. Draw a net of the cylinder shown.

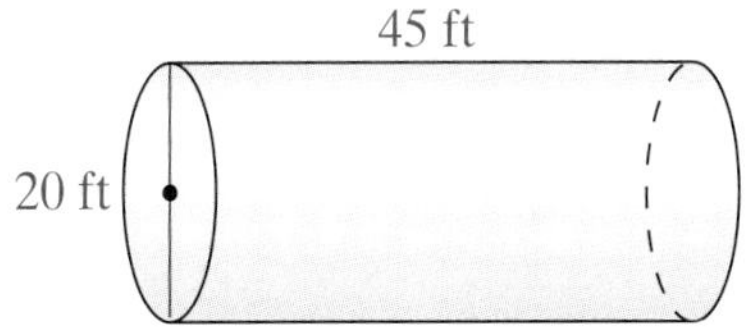

    b. Find the surface area of the cylinder to the nearest tenth. Show your work.

47. You treat a friend to dinner. The cost of the food items from the menu total \$20.46. A 5% sales tax on the food items will be added. Also, you want to give a tip of 25% (before tax) for excellent service.
    a. How much is the sales tax?
    b. How much is the tip?
    c. What is the total cost of the dinner?

Real-World Snapshots

Against the Odds?

Applying Probability Your friend claims to be a great coin flipper who gets heads 50% of the time. Without doing any math, you know this is not a special skill—the results are pure chance. Suppose another friend claims to be a great free-throw shooter because of a 30% free-throw success rate. This claim is harder to evaluate. How can you tell if it's luck or skill?

Put It All Together

Materials compass, ruler, calculator

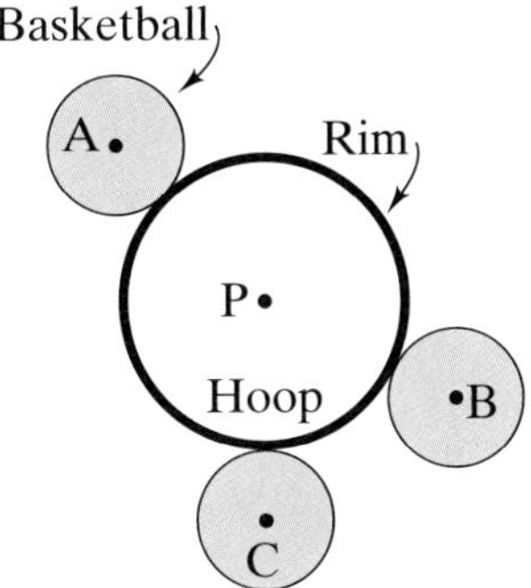

Figure 1

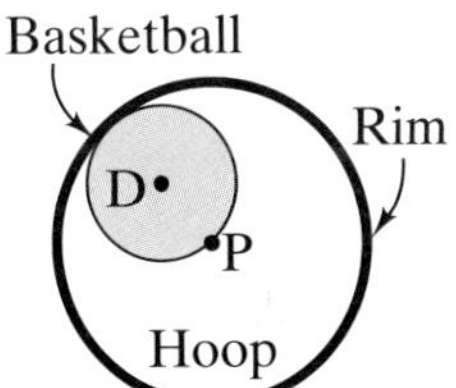

Figure 2

1. Suppose that your friend can hit the rim of the basket every time. Figure 1 shows the basket from above. Shots A, B and C just barely touch the rim.
   a. Copy Figure 1. Draw a circle centered on point P that connects the centers of balls A, B, and C. This is the *landing zone*. The center of the ball is within this circle for each shot.
   b. **Research** Find the radius of a men's basketball and of a basketball hoop. Calculate the area of the landing zone.
2. A "swish" shot passes through the net without touching the rim. Figure 2 shows ball D swishing through the net, falling just within the rim.
   a. Copy Figure 2. Draw two more balls (E and F) that also fall just within the rim.
   b. Draw a circle centered on point P that connects the centers of balls D, E, and F. This is the target zone. The center of the ball will be within this circle every time the ball "swishes" the net.
   c. Calculate the area of the target zone.
3. a. Suppose you are shooting baskets at random. Find the probability that a ball hitting the landing zone will also be in the target zone as follows:

$$\text{Probability of "swish"} = \frac{\text{area of target zone}}{\text{area of landing zone}}$$

   Calculate this probability. Convert it to a percent.
   b. Calculate the probability of making a free-throw when the only baskets that count are swishes. Assume all shots hit the landing zone.
   c. **Writing in Math** Is someone who has a 30% success rate great at making free throws? Explain.

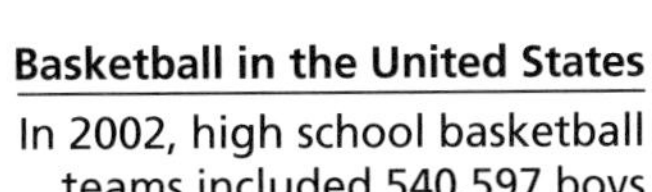

Basketball in the United States

In 2002, high school basketball teams included 540,597 boys and 456,169 girls.

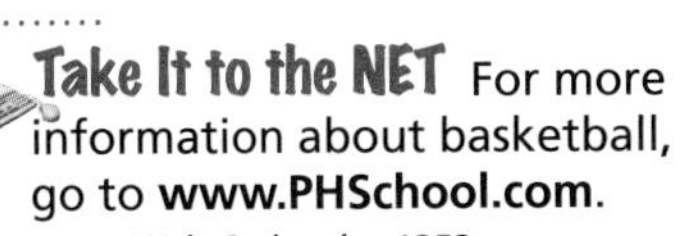

Take It to the NET For more information about basketball, go to **www.PHSchool.com**.
Web Code: abe-1253

Chapter Projects

Board Walk

Chapter 1 Decimals and Integers

What makes a board game so much fun? You have challenges like road blocks or false paths that make you backtrack. Then you land on a lucky square that lets you leap forward past your opponent. Best of all, you are with your friends as you play!

Create a Board Game For this chapter project, you will use integers to create a game. Then you will play your game with friends or family for a trial run. Finally you will decorate your game and bring it to class to play.

Take It to the NET Go to **www.PHSchool.com** for information to help you complete your project.
Web Code: abd-0161

READ ALL ABOUT IT!

Chapter 2 Equations and Inequalities

Flexible hours! Great pay! Work before or after school! Newspaper deliverers needed! Suppose to earn extra money you get a job delivering newspapers in your neighborhood. You plan to save the money you make so that you can buy yourself brand new snow skiing gear.

Make a Savings Plan In this chapter, you will figure out how much time you can commit to your job, how much money you can earn per week, and how much money you need to make per week in order to reach your savings goal. As part of your final project, you will write a letter to your boss at the newspaper office describing your level of commitment as a newspaper deliverer.

Take It to the NET Go to **www.PHSchool.com** for information to help you complete your project.
Web Code: abd-0261

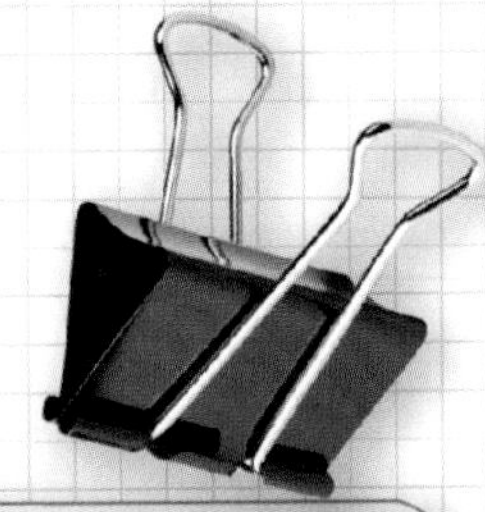

Making the Measure

Chapter 3 Exponents, Factors, and Fractions

In the high jump, as in most sports, a consistent system of measurement allows athletes to make comparisons. It took the decree of a king to create one such system!

Back in the 12th century, King Henry I of England decided that a yard was the distance from the tip of his nose to the end of his thumb. How far is it from the tip of your nose to the end of your thumb? Is it more than a yard or less? Is it the same distance for everyone?

Invent Your Own Ruler For the chapter project, you will design a new system for measuring distance. Your final project will be a new ruler, together with a report on its usefulness.

Take It to the NET Go to **www.PHSchool.com** for information to help you complete your project.
Web Code: abd-0361

Toss and Turn

Chapter 4 Operations With Fractions

Did you ever make pancakes? The recipe can be pretty simple–an egg, some pancake mix, milk, and maybe some oil. Or forget the mix and start from scratch! Either way, you can vary the ingredients to suit your tastes. Do you want to include some wheat germ? How about some pecans, or maybe some fruit? Bananas are always in season!

Write Your Own Recipe For the chapter project, you will write your own recipe for pancakes. Your final project will be a recipe that will feed everyone in your class.

Take It to the NET Go to **www.PHSchool.com** for information to help you complete your project.
Web Code: abd-0461

Weighty Matters

Chapter 5 Ratios, Rates, and Proportions

Have you ever loved a pet so much that you wanted a statue made of it? Imagine a statue of your pet on the front steps of your home. "Gee, what a wise way to spend hard-earned money," your admiring neighbors would say. Or maybe not. In addition to being expensive, these statues would also be heavy. For instance, a 35-lb dog cast in gold would weigh about 670 lb.

Using Specific Gravity For the chapter project, you will find the weight of different animals and the weight of different metals. Your final project will be a table of animals with their weights, the weight of their statues in different materials, and the cost of the statues.

Take It to the NET Go to **www.PHSchool.com** for information to help you complete your project.
Web Code: abd-0561

Chapter 6 Percents

Your world is spinning. You are screaming. And you are loving every minute of it! Even though you are scared, you know that you will come to a safe stop at the end of the ride.

A successful amusement park attraction must be both fun and safe. Planners of amusement parks use a lot of math to create thrills but avoid any spills.

Take a Survey For the chapter project, you will decide which rides are most likely to be most popular. Your final product will be a recommendation about which rides to include in a proposed amusement park for your town.

Take It to the NET Go to **www.PHSchool.com** for information to help you complete your project.
Web Code: abd-0661

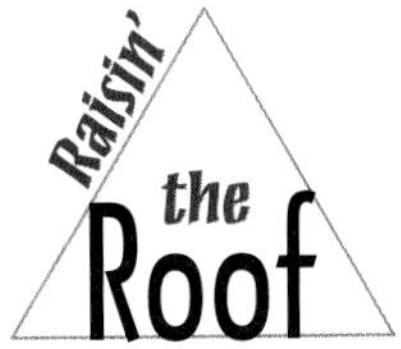

Chapter 7 Geometry

Look around you. Triangles are everywhere in construction! You see them in bridges, in buildings, in scaffolding: even in bicycle frames! This project will give you a greater appreciation of the importance of triangles in construction. You might also develop a taste for raisins!

Build a Tower For the chapter project, you will use toothpicks and raisins to build geometric shapes. Your final product will be a tower strong enough to support a baseball.

Take It to the NET Go to **www.PHSchool.com** for information to help you complete your project.
Web Code: abd-0761

SHAPE UP AND SHIP OUT

Chapter 8 Geometry and Measurement

Space is money! So before cargo is prepared for shipment in large containers, it is packaged in smaller containers based on its size and shape.

Cans of tuna are examples of items you buy in cylindrical containers. Would you pack two cylinders side-by-side or one above the other? One arrangement wastes cardboard! But which one?

Design Boxes for Shipping Cylinders For the chapter project, you will design boxes to hold cylindrical items. Your final product will be a model of a box that holds six cylinders.

Take It to the NET Go to **www.PHSchool.com** for information to help you complete your project.
Web Code: abd-0861

happy *landings*

Chapter 9 Patterns and Rules

Imagine this–you have just opened your parachute and you are floating through the air. Exciting, huh? How long it takes you to come to the ground can be predicted because the change in height versus time occurs in a predictable pattern. Many other things change in a predictable pattern, for instance, the height of a burning candle and the growth of money in a bank account.

Graphing Data For the chapter project, you will find how fast a container of water will empty if there is a hole in it. Your final project will be a graph of the data you collect.

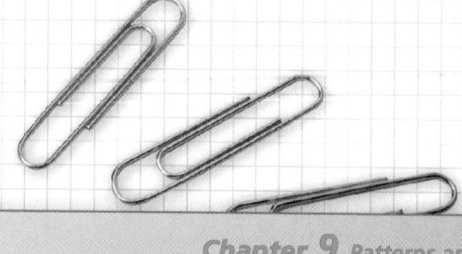

Take It to the NET Go to **www.PHSchool.com** for information to help you complete your project.
Web Code: abd-0961

People's *choice*

Chapter 10 Graphing in the Coordinate Plane

You're an advertising executive, and you want to know which of three television shows is the most popular. So you plan to conduct a poll of viewers.

But how many viewers do you survey? Polling is expensive, so you don't want to poll too many. Polling too few viewers might give you the wrong information. Here's your chance to explore the process!

Finding a Sample Size Fill a container with three different kinds of beans. Use the beans to find the sample size that best predicts the percent of each kind of bean in the container.

Take It to the NET Go to **www.PHSchool.com** for information to help you complete your project.
Web Code: abd-1061

Chapter 11 Displaying and Analyzing Data

Chances are there's at least one person in a large crowd who has the same birthday as you! How many people do you think have the same favorite food? How many like the same television show? What kinds of cars do the people in the crowd have? Pollsters face questions like these all the time, and they take surveys to help answer them.

Estimate the Size of a Crowd and Take a Survey For the chapter project, you will use averages to estimate the size of a crowd. You will also take a survey and present your results in a graph.

Take It to the NET Go to **www.PHSchool.com** for information to help you complete your project.

Web Code: abd-1161

Everybody Wins

Chapter 12 Using Probability

Remember the game "Rock, Paper, Scissors"? It is an unusual game because paper wins over rock, rock wins over scissors, and scissors win over paper. You can use mathematics to create and investigate a situation with similar characteristics.

Make Three Number Cubes For this chapter project, you will design three number cubes A, B, and C, which have a surprising property: A usually beats B, B usually beats C, and C usually beats A. Your final step will be to construct your cubes.

Take It to the NET Go to **www.PHSchool.com** for information to help you complete your project.

Web Code: abd-1261

Chapter 1 Extra Practice

Lesson 1-1 Use any estimation strategy to estimate.

1. $2.7236 - 0.6512$ **2.** $2.4 + 0.86$ **3.** $106.3 \div 7.92$ **4.** 7.06×9.23

Lesson 1-2 Find each sum or difference.

5. $5.87 + 2.41$ **6.** $9.31 - 4.08$ **7.** $7.2 + 1.907$ **8.** $4.86 - 2.161$

Lesson 1-3 Find each product or quotient.

9. 2.9×1.7 **10.** $6.09 \cdot 1.3$ **11.** $30.6 \div 3.6$ **12.** $44.856 \div 7.12$

Lesson 1-4 Write a number that makes each statement true.

13. ■ L $=$ 90 mL **14.** 0.6 mL $=$ ■ L **15.** ■ mg $=$ 2.7 kg **16.** ■ km $=$ 620,000 m

Lesson 1-5 Use the problem-solving plan to solve the problem.

17. Find two whole numbers whose product is 117 and whose quotient is 13.

Lesson 1-6 Compare using <, >, or =.

18. $|-3|$ ■ $|-2|$ **19.** $|10|$ ■ $|-10|$ **20.** $|-19|$ ■ $|9|$ **21.** $|-11|$ ■ $|-12|$

Lesson 1-7 Find the value of each expression.

22. $-110 + 5 - (-5)$ **23.** $3(-6 \div 3)$ **24.** $(-3)(-2)(-1)$ **25.** $2(-2) - 4$

26. $|-9| + 8 - (-1)$ **27.** $-7 + |12 - 8|$ **28.** $4 + 11 - (-13)$ **29.** $-14 \div (-7)$

Lesson 1-8 Find each product or quotient.

30. $-5 \cdot (-9)$ **31.** $11 \cdot (-3)$ **32.** $-45 \div (-9)$ **33.** $\frac{-121}{11}$

Lesson 1-9 Find the value of each expression.

34. $2(8 - 4.5)$ **35.** $24 - (3 + 1.9)$ **36.** $3.14(2.1 + 7.5)$ **37.** $3(6.1 + 0.461)$

38. $(18 - 2.4)(0.7)$ **39.** $8.3 \cdot 6.9 - 4.7$ **40.** $(5.3 - 0.9) \div 1.1$ **41.** $2.7 \cdot (3.1 - 0.7)$

Lesson 1-10 Find the mean, median, and mode for each situation.

42. prices of different brands of cameras
\$150, \$100, \$240, \$220, \$195, \$225

43. number of seconds to run the 100-meter dash
9, 13, 14, 11, 12, 12, 15, 14, 10, 13, 9, 12

Chapter 2 Extra Practice

Extra Practice

Lesson 2-1 Write an algebraic expression for each word phrase.

1. The difference of a number n and 3
2. 17 more than s students
3. 5 fewer than d days
4. 6 more than a number n divided by 2
5. Copy and complete the table at the right. Substitute the value on the left for the variable in the expression at the top of each column. Then evaluate.

x	$3(x - 1)$	$3x - 1$	$3x + 1$
5	■	■	■
2	■	■	■

Lesson 2-2 Solve each equation using mental math.

6. $5b = 30$
7. $n + 5 = 17$
8. $m - 8 = 15$
9. $\frac{z}{3} = 9$

Lesson 2-3 Solve each equation. Then check your answer.

10. $t - 13 = -29$
11. $17 + d = -7$
12. $d + 112 = 159$
13. $y - 68 = 94$

Lesson 2-4 Solve each equation. Then check your answer.

14. $\frac{m}{5} = -15$
15. $-7y = -42$
16. $0.4t = 16$
17. $\frac{x}{12} = -8$

Lesson 2-5 Solve each equation using number sense.

18. $7t + 5 = 40$
19. $2d - 12 = 18$
20. $5w - 18 = 7$
21. $\frac{z}{4} + 5 = 15$

Lesson 2-6 Solve each equation. Then check your answer.

22. $\frac{r}{-6} + 4 = 3$
23. $12m + 24 = 0$
24. $-6g - 9 = 15$
25. $\frac{k}{-3} - 2 = -20$

Lesson 2-7 Use the problem-solving strategy *Write an Equation* to solve the problem.

26. **Shopping** A pair of running shoes costs \$37 less than twice the cost of a pair of basketball sneakers. The basketball sneakers cost \$48.50. How much do the running shoes cost? Check your answer in the original problem.

Lessons 2-8 through 2-10 Solve each inequality. Graph the solution.

27. $y + 5 \geq 11$
28. $p + 7 < -3$
29. $a - 9 \leq 1$
30. $d - 3 > -13$
31. $3y \geq 33$
32. $\frac{p}{7} < -2$
33. $\frac{a}{-8} \leq -7$
34. $4d > -36$

Chapter 3 Extra Practice

Lesson 3-1 **Simplify. Use a calculator, paper and pencil, or mental math.**

1. 100^1
2. 5^3
3. $(-5)^4$
4. -6^2
5. $(12 - 5)^3$

Lesson 3-2 **Write in scientific notation.**

6. 5,000
7. 160,000
8. 4,700,000
9. 7,900,000,000

Lesson 3-3 **Test whether each number is divisible by 2, 3, 4, 5, 8, 9, or 10. Some numbers may be divisible by more than one number.**

10. 36
11. 324
12. 150
13. 840
14. 2,235

Lesson 3-4 **Use the prime factorization to find the GCF of each pair of numbers.**

15. 35, 49
16. 11, 12
17. 28, 40
18. 17, 34
19. 16, 26
20. 16, 86

Lesson 3-5 **Write each fraction in simplest form.**

21. $\frac{21}{24}$
22. $\frac{65}{100}$
23. $\frac{15}{75}$
24. $\frac{40}{80}$
25. $\frac{72}{108}$
26. $\frac{110}{225}$

Lesson 3-6 **Compare each pair of fractions. Use <, >, or =.**

27. $\frac{1}{4}$ ■ $\frac{2}{9}$
28. $\frac{3}{7}$ ■ $\frac{1}{2}$
29. $\frac{2}{5}$ ■ $\frac{4}{10}$
30. $\frac{5}{6}$ ■ $\frac{7}{8}$
31. $\frac{3}{5}$ ■ $\frac{2}{3}$

Lesson 3-7 **Use the problem-solving strategies *Solve a Simpler Problem* and *Look for a Pattern* to solve the problem.**

32. Find the sum of the first one hundred even numbers. That is, find the sum of $2 + 4 + 6 + 8 + \ldots + 200$.

Lessons 3-8 and 3-9 **Write each mixed number as an improper fraction. Write each fraction as a decimal.**

33. $7\frac{7}{8}$
34. $3\frac{5}{7}$
35. $3\frac{1}{4}$
36. $4\frac{2}{5}$
37. $10\frac{1}{6}$
38. $2\frac{2}{5}$
39. $\frac{4}{5}$
40. $\frac{1}{9}$
41. $\frac{7}{8}$
42. $\frac{13}{4}$
43. $\frac{28}{8}$
44. $\frac{100}{6}$

Lesson 3-10 **Order from least to greatest.**

45. $\frac{9}{12}, 0.35, \frac{3}{6}, -1.0$
46. $-1.8, \frac{1}{4}, \frac{1}{3}, 3.5$
47. $\frac{10}{11}, 0.\overline{6}, \frac{1}{2}, 0.375$

Chapter 4 Extra Practice

Lesson 4-1 **Use benchmarks to estimate each sum or difference.**

1. $\frac{2}{5} + \frac{7}{9}$ **2.** $15\frac{1}{5} - 5\frac{4}{7}$ **3.** $71\frac{1}{5} - 5\frac{2}{3}$ **4.** $99\frac{9}{19} + \frac{1}{5}$

Lessons 4-2 and 4-3 **Find each sum or difference.**

5. $\frac{2}{3} + \frac{2}{3}$ **6.** $\frac{7}{10} - \frac{3}{10}$ **7.** $\frac{7}{12} - \frac{1}{4}$ **8.** $\frac{1}{6} + \frac{3}{4}$

9. $4\frac{3}{8} + 2\frac{5}{8}$ **10.** $5\frac{2}{5} - 1\frac{4}{5}$ **11.** $11 - 3\frac{1}{8}$ **12.** $7\frac{2}{5} + 3\frac{1}{4}$

Lessons 4-4 and 4-5 **Find each product or quotient.**

13. $\frac{3}{8} \cdot \frac{2}{5}$ **14.** $\frac{1}{4}$ of $\frac{4}{5}$ **15.** $\frac{5}{6}$ of 30 **16.** $2\frac{7}{8} \cdot \frac{4}{5}$

17. $\frac{3}{5} \div \frac{1}{5}$ **18.** $9 \div \frac{3}{4}$ **19.** $\frac{5}{6} \div \frac{3}{8}$ **20.** $3\frac{2}{3} \div 2\frac{1}{2}$

Lesson 4-6 **Solve each equation.**

21. $b + \frac{1}{4} = \frac{5}{8}$ **22.** $\frac{2}{7} = y - \frac{1}{2}$ **23.** $18 = \frac{1}{5}b$

24. $\frac{w}{3} = 15$ **25.** $\frac{1}{4}c - 2 = \frac{3}{4}$ **26.** $\frac{4}{5} = z - \frac{3}{10}$

Lesson 4-7 **Use the problem-solving strategy *Try, Check, and Revise* or *Work Backward* to solve the problem. Check your answer.**

27. Schedules After school you spend $1\frac{1}{4}$ h at an extra-help session and then $\frac{3}{4}$ h at a friend's house. It takes you 10 min to get home. You need to be home at 5:45 P.M. What time does school end?

Lesson 4-8 **Complete.**

28. $\frac{3}{4}$gal = ■ c **29.** 4,500 lb = ■ t **30.** $\frac{3}{8}$ mi = ■ yd

31. $12\frac{2}{3}$ lb = ■ oz **32.** $6\frac{1}{2}$ t = ■ lb **33.** 2 yd, 1 ft = ■ yd

Lesson 4-9 **Choose the more precise measurement.**

34. 25 g, 2.55 kg **35.** 2 t, $5\frac{1}{4}$ lb **36.** 28 pt, 15 qt

37. 7 L, 35.95 mL **38.** 0.75 g, 1,000 mg **39.** 120 min, 2 h

Chapter 5

Extra Practice

Lesson 5-1 Write each ratio in two other ways.

1. $\frac{2}{3}$
2. 3:5
3. 4 to 7
4. 15:5
5. $\frac{25}{50}$

Lesson 5-2 Find each unit price. Then determine the better buy.

6. detergent: 32 fl oz for \$2.29; 48 fl oz for \$3.19
7. cereal: 12 oz for \$3.95; 16 oz for \$4.80
8. sports drink: 2 pt for \$2.49; 6 pt for \$7.14
9. milk: 1 gal for \$1.99; 3 gal for \$5.69
10. pasta: 8 oz for \$1.29; 32 oz for \$4.99
11. fish: 2 lb for \$13.98; 3 lb for \$17.97
12. fabric: 3 yd for \$12.48; 5 yd for \$20.30
13. rice: 2 lb for \$1.89; 8 lb for \$6.79
14. juice: 2 L for \$5.99; 0.5 L for \$1.25

Lesson 5-3 Use the problem-solving strategy *Draw a Diagram* or *Solve a Simpler Problem* to solve the problem.

15. **Chess** At the first meeting of the Chess Club, the nine members decide to have a tournament in which each player plays a game against every other player. How many games will there be?

Lesson 5-4 Determine whether the ratios in each pair are proportional by using cross products.

16. $\frac{4}{3}, \frac{12}{9}$
17. $\frac{8}{5}, \frac{11}{7}$
18. $\frac{21}{6}, \frac{7}{2}$
19. $\frac{6}{24}, \frac{2}{4}$
20. $\frac{50}{6}, \frac{3}{2}$

Lesson 5-5 Solve each proportion using cross products.

21. $\frac{12}{a} = \frac{3}{5}$
22. $\frac{n}{12} = \frac{4}{16}$
23. $\frac{7}{8} = \frac{n}{4}$
24. $\frac{7}{10} = \frac{14}{a}$
25. $\frac{7}{n} = \frac{17.5}{5}$

Lesson 5-6 Each pair of figures is similar. Find the value of each variable.

26.

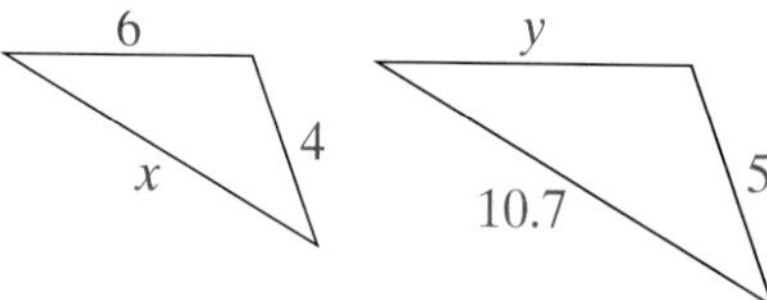

27.

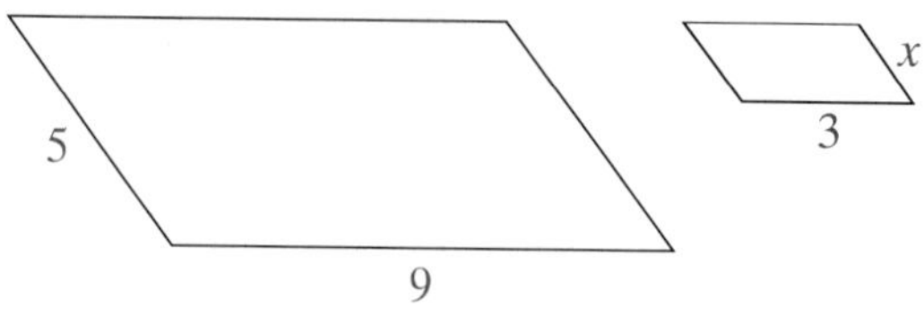

Lesson 5-7 The scale on a drawing is 0.5 in. : 15 ft. Find the actual length for each drawing length. Round to the nearest tenth, if necessary.

28. 15 in.
29. 20 in.
30. 10 in.
31. 40 in.
32. 15.5 in.
33. 1.25 in.

Chapter 6 Extra Practice

Lesson 6-1 **Write each ratio as a percent.**

1. $\frac{4}{5}$ **2.** $\frac{11}{5}$ **3.** $\frac{3}{25}$ **4.** $\frac{19}{20}$ **5.** $\frac{1}{10}$ **6.** $\frac{3}{2}$

Lesson 6-2 **Write each percent as a decimal.**

7. 37.5% **8.** 11.375% **9.** 2.55% **10.** 9% **11.** 1.111% **12.** 97.05%

Lesson 6-3 **Write each percent as a fraction in simplest form.**

13. 225% **14.** 0.1% **15.** 0.07% **16.** 398% **17.** 156% **18.** 0.2%

Lesson 6-4 **Find each answer using mental math.**

19. 30% of 285 **20.** 51% of 326 **21.** 9% of 1,250 **22.** 49% of 88 **23.** 101% of 150

Lesson 6-5 **Write a proportion and solve.**

24. 54 is what percent of 135? **25.** What percent of 48 is 2.4? **26.** What percent of 200 is 120?

27. 8 is what percent of 20? **28.** 32.5 is what percent of 130? **29.** What percent of 150 is 27?

Lesson 6-6 **Write and solve an equation to find the part of a whole.**

30. 30% of 250 is what number? **31.** What number is 90% of 70? **32.** 45% of 200 is what number?

33. What number is 7% of 88? **34.** 4% of 200 is what number? **35.** What number is 22% of 1?

Lesson 6-7 **Find each payment.**

36. \$75 with a 5% sales tax **37.** \$219 with a 3.5% sales tax **38.** \$85.65 with a 3% sales tax

Lesson 6-8 **Find each percent of change. Round to the nearest tenth. State whether the change is an increase or a decrease.**

39. 25 to 40 **40.** 95 to 45 **41.** 108 to 110 **42.** 50 to 95 **43.** 125 to 75

44. 8.5 to 10 **45.** 100 to 15 **46.** 63.5 to 20 **47.** 111 to 150 **48.** 25.9 to 30.2

Lesson 6-9 **Use the problem-solving strategy *Write an Equation* to solve the problem.**

49. Discounts A book store pays \$4.25 for paperback books and charges \$9.95. What is the maximum percent of discount the store can offer, while making a profit of \$2 on each book? Check your answer.

Extra Practice

Lesson 7-1 Name each segment, ray, or line.

1. 

2. 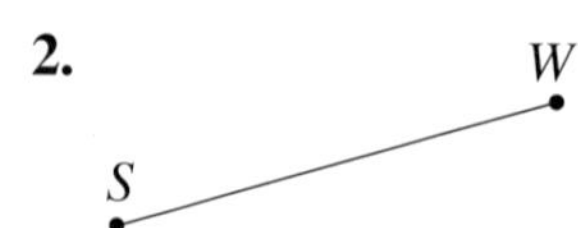

3. 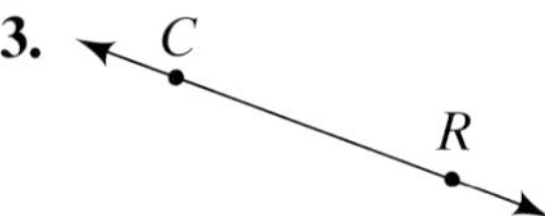

Lesson 7-2 Find the measures of the complement and the supplement of each angle.

4. $m\angle A = 25°$

5. $m\angle U = 15°$

6. $m\angle T = 85°$

7. $m\angle C = 46°$

Lesson 7-3 Copy each segment. Then construct its perpendicular bisector.

8. 

9. 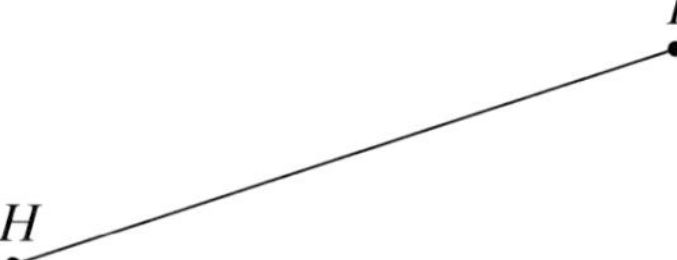

Lesson 7-4 Find x in each triangle.

10. 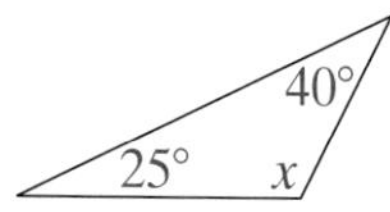

11. 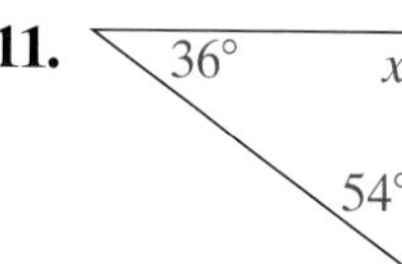

12. 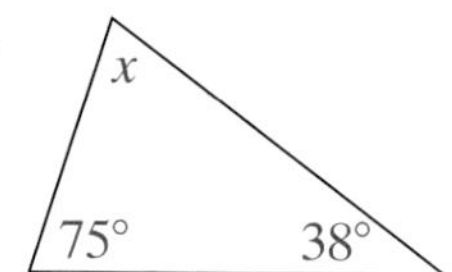

Lesson 7-5 Classify each polygon. Then name the congruent sides and angles.

13. 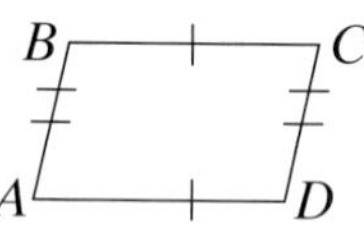

14. 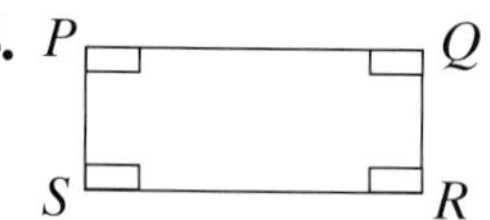

15. 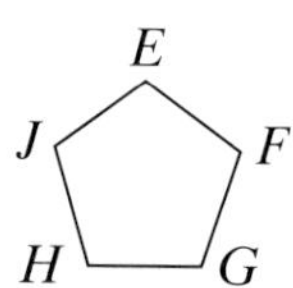

16. 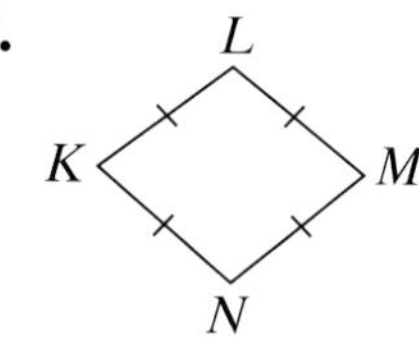

Lesson 7-6 Use the problem-solving strategies *Make a Table* and *Look for a Pattern* to solve the problem. Check your answer.

17. What is the sum of the angles of a decagon?

Lesson 7-7 $\triangle ABD \cong \triangle CED$. Complete each congruence statement.

18. $\angle A \cong$ ■

19. $\angle D \cong$ ■

20. $\overline{AD} \cong$ ■

21. $\overline{AB} \cong$ ■

Lessons 7-8 and 7-9 Circles and Circle Graphs

22. **Surveys** In a survey of 500 people, 86 of them preferred Brand A. Find the measure of the central angle that you would draw to represent Brand A in a circle graph.

Chapter 8 Extra Practice

Lesson 8-1 **Estimate the area of each shaded region. Each square represents 100 ft^2.**

1. 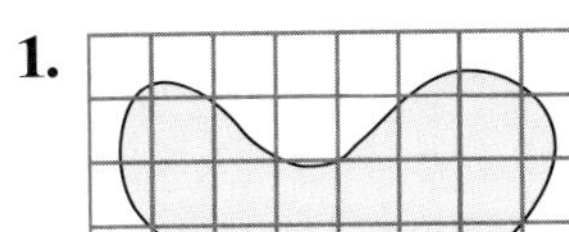

2. 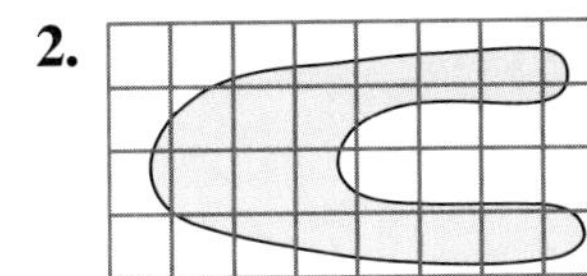

3. 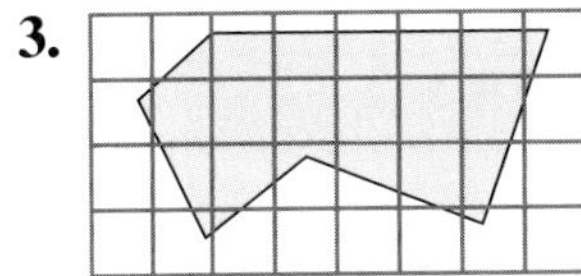

Lessons 8-2 and 8-3 **Find the area of each parallelogram or trapezoid.**

4. 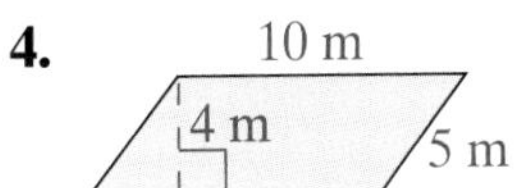

5. 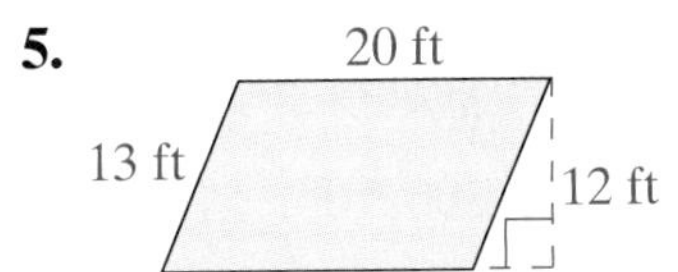

6. 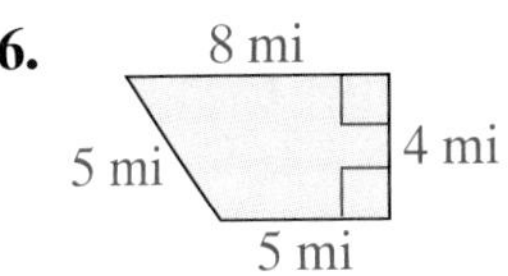

Lesson 8-4 **Use $\pi \approx 3.14$ to estimate the circumference and area for each circle.**

7. $d = 1.5$ km
8. $r = 6$ cm
9. $r = 9$ m
10. $d = 20$ in.

Lesson 8-5 **Simplify each square root.**

11. $\sqrt{1}$
12. $\sqrt{4}$
13. $\sqrt{49}$
14. $\sqrt{81}$
15. $\sqrt{900}$
16. $\sqrt{3,600}$

Lesson 8-6 **Find each missing length.**

17. 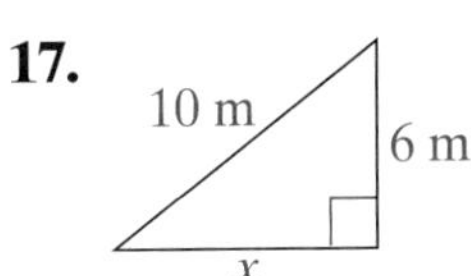

18. 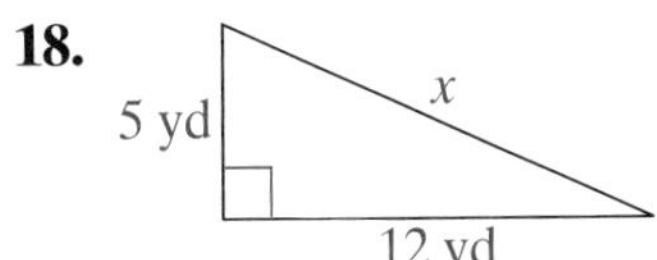

19. 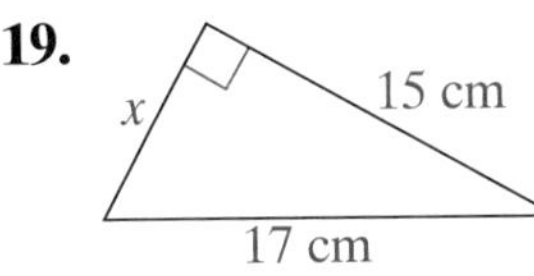

Lessons 8-7 and 8-8 **Name each figure. Find the surface area of the figures in Exercises 20 and 22.**

20. 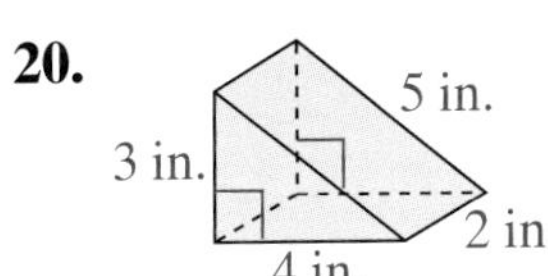

21. 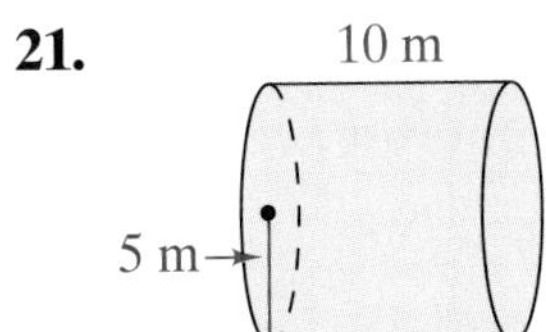

22. 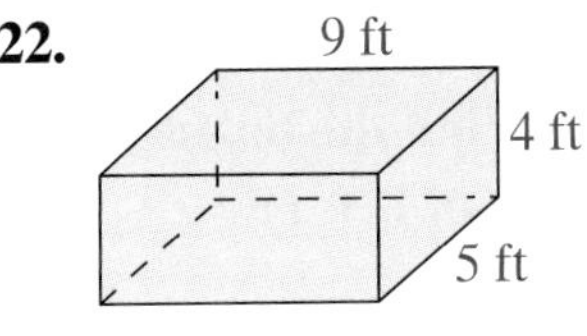

Lesson 8-9 **Volume of Rectangular Prisms and Cylinders**

23. Find the volume of the figures in Exercises 21 and 22.

Lesson 8-10 **Use the problem-solving strategy *Try, Check,* and *Revise* or *Write an Equation* to solve the problem.**

24. One leg of a right triangle measures 9 mm. The hypotenuse measures 15 mm. Find the length of the other leg.

Chapter 9 Extra Practice

Lessons 9-1 and 9-3 **Graph the data in each table. In Exercise 3, first find the values of the variables.**

1.

Hours of Study	Science Test Score
1	72
2	77
3	89
4	92

2.

Time (mo)	Savings (dollars)
2	125
4	295
6	420
8	625

3.

A	B
15	45
17	51
19	57
23	q
p	81

Lesson 9-2 **Identify each sequence as *arithmetic, geometric, both,* or *neither.***

4. 7, 10, 13, 16, . . .

5. 800, 400, 200, 100, . . .

6. 50, 25, 48, 24, . . .

Lesson 9-4 **Write a rule for the function represented by each table.**

7.

x	y
0	0
1	6
2	12
3	18

8.

x	y
0	−2
1	−1
2	0
3	1

9.

x	y
0	1
1	4
2	7
3	10

10.

x	y
0	10
1	8
2	6
3	4

Lesson 9-5 **Graph each function. Use input values of 1, 2, 3, 4, and 5.**

11. Output = Input + 5

12. Output = 8 − Input

13. Output = Input^2

Lesson 9-6 **Interpreting Graphs**

14. On her trip to the library, Arlene walked two blocks to the bus stop in five minutes. She rodes the bus for 15 min. The bus stopped three times, for one minute each time. Sketch a graph to represent Arlene's trip.

Lesson 9-7 **Find the balance in each compound interest account. Use the formula $B = p(1 + r)^t$.**

15. \$1,000 principal
5% annual interest rate
4 years

16. \$700 principal
4% annual interest rate
12 years

17. \$1,500 principal
5.5% annual interest rate
7 years

Lesson 9-8 ***Write an Equation*** **to solve the problem. Check your answer.**

18. **Cars** An auto mechanic charged a customer \$265 for repairs. The cost of parts was \$105, and the mechanic charged \$40 per hour for labor. How many hours did it take the mechanic to fix the car?

Chapter 10

Extra Practice

Lessons 10-1 and 10-3 **Use the graph for Exercises 1–6.**

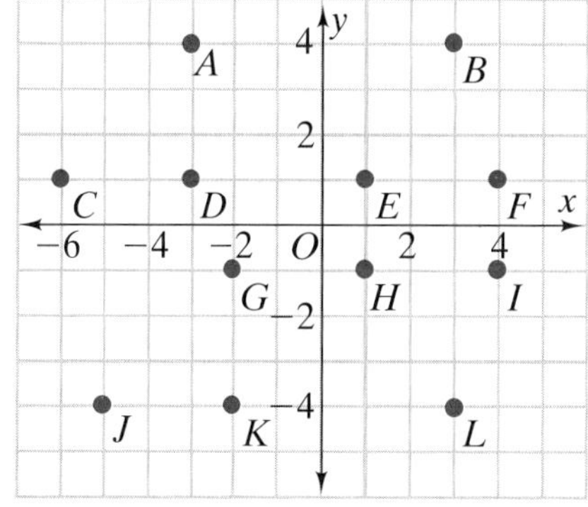

Name the point with the given coordinates.

1. $(-2, -1)$ **2.** $(1, 1)$ **3.** $(3, 4)$

Find the slope of the line through the points.

4. A and E **5.** G and E **6.** B and F

Lesson 10-2 **Tell whether each ordered pair is a solution of $y = x + 18$.**

7. $(2, 20)$ **8.** $(22, 4)$ **9.** $(36, -18)$

Lesson 10-4 **Make a table of values for each equation. Use integer values of x from -3 to 3. Then graph each equation.**

10. $y = x^2$ **11.** $y = x^2 - 4$ **12.** $y = 3x^2$ **13.** $y = 4|x|$

Lesson 10-5 **Use the problem-solving strategies *Make a Table* and *Make a Graph* to solve the problem.**

14. Animals A foal was 100 lb when it was born. It weighed 160 lb at 4 weeks and 220 lb at 8 weeks. At that rate of increase, about how many pounds will the foal weigh at 14 weeks?

Lesson 10-6 **Write a rule for the translation shown in each graph.**

15.

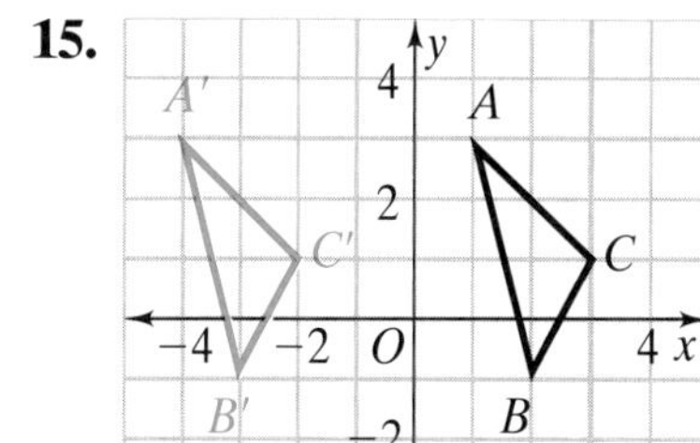

16.

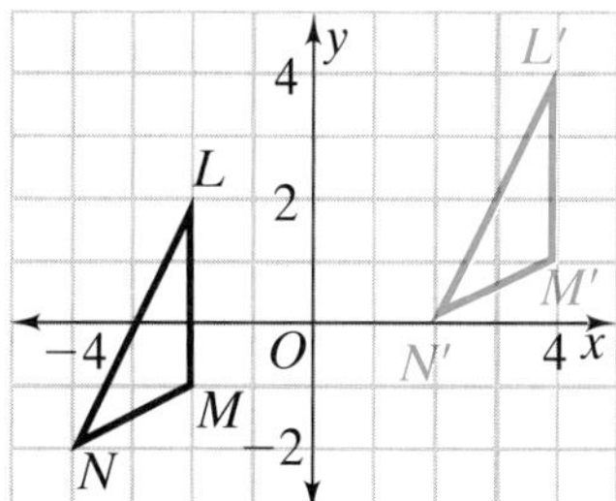

17.

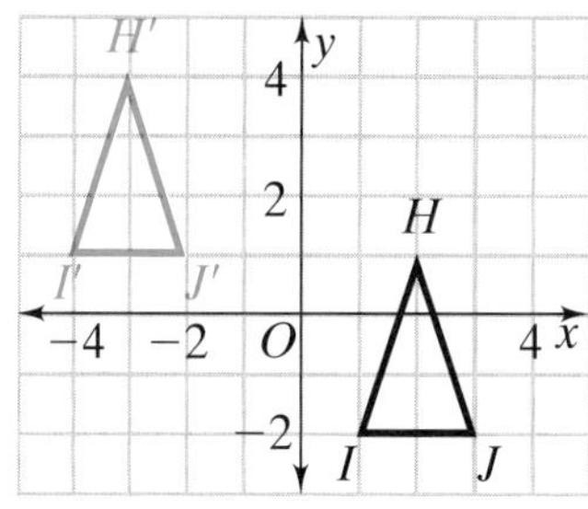

Lesson 10-7 **Use the graph from Exercises 1–6 to answer Exercise 18.**

18. Is the triangle formed by points E, B, and F a reflection, a rotation, or a translation of the triangle formed by points H, L, and I? Explain.

Lesson 10-8 **Rotations**

19. a. Graph the square $ABCD$ with vertices $A(2, -3)$, $B(4, -5)$, $C(6, -3)$, and $D(4, -1)$. Then connect the vertices in order.

b. Draw the image of $ABCD$ after a rotation of 180° about point A.

c. Write the new coordinates of the vertices of $ABCD$.

Chapter 11

Extra Practice

Lesson 11-1 Use the data below for Exercises 1 and 2.
high temperatures (°F): 85, 88, 91, 84, 90, 85, 84, 90, 88, 86, 85, 92, 85, 86, 88

1. Make a frequency table.

2. Make a line plot.

Lesson 11-2 Use the graph for Exercises 3–5.

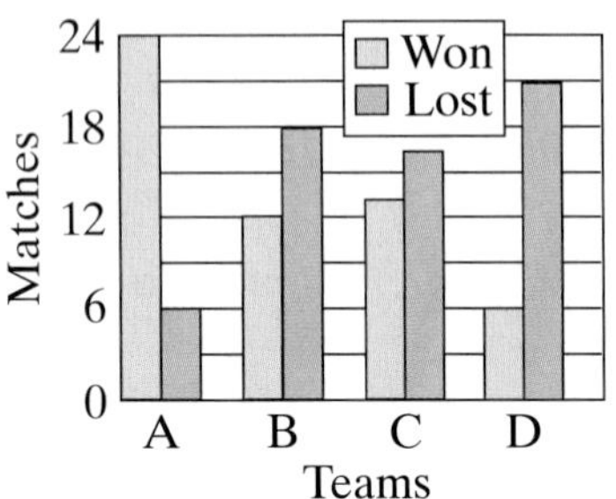

3. Which team has won the most matches?

4. Which team has won the fewest matches?

5. About how many more matches has Team A won than Team D?

Lesson 11-3 The table shows the number of stories of some tall buildings in the United States. Use the table to answer Exercises 6 and 7.

Number of Stories				
73	44	57	64	48
60	55	51	77	40
80	72	60	82	57

6. Draw a stem-and-leaf plot for the data.

7. What is the range of the data?

Lesson 11-4 Solve the problem by using the problem-solving strategies ***Use Logical Reasoning*** **and** ***Make a Table.***

8. Jobs Keesha, Jared, and Antoine are a nurse, an accountant, and an electrician. Jared is the brother of the accountant. Antoine has never met the accountant or the electrician. Which person has each job?

Lesson 11-5 Random Samples and Surveys

9. Write a fair survey question and a biased survey question.

Lesson 11-6 Estimating Population Size

10. Suppose 25 sea gulls were marked in a nesting area. Later, 500 sea gulls were counted, 19 of which were marked. Estimate the population.

Lesson 11-7 The graph shows the growth of household VCR purchases.

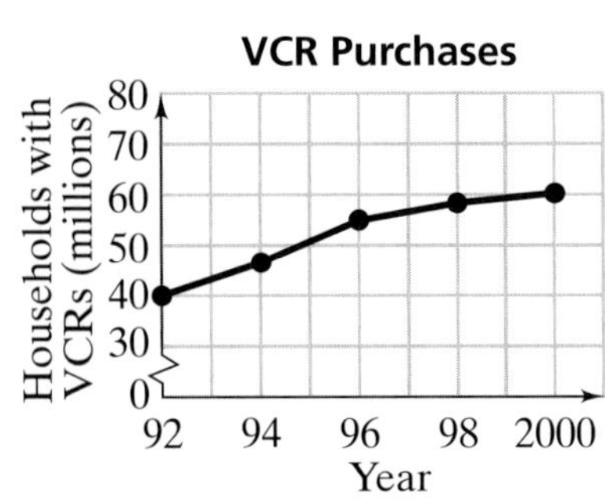

11. Decide whether the graph appears misleading. If so, explain how the graph creates the misleading impression.

Lesson 11-8 The data show the heights and weights of some 7-year-olds.

Height	40 in.	39 in.	42 in.	45 in.	48 in.	43 in.	41 in.
Weight	56 lb	52 lb	62 lb	75 lb	72 lb	67 lb	62 lb

12. Make a scatter plot of the data. Describe any trend you see in the data.

Chapter 12 Extra Practice

Lesson 12-1 **You roll a number cube. Find the odds in favor of each outcome.**

1. rolling a 2
2. rolling a 3 or 5
3. rolling a 2, 4, or 6

Lesson 12-2 **Experimental Probability**

4. A quality control engineer at a factory inspected 300 glow sticks for quality. The engineer found 15 defective glow sticks. What is the experimental probability that a glow stick is defective?

Lesson 12-3 **Use the problem-solving strategy *Make an Organized List* or *Simulate a Problem* to solve the problem.**

5. Crispy Cereal offers one free prize in every box: a baseball card, a keychain, or a bracelet. If you buy 3 boxes, what is the probability of *not* getting a baseball card?

Lesson 12-4 **Make a table to show the sample space for each situation. Then find the number of outcomes.**

6. You toss three coins.
7. You spin a number 1 to 6 and toss a coin.
8. You choose one letter from each of the two sets of letters E, F, G, H and A, B, C.
9. **a.** You flip two coins and spin a spinner with three congruent sections colored red, white, and blue. Draw a tree diagram to find the sample space.
   b. Find P(2 heads and blue) and P(at least 1 tail and red).

Lesson 12-5 **A bag contains 6 green marbles, 8 blue marbles, and 3 red marbles. Find *P(B)* after *A* has happened.**

10. A: Draw a green marble. Keep it. B: Draw a red marble.
11. A: Draw a blue marble. Replace it. B: Draw a red marble.
12. A box contains the letters S T A T I S T I C S. Suppose you select two letters, one after the other without replacement. Find $P(S$, then $T)$.

Lessons 12-6 and 12-7 **State whether the situation is a *permutation* or a *combination*. Then answer the question.**

13. In how many ways can a committee of 2 be chosen from 5 members?
14. In how many ways can a president and a treasurer be selected from a club of 5 members?

Skills Handbook

Comparing and Ordering Whole Numbers

The numbers on a number line are in order from least to greatest.

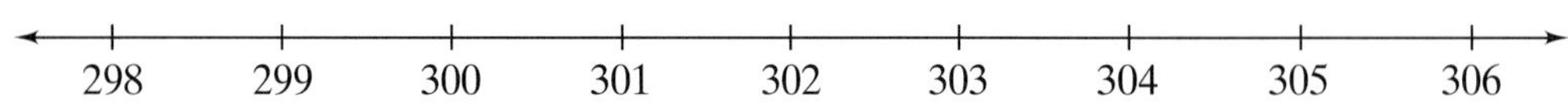

You can use a number line to compare whole numbers. Use the symbols $>$ (is greater than) and $<$ (is less than).

1 EXAMPLE

Use $>$ or $<$ to compare the numbers.

a. 303 ■ 299

303 is to the right of 299.

$303 > 299$

b. 301 ■ 305

301 is to the left of 305.

$301 < 305$

The value of a digit depends on its place in a number. Compare digits starting from the left.

2 EXAMPLE

Use $>$ or $<$ to compare the numbers.

a. 12,060,012,875 ■ 12,060,012,675

8 hundreds $>$ 6 hundreds, so
12,060,012,875 $>$ 12,060,012,675

b. 465,320 ■ 4,653,208

0 millions $<$ 4 millions, so
465,320 $<$ 4,653,208

EXERCISES

Use $>$ or $<$ to compare the numbers.

1. 3,660 ■ 360 **2.** 74,328 ■ 74,238 **3.** 88,010 ■ 8,101 **4.** 87,524 ■ 9,879

5. 295,286 ■ 295,826 **6.** 829,631 ■ 842,832 **7.** 932,401 ■ 932,701 **8.** 60,000 ■ 500,000

9. 1,609,372,002 ■ 609,172,002 **10.** 45,248,315,150 ■ 45,283,718,150

Write the numbers from least to greatest.

11. 3,747; 3,474; 3,774; 3,347; 3,734 **12.** 70,903; 70,309; 73,909; 73,090

13. 32,056,403; 302,056,403; 30,265,403; 30,256,403 **14.** 884,172; 881,472; 887,142; 881,872

Rounding Whole Numbers

You can use number lines to help you round numbers.

1 EXAMPLE

a. Round 7,510 to the nearest thousand.

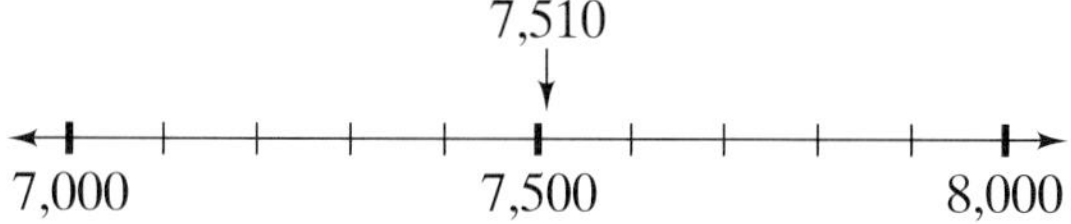

7,510 is between 7,000 and 8,000.

7,510 rounds to 8,000.

b. Round 237 to the nearest ten.

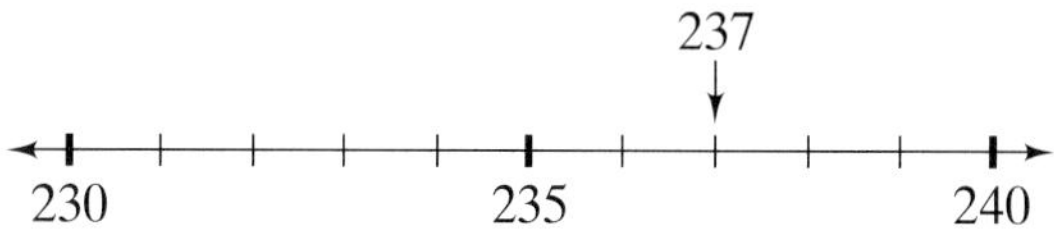

237 is between 230 and 240.

237 rounds to 240.

To round a number to a particular place, look at the digit to the right of that place. If the digit is less than 5, round down. If the digit is 5 or more, round up.

2 EXAMPLE

Round to the place of the underlined digit.

a. 3,4<u>6</u>3,280

The digit to the right of the 6 is 3, so 3,463,280 rounds down to 3,460,000.

b. 28<u>9</u>,543

The digit to the right of the 9 is 5, so 289,543 rounds up to 290,000.

EXERCISES

Round to the nearest ten.

1. 42 **2.** 89 **3.** 671 **4.** 3,482 **5.** 7,029 **6.** 661,423

Round to the nearest thousand.

7. 5,800 **8.** 3,100 **9.** 44,500 **10.** 9,936 **11.** 987 **12.** 313,591

13. 5,641 **14.** 37,896 **15.** 82,019 **16.** 808,155 **17.** 34,501 **18.** 650,828

Round to the place of the underlined digit.

19. 68,<u>8</u>52 **20.** <u>4</u>51,006 **21.** 3,40<u>6</u>,781 **22.** 2<u>8</u>,512,030 **23.** 71,2<u>2</u>5,003

24. 96,<u>3</u>59 **25.** 4<u>0</u>1,223 **26.** <u>8</u>,902 **27.** 3,67<u>7</u> **28.** 2,551,<u>7</u>50

29. 6<u>8</u>,663 **30.** 70<u>1</u>,803,229 **31.** 56<u>5</u>,598 **32.** 32,<u>8</u>10 **33.** 1,<u>0</u>46,300

Multiplying Whole Numbers

When you multiply by a two-digit number, first multiply by the ones and then multiply by the tens. Add the products.

1 EXAMPLE

Multiply 62 × 704.

Step 1

$$\begin{array}{r} 704 \\ \times\ 62 \\ \hline 1408 \end{array}$$

Step 2

$$\begin{array}{r} 704 \\ \times\ 62 \\ \hline 1408 \\ 42240 \end{array}$$

Step 3

$$\begin{array}{r} 704 \\ \times\ 62 \\ \hline 1408 \\ +\ 42240 \\ \hline 43{,}648 \end{array}$$

2 EXAMPLE

Find each product.

a. 93 × 6

$$\begin{array}{r} 93 \\ \times\ 6 \\ \hline 558 \end{array}$$

b. 25 × 48

$$\begin{array}{r} 48 \\ \times\ 25 \\ \hline 240 \\ +\ 960 \\ \hline 1{,}200 \end{array}$$

c. 80 × 921

$$\begin{array}{r} 921 \\ \times\ 80 \\ \hline 73{,}680 \end{array}$$

EXERCISES

Find each product.

1. $\begin{array}{r} 74 \\ \times\ 6 \\ \hline \end{array}$ **2.** $\begin{array}{r} 35 \\ \times\ 9 \\ \hline \end{array}$ **3.** $\begin{array}{r} 53 \\ \times\ 7 \\ \hline \end{array}$ **4.** $\begin{array}{r} 80 \\ \times\ 8 \\ \hline \end{array}$ **5.** $\begin{array}{r} 98 \\ \times\ 4 \\ \hline \end{array}$ **6.** $\begin{array}{r} 65 \\ \times\ 8 \\ \hline \end{array}$

7. $\begin{array}{r} 512 \\ \times\ 3 \\ \hline \end{array}$ **8.** $\begin{array}{r} 407 \\ \times\ 9 \\ \hline \end{array}$ **9.** $\begin{array}{r} 225 \\ \times\ 6 \\ \hline \end{array}$ **10.** $\begin{array}{r} 340 \\ \times\ 5 \\ \hline \end{array}$ **11.** $\begin{array}{r} 816 \\ \times\ 7 \\ \hline \end{array}$ **12.** $\begin{array}{r} 603 \\ \times\ 3 \\ \hline \end{array}$

13. $\begin{array}{r} 70 \\ \times\ 36 \\ \hline \end{array}$ **14.** $\begin{array}{r} 41 \\ \times\ 55 \\ \hline \end{array}$ **15.** $\begin{array}{r} 38 \\ \times\ 49 \\ \hline \end{array}$ **16.** $\begin{array}{r} 601 \\ \times\ 87 \\ \hline \end{array}$ **17.** $\begin{array}{r} 271 \\ \times\ 34 \\ \hline \end{array}$ **18.** $\begin{array}{r} 450 \\ \times\ 67 \\ \hline \end{array}$

19. 6 × 82 **20.** 405 × 5 **21.** 81 × 9 **22.** 3 × 274 **23.** 553 × 4

24. 60 × 84 **25.** 52 × 17 **26.** 31 × 90 **27.** 78 × 52 **28.** 43 × 66

29. 826 × 3 **30.** 702 × 4 **31.** 5 × 128 **32.** 6 × 339 **33.** 781 × 7

Dividing Whole Numbers

First estimate the quotient by rounding the divisor, the dividend, or both. When you divide, after you bring down a digit, you must write a digit in the quotient.

EXAMPLE

Find each quotient.

a. $741 \div 8$

Estimate:
$720 \div 8 \approx 90$

$$\begin{array}{r} 92\text{ R5} \\ 8\overline{)741} \\ -72 \\ \hline 21 \\ -16 \\ \hline 5 \end{array}$$

b. $838 \div 43$

Estimate:
$800 \div 40 \approx 20$

$$\begin{array}{r} 19\text{ R21} \\ 43\overline{)838} \\ -43 \\ \hline 408 \\ -387 \\ \hline 21 \end{array}$$

c. $367 \div 9$

Estimate:
$360 \div 9 \approx 40$

$$\begin{array}{r} 40\text{ R7} \\ 9\overline{)367} \\ -360 \\ \hline 7 \end{array}$$

EXERCISES

Divide.

1. $4\overline{)61}$	**2.** $8\overline{)53}$	**3.** $7\overline{)90}$	**4.** $3\overline{)84}$	**5.** $6\overline{)81}$
6. $6\overline{)469}$	**7.** $3\overline{)653}$	**8.** $8\overline{)645}$	**9.** $9\overline{)231}$	**10.** $4\overline{)415}$
11. $60\overline{)461}$	**12.** $40\overline{)213}$	**13.** $70\overline{)517}$	**14.** $30\overline{)432}$	**15.** $80\overline{)276}$
16. $43\overline{)273}$	**17.** $52\overline{)281}$	**18.** $69\overline{)207}$	**19.** $38\overline{)121}$	**20.** $81\overline{)433}$
21. $94\overline{)1{,}368}$	**22.** $62\overline{)1{,}147}$	**23.** $55\overline{)2{,}047}$	**24.** $85\overline{)1{,}450}$	**25.** $46\overline{)996}$
26. $94 \div 4$	**27.** $66 \div 9$	**28.** $90 \div 5$	**29.** $69 \div 6$	**30.** $58 \div 8$
31. $323 \div 5$	**32.** $849 \div 7$	**33.** $404 \div 8$	**34.** $934 \div 3$	**35.** $619 \div 6$
36. $777 \div 50$	**37.** $528 \div 20$	**38.** $443 \div 40$	**39.** $312 \div 40$	**40.** $335 \div 60$
41. $382 \div 72$	**42.** $580 \div 68$	**43.** $279 \div 43$	**44.** $232 \div 27$	**45.** $331 \div 93$
46. $614 \div 35$	**47.** $423 \div 28$	**48.** $489 \div 15$	**49.** $1{,}134 \div 51$	**50.** $1{,}103 \div 26$

Place Value and Decimals

Each digit in a decimal has both a place and a value. The value of any place is one tenth the value of the place to its left. In the chart below, the digit 5 is in the hundredths place. So its value is 5 hundredths.

thousands	hundreds	tens	ones	.	tenths	hundredths	thousandths	ten-thousandths	hundred-thousandths
2	8	3	6	.	7	5	0	1	4

EXAMPLE

a. In what place is the digit 8?

hundreds

b. What is the value of the digit 8?

8 hundreds

EXERCISES

Use the chart above. Write the place of each digit.

1. 3 **2.** 4 **3.** 6 **4.** 7 **5.** 1 **6.** 0

Use the chart above. Write the value of each digit.

7. 3 **8.** 4 **9.** 6 **10.** 7 **11.** 1 **12.** 0

Write the value of the digit 6 in each number.

13. 0.162 **14.** 0.016 **15.** 13.672 **16.** 1,640.8 **17.** 62.135

18. 26.34 **19.** 6,025.9 **20.** 0.6003 **21.** 2,450.65 **22.** 615.28

23. 3.16125 **24.** 1.20641 **25.** 0.15361 **26.** 1.55736 **27.** 0.20516

Write the value of the underlined digit.

28. $2\underline{4}.0026$ **29.** $14.9\underline{3}1$ **30.** $5.78\underline{9}4$ **31.** $0.\underline{8}7$ **32.** $10.056\underline{3}$

Reading and Writing Decimals

A place value chart can help you read and write decimals. When there are no ones, write a zero before the decimal point.

billions	hundred millions	ten millions	millions	hundred thousands	ten thousands	thousands	hundreds	tens	ones	.	tenths	hundredths	thousandths	ten-thousandths	hundred-thousandths	millionths	**Read**
									0	.	0	7					7 hundredths
								2	3	.	0	1	4				23 and 14 thousandths
3	0	0	0	0	0	0	0	0	0	.	8						3 billion and 8 tenths
									5	.	0	0	0	1	0	2	5 and 102 millionths

EXAMPLE

a. Write thirteen ten-thousandths in numerals.

Ten-thousandths is 4 places after the decimal point. So, the decimal will have 4 places after the decimal point. The number is 0.0013.

b. Write 1.025 in words.

The digit 5 is in the thousandths place. So, 1.025 is one and twenty-five thousandths.

EXERCISES

Write a number for the given words.

1. three hundredths

2. twenty-one millions

3. six and two hundredths

4. two billion and six tenths

5. two and five hundredths

6. five thousand twelve

7. seven millionths

8. forty-one ten-thousandths

9. eleven thousandths

10. one and twenty-five millionths

11. three hundred four thousandths

Write each number in words.

12. 5,700.4

13. 3,000,000.09

14. 12.000069

15. 900.02

16. 25.00007

17. 0.00015

Rounding Decimals

You can use number lines to help you round decimals.

1 EXAMPLE

a. Round 1.627 to the nearest tenth.

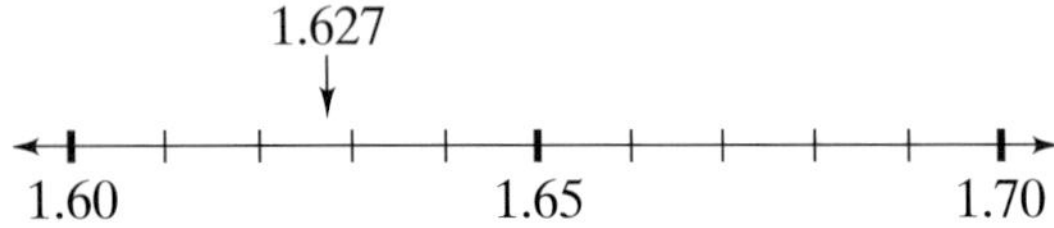

1.627 is between 1.6 and 1.7.

1.627 rounds to 1.6.

b. Round 0.248 to the nearest hundredth.

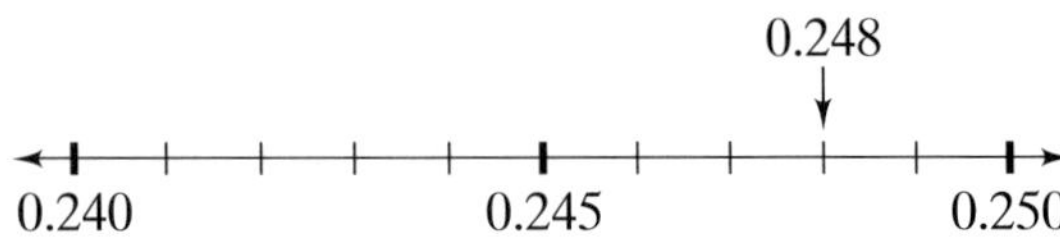

0.248 is between 0.24 and 0.25.

0.248 rounds to 0.25.

To round a number to a particular place, look at the digit to the right of that place. If the digit is less than 5, round down. If the digit is 5 or more, round up.

2 EXAMPLE

a. Round 2.4301 to the nearest whole number.

The digit to the right of 2 is 4, so 2.4301 rounds down to 2.

b. Round 0.0515 to the nearest thousandth.

The digit to the right of 1 is 5, so 0.0515 rounds up to 0.052.

EXERCISES

Round to the nearest tenth.

1. 2.75 **2.** 3.816 **3.** 19.72 **4.** 401.1603 **5.** 499.491 **6.** 3.949

7. 4.67522 **8.** 20.397 **9.** 399.956 **10.** 129.98 **11.** 96.4045 **12.** 125.66047

Round to the nearest hundredth.

13. 31.723 **14.** 14.869 **15.** 1.78826 **16.** 0.1119 **17.** 736.941 **18.** 9.6057

19. 0.699 **20.** 4.231 **21.** 12.09531 **22.** 5.77125 **23.** 0.9195 **24.** 4.0033

Round to the nearest thousandth.

25. 0.4387 **26.** 0.0649 **27.** 3.4953 **28.** 8.07092 **29.** 0.6008 **30.** 6.0074

Round to the nearest whole number.

31. 3.942 **32.** 10.4 **33.** 79.52 **34.** 105.3002 **35.** 431.23 **36.** 0.4962

Multiplying Decimals

When you multiply decimals, first multiply as if the factors were whole numbers. Then, count the decimal places in both factors to find how many places are needed in the product.

1 EXAMPLE

Multiply 2.5 × 1.8.

$$\begin{array}{rl} 1.8 & \leftarrow \text{one decimal place} \\ \times\ 2.5 & \leftarrow \text{one decimal place} \\ \hline 90 & \\ +\ 360 & \\ \hline 4.50 & \leftarrow \text{two decimal places} \end{array}$$

2 EXAMPLE

Find each product.

a. 0.7 × 1.02

$$\begin{array}{r} 1.02 \\ \times\ 0.7 \\ \hline 0.714 \end{array}$$

b. 0.03 × 407

$$\begin{array}{r} 407 \\ \times\ 0.03 \\ \hline 12.21 \end{array}$$

c. 0.62 × 2.45

$$\begin{array}{r} 2.45 \\ \times\ 0.62 \\ \hline 490 \\ +\ 14700 \\ \hline 1.5190 \end{array}$$

d. 75 × 3.06

$$\begin{array}{r} 3.06 \\ \times\ 75 \\ \hline 1530 \\ +\ 21420 \\ \hline 229.50 \end{array}$$

EXERCISES

Multiply.

1. $\begin{array}{r} 0.3 \\ \times\ 8 \\ \hline \end{array}$ **2.** $\begin{array}{r} 5 \\ \times\ 0.06 \\ \hline \end{array}$ **3.** $\begin{array}{r} 0.04 \\ \times\ 7 \\ \hline \end{array}$ **4.** $\begin{array}{r} 6 \\ \times\ 0.8 \\ \hline \end{array}$ **5.** $\begin{array}{r} 3.1 \\ \times\ 0.05 \\ \hline \end{array}$ **6.** $\begin{array}{r} 14 \\ \times\ 0.2 \\ \hline \end{array}$

7. $\begin{array}{r} 3.1 \\ \times\ 6 \\ \hline \end{array}$ **8.** $\begin{array}{r} 0.05 \\ \times\ 43 \\ \hline \end{array}$ **9.** $\begin{array}{r} 0.27 \\ \times\ 5 \\ \hline \end{array}$ **10.** $\begin{array}{r} 72 \\ \times\ 0.6 \\ \hline \end{array}$ **11.** $\begin{array}{r} 0.8 \\ \times\ 312 \\ \hline \end{array}$ **12.** $\begin{array}{r} 4.56 \\ \times\ 7 \\ \hline \end{array}$

13. 5 × 2.41 **14.** 704 × 0.3 **15.** 9 × 1.35 **16.** 1.2 × 0.3

17. 0.04 × 2.5 **18.** 6.6 × 0.3 **19.** 15.1 × 0.02 **20.** 0.8 × 31.3

21. 0.07 × 25.1 **22.** 42.2 × 0.9 **23.** 0.6 × 30.02 **24.** 0.05 × 11.8

25. 71.13 × 0.4 **26.** 48 × 2.1 **27.** 6.3 × 85 **28.** 0.42 × 98

29. 76 × 3.3 **30.** 0.77 × 51 **31.** 5.2 × 4.8 **32.** 0.12 × 6.1

Zeros in the Product

When you multiply with decimals, start at the right of the product to count the number of decimal places. Sometimes you need to write extra zeros to the left of a product before you can place the decimal point.

1 EXAMPLE

Multiply 0.03×0.51.

Step 1

$$\begin{array}{r} 0.51 \\ \times\ 0.03 \\ \hline 153 \end{array}$$

← two decimal places
← two decimal places
← four decimal places

Step 2

$$\begin{array}{r} 0.51 \\ \times\ 0.03 \\ \hline 0.0153 \end{array}$$

← Put extra zeros to the left. Then place the decimal point.

2 EXAMPLE

Find each product.

a. 0.2×0.3

$$\begin{array}{r} 0.3 \\ \times\ 0.2 \\ \hline 0.06 \end{array}$$

b. 0.5×0.04

$$\begin{array}{r} 0.04 \\ \times\ 0.5 \\ \hline 0.020 \end{array}$$

c. 4×0.02

$$\begin{array}{r} 0.02 \\ \times\ 4 \\ \hline 0.08 \end{array}$$

d. 0.02×0.45

$$\begin{array}{r} 0.45 \\ \times\ 0.02 \\ \hline 0.0090 \end{array}$$

EXERCISES

Multiply.

1. $\begin{array}{r} 0.1 \\ \times\ 0.6 \\ \hline \end{array}$
2. $\begin{array}{r} 0.4 \\ \times\ 0.2 \\ \hline \end{array}$
3. $\begin{array}{r} 0.05 \\ \times\ 0.06 \\ \hline \end{array}$
4. $\begin{array}{r} 0.01 \\ \times\ 8 \\ \hline \end{array}$

5. $\begin{array}{r} 0.7 \\ \times\ 0.02 \\ \hline \end{array}$
6. $\begin{array}{r} 0.03 \\ \times\ 0.4 \\ \hline \end{array}$
7. $\begin{array}{r} 0.03 \\ \times\ 0.9 \\ \hline \end{array}$
8. $\begin{array}{r} 0.06 \\ \times\ 0.5 \\ \hline \end{array}$

9. $\begin{array}{r} 0.2 \\ \times\ 0.02 \\ \hline \end{array}$
10. $\begin{array}{r} 7 \\ \times\ 0.01 \\ \hline \end{array}$
11. $\begin{array}{r} 0.05 \\ \times\ 0.05 \\ \hline \end{array}$
12. $\begin{array}{r} 0.6 \\ \times\ 0.06 \\ \hline \end{array}$

13. 0.4×0.08
14. 0.07×0.05
15. 0.03×0.03
16. 0.09×0.05
17. 0.5×0.08
18. 0.06×0.7
19. 0.07×0.01
20. 0.16×0.2
21. 0.01×0.74
22. 0.47×0.08
23. 0.76×0.1
24. 0.19×0.3
25. 0.5×0.17
26. 0.31×0.08
27. 0.14×0.05
28. 0.07×0.85
29. 0.45×0.06
30. 0.4×0.23
31. 0.17×0.06
32. 0.3×0.24
33. 0.67×0.09
34. 0.08×0.39
35. 0.3×0.27
36. 0.19×0.05

Dividing a Decimal by a Whole Number

When you divide a decimal by a whole number, first divide as if the numbers were whole numbers. Then put a decimal point in the quotient directly above the decimal point in the dividend.

1 EXAMPLE

Divide 0.256 ÷ 8.

Step 1

$$\begin{array}{r} 32 \\ 8\overline{)0.256} \\ -24 \\ \hline 16 \\ -16 \\ \hline 0 \end{array}$$

Step 2

$$\begin{array}{r} 0.032 \\ 8\overline{)0.256} \\ -24 \\ \hline 16 \\ -16 \\ \hline 0 \end{array}$$

← **Put extra zeros to the left. Then place the decimal point.**

2 EXAMPLE

Find each quotient.

a. 12.6 ÷ 6

$$\begin{array}{r} 2.1 \\ 6\overline{)12.6} \\ -12 \\ \hline 06 \\ -6 \\ \hline 0 \end{array}$$

b. 37.26 ÷ 81

$$\begin{array}{r} 0.46 \\ 81\overline{)37.26} \\ -324 \\ \hline 486 \\ -486 \\ \hline 0 \end{array}$$

c. 0.666 ÷ 9

$$\begin{array}{r} 0.074 \\ 9\overline{)0.666} \\ -63 \\ \hline 36 \\ -36 \\ \hline 0 \end{array}$$

EXERCISES

Divide.

1. $4\overline{)28.56}$ **2.** $5\overline{)16.5}$ **3.** $9\overline{)6.984}$ **4.** $6\overline{)91.44}$ **5.** $4\overline{)35.16}$

6. $81\overline{)33.291}$ **7.** $22\overline{)2.42}$ **8.** $26\overline{)1723.8}$ **9.** $83\overline{)15.272}$ **10.** $39\overline{)26.91}$

11. 22.2 ÷ 3 **12.** 1.2 ÷ 4 **13.** 4.65 ÷ 5 **14.** 7.11 ÷ 9

15. 17.52 ÷ 2 **16.** 10.53 ÷ 9 **17.** 14.49 ÷ 7 **18.** 37.14 ÷ 6

19. 0.0324 ÷ 9 **20.** 0.1352 ÷ 8 **21.** 0.0882 ÷ 6 **22.** 0.8682 ÷ 6

23. 79.599 ÷ 13 **24.** 45.918 ÷ 18 **25.** 59.7 ÷ 15 **26.** 74.664 ÷ 12

27. 12.342 ÷ 22 **28.** 29.792 ÷ 32 **29.** 22.568 ÷ 26 **30.** 11.340 ÷ 36

Powers of Ten

You can use shortcuts when multiplying and dividing by powers of ten.

When you multiply by...	move the decimal point...	When you divide by...	move the decimal point...
1,000	3 places to the right.	1,000	3 places to the left.
100	2 places to the right.	100	2 places to the left.
10	1 place to the right.	10	1 place to the left.
0.1	1 place to the left.	0.1	1 place to the right.
0.01	2 places to the left.	0.01	2 places to the right.

EXAMPLE

Multiply or divide.

a. 0.3×0.01

0.00.3 ← Move the decimal point 2 places to the left.

$0.3 \times 0.01 = 0.003$

b. $0.18 \div 1{,}000$

0.000.18 ← Move the decimal point 3 places to the left.

$0.18 \div 1{,}000 = 0.00018$

EXERCISES

Multiply.

1. 3.2×0.01 **2.** $1{,}000 \times 0.12$ **3.** 0.7×0.1 **4.** 0.01×6.2

5. 0.09×100 **6.** 23.6×0.01 **7.** 5.2×10 **8.** $0.08 \times 1{,}000$

9. 100×0.05 **10.** 0.1×0.24 **11.** 18.03×0.1 **12.** 6.1×100

Divide.

13. $82.3 \div 0.1$ **14.** $0.4 \div 1{,}000$ **15.** $5.02 \div 0.01$ **16.** $16.5 \div 100$

17. $236.7 \div 0.1$ **18.** $45.28 \div 10$ **19.** $0.9 \div 1{,}000$ **20.** $1.03 \div 0.01$

21. $42.6 \div 0.1$ **22.** $203.05 \div 0.01$ **23.** $4.7 \div 10$ **24.** $0.07 \div 100$

Multiply or divide.

25. 0.32×0.1 **26.** $0.03 \div 100$ **27.** $2.6 \div 0.1$ **28.** $12.6 \times 1{,}000$

29. $0.8 \div 1{,}000$ **30.** 0.01×6.7 **31.** 100×0.15 **32.** $23.5 \div 10$

Zeros in Decimal Division

When you are dividing by a decimal, sometimes you need to use extra zeros in the dividend, the quotient, or both.

EXAMPLE

Find each quotient.

a. 0.14 ÷ 0.04

Multiply by 100.

```
        3.5
0.04.)0.14.0
      -12
        20
       -20
         0
```

b. 0.00434 ÷ 0.07

Multiply by 100.

```
        0.062
0.07.)0.00.434
          -42
           14
          -14
            0
```

c. 0.045 ÷ 3.6

Multiply by 10.

```
      0.0125
3.6.)0.0.4500
        -36
         90
        -72
        180
       -180
          0
```

EXERCISES

Divide.

1. $0.4\overline{)0.001}$ **2.** $0.05\overline{)0.0023}$ **3.** $0.02\overline{)0.000162}$

4. $0.6\overline{)0.0015}$ **5.** $1.2\overline{)0.078}$ **6.** $0.34\overline{)0.00119}$

7. $0.12\overline{)0.009}$ **8.** $2.5\overline{)0.021}$ **9.** 0.0017 ÷ 0.02

10. 0.003 ÷ 0.6 **11.** 0.01099 ÷ 0.7 **12.** 0.104 ÷ 0.05

13. 0.0945 ÷ 0.09 **14.** 0.00045 ÷ 0.3 **15.** 0.052 ÷ 0.8

16. 0.142 ÷ 0.04 **17.** 0.034 ÷ 0.05 **18.** 0.0019 ÷ 0.2

19. 0.9 ÷ 0.2 **20.** 0.000175 ÷ 0.07 **21.** 0.0084 ÷ 1.4

22. 0.259 ÷ 3.5 **23.** 0.00468 ÷ 0.52 **24.** 0.00056 ÷ 0.16

25. 0.0612 ÷ 7.2 **26.** 0.17701 ÷ 3.1 **27.** 0.00063 ÷ 0.18

28. 0.011 ÷ 0.25 **29.** 0.3069 ÷ 9.3 **30.** 0.000924 ÷ 0.44

31. 0.03234 ÷ 0.35 **32.** 0.00123 ÷ 8.2 **33.** 0.03225 ÷ 0.75

34. 0.006 ÷ 0.75 **35.** 0.73 ÷ 0.25 **36.** 0.68 ÷ 0.002

37. 0.398 ÷ 0.05 **38.** 0.0004 ÷ 0.002 **39.** 0.125 ÷ 0.005

Adding and Subtracting Fractions With Like Denominators

When you add or subtract fractions with the same denominator, first add or subtract the numerators. Write the answer over the denominator. If necessary, change the answer to simplest form.

1 EXAMPLE

Add or subtract. Write the answer in simplest form.

a. $\frac{5}{16} + \frac{3}{16}$

$$\begin{array}{r} \frac{5}{16} \\ +\frac{3}{16} \\ \hline \frac{8}{16} = \frac{1}{2} \end{array}$$

b. $\frac{7}{8} - \frac{1}{8}$

$$\begin{array}{r} \frac{7}{8} \\ -\frac{1}{8} \\ \hline \frac{6}{8} = \frac{3}{4} \end{array}$$

c. $\frac{3}{5} + \frac{2}{5}$

$\frac{3}{5} + \frac{2}{5} = \frac{5}{5} = 1$

To add or subtract mixed numbers, add or subtract the fractions first. Then add or subtract the whole numbers. If necessary, change the answer to simplest form.

2 EXAMPLE

a. $2\frac{5}{8} + 3\frac{1}{8}$

$$\begin{array}{r} 2\frac{5}{8} \\ +3\frac{1}{8} \\ \hline 5\frac{6}{8} = 5\frac{3}{4} \end{array}$$

b. $4\frac{3}{4} - 1\frac{1}{4}$

$$\begin{array}{r} 4\frac{3}{4} \\ -1\frac{1}{4} \\ \hline 3\frac{2}{4} = 3\frac{1}{2} \end{array}$$

c. $5\frac{5}{6} + 2\frac{5}{6}$

$$\begin{aligned} 5\frac{5}{6} + 2\frac{5}{6} &= 7\frac{10}{6} \\ &= 7 + 1 + \frac{4}{6} \\ &= 8\frac{2}{3} \end{aligned}$$

EXERCISES

Add or subtract. Write the answers in simplest form.

1. $\begin{array}{r} \frac{2}{5} \\ +\frac{2}{5} \\ \hline \end{array}$ **2.** $\begin{array}{r} \frac{2}{6} \\ -\frac{1}{6} \\ \hline \end{array}$ **3.** $\begin{array}{r} \frac{2}{7} \\ +\frac{2}{7} \\ \hline \end{array}$ **4.** $\begin{array}{r} 9\frac{1}{3} \\ -8\frac{1}{3} \\ \hline \end{array}$ **5.** $\begin{array}{r} 8\frac{6}{7} \\ -4\frac{2}{7} \\ \hline \end{array}$ **6.** $\begin{array}{r} 3\frac{1}{10} \\ +1\frac{3}{10} \\ \hline \end{array}$

7. $\frac{3}{8} + \frac{2}{8}$ **8.** $\frac{3}{6} - \frac{1}{6}$ **9.** $\frac{6}{8} - \frac{3}{8}$ **10.** $\frac{2}{9} + \frac{1}{9}$ **11.** $\frac{4}{5} - \frac{1}{5}$

12. $\frac{3}{4} + \frac{1}{4}$ **13.** $\frac{9}{10} - \frac{3}{10}$ **14.** $8\frac{7}{10} + 2\frac{3}{10}$ **15.** $1\frac{4}{5} + 3\frac{3}{5}$ **16.** $2\frac{2}{9} + 3\frac{4}{9}$

17. $3\frac{2}{5} + 8\frac{1}{5}$ **18.** $8\frac{5}{8} - 3\frac{3}{8}$ **19.** $1\frac{1}{12} + 5\frac{5}{12}$ **20.** $9\frac{7}{10} - 2\frac{3}{10}$ **21.** $9\frac{3}{4} + 1\frac{3}{4}$

Metric Units of Length

The basic unit of length in the metric system is the meter. All the other units are based on the meter. In the chart below, each unit is 10 times the value of the unit to its left.

Unit	Millimeter	Centimeter	Decimeter	Meter	Decameter	Hectometer	Kilometer
Symbol	mm	cm	dm	m	dam	hm	km
Value	0.001 m	0.01 m	0.1 m	1 m	10 m	100 m	1,000 m

To change a measure from one unit to another, start by using the chart to find the relationship between the two units.

EXAMPLE

Complete each equation.

a. 0.8 km = ■ m

1 km = 1,000 m

0.8 × 1,000 = 800 ← **To change km to m, multiply by 1,000.**

0.8 km = 800 m

b. 17.2 mm = ■ cm

1 mm = 0.1 cm

17.2 × 0.1 = 1.72 ← **To change mm to cm, multiply by 0.1.**

17.2 mm = 1.72 cm

c. ■ cm = 2.1 km

1 km = 100,000 cm

2.1 × 100,000 = 210,000 ← **To change km to cm, multiply by 100,000.**

210,000 cm = 2.1 km

d. ■ m = 5,200 cm

1 cm = 0.01 m

5,200 × 0.01 = 52 ← **To change cm to m, multiply by 0.01.**

52 m = 5,200 cm

EXERCISES

Complete each equation.

1. 1mm = ■ cm
2. 1 m = ■ km
3. 1 mm = ■ m
4. 1 cm = ■ m

5. 1.2 cm = ■ km
6. ■ km = 45,000 mm
7. ■ m = 30 km

8. 6.2 cm = ■ mm
9. 3.3 km = ■ m
10. 0.6 mm = ■ cm

11. 72 cm = ■ m
12. 180 m = ■ mm
13. ■ cm = 13 km

14. ■ m = 530 cm
15. 4,900 mm = ■ m
16. ■ cm = 24 m

17. ■ km = 106,000 cm
18. 259,000 mm = ■ m
19. 1,200,000 mm = ■ km

Metric Units of Capacity

The basic unit of capacity in the metric system is the liter. All the other units are based on the liter. In the chart below, each unit is 10 times the value of the unit on the left. Note that we use a capital L as the abbreviation for *liter* to avoid confusion with the number 1.

Unit	Milliliter	Centiliter	Deciliter	Liter	Decaliter	Hectoliter	Kiloliter
Symbol	mL	cL	dL	L	daL	hL	kL
Value	0.001 L	0.01 L	0.1 L	1 L	10 L	100 L	1,000 L

To change a measure from one unit to another, start by using the chart to find the relationship between the two units.

EXAMPLE

Complete each equation.

a. 245 mL = ■ L

1 mL = 0.001 L

245 × 0.001 = 0.245 ← **To change mL to L, multiply by 0.001.**

245 mL = 0.245 L

b. ■ mL = 4.5 kL

1 kL = 1,000,000 mL

4.5 × 1,000,000 = 4,500,000 ← **To change kL to mL, multiply by 1,000,000.**

4,500,000 mL = 4.5 kL

EXERCISES

Complete each equation.

1. 1 L = ■ mL
2. 1 mL = ■ kL
3. 1 kL = ■ L
4. 1 kL = ■ mL
5. 200 L = ■ kL
6. 1.3 kL = ■ mL
7. ■ L = 30 kL
8. ■ kL = 5.2 L
9. 180 mL = ■ L
10. ■ kL = 240 L
11. 0.6 mL = ■ L
12. ■ kL = 106,000 L
13. 72 kL = ■ mL
14. ■ mL = 1.5 kL
15. ■ kL = 450,000 mL
16. 4,900 L = ■ kL
17. ■ kL = 200,000 mL
18. ■ L = 8 mL
19. 4.2 L = ■ mL
20. 57,000,000 mL = ■ L
21. 28,000 kL = ■ L
22. ■ mL = 9,000 L
23. 4,000 L = ■ mL
24. 870 L = ■ kL

Metric Units of Mass

The basic unit of mass in the metric system is the gram. All the other units are based on the gram. In the chart below, each unit is 10 times the value of the unit to its left.

Unit	Milligram	Centigram	Decigram	Gram	Decagram	Hectogram	Kilogram
Symbol	mg	cg	dg	g	dag	hg	kg
Value	0.001 g	0.01 g	0.1 g	1 g	10 g	100 g	1,000 g

To change a measure from one unit to another, start by using the chart to find the relationship between the two units.

EXAMPLE

Complete each equation.

a. 2.3 kg = ■ g

1 kg = 1,000 g

2.3 × 1,000 = 2,300 ← **To change kg to g, multiply by 1,000.**

2.3 kg = 2,300 g

b. ■ g = 250 mg

1 mg = 0.001 = 0.25

250 × 0.001 = 0.25 ←**To change mg to g, multiply by 0.001.**

0.25 g = 250 mg

EXERCISES

Complete each equation.

1. 1 mg = ■ g

2. 1 g = ■ kg

3. 1 mg = ■ kg

4. 1 g = ■ mg

5. 1 kg = ■ g

6. 1 kg = ■ mg

7. ■ g = 8 mg

8. 1,500 mg = ■ kg

9. ■ kg = 200,000 g

10. 72 g = ■ kg

11. ■ mg = 5.2 kg

12. 180 mg = ■ g

13. ■ mg = 3.7 g

14. 0.6 mg = ■ g

15. 370 g = ■ kg

16. ■ kg = 300,000 mg

17. 900 g = ■ mg

18. ■ kg = 5.7 mg

19. 120 g = ■ kg

20. ■ kg = 440 g

21. ■ kg = 1,006,000 mg

22. 0.009 kg = ■ mg

23. 0.2 mg = ■ g

24. 8.6 kg = ■ g

25. 800 g = ■ mg

26. 1.7 kg = ■ g

27. ■ mg = 6.2 kg

Tables

Table 1 Measures

Metric	Customary
Length	**Length**
10 millimeters (mm) = 1 centimeter (cm) 100 cm = 1 meter (m) 1,000 mm = 1 m 1,000 m = 1 kilometer (km)	12 inches (in.) = 1 foot (ft) 36 in. = 1 yard (yd) 3 ft = 1 yd 5,280 ft = 1 mile (mi) 1,760 yd = 1 mi
Area	**Area**
100 square millimeters (mm^2) = 1 square centimeter (cm^2) 10,000 cm^2 = 1 square meter (m^2)	144 square inches $(in.^2)$ = 1 square foot (ft^2) 9 ft^2 = 1 square yard (yd^2) 4,840 yd^2 = 1 acre
Volume	**Volume**
1,000 cubic millimeters (mm^3) = 1 cubic centimeter (cm^3) 1,000,000 cm^3 = 1 cubic meter (m^3)	1,728 cubic inches $(in.^3)$ = 1 cubic foot (ft^3) 27 ft^3 = 1 cubic yard (yd^3)
Mass	**Mass**
1,000 milligrams (mg) = 1 gram (g) 1,000 g = 1 kilogram (kg)	16 ounces (oz) = 1 pound (lb) 2,000 lb = 1 ton (t)
Liquid Capacity	**Liquid Capacity**
1,000 milliliters (mL) = 1 liter (L)	8 fluid ounces (fl oz) = 1 cup (c) 2 c = 1 pint (pt) 2 pt = 1 quart (qt) 4 qt = 1 gallon (gal)

Time
1 minute (min) = 60 seconds (s) 1 hour (h) = 60 min 1 day (d) = 24 h 1 year (yr) = 365 d

Table 2 Reading Math Symbols

Symbol	Meaning	Page
$\approx$	is approximately equal to	p. 5
$-$	minus (subtraction)	p. 5
$=$	is equal to	p. 6
$+$	plus (addition)	p. 6
$\times, \cdot$	times (multiplication)	p. 6
$\stackrel{?}{=}$	Is the statement true?	p. 12
$(\ )$	parentheses for grouping	p. 12
$\div$	divide (division)	p. 19
$\neq$	is not equal to	p. 22
$\lvert a \rvert$	absolute value of *a*	p. 33
$-a$	opposite of *a*	p. 33
$>$	is greater than	p. 34
$<$	is less than	p. 34
$\geq$	is greater than or equal to	p. 41
$\leq$	is less than or equal to	p. 41
$[\ ]$	brackets for grouping	p. 51
a^n	*n*th power of *a*	p. 131
^	raised to a power (calculator key)	p. 132
$\frac{1}{a}$	reciprocal of *a*	p. 207
$^\circ$	degree(s)	p. 228
$a : b$	ratio of *a* to *b*	p. 241
$\sim$	is similar to	p. 267
$\triangle ABC$	triangle with vertices *ABC*	p. 267
$\angle A$	angle with vertex *A*	p. 268
%	percent	p. 291
$\overleftrightarrow{AB}$	line *AB*	p. 347
$\overrightarrow{AB}$	ray *AB*	p. 347
$\overline{AB}$	segment *AB*	p. 347
$\parallel$	is parallel to	p. 348
$\angle ABC$	angle with sides *BA* and *BC*	p. 351
$m\angle ABC$	measure of angle *ABC*	p. 351
$\perp$	is perpendicular to	p. 357
$\cong$	is congruent to	p. 378
AB	length of segment $\overline{AB}$	p. 380
d	diameter	p. 383
r	radius	p. 383
$\overset{\frown}{AB}$	arc *AB*	p. 384
ℓ	slant, length	p. 407
w	width	p. 407
A	area	p. 408
b	base length	p. 408
h	height	p. 408
b_1, b_2	base lengths of a trapezoid	p. 413
C	circumference	p. 419
π	pi, an irrational number approximately equal to 3.14	p. 419
$\sqrt{x}$	nonnegative square root of *x*	p. 426
B	area of base	p. 449
V	volume	p. 449
$\ldots$	and so on	p. 474
P	perimeter	p. 507
(a, b)	ordered pair with *x*-coordinate *a* and *y*-coordinate *b*	p. 521
$F \to F'$	*F* maps onto *F'*	p. 549
A'	image of *A*, *A* prime	p. 549
$P(\text{event})$	probability of the event	p. 629
$n!$	*n* factorial	p. 661

Tables

Table 3 Squares and Square Roots

Number n	Square n^2	Positive Square Root $\sqrt{n}$	Number n	Square n^2	Positive Square Root $\sqrt{n}$
1	1	1.000	**51**	2,601	7.141
2	4	1.414	**52**	2,704	7.211
3	9	1.732	**53**	2,809	7.280
4	16	2.000	**54**	2,916	7.348
5	25	2.236	**55**	3,025	7.416
6	36	2.449	**56**	3,136	7.483
7	49	2.646	**57**	3,249	7.550
8	64	2.828	**58**	3,364	7.616
9	81	3.000	**59**	3,481	7.681
10	100	3.162	**60**	3,600	7.746
11	121	3.317	**61**	3,721	7.810
12	144	3.464	**62**	3,844	7.874
13	169	3.606	**63**	3,969	7.937
14	196	3.742	**64**	4,096	8.000
15	225	3.873	**65**	4,225	8.062
16	256	4.000	**66**	4,356	8.124
17	289	4.123	**67**	4,489	8.185
18	324	4.243	**68**	4,624	8.246
19	361	4.359	**69**	4,761	8.307
20	400	4.472	**70**	4,900	8.367
21	441	4.583	**71**	5,041	8.426
22	484	4.690	**72**	5,184	8.485
23	529	4.796	**73**	5,329	8.544
24	576	4.899	**74**	5,476	8.602
25	625	5.000	**75**	5,625	8.660
26	676	5.099	**76**	5,776	8.718
27	729	5.196	**77**	5,929	8.775
28	784	5.292	**78**	6,084	8.832
29	841	5.385	**79**	6,241	8.888
30	900	5.477	**80**	6,400	8.944
31	961	5.568	**81**	6,561	9.000
32	1,024	5.657	**82**	6,724	9.055
33	1,089	5.745	**83**	6,889	9.110
34	1,156	5.831	**84**	7,056	9.165
35	1,225	5.916	**85**	7,225	9.220
36	1,296	6.000	**86**	7,396	9.274
37	1,369	6.083	**87**	7,569	9.327
38	1,444	6.164	**88**	7,744	9.381
39	1,521	6.245	**89**	7,921	9.434
40	1,600	6.325	**90**	8,100	9.487
41	1,681	6.403	**91**	8,281	9.539
42	1,764	6.481	**92**	8,464	9.592
43	1,849	6.557	**93**	8,649	9.644
44	1,936	6.633	**94**	8,836	9.695
45	2,025	6.708	**95**	9,025	9.747
46	2,116	6.782	**96**	9,216	9.798
47	2,209	6.856	**97**	9,409	9.849
48	2,304	6.928	**98**	9,604	9.899
49	2,401	7.000	**99**	9,801	9.950
50	2,500	7.071	**100**	10,000	10.000

Formulas and Properties

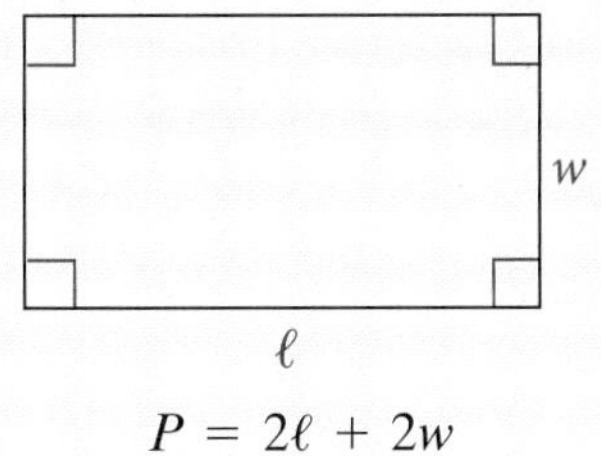

$P = 2\ell + 2w$
$A = \ell w$

Rectangle

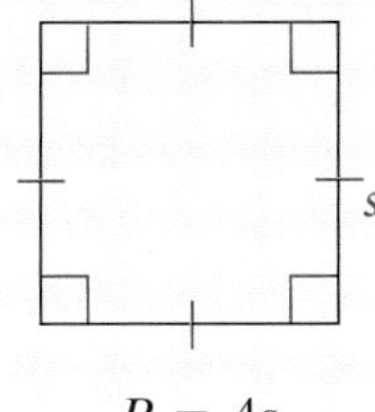

$P = 4s$
$A = s^2$

Square

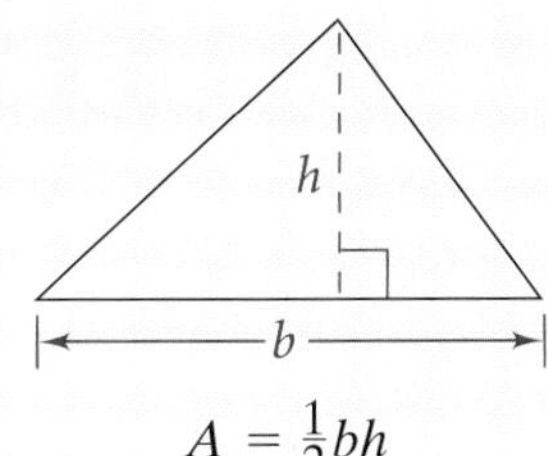

$A = \frac{1}{2}bh$

Triangle

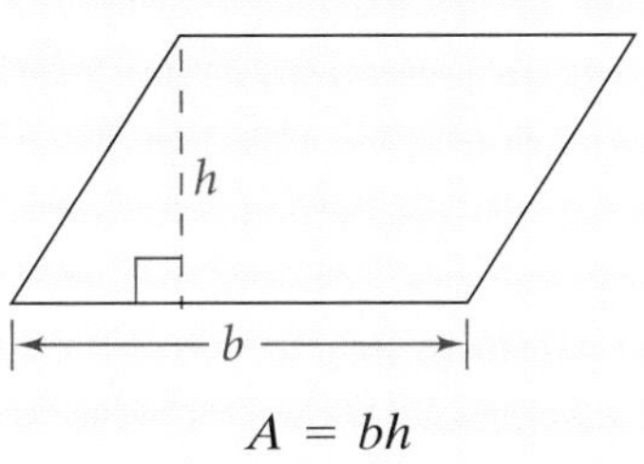

$A = bh$

Parallelogram

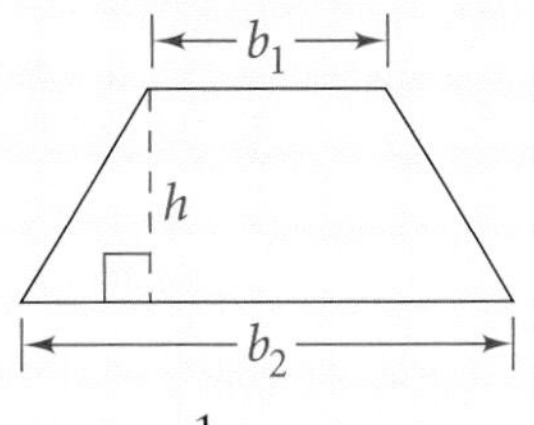

$A = \frac{1}{2}(b_1 + b_2)h$

Trapezoid

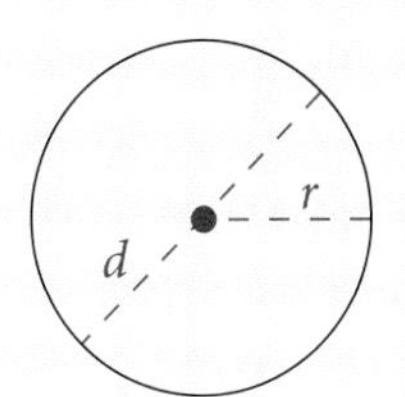

$C = 2\pi r$ or $C = \pi d$
$A = \pi r^2$

Circle

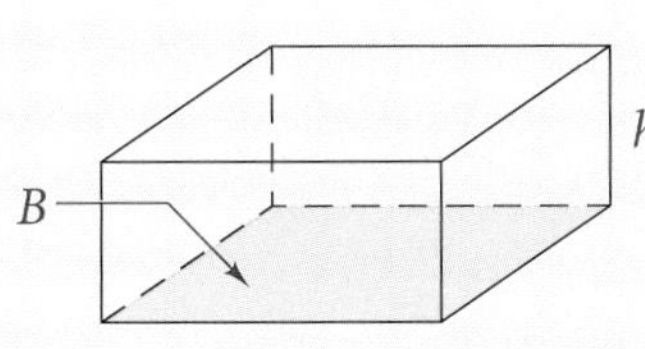

$V = Bh$

Rectangular Prism

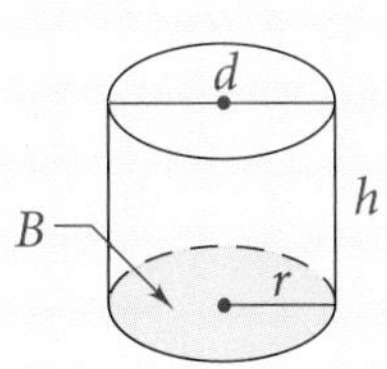

$V = Bh$

Cylinder

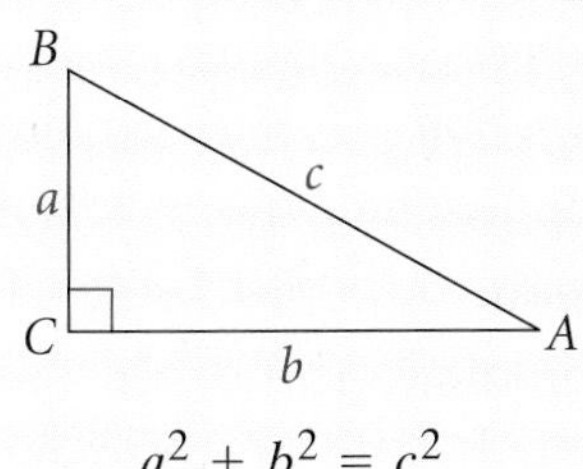

$a^2 + b^2 = c^2$

Pythagorean Theorem

Formulas and Properties

Properties of Real Numbers

Unless otherwise stated, the variables a, b, c, and d used in these properties can be replaced with any number represented on a number line.

Identity Properties

Addition $a + 0 = a$ and $0 + a = a$

Multiplication $a \cdot 1 = a$ and $1 \cdot a = a$

Commutative Properties

Addition $a + b = b + a$

Multiplication $a \cdot b = b \cdot a$

Associative Properties

Addition $(a + b) + c = a + (b + c)$

Multiplication $(a \cdot b) \cdot c = a \cdot (b \cdot c)$

Inverse Properties

Addition

$a + (-a) = 0$ and $-a + a = 0$

Multiplication

$a \cdot \frac{1}{a} = 1$ and $\frac{1}{a} \cdot a = 1$ $(a \neq 0)$

Distributive Properties

$a(b + c) = ab + ac$ $(b + c)a = ba + ca$

$a(b - c) = ab - ac$ $(b - c)a = ba - ca$

Properties of Equality

Addition If $a = b$, then $a + c = b + c$.

Subtraction If $a = b$, then $a - c = b - c$.

Multiplication If $a = b$, then $a \cdot c = b \cdot c$.

Division If $a = b$, and $c \neq 0$, then $\frac{a}{c} = \frac{b}{c}$.

Substitution If $a = b$, then b can replace a in any expression.

Reflexive $a = a$

Symmetric If $a = b$, then $b = a$.

Transitive If $a = b$ and $b = c$, then $a = c$.

Cross-Products Property

$\frac{a}{c} = \frac{b}{d}$ is equivalent to $ad = bc$.

Zero-Product Property

If $ab = 0$, then $a = 0$ or $b = 0$.

Closure Property

$a + b$ is a unique real number.

ab is a unique real number.

Density Property

Between any two rational numbers, there is at least one other rational number.

Properties of Inequality

Addition If $a > b$, then $a + c > b + c$.
If $a < b$, then $a + c < b + c$.

Subtraction If $a > b$, then $a - c > b - c$.
If $a < b$, then $a - c < b - c$.

Multiplication

If $a > b$ and $c > 0$, then $ac > bc$.

If $a < b$ and $c > 0$, then $ac < bc$.

If $a > b$ and $c < 0$, then $ac < bc$.

If $a < b$ and $c < 0$, then $ac > bc$.

Division

If $a > b$ and $c > 0$, then $\frac{a}{c} > \frac{b}{c}$.

If $a < b$ and $c > 0$, then $\frac{a}{c} < \frac{b}{c}$.

If $a > b$ and $c < 0$, then $\frac{a}{c} < \frac{b}{c}$.

If $a < b$ and $c < 0$, then $\frac{a}{c} > \frac{b}{c}$.

Transitive If $a > b$ and $b > c$, then $a > c$.

English/Spanish Illustrated Glossary

EXAMPLES

Absolute value (p. 34) The absolute value of a number is its distance from 0 on a number line.

Valor absoluto (p. 34) El valor absoluto de un número es su distancia del 0 en una recta numérica.

-7 is 7 units from 0, so $|-7| = 7$.

Acute angle (p. 352) An acute angle is an angle with a measure between 0° and 90°.

Ángulo agudo (p. 352) Un ángulo agudo es un ángulo que mide entre 0° y 90°.

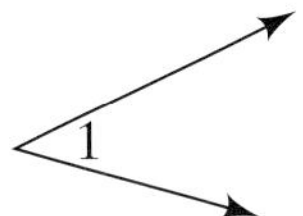

$0° < m\angle 1 < 90°$

Acute triangle (p. 364) An acute triangle has three acute angles.

Triángulo acutángulo (p. 364) Un triángulo acutángulo tiene tres ángulos agudos.

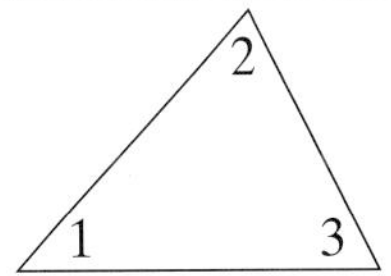

$\angle 1$, $\angle 2$, and $\angle 3$ are acute.

Addition Property of Equality (p. 83) The Addition Property of Equality states that if the same value is added to each side of an equation, the results are equal.

Propiedad aditiva de la igualdad (p. 83) La propiedad aditiva de la igualdad establece que si se suma el mismo valor a cada lado de una ecuación, los resultados son iguales.

Since $\frac{20}{2} = 10$, $\frac{20}{2} + 3 = 10 + 3$.
If $a = b$, then $a + c = b + c$.

Additive inverse (p. 39) Two numbers whose sum is 0 are additive inverses.

Inverso aditivo (p. 39) Dos números cuya suma es 0 son inversos aditivos.

$(-5) + 5 = 0$

Adjacent angles (p. 353) Adjacent angles share a vertex and a side but have no interior points in common.

Ángulos adyacentes (p. 353) Los ángulos adyacentes comparten un vértice y un lado, pero no tienen puntos interiores en común.

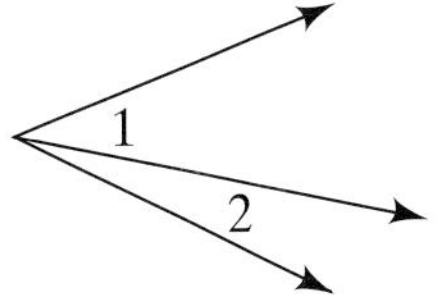

$\angle 1$ and $\angle 2$ are adjacent angles.

Algebraic expression (p. 71) An algebraic expression is a mathematical phrase that uses variables, numbers, and operation symbols.

Expresión algebraica (p. 71) Una expresión algebraica es un enunciado matemático que usa variables, números y símbolos de operaciones.

$2x - 5$ is an algebraic expression.

EXAMPLES

Angle (p. 351) An angle is formed by two rays with a common endpoint called a vertex.

Ángulo (p. 351) Un ángulo está formado por dos rayos que tienen un punto final común llamado vértice.

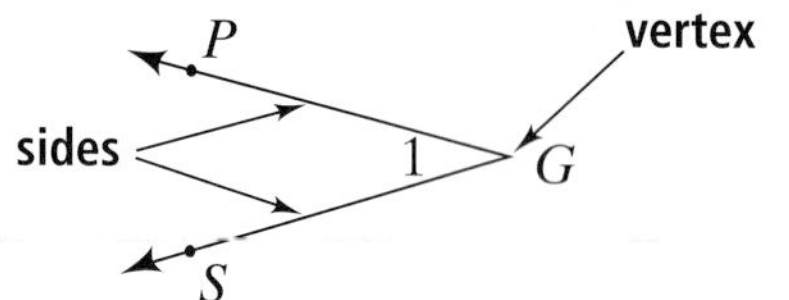

$\angle 1$ is made up of $\overrightarrow{GP}$ and $\overrightarrow{GS}$ with common endpoint G.

Angle bisector (p. 358) An angle bisector is a ray that divides an angle into angles of equal measure.

Bisectriz de un ángulo (p. 358) La bisectriz de un ángulo es un rayo que divide un ángulo en ángulos de igual medida.

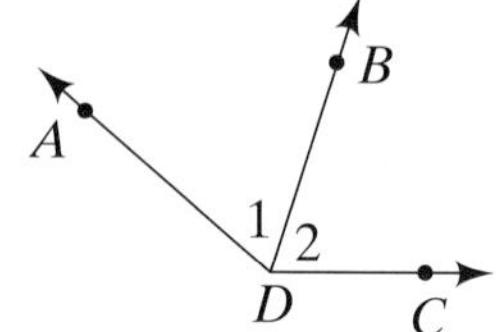

$\overrightarrow{DB}$ bisects $\angle ADC$, so $\angle 1 \cong \angle 2$.

Angle of rotation (p. 560) The angle of rotation is the angle measure that a figure rotates to fit exactly on top of itself.

Ángulo de rotación (p. 560) El ángulo de rotación es la medida angular que rota una figura para calzar exactamente sobre ella misma.

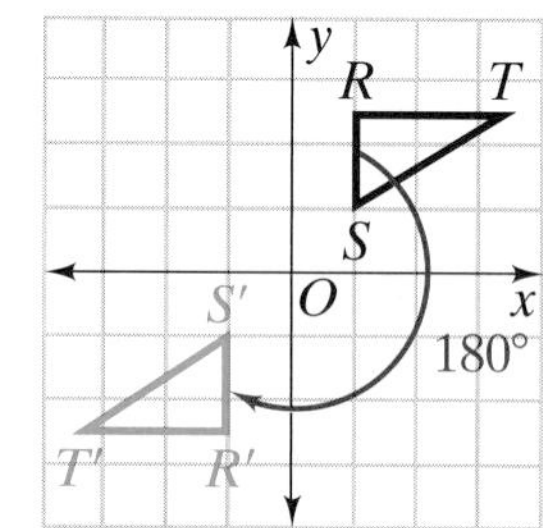

$\triangle RST$ has been rotated 180° to $\triangle R'S'T'$.

Arc (p. 358) An arc is part of a circle.

Arco (p. 358) Un arco es parte de un círculo.

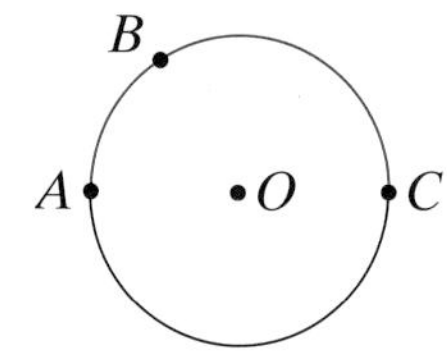

$\overset{\frown}{AB}$ is an arc of circle O. $\overset{\frown}{ABC}$ is a semicircle of circle O.

Area (p. 404) The area of a figure is the number of square units it encloses.

Área (p. 404) El área de una figura es el número de unidades cuadradas que contiene.

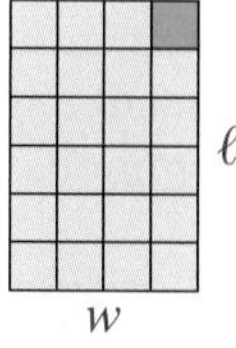

The area of each square is 1 ft^2. $\ell = 6$ ft and $w = 4$ ft, so the area is 24 ft^2.

Arithmetic sequence (p. 474) In an arithmetic sequence, each term is the result of adding a fixed number (called the common difference) to the previous term.

Progresión aritmética (p. 474) En una progresión aritmética, cada término es el resultado de sumar un número fijo al término anterior.

The sequence 4, 10, 16, 22, 28, . . . is an arithmetic sequence. You add 6 to each term to find the next term.

EXAMPLES

Associative Property of Addition (p. 12) The Associative Property of Addition states that changing the grouping of the addends does not change the sum.

Propiedad asociativa de la suma (p. 12) La propiedad asociativa de la suma establece que cambiar la agrupación de los sumandos no cambia la suma.

$(2 + 3) + 7 = 2 + (3 + 7)$

$(a + b) + c = a + (b + c)$

Associative Property of Multiplication (p. 18) The Associative Property of Multiplication states that changing the grouping of factors does not change the product.

Propiedad asociativa de la multiplicación (p. 18) La propiedad asociativa de la multiplicación establece que cambiar la agrupación de los factores no altera el producto.

$(3 \cdot 4) \cdot 5 = 3 \cdot (4 \cdot 5)$

$(a \cdot b) \cdot c = a \cdot (b \cdot c)$

B

Balance (p. 500) The balance of an account is the principal plus the interest earned.

Saldo (p. 500) El saldo de una cuenta es el capital más los intereses ganados.

You deposit \$100 and earn \$5 interest. Your balance is \$105.

Base (p. 131) When a number is written in exponential form, the number that is used as a factor is the base.

Base (p. 131) Cuando un número se escribe en forma exponencial, el número que se usa como factor es la base.

$5^4 = 5 \times 5 \times 5 \times 5$

└ base

Bases of three-dimensional figures (pp. 437, 438) See *Cone*, *Cylinder*, *Prism*, and *Pyramid*.

Bases de figuras tridimensionales (pp. 437, 438) Ver *Cone*, *Cylinder*, *Prism* y *Pyramid*.

Bases of two-dimensional figures (pp. 407, 408, 414) See *Parallelogram*, *Triangle*, and *Trapezoid*.

Bases de figuras bidimensionales (pp. 407, 408, 414) Ver *Parallelogram*, *Triangle* y *Trapezoid*.

EXAMPLES

Benchmark (p. 187) A benchmark is a convenient number used to replace fractions that are less than 1.

Punto de referencia (p. 187) Un punto de referencia es un número conveniente que se usa para reemplazar fracciones menores que 1.

Using benchmarks, you would estimate $\frac{5}{6} + \frac{4}{9}$ as $1 + \frac{1}{2}$.

Biased question (p. 597) A biased question is a question that makes one answer appear better than another.

Pregunta tendenciosa (p. 597) Una pregunta tendenciosa es una pregunta que hace que una respuesta parezca mejor que otra.

"Do you prefer good food or junk food?"

Box-and-whisker plot (p. 586) A box-and-whisker plot is a graph that summarizes a data set along a number line. There is a box in the middle and whiskers at either side.

Gráfica de caja y brazos (p. 586) Una gráfica de caja y brazos es un diagrama que resume un conjunto de datos usando una recta línea. Hay una caja en el centro y extensiones a cada lado.

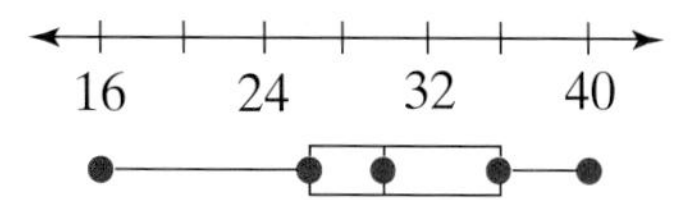

The box-and-whisker plot uses these data: 16 19 26 26 27 29 30 31 34 34 38 39 40

The lower quartile is 26. The median is 30. The upper quartile is 36.

Capture/recapture (p. 602) Capture/recapture is a sampling technique that uses proportions to estimate animal populations.

Captura/recaptura (p. 602) Captura/recaptura es una técnica de muestreo que usa las proporciones para estimar poblaciones animales.

Cell (p. 579) A cell is a box where a row and a column meet.

Celda (p. 579) Una celda es una caja donde se unen una fila y una columna.

	A	B	C	D	E
1	0.50	0.70	0.60	0.50	2.30
2	1.50	0.50	2.75	2.50	7.25

Column C and row 2 meet at the shaded box, cell C2.

Center of a circle (p. 383) A circle is named by its center.

Centro de un círculo (p. 383) Un círculo es denominado por su centro.

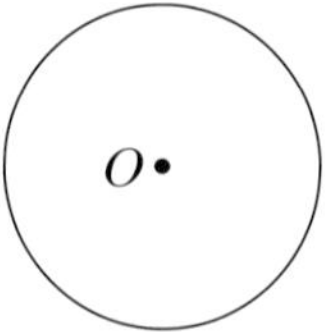

Circle O

EXAMPLES

Center of a sphere (p. 438) See *Sphere*.

Centro de una esfera (p. 438) Ver *Sphere*.

Center of rotation (p. 559) The center of rotation is a fixed point about which a figure is rotated.

Centro de rotación (p. 559) El centro de rotación es un punto fijo alrededor del cual rota una figura.

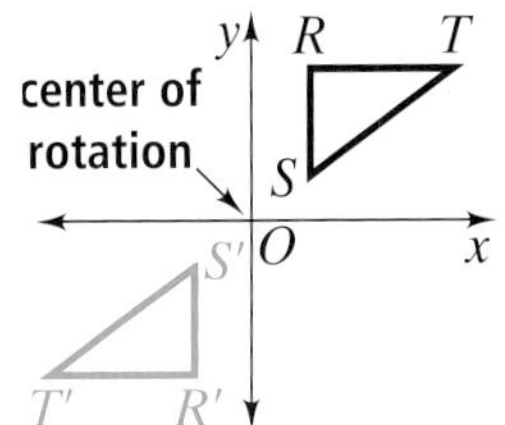

O is the center of rotation.

Central angle (p. 383) A central angle is an angle with its vertex at the center of a circle.

Ángulo central (p. 383) Un ángulo central es un ángulo que tiene el vértice en el centro de un círculo.

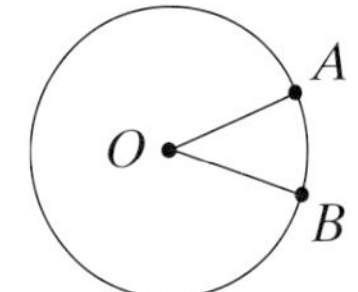

$\angle AOB$ is a central angle of circle *O*.

Chord (p. 383) A chord is a segment that has both endpoints on the circle.

Cuerda (p. 383) Una cuerda es un segmento que tiene ambos extremos sobre el círculo.

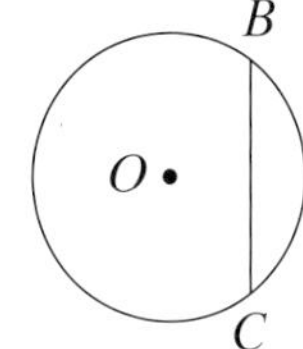

$\overline{CB}$ is a chord of circle *O*.

Circle (p. 383) A circle is the set of points in a plane that are all the same distance from a given point called the center.

Círculo (p. 383) Un círculo es el conjunto de puntos de un plano que están a la misma distancia de un punto dado llamado centro.

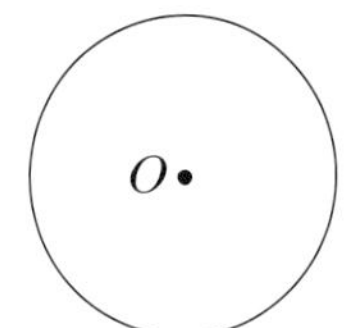

Circle graph (p. 388) A circle graph is a graph of data where a circle represents the whole.

Gráfica circular (p. 388) Una gráfica circular es una gráfica de datos donde un círculo representa el todo.

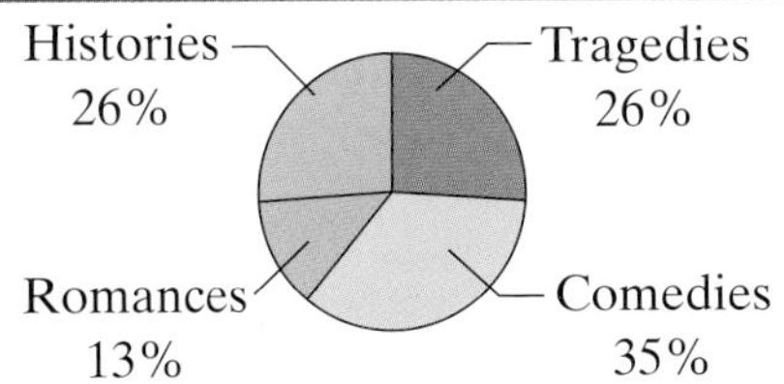

The circle graph represents the types of plays William Shakespeare wrote.

EXAMPLES

Circumference (p. 419) Circumference is the distance around a circle. You calculate the circumference of a circle by multiplying the diameter by π.

Circunferencia (p. 419) La circunferencia es la distancia alrededor de un círculo. La circunferencia de un círculo se calcula multiplicando el diámetro por π.

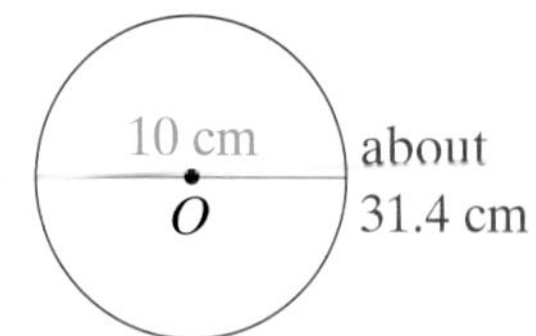

The circumference of a circle with a diameter of 10 cm is 10π, or approximately 31.4 cm.

Combination (p. 664) A combination is a grouping of objects in which the order of the objects does not matter.

Combinación (p. 664) Una combinación es una agrupación de objetos en que el orden de los objetos no tiene importancia.

You choose two vegetables from carrots, peas, and spinach. The possible combinations are: carrots and peas, carrots and spinach, and peas and spinach.

Commission (p. 324) A commission is pay that is equal to a percent of sales.

Comisión (p. 324) Una comisión es un pago que es igual a un porcentaje de las ventas.

A salesperson receives a 6% commission on sales of $200. Her commission is $12.

Commutative Property of Addition (p. 12) The Commutative Property of Addition states that changing the order of the addends does not change the sum.

Propiedad conmutativa de la suma (p. 12) La propiedad conmutativa de la suma establece que al cambiar el orden de los sumandos no se altera la suma.

$3 + 1 = 1 + 3$

$a + b = b + a$

Commutative Property of Multiplication (p. 18) The Commutative Property of Multiplication states that changing the order of the factors does not change the product.

Propiedad conmutativa de la multiplicación (p. 18) La propiedad conmutativa de la multiplicación establece que al cambiar el orden de los factores no se altera el producto.

$6 \cdot 3 = 3 \cdot 6$

$a \cdot b = b \cdot a$

Compass (p. 358) A compass is a geometric tool used to draw circles or arcs.

Compás (p. 358) Un compás es una herramienta que se usa en geometría para dibujar círculos o arcos.

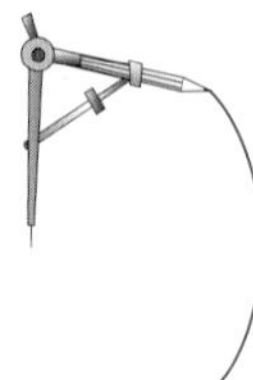

Compatible numbers (p. 6) Compatible numbers are numbers that are easy to compute mentally.

Números compatibles (p. 6) Los números compatibles son números con los que se puede calcular mentalmente con facilidad.

Estimate $151 \div 14.6$.

$151 \approx 150$, $14.6 \approx 15$

$150 \div 15 = 10$

$151 \div 14.6 \approx 10$

EXAMPLES

Complement (p. 630) The complement of an event is the collection of outcomes not contained in the event.

Complemento (p. 630) El complemento de un suceso es la colección de resultados que el suceso no incluye.

The event *no rain* is the complement of the event *rain*.

Complementary (p. 352) Two angles are complementary if the sum of their measures is 90°.

Complementario (p. 352) Dos ángulos son complementarios si la suma de sus medidas es 90°.

$\angle BCA$ and $\angle CAB$ are complementary angles.

Composite number (p. 146) A composite number is a whole number greater than 1 that has more than two factors.

Número compuesto (p. 146) Un número compuesto es un número entero mayor que 1, que tiene más de dos factores.

24 is a composite number. Its factors are 1, 2, 3, 4, 6, 8, 12, and 24.

Compound event (p. 653) A compound event is an event that consists of two or more events. The probability of a compound event can be found by multiplying the probability of one event by the probability of a second event.

Suceso compuesto (p. 653) Un suceso compuesto es un suceso que está formado por dos o más sucesos. La probabilidad de un suceso compuesto se puede hallar al multiplicar la probabilidad de un suceso por la probabilidad de un segundo suceso.

If $P(A) = \frac{1}{3}$ and $P(B) = \frac{1}{2}$, then $P(A \text{ and } B) = \frac{1}{6}$.

Compound interest (p. 500) Compound interest is interest paid on the original principal and on any interest that has been left in the account. You can use the formula $B = p(1 + r)^t$ where B is the balance in the account, p is the principal, r is the annual interest rate, and t is the time in years that the account earns interest.

Interés compuesto (p. 500) El interés compuesto es el interés que se paga sobre el principal original y sobre cualquier interés que ha quedado en la cuenta. Se puede usar la fórmula $B = p(1 + r)^t$ donde B es el saldo en la cuenta, p es el principal, r es la tasa de interés anual y t es el tiempo en años en que la cuenta gana interés.

You deposit \$500 in an account earning 5% annual interest.

The balance after six years is $500\ (1 + 0.05)^6$, or \$670.05.

Cone (p. 438) A cone is a three-dimensional figure with one circular base and one vertex.

Cono (p. 438) Un cono es una figura tridimensional con una base circular y un vértice.

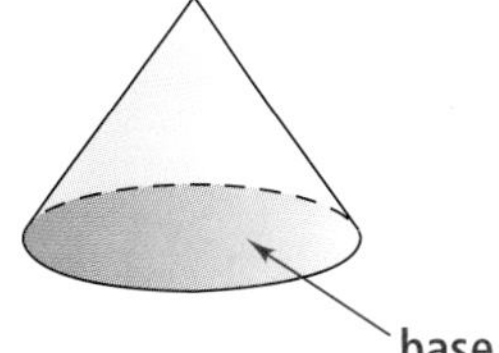

EXAMPLES

Congruent angles (p. 353) Congruent angles are angles that have the same measure.

Ángulos congruentes (p. 353) Los ángulos congruentes son ángulos que tienen la misma medida.

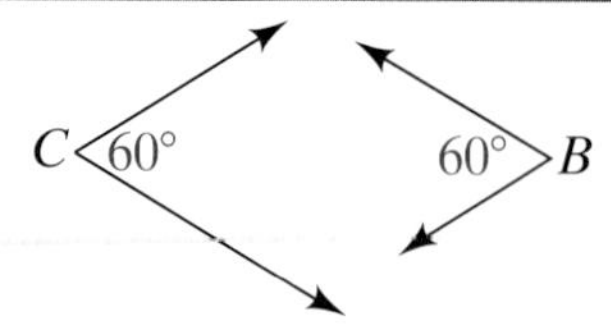

$\angle B \cong \angle C$

Congruent polygons (p. 378) Congruent polygons are polygons with the same size and shape.

Polígonos congruentes (p. 378) Los polígonos congruentes son polígonos que tienen el mismo tamaño y forma.

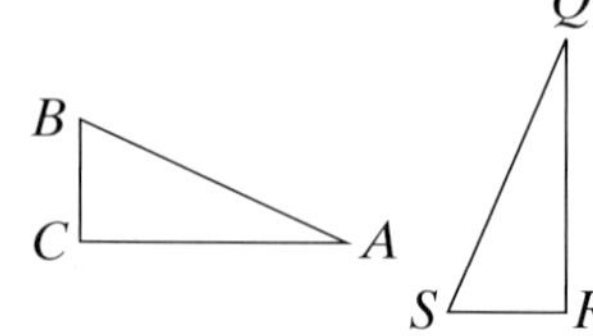

$\triangle ABC \cong \triangle QSR$

Congruent sides (p. 363) Congruent sides have the same length.

Lados congruentes (p. 363) Los lados congruentes tienen la misma longitud.

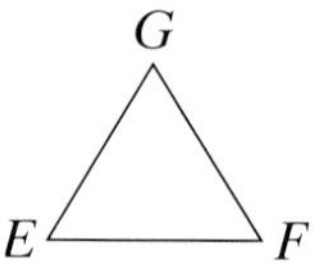

$\triangle EFG$ is an equilateral triangle.
$\overline{EF} \cong \overline{FG} \cong \overline{GE}$

Conjecture (p. 475) A conjecture is a prediction that suggests what can be expected to happen.

Conjetura (p. 475) Una conjetura es una predicción que sugiere lo que se puede esperar que ocurra.

Every clover has three leaves.

Coordinate plane (p. 521) A coordinate plane is formed by a horizontal number line called the x-axis and a vertical number line called the y-axis.

Plano de coordenadas (p. 521) Un plano de coordenadas está formado por una recta numérica horizontal llamada eje de x y por una recta numérica vertical llamada eje de y.

Corresponding parts (p. 378) Corresponding parts of congruent polygons are congruent.

Partes correspondientes (p. 378) Las partes correspondientes de los polígonos congruentes son congruentes.

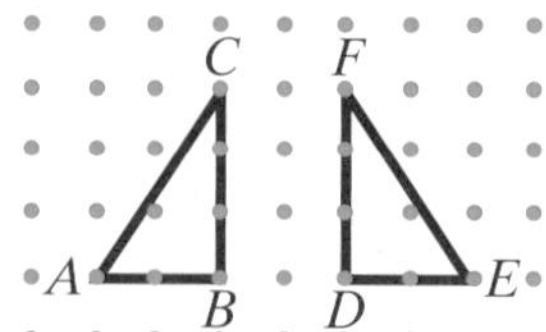

$\overline{AB} \cong \overline{ED}, \overline{BC} \cong \overline{DF}, \overline{CA} \cong \overline{FE}$
$\angle A \cong \angle E, \angle B \cong \angle D, \angle C \cong \angle F$
$\triangle ABC \cong \triangle EDF$

EXAMPLES

Counting principle (p. 648) If there are m ways of making one choice from a first situation and n ways of making a choice from a second situation, then there are $m \times n$ ways to make the first choice followed by the second.

Principio de conteo (p. 648) Si hay m maneras de hacer una elección para una primera situación y n maneras de hacer una elección para una segunda situación, entonces hay $m \times n$ maneras de hacer la primera elección seguida de la segunda.

Toss a coin and roll a standard number cube. The total number of possible outcomes is $2 \times 6 = 12$.

Cross products (p. 257) For two ratios, the cross products are found by multiplying the denominator of one ratio by the numerator of the other ratio.

Productos cruzados (p. 257) En dos razones, los productos cruzados se hallan al multiplicar el denominador de una razón por el numerador de la otra razón.

In the proportion $\frac{2}{5} = \frac{10}{25}$, the cross products are $2 \cdot 25$ and $5 \cdot 10$.

Cube (p. 437) A cube is a rectangular prism whose faces are all squares.

Cubo (p. 437) Un cubo es un prisma rectangular cuyas caras son todas cuadrados.

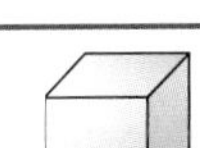
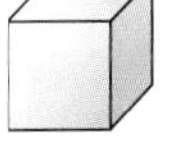

Cubic unit (p. 449) A cubic unit is a cube whose edges are one unit long.

Unidad cúbica (p. 449) Una unidad cúbica es un cubo cuyos lados tienen una unidad de longitud.

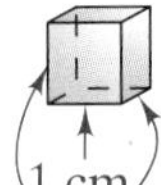

Cylinder (p. 438) A cylinder is a three-dimensional figure with two congruent parallel bases that are circles.

Cilindro (p. 438) Un cilindro es una figura tridimensional con dos bases congruentes paralelas que son círculos.

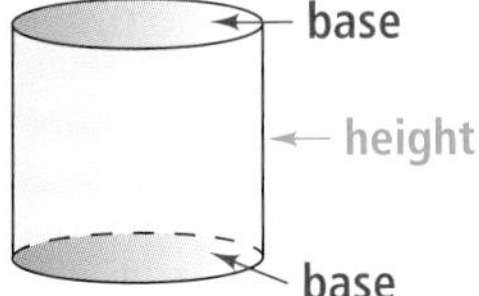

D

Decagon (p. 369) A decagon is a polygon with 10 sides.

Decágono (p. 369) Un decágono es un polígono que tiene 10 lados.

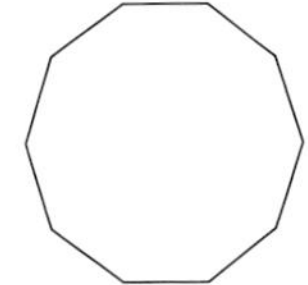

	EXAMPLES
Dependent events (p. 655) Two events are dependent events if the occurrence of one event affects the probability of the occurrence of the other event. **Sucesos dependientes (p. 655)** Dos sucesos son dependientes si el acontecimiento de uno afecta la probabilidad de que el otro ocurra.	Suppose you draw two marbles, one after the other, from a bag. If you do *not* replace the first marble before drawing the second marble, the events are dependent.
Diameter (p. 383) A diameter is a segment that passes through the center of a circle and has both endpoints on the circle. **Diámetro (p. 383)** Un diámetro es un segmento que pasa por el centro de un círculo y que tiene ambos extremos sobre el círculo.	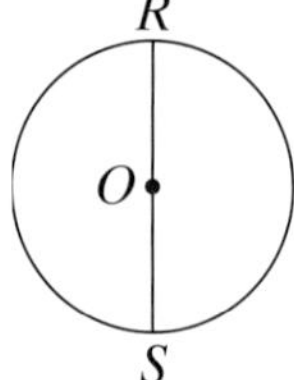 $\overline{RS}$ is a diameter of circle O.
Discount (p. 329) The difference between the original price and the sale price of an item is called the discount. **Descuento (p. 329)** Se llama descuento a la diferencia entre el precio de un artículo y su precio de venta.	A \$20 book is discounted by \$2.50 to sell for \$17.50.
Distributive Property (p. 51) The Distributive Property shows how multiplication affects an addition or subtraction: $a(b + c) = ab + ac$. **Propiedad distributiva (p. 51)** La propiedad distributiva muestra cómo la multiplicación afecta a una suma o a una resta: $a(b + c) = ab + ac$.	$2\left(3 + \frac{1}{2}\right) = 2 \cdot 3 + 2 \cdot \frac{1}{2}$ $8(5 - 3) = 8 \cdot 5 - 8 \cdot 3$
Divisible (p. 141) A whole number is divisible by a second whole number if the first number can be divided by the second number with a remainder of 0. **Divisible (p. 141)** Un número entero es divisible por un segundo número entero si el primer número se puede dividir por el segundo número y el residuo es 0.	16 is divisible by 1, 2, 4, 8, and 16.
Division Property of Equality (p. 88) The Division Property of Equality states that if both sides of an equation are divided by the same nonzero number, the results are equal. **Propiedad de división de la igualdad (p. 88)** La propiedad de división de la igualdad establece que si ambos lados de una ecuación se dividen por el mismo número distinto de cero, los resultados son iguales.	Since $3(2) = 6, 3(2) \div 2 = 6 \div 2$. If $a = b$ and $c \neq 0$, then $\frac{a}{c} = \frac{b}{c}$.

EXAMPLES

Double bar graph (p. 580) A double bar graph is a graph that uses bars to compare two sets of data.

Gráfica de doble barra (p. 580) Una gráfica de doble barra es una gráfica que usa barras para comparar dos conjuntos de datos.

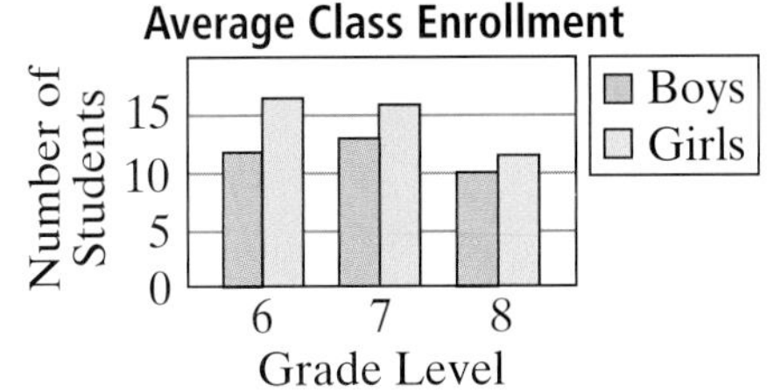

This double bar graph shows class size for grades 6, 7, and 8 for boys and girls.

Double line graph (p. 580) A double line graph is a graph that compares changes over time for two sets of data.

Gráfica de doble línea (p. 580) Una gráfica de doble línea es una gráfica que compara los cambios de dos conjuntos de datos a través del tiempo.

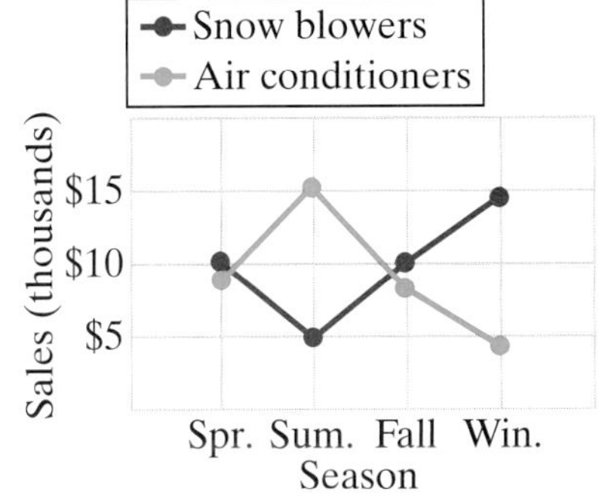

This double line graph represents seasonal air conditioner and snow blower sales (in thousands of dollars) for a large department store chain.

E

Edge (p. 437) An edge is a segment formed by the intersection of two faces of a three-dimensional figure.

Arista (p. 437) Una arista es un segmento formado por la intersección de dos caras de una figura tridimensional.

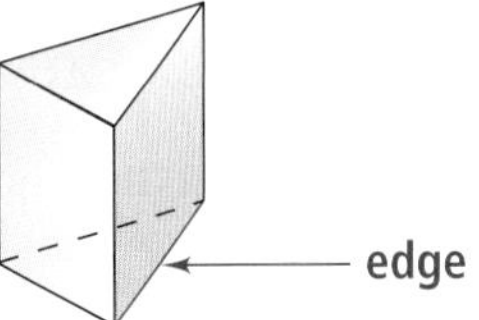

Equal ratios (p. 242) Equal ratios name the same number. Equal ratios written as fractions are equivalent fractions.

Razones iguales (p. 242) Las razones iguales indican el mismo número. Las razones iguales escritas como fracciones son fracciones equivalentes.

The ratios $\frac{4}{7}$ and $\frac{8}{14}$ are equal.

Equation (p. 77) An equation is a mathematical sentence with an equal sign.

Ecuación (p. 77) Una ecuación es una oración matemática con un signo igual.

$27 \div 9 = 3$ and $x + 10 = 8$ are examples of equations.

EXAMPLES

Equilateral triangle (p. 363) An equilateral triangle is a triangle with three congruent sides.

Triángulo equilátero (p. 363) Un triángulo equilátero es un triángulo que tiene tres lados congruentes.

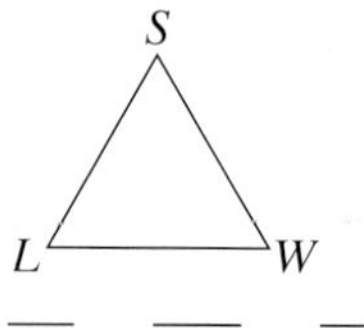

$\overline{SL} \cong \overline{LW} \cong \overline{WS}$

Equivalent fractions (p. 151) Equivalent fractions are fractions that name the same amount.

Fracciones equivalentes (p. 151) Las fracciones equivalentes son fracciones que indican la misma cantidad.

$\frac{1}{2}$ and $\frac{25}{50}$ are equivalent fractions.

Evaluating expressions (p. 92) To evaluate an expression, replace each variable with a number. Then follow the Order of Operations.

Evaluación de una expresión (p. 92) Para evaluar una expresión, se reemplaza cada variable con un número. Luego se sigue el orden de las operaciones.

To evaluate the expression $3x + 2$ for $x = 4$, substitute 4 for x.
$3x + 2 = 3(4) + 2 = 14$

Event (p. 629) A collection of possible outcomes is an event.

Suceso (p. 629) Un suceso es un grupo de resultados posibles.

When you toss a coin, "heads" and "tails" are possible outcomes.

Experimental probability (p. 636) For a series of trials, the experimental probability of an event is the ratio of the number of times an event occurs to the total number of trials.

$$P(\text{event}) = \frac{\text{number of times an event occurs}}{\text{total number of trials}}$$

Probabilidad experimental (p. 636) En una serie de pruebas, la probabilidad experimental de un suceso es la razón del número de veces que ocurre un suceso al número total de pruebas.

$$\text{P(suceso)} = \frac{\text{número de veces que ocurre un suceso}}{\text{número total de pruebas}}$$

A basketball player makes 19 baskets in 28 attempts. The experimental probability that the player makes a basket is $\frac{19}{28} \approx 68\%$.

Exponent (p. 131) An exponent tells how many times a number, or base, is used as a factor.

Exponente (p. 131) Un exponente dice cuántas veces se usa como factor un número, o base.

exponent

$3^4 = 3 \times 3 \times 3 \times 3$
Read 3^4 as *three to the fourth power.*

F

Face (p. 437) A face is a flat surface of a three-dimensional figure that is shaped like a polygon.

Cara (p. 437) Una cara es una superficie plana de una figura tridimensional que tiene la forma de un polígono.

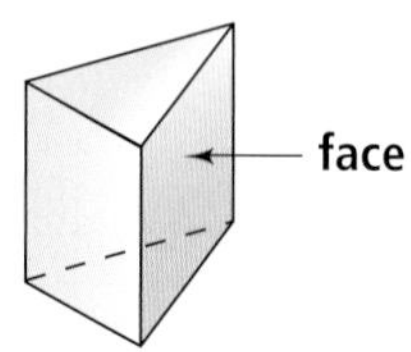

EXAMPLES

Factor (p. 146) A factor is a whole number that divides another whole number with a remainder of 0.

Divisor (p. 146) Un divisor es un número entero que divide a otro número entero y el residuo es 0.

1, 2, 3, 4, 6, 12, 18, and 36 are factors of 36.

Factorial (p. 661) A factorial is the product of all positive integers less than or equal to a number. The symbol for factorial is an exclamation point.

Factorial (p. 661) Una factorial es el producto de todos los enteros positivos menores o iguales que un número. El símbolo de factorial es un signo de cierre de exclamación.

$5! = 5 \times 4 \times 3 \times 2 \times 1 = 120$

Formula (p. 507) A formula is a rule that shows the relationship between two or more quantities.

Fórmula (p. 507) Una fórmula es una regla que muestra la relación entre dos o más cantidades.

The formula $P = 2l + 2w$ gives the perimeter of a rectangle in terms of its length and width.

Frequency table (p. 573) A frequency table is a table that lists each item in a data set with the number of times the item occurs.

Tabla de frecuencia (p. 573) Una tabla de frecuencia es una tabla que registra todos los elementos de un conjunto de datos y el número de veces que ocurre cada uno.

Household Telephones

Phones	Tally	Frequency
1	𝍸 III	8
2	𝍸 I	6
3	IIII	4

This frequency table shows the number of household telephones for a class of students.

Function (p. 484) A function is a relationship that assigns exactly one output value for each input value.

Función (p. 484) Una función es una relación que asigna exactamente un valor resultante a cada valor inicial.

Salary s is a function of the number of hours worked w. If you earn \$6/h, then your salary can be expressed by the function $s = 6w$.

G

Geometric sequence (p. 475) In a geometric sequence, each term is the result of multiplying the previous term by a fixed number (called the common ratio).

Progresión geométrica (p. 475) En una progresión geométrica, cada término es el resultado de la multiplicación del término anterior por un número fijo llamado rayón común.

The sequence 1, 3, 9, 27, 81, . . . is a geometric sequence. You multiply each term by 3 to find the next term.

EXAMPLES

Graph of an equation (p. 528) The graph of an equation is the graph of all the points with coordinates that are solutions of the equation.

Gráfica de una ecuación (p. 528) La gráfica de una ecuación es la gráfica de todos los puntos cuyas coordenadas son soluciones a la ecuación.

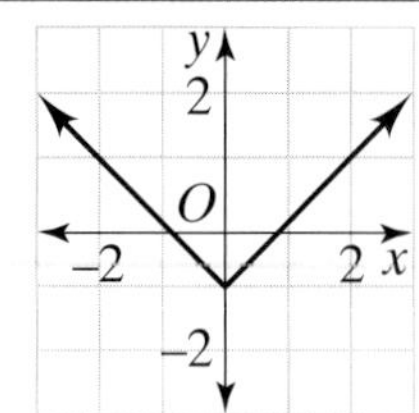

The coordinates of all the points on the graph satisfy the equation $y = |x| - 1$.

Greatest common factor (GCF) (p. 147) The greatest common factor of two or more numbers is the greatest number that is a factor of all of the numbers.

Máximo común divisor (MCD) (p. 147) El máximo común divisor de dos o más números es el mayor número que es divisor de todos los números.

The GCF of 12 and 30 is 6.

H

Height of three-dimensional figures (pp. 437, 438) See *Cylinder* and *Prism.*

Altura de figuras tridimensionales (pp. 437, 438) Ver *Cylinder* y *Prism.*

Height of two-dimensional figures (pp. 407, 408, 413) See *Parallelogram, Triangle,* and *Trapezoid.*

Altura de figuras bidimensionales (pp. 407, 408, 413) Ver *Parallelogram, Triangle* y *Trapezoid.*

Hexagon (p. 369) A hexagon is a polygon with six sides.

Hexágono (p. 369) Un hexágono es un polígono que tiene seis lados.

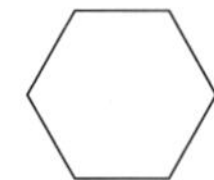

EXAMPLES

Histogram (p. 574) A histogram is a bar graph with no spaces between the bars. The height of each bar shows the frequency of data within that interval.

Histograma (p. 574) Un histograma es una gráfica de barras sin espacio entre las barras. La altura de cada barra muestra la frecuencia de los datos dentro del intervalo.

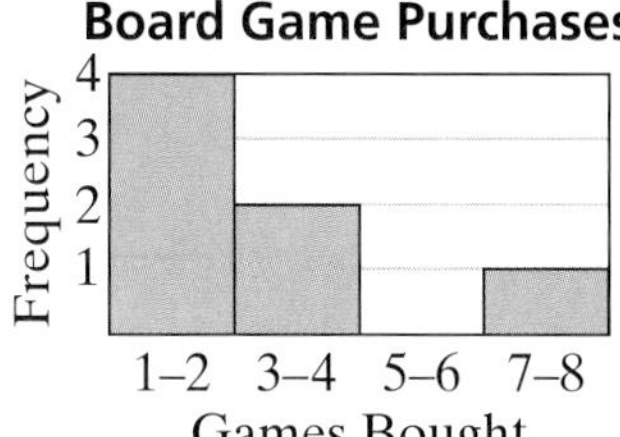

The histogram gives the frequency of board game purchases at a local toy store.

Horizontal (p. 523) Horizontal lines are parallel to the x-axis.

Horizontal (p. 523) Las rectas horizontales son paralelas al eje de x.

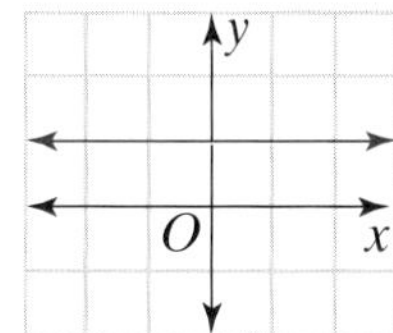

Hypotenuse (p. 432) In a right triangle, the hypotenuse is the longest side, which is opposite the right angle.

Hipotenusa (p. 432) En un triángulo rectángulo, la hipotenusa es el lado más largo, que es el lado opuesto al ángulo recto.

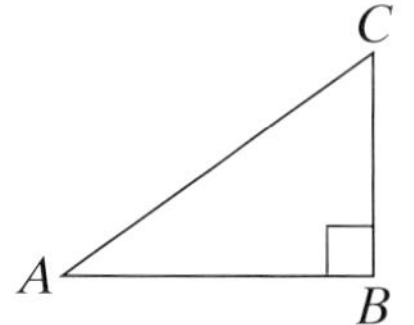

$\overline{AC}$ is the hypotenuse of $\triangle ABC$.

Identity Property of Addition (p. 12) The Identity Property of Addition states that the sum of 0 and a is a.

Propiedad de identidad de la suma (p. 12) La propiedad de identidad de la suma establece que la suma de cero y a es a.

$7 + 0 = 7$

$a + 0 = a$

Identity Property of Multiplication (p. 18) The Identity Property of Multiplication states that the product of 1 and a is a.

Propiedad de identidad de la multiplicación (p. 18) La propiedad de identidad de la multiplicación establece que el producto de 1 y a es a.

$7 \cdot 1 = 7$

$a \cdot 1 = a$

Image (p. 549) An image is the result of a transformation of a point, line, or figure.

Imagen (p. 549) Una imagen es el resultado de una transformación de un punto, una recta o una figura.

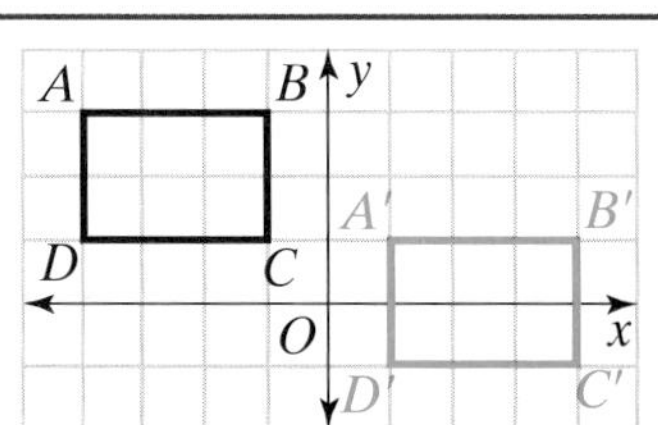

$A'B'C'D'$ is the image of $ABCD$.

English/Spanish Glossary

EXAMPLES

Improper fraction (p. 164) An improper fraction has a numerator that is greater than or equal to its denominator.

Fracción impropia (p. 164) Una fracción impropia tiene un numerador mayor o igual que su denominador.

$\frac{24}{15}$ and $\frac{16}{16}$ are improper fractions.

Independent events (p. 654) Two events are independent events if the occurrence of one event does not affect the probability of the occurrence of the other.

Sucesos independientes (p. 654) Dos sucesos son independientes si el acontecimiento de uno no afecta la probabilidad de que el otro suceso ocurra.

Suppose you draw two marbles, one after the other, from a bag. If you replace the first marble before drawing the second marble, the events are independent.

Indirect measurement (p. 269) Indirect measurement uses proportions and similar triangles to measure distances that would be difficult to measure directly.

Medición indirecta (p. 269) La medición indirecta usa proporciones y triángulos semejantes para medir las distancias que serían difíciles de medir directamente.

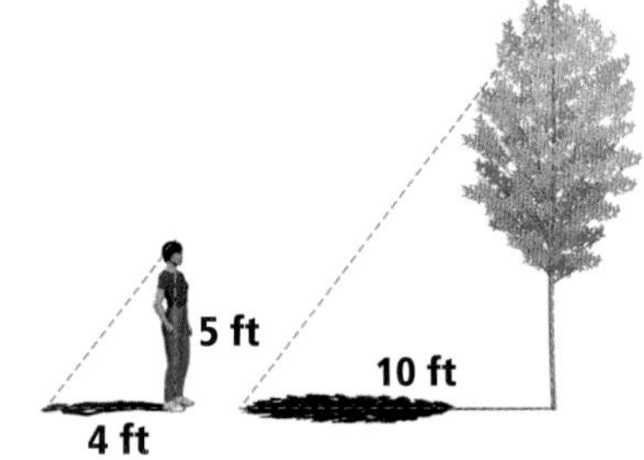

A 5-ft-tall person standing near a tree has a shadow 4 ft long. The tree has a shadow 10 ft long. The height of the tree is 12.5 ft.

Inductive reasoning (p. 475) Inductive reasoning involves looking for a pattern and writing a rule to describe the pattern in a sequence.

Razonamiento inductivo (p. 475) El razonamiento inductivo implica buscar un patrón y escribir una regla para describir el patrón en una secuencia.

By inductive reasoning, the next number in the pattern 2, 4, 6, 8, . . . is 10.

Inequality (p. 107) An inequality is a mathematical sentence that contains one of the signs $<, >, \leq, \geq$, or $\neq$.

Desigualdad (p. 107) Una desigualdad es una oración matemática que contiene uno de los signos $<, >, \leq, \geq$ o $\neq$.

$x < -5, x > 8, x \leq 1, x \geq -11, x \neq 7$

Integers (p. 34) Integers are the set of positive whole numbers, their opposites, and 0.

Enteros (p. 34) Los enteros son el conjunto de números enteros positivos, sus opuestos y el 0.

$\ldots -3, -2, -1, 0, 1, 2, 3, \ldots$

Intersecting lines (p. 348) Intersecting lines have exactly one point in common.

Rectas que se intersecan (p. 348) Las rectas que se intersecan tienen exactamente un punto en común.

	EXAMPLES
Inverse operations (p. 83) Inverse operations are operations that undo each other. **Operaciones inversas (p. 83)** Las operaciones inversas son las operaciones que se anulan entre ellas.	Addition and subtraction are inverse operations.
Irrational number (p. 428) An irrational number is a number that cannot be written as the ratio of two integers. In decimal form, an irrational number cannot be written as a terminating or repeating decimal. **Número irracional (p. 428)** Un número irracional es un número que no se puede escribir como una razón de dos enteros. Como decimal, un número irracional no se puede escribir como decimal finito o periódico.	The numbers π and 2.41592653 . . . are irrational numbers.
Irregular polygon (p. 370) An irregular polygon is a polygon with sides that are not all congruent and/or angles that are not all congruent. **Polígono irregular (p. 370)** Un polígono irregular es un polígono que tiene lados que no son todos congruentes y/o ángulos que no son todos congruentes.	K L N M *KLMN* is an irregular polygon.
Isosceles triangle (p. 363) An isosceles triangle is a triangle with at least two congruent sides. **Triángulo isósceles (p. 363)** Un triángulo isósceles es un triángulo que tiene al menos dos lados congruentes.	L M B $\overline{LM} \cong \overline{LB}$

L

Least common denominator (LCD) (p. 156) The least common denominator of two or more fractions is the least common multiple (LCM) of their denominators. **Mínimo común denominador (MCD) (p. 156)** El mínimo común denominador de dos o más fracciones es el mínimo común múltiplo (MCD) de sus denominadores.	The LCD of the fractions $\frac{3}{8}$ and $\frac{7}{10}$ is 40.
Least common multiple (LCM) (p. 145) The least common multiple of two or more numbers is the least multiple that is common to all of the numbers. **Mínimo común múltiplo (MCM) (p. 145)** El mínimo común múltiplo de dos o más números es el menor múltiplo que es común con todos los números.	The LCM of 15 and 6 is 30.

EXAMPLES

Legend (p. 580) A legend, or key, identifies data that are compared.

Leyenda (p. 580) Una leyenda, o clave, identifica categorías en una gráfica.

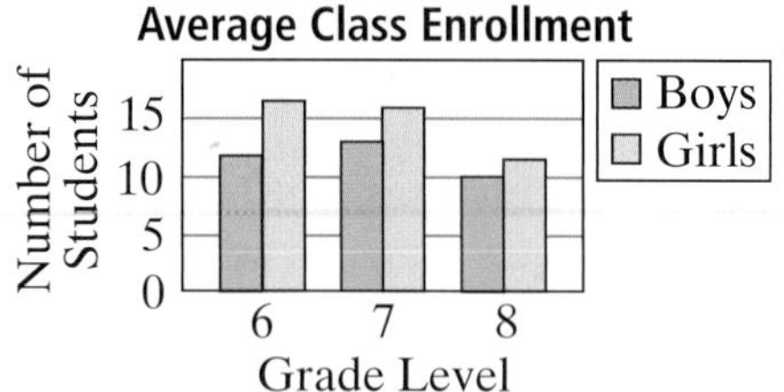

Legs of a right triangle (p. 432) The legs of a right triangle are the two shorter sides of the triangle.

Catetos de un triángulo rectángulo (p. 432) Los catetos de un triángulo rectángulo son los dos lados más cortos del triángulo.

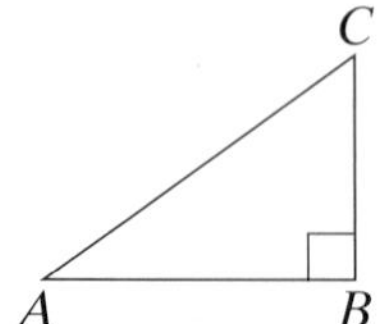

$\overline{AB}$ and $\overline{BC}$ are the legs of $\triangle ABC$.

Line (p. 347) A line is a series of points that extends in two opposite directions without end.

Recta (p. 347) Una recta es una serie de puntos que se extiende indefinidamente en dos direcciones opuestas.

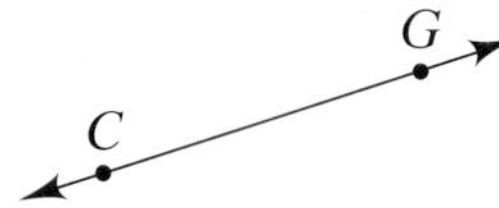

$\overleftrightarrow{CG}$ is shown.

Linear equation (p. 528) An equation is a linear equation when the graph of its solutions is a line.

Ecuación lineal (p. 528) Una ecuación es lineal cuando la gráfica de sus soluciones es una línea.

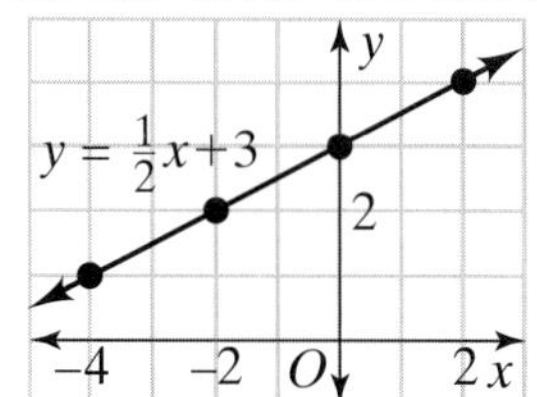

$y = \frac{1}{2}x + 3$ is a linear equation because the graph of its solutions is a line.

Line of reflection (p. 555) A line of reflection is a line over which a figure is reflected.

Eje de reflexión (p. 555) Un eje de reflexión es una recta sobre la cual se refleja una figura.

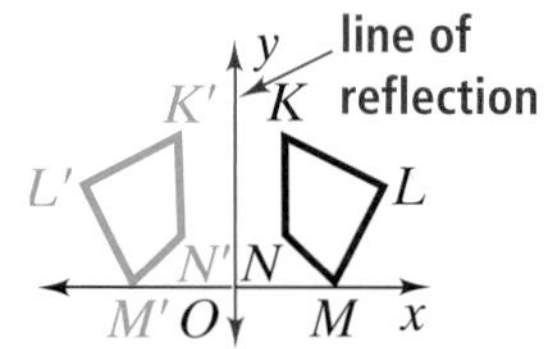

KLMN is reflected over the *y*-axis.

Line of symmetry (p. 554) A line of symmetry divides a figure into mirror images.

Eje de simetría (p. 554) Un eje de simetría divide una figura en imágenes reflejas.

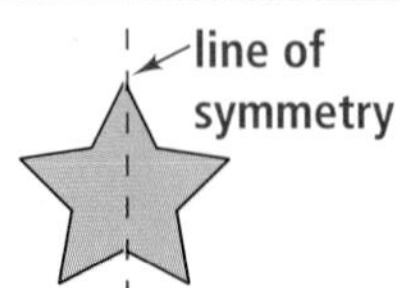

EXAMPLES

Line plot (p. 573) A line plot is a graph that shows the shape of a data set by stacking X's above each data value on a number line.

Diagrama de puntos (p. 573) Un diagrama de puntos es una gráfica que muestra la forma de un conjunto de datos agrupando X sobre cada valor de una recta numérica.

Pets Owned by Students

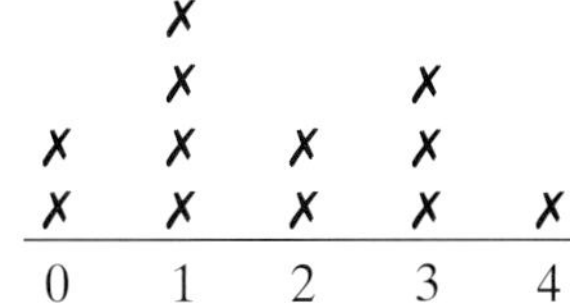

The line plot shows the number of pets owned by each of 12 students.

Markup (p. 328) The markup is the difference between the selling price and the original cost.

Sobrecosto (p. 328) El sobrecosto es la diferencia entre el precio de venta y el costo original.

A store buys a shirt for \$15 and sells it for \$25. The markup is \$10.

Mean (p. 56) The mean of a set of data values is the sum of the data divided by the number of data items.

Media (p. 56) La media de un conjunto de valores de datos es la suma de los datos dividida por el número de datos.

The mean temperature (°F) for the set of temperatures 44, 52, 48, 55, 61, and 67 is $\frac{44 + 52 + 48 + 55 + 61 + 67}{6} = 54.5°$ F.

Median (p. 57) The median of a data set is the middle value when the data are arranged in numerical order. When there is an even number of data values, the median is the mean of the two middle values.

Mediana (p. 57) La mediana de un conjunto de datos es el valor del medio cuando los datos están organizados en orden numérico. Cuando hay un número par de valores de datos, la mediana es la media de los dos valores del medio.

Temperatures (°F) for five days arranged in order are 44, 48, 52, 55, and 58. The median temperature is 52°F because it is the middle number in the set of data.

Midpoint (p. 357) The midpoint of a segment is the point that divides the segment into two segments of equal length.

Punto medio (p. 357) El punto medio de un segmento es el punto que divide el segmento en dos segmentos de igual longitud.

X M Y

$XM = YM$. M is the midpoint of $\overline{XY}$.

Mixed number (p. 164) A mixed number is the sum of a whole number and a fraction.

Número mixto (p. 164) Un número mixto es la suma de un número entero y una fracción.

$3\frac{11}{16}$ is a mixed number.

$3\frac{11}{16} = 3 + \frac{11}{16}$

English/Spanish Glossary

EXAMPLES

Mode (p. 58) The mode of a data set is the item that occurs with the greatest frequency.

Moda (p. 58) La moda de un conjunto de datos es el dato que sucede con mayor frecuencia.

The mode of the set of prices \$2.50, \$2.75, \$3.60, \$2.75, and \$3.70 is \$2.75.

Multiple (p. 145) A multiple of a number is the product of that number and any nonzero whole number.

Múltiplo (p. 145) Un múltiplo de un número es el producto de ese número y cualquier número entero diferente de cero.

The number 39 is a multiple of 13.

Multiplication Property of Equality (p. 89) The Multiplication Property of Equality states that if each side of an equation is multiplied by the same number, the results are equal.

Propiedad multiplicativa de la igualdad (p. 89) La propiedad multiplicativa de la igualdad establece que si cada lado de una ecuación se multiplica por el mismo número, los resultados son iguales.

Since $\frac{12}{2} = 6$, $\frac{12}{2} \cdot 2 = 6 \cdot 2$.
If $a = b$, then $a \cdot c = b \cdot c$.

Negative trend (p. 614) There is a negative trend between two sets of data if one set of values tends to increase while the other set tends to decrease.

Tendencia negativa (p. 614) Hay una tendencia negativa entre dos conjuntos de datos si un conjunto de valores tiende a aumentar, mientras el otro conjunto tiende a disminuir.

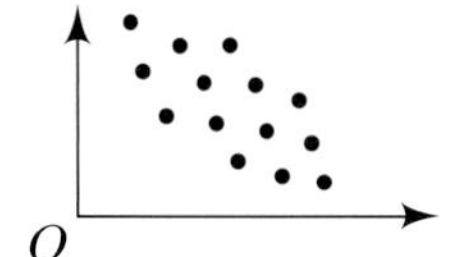

Net (p. 442) A net is a two-dimensional pattern that can be folded to form a three-dimensional figure.

Plantilla (p. 442) Una plantilla es un patrón bidimensional que se puede doblar para formar una figura tridimensional.

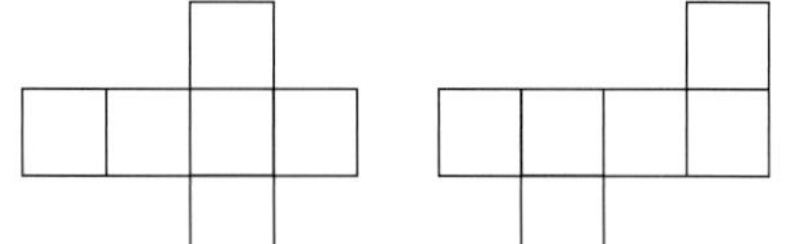

These are nets for a cube.

Nonlinear equation (p. 540) The graph of a nonlinear equation is not a straight line.

Ecuación no lineal (p. 540) La gráfica de una ecuación no lineal no es una recta.

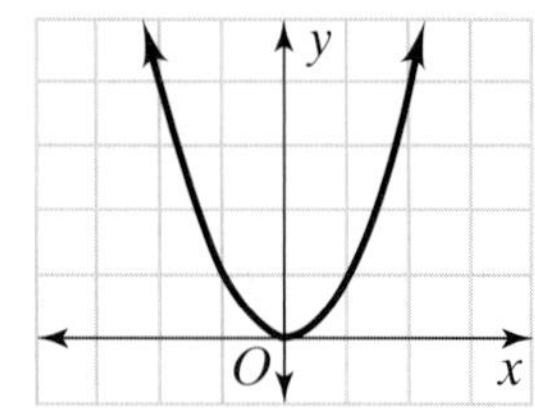

$y = x^2$ is an example of a nonlinear equation.

EXAMPLES

No trend (p. 614) There is no trend between two sets of data if the points show no relationship to each other.

Sin tendencia (p. 614) Sin tendencia entre dos conjuntos de datos significa que no hay relación alguna entre los puntos.

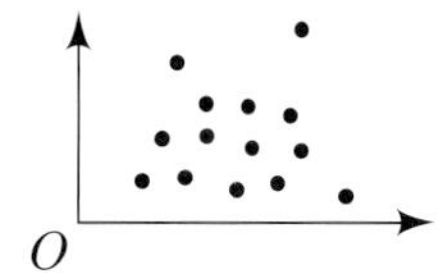

Obtuse angle (p. 352) An obtuse angle is an angle with a measure greater than 90° and less than 180°.

Ángulo obtuso (p. 352) Un ángulo obtuso es un ángulo que mide más de 90° y menos de 180°.

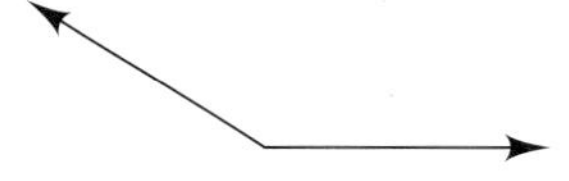

Obtuse triangle (p. 364) An obtuse triangle is a triangle with one obtuse angle.

Triángulo obtusángulo (p. 364) Un triángulo obtusángulo es un triángulo que tiene un ángulo obtuso.

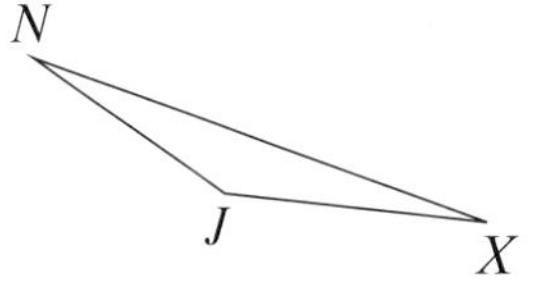

Octagon (p. 369) An octagon is a polygon with eight sides.

Octágono (p. 369) Un octágono es un polígono que tiene ocho lados.

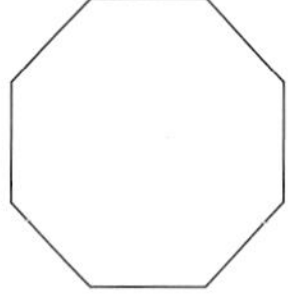

Odds (p. 631) When outcomes are equally likely, odds are expressed as the following ratios:

odds in favor of an event = number of favorable outcomes : number of unfavorable outcomes
odds against an event = number of unfavorable outcomes : number of favorable outcomes

Posibilidades (p. 631) Cuando los resultados son igualmente posibles, las posibilidades se expresan como las siguientes razones:

posibilidades *en favor* de un suceso = número de resultados favorables : número de resultados desfavorables
posibilidades *en contra* de un suceso = número de resultados desfavorables : número de resultados favorables

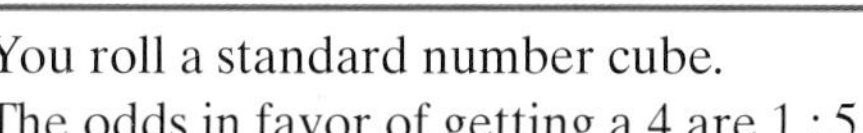
You roll a standard number cube.

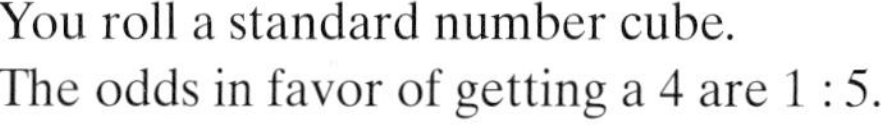
The odds in favor of getting a 4 are 1 : 5.

Open sentence (p. 77) An open sentence is an equation with one or more variables.

Proposición abierta (p. 77) Una proposición abierta es una ecuación con una o más variables.

$b - 7 = 12$

EXAMPLES

Opposites (p. 34) Opposites are two numbers that are the same distance from 0 on a number line, but in opposite directions.

Opuestos (p. 34) Opuestos son dos números que están a la misma distancia del 0 en una recta numérica, pero en direcciones opuestas.

17 and -17 are opposites.

Ordered pair (p. 521) An ordered pair identifies the location of a point. The x-coordinate shows a point's position left or right of the y-axis. The y-coordinate shows a point's position up or down from the x-axis.

Par ordenado (p. 521) Un par ordenado identifica la ubicación de un punto. La coordenada x muestra la posición de un punto a la izquierda o derecha del eje de y. La coordenada y muestra la posición de un punto arriba o abajo del eje de x.

The x-coordinate of the point $(-2, 1)$ is -2, and the y-coordinate is 1.

Order of Operations (pp. 50, 132)
1. Work inside grouping symbols.
2. Do all work with exponents.
3. Multiply and divide in order from left to right.
4. Add and subtract in order from left to right.

Orden de las operaciones (pp. 50, 132)
1. Trabaja dentro de los signos de agrupación.
2. Trabaja con los exponentes.
3. Multiplica y divide en orden de izquierda a derecha.
4. Suma y resta en orden de izquierda a derecha.

$2^3(7 - 4) = 2^3 \cdot 3 = 8 \cdot 3 = 24$

Origin (p. 521) The origin is the point of intersection of the x- and y-axes on a coordinate plane.

Origen (p. 521) El origen es el punto de intersección de los ejes de x y de y en un plano de coordenadas.

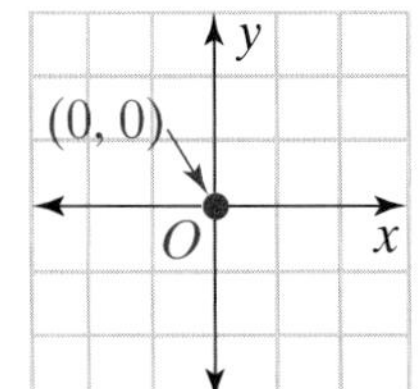

The ordered pair that describes the origin is $(0, 0)$.

Outcome (p. 629) An outcome is any of the possible results that can occur in an experiment.

Resultado (p. 629) Un resultado es cualquiera de los posibles desenlaces que pueden ocurrir en un experimento.

The outcomes of rolling a standard number cube are 1, 2, 3, 4, 5, and 6.

Outlier (p. 57) An outlier is a data item that is much higher or much lower than the other items in a data set.

Valor extremo (p. 57) Un valor extremo es un dato que es mucho más alto o más bajo que los demás datos en un conjunto de datos.

An outlier in the data set 6, 7, 9, 10, 11, 12, 14, and 52 is 52.

EXAMPLES

Parallel lines (p. 348) Parallel lines are lines in the same plane that never intersect.

Rectas paralelas (p. 348) Las rectas paralelas son rectas en el mismo plano que nunca se intersecan.

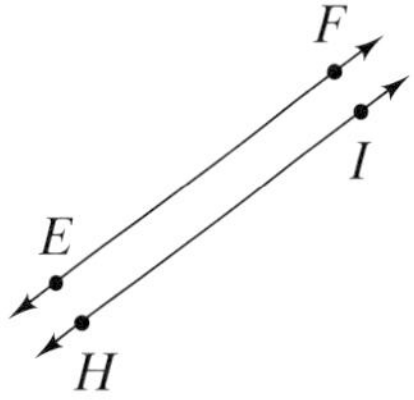

$\overleftrightarrow{EF}$ is parallel to $\overleftrightarrow{HI}$.

Parallelogram (p. 370) A parallelogram is a quadrilateral with both pairs of opposite sides parallel.

Paralelogramo (p. 370) Un paralelogramo es un cuadrilátero cuyos pares de lados opuestos son paralelos.

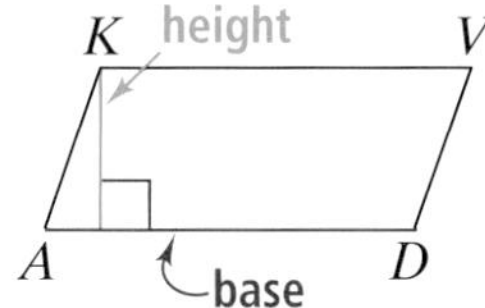

$\overline{KV}$ is parallel to $\overline{AD}$ and $\overline{AK}$ is parallel to $\overline{DV}$, so $KVDA$ is a parallelogram.

Pentagon (p. 369) A pentagon is a polygon with five sides.

Pentágono (p. 369) Un pentágono es un polígono que tiene cinco lados.

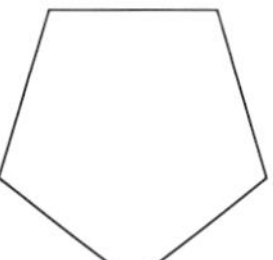

Percent (p. 291) A percent is a ratio that compares a number to 100.

Porcentaje (p. 291) Un porcentaje es una razón que compara un número con 100.

$\frac{25}{100} = 25\%$

Percent of change (p. 327) The percent of change is the percent a quantity increases or decreases from its original amount.

Porcentaje de cambio (p. 327) El porcentaje de cambio es el porcentaje que aumenta o disminuye una cantidad a partir de su cantidad original.

The number of employees increases from 14 to 21. The percent of change is $\frac{21 - 14}{14} = 50\%$.

Perfect square (p. 426) A perfect square is a number that is the square of an integer.

Cuadrado perfecto (p. 426) Un cuadrado perfecto es un número que es el cuadrado de un entero.

Since $25 = 5^2$, 25 is a perfect square.

Perimeter (p. 403) The perimeter of a figure is the distance around the figure.

Perímetro (p. 403) El perímetro de una figura es la distancia alrededor de la figura.

A 4 ft B
2 ft 2 ft
D 4 ft C

The perimeter of rectangle $ABCD$ is 12 ft.

EXAMPLES

Permutation (p. 660) A permutation is an arrangement of objects in a particular order.

Permutación (p. 660) Una permutación es un arreglo de objetos en un orden particular.

The permutations of the letters W, A, and X are WAX, WXA, AXW, AWX, XWA, and XAW.

Perpendicular bisector (p. 357) A perpendicular bisector is a segment bisector that is perpendicular to the segment.
Mediatriz (p. 357) Una mediatriz es una bisectriz de un segmento que es perpendicular a ese segmento.

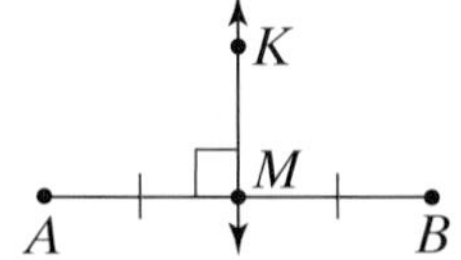

$\overleftrightarrow{MK} \perp \overline{AB}$, $AM = MB$. $\overleftrightarrow{MK}$ is the perpendicular bisector of $\overline{AB}$.

Perpendicular lines (p. 357) Perpendicular lines intersect to form right angles.

Rectas perpendiculares (p. 357) Las rectas perpendiculares se intersecan para formar ángulos rectos.

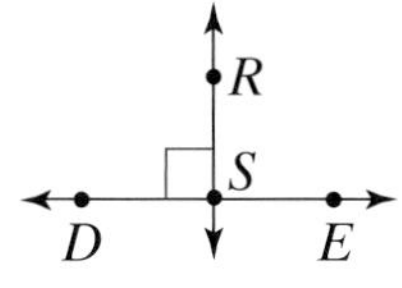

$\overleftrightarrow{DE} \perp \overleftrightarrow{RS}$

Pi (p. 419) Pi (π) is the ratio of the circumference C of any circle to its diameter d.

Pi (p. 419) Pi (π) es la razón de la circunferencia C de cualquier círculo a su diámetro d.

C d $\pi = \frac{C}{d}$

Plane (p. 348) A plane is a flat surface that extends indefinitely in all directions.

Plano (p. 348) Un plano es una superficie plana que se extiende indefinidamente en todas las direcciones.

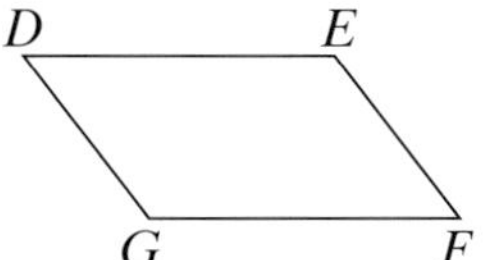

DEFG is a plane.

Point (p. 347) A point is a location that has no size.

Punto (p. 347) Un punto es una ubicación que no tiene tamaño.

• *A*

A is a point.

Polygon (p. 268) A polygon is a closed figure formed by three or more line segments that do not cross.

Polígono (p. 268) Un polígono es una figura cerrada que está formada por tres o más segmentos de recta que no se cruzan.

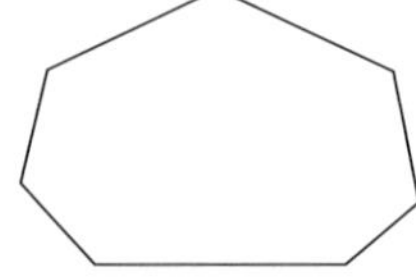

Population (p. 596) A population is a group of objects or people about which information is wanted.

Población (p. 596) Una población es un grupo de objetos o personas sobre el que se busca información.

A class of 25 students is a sample of the population of a school.

EXAMPLES

Positive trend (p. 614) There is a positive trend between two sets of data if one set of values tends to increase while the other set tends to increase.

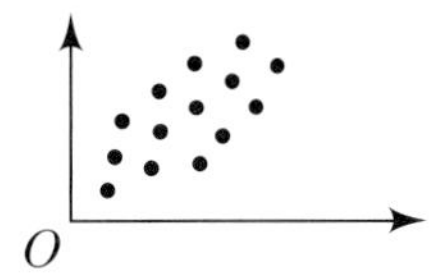

Tendencia positiva (p. 614) Existe una tendencia positiva entre dos conjuntos de datos si un conjunto de valores tiende a aumentar mientras el otro conjunto también tiende a aumentar.

Power (p. 132) A power is a number that can be expressed using an exponent.

3^4, 5^2, and 2^{10} are powers.

Potencia (p. 132) Una potencia es un número que se puede expresar usando un exponente.

Precision (p. 227) Precision refers to the exactness of a measurement, determined by the unit of measure.

$\frac{1}{16}$ in. is a smaller unit than $\frac{1}{4}$ in., so $\frac{1}{16}$ in. is more precise than $\frac{1}{4}$ in.

Precisión (p. 227) La precisión se refiere a la exactitud de una medida, determinada por la unidad de medida.

Prime factorization (p. 146) Writing a composite number as the product of its prime factors is the prime factorization of the number.

The prime factorization of 12 is $2 \cdot 2 \cdot 3$, or $2^2 \cdot 3$.

Descomposición en factores primos (p. 146) Escribir un número compuesto como el producto de sus factores primos es la descomposición en factores primos del número.

Prime notation (p. 549) Prime notation is used to identify an image point.

Point $F'(4, 1)$ is the image of point $F(4, 3)$ after a translation.

Notación prima (p. 549) La notación prima se usa para identificar un punto de imagen.

Prime number (p. 146) A prime number is a whole number with exactly two factors, 1 and the number itself.

13 is a prime number because its only factors are 1 and 13.

Número primo (p. 146) Un número primo es un entero que tiene exactamente dos factores, 1 y el mismo número.

Principal (p. 499) Principal is the original amount deposited or borrowed.

You deposit $500 in a savings account. Your principal is $500.

Capital (p. 499) El capital es el monto original que se deposita o se toma prestado.

EXAMPLES

Prism (p. 437) A prism is a three-dimensional figure with two parallel and congruent polygonal faces, called bases. A prism is named for the shape of its base.

Prisma (p. 437) Un prisma es una figura tridimensional que tiene dos caras poligonales paralelas y congruentes llamadas bases. Un prisma recibe su nombre por la forma de su base.

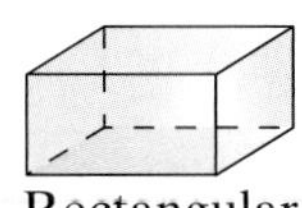

Rectangular Prism

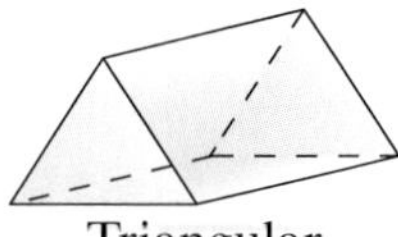

Triangular Prism

Probability (pp. 629, 636) Probability is used to describe the likeliness that an event will happen. See *Experimental probability* and *Theoretical probability*.

Probabilidad (pp. 629, 636) La probabilidad se usa para describir la posibilidad de que ocurra un suceso. Ver *Experimental probability* y *Theoretical probability.*

Proportion (p. 256) A proportion is an equation stating that two ratios are equal.

Proporción (p. 256) Una proporción es una ecuación que establece que dos razones son iguales.

$\frac{3}{12} = \frac{9}{36}$ is a proportion.

Pyramid (p. 438) A pyramid is a three-dimensional figure with triangular faces that meet at a vertex and a base that is a polygon. A pyramid is named for the shape of its base.

Pirámide (p. 438) Una pirámide es una figura tridimensional que tiene caras triangulares que coinciden en un vértice y una base que es un polígono. Una pirámide recibe su nombre por la forma de su base.

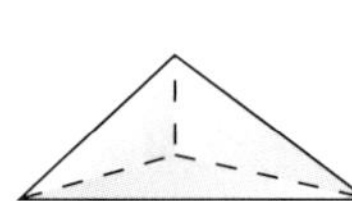

Triangular Pyramid

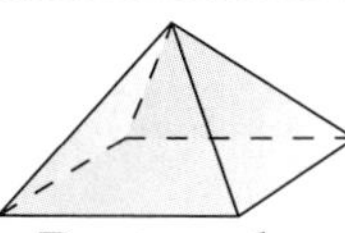

Rectangular Pyramid

Pythagorean Theorem (p. 432) In any right triangle, the sum of the squares of the lengths of the legs (a and b) is equal to the square of the length of the hypotenuse (c): $a^2 + b^2 = c^2$.

Teorema de Pitágoras (p. 432) En cualquier triángulo rectángulo, la suma del cuadrado de la longitud de los catetos (a y b) es igual al cuadrado de la longitud de la hipotenusa (c): $a^2 + b^2 = c^2$.

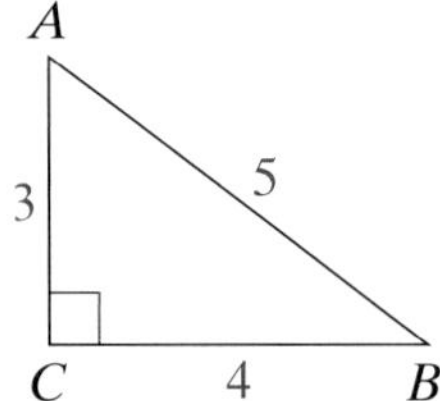

The right triangle has leg lengths 3 and 4 and hypotenuse length 5.
$3^2 + 4^2 = 5^2$

Q

EXAMPLES

Quadrants (p. 522) The x- and y-axes divide the coordinate plane into four regions called quadrants.

Cuadrantes (p. 522) Los ejes de x y de y dividen el plano de coordenadas en cuatro regiones llamadas cuadrantes.

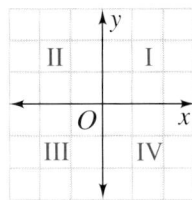

The quadrants are labeled I, II, III, and IV.

Quadrilateral (p. 369) A quadrilateral is a polygon with four sides.

Cuadrilátero (p. 369) Un cuadrilátero es un polígono que tiene cuatro lados.

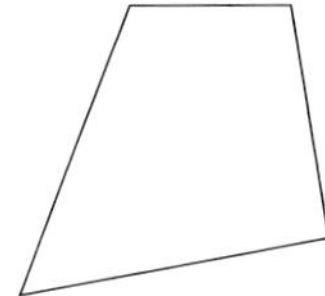

R

Radius (p. 383) A radius of a circle is a segment that connects the center of a circle to the circle.

Radio (p. 383) Un radio de un círculo es un segmento que conecta el centro del círculo con el círculo.

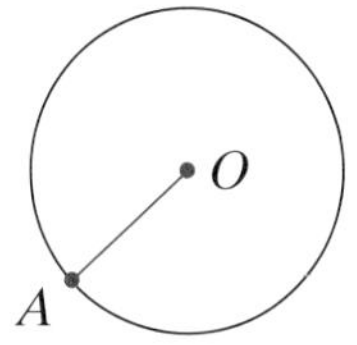

$\overline{OA}$ is a radius of circle O.

Random sample (p. 596) In a random sample, each member of the population has an equal chance of being selected.

Muestra aleatoria (p. 596) En una muestra aleatoria, cada miembro de la población tiene la misma posibilidad de ser elegido.

For the population *customers at a mall*, a random sample would be every 20th customer entering in a 2-hour period.

Range (p. 41) The range of a data set is the difference between the greatest and the least values.

Rango (p. 41) El rango de un conjunto de datos es la diferencia entre los valores mayor y menor.

Data set: 62, 109, 234, 35, 96, 49, 201
Range: $201 - 35 = 166$

Rate (p. 246) A rate is a ratio that compares two quantities measured in different units.

Tasa (p. 246) Una tasa es una razón que compara dos cantidades medidas en diferentes unidades.

You read 116 words in 1 min.
Your reading rate is $\frac{116 \text{ words}}{1 \text{ min}}$.

EXAMPLES

Ratio (p. 241) A ratio is a comparison of two quantities by division.

Razón (p. 241) Una razón es una comparación de dos cantidades mediante la división.

There are three ways to write a ratio: 9 to 10, 9 : 10, and $\frac{9}{10}$.

Rational number (p. 173) A rational number is a number that can be written as a quotient of two integers, where the divisor is not 0.

Número racional (p. 173) Un número racional es un número que se puede escribir como cociente de dos enteros, donde el divisor es diferente de cero.

$\frac{1}{3}$, -5, 6.4, 0.666 . . . , $-2\frac{4}{5}$, 0, and $\frac{7}{3}$ are rational numbers.

Ray (p. 347) A ray is part of a line, with one endpoint and all the points of the line on one side of the endpoint.

Rayo (p. 347) Un rayo es una parte de una recta que tiene un extremo y todos los puntos de la recta a un lado del extremo.

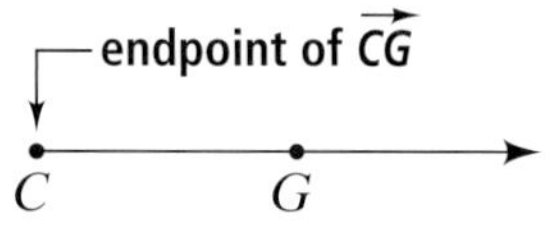

endpoint of $\overrightarrow{CG}$

C G

$\overrightarrow{CG}$ represents a ray.

Reciprocal (p. 207) Two numbers are reciprocals if their product is 1.

Recíproco (p. 207) Dos números son recíprocos si su producto es 1.

The numbers $\frac{4}{9}$ and $\frac{9}{4}$ are reciprocals.

Rectangle (p. 370) A rectangle is a parallelogram with four right angles.

Rectángulo (p. 370) Un rectángulo es un paralelogramo que tiene cuatro ángulos rectos.

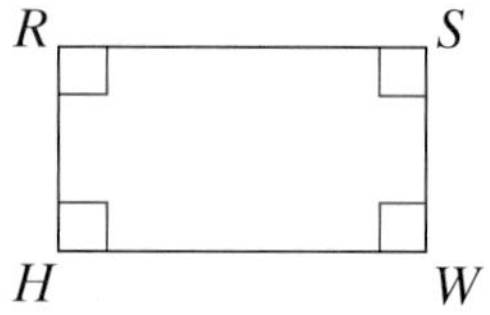

R S

H W

Reflection (p. 555) A reflection, or flip, is a transformation that flips a figure over a line of reflection.

Reflexión (p. 555) Una reflexión es una transformación que voltea una figura sobre un eje de reflexión.

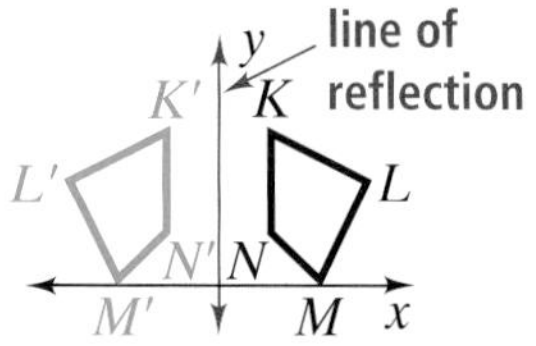

y line of reflection
K′ K
L′ L
N′ N
M′ M x

$K'L'M'N'$ is a reflection of $KLMN$ over the y-axis.

Regular polygon (p. 370) A regular polygon is a polygon with all sides congruent and all angles congruent.

Polígono regular (p. 370) Un polígono regular es un polígono que tiene todos los lados y todos los ángulos congruentes.

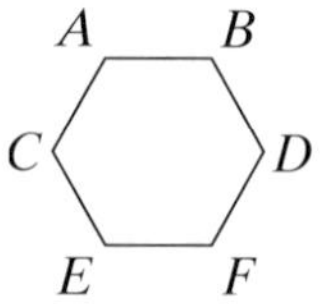

A B
C D
E F

$ABDFEC$ is a regular hexagon.

EXAMPLES

Repeating decimal (p. 169) A repeating decimal is a decimal that repeats without end. The repeating block can be one or more digits.

Decimal periódico (p. 169) Un decimal periódico es un decimal que repite los mismos dígitos interminablemente. El bloque que se repite puede ser un dígito o más de un dígito.

$0.888\ldots = .0\overline{8}$

$0.272727\ldots = 0.\overline{27}$

Rhombus (p. 370) A rhombus is a parallelogram with four congruent sides.

Rombo (p. 370) Un rombo es un paralelogramo que tiene cuatro lados congruentes.

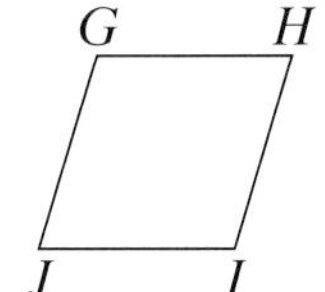

Right angle (p. 352) A right angle is an angle with a measure of 90°.

Ángulo recto (p. 352) Un ángulo recto es un ángulo que mide 90°.

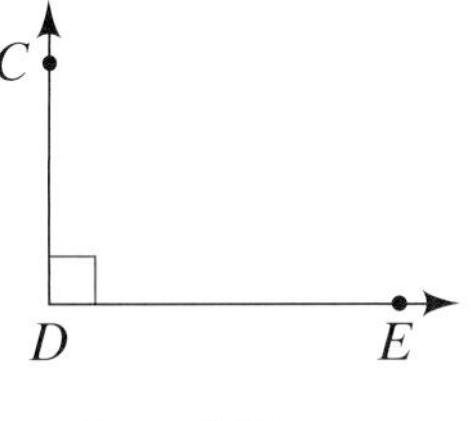

$m\angle D = 90°$

Right triangle (p. 364) A right triangle is a triangle with one right angle.

Triángulo rectángulo (p. 364) Un triángulo rectángulo es un triángulo que tiene un ángulo recto.

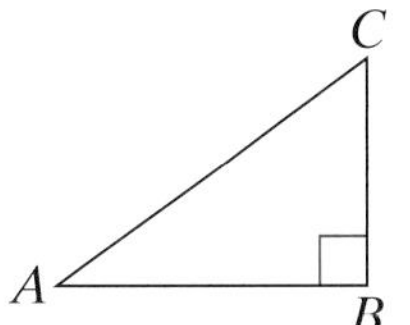

Since $\angle B$ is a right angle, $\triangle ABC$ is a right triangle.

Rotation (p. 559) A rotation is a transformation that turns a figure about a fixed point O, called the center of rotation.

Rotación (p. 559) Una rotación es una transformación que gira una figura sobre un punto fijo O, llamado centro de rotación.

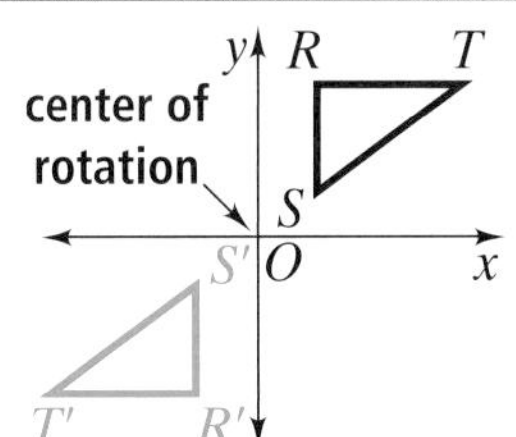

$\triangle RST$ has been rotated about the origin O to $\triangle R'S'T'$.

Rotational symmetry (p. 559) A figure has rotational symmetry if it can be rotated 180° or less and match the original figure.

Simetría rotacional (p. 559) Una figura tiene simetría rotacional si se puede rotar 180° o menos y calzar sobre la figura original.

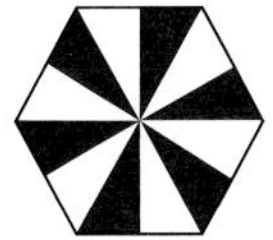

This figure has 60° rotational symmetry.

EXAMPLES

Sample space (p. 647) Sample space is the collection of all possible outcomes in a probability experiment.

Espacio muestral (p. 647) El espacio muestral es el total de todos los resultados posibles en un experimento de probabilidad.

The sample space for tossing two coins is HH, HT, TH, TT.

Scale (p. 275) A scale is the ratio that compares a length in a drawing to the corresponding length in the actual object.

Escala (p. 275) Una escala es la razón que compara la longitud en un dibujo con la longitud correspondiente en el objeto real.

A 25-mi road is 1 in. long on a map. The scale can be written three ways: 1 in. : 25 mi, $\frac{1 \text{ in.}}{25 \text{ mi}}$, 1 in. = 25 mi.

Scale drawing (p. 275) A scale drawing is an enlarged or reduced drawing of an object that is similar to the actual object.

Dibujo a escala (p. 275) Un dibujo a escala es un dibujo aumentado o reducido de un objeto que es semejante al objeto real.

Maps and floor plans are scale drawings.

Scalene triangle (p. 363) A scalene triangle is a triangle with no congruent sides.

Triángulo escaleno (p. 363) Un triángulo escaleno es un triángulo cuyos lados no son congruentes.

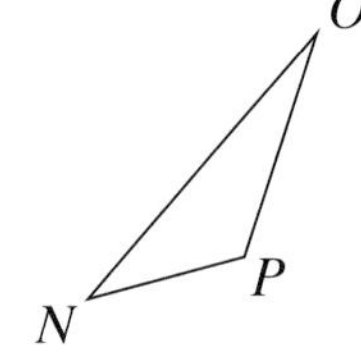

Scatter plot (p. 613) A scatter plot is a graph that relates two sets of data.

Diagrama de dispersión (p. 613) Un diagrama de dispersión es una gráfica que relaciona dos conjuntos de datos.

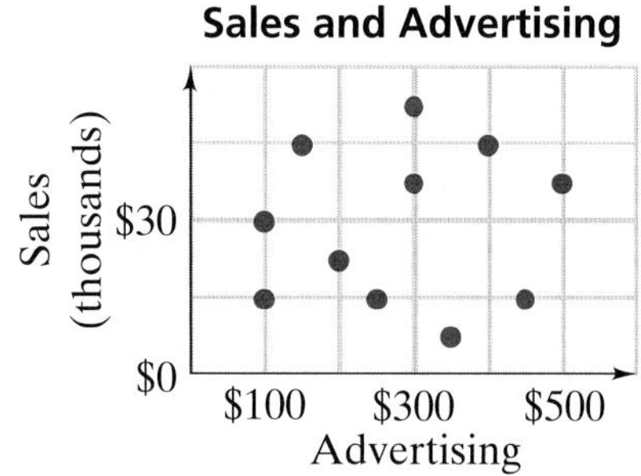

The scatter plot shows amounts spent by several companies on advertising (in dollars) versus product sales (in thousands of dollars).

Scientific notation (p. 137) A number in scientific notation is written as the product of two factors. The first factor is a number greater than or equal to 1 and less than 10; the second factor is a power of 10.

Notación científica (p. 137) Un número en notación científica se escribe como el producto de dos factores. El primer factor es un número mayor o igual a 1 y menor que 10; el segundo factor es una potencia de 10.

37,000,000 is written as 3.7×10^7 in scientific notation.

EXAMPLES

Segment (p. 347) A segment has two endpoints and all the points of the line between the points.

Segmento (p. 347) Un segmento tiene dos extremos y todos los puntos de la recta entre los puntos extremos.

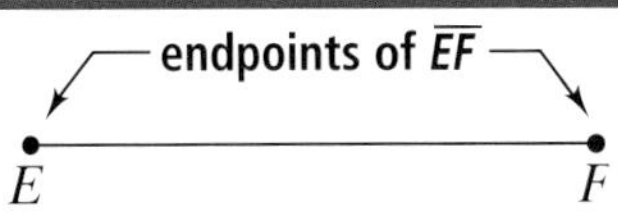

$\overline{EF}$ represents the segment shown.

Segment bisector (p. 357) A segment bisector is a line, segment, or ray that goes through the midpoint of a segment.

Mediatriz de un segmento (p. 357) Una mediatriz de un segmento es una recta, segmento o rayo que pasa por el punto medio de un segmento.

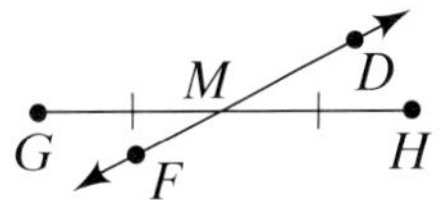

$GM = MH$. $\overleftrightarrow{FD}$ is a bisector of $\overline{GH}$.

Sequence (p. 474) A sequence is a set of numbers that follow a pattern.

Secuencia (p. 474) Una secuencia es un conjunto de números que sigue un patrón.

3, 6, 9, 12, 15, . . . is a sequence.

Similar polygons (p. 268) Two polygons are similar if their corresponding angles have the same measure and the lengths of their corresponding sides are proportional.

Polígonos semejantes (p. 268) Dos polígonos son semejantes si sus ángulos correspondientes tienen la misma medida y las longitudes de sus lados correspondientes son proporcionales.

$\triangle ABC \sim \triangle RTS$

Simple interest (p. 499) Simple interest is interest calculated only on the principal. Use the formula $I = prt$ where I is the interest, p is the principle, r is the annual interest rate, and t is time in years.

Interés simple (p. 499) El interés simple se calcula sólo en relación al principal. Se usa la fórmula $I = prt$ donde I es el interés, p es el principal, r es la tasa de interés anual y t es el tiempo en años.

The simple interest earned on \$200 invested at 5% annual interest for three years is \$200 · 0.05 · 6, or \$30.

Simplest form (p. 152) A fraction is in simplest form when the numerator and denominator have no common factors other than 1.

Mínima expresión (p. 152) Una fracción está en su mínima expresión cuando el numerador y el denominador no tienen otro factor común más que el uno.

The simplest form of $\frac{3}{9}$ is $\frac{1}{3}$.

Skew lines (p. 348) Skew lines lie in different planes. They are neither parallel nor intersecting.

Rectas cruzadas (p. 348) Las rectas cruzadas están en planos diferentes. No son paralelas ni se intersecan.

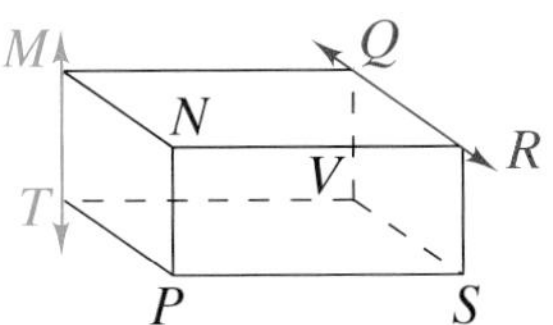

$\overleftrightarrow{MT}$ and $\overleftrightarrow{QR}$ are skew lines.

EXAMPLES

Slope of a line (p. 533) Slope is a ratio that describes the steepness of a line.
Slope $= \frac{\text{rise}}{\text{run}}$

Pendiente de una recta (p. 533) La pendiente es la razón que describe la inclinación de una recta.

Pendiente $= \frac{\text{cambio vertical}}{\text{cambio horizontal}}$

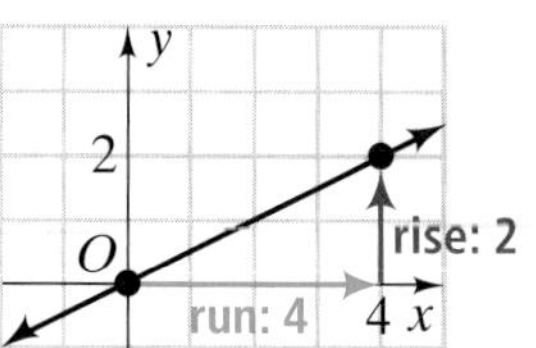

The slope of the given line is $\frac{2}{4} = \frac{1}{2}$.

Solution (pp. 77, 107) A solution is any value or values that make an equation or inequality true.

Solución (pp. 77, 107) Una solución es cualquier valor o valores que hacen que una ecuación o una desigualdad sea verdadera.

4 is the solution of $x + 5 = 9$.

7 is a solution of $x < 15$.

Sphere (p. 438) A sphere is the set of all points in space that are the same distance from a center point.

Esfera (p. 438) Una esfera es el conjunto de todos los puntos en el espacio que están a la misma distancia de un punto central.

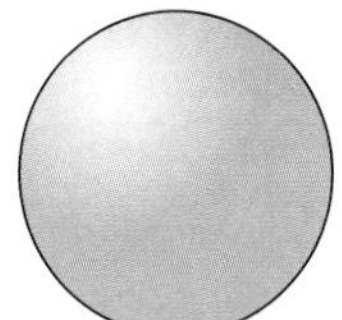

Spreadsheet (p. 579) A spreadsheet is a tool used for organizing and analyzing data. Spreadsheets are arranged in numbered rows and lettered columns.

Hoja de cálculo (p. 579) Una hoja de cálculo es una herramienta que se usa para organizar y analizar datos. Las hojas de cálculo se organizan en filas numeradas y columnas en orden alfabético.

	A	B	C	D	E
1	0.50	0.70	0.60	0.50	2.30
2	1.50	0.50	2.75	2.50	7.25

In the spreadsheet, column C and row 2 meet at the shaded box, cell C2.

Square (p. 370) A square is a parallelogram with four right angles and four congruent sides.

Cuadrado (p. 370) Una cuadrado es un paralelogramo que tiene cuatro ángulos rectos y cuatro lados congruentes.

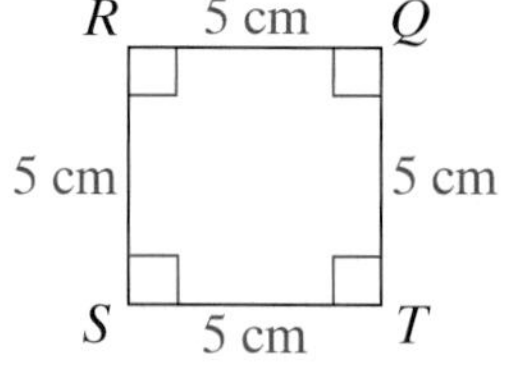

$QRST$ is a square. $\angle Q$, $\angle R$, $\angle S$, and $\angle T$ are right angles, and $\overline{QR} \cong \overline{RS} \cong \overline{ST} \cong \overline{TQ}$.

Square root (p. 426) Finding the square root of a number is the inverse of squaring a number.

Raíz cuadrada (p. 426) Hallar la raíz cuadrada de un número es el inverso de elevar un número al cuadrado.

$\sqrt{9} = 3$ because $3^2 = 9$.

EXAMPLES

Stem-and-leaf plot (p. 585) A stem-and-leaf plot is a graph that uses the digits of each number to show the shape of the data. Each data value is broken into a "stem" (digit or digits on the left) and a "leaf" (digit or digits on the right).

Diagrama de tallo y hojas (p. 585) Un diagrama de tallo y hojas es una gráfica en la que se usan los dígitos de cada número para mostrar la forma de los datos. Cada valor de los datos se divide en "tallo" (dígito o dígitos a la izquierda) y "hojas" (dígito o dígitos a la derecha).

stem	leaves
27	7
28	5 6 8
29	6 9
30	8

Key: 27 | 7 means 27.7

This stem-and-leaf plot displays recorded times in a race. The stem represents the whole number of seconds. The leaves represent tenths of a second.

Straight angle (p. 352) A straight angle is an angle with a measure of 180°.

Ángulo llano (p. 352) Un ángulo llano es un ángulo que mide 180°.

$m\angle TPL = 180°$

180°

T P L

Subtraction Property of Equality (p. 120) The Subtraction Property of Equality states that if the same number is subtracted from each side of an equation, the results are equal.

Propiedad sustractiva de la igualdad (p. 120) La propiedad sustractiva de la igualdad establece que si se resta el mismo número a cada lado de una ecuación, los resultados son iguales.

Since $\frac{20}{2} = 10, \frac{20}{2} - 3 = 10 - 3$.
If $a = b$, then $a - c = b - c$.

Supplementary (p. 352) Supplementary angles are two angles whose measures add to 180°.

Suplementario (p. 352) Los ángulos suplementarios son dos ángulos cuyas medidas suman 180°.

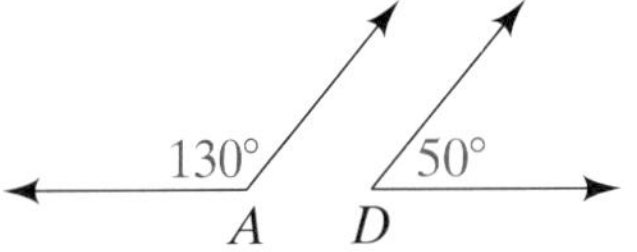

$\angle A$ and $\angle D$ are supplementary angles.

Surface area of a prism (p. 443) The surface area of a prism is the sum of the areas of its faces.

Área total de un prisma (p. 443) El área total de un prisma es la suma de las áreas de sus caras.

Each square = 1 in.^{2}

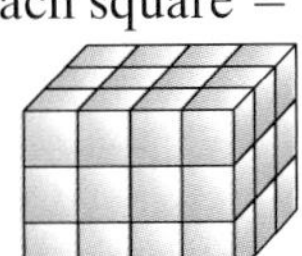

$4 \cdot 12 \text{ in.}^2 + 2 \cdot 9 \text{ in.}^2 = 66 \text{ in.}^2$

EXAMPLES

Symmetry (p. 554) A figure has symmetry when one side is the mirror image of the other side.

Simetría (p. 554) Una figura tiene simetría cuando un lado es la imagen refleja del otro lado.

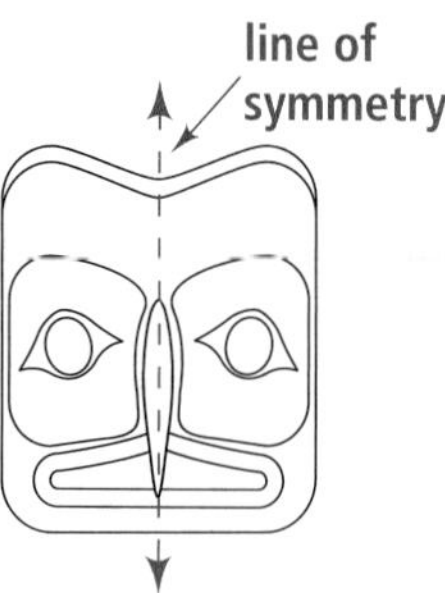

The left and right sides of the mask are mirror images of each other.

Terminating decimal (p. 168) A terminating decimal is a decimal that stops, or terminates.

Decimal finito (p. 168) Un decimal finito es un decimal que termina.

Both 0.6 and 0.7265 are terminating decimals.

Theoretical probability (p. 629) The formula used to compute the theoretical probability of an event is

$P(\text{event}) = \frac{\text{number of favorable outcomes}}{\text{total number of possible outcomes}}$.

Probabilidad teórica (p. 629) La fórmula que se usa para calcular la probabilidad teórica de un suceso es

$P\,(\text{suceso}) = \frac{\text{número favorable de resultados}}{\text{número total de resultados posibles}}$.

Suppose you select a letter from the letters H, A, P, P, and Y. The theoretical probability of selecting a P is $\frac{2}{5}$.

Three-dimensional figure (p. 437) Three-dimensional figures are figures that do not lie in a plane.

Figura tridimensional (p. 437) Las figuras tridimensionales son figuras que no están en un solo plano.

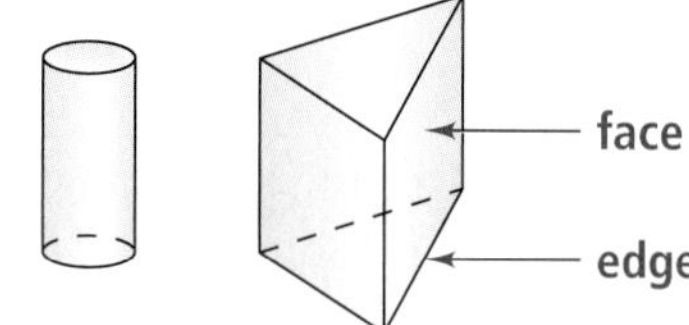

Tip (p. 322) A tip is a percent of a bill given to a person providing a service.

Propina (p. 322) Una propina es un porcentaje de una cuenta que se le da a una persona por el servicio prestado.

A lunch bill is $18. You leave a 20% tip of $3.60.

EXAMPLES

Transformations (p. 549) A transformation is a change of the position, shape, or size of a figure. Three types of transformations that change position only are translations, reflections, and rotations.

Transformaciones (p. 549) Una transformación es un cambio de posición, forma o tamaño de una figura. Tres tipos de transformaciones que cambian la posición son las traslaciones, las reflexiones y las rotaciones.

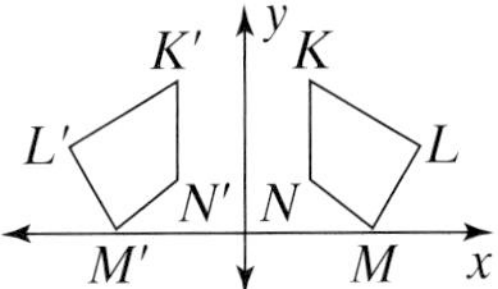

$K'L'M'N'$ is a reflection, or flip, of $KLMN$ across the y-axis.

Translation (p. 549) A translation is a transformation that moves every point of a figure the same distance and in the same direction.

Traslación (p. 549) Una traslación es una transformación que mueve cada punto de una figura la misma distancia y en la misma dirección.

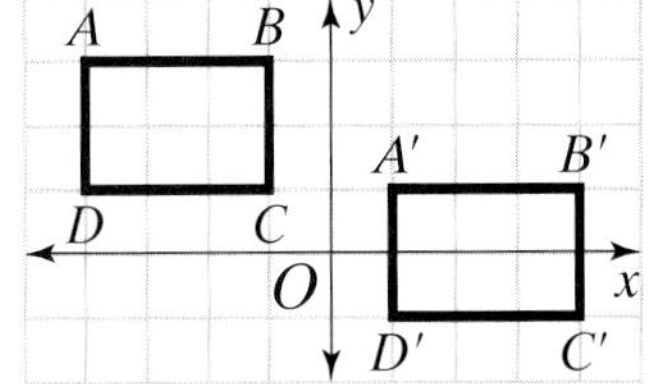

$A'B'C'D'$ is a translation image of $ABCD$.

Trapezoid (p. 370) A trapezoid is a quadrilateral with exactly one pair of parallel sides.

Trapecio (p. 370) Un trapecio es un cuadrilátero que tiene exactamente un par de lados paralelos.

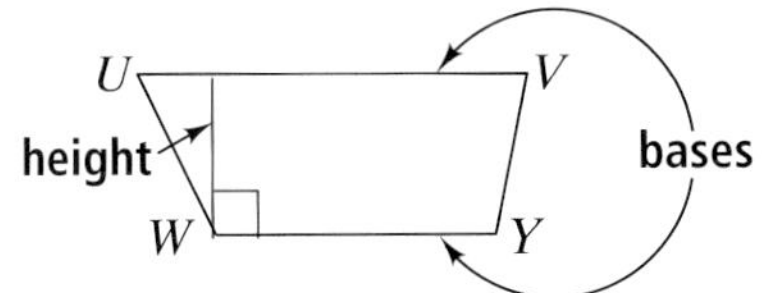

$\overline{UV}$ is parallel to $\overline{WY}$.

Trend (p. 614) A trend is a relationship between two sets of data. See *Positive trend*, *Negative trend*, and *No trend*.

Tendencia (p. 614) Una tendencia es una relación entre dos conjuntos de datos. Ver *Positive trend*, *Negative trend* y *No trend*.

Triangle (p. 363) A triangle is a polygon with three sides.

Triángulo (p. 363) Un triángulo es un polígono que tiene tres lados.

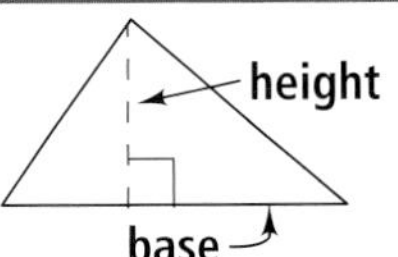

Unit price (p. 247) A unit price is a unit rate that gives the cost of one item.

Precio unitario (p. 247) Un precio unitario es una tasa unitaria que da el costo de un artículo.

$\frac{\$5.98}{10.2 \text{ fl oz}} = \$.59/\text{fl oz}$

EXAMPLES

Unit rate (p. 246) The rate for one unit of a given quantity is called the unit rate.

Tasa unitaria (p. 246) La tasa para una unidad de una cantidad dada se llama tasa unitaria.

If you drive 130 mi in 2 h, your unit rate is $\frac{65 \text{ mi}}{1 \text{ h}}$, or 65 mi/h.

Variable (p. 71) A variable is a letter that stands for a number. The value of an algebraic expression varies, or changes, depending upon the value given to the variable.

Variable (p. 71) Una variable es una letra que representa un número. El valor de una expresión algebraica varía, o cambia, dependiendo del valor que se le dé a la variable.

x is a variable in the equation $9 + x = 7$.

Variable expression (p. 92) A variable expression is a group of numbers, variables, and operations.

Expresión variable (p. 92) Una expresión variable es un grupo de números, variables y operaciones.

$7 + x, 2y - 4, \frac{3}{5}g, \frac{7}{k}$

Vertex of an angle (p. 351) The vertex of an angle is the point of intersection of two sides of an angle or figure.

Vértice de un ángulo (p. 351) El vértice de un ángulo es el punto de intersección de dos lados de un ángulo o figura.

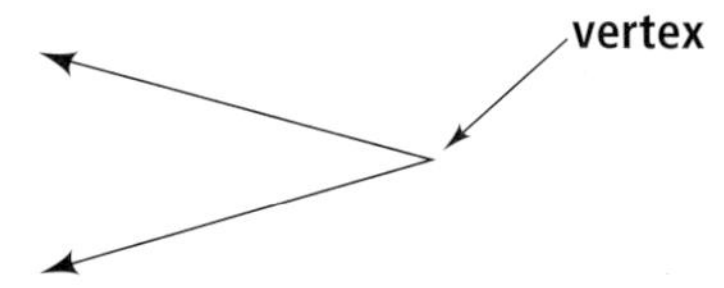

Vertex of a polygon (p. 351) The vertex of a polygon is any point where two sides of a polygon meet.

Vértice de un polígono (p. 351) El vértice de un polígono es cualquier punto donde se encuentran dos lados de un polígono.

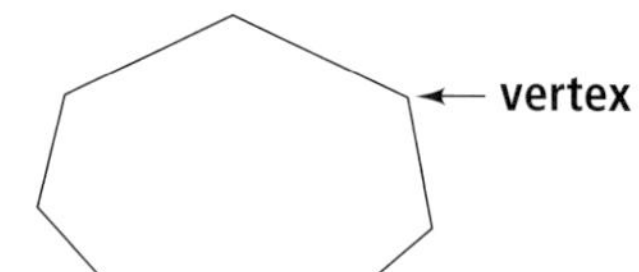

Vertical (p. 523) Vertical lines are parallel to the y-axis.

Vertical (p. 523) Las rectas verticales son paralelas al eje de y.

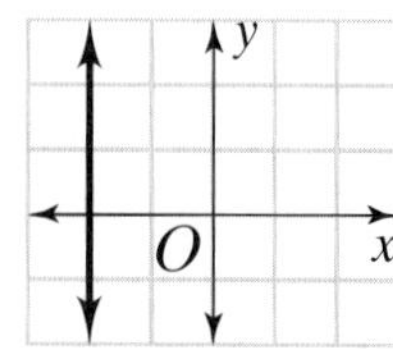

Vertical angles (p. 353) Vertical angles are formed by two intersecting lines. Vertical angles are opposite each other.

Ángulos verticales (p. 353) Los ángulos verticales están formados por dos rectas que se intersecan. Los ángulos verticales son opuestos entre sí.

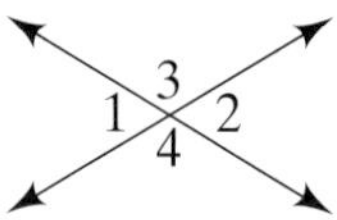

$\angle 1$ and $\angle 2$ are vertical angles, as are $\angle 3$ and $\angle 4$.

EXAMPLES

Volume (p. 449) The volume of a three-dimensional figure is the number of cubic units needed to fill the space inside the figure.

Volumen (p. 449) El volumen de una figura tridimensional es el número de unidades cúbicas que se necesitan para llenar el espacio dentro de la figura.

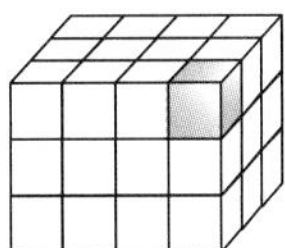

The volume of the rectangular prism is 36 in.^{3}.

X

***x*-axis (p. 521)** The *x*-axis is the horizontal number line that, together with the *y*-axis, form the coordinate plane.

Eje de *x* (p. 521) El eje de *x* es la recta numérica horizontal que, junto con el eje de *y*, forma el plano de coordenadas.

***x*-coordinate (p. 521)** The *x*-coordinate is the first number in an ordered pair. It tells the number of horizontal units a point is from the origin, *O*.

Coordenada *x* (p. 521) La coordenada *x* es el primer número en un par ordenado. Indica el número de unidades horizontales a las que un punto está del orígen, *O*.

The *x*-coordinate is -2 for the ordered pair $(-2, 1)$.
The *x*-coordinate is 2 units to the left of the origin.

Y

***y*-axis (p. 521)** The *y*-axis is the vertical number line that, together with the *x*-axis, forms the coordinate plane.

Eje de *y* (p. 521) El eje de *y* es la recta numérica vertical que, junto con el eje de *x*, forma el plano de coordenadas.

***y*-coordinate (p. 521)** The *y*-coordinate is the second number in an ordered pair. It tells the number of vertical units a point is from the origin, *O*.

Coordenada *y* (p. 521) La coordenada *y* es el segundo número en un par ordenado. Indica el número de unidades verticales a las que un punto está del orígen, *O*.

The *y*-coordinate is 1 for the ordered pair $(-2, 1)$. The *y*-coordinate is 1 unit up from the *x*-axis.

EXAMPLES

Zero Product Property (p. 18) The Zero Product Property states that the product of 0 and any number is 0.

$6 \cdot 0 = 0$

$a \cdot 0 = 0$

Propiedad del cero (p. 18) La propiedad del cero establece que el producto de cero y cualquier número es cero.

Answers to Instant Check System™

Chapter 1

Diagnosing Readiness p. 4

1. < **2.** > **3.** < **4.** > **5.** > **6.** < **7.** 37 **8.** 74 **9.** 562 **10.** 280 **11.** three tenths **12.** six thousandths **13.** nine ones **14.** three hundredths **15.** seven ten-thousandths **16.** four hundred twenty-one and five tenths **17.** five thousand six and twenty-five hundredths **18.** fifteen and four thousandths **19.** three hundred twenty-nine thousandths **20.** seven hundred ten and four hundred thirteen thousandths **21.** 34.12 **22.** 278.79 **23.** 3.60 **24.** 81.80 **25.** 17.00

Lesson 1-1 pp. 5–7

Check Skills You'll Need **1.** 3,500 **2.** 24,110 **3.** 50 **4.** 130,000 **5.** 400 **6.** 5,000 **7.** 200,000 **8.** 83,000 **9.** 1,000 **10.** 3,510; 3,500; 4,000

Check Understanding **1.** about 1 m **2a.** about 24 **b.** about 55 **3.** about $14 **4a.** 48 is a multiple of 8 **b.** About 3 CDs; category B CDs are about $16 each and 48 is a multiple of 16 that is close to $50.25. **c.** No; you can overestimate if you round to a lower number.

Lesson 1-2 pp. 11–13

Check Skills You'll Need **1.** < **2.** > **3.** < **4.** < **5.** > **6.** >

Check Understanding **1a.** The decimal point is after 10, so 7.42
10.00
b. 26.601 **2.** 9.077 **3a.** 3°F **b.** 3.4°F **4a.** 10.3 **b.** 9.0 **c.** 16.1

Lesson 1-3 pp. 17–19

Check Skills You'll Need **1.** 5 **2.** 8 **3.** 13 **4.** 7

Check Understanding **1a.** 33.3 **b.** 11.583 **2a.** 63 **b.** 0 **c.** 18.2 **d.** Answers may vary. Sample: Assoc. Prop. of Multiplication; multiply 2.5 and 2 first to get the whole number 5 which is easier to multiply by 4.3. **3a.** 2.3 **b.** 10.6 **c.** 14.7 **4a.** 0.0225 **b.** 25 **c.** 0.35

Lesson 1-4 pp. 23–25

Check Skills You'll Need **1.** 2.5 **2.** 4,567 **3.** 3 **4.** 4.58 **5.** 2.9097 **6.** 0.01809 **7.** 0.0467 **8.** 70

Check Understanding **1a.** Gram; it is closer to the weight of paper clips than a bunch of bananas. **b.** Millimeter; it is similar to the thickness of a paper clip. **c.** Milliliter; it holds less than a teaspoon. **d.** Meter; a fence is not long enough to use kilometers. **2a.** 28 cm **b.** 500 mg **3a.** 0.789 **b.** 4.59 **c.** 0.324 **4a.** 3.015 m **b.** 2,198 mL **c.** Kilograms; it would be a very large number of grams.

Checkpoint Quiz 1 **1.** $10 **2.** $11 **3.** 24.6342 **4.** 14.3448 **5.** 12.1584 **6.** 0.096 **7.** 12.5 **8.** 07.068 kg **9.** 1,408 cm **10.** 6.45 lb

Lesson 1-5 pp. 30–31

Check Skills You'll Need **1.** 189 **2.** 124 **3.** 784 **4.** 122 **5.** 216 **6.** 520 **7.** 50

Check Understanding **1a.** Check students' work. **b.** There are 13 tables that seat 5 and 3 tables that seat 8.

Lesson 1-6 pp. 34–35

Check Skills You'll Need **1.** 29, 41, 51, 54 **2.** 203, 230, 233, 302 **3.** 111, 121, 212, 222 **4.** 970, 975, 982, 985

Check Understanding **1a.** 8 **b.** −13 **c.** 22 **2a.** 8 **b.** −1 and 1 **3a.** < **b.** > **c.** < **4.** −4, −1, 2, 3

Lesson 1-7 pp. 39–41

Check Skills You'll Need **1.** 5 **2.** 2 **3.** 5 **4.** 7 **5.** 8 **6.** 7 **7.** 5 **8.** 5 **9.** 0

Check Understanding **1a.** 2 **b.** −3 **c.** −7 **d.** Comm. Prop. of Add. **2a.** −9 **b.** −5 **c.** −8 **3a.** −162 **b.** −18 **c.** −9 **d.** 9 + (−6) = 3; then 3 + 8 = 11 **4a.** −4 **b.** 4 **c.** −3 **d.** −7 **5a.** 100 **b.** 34
c.
−120 −80 −40 0 40 80 120

Lesson 1-8 pp. 45–47

Check Skills You'll Need **1.** 30 **2.** −12 **3.** −36 **4.** 56 **5.** −54 **6.** −4

Check Understanding **1a.** −12 **b.** −120 **c.** 72 **d.** 7 **2a.** −7 **b.** 4 **c.** 8 **d.** −11 **3.** −524 ft/h

Checkpoint Quiz 2 **1.** > **2.** < **3.** = **4.** 4 **5.** −9 **6.** −3 **7.** −29 **8.** 93 **9.** −7 **10.** 22 pages

Lesson 1-9 pp. 50–52

Check Skills You'll Need **1.** 12.1 **2.** 18 **3.** 20 **4.** 16.3 **5.** double the value of 6.8 − 2.3

Check Understanding 1a. −15 b. 0 c. −9 2. 77.5 in.^{2} 3a. 168 b. 126 c. 288 d. 644 e. Yes; it is an example of the Comm. Prop. of Mult. 4a. 48.4 b. 19.5 c. 101.2

Lesson 1-10 — pp. 56–58

Check Skills You'll Need 1. 13 2. −4 3. 26 4. 5 5. 10 6. 140

Check Understanding 1. 224 2. 40.8 watts 3a. −18; the outlier lowers the mean. b. 9.7; the outlier raises the mean. 4a. 3.15; the outlier is 10. b. the median; because the outlier influences the mean c. 42; about 45.5 5a. 17 b. no mode c. pen

Chapter 2

Diagnosing Readiness — p. 70

1. 4.414 2. 8.6 3. 0.79 4. 15.21 5. 2.7 6. 22.96 7. < 8. < 9. = 10. < 11. −8 12. 0 13. −40 14. 8 15. −36 16. 4 17. 42 18. −6 19. 20 20. 1 21. 1 22. 6 23. 7 24. 38

Lesson 2-1 — pp. 71–73

Check Skills You'll Need 1. 11 2. 10 3. −10 4. 3 5. 22 6. −12 7. 4 8. −2

Check Understanding 1a. 13 b. 38 c. 0 2a. $p - 16$ b. $6 + h$ 3a. Answers may vary. Sample: five more than a number b. Answers may vary. Sample: a number divided by three c. Answers may vary. Sample: fifty less than a number 4. $9t$

Lesson 2-2 — pp. 77–79

Check Skills You'll Need 1. $y + 4$ 2. $v - 6$ 3. $8p$ 4. $t - 6$ 5. $2x$ 6. $\frac{k}{9}$

Check Understanding 1. 8 2a. −9 b. −16 c. 32 d. 10 3a. about 48 b. about 26 boxes

Lesson 2-3 — pp. 83–85

Check Skills You'll Need 1. about 9 2. about 18 3. about 7 4. about 32 5. about 25 6. about 29

Check Understanding 1a. 168 b. 57 c. 327 2. $26.95 3a. 73 b. −132 c. 119 d. Yes; in either case, you subtract 114 from both sides. 4. $p - 2.4 = 26.75$; $29.15

Lesson 2-4 — pp. 88–92

Check Skills You'll Need 1. 12 2. −7 3. 84 4. −13 5. −26 6. 2 7. 4 8. −25 9. −27

Check Understanding 1a. −7.2 b. 9 c. 3 2a. $6d = 96$ and $0.06d = 0.96$ have the same solution, $d = 16$, so the equations are the same. b. $5t = 110$; $22 3a. 744 b. −390 c. 126.5

Checkpoint Quiz 1 1. $x - 4$ 2. $3x$ 3. $\frac{4}{x}$ 4. $x + 9$ 5. −4 6. 2 7. −9 8. 48 9. 20 10. 36

Lesson 2-5 — pp. 93–95

Check Skills You'll Need 1. 13 2. 24 3. 7 4. $m - 5$ 5. $2p$ 6. $d + 5$

Check Understanding 1. Let p = the number of slices in the entire pizza; $\frac{p}{3} - 2$ 2a. $0.79m + 1.25$; $6.78 b. $0.79 + 1.25p$; $9.54 3a. 4 b. 5 c. 11 4a. $1.50 + \frac{z}{3} = 6$; $13.50 b. five 3-point baskets

Lesson 2-6 — pp. 98–99

Check Skills You'll Need 1. 6 2. −5 3. 9 4. −64 5. 6 6. −18 7. −24 8. 35 9. 60

Check Understanding 1a. 28 b. 1 c. 12 2a. 200 b. −136 c. 26 d. They are reversed.

Lesson 2-7 — pp. 102–103

Check Skills You'll Need 1. $n - 7 = 12$; 19 2. $9 + n = 36$; 27 3. $27 = n - 10$; 37 4. $n + 17 = 5$; −12

Check Understanding 1. 16 bulbs 2a. 3 sea otters b. $2s + 7 = 19$

Lesson 2-8 — pp. 107–111

Check Skills You'll Need 1. > 2. > 3. > 4. > 5. < 6. > 7. > 8. = 9. >

Check Understanding 1a. −2, 1 b. −6 c. Yes; −4 = −4 2a.

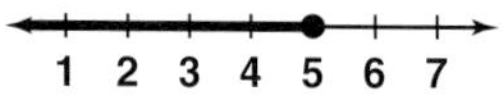

1 2 3 4 5 6 7

b.

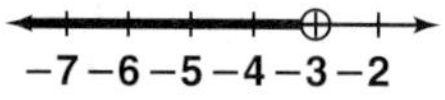

−7 −6 −5 −4 −3 −2

c.

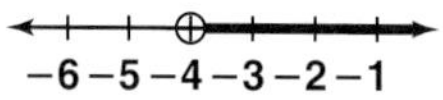

−6 −5 −4 −3 −2 −1

d.

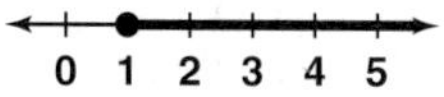

0 1 2 3 4 5

3a. $x \geq -3$ b. $x < 4$ 4. $t \leq 32$

Checkpoint Quiz 2 1. 5 2. 40 3. 2 4. −9 5. Let n = a number; $2n - 6 = 10$; 8 6. Let c = the cost of a skirt; $12 + 2c = 38$; $13

7.

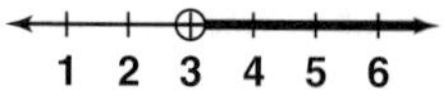

1 2 3 4 5 6

8.

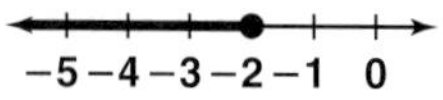

−5 −4 −3 −2 −1 0

9.

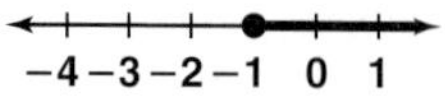

−4 −3 −2 −1 0 1

10.

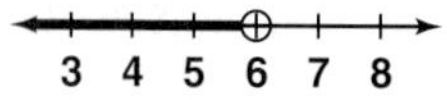

3 4 5 6 7 8

Lesson 2-9 — pp. 112–113

Check Skills You'll Need 1. −6 2. 1 3. 9 4. 15 5. 16 6. 7

Check Understanding 1a. $x > 14$;

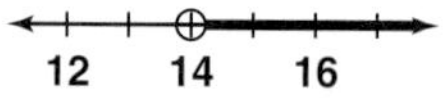

12 14 16

b. $y < 7$; 

c. $w \leq -1$; 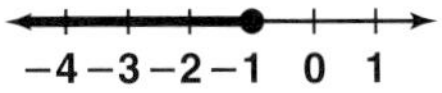

2a. $x > -4$; 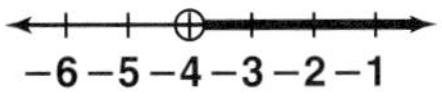

b. $y < 1$; 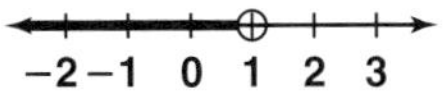

c. $w \leq -9$; 

d. 5 **3.** more than 91 points

Lesson 2-10 pp. 116–118

Check Skills You'll Need **1.** 5 **2.** −10 **3.** −4 **4.** 40 **5.** 16 **6.** −28

Check Understanding **1a.** Answers may vary. Sample: $70 \cdot 85 \leq 6{,}000$ **b.** Answers may vary. Sample: A forklift can safely carry a load weighing less than 6,000 lb. **c.** 416 min

2a. $p > -9$; 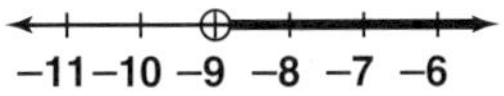

b. $m \leq 3$; 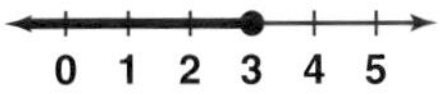

c. $n > -3$; 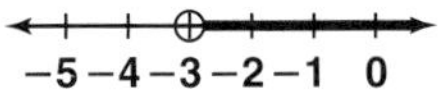

3a. $k > 20$ **b.** $p \leq -42$ **c.** $m \leq -54$

Chapter 3

Diagnosing Readiness p. 130

1. 5.5 **2.** 1.423 **3.** 3.89 **4.** 677.447 **5.** −36 **6.** 9 **7.** −9 **8.** 4 **9.** 22 **10.** 2 **11.** 1 **12.** −8 **13.** −5 **14.** 10 **15.** −14 **16.** −6 **17.** −72 **18.** $h \leq -9$ **19.** $t > -6$ **20.** $m < -21$ **21.** $k \geq -10$

Lesson 3-1 pp. 131–133

Check Skills You'll Need **1.** 2 **2.** 12 **3.** 20 **4.** −1 **5.** 11.5 **6.** 8 **7.** Multiplying the number by itself produces a larger result.

Check Understanding **1a.** 5^5 **b.** a^3 **2a.** 243 **b.** 1,000,000,000 **c.** 9.61 **d.** 1.728 **3a.** 12 **b.** 12 **c.** 62 **d.** 5 [×] [(] 9 [−] 2 [)] [^] 3 [=] **4a.** −8 **b.** −8 **c.** −81 **d.** 81 **e.** Yes; multiplying a negative number by another negative number always results in a positive number.

Lesson 3-2 pp. 136–137

Check Skills You'll Need **1.** 27 **2.** 16 **3.** 100,000 **4.** 1 **5.** 10 **6.** 256 **7.** 10^7 is closer to a million.

Check Understanding **1a.** 3.96×10^8 **b.** No; 107 is not between 1 and 10. **2a.** 120 **b.** 332,000 **c.** 6,443,000,000

Lesson 3-3 pp. 141–142

Check Skills You'll Need **1.** 4 **2.** 3 **3.** 5 **4.** −15 **5.** 124 **6.** 132

Check Understanding **1a.** Yes; 160 ends in 5 or 0. **b.** No; 76 does not end in 0. **c.** Yes; 60 is divisible by 4. **d.** Yes; 856 is divisible by 8. **e.** Yes; if a number is divisible by both 2 and 5 it ends in 0, so it is divisible by 10. **2a.** No; $2 + 6 + 2 = 10$, which is not divisible by 3. **b.** Yes; $1 + 3 + 4 + 4 + 9 = 21$, which is divisible by 3. **c.** No; $5 + 8 + 6 = 19$, which is not divisible by 9. **d.** No; $3 + 0 + 7 + 5 + 6 = 21$, which is not divisible by 9. **3.** Joshua

Lesson 3-4 pp. 145–147

Check Skills You'll Need **1.** Yes; 48 ends in 8. **2.** Yes; $4 + 8 = 12$, which is divisible by 3. **3.** Yes; 48 is divisible by 4. **4.** No; 48 does not end in 0 or 5. **5.** Yes; 48 is divisible by 2 and by 3. **6.** Yes; 48 is divisible by 8.

Check Understanding **1a.** 20 **b.** 35 **c.** 60 **d.** Answers may vary. Sample: A multiple is a product of a given number and a non-zero whole number. **2a.** 1, 2, 3, 6, 7, 14, 21, 42 **b.** 1 and 2 **3a.** composite **b.** composite **c.** prime **d.** 2 **e.** 2 **4.** $72 = 2^3 \cdot 3^2$ **5.** 8

Lesson 3-5 pp. 151–155

Check Skills You'll Need **1.** 2 **2.** 1 **3.** 12 **4.** 5 **5.** 5 **6.** 1 **7.** Answers may vary. Sample: When you divide any number by itself, the result is 1.

Check Understanding **1a.** Answers may vary. Sample: $\frac{8}{10}, \frac{12}{15}$ **b.** Answers may vary. Sample: $\frac{4}{2}, \frac{6}{3}, \frac{8}{4}$ **2a.** Answers may vary. Sample: $\frac{9}{15}, \frac{3}{5}$ **b.** No; $\frac{2}{4} = \frac{1}{2}$ but $\frac{8}{8} = \frac{2}{2}$. **3.** $\frac{2}{3}$ **4a.** $\frac{2}{5}$ **b.** Answers may vary. Sample: The LCM will be larger than the numerator or the denominator so you will not be able to simplify the fraction.

Checkpoint Quiz 1 **1.** 75 **2.** 16 **3.** 54 **4.** 3.05×10^7 **5.** 20,100 **6.** 4.611×10^7 **7.** Answers may vary. Sample: 132 and 42 **8.** $\frac{1}{2}$ **9.** $\frac{7}{10}$ **10.** $\frac{5}{8}$

Lesson 3-6 pp. 156–157

Check Skills You'll Need **1.** 12 **2.** 30 **3.** 20 **4.** 8 **5.** 14 **6.** 45

Check Understanding **1a.** < **b.** < **c.** > **2a.** $\frac{3}{8}, \frac{2}{5}, \frac{1}{2}$ **b.** $\frac{1}{3}, \frac{7}{12}, \frac{6}{9}$ **c.** $\frac{1}{15}, \frac{1}{5}, \frac{2}{6}$ **d.** Reducing the fractions gives $\frac{2}{5}, \frac{3}{5}$, and $\frac{1}{5}$, which already have a common denominator.

Lesson 3-7 pp. 160–161

Check Skills You'll Need **1.** 16 **2.** 625 **3.** 343 **4.** 243 **5.** 4 **6.** 64

Check Understanding **1a.** 8, 4, 2, 6, 8, 4, 2, 6, . . . **b.** 2

Lesson 3-8 pp. 164–165

Check Skills You'll Need **1.** $\frac{3}{5}$ **2.** $\frac{5}{6}$ **3.** $\frac{2}{3}$ **4.** $\frac{3}{4}$ **5.** $\frac{5}{12}$ **6.** $\frac{2}{2}$

Check Understanding **1.** $\frac{15}{4}$ **2.** $\frac{21}{8}$ **3a.** Divide the numerator and denominator by the GCF to reduce the fraction in one step. **b.** $1\frac{1}{4}$

Lesson 3-9 pp. 168–170

Check Skills You'll Need **1.** $\frac{4}{5}$ **2.** $\frac{1}{5}$ **3.** $\frac{1}{4}$ **4.** $\frac{7}{10}$ **5.** $\frac{2}{3}$ **6.** $\frac{1}{8}$

Check Understanding **1a.** 0.8 **b.** Yes; for the fraction $\frac{4}{5}$, the quotient is $0.8\frac{0}{5}$, which is 0.8. **2a.** $0.\overline{18}$ **b.** $0.\overline{3}$ **c.** $0.\overline{3}$ **d.** $0.\overline{5}$ **e.** No; digits do not repeat as a block. **3a.** $1\frac{91}{250}$ **b.** $2\frac{12}{25}$ **c.** $\frac{3}{5}$ **d.** $\frac{11}{40}$ **4.** $\frac{7}{8}$, 0.862, $\frac{8}{15}$, 0.35

Lesson 3-10 pp. 173–176

Check Skills You'll Need **1.** > **2.** = **3.** < **4.** = **5.** > **6.** <

Check Understanding **1a.** < **b.** < **c.** > **2a.** < **b.** > **c.** < **d.** Answers may vary. Sample: It is less than the tenths place of −4.7, even though −4.4 is greater than −4.7. **3a.** $-\frac{5}{8}$, −0.1, $\frac{2}{3}$, 2.2 **b.** 0.025, $\frac{1}{32}$, $\frac{1}{8}$, 0.625 **c.** Answers may vary. Rounding $-\frac{2}{9}$ to the nearest tenth is −0.2, but −0.2 is already in the set of numbers.

Checkpoint Quiz 2 **1.** > **2.** < **3.** = **4.** > **5.** $4\frac{5}{6}$ **6.** $\frac{37}{9}$ **7.** $16\frac{2}{5}$ **8.** $\frac{17}{6}$ **9.** 0.0112; 0.004; 0.0001 **10.** −0.45, $-\frac{4}{9}$, $\frac{7}{8}$, $\frac{9}{5}$, 1.89

Chapter 4

Diagnosing Readiness p. 186

1. −40 **2.** −24 **3.** 100 **4.** 18 **5.** −45 **6.** 60 **7.** −3 **8.** 20 **9.** 5 **10.** 26 **11.** 22 **12.** 3 **13.** 8 **14.** 45 **15.** 5 **16.** 108 **17.** 3 **18.** 4 **19.** 4 **20.** 9 **21.** 9 **22.** 21 **23.** 12 **24.** 9

Lesson 4-1 pp. 187–188

Check Skills You'll Need **1.** > **2.** = **3.** < **4.** > **5.** = **6.** >

Check Understanding **1a.** about $\frac{1}{2}$ **b.** about $\frac{1}{2}$ **c.** about $\frac{1}{2}$ **d.** See if the numerator is half of, or more or less than half of, the denominator. **2.** about 4 lb **3a.** about 20 **b.** about 48 **4a.** about 6 **b.** about 6 **c.** Low; $1\frac{4}{5}$ rounds to 2, resulting in a smaller quotient.

Lesson 4-2 pp. 192–193

Check Skills You'll Need **1.** 4 **2.** 8 **3.** 24 **4.** 1 **5.** 28 **6.** 5 **7.** Answers may vary. Sample: $\frac{1}{4}$, $\frac{2}{8}$, $\frac{8}{32}$

Check Understanding **1a.** $\frac{4}{5}$ **b.** $1\frac{1}{4}$ **2a.** $\frac{11}{24}$ **b.** $\frac{11}{12}$ **c.** $1\frac{2}{15}$ **3a.** $\frac{5}{8}$ **b.** $\frac{1}{2}$

Lesson 4-3 pp. 197–198

Check Skills You'll Need **1.** < **2.** < **3.** < **4.** > **5.** < **6.** > **7.** the smaller the denominator, the greater the value

Check Understanding **1a.** $4\frac{1}{3}$ **b.** $5\frac{4}{5}$ **c.** You add the fractions and then add the whole numbers. **2a.** $3\frac{11}{12}$ **b.** $12\frac{1}{24}$ **c.** Rename when the sum of the fractions is greater than 1. **3a.** $1\frac{3}{4}$ **b.** $1\frac{1}{2}$ **c.** when you are subtracting a larger fraction

Checkpoint Quiz 1 **1.** about 6 in. **2.** about 14 in. **3.** about 5 in. **4.** $\frac{1}{6}$ **5.** 2 **6.** $5\frac{9}{10}$ **7.** $8\frac{19}{20}$ **8.** $\frac{2}{9}$ **9.** $11\frac{5}{8}$ **10.** $21\frac{5}{8}$ in.

Lesson 4-4 pp. 202–204

Check Skills You'll Need **1.** $\frac{13}{5}$ **2.** $\frac{13}{2}$ **3.** $\frac{19}{4}$ 4. $\frac{35}{4}$ **5.** $\frac{38}{3}$ **6.** $\frac{82}{9}$ **7.** $9\frac{1}{3}$

Check Understanding **1a.** $\frac{3}{20}$ **b.** $\frac{2}{3}$ **c.** $\frac{8}{15}$ **2.** $\frac{3}{10}$ **3a.** 15 **b.** 12 **c.** Less; you are finding a fraction of 28. **4a.** $10\frac{19}{24}$ **b.** $4\frac{17}{25}$

Lesson 4-5 pp. 207–208

Check Skills You'll Need **1.** $\frac{2}{7}$ **2.** $\frac{5}{18}$ **3.** $\frac{13}{60}$ **4.** 35 **5.** $1\frac{1}{35}$ **6.** 4

Check Understanding **1a.** 14 **b.** $\frac{5}{6}$ **2a.** $1\frac{25}{44}$ **b.** $\frac{3}{4}$ **3a.** $4\frac{13}{20}$ **b.** $\frac{14}{33}$ **c.** yes; $10 \div 2 = 5$, $10 \cdot \frac{1}{2} = 5$

Lesson 4-6 pp. 213–214

Check Skills You'll Need **1.** 10 **2.** 16 **3.** 11 **4.** 6 **5.** 8 **6.** 3 **7.** Add. Prop. of Equal., Div. Prop. of Equal.

Check Understanding **1a.** $2\frac{3}{8}$ **b.** $\frac{1}{2}$ **2a.** 15 **b.** 24 **3a.** 32 **b.** 20 **c.** No; multiplying before adding gives an incorrect answer.

Lesson 4-7 pp. 218–219

Check Skills You'll Need **1.** $\frac{7}{9}$ **2.** $1\frac{1}{21}$ **3.** $1\frac{5}{44}$ **4.** $1\frac{1}{4}$ **5.** 1 **6.** $2\frac{4}{15}$ **7.** numerators are added like integers; denominators stay the same

Check Understanding **1.** 6:40 P.M.

Lesson 4-8 pp. 222–223

Check Skills You'll Need **1.** $\frac{1}{2}$ **2.** $\frac{3}{4}$ **3.** $\frac{3}{10}$ **4.** $1\frac{11}{12}$ **5.** 12 **6.** $\frac{2}{7}$ **7.** Yes; $s = 32$ in each equation.

Check Understanding **1.** $1\frac{7}{12}$ ft **2.** $6\frac{1}{4}$ servings **3a.** 74 oz **b.** It takes more smaller units to equal the larger units. It takes fewer larger units to equal the smaller units.

Checkpoint Quiz 2 **1.** $\frac{2}{7}$ **2.** $\frac{2}{3}$ **3.** $6\frac{2}{3}$ **4.** $3\frac{1}{4}$ **5.** 20 **6.** $28\frac{3}{4}$ **7.** −32 **8.** $2\frac{1}{3}$ **9.** 25 **10.** 12

Lesson 4-9 pp.227–229

Check Skills You'll Need **1.** \$4.50 **2.** \$13.00 **3.** \$3.50 **4.** \$13.50 **5.** \$24.50 **6.** \$54.00

Check Understanding **1a.** $\frac{1}{8}$ in. **b.** $\frac{1}{16}$ in. **c.** No; $\frac{1}{16}$ in. is smaller than $\frac{1}{8}$ in. **2a.** 25.5 g **b.** 13 in. **c.** 13.25 L **d.** No; an inch is a smaller unit of measure. **3a.** 44 m **b.** 14.1 g **c.** 4 L

Chapter 5

Diagnosing Readiness p. 240

1. 14.4 **2.** 1.775 **3.** 47.7 **4.** 7.41 **5.** 3.39 **6.** 5.9575 **7.** 114.66 **8.** 10.52 **9.** 8 **10.** 60 **11.** 2 **12.** $\frac{1}{7}$ **13.** $\frac{1}{7}$ **14.** 11 **15.** 75 **16.** 24 **17.** > **18.** < **19.** = **20.** > **21.** = **22.** < **23.** $\frac{3}{4}$ **24.** $\frac{1}{2}$ **25.** $\frac{7}{8}$ **26.** $\frac{3}{8}$ **27.** $\frac{1}{3}$ **28.** $\frac{5}{9}$ **29.** $\frac{2}{3}$ **30.** $\frac{2}{7}$

Lesson 5-1 p. 241

Check Skills You'll Need **1.** $\frac{1}{2}$ **2.** $\frac{7}{9}$ **3.** $\frac{4}{7}$ **4.** $\frac{1}{3}$ **5.** $\frac{1}{8}$ **6.** $\frac{5}{7}$

Check Understanding **1a.** 7 to 12, 7 : 12, $\frac{7}{12}$ **b.** 5 to 7, 5 : 7, $\frac{5}{7}$ **2a.** 2.33 **b.** Answers may vary. Sample: when both numbers are non-negative and the first number is less than the second **3a.** Answers may vary. Sample: $\frac{5}{8}$, $\frac{20}{32}$ **4a.** The GCF of its numerator and denominator is 1. **b.** $\frac{7}{11}$

Lesson 5-2 p. 246

Check Skills You'll Need **1.** $\frac{3}{5}$ **2.** $\frac{1}{9}$ **3.** $\frac{4}{7}$ **4.** $\frac{3}{4}$ **5.** $\frac{11}{8}$ **6.** $\frac{8}{9}$

Check Understanding **1.** 70 heartbeats per min **2a.** 45 words/min **b.** Answers may vary. Sample: Since 2h 30 min = 150 min, multiplying the unit rate by 150 will give a result of 6,750 words in 2h 30 min. **3a.** \$7.00 **b.** \$.60 **4a.** \$.064/fl oz, \$.056/fl oz; the 64-fl-oz choice is the better buy. **b.** \$.093/oz, \$.075/oz; the 14.5-oz choice is the better buy.

Lesson 5-3 p. 252

Check Skills You'll Need **1.** −12 **2.** 4 **3.** −9 **4.** 5 **5.** −7 **6.** 20 **7.** −7

Check Understanding **1a.** Check students' work. **b.** 8 d

Checkpoint Quiz 1 **1.** 7 to 52, $\frac{7}{52}$ **2.** $\frac{2}{3}$ **3.** $\frac{1}{3}$ **4.** 12 to 7 **5.** 2 : 3 **6.** 42 words/min **7.** 9 points/game **8.** \$.2633, \$.2475; the second item is the better buy. **9.** \$7.80, \$6.57; the second item is the better buy. **10.** 15 pizzas

Lesson 5-4 p. 256

Check Skills You'll Need **1.** > **2.** = **3.** < **4.** > **5.** < **6.** =

Check Understanding **1a.** Yes; both ratios equal $\frac{2}{3}$. **b.** no; $\frac{5}{6} \neq \frac{5}{7}$ **c.** Yes; both ratios equal $\frac{3}{5}$. **2a.** Yes; a common multiplier is 5. **b.** no **c.** Yes; a common multiplier is 5. **d.** $\frac{15}{60} = \frac{15 \div 15}{60 \div 15} = \frac{1}{4}$, $\frac{75}{300} = \frac{75 \div 75}{300 \div 75} = \frac{1}{4}$ **3a.** yes; 48 = 48 **b.** yes; 36 = 36 **c.** no; 36 ≠ 40

Lesson 5-5 p. 260

Check Skills You'll Need **1.** 8 km/d **2.** 16 ft/s **3.** 62 mi/h **4.** 25 push-ups/min **5.** 60 words/min **6.** 3 examples/min **7.** Check students' work.

Check Understanding **1a.** \$6.37 **b.** \$119.51 **2a.** 9 **b.** 2 **c.** 10 **d.** Answers may vary. Sample: With a common factor you can solve the problem by just multiplying or dividing two numbers. **3a.** 16 **b.** 24 **c.** 180 **d.** Yes; answers may vary. Sample: Both proportions have the same cross products, $25x = 570$.

Lesson 5-6 p. 267

Check Skills You'll Need **1.** 6 **2.** 6 **3.** 8 **4.** 12 **5.** 72 **6.** 1.5

Check Understanding **1.** Yes; *DEFG* ~ *LMNO*; corresponding angles have equal measure, and the ratio of all pairs of corresponding sides is $\frac{1}{2}$.

2. 40; answers may vary. Sample: Since the triangles are similar, the ratios of the corresponding sides are all equal. **3a.** 36 ft **b.** 20 ft

Checkpoint Quiz 2 **1.** no **2.** yes **3.** no **4.** yes **5.** \$8.40 **6.** \$16.50 **7.** 120° **8.** 26° **9.** 9 **10.** 12

Lesson 5-7 p. 275

Check Skills You'll Need **1.** 8 **2.** 15 **3.** 3 **4.** 18 **5.** 7 **6.** 1

Check Understanding **1.** 15 m **2a.** about 206 km **b.** about 146 km **3.** 1 in. : 18 in.

Chapter 6

Diagnosing Readiness p. 290

1. 5 **2.** 14 **3.** 5 **4.** 30 **5.** 800 **6.** 8.4 **7.** 3 **8.** $\frac{17}{20}$ **9.** $\frac{2}{5}$ **10.** $\frac{17}{25}$ **11.** $\frac{5}{4}$ **12.** $\frac{1}{100}$ **13.** 12 **14.** 55 **15.** 20 **16.** 80 **17.** 2.16 **18.** 200

Lesson 6-1 pp. 291–292

Check Skills You'll Need **1–6.** Answers may vary. Samples are given: **1.** $\frac{4}{10}$, $\frac{6}{15}$ **2.** $\frac{26}{100}$, $\frac{39}{150}$ **3.** $\frac{6}{50}$, $\frac{9}{75}$ **4.** $\frac{2}{20}$, $\frac{3}{30}$ **5.** $\frac{34}{40}$, $\frac{51}{60}$ **6.** $\frac{6}{8}$, $\frac{9}{12}$

Check Understanding **1.** $\frac{54}{100}$; 54%

2a. 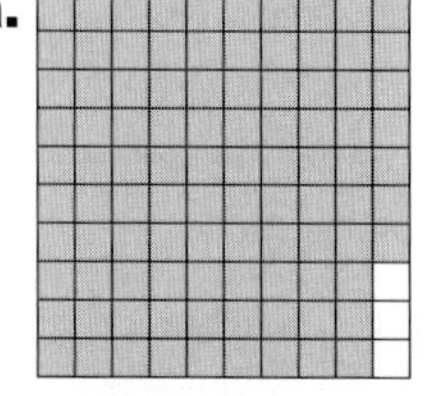 **b.** 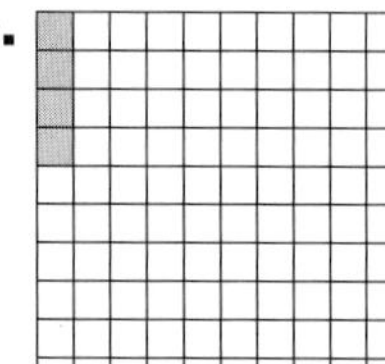

c.

3a. $\frac{3}{4}$; 75% **b.** $\frac{1}{2}$; 50% **c.** $\frac{7}{10}$; 70% **d.** 20 squares **4a.** 24% **b.** 75% **c.** 2% **d.** 45% **e.** Answers may vary. Sample: Write each ratio as a percent, and compare the two percents.

Lesson 6-2 pp. 295–297

Check Skills You'll Need **1.** 0.3125 **2.** 0.125 **3.** 0.275 **4.** $0.8\overline{3}$ **5.** $0.\overline{4}$ **6.** $0.1\overline{3}$ **7.** $\frac{1}{3} = 0.\overline{3} = 0.3\overline{3}$, so $\frac{1}{3} = 0.3\overline{3}$.

Check Understanding **1a.** 7% **b.** 60.7% **c.** 90% **d.** 25% **2a.** 0.35 **b.** 0.125 **c.** 0.09 **d.** 0.078 **3a.** 29%, $\frac{3}{10}$, $\frac{11}{25}$, 0.74 **b.** 0.08, 15%, $\frac{7}{20}$, 50% **4a.** 60% **b.** 12% **c.** 52.5% **d.** 68.8% **5a.** $\frac{19}{20}$ **b.** $\frac{2}{25}$ **c.** $\frac{79}{100}$ **d.** $\frac{1}{10}$ **e.** 1, 2, 4, 5, 10, 20, 25, 50, 100

Lesson 6-3 p. 301

Check Skills You'll Need **1.** 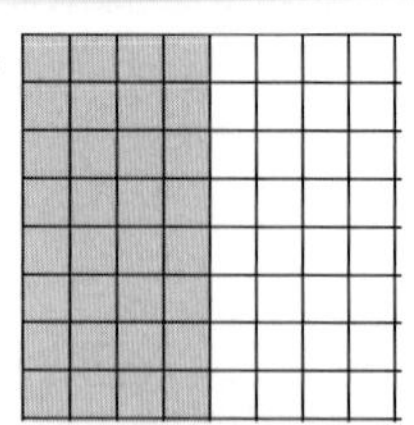

2. **3.** 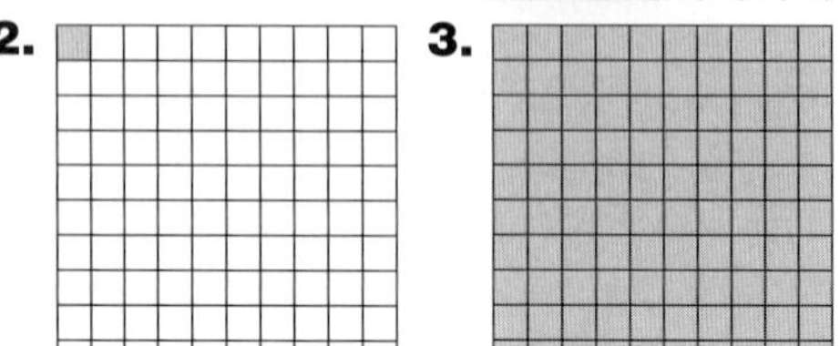

4. 1% **5.** 98% **6.** 95% **7.** 8%

Check Understanding **1.** 1.25; $\frac{5}{4}$ or $1\frac{1}{4}$ **2.** 0.0035; $\frac{7}{2{,}000}$ **3a.** 341.67% **b.** 280% **c.** 171% **d.** 400.5% **4.** 0.46%

Lesson 6-4 p. 305

Check Skills You'll Need **1.** 1,200 **2.** 915 **3.** 1,350 **4.** 63 **5.** 70.2 **6.** 29.7 **7.** Answers may vary. Sample: To find 38 × 15, you can use the fact that 38 = 40 − 2. So, 38 × 15 = 40 × 15 − 2 × 15 = 600 − 30 = \$570.

Check Understanding **1a.** 58.5 **b.** Answers may vary. Sample: You would probably use a fraction when the percent can be written as a fraction that is compatible with the other number. You would use a decimal for all other cases. **2.** 18 seventh-grade students **3a.** 960 **b.** 2,376 **c.** 216 **d.** 1,464 **4a.** about 60 **b.** about 100 **c.** about 600 **d.** about 500

Checkpoint Quiz 1 **1.** 0.45; $\frac{9}{20}$ **2.** 1.35; $1\frac{7}{20}$ **3.** 0.0098; $\frac{49}{5{,}000}$ **4.** 56% **5.** 20% **6.** 0.4% **7.** 16.82 **8.** 30.4 **9.** 0.24 **10.** 35%

Lesson 6-5 p. 311

Check Skills You'll Need **1.** 8 **2.** 15 **3.** 87.5 **4.** 100 **5.** 56 **6.** 36 **7.** Answers may vary. Sample: The cross products are equal, so $100n = 60 \cdot 75$, or $100n = 4{,}500$. So $n = \frac{4{,}500}{100} = 45$.

Check Understanding **1a.** 25% **b.** 28.8% **c.** No; 44 is less than 100% of 80, while 80 is more than 100% of 44. **2a.** Answers may vary. Sample: The "whole" is the denom. and the "part" is the numerator. **b.** 12.5% **3a.** 75 **b.** 60 **c.** Smaller; 70

is 125% of that number, so 70 is greater than the number. **4a.** 250 **b.** 240 **c.** No; the sum is greater than 100%.

Lesson 6-6 pp. 318–319

Check Skills You'll Need **1.** $3x = 51$; 17 **2.** $\frac{x}{4} = 12$; 48 **3.** $70 = 5x$; 14 **4.** $5 = \frac{x}{11}$; 55 **5.** $100x = 33$; 0.33 **6.** $\frac{x}{10} = 6$; 60

Check Understanding **1.** 16.2 **2.** 150 **3.** 20%

Lesson 6-7 pp. 322–326

Check Skills You'll Need **1.** 1.05; $1\frac{1}{20}$ **2.** 1.18; $1\frac{9}{50}$ **3.** 2.5; $2\frac{1}{2}$ **4.** 0.005; $\frac{1}{200}$ **5.** 0.003; $\frac{3}{1,000}$ **6.** 0.008; $\frac{1}{125}$

Check Understanding **1a.** Yes; the total cost is \$193.97. **b.** \$39 **2a.** about \$8.70 **b.** about \$9.30 **c.** about \$7.50 **d.** about \$4.50 **e.** Find 10%, then double it. **3a.** \$12.29; the difference is caused by a "rounding error." **b.** \$15.75 **4.** \$192 **5.** \$849

Checkpoint Quiz 2 **1.** $58.\overline{3}$% **2.** 16 **3.** 84% **4.** 135 **5.** 45% **6.** 68.4 **7.** 222 **8.** 540 **9.** \$77 **10.** \$60.69

Lesson 6-8 pp. 327–329

Check Skills You'll Need **1.** 50 **2.** 75 **3.** 81.25% **4.** 40% **5.** 80 **6.** 60%

Check Understanding **1a.** 1.9% **b.** The percent of increase is different because the original amount is different. **2a.** 99.4% **b.** 35.1% **c.** Answers may vary. Sample: Yes; if you buy an item for \$1 and sell it for \$3, the percent of markup is 200%. **3.** 40%

Lesson 6-9 pp. 333–335

Check Skills You'll Need **1.** 19.2 **2.** 300 **3.** 27.38 **4.** 25.175 **5.** 0.004 **6.** 4,229.7

Check Understanding **1.** When not on sale, the \$450 couch costs \$600 (because $\$600 \cdot 0.75 = \$450$). Comparing \$600 to \$750, the percent of discount is $\frac{150}{750} = 20\%$. **2a.** 250% markup **b.** 47.6% discount

Chapter 7

Diagnosing Readiness p. 346

1. < **2.** > **3.** < **4.** > **5.** 2 **6.** 15 **7.** 12 **8.** 105 **9.** 5 **10.** 94 **11.** 80 **12.** 16 **13.** 111 **14.** 46 **15.** 108 **16.** 86.4 **17.** 16.2 **18.** 64.8

Lesson 7-1 p. 347–348

Check Skills You'll Need **1.** −4 −2 0 2 **2.** −3 −2 −1 0 1 **3.** −2 0 2 **4.** 0 2 4 6 **5.** −3 −2 −1 0 1 **6.** −1 0 1 2 3 4

Check Understanding **1a.** $\overrightarrow{PD}$ **b.** $\overline{RS}$ **c.** $\overleftrightarrow{AV}$ **2a.** $\overline{EF}$, $\overline{HD}$ **b.** $\overline{AB}$, $\overline{EB}$, $\overline{CB}$, $\overline{AB}$, $\overline{HG}$, $\overline{HD}$, **c.** $\overline{FC}$, $\overline{EF}$, $\overline{BC}$, $\overline{HD}$ **d.** No, they are parallel.

Lesson 7-2 pp. 351–353

Check Skills You'll Need **1.** 3 **2.** 70 **3.** 23 **4.** 140 **5.** 74 **6.** 8

Check Understanding **1.** 15° **2a.** right **b.** acute **c.** obtuse **3a.** 53° **b.** Yes; you have to add a larger angle to make a 180° angle than to make a 90° angle. **4a.** 108°; 72°; 108° **b.** 360°

Lesson 7-3 pp. 357–359

Check Skills You'll Need **1.** $\overline{VW}$ **2.** $\overrightarrow{FG}$ **3.** $\overrightarrow{BD}$ **4.** $\overleftrightarrow{CL}$ **5.** $\overrightarrow{RM}$ **6.** $\overline{XT}$

Check Understanding **1a.** No; a segment has only one midpoint. **b.** drawing not to scale

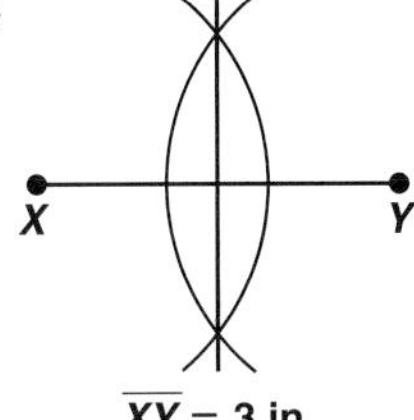

2a. Answers may vary. Sample:

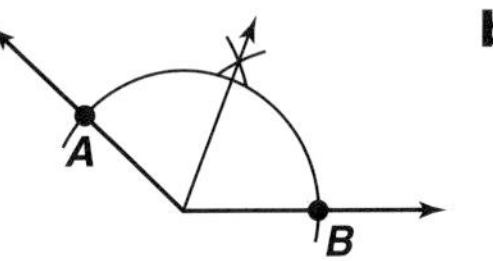

b. 33°

Lesson 7-4 pp. 363–367

Check Skills You'll Need **1.** right **2.** obtuse **3.** acute

Check Understanding **1a.** equilateral, isosceles **b.** scalene **c.** isosceles **2a.** right **b.** acute **3a.** 22° **b.** 45°

Checkpoint Quiz 1 **1.** $\overrightarrow{XZ}$ **2.** $\overleftrightarrow{NM}$ **3.** $\overrightarrow{BA}$ **4.** $\overline{KV}$ **5.** 78°; 168° **6.** 43°; 133° **7.** 25°; 115° **8.** 7°; 97° **9.** 70° **10.**

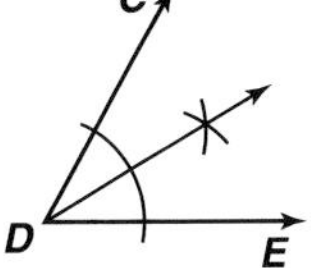

Instant Check System™ Answers

Lesson 7-5 pp. 369–370

Check Skills You'll Need **1.** scalene **2.** equilateral, isosceles **3.** isosceles **4.** isosceles **5.** scalene **6.** equilateral, isosceles

Check Understanding **1a.** octagon; irregular **b.** triangle; regular **2a.** hexagons, triangles, trapezoids, parallelograms, rhombuses, pentagons **b.** squares, triangles, rhombuses, hexagons, pentagons, decagons **3a.**

b. No; a square has 4 congruent sides as does a rhombus.

Lesson 7-6 pp. 374–375

Check Skills You'll Need **1.** 63°; 153° **2.** 7°; 97° **3.** 77°; 167° **4.** 48°; 138° **5.** 56°; 146° **6.** 83°; 173°

Check Understanding **1.** 78 blocks

Lesson 7-7 pp. 378–382

Check Skills You'll Need **1.** 97° **2.** 30° **3.** 64°

Check Understanding **1.** Congruent; corresponding sides and corresponding angles have the same measure. **2.** No; the sides are different lengths. **3a.** $\overline{AB} \cong \overline{FG}$; $\overline{BC} \cong \overline{GH}$; $\overline{CD} \cong \overline{HI}$; $\overline{DA} \cong \overline{IF}$; $\angle A \cong \angle F$; $\angle B \cong \angle G$; $\angle C \cong \angle H$; $\angle D \cong \angle I$ **b.** 15.5; 139°

Checkpoint Quiz 2 **1.** **2.**

3.

4. Congruent; all corresponding sides and corresponding angles are congruent. **5.** 9 steps; after she gets to the middle step she has −2 + 4 − 3 + 5, or 4 steps left to go. So there are 4 steps before and 4 steps after the middle step. The total number of steps is 4 + 1 + 4 = 9.

Lesson 7-8 pp. 383–384

Check Skills You'll Need **1.** $\overline{FR}$ **2.** $\overrightarrow{ZJ}$ **3.** $\overleftrightarrow{NK}$ **4.** $\overline{FR}$ could be named as $\overline{RF}$, and $\overleftrightarrow{NK}$ can be renamed as $\overleftrightarrow{KN}$.

Check Understanding **1a.** $\overline{PW}$, $\overline{PT}$, $\overline{PS}$, $\overline{PR}$ are radii. $\overline{TR}$, $\overline{WS}$ are diameters. $\overline{TS}$, $\overline{TR}$, $\overline{WS}$ are all chords. $\angle TPW$, $\angle TPR$, $\angle TPS$, $\angle SPR$, $\angle SPW$, $\angle WPR$ are all central angles. **b.** Yes; a chord has both endpoints on the circle. **2.** $\overset{\frown}{ZY}$, $\overset{\frown}{ZYX}$, $\overset{\frown}{YZX}$ **3.** $\overset{\frown}{CDE}$, $\overset{\frown}{CE}$

Lesson 7-9 pp. 388–389

Check Skills You'll Need **1.** 90 **2.** 216 **3.** 259.2 **4.** 64.8 **5.** 342 **6.** 194.4

Check Understanding **1.** about \$0.5 billion **2a.** 144° **b.**

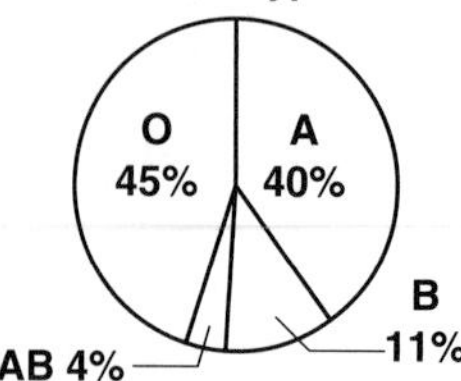

Chapter 8

Diagnosing Readiness p. 402

1. 3.14 **2.** 123 **3.** 3.14 **4.** 3,140 **5.** 108 **6.** 4 **7.** 97 **8.** 24 **9.** 144 **10.** 3 **11.** 9 **12.** 58° **13.** 50° **14.** 63° **15.** 125°

Lesson 8-1 pp. 403–404

Check Skills You'll Need **1.** 72 **2.** 4 **3.** 84 **4.** 5 **5.** 48 **6.** $2\frac{1}{6}$

Check Understanding **1a.** feet **b.** inches **c.** inches **d.** feet **2.** 18 in.; answers may vary. Sample: The length would be less than a yard. **3a.** Answers may vary. Sample: about 92 yd^2 **b.** Answers may vary. Sample: You could find the dimensions of the rectangle that encloses the figure and then find the perimeter of the rectangle.

Lesson 8-2 pp. 407–410

Check Skills You'll Need **1.** 6 **2.** 10 **3.** 2 **4.** 8 **5.** $7\frac{1}{2}$ **6.** $4\frac{1}{2}$

Check Understanding **1a.** 6 m^2 **b.** 27 $in.^2$ **2a.** 216 m^2 **b.** 48 cm^2 **3.** 15 cm^2

Lesson 8-3 pp. 413–415

Check Skills You'll Need **1.** 75 cm^2 **2.** 72 mi^2 **3.** 135 m^2

Check Understanding **1a.** 34.1 m^2 **b.** 165 cm^2 **c.** Answers may vary. Sample: You can divide the trapezoid into 2 triangles by drawing a diagonal. Then find the sum of the areas of the triangles. **2.** 13,000 yd^2

Lesson 8-4 pp. 419–424

Check Skills You'll Need **1.** 1 **2.** 81 **3.** 121 **4.** 18 **5.** 144 **6.** 320

Check Understanding **1a.** 28.3 m **b.** 20.4 m **c.** 125.6 cm or 125.7 cm

Check Understanding **2a.** 452 m^2 **b.** 201 mm^2 **c.** 64 cm^2 **d.** Divide the diameter by 2 to find the radius and then use the formula for area of a circle. **3.** 706.9 ft^2

Checkpoint Quiz 1 **1.** 420 km^2 **2.** 360 km^2 **3.** 54 m^2 **4.** 240 in.^{2} **5.** 371 m^2 **6.** 160 m^2 **7.** 60 yd^2 **8.** 90 m^2 **9.** 50.3 in.; 201.1 in.^{2} **10.** 44.0 ft; 153.9 ft^2

Lesson 8-5 pp. 426–428

Check Skills You'll Need **1.** 64 **2.** 144 **3.** 4 **4.** 49 **5.** 16 **6.** 25 **7.** Multiply the number by itself.

Check Understanding **1.** 8 **2.** 6 ft **3a.** No; each side should be about 4.5 ft. **b.** about 8 **4a.** irrational **b.** rational **c.** rational **d.** rational

Lesson 8-6 pp. 432–433

Check Skills You'll Need **1.** 2 **2.** 4 **3.** 6 **4.** 7 **5.** 10 **6.** 8

Check Understanding **1.** 17 in. **2a.** No; you are squaring the numbers, so the length of *a* will increase by more than 2 m. **b.** 24 mi **3.** 65 m

Lesson 8-7 pp. 437–438

Check Skills You'll Need **1.** **2.**

3. **4.**

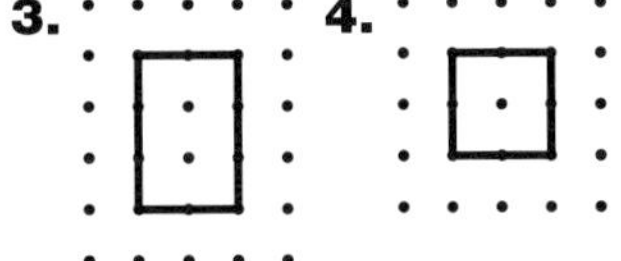

Check Understanding **1.** rectangle; rectangular prism **2a.** triangular prism **b.** cone **3.**

Lesson 8-8 pp. 442–444

Check Skills You'll Need **1.** 48 m^2 **2.** 6 ft^2 **3.** 200 cm^2

Check Understanding **1.** Answers may vary. Sample:

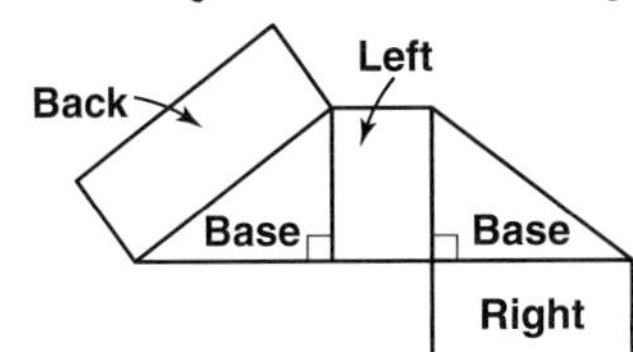

2. 328 ft^2 **3a.** 3,455.8 m^2 **b.** A net of any cylinder contains two circles and a rectangle. The dimensions of these can vary.

Lesson 8-9 pp. 449–454

Check Skills You'll Need **1.** 113 m^2 **2.** 177 in.^{2} **3.** 28 cm^2

Check Understanding **1a.** 1,755 in.^{3} **b.** 125 ft^3 **2.** 1,583 m^3 **3a.** 6,000 cm^3; 6,107 cm^3 **b.** It will be a little large.

Checkpoint Quiz 2 **1.** $8 < \sqrt{77} < 9$ **2.** 39 cm **3.** 4 yd **4.** 8 m **5.** sphere **6.** cone **7.** 36 in.^{2} **8.** 2,884 m^2 **9.** 180 cm^3 **10.** 6,773 in.^{3}

Lesson 8-10 pp. 455–456

Check Skills You'll Need **1.** 15 **2.** 36 **3.** 80 **4.** 20 **5.** $10\frac{2}{5}$ **6.** $\frac{1}{3}$

Check Understanding **1a.** Check students' work. **b.** 210 ft

Chapter 9

Diagnosing Readiness p. 468

1. 6.9 **2.** −40.8 **3.** 52.4 **4.** 1.5 **5.** 5 **6.** 5 **7.** $4\frac{3}{4}$ **8.** $2\frac{3}{4}$ **9.** 0 **10.** 32 **11.** −3 **12.** $64\frac{1}{4}$ **13.** 36 **14.** 343 **15.** $24\frac{3}{8}$ **16.** $2\frac{2}{3}$ **17.** 0.04 **18.** 0.12 **19.** 0.0358 **20.** 0.0405 **21.** 0.103

Lesson 9-1 pp. 469–471

Check Skills You'll Need **1–6.**

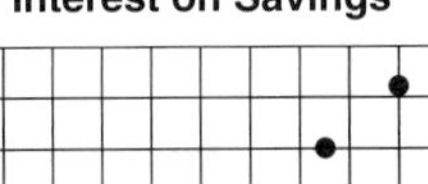

7. $-5.6, -5.\overline{5}, -\frac{5}{6}, 2.98, 3\frac{1}{3}$

Check Understanding **1a.**

Interest on Savings

Interest Earned ($): 0, 10, 20, 30

Amount Saved ($): 200, 400, 600, 800

b. Answers may vary. Sample: An interval of \$5; it is easier to count in 5's than in 4's. **2.** Graphs may vary. Sample:

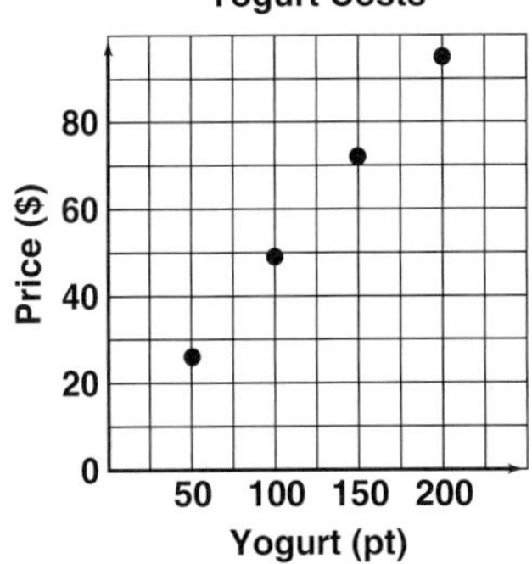

3. about \$2.10 **4a.** about 175°F **b.** temperatures below 0°C

Lesson 9-2 pp. 474–476

Check Skills You'll Need **1.** 0 **2.** −1 **3.** −2 **4.** −3 **5.** −4 **6.** −5

Check Understanding **1a.** Start with 44 and add −9 repeatedly; 8, −1, −10. **b.** Yes; each term is found by adding −11 to the previous term. **2a.** Start with 1,000 and multiply by $\frac{1}{10}$ repeatedly; 1, $\frac{1}{10}$, $\frac{1}{100}$. **b.** Yes; each term is found by multiplying the previous term by $-\frac{1}{4}$. **3a.** neither **b.** neither **c.** arithmetic

Lesson 9-3 pp. 480–481

Check Skills You'll Need **1.** −10 **2.** 16 **3.** −27 **4.** 20 **5.** 82 **6.** 1 **7.** Answers may vary. Sample: +10, · 6, −(−10), or ÷ $\frac{1}{6}$

Check Understanding **1a.**

Fresh Fish (lb)	Price (\$)
1	6.50
2	13.00
3	19.50
4	26.00
5	32.50

b. \$130.00 **c.** Answers may vary. Sample: Each row can be checked for a pattern. Finding the same pattern in each row builds confidence that the pattern is the correct rule for any value. **2.** $x = 6, y = 242$ **3a.** $n - 9$; 91 **b.** 10,000

Lesson 9-4 pp. 484–488

Check Skills You'll Need **1.** 9 **2.** 1 **3.** −1 **4.** 5 **5.** 0 **6.** 2 **7.** −1

Check Understanding **1a.** $d = 62t$ **b.** arithmetic **2.** $y = 4x + 1$ **3.**

x	y
0	−4
1	−2
2	0
3	2

Checkpoint Quiz 1 **1.** Start with 7 and add 7 repeatedly; 35, 42, 49. **2.** Start with 250 and add −30 repeatedly; 130, 100, 70 **3.** Start with 2, then add 3, 6, 12, 24 and so on; 47, 95, 191. **4.** Start with −4 and multiply by −3 repeatedly; −324, 972, −2,916. **5.** arithmetic; arithmetic; neither; geometric **6.** $m = 16, n = 9$ **7.**

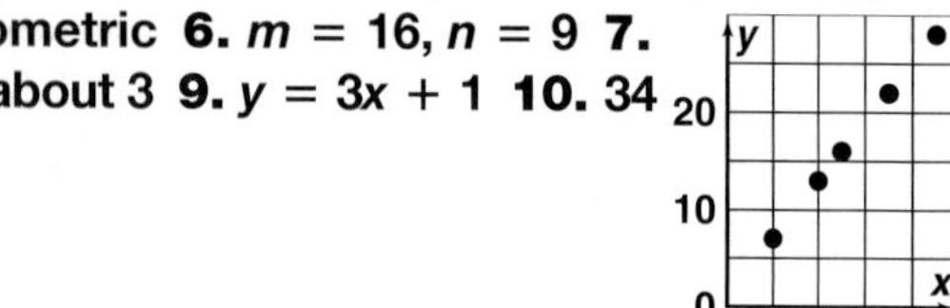

8. about 3 **9.** $y = 3x + 1$ **10.** 34

Lesson 9-5 pp. 489–490

Check Skills You'll Need **1.**

x	y
0	0
1	2
2	4
3	6

2.

x	y
0	0
1	−1
2	−2
3	−3

3.

x	y
0	−2
1	2
2	6
3	10

4.

x	y
0	5
1	6
2	7
3	8

5.

x	y
0	0
1	$\frac{1}{2}$
2	1
3	$1\frac{1}{2}$

6.

x	y
0	0
1	−3
2	−6
3	−9

Check Understanding **1.**

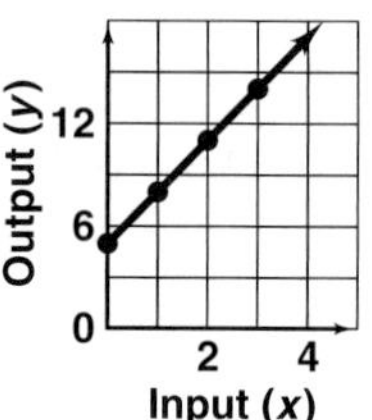

2a. $c = 0.13m$; \$1.95

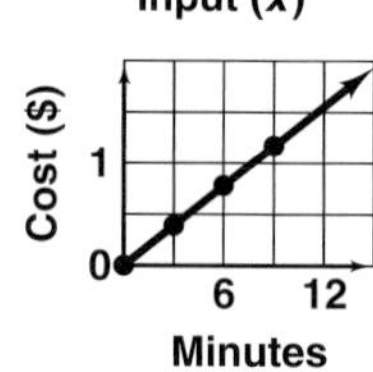

b. No; the function $y = x + 1$ is an example of a function that has an output of 1 for an input of 0.

Lesson 9-6 pp. 494–495

Check Skills You'll Need **1.** 80 mi **2.** 100 mi **3.** 200 mi **4.** 140 mi **5.** 10 mi **6.** 20 mi **7.** a straight line through (0, 0)

Check Understanding **1a.** Answers may vary. Sample: You walk two blocks at a fast pace, then stop for 12 min. Then you walk 2 blocks at a slower pace, then 1 block at the faster pace. **b.** Between 0 and 4 min, and 32 and 36 min; the steeper parts of the graph show faster speed.

2a.

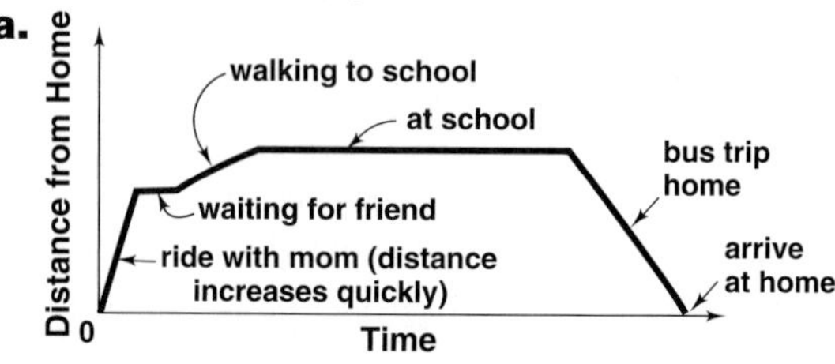

b. The graph is different only where it shows the bus trip home. **3a.**

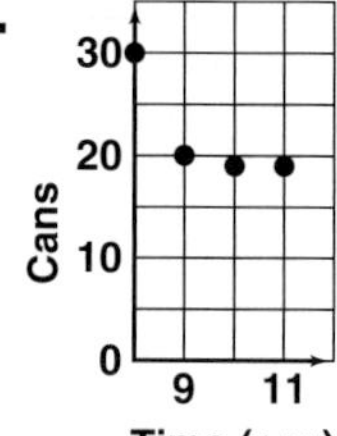

b. No; you do not know what time the sales took place and a sale cannot be for part of a can.

Lesson 9-7 pp. 499–502

Check Skills You'll Need **1.** 0.04 **2.** 0.09 **3.** 0.02 **4.** 0.065 **5.** 0.0509 **6.** 0.1821

Check Understanding **1a.** \$44.00 **b.** principal, annual rate, and number of years **2.**

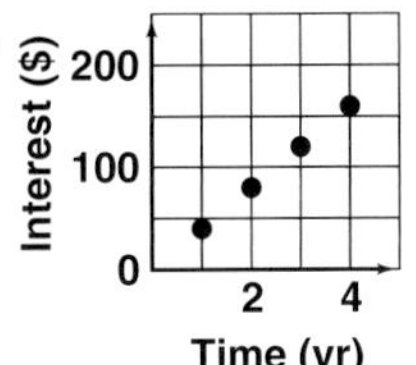

3. \$4,943.49

Checkpoint Quiz 2 **1.**

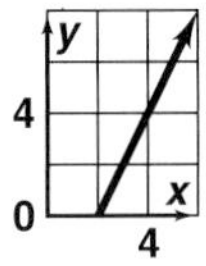

2.

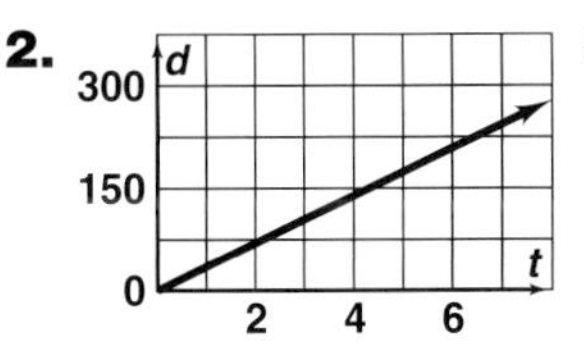

3.

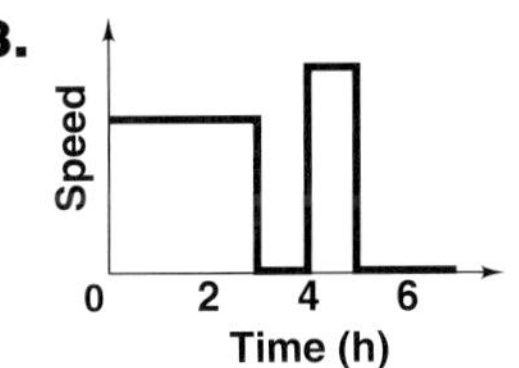

4.

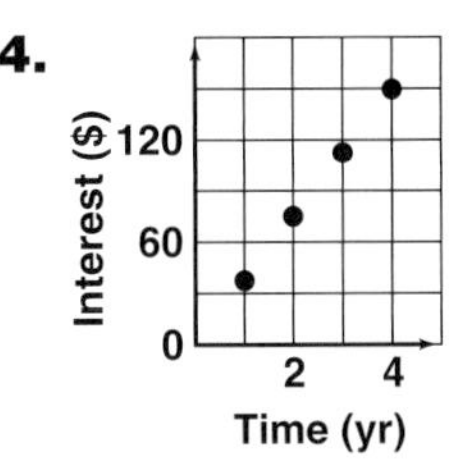

5. \$1,009.53

Lesson 9-8 pp. 503–504

Check Skills You'll Need **1.** 12 **2.** 18 **3.** −13 **4.** 3 **5.** 10 **6.** −19

Check Understanding **1.** 5,240 Cal; 4,585 Cal **2.** 9 omnitheatre shows

Lesson 9-9 pp. 507–508

Check Skills You'll Need **1.** 14 **2.** −2 **3.** $2\frac{2}{3}$ **4.** −20 **5.** −32 **6.** 4.2

Check Understanding **1a.** $x = \frac{y + 4}{2}$

b. $y = 2x - 4$ $\quad x = \frac{y + 4}{2}$

$20 = 2(12) - 4$ $\quad 12 = \frac{20 + 4}{2}$

$20 = 20$ ✔ $\quad 12 = 12$ ✔

c. The Distributive Property **2.** 6%

Chapter 10

Diagnosing Readiness p. 520

1.

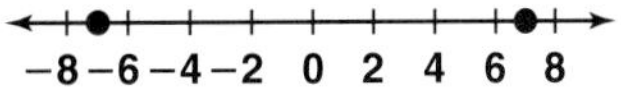

2.

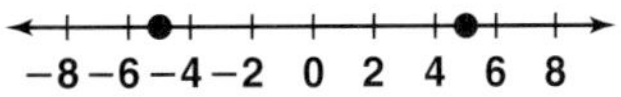

3.

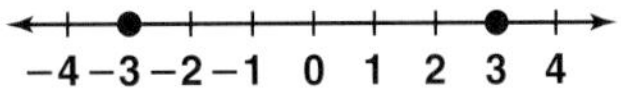

4.

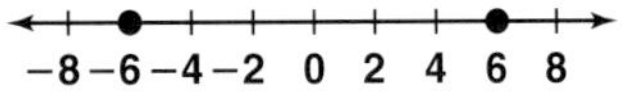

5. 63 **6.** −10 **7.** 6 **8.** 0 **9.** 10 **10.** 19 **11.** 9 **12.** −13 **13.** 125 **14.** 64 **15.** 1,331 **16.** 10,000 **17.** $\frac{6}{7}$ **18.** $\frac{5}{6}$ **19.** $\frac{5}{9}$ **20.** $\frac{10}{19}$ **21.** acute **22.** right **23.** obtuse **24.** straight **25.** obtuse **26.** acute

Lesson 10-1 pp. 521–523

Check Skills You'll Need **1.**

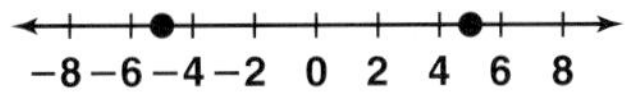

2.

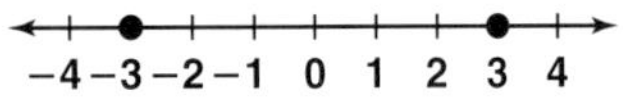

3.

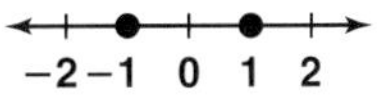

4.

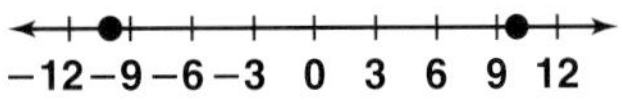

5.

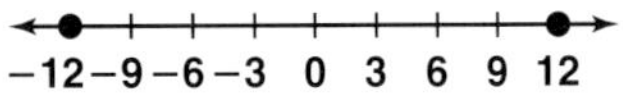

6.

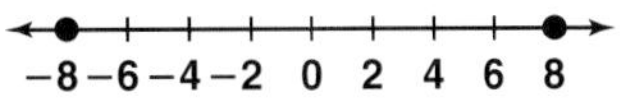

Check Understanding **1a.** $A(-2, 3)$, $B(2, -3)$, $C(-2, -3)$ **b.** $(0, 0)$ **2a–c.**

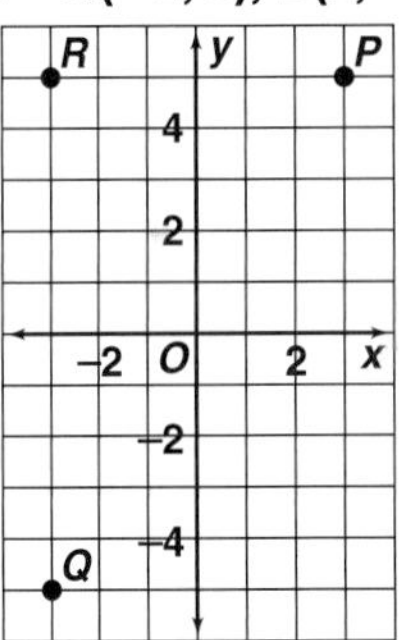

d. P: I; Q: III; R: II

3a. horizontal

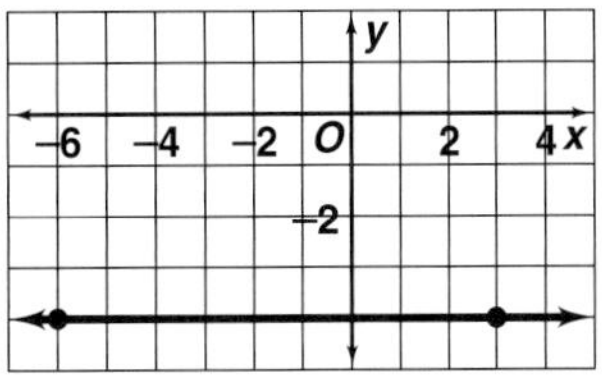

Instant Check System™ Answers

b. 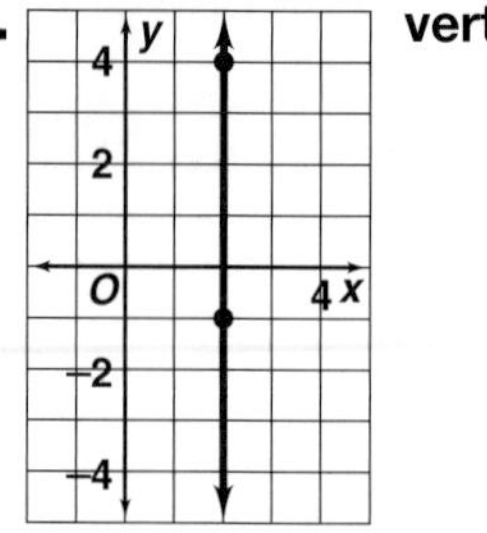

vertical

c. They are the same; they are the same.

Lesson 10-2 pp. 527–528

Check Skills You'll Need **1.** 9 **2.** 15 **3.** 8 **4.** 10 **5.** 4 **6.** 5 **7.** no; $(3 + 4) - 2 = 3 + (4 - 2)$

Check Understanding **1a.** yes **b.** no **c.** no

3b. 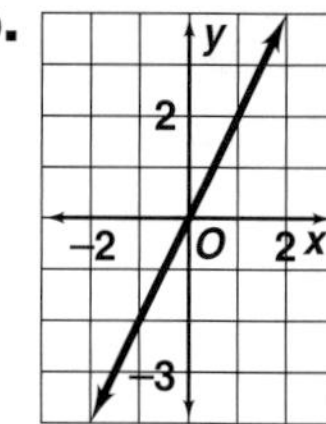

c. A linear equation has an infinite number of solutions, because there is an infinite number of points on the graph of the equation.

Lesson 10-3 pp. 533–535

Check Skills You'll Need **1.** $\frac{3}{4}$ **2.** $\frac{4}{5}$ **3.** $-\frac{2}{3}$ **4.** $\frac{1}{3}$ **5.** -5

Check Understanding **1a.** -2 **b.** -2; the slope is always the same. **2a.** $-\frac{1}{2}$ **b.** Roof *B;* the slope of roof *A* is $\frac{1}{4}$, and the slope of roof *B* is $\frac{5}{6}$. Since $\frac{5}{6} > \frac{1}{4}$, roof *B* is steeper than roof *A.* **3a.** yes;

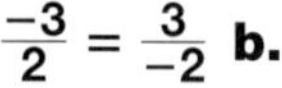
$\frac{-3}{2} = \frac{3}{-2}$ **b.** 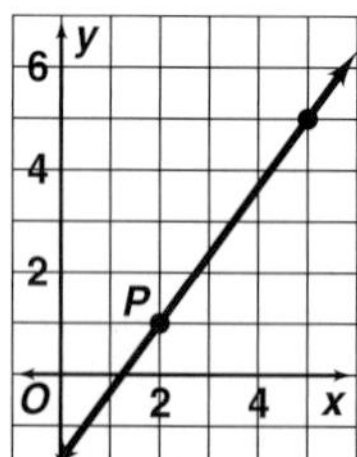

Checkpoint Quiz 1 **1.** vertical **2.** horizontal **3.** vertical **4.** 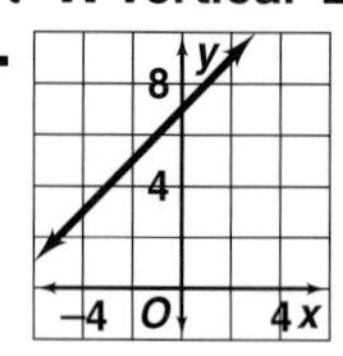

5. 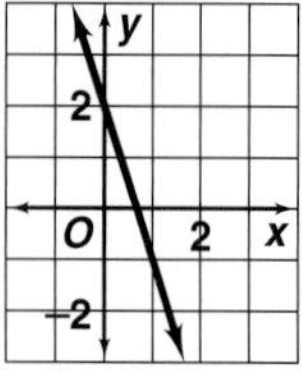

6. 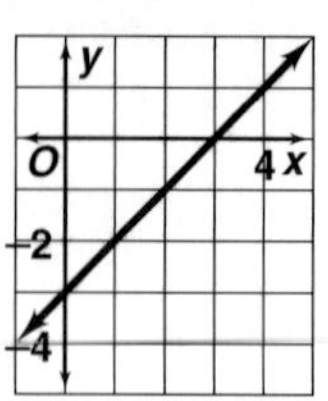

7. $-\frac{3}{2}$ **8.** 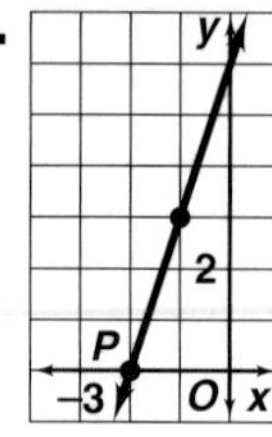

9. 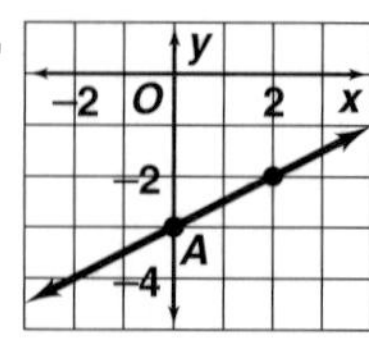

10. 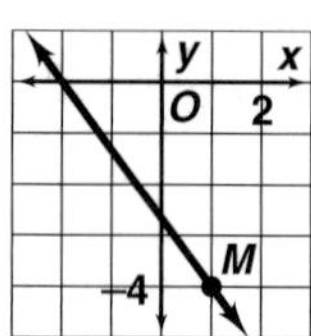

Lesson 10-4 pp. 540–541

Check Skills You'll Need **1–6.** Answers may vary. Samples are given. **1.** (0, 12), (−2, 10), (3, 15) **2.** (0, −20), (5, −15), (−10, −30) **3.** (0, 0), (1, 15), (−2, −30) **4.** (0, −2), (2, 4), (−1, −5) **5.** (0, 4), (4, 0), (−3, 7) **6.** (0, 2), (1, 7), (−2, −8)

Check Understanding **1a.**

x	−3	−2	−1	0	1	2	3
y	18	8	2	0	2	8	18

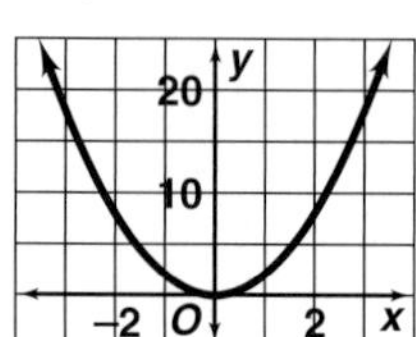

2.

x	−2	−1	0	1	2
y	4	2	0	2	4

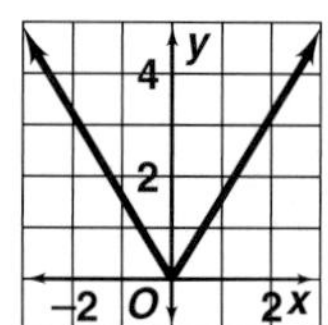

Lesson 10-5 pp. 544–545

Check Skills You'll Need **1.** 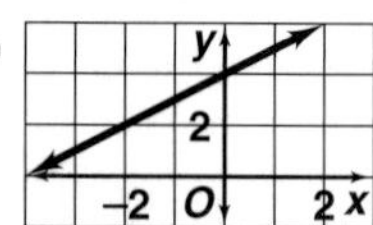

2. 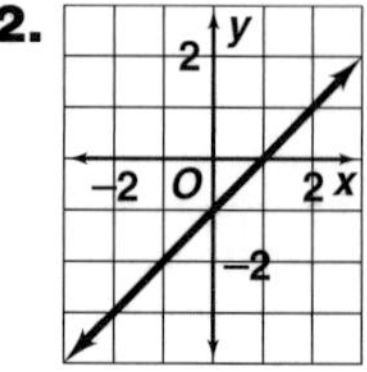

3. **4.** 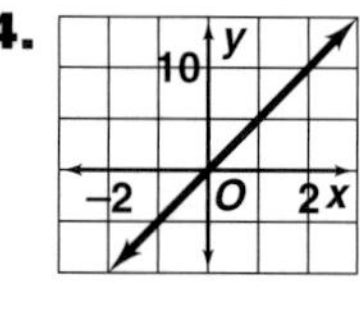

5. 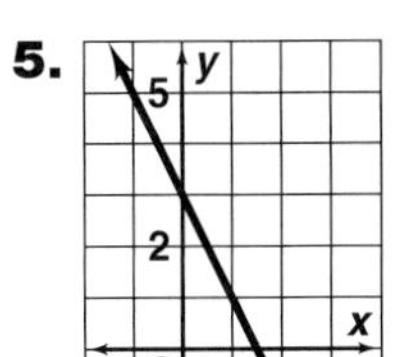
6. 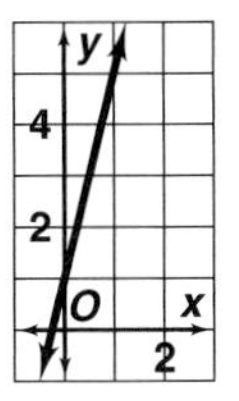
7.

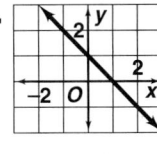

8. 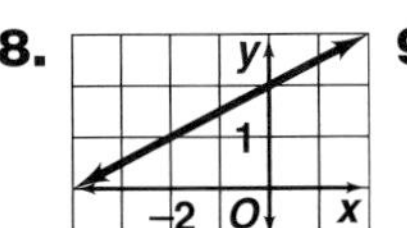
9. 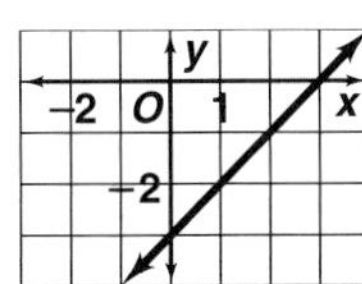

Check Understanding **1.** about 6.5 in.

Lesson 10-6 pp. 549–551

Check Skills You'll Need **1–4.** 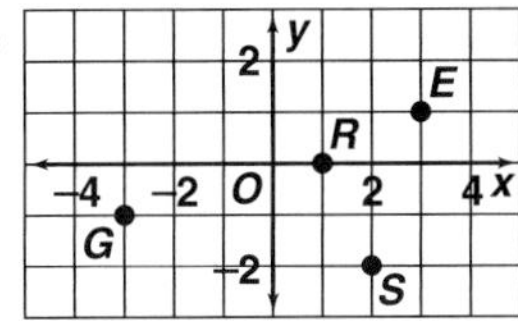

5. Answers may vary. Sample: Two coordinates are needed to place the point both horizontally and vertically.

Check Understanding **1a.** $(-3, -3)$ **b.** Horizontal translations do not change the y-coordinate, and vertical translations do not change the x-coordinate. **2.** 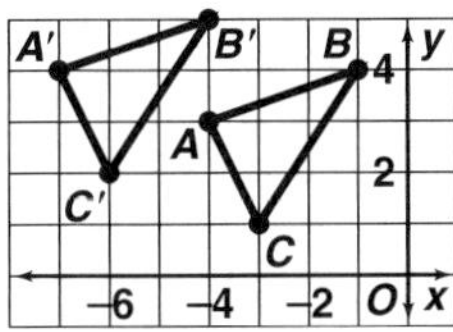

$A(-4, 3)$, $B(-1, 4)$, $C(-3, 1) \rightarrow A'(-7, 4)$, $B'(-4, 5)$, $C'(-6, 2)$ **3a.** $(x, y) \rightarrow (x + 4, y + 4)$ **b.** -2; 6

Lesson 10-7 pp. 554–555

Check Skills You'll Need **1.** $(-1, 1)$ **2.** $(-5, -1)$ **3.** $(-6, 5)$ **4.** $(-8, 4)$ **5.** left 2; down 2

Check Understanding **1.** 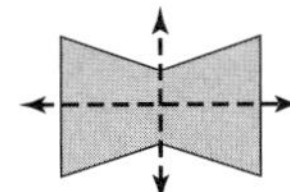

2a–b. 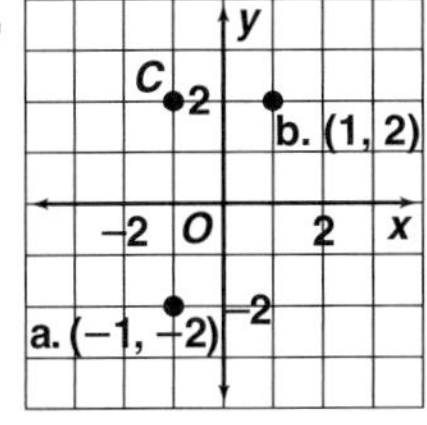

3a. 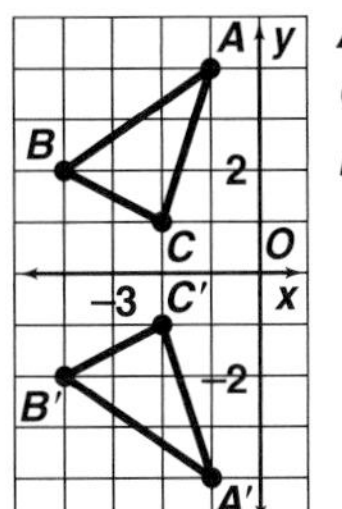
$A(-1, 4)$, $B(-4, 2)$, $C(-2, 1) \rightarrow A'(-1, -4)$, $B'(-4, -2)$, $C'(-2, -1)$

b. The x-coordinates stay the same, the y-coordinates are opposites.

Checkpoint Quiz 2 **1.** 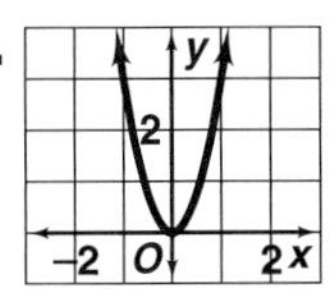

2. 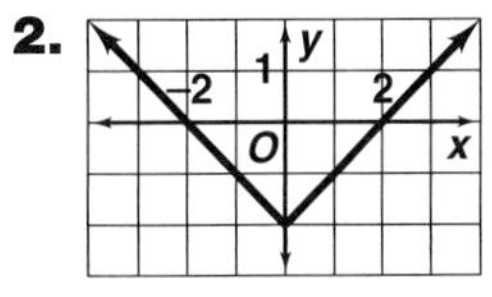
3. 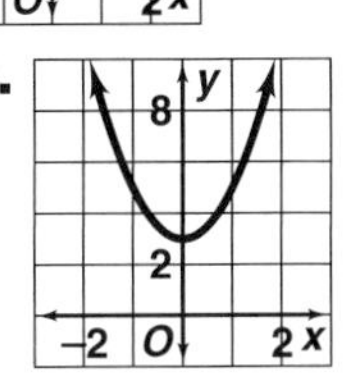

4. \$50 **5.** $(-3, 9)$ **6.** $(12, 6)$ **7.** $(3, 0)$ **8.** $(1, 4)$ **9.** $(3, 1)$ **10.** $(6, 4)$

Lesson 10-8 pp. 559–560

Check Skills You'll Need **1.** acute

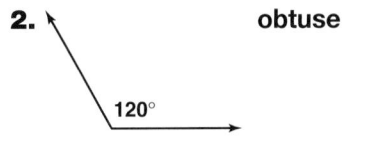

60°

2. obtuse

120°

3. right

90°

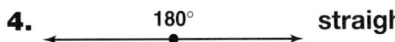

4. 180° straight

Check Understanding **1a.** Yes, the figure has rotational symmetry. You can rotate it 72° and match the original figure. **b.** No, the figure does not have rotational symmetry. You cannot match the original figure by rotating it 180° or less. **2a.** yes; 120° **b.** No; the size of the angle stays the same no matter how large the figure.
3a. 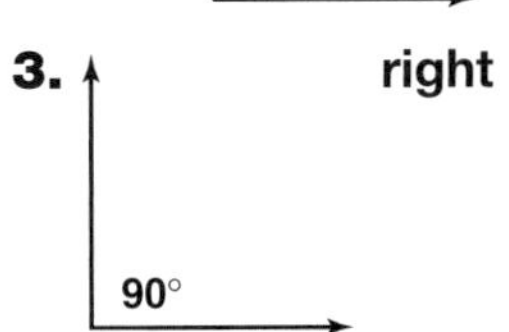
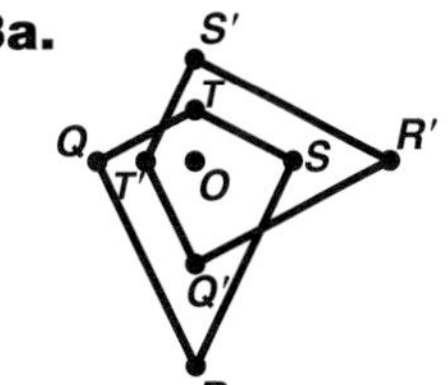

3b. 180°; 360°

Chapter 11

Diagnosing Readiness p. 572

1. 13, 30, 31, 32, 33, 34 **2.** 119, 121, 125, 129, 137 **3.** 10.2, 10.9, 11.1, 11.3, 11.5 **4.** −5, −4, −3, −1, 0, 2 **5.** 12 **6.** 32 **7.** 67 **8.** 8.5 **9.** 18 **10.** 14 **11.** 68 **12.** 108 **13–16.**

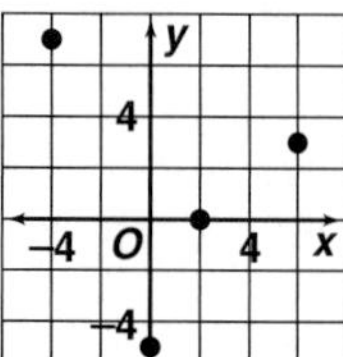

Lesson 11-1 p. 573–574

Check Skills You'll Need **1.** 16, 22, 23, 45, 52, 61, 87, 91 **2.** 4.1, 4.13, 4.15, 4.2, 4.3 **3.** 108, 116, 125, 132, 132, 191 **4.** 7.08, 7.25, 7.3, 7.62, 7.9

Check Understanding **1.**

U.S. Representatives for 22 States

Number of Represen-tatives	Tally	Frequency
1	𝍸	5
2	II	2
3	IIII	4
4	II	2
5	III	3
6		0
7	II	2
8	II	2
9	II	2

2. 3; 12; there are 12 *x*'s above the 3.

Lesson 11-2 pp. 579–581

Check Skills You'll Need

1.

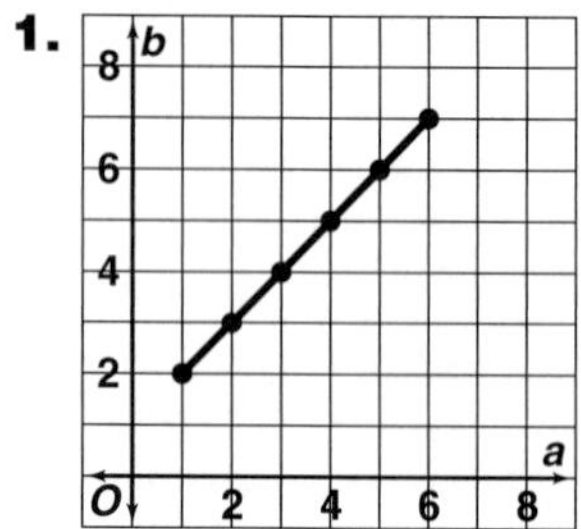

2.

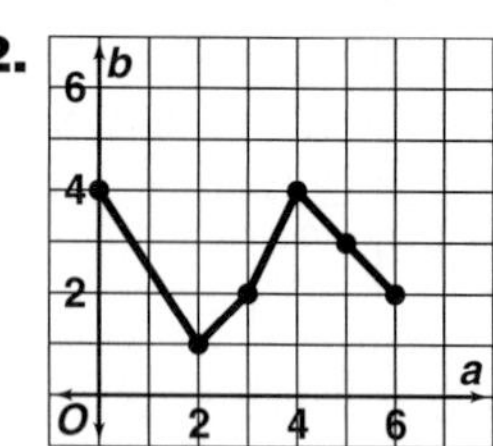

Check Understanding **1a.** 78.8; 78.8 million households with VCRs in 1996 **b.** B3 **2.** 1994, 1996, 1998, and 2000 **3a.** 1994 and 1996 **b.** Use a double line graph to show a trend, and use a double bar graph to compare values.

Lesson 11-3 p. 585–590

Check Skills You'll Need **1.** 42 **2.** 31 **3.** 3.15 **4.** 6.4 **5.** 122.5 **6.** 231

Check Understanding **1a.** 6 tenths **b.** The number shows up twice in the data. **c.** Wind Speeds Recorded During Storm (mph)

Stem	Leaves
0	9
1	4 6 8
2	5 5 9
3	0 3 4 8

Key: 1 | 4 means 14

2a. Charlotte, NC **b.** Charlotte, NC; Portland, ME **c.** Charlotte, 1.7 in.; Portland, 2.3 in.

3a.

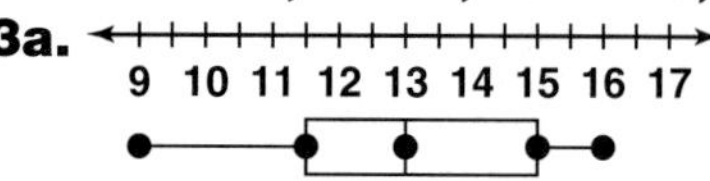

b. No; depending on the data set, the median may not be in the middle because it is not an average.

Checkpoint Quiz 1 **1.**

Number	Tally	Frequency
1	II	2
2	II	2
3	II	2
4	II	2
5	III	3
6	I	1
7	II	2
8	II	2
9	I	1

```
                x
x  x  x  x  x       x  x
x  x  x  x  x   x   x  x  x
1  2  3  4  5   6   7  8  9
```

2. Graphs and explanations may vary. Sample:

Art Show Attendance

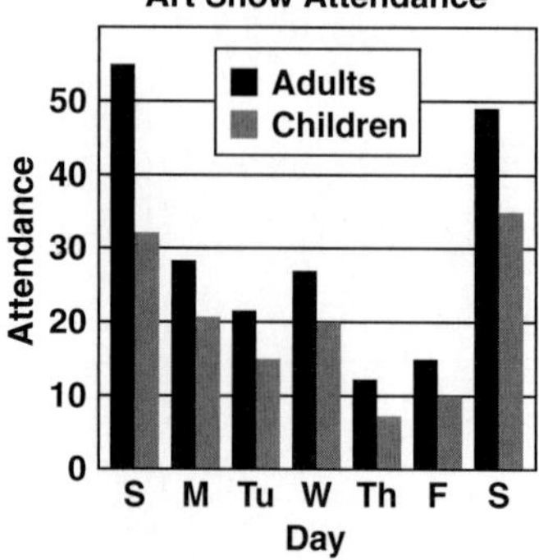

I chose a double bar graph so I could compare both sets of data.

3. 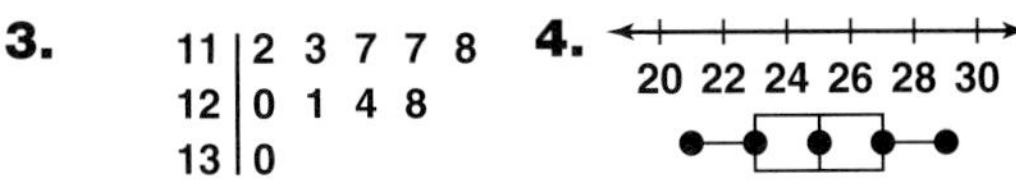

Key: 11 | 2 means 112

5. 18; 8

Lesson 11-4 p. 592–593

Check Skills You'll Need **1.**

Heights	Tally	Frequency
52	|||	3
53	||	2
54		0
55	|||	3
56	𝍸	5
57	|||	3
58	||	2
59	|	1
60	|	1

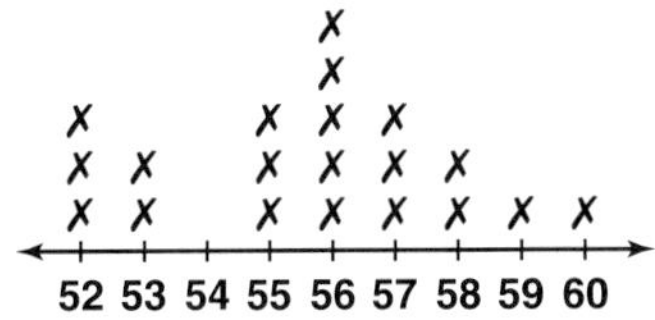

2.

Ages	Tally	Frequency
58	|	1
59		0
60		0
61		0
62	|||	3
63	||||	4
64	||	2
65	||||	4
66		0
67	|	1
68	||	2
69	||	2
70		0
71	|	1

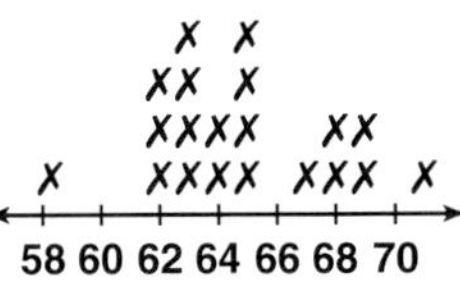

Check Understanding **1.** Mary, Donna, Susan, Genevieve

Lesson 11-5 p. 596–597

Check Skills You'll Need **1.** 80% **2.** 25% **3.** 70% **4.** 33.3% **5.** 99.9% **6.** 100%

Check Understanding **1a.** Answers may vary. Sample: **b.** you won't just get people shopping after work **c.** Answers may vary. Sample: Take a random sample from the local phone book and survey every 20th person. **2a.** Biased; the question implies that anchovies are slimy and vegetables are healthy. **b.** Fair; the question makes no assumptions about pizza toppings.

Lesson 11-6 p. 602–603

Skills You'll Need **1.** 10 **2.** 2.9 **3.** 44 **4.** 1.8 **5.** 9 **6.** 8 **7.** 2.5 **8.** 1

Check Understanding 1a. about 1,875 deer **b.** about 2,571 deer **c.** It decreases.

Lesson 11-7 p. 606–608

Check Skills You'll Need **1.** 117.8; 118; 123 **2.** 56; 50; 50 **3.** 2.3; 2.2; none **4.** 57; 46; 39

Check Understanding **1.** Graph (a); the graph makes it look like the time was at least 4 times greater. **2a.** 15–30 yr **b.**

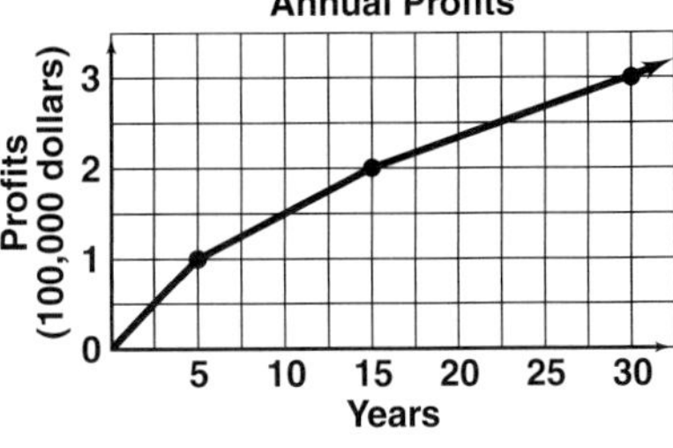

3a. 1; 1 **b.** Median; outliers do not affect the median. **4a.** 599 Cal **b.** about 46 g **c.** Answers may vary. Sample: "Home of the Under-500-Calorie Kiddie Burger."

Lesson 11-8 pp. 613–618

Check Skills You'll Need 1–6.

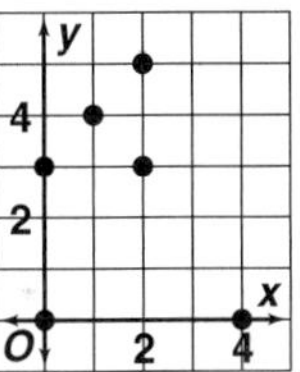

Check Understanding

1a.

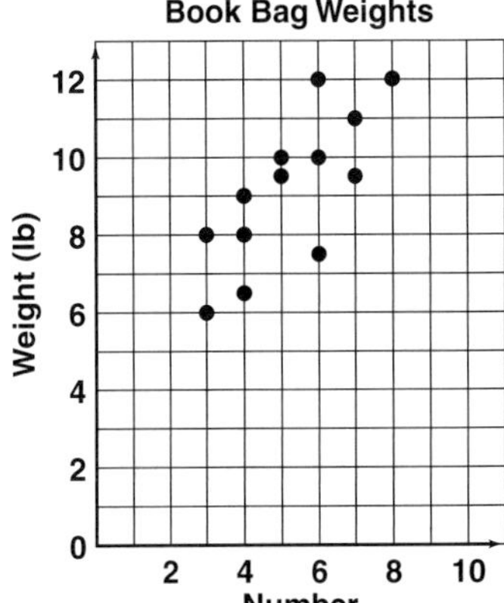

b. about 3 books **c.** Answers may vary. Sample: About 14 lb; find a line that is close to most points and find where 10 books would fall on the line. **2.** Negative trend; as the number of leaves increase, the amount of sunlight beneath the tree will tend to decrease.

Checkpoint Quiz 2 **1.** Elsa: green towel and beach ball; Anna: blue towel and sandwiches; LaToya: red towel and iced tea **2.**

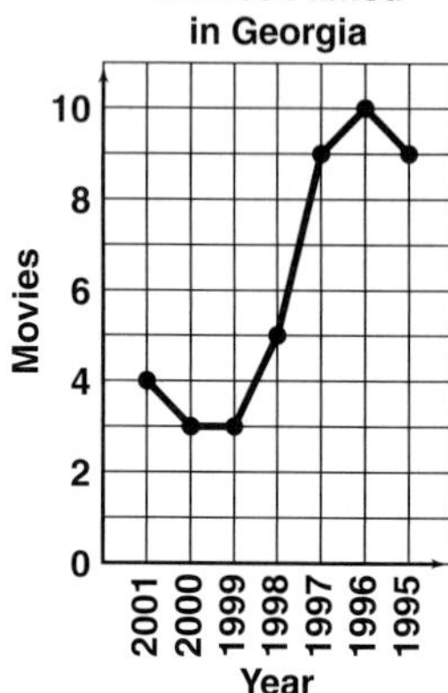

3. Check students' work. **4.** about 172 turtles **5.** A

Chapter 12

Diagnosing Readiness p. 628

1. $\frac{3}{8}$ **2.** $\frac{10}{27}$ **3.** $\frac{3}{13}$ **4.** $\frac{2}{5}$ **5.** $\frac{8}{11}$ **6.** $\frac{1}{4}$ **7.** $\frac{3}{7}$ **8.** $\frac{4}{9}$ **9.** 9 **10.** 43.75 **11.** 5 **12.** 43.75 **13.** 64 **14.** 10.5 **15.** 46% **16.** 26.5% **17.** 7% **18.** 25.6% **19.** 82% **20.** 2% **21.** 80% **22.** 45.5% **23.** 57.1% **24.** 40% **25.** 48.9% **26.** 40%

Lesson 12-1 pp. 629–632

Check Skills You'll Need **1.** 0.62; 62% **2.** 0.95; 95% **3.** 0.275; 27.5% **4.** 1.1; 110% **5.** Answers may vary. Sample: Divide the percent by 100.

Check Understanding **1.** $\frac{3}{5}$; 0.6; 60% **2a.** $\frac{1}{3}$ **b.** 0 **c.** Answers may vary. Sample: Roll a number less than 10. **3a.** $\frac{5}{6}$; $0.8\overline{3}$; $83.\overline{3}\%$ **b.** $\frac{2}{3}$; $0.\overline{6}$; $66.\overline{6}\%$ **4.** 1 : 4

Lesson 12-2 pp. 636–638

Check Skills You'll Need **1.** $\frac{1}{6}$; $0.1\overline{6}$; about 16.7% **2.** $\frac{1}{2}$; 0.5; 50% **3.** 0; 0; 0% **4.** Answers may vary. Sample: An outcome is a single result, an event can be a group of results.

Check Understanding **1.** $\frac{5}{12}$ **2a.** No; experimental results may differ for other batches of bicycles.

$\frac{1}{6}$

b. 105 bikes **3a.** **b.** 5 coins; you would use one coin for each of the five babies.

Lesson 12-3 pp. 643–644

Check Skills You'll Need **1.** $\frac{1}{4}$ **2.** $\frac{12}{25}$ **3.** $\frac{19}{25}$

Check Understanding **1a.** Answers may vary. Sample: Method 1 is easier for this problem because you only have to list 16 outcomes versus simulating the problem and recording results. **b.** Answers may vary. Sample: 0.25

Lesson 12-4 pp. 647–652

Check Skills You'll Need **1.** $2^2 \cdot 3$ **2.** $2 \cdot 7$ **3.** $2^2 \cdot 5$ **4.** $2^3 \cdot 3^2$ **5.** Answers may vary. Sample: A factor tree helps organize the steps and keeps track of the prime factors.

Check Understanding **1.**

	H	T
H	HH	HT
T	TH	TT

; $\frac{1}{4}$

2a.

Vessel	Stream	Outcomes
Kayak	N	K, N
	NW	K, NW
	NE	K, NE
Canoe	N	C, N
	NW	C, NW
	NE	C, NE
Rowboat	N	R, N
	NW	R, NW
	NE	R, NE

b. $\frac{1}{3}$ **3a.** 35 sandwiches **b.** $\frac{1}{5}$

Checkpoint Quiz 1 **1.** $\frac{2}{5}$; 0.4; 40% **2.** $\frac{4}{5}$; 0.8; 80% **3a.** $\frac{32}{119}$ **b.** $\frac{20}{119}$ **4a.** Check students' work. **b.** A simulation represents experimental probability because you use data. An organized list represents theoretical probability because it lists all possible outcomes.

5a. PP, PB, PR, PG
BB, BR, BG, BP
GG, GP, GB, GR
RR, RB, RP, RG

b. $\frac{1}{16}$ **c.** $\frac{1}{16}$

Lesson 12-5 pp. 653–655

Check Skills You'll Need **1.** $\frac{9}{16}$ **2.** $\frac{6}{25}$ **3.** $\frac{1}{20}$ **4.** $\frac{6}{49}$ **5.** $\frac{1}{2}$ **6.** $\frac{1}{10}$ **7.** $\frac{1}{3}$ **8.** $\frac{4}{11}$

Check Understanding **1.** $\frac{1}{4}$ **2a.** $\frac{1}{36}$ **b.** $\frac{1}{9}$ **3.** $\frac{1}{10}$ **4.** The number of favorable outcomes is 1, and the number of possible outcomes is 25.

Lesson 12-6 pp. 660–661

Check Skills You'll Need **1.** 132 **2.** 380 **3.** 90 **4.** 156 **5.** 336 **6.** 720 **7.** 60 **8.** 120

Check Understanding **1.** 720 **2a.** 7! = 5,040 **b.** No; 3! + 2! = 8; 5! = 120 **3.** The example only selects 3 teams from the 16 choices, so the answer is 16 × 15 × 14, not 16!.

Lesson 12-7 pp. 664–668

Check Skills You'll Need **1.** 24 **2.** 6 **3.** 720 **4.** The arrangement may form a word.

Check Understanding **1.** 3 **2.** 6

Checkpoint Quiz 2 **1.** $\frac{3}{49}$ **2.** $\frac{2}{49}$ **3.** $\frac{5}{49}$ **4.** $\frac{2}{49}$ **5.** $\frac{3}{56}$ **6.** $\frac{3}{14}$ **7.** $\frac{1}{14}$ **8.** 720 ways **9.** 15 combinations **10a.** ABCD, ABDC, ACBD, ACDB, ADBC, ADCB, BACD, BADC, BCAD, BCDA, BDAC, BDCA, CABD, CADB, CBAD, CBDA, CDAB, CDBA, DABC, DACB, DBAC, DBCA, DCAB, DCBA **b.** 6 combinations

Selected Answers

Chapter 1

Lesson 1-1 pp. 7–9

EXERCISES **1.** about 11 **3.** about 19 **7.** about 60 **9.** about 891 **13.** about 660 mi **15.** about 19 **17.** about 14 **21.** about 4 **23.** about 10 **33.** about 3 mi/h more **37.** about $2 **39.** about $4 **41.** about $56 **43.** Anchorage 45 in., El Paso 24 in., Indianapolis 120 in., Miami 180 in., Pago Pago 600 in., San Jose 210 in., South Pole Sta. 0 in. **57.** 4; 40; 403; 4,004 **59.** two hundred forty-eight and nine tenths **61.** four and twenty-eight hundredths

Lesson 1-2 pp. 13–15

EXERCISES **1.** 7.46 **3.** 105.8 **11.** 1.88 m **13.** 7.2 **15.** 14.71 **19.** 43.5 **21.** 39.5 **25.** 0.0645 **27.** 4.13 **31a.** $1.75 **b.** $8.75 **c.** $8.25 **33.** 4.67 in. **35.** Comm. Prop. of Add. **37.** Ident. Prop. of Add. **39.** $13.85 **43.** > **45.** < **59.** about 4 **61.** nine hundredths **63.** eight thousandths

Lesson 1-3 pp. 20–22

EXERCISES **1.** 0.14 **3.** 0.15 **9.** 4.2 mi **11.** 0 **13.** 21.5 **17.** 2.7 **19.** 21 **23.** $4.75 **25.** 0.075 **27.** 740 **33.** 0.009 **35.** 502 **37a.** $1.73 **b.** 4 L **c.** You multiply in (a) and divide in (b). **39.** 0; Zero Prop. **41.** 3; Comm. Prop. of Mult. **45a.** 490 **b.** 1.3 **c.** 64 **d.** Divide the product by the given factor. You can check by multiplying the two factors to see if you get the product. **47.** 71.3 **49.** 134.68 **57a.** 4 **b.** 40 **c.** 400 **d.** It gets larger. **59a.** between 106 and 116 cm **b.** no **61.** 3,184.71 **63.** 2,187.50 **71.** 1.643 **73.** 20.19 **75.** 7 tens **77.** 7 tenths

Lesson 1-4 pp. 26–28

EXERCISES **1.** Centimeters; a book is not even close to a meter. **3.** Gram; a pumpkin seed is close to the weight of a paper clip. **7.** 250 mL **9.** 3.7 kg **11.** 900 **13.** 58,000 **17.** 23.051 km **19.** 6,477 mL **23.** 240 mL **25.** grams **27.** decaliter **29.** 5 mugs **33.** D **35.** F **49.** 0 **51.** 210.9 **55.** 6.501

Lesson 1-5 pp. 32–33

EXERCISES **1.** 7 and 21 **3.** 130 pigs, 90 chickens **5.** 14 yr old **7.** troposphere, stratosphere, mesosphere, thermosphere, exosphere **19.** 31,700 **21.** 10 **23.** 1

Lesson 1-6 pp. 36–38

EXERCISES **1.** 1 **3.** −15 **11.** 10 **13.** 16 **21.** > **23.** < **29.** −6, −4, −2, 3, 8 **31.** −7, −3, 1, 2, 10 **35.** −12, −7, −4, −3, +2, +4 **37.** −8 **39.** 2

41. −4 −3 −2 −1 0 1 2 3 4

43. −8 −6 −4 −2 0 2 4 6 8

45. −8 **47.** −1,345

49a. −10 −5 0 5 10 15 20 25 30

b. from left to right: Barrow, Duluth, Caribou, Bismark, Omaha **51.** Barrow; Bismark **53.** < **55.** > **65.** 7 **67.** 2 **81.** 0.02678 **83.** Comm. Prop. of Add. **85.** Assoc. Prop. of Add.

Lesson 1-7 pp. 42–44

EXERCISES **1.** −9 **3.** 1 **13.** 38 **15.** −6 **25.** 7°F **27.** 0 **29.** 25 **39.** 26 **41.** 12 **45.** −10 **47.** 15 **53.** $9 **55.** −1 + 4 = 3 **57.** 3 + (−7) = −4 **59.** Anchorage: 124°F, El Paso: 117°F, Indianapolis: 132°F, Miami: 72°F, Pago Pago: 31°F, San Jose: 43°F, South Pole Sta.: 113°F **61.** negative **63.** positive **65.** A **67.** C **69.** 6:00 P.M. **71.** 1:00 A.M. **83.** > **85.** < **89.** 17 **91.** 43

Lesson 1-8 pp. 47–49

EXERCISES **1.** 26 **3.** 30 **13.** −3 **15.** 10 **25.** −38 m/min **27.** *G* **29.** *B* **33a.** −$16 **b.** $22 **45.** negative **47.** negative **51.** −3 **61.** 9 **63.** 5 **65.** 14 cm

Lesson 1-9 pp. 52–54

EXERCISES **1.** 11 **3.** 3 **11.** 13,500 ft^2 **13.** 546 **15.** 696 **25.** −3; −3; 21 **27.** 7; −49 **29a.** $20 \times 28.5 = 20(28 + .5) = 560 + 10 = 570$ **b.** 570 $in.^2$ **31.** $29.40 **33.** + **35.** + **37.** $3(5 + 5) = 3 \cdot 5 + 3 \cdot 5 = 30$ cm^2 **39a.** $31.50 **b.** $28.50 **c.** $60 **43.** $4 \cdot 4 \div (4 + 4) = 2$ **53.** −48 **55.** 63 **57.** 1.3 **59.** 24.8

Lesson 1-10 pp. 58–60

EXERCISES **1.** 8 **3.** 1 **5.** $4.60 **7.** 307.2 mi **9.** 46; it decreases the mean of the data. **11.** 14.7; it raises the mean of the data. **13.** 41 **15.** −1.5 **17.** 51 and 58 **19.** 2; 2; 1 and 2 **21a.** 12.7 yr **b.** 12 yr **c.** 12 and 15 yr **d.** Median; 20 may be considered an outlier. **27.** $4.57 **29.** 3.49; 6.1; 3.2 **41.** 27 **43.** 2 **45.** 123, 213, 213, 231, 312, 321

Chapter Review pp. 62–63

1. Distr. Prop. **2.** Assoc. Prop. of Add. **3.** absolute value **4.** mode **5.** order of operations

Exercises 6–9. Answers may vary. Samples are given.

6. 7; compatible numbers **7.** 52, rounding **8.** 63, rounding **9.** 6; front-end estimation **10.** It is most useful for finding quotients because it works with multiples. **11.** 3.7 **12.** 0.567 **13.** 0.73 **14.** 16.875 **15.** 7.31 lb **16.** 0.456 **17.** 14,200 **18.** 340 **19.** Answers may vary. Sample: Fill the 13-L container and pour it into the 5-L container, leaving 8 L in the 13-L container. Pour this 8 L into the 11-L container. Pour the 5 L back into the 24-L container. Repeat filling of 13-L container, pouring into 5-L container and return to 24-L container. The 11-L, 13-L, and 24-L containers each hold 8 L. **20.** $<$ **21.** $=$ **22.** $>$ **23.** $>$ **24.** -22 **25.** 29 **26.** -30 **27.** -25 **28.** 3.425 **29.** 13.13 **30.** 2; 2; 2

Chapter 2

Lesson 2-1 pp. 73–75

EXERCISES **1.** 42 **3.** 3 **27.** 12 **29.** 8.5 **35.** 3.7 **37.** 1.4 **43.** $440p$ **53.** 11.9 **55.** 122 **57.** 699

Lesson 2-2 pp. 79–81

EXERCISES **1.** 16 **3.** 104 **9.** -6 **11.** 3 **21.** about 19 **23.** about 36 **27.** 90 ft **29.** about 54 **31.** about 222 **39.** about 10 in. **41.** 6 **43.** 30 **45.** about 3 bowling pins **61.** 72 **63.** 11 **67.** 5 **69.** -4 **73.** 125 children and 45 adults

Lesson 2-3 pp. 85–87

EXERCISES **1.** -49 **3.** 43 **9.** $344 = a - 1{,}117$; 1,461 m/s **11.** 27 **13.** 472 **19.** $15 + p = 33$; 18 points **21.** 119 **23.** -9 **31.** $7 = g - 6$; 13 yr **33.** D **35.** C

Lesson 2-4 pp. 90–92

EXERCISES **1.** -47 **3.** -68 **11.** 4 h **13.** 28 **15.** -60 **23.** $15{,}830 = 8a$; $a \approx 1{,}979$ lb of apples **25.** -3 **27.** -6 **35.** $12x = -36$; -36 is the multiple of 12 that is closest to -38; $x \approx -3$ **37.** -43.26 **39.** 128.7 **57.** 16 **59.** 63 **61.** Ident. Prop. of Mult.

Lesson 2-5 pp. 96–97

EXERCISES **1.** $3p - 2$ **3.** Let p = number of pages; $\frac{p}{2} - 7$ **7.** Let m = number of months; $40m + 35$; \$435 **9.** 10 **11.** 3 **15.** 7 wk **17.** 11 **19.** 45 **25.** \$40 is the hourly rate, h is the number of hours the electrician works, \$35 is the fee for a house call, and \$115 is the total bill. The electrician works 2 h. **27.** \$12 **29.** 10 **37.** 72 **39.** 60 **41.** 179

Lesson 2-6 pp. 100–101

EXERCISES **1.** -3 **3.** 8 **19.** 54 **21.** -6 **25.** Let n = number of extra nights; $3.95 + 1.25n = 7.70$; 3 extra nights **27.** Let h = number of hours; $20h - 3 = 117$; 6 h **29.** -140 **31.** 39 **37.** 30 = the DJ's hourly wage; x = hours the DJ works; 65 = cost of decorations; 170 = amount of money budgeted **39.** Let m = number of miles driven; $38 + 0.30m = 74$; 120 mi **51.** -9 **53.** 3

Lesson 2-7 pp. 104–105

EXERCISES **1.** $17 = 5m - 3$; 4 mysteries **3.** $2{,}800 = 1{,}000 + 30w$; 60 wk **7.** 10,053 tickets **9.** Yes; to solve $15g = 150$ you must divide 150 by 15, or $\frac{150}{15}$. The solution for both is $g = 10$. **11.** 3,614 ft **13.** \$464.55 **21.** $\frac{n}{5} = -7$; -35 **23.** 8 **25.** -13

Lesson 2-8 pp. 109–111

EXERCISES **1.** -2 **3.** -12

7. 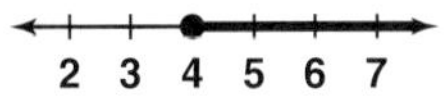

9. 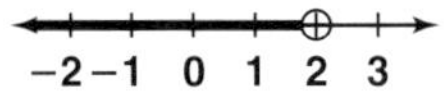

15. $x \le 6$ **17.** $x \ge -1$ **19.** $r \ge 30$ **21.** $s \le 65$ **23.** $-1, 1, 2$ **25.** 3 **27.** $w \le 3$

31. $\ell < 5$; 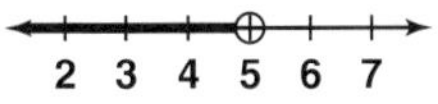

33. $a \ge 17$; 

49. 40 **51.** -17.5 **57.** $-4, -2, -1, 2, 4, 7$ **59.** $-5, -2, 0, 7, 10$

Lesson 2-9 pp. 114–115

EXERCISES **1.** $h < 34$; 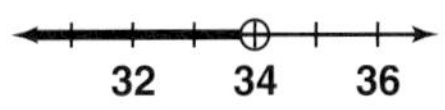

3. $a < 9$; 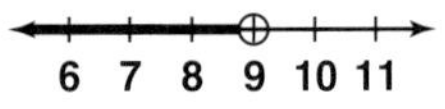

19. $p + 132 \le 225$; $p \le 93$ **21.** $\ell + 32{,}000 < 75{,}000$; $\ell < 43{,}000$ **23.** $c < -4.6$ **25.** $t \ge 7$ **31.** $d + 2.1 > 2.25$; $d > 0.15$ **33.** $15 + n > 10$; $n > -5$ **35.** $n - 6 \le -7$; $n \le -1$ **37.** at least 11 in. **47.** $r < 125$

Lesson 2-10 pp. 119–120

EXERCISES **1.** $6p \geq 296$; at least 50 pages **3.** $6a \leq 27$; at most 4 apple pies **5.** $p > 12$;
10 11 12 13 14 15

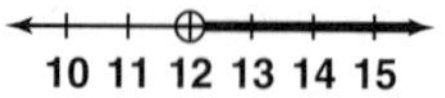

7. $x < -8$;
−11 −10 −9 −8 −7 −6

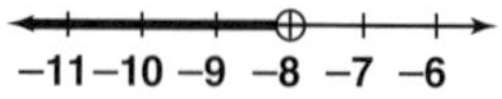

21. $t > 50$ **23.** $h < -30$ **25.** $g < 0.7$ **27.** $n \geq 7$ **29.** To solve $-5x < 25$, divide each side by -5 and reverse the inequality symbol. To solve $5x < 25$, divide both sides by 5, but do not reverse the symbol. **31.** 3 hot dogs **33.** 4 bags of peanuts; \$0.50 **35.** $-3x > 12$; $x < -4$ **37.** $\frac{x}{-9} < 10$; $x > -90$ **49.** $m \geq -9$ **51.** $h > -8$ **53.** −56 **55.** 54

Chapter Review pp. 122–123

1. E **2.** B **3.** C **4.** F **5.** G **6.** 5 **7.** 6 **8.** 13 **9.** 4 **10.** 5.5c **11.** −7 **12.** 20 **13.** 4 **14.** 72 **15.** 23 **16.** 5 **17.** 35 **18.** 21 **19.** 24 **20.** 84 **21.** 99 **22.** −12 **23.** 52 **24.** 5 **25.** 43 **26.** −54 **27.** 1 **28.** 12 **29.** −3 **30.** $140 + 35w = 1{,}050$; 26 wk **31.** $116t - 25 = 352$; \$3.25

32. $t \leq 10$;
7 8 9 10 11 12

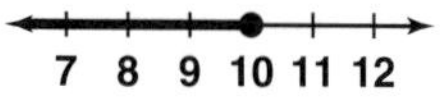

33. $r < 5$;
2 3 4 5 6 7

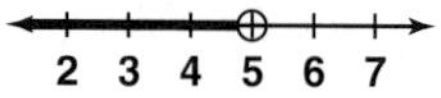

34. $h < -22$;
−24 −22 −20

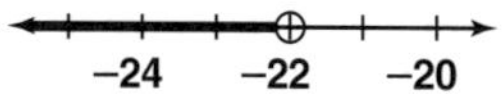

35. $n \leq 1$;
−2 −1 0 1 2 3

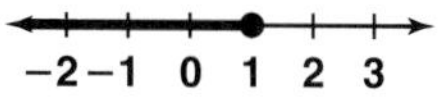

36. $g > 17$;
15 17 19

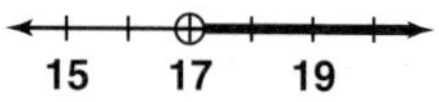

37. $t \geq -10$;
−12 −10 −8

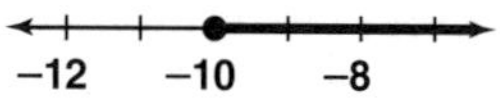

38. $m \geq -7$;
−9 −8 −7 −6 −5 −4

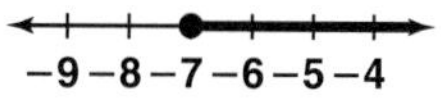

39. $p < -4$;
−7 −6 −5 −4 −3 −2

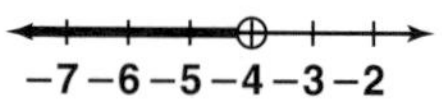

40. $p \geq -15$;
−17 −15 −13

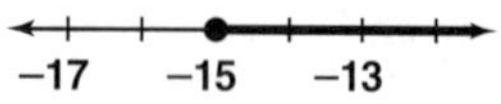

41. $x < 14$;
12 14 16

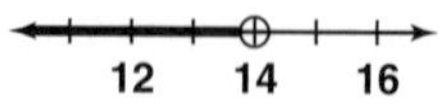

Chapter 3

Lesson 3-1 pp. 133–135

EXERCISES **1.** 6^3 **3.** 7^5 **7.** 81 **9.** 0.000064 **11a.** 0.216 in.^{3} **b.** 0.6 [^] 3 [=] or 0.6 [y^x] 3 [=] **13.** 39 **15.** 37 **21.** −216 **23.** −2,187 **27.** 137 **29.** 89 **39.** C **41.** A **43.** The exponent is equal to the number of zeros. **45.** 13 **47.** −64 **51a.** 0 **b.** 1, 1, 1, 1, 1 **53a.** 5 **b.** 25 **c.** Answers may vary. Sample: "5 squared" is the number of units of area if 5 is the length of a side. **65.** $n > 3$ **67.** $z \geq -12$ **69.** 40 **71.** −7

Lesson 3-2 pp. 138–139

EXERCISES **1.** 7.5×10^3 **3.** 1.25×10^3 **9.** 3,400 **11.** 8,210 **21.** 35.4 is not between 1 and 10. **23.** 0.387 is not between 1 and 10. **25.** 1.290×10^{22}, 3.303×10^{23}, 6.421×10^{23}, 4.869×10^{24}, 5.976×10^{24}, 8.686×10^{25}, 1.024×10^{26}, 5.688×10^{26}, 1.900×10^{27} **27.** 3.26×10^{11} **29.** 1.2285×10^5 **33.** 3.3×10^2 h **35.** 5,880,000,000,000 mi **37.** Answers may vary. Sample: The decimal point moves 8 places to the left in 725,000,000 to get 7.25, so the exponent is 8; $725{,}000{,}000 = 7.25 \times 10^8$. **39.** 1,203,000,000,000,000 **41.** The first colony is growing faster, because $2.2 \times 10^6 > 6.3 \times 10^5$. **49.** 72 **51.** $c < 2$ **53.** $w \geq -18$

Lesson 3-3 pp. 143–144

EXERCISES **1.** No; 571 does not end in 0, 2, 4, 6, or 8. **3.** Yes; 3,650 ends in 0. **17.** top: green; middle: red; bottom: yellow **19.** 2, 3, 5, 10 **21.** 2, 3, 4 **29a.** 66, 785 **b.** 66, 785 **c.** If a number is divisible by both 2 and 3, then it is divisible by 6. **31.** No; 12 is divisible by 2 but 21 is not. **33.** No; 1,800 is divisible by 8 but 8,100 is not. **35.** 7 **37.** 2 **47.** 3.48×10^5 **49.** 6.125×10^3

Lesson 3-4 pp. 148–149

EXERCISES **1.** 12 **3.** 40 **11.** in 21 days **13.** 1, 23 **15.** 1, 2, 31, 62 **23.** composite **25.** neither **27.** $3^2 \cdot 5$ **29.** $2^2 \cdot 3 \cdot 7$ **37.** 2 **39.** 16 **45.** prime **47.** composite **53.** $2 \cdot 43$ **55.** $2 \cdot 3 \cdot 5 \cdot 7$ **61.** 25 seats **63.** 1 **65.** 50 **67a.** 6; it is the GCF; 6 is the product of the common factors of 18 and 24. **b.** 72; it is the LCM; 72 is the least multiple common to 18 and 24. **75.** −13 **77.** −55 **79.** −13, −10, −7

Lesson 3-5 153–155

EXERCISES **17.** $\frac{3}{4}$ **19.** $\frac{11}{13}$ **25.** $\frac{53}{103}$ **27.** 40 **29.** 20 **31a.** $\frac{3}{4}$ in. **b.** $\frac{6}{8}$ in. **c.** Part b; a buttonhole that is $\frac{3}{4}$ in. is too narrow. **37.** D **39.** Novels $\frac{3}{5}$, Biographies $\frac{4}{15}$, Science Fiction $\frac{2}{15}$ **41.** 21 **43.** 24 **45.** School $\frac{7}{24}$, Job $\frac{1}{8}$, Homework/TV $\frac{1}{6}$, Sleeping $\frac{1}{3}$, Eating $\frac{1}{12}$ **55.** $\frac{17}{125}$ **57.** 30 **59.** 17.62 **61.** 43.49

Lesson 3-6 pp. 157–159

EXERCISES **1.** < **3.** < **13.** $\frac{2}{3}, \frac{3}{4}, \frac{5}{6}$ **15.** $\frac{4}{9}, \frac{1}{2}, \frac{2}{3}$ **23.** > **25.** > **27.** what they do **29.** what they do, what they say, what they hear **31.** $\frac{3}{4} > \frac{7}{10}$ **33.** If two fractions have the same numerator, then the fraction with the smaller denominator is greater. **35.** B **37.** C **39.** $\frac{1}{3}, \frac{4}{6}, 1$ **41.** $\frac{4}{3}, 2, \frac{5}{2}$

43. $2\frac{3}{4}$ h **45.** $1\frac{2}{9}$, $1\frac{4}{15}$ **47.** The cheese pizza was most popular because it had the least left over $\left(\frac{5}{8} < \frac{2}{3}, \frac{5}{8} < \frac{3}{9}\right)$. **57.** 3 **59.** 2.82 **61.** 114.594

Lesson 3-7 pp. 162–163

EXERCISES **1a.** 7, 9, 3, 1, 7, 9, 3, 1, . . . **b.** 7 **3.** −1 **5.** 63 games **7.** 13 ways **9.** 7 days **11.** 350 cal **13.** 111,111,111,111,111,111,110 **19.** 56 **21.** 33 **23.** Yes; 2 + 1 + 6 = 9, which is divisible by 3. **25.** No; 315 is divisible by 3, but not 2. **27.** 11 **29.** 60

Lesson 3-8 pp. 166–167

EXERCISES **1.** $\frac{19}{8}$ **3.** $\frac{13}{12}$ **17.** $8\frac{1}{3}$ **19.** $2\frac{7}{12}$ **27.** $4\frac{1}{2}$ mi **29.** $4\frac{1}{2}$ **31.** $4\frac{2}{5}$ **39.** $\frac{95}{2}$, $47\frac{1}{2}$ **41.** $1\frac{5}{8}$, $\frac{13}{8}$ **43.** $\frac{26}{3}$ **45.** $\frac{43}{7}$ **49.** $\frac{26}{8}$, $3\frac{1}{4}$ **59.** −13 **61.** 9 **63.** −12 **65.** 4

Lesson 3-9 pp. 170–172

EXERCISES **1.** 0.4 **3.** 0.375 **17.** $\frac{1}{8}$ **19.** $2\frac{1}{2}$ **25.** $\frac{7}{8}$, 0.83, $\frac{9}{22}$, 0.4 **27.** 0.67, $\frac{2}{3}$, $\frac{7}{12}$, 0.58, $\frac{5}{9}$ **29.** sea star, scallop, red water mite, mosquito **31.** $1\frac{1}{100}$, 1.0101, $1.\overline{01}$

33a–b.

Seed Type	Fraction	Decimal
A	$\frac{5}{16}$	0.31
B	$\frac{1}{4}$	0.25
C	$\frac{1}{2}$	0.5
D	$\frac{17}{35}$	0.49
E	$\frac{9}{26}$	0.35
F	$\frac{1}{3}$	0.33
G	$\frac{14}{55}$	0.25
H	$\frac{18}{35}$	0.51
I	$\frac{8}{15}$	0.53

c. about $\frac{1}{2}$: C, D, H, I about $\frac{1}{3}$: A, E, F about $\frac{1}{4}$: B, G **d.** Seed types C, D, H, I are preferred because they sprout more frequently than the others. **35.** N.Y.: $\frac{4,690}{18,976}$, Tex.: $\frac{5,887}{20,852}$, Calif.: $\frac{9,250}{33,872}$, Fla.: $\frac{3,646}{15,982}$, Ohio: $\frac{2,888}{11,353}$ **37.** Fla., N.Y., Ohio, Calif., Tex. **49.** $\frac{5}{3}$ **51.** $\frac{58}{9}$ **55.** 0.05 **57.** 35

Lesson 3-10 pp. 175–176

EXERCISES **1.** > **3.** < **7.** > **9.** < **13.** −1.0, $-\frac{3}{4}$, 0.25, $\frac{3}{2}$ **15.** −1.5, $\frac{1}{2}$, 0.545, $\frac{6}{11}$ 1 **17a.** −\$40.91 **b.** \$122.18, \$81.27, \$56.27, \$54.09, \$12.37, −\$3.13, −\$35.63, −\$40.91 **21.** < **23.** C **25.** D **35.** $\frac{2}{5}$, $\frac{21}{25}$, $0.9\overline{3}$, 1.99 **37.** $\frac{1}{2}$ **39.** $\frac{3}{8}$

Chapter Review pp. 178–179

1. exponent **2.** prime **3.** factors **4.** equivalent fraction **5.** GCF **6.** −16 **7.** −64 **8.** 125 **9.** 60 **10.** 7.123×10^6 **11.** 906,000 **12.** 8.19×10^4 **13.** 601,500,000 **14.** 2, 3, 4, 8 **15.** 2, 4, 8 **16.** 2, 3, 5, 9, 10 **17.** 2 **18.** 2, 4, 8, 10 **19.** 2, 3, 5, 10 **20.** $2 \cdot 3 \cdot 7$ **21.** $2 \cdot 3 \cdot 13$ **22.** $2 \cdot 3^2 \cdot 5$ **23.** $2^2 \cdot 23$ **24.** 5^3 **25.** 210 days from now. **26.** $\frac{1}{6}$, $\frac{1}{4}$, $\frac{1}{3}$ **27.** $\frac{1}{4}$, $\frac{3}{8}$, $\frac{2}{5}$ **28.** $\frac{3}{8}$, $\frac{1}{2}$, $\frac{5}{6}$ **29.** $\frac{5}{9}$, $\frac{7}{12}$, $\frac{2}{3}$ **30.** twice **31.** 6 **32.** $2\frac{1}{4}$ **33.** $6\frac{2}{3}$ **34.** 25 **35.** 7 **36.** $0.\overline{3}$ **37.** $0.\overline{5}$ **38.** 2.5 **39.** 0.8 **40.** 0.08 **41.** $-\frac{7}{8}$, $0.\overline{3}$, $\frac{3}{4}$ **42.** $-\frac{4}{11}$, −0.3, 2.7 **43.** $-\frac{5}{6}$, −0.5, 2.2

Chapter 4

Lesson 4-1 pp. 188–190

EXERCISES **1.** about $\frac{1}{2}$ **3.** about $\frac{1}{2}$ **9.** about 10 **10.** about 3 **11.** about 5 **17.** about 8 **19.** about 15 **25.** about 4 **27.** about 4 **33.** about $1\frac{1}{2}$ t **35.** about $\frac{1}{2}$ t **37.** about 9 **39.** about 4 **45a.** about 0 **b.** about $\frac{1}{2}$ **c.** Part (b); $\frac{2}{5}$ is closer to $\frac{1}{2}$ **55.** 3^3 **57.** $2^3 \cdot 7$ **58.** $2 \cdot 29$ **63.** −32 **65.** 75

Lesson 4-2 pp. 194–196

EXERCISES **1.** $\frac{5}{7}$ **3.** $1\frac{1}{8}$ **17.** $\frac{3}{5}$ **19.** $\frac{1}{2}$ **25.** $\frac{1}{2}$ **27.** $\frac{13}{16}$ **35.** The student added the denominators; $\frac{5}{8}$. **37.** $\frac{7}{12}$ **39.** $\frac{5}{6}$ **43.** $\frac{1}{3} - \frac{1}{4} = \frac{1}{12}$ **45a.** $\frac{7}{12}$ of the students **b.** yes; $\frac{7}{12} > \frac{1}{2}$ **47.** $\frac{2}{7}$ **49.** $\frac{1}{2}$ **53.** $\frac{7}{20}$ **69.** $-\frac{9}{16}$, −0.5, $\frac{8}{7}$, 1.6 **71.** \$35.14, \$36.00; \$37.00

Lesson 4-3 pp. 199–201

EXERCISES **1.** $8\frac{1}{5}$ **3.** 8 **17.** $6\frac{1}{2}$ **19.** $7\frac{3}{8}$ **25a.** [(] 4 [+] 1 [÷] 8 [)] [−] [(] 1 [+] 3 [÷] 4 [)] [=] **b.** $2\frac{3}{8}$ **27.** $3\frac{1}{15}$ **29.** $27\frac{1}{2}$ **39.** $6\frac{3}{7}$; the student renamed $10\frac{1}{7}$ as $9\frac{11}{7}$ instead of $9\frac{8}{7}$. **41a.** $10\frac{5}{8}$ c.i. **b.** \$85.00 **43.** $\frac{5}{8}$ mi **55.** $x \leq 0$ **57.** $x < -1$ **59.** 115 **61.** 248

Lesson 4-4 pp. 205–206

EXERCISES **1.** $\frac{1}{3}$ **3.** $\frac{5}{18}$ **9.** $\frac{1}{10}$ **11.** $\frac{4}{11}$ **17.** 3 **19.** 12 **29.** Student did not write mixed numbers as improper fractions before multiplying; $3\frac{7}{15}$. **31.** $\frac{1}{8}$ **33.** $\frac{7}{16}$ **53.** 6 **55.** 200 **59.** about 76 **61.** about 270

Lesson 4-5	pp. 209–211

EXERCISES **1.** $\frac{1}{4}$ **3.** $2\frac{2}{5}$ **15.** $\frac{5}{6}$ **17.** $2\frac{5}{6}$ **19.** 6 d **21.** 12 ft **23.** 24 **25.** $\frac{1}{12}$ **33.** $\frac{3}{100}$ **35.** $8\frac{1}{3}$ **41.** Your friend found the reciprocal of $\frac{3}{8}$; $\frac{8}{43}$. **43.** $9\frac{4}{5}$ **45.** $1\frac{1}{2}$ **51.** (13 + 7 ÷ 8) ÷ (6 + 1 ÷ 6) = $2\frac{1}{4}$ **67.** > **69.** 42 **71.** 7

Lesson 4-6	pp. 215–216

EXERCISES **1.** $4\frac{3}{4}$ **3.** 4 **13.** 4 **15.** 60 **19.** $7\frac{1}{3}$ **21.** $\frac{5}{12}$ **25.** 1 **27.** $\frac{5}{9}$ **29.** The student should have subtracted $\frac{1}{2}$ from each side; $2\frac{1}{2}$. **45.** $5\frac{9}{10}$ **47.** 7 **55.** $p \geq 16$

0 4 8 12 16 20 24

57. $d < 30$

0 10 20 30 40 50

61. $\frac{1}{3}x$ **63.** $8p$

Lesson 4-7	pp. 219–221

EXERCISES **1.** 212 people **3.** 3:30 P.M. **5.** 3 dimes and 7 nickels **7.** 5 h **9.** $32 **11.** 2 yr **13.** Year 7 **15.** Put 2-mg and 9-mg weights and wire on one side; put 5-mg and 7-mg weights on other side and see if scale balances. **23.** $7\frac{1}{3}$ **25.** $1\frac{1}{4}$ **29.** $0.\overline{142857}$ **31.** $0.4\overline{6}$

Lesson 4-8	pp. 223–225

EXERCISES **1.** $4\frac{1}{2}$ **3.** 5 **7.** 6 **9.** $3\frac{1}{4}$ **19.** mult. **21.** mult. **27.** In.; a pencil is less than a foot. **29.** gal; largest unit of capacity **33.** $\frac{1}{4}$ **35.** 21 **57.** $n - 10 = 15$; 25 **59.** $5n = 33$; $6\frac{3}{5}$ **61.** 68 cm

Lesson 4-9	pp. 229–230

EXERCISES **1.** mm **3.** $11\frac{15}{16}$ in. **5.** 56 lb **13.** 14 g **15.** 11.0 yd **19.** 1.9 cm **21.** mL **23.** oz **29.** 11.06 m **31.** 9 in. **35.** 541 ft **47.** 5.0×10^3 **49.** 1.6×10^5 **55.** 75 **57.** 36

Chapter Review	pp. 232–233

1. reciprocal **2.** benchmark **3.** precision **4.** benchmark; precision **5.** about 1 **6.** about $\frac{1}{2}$ **7.** about 30 **8.** about 3 **9.** about 8 mi **10.** $\frac{5}{8}$ **11.** $3\frac{1}{12}$ **12.** $6\frac{13}{15}$ **13.** $15\frac{5}{12}$ **14.** $\frac{1}{4}$ **15.** $\frac{9}{10}$ **16.** 9 **17.** $94\frac{23}{24}$ **18.** $\frac{1}{2}$ **19.** 6 **20.** $3\frac{3}{5}$ **21.** $\frac{5}{18}$ **22.** $1\frac{1}{10}$ **23.** $8\frac{1}{2}$ **24.** 50 **25.** 27 **25.** 90 **27.** 10 **28.** $\frac{1}{3}s = 89$; 267 students **29.** $39.76 **30.** $3\frac{1}{2}$ **31.** $1\frac{1}{2}$ **32.** 5 **33.** 2 **34.** 4,000 **35.** 7 **36.** 12 c **37.** 5.5 L **38.** 8.75 m **39.** 23 h **40.** 25 g **41.** $11\frac{3}{16}$ in. **42.** 7 g **43.** 13 yd **44.** 11.6 cm **45.** 21.00 lb **46.** 5 L **47.** 5.13 m

Chapter 5

Lesson 5-1	pp. 243–245

EXERCISES **1.** 5 to 2, 5 : 2, $\frac{5}{2}$ **3.** 1 to 4, 1 : 4, $\frac{1}{4}$ **5.** 3.6 **7.** 0.48 **13.** $\frac{11}{3}$ **15.** $\frac{2}{7}$ **17.** $\frac{25}{1}$ **21.** equal **23.** not equal **27.** Room 101 and Room 107 **29a.** $\frac{13}{18}$ **b.** $\frac{169}{324}$ **c.** Answers may vary. Sample: The ratio of the areas equals the square of the ratio of the sides. **31a.** 8 : 4, 7.5 : 3, 3.5 : 1 **b.** 10 qt antifreeze, 5 qt water **39.** 45 **41.** about 32,000 **43.** about 6

Lesson 5-2	pp. 248–250

EXERCISES **1.** 300 mi/h **3.** $5.80/h **7.** 4.35 m/s **9.** 1.12 mi/min **13.** $15 **15.** $24 **19.** $3/yd^2 **21.** $4.11/lb **23.** $.06/fl oz, $.05/fl oz; the second detergent is the better buy. **25a.** 27 students/1 teacher **b.** No; the student-to-teacher ratio would be 950 students/40 teachers, or 23.75 students/1 teacher. **27.** 5,000 gal **29a.** 1 person/mi^2 **31.** 10.35 m/s **33.** $.49/yd, $.65/yd; the first ribbon is the better buy. **35.** $1.85/qt **37.** $.09/oz **49.** 27 **51.** 279,936 **57.** $a < 5$;

3 4 5 6

59. $x \leq -8$;

−8 −7 −6

Lesson 5-3	pp. 253–255

EXERCISES **1.** 31 games **3.** 21 games **5.** $268.92 **7.** 4 wk **19.** 7 less than *x* **21.** *y* divided by 2 **25.** three fourths of *s* plus twice *r* **27.** 3 **29.** 6

Lesson 5-4	pp. 258–259

EXERCISES **1.** yes **3.** yes **9.** yes **11.** no **17.** yes **19.** no **25.** No; $\frac{4}{5}$ and $\frac{16}{25}$ are not proportional because $4 \times 25 \neq 5 \cdot 16$. **27.** no **29.** yes **31.** $\frac{b}{h} = \frac{20}{15} = \frac{12}{9}$ is a proportion. **41.** −2 **43.** 15.25; 16.5

Lesson 5-5	pp. 262–265

EXERCISES **1.** $10.32 **3.** 2.5 lb **7.** 6 **9.** 6 **17.** 10 **18.** 85.75 **19.** 6 **25.** 525 mosquitoes **27.** 624 ants **29.** 17,100,000 votes **31.** 448 **33.** 4 **37.** $10\frac{1}{2}$ h **41.** 21.7 **43.** 9.3 **49a.** 72 beats/min **b.** 24 **63.** no **65.** yes **69.** 17 : 9, $\frac{17}{9}$ **71.** 16 to 7, 16 : 7 **75.** −12, −3, 10, 16 **77.** −5, −1, 0, 2, 5

Lesson 5-6 pp. 269–272

EXERCISES **1.** $\triangle XYZ \sim \triangle TVK$ because corresponding angles are equal, and corresponding sides are proportional. **3.** 12 ft **5.** 92° **7.** 37.5 ft **9.** 2.8 **11.** 24.7 **15a.** $\frac{PQ}{ST} = \frac{QR}{TR}$ **b.** 2.88 km **c.** Yes; since $\overline{PR}$ and $\overline{SR}$ are corresponding sides in similar triangles, you can solve a proportion to find *d*. **d.** No; since $\overline{SR}$ and $\overline{QR}$ are not corresponding sides in similar triangles, you cannot set up a proportion to find *d*. **17.** 24 in. **19.** 15 **21.** 20 **23.** 99 cm **25.** 42 **27.** 26 **37.** 25 yd **39.** 20.1 in. **43.** $\frac{11}{4}$ **45.** $\frac{53}{12}$ **51.** −14 **53.** −6

Lesson 5-7 pp. 277–279

EXERCISES **1.** 70 ft **3.** 20 ft **7.** about 48 mi **9.** about 48 mi **11.** 1 in. : 15 ft **13.** 30 km **15.** 105 km **19.** Set up and solve the proportion $\frac{2 \text{ in.}}{17 \text{ ft}} = \frac{x \text{ in.}}{51 \text{ ft}}$. $2 \cdot 51 = 17x$, $x = 6$. The drawn object should be 6 in. long. **21. a.** $\frac{1}{4}$ in.

b.

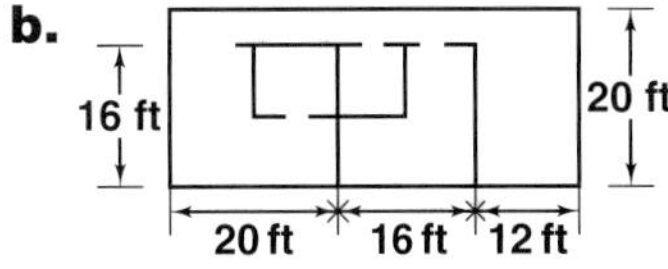

23. 7.2 km **25.** 18.7 km **27.** 1 cm : 0.71 mm **29a.** 1 in. : 6 in. **b.** 32 in.

Chapter Review pp. 282–283

1. a scale drawing **2.** unit price **3.** rate **4.** scale **5.** similar 6. $\frac{3}{10}$ **7.** $\frac{16}{5}$ **8.** 3 : 1 **9.** 15 to 4 **10.** $\frac{1}{4}$ **11.** $\frac{39}{97}$, 39 to 97, 39 : 97 **12.** 6 passengers/car **13.** 75 cal/serving **14.** \$.28/oz, \$.31/oz; the 10-oz size is the better buy. **15.** 437.5 **16.** $16\frac{2}{3}$ min **17.** 12 **18.** 25 **19.** 3 **20.** 136 **21.** $\frac{5}{3} = \frac{x}{250{,}000}$; 417,000 board feet **22.** 15 ft **23.** 45 **24.** $x = 45$, $y = 36$ **25.** 3,996 mi 26. 0.75 in.

Chapter 6

Lesson 6-1 pp. 293–294

EXERCISES **1.** $\frac{64}{100}$; 64% **3.** $\frac{60}{100}$; 60%

5. **7.**

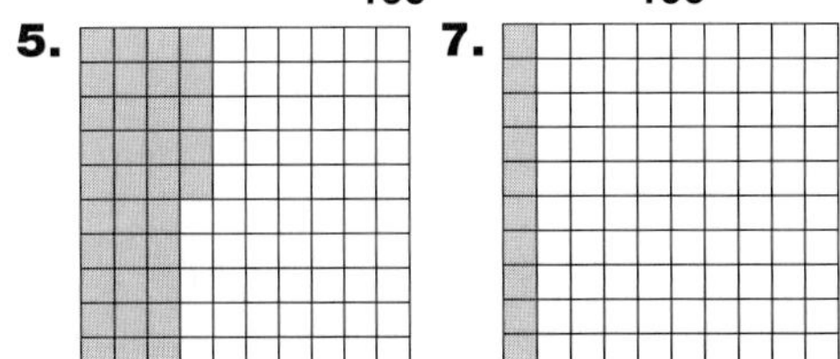

13. $\frac{1}{10}$, 10% **15.** 60% **17.** 84% **25.** 70% **27.** 9% **29.** 75% **31.** 95% **33.** $\frac{9}{25}$, 36% **35.** $\frac{28}{100}$, 28% **37.** 60% < 70%, so $\frac{3}{5} < \frac{7}{10}$ **39.** 50% > 46%, so $\frac{1}{2} > \frac{23}{50}$ **49.** $4\frac{8}{9}$ **51.** $36\frac{13}{20}$ **53.** $0.1\overline{6}$ **55.** $0.\overline{5}$

Leson 6-2 pp. 298–300

EXERCISES **1.** 52% **3.** 9% **7.** 0.88 **9.** 0.03 **11.** 12%, 0.25, $\frac{1}{2}$ **13.** $\frac{4}{5}$, 0.81, 90% **17.** 90% **19.** 8.3% **25.** $\frac{3}{50}$ **27.** $\frac{9}{20}$ **31.** > **33.** < **37a.** $\frac{7}{50}$, 0.14; $\frac{17}{50}$, 0.34; $\frac{7}{20}$, 0.35 **b.** Magnesium: 86%; Iron: 66%; Vitamin B6: 65% **39.** $66\frac{2}{3}$% **41.** $\frac{1}{6}$ **43.** $\frac{1}{40}$ **47a.** 12.5% **b.** 1 slice **51.** D **65.** $1\frac{4}{5}$ **67.** $\frac{1}{250}$ **73.** 28 **75.** 0.918

Lesson 6-3 pp. 302–304

EXERCISES **1.** 1.8; $1\frac{4}{5}$ **3.** 1.75; $1\frac{3}{4}$ **13.** 475% **15.** 101% **31.** 190% **33.** 1.26; $1\frac{13}{50}$

35. **37.**

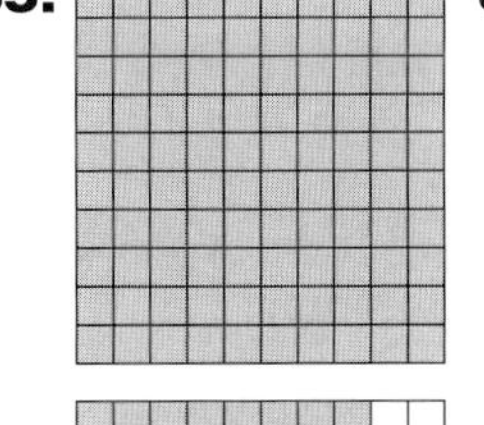

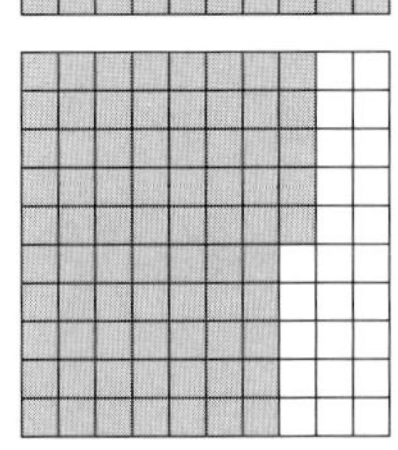

39. 155% **42.** 187.5% **45.** Yes; it is reasonable that $\frac{1}{2}$ of 1% of the seeds did not grow. **47.** If you surpass the goal by $\frac{1}{5}$ of the amount of the goal, then you have reached $1\frac{1}{5}$ of the goal, or 120% of the goal. **56.** [2] Divide 1 by the total number of school days, 180. Change the decimal to a percent. $\frac{1}{180} = 0.00555\ldots = 0.555\ldots\% \approx 0.6\%$ [1] minor error OR answer only **58.** $\frac{3}{8}$ **65.** 24 **67.** 245

Lesson 6-4 pp. 307–310

EXERCISES **1.** 5.4 **3.** 7 **15.** 58.96 **17.** 474 **25.** about 30 **27.** about 80 **33.** Yes; 0.32 × 96 = 0.01 × 32 × 96 = 32 × 0.96, so 32% of 96 = 96% of 32. **35a.** 70% **b.** \$3.98 per yd **37.** \$9.74 **39.** 4.5 **41.** 12 **53.** about 60 **55.** about 55 **59.** 21 questions **71.** 92% **73.** 20 **75.** 33.6 **77.** $6\frac{3}{10}$

Lesson 6-5 pp. 314–316

EXERCISES **1.** 75% **3.** 92% **9.** 25% **11.** 70%

13. 75 **15.** 25 **21.** $249 **23.** $\frac{90}{n} = \frac{40}{100}$; $n = 225$
26. $\frac{139.1}{n} = \frac{65}{100}$; $n = 214$ **29.** 12 runners **31.** C
33. B **35.** 340 **37.** 12.5% **53.** 80.64 **55.** 39.56
59. $\frac{4}{5}$ **61.** $\frac{1}{20}$ **65.** $5x + 2 = 37$; 7

Lesson 6-6 pp. 319–321

EXERCISES **1.** $0.18 \cdot 90 = x$; 16.2 **3.** $x = 0.05 \cdot 522$; 26.1 **9.** 360 Cal **11.** $0.40x = 30$; 75
13. $0.48x = 216$; 450 **19.** 50°F **21.** $625x = 550$; 88% **23.** $18 = 48x$; 37.5% **29.** 45 students **31.** D
33. B **39.** 68.8% **41.** 57.5% **61.** $6\frac{1}{4}$ **63.** 44
65. 1, 3, 5, 15, 25, 75

Lesson 6-7 pp. 324–326

EXERCISES **1.** $37.79 **3.** $85.46 **5.** $121.98
7. about $4.60 **9.** about $4.20 **11.** $42.90
13. $13.87 **15.** $200 **17.** $27 **19.** $789 **21.** $490
23. 3% **25.** $6,200 **29.** $98.50 **37.** 34 miles per gallon **39.** −4 **41.** −48

Lesson 6-8 pp. 330–332

EXERCISES **1.** 25% **3.** 100% **9.** 16.5% **11.** 50%
13. 120% **17.** 10% **19.** 20% **25.** 50% increase
27. 10% decrease **33.** 6.3% discount
35.

	A	B	C	D
1	Yr	Sales	Change ($)	Change (%)
2	1	200,000	—	—
3	2	240,000	40,000	20%
4	3	300,000	60,000	25%
5	4	330,000	30,000	10%

37. about 15.7% **39a.** 300% **b.** 3,072 **41.** $53.30
43. $200.20 **45.** about 108.0% **57.** $471.30 **59.** $0.\overline{6}$ **61.** $0.\overline{7}$ **64.** 0

Lesson 6-9 pp. 335–336

EXERCISES **1.** 20% discount **3.** 22.7% discount
7. 7 cm by 14 cm **17.** 40.9% decrease **19.** 12.9% increase **23.** 660 **25.** 210

Chapter Review pp. 338–339

1. C **2.** E **3.** F **4.** B **5.** A **6.** 0.65; $\frac{13}{20}$ **7.** 0.02; $\frac{1}{50}$
8. 0.018; $\frac{9}{500}$ **9.** 0.625; $\frac{5}{8}$ **10.** 37.5% **11.** 16%
12. 3% **13.** 42.5% **14.** 143% **15.** 1.4% **16.** 275%
17. 0.8% **18.** 44.28 **19.** 6.56 **20.** 97.2 **21.** 70%
22. 47.5 **23.** 252 **24.** 12 **25.** 72 **26.** 20%
27. $57.60 **28.** about $13.15 **29.** $268 **30.** $225
31. 17% decrease **32.** 20% increase **33.** 15% increase **34.** 31% decrease **35.** If the original amount is less than the new amount, it is an increase; if the original amount is more than the new amount, it is a decrease.

Chapter 7

Lesson 7-1 pp. 348–349

EXERCISES **1.** $\overline{LC}$ **3.** $\overleftrightarrow{KE}$ **11.** $\overline{BF}$, $\overline{CG}$, $\overline{HG}$, $\overline{EF}$
13. $\overline{EA}$, $\overline{HD}$, $\overline{AB}$, $\overline{DC}$ **15.** A, D **17.** Q, W
23. parallel **33.** 16% decrease **35.** 11% decrease

Lesson 7-2 pp. 354–356

EXERCISES **1.** 50° **3.** 115° **7.** acute **9.** obtuse
11. obtuse **13.** 85°, 175° **15.** 40°; 130° **21.** 57°
23. 66.5°; 156.5° **25.** 42.1°; 132.1° **29.** about 65°
33. ∠ABE and ∠EBG; ∠FBH and ∠HBC **35.** acute
43. $42.55 **45.** 14.4 km **47.** 24 km

Lesson 7-3 pp. 359–361

EXERCISES **1.** Drawing not to scale

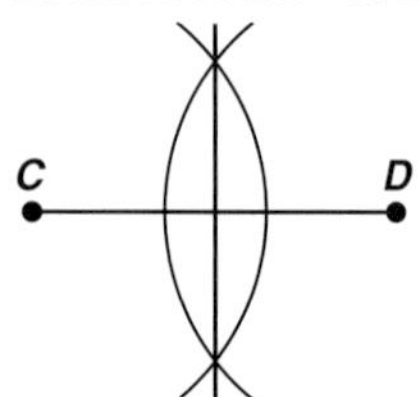

3. Answers may vary. Sample: (drawing not to scale)

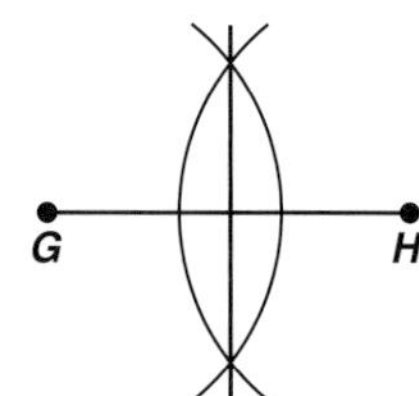

5. Drawing not to scale

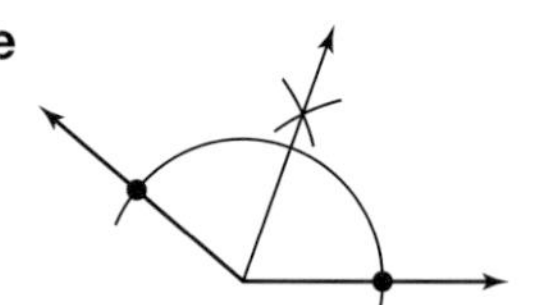

7. 24° **9.** 8 in. **11.** 5 ft **15.** *m*
17a–b. C F E D **19.** 22.5°
21. 60° **23.** 4 Iron **37.** $32.60 **39.** $\frac{6}{13}$; 6 to 13
41. 16 : 25; 16 to 25

Lesson 7-4 pp. 365–367

EXERCISES **1.** isosceles **3.** equilateral, isosceles **7.** obtuse **9.** right **13.** 80° **15.** 40° **19.** acute **21.** right **23.** isosceles triangle **25.** equilateral, isosceles **27.** isosceles **39.** 1.37; $\frac{137}{100}$ **41.** 1.75; $\frac{7}{4}$ **43.** 0.4375 **45.** $1.\overline{6}$

Lesson 7-5 pp. 371–373

EXERCISES **1.** The pentagon is regular because all sides are congruent and all angles are congruent. **3.** The quadrilateral is irregular because not all the sides are congruent. **5.** squares, trapezoids, triangles, pentagons **7.**

9. parallelogram; $\overline{AB}$ is parallel to $\overline{DC}$ and $\overline{AD}$ is parallel to $\overline{BC}$. **11.** **13.**

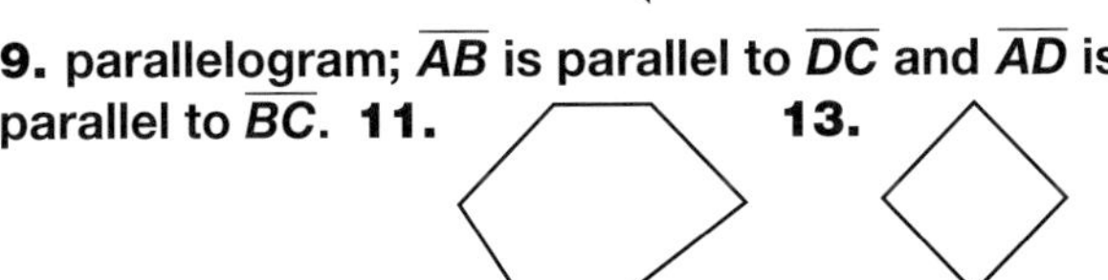

15a.

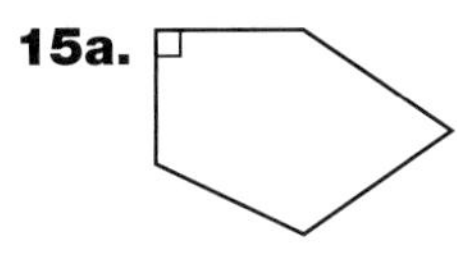

b. No; three right angles would result in 2 pairs of parallel sides.

17.

27. about 6 **29.** about $\frac{1}{2}$ **31.** prime **33.** composite; $3^3 \cdot 239$

Lesson 7-6 pp. 375–377

EXERCISES **1.** 45 black tiles **3.** 21 segments **5.** 13 dimes, 1 quarter; 8 dimes, 3 quarters; 3 dimes, 5 quarters **7.** 77 diagonals **9.** 3 small tables and 5 large tables **11.** Rosa plays the piano, Alberto plays the drums, and Lewis plays the guitar.

21.

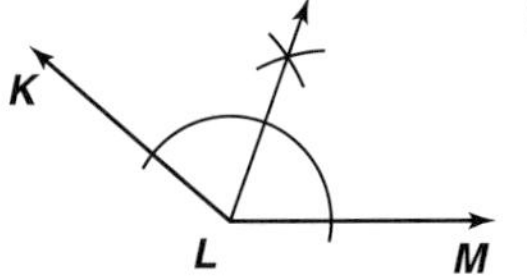

23. 60% **25.** 113.6%

Lesson 7-7 pp. 380–382

EXERCISES **1.** Congruent; corresponding sides and corresponding angles have the same measure. **3.** Not congruent; not all corresponding sides and angles are congruent. **5.** yes **7a.** $\overline{HG} \cong \overline{NM}$; $\overline{GF} \cong \overline{ML}$; $\overline{DF} \cong \overline{KL}$; $\overline{DH} \cong \overline{KN}$; $\angle H \cong \angle N$; $\angle G \cong \angle M$; $\angle F \cong \angle L$; $\angle D \cong \angle K$ **b.** $m\angle H = 111°$; $m\angle F = 69°$; $m\angle M = 111°$; $KL = 20$; $KL = 20$ **9a.** $\overline{ED} \cong \overline{KJ}$; $\overline{DC} \cong \overline{JI}$; $\overline{CB} \cong \overline{IH}$; $\overline{BA} \cong \overline{HG}$; $\overline{AF} \cong \overline{GL}$; $\overline{FE} \cong \overline{LK}$; $\angle E \cong \angle K$; $\angle D \cong \angle J$; $\angle C \cong \angle I$; $\angle B \cong \angle H$; $\angle A \cong \angle G$; $\angle F \cong \angle L$ **13.** $\triangle SRT$ **15.** $\triangle FDE$ **17.** $\angle C$ **19.** $\angle ABD$ **29.** acute **31.** obtuse **33.** 4.5

Lesson 7-8 pp. 385–386

EXERCISES **1.** M **3.** $\overline{JL}$ **7.** $\overline{OC}, \overline{OK}, \overline{OD}$ **9.** $\overline{CD}$ **11.** $\overset{\frown}{TR}, \overset{\frown}{RS}, \overset{\frown}{ST}$ **13.** $\overset{\frown}{CD}, \overset{\frown}{DB}, \overset{\frown}{CB}$ **15.** $\overline{FG}, \overline{EF}$ **17.** $\overline{FH}$ **33.** 110° **35.** $5\frac{9}{14}$ **37.** $-3\frac{11}{12}$

Lesson 7-9 pp. 390–392

EXERCISES **1.** sleeping **3.** 71% **5.** 40° **7.** 122° **13.**

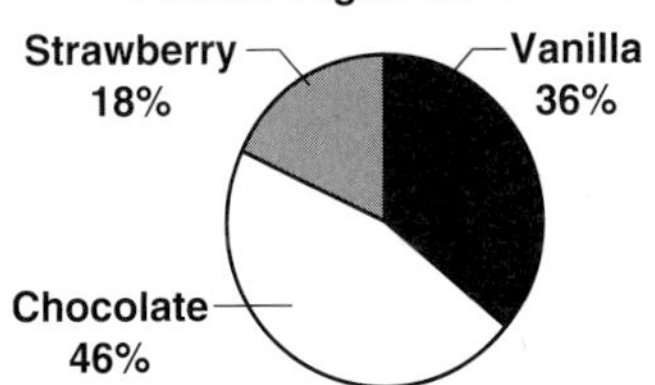

15. Mexico **17.** 11.6 million people **19.**

Students Volunteering
5 days 8%
4 days 8%
1 day 44%
3 days 20%
2 days 20%

21. 108°, 45% **23.** $\frac{3}{10}$ (108°); 144° $\left(\frac{2}{5}\right)$; 18° $\left(\frac{1}{20}\right)$ **35.** 350% **37.** 45% **39.** $10\frac{7}{18}$ **41.** $\frac{5}{8}$

Chapter Review pp. 394–395

1. parallel **2.** pentagon **3.** complementary **4.** scalene **5.** acute **6.** 35°, 125° **7.** 63°, 153° **8.** 3°, 93° **9.** 78°, 168°

10.

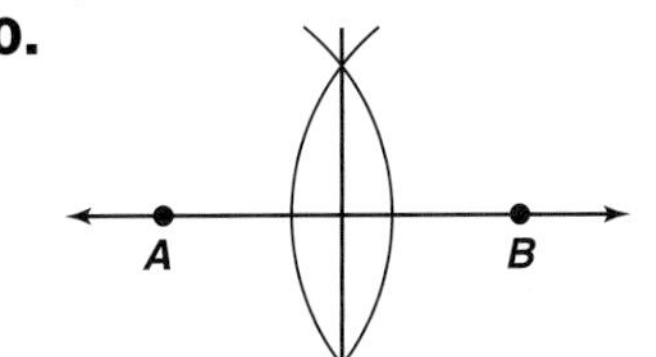

11.

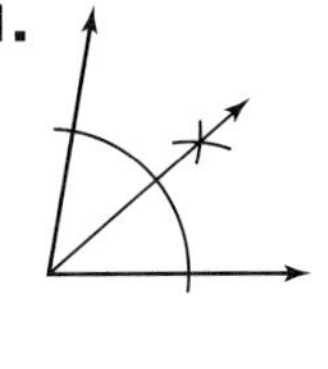

12. 120°; isosceles; obtuse **13.** 60°; acute; equilateral **14.** 31°; right; scalene **15.** pentagon; regular **16.** square; regular **17.** octagon; irregular **18.** 66 white triangles **19a.** $\overline{AB} \cong \overline{MN}$; $\overline{BC} \cong \overline{NP}$; $\overline{AC} \cong \overline{MP}$; $\angle A \cong \angle M$; $\angle B \cong$

$\angle N$; $\angle C \cong \angle P$ **b.** $m\angle M = 30°$; $m\angle B = 104°$; $m\angle C = m\angle P = 46°$; $MN = 17$; $AC = 22$; $BC = 12$ **20.** $\overline{TW}, \overline{TY}, \overline{TK}, \overline{TM}$ **21.** $\overline{MY}$ **22.** T **23.** $\overset{\frown}{WY}, \overset{\frown}{MV}, \overset{\frown}{KY}$ **24.** $\overset{\frown}{WYK}, \overset{\frown}{YKMW}, \overset{\frown}{KMWY}, \overset{\frown}{MWYK}, \overset{\frown}{WYKM}$

Chapter 8

Lesson 8-1 pp. 359–361

EXERCISES **1.** inch **3.** feet **7.** 6 in.; it is less than a foot. **9.** 2 in.; the tail is less than a foot. **11.** about 625 mi^2 **13.** about 5 cm **15.** about 2 cm **17.** Lay the string around the edge of the puzzle piece. Mark the length and then measure the string. **19.** m **21.** m^2 or km^2 **23.** about $\frac{1}{2}$ in. **25.** about 1 in. **33.** 150% increase **35.** 44.4% decrease **39.** 28 **41.** 10

Lesson 8-2 pp. 410–412

EXERCISES **1.** 60 m^2 **3.** 108 cm^2 **7.** 56 cm^2 **9.** 270 m^2 **13.** 17.5 m^2 **15.** 84 $in.^2$ **17.** 20 cm^2 **19.** 12 $in.^2$ **21.** 7.75 ft^2 **23.** 41,800 mi^2 **25.** The area doubles. $A_1 = \frac{1}{2}bh$; $A_2 = \frac{1}{2}(2b)h = bh$. The area of A_2 is twice A_1. **27.** 27.68 km^2 **37.** 1.35; $1\frac{7}{20}$ **39.** 0.0003; $\frac{3}{10{,}000}$ **41.** $\frac{10}{21}$ **43.** $\frac{1}{2}$

Lesson 8-3 pp. 416–418

EXERCISES **1.** 144 m^2 **3.** 110,622 mi^2 **5.** 831.96 m^2 **7.** 124 $in.^2$ **11.** 121.5 $in.^2$ **13.** $5\frac{3}{4}$ ft^2 **15.** 198 ft^2 **17.** 3,300 cm^2; 260 cm **25.** \$480.18 **27.** 55 **29.** 18

Lesson 8-4 pp. 422–424

EXERCISES **1.** 157.0 cm or 157.1 cm **3.** 84.8 m **7.** 113 $in.^2$ **9.** 1,963 cm^2 **17a.** 314 ft^2 **b.** 380 ft^2 **19.** 424 m **21.** 4.4 cm; 1.54 cm^2 **23.** 37.7 ft; 113.1 ft^2 **25.** about 188 in.; about 2,827 $in.^2$ **27.** about 10 m **29.** about 16 ft **33a.** 98.52 m^2 **b.** 98.47 m^2 **c.** Kenny's; using the π key is more accurate, so 98.57 rounds to 99. **45.** $\angle T$ **47.** 30° **49.** 119°

Lesson 8-5 pp. 428–430

EXERCISES **1.** 4 **3.** 6 **11.** 20 yd **13.** about 4 **15.** about 6 **19.** irrational **21.** rational **27.** rational **29.** rational, whole, integer **39.** 8 km **41.** 11 ft **53.** 2 **55.** 11.25 **57.** 28 **59.** 6

Lesson 8-6 pp. 434–436

EXERCISES **1.** 13 m **3.** 17 m **11.** 15 in. **13.** 51.9 cm **19.** 127.3 ft **21.** 10 ft **23.** 13.6 m **25.** 23.3 ft **31.** 23.4 ft **33.** 7 km **35a.** Check to see if the sum of the squares of the two shortest sides equals the square of the longest side.

$$10^2 + 24^2 \stackrel{?}{=} 26^2$$
$$100 + 576 \stackrel{?}{=} 676$$
$$676 = 676$$

It is a right triangle.

b. It is not a right triangle because
$144 + 256 \neq 441$
$400 \neq 441$
45. 5 **47.** 2 **51.** $n = .60(40)$; 24

Lesson 8-7 pp. 439–440

EXERCISES **1.** rectangle; rectangular prism **3.** pentagon; pentagonal prism **7.** cylinder **9.** sphere **13.** 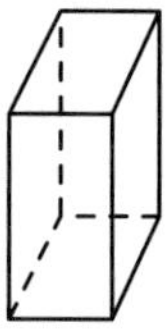 **15.**  **19.** cone **21.** sphere **23.** $\overline{MA}, \overline{BP}, \overline{KA}, \overline{KB}$ **25.** $\overline{MD}, \overline{DP}, \overline{KP}, \overline{KM}, \overline{KD}$ **27.** 3.5 m^2; 24 m^2; 21 m^2; 12 m^2 **37.** 11 m

Lesson 8-8 pp. 444–447

EXERCISES Exercises 1–4. Nets may vary. Samples are given. **1.**

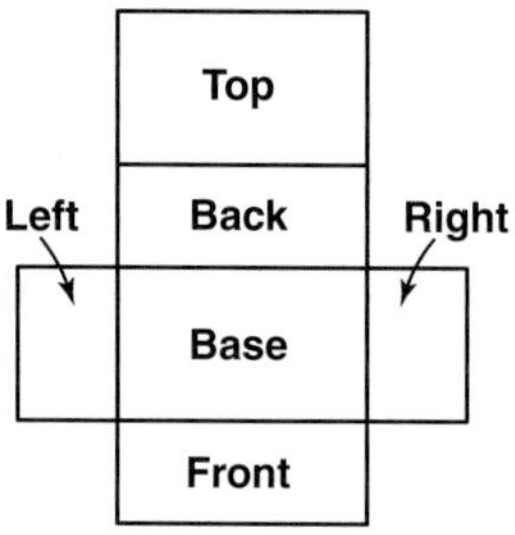

3.

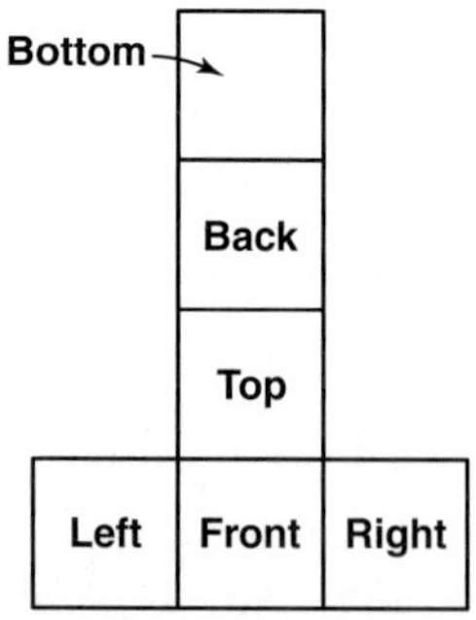

5. 264 m^2 **7.** 188 m^2 **15.** 785.4 cm^2 **17.** 2,269.8 m^2 **19.** cylinder; about 5,089.4 $in.^2$ **25.** 245 cm^2 **27.** 2,111 m^2 **29.** You cannot interchange the values of r and h. **31.** 106.8 $in.^2$ **33.** 70.7 cm^2 **43.** 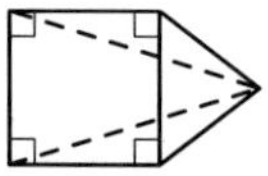

45. $\overline{RS}, \overline{SU}, \overline{TU}$, or $\overline{RT}$ **47.** $\overline{OR}, \overline{OS}, \overline{OT}, \overline{OU}$

Lesson 8-9 pp. 451–454

EXERCISES **1.** 166.375 in.^{3} **3.** 896 cm^3 **7.** 1,131 m^3 **9.** 352 m^3 **11.** 4,580 cm^3 **13.** about 84 in.^{3}; 88 in.^{3} **15.** about 280 in.^{3}; 250 in.^{3} **17.** 6.5 cm **19.** 18 in. **23.** 2 ft **25.** 6 cm **27a.** 24 in.^{3} **b.** 12 in.^{3} **c.** $V = Bh_2 = \left(\frac{1}{2}bh_1\right) \cdot h_2$ $= \left(\frac{1}{2} \cdot 3 \cdot 4\right) \cdot 2 = 12$ in.^{3} **37.** 527.5 m^2 **39.** 50°; 140° **41.** 53°; 143°

Lesson 8-10 pp. 457–458

EXERCISES **1.** 38 ft × 38 ft **3.** 20 cm **7a.** $\overline{GA}$ **b.** $\overline{AB}$ and $\overline{BC}$; $\overline{AC}$ and $\overline{GC}$ **c.** 35 in.; 37 in. **9.** $5.45 **17.** acute **19.** acute **23.** 650,000 **25.** 52,600,000

Chapter Review pp. 460–461

1. edge **2.** hypotenuse **3.** prism **4.** circumference **5.** cone **6.** 400 in.^{2} **7.** 7 in.; the width is less than a foot. **8.** 10.5 m^2 **9.** 38 cm^2 **10.** 160 ft^2 **11.** 25.1 in.; 50.3 in.^{2} **12.** 44 mi; 153.9 mi^2 **13.** 22 m; 38.5 m^2 **14.** 6 in. **15.** $6 < \sqrt{45} < 7$ **16.** 39 yd **17.** 22 in.^{2}; 6 in.^{3} **18.** 288 m^2; 324 m^3 **19.** 747.7 yd^2; 1,539.4 yd^3 **20.** 3 ft × 6 ft **21.** 21 cm × 7 cm × 14 cm

Chapter 9

Lesson 9-1 pp. 471–473

EXERCISES **1.**

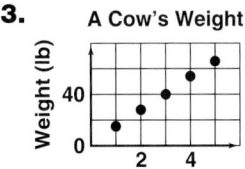

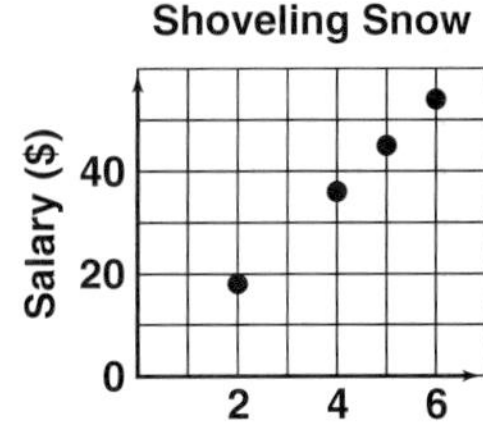

3. A Cow's Weight

Weight (lb) 40 0 2 4

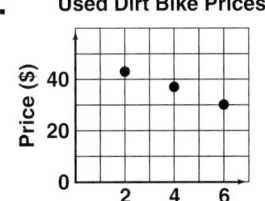

5. Used Dirt Bike Prices

Price ($) 40 20 0 2 4 6

7. about 10 yr old **9.** about 3 yr **11.** about $8 **13a.**

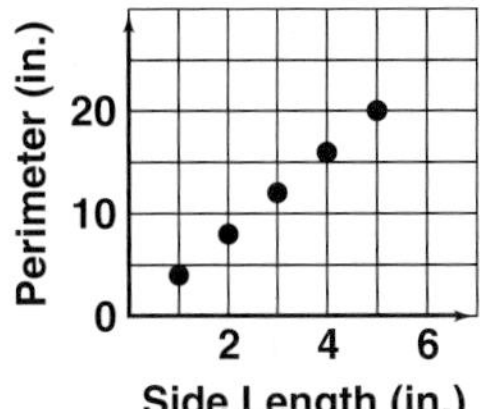

b. about 2.4 in. **c.** about 14 in.

15.

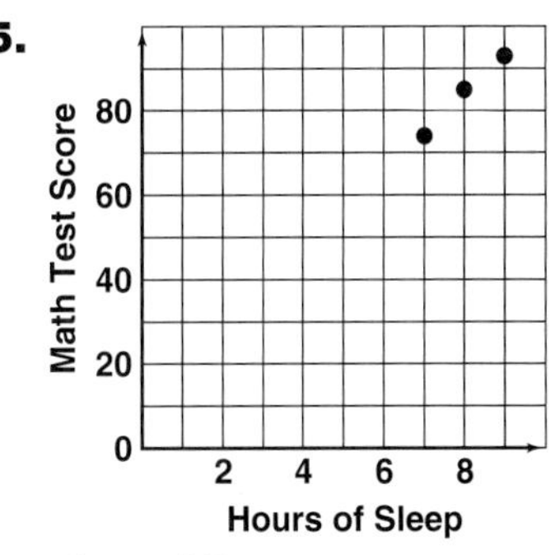

about 65

17.

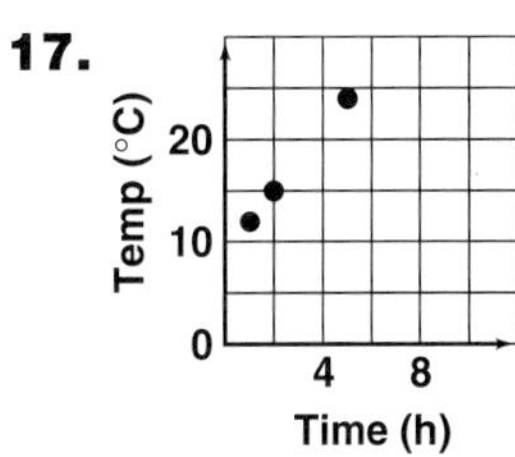

33°C

27. 0.38 **29.** 1.5 **31.** 3 **33.** −11

Lesson 9-2 pp. 476–478

EXERCISES **1.** Start with 5 and add 5 repeatedly; 25, 30, 35. **3.** Start with 34 and add −5 repeatedly; 14, 9, 4. **13.** neither **15.** geometric **19.** neither **21a.** 2, 3, 5, 8, 13, 21, 34 **b.** neither **23.** Start with 4 and multiply by −2 repeatedly; 64, −128, 256. **25.** Start with −2 and multiply by 2 repeatedly; −32, −64, −128. **31.** neither; arithmetic; neither; neither; neither **33.** 123,456 × 9 = 1,111,104 **35.** Start with 1 and add 0.5 repeatedly. **37.** Start with 10 and add −0.7 repeatedly. **43a.** 15 cm^2 **b.** 60 cm^2 **c.** When a rectangle's dimensions are doubled, its area is multiplied by 4.

45a.
row 4   1 2 3 4 3 2 1
row 5   1 2 3 4 5 4 3 2 1
row 6   1 2 3 4 5 6 5 4 3 2 1
row 7   1 2 3 4 5 6 7 6 5 4 3 2 1

b. 1; 4; 9; 16; 25; 36; 49 **c.** The sum of the numbers of row n is n^2. **d.** 400 **47.** 1 **57.** 12.5 mi **59.** 125 mi **61.** $\frac{6}{1}$ **63.** $\frac{1}{5}$

Lesson 9-3 pp. 482–483

EXERCISES **1.**

Cans of Soup	Number of Servings
3	9
4	12
5	15
6	18
7	21

3.

Change in a Parking Meter ($)	Time Allowed to Park (h)
.25	0.5
.50	1
.75	1.5
1.25	2.5

5. $m = 180, n = 20$ **7.** $s = 140, t = 184$ **9.** $n - 20$; 80 **11.** $-3n$; -300 **15.**

Time (h)	0.5	1	1.5	2
Cost ($)	12.50	25	37.50	50

17a.

x	0	1	2	3	4	5
y	−1	2	5	8	11	14

b. Multiply x by 3 and subtract 1. **19.** $x = 0.5, y = 10{,}000$ **21.**

Side Length (in.)	Area (in.²)
2	4
3	9
5	25
8	64
10	100
12	144

33. 15 **35.** 21 **37.** −180 **39.** 121

Lesson 9-4 pp. 486–488

EXERCISES **1.** $d = 30t$ **3.** $c = 12t$ **5.** $y = x + 4$ **7.** $y = -9x + 1$ **11.**

x	y
0	12
1	10
2	8
3	6

13.

x	y
0	0
1	$\frac{1}{2}$
2	1
3	$\frac{3}{2}$

21. yes; one output for each input **23a.** $w = 150m$ **b.** 1,200 words **c.** 19 min **d.** Input; words are given as a function of minutes. **25.** −2 **27.** $-\frac{2}{3}$ **29.** $y = \frac{1}{2}x$ **31.** $y = \frac{1}{2}x + 1$ **45.** 57.1% **47.** 0.96 **49.** 72

Lesson 9-5 pp. 490–492

EXERCISES **1.**

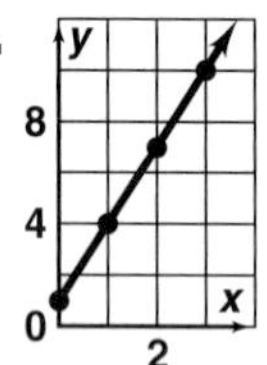

3. $S = 6t$; $60

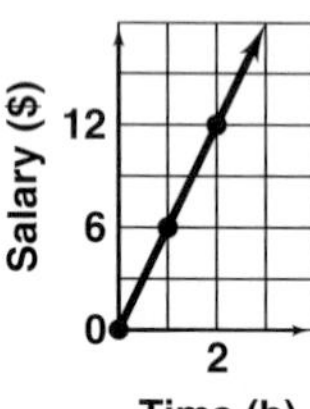

5. $d = 320t$; 3,200 mi

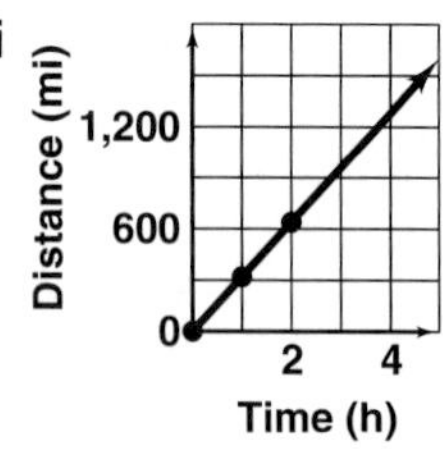

7.

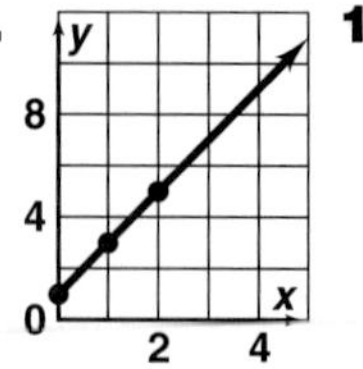

11. C **13.** B **15a.** c = 380y **b.** $10,640 **17.** 10 **19.** 0 **29.** > **31.** < **33.** 10,478.6 **35.** 0.04

Lesson 9-6 pp. 496–498

EXERCISES **1.** You walk at a steady pace traveling 6 blocks in 16 min.

3.

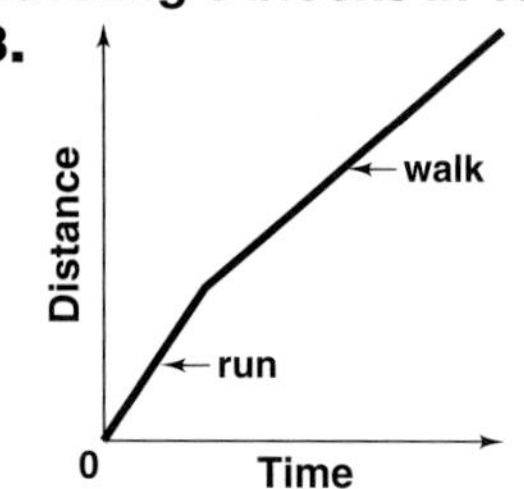

5.

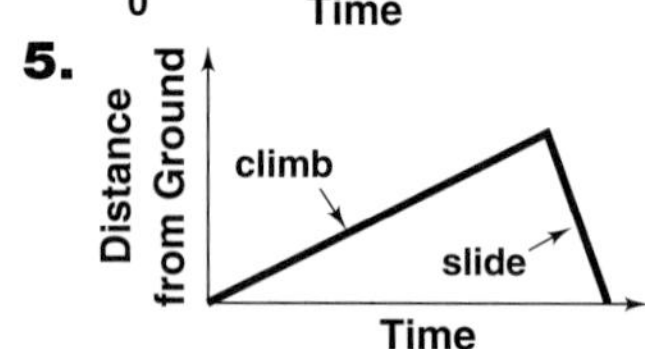

7. You should not connect the points because you sell only whole-number glasses of lemonade.

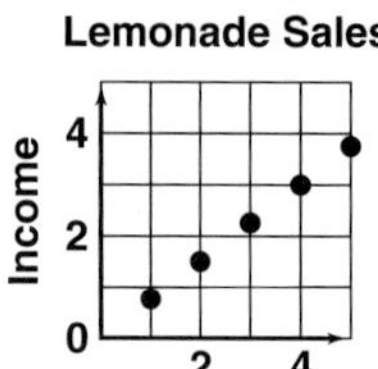

9a.

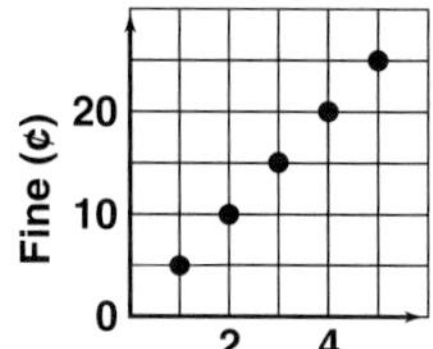

b. No; the fine is calculated from whole-numbers of days. **11.** B **13.** A **15.**

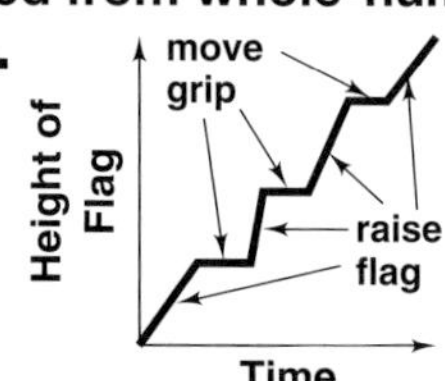

17. Paulo walked the distance of 6 blocks in the shortest period of time, so Paulo walked the fastest. **19.**

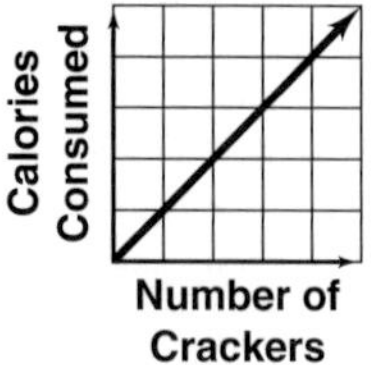

29. 15 ft^2 **31.** 57 $in.^2$ **33.** $33\frac{1}{3}\%$ **35.** 30

Lesson 9-7 pp. 501–502

EXERCISES **1.** $71.40 **3.** $51.00

5.

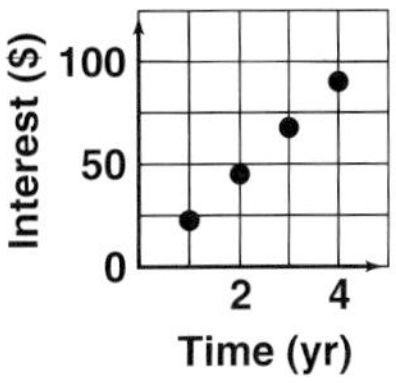

7.

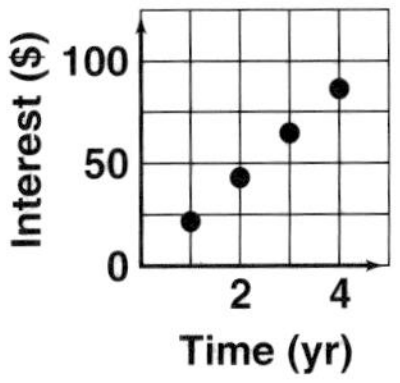

11. \$1,643.94 **13.** \$1,413.81 **15.** \$543.14 **17.** \$37.50 **19.** \$18.00 **21a.** B **b.** C **c.** A **d.** E **23.** Longer term CDs will have a higher interest rate, but the principal will be locked up longer. **29.** −7 **31.** −14 **33.** 5

Lesson 9-8 pp. 504–506

EXERCISES **1.** 23 gal, 12 gal **3.** 23,043 swimsuits; 16,521 swimsuits **5.** 1 lb, 3 lb, 9 lb **7.** 20 diagonals **9.** 24 shells, 22 shells, 20 shells, 18 shells, 16 shells **17.** 12 **19.** $-\frac{1}{2}$ **29.** Start with 9 and add 2.3 repeatedly; 18.2, 20.5, 22.8.

Lesson 9-9 pp. 509–510

EXERCISES **1.** $y = \frac{x}{z}$ **3.** $r = \frac{p + 5}{3}$ **11.** 2.8% **13a.** $c = 0.07s$ **b.** \$120,000 **15.** $w = \frac{V}{\ell h}$ **17.** $C = \frac{5}{9}(F - 32)$ **21.** $y = \frac{1}{3}x - 2$ or $y = \frac{x - 6}{3}$ **23.** $n = \frac{w - 5m}{3}$ **27.** about 11,451 times at bat **29a.** \$427.50 **b.** 8 h **39.** 14.4 m **41.** acute **43.** obtuse

Chapter Review pp. 512–513

1. arithmetic **2.** function **3.** principal **4.** compound **5.** conjecture

6.

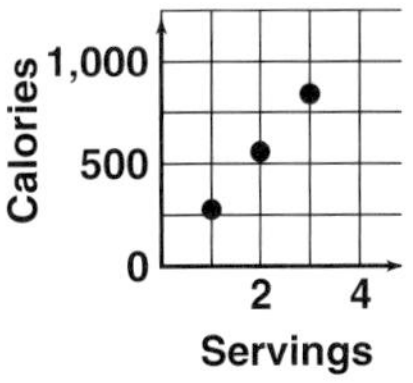

7.

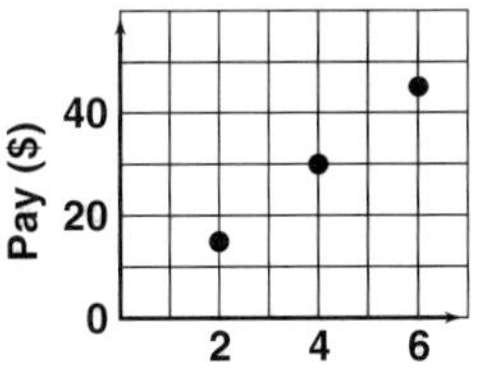

8. \$82.50 **9.** Arithmetic; start with 2 and add 8 repeatedly; 34, 42, 50. **10.** Geometric; start with 48 and multiply by $\frac{1}{12}$ repeatedly; $\frac{1}{36}$, $\frac{1}{432}$, $\frac{1}{5{,}184}$. **11.** Neither; start with 1 and add 1, 3, 9, 27, and so on; 121, 364, 1,093.

12a.

Term	1	2	3	4	5	6
Value	−6	−12	−18	−24	−30	−36

b. $-6n$; −600 **13a.**

x	y
0	3
2	4
4	5
6	6

b. $y = \frac{1}{2}x + 3$

14a. $y = 2x + 2$ **b.**

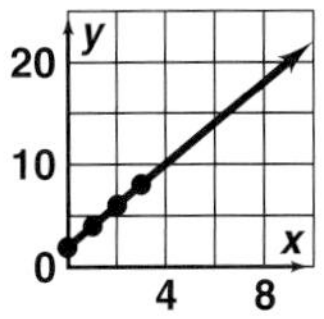

15. 7, 5, 3, 1, −1 **16.** Answers may vary. Sample: You travel for 2 h at a constant rate of 50 mi/h. You stop for 4 h, and then return to your starting place at a constant rate of 50 mi/h.

17.

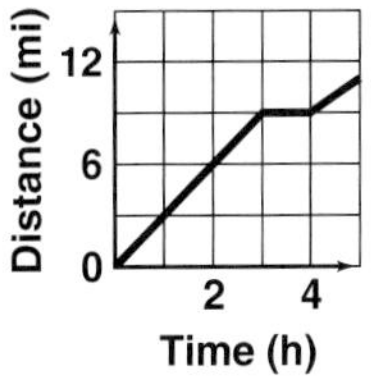

18. Answers may vary. Sample: Simple interest is calculated only on the principal; compound interest is calculated by the principal and any interest that has been earned. **19.** \$450 **20.** \$3,298.49 **21.** \$3.50 **22.** $x = \frac{z - y}{3}$ **23.** $x = -\frac{k}{4yz}$ **24.** $x = 9\left(\frac{z}{3} + 4\right)$, or $x = 3z + 36$

Chapter 10

Lesson 10-1 pp. 524–525

EXERCISES **1.** (0, 5) **3.** (−5, 3)

7–12.

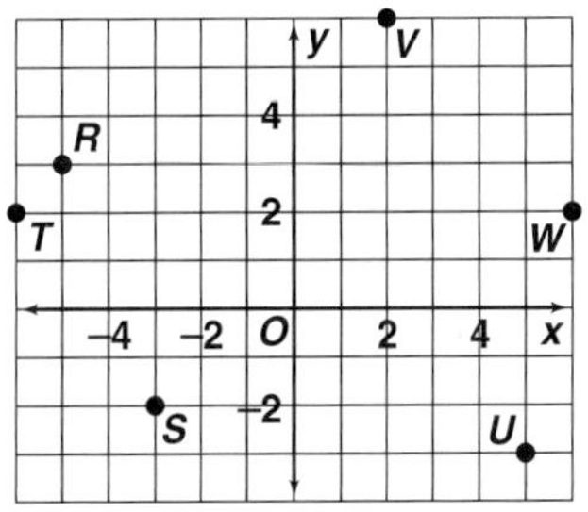

13.

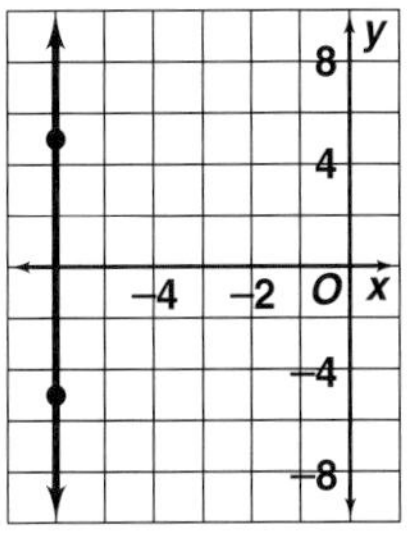

vertical

15.

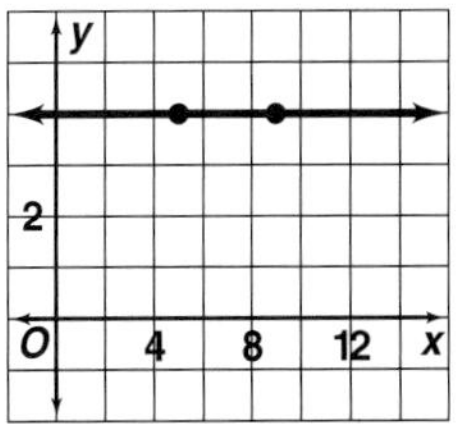

horizontal

19. horizontal **21.** horizontal **25a.** 150 beats, 450 beats, 750 beats **b.**

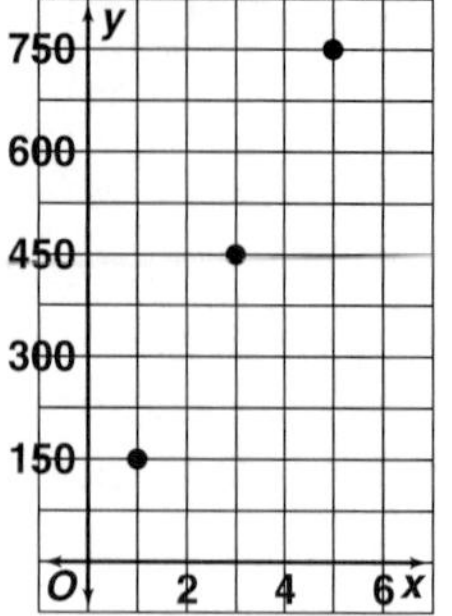

27a.

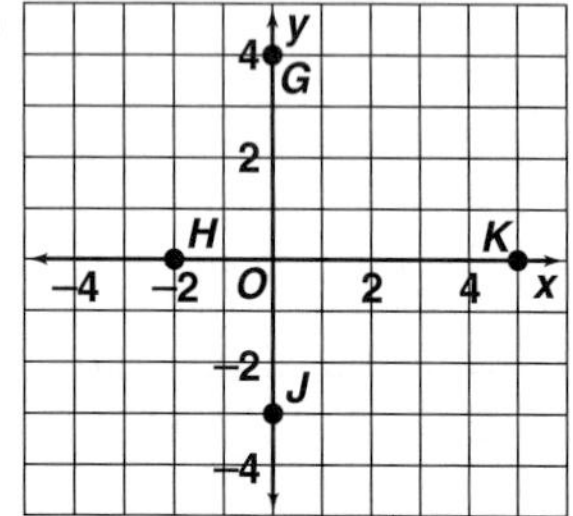

H and *K* are on the *x*-axis; *G* and *J* are on the *y*-axis. **b.** *x*-axis; *y*-axis **29.** III **41.** 11 **43.** 20 **45.** 16.7% **47.** 10.3%

Lesson 10-2 pp. 529–531

EXERCISES 1. no **3.** no **17.**

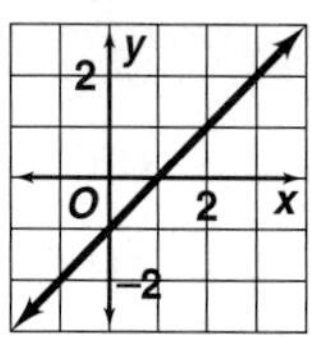

19.

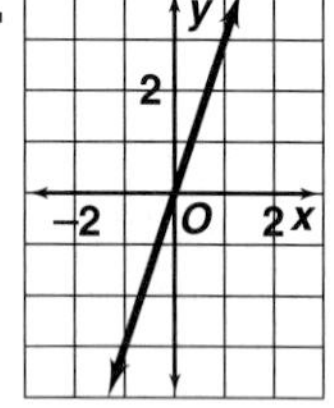

29a.

x	*x* − 7	*y*	(*x*, *y*)
0	0 − 7	−7	(0, −7)
−3	−3 − 7	−10	(−3, −10)
10	10 − 7	3	(10, 3)

b.

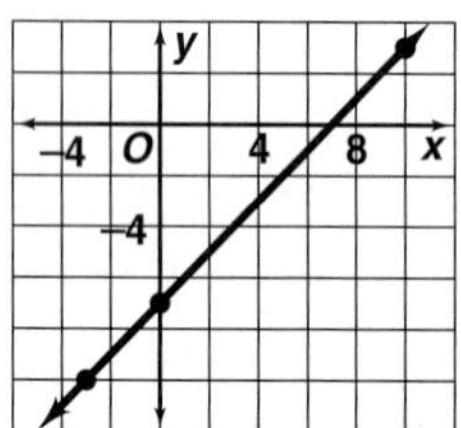

31a. Negative *x*-values; you cannot have a negative number of hives.

b.

x	50*x*	*y*	(*x*, *y*)
0	50(0)	0	(0, 0)
2	50(2)	100	(2, 100)
4	50(4)	200	(4, 200)

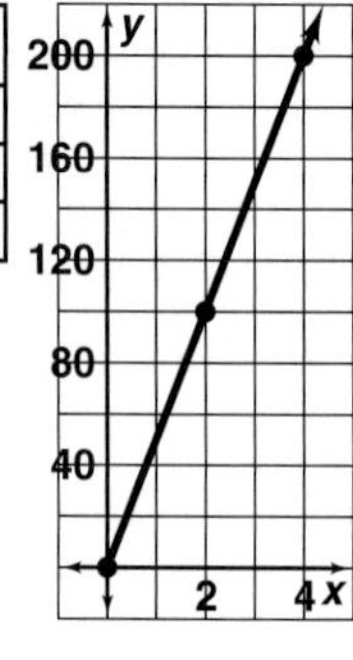

33. II **35.** none **41.** $-3 + 3 = 0 \neq 3$; $-2(-3) = 6 \neq 3$

43. **45.**

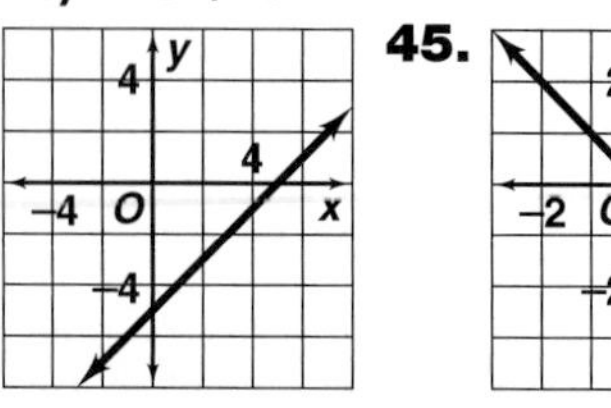

47. *q* **61.** 7.9 in. **63.** obtuse **65.** straight **67.** obtuse

Lesson 10-3 pp. 535–538

EXERCISES 1. $\frac{1}{2}$ **3.** $-\frac{1}{3}$ **5.** $\frac{5}{4}$

7.

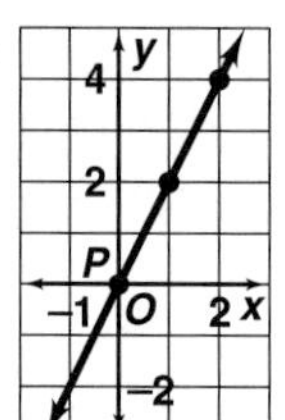

9.

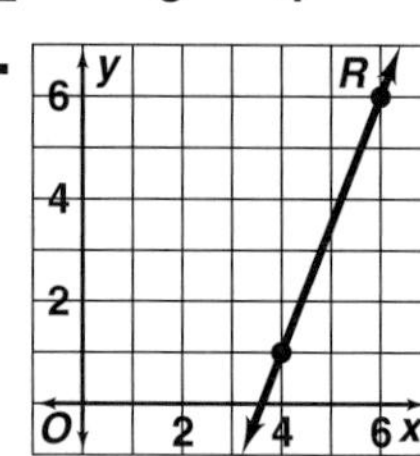

13a. *j* **b.** *j*: −2; *k*: $\frac{2}{3}$ **15.** No; the slope of the ramp is $\frac{33}{80}$, while the slope of the guidelines is $\frac{1}{12}$. Since $\frac{33}{80} > \frac{1}{12}$, the ramp does not meet the guidelines. **17.** $-\frac{1}{4}$ **19.** $-\frac{5}{7}$ **23a.** $24,000 **b.** −2 **c.** Every year the value of the car decreases $2,000. **25.** 5 sections; 4 sections; there are 5 segments that rise from left to right and 4 that go down from left to right.

27.

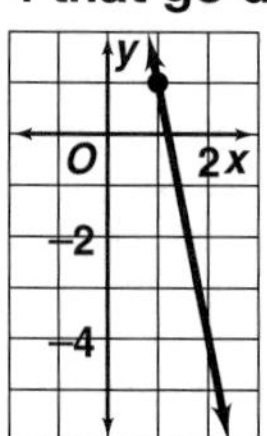

29.

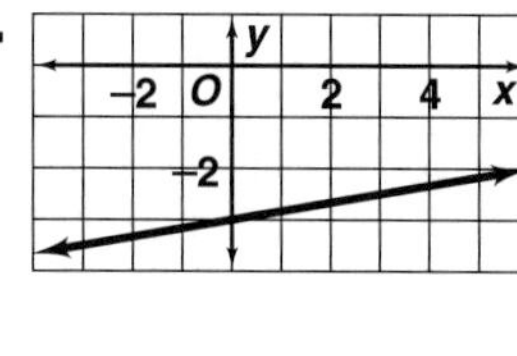

37. 75%, $\frac{7}{9}$, 0.78 **39.**

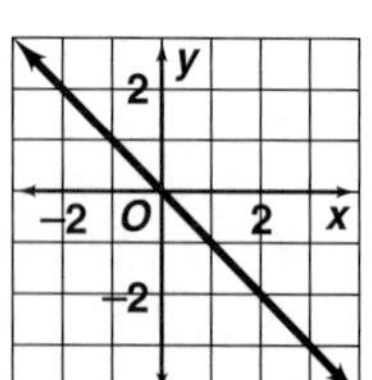

41. 60 **43.** 90°

Lesson 10-4 pp. 542–543

EXERCISES 1.

x	−3	−2	−1	0	1	2	3
y	9	4	1	0	1	4	9

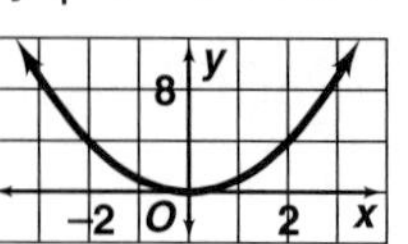

3.

x	−3	−2	−1	0	1	2	3
y	11	6	3	2	3	6	11

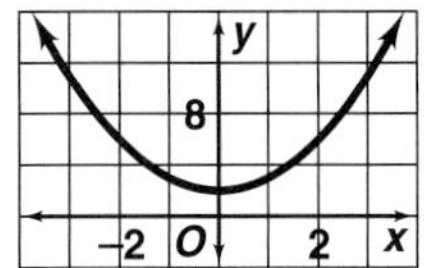

19. parabola **21.** absolute value

25a.

t	$16t^2$	d	(t, d)
0	$16(0)^2$	0	(0, 0)
1	$16(1)^2$	16	(1, 16)
3	$16(3)^2$	144	(3, 144)
5	$16(5)^2$	400	(5, 400)

b.

27. A **29.** F

31.

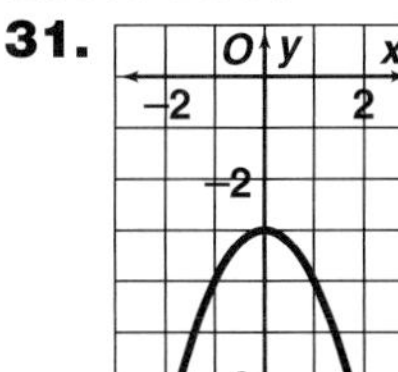

33.

37a.

x	$-\lvert x\rvert$	y	(x, y)
−3	$-\lvert-3\rvert$	−3	(−3, −3)
−1	$-\lvert-1\rvert$	−1	(−1, −1)
0	$-\lvert 0\rvert$	0	(0, 0)
1	$-\lvert 1\rvert$	−1	(1, −1)
3	$-\lvert 3\rvert$	−3	(3, −3)

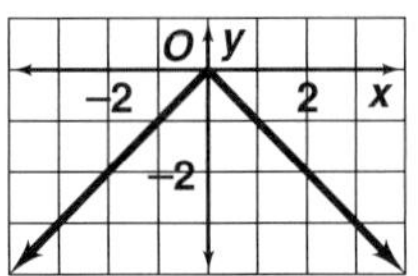

b. No; for nonzero values of *x*, the *y*-values are negative. **49.** $\overline{AB}$; $\overline{CB}$; $\overline{DB}$; $\overline{AC}$ **51.** $\overline{EA}$; $\overline{EB}$; $\overline{EC}$; $\overline{ED}$ **53.** 5.0 mm **55.** 8.75 m

Lesson 10-5 pp. 545–547

EXERCISES 1. \$9 **3.** \$24 **7.** 928 tiles **9.** $\frac{1}{8}$

Lesson 10-6 pp. 552–553

EXERCISES 1. (1, −2) **3.** (−5, −3)

7.

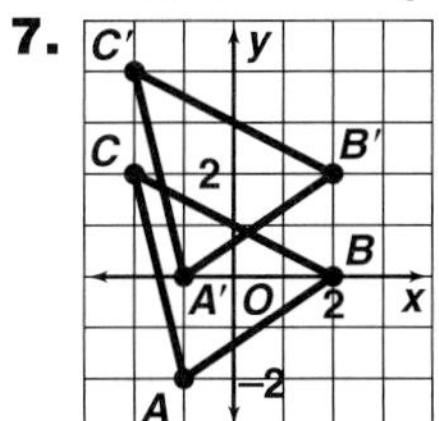

A(−1, −2), *B*(2, 0), *C*(−2, 2) → *A*′(−1, 0), *B*′(2, 2), *C*′(−2, 4)

9.

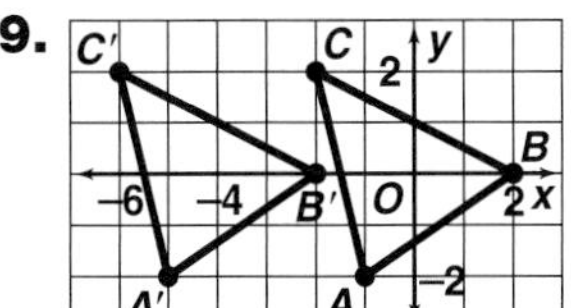

A(−1, −2), *B*(2, 0), *C*(−2, 2) → *A*′(−5, −2), *B*′(−2, 0), *C*′(−6, 2) **13.** (*x*, *y*) → (*x* + 5, *y* + 4) **15.** *P*′(2, 4), *L*′(−1, 4), *N*′(2, 1); (*x*, *y*) → (*x* + 4, *y* + 3) **17.** *M*′(6, 4); (*x*, *y*) → (*x* + 3, *y* − 1) **19.** C′(−1, −3); (*x*, *y*) → (*x* + 1, *y* + 2) **21a–b.** Answers may vary. Samples are given. **a.** up 2, right 1 **b.** up 2, right 1; up 1, right 2; up 1, right 2 **23.** right 3; up 1 **33.** −35 **35.** no **37.** no **39.** no

Lesson 10-7 pp 556–558

EXERCISES 1.

3.

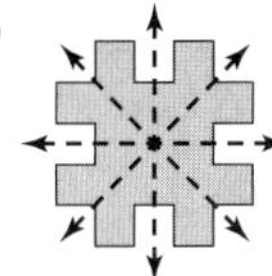

5. (3, −8) **7.** (−3, 6) **15.** *A*′(1, 1) **17.** *C*′(5, −2)

19.

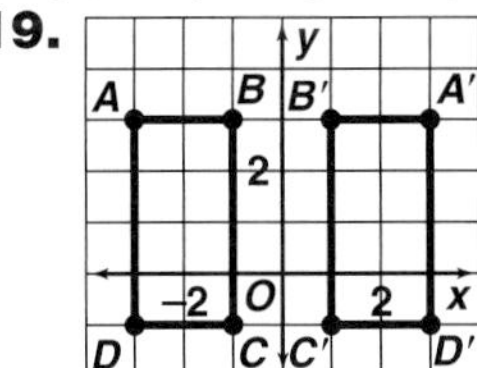

A(−3, 3), *B*(−1, 3), *C*(−1, −1), *D*(−3, −1) → *A*′(3, 3), *B*′(1, 3), *C*′(1, −1), *D*′(3, −1) **21.** Answers may vary. Sample: A E I V **23.** *B* and *E* **25.** The *y*-coordinate stays the same and the *x*-coordinate is multiplied by −1. **27.** reflection; *y*-axis **29.** translation; (*x*, *y*) → (*x* + 5, *y* − 3) **31.** (3, 1), (−3, −1) **33.** (2, −1), (−2, 1) **47.** 60 **49.** 14 **53.** $x \geq 1$

Lesson 10-8 pp. 561–562

Exercises 1. no **3.** yes **5.** no

7.

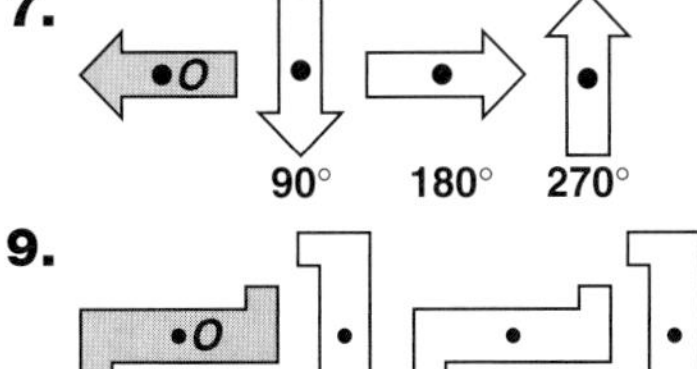

9.

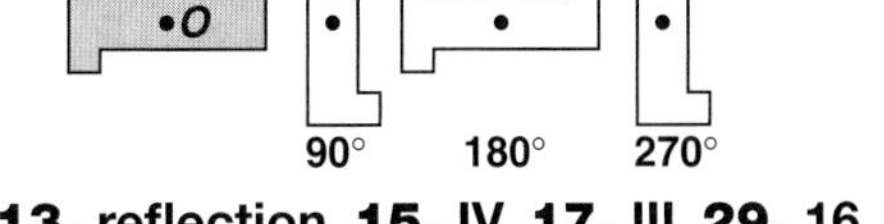

13. reflection **15.** IV **17.** III **29.** 16 **31.** 27.5 **35.** 40.078 **37.** 15.54

Selected Answers

Chapter Review pp. 564–565

1. reflection **2.** center of rotation **3.** solution **4.** ordered pair **5.** linear equation

6. 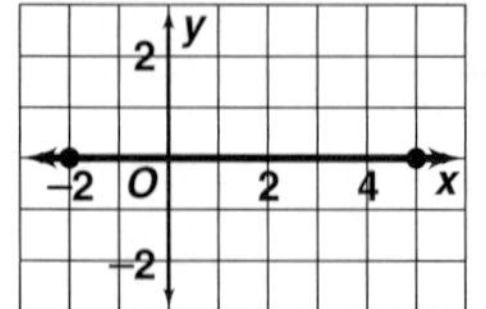 horizontal

7. 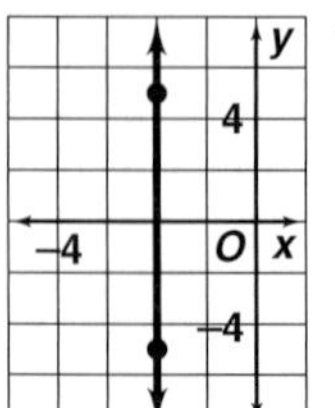 vertical

8. 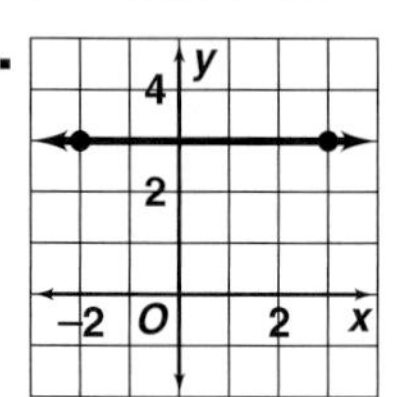 horizontal

9–12. Answers may vary. Samples are given. **9.** (0, 3), (−2, 1), (5, 8) **10.** (0, −5), (5, 0), (−1, −6) **11.** (0, 1), (2, 5), (−3, −5) **12.** (0, −2), (4, −6), (−3, 1) **13.** 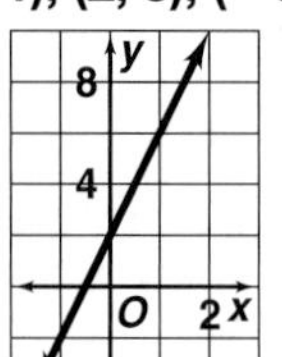 **14.** 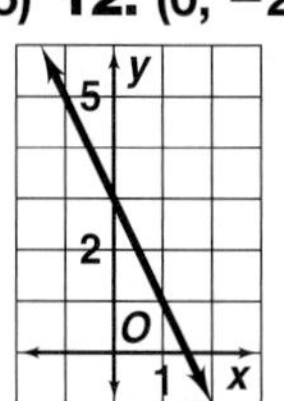 **15.** 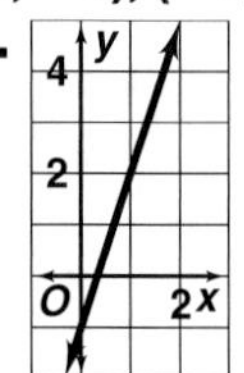

16. 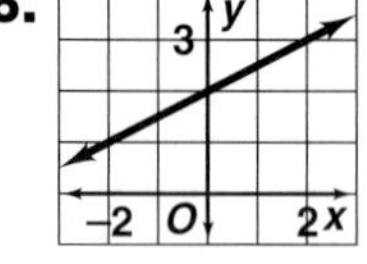 **17.** 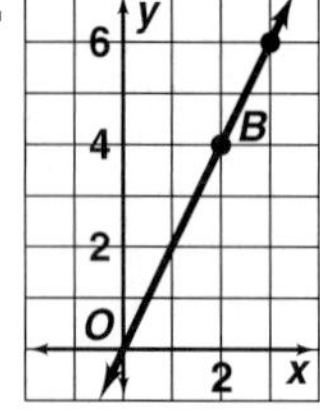

18. 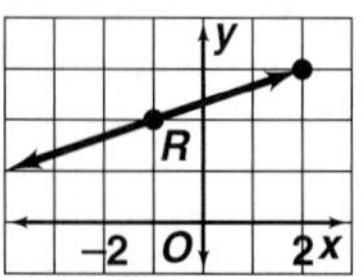 **19.** 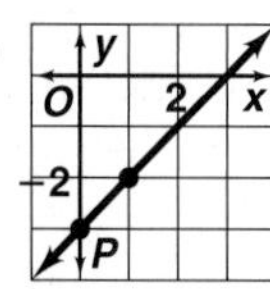

20. 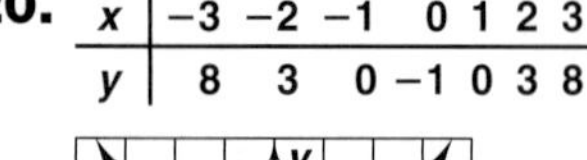

x	−3	−2	−1	0	1	2	3
y	8	3	0	−1	0	3	8

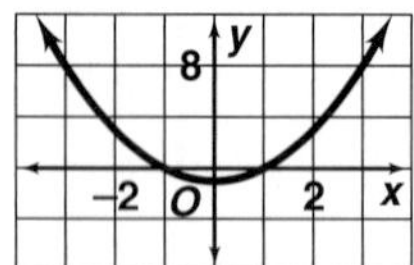

21. 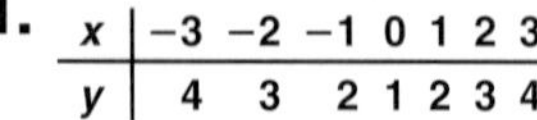

x	−3	−2	−1	0	1	2	3
y	4	3	2	1	2	3	4

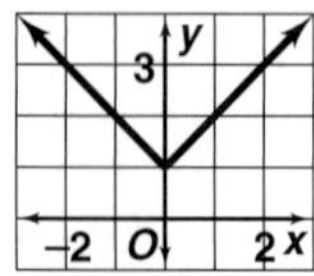

22.

x	−3	−2	−1	0	1	2	3
y	16	6	0	−2	0	6	16

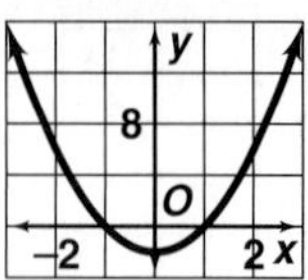

23.

x	−3	−2	−1	0	1	2	3
y	12	8	4	0	4	8	12

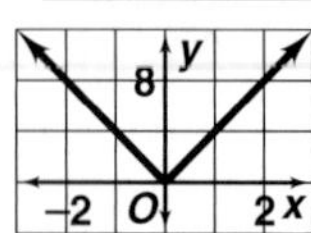

24. 30 mi **25.** $A(3, -1)$, $B(1, 1)$, $C(4, 4) \rightarrow A'(3, -3)$, $B'(1, -1)$, $C'(4, 2)$ **26.** $A(3, -1)$, $B(1, 1)$, $C(4, 4) \rightarrow A'(0, -1)$, $B'(-2, 1)$, $C'(1, 4)$ **27.** $A(3, -1)$, $B(1, 1)$, $C(4, 4) \rightarrow A'(6, -6)$, $B'(4, -4)$, $C'(7, -1)$

28. 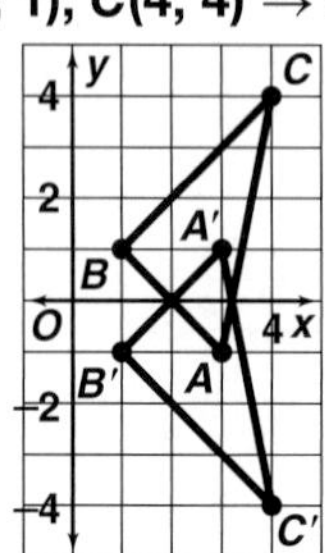 $A(3, -1)$, $B(1, 1)$, $C(4, 4) \rightarrow A'(3, 1)$, $B'(1, -1)$, $C'(4, -4)$

29. yes; 90°, 180°, 270°

30. yes; 180°

Chapter 11

Lesson 11-1 pp. 576–578

EXERCISES 1.

Tickets Sold	Tally	Frequency
45	||	2
46	||||	4
47		0
48	||	2
49	|	1
50	|||	3
51	||	2
52		0
53	|	1

3.

Student Ages	Tally	Frequency
11	||||	4
12	~~||||~~	5
13	~~||||~~	5
14	|||	3

5. 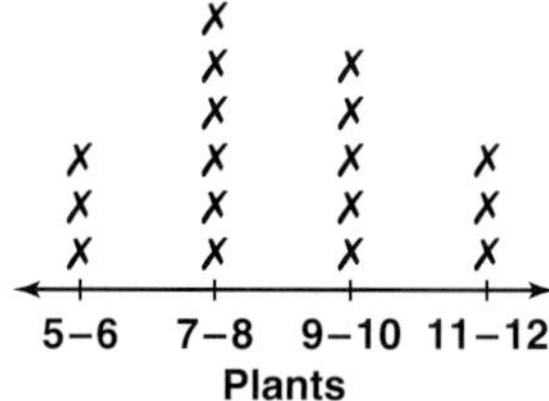

7.

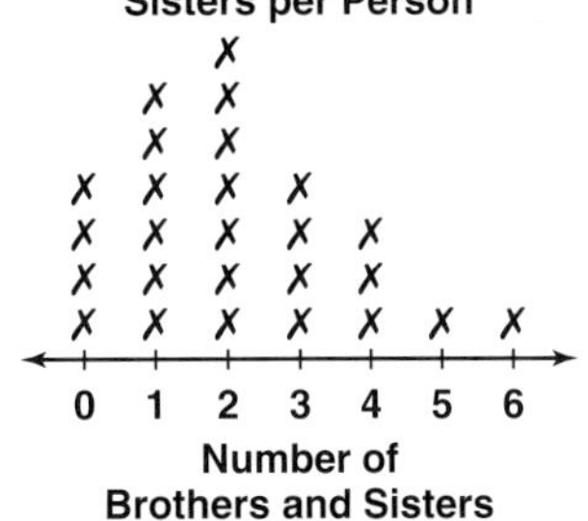

9.

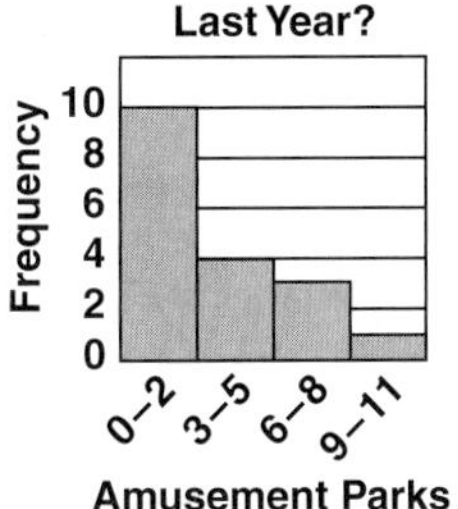

11.

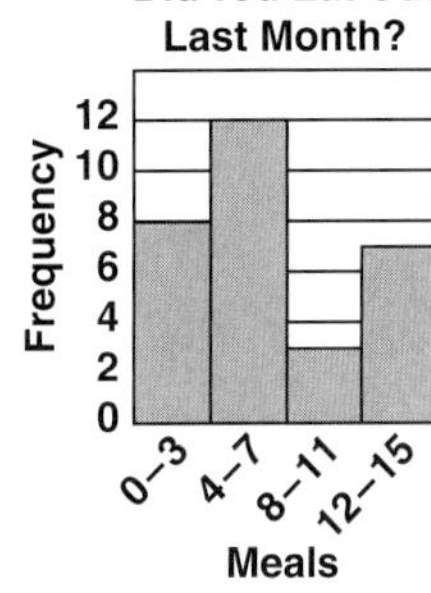

13. 4 customers

17. 4–5; 15 responses **19.** about 49 people **21.** times flown in an airplane

31.

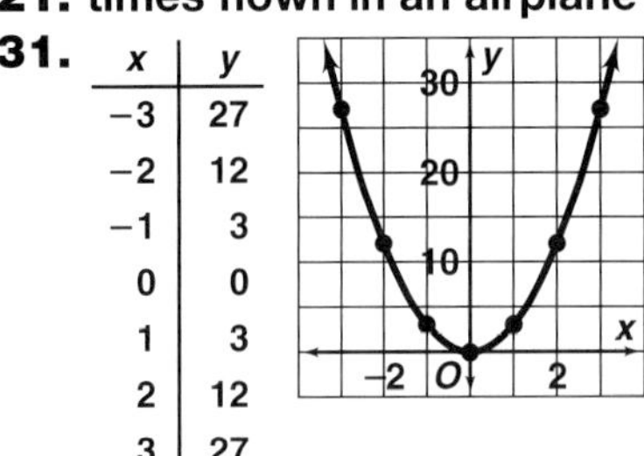

x	y
−3	27
−2	12
−1	3
0	0
1	3
2	12
3	27

33. $120

Lesson 11-2 pp. 581–584

EXERCISES **1.** Dog **3.** 46 **5.** 26 **7.** D3 **9.** B3 **11.** Corpus Christi, TX; Albany, NY **13.** Sante Fe, NM, and Albany, NY **17.** 1980–1990 **19.** 1970–1990 **21.** Answers may vary. Sample: Perhaps the price of autos rose, so more people may have started riding bikes. **23.** about 2,400,000 **25.** every year **27.** about 200,000 books **29.** onions **31.** pickles

43.

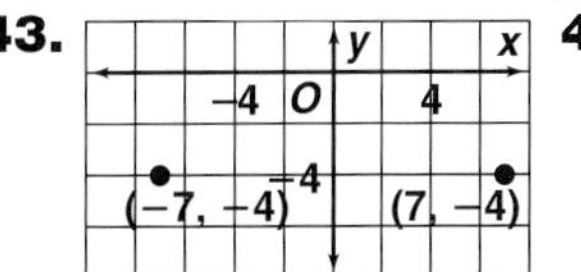

45. 3 **47.** −8

Lesson 11-3 pp. 587–590

EXERCISES **1.**

1.85

3.

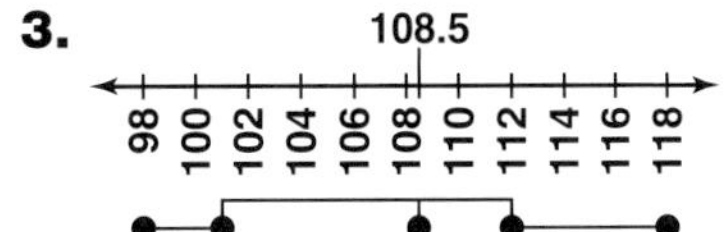

5. Male students are taller than female students. **7.** 70 in. **9.**

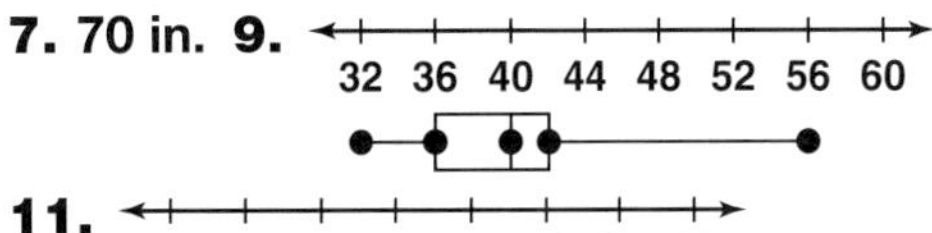

11.

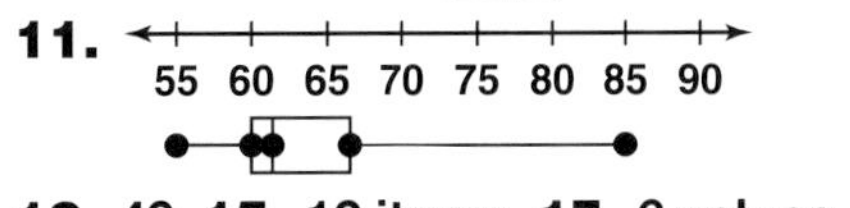

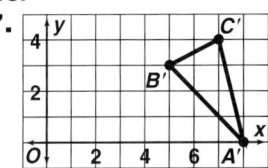

13. 49 **15.** 12 items **17.** 6 values **19.** tenths **21.** 6 people **25.** 93 **33.** No; the interval only shows 16–20 pennies.

35.

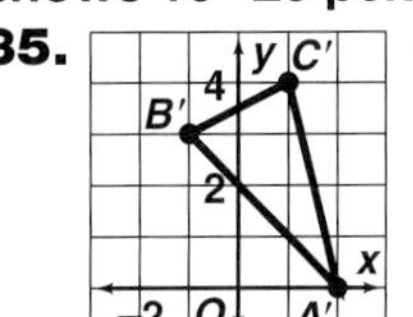

37.

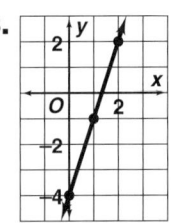

Lesson 11-4 pp. 593–595

EXERCISES **1.** soccer balls; footballs **3.** Mandela **5.** Keesha = Spanish; Frieda = Italian, Pascal = French, Jared = German, Mika = Chinese **7.** 22.5 ft **9a.** Ludberg, Chester, Topson, Dornville **b.** 16.5 mi **11.** 7 students **15.** 138 whole numbers

21.

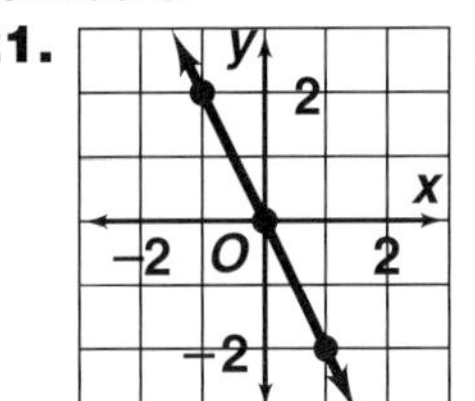

23.

27. 10 **29.** 3

Lesson 11-5 pp. 598–600

EXERCISES **1b.** Teenagers entering a grocery store won't already be snacking and can think of more possible snacks. This sample is more likely to be random. **3a.** Students from different grades will be exposed to different books. This sample is more likely to be random. **5.** Biased; the question uses the words *invigorating* and *couch potato.* **7.** Fair; the question makes no assumptions. **11.** "Are you a college student?" **17.** Get a list of bus drivers from each company and call every 10th driver. **21.** Survey B; survey A is biased because it uses the terms *noisy* and *over-priced;* survey B is not biased because it makes no assumptions. **29.** 23 students **33.**

35. $\ell = \frac{p - 2w}{2}$

Lesson 11-6 pp. 603–605

EXERCISES **1.** about 1,823 deer **3.** about 2,273 deer **11.** about 13,661 bass **13.** about 9,147 penguins **15.** about 9,748 rabbits **17.** about 496 catfish **23a.** about 357 squirrels **b.** It would make the estimate appear too large.

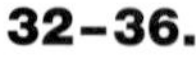
32–36.

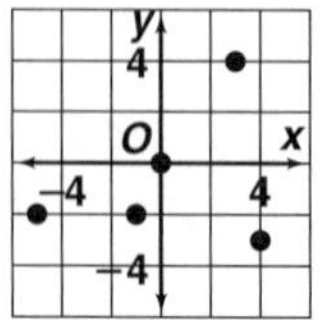

37. start with 3 and repeatedly add 5; 23, 28, 33
39. start with 27 and repeatedly subtract 11; −17, −28, −39

Lesson 11-7 pp. 608–611

EXERCISES **1a.** The graph gives the impression that the price of widgets will decrease by $\frac{1}{2}$ from 2000–2004. **b.** The scale on the *y*-axis starts at 7.

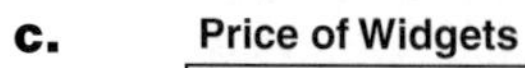
c.

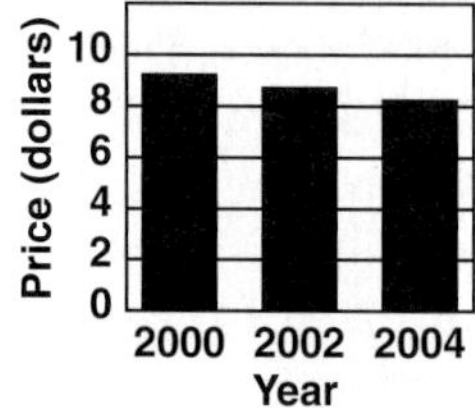

3a. The graph gives the impression that the rates stayed the same. **b.** The intervals are very large.
c.

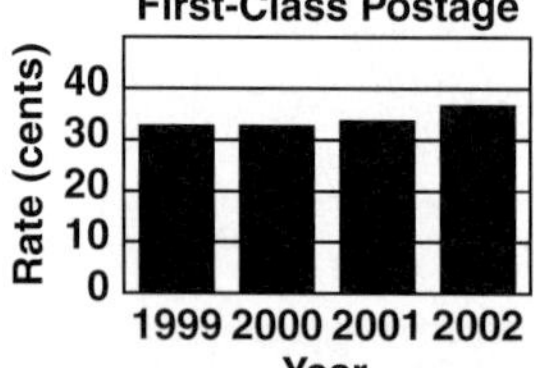

5a. mean **b.** mode

7a. yes **b.** She won two of three games. **9.** The *y* axis starts with 8 instead of 0. The title is also misleading since grapes are not everybody's favorite. **11a.** The graph gives the impression that profits have been increasing. **b.** It reverses the scale on the *x*-axis.
c.

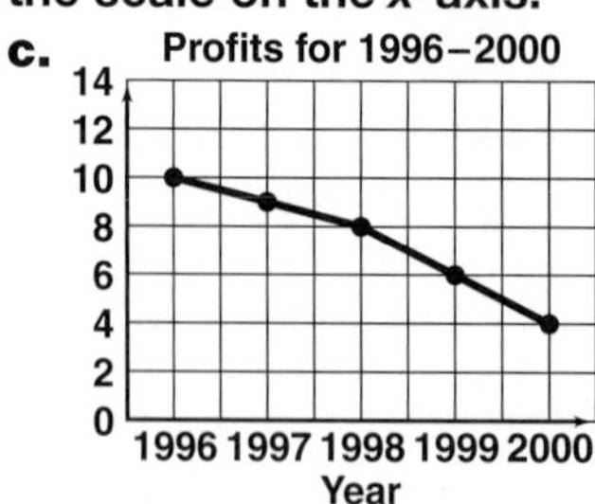

13. Yes; $\frac{97}{200}$ is only 49%, not 97%.

15c.

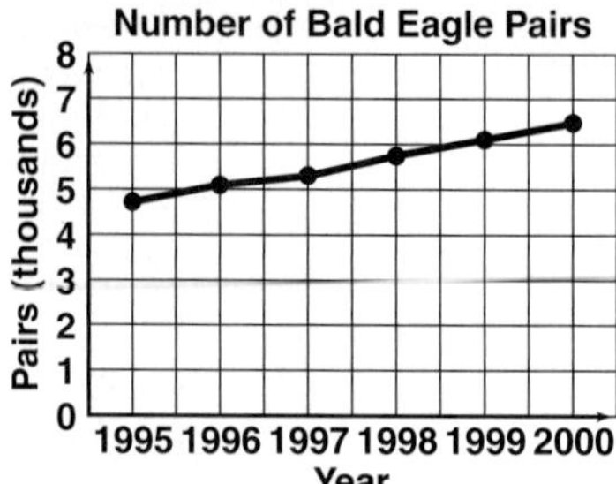

25.

Number	Tally	Frequency
11–13	III	3
14–16	III	3
17–19	I	1
20–22		0
23–25		0
26–28	I	1

27.

Number	Tally	Frequency
61	I	1
62	II	2
63	III	3
64	I	1
65		0
66	I	1
67	I	1

29.

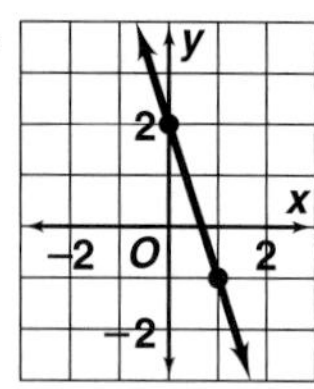

31.

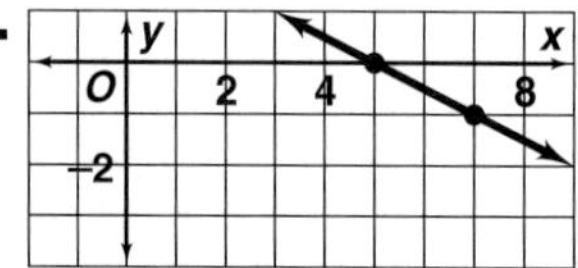

33. $-\frac{1}{3}$ **35.** −2

Lesson 11-8 pp. 615–618

EXERCISES **1.**

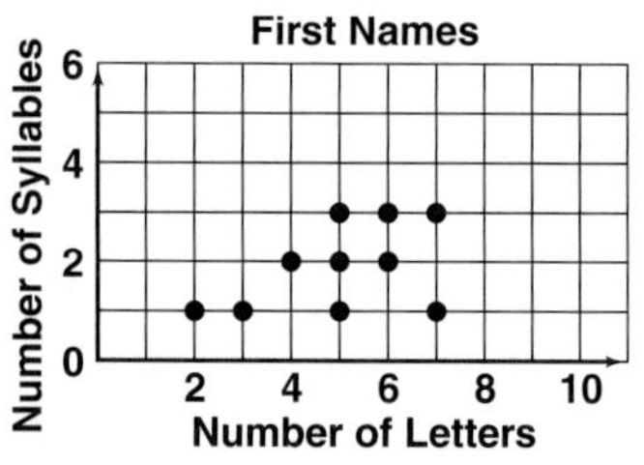

3.

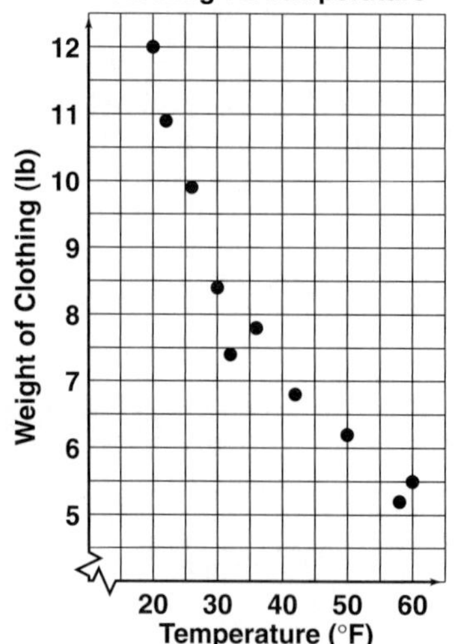

7. no trend **9.** no trend **13a.** Answers may vary. Sample: Attendance (millions); Average Ticket Cost (dollars) **b.** *x*-axis: 20¢; *y*-axis: 50 (million) **15.** As attendance increased, average ticket cost would also; no; as one data increases so does the other. **17.** Negative; as the number of hours watching TV increases, the time spent studying will probably decrease. **19.** Negative; losing teams replace their coaches more often than winning teams do. **25.** Yes; it seems that as the wolf population increases, the moose population decreases. **33.** No; the question makes no assumptions about either season.

35.

3	7
4	
5	
6	8
7	5 8 9
8	4 6 8
9	2 4 6
10	1 3

3 | 7 means 3.7

37.

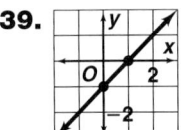

39.

Chapter Review pp. 620–621

1. stem-and-leaf plot **2.** negative **3.** legend **4.** line plot **5.** population

6.

Number of Hours of TV (weekly)

Hours	Tally	Frequency
3	I	1
4	II	2
5	𝍸	5
6	𝍸	5
7	IIII	4
8	II	2
9	I	1

Temperatures

1	6 9
2	3 7 7 9
3	6
4	0 0 0 5 7 7 8
5	0 0 1 4 5 8
6	0 0 0 1 6 9
7	0

7a. counts to 20 **b.** counts to 20

8.

Temperatures

1	6 9
2	3 7 7 9
3	6
4	0 0 0 5 7 7 8
5	0 0 1 4 5 8
6	0 0 0 1 6 9
7	0

Key: 1 | 6 means 16

9. Antonia: fish; Becca: parrot; Corwin: turtle **10.** Fair; the question makes no assumptions about the activity. **11.** Biased; the question assumes the ocean is calm and soothing. **12.** about 368 wolves **13.** The *y*-axis starts at 93, so it appears that the student who studied 6 h did twice as well as the student who studied 4 h. **14.** no trend **15.** negative

Chapter 12

Lesson 12-1 pp. 632–634

EXERCISES **1.** $\frac{1}{12}$; $0.08\overline{3}$; about 83% **3.** $\frac{1}{2}$; 0.5; 50% **9.** $\frac{1}{5}$ **11.** $\frac{1}{2}$ **17.** 1 : 5 **19.** 1 : 1 **21.** $\frac{3}{4}$ **23.** $\frac{1}{2}$ **25a.** 0.7 **b.** 35% **27.** 0.06 **29.** 0.04 **33a.** $\frac{2}{7}$ **b.** $\frac{5}{7}$ **c.** 1 **d.** 1 **43.** no trend **45.** negative trend **47.** Fair; question is not biased because there are no biased terms.

Lesson 12-2 pp. 638–641

EXERCISES **1.** $\frac{1}{2}$ **3.** $\frac{18}{25}$ **5.** $\frac{3}{20}$ **7.** $\frac{1}{5}$ **9.** $\frac{13}{320}$ **19.** $\frac{6}{25}$ **21.** $\frac{2}{25}$ **23.** $\frac{7}{25}$ **25.** C; you guess 2 numbers from a group of 6, so you should use a group of 6 cards. **27.** B; there are two choices for each question so use 6 coins since each question has 2 outcomes. **29.** $\frac{5}{26}$ **31.** $\frac{13}{26}$ or $\frac{1}{2}$ **41.** $\frac{2}{9}$ **43.** $\frac{7}{9}$

Lesson 12-3 pp. 644–646

EXERCISES **1–3.** Check students' work. **5a.** $6,675 **b.** $5,743.50 **11.** 37 **15.** B **17.** $\frac{1}{8}$; 0.125; 12.5% **21.** (−2, −3)

Lesson 12-4 pp. 649–652

EXERCISES **9.** 96 ways **11.** $\frac{1}{8}$ **13.** 0 **17.** 81 **19.** 32 **21.** $\frac{1}{4}$ **23.** $\frac{1}{2}$

27.

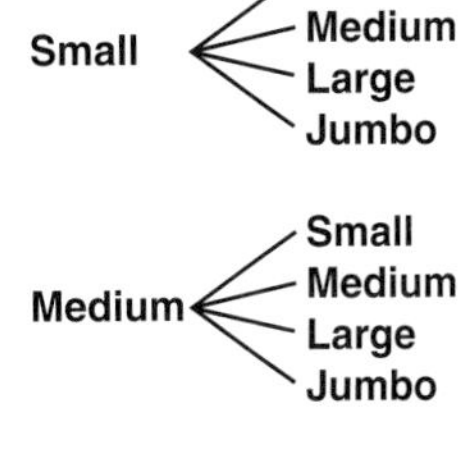

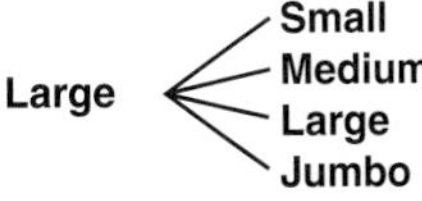

29. Yes; there are 24 possible orders, so the probability for each order is $\frac{1}{24}$. **37.** The colors are W, L, V, and R and the background scenes are O, K, U, and D. An organized list of outcomes is

Selected Answers

WO, WK, WU, WD, LO, LK, LU, LD, VO, VK, VU, VD, RO, RK, RU, RD.

Lesson 12-5 pp. 656–658

EXERCISES 1. $\frac{1}{36}$ **3.** $\frac{1}{12}$ **7.** $\frac{1}{64}$ **9.** 0 **11.** $\frac{1}{7}$ **13.** $\frac{2}{7}$ **17.** $\frac{1}{38}$ **19.** $\frac{8}{243}$ **21.** $\frac{4}{81}$ by 1. **25.** $\frac{1}{25}$ **27.** $\frac{62}{595}$

35.

	1	2	3
H	H1	H2	H3
T	T1	T2	T3

37. 126°

Lesson 12-6 pp. 662–663

EXERCISES 1. 120 **3.** 6 **7.** 3! = 6 **9.** 4! = 24 **15.** 42 **17.** 30 **21.** 2,730 ways **23.** 24 **25.** 5,040 **29.** 17,576 passwords **31.** 4 **33.** 840

Lesson 12-7 pp. 665–668

EXERCISES 1. 6 **3.** 3 **5.** 3 **7.** 15 **9.** 6 **11.** 3 **15.** 30 **19.** BEO, BEP, BER, BEW, BOP, BOR, BOW, EOP, EOR, EOW, BPR, BPW, BRW, OPR, OPW, EPR, EPW, ERW, PRW, ORW **23.** combination; 56 sets **25.** permutation; 24 orders **29.** 10 combinations **41.** 4! = 24 **43.** 6! = 720

47.

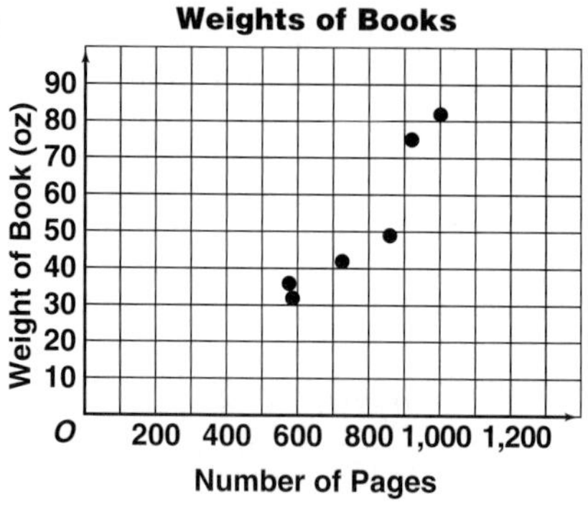

Chapter Review pp. 670–671

1. combination **2.** event **3.** independent **4.** odds **5.** Experimental **6.** $\frac{1}{7}$ **7.** $\frac{2}{7}$ **8.** $\frac{6}{7}$ **9.** $\frac{1}{7}$ **10.** $\frac{5}{7}$ **11.** $\frac{2}{7}$ **12a.** $\frac{1}{50}$ **b.** 32 **13.** Check students' work. **14a.** OSC, OST, OBC, OBT, ASC, AST, ABC, ABT; $\frac{1}{8}$ **b.** Check students' work.

15a.

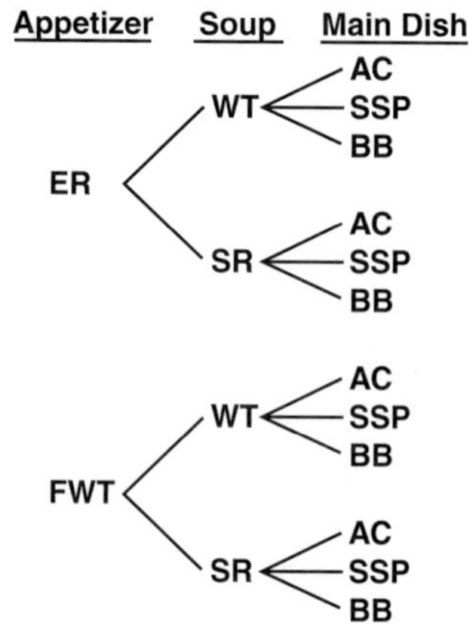

b. $\frac{1}{12}$ **16.** 12 dinners **17.** $\frac{15}{91}$ **18.** $\frac{24}{91}$ **19.** $\frac{4}{13}$ **20.** 5 teams **21.** 24 ways

Extra Practice

Chapter 1 p. 684

Exercises 1, 3, 5. Answers may vary. Samples: **1.** 2 **3.** 13 **5.** 8.28 **7.** 9.107 **9.** 4.93 **11.** 8.5 **13.** 0.09 **15.** 2,700,000 **17.** 3, 39 **19.** = **21.** < **23.** −6 **25.** −8 **31.** −33 **33.** −11 **35.** 19.1 **37.** 19.683 **43.** 12; 12; 12

Chapter 2 p. 685

1. $n - 3$ **3.** $d - 5$ **7.** 12 **9.** 27 **11.** −24 **13.** 162 **15.** 6 **17.** −96 **19.** 15 **21.** 40 **23.** −2 **25.** 54 **27.** $y \geq 6$;

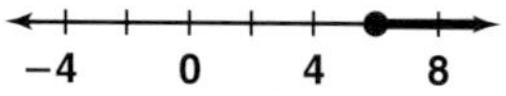

29. $a \leq 10$;

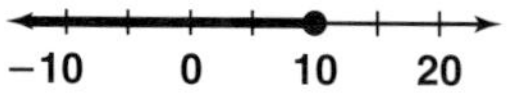

Chapter 3 p. 686

1. 100 **3.** 625 **7.** 1.6×10^5 **9.** 7.9×10^9 **11.** 2, 3, 4, 9 **13.** 2, 3, 4, 5, 8, 10 **15.** 7 **17.** 4 **21.** $\frac{7}{8}$ **23.** $\frac{1}{5}$ **27.** > **29.** = **33.** $\frac{63}{8}$ **35.** $\frac{13}{4}$ **45.** −1.0, 0.35, $\frac{3}{6}$, $\frac{9}{12}$ **47.** 0.375, $\frac{1}{2}$, $0.\overline{6}$, $\frac{10}{11}$

Chapter 4 p. 687

Exercises 1–8. Answers may vary. Samples: **1.** 1 **3.** 65 **5.** $1\frac{1}{3}$ **7.** $\frac{1}{3}$ **13.** $\frac{3}{20}$ **15.** 25 **21.** $\frac{3}{8}$ **23.** 90 **27.** 3:35 P.M. **29.** $2\frac{1}{4}$ **31.** $202\frac{2}{3}$ **35.** $5\frac{1}{4}$ lb **37.** 35.95 mL

Chapter 5 p. 688

1. 2 : 3; 2 to 3 **3.** $\frac{4}{7}$; 4 : 7 **7.** 16 oz for \$4.80 **9.** 3 gal for \$5.69 **15.** 36 games **17.** no **19.** no **21.** 20 **23.** 3.5 **27.** $1\frac{2}{3}$ **29.** 600 ft **31.** 1,200 ft

Chapter 6 p. 689

1. 80% **3.** 12% **7.** 0.375 **9.** 0.0255 **13.** $2\frac{1}{4}$ **15.** $\frac{7}{10,000}$ **19.** 85.5 **21.** 112.5 **25.** 5% **27.** 40% **31.** 63 **33.** 6.16 **37.** \$226.67 **39.** 60% increase **41.** 1.9% increase **49.** about 37%

Chapter 7 p. 690

1. $\overrightarrow{YZ}$ **3.** $\overleftrightarrow{CR}$ **5.** 75°; 165° **7.** 44°; 134°

9.

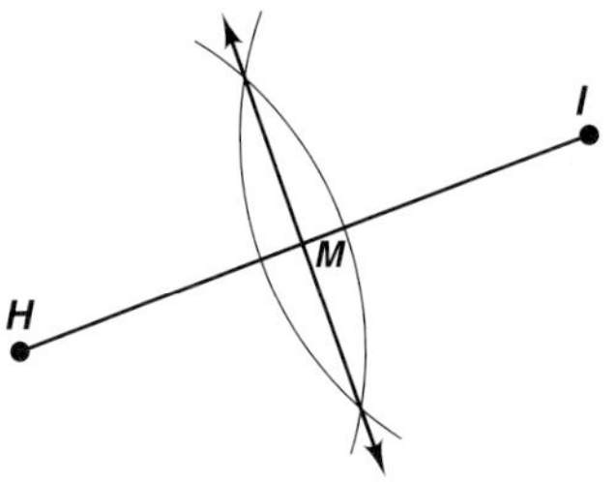

11. 90° **13.** parallelogram; $\overline{AB}$ and $\overline{CD}$, $\overline{BC}$ and $\overline{AD}$; ∠B and ∠D, ∠A and ∠C **15.** pentagon: $\overline{EF}$, $\overline{FG}$, $\overline{GH}$, $\overline{HJ}$, and $\overline{JE}$; ∠E, ∠F, ∠G, ∠H, and ∠J **17.** 1,440° **19.** ∠D **21.** $\overline{CE}$

Chapter 8 p. 691

1. about 1,400 ft^2 **3.** about 15 ft^2 **5.** 240 ft^2 **7.** 4.71 km; 1.8 km^2 **9.** 56.5 m; 254.3 m^2 **11.** 1 **13.** 7 **17.** 8 m **19.** 8 cm **21.** cylinder **23.** 785 m^3; 180 ft^3

Chapter 9 p. 692

1.

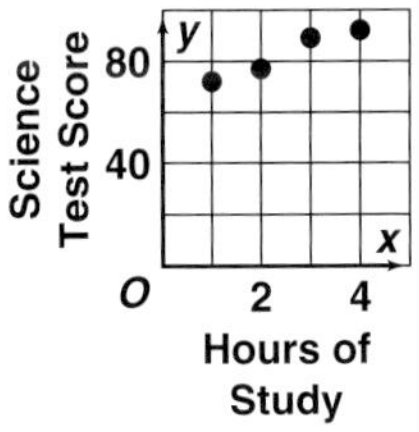

3. $p = 27$, $q = 69$

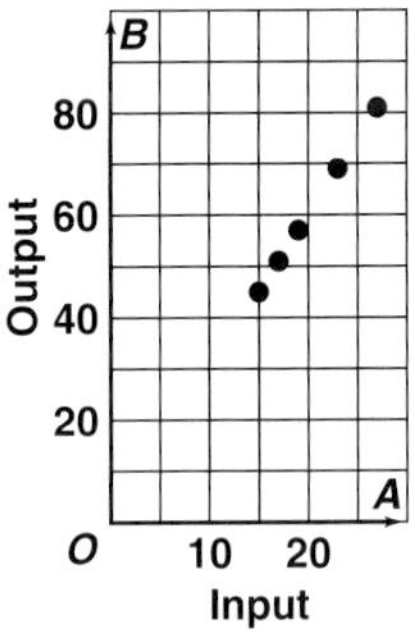

5. geometric **7.** $y = 6x$ **9.** $y = 3x + 1$

11.

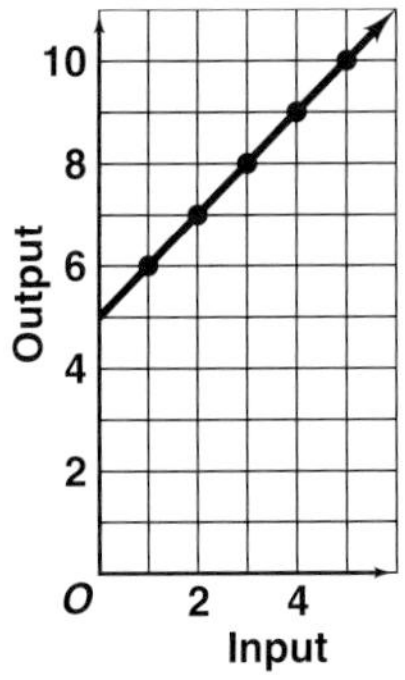

13.

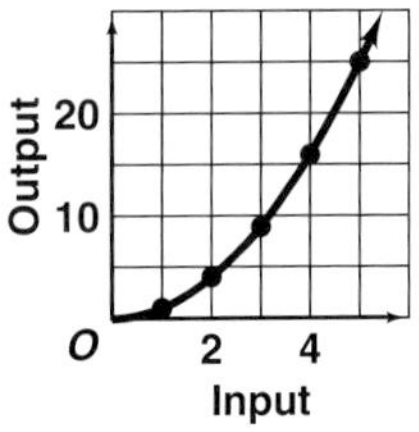

15. $1,215.51 **17.** $2,182.02

Chapter 10 p. 693

1. G **3.** B **5.** $\frac{2}{3}$ **7.** yes **9.** no

11.

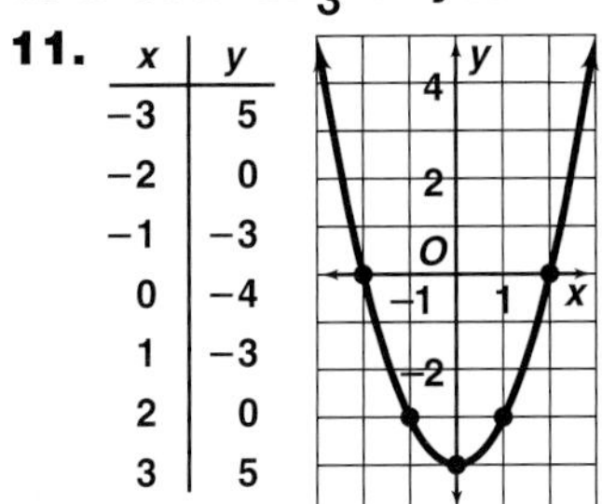

x	y
−3	5
−2	0
−1	−3
0	−4
1	−3
2	0
3	5

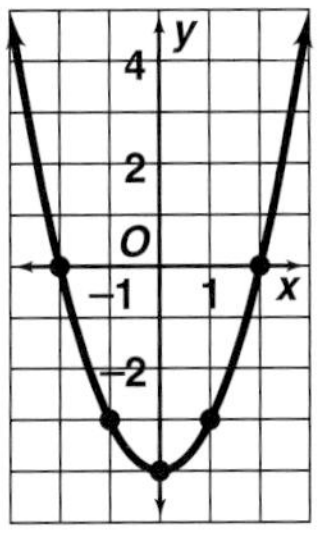

13.

x	y
−3	12
−2	8
−1	4
0	0
1	4
2	8
3	12

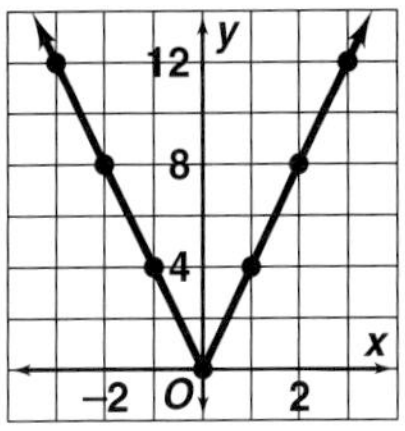

15. $(x, y) \rightarrow (x - 5, y)$ **17.** $(x, y) \rightarrow (x - 5, y + 3)$

19. a–b.

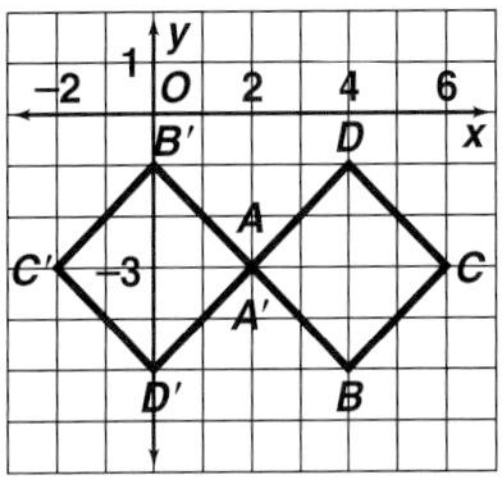

c. (2, −3), (0, −1), (−2, −3), (0, −5)

Chapter 11 p. 694

1.

Temp.	Tally	Frequency
84	||	2
85	||||	4
86	||	2
87		0
88	|||	3
89		0
90	||	2
91	|	1
92	|	1

3. A **5.** 18 **7.** 42

9. Check students' work. **11.** Misleading; the title says VCR purchases, but the graph only shows households with VCRs.

Chapter 12 p. 695

1. $\frac{1}{5}$ **3.** 1 **5.** $\frac{8}{27}$

9.a.

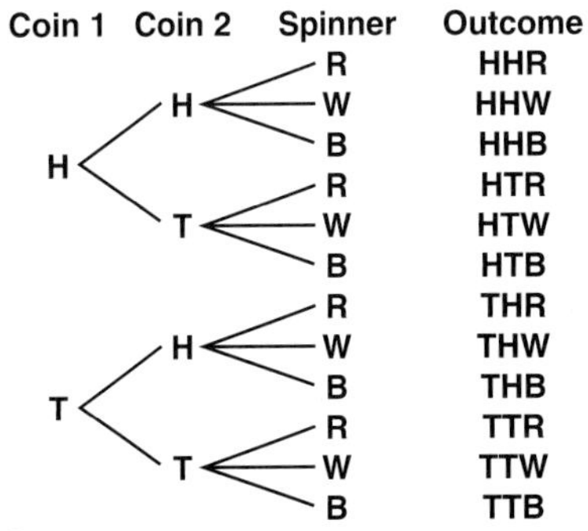

b. $\frac{1}{12}$; $\frac{1}{4}$

11. $\frac{3}{17}$ **13.** combination; 10

Skills Handbook

Comparing and Ordering Whole Numbers p. 696

1. > **3.** > **5.** < **7.** < **9.** > **11.** 3,347; 3,474; 3,734; 3,747; 3,774 **13.** 30,256,403; 30,265,403; 32,056,403; 302,056,403

Rounding Whole Numbers p. 697

1. 40 **3.** 670 **5.** 7,030 **7.** 6,000 **9.** 44,000 **11.** 1,000 **13.** 6,000 **15.** 82,000 **17.** 35,000 **19.** 68,900 **21.** 3,407,000 **23.** 71,230,000 **25.** 400,000 **27.** 3,680 **29.** 69,000 **31.** 566,000 **33.** 1,000,000

Multiplying Whole Numbers p. 698

1. 444 **3.** 371 **5.** 392 **7.** 1,536 **9.** 1,350 **11.** 5,712 **13.** 2,520 **15.** 1,862 **17.** 9,214 **19.** 492 **21.** 729 **23.** 2,208 **25.** 884 **27.** 4,056 **29.** 2,478 **31.** 640 **33.** 5,467

Dividing Whole Numbers p. 699

1. 15 R1 **3.** 12 R6 **5.** 13 R3 **7.** 217 R2 **9.** 25 R6 **11.** 7 R41 **13.** 7 R27 **15.** 3 R36 **17.** 5 R21 **19.** 3 R7 **21.** 14 R52 **23.** 37 R12 **25.** 21 R30 **27.** 7 R3 **29.** 11 R3 **31.** 64 R3 **33.** 50 R4 **35.** 103 R1 **37.** 26 R8 **39.** 7 R32 **41.** 5 R22 **43.** 6 R21 **45.** 3 R52 **47.** 15 R3 **49.** 22 R12

Place Value and Decimals p. 700

1. tens **3.** ones **5.** ten-thousandths **7.** 3 tens **9.** 6 ones **11.** 1 ten-thousandth **13.** 6 hundredths **15.** 6 tenths **17.** 6 tens **19.** 6 thousands **21.** 6 tenths **23.** 6 hundredths **25.** 6 ten-thousandths **27.** 6 hundred-thousandths **29.** 3 hundredths **31.** 8 tenths

Reading and Writing Decimals p. 701

1. 0.03 **3.** 6.02 **5.** 2.05 **7.** 0.000007 **9.** 0.011 **11.** 0.304 **13.** three million and nine hundredths **15.** nine hundred and two hundredths **17.** fifteen hundred-thousandths

Rounding Decimals p. 702

1. 2.8 **3.** 19.7 **5.** 499.5 **7.** 4.7 **9.** 400.0 **11.** 96.4 **13.** 31.72 **15.** 1.79 **17.** 736.94 **19.** 0.70 **21.** 12.10 **23.** 0.92 **25.** 0.439 **27.** 3.495 **29.** 0.601 **31.** 4 **33.** 80 **35.** 431

Multiplying Decimals p. 703

1. 2.4 **3.** 0.28 **5.** 0.155 **7.** 18.6 **9.** 1.35 **11.** 249.6 **13.** 12.05 **15.** 12.15 **17.** 0.1 **19.** 0.302 **21.** 1.757 **23.** 18.012 **25.** 28.452 **27.** 535.5 **29.** 250.8 **31.** 24.96

Zeros in the Product p. 704

1. 0.06 **3.** 0.003 **5.** 0.014 **7.** 0.027 **9.** 0.004 **11.** 0.0025 **13.** 0.032 **15.** 0.0009 **17.** 0.04 **19.** 0.0007 **21.** 0.0074 **23.** 0.076 **25.** 0.085 **27.** 0.007 **29.** 0.027 **31.** 0.0102 **33.** 0.0603 **35.** 0.081

Dividing a Decimal by a Whole Number p. 705

1. 7.14 **3.** 0.776 **5.** 8.79 **7.** 0.11 **9.** 0.184 **11.** 7.4 **13.** 0.93 **15.** 8.76 **17.** 2.07 **19.** 0.0036 **21.** 0.0147 **23.** 6.123 **25.** 3.98 **27.** 0.561 **29.** 0.868

Powers of Ten p. 706

1. 0.032 **3.** 0.07 **5.** 9 **7.** 52 **9.** 5 **11.** 1.803 **13.** 823 **15.** 502 **17.** 2,367 **19.** 0.0009 **21.** 426 **23.** 0.47 **25.** 0.032 **27.** 26 **29.** 0.0008 **31.** 15

Zeros in Decimal Division p. 707

1. 0.0025 **3.** 0.0081 **5.** 0.065 **7.** 0.075 **9.** 0.085 **11.** 0.0157 **13.** 1.05 **15.** 0.065 **17.** 0.68 **19.** 4.5 **21.** 0.006 **23.** 0.009 **25.** 0.0085 **27.** 0.0035 **29.** 0.033 **31.** 0.0924 **33.** 0.043 **35.** 2.92 **37.** 7.96 **39.** 25

Adding and Subtracting Fractions With Like Denominators p. 708

1. $\frac{4}{5}$ **3.** $\frac{4}{7}$ **5.** $4\frac{4}{7}$ **7.** $\frac{5}{8}$ **9.** $\frac{3}{8}$ **11.** $\frac{3}{5}$ **13.** $\frac{3}{5}$ **15.** $5\frac{2}{5}$ **17.** $11\frac{3}{5}$ **19.** $6\frac{1}{2}$ **21.** $11\frac{1}{2}$

Metric Units of Length p. 709

1. 0.1 **3.** 0.001 **5.** 0.000012 **7.** 30,000 **9.** 3,300 **11.** 0.72 **13.** 1,300,000 **15.** 4.9 **17.** 1.06 **19.** 1.2

Metric Units of Capacity p. 710

1. 1,000 **3.** 1,000 **5.** 0.2 **7.** 30,000 **9.** 0.18 **11.** 0.0006 **13.** 72,000,000 **15.** 0.45 **17.** 0.2 **19.** 4,200 **21.** 28,000,000 **23.** 4,000,000

Metric Units of Mass p. 711

1. 0.001 **3.** 0.000001 **5.** 1,000 **7.** 0.008 **9.** 200 **11.** 5,200,000 **13.** 3,700 **15.** 0.37 **17.** 900,000 **19.** 0.12 **21.** 1.006 **23.** 0.0002 **25.** 800,000 **27.** 6,200,000

Index

A

Absolute value, 34–35, 63
Absolute value equation, 541, 542
Activity. *See* Investigation
Acute angle, 352, 355, 356, 363, 366, 382
Acute triangle, 364
Addition
- Associative Property of, 12, 13, 43, 62
- Commutative Property of, 12, 13, 43, 62
- of decimals, 11, 13–15, 62, 70, 130
- of fractions, 192–196, 232, 708
- Identity Property of, 12, 43
- of integers, 39–40, 42–44, 63, 70, 186
- of mixed numbers, 197–198, 199–201, 212
- for solving equations, 83–84, 85–87, 186, 213, 215–216, 233
- for solving inequalities, 112–115

Addition Property
- of Equality, 83–84, 213
- of Inequality, 112

Additive inverse, 39
Adjacent angles, 353, 377
Algebra
- adding and subtracting integers, 39–44, 63, 70, 186
- applications of percent, 322–326
- comparing and ordering integers, 4, 34–38, 70, 346, 520, 696
- counting principle, 648
- estimating population size, 602–605, 622
- evaluating and writing algebraic expressions, 71–75, 468, 520
- exercises that use, 111, 134, 135, 139, 144, 149, 154, 155, 159, 163, 167, 172, 175, 190, 195, 201, 205, 206, 210, 211, 216, 221, 225, 234, 245, 264, 269, 277, 316, 326, 332, 336, 353, 355, 356, 365, 366, 386, 402, 418, 430, 498, 502, 506, 525, 538, 547, 553, 558, 562, 572, 583, 588, 589, 628, 633, 640, 663
- finding percent of change, 327–332, 339, 340, 350
- finding slope of a line, 533–538
- function rules, 484–488
- graphing and writing inequalities, 107–111
- graphing functions, 489–492, 513, 514
- graphing linear equations, 527–531
- graphing points in four quadrants, 521–525, 572, 605
- interpreting graphs, 494–498
- in Mixed Reviews, 111, 135, 139, 144, 149, 155, 159, 163, 167, 201, 206, 211, 216, 221, 225, 245, 250, 255, 259, 272, 279, 310, 316, 326, 332, 336, 350, 386, 406, 430, 436, 498, 502, 506, 525, 538, 547, 553, 558, 562, 578, 584, 590, 595, 600, 605, 611, 618, 634, 641, 646, 652
- multiplying and dividing integers, 4, 45–49, 63, 70, 130, 186
- nonlinear relationships, 540–543, 565
- number sequences, 474–478, 512, 605
- patterns and tables, 480–483
- proportions. *See* Proportion
- solving equations by adding or subtracting, 83–87, 186, 213, 215–216, 233
- solving equations by multiplying or dividing, 88–92, 186, 214, 215–216, 233, 240
- solving equations with fractions, 213–216, 290, 468
- solving equations with Number Sense, 77–81, 94–97, 122, 186
- solving inequalities by adding or subtracting, 112–115
- solving inequalities by multiplying or dividing, 116–120, 130
- solving percent problems using equations, 318–321, 339
- solving percent problems using proportions, 311–316, 339
- solving two-step equations, 98–101, 123, 130, 186, 214–216, 468
- transforming formulas, 507–510, 513
- two-step problems, 93–101

Algebraic expression, 71–75
- defined, 71, 122
- evaluating, 72, 73–75, 122, 468, 520
- writing, 72–75, 468, 520

Algebra tiles, 82
Analysis
- of circle graph, 388–389
- data analysis. *See* Data analysis
- dimensional analysis, 251
- error analysis, 8, 91, 119, 148, 154, 194, 199, 205, 210, 212, 215, 224, 245, 263, 315, 349, 355, 446, 472, 529, 536, 557, 560
- exercise that uses, 616
- of games, 654

Angle(s)
- acute, 352, 355, 356, 363, 366, 382
- adjacent, 353, 377
- central, 383, 384, 385, 395
- classifying, 352, 355, 382, 520
- complementary, 352–353, 355, 356, 361, 367, 394, 395
- congruent, 353, 362, 373
- defined, 351
- identifying, 352
- measuring, 345, 351–352, 353–355, 364–367, 389, 396, 398–399, 402, 520
- obtuse, 352, 355, 359, 362, 363, 382
- pairs of, 352–356
- Real-World Snapshots, 345, 398–399
- right, 352, 355, 363, 382
- of rotation, 560, 561, 565
- straight, 352, 355, 382
- supplementary, 352–353, 355, 356, 361, 367, 394, 395
- in triangles, 364–365
- vertex of, 351
- vertical, 353, 354, 355

Angle bisector, 358–359, 360, 361, 394
Angle sum of triangles, 364
Annual interest rate, 499–502
Applications. *See* Real-World Applications
Arc
- defined, 358
- naming, 384, 385, 386

Area, 404–424, 460–461
- of circles, 420–424, 444
- defined, 404, 460
- estimating, 404–406, 460
- of irregular figures, 415–418, 460
- of parallelograms, 407–408, 410–412, 460
- of rectangles, 6, 404, 406, 444
- of squares, 427
- surface. *See* Surface area
- of trapezoids, 413–414, 416–418, 460
- of triangles, 408–412, 460

Arithmetic sequence, 474–475, 476–478, 512, 605
Arrow notation, 550, 565
Assessment
- Chapter Reviews, 62–63, 122–123, 178–179, 232–233, 282–283, 338–339, 394–395, 460–461, 512–513, 564–565, 620–621, 670–671
- Chapter Tests, 64, 124, 180, 234, 284, 340, 396, 462, 514, 566, 622, 672
- Checkpoint Quizzes, 28, 49, 92, 111, 155, 176, 201, 225, 255, 272, 310, 326, 367, 382, 424, 454, 488, 502, 538, 558, 590, 618, 652, 668
- Cumulative Reviews, 125, 235, 341, 463, 567, 673–675
- open-ended, 14, 16, 37, 53, 59, 74, 86, 91, 124, 270, 273, 294, 315, 385, 386, 429, 446, 491, 525, 532, 548, 556, 562, 577, 599, 611, 618, 632, 635, 666
- Test Prep, 9, 15, 22, 27, 33, 38, 40, 44, 49, 54, 60, 65, 75, 81, 87, 88, 92, 97, 101, 105, 111, 115, 120, 125, 135, 139, 144, 149, 152, 155, 159, 163, 167, 172, 176, 181, 190, 196, 198, 200, 206, 211, 216, 221, 225, 230, 235, 245, 250, 255, 256, 259, 264–265, 271–272, 276, 279, 285, 294, 300, 304, 310, 316, 321, 326, 332, 336, 341, 350, 354, 356, 361, 367, 373, 377, 382, 386, 392, 397, 406, 412, 418, 424, 430, 432, 436, 440, 447, 453, 458, 463, 473, 478, 481, 483, 488, 492, 498, 502, 506, 510, 515, 525, 531, 537–538, 540, 543, 547, 553, 558, 562, 567, 578, 584, 589, 595, 599–600, 605, 611, 617–618, 623, 633–634, 641, 646, 651, 658, 663, 667, 673–675

See also Chapter Projects: Instant Check System; Mixed Review; Test-Taking Strategies
Associative Property
of Addition, 12, 13, 43, 62
of Multiplication, 18, 62
Average. *See* Mean
Axes, of graph, 521

B

Balance, 500, 501, 502, 513
Bar graph
defined, 580
double, 580–584, 620
Base
of cone, 438, 461
of cylinder, 438
of an exponent, 131
of parallelogram, 407
of prism, 437, 439
of pyramid, 438
of three-dimensional figures, 437, 438, 439
of trapezoid, 413
of triangle, 408
of two-dimensional figures, 407, 408, 413
Benchmark, 187–188, 189, 232
Biased question, 597, 598, 599, 621, 622
Bisector, 357–361
angle, 358–359, 360, 361, 394
folding, 357
perpendicular, 357–358, 359
segment, 357–358, 360, 394
Box-and-whisker plot, 586–590, 621

C

Calculator
with decimals, 169, 171
exercises that use, 8, 55, 86, 91, 132, 133, 134, 171, 190, 195, 199, 210, 250, 297, 458, 472, 478, 539
with exponents, 132, 136, 137
for finding angle measures, 389
for finding area of circle, 421
for finding circumference, 420
for finding interest, 501
fraction, 212
with fractions, 168, 171, 195, 199, 210
graphing. *See* Graphing calculator
for grouping symbols, 55
hints, 132, 133, 137, 169, 661, 667
with mixed numbers, 204
with Pythagorean Theorem, 433
scientific, 55, 133
for scientific notation, 136, 137
for simplifying expressions, 55, 133, 134
using, 55
Capacity
customary units of, 222–225
metric units of, 23–27, 710
See also Volume
Capture/recapture method, 602–605
Careers
amusement park designer, 265
archaeologist, 515
architect, 350
artist, 506
atmospheric scientist, 244
botanist, 490
bricklayer, 509
career day and, 665
coach, 151
computer-aided spacesuit designer, 279
costume designer, 583
detective, 28
fabric designers, 385
financial planner, 530
florist, 53
journalist, 154
librarian, 89
marine biologist, 210
math teacher, 522
park ranger, 599
pediatrician, 19
physical therapist, 355
pollster, 600
rescue swimmer, 411
biological scientist, 331
sculptor, 427
songwriter, 196
surveyor, 270
tailor, 650
tour boat driver, 662
veterinarian, 78
waiter or waitress, 323
See also Math at Work
Cartesian plane, 521. *See also* Coordinate plane
Cell, 579, 581
Center
of circle, 383, 385
of dilation, 273
of rotation, 559, 560
of sphere, 438
Centimeter, 23, 24
Central angle, 383, 384, 385, 395
Central tendency. *See* Measures of central tendency
Challenge, 9, 15, 22, 27, 33, 38, 44, 48, 54, 60, 74, 80–81, 87, 92, 97, 101, 105, 110, 115, 120, 135, 139, 144, 149, 154, 159, 162, 167, 172, 175, 190, 195, 200, 206, 211, 215, 221, 224, 230, 245, 250, 254, 259, 264, 271, 278–279, 294, 300, 303, 309, 315, 321, 325, 332, 336, 349, 356, 361, 366–367, 373, 377, 381, 385–386, 392, 406, 412, 418, 423, 429, 436, 440, 447, 453, 458, 473, 478, 483, 487, 492, 498, 502, 505, 510, 525, 530, 537, 543, 546, 553, 557, 562, 578, 583–584, 589, 595, 599, 604–605, 611, 617, 633, 640, 646, 651, 658, 663, 677
Change, percent of, 327–332, 339, 340, 350
Chapter Projects, 678–683
Build a Tower, 681
Design Boxes for Shipping Cylinders, 681
Estimate the Size of a Crowd and Take a Survey, 683
Find a Sample Size, 682
Graphing Data, 682
Invent Your Own Ruler, 679
Make a Board Game, 678
Make Three Number Cubes, 683
Take a Survey, 680
Using Specific Gravity, 680
Write Your Own Recipe, 679
Chapter Reviews. *See* Assessment
Chapter Tests. *See* Assessment
Checkpoint Quizzes. *See* Assessment
Check Skills You'll Need. *See* Instant Check System
Check Understanding. *See* Instant Check System
Choose a Method, 25, 49, 99, 147, 209, 262, 329, 354, 416, 508, 541, 575, 656
Chord, 383, 384, 385, 386, 395
Circle, 383–386, 419–424
area of, 420–424, 444
central angle of, 383, 384, 385, 395
circumference of, 419–420, 422–424, 461
defined, 383, 395
diameter of, 383, 384, 385, 386, 395
identifying parts of, 383–386
radius of, 383, 384, 385, 395, 420
Circle graph, 388–392
analyzing, 388–389
constructing, 389
defined, 388, 395
sectors of, 389
Circumference, 419–420, 422–424, 461
Classification
of angles, 352, 355, 382, 520
of numbers, 427–430
of polygons, 369–370, 395
of triangles, 363–364, 365, 366
Clustering, 8
Combination, 664–668, 671
Comics, 138, 299, 372, 429, 537
Commission, 324, 325, 339
Common multiplier, 257
Communication. *See* Investigation; Reasoning; Writing in Math
Commutative Property
of Addition, 12, 13, 43, 62
of Multiplication, 18, 62
Comparing
decimals, 174, 175, 295
fractions, 156–159, 240
integers, 4, 35–38, 70, 346, 520
negative rational numbers, 173–174
percents and decimals, 295
symbols for, 107, 109, 110, 156
unit prices, 247–250, 251
whole numbers, 696
writing to compare, 266
Compass, 358, 359, 362, 386, 389, 394
Compatible numbers, 6, 62, 78, 188
Compensation, 16

Complement, 630–631
Complementary angles, 352–353, 355, 356, 361, 367, 394, 395
Composite number, 146, 148, 179, 373
Compound event, 653–658
Compound inequality, 110
Compound interest, 500–502, 513
Computer
creating similar figures with, 273
Real-World Applications of, 299, 506, 587
spreadsheets, 76, 501, 579–584, 622, 642
Concept map, 425
Cone, 438, 439, 461
Congruent angles, 353, 362, 373
Congruent figures, 378–382
corresponding parts in, 378, 381, 395
identifying, 379
working with, 380
Congruent polygons, 378–382, 395
Congruent sides of triangle, 363, 367
Conjecture, 475, 476, 477, 478
Connections. *See* Interdisciplinary Connections; Real-World Applications
Connections to math strands. *See* Algebra; Data analysis; Geometry; Measurement; Patterns; Probability
Constant, 534
Construction
of angle bisectors, 358–359
of circle graphs, 389
of congruent angles, 362
of parallel lines, 362
of perpendicular bisector, 358
of segment bisector, 357
Conversions
customary system, 222–225, 233, 234
metric system, 24–28, 63, 64, 709–711
Cooperative Learning. *See* Investigation
Coordinate, 522–525, 526, 563, 564
applying, 519, 568–569
Real-World Snapshots, 519, 568–569
writing, 522
x-coordinate, 521, 522
y-coordinate, 521, 522
Coordinate plane, 521–526
defined, 521
geometry in, 526
graphing points on, 521–525, 572, 605
patterns in, 523
quadrants in, 522–525
Corresponding parts, 378, 381, 395
Corresponding sides, 267, 268
Counting principle, 648–652, 671
Critical thinking. *See* Reasoning
Cross-curriculum exercises. *See* Interdisciplinary connections
Cross products
solving proportions using, 261–262, 263, 264, 283
using, 257–259
Cross-Products Property, 257–258
Cube, 437
Cubic unit, 449
Cumulative Reviews. *See* Assessment
Customary system of measurement, 222–225, 233, 402
for capacity, 223–225
choosing appropriate units of measure in, 403–404, 405
conversions in, 222–225, 233, 234
estimating in, 226, 230
for length, 222–225, 403–404, 405–406
for weight (mass), 223–225
Cylinder
bases of, 438
defined, 438
height of, 438
surface area of, 445–447, 461
volume of, 450–454, 461

D

Data
collecting, 576, 581, 589, 591, 597
using to persuade, 606–611
Data analysis, 57, 195, 309, 604, 616, 617, 639
applying, 571, 624–625
box-and-whisker plot, 586–590, 621
circle graph, 388–392, 395
comparisons. *See* Comparing
double bar graph, 580–584, 619, 620
double line graph, 580–584, 620, 622
frequency table, 573–578, 592, 611, 620, 652
histogram, 574–578, 590, 620
line plot, 573–578, 592, 620, 638
mean, median, and mode, 56–60, 63, 65, 572, 586, 589, 606, 607–608
misleading graphs, 606–611
misleading statistics, 607–611
range, 41, 590
Real-World Snapshots, 571, 624–625
scatter plots, 613–618, 621, 622, 634, 668
spreadsheet, 76, 501, 579–584, 622, 642
stem-and-leaf plot, 585–590, 619, 621, 641
survey, 597–600, 618, 680, 683
tables. *See* Table
trends, 614–618, 621, 634
Data File, 3, 8, 69, 110, 129, 153, 158, 172, 185, 200, 224, 239, 249, 264, 289, 299, 315, 331, 345, 355, 360, 401, 445, 452, 467, 473, 491, 519, 530, 537, 571, 588, 610, 627, 639, 657
Data Updates. *See* Internet links
Decagons, 369
Decameter, 24
Decimal(s)
adding, 11, 13–15, 62, 70, 130
changing to fractions, 170, 290
comparing, 174, 175, 295
dividing, 19–22, 62, 240, 705, 707
estimating with, 11, 12, 13, 15, 19, 62, 206, 250
fractions and, 168–172
modeling, 17, 295
multiplying, 17–18, 20–22, 62, 240, 402, 703
ordering, 170, 171, 296
percent and, 295–296, 298–300, 302–304, 338, 367, 468, 628
place value and, 4, 700
reading and writing, 701
repeating, 169, 170–172, 174, 179, 367, 427
rounding, 4, 702
subtracting, 11–12, 13–15, 62, 70, 130
terminating, 168–169, 174, 179, 427
writing ratios as, 242, 243
Decimal points, aligning, 11, 12, 62
Decimeter, 24
Decrease, percent of, 329, 330, 331, 340, 350, 406
Deductive Reasoning. *See* Reasoning
Denominator, 151, 152
common, 192–193
different, 193
least common (LCD), 156–157, 179, 193
like, 708
See also Fraction(s)
Dependent event, 655–658, 671
Depreciation, percent of, 331
Descartes, Rene, 521, 522
Diagnosing Readiness, 4, 70, 130, 186, 240, 290, 346, 402, 468, 520, 572, 628
Diagonal, 373
Diagram
drawing, 31, 252–255, 374–377, 393, 431
tree, 648, 650, 651, 656, 671
Venn, 591
Diameter, 384, 385, 386, 395
defined, 383
estimating, 423
Difference
compensation and, 16
estimating, 5–6, 7, 8
See also Subtraction
Dilation, 273
Dimensional analysis, 251
Discounts
percent of, 329, 330, 333–336, 339
successive, 333
Discrete Mathematics
combination, 664–668, 671
counting principle, 648–652, 671
factorial, 661, 662, 668
permutation, 660–663, 671
tree diagram, 648, 650
Disjoint events, 657
Distributive Property, 51–54, 63, 64, 130, 673
Dividend, 19
Divisibility tests, 141–144, 178
Divisible, 141, 178
Division
of decimals, 19–22, 62, 240, 705, 707
of fractions, 207–211, 232

of integers, 4, 46–49, 63, 70, 130, 186
of mixed numbers, 208–211, 212
solving equations by, 89, 90–92, 186, 214, 215–216, 233, 240
for solving inequalities, 117–118, 119–120, 130
of whole numbers, 4, 699

Division Property
of Equality, 88–89, 90–92
of Inequality, 117

Divisor, 19

Double bar graph, 580–584, 620

Double line graph, 580–584, 620, 622

***Draw a Diagram* Problem-Solving Strategy,** 31, 252–255, 374–377, 393

E

Earhart, Amelia, 491

Edge, 437

Enrichment. *See* Extension; Stretch Your Thinking

Equality
Addition Property of, 83–84, 213
Division Property of, 88–89, 90–92
Multiplication Property of, 90–92
Subtraction Property of, 84–85, 213

Equal ratios, 242–245, 292–294

Equation
absolute value, 541, 542
addition, 82
defined, 77, 122
graph of, 528, 529–530, 564
linear. *See* Linear equations
modeling, 82, 213
multiplication, 82
nonlinear, 540–543, 565
as Problem-Solving Strategy, 102–105, 333–336, 455–458, 503–506
solutions to, 77–81, 82, 527, 564
solving by adding, 83–84, 85–87, 186, 213, 215–216, 233
solving by multiplying or dividing, 88–92, 186, 214, 215–216, 233, 240, 290
solving by subtracting, 84–87, 213, 215–216, 233
solving percent problems using, 318–321, 339
solving using algebra tiles, 82
solving using fractions, 213–216, 290, 468
solving using Mental Math, 78, 79, 80, 351
solving using Number Sense, 77–81, 94–97, 122, 186
solving using substitution, 78, 541
two-step, 93–101, 123, 130, 186, 214–216, 468
writing, 73, 78, 84, 85, 89, 94, 95, 102–105, 203, 214, 318, 319, 324, 333–336, 455–458, 490, 503–506

Equilateral triangle, 363, 366

Equivalent fractions, 151–152, 153–155, 156

Error Analysis, 8, 91, 119, 148, 154, 194, 199, 205, 210, 212, 215, 224, 245, 263, 315, 349, 355, 446, 472, 529, 536, 557, 560

Estimation, 5–9, 62
of area, 404–406, 460
choosing reasonable estimates, 24, 404, 405
with decimals, 11, 12, 13, 15, 19, 62, 206, 250
of diameter, 423
in different systems, 230
exact answers and, 5
exercises that use, 7–9, 15, 19, 26, 33, 49, 64, 74, 91, 135, 171, 189–190, 193, 198, 235, 263, 290, 373, 405–406, 469, 472, 498, 501, 582, 583, 673, 674
with fractions, 187–190, 203, 210, 232
front-end, 6, 7
of interest, 501
of length, 403–404, 405–406
in measurement, 226, 230
with metric units, 24, 230, 405
with mixed numbers, 188–190, 197, 198, 204
of percentage, 294, 297, 307, 308, 309
of population size, 602–605, 622
of product, 6, 7, 188, 189
of quotients, 7, 188, 189
from scale drawings, 275
of solutions to equations, 77, 78–79, 78–81, 91
of square roots, 427, 428
of sums or differences, 5–6, 7, 8
as Test-Taking Strategy, 511
using graphs, 470–473
using Number Sense for, 77, 78
using to find part of a whole, 307, 309

Estimation project, 683

Estimation strategies
clustering, 8
compatible numbers, 7, 62, 78, 188
front-end, 6, 7
rounding, 5–6

Evaluating expressions, 72, 73–75, 122, 468, 520

Event
compound, 653–658
defined, 629
dependent, 655–658, 671
independent, 653–658
probability of. *See* Probability
simulating, 638, 640, 641

Experimental probability, 635, 636–641
defined, 636, 670
finding, 636–637, 670
formula for, 637, 670

Exponent, 131–140
defined, 131, 178
exploring, 131
negative, 140
simplifying expressions with, 132–135, 468, 520
writing expressions using, 131–132, 133–135
writing numbers with, 131–132, 133–135

Expression
algebraic, 71–75, 122, 468, 520
simplifying, 55, 132–135
two-step, 93–94

Extension
Constructing Angles and Parallel Lines, 362
Dimensional Analysis, 251
Estimating in Different Systems, 230
Geometry in the Coordinate Plane, 526
Mental Math: Compensation, 16
Negative Exponents, 140
Patterns in Three-Dimensional Figures, 448
Three Views of an Object, 441
Venn Diagrams, 591
See also Technology; Challenge

Extra Practice, 684–695. *See also* Mixed Review

F

Face, 437

Factor
defined, 146, 179
finding, 146, 148
greatest common (GCF), 147, 148, 149, 152, 165, 186, 203, 243
scale, 273
using to write equivalent fractions, 152, 153

Factorial, 661, 662, 668

Factorization, prime, 145–149, 179, 373, 647

Factor tree, 146

Fibonnaci sequence, 477

Figures
changing position of, 548
naming, 438, 439
similar, 267–272, 283
translating, 549–553, 565, 646
See also Three-dimensional figures; Two-dimensional figures; *names of individual figures*

Flip, 548

Formulas, 715
for area of a circle, 421
for area of a parallelogram, 407–408, 460
for area of a square, 427
for area of a trapezoid, 414, 460
for area of a triangle, 409, 460
for circumference of a circle, 419, 461
for compound interest, 500
defined, 507, 513
for probability, 637, 670
for simple interest, 499
in spreadsheets, 76
transforming, 507–510, 513
for volume of a cylinder, 450, 461
for volume of a prism, 449–450, 461

Fraction(s), 151–159
adding, 191–196, 232, 708
applying, 129, 182–183, 185, 236–237
benchmarks with, 187–188, 189, 232
changing decimals to, 170, 290
codes representing, 142

comparing, 156–159, 240
dividing, 207–211, 232
equivalent, 151–152, 153–155, 156
estimating with, 187–190, 203, 210, 232
improper, 164–167, 179
with like denominators, 708
modeling, 151, 153, 156, 158, 164, 191, 192, 193, 194–195, 202, 207, 213
multiplying, 202–206, 232
ordering, 156–159, 168, 170, 171, 240, 296
percent and, 294, 296, 297–300, 302–304, 306, 338, 367, 628
Real-World Snapshots, 129, 182–183, 185, 236–237
reciprocal of, 207, 232
relating to decimals, 168–172
simplest form of, 152, 153, 155, 166, 179, 367, 639, 640
simplifying, 152–155, 240, 520
solving equations with, 213–216, 290, 468
subtraction, 191–196, 708
See also Mixed numbers

Fraction bars, 51

Fraction calculator, 212

Frequency table, 573–578
defined, 573, 620
exercises that use, 576, 577, 592, 611, 620, 652
making, 573–574

Front-end estimation, 6, 7

Fuller, R. Buckminster, 352

Function(s), 484–498
defined, 484, 513
evaluating, 485
graphing, 489–498, 513
three views of, 493

Function rules, 484–488, 490, 491–492, 504–505, 514, 583, 584, 611

Function tables, 485, 486, 487, 489–492, 514

G

Games
Practice, 75, 163, 304, 430, 547, 634
probability in, 634, 654, 655, 670
Real-World Applications of, 42, 143, 339, 495, 670

GCF (greatest common factor), 147, 148, 149, 152, 165, 186, 203, 243

Geodesic dome, 352

Geometric models, 17, 50, 88, 94, 95, 151, 153, 164, 202, 242, 246, 247, 291, 292, 295, 298

Geometric patterns, 162, 220, 245, 374–375, 377, 395, 396, 447, 448, 449, 505, 584, 645

Geometric sequence, 475, 476–478, 512

Geometry
angles, 351–356
area. *See* Area
bisectors, 357–361, 394
circle graphs, 388–392, 395
circles. *See* Circle
congruence, 353, 362, 373, 378–382, 395
in coordinate plane, 526. *See also* Coordinate plane
creating similar figures, 273
exercises that use, 15, 32, 33, 53, 101, 135, 195, 200, 210, 254, 259, 269, 270, 335, 435, 457, 472, 476, 477, 478, 483, 492, 497, 505, 510, 530, 546, 605, 623, 657
lines, 347–350
maps and scale drawings, 275–279, 283, 286–287
parallelograms. *See* Parallelogram
patterns in, 374–377, 395
perimeters. *See* Perimeter
planes, 348–350. *See also* Coordinate plane
polygons, 369–373
prisms. *See* Prism
quadrilaterals, 369–373
rectangles. *See* Rectangle
similar figures, 267–272, 283
squares. *See* Square
three-dimensional figures. *See* Three-dimensional figures
trapezoids. *See* Trapezoid
triangles. *See* Triangle
volume. *See* Volume

Geometry software, 273

Goniometer, 355

Glossary/Study guide 717–754

Gram, 23

Graph, 469–473, 521–558
bar, 580
circle, 388–392, 395
describing, 494, 496
double bar, 580–584, 620
double line, 580–584, 620, 622
of equation, 527–531
estimating on, 470–473
extending, 471
horizontal lines on, 523, 524, 564
interpreting, 494–498
misleading, 606–611
percent data from, 305
scale on, 469–470, 512
scatter plots, 613–618, 621, 622, 634, 668
sketching, 495, 496, 497
stem-and-leaf plot, 585–590, 621, 641
vertical lines in, 523, 524, 564
x-axis of, 521
y-axis of, 521
See also Coordinate plane

Graphing
absolute value equations, 541
equations, 528, 564
functions, 489–498, 513, 514
inequalities, 108, 109–111, 112, 113, 114, 123, 125
integers, 35
interval, 469–470, 512
linear equations, 527–531
nonlinear equations, 540–543, 565
parabolas, 540, 542
points, 521–525, 572, 605
reflections, 555, 556–557, 565, 584, 675
translations, 549–557, 565, 646, 675
triangles, 526

Graphing calculator
exploring slope using, 539
Graph feature, 493
hints, 661, 667
Math feature, 661, 667
Table feature, 493
three views of a function, 493
Trace feature, 539, 541
Window feature, 493
Zoom feature, 539, 541

Graphing project, 682

Gravity, specific, 680

Greatest common factor (GCF), 147, 148, 149, 152, 165, 186, 203, 243

Group, working in. *See* Investigation

Grouping symbols, 51–54, 55

H

Harrison, William, 293

Hectometer, 24

Height
of cylinder, 438
of parallelogram, 407
of prism, 437
of three-dimensional figures, 437, 438
of trapezoid, 413
of triangle, 408
of two-dimensional figures, 407, 408, 413

Hexagon, 369, 370, 386

Hexagonal prism, 438

Histogram, 574–578
defined, 574, 620
drawing, 574–575
exercises that use, 576, 577, 578, 590, 620

Horizontal line, 523, 524, 564

Hypotenuse, 432–433, 434–436, 461, 526

I

Identity Property
of Addition, 12, 43
of Multiplication, 18

Image, 549

Improper fraction, 164–167
defined, 164, 179
writing, 165
writing as mixed numbers, 165–167
writing mixed numbers as, 164–167

Increase, percent of, 327–328, 350, 406

Independent event, 653–658

Indirect measurement, 269

Inductive reasoning. *See* Reasoning

Inequalities, 107–120
Addition Property of, 112
applying, 69, 126–127
compound, 110
defined, 107, 123
Division Property of, 117
exploring, 116
graphing, 108, 109–111, 112, 113, 114, 123
identifying solutions of, 107
Multiplication Property of, 118

Index

patterns in solving, 116
Real-World Snapshots, 69, 126–127
solutions of, 107, 109–111, 123, 124
solving by adding or subtracting, 112–115
solving by dividing, 117–118, 119–120, 130
solving by multiplying, 118–120, 130
Subtraction Property of, 113
writing, 108–111, 123

Input/output pairs, 485

Instant Check System
answers to, 755–771
Check Skills You'll Need, 5, 11, 17, 23, 30, 34, 39, 45, 50, 56, 71, 77, 83, 88, 93, 98, 102, 107, 112, 116, 131, 136, 141, 145, 151, 156, 160, 164, 168, 173, 187, 192, 197, 202, 207, 213, 218, 222, 227, 241, 246, 252, 256, 260, 267, 275, 291, 295, 301, 305, 311, 318, 322, 327, 333, 347, 351, 357, 363, 369, 374, 378, 383, 388, 403, 407, 413, 419, 426, 432, 437, 442, 449, 455, 469, 474, 480, 484, 489, 494, 499, 503, 507, 521, 527, 533, 540, 544, 549, 554, 559, 573, 579, 585, 592, 596, 602, 606, 613, 629, 636, 643, 647, 653, 660, 664
Check Understanding, 5, 6, 7, 11, 12, 13, 17, 18, 19, 23, 24, 25, 31, 34, 35, 40, 41, 46, 47, 51, 52, 56, 57, 58, 72, 73, 78, 79, 84, 85, 89, 90, 93, 94, 95, 98, 99, 103, 107, 108, 109, 112, 113, 117, 118, 132, 133, 137, 141, 142, 145, 146, 147, 151, 152, 156, 157, 161, 165, 169, 170, 173, 174, 187, 188, 192, 193, 197, 198, 203, 204, 207, 208, 213, 214, 219, 222, 223, 228, 229, 242, 243, 246, 247, 248, 253, 256, 257, 258, 260, 261, 268, 269, 275, 276, 291, 292, 296, 297, 301, 302, 306, 307, 311, 312, 313, 318, 319, 322, 323, 324, 328, 329, 334, 347, 348, 351, 352, 353, 358, 359, 363, 364, 365, 370, 371, 375, 379, 380, 384, 388, 389, 403, 404, 408, 409, 410, 414, 415, 420, 421, 426, 427, 428, 433, 437, 438, 442, 443, 444, 449, 450, 451, 456, 469, 470, 471, 475, 476, 480, 481, 484, 485, 489, 490, 494, 495, 499, 500, 503, 504, 507, 508, 522, 523, 527, 528, 534, 535, 540, 541, 545, 549, 550, 551, 555, 559, 560, 573, 574, 575, 579, 580, 581, 585, 586, 587, 593, 597, 603, 606, 607, 608, 613, 614, 629, 630, 631, 637, 638, 644, 647, 648, 649, 654, 655, 660, 661, 664, 665
Checkpoint Quiz, 28, 49, 92, 111, 155, 176, 201, 225, 255, 272, 310, 326, 367, 382, 424, 454, 488, 502, 538, 558, 590, 618, 652, 668
Diagnosing Readiness, 4, 70, 130, 186, 240, 290, 346, 402, 468, 520, 572, 628

Integers
absolute value of, 34–35, 63
adding, 39–40, 42–44, 63, 70, 186
applying, 3, 66–67
comparing, 4, 35–38, 70, 346, 520
defined, 34, 63, 173
dividing, 4, 46–49, 63, 70, 130, 186
graphing, 35, 520
multiplying, 4, 45–46, 47–49, 63, 70, 130, 186
ordering, 35–38, 520, 696
parity of, 65
Real-World Snapshots, 3, 66–67
subtracting, 41–44, 63, 70, 186
using Distributive Property with, 52, 63, 64, 130

Interdisciplinary Connections
anatomy, 153, 250, 257
archaeology, 423, 515
architecture, 53, 277, 278, 283, 348, 352, 363, 371, 438
art, 54, 271, 281, 427, 461, 551
astronomy, 137, 138, 139, 181
biology, 86, 139, 171, 203, 210, 220, 243, 297, 477, 602–603, 617, 621
botany, 171, 490
chemistry, 169, 244, 514
engineering, 331, 417
geography, 26, 36, 132, 138, 171, 206, 215, 217, 224, 225, 249, 276, 277, 293, 404, 406, 411, 414, 417, 588, 591, 594
geology, 594
government, 293, 302, 314, 328, 631, 633
history, 263, 293, 423, 573, 596
journalism, 154
languages, 32, 157, 309, 594
music, 7, 11, 48, 189, 242, 312, 320, 329, 331, 388, 417, 446, 482, 617, 667
physical science, 32, 259
physics, 47, 86, 87, 181, 542
science, 43, 59, 134, 205, 389, 429, 483, 514, 524, 557, 632, 638, 640
social studies, 242, 254, 335, 422, 573
zoology, 175

Interest, 499–502
compound, 500–502, 513
simple, 499–500, 501–502, 513

Internet links
Chapter Projects, 678–683
Chapter Tests, 64, 124, 180, 234, 284, 340, 396, 462, 514, 566, 622, 672
Lesson Quizzes, 9, 15, 22, 27, 33, 38, 44, 49, 54, 60, 75, 81, 87, 92, 97, 101, 105, 111, 115, 120, 135, 139, 144, 149, 155, 159, 163, 167, 172, 176, 190, 196, 200, 206, 211, 216, 221, 225, 230, 245, 250, 255, 259, 264, 271, 279, 294, 300, 304, 310, 316, 321, 326, 332, 336, 350, 356, 361, 367, 373, 377, 382, 386, 392, 406, 412, 418, 424, 430, 436, 440, 447, 453, 458, 473, 478, 483, 488, 492, 498, 502, 506, 510, 525, 531, 537, 543, 547, 553, 558, 562, 578, 584, 589, 595, 600, 605, 611, 617, 634, 641, 646, 651, 658, 663, 677
Math at Work, 28, 196, 265, 350, 506, 600
Real-World Snapshots, 66–67, 126–127, 182–183, 236–237, 342–343, 398–399, 464–465, 516–517, 568–569, 624–625, 676–677
Vocabulary Quizzes, 62, 122, 178, 232, 282, 338, 394, 460, 512, 564, 620, 670
See also Chapter Projects; Math at Work; Real-World Snapshots

Intersecting lines, 348, 349, 350

Interval
on graphs, 469–470, 512
misleading, 607–611

Inverse operation, 39, 46, 83, 89, 123

Investigation
Algebraic Expressions, 71
Angles of a Triangle, 364
Area of a Parallelogram, 407
Area of a Trapezoid, 413
A Survey of Birthday Data, 241
Collecting Data, 576
Combining Operations, 50
Estimates and Exact Answers, 5
Experimenting with Probability, 636
Exploring Arrangements, 660
Exploring Congruent Figures, 378
Exploring Estimation, 77
Exploring Experimental Probability, 635
Exploring Exponents, 131
Exploring Inequalities, 116
Exploring Multiple Events, 653
Exploring Patterns in the Coordinate Plane, 523
Exploring Percent of Change, 327
Exploring Slides, Flips, and Turns, 548
Exploring Slope, 533
Exploring Tessellations, 551
Exploring the Pythagorean Theorem, 431
Finding a Pattern, 474
Folding Bisectors, 357
Graphing a Function, 489
Making Graphs, 581
Making a Scale Drawing, 277
Modeling Decimal Multiplication, 17
Modeling Equations, 82, 213
Modeling Multiplication of Fractions, 202
Ordering Fractions, 168
Plan a Trip, 280
Powers of 10, 136
Precision in Measurements, 227
Relating Area of a Circle to the Radius, 420
Relating Fractions, Decimals, and Percents, 295
Exploring Similar Figures, 267
Squares and Square Roots, 426
Using Fraction Models, 191
Using Percent Data from a Graph, 305
Writing Unbiased Questions, 597

Irrational number, 428–430, 461

Irregular figure, area of, 415–418, 460

Irregular polygon, 370, 372

Isosceles triangle, 363, 367

J

Justification, 13, 18, 52, 177, 307, 353, 366, 368, 379, 380, 497
See also Writing in Math

K

Kilogram, 23
Kilometer, 23, 24

L

Leaf, 585. *See also* Stem-and-leaf plot
Least common denominator (LCD), 156–157, 179, 193
Least common multiple (LCM)
  defined, 145
  finding, 145–146, 148
  using to solve two-step equations, 214–215
Leg, of right triangle, 432, 433, 434–436, 461
Legend (key), 580
Length
  customary units of, 222–225, 403–404, 405–406
  estimating, 403–404, 405–406
  of hypotenuse of triangle, 432–433, 434–436, 461, 526
  of legs of triangle, 433, 434–436, 461
  metric units of, 23, 405, 709
  missing, 268–269
Lesson investigation
  Algebraic Expressions, 71
  Angles of a Triangle, 364
  Area of a Parallelogram, 407
  Area of a Trapezoid, 413
  Combining Operations, 50
  Estimates and Exact Answers, 5
  Experimenting with Probability, 636
  Exploring Arrangements, 660
  Exploring Congruent Figures, 378
  Exploring Estimation, 77
  Exploring Exponents, 131
  Exploring Inequalities, 116
  Exploring Multiple Events, 653
  Exploring Patterns in the Coordinate Plane, 523
  Exploring Percent of Change, 327
  Exploring Slope, 533
  Exploring Tessellations, 551
  Finding a Pattern, 474
  Folding Bisectors, 357
  Graphing a Function, 489
  Making a Scale Drawing, 277
  Making Graphs, 581
  Modeling Decimal Multiplication, 17
  Ordering Fractions, 168
  Powers of 10, 136
  Precision in Measurements, 227
  Relating the Area of a Circle to the Radius, 420
  Relating Fractions, Decimals and Percents, 295
  Squares and Square Roots, 426
  A Survey of Birthday Data, 241
  Using Percent Data From a Graph, 305
  Writing Unbiased Questions, 597
Line, 347–350
  defined, 347
  drawing, 535
  horizontal, 523, 524, 564
  intersecting, 348, 349, 350
  parallel, 348, 349, 350, 362, 394
  perpendicular, 357
  of reflection, 555
  skew, 348, 394
  slope of, 533–539, 565
  of symmetry, 554–555, 675
  vertical, 523, 524, 564
Linear equations
  defined, 528, 564
  graphing, 527–531
Line graph, 580–584, 620
Line plot, 573–578
  defined, 573, 620
  exercises that use, 576, 577, 578, 592, 620
  making, 573–574, 575
Liter, 23
Logical reasoning. *See* Reasoning
Logic Table, 592–594
***Look for a Pattern* Problem-Solving Strategy,** 160–163, 374–377, 395
Lowest terms. *See* Simplest form

M

***Make a Graph* Problem-Solving Strategy,** 544–547
***Make an Organized List* Problem-Solving Strategy,** 643–646, 671
***Make a Table* Problem-Solving Strategy,** 31, 544–547, 592–595, 621
Manipulatives
  algebra tiles, 82
  centimeter graph paper, 431
  centimeter ruler, 276, 277, 278
  compass, 358, 359, 362, 386, 389, 394
  construction paper, 304
  dot paper, 371, 372, 382, 437
  graph paper, 17, 50, 371, 372, 382, 406, 407, 426, 431, 438, 439, 447, 547, 646
  index cards, 75, 430
  number cubes, 75, 533, 629, 630, 631, 632, 634, 636, 639, 646, 649, 650, 651, 654, 656, 663, 683
  paper, 202
  protractor, 351, 389, 559
  ruler, 276, 278, 373, 679
  spinner, 632, 639, 641, 649, 650, 651, 652, 658, 672, 673
  straightedge, 349, 358, 362
  tape measure, 12
  tracing paper, 357
  unit cubes, 426, 448
  See also Calculator; Graphing calculator
Maps, 275–279
  concept, 425
  exercises that use, 232, 277, 284, 341, 567
  finding distance on, 276
  Real-World Applications of, 232, 284, 341, 567
  scale of, 277, 280, 283
  trip planning with, 280
Markup, 328, 330, 332, 334, 339, 377
Mass
  customary units of, 223–225
  metric units of, 23, 711
Math at Work
  amusement park designer, 265
  architect, 350
  artist, 506
  detective, 28
  pollster, 600
  songwriter, 196
  See also Careers
Mathematical Techniques. *See* Estimation; Mental Math; Number Sense; Problem Solving
Math in the Media, 138, 299, 372, 429, 537
Mean, 56–57, 58–60, 63, 65, 606, 607–608
Measurement, 222–229, 712
  of angles, 345, 351–352, 353–355, 364–367, 389, 396, 398–399, 402, 520
  customary system of. *See* Customary system of measurement
  exercises that use, 12, 63, 201, 208, 224, 269, 457, 461, 482, 486, 505, 594, 645
  indirect, 269, 270
  in metric units. *See* Metric units
  precision in, 227–229, 233
  units of. *See* Unit of measurement
Measures of central tendency, 56–60
  mean, 56–57, 58–60, 63, 65, 606, 607–608
  median, 57, 58–60, 63, 65, 572, 586, 589, 607–608
  mode, 58–60, 63, 608
Median, 57, 58–60, 63, 65, 572, 586, 589, 607–608
Mental Math, 13, 18, 20–21, 28, 50, 52, 53, 64, 78, 80–81, 86, 91, 132, 133, 134, 149, 190, 195, 197, 201, 211, 250, 261, 284, 307, 406, 410, 481, 484, 552, 554, 557, 561, 654
  compensation, 16
  solving equations using, 78, 79, 80, 351
  solving proportions using, 263
  using to find part of a whole, 306–307, 308
Meter, 23, 24
Metric units, 23–28, 709–711
  of capacity, 23, 710
  choosing, 23, 233
  combining, 25
  converting, 24–25, 26–28, 64
  estimating in, 24, 230, 405
  of length, 23, 405, 709
  of mass, 23, 711
Midpoint, 357, 360, 361
Milligram, 23
Milliliter, 23
Millimeter, 23, 24
Misleading graph, 606–611
Misleading statistics, 607–611
Missing measure, 268–269
Mixed numbers
  adding, 197–198, 199–201, 212

defined, 164, 179
dividing, 208–211, 212
estimating with, 188–190, 197, 198, 204
multiplying, 204–206, 212
subtracting, 198–201
writing as improper fractions, 164–167
writing as percents, 302, 338–339
writing improper fractions as, 165–167
See also Fraction(s)

Mixed Review, 9, 15, 22, 28, 33, 38, 44, 49, 54, 60, 75, 81, 87, 92, 97, 101, 105, 111, 115, 120, 135, 139, 144, 149, 155, 159, 163, 167, 172, 176, 190, 196, 201, 206, 211, 216, 221, 225, 230, 245, 250, 255, 259, 265, 272, 279, 294, 300, 304, 310, 316, 321, 326, 332, 336, 350, 356, 361, 367, 373, 377, 382, 386, 392, 406, 412, 418, 424, 430, 436, 440, 447, 454, 458, 473, 478, 483, 488, 492, 498, 502, 506, 510, 525, 531, 538, 543, 547, 553, 558, 562, 578, 584, 590, 595, 600, 605, 611, 618, 634, 641, 646, 652, 658, 663, 668

Mode, 58–60, 63, 608

Modeling
algebra tiles, 82
decimals, 17, 295
exercises that use, 42, 43, 53, 64, 104, 153, 158, 167, 180, 191, 194, 293, 294, 303, 314, 316, 339, 340, 426, 505
fractions, 151, 153, 156, 158, 164, 191, 192, 193, 194–195, 202, 207, 213
geometric, 17, 50, 88, 94, 95, 151, 153, 164, 202, 242, 246, 247, 291, 292, 295, 298
number line, 16, 24, 34–35, 39, 40, 41, 45, 108, 112, 145, 156, 164, 173, 187, 207, 296
percent, 291, 292, 293, 295, 298, 311–313, 314, 316
proportions, 311–313, 314, 316
rates, 246, 247
ratios, 242
for solving equations, 78, 82, 83, 84, 85, 88, 89, 94, 95, 102–103, 203, 213, 214, 318, 319, 324, 333–334, 503–504
for solving inequalities, 109, 112, 113, 117
verbal, 72, 73, 78, 84, 85, 89, 94, 95, 102–103, 109, 113, 117, 203, 214, 318, 319, 324, 333–334, 490, 503–504, 602, 621, 660–661, 665
Real-World Applications of, 276
scale, 276, 286–287

Money
minting of, 75
principal and interest, 499–502, 513
Real-World Applications of, 16, 21, 27, 32, 36, 42, 48, 54, 64, 75, 86, 87, 89, 91, 96, 99, 104, 124, 159, 175, 214, 220, 254, 285, 293, 308, 313, 335, 337, 376, 487, 530, 546, 558, 590, 645, 675

More Than One Way, 25, 99, 147, 209, 262, 329, 354, 416, 508, 541, 575, 656

Multiple
defined, 145, 179
least common (LCM), 145–146, 148, 214–215
using to write equivalent fractions, 151, 153

Multiplication
Associative Property of, 18, 62
to change metric units, 24
Commutative Property of, 18, 62
of decimals, 17–18, 20–22, 62, 240, 402, 703
of fractions, 202–206, 232
Identity Property of, 18
of integers, 4, 45–46, 47–49, 63, 70, 130, 186
of mixed numbers, 204–206, 212
solving equations by, 88–92, 186, 214, 215–216, 233, 240
solving inequalities by, 118–120, 130
of whole numbers, 698
Zero Product Property of, 18

Multiplication Property
of Equality, 90–92
of Inequalities, 118

Multiplier, common, 257

N

Need Help?, 19, 32, 34, 39, 95, 104, 112, 136, 146, 161, 173, 188, 193, 203, 213, 219, 243, 253, 292, 296, 306, 307, 318, 353, 360, 365, 375, 403, 405, 407, 408, 413, 419, 433, 457, 475, 486, 500, 505, 510, 522, 528, 535, 545, 583, 586, 593, 603, 645, 647, 665

Negative exponent, 140

Negative rational numbers, 173–174

Negative slope, 534

Negative trend, 614–618, 621

Net, 442–447, 461
defined, 442
drawing, 442, 443, 444, 461
finding surface areas using, 443–447, 461

Nonlinear equation, 540–543, 565

Notation
arrow, 565, 675
prime (A'), 549
scientific, 136–139, 140, 178, 181

No trend, 614–618, 621

Number(s)
classifying, 427–430
compatible, 6, 7, 62, 78, 188
composite, 146, 148, 179, 373
finding percent of, 305–310, 346
irrational, 428–430, 461
prime, 146, 148, 179, 181, 373
random, 642
rational, 173–176, 179, 427
in scientific notation, 136–139, 140, 178, 181
in standard form, 137–139, 140
writing with exponents, 131–132, 133–135
See also Integers; Mixed numbers; Whole numbers

Number line
adding integers on, 39–40
graphing inequalities on, 108, 109, 110, 112, 113, 125
graphing integers on, 35
modeling with, 16, 24, 45, 145, 156, 173, 187, 207
multiplying integers on, 45
ordering percents, fractions, and decimals on, 296
subtracting integers on, 41
understanding mixed numbers and improper fractions, 164

Number patterns, 160–161, 162, 332, 336, 474–475, 476–478, 480–481, 482, 483, 512, 605

Number properties, 12–13, 43, 51–54, 62, 63, 64, 83–92, 90–92, 112, 113, 117, 118, 130, 213, 673, 715–717

Number Sense, 7, 11, 15, 21, 35, 41, 43, 44, 94, 95, 122, 131, 136, 144, 146, 149, 153, 162, 166, 174, 175, 188, 190, 197, 200, 204, 210, 218, 223, 226, 242, 247, 261, 292, 294, 297, 299, 308, 311, 312, 315, 391, 412, 448, 524, 527, 529, 537, 540, 543, 550, 555, 560, 595, 638, 657, 665
developing, 160–161
for estimating, 77, 78
using to solve equations, 77–81, 94–97, 122, 186
using to solve two-step equations, 94–97, 186

Number sequences
arithmetic sequence, 474–475, 476–478, 512, 605
Fibonacci sequence, 477
geometric sequence, 475, 476–478, 512

Number theory, 145, 146, 147

Numerator, 151, 152. *See also* Fraction(s)

O

Obtuse angle, 352, 355, 359, 362, 363, 382

Obtuse triangle, 364

Octagon, 369

Odds, 631

Open-ended, 14, 16, 37, 53, 59, 74, 86, 91, 124, 270, 273, 294, 315, 385, 386, 429, 446, 491, 525, 532, 548, 556, 562, 577, 599, 611, 618, 632, 635

Open sentence, 77, 122

Operations. *See* Order of Operations

Opposites, 34, 63

Ordered pair, 521, 523, 524, 527, 529, 564

Ordering
decimals, 170, 171, 296
fractions, 156–159, 168, 170, 171, 240, 296
integers, 35–38, 520, 696
percents, 296
rational numbers, 174–176
whole numbers, 696

Order of Operations, 50–54, 63, 70, 130, 132, 402
defined, 50, 63

simplifying expressions with exponents using, 132–135, 468, 520
Origin, 521
Outcome, 629–634
Outlier, 57, 58, 59, 63

P

Packaging, 451, 452
Parabola, 540, 542
Parallel lines, 348, 349, 350, 362, 394
Parallelogram
area of, 407–408, 410–412, 460
base of, 407
defined, 371, 407
height of, 407
Parity, 65
Patterns
applying, 467, 516–517
in a coordinate plane, 523
exercises that use, 21, 134, 158, 162, 210, 245, 254, 295, 331, 335, 431, 448, 457, 458, 477, 483
finding in arithmetic sequences, 474
geometric, 162, 220, 245, 374–375, 377, 395, 396, 447, 448, 449, 505, 584, 645
graphs and, 469–473
looking for, 160–163, 374–377, 395
number, 160–161, 162, 332, 336, 474–475, 476–478, 480–483, 512, 605
Real-World Snapshots, 467, 516–517
in solving inequalities, 116
tables and, 480–483
in three-dimensional figures, 448
Pentagon, 369, 370
Percent, 291–332, 338–339, 342–343
applications of, 322–326
of change, 327–332, 339, 340, 350
commissions, 323–324, 325, 339, 340
decimals and, 295–296, 298–300, 302–304, 338, 367, 468, 628
of decrease, 329, 330, 331, 340, 350, 406
defined, 291, 338
of depreciation, 331
of discount, 329, 330, 333–336, 339
estimating, 294, 297, 307, 308, 309
finding percent of a number, 305–310, 346
fractions and, 294, 296, 297–300, 302–304, 306, 338, 367, 628
greater than 100 or less than 1, 301–304
of increase, 327–328, 340, 350, 406
of markup, 328, 330, 332, 334, 339, 377
modeling, 291, 292, 293, 295, 298, 303, 311, 312, 314–316
Real-World Snapshots, 289, 342–343
sales tax, 314, 322, 324, 325, 336
tips, 33, 322–323, 324–325, 326, 356
using data from a graph, 305
using to find part of a whole, 305–306, 346
writing mixed numbers as, 302, 338–339
writing using equal ratios, 291, 292–294
Percent problems
solving using equations, 318–321, 339
solving using proportions, 311–316, 339
Perfect square, 426–427
Perimeter
of rectangles, 15, 406
of triangles, 15
Permutation, 660–663, 671
Perpendicular bisector, 357–358, 359
Perpendicular lines, 357
Persuasion
using data for, 606–611
writing for, 612
Pi (π), 419, 423
Place value, 700
Plane, 348–350. *See also* Coordinate plane
Point
decimal, 11, 12, 62, 347
graphing, 521–525, 572, 605
midpoint, 357, 360, 361
rotation about, 560
Polygon, 369–373
classifying, 369–370, 395
congruent, 378–382, 395
defined, 268, 369, 395
drawing, 371, 372
identifying, 370, 371–372, 395
irregular, 370, 372
regular, 370, 372, 395
similar, 267–272, 273, 283
vertex of, 438, 461
Polyhedron. *See* Three-dimensional figures
Population
defined, 596
estimating size of, 602–605, 622
Real-World Applications of, 249, 336, 458, 544, 602–605, 617
Positive slope, 534
Positive trend, 614–618, 621
Powers
defined, 132, 178
with negatives, simplifying, 133
of 10, 136, 137, 706
See also Exponent
Practice games, 75, 163, 304, 430, 547, 634
Precision, 227–230
defined, 227, 233
finding, 228
in measurements, 227–229, 233
rounding and, 228
Prediction
exercises that use, 639, 640
using probability, 602, 637
of population size, 602, 637
using graphs, 471, 472, 473
making from a line graph, 471, 472, 473, 613
Price, unit, 247–250, 251, 282
Prime factorization, 145–149, 179, 373, 647
Prime notation (A'), 549
Prime number, 146, 148, 179, 181, 373
Principal, 499, 513
Prism
bases of, 437, 439
defined, 437
drawing, 438
height of, 437
hexagonal, 438
identifying, 437–438
rectangular, 449–454
surface area of, 443, 445–447, 461
triangular, 442, 443
volume of, 449–450, 451–454, 461
Probability, 629–668
applying, 627, 676–677
combination, 664–668, 671
of complement, 630–631
of dependent events, 655–658, 671
exercises that use, 632–634, 635, 638–641, 642, 644–646, 649–652, 656–658, 659, 662–663, 665–668, 670–672
experimental, 635, 636–641, 670
finding, 629–630, 641
of independent events, 653–658
odds, 631
outcome, 629–634
permutation, 660–663, 671
Real-World Snapshots, 627, 676–677
sample spaces, 647–652, 671
simulations, 638, 640, 641, 643–646
theoretical, 629, 670
using to predict, 602, 637
writing as decimal, fraction, or percent, 629, 631, 632, 646
Problem Solving
changing units of weight, 223
comparing and ordering fractions, 157
comparing two sets of data, 576
dividing fractions, 208
dividing integers, 47
finding area of a circle, 421
finding area of a triangle, 410
finding combinations, 664
finding commissions, 324
finding compound interest, 500
finding experimental probability, 637
finding missing lengths, 268–269
finding percent using proportions, 312
finding slope, 534–535
finding tips, 323
finding unit rates, 247
finding volume of a cylinder, 451
finding whole using proportions, 313
graphing functions, 490
identifying arcs of a circle, 395
making graphs, 470
misleading data, 608
multiplying fractions, 203
percents and fractions, 297
problems involving scale, 276
rotational symmetry, 560
sketching graphs, 495
solving equations by adding, 84
solving equations by dividing, 89
solving equations by subtracting, 85
solving for a variable, 507, 509–510, 513
solving inequalities by dividing, 117
solving inequalities by subtracting, 113
subtracting fractions, 193
in two different ways, 218–219, 252–253, 455–456
using divisibility tests, 142

using formulas for, 507–509
using geometric and other sequences, 476
using multiple strategies, 544–545
using Number Sense, 95
using order of operations, 51
using percents greater than 100 or less than 1, 302
using percents to find part of a whole, 306
using Problem-Solving Plan, 30–31, 81
using Pythagorean Theorem, 433
using scale drawings, 275–279
word problems, 106, 217, 317, 479, 601, 659
working with congruent figures, 379
writing algebraic expressions, 73
writing equations, 102–105, 333–336, 455–458, 503–506
writing function rules, 484–485
writing inequalities, 109
writing numbers with exponents, 132
writing rules for translations, 551

Problem-Solving Plan, 30–33, 81

Problem-Solving Strategies
choosing, 31, 32–33, 104, 161–162, 220–221, 254, 335–336, 376–377, 457–458, 505, 546
Draw a Diagram, 252–255, 269, 374–377, 393
exercises that use, 32–33, 104, 254
Look for a Pattern, 160–163, 374–377, 395
Make a Graph, 544–547
Make an Organized List, 643–646, 671
Make a Table, 31, 544–547, 592–595, 621
Simulate a Problem, 643–646
Solve a Simpler Problem, 160–163, 252–255
Try, Check, and Revise, 31, 218–221, 455–458
Use Logical Reasoning, 592–595, 621
Work Backward, 218–221, 233, 508
Write an Equation, 102–105, 333–336, 455–458, 503–506

Product
estimating, 6, 7, 188, 189
zeros in, 704
See also Cross product; Multiplication

Projects. *See* Chapter Projects

Properties, 715–717
of Addition, 12–13, 43, 62
Cross-Property, 257–258
Distributive, 51–54, 63, 64, 130, 673
of Equality, 83–92, 213
of Inequality, 112, 113, 117, 118
of Multiplication, 18, 62, 90–92, 118

Proportion
defined, 256, 283
finding distance, 276
finding the whole using, 312–313
modeling, 311–313, 314, 316
ratios. *See* Ratio
solving, 256–259, 346, 572, 602–605
solving percent problems using, 311–316, 339
solving using cross products, 261–262, 263, 264, 283
solving using Mental Math, 263
solving using unit rates, 260, 262
solving using variables, 261, 346

Proportional reasoning, 260–265, 290, 628

Protractor, 351, 389, 559

Pyramid
base of, 438
defined, 438
edges of, 440
vertex of, 438

Pythagorean Theorem, 431–436, 461

Q

Quadrant, 522–525

Quadrilateral, 369–373
defined, 369
drawing, 371, 373
special, identifying, 370–371, 372

Quartile, 801

Question, biased, 597, 598, 599, 621, 622

Quotient, 19
estimating, 188, 189
See also Division

R

Radical sign, 426

Radius, 383, 384, 385, 395, 420

Random number, 642

Random sample, 596–600

Range, 41, 590

Rate, 246–250, 282
modeling, 246, 247

Ratio, 241–245, 282
applying, 239, 286–287
defined, 241, 282
equal, 242–245, 292–294
modeling, 242
Real-World Snapshots, 239, 286–287
testing, 256–257, 258–259
writing, 241–242, 243
writing as decimals, 242, 243
writing as percent, 291, 292–294
writing in simplest form, 256, 628

Rational numbers, 173–176
defined, 173, 179, 427
negative, 173–174
ordering, 174–176
See also Decimal(s); Fraction(s); Integers; Whole numbers

Rays, 347–348, 349

Reading Comprehension, 60, 65, 75, 155, 181, 206, 225, 279, 285, 326, 352, 356, 397, 406, 498, 515, 531, 589, 623, 641

Reading Math, 6, 23, 24, 46, 51, 57, 90, 107, 110, 131, 156, 169, 170, 174, 192, 204, 206, 215, 222, 228, 260, 275, 291, 315, 333, 352, 384, 414, 421, 426, 449, 475, 477, 484, 507, 521, 523, 533, 534, 549, 550, 559, 574, 597, 629, 631, 657, 660
Learning to Read Your Textbook, 10
Learning Vocabulary, 274, 387, 532
Making Concept Maps, 425
Reading a Math Lesson, 150
Word Problems, 106, 217, 317, 479, 601, 659

Real-World Applications
advertising, 53, 87, 199, 308, 566, 608
amusement parks, 115, 384
animals, 13, 14, 60, 63, 78, 103, 144, 145, 175, 188, 200, 220, 243, 262, 278, 457, 538, 544, 546, 591, 602–603, 604, 605, 617, 618, 643
antique cycles, 30
appliances, 639
aquariums, 453, 538
auctions, 303
avalanche forecasting, 534
aviation, 71, 97, 250, 263, 411, 491, 552
awards, 315
ballooning, 139, 284, 646
banking, 21, 48, 76, 99, 154, 159, 175, 234, 500, 501, 502, 509, 513, 514
baseball, 9, 80, 87, 434, 509, 574, 639
basketball, 86, 95, 115, 151, 253, 306, 320, 514, 553, 627, 637, 641, 657, 676–677
beekeeping, 529
bicycles, 423
billiards, 42
birds, 27, 74, 157, 203
boats and boating, 195, 275, 435, 455, 648
books, 22, 84, 89, 105, 294, 303, 308, 317, 319, 325, 335, 473, 496, 577, 582, 613
bowling, 64, 80, 94, 609
bridge, 360
broadcasting, 657, 659
budgeting, 313, 392
buildings, 349, 381
business, 53, 74, 145, 162, 215, 221, 262, 264, 330, 331, 505, 545, 583, 584
camping, 435, 446
careers, 665
carpentry, 32, 159, 167, 193, 194, 196, 222, 250, 349, 376, 410, 457
cars, 58, 90, 101, 152, 161, 194, 244, 245, 260, 281, 284, 315, 480, 482, 484, 504, 536, 545, 562, 567, 672
chess, 553
circus ring, 421
city planning, 355, 391
class trip, 396
climate, 8, 14, 35, 37, 38, 41, 43, 44, 58, 80, 154, 201, 303, 320, 586
clocks, 561
clothing, 13, 104, 166, 226, 234, 250, 279, 293, 310, 314, 329, 331, 333, 335, 340, 511, 598, 630, 650, 664–665
codes, 142
coins, 104, 631
commissions, 324, 339, 340
computer animation, 551
computers, 217, 299, 506, 587
Congress, 302
conservation, 411
Constitution, 573
construction, 51, 53, 199, 435, 461, 509

consumer issues, 9, 20, 22, 59, 105, 106, 114, 119, 323, 331, 335, 504
cooking, 7, 23, 26, 119, 125, 159, 166, 211, 228, 244, 272, 281, 336, 650
crafts, 27, 28, 330, 463
cross-country racing, 198, 565
cross-training, 476
cycling, 22, 64, 84, 223, 266, 331, 423, 492, 496, 504, 667
data collection, 576, 581, 589, 591, 597
decorating, 64, 100, 258, 291
design, 26, 386, 417, 560
dining, 356, 361
dinosaurs, 278
discounts, 234, 329, 330, 331, 333–336, 339
eagle rays, 5
earnings, 9, 32, 73, 74, 92, 100, 131, 162, 220, 234, 264, 265, 308, 310, 313, 324, 325, 330, 331, 397, 473, 476, 491, 510, 622
eology, 604
education, 44, 100, 114, 196, 249, 264, 284, 292, 299, 304, 309, 314, 320, 337, 453, 515, 620, 650
energy consumption, 397
entertainment, 20, 65, 81, 89, 91, 100, 102–103, 104, 115, 119, 149, 167, 205, 218–219, 302, 321, 330, 337, 341, 384, 406, 421, 433, 505, 577, 583, 616
environment, 303, 309, 411, 610
exercise, 47, 49, 64, 96, 97, 148, 162, 205, 234, 472, 513, 530, 672
families, 654
farming, 32, 111
fashion, 143, 293
fishing, 113
fitness, 20, 64, 97, 148, 166, 205, 234, 472, 513, 530, 672
flags, 242, 271
flowers, 668
food, 20, 26, 59, 63, 79, 88, 95, 97, 105, 109, 119, 124, 159, 165, 166, 190, 195, 208, 211, 234, 250, 264, 272, 281, 284, 297, 300, 301, 319, 320, 330, 341, 506, 531, 543, 567, 583, 609, 612, 649, 671
football, 37, 58, 64, 418
forestry, 309
freight, 8
fund-raising, 73, 104, 105, 106, 124, 220, 316, 320, 331, 513, 546, 588, 593, 609, 645
games, 42, 143, 339, 495, 654, 655, 670
gardening, 87, 103, 106, 321, 456, 529
gasoline, 9, 90, 194, 281, 284, 480, 482, 504
golf, 36, 37, 42, 344, 398, 399, 667
grades, 195, 292, 299, 309, 320, 337, 515
groceries, 63, 124, 179, 311, 330
grooming, 325
gross domestic product, 584
gymnastics, 13, 147, 220, 283
hamsters, 546
health, 12, 56, 86, 162, 264, 577, 622
height, 587
hiking, 48, 199, 224, 226, 341, 666
hobbies, 20, 48, 546, 574, 661
hockey, 235, 421, 661, 675
home improvement, 546
home repairs, 96, 514
indrustrial arts, 428
industry, 446, 582
insurance, 339
interior design, 417
Internet providers, 506
investments, 48, 85, 120
jewelry, 334
jobs, 100, 131, 219, 234, 254, 314, 331, 340, 376, 473, 476, 506, 537, 594
jogging, 97, 166, 205, 234, 503, 513, 530
kaleidoscopes, 6
kites, 594
ladders, 462
land, 536
landscaping, 21
leisure, 56
libraries, 89, 105, 200, 303, 315, 317, 376, 487, 496, 582
light, 139
loans, 42, 255, 501, 514
long jump, 114
mail, 180
machinery, 117
manufacturing, 379, 445, 446, 598, 637, 639
maps, 232, 283, 284, 341, 567
markup, 328, 330, 331, 332, 334
masonry, 124, 234
meal planning, 208, 234
measurement, 208
medicine, 610
memorabilia, 303
models, 276, 645
money, 16, 21, 27, 32, 36, 42, 48, 54, 64, 75, 86, 87, 89, 91, 96, 99, 104, 124, 159, 175, 180, 214, 220, 254, 285, 293, 308, 313, 335, 337, 376, 487, 530, 546, 558, 590, 593, 645, 675
mountain climbing, 47, 230
mountains, 594
movies, 104, 114
moving, 79
museums, 54, 504, 546
nature, 27, 262, 477, 559
navigation, 435
nutrition, 19, 26, 109, 115, 243, 246, 297, 299, 300, 301, 491, 497, 582, 585, 609, 671
Olympics, 101, 282, 609, 661
origami, 281, 360
packaging, 28, 80, 143, 446, 452
painting, 258, 281, 667
parks, 81, 412, 434, 599
parties, 97, 99, 100, 165, 200, 235, 281
pets, 63, 78, 538
photography, 144, 554
physical therapy, 355
planning, 210, 218, 280, 355, 391, 662
plants, 138, 490
politics, 599
pools, 422
population density, 249
population growth, 336, 582
postage, 337
prizes, 644, 672
produce, 64
profit, 122, 607
projects, 189
public service, 79
publishing, 473
quality control, 672
quilting, 410, 463
racing, 120, 166, 198, 247, 249, 497, 565
ramps, 536
real estate, 417, 509, 578
recreation, 319, 340, 433, 435, 446, 527
recycling, 231
rescue, 411
research, 127, 280, 286, 315
restaurants, 33, 81, 88, 218, 323, 339, 340, 675
rides, 119
robotics, 525
salary, 9, 32, 73, 74, 92, 96, 100, 131, 162, 220, 234, 264, 265, 308, 310, 313, 324, 325, 330, 331, 397, 473, 476, 491, 498, 510, 646
sales, 6, 9, 20, 21, 22, 234, 303, 308, 309, 310, 314, 324, 325, 326, 328, 329, 333, 336, 340, 505, 509, 622
savings, 14, 21, 86, 99, 114, 123, 159, 500, 501, 502, 505, 508, 509, 513, 514, 545
schools, 233, 314
scuba diving, 48
sculpting, 427
sewing, 308
shipping, 143, 281
ships, 124, 180, 435
shopping, 6, 20, 22, 58, 63, 80, 101, 105, 106, 111, 114, 115, 119, 124, 125, 216, 220, 233, 235, 247–248, 250, 251, 255, 260, 262, 283, 322, 324, 325, 326, 328, 329, 335, 337, 339, 340, 391, 494
skateboards, 84
skating, 14
skiing, 162, 318
skydiving, 542
soccer, 124, 161, 662
softball, 22, 74, 105, 216, 244
speed of light, 181
speedreading, 487
sports, 22, 36, 37, 42, 58, 80, 84, 86, 87, 89, 95, 101, 105, 110, 113, 114, 115, 120, 124, 147, 161, 188, 195, 198, 216, 220, 223, 244, 247, 249, 253, 272, 282, 306, 315, 318, 330, 336, 340, 418, 421, 434, 435, 476, 497, 503, 504, 509, 514, 553, 565, 574, 593, 609, 637, 639, 641, 657, 661, 662, 665, 667, 675
stationery, 332
stocks, 85
submarines, 47
supplies, 53, 94, 315, 436
support cables, 462
surveying, 270
surveys (opinion polls), 170, 256, 391
swimming, 49, 188, 340, 665
table tennis, 253
tailoring, 650
taxes, 314, 322, 324, 325, 336
technology, 134, 339, 422
telephones, 32, 96, 121, 210, 470, 490
television, 579, 580, 581

temperature, 36, 37, 38, 41, 42, 43, 44, 59, 104, 230, 235, 320, 471 483, 511
tennis, 22, 435
tests, 114
theater, 91, 114, 321
tickets, 81, 102, 106
time, 219, 314, 497
time zones, 43, 591
tipping, 33, 322–323, 325, 326, 356
tourism, 649, 659, 662
toys, 162, 331, 470, 637
track and field, 666
traffic, 179, 366
transportation, 7, 58, 90, 97, 101, 124, 196, 323, 495, 552, 567, 599
travel, 8, 97, 101, 124, 152, 175, 194, 200, 226, 250, 263, 280, 376, 390, 484, 491, 504, 659
trees, 91, 614, 652
tutoring, 234
utilities, 284
volunteering, 391
weather, 8, 14, 35, 41, 42, 43, 44, 58, 80, 104, 154, 201, 230, 303, 320, 586, 645
weight, 80, 114, 117, 119, 189, 221, 234, 271, 505, 506
whirlpools, 427
wildlife population, 544, 602–605, 610, 617
wood, 283
work, 314

Real-World Snapshots
angle measures, 345, 398–399
coordinates, 519, 568–569
data analysis, 571, 624–625
fractions, 129, 182–183, 185, 236–237
inequalities, 69, 126–127
integers, 3, 66–67
patterns, 467, 516–517
percents, 289, 342–343
probability, 627, 676–677
ratios, 239, 286–287
volume, 401, 464–465

Reasonableness of solutions, 11, 19, 31, 117, 193, 197, 198, 203, 204, 208, 297, 306, 495, 500, 504, 545

Reasoning, 7, 15, 18, 20, 21, 22, 25, 27, 38, 40, 44, 48, 57, 59, 66, 74, 76, 85, 87, 89, 92, 94, 95, 99, 107, 110, 113, 115, 117, 119, 127, 132, 133, 134, 135, 137, 141, 145, 146, 148, 149, 152, 153, 157, 159, 165, 168, 169, 172, 174, 180, 183, 187, 190, 193, 198, 208, 213, 214, 215, 222, 228, 236, 243, 244, 245, 247, 249, 257, 259, 261, 263, 264, 268, 270, 278, 286, 292, 295, 300, 306, 309, 312, 313, 323, 328, 332, 335, 348, 353, 358, 360, 366, 367, 371, 372, 381, 384, 385, 390, 392, 404, 407, 411, 412, 413, 421, 423, 431, 436, 444, 446, 448, 451, 452, 457, 469, 471, 473, 475, 477, 478, 480, 484, 487, 490, 494, 495, 497, 499, 502, 507, 523, 524, 528, 535, 539, 549, 574, 577, 578, 581, 582, 583, 586, 587, 588, 591, 595, 597, 598, 599, 604, 606, 607, 608, 609, 610, 614, 616, 617, 622, 630, 633, 635, 637, 640, 642, 650, 651, 652, 655, 658, 661, 666
deductive, 13, 18, 20, 110, 149, 218–219, 592–593, 594, 621, 622
inductive, 21, 71, 81, 131, 134, 136, 160–162, 163, 196, 210, 211, 220, 335, 336, 342–343, 374–375, 376, 377, 474–478, 480–483, 488, 506, 512, 514, 595
justifying steps, 18, 52, 177, 307, 353, 354, 366, 368, 497
logical, 592–595, 621
making conjectures, 475, 476, 477, 478
proportional, 260–265, 290, 628
validating conclusions, 11, 19, 31, 103, 117, 161, 193, 197, 198, 203, 208, 219, 253, 297, 306, 334, 375, 456, 495, 500, 503, 504, 545, 593, 644. *See also* Justification
See also Error Analysis; Justification; Problem Solving Strategies

Reciprocal, 207, 232

Rectangle
area of, 6, 404, 406, 444
defined, 370
perimeter of, 15, 406

Rectangular prism, 449–454

Reflection, 555–558
defined, 555, 565
graphing, 555, 557, 565, 584, 675
line of, 555

Regular polygon, 370, 372, 395

Repeating decimal, 169, 170–172, 174, 179, 367, 427

Representation. *See* Modeling

Revere, Paul, 189

Review. *See* Assessment; Extra Practice; Mixed Review; Need Help?; Skills Handbook

Rhombus, 370, 373

Right angle, 352, 355, 363, 364, 382

Right triangle, 431–436
defined, 364
finding length of hypotenuse of, 432–433, 434–436, 461, 526
finding length of legs of, 433, 434–436, 461

Rise, 533

Roman Numerals, 15

Roosevelt, Franklin D., 263

Root, square, 426–427, 428–430, 461, 714

Rotation, 559–562
angle of, 560, 561, 565
center of, 559, 560
defined, 559, 565
about a point, 560

Rotational symmetry, 559–560, 561, 562, 565

Rounding
decimals, 4, 702
estimating by, 5–6
exercises that use, 4, 7, 33, 75, 228, 702
precision and, 228
whole numbers, 697

Rules
function, 484–488, 490, 491–492, 504–505, 514, 583, 584, 611
for translations, 550–551, 552

Run, 533

S

Sales tax, 314, 322, 324, 325, 336

Sample, random, 596–600

Sample size, 682

Sample space, 647–652, 671

Scale
defined, 275, 283
finding, 276, 286–287
on graphs, 469–470, 512
of maps, 277, 280, 283
modeling, 276, 286–287

Scale drawing, 275–279
defined, 275, 283
exercises that use, 356
making, 277
problem solving using, 275–279, 283

Scale factor, 273

Scalene triangle, 363

Scatter plot, 613–618, 622
defined, 613, 621
describing trends in, 614, 634, 668
drawing, 613, 615
interpreting, 614

Scientific calculator
with order of operations, 133
using, 55

Scientific notation, 136–139, 181
defined, 137, 178
negative exponents in, 140
writing in, 137

Segment, 347–348, 349, 359

Segment bisector, 357–358, 360, 394

Selected Answers, 772–792

Semicircle, 384

Sequence, 474–478, 512
arithmetic, 474–475, 476–478, 512, 605
defined, 474, 512
Fibonnaci, 477
geometric, 475, 476–478, 512

Sides
congruent, 363, 367
corresponding, 267, 268

Similar polygons, 267–272, 283
creating, 273
defined, 268, 283
verifying similarity of, 268

Simple interest, 499–500, 501–502, 513

Simpler problem, solving, 160–163, 252–255

Simplest form
of fraction, 152, 153, 155, 166, 179, 367, 638, 639, 640
of ratio, 256, 628

***Simulate a Problem* Problem-Solving Strategy,** 643–646

Simulation, 638, 640, 641, 643–646

Skew line, 348, 394

Skills Handbook, 696–711

adding and subtracting fractions with like denominators, 708
comparing and ordering whole numbers, 696
dividing a decimal by a whole number, 705
dividing whole numbers, 699
metric units of capacity, 710
metric units of length, 709
metric units of mass, 711
multiplying decimals, 703
multiplying whole numbers, 698
place value and decimals, 700
powers of 10, 706
reading and writing decimals, 701
rounding decimals, 702
rounding whole numbers, 697
zeros in decimal division, 707
zeros in the product, 704

Slide, 548

Slope of a line, 533–539, 565
constant, 534
defined, 533
exploring, 533, 539
finding, 533–538
negative, 534
positive, 534

Software, 273

Solid figures. *See* Three-dimensional figures

Solution
defined, 77, 122, 527, 564
to equations, 77–81, 82, 527, 564
estimating, 77, 78–81, 91
of inequalities, 107, 109–111, 123, 124

***Solve a Simpler Problem* Problem-Solving Strategy,** 160–163, 252–255

Spatial visualization
drawing a diagram, 31, 252–255, 374–377, 393, 431
drawing tessellations, 551
drawing and visualizing solids, 437–440, 441
modeling volume, 449, 453
sketching nets, 442, 444, 461
visualizing packaging, 451, 452
See also Manipulatives; Modeling

Specific gravity, 680

Sphere, 438

Spreadsheet, 76, 501, 579–584
defined, 579
exercises that use, 581, 583, 622, 642
formulas in, 76
using, 76, 579–580

Square
area of, 427
defined, 370
perfect, 426–427

Square number, 131–135, 426–427, 461

Square root, 426–427, 428–430, 461, 714

Standard form, 137–139, 140

Standardized Test Preparation. *See* Assessment

Statistics
box-and-whisker, 586–590, 621
drawing a scatter plot, 613, 615, 616, 618, 622
histogram, 574–578
measures of central tendency, 56–60, 63, 65, 572, 586, 589, 606, 607, 608, 609
misleading graph, 606–611
probability, 629–659, 662, 663, 668, 670, 671, 672
using appropriate, 578, 589, 596–599, 606–610
See also Data; Data analysis; Graphing; Survey

Stem, 585

Stem-and-leaf plot, 585–590, 621, 641

Stevenson, Robert Louis, 308

Straight angle, 352, 355, 382

Straightedge, 349, 358, 362

Stretch Your Thinking, 9, 15, 22, 27, 33, 38, 44, 48, 54, 60, 66, 74, 81, 87, 92, 97, 101, 105, 110, 115, 120, 135, 139, 144, 149, 154, 159, 162, 167, 172, 175, 190, 195, 200, 206, 211, 215, 221, 224, 230, 245, 250, 254, 259, 264, 271, 279, 294, 300, 304, 309, 315, 321, 325, 332, 336, 349, 356, 361, 367, 373, 377, 381, 386, 392, 406, 412, 418, 423, 429, 436, 440, 447, 453, 458, 473, 478, 483, 487, 492, 498, 502, 505, 510, 525, 530, 537, 543, 546, 553, 557, 562, 578, 584, 589, 595, 599, 605, 611, 617, 633, 640, 646, 651, 658, 663, 667

Study guide. *See* Glossary

Substitution, solving equations using, 78, 541

Subtraction
of decimals, 11–12, 13–15, 62, 70, 130
of fractions, 191–196, 708
of integers, 41–44, 63, 70, 186
of mixed numbers, 198–201
solving equations using, 84–87, 213, 215–216, 233
solving inequalities using, 112–115

Subtraction Property
of Equality, 84–85, 213
of Inequality, 113

Successive discount, 333

Sum
compensation and, 16
estimating, 5–6, 7, 8
See also Addition

Supplementary angles, 352–353, 355, 356, 361, 367, 394, 395

Surface area, 442–447, 461, 462
of cylinder, 444–447, 461
drawing a net, 442, 444, 461
finding using nets, 443–447, 461
of prism, 443, 445–447, 461
of solid, 443

Survey, 597–600, 618, 680, 683

Symbols, 713
in comparisons, 107, 109, 110, 156
for congruence, 378
grouping, 51–54, 55
for repeating decimals, 169
for similarity, 267
for square root, 426

Symmetry, 554–558
defined, 554
line of, 554–555, 675
rotational, 559–560, 561, 562, 565

T

Table, 480–483
frequency, 573–578, 592, 611, 620, 652
function, 485, 486, 487, 489–492, 514
as Problem-Solving Strategy, 31, 544–547, 592–595, 621
representing functions in, 485, 486, 487, 489–492, 514
representing patterns in, 480–481
using with a sequence, 481
of values, 528, 542
writing rules using, 481

Take It to the Net. *See* Internet links

Technology
Creating Similar Figures, 273
exercises that use, 134, 339, 422, 525
Exploring Slope, 539
Goniometer, 355
hint, 580
Random Numbers, 642
Three Views of a Function, 493
Using a Fraction Calculator, 212
Using a Scientific Calculator, 55
Using Spreadsheets, 76
See also Calculator; Computer; Graphing calculator

Ten, powers of, 136, 137, 706

Term of a sequence, 481, 482

Terminating decimal, 168–169, 174, 179, 427

Tessellation, 551

Test. *See* Assessment

Test Prep. *See* Assessment

Test-Prep Tips, 40, 88, 152, 198, 256, 276, 327, 354, 432, 481, 540, 605, 666

Test-Taking Strategies
answering gridded-response questions, 61
answering the question asked, 619
answering true/false questions, 563
drawing a diagram, 393
eliminating answers, 669
estimating answers, 511
finding multiple correct answers, 459
reading comprehension questions, 231
using variables, 281
work backward, 337
writing extended responses, 177
writing short responses, 121

Theoretical probability, 629, 670

Three-dimensional figures
base of, 437, 438, 439, 461
drawing, 438, 439, 441
edge of, 437

face of, 437
height of, 437, 438
identifying, 437–440
net of, 442, 444, 461
patterns in, 448
prisms. *See* Prism
surface area of, 443
three views of, 441
volume of. *See* Volume

Time, 219, 314, 497

Tips, 33, 322–323, 324–325, 326, 339, 356

Transformation, 549, 565

Translation, 549–553
defined, 549, 565
graphing, 549–550, 565, 646, 675
writing rules for, 550–551, 552

Trapezoid
area of, 413–414, 416–418, 460
bases of, 413
defined, 370, 413
drawing, 371
height of, 413
similar, 268

Tree diagram, 648, 650, 651, 656, 671

Trend, 614–618, 621, 634, 668

Triangle, 363–367
acute, 364
angle sum of, 364
area of, 408–412, 460
base of, 408
classifying, 363–364, 365, 366
congruent sides of, 363, 367
equilateral, 363, 366
graphing in coordinate plane, 526
height of, 408
hypotenuse of, 432–433, 434–436, 461, 526
isosceles, 363, 367
legs of, 432, 433, 434–436, 461
measures of angles in, 364–367, 402
obtuse, 364
perimeter of, 15
right. *See* Right triangle
scalene, 363
similar, 268, 269

Triangular prism, 442, 443

Trip planning, 280

***Try, Check, and Revise* Problem-Solving Strategy,** 31, 218–221, 455–458

Turn, 548

Two-dimensional figures
base of, 407, 408, 413
height of, 407, 408, 413

Two-step equation, 93–101
exploring, 93–97
solving, 94–101, 123, 130, 186, 214–216, 468

Two-step problems, 93–101

U

Unit of measurement, 712
for capacity, 23, 223–225, 710
converting, 24–28, 63, 64, 222–225, 233, 234, 235, 709–711
choosing, 403
for length, 23, 222–223, 403–404, 405–406, 709
for mass, 23, 223–225, 711
metric. *See* Metric units
precision and, 226–229, 233
for volume, 23, 223–225, 710
for weight, 223–225

Unit price, 247–250, 251, 282

Unit rate
finding, 246–247, 248–250
solving proportions using, 260, 262
writing, 246–247, 282–283

***Use Logical Reasoning* Problem-Solving Strategy,** 592–595, 621

V

Value
absolute, 34–35, 63, 541
place, 700
table of, 528, 542
of variables, 481, 483

Validating conclusions. *See* Reasoning

Variable
defined, 71, 122, 124
finding values of, 481, 483
solving for, 507, 509–510, 513
solving proportions using, 261, 346
using, 281

Variable expression. *See* Algebraic expression

Venn diagram, 591

Verbal model
for problem solving, 72, 73, 78, 84, 85, 89, 94, 95, 102–103, 109, 113, 117, 213, 214, 318, 319, 324, 333–334, 490, 503–504, 602, 621, 660–661, 665

Vertex
of angle, 351
of cone, 438, 461
defined, 351
of polygon, 438, 461
of pyramid, 438

Vertical angle, 353, 354, 355

Vertical line, 523, 524, 564

Views
of functions, 493
of three-dimensional figures, 441

Visual thinking. *See* Spatial visualization

Vocabulary, learning, 274, 387, 532

Volume, 449–454, 461, 462
applying, 401, 464–465
customary units of, 223–225
of cylinders, 450–454, 461
defined, 449
metric units of, 23, 710
modeling, 449, 453
of prisms, 449–450, 451–454, 461
Real-World Snapshots, 401, 464–465

W

Weight
customary units of, 223–225
Real-World Applications, 80, 114, 117, 119, 189, 221, 234, 271, 505

Whole numbers, 34, 696–699
comparing and ordering, 4, 696
dividing, 4, 699
dividing decimals by, 705
multiplying, 698
multiplying fractions by, 204
rounding, 697
See also Integers; Mixed numbers; Whole numbers

Woods, Tiger, 37

Word phrase, 72

Word problem, 106, 217, 317, 479, 601, 659. *See also* Problem Solving

***Work Backward* Problem-Solving Strategy,** 218–221, 233, 508

Work Backward Test-Taking Strategy, 337

Work Together. *See* Investigation

***Write an Equation* Problem-Solving Strategy,** 102–105, 333–336, 455–458, 503–506

Writing in Math, 8, 14, 21, 26, 37, 43, 48, 54, 59, 62, 64, 66, 74, 76, 80, 86, 91, 96, 100, 104, 110, 115, 119, 124, 127, 134, 139, 143, 148, 153, 158, 162, 167, 172, 175, 180, 189, 195, 199, 205, 210, 215, 221, 224, 230, 234, 236, 244, 249, 254, 259, 263, 266, 270, 273, 277, 284, 293, 300, 303, 309, 315, 320, 325, 331, 335, 339, 340, 349, 355, 360, 366, 368, 372, 376, 381, 385, 391, 396, 405, 411, 417, 420, 423, 429, 431, 435, 439, 445, 452, 458, 462, 472, 477, 482, 486, 491, 497, 502, 505, 509, 514, 524, 530, 536, 543, 546, 548, 552, 556, 561, 566, 578, 582, 583, 588, 594, 598, 599, 604, 610, 616, 622, 633, 639, 642, 645, 650, 657, 663, 667, 672
Writing to Compare, 266
Writing to Explain, 29
Writing to Justify, 368
Writing to Persuade, 612

X

***x*-axis,** 521

***x*-coordinate,** 521, 522

Y

***y*-axis,** 521

***y*-coordinate,** 521, 522

Z

Zero
in decimal division, 707
in decimals, 19–20
dividing by, 20
in product, 704

Zero Product Property, 18

Acknowledgments

Staff Credits

The people who made up the *Prentice Hall Mathematics Courses 1, 2, and 3 team*—representing design services, editorial, editorial services, market research, education technology, production services, product services, project office, and publishing processes—are listed below. Bold type denotes the core team members.

Amy Acer, Leora Adler, Scott Andrews, Carolyn Artin, Barbara Bertell, Suzanne Biron, Stephanie Bradley, **Judith Buice,** Christine Cannon, Ronit Carter, Justin Collins, Bob Cornell, Patricia Crotty, Patrick Culleton, Carol Dance, Sheila DeFazio, Marian DeLollis, Jo DiGiustini, Delphine Dupee, Emily Ellen, **Janet Fauser,** Debby Faust, Suzanne Feliciello, Steve Fenton, Michael Ferrio, Jonathan Fisher, Barbara Hardt, Richard Heater, Kerri Hoar, Jayne Holman, Karen Holtzman, Kate House, Alan Hull, **Nancy Jones,** Judie Jozokos, Melissa Kent, Russ Lappa, Lisa LaVallee, Christine Lee, Carolyn Lock, Rebecca Loveys, Catherine Maglio, **Cheryl Mahan,** Barry Maloney, Chris Maniatis, **Tim McDonald,** Autumn Mellor, Eve Melnechuk, Terri Mitchell, Janet Morris, Sandra Morris, Kyai Mullei, **Cindy Noftle,** Marsha Novak, Greg Oles, Marie Opera, Jill Ort, Michael Oster, Christopher Ott, Steve Ouellette, Joan Paley, Dorothy Preston, Roberto Portocarrero, John Reece, Sandy Roedel-Baker, Rashid Ross, Irene Rubin, Alan Ruffin, Donna Russo, John Saxe, JoAnne Sgroi, Vicky Shen, Dennis Slattery, Lisa Smith-Ruvalcaba, **Nancy Smith,** Emily Soltanoff, Debby Sommer, David Spangler, Cynthia Speranza, Karen Swanson, Mark Tricca, Michael Vogel, Nate Walker, Lisa Walston, Roberta Warshaw, Matthew Wilson, Helen Young, **Carol Zacny**

Cover Design

Peter Brooks, Brainworx Studios

Cover Photos

t, Corbis Images/PictureQuest; **b,** Paul Frankian/Index Stock Imagery, Inc.

Technical Illustration

Nesbitt Graphics, Inc.

Photo Research

Sharon Donahue, Sue McDermott, Kathy Beaura Ringrose

Illustration

Argosy Publishing: 153
Ken Batelman: 100, 229, 254, 629
Das Grup: 649, 651
Dorling Kindersley: 67, 286-287, 568-569
Joel Dubin: 496, 498, 657
John Edwards, Inc.: 72, 85, 87, 271, 278, 630, 640
Ed Gazdi: 143
Trevor Johnston: 225, 327, 446
Kelly Graphics: 56, 384, 388
Carla Kiwior: 200
Mary Elizabeth McNeil: 80, 223
Brucie Rosch: 8, 53, 83, 94,104, 208, 249, 257, 278, 291, 443, 452, 502, 604, 633
John Schreiner: 119, 325, 653
Wilkinson Studios: 451, 667
J/B Woolsey: 51, 88, 194, 245, 247, 248, 269, 275
XNR Productions: 35, 41, 43, 155, 171, 249, 271, 276, 277, 280, 411, 414, 417, 505, 588

Photography

Front matter: Page vii, Doug Wilson/Alamy; **viii,** Ariel Skelley/Corbis Stock Market; **ix,** David Aubrey/Corbis; **x,** Douglas Faulkner/Corbis Stock Market; **xi,** NASA; **xii,** Charles O'Rear/Corbis; **xiii,** Richard Pasley/Stock Boston; **xiv,** K.M. Westermann/Corbis; **xv,** Jeff Greenberg/PhotoEdit; **xvi,** George Hall/Corbis; **xvii,** Anton Vengo/SuperStock, Inc.; **xviii,** Andy Sacks/Getty Images, Inc.; **xx-xxiii** all, Richard Haynes

Chapter 1 Pages 2, Art Wolfe/Photo Researchers, Inc.; **4,** Photo Researchers, Inc.; **5 t,** Art Wolfe/Photo Researchers, Inc.; **5 b,** Norbert Wu; **6,** Russ Lappa; **7,** Pearson Education; **8,** North Wind Pictures; **10,** Laura Dwight/Corbis; **11,** Art Wolfe/Photo Researchers, Inc. **12,** Russ Lappa; **14 t,** David Young Wolff/PhotoEdit; **14 bl,** Andrew McKim/Masterfile Corporation; **14 br,** DK Picture Library; **17,** Art Wolfe/Photo Researchers, Inc.; **19,** Eyewire/Getty Images, Inc.; **21,** Rachel Epstein/PhotoEdit; **22,** Arthur Tilley/Getty Images, Inc.; **23 tl,** Art Wolfe/Photo Researchers, Inc.; **23 tr,** Prentice Hall; **23 mr,** Guy Ryecart/DK Picture Library; **23 br,** DK Picture Library; **25 all,** Richard Haynes; **26,** Courtesy of the U.S. Geological Survey; **27,** Russ Pool; **28,** Frank Siteman/Monkmeyer; **30,** Art Wolfe/Photo Researchers, Inc.; **31,** Kindra Clineff/The Picture Cube/Index Stock Imagery, Inc.; **32,** Phil McCarten/PhotoEdit; **34,** Art Wolfe/Photo Researchers, Inc.; **37,** Reuters NewMedia, Inc./Corbis; **39,** Art Wolfe/Photo Researchers, Inc.; **43,** Dan Suzio/Photo Researchers, Inc.; **45,** Art Wolfe/Photo Researchers, Inc.; **47,** Gary Brettnacher/Getty Images, Inc.; **48,** Peter Pinnock/Getty Images, Inc.; **50,** Art Wolfe/Photo Researchers, Inc.; **53,** Doug Wilson/Alamy; **54,** Robert Frerck/Woodfin Camp; **56,** Art Wolfe/Photo Researchers, Inc.; **59,** Gordon Clayton/DK Picture Library; **60,** AP/Wide World Photos; **62,** Art Wolfe/Photo Researchers, Inc.; **64,** Art Wolfe/Photo Researchers, Inc.; **66,** Photo Franca Principe, IMSS; **67,** Digital Vision/Getty Images, Inc.

Chapter 2 Pages 68-69, David L. Ryan/Merlin-Net.com; **70,** Photo Researchers, Inc.; **71 t,** David L. Ryan/Merlin-Net.com; **71 b,** Corbis; **73,** David Young-Wolff/PhotoEdit; **74 br,** Tom Pettyman/PhotoEdit; **74 tl,** Francois Gohier/Ardea; **75,** Prentice Hall; **77 t,** David L. Ryan/Merlin-Net.com; **77 bl,** Corbis; **77 br,** Reuters NewMedia, Inc./Corbis; **78,** Ariel Skelley/Corbis Stock Market; **80,** PhotoDisc/Getty Images, Inc.; **83,** David L. Ryan/Merlin-Net.com; **85,** Newsmakers/Getty Images, Inc.; **86,** Dr. Jeremy Burgess/Photo Researchers, Inc.; **88,** David L. Ryan/Merlin-Net.com; **89,** John Henley/Corbis Stock Market; **91,** Will Hart; **93,** David L. Ryan/Merlin-Net.com; **94,** Michael Newman/PhotoEdit; **97,** David Young-Wolff/PhotoEdit; **98,** David L. Ryan/Merlin-Net.com; **99 all,** Richard Haynes; **100,** Patrick Clark/Getty Images, Inc.; **102,** David L. Ryan/Merlin-Net.com; **103,** Friedrich Von Horsten/Animals Animals/Earth Scenes; **105,** G. Brad Lewis/Photo Resource Hawaii; **106,** Matthew Ward/ DK Picture Library; **107,** David L. Ryan/Merlin-Net.com; **109,** Russ Lappa; **110 l,** SuperStock, Inc.; **110 m,** D. & J. Heaton/Stock Boston; **110 r,** Michael Newman/PhotoEdit; **112,**

David L. Ryan/Merlin-Net.com; **113,** Chip Henderson/Index Stock Imagery, Inc.; **114,** Kevin R. Morris/Corbis; **116,** David L. Ryan/Merlin-Net.com; **117,** Antonio Mo/Getty Images, Inc.; **120 l,** Santokh Kochar/Getty Images, Inc.; **120 m,** G.K. & Vikki Hart/Getty Images, Inc.; **120 r,** David Buffington/Getty Images, Inc.; **122,** David L. Ryan/Merlin-Net.com; **124,** David L. Ryan/Merlin-Net.com; **126 t,** Steve Shott/DK Picture Library; **126-127,** Ron Kimball/Premium Stock/PictureQuest; **127 tl,** Steve Shott/DK Picture Library; **127 tr,** DK Picture Library; **127 mr,** Russ Lappa; **127 m,** Russ Lappa; **127 mr,** Russ Lappa; **127 b,** Russ Lappa.

Chapter 3 Pages 128-129, A. & J. Visaoe/Peter Arnold, Inc.; **130,** Lawrence Migdale/Photo Researchers, Inc.; **131 t,** A. & J. Visaoe/Peter Arnold, Inc.; **131 b,** Getty Images, Inc.; **134,** Andrew Syred/Photo Researchers, Inc.; **136, A.** & J. Visaoe/Peter Arnold, Inc.; **137,** NASA/Finley Holiday Films; **138,** FOXTROT ©1992 Bill Amend. Reprinted with permission of Universal Press Syndicate. All rights reserved.; **139,** Corbis; **141,** A. & J. Visaoe/Peter Arnold, Inc.; **142,** Bettmann/Corbis; **145 t,** A. & J. Visaoe/Peter Arnold, Inc.; **145 b,** D.J. Peters/AP/Wide World Photos; **147 all,** Richard Haynes; **149,** G.D.T./Getty Images, Inc.; **151 t,** A. & J. Visaoe/Peter Arnold, Inc.; **151 b,** Elsa/Allsport/Getty Images, Inc.; **154,** Jeff Greenberg/PhotoEdit; **156,** A. & J. Visaoe/Peter Arnold, Inc.; **157,** 1995, David Weintraub/Photo Researchers, Inc.; **158 t,** Peter Turnley/Corbis; **158 b,** Prentice Hall; **160,** A. & J. Visaoe/Peter Arnold, Inc.; **162 t,** Enzo & Paolo Ragazzini/Corbis; **162 b,** Stephen Oliver/DK Picture Library; **163 l,** Russ Lappa; **163 r,** Richard Haynes; **164 t,** A. & J. Visaoe/Peter Arnold, Inc.; **164 b,** DK Picture Library; **166,** The Image Works; **168 t,** A. & J. Visaoe/Peter Arnold, Inc.; **168 b,** DK Picture Library; **171,** Janet Foster/Masterfile Corporation; **173,** A. & J. Visaoe/Peter Arnold, Inc.; **175,** David Aubrey/Corbis; **178,** A. & J. Visaoe/Peter Arnold, Inc.; **180,** A. & J. Visaoe/Peter Arnold, Inc.; **182 tl,** DK Picture Library; **182 tm,** Courtesy of Sony; **182 tr,** Steve Cole/PhotoDisc/Getty Images, Inc.; **182 b,** Jim Corwin/Stock Connection/PictureQuest; **182-183,** Abe Rezny/The Image Works.

Chapter 4 Pages 184-185, Bruce M. Herman/Photo Researchers, Inc.; 186, Richard Hutchings/PhotoEdit; **187,** Bruce M. Herman/Photo Researchers, Inc.; **189,** Peter Vanderwarker/Stock Boston; **192,** Bruce M. Herman/Photo Researchers, Inc.; **193,** Addison Geary; **195 t,** Tom Stewart/Corbis; **195 m,** John A. Rizzo/Getty Images, Inc.; **195 b,** John A. Rizzo/Getty Images, Inc.; **196,** Tom Stewart/Corbis; **197,** Bruce M. Herman/Photo Researchers, Inc.; **199,** Tom Stewart/Corbis; **202,** Bruce M. Herman/Photo Researchers, Inc.; **203,** Robert Tyrell; **205,** Kwame Zikomo/SuperStock, Inc.; **207,** Bruce M. Herman/Photo Researchers, Inc.; **209 all,** Richard Haynes; **210,** Douglas Faulkner/Corbis Stock Market; **213,** Bruce M. Herman/Photo Researchers, Inc.; **214,** Eric Poggenpohl/Folio; **218 t,** Bruce M. Herman/Photo Researchers, Inc.; **218 b,** Tony Arruza/Getty Images, Inc.; **220,** Gallo Images/Corbis; **222,** Bruce M. Herman/Photo Researchers, Inc.; **223,** Karl Weatherly/Getty Images, Inc.; **224,** Jay Dickman/Corbis; **227 t,** Bruce M. Herman/Photo Researchers, Inc.; **227 b,** DK Picture Library; **228,** Russ Lappa; **231,** Jeri Gleiter/Getty Images, Inc.; **232,** Bruce M. Herman/Photo Researchers, Inc.; **234,** Bruce M. Herman/Photo Researchers, Inc.; **236-237,** Jose Fuste Raga/Corbis; **237 tl,** Rainer Grosskopf/Getty Images, Inc.; **237 tr,** Barbara Magnuson Larry Kimball/Visuals Unlimited.

Chapter 5 Pages 238-239, Dave G. Houser/Corbis; **240,** Mark Richards/PhotoEdit; **241,** Dave G. Houser/Corbis; **242,** Tony Freeman/PhotoEdit; **242 inset,** Mark Burnett/Stock Boston; **244,** Mark Richards/PhotoEdit; **246,** Dave G. Houser/Corbis; **247,** Andy Lyons/Getty Images, Inc.; **249,** Steve Gorton/DK Picture Library; **252 t,** Dave G. Houser/Corbis; **252 b,** Bryan Peterson/Getty Images, Inc.; **254,** Marc Asnin/Corbis Saba; **256,** Dave G. Houser/Corbis; **259,** NASA/Roger Ressmeyer/Corbis; **260 t,** Dave G. Houser/Corbis; **260 b,** DK Picture Library; **262** all, Richard Haynes; **263,** Corbis; **264,** Frank Siteman/Stock Boston; **265,** Disneyland Paris' Le Orbitron 1990-1991 Functional motorized study/display model Dimensional Designer Doug Hartwell ©Walt Disney Imagineering; **267,** Dave G. Houser/Corbis; **270,** Michael Keller/Corbis Stock Market; **275,** Dave G. Houser/Corbis; **276,** Russ Lappa; **280,** AP/Wide World Photos; **282,** Dave G. Houser/Corbis; **284,** Dave G. Houser/Corbis; **287,** www.rubberball.com.

Chapter 6 Pages 288-289, Ken Musgrave; **290,** Adam Smith Productions/Corbis; **291,** Ken Musgrave; **295,** Ken Musgrave; **297,** Peter Johnson/Corbis; **299 t,** DK Picture Library; **299 b,** Hillary Price; **300 all,** DK Picture Library; **301,** Ken Musgrave; **303,** Ron Thomas/Getty Images, Inc.; **304,** Richard Haynes; **305,** Ken Musgrave; **307,** Richard Haynes; **309,** UNEP/Rougier/The Image Works; **311 t,** Ken Musgrave; **311 b,** Paul Chesley/Getty Images, Inc.; **312,** Bob Daemmrich/Stock Boston; **315,** Bob Daemmrich/Stock Boston; **318,** Ken Musgrave; **319,** David Young-Wolff/PhotoEdit; **320,** Bob Daemmrich/The Image Works; **322,** Ken Musgrave; **323,** Bernard Wolf/PhotoEdit; **327,** Ken Musgrave; **329 all,** Richard Haynes; **331,** Photo Researchers, Inc.; **333,** Ken Musgrave; **334,** Charles O'Rear/Corbis; **335,** Owen Franken/Stock Boston; 338, Ken Musgrave; **340,** Ken Musgrave; **342 all,** Courtesy of the U.S. Geological Survey; **343 t,** David Nicholls; **343 m,** Courtesy of the U.S. Geological Survey; **343 b,** Courtesy of the U.S. Geological Survey.

Chapter 7 Pages 344-345, Photo by Bill Barley, ©1997; **346,** Bill Horsman/Stock Boston; **347,** Photo by Bill Barley, ©1997; **348,** Rafael Macia/Photo Researchers, Inc.; 349, James Marshall/Corbis Stock Market; **350,** Peter Beck/Corbis; **351,** Photo by Bill Barley, ©1997; **352,** Richard Pasley/Stock Boston; **354 all,** Richard Haynes; **355,** Prentice Hall; **356 t,** DK Picture Library; 356 bl, National Fish and Wildlife Forensics Lab; **356 br,** National Fish and Wildlife Forensics Lab; **357,** Photo by Bill Barley, ©1997; **358,** Courtesy of Wellesley College Library, Special Collections, photo by George McLean; **360 all,** Russ Lappa; **363 t,** Photo by Bill Barley, ©1997; **363 b,** William S. Helsel/Stone/Getty Images, Inc.; **366,** Paul Hermansen/Getty Images, Inc.; **369,** Photo by Bill Barley, ©1997; **371,** Bill Aron/PhotoEdit; **372 tl,** Felicia Martinez/PhotoEdit; **372 tm,** Max Alexander/DK Picture Library; **372 tr,** Design by Jean-Charles Guillois and Ines Levy; **372 ml,** Paul Trummer/Getty Images, Inc.; **372 mr,** Cavagnaro/Visuals Unlimited; **372 b,** 1995 by NEA, Inc. Thaves 6-13; **374 t,** Photo by Bill Barley, ©1997; **374 b,** Michael Newman/PhotoEdit; **376,** David M. Grossman/Photo Researchers, Inc.; **378,** Photo by Bill Barley, ©1997; **379,** Kenneth Murray/Photo Researchers, Inc.; **383 t,** Photo by Bill Barley, ©1997; **383 b,** Spencer Grant/PhotoEdit; **385,** James L. Amos/Corbis; **383,** Photo by Bill Barley, ©1997; **389,** NASA; **391,** Ed Young/Photo Researchers, Inc.; **394,** Photo by Bill Barley, ©1997; **396,** Photo by Bill Barley, ©1997; **398 t,** Jack Hollingsworth/Getty Images, Inc.; **398 bl,** Courtesy, Professional Miniature Golf Association, Michael Meservy; **398-399,** Richard Hamilton Smith/Corbis; **399,** SW Productions/Getty Images, Inc.

Chapter 8 Pages 400-401, Michael Grecco/Stock Boston; **402,** Michael Prince/Corbis; **403,** Michael Grecco/Stock Boston; **406,** Matsumoto/Explorer/Photo Researchers, Inc.; **407,** Michael Grecco/Stock Boston; **410,** PhotoEdit; **411,** Patrick Montgomery/U.S. Coast Guard; **413,** Michael Grecco/Stock Boston; **414 l,** Buddy Mays/Corbis; **414 inset,** Colin Keates/DK

Picture Library; **416 all,** Richard Haynes; **417,** C Squared Studios/Getty Images, Inc.; **419 t,** Michael Grecco/Stock Boston; **419 b,** Prentice Hall; **423,** Lawrence Migdal/Stock Boston; **426,** Michael Grecco/Stock Boston; **427,** K.M. Westermann/Corbis; **429,** FOXTROT ©1992 Bill Amend. Reprinted with permission of Universal Press Syndicate. All rights reserved; **430,** Richard Haynes; **432,** Michael Grecco/Stock Boston; **433,** PhotoEdit; **434,** Barrie Rokeach/Getty Images, Inc.; **435,** Michael J. Howell/Stock Boston; **437 t,** Michael Grecco/Stock Boston; **437 b,** David Parker/Photo Researchers, Inc.; **438,** Russ Lappa; **439 l,** Spike Mafford/Getty Images, Inc.; **439 m,** John Lei/Stock Boston; **439 r,** Davies & Starr/Getty Images, Inc.; **441 all,** Russ Lappa; **442,** Michael Grecco/Stock Boston; **444,** Richard Haynes; **446 l,** Syracuse Newspapers/Michelle Gabel/The Image Works; **446 r,** Amy Etra/PhotoEdit; **449,** Michael Grecco/Stock Boston; **453,** PhotoEdit; **455 t,** Michael Grecco/Stock Boston; **455 b,** Bob Daemmrich; **457 l,** Siede Preis/Getty Images, Inc.; **457 m,** Spencer Grant/PhotoEdit; **457 r,** Siede Preis/Getty Images, Inc.; 460, Michael Grecco/Stock Boston; **462,** Michael Grecco/Stock Boston; **464 l,** Chris Brown/Stock Boston/PictureQuest; **464-465,** T.J. Florian/PictureQuest; **465 m,** Phil Kember/Index Stock Imagery/PictureQuest; **465 r,** Digital Vision/Getty Images, Inc.

Chapter 9 Pages 466-467, Charles Bush; **468,** David Frazier/Photo Researchers, Inc.; **469,** Charles Bush; **470,** Russ Lappa; **471,** Elena Rooraid/PhotoEdit; **472,** Bob Daemmrich/Stock Boston; **474,** Charles Bush; **477,** Mark Antman/The Image Works; **480 t,** Charles Bush; **480 b,** Spencer Grant/PhotoEdit; **483 l,** Cheryl Hogue/Visuals Unlimited; **483 r,** Russ Lappa; **484,** Charles Bush; **487,** Michael Newman/PhotoEdit; **489,** Charles Bush; **490,** Mark Bernett/Stock Boston; **491,** Bettmann/Corbis; **494,** Charles Bush; **495,** Jeff Greenberg/PhotoEdit; **496,** Lowe Art Museum, University of Miami/SuperStock, Inc.; **497 t,** Nancy Ney/Corbis; 497 m, Larry Williams/Corbis; **497 b,** Allen Lee Page/Corbis; **497 bl,** Robert Dowling/Corbis; **497 bm,** Lawrence Migdale/Stock Boston; **497 br,** John Kaprielian/Photo Researchers, Inc.; **499,** Charles Bush; **501,** Ariel Skelley/Corbis; **503 t,** Charles Bush; **503 b,** Brian Bailey/Getty Images, Inc.; 504, Bob Daemmrich/The Image Works; **505,** Ronan Beste/ Animals Animals/Earth Scenes; **506,** Chris Marona/Photo Researchers, Inc.; **507,** Charles Bush; **508 all,** Richard Haynes; **509,** Richard Hutchings/Photo Researchers, Inc.; **512,** Charles Bush; **514,** Charles Bush; **516 l,** Harold Wilion/Index Stock Imagery/PictureQuest; **516-517,** Neil Fletcher/DK Picture Library; **517 t,** Ruth A. Adams/Index Stock Imagery/PictureQuest.

Chapter 10 Pages 518-519, NASA/Masterfile Corporation; **520,** Inga Spence/Visuals Unlimited; **521,** NASA/Masterfile Corporation; **522,** James Marshall/The Image Works; **524,** John R. Bracegirdle/Getty Images, Inc.; **527 t,** NASA/Masterfile; **527 b,** Dave Nagel/Getty Images, Inc.; **529,** Lynda Richardson/Corbis; **530,** EyeWire Collection/Getty Images, Inc.; **531,** Annie Hunter; **533,** NASA/Masterfile Corporation; **534,** Corbis; **535,** Bruce Burkhardt/Corbis; **536 tl,** Peter Guttman/Corbis; **536 tr,** Adam Jones/Photo Researchers, Inc.; **536 b,** Prentice Hall; **537,** BIZARRO ©1997 by Dan Piraro. Reprinted with permission of UNIVERSAL PRESS SYNDICATE. All rights reserved.; **540 t,** NASA/Masterfile Corporation; 540 bl, Colorsport; **540 br,** Ryan McVay/Getty Images, Inc.; **541 all,** Richard Haynes; **542,** Steve Fitchett/Getty Images, Inc.; **544 t,** NASA/Masterfile Corporation; **544 b,** Jeff Lepore/Photo Researchers, Inc.; **547,** Richard Haynes; **549,** NASA/Masterfile Corporation; **552,** George Hall/Corbis; **554 t,** NASA/Masterfile Corporation; **554 m,** Nuridsany et Perennou/Photo Researchers, Inc.; **554 bl,** Charles Kennard/Stock Boston; **554 br,** Jerome Wexler/Photo Researchers, Inc.; **557,** Sturgis McKeever/Photo Researchers, Inc.; **559 t,** NASA/Masterfile Corporation; **559 m,** Foto World/Getty Images, Inc.; **559 b,** Rod Planck/Tom Stack & Associates, Inc.; **560,** Prentice Hall; **564,** NASA/Masterfile Corporation; **566,** NASA/Masterfile Corporation; **568-569 all,** LUCASFILM LTD. Star War: Episode II - Attack of the Clones © 2002 Lucasfilm Ltd. & TM. All rights reserved. Used under authorization. Unauthorized duplication is a violation of applicable law. No internet use.

Chapter 11 Pages 570-571, John Hickey/The Buffalo News; **572,** 2000 by Consumers Union of the United States, Inc., Yonkers, New York 10703-1057, a non profit organization. Reprinted with permission from the March 2000 issue of Consumer Reports, for educational purposes only; **573,** John Hickey/The Buffalo News; **574,** DK Picture Library; **575 all,** Richard Haynes; **576,** Dennis MacDonald/PhotoEdit; **579,** John Hickey/The Buffalo News; **580,** Chris Casaburi; **582,** Ryan McVay/Getty Images, Inc.; **583,** Mike Okoniewski/The Image Works; **585,** John Hickey/The Buffalo News; **587,** Anton Vengo/SuperStock, Inc.; **589,** AP/Wide World Photos; **591,** Siede Preis/Getty Images, Inc.; **592 t,** John Hickey/The Buffalo News; **592 tl,** Angelo Cavalli/Image Bank/Getty Images, Inc.; **592 tml,** Tom Dietrich/Getty Images, Inc.; **592 bml,** Dennis MacDonald/PhotoEdit; **592 bl,** Owaki-Kulla/Corbis; **596 t,** John Hickey/The Buffalo News; **596 bl,** Bettman/Corbis; **596 br,** Bettman/Corbis; **599,** Karen Preuss/The Image Works; **600,** Michael Newman/PhotoEdit; **602 t,** John Hickey/The Buffalo News; **602 b,** Jim Brandenburg/Minden Pictures; **604,** Amos Nachuom/Corbis; **606 t,** John Hickey/The Buffalo News; **606 b,** Tony Freeman/PhotoEdit; **608 t,** Patricia Brabant/Getty Images, Inc.; **608 b,** John A. Rizzo/Getty Images, Inc.; **609,** Corel Corperation; **613,** John Hickey/The Buffalo News; **614,** David Weintraub/Photo Researchers, Inc.; **616,** David Young-Wolff/PhotoEdit; **620,** John Hickey/The Buffalo News; **622,** John Hickey/The Buffalo News; **624 t,** Randy Ury/Corbis; **624-625,** Jeff Maloney/Getty Images, Inc.; **625 t,** Philip Gatward/ DK Picture Library.

Chapter 12 Pages 626-627, Pictor International, Ltd./PictureQuest; **628,** Andy Sacks/Getty Images, Inc.; **629,** Pictor International, Ltd./PictureQuest; **631 b,** Prentice Hall; **633,** Michael Geissinger/The Image Works; **636,** Pictor International, Ltd./PictureQuest; **637,** Wally Santana/AP/Wide World Photos; **638,** Paul Barton/Corbis; **639,** David Young-Wolff/PhotoEdit; 640, Bill Bachman/Stock Boston; **641,** David Young-Wolff/PhotoEdit; **643 t,** Pictor International, Ltd./PictureQuest; **643 b,** Randall Hyman; **645,** Russ Lappa; **646,** Reuters NewMedia Inc./Corbis; **647,** Pictor International, Ltd./PictureQuest; **648,** Hughes Martin/Corbis; **650,** TRBPhoto/Getty Images, Inc.; **653,** Pictor International, Ltd./PictureQuest; **654,** Camille Tokerud/Photo Researchers, Inc.; **656 all,** Richard Haynes; **660 t,** Pictor International, Ltd./PictureQuest; **660 b,** Getty Images, Inc.; **661,** Robert Laberge/Getty Images, Inc.; **662,** Joseph Sohm/ChromoSohm, Inc./Corbis; **664,** Pictor International, Ltd./PictureQuest; **666,** Russ Lappa; **670,** Pictor International, Ltd./PictureQuest; **672,** Pictor International, Ltd./PictureQuest; **676 t,** Ken Chernus/Getty Images, Inc.; **676-677,** Larry Dale Gordon/Getty Images, Inc.; **677 r,** Tony Bee/PictureQuest.